Crime State Rankings 2010
Crime Across America

Kathleen O'Leary Morgan

and

Scott Morgan

with

Rachel Boba

CQ PRESS

A Division of SAGE
Washington, D.C.

CQ Press
2300 N Street, NW, Suite 800
Washington, DC 20037

Phone: 202-729-1900; toll-free, 1-866-4CQ-PRESS (1-866-427-7737)

Web: www.cqpress.com

Cover design: Silverander Communications

Printed and bound in the United States of America

14   13   12   11   10   1   2   3   4   5

ISSN 1077-4408
ISBN 978-1-60426-618-4

Contents

Detailed Table of Contents

Introduction and Methodology

Crime State Rankings 2010 analyzes the latest available (2008) FBI crime data for the United States. It uses criminal justice data to compare and rank the fifty states and the District of Columbia in a variety of ways to provide easily understandable information to federal, state, and local officials and citizens. This introductory section includes a description of the crime data used in the book and the methodology used for the rankings, a distribution analysis of comparison scores and crime rates of selected variables, and additional information and caveats regarding the results. The remainder of the book contains state-by-state tables that present analysis of reported crime incidents, rates, and trends; consumer fraud and identity theft; prison and corrections populations and facilities; law enforcement personnel and expenditures; juvenile crime; drugs and alcohol abuse and treatment programs; and arrests and crime clearances. In all, more than 500 tables provide answers to hundreds of questions about reported crime and criminal justice information.

Purpose of This Book

The purpose of *Crime State Rankings 2010* is to serve as a resource for state and local officials, law enforcement officials, and the community, as governors, mayors, and concerned citizens often seek straightforward, organized criminal justice information to understand and begin to address public safety issues in their own states and local communities. Along with the wealth of descriptive information presented here, this book also provides a unique approach by which individuals can compare states' reported crime rates (per 100,000 persons) to the national level of reported crime (comparison score) and to other states (rankings).

In previous editions, the terms "safest" and "dangerous" were used to describe the states with lowest and highest rankings. These terms are no longer used because perceptions of safety and danger are just that—perceptions. It is important to note that the analyses in this book are purely descriptive. At no time do we attempt to explain why there are differences between and among states. These explanations are beyond the scope of this book and are currently being pursued by criminologists and other social science researchers.

To enhance the usefulness of *Crime State Rankings 2010*, this edition includes a chapter that offers histograms of the results of selected analyses along with measures of central tendency, such as median, mean, standard deviation, and minimum and maximum values. This analysis is provided so that readers can better understand the overall distribution of values of a variable (for example, homicide rate) for the fifty states and the District of Columbia as well as how a particular state compares to the others.

The Data and Its Limitations

While also using information from the Bureau of Justice Statistics, the Census Bureau, and the Drug Enforcement Administration, a significant amount of the data featured in *Crime State Rankings 2010* comes from the FBI publication *Crime in the United States*, which is available every fall for the previous year. This report is based on data from the Uniform Crime Reporting (UCR) Program, which provides national standards for the uniform classification of crimes, clearances, and arrests (for further details, visit the FBI's Web site at www.fbi.gov/ucr). Notably, the UCR crime definitions are distinct and do not conform to federal or state laws; however, they do provide systematically collected data on the types of crimes that are often of the most concern. More than 17,000 city, university and college, county, state, tribal, and federal law enforcement agencies voluntarily provide information representing 94.9 percent of the population (in 2008) to their respective states, which then provide the information to the FBI.

While there are well-documented criticisms of the UCR data that must be considered when using these data for any purpose, these criticisms should not preclude officials, practitioners, and others from using the data to understand increases and decreases in crime and guide policy decisions. The UCR data consist of both aggregate counts of selected crimes (Part I crimes only) and aggregate counts of all arrests (Part I crimes as well as all others). Part I crimes include murder, rape, robbery, aggravated assault, burglary, larceny-theft, motor vehicle theft, and arson. The FBI does not report aggregate counts of Part II crimes—such as simple assault, fraud, prostitution, and DUI—only arrests. In addition, UCR procedures require that individual police departments use a hierarchical coding system for Part I crimes, which means if two crimes happen during one incident, only one is counted. For example, if one person is the victim of both rape and robbery, only the rape will be counted.

Another, and likely the most, important consideration when interpreting crime statistics based on UCR data is that these data contain only those crimes that have been reported to or discovered by police (that is, crimes "known to law enforcement")—not all crime that has occurred. In fact, the Bureau of Justice Statistics (BJS) estimates from the National Crime Victimization Survey (NCVS) that violent crime is reported between 40 to 50 percent of the time and that property crime is reported between 30 to 40 percent of the time (BJS, 2008). The result of the factors discussed here is that Part I crime statistics represent only a portion of the actual crime that has occurred.

Additional criticisms of the UCR data include inaccuracy due to inputting errors and handling of missing data (Lynch & Jarvis, 2008; Maltz, 1999); pressure on some law enforcement agencies to "doctor" the numbers; and the use of aggregate numbers that mask other factors such as time of day, location, and circumstance of the crime. Yet, the UCR data are the most comprehensive and consistently collected data on crime in our country. Examining these data at the state level provides a birds-eye view of crime, as states themselves are diverse in their characteristics (for example, population density, rural versus urban areas, and topography), and levels of crime vary within states. In most cases, analysis of UCR data begins the conversation about crime issues, and additional in-depth analysis in metropolitan areas, cities, and neighborhoods is required to truly understand the nature and context of crime problems (Boba, 2008).

Methodology

The methodology used to produce the statistics presented in this book is fairly straightforward. In the first analysis—unique to this book—a comparison score is calculated for each state that is a summary of the percent differences of the reported crime rate from the national rate of six crime types (the formula is described below). The rest of the analyses are simple calculations of frequency, percent, rate, and percent change of reported crime and other criminal justice information.

In each analysis, the states are presented in alphabetical order as well as by their rank from highest to lowest for each variable under examination. In the case of a tie, rankings are listed alphabetically. Parentheses indicate negative numbers and rates (except in the data distribution charts in which negative signs are used). Data reported as "NA" are not available or could not be calculated. The national totals and rates appearing at the top of each table are for the entire United States.

"Comparison Score" Methodology

The methodology for determining the state comparison crime rate rankings involves a multistep process in which the reported crime across six crime categories—murder, rape, robbery, aggravated assault, burglary, and motor vehicle theft—per 100,000 population rates are compared to the national reported crime per 100,000 population rates and then indexed to create a summary score and ranking across six areas of reported violent and property crime. Larceny-theft is not included in this analysis because the FBI and an advisory board of criminologists concluded in 2004 that the Crime Index (the six crimes listed above and larceny-theft) was inflated by the high number of larceny-thefts and was no longer a true indicator of crime. Although the FBI

has not yet developed a solution, our methodology considers the listed six crimes only. Please note that in 2008, larceny-theft comprised 59 percent of all reported crimes.

The following are steps for the "comparison score" calculation and an example that illustrates the calculations:

1. For each of the 6 categories of reported crime, the crime rate per 100,000 residents of a state is calculated from the reported crime and population data provided to the FBI by local law enforcement agencies. For example, the per capita reported murder rate per 100,000 persons for Nevada is 6.3: Nevada's murder count for 2008, 163, is divided by its population, 2,600,167, and then multiplied by 100,000 to arrive at 6.3.

2. The percent difference between the state rate and the national rate for each of the six crimes is then computed. The use of percent difference for each crime separately eliminates weighting more frequent crimes more heavily (that is, typically there are many more property crimes than violent crimes). The formula for this calculation is:

$$\frac{\text{State Rate} - \text{National Rate}}{\text{National Rate}} \times 100$$

3. The number is then scaled to be one-sixth (.1667) of the index to make it comparable to scores in the previous editions of this book. A number of years ago, we weighted each of the six crimes based on the results of a telephone survey that determined which crimes were of greatest concern to Americans. The polls indicated that most Americans believed crimes such as burglary are more likely to happen in their lives than more heinous crimes such as murder. Thus, burglary received the highest weight, and murder received the lowest weight in the formula. However, we discontinued the polling and consequently eliminated the weights. We left this stage in the methodology, however, giving each crime equal weight so that future scores would be more closely comparable to the scores with the weighted factors.

4. The final comparison score for each state is the sum of its individual scores for the six crimes. In this example, Nevada's final comparison score is 51.6. The interpretation of these scores is that the higher a state comparison score, the further it is above the national score; the lower the comparison score, the further it is below the national score; and a comparison score of zero is equal to the national score.

Example: Nevada

	Murder	Rape	Robbery	Aggravated Assault	Burglary	Motor Vehicle Theft
State Rate	6.3	42.4	248.9	426.9	929.0	611.6
National Rate	5.4	29.3	145.3	274.6	730.8	314.7
Percent Difference	16.7%	44.7%	71.3%	55.5%	27.1%	94.3%
Weighting Factor	.1667	.1667	.1667	.1667	.1667	.1667
Resulting Score	2.8	7.5	11.9	9.2	4.5	15.7

5. The comparison scores are sorted from highest to lowest to produce the rankings. Note that the rankings do not indicate the actual difference between the scores, only their order.

This methodology results in a comparison score for each state that compares its rate to the national rates, providing a means of comparison among states in terms of how much higher or lower each state is than the national average.

References

Boba, R. (2008). *Crime analysis with crime mapping.* Thousand Oaks, Calif.: SAGE Publications.

Bureau of Justice Statistics [BJS] (2008). *Percent of total crime reported to the police.* Retrieved October 7, 2008 from www.ojp.usdoj.gov/bjs/glance/tables/reportingtypetab.htm.

FBI (2009). www.fbi.gov and www.fbi.gov/ucr/cius2007/about/table_methodology.html.

Lynch, J.P. and Jarvis, J.P. (2008). Missing data and imputation in the Uniform Crime Reports and the effects on national estimates. *Journal of Contemporary Criminal Justice,* 24: 69–85.

Maltz, M. (1999). *Bridging gaps in police crime data.* Technical Report. Washington, D.C.: Bureau of Justice Statistics.

Distribution Analysis

This section of *Crime State Rankings 2010* presents charts depicting the distributions of selected analyses contained in this book. The purpose of this section is to provide a mechanism of comparison beyond the rankings. Along with each histogram, measures of central tendency such as median, mean, standard deviation, and minimum and maximum values are reported to further describe the distribution of each analysis.

Each histogram is formatted as an area chart for easier viewing. Along the bottom (x-axis), the values depict ranges for which the state's values are totaled and along the left (y-axis) the number of states with values in that range is shown. Additional statistics are provided to show each distribution's measures of central tendency. The median indicates the middle value of the distribution, which means that 50 percent of the states have scores or rates above and the other 50 percent have scores or rates below that value. The mean is the average value of the distribution, and the standard deviation, in general, is the measure of spread of all the values from the mean. The minimum and maximum values are the lowest and highest values of the distribution, respectively. Note that all these statistics are different for each data distribution.

These statistics are based on the normal curve, so one standard deviation above and below the mean contains 68 percent of the states, two standard deviations above and below the mean contain 95 percent of the states, and three standard deviations above and below the mean contains 99.7 percent of the states. The purpose of these statistics is descriptive, and together they assist readers in understanding the values of all the states together as well as where an individual state sits relative to the others. For example, in Figure 1 the statistics for the state comparison scores are interpreted as follows:

- The lowest comparison score for states is –57.6.
- The highest comparison score for states is 51.6.
- The range of scores (maximum minus minimum) is 109.2.
- 50 percent of the states have comparison scores lower than –13.9, and 50 percent have scores higher than –13.9.

- The average comparison score for states is –9.7, and the standard deviation is 29.8.
- 68 percent of the states have scores between –39.5 and 20.1.
- 95 percent of the states have scores between –69.2 and 49.9.
- 99.7 percent of the states have scores between –99.0 and 79.7 (The fact that the lower end of this and the previous range are less than the minimum value of the distribution indicate the distribution is skewed.)

Also in Figure 1, when assessing one state, for example North Carolina, its value of 11.98 reveals that it is in the higher than 50 percent of all the scores (above the median of –13.9) range and falls within the first standard deviation of the mean with 68 percent of the other scores (between –39.5 and 20.1).

The remainder of this section presents histograms and noted statistics for the analyses listed here:

1. State Comparison Scores
2. State Murder Rates
3. State Rape Rates
4. State Robbery Rates
5. State Aggravated Assault Rates
6. State Burglary Rates
7. State Auto Theft Rates
8. State Larceny Theft Rates

A word of caution: The distribution analysis histograms and statistics are provided to help understand the nature of the values within each analysis, but the analyses are still based on data that must be interpreted within the constraints noted earlier. These charts are only descriptions of the data and do not provide predictions or explanations of why these values are different.

Figure 1   State Comparison Scores

Frequency of States

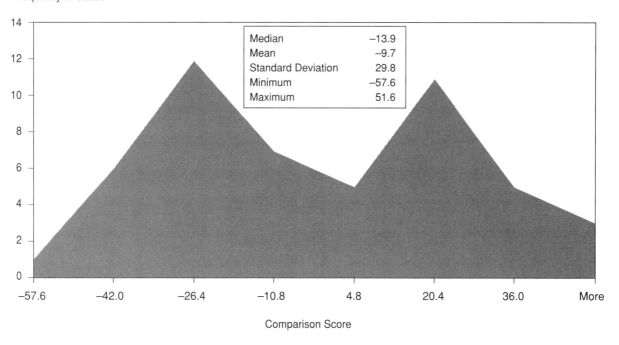

Median	−13.9
Mean	−9.7
Standard Deviation	29.8
Minimum	−57.6
Maximum	51.6

Comparison Score

Figure 2   State Murder Rates

Frequency of States

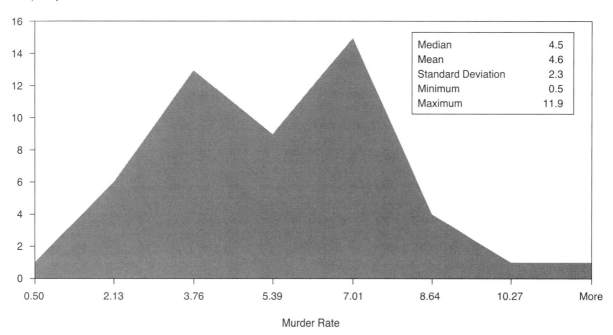

Median	4.5
Mean	4.6
Standard Deviation	2.3
Minimum	0.5
Maximum	11.9

Murder Rate

Figure 3 State Rape Rates

Frequency of States

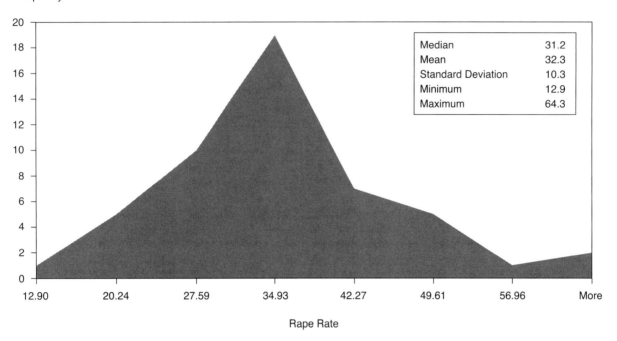

Median	31.2
Mean	32.3
Standard Deviation	10.3
Minimum	12.9
Maximum	64.3

Rape Rate

Figure 4 State Robbery Rates

Frequency of States

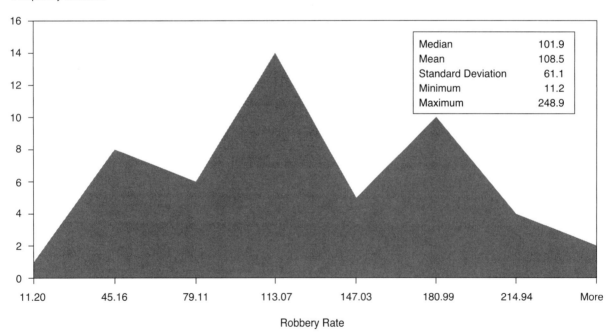

Median	101.9
Mean	108.5
Standard Deviation	61.1
Minimum	11.2
Maximum	248.9

Robbery Rate

Figure 5   State Aggravated Assault Rates

Frequency of States

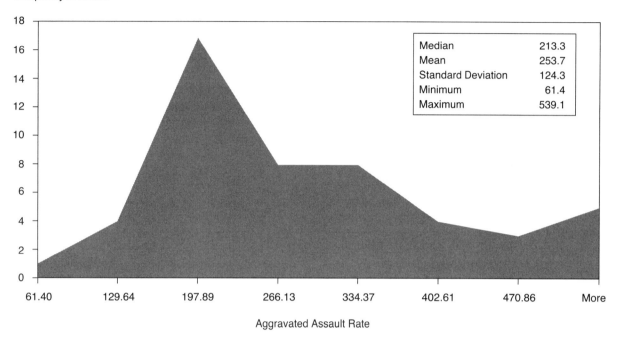

Median	213.3
Mean	253.7
Standard Deviation	124.3
Minimum	61.4
Maximum	539.1

Aggravated Assault Rate

Figure 6   State Burglary Rates

Frequency of States

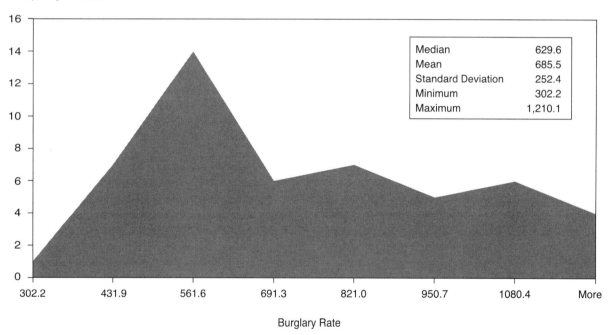

Median	629.6
Mean	685.5
Standard Deviation	252.4
Minimum	302.2
Maximum	1,210.1

Burglary Rate

Figure 7 State Auto Theft Rates

Frequency of States

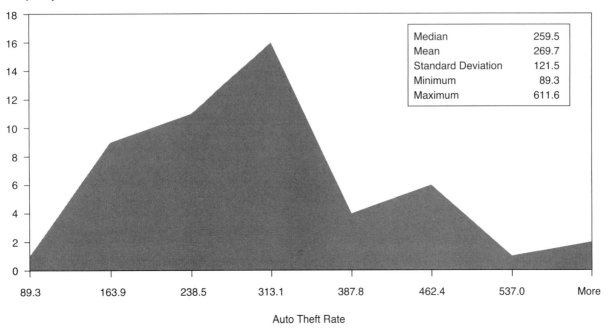

Median	259.5
Mean	269.7
Standard Deviation	121.5
Minimum	89.3
Maximum	611.6

Auto Theft Rate

Figure 8 State Larceny Theft Rates

Frequency of States

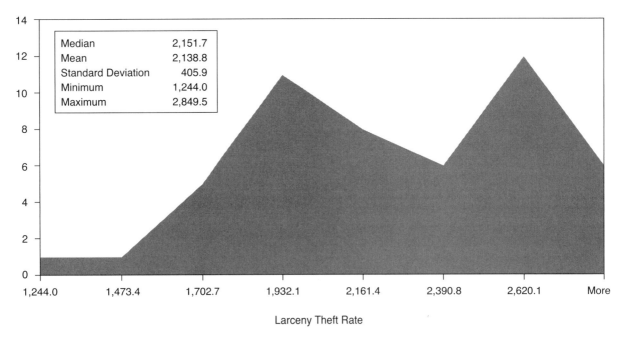

Median	2,151.7
Mean	2,138.8
Standard Deviation	405.9
Minimum	1,244.0
Maximum	2,849.5

Larceny Theft Rate

The 2010 State Crime Rate Rankings

ALPHA ORDER

RANK	STATE	SUM	09 RANK	CHANGE
40	Alabama	16.57	38	-2
37	Alaska	13.15	44	7
42	Arizona	17.46	43	1
41	Arkansas	16.81	40	-1
36	California	13.11	37	1
24	Colorado	(16.68)	24	0
16	Connecticut	(32.16)	10	-6
44	Delaware	28.09	34	-10
45	Florida	30.23	46	1
39	Georgia	15.62	39	0
23	Hawaii	(21.06)	23	0
5	Idaho	(46.52)	11	6
31	Illinois	3.95	31	0
26	Indiana	(12.33)	26	0
10	Iowa	(37.77)	8	-2
27	Kansas	(8.19)	29	2
22	Kentucky	(21.35)	22	0
48	Louisiana	36.24	49	1
4	Maine	(53.73)	3	-1
43	Maryland	27.12	42	-1
21	Massachusetts	(22.40)	21	0
34	Michigan	12.74	41	7
14	Minnesota	(34.04)	18	4
28	Mississippi	(5.62)	27	-1
32	Missouri	10.81	32	0
7	Montana	(44.19)	6	-1
20	Nebraska	(25.88)	19	-1
50	Nevada	51.59	50	0
1	New Hampshire	(57.61)	1	0
19	New Jersey	(29.81)	16	-3
49	New Mexico	42.64	47	-2
15	New York	(32.19)	15	0
33	North Carolina	11.98	33	0
3	North Dakota	(54.61)	4	1
30	Ohio	(2.76)	28	-2
38	Oklahoma	13.18	35	-3
17	Oregon	(30.07)	20	3
25	Pennsylvania	(15.52)	25	0
18	Rhode Island	(29.84)	9	-9
47	South Carolina	35.68	48	1
9	South Dakota	(37.84)	5	-4
46	Tennessee	30.31	45	-1
35	Texas	13.03	36	1
12	Utah	(36.77)	17	5
2	Vermont	(54.76)	2	0
13	Virginia	(35.18)	14	1
29	Washington	(4.34)	30	1
11	West Virginia	(37.33)	12	1
8	Wisconsin	(38.50)	13	5
6	Wyoming	(45.69)	7	1

RANK ORDER

RANK	STATE	SUM	09 RANK	CHANGE
1	New Hampshire	(57.61)	1	0
2	Vermont	(54.76)	2	0
3	North Dakota	(54.61)	4	1
4	Maine	(53.73)	3	-1
5	Idaho	(46.52)	11	6
6	Wyoming	(45.69)	7	1
7	Montana	(44.19)	6	-1
8	Wisconsin	(38.50)	13	5
9	South Dakota	(37.84)	5	-4
10	Iowa	(37.77)	8	-2
11	West Virginia	(37.33)	12	1
12	Utah	(36.77)	17	5
13	Virginia	(35.18)	14	1
14	Minnesota	(34.04)	18	4
15	New York	(32.19)	15	0
16	Connecticut	(32.16)	10	-6
17	Oregon	(30.07)	20	3
18	Rhode Island	(29.84)	9	-9
19	New Jersey	(29.81)	16	-3
20	Nebraska	(25.88)	19	-1
21	Massachusetts	(22.40)	21	0
22	Kentucky	(21.35)	22	0
23	Hawaii	(21.06)	23	0
24	Colorado	(16.68)	24	0
25	Pennsylvania	(15.52)	25	0
26	Indiana	(12.33)	26	0
27	Kansas	(8.19)	29	2
28	Mississippi	(5.62)	27	-1
29	Washington	(4.34)	30	1
30	Ohio	(2.76)	28	-2
31	Illinois	3.95	31	0
32	Missouri	10.81	32	0
33	North Carolina	11.98	33	0
34	Michigan	12.74	41	7
35	Texas	13.03	36	1
36	California	13.11	37	1
37	Alaska	13.15	44	7
38	Oklahoma	13.18	35	-3
39	Georgia	15.62	39	0
40	Alabama	16.57	38	-2
41	Arkansas	16.81	40	-1
42	Arizona	17.46	43	1
43	Maryland	27.12	42	-1
44	Delaware	28.09	34	-10
45	Florida	30.23	46	1
46	Tennessee	30.31	45	-1
47	South Carolina	35.68	48	1
48	Louisiana	36.24	49	1
49	New Mexico	42.64	47	-2
50	Nevada	51.59	50	0

I. ARRESTS

Important Note Regarding Arrest Numbers

The state arrest numbers reported by the FBI and shown on pages 3 to 38 are only from those law enforcement agencies that submitted complete arrests reports for 12 months in 2008. The arrest rates were calculated by the editors using population totals provided by the FBI for those jurisdictions reporting. Reports from law enforcement agencies in Illinois, Kentucky, and the District of Columbia were insufficient to calculate rates. Reports from New York and Mississippi represented less than half of their state population. Rates for these states should be interpreted with caution.

Reported Arrests in 2008

National Total = 11,859,179 Reported Arrests*

ALPHA ORDER

RANK	STATE	ARRESTS	% of USA
20	Alabama	212,192	1.8%
44	Alaska	38,294	0.3%
8	Arizona	334,238	2.8%
29	Arkansas	138,372	1.2%
1	California	1,547,811	13.1%
18	Colorado	221,175	1.9%
30	Connecticut	123,405	1.0%
41	Delaware	42,641	0.4%
2	Florida	1,149,818	9.7%
15	Georgia	268,869	2.3%
39	Hawaii	52,818	0.4%
37	Idaho	71,854	0.6%
23	Illinois	172,433	1.5%
19	Indiana	220,709	1.9%
31	Iowa	116,614	1.0%
35	Kansas	80,352	0.7%
45	Kentucky	35,973	0.3%
28	Louisiana	140,519	1.2%
38	Maine	57,060	0.5%
13	Maryland	300,165	2.5%
26	Massachusetts	149,582	1.3%
14	Michigan	276,904	2.3%
21	Minnesota	204,367	1.7%
33	Mississippi	108,280	0.9%
9	Missouri	332,126	2.8%
47	Montana	32,378	0.3%
34	Nebraska	89,301	0.8%
24	Nevada	166,395	1.4%
40	New Hampshire	43,634	0.4%
7	New Jersey	386,427	3.3%
36	New Mexico	78,500	0.7%
12	New York	300,683	2.5%
5	North Carolina	413,895	3.5%
48	North Dakota	27,896	0.2%
16	Ohio	249,113	2.1%
25	Oklahoma	161,466	1.4%
27	Oregon	147,653	1.2%
4	Pennsylvania	483,711	4.1%
46	Rhode Island	35,157	0.3%
22	South Carolina	177,424	1.5%
49	South Dakota	27,721	0.2%
11	Tennessee	309,981	2.6%
3	Texas	1,141,646	9.6%
32	Utah	114,017	1.0%
50	Vermont	13,533	0.1%
10	Virginia	331,159	2.8%
17	Washington	228,993	1.9%
42	West Virginia	41,681	0.4%
6	Wisconsin	411,968	3.5%
43	Wyoming	40,979	0.3%

RANK ORDER

RANK	STATE	ARRESTS	% of USA
1	California	1,547,811	13.1%
2	Florida	1,149,818	9.7%
3	Texas	1,141,646	9.6%
4	Pennsylvania	483,711	4.1%
5	North Carolina	413,895	3.5%
6	Wisconsin	411,968	3.5%
7	New Jersey	386,427	3.3%
8	Arizona	334,238	2.8%
9	Missouri	332,126	2.8%
10	Virginia	331,159	2.8%
11	Tennessee	309,981	2.6%
12	New York	300,683	2.5%
13	Maryland	300,165	2.5%
14	Michigan	276,904	2.3%
15	Georgia	268,869	2.3%
16	Ohio	249,113	2.1%
17	Washington	228,993	1.9%
18	Colorado	221,175	1.9%
19	Indiana	220,709	1.9%
20	Alabama	212,192	1.8%
21	Minnesota	204,367	1.7%
22	South Carolina	177,424	1.5%
23	Illinois	172,433	1.5%
24	Nevada	166,395	1.4%
25	Oklahoma	161,466	1.4%
26	Massachusetts	149,582	1.3%
27	Oregon	147,653	1.2%
28	Louisiana	140,519	1.2%
29	Arkansas	138,372	1.2%
30	Connecticut	123,405	1.0%
31	Iowa	116,614	1.0%
32	Utah	114,017	1.0%
33	Mississippi	108,280	0.9%
34	Nebraska	89,301	0.8%
35	Kansas	80,352	0.7%
36	New Mexico	78,500	0.7%
37	Idaho	71,854	0.6%
38	Maine	57,060	0.5%
39	Hawaii	52,818	0.4%
40	New Hampshire	43,634	0.4%
41	Delaware	42,641	0.4%
42	West Virginia	41,681	0.4%
43	Wyoming	40,979	0.3%
44	Alaska	38,294	0.3%
45	Kentucky	35,973	0.3%
46	Rhode Island	35,157	0.3%
47	Montana	32,378	0.3%
48	North Dakota	27,896	0.2%
49	South Dakota	27,721	0.2%
50	Vermont	13,533	0.1%
	District of Columbia**	NA	NA

Source: Reported data from the Federal Bureau of Investigation
   "Crime in the United States 2008" (Uniform Crime Reports, September 14, 2009, http://www.fbi.gov/ucr/ucr.htm)
*By law enforcement agencies submitting complete reports to the F.B.I. for 12 months in 2008. The F.B.I. estimates 14,005,615 reported and unreported arrests occurred in 2008. See important note at beginning of this chapter.
**Not available.

Reported Arrest Rate in 2008

National Rate = 4,759.1 Reported Arrests per 100,000 Population*

ALPHA ORDER

RANK	STATE	RATE
12	Alabama	5,624.0
10	Alaska	5,745.7
16	Arizona	5,210.5
9	Arkansas	5,756.5
33	California	4,234.2
17	Colorado	5,073.3
40	Connecticut	3,824.4
19	Delaware	4,883.9
5	Florida	6,285.1
27	Georgia	4,484.7
26	Hawaii	4,612.1
18	Idaho	5,006.7
NA	Illinois**	NA
24	Indiana	4,737.7
35	Iowa	4,216.3
32	Kansas	4,238.4
NA	Kentucky**	NA
11	Louisiana	5,684.5
31	Maine	4,341.8
15	Maryland	5,384.8
48	Massachusetts	2,570.2
46	Michigan	3,195.7
38	Minnesota	4,027.7
1	Mississippi	8,278.2
8	Missouri	5,992.0
43	Montana	3,471.7
13	Nebraska	5,464.6
4	Nevada	6,536.8
34	New Hampshire	4,226.0
25	New Jersey	4,625.0
14	New Mexico	5,429.0
45	New York	3,259.9
7	North Carolina	6,258.9
22	North Dakota	4,804.8
42	Ohio	3,628.1
28	Oklahoma	4,438.2
36	Oregon	4,045.6
39	Pennsylvania	4,024.1
44	Rhode Island	3,345.8
37	South Carolina	4,033.1
29	South Dakota	4,398.7
6	Tennessee	6,264.7
20	Texas	4,883.7
23	Utah	4,797.0
47	Vermont	2,654.7
30	Virginia	4,390.0
21	Washington	4,809.6
41	West Virginia	3,757.3
3	Wisconsin	7,435.5
2	Wyoming	7,761.0

RANK ORDER

RANK	STATE	RATE
1	Mississippi	8,278.2
2	Wyoming	7,761.0
3	Wisconsin	7,435.5
4	Nevada	6,536.8
5	Florida	6,285.1
6	Tennessee	6,264.7
7	North Carolina	6,258.9
8	Missouri	5,992.0
9	Arkansas	5,756.5
10	Alaska	5,745.7
11	Louisiana	5,684.5
12	Alabama	5,624.0
13	Nebraska	5,464.6
14	New Mexico	5,429.0
15	Maryland	5,384.8
16	Arizona	5,210.5
17	Colorado	5,073.3
18	Idaho	5,006.7
19	Delaware	4,883.9
20	Texas	4,883.7
21	Washington	4,809.6
22	North Dakota	4,804.8
23	Utah	4,797.0
24	Indiana	4,737.7
25	New Jersey	4,625.0
26	Hawaii	4,612.1
27	Georgia	4,484.7
28	Oklahoma	4,438.2
29	South Dakota	4,398.7
30	Virginia	4,390.0
31	Maine	4,341.8
32	Kansas	4,238.4
33	California	4,234.2
34	New Hampshire	4,226.0
35	Iowa	4,216.3
36	Oregon	4,045.6
37	South Carolina	4,033.1
38	Minnesota	4,027.7
39	Pennsylvania	4,024.1
40	Connecticut	3,824.4
41	West Virginia	3,757.3
42	Ohio	3,628.1
43	Montana	3,471.7
44	Rhode Island	3,345.8
45	New York	3,259.9
46	Michigan	3,195.7
47	Vermont	2,654.7
48	Massachusetts	2,570.2
NA	Illinois**	NA
NA	Kentucky**	NA
	District of Columbia**	NA

Source: CQ Press using reported data from the Federal Bureau of Investigation
   "Crime in the United States 2008" (Uniform Crime Reports, September 14, 2009, http://www.fbi.gov/ucr/ucr.htm)
*By law enforcement agencies submitting complete reports to the F.B.I. for 12 months in 2008. These rates based on population estimates for areas under the jurisdiction of those agencies reporting. Arrest rate based on the F.B.I. estimate of total arrests is 4,637.7 reported and unreported arrests per 100,000 population. See important note at beginning of this chapter.
**Not available.

Reported Arrests for Crime Index Offenses in 2008

National Total = 1,965,272 Reported Arrests*

<u>ALPHA ORDER</u>

RANK	STATE	ARRESTS	% of USA
23	Alabama	31,037	1.6%
42	Alaska	6,229	0.3%
10	Arizona	51,130	2.6%
31	Arkansas	20,186	1.0%
1	California	295,781	15.1%
22	Colorado	31,661	1.6%
28	Connecticut	23,075	1.2%
36	Delaware	9,688	0.5%
2	Florida	202,682	10.3%
12	Georgia	48,891	2.5%
43	Hawaii	5,842	0.3%
40	Idaho	8,434	0.4%
20	Illinois	32,083	1.6%
18	Indiana	38,878	2.0%
32	Iowa	18,180	0.9%
37	Kansas	9,678	0.5%
39	Kentucky	8,517	0.4%
25	Louisiana	28,978	1.5%
38	Maine	9,060	0.5%
9	Maryland	51,148	2.6%
24	Massachusetts	30,945	1.6%
14	Michigan	47,564	2.4%
19	Minnesota	34,857	1.8%
33	Mississippi	13,055	0.7%
7	Missouri	57,781	2.9%
44	Montana	5,469	0.3%
35	Nebraska	11,569	0.6%
27	Nevada	24,058	1.2%
46	New Hampshire	3,789	0.2%
13	New Jersey	48,613	2.5%
34	New Mexico	12,467	0.6%
6	New York	62,235	3.2%
5	North Carolina	79,250	4.0%
48	North Dakota	3,383	0.2%
15	Ohio	42,269	2.2%
29	Oklahoma	22,985	1.2%
21	Oregon	32,046	1.6%
4	Pennsylvania	86,632	4.4%
45	Rhode Island	4,632	0.2%
26	South Carolina	25,447	1.3%
49	South Dakota	3,247	0.2%
8	Tennessee	53,332	2.7%
3	Texas	165,017	8.4%
30	Utah	20,769	1.1%
50	Vermont	2,170	0.1%
16	Virginia	40,540	2.1%
17	Washington	39,295	2.0%
41	West Virginia	6,339	0.3%
11	Wisconsin	50,475	2.6%
47	Wyoming	3,706	0.2%

<u>RANK ORDER</u>

RANK	STATE	ARRESTS	% of USA
1	California	295,781	15.1%
2	Florida	202,682	10.3%
3	Texas	165,017	8.4%
4	Pennsylvania	86,632	4.4%
5	North Carolina	79,250	4.0%
6	New York	62,235	3.2%
7	Missouri	57,781	2.9%
8	Tennessee	53,332	2.7%
9	Maryland	51,148	2.6%
10	Arizona	51,130	2.6%
11	Wisconsin	50,475	2.6%
12	Georgia	48,891	2.5%
13	New Jersey	48,613	2.5%
14	Michigan	47,564	2.4%
15	Ohio	42,269	2.2%
16	Virginia	40,540	2.1%
17	Washington	39,295	2.0%
18	Indiana	38,878	2.0%
19	Minnesota	34,857	1.8%
20	Illinois	32,083	1.6%
21	Oregon	32,046	1.6%
22	Colorado	31,661	1.6%
23	Alabama	31,037	1.6%
24	Massachusetts	30,945	1.6%
25	Louisiana	28,978	1.5%
26	South Carolina	25,447	1.3%
27	Nevada	24,058	1.2%
28	Connecticut	23,075	1.2%
29	Oklahoma	22,985	1.2%
30	Utah	20,769	1.1%
31	Arkansas	20,186	1.0%
32	Iowa	18,180	0.9%
33	Mississippi	13,055	0.7%
34	New Mexico	12,467	0.6%
35	Nebraska	11,569	0.6%
36	Delaware	9,688	0.5%
37	Kansas	9,678	0.5%
38	Maine	9,060	0.5%
39	Kentucky	8,517	0.4%
40	Idaho	8,434	0.4%
41	West Virginia	6,339	0.3%
42	Alaska	6,229	0.3%
43	Hawaii	5,842	0.3%
44	Montana	5,469	0.3%
45	Rhode Island	4,632	0.2%
46	New Hampshire	3,789	0.2%
47	Wyoming	3,706	0.2%
48	North Dakota	3,383	0.2%
49	South Dakota	3,247	0.2%
50	Vermont	2,170	0.1%
	District of Columbia**	NA	NA

Source: CQ Press using reported data from the Federal Bureau of Investigation
   "Crime in the United States 2008" (Uniform Crime Reports, September 14, 2009, http://www.fbi.gov/ucr/ucr.htm)
*By law enforcement agencies submitting complete reports to the F.B.I. for 12 months in 2008. The F.B.I. estimates 2,282,256 reported and unreported arrests for crime index offenses occurred in 2008. Crime index offenses consist of murder, forcible rape, robbery, aggravated assault, burglary, larceny-theft, motor vehicle theft, and arson. See important note at beginning of this chapter. **Not available.

Reported Arrest Rate for Crime Index Offenses in 2008

National Rate = 788.7 Reported Arrests per 100,000 Population*

ALPHA ORDER

RANK	STATE	RATE
18	Alabama	822.6
9	Alaska	934.6
21	Arizona	797.1
15	Arkansas	839.8
20	California	809.1
22	Colorado	726.2
24	Connecticut	715.1
3	Delaware	1,109.6
4	Florida	1,107.9
19	Georgia	815.5
45	Hawaii	510.1
34	Idaho	587.7
NA	Illinois**	NA
16	Indiana	834.6
31	Iowa	657.3
44	Kansas	510.5
NA	Kentucky**	NA
2	Louisiana	1,172.3
28	Maine	689.4
10	Maryland	917.6
42	Massachusetts	531.7
40	Michigan	548.9
29	Minnesota	687.0
7	Mississippi	998.1
6	Missouri	1,042.4
35	Montana	586.4
25	Nebraska	707.9
8	Nevada	945.1
48	New Hampshire	367.0
37	New Jersey	581.8
14	New Mexico	862.2
30	New York	674.7
1	North Carolina	1,198.4
36	North Dakota	582.7
33	Ohio	615.6
32	Oklahoma	631.8
12	Oregon	878.0
23	Pennsylvania	720.7
46	Rhode Island	440.8
38	South Carolina	578.4
43	South Dakota	515.2
5	Tennessee	1,077.8
26	Texas	705.9
13	Utah	873.8
47	Vermont	425.7
41	Virginia	537.4
17	Washington	825.3
39	West Virginia	571.4
11	Wisconsin	911.0
27	Wyoming	701.9

RANK ORDER

RANK	STATE	RATE
1	North Carolina	1,198.4
2	Louisiana	1,172.3
3	Delaware	1,109.6
4	Florida	1,107.9
5	Tennessee	1,077.8
6	Missouri	1,042.4
7	Mississippi	998.1
8	Nevada	945.1
9	Alaska	934.6
10	Maryland	917.6
11	Wisconsin	911.0
12	Oregon	878.0
13	Utah	873.8
14	New Mexico	862.2
15	Arkansas	839.8
16	Indiana	834.6
17	Washington	825.3
18	Alabama	822.6
19	Georgia	815.5
20	California	809.1
21	Arizona	797.1
22	Colorado	726.2
23	Pennsylvania	720.7
24	Connecticut	715.1
25	Nebraska	707.9
26	Texas	705.9
27	Wyoming	701.9
28	Maine	689.4
29	Minnesota	687.0
30	New York	674.7
31	Iowa	657.3
32	Oklahoma	631.8
33	Ohio	615.6
34	Idaho	587.7
35	Montana	586.4
36	North Dakota	582.7
37	New Jersey	581.8
38	South Carolina	578.4
39	West Virginia	571.4
40	Michigan	548.9
41	Virginia	537.4
42	Massachusetts	531.7
43	South Dakota	515.2
44	Kansas	510.5
45	Hawaii	510.1
46	Rhode Island	440.8
47	Vermont	425.7
48	New Hampshire	367.0
NA	Illinois**	NA
NA	Kentucky**	NA
	District of Columbia**	NA

Source: CQ Press using reported data from the Federal Bureau of Investigation
  "Crime in the United States 2008" (Uniform Crime Reports, September 14, 2009, http://www.fbi.gov/ucr/ucr.htm)
*By law enforcement agencies submitting complete reports to the F.B.I. for 12 months in 2008. These rates based on population estimates for areas under the jurisdiction of those agencies reporting. Arrest rate based on the F.B.I. estimate of reported and unreported arrests for crime index offenses is 750.6 arrests per 100,000 population. See important note at beginning of this chapter. **Not available.

Reported Arrests for Violent Crime in 2008

National Total = 510,195 Reported Arrests*

ALPHA ORDER					RANK ORDER			
RANK	STATE	ARRESTS	% of USA		RANK	STATE	ARRESTS	% of USA
23	Alabama	6,541	1.3%		1	California	125,235	24.5%
35	Alaska	2,121	0.4%		2	Florida	52,740	10.3%
15	Arizona	9,226	1.8%		3	Texas	34,235	6.7%
30	Arkansas	4,749	0.9%		4	Pennsylvania	25,776	5.1%
1	California	125,235	24.5%		5	North Carolina	18,852	3.7%
25	Colorado	6,208	1.2%		6	New Jersey	13,948	2.7%
27	Connecticut	5,934	1.2%		7	Tennessee	13,626	2.7%
33	Delaware	2,942	0.6%		8	New York	13,320	2.6%
2	Florida	52,740	10.3%		9	Maryland	13,001	2.5%
13	Georgia	11,489	2.3%		10	Missouri	12,520	2.5%
41	Hawaii	1,319	0.3%		11	Massachusetts	12,474	2.4%
40	Idaho	1,425	0.3%		12	Michigan	12,398	2.4%
16	Illinois	8,711	1.7%		13	Georgia	11,489	2.3%
17	Indiana	8,351	1.6%		14	Louisiana	9,236	1.8%
31	Iowa	4,230	0.8%		15	Arizona	9,226	1.8%
34	Kansas	2,491	0.5%		16	Illinois	8,711	1.7%
39	Kentucky	1,817	0.4%		17	Indiana	8,351	1.6%
14	Louisiana	9,236	1.8%		18	Wisconsin	8,050	1.6%
45	Maine	735	0.1%		19	Virginia	7,457	1.5%
9	Maryland	13,001	2.5%		20	South Carolina	7,270	1.4%
11	Massachusetts	12,474	2.4%		21	Washington	6,943	1.4%
12	Michigan	12,398	2.4%		22	Ohio	6,808	1.3%
28	Minnesota	5,612	1.1%		23	Alabama	6,541	1.3%
38	Mississippi	1,946	0.4%		24	Nevada	6,516	1.3%
10	Missouri	12,520	2.5%		25	Colorado	6,208	1.2%
44	Montana	852	0.2%		26	Oklahoma	5,956	1.2%
37	Nebraska	1,967	0.4%		27	Connecticut	5,934	1.2%
24	Nevada	6,516	1.3%		28	Minnesota	5,612	1.1%
47	New Hampshire	624	0.1%		29	Oregon	4,844	0.9%
6	New Jersey	13,948	2.7%		30	Arkansas	4,749	0.9%
32	New Mexico	3,464	0.7%		31	Iowa	4,230	0.8%
8	New York	13,320	2.6%		32	New Mexico	3,464	0.7%
5	North Carolina	18,852	3.7%		33	Delaware	2,942	0.6%
50	North Dakota	408	0.1%		34	Kansas	2,491	0.5%
22	Ohio	6,808	1.3%		35	Alaska	2,121	0.4%
26	Oklahoma	5,956	1.2%		36	Utah	2,044	0.4%
29	Oregon	4,844	0.9%		37	Nebraska	1,967	0.4%
4	Pennsylvania	25,776	5.1%		38	Mississippi	1,946	0.4%
43	Rhode Island	876	0.2%		39	Kentucky	1,817	0.4%
20	South Carolina	7,270	1.4%		40	Idaho	1,425	0.3%
48	South Dakota	465	0.1%		41	Hawaii	1,319	0.3%
7	Tennessee	13,626	2.7%		42	West Virginia	1,280	0.3%
3	Texas	34,235	6.7%		43	Rhode Island	876	0.2%
36	Utah	2,044	0.4%		44	Montana	852	0.2%
49	Vermont	456	0.1%		45	Maine	735	0.1%
19	Virginia	7,457	1.5%		46	Wyoming	633	0.1%
21	Washington	6,943	1.4%		47	New Hampshire	624	0.1%
42	West Virginia	1,280	0.3%		48	South Dakota	465	0.1%
18	Wisconsin	8,050	1.6%		49	Vermont	456	0.1%
46	Wyoming	633	0.1%		50	North Dakota	408	0.1%
						District of Columbia**	NA	NA

Source: Reported data from the Federal Bureau of Investigation
   "Crime in the United States 2008" (Uniform Crime Reports, September 14, 2009, http://www.fbi.gov/ucr/ucr.htm)
*By law enforcement agencies submitting complete reports to the F.B.I. for 12 months in 2008. The F.B.I. estimates 594,911 reported and unreported arrests for violent crimes occurred in 2008. Violent crimes are offenses of murder, forcible rape, robbery, and aggravated assault. See important note at beginning of this chapter.
**Not available.

Reported Arrest Rate for Violent Crime in 2008

National Rate = 204.7 Reported Arrests per 100,000 Population*

ALPHA ORDER

RANK ORDER

RANK	STATE	RATE		RANK	STATE	RATE
18	Alabama	173.4		1	Louisiana	373.6
4	Alaska	318.2		2	California	342.6
28	Arizona	143.8		3	Delaware	337.0
14	Arkansas	197.6		4	Alaska	318.2
2	California	342.6		5	Florida	288.3
30	Colorado	142.4		6	North Carolina	285.1
16	Connecticut	183.9		7	Tennessee	275.4
3	Delaware	337.0		8	Nevada	256.0
5	Florida	288.3		9	New Mexico	239.6
15	Georgia	191.6		10	Maryland	233.2
36	Hawaii	115.2		11	Missouri	225.9
38	Idaho	99.3		12	Pennsylvania	214.4
NA	Illinois**	NA		13	Massachusetts	214.3
17	Indiana	179.3		14	Arkansas	197.6
22	Iowa	152.9		15	Georgia	191.6
32	Kansas	131.4		16	Connecticut	183.9
NA	Kentucky**	NA		17	Indiana	179.3
1	Louisiana	373.6		18	Alabama	173.4
48	Maine	55.9		19	New Jersey	166.9
10	Maryland	233.2		20	South Carolina	165.3
13	Massachusetts	214.3		21	Oklahoma	163.7
29	Michigan	143.1		22	Iowa	152.9
37	Minnesota	110.6		23	Mississippi	148.8
23	Mississippi	148.8		24	Texas	146.4
11	Missouri	225.9		25	Washington	145.8
41	Montana	91.4		26	Wisconsin	145.3
33	Nebraska	120.4		27	New York	144.4
8	Nevada	256.0		28	Arizona	143.8
47	New Hampshire	60.4		29	Michigan	143.1
19	New Jersey	166.9		30	Colorado	142.4
9	New Mexico	239.6		31	Oregon	132.7
27	New York	144.4		32	Kansas	131.4
6	North Carolina	285.1		33	Nebraska	120.4
46	North Dakota	70.3		34	Wyoming	119.9
39	Ohio	99.2		35	West Virginia	115.4
21	Oklahoma	163.7		36	Hawaii	115.2
31	Oregon	132.7		37	Minnesota	110.6
12	Pennsylvania	214.4		38	Idaho	99.3
44	Rhode Island	83.4		39	Ohio	99.2
20	South Carolina	165.3		40	Virginia	98.9
45	South Dakota	73.8		41	Montana	91.4
7	Tennessee	275.4		42	Vermont	89.5
24	Texas	146.4		43	Utah	86.0
43	Utah	86.0		44	Rhode Island	83.4
42	Vermont	89.5		45	South Dakota	73.8
40	Virginia	98.9		46	North Dakota	70.3
25	Washington	145.8		47	New Hampshire	60.4
35	West Virginia	115.4		48	Maine	55.9
26	Wisconsin	145.3		NA	Illinois**	NA
34	Wyoming	119.9		NA	Kentucky**	NA
					District of Columbia**	NA

Source: CQ Press using reported data from the Federal Bureau of Investigation
    "Crime in the United States 2008" (Uniform Crime Reports, September 14, 2009, http://www.fbi.gov/ucr/ucr.htm)
*By law enforcement agencies submitting complete reports to the F.B.I. for 12 months in 2008. These rates based on population estimates for areas under the jurisdiction of those agencies reporting. Arrest rate based on the F.B.I. estimate of reported and unreported arrests for violent crimes is 195.7 arrests per 100,000 population. See important note at beginning of this chapter.
**Not available.

Reported Arrests for Murder in 2008

National Total = 10,770 Reported Arrests*

ALPHA ORDER

RANK	STATE	ARRESTS	% of USA
9	Alabama	315	2.9%
40	Alaska	22	0.2%
10	Arizona	310	2.9%
26	Arkansas	118	1.1%
1	California	1,850	17.2%
22	Colorado	155	1.4%
28	Connecticut	110	1.0%
38	Delaware	32	0.3%
2	Florida	882	8.2%
8	Georgia	320	3.0%
41	Hawaii	18	0.2%
42	Idaho	14	0.1%
6	Illinois	364	3.4%
16	Indiana	268	2.5%
34	Iowa	50	0.5%
35	Kansas	47	0.4%
33	Kentucky	55	0.5%
20	Louisiana	183	1.7%
47	Maine	8	0.1%
12	Maryland	307	2.9%
31	Massachusetts	77	0.7%
24	Michigan	142	1.3%
27	Minnesota	111	1.0%
25	Mississippi	135	1.3%
7	Missouri	356	3.3%
46	Montana	11	0.1%
37	Nebraska	43	0.4%
23	Nevada	146	1.4%
49	New Hampshire	5	0.0%
14	New Jersey	276	2.6%
32	New Mexico	71	0.7%
15	New York	273	2.5%
4	North Carolina	578	5.4%
50	North Dakota	3	0.0%
19	Ohio	186	1.7%
21	Oklahoma	160	1.5%
30	Oregon	95	0.9%
5	Pennsylvania	576	5.3%
45	Rhode Island	12	0.1%
17	South Carolina	198	1.8%
44	South Dakota	13	0.1%
13	Tennessee	304	2.8%
3	Texas	863	8.0%
35	Utah	47	0.4%
47	Vermont	8	0.1%
11	Virginia	309	2.9%
29	Washington	104	1.0%
39	West Virginia	31	0.3%
18	Wisconsin	195	1.8%
42	Wyoming	14	0.1%

RANK ORDER

RANK	STATE	ARRESTS	% of USA
1	California	1,850	17.2%
2	Florida	882	8.2%
3	Texas	863	8.0%
4	North Carolina	578	5.4%
5	Pennsylvania	576	5.3%
6	Illinois	364	3.4%
7	Missouri	356	3.3%
8	Georgia	320	3.0%
9	Alabama	315	2.9%
10	Arizona	310	2.9%
11	Virginia	309	2.9%
12	Maryland	307	2.9%
13	Tennessee	304	2.8%
14	New Jersey	276	2.6%
15	New York	273	2.5%
16	Indiana	268	2.5%
17	South Carolina	198	1.8%
18	Wisconsin	195	1.8%
19	Ohio	186	1.7%
20	Louisiana	183	1.7%
21	Oklahoma	160	1.5%
22	Colorado	155	1.4%
23	Nevada	146	1.4%
24	Michigan	142	1.3%
25	Mississippi	135	1.3%
26	Arkansas	118	1.1%
27	Minnesota	111	1.0%
28	Connecticut	110	1.0%
29	Washington	104	1.0%
30	Oregon	95	0.9%
31	Massachusetts	77	0.7%
32	New Mexico	71	0.7%
33	Kentucky	55	0.5%
34	Iowa	50	0.5%
35	Kansas	47	0.4%
35	Utah	47	0.4%
37	Nebraska	43	0.4%
38	Delaware	32	0.3%
39	West Virginia	31	0.3%
40	Alaska	22	0.2%
41	Hawaii	18	0.2%
42	Idaho	14	0.1%
42	Wyoming	14	0.1%
44	South Dakota	13	0.1%
45	Rhode Island	12	0.1%
46	Montana	11	0.1%
47	Maine	8	0.1%
47	Vermont	8	0.1%
49	New Hampshire	5	0.0%
50	North Dakota	3	0.0%
	District of Columbia**	NA	NA

Source: Reported data from the Federal Bureau of Investigation
"Crime in the United States 2008" (Uniform Crime Reports, September 14, 2009, http://www.fbi.gov/ucr/ucr.htm)
*By law enforcement agencies submitting complete reports to the F.B.I. for 12 months in 2008. The F.B.I. estimates 12,955 reported and unreported arrests for murder occurred in 2008. Murder includes nonnegligent manslaughter. See important note at beginning of this chapter.
**Not available.

Reported Arrest Rate for Murder in 2008

National Rate = 4.3 Reported Arrests per 100,000 Population*

ALPHA ORDER				RANK ORDER		
RANK	STATE	RATE		RANK	STATE	RATE
3	Alabama	8.3		1	Mississippi	10.3
25	Alaska	3.3		2	North Carolina	8.7
14	Arizona	4.8		3	Alabama	8.3
12	Arkansas	4.9		4	Louisiana	7.4
11	California	5.1		5	Missouri	6.4
22	Colorado	3.6		6	Tennessee	6.1
24	Connecticut	3.4		7	Indiana	5.8
20	Delaware	3.7		8	Nevada	5.7
14	Florida	4.8		9	Maryland	5.5
10	Georgia	5.3		10	Georgia	5.3
39	Hawaii	1.6		11	California	5.1
45	Idaho	1.0		12	Arkansas	4.9
NA	Illinois**	NA		12	New Mexico	4.9
7	Indiana	5.8		14	Arizona	4.8
38	Iowa	1.8		14	Florida	4.8
33	Kansas	2.5		14	Pennsylvania	4.8
NA	Kentucky**	NA		17	South Carolina	4.5
4	Louisiana	7.4		18	Oklahoma	4.4
46	Maine	0.6		19	Virginia	4.1
9	Maryland	5.5		20	Delaware	3.7
42	Massachusetts	1.3		20	Texas	3.7
39	Michigan	1.6		22	Colorado	3.6
34	Minnesota	2.2		23	Wisconsin	3.5
1	Mississippi	10.3		24	Connecticut	3.4
5	Missouri	6.4		25	Alaska	3.3
43	Montana	1.2		25	New Jersey	3.3
31	Nebraska	2.6		27	New York	3.0
8	Nevada	5.7		28	West Virginia	2.8
47	New Hampshire	0.5		29	Ohio	2.7
25	New Jersey	3.3		29	Wyoming	2.7
12	New Mexico	4.9		31	Nebraska	2.6
27	New York	3.0		31	Oregon	2.6
2	North Carolina	8.7		33	Kansas	2.5
47	North Dakota	0.5		34	Minnesota	2.2
29	Ohio	2.7		34	Washington	2.2
18	Oklahoma	4.4		36	South Dakota	2.1
31	Oregon	2.6		37	Utah	2.0
14	Pennsylvania	4.8		38	Iowa	1.8
44	Rhode Island	1.1		39	Hawaii	1.6
17	South Carolina	4.5		39	Michigan	1.6
36	South Dakota	2.1		39	Vermont	1.6
6	Tennessee	6.1		42	Massachusetts	1.3
20	Texas	3.7		43	Montana	1.2
37	Utah	2.0		44	Rhode Island	1.1
39	Vermont	1.6		45	Idaho	1.0
19	Virginia	4.1		46	Maine	0.6
34	Washington	2.2		47	New Hampshire	0.5
28	West Virginia	2.8		47	North Dakota	0.5
23	Wisconsin	3.5		NA	Illinois**	NA
29	Wyoming	2.7		NA	Kentucky**	NA
					District of Columbia**	NA

Source: CQ Press using reported data from the Federal Bureau of Investigation
"Crime in the United States 2008" (Uniform Crime Reports, September 14, 2009, http://www.fbi.gov/ucr/ucr.htm)
*By law enforcement agencies submitting complete reports to the F.B.I. for 12 months in 2008. These rates based on population estimates for areas under the jurisdiction of those agencies reporting. Arrest rate based on the F.B.I. estimate of reported and unreported arrests for murder is 4.3 arrests per 100,000 population. See important note at beginning of this chapter.
**Not available.

Reported Arrests for Rape in 2008

National Total = 18,686 Reported Arrests*

ALPHA ORDER

RANK	STATE	ARRESTS	% of USA
17	Alabama	356	1.9%
44	Alaska	54	0.3%
29	Arizona	185	1.0%
28	Arkansas	194	1.0%
1	California	2,088	11.2%
12	Colorado	453	2.4%
26	Connecticut	244	1.3%
34	Delaware	138	0.7%
3	Florida	1,770	9.5%
20	Georgia	313	1.7%
38	Hawaii	102	0.5%
38	Idaho	102	0.5%
13	Illinois	452	2.4%
25	Indiana	262	1.4%
36	Iowa	108	0.6%
30	Kansas	183	1.0%
49	Kentucky	33	0.2%
27	Louisiana	238	1.3%
40	Maine	72	0.4%
14	Maryland	404	2.2%
21	Massachusetts	310	1.7%
7	Michigan	578	3.1%
37	Minnesota	106	0.6%
32	Mississippi	165	0.9%
8	Missouri	548	2.9%
50	Montana	25	0.1%
33	Nebraska	146	0.8%
24	Nevada	263	1.4%
42	New Hampshire	69	0.4%
15	New Jersey	372	2.0%
35	New Mexico	129	0.7%
9	New York	543	2.9%
10	North Carolina	520	2.8%
46	North Dakota	45	0.2%
11	Ohio	487	2.6%
19	Oklahoma	316	1.7%
23	Oregon	276	1.5%
4	Pennsylvania	1,167	6.2%
43	Rhode Island	58	0.3%
22	South Carolina	289	1.5%
45	South Dakota	53	0.3%
18	Tennessee	344	1.8%
2	Texas	2,034	10.9%
31	Utah	181	1.0%
41	Vermont	71	0.4%
16	Virginia	370	2.0%
6	Washington	675	3.6%
48	West Virginia	40	0.2%
5	Wisconsin	710	3.8%
46	Wyoming	45	0.2%

RANK ORDER

RANK	STATE	ARRESTS	% of USA
1	California	2,088	11.2%
2	Texas	2,034	10.9%
3	Florida	1,770	9.5%
4	Pennsylvania	1,167	6.2%
5	Wisconsin	710	3.8%
6	Washington	675	3.6%
7	Michigan	578	3.1%
8	Missouri	548	2.9%
9	New York	543	2.9%
10	North Carolina	520	2.8%
11	Ohio	487	2.6%
12	Colorado	453	2.4%
13	Illinois	452	2.4%
14	Maryland	404	2.2%
15	New Jersey	372	2.0%
16	Virginia	370	2.0%
17	Alabama	356	1.9%
18	Tennessee	344	1.8%
19	Oklahoma	316	1.7%
20	Georgia	313	1.7%
21	Massachusetts	310	1.7%
22	South Carolina	289	1.5%
23	Oregon	276	1.5%
24	Nevada	263	1.4%
25	Indiana	262	1.4%
26	Connecticut	244	1.3%
27	Louisiana	238	1.3%
28	Arkansas	194	1.0%
29	Arizona	185	1.0%
30	Kansas	183	1.0%
31	Utah	181	1.0%
32	Mississippi	165	0.9%
33	Nebraska	146	0.8%
34	Delaware	138	0.7%
35	New Mexico	129	0.7%
36	Iowa	108	0.6%
37	Minnesota	106	0.6%
38	Hawaii	102	0.5%
38	Idaho	102	0.5%
40	Maine	72	0.4%
41	Vermont	71	0.4%
42	New Hampshire	69	0.4%
43	Rhode Island	58	0.3%
44	Alaska	54	0.3%
45	South Dakota	53	0.3%
46	North Dakota	45	0.2%
46	Wyoming	45	0.2%
48	West Virginia	40	0.2%
49	Kentucky	33	0.2%
50	Montana	25	0.1%
	District of Columbia**	NA	NA

Source: Reported data from the Federal Bureau of Investigation
"Crime in the United States 2008" (Uniform Crime Reports, September 14, 2009, http://www.fbi.gov/ucr/ucr.htm)
*By law enforcement agencies submitting complete reports to the F.B.I. for 12 months in 2008. The F.B.I. estimates 22,584 reported and unreported arrests for rape occurred in 2008. Forcible rape is the carnal knowledge of a female forcibly and against her will. Assaults or attempts to commit rape by force or threat of force are included. See important note at beginning of this chapter. **Not available.

Reported Arrest Rate for Rape in 2008

National Rate = 7.5 Reported Arrests per 100,000 Population*

ALPHA ORDER

RANK	STATE	RATE
13	Alabama	9.4
21	Alaska	8.1
46	Arizona	2.9
21	Arkansas	8.1
36	California	5.7
6	Colorado	10.4
25	Connecticut	7.6
1	Delaware	15.8
9	Florida	9.7
41	Georgia	5.2
14	Hawaii	8.9
29	Idaho	7.1
NA	Illinois**	NA
37	Indiana	5.6
44	Iowa	3.9
9	Kansas	9.7
NA	Kentucky**	NA
12	Louisiana	9.6
38	Maine	5.5
28	Maryland	7.2
40	Massachusetts	5.3
32	Michigan	6.7
NA	Minnesota**	NA
5	Mississippi	12.6
8	Missouri	9.9
47	Montana	2.7
14	Nebraska	8.9
7	Nevada	10.3
32	New Hampshire	6.7
43	New Jersey	4.5
14	New Mexico	8.9
35	New York	5.9
23	North Carolina	7.9
24	North Dakota	7.8
29	Ohio	7.1
17	Oklahoma	8.7
25	Oregon	7.6
9	Pennsylvania	9.7
38	Rhode Island	5.5
34	South Carolina	6.6
20	South Dakota	8.4
31	Tennessee	7.0
17	Texas	8.7
25	Utah	7.6
3	Vermont	13.9
42	Virginia	4.9
2	Washington	14.2
45	West Virginia	3.6
4	Wisconsin	12.8
19	Wyoming	8.5

RANK ORDER

RANK	STATE	RATE
1	Delaware	15.8
2	Washington	14.2
3	Vermont	13.9
4	Wisconsin	12.8
5	Mississippi	12.6
6	Colorado	10.4
7	Nevada	10.3
8	Missouri	9.9
9	Florida	9.7
9	Kansas	9.7
9	Pennsylvania	9.7
12	Louisiana	9.6
13	Alabama	9.4
14	Hawaii	8.9
14	Nebraska	8.9
14	New Mexico	8.9
17	Oklahoma	8.7
17	Texas	8.7
19	Wyoming	8.5
20	South Dakota	8.4
21	Alaska	8.1
21	Arkansas	8.1
23	North Carolina	7.9
24	North Dakota	7.8
25	Connecticut	7.6
25	Oregon	7.6
25	Utah	7.6
28	Maryland	7.2
29	Idaho	7.1
29	Ohio	7.1
31	Tennessee	7.0
32	Michigan	6.7
32	New Hampshire	6.7
34	South Carolina	6.6
35	New York	5.9
36	California	5.7
37	Indiana	5.6
38	Maine	5.5
38	Rhode Island	5.5
40	Massachusetts	5.3
41	Georgia	5.2
42	Virginia	4.9
43	New Jersey	4.5
44	Iowa	3.9
45	West Virginia	3.6
46	Arizona	2.9
47	Montana	2.7
NA	Illinois**	NA
NA	Kentucky**	NA
NA	Minnesota**	NA
	District of Columbia**	NA

Source: CQ Press using reported data from the Federal Bureau of Investigation
"Crime in the United States 2008" (Uniform Crime Reports, September 14, 2009, http://www.fbi.gov/ucr/ucr.htm)
*By law enforcement agencies submitting complete reports to the F.B.I. for 12 months in 2008. These rates based on population estimates for areas under the jurisdiction of those agencies reporting. Arrest rate based on the F.B.I. estimate of reported and unreported arrests for rape is 7.4 arrests per 100,000 population. See important note at beginning of this chapter.
**Not available.

Reported Arrests for Robbery in 2008

National Total = 112,608 Reported Arrests*

ALPHA ORDER

RANK	STATE	ARRESTS	% of USA
17	Alabama	2,047	1.8%
40	Alaska	275	0.2%
18	Arizona	2,044	1.8%
31	Arkansas	623	0.6%
1	California	22,391	19.9%
28	Colorado	926	0.8%
25	Connecticut	1,245	1.1%
30	Delaware	713	0.6%
2	Florida	11,870	10.5%
9	Georgia	2,958	2.6%
38	Hawaii	393	0.3%
45	Idaho	97	0.1%
11	Illinois	2,922	2.6%
20	Indiana	1,930	1.7%
36	Iowa	404	0.4%
39	Kansas	285	0.3%
32	Kentucky	598	0.5%
27	Louisiana	1,035	0.9%
42	Maine	184	0.2%
5	Maryland	4,443	3.9%
16	Massachusetts	2,065	1.8%
13	Michigan	2,488	2.2%
24	Minnesota	1,286	1.1%
33	Mississippi	572	0.5%
14	Missouri	2,419	2.1%
46	Montana	47	0.0%
37	Nebraska	397	0.4%
21	Nevada	1,835	1.6%
43	New Hampshire	150	0.1%
6	New Jersey	4,371	3.9%
35	New Mexico	417	0.4%
8	New York	3,393	3.0%
7	North Carolina	4,364	3.9%
49	North Dakota	25	0.0%
12	Ohio	2,615	2.3%
29	Oklahoma	831	0.7%
26	Oregon	1,187	1.1%
4	Pennsylvania	7,412	6.6%
41	Rhode Island	259	0.2%
23	South Carolina	1,383	1.2%
48	South Dakota	31	0.0%
10	Tennessee	2,934	2.6%
3	Texas	8,199	7.3%
34	Utah	495	0.4%
50	Vermont	21	0.0%
15	Virginia	2,194	1.9%
22	Washington	1,637	1.5%
44	West Virginia	143	0.1%
19	Wisconsin	1,981	1.8%
47	Wyoming	35	0.0%

RANK ORDER

RANK	STATE	ARRESTS	% of USA
1	California	22,391	19.9%
2	Florida	11,870	10.5%
3	Texas	8,199	7.3%
4	Pennsylvania	7,412	6.6%
5	Maryland	4,443	3.9%
6	New Jersey	4,371	3.9%
7	North Carolina	4,364	3.9%
8	New York	3,393	3.0%
9	Georgia	2,958	2.6%
10	Tennessee	2,934	2.6%
11	Illinois	2,922	2.6%
12	Ohio	2,615	2.3%
13	Michigan	2,488	2.2%
14	Missouri	2,419	2.1%
15	Virginia	2,194	1.9%
16	Massachusetts	2,065	1.8%
17	Alabama	2,047	1.8%
18	Arizona	2,044	1.8%
19	Wisconsin	1,981	1.8%
20	Indiana	1,930	1.7%
21	Nevada	1,835	1.6%
22	Washington	1,637	1.5%
23	South Carolina	1,383	1.2%
24	Minnesota	1,286	1.1%
25	Connecticut	1,245	1.1%
26	Oregon	1,187	1.1%
27	Louisiana	1,035	0.9%
28	Colorado	926	0.8%
29	Oklahoma	831	0.7%
30	Delaware	713	0.6%
31	Arkansas	623	0.6%
32	Kentucky	598	0.5%
33	Mississippi	572	0.5%
34	Utah	495	0.4%
35	New Mexico	417	0.4%
36	Iowa	404	0.4%
37	Nebraska	397	0.4%
38	Hawaii	393	0.3%
39	Kansas	285	0.3%
40	Alaska	275	0.2%
41	Rhode Island	259	0.2%
42	Maine	184	0.2%
43	New Hampshire	150	0.1%
44	West Virginia	143	0.1%
45	Idaho	97	0.1%
46	Montana	47	0.0%
47	Wyoming	35	0.0%
48	South Dakota	31	0.0%
49	North Dakota	25	0.0%
50	Vermont	21	0.0%
	District of Columbia**	NA	NA

Source: Reported data from the Federal Bureau of Investigation
"Crime in the United States 2008" (Uniform Crime Reports, September 14, 2009, http://www.fbi.gov/ucr/ucr.htm)
*By law enforcement agencies submitting complete reports to the F.B.I. for 12 months in 2008. The F.B.I. estimates 129,403 reported and unreported arrests for robbery occurred in 2008. Robbery is the taking or attempting to take anything of value by force or threat of force. See important note at beginning of this chapter.
**Not available.

Reported Arrest Rate for Robbery in 2008

National Rate = 45.2 Reported Arrests per 100,000 Population*

ALPHA ORDER

RANK	STATE	RATE
9	Alabama	54.3
16	Alaska	41.3
26	Arizona	31.9
31	Arkansas	25.9
7	California	61.3
36	Colorado	21.2
17	Connecticut	38.6
1	Delaware	81.7
5	Florida	64.9
11	Georgia	49.3
24	Hawaii	34.3
43	Idaho	6.8
NA	Illinois**	NA
15	Indiana	41.4
39	Iowa	14.6
38	Kansas	15.0
NA	Kentucky**	NA
14	Louisiana	41.9
41	Maine	14.0
2	Maryland	79.7
21	Massachusetts	35.5
30	Michigan	28.7
32	Minnesota	25.3
12	Mississippi	43.7
13	Missouri	43.6
45	Montana	5.0
34	Nebraska	24.3
3	Nevada	72.1
40	New Hampshire	14.5
10	New Jersey	52.3
29	New Mexico	28.8
19	New York	36.8
4	North Carolina	66.0
47	North Dakota	4.3
18	Ohio	38.1
35	Oklahoma	22.8
25	Oregon	32.5
6	Pennsylvania	61.7
33	Rhode Island	24.6
27	South Carolina	31.4
46	South Dakota	4.9
8	Tennessee	59.3
22	Texas	35.1
37	Utah	20.8
48	Vermont	4.1
28	Virginia	29.1
23	Washington	34.4
42	West Virginia	12.9
20	Wisconsin	35.8
44	Wyoming	6.6

RANK ORDER

RANK	STATE	RATE
1	Delaware	81.7
2	Maryland	79.7
3	Nevada	72.1
4	North Carolina	66.0
5	Florida	64.9
6	Pennsylvania	61.7
7	California	61.3
8	Tennessee	59.3
9	Alabama	54.3
10	New Jersey	52.3
11	Georgia	49.3
12	Mississippi	43.7
13	Missouri	43.6
14	Louisiana	41.9
15	Indiana	41.4
16	Alaska	41.3
17	Connecticut	38.6
18	Ohio	38.1
19	New York	36.8
20	Wisconsin	35.8
21	Massachusetts	35.5
22	Texas	35.1
23	Washington	34.4
24	Hawaii	34.3
25	Oregon	32.5
26	Arizona	31.9
27	South Carolina	31.4
28	Virginia	29.1
29	New Mexico	28.8
30	Michigan	28.7
31	Arkansas	25.9
32	Minnesota	25.3
33	Rhode Island	24.6
34	Nebraska	24.3
35	Oklahoma	22.8
36	Colorado	21.2
37	Utah	20.8
38	Kansas	15.0
39	Iowa	14.6
40	New Hampshire	14.5
41	Maine	14.0
42	West Virginia	12.9
43	Idaho	6.8
44	Wyoming	6.6
45	Montana	5.0
46	South Dakota	4.9
47	North Dakota	4.3
48	Vermont	4.1
NA	Illinois**	NA
NA	Kentucky**	NA
	District of Columbia**	NA

Source: CQ Press using reported data from the Federal Bureau of Investigation
"Crime in the United States 2008" (Uniform Crime Reports, September 14, 2009, http://www.fbi.gov/ucr/ucr.htm)
*By law enforcement agencies submitting complete reports to the F.B.I. for 12 months in 2008. These rates based on population estimates for areas under the jurisdiction of those agencies reporting. Arrest rate based on the F.B.I. estimate of reported and unreported arrests for robbery is 42.6 arrests per 100,000 population. See important note at beginning of this chapter.
**Not available.

Reported Arrests for Aggravated Assault in 2008

National Total = 368,131 Reported Arrests*

<table>
<tr><td colspan="4">ALPHA ORDER</td><td colspan="4">RANK ORDER</td></tr>
<tr><td>RANK</td><td>STATE</td><td>ARRESTS</td><td>% of USA</td><td>RANK</td><td>STATE</td><td>ARRESTS</td><td>% of USA</td></tr>
<tr><td>27</td><td>Alabama</td><td>3,823</td><td>1.0%</td><td>1</td><td>California</td><td>98,906</td><td>26.9%</td></tr>
<tr><td>35</td><td>Alaska</td><td>1,770</td><td>0.5%</td><td>2</td><td>Florida</td><td>38,218</td><td>10.4%</td></tr>
<tr><td>15</td><td>Arizona</td><td>6,687</td><td>1.8%</td><td>3</td><td>Texas</td><td>23,139</td><td>6.3%</td></tr>
<tr><td>28</td><td>Arkansas</td><td>3,814</td><td>1.0%</td><td>4</td><td>Pennsylvania</td><td>16,621</td><td>4.5%</td></tr>
<tr><td>1</td><td>California</td><td>98,906</td><td>26.9%</td><td>5</td><td>North Carolina</td><td>13,390</td><td>3.6%</td></tr>
<tr><td>20</td><td>Colorado</td><td>4,674</td><td>1.3%</td><td>6</td><td>Tennessee</td><td>10,044</td><td>2.7%</td></tr>
<tr><td>24</td><td>Connecticut</td><td>4,335</td><td>1.2%</td><td>7</td><td>Massachusetts</td><td>10,022</td><td>2.7%</td></tr>
<tr><td>33</td><td>Delaware</td><td>2,059</td><td>0.6%</td><td>8</td><td>Missouri</td><td>9,197</td><td>2.5%</td></tr>
<tr><td>2</td><td>Florida</td><td>38,218</td><td>10.4%</td><td>9</td><td>Michigan</td><td>9,190</td><td>2.5%</td></tr>
<tr><td>12</td><td>Georgia</td><td>7,898</td><td>2.1%</td><td>10</td><td>New York</td><td>9,111</td><td>2.5%</td></tr>
<tr><td>42</td><td>Hawaii</td><td>806</td><td>0.2%</td><td>11</td><td>New Jersey</td><td>8,929</td><td>2.4%</td></tr>
<tr><td>38</td><td>Idaho</td><td>1,212</td><td>0.3%</td><td>12</td><td>Georgia</td><td>7,898</td><td>2.1%</td></tr>
<tr><td>19</td><td>Illinois</td><td>4,973</td><td>1.4%</td><td>13</td><td>Maryland</td><td>7,847</td><td>2.1%</td></tr>
<tr><td>16</td><td>Indiana</td><td>5,891</td><td>1.6%</td><td>14</td><td>Louisiana</td><td>7,780</td><td>2.1%</td></tr>
<tr><td>29</td><td>Iowa</td><td>3,668</td><td>1.0%</td><td>15</td><td>Arizona</td><td>6,687</td><td>1.8%</td></tr>
<tr><td>34</td><td>Kansas</td><td>1,976</td><td>0.5%</td><td>16</td><td>Indiana</td><td>5,891</td><td>1.6%</td></tr>
<tr><td>39</td><td>Kentucky</td><td>1,131</td><td>0.3%</td><td>17</td><td>South Carolina</td><td>5,400</td><td>1.5%</td></tr>
<tr><td>14</td><td>Louisiana</td><td>7,780</td><td>2.1%</td><td>18</td><td>Wisconsin</td><td>5,164</td><td>1.4%</td></tr>
<tr><td>46</td><td>Maine</td><td>471</td><td>0.1%</td><td>19</td><td>Illinois</td><td>4,973</td><td>1.4%</td></tr>
<tr><td>13</td><td>Maryland</td><td>7,847</td><td>2.1%</td><td>20</td><td>Colorado</td><td>4,674</td><td>1.3%</td></tr>
<tr><td>7</td><td>Massachusetts</td><td>10,022</td><td>2.7%</td><td>21</td><td>Oklahoma</td><td>4,649</td><td>1.3%</td></tr>
<tr><td>9</td><td>Michigan</td><td>9,190</td><td>2.5%</td><td>22</td><td>Virginia</td><td>4,584</td><td>1.2%</td></tr>
<tr><td>26</td><td>Minnesota</td><td>4,109</td><td>1.1%</td><td>23</td><td>Washington</td><td>4,527</td><td>1.2%</td></tr>
<tr><td>40</td><td>Mississippi</td><td>1,074</td><td>0.3%</td><td>24</td><td>Connecticut</td><td>4,335</td><td>1.2%</td></tr>
<tr><td>8</td><td>Missouri</td><td>9,197</td><td>2.5%</td><td>25</td><td>Nevada</td><td>4,272</td><td>1.2%</td></tr>
<tr><td>43</td><td>Montana</td><td>769</td><td>0.2%</td><td>26</td><td>Minnesota</td><td>4,109</td><td>1.1%</td></tr>
<tr><td>36</td><td>Nebraska</td><td>1,381</td><td>0.4%</td><td>27</td><td>Alabama</td><td>3,823</td><td>1.0%</td></tr>
<tr><td>25</td><td>Nevada</td><td>4,272</td><td>1.2%</td><td>28</td><td>Arkansas</td><td>3,814</td><td>1.0%</td></tr>
<tr><td>47</td><td>New Hampshire</td><td>400</td><td>0.1%</td><td>29</td><td>Iowa</td><td>3,668</td><td>1.0%</td></tr>
<tr><td>11</td><td>New Jersey</td><td>8,929</td><td>2.4%</td><td>30</td><td>Ohio</td><td>3,520</td><td>1.0%</td></tr>
<tr><td>32</td><td>New Mexico</td><td>2,847</td><td>0.8%</td><td>31</td><td>Oregon</td><td>3,286</td><td>0.9%</td></tr>
<tr><td>10</td><td>New York</td><td>9,111</td><td>2.5%</td><td>32</td><td>New Mexico</td><td>2,847</td><td>0.8%</td></tr>
<tr><td>5</td><td>North Carolina</td><td>13,390</td><td>3.6%</td><td>33</td><td>Delaware</td><td>2,059</td><td>0.6%</td></tr>
<tr><td>50</td><td>North Dakota</td><td>335</td><td>0.1%</td><td>34</td><td>Kansas</td><td>1,976</td><td>0.5%</td></tr>
<tr><td>30</td><td>Ohio</td><td>3,520</td><td>1.0%</td><td>35</td><td>Alaska</td><td>1,770</td><td>0.5%</td></tr>
<tr><td>21</td><td>Oklahoma</td><td>4,649</td><td>1.3%</td><td>36</td><td>Nebraska</td><td>1,381</td><td>0.4%</td></tr>
<tr><td>31</td><td>Oregon</td><td>3,286</td><td>0.9%</td><td>37</td><td>Utah</td><td>1,321</td><td>0.4%</td></tr>
<tr><td>4</td><td>Pennsylvania</td><td>16,621</td><td>4.5%</td><td>38</td><td>Idaho</td><td>1,212</td><td>0.3%</td></tr>
<tr><td>44</td><td>Rhode Island</td><td>547</td><td>0.1%</td><td>39</td><td>Kentucky</td><td>1,131</td><td>0.3%</td></tr>
<tr><td>17</td><td>South Carolina</td><td>5,400</td><td>1.5%</td><td>40</td><td>Mississippi</td><td>1,074</td><td>0.3%</td></tr>
<tr><td>48</td><td>South Dakota</td><td>368</td><td>0.1%</td><td>41</td><td>West Virginia</td><td>1,066</td><td>0.3%</td></tr>
<tr><td>6</td><td>Tennessee</td><td>10,044</td><td>2.7%</td><td>42</td><td>Hawaii</td><td>806</td><td>0.2%</td></tr>
<tr><td>3</td><td>Texas</td><td>23,139</td><td>6.3%</td><td>43</td><td>Montana</td><td>769</td><td>0.2%</td></tr>
<tr><td>37</td><td>Utah</td><td>1,321</td><td>0.4%</td><td>44</td><td>Rhode Island</td><td>547</td><td>0.1%</td></tr>
<tr><td>49</td><td>Vermont</td><td>356</td><td>0.1%</td><td>45</td><td>Wyoming</td><td>539</td><td>0.1%</td></tr>
<tr><td>22</td><td>Virginia</td><td>4,584</td><td>1.2%</td><td>46</td><td>Maine</td><td>471</td><td>0.1%</td></tr>
<tr><td>23</td><td>Washington</td><td>4,527</td><td>1.2%</td><td>47</td><td>New Hampshire</td><td>400</td><td>0.1%</td></tr>
<tr><td>41</td><td>West Virginia</td><td>1,066</td><td>0.3%</td><td>48</td><td>South Dakota</td><td>368</td><td>0.1%</td></tr>
<tr><td>18</td><td>Wisconsin</td><td>5,164</td><td>1.4%</td><td>49</td><td>Vermont</td><td>356</td><td>0.1%</td></tr>
<tr><td>45</td><td>Wyoming</td><td>539</td><td>0.1%</td><td>50</td><td>North Dakota</td><td>335</td><td>0.1%</td></tr>
<tr><td colspan="4"></td><td>District of Columbia**</td><td></td><td>NA</td><td>NA</td></tr>
</table>

Source: Reported data from the Federal Bureau of Investigation
"Crime in the United States 2008" (Uniform Crime Reports, September 14, 2009, http://www.fbi.gov/ucr/ucr.htm)
*By law enforcement agencies submitting complete reports to the F.B.I. for 12 months in 2008. The F.B.I. estimates 429,969 reported and unreported arrests for aggravated assault occurred in 2008. Aggravated assault is an attack for the purpose of inflicting severe bodily injury. See important note at beginning of this chapter.
**Not available.

Reported Arrest Rate for Aggravated Assault in 2008

National Rate = 147.7 Reported Arrests per 100,000 Population*

ALPHA ORDER				RANK ORDER		
RANK	STATE	RATE		RANK	STATE	RATE
27	Alabama	101.3		1	Louisiana	314.7
3	Alaska	265.6		2	California	270.6
24	Arizona	104.2		3	Alaska	265.6
12	Arkansas	158.7		4	Delaware	235.8
2	California	270.6		5	Florida	208.9
21	Colorado	107.2		6	Tennessee	203.0
15	Connecticut	134.3		7	North Carolina	202.5
4	Delaware	235.8		8	New Mexico	196.9
5	Florida	208.9		9	Massachusetts	172.2
17	Georgia	131.7		10	Nevada	167.8
39	Hawaii	70.4		11	Missouri	165.9
34	Idaho	84.5		12	Arkansas	158.7
NA	Illinois**	NA		13	Maryland	140.8
19	Indiana	126.5		14	Pennsylvania	138.3
16	Iowa	132.6		15	Connecticut	134.3
24	Kansas	104.2		16	Iowa	132.6
NA	Kentucky**	NA		17	Georgia	131.7
1	Louisiana	314.7		18	Oklahoma	127.8
48	Maine	35.8		19	Indiana	126.5
13	Maryland	140.8		20	South Carolina	122.7
9	Massachusetts	172.2		21	Colorado	107.2
23	Michigan	106.1		22	New Jersey	106.9
38	Minnesota	81.0		23	Michigan	106.1
37	Mississippi	82.1		24	Arizona	104.2
11	Missouri	165.9		24	Kansas	104.2
36	Montana	82.5		26	Wyoming	102.1
34	Nebraska	84.5		27	Alabama	101.3
10	Nevada	167.8		28	Texas	99.0
47	New Hampshire	38.7		29	New York	98.8
22	New Jersey	106.9		30	West Virginia	96.1
8	New Mexico	196.9		31	Washington	95.1
29	New York	98.8		32	Wisconsin	93.2
7	North Carolina	202.5		33	Oregon	90.0
43	North Dakota	57.7		34	Idaho	84.5
46	Ohio	51.3		34	Nebraska	84.5
18	Oklahoma	127.8		36	Montana	82.5
33	Oregon	90.0		37	Mississippi	82.1
14	Pennsylvania	138.3		38	Minnesota	81.0
45	Rhode Island	52.1		39	Hawaii	70.4
20	South Carolina	122.7		40	Vermont	69.8
42	South Dakota	58.4		41	Virginia	60.8
6	Tennessee	203.0		42	South Dakota	58.4
28	Texas	99.0		43	North Dakota	57.7
44	Utah	55.6		44	Utah	55.6
40	Vermont	69.8		45	Rhode Island	52.1
41	Virginia	60.8		46	Ohio	51.3
31	Washington	95.1		47	New Hampshire	38.7
30	West Virginia	96.1		48	Maine	35.8
32	Wisconsin	93.2		NA	Illinois**	NA
26	Wyoming	102.1		NA	Kentucky**	NA
					District of Columbia**	NA

Source: CQ Press using reported data from the Federal Bureau of Investigation
 "Crime in the United States 2008" (Uniform Crime Reports, September 14, 2009, http://www.fbi.gov/ucr/ucr.htm)
*By law enforcement agencies submitting complete reports to the F.B.I. for 12 months in 2008. These rates based on population estimates for areas under the jurisdiction of those agencies reporting. Arrest rate based on the F.B.I. estimate of reported and unreported arrests for aggravated assault is 141.4 arrests per 100,000 population. See important note at beginning of this chapter. **Not available.

Reported Arrests for Property Crime in 2008

National Total = 1,455,077 Reported Arrests*

ALPHA ORDER

RANK	STATE	ARRESTS	% of USA
22	Alabama	24,496	1.7%
44	Alaska	4,108	0.3%
9	Arizona	41,904	2.9%
31	Arkansas	15,437	1.1%
1	California	170,546	11.7%
21	Colorado	25,453	1.7%
29	Connecticut	17,141	1.2%
39	Delaware	6,746	0.5%
2	Florida	149,942	10.3%
12	Georgia	37,402	2.6%
43	Hawaii	4,523	0.3%
38	Idaho	7,009	0.5%
23	Illinois	23,372	1.6%
18	Indiana	30,527	2.1%
32	Iowa	13,950	1.0%
37	Kansas	7,187	0.5%
40	Kentucky	6,700	0.5%
24	Louisiana	19,742	1.4%
36	Maine	8,325	0.6%
11	Maryland	38,147	2.6%
26	Massachusetts	18,471	1.3%
14	Michigan	35,166	2.4%
19	Minnesota	29,245	2.0%
33	Mississippi	11,109	0.8%
7	Missouri	45,261	3.1%
42	Montana	4,617	0.3%
34	Nebraska	9,602	0.7%
28	Nevada	17,542	1.2%
46	New Hampshire	3,165	0.2%
15	New Jersey	34,665	2.4%
35	New Mexico	9,003	0.6%
6	New York	48,915	3.4%
5	North Carolina	60,398	4.2%
48	North Dakota	2,975	0.2%
13	Ohio	35,461	2.4%
30	Oklahoma	17,029	1.2%
20	Oregon	27,202	1.9%
4	Pennsylvania	60,856	4.2%
45	Rhode Island	3,756	0.3%
27	South Carolina	18,177	1.2%
49	South Dakota	2,782	0.2%
10	Tennessee	39,706	2.7%
3	Texas	130,782	9.0%
25	Utah	18,725	1.3%
50	Vermont	1,714	0.1%
16	Virginia	33,083	2.3%
17	Washington	32,352	2.2%
41	West Virginia	5,059	0.3%
8	Wisconsin	42,425	2.9%
47	Wyoming	3,073	0.2%

RANK ORDER

RANK	STATE	ARRESTS	% of USA
1	California	170,546	11.7%
2	Florida	149,942	10.3%
3	Texas	130,782	9.0%
4	Pennsylvania	60,856	4.2%
5	North Carolina	60,398	4.2%
6	New York	48,915	3.4%
7	Missouri	45,261	3.1%
8	Wisconsin	42,425	2.9%
9	Arizona	41,904	2.9%
10	Tennessee	39,706	2.7%
11	Maryland	38,147	2.6%
12	Georgia	37,402	2.6%
13	Ohio	35,461	2.4%
14	Michigan	35,166	2.4%
15	New Jersey	34,665	2.4%
16	Virginia	33,083	2.3%
17	Washington	32,352	2.2%
18	Indiana	30,527	2.1%
19	Minnesota	29,245	2.0%
20	Oregon	27,202	1.9%
21	Colorado	25,453	1.7%
22	Alabama	24,496	1.7%
23	Illinois	23,372	1.6%
24	Louisiana	19,742	1.4%
25	Utah	18,725	1.3%
26	Massachusetts	18,471	1.3%
27	South Carolina	18,177	1.2%
28	Nevada	17,542	1.2%
29	Connecticut	17,141	1.2%
30	Oklahoma	17,029	1.2%
31	Arkansas	15,437	1.1%
32	Iowa	13,950	1.0%
33	Mississippi	11,109	0.8%
34	Nebraska	9,602	0.7%
35	New Mexico	9,003	0.6%
36	Maine	8,325	0.6%
37	Kansas	7,187	0.5%
38	Idaho	7,009	0.5%
39	Delaware	6,746	0.5%
40	Kentucky	6,700	0.5%
41	West Virginia	5,059	0.3%
42	Montana	4,617	0.3%
43	Hawaii	4,523	0.3%
44	Alaska	4,108	0.3%
45	Rhode Island	3,756	0.3%
46	New Hampshire	3,165	0.2%
47	Wyoming	3,073	0.2%
48	North Dakota	2,975	0.2%
49	South Dakota	2,782	0.2%
50	Vermont	1,714	0.1%
	District of Columbia**	NA	NA

Source: Reported data from the Federal Bureau of Investigation
   "Crime in the United States 2008" (Uniform Crime Reports, September 14, 2009, http://www.fbi.gov/ucr/ucr.htm)
*By law enforcement agencies submitting complete reports to the F.B.I. for 12 months in 2008. The F.B.I. estimates 1,687,345 reported and unreported arrests for property crime occurred in 2008. Property crimes are offenses of burglary, larceny-theft, motor vehicle theft, and arson. See important note at beginning of this chapter.
**Not available.

Reported Arrest Rate for Property Crime in 2008

National Rate = 583.9 Reported Arrests per 100,000 Population*

ALPHA ORDER

RANK	STATE	RATE
16	Alabama	649.3
21	Alaska	616.4
15	Arizona	653.2
17	Arkansas	642.2
36	California	466.5
23	Colorado	583.8
27	Connecticut	531.2
8	Delaware	772.7
3	Florida	819.6
19	Georgia	623.9
43	Hawaii	395.0
34	Idaho	488.4
NA	Illinois**	NA
14	Indiana	655.3
32	Iowa	504.4
44	Kansas	379.1
NA	Kentucky**	NA
6	Louisiana	798.6
18	Maine	633.5
12	Maryland	684.3
47	Massachusetts	317.4
42	Michigan	405.9
25	Minnesota	576.4
2	Mississippi	849.3
4	Missouri	816.6
33	Montana	495.1
22	Nebraska	587.6
11	Nevada	689.1
48	New Hampshire	306.5
40	New Jersey	414.9
20	New Mexico	622.6
28	New York	530.3
1	North Carolina	913.3
30	North Dakota	512.4
29	Ohio	516.5
35	Oklahoma	468.1
10	Oregon	745.3
31	Pennsylvania	506.3
45	Rhode Island	357.4
41	South Carolina	413.2
38	South Dakota	441.4
5	Tennessee	802.5
26	Texas	559.5
7	Utah	787.8
46	Vermont	336.2
39	Virginia	438.6
13	Washington	679.5
37	West Virginia	456.0
9	Wisconsin	765.7
24	Wyoming	582.0

RANK ORDER

RANK	STATE	RATE
1	North Carolina	913.3
2	Mississippi	849.3
3	Florida	819.6
4	Missouri	816.6
5	Tennessee	802.5
6	Louisiana	798.6
7	Utah	787.8
8	Delaware	772.7
9	Wisconsin	765.7
10	Oregon	745.3
11	Nevada	689.1
12	Maryland	684.3
13	Washington	679.5
14	Indiana	655.3
15	Arizona	653.2
16	Alabama	649.3
17	Arkansas	642.2
18	Maine	633.5
19	Georgia	623.9
20	New Mexico	622.6
21	Alaska	616.4
22	Nebraska	587.6
23	Colorado	583.8
24	Wyoming	582.0
25	Minnesota	576.4
26	Texas	559.5
27	Connecticut	531.2
28	New York	530.3
29	Ohio	516.5
30	North Dakota	512.4
31	Pennsylvania	506.3
32	Iowa	504.4
33	Montana	495.1
34	Idaho	488.4
35	Oklahoma	468.1
36	California	466.5
37	West Virginia	456.0
38	South Dakota	441.4
39	Virginia	438.6
40	New Jersey	414.9
41	South Carolina	413.2
42	Michigan	405.9
43	Hawaii	395.0
44	Kansas	379.1
45	Rhode Island	357.4
46	Vermont	336.2
47	Massachusetts	317.4
48	New Hampshire	306.5
NA	Illinois**	NA
NA	Kentucky**	NA
	District of Columbia**	NA

Source: CQ Press using reported data from the Federal Bureau of Investigation
   "Crime in the United States 2008" (Uniform Crime Reports, September 14, 2009, http://www.fbi.gov/ucr/ucr.htm)
*By law enforcement agencies submitting complete reports to the F.B.I. for 12 months in 2008. These rates based on population estimates for areas under the jurisdiction of those agencies reporting. Arrest rate based on the F.B.I. estimate of reported and unreported arrests for property crime is 554.9 arrests per 100,000 population. See important note at beginning of this chapter.
**Not available.

Reported Arrests for Burglary in 2008

National Total = 267,687 Reported Arrests*

<table>
<tr><td colspan="4">ALPHA ORDER</td><td colspan="4">RANK ORDER</td></tr>
<tr><td>RANK</td><td>STATE</td><td>ARRESTS</td><td>% of USA</td><td>RANK</td><td>STATE</td><td>ARRESTS</td><td>% of USA</td></tr>
<tr><td>19</td><td>Alabama</td><td>4,110</td><td>1.5%</td><td>1</td><td>California</td><td>56,409</td><td>21.1%</td></tr>
<tr><td>44</td><td>Alaska</td><td>457</td><td>0.2%</td><td>2</td><td>Florida</td><td>31,468</td><td>11.8%</td></tr>
<tr><td>14</td><td>Arizona</td><td>5,086</td><td>1.9%</td><td>3</td><td>Texas</td><td>19,693</td><td>7.4%</td></tr>
<tr><td>27</td><td>Arkansas</td><td>2,992</td><td>1.1%</td><td>4</td><td>North Carolina</td><td>14,459</td><td>5.4%</td></tr>
<tr><td>1</td><td>California</td><td>56,409</td><td>21.1%</td><td>5</td><td>Pennsylvania</td><td>10,310</td><td>3.9%</td></tr>
<tr><td>26</td><td>Colorado</td><td>2,993</td><td>1.1%</td><td>6</td><td>New York</td><td>7,893</td><td>2.9%</td></tr>
<tr><td>29</td><td>Connecticut</td><td>2,846</td><td>1.1%</td><td>7</td><td>Maryland</td><td>7,411</td><td>2.8%</td></tr>
<tr><td>37</td><td>Delaware</td><td>1,102</td><td>0.4%</td><td>8</td><td>Missouri</td><td>7,085</td><td>2.6%</td></tr>
<tr><td>2</td><td>Florida</td><td>31,468</td><td>11.8%</td><td>9</td><td>Georgia</td><td>6,654</td><td>2.5%</td></tr>
<tr><td>9</td><td>Georgia</td><td>6,654</td><td>2.5%</td><td>10</td><td>New Jersey</td><td>6,419</td><td>2.4%</td></tr>
<tr><td>42</td><td>Hawaii</td><td>601</td><td>0.2%</td><td>11</td><td>Michigan</td><td>6,251</td><td>2.3%</td></tr>
<tr><td>39</td><td>Idaho</td><td>938</td><td>0.4%</td><td>12</td><td>Tennessee</td><td>6,221</td><td>2.3%</td></tr>
<tr><td>28</td><td>Illinois</td><td>2,894</td><td>1.1%</td><td>13</td><td>Ohio</td><td>6,211</td><td>2.3%</td></tr>
<tr><td>18</td><td>Indiana</td><td>4,475</td><td>1.7%</td><td>14</td><td>Arizona</td><td>5,086</td><td>1.9%</td></tr>
<tr><td>32</td><td>Iowa</td><td>1,907</td><td>0.7%</td><td>15</td><td>Washington</td><td>4,895</td><td>1.8%</td></tr>
<tr><td>38</td><td>Kansas</td><td>1,054</td><td>0.4%</td><td>16</td><td>Wisconsin</td><td>4,664</td><td>1.7%</td></tr>
<tr><td>35</td><td>Kentucky</td><td>1,220</td><td>0.5%</td><td>17</td><td>Virginia</td><td>4,624</td><td>1.7%</td></tr>
<tr><td>20</td><td>Louisiana</td><td>3,840</td><td>1.4%</td><td>18</td><td>Indiana</td><td>4,475</td><td>1.7%</td></tr>
<tr><td>33</td><td>Maine</td><td>1,352</td><td>0.5%</td><td>19</td><td>Alabama</td><td>4,110</td><td>1.5%</td></tr>
<tr><td>7</td><td>Maryland</td><td>7,411</td><td>2.8%</td><td>20</td><td>Louisiana</td><td>3,840</td><td>1.4%</td></tr>
<tr><td>21</td><td>Massachusetts</td><td>3,725</td><td>1.4%</td><td>21</td><td>Massachusetts</td><td>3,725</td><td>1.4%</td></tr>
<tr><td>11</td><td>Michigan</td><td>6,251</td><td>2.3%</td><td>22</td><td>South Carolina</td><td>3,552</td><td>1.3%</td></tr>
<tr><td>24</td><td>Minnesota</td><td>3,388</td><td>1.3%</td><td>23</td><td>Nevada</td><td>3,492</td><td>1.3%</td></tr>
<tr><td>31</td><td>Mississippi</td><td>2,248</td><td>0.8%</td><td>24</td><td>Minnesota</td><td>3,388</td><td>1.3%</td></tr>
<tr><td>8</td><td>Missouri</td><td>7,085</td><td>2.6%</td><td>25</td><td>Oklahoma</td><td>3,114</td><td>1.2%</td></tr>
<tr><td>46</td><td>Montana</td><td>360</td><td>0.1%</td><td>26</td><td>Colorado</td><td>2,993</td><td>1.1%</td></tr>
<tr><td>40</td><td>Nebraska</td><td>908</td><td>0.3%</td><td>27</td><td>Arkansas</td><td>2,992</td><td>1.1%</td></tr>
<tr><td>23</td><td>Nevada</td><td>3,492</td><td>1.3%</td><td>28</td><td>Illinois</td><td>2,894</td><td>1.1%</td></tr>
<tr><td>45</td><td>New Hampshire</td><td>437</td><td>0.2%</td><td>29</td><td>Connecticut</td><td>2,846</td><td>1.1%</td></tr>
<tr><td>10</td><td>New Jersey</td><td>6,419</td><td>2.4%</td><td>30</td><td>Oregon</td><td>2,816</td><td>1.1%</td></tr>
<tr><td>36</td><td>New Mexico</td><td>1,215</td><td>0.5%</td><td>31</td><td>Mississippi</td><td>2,248</td><td>0.8%</td></tr>
<tr><td>6</td><td>New York</td><td>7,893</td><td>2.9%</td><td>32</td><td>Iowa</td><td>1,907</td><td>0.7%</td></tr>
<tr><td>4</td><td>North Carolina</td><td>14,459</td><td>5.4%</td><td>33</td><td>Maine</td><td>1,352</td><td>0.5%</td></tr>
<tr><td>49</td><td>North Dakota</td><td>281</td><td>0.1%</td><td>34</td><td>Utah</td><td>1,342</td><td>0.5%</td></tr>
<tr><td>13</td><td>Ohio</td><td>6,211</td><td>2.3%</td><td>35</td><td>Kentucky</td><td>1,220</td><td>0.5%</td></tr>
<tr><td>25</td><td>Oklahoma</td><td>3,114</td><td>1.2%</td><td>36</td><td>New Mexico</td><td>1,215</td><td>0.5%</td></tr>
<tr><td>30</td><td>Oregon</td><td>2,816</td><td>1.1%</td><td>37</td><td>Delaware</td><td>1,102</td><td>0.4%</td></tr>
<tr><td>5</td><td>Pennsylvania</td><td>10,310</td><td>3.9%</td><td>38</td><td>Kansas</td><td>1,054</td><td>0.4%</td></tr>
<tr><td>41</td><td>Rhode Island</td><td>777</td><td>0.3%</td><td>39</td><td>Idaho</td><td>938</td><td>0.4%</td></tr>
<tr><td>22</td><td>South Carolina</td><td>3,552</td><td>1.3%</td><td>40</td><td>Nebraska</td><td>908</td><td>0.3%</td></tr>
<tr><td>49</td><td>South Dakota</td><td>281</td><td>0.1%</td><td>41</td><td>Rhode Island</td><td>777</td><td>0.3%</td></tr>
<tr><td>12</td><td>Tennessee</td><td>6,221</td><td>2.3%</td><td>42</td><td>Hawaii</td><td>601</td><td>0.2%</td></tr>
<tr><td>3</td><td>Texas</td><td>19,693</td><td>7.4%</td><td>43</td><td>West Virginia</td><td>583</td><td>0.2%</td></tr>
<tr><td>34</td><td>Utah</td><td>1,342</td><td>0.5%</td><td>44</td><td>Alaska</td><td>457</td><td>0.2%</td></tr>
<tr><td>48</td><td>Vermont</td><td>300</td><td>0.1%</td><td>45</td><td>New Hampshire</td><td>437</td><td>0.2%</td></tr>
<tr><td>17</td><td>Virginia</td><td>4,624</td><td>1.7%</td><td>46</td><td>Montana</td><td>360</td><td>0.1%</td></tr>
<tr><td>15</td><td>Washington</td><td>4,895</td><td>1.8%</td><td>47</td><td>Wyoming</td><td>334</td><td>0.1%</td></tr>
<tr><td>43</td><td>West Virginia</td><td>583</td><td>0.2%</td><td>48</td><td>Vermont</td><td>300</td><td>0.1%</td></tr>
<tr><td>16</td><td>Wisconsin</td><td>4,664</td><td>1.7%</td><td>49</td><td>North Dakota</td><td>281</td><td>0.1%</td></tr>
<tr><td>47</td><td>Wyoming</td><td>334</td><td>0.1%</td><td>49</td><td>South Dakota</td><td>281</td><td>0.1%</td></tr>
<tr><td></td><td></td><td></td><td></td><td colspan="2">District of Columbia**</td><td>NA</td><td>NA</td></tr>
</table>

Source: Reported data from the Federal Bureau of Investigation
"Crime in the United States 2008" (Uniform Crime Reports, September 14, 2009, http://www.fbi.gov/ucr/ucr.htm)
*By law enforcement agencies submitting complete reports to the F.B.I. for 12 months in 2008. The F.B.I. estimates 308,479 reported and unreported arrests for burglary occurred in 2008. Burglary is the unlawful entry of a structure to commit a felony or theft. Attempts are included. See important note at beginning of this chapter.
**Not available.

Reported Arrest Rate for Burglary in 2008

National Rate = 107.4 Reported Arrests per 100,000 Population*

ALPHA ORDER

RANK	STATE	RATE
13	Alabama	108.9
33	Alaska	68.6
26	Arizona	79.3
11	Arkansas	124.5
5	California	154.3
32	Colorado	68.7
18	Connecticut	88.2
9	Delaware	126.2
2	Florida	172.0
12	Georgia	111.0
44	Hawaii	52.5
35	Idaho	65.4
NA	Illinois**	NA
16	Indiana	96.1
31	Iowa	68.9
41	Kansas	55.6
NA	Kentucky**	NA
4	Louisiana	155.3
14	Maine	102.9
7	Maryland	133.0
36	Massachusetts	64.0
30	Michigan	72.1
34	Minnesota	66.8
3	Mississippi	171.9
8	Missouri	127.8
48	Montana	38.6
41	Nebraska	55.6
6	Nevada	137.2
47	New Hampshire	42.3
28	New Jersey	76.8
24	New Mexico	84.0
20	New York	85.6
1	North Carolina	218.6
45	North Dakota	48.4
17	Ohio	90.5
20	Oklahoma	85.6
27	Oregon	77.2
19	Pennsylvania	85.8
29	Rhode Island	73.9
25	South Carolina	80.7
46	South Dakota	44.6
10	Tennessee	125.7
22	Texas	84.2
40	Utah	56.5
39	Vermont	58.8
38	Virginia	61.3
15	Washington	102.8
43	West Virginia	52.6
22	Wisconsin	84.2
37	Wyoming	63.3

RANK ORDER

RANK	STATE	RATE
1	North Carolina	218.6
2	Florida	172.0
3	Mississippi	171.9
4	Louisiana	155.3
5	California	154.3
6	Nevada	137.2
7	Maryland	133.0
8	Missouri	127.8
9	Delaware	126.2
10	Tennessee	125.7
11	Arkansas	124.5
12	Georgia	111.0
13	Alabama	108.9
14	Maine	102.9
15	Washington	102.8
16	Indiana	96.1
17	Ohio	90.5
18	Connecticut	88.2
19	Pennsylvania	85.8
20	New York	85.6
20	Oklahoma	85.6
22	Texas	84.2
22	Wisconsin	84.2
24	New Mexico	84.0
25	South Carolina	80.7
26	Arizona	79.3
27	Oregon	77.2
28	New Jersey	76.8
29	Rhode Island	73.9
30	Michigan	72.1
31	Iowa	68.9
32	Colorado	68.7
33	Alaska	68.6
34	Minnesota	66.8
35	Idaho	65.4
36	Massachusetts	64.0
37	Wyoming	63.3
38	Virginia	61.3
39	Vermont	58.8
40	Utah	56.5
41	Kansas	55.6
41	Nebraska	55.6
43	West Virginia	52.6
44	Hawaii	52.5
45	North Dakota	48.4
46	South Dakota	44.6
47	New Hampshire	42.3
48	Montana	38.6
NA	Illinois**	NA
NA	Kentucky**	NA
	District of Columbia**	NA

Source: CQ Press using reported data from the Federal Bureau of Investigation
  "Crime in the United States 2008" (Uniform Crime Reports, September 14, 2009, http://www.fbi.gov/ucr/ucr.htm)
*By law enforcement agencies submitting complete reports to the F.B.I. for 12 months in 2008. These rates based on population estimates for areas under the jurisdiction of those agencies reporting. Arrest rate based on the F.B.I. estimate of reported and unreported arrests for burglary is 101.5 arrests per 100,000 population. See important note at beginning of this chapter.
**Not available.

Reported Arrests for Larceny-Theft in 2008

National Total = 1,092,018 Reported Arrests*

ALPHA ORDER

RANK	STATE	ARRESTS	% of USA
22	Alabama	19,192	1.8%
44	Alaska	3,337	0.3%
9	Arizona	33,963	3.1%
31	Arkansas	11,967	1.1%
3	California	95,447	8.7%
21	Colorado	20,936	1.9%
28	Connecticut	13,466	1.2%
39	Delaware	5,403	0.5%
1	Florida	109,021	10.0%
11	Georgia	28,467	2.6%
43	Hawaii	3,467	0.3%
37	Idaho	5,802	0.5%
24	Illinois	15,889	1.5%
19	Indiana	23,865	2.2%
32	Iowa	11,349	1.0%
38	Kansas	5,678	0.5%
40	Kentucky	5,268	0.5%
25	Louisiana	14,812	1.4%
36	Maine	6,580	0.6%
15	Maryland	26,879	2.5%
26	Massachusetts	13,906	1.3%
17	Michigan	25,696	2.4%
18	Minnesota	24,188	2.2%
33	Mississippi	8,275	0.8%
8	Missouri	34,447	3.2%
42	Montana	3,973	0.4%
34	Nebraska	8,242	0.8%
30	Nevada	12,712	1.2%
46	New Hampshire	2,596	0.2%
14	New Jersey	26,932	2.5%
35	New Mexico	7,336	0.7%
6	New York	38,595	3.5%
5	North Carolina	44,112	4.0%
48	North Dakota	2,497	0.2%
12	Ohio	27,928	2.6%
29	Oklahoma	13,046	1.2%
20	Oregon	22,590	2.1%
4	Pennsylvania	46,384	4.2%
45	Rhode Island	2,794	0.3%
27	South Carolina	13,725	1.3%
49	South Dakota	2,342	0.2%
10	Tennessee	30,894	2.8%
2	Texas	104,395	9.6%
23	Utah	16,821	1.5%
50	Vermont	1,308	0.1%
13	Virginia	27,101	2.5%
16	Washington	25,769	2.4%
41	West Virginia	4,263	0.4%
7	Wisconsin	35,698	3.3%
47	Wyoming	2,592	0.2%

RANK ORDER

RANK	STATE	ARRESTS	% of USA
1	Florida	109,021	10.0%
2	Texas	104,395	9.6%
3	California	95,447	8.7%
4	Pennsylvania	46,384	4.2%
5	North Carolina	44,112	4.0%
6	New York	38,595	3.5%
7	Wisconsin	35,698	3.3%
8	Missouri	34,447	3.2%
9	Arizona	33,963	3.1%
10	Tennessee	30,894	2.8%
11	Georgia	28,467	2.6%
12	Ohio	27,928	2.6%
13	Virginia	27,101	2.5%
14	New Jersey	26,932	2.5%
15	Maryland	26,879	2.5%
16	Washington	25,769	2.4%
17	Michigan	25,696	2.4%
18	Minnesota	24,188	2.2%
19	Indiana	23,865	2.2%
20	Oregon	22,590	2.1%
21	Colorado	20,936	1.9%
22	Alabama	19,192	1.8%
23	Utah	16,821	1.5%
24	Illinois	15,889	1.5%
25	Louisiana	14,812	1.4%
26	Massachusetts	13,906	1.3%
27	South Carolina	13,725	1.3%
28	Connecticut	13,466	1.2%
29	Oklahoma	13,046	1.2%
30	Nevada	12,712	1.2%
31	Arkansas	11,967	1.1%
32	Iowa	11,349	1.0%
33	Mississippi	8,275	0.8%
34	Nebraska	8,242	0.8%
35	New Mexico	7,336	0.7%
36	Maine	6,580	0.6%
37	Idaho	5,802	0.5%
38	Kansas	5,678	0.5%
39	Delaware	5,403	0.5%
40	Kentucky	5,268	0.5%
41	West Virginia	4,263	0.4%
42	Montana	3,973	0.4%
43	Hawaii	3,467	0.3%
44	Alaska	3,337	0.3%
45	Rhode Island	2,794	0.3%
46	New Hampshire	2,596	0.2%
47	Wyoming	2,592	0.2%
48	North Dakota	2,497	0.2%
49	South Dakota	2,342	0.2%
50	Vermont	1,308	0.1%
	District of Columbia**	NA	NA

Source: Reported data from the Federal Bureau of Investigation
"Crime in the United States 2008" (Uniform Crime Reports, September 14, 2009, http://www.fbi.gov/ucr/ucr.htm)
*By law enforcement agencies submitting complete reports to the F.B.I. for 12 months in 2008. The F.B.I. estimates 1,266,706 reported and unreported arrests for larceny-theft occurred in 2008. Larceny-theft is the unlawful taking of property without use of force, violence, or fraud. Attempts are included. Motor vehicle thefts are excluded. See important note at beginning of this chapter. **Not available.

Reported Arrest Rate for Larceny-Theft in 2008

National Rate = 438.2 Reported Arrests per 100,000 Population*

ALPHA ORDER

RANK	STATE	RATE
14	Alabama	508.7
17	Alaska	500.7
12	Arizona	529.5
20	Arkansas	497.8
45	California	261.1
23	Colorado	480.2
30	Connecticut	417.3
8	Delaware	618.8
10	Florida	595.9
25	Georgia	474.8
41	Hawaii	302.7
33	Idaho	404.3
NA	Illinois**	NA
13	Indiana	512.3
31	Iowa	410.3
42	Kansas	299.5
NA	Kentucky**	NA
9	Louisiana	599.2
17	Maine	500.7
22	Maryland	482.2
48	Massachusetts	238.9
43	Michigan	296.6
24	Minnesota	476.7
4	Mississippi	632.6
6	Missouri	621.5
28	Montana	426.0
16	Nebraska	504.4
19	Nevada	499.4
47	New Hampshire	251.4
39	New Jersey	322.3
15	New Mexico	507.3
29	New York	418.4
2	North Carolina	667.1
27	North Dakota	430.1
32	Ohio	406.7
38	Oklahoma	358.6
7	Oregon	619.0
34	Pennsylvania	385.9
44	Rhode Island	265.9
40	South Carolina	312.0
36	South Dakota	371.6
5	Tennessee	624.4
26	Texas	446.6
1	Utah	707.7
46	Vermont	256.6
37	Virginia	359.3
11	Washington	541.2
35	West Virginia	384.3
3	Wisconsin	644.3
21	Wyoming	490.9

RANK ORDER

RANK	STATE	RATE
1	Utah	707.7
2	North Carolina	667.1
3	Wisconsin	644.3
4	Mississippi	632.6
5	Tennessee	624.4
6	Missouri	621.5
7	Oregon	619.0
8	Delaware	618.8
9	Louisiana	599.2
10	Florida	595.9
11	Washington	541.2
12	Arizona	529.5
13	Indiana	512.3
14	Alabama	508.7
15	New Mexico	507.3
16	Nebraska	504.4
17	Alaska	500.7
17	Maine	500.7
19	Nevada	499.4
20	Arkansas	497.8
21	Wyoming	490.9
22	Maryland	482.2
23	Colorado	480.2
24	Minnesota	476.7
25	Georgia	474.8
26	Texas	446.6
27	North Dakota	430.1
28	Montana	426.0
29	New York	418.4
30	Connecticut	417.3
31	Iowa	410.3
32	Ohio	406.7
33	Idaho	404.3
34	Pennsylvania	385.9
35	West Virginia	384.3
36	South Dakota	371.6
37	Virginia	359.3
38	Oklahoma	358.6
39	New Jersey	322.3
40	South Carolina	312.0
41	Hawaii	302.7
42	Kansas	299.5
43	Michigan	296.6
44	Rhode Island	265.9
45	California	261.1
46	Vermont	256.6
47	New Hampshire	251.4
48	Massachusetts	238.9
NA	Illinois**	NA
NA	Kentucky**	NA
	District of Columbia**	NA

Source: CQ Press using reported data from the Federal Bureau of Investigation
"Crime in the United States 2008" (Uniform Crime Reports, September 14, 2009, http://www.fbi.gov/ucr/ucr.htm)
*By law enforcement agencies submitting complete reports to the F.B.I. for 12 months in 2008. These rates based on population estimates for areas under the jurisdiction of those agencies reporting. Arrest rate based on the F.B.I. estimate of reported and unreported arrests for larceny-theft is 416.6 arrests per 100,000 population. See important note at beginning of this chapter.
**Not available.

Reported Arrests for Motor Vehicle Theft in 2008

National Total = 84,208 Reported Arrests*

ALPHA ORDER

RANK	STATE	ARRESTS	% of USA
22	Alabama	1,067	1.3%
39	Alaska	268	0.3%
9	Arizona	2,593	3.1%
34	Arkansas	417	0.5%
1	California	17,203	20.4%
19	Colorado	1,298	1.5%
27	Connecticut	711	0.8%
44	Delaware	171	0.2%
2	Florida	9,073	10.8%
11	Georgia	2,091	2.5%
33	Hawaii	424	0.5%
41	Idaho	185	0.2%
4	Illinois	4,514	5.4%
13	Indiana	1,970	2.3%
30	Iowa	553	0.7%
36	Kansas	372	0.4%
45	Kentucky	150	0.2%
24	Louisiana	920	1.1%
38	Maine	330	0.4%
7	Maryland	3,292	3.9%
28	Massachusetts	707	0.8%
8	Michigan	2,919	3.5%
16	Minnesota	1,479	1.8%
31	Mississippi	485	0.6%
6	Missouri	3,343	4.0%
40	Montana	227	0.3%
35	Nebraska	374	0.4%
20	Nevada	1,118	1.3%
50	New Hampshire	85	0.1%
25	New Jersey	917	1.1%
37	New Mexico	350	0.4%
12	New York	1,992	2.4%
15	North Carolina	1,511	1.8%
43	North Dakota	175	0.2%
21	Ohio	1,081	1.3%
29	Oklahoma	591	0.7%
17	Oregon	1,452	1.7%
5	Pennsylvania	3,479	4.1%
46	Rhode Island	138	0.2%
26	South Carolina	772	0.9%
48	South Dakota	115	0.1%
10	Tennessee	2,324	2.8%
3	Texas	5,962	7.1%
32	Utah	460	0.5%
49	Vermont	87	0.1%
23	Virginia	1,052	1.2%
18	Washington	1,412	1.7%
42	West Virginia	179	0.2%
14	Wisconsin	1,664	2.0%
47	Wyoming	125	0.1%

RANK ORDER

RANK	STATE	ARRESTS	% of USA
1	California	17,203	20.4%
2	Florida	9,073	10.8%
3	Texas	5,962	7.1%
4	Illinois	4,514	5.4%
5	Pennsylvania	3,479	4.1%
6	Missouri	3,343	4.0%
7	Maryland	3,292	3.9%
8	Michigan	2,919	3.5%
9	Arizona	2,593	3.1%
10	Tennessee	2,324	2.8%
11	Georgia	2,091	2.5%
12	New York	1,992	2.4%
13	Indiana	1,970	2.3%
14	Wisconsin	1,664	2.0%
15	North Carolina	1,511	1.8%
16	Minnesota	1,479	1.8%
17	Oregon	1,452	1.7%
18	Washington	1,412	1.7%
19	Colorado	1,298	1.5%
20	Nevada	1,118	1.3%
21	Ohio	1,081	1.3%
22	Alabama	1,067	1.3%
23	Virginia	1,052	1.2%
24	Louisiana	920	1.1%
25	New Jersey	917	1.1%
26	South Carolina	772	0.9%
27	Connecticut	711	0.8%
28	Massachusetts	707	0.8%
29	Oklahoma	591	0.7%
30	Iowa	553	0.7%
31	Mississippi	485	0.6%
32	Utah	460	0.5%
33	Hawaii	424	0.5%
34	Arkansas	417	0.5%
35	Nebraska	374	0.4%
36	Kansas	372	0.4%
37	New Mexico	350	0.4%
38	Maine	330	0.4%
39	Alaska	268	0.3%
40	Montana	227	0.3%
41	Idaho	185	0.2%
42	West Virginia	179	0.2%
43	North Dakota	175	0.2%
44	Delaware	171	0.2%
45	Kentucky	150	0.2%
46	Rhode Island	138	0.2%
47	Wyoming	125	0.1%
48	South Dakota	115	0.1%
49	Vermont	87	0.1%
50	New Hampshire	85	0.1%
	District of Columbia**	NA	NA

Source: Reported data from the Federal Bureau of Investigation
"Crime in the United States 2008" (Uniform Crime Reports, September 14, 2009, http://www.fbi.gov/ucr/ucr.htm)
*By law enforcement agencies submitting complete reports to the F.B.I. for 12 months in 2008. The F.B.I. estimates 98,035 reported and unreported arrests for motor vehicle theft occurred in 2009. Motor vehicle theft includes the theft or attempted theft of a self-propelled vehicle. Excludes motorboats, construction equipment, airplanes, and farming equipment. See important note at beginning of this chapter. **Not available.

Reported Arrest Rate for Motor Vehicle Theft in 2008

National Rate = 33.8 Reported Arrests per 100,000 Population*

ALPHA ORDER

RANK	STATE	RATE
22	Alabama	28.3
9	Alaska	40.2
8	Arizona	40.4
38	Arkansas	17.3
4	California	47.1
18	Colorado	29.8
30	Connecticut	22.0
33	Delaware	19.6
3	Florida	49.6
14	Georgia	34.9
13	Hawaii	37.0
45	Idaho	12.9
NA	Illinois**	NA
7	Indiana	42.3
32	Iowa	20.0
33	Kansas	19.6
NA	Kentucky**	NA
11	Louisiana	37.2
24	Maine	25.1
2	Maryland	59.1
46	Massachusetts	12.1
15	Michigan	33.7
20	Minnesota	29.1
12	Mississippi	37.1
1	Missouri	60.3
25	Montana	24.3
28	Nebraska	22.9
6	Nevada	43.9
48	New Hampshire	8.2
47	New Jersey	11.0
26	New Mexico	24.2
31	New York	21.6
29	North Carolina	22.8
16	North Dakota	30.1
42	Ohio	15.7
40	Oklahoma	16.2
10	Oregon	39.8
21	Pennsylvania	28.9
44	Rhode Island	13.1
37	South Carolina	17.5
36	South Dakota	18.2
5	Tennessee	47.0
23	Texas	25.5
35	Utah	19.4
39	Vermont	17.1
43	Virginia	13.9
19	Washington	29.7
41	West Virginia	16.1
17	Wisconsin	30.0
27	Wyoming	23.7

RANK ORDER

RANK	STATE	RATE
1	Missouri	60.3
2	Maryland	59.1
3	Florida	49.6
4	California	47.1
5	Tennessee	47.0
6	Nevada	43.9
7	Indiana	42.3
8	Arizona	40.4
9	Alaska	40.2
10	Oregon	39.8
11	Louisiana	37.2
12	Mississippi	37.1
13	Hawaii	37.0
14	Georgia	34.9
15	Michigan	33.7
16	North Dakota	30.1
17	Wisconsin	30.0
18	Colorado	29.8
19	Washington	29.7
20	Minnesota	29.1
21	Pennsylvania	28.9
22	Alabama	28.3
23	Texas	25.5
24	Maine	25.1
25	Montana	24.3
26	New Mexico	24.2
27	Wyoming	23.7
28	Nebraska	22.9
29	North Carolina	22.8
30	Connecticut	22.0
31	New York	21.6
32	Iowa	20.0
33	Delaware	19.6
33	Kansas	19.6
35	Utah	19.4
36	South Dakota	18.2
37	South Carolina	17.5
38	Arkansas	17.3
39	Vermont	17.1
40	Oklahoma	16.2
41	West Virginia	16.1
42	Ohio	15.7
43	Virginia	13.9
44	Rhode Island	13.1
45	Idaho	12.9
46	Massachusetts	12.1
47	New Jersey	11.0
48	New Hampshire	8.2
NA	Illinois**	NA
NA	Kentucky**	NA
	District of Columbia**	NA

Source: CQ Press using reported data from the Federal Bureau of Investigation
  "Crime in the United States 2008" (Uniform Crime Reports, September 14, 2009, http://www.fbi.gov/ucr/ucr.htm)
*By law enforcement agencies submitting complete reports to the F.B.I. for 12 months in 2008. These rates based on population estimates for areas under the jurisdiction of those agencies reporting. Arrest rate based on the F.B.I. estimate of reported and unreported arrests for motor vehicle theft is 32.2 arrests per 100,000 population. See important note at beginning of this chapter.
**Not available.

Reported Arrests for Arson in 2008

National Total = 11,164 Reported Arrests*

ALPHA ORDER				RANK ORDER			
RANK	STATE	ARRESTS	% of USA	RANK	STATE	ARRESTS	% of USA
28	Alabama	127	1.1%	1	California	1,487	13.3%
44	Alaska	46	0.4%	2	Texas	732	6.6%
17	Arizona	262	2.3%	3	Pennsylvania	683	6.1%
40	Arkansas	61	0.5%	4	Maryland	565	5.1%
1	California	1,487	13.3%	5	New York	435	3.9%
19	Colorado	226	2.0%	6	Wisconsin	399	3.6%
29	Connecticut	118	1.1%	7	New Jersey	397	3.6%
37	Delaware	70	0.6%	8	Missouri	386	3.5%
9	Florida	380	3.4%	9	Florida	380	3.4%
22	Georgia	190	1.7%	10	Oregon	344	3.1%
47	Hawaii	31	0.3%	11	North Carolina	316	2.8%
33	Idaho	84	0.8%	12	Virginia	306	2.7%
36	Illinois	75	0.7%	13	Michigan	300	2.7%
21	Indiana	217	1.9%	14	Oklahoma	278	2.5%
25	Iowa	141	1.3%	15	Washington	276	2.5%
34	Kansas	83	0.7%	16	Tennessee	267	2.4%
39	Kentucky	62	0.6%	17	Arizona	262	2.3%
24	Louisiana	170	1.5%	18	Ohio	241	2.2%
38	Maine	63	0.6%	19	Colorado	226	2.0%
4	Maryland	565	5.1%	20	Nevada	220	2.0%
26	Massachusetts	133	1.2%	21	Indiana	217	1.9%
13	Michigan	300	2.7%	22	Georgia	190	1.7%
22	Minnesota	190	1.7%	22	Minnesota	190	1.7%
32	Mississippi	101	0.9%	24	Louisiana	170	1.5%
8	Missouri	386	3.5%	25	Iowa	141	1.3%
41	Montana	57	0.5%	26	Massachusetts	133	1.2%
35	Nebraska	78	0.7%	27	South Carolina	128	1.1%
20	Nevada	220	2.0%	28	Alabama	127	1.1%
42	New Hampshire	47	0.4%	29	Connecticut	118	1.1%
7	New Jersey	397	3.6%	30	New Mexico	102	0.9%
30	New Mexico	102	0.9%	30	Utah	102	0.9%
5	New York	435	3.9%	32	Mississippi	101	0.9%
11	North Carolina	316	2.8%	33	Idaho	84	0.8%
48	North Dakota	22	0.2%	34	Kansas	83	0.7%
18	Ohio	241	2.2%	35	Nebraska	78	0.7%
14	Oklahoma	278	2.5%	36	Illinois	75	0.7%
10	Oregon	344	3.1%	37	Delaware	70	0.6%
3	Pennsylvania	683	6.1%	38	Maine	63	0.6%
42	Rhode Island	47	0.4%	39	Kentucky	62	0.6%
27	South Carolina	128	1.1%	40	Arkansas	61	0.5%
45	South Dakota	44	0.4%	41	Montana	57	0.5%
16	Tennessee	267	2.4%	42	New Hampshire	47	0.4%
2	Texas	732	6.6%	42	Rhode Island	47	0.4%
30	Utah	102	0.9%	44	Alaska	46	0.4%
50	Vermont	19	0.2%	45	South Dakota	44	0.4%
12	Virginia	306	2.7%	46	West Virginia	34	0.3%
15	Washington	276	2.5%	47	Hawaii	31	0.3%
46	West Virginia	34	0.3%	48	North Dakota	22	0.2%
6	Wisconsin	399	3.6%	48	Wyoming	22	0.2%
48	Wyoming	22	0.2%	50	Vermont	19	0.2%
					District of Columbia**	NA	NA

Source: Reported data from the Federal Bureau of Investigation
   "Crime in the United States 2008" (Uniform Crime Reports, September 14, 2009, http://www.fbi.gov/ucr/ucr.htm)
*By law enforcement agencies submitting complete reports to the F.B.I. for 12 months in 2008. The F.B.I. estimates 14,125 reported and unreported arrests for arson occurred in 2008. Arson is the willful burning of or attempt to burn a building, vehicle, or another's personal property. See important note at beginning of this chapter.
**Not available.

Reported Arrest Rate for Arson in 2008

National Rate = 4.5 Reported Arrests per 100,000 Population*

ALPHA ORDER

RANK	STATE	RATE
40	Alabama	3.4
11	Alaska	6.9
31	Arizona	4.1
46	Arkansas	2.5
31	California	4.1
18	Colorado	5.2
35	Connecticut	3.7
4	Delaware	8.0
48	Florida	2.1
41	Georgia	3.2
45	Hawaii	2.7
14	Idaho	5.9
NA	Illinois**	NA
24	Indiana	4.7
19	Iowa	5.1
28	Kansas	4.4
NA	Kentucky**	NA
11	Louisiana	6.9
20	Maine	4.8
1	Maryland	10.1
47	Massachusetts	2.3
38	Michigan	3.5
35	Minnesota	3.7
5	Mississippi	7.7
9	Missouri	7.0
13	Montana	6.1
20	Nebraska	4.8
3	Nevada	8.6
26	New Hampshire	4.6
20	New Jersey	4.8
8	New Mexico	7.1
24	New York	4.7
20	North Carolina	4.8
34	North Dakota	3.8
38	Ohio	3.5
6	Oklahoma	7.6
2	Oregon	9.4
16	Pennsylvania	5.7
27	Rhode Island	4.5
44	South Carolina	2.9
9	South Dakota	7.0
17	Tennessee	5.4
42	Texas	3.1
29	Utah	4.3
35	Vermont	3.7
31	Virginia	4.1
15	Washington	5.8
42	West Virginia	3.1
7	Wisconsin	7.2
30	Wyoming	4.2

RANK ORDER

RANK	STATE	RATE
1	Maryland	10.1
2	Oregon	9.4
3	Nevada	8.6
4	Delaware	8.0
5	Mississippi	7.7
6	Oklahoma	7.6
7	Wisconsin	7.2
8	New Mexico	7.1
9	Missouri	7.0
9	South Dakota	7.0
11	Alaska	6.9
11	Louisiana	6.9
13	Montana	6.1
14	Idaho	5.9
15	Washington	5.8
16	Pennsylvania	5.7
17	Tennessee	5.4
18	Colorado	5.2
19	Iowa	5.1
20	Maine	4.8
20	Nebraska	4.8
20	New Jersey	4.8
20	North Carolina	4.8
24	Indiana	4.7
24	New York	4.7
26	New Hampshire	4.6
27	Rhode Island	4.5
28	Kansas	4.4
29	Utah	4.3
30	Wyoming	4.2
31	Arizona	4.1
31	California	4.1
31	Virginia	4.1
34	North Dakota	3.8
35	Connecticut	3.7
35	Minnesota	3.7
35	Vermont	3.7
38	Michigan	3.5
38	Ohio	3.5
40	Alabama	3.4
41	Georgia	3.2
42	Texas	3.1
42	West Virginia	3.1
44	South Carolina	2.9
45	Hawaii	2.7
46	Arkansas	2.5
47	Massachusetts	2.3
48	Florida	2.1
NA	Illinois**	NA
NA	Kentucky**	NA
	District of Columbia**	NA

Source: CQ Press using reported data from the Federal Bureau of Investigation
   "Crime in the United States 2008" (Uniform Crime Reports, September 14, 2009, http://www.fbi.gov/ucr/ucr.htm)
*By law enforcement agencies submitting complete reports to the F.B.I. for 12 months in 2008. These rates based on population estimates for areas under the jurisdiction of those agencies reporting. Arrest rate based on the F.B.I. estimate of reported and unreported arrests for arson is 4.6 arrests per 100,000 population. See important note at beginning of this chapter.
**Not available.

Reported Arrests for Weapons Violations in 2008

National Total = 146,347 Reported Arrests*

<table>
<thead>
<tr><th colspan="4">ALPHA ORDER</th><th colspan="4">RANK ORDER</th></tr>
<tr><th>RANK</th><th>STATE</th><th>ARRESTS</th><th>% of USA</th><th>RANK</th><th>STATE</th><th>ARRESTS</th><th>% of USA</th></tr>
</thead>
<tbody>
<tr><td>27</td><td>Alabama</td><td>1,546</td><td>1.1%</td><td>1</td><td>California</td><td>31,800</td><td>21.7%</td></tr>
<tr><td>42</td><td>Alaska</td><td>345</td><td>0.2%</td><td>2</td><td>Texas</td><td>11,667</td><td>8.0%</td></tr>
<tr><td>14</td><td>Arizona</td><td>3,681</td><td>2.5%</td><td>3</td><td>Florida</td><td>8,092</td><td>5.5%</td></tr>
<tr><td>30</td><td>Arkansas</td><td>1,330</td><td>0.9%</td><td>4</td><td>North Carolina</td><td>7,434</td><td>5.1%</td></tr>
<tr><td>1</td><td>California</td><td>31,800</td><td>21.7%</td><td>5</td><td>New Jersey</td><td>5,059</td><td>3.5%</td></tr>
<tr><td>21</td><td>Colorado</td><td>2,054</td><td>1.4%</td><td>6</td><td>Wisconsin</td><td>4,997</td><td>3.4%</td></tr>
<tr><td>29</td><td>Connecticut</td><td>1,399</td><td>1.0%</td><td>7</td><td>Georgia</td><td>4,935</td><td>3.4%</td></tr>
<tr><td>39</td><td>Delaware</td><td>477</td><td>0.3%</td><td>8</td><td>Michigan</td><td>4,617</td><td>3.2%</td></tr>
<tr><td>3</td><td>Florida</td><td>8,092</td><td>5.5%</td><td>9</td><td>Pennsylvania</td><td>4,576</td><td>3.1%</td></tr>
<tr><td>7</td><td>Georgia</td><td>4,935</td><td>3.4%</td><td>10</td><td>Maryland</td><td>4,328</td><td>3.0%</td></tr>
<tr><td>44</td><td>Hawaii</td><td>199</td><td>0.1%</td><td>11</td><td>Illinois</td><td>4,117</td><td>2.8%</td></tr>
<tr><td>35</td><td>Idaho</td><td>625</td><td>0.4%</td><td>12</td><td>Missouri</td><td>4,058</td><td>2.8%</td></tr>
<tr><td>11</td><td>Illinois</td><td>4,117</td><td>2.8%</td><td>13</td><td>Virginia</td><td>4,035</td><td>2.8%</td></tr>
<tr><td>23</td><td>Indiana</td><td>1,921</td><td>1.3%</td><td>14</td><td>Arizona</td><td>3,681</td><td>2.5%</td></tr>
<tr><td>38</td><td>Iowa</td><td>519</td><td>0.4%</td><td>15</td><td>New York</td><td>3,379</td><td>2.3%</td></tr>
<tr><td>34</td><td>Kansas</td><td>731</td><td>0.5%</td><td>16</td><td>Tennessee</td><td>3,238</td><td>2.2%</td></tr>
<tr><td>37</td><td>Kentucky</td><td>611</td><td>0.4%</td><td>17</td><td>Ohio</td><td>2,999</td><td>2.0%</td></tr>
<tr><td>25</td><td>Louisiana</td><td>1,748</td><td>1.2%</td><td>18</td><td>Washington</td><td>2,879</td><td>2.0%</td></tr>
<tr><td>41</td><td>Maine</td><td>356</td><td>0.2%</td><td>19</td><td>Minnesota</td><td>2,269</td><td>1.6%</td></tr>
<tr><td>10</td><td>Maryland</td><td>4,328</td><td>3.0%</td><td>20</td><td>Oklahoma</td><td>2,131</td><td>1.5%</td></tr>
<tr><td>28</td><td>Massachusetts</td><td>1,405</td><td>1.0%</td><td>21</td><td>Colorado</td><td>2,054</td><td>1.4%</td></tr>
<tr><td>8</td><td>Michigan</td><td>4,617</td><td>3.2%</td><td>22</td><td>Nevada</td><td>2,051</td><td>1.4%</td></tr>
<tr><td>19</td><td>Minnesota</td><td>2,269</td><td>1.6%</td><td>23</td><td>Indiana</td><td>1,921</td><td>1.3%</td></tr>
<tr><td>33</td><td>Mississippi</td><td>1,003</td><td>0.7%</td><td>24</td><td>Oregon</td><td>1,777</td><td>1.2%</td></tr>
<tr><td>12</td><td>Missouri</td><td>4,058</td><td>2.8%</td><td>25</td><td>Louisiana</td><td>1,748</td><td>1.2%</td></tr>
<tr><td>48</td><td>Montana</td><td>121</td><td>0.1%</td><td>26</td><td>South Carolina</td><td>1,682</td><td>1.1%</td></tr>
<tr><td>32</td><td>Nebraska</td><td>1,108</td><td>0.8%</td><td>27</td><td>Alabama</td><td>1,546</td><td>1.1%</td></tr>
<tr><td>22</td><td>Nevada</td><td>2,051</td><td>1.4%</td><td>28</td><td>Massachusetts</td><td>1,405</td><td>1.0%</td></tr>
<tr><td>49</td><td>New Hampshire</td><td>88</td><td>0.1%</td><td>29</td><td>Connecticut</td><td>1,399</td><td>1.0%</td></tr>
<tr><td>5</td><td>New Jersey</td><td>5,059</td><td>3.5%</td><td>30</td><td>Arkansas</td><td>1,330</td><td>0.9%</td></tr>
<tr><td>36</td><td>New Mexico</td><td>619</td><td>0.4%</td><td>31</td><td>Utah</td><td>1,200</td><td>0.8%</td></tr>
<tr><td>15</td><td>New York</td><td>3,379</td><td>2.3%</td><td>32</td><td>Nebraska</td><td>1,108</td><td>0.8%</td></tr>
<tr><td>4</td><td>North Carolina</td><td>7,434</td><td>5.1%</td><td>33</td><td>Mississippi</td><td>1,003</td><td>0.7%</td></tr>
<tr><td>45</td><td>North Dakota</td><td>166</td><td>0.1%</td><td>34</td><td>Kansas</td><td>731</td><td>0.5%</td></tr>
<tr><td>17</td><td>Ohio</td><td>2,999</td><td>2.0%</td><td>35</td><td>Idaho</td><td>625</td><td>0.4%</td></tr>
<tr><td>20</td><td>Oklahoma</td><td>2,131</td><td>1.5%</td><td>36</td><td>New Mexico</td><td>619</td><td>0.4%</td></tr>
<tr><td>24</td><td>Oregon</td><td>1,777</td><td>1.2%</td><td>37</td><td>Kentucky</td><td>611</td><td>0.4%</td></tr>
<tr><td>9</td><td>Pennsylvania</td><td>4,576</td><td>3.1%</td><td>38</td><td>Iowa</td><td>519</td><td>0.4%</td></tr>
<tr><td>40</td><td>Rhode Island</td><td>391</td><td>0.3%</td><td>39</td><td>Delaware</td><td>477</td><td>0.3%</td></tr>
<tr><td>26</td><td>South Carolina</td><td>1,682</td><td>1.1%</td><td>40</td><td>Rhode Island</td><td>391</td><td>0.3%</td></tr>
<tr><td>47</td><td>South Dakota</td><td>129</td><td>0.1%</td><td>41</td><td>Maine</td><td>356</td><td>0.2%</td></tr>
<tr><td>16</td><td>Tennessee</td><td>3,238</td><td>2.2%</td><td>42</td><td>Alaska</td><td>345</td><td>0.2%</td></tr>
<tr><td>2</td><td>Texas</td><td>11,667</td><td>8.0%</td><td>43</td><td>West Virginia</td><td>268</td><td>0.2%</td></tr>
<tr><td>31</td><td>Utah</td><td>1,200</td><td>0.8%</td><td>44</td><td>Hawaii</td><td>199</td><td>0.1%</td></tr>
<tr><td>50</td><td>Vermont</td><td>18</td><td>0.0%</td><td>45</td><td>North Dakota</td><td>166</td><td>0.1%</td></tr>
<tr><td>13</td><td>Virginia</td><td>4,035</td><td>2.8%</td><td>46</td><td>Wyoming</td><td>136</td><td>0.1%</td></tr>
<tr><td>18</td><td>Washington</td><td>2,879</td><td>2.0%</td><td>47</td><td>South Dakota</td><td>129</td><td>0.1%</td></tr>
<tr><td>43</td><td>West Virginia</td><td>268</td><td>0.2%</td><td>48</td><td>Montana</td><td>121</td><td>0.1%</td></tr>
<tr><td>6</td><td>Wisconsin</td><td>4,997</td><td>3.4%</td><td>49</td><td>New Hampshire</td><td>88</td><td>0.1%</td></tr>
<tr><td>46</td><td>Wyoming</td><td>136</td><td>0.1%</td><td>50</td><td>Vermont</td><td>18</td><td>0.0%</td></tr>
<tr><td></td><td></td><td></td><td></td><td></td><td>District of Columbia**</td><td>NA</td><td>NA</td></tr>
</tbody>
</table>

Source: Reported data from the Federal Bureau of Investigation
   "Crime in the United States 2008" (Uniform Crime Reports, September 14, 2009, http://www.fbi.gov/ucr/ucr.htm)
*By law enforcement agencies submitting complete reports to the F.B.I. for 12 months in 2008. The F.B.I. estimates 179,661 reported and unreported arrests for weapons violations occurred in 2008. Weapons violations include illegal carrying and possession. See important note at beginning of this chapter.
**Not available.

Reported Arrest Rate for Weapons Violations in 2008

National Rate = 58.7 Reported Arrests per 100,000 Population*

ALPHA ORDER

RANK	STATE	RATE
32	Alabama	41.0
20	Alaska	51.8
15	Arizona	57.4
16	Arkansas	55.3
3	California	87.0
24	Colorado	47.1
29	Connecticut	43.4
17	Delaware	54.6
26	Florida	44.2
4	Georgia	82.3
45	Hawaii	17.4
28	Idaho	43.5
NA	Illinois**	NA
31	Indiana	41.2
44	Iowa	18.8
33	Kansas	38.6
NA	Kentucky**	NA
9	Louisiana	70.7
39	Maine	27.1
6	Maryland	77.6
42	Massachusetts	24.1
19	Michigan	53.3
25	Minnesota	44.7
7	Mississippi	76.7
8	Missouri	73.2
46	Montana	13.0
10	Nebraska	67.8
5	Nevada	80.6
47	New Hampshire	8.5
12	New Jersey	60.5
30	New Mexico	42.8
37	New York	36.6
1	North Carolina	112.4
38	North Dakota	28.6
27	Ohio	43.7
14	Oklahoma	58.6
23	Oregon	48.7
35	Pennsylvania	38.1
36	Rhode Island	37.2
34	South Carolina	38.2
43	South Dakota	20.5
11	Tennessee	65.4
22	Texas	49.9
21	Utah	50.5
48	Vermont	3.5
18	Virginia	53.5
12	Washington	60.5
41	West Virginia	24.2
2	Wisconsin	90.2
40	Wyoming	25.8

RANK ORDER

RANK	STATE	RATE
1	North Carolina	112.4
2	Wisconsin	90.2
3	California	87.0
4	Georgia	82.3
5	Nevada	80.6
6	Maryland	77.6
7	Mississippi	76.7
8	Missouri	73.2
9	Louisiana	70.7
10	Nebraska	67.8
11	Tennessee	65.4
12	New Jersey	60.5
12	Washington	60.5
14	Oklahoma	58.6
15	Arizona	57.4
16	Arkansas	55.3
17	Delaware	54.6
18	Virginia	53.5
19	Michigan	53.3
20	Alaska	51.8
21	Utah	50.5
22	Texas	49.9
23	Oregon	48.7
24	Colorado	47.1
25	Minnesota	44.7
26	Florida	44.2
27	Ohio	43.7
28	Idaho	43.5
29	Connecticut	43.4
30	New Mexico	42.8
31	Indiana	41.2
32	Alabama	41.0
33	Kansas	38.6
34	South Carolina	38.2
35	Pennsylvania	38.1
36	Rhode Island	37.2
37	New York	36.6
38	North Dakota	28.6
39	Maine	27.1
40	Wyoming	25.8
41	West Virginia	24.2
42	Massachusetts	24.1
43	South Dakota	20.5
44	Iowa	18.8
45	Hawaii	17.4
46	Montana	13.0
47	New Hampshire	8.5
48	Vermont	3.5
NA	Illinois**	NA
NA	Kentucky**	NA
	District of Columbia**	NA

Source: CQ Press using reported data from the Federal Bureau of Investigation
   "Crime in the United States 2008" (Uniform Crime Reports, September 14, 2009, http://www.fbi.gov/ucr/ucr.htm)
*By law enforcement agencies submitting complete reports to the F.B.I. for 12 months in 2008. These rates based on population estimates for areas under the jurisdiction of those agencies reporting. Arrest rate based on the F.B.I. estimate of reported and unreported arrests for weapons violations is 59.1 arrests per 100,000 population. See important note at beginning of this chapter. **Not available.

Reported Arrests for Driving Under the Influence in 2008

National Total = 1,171,935 Reported Arrests*

<table>
<tr><td colspan="4"><u>ALPHA ORDER</u></td><td colspan="4"><u>RANK ORDER</u></td></tr>
<tr><th>RANK</th><th>STATE</th><th>ARRESTS</th><th>% of USA</th><th>RANK</th><th>STATE</th><th>ARRESTS</th><th>% of USA</th></tr>
<tr><td>23</td><td>Alabama</td><td>14,991</td><td>1.3%</td><td>1</td><td>California</td><td>214,828</td><td>18.3%</td></tr>
<tr><td>41</td><td>Alaska</td><td>5,538</td><td>0.5%</td><td>2</td><td>Texas</td><td>90,066</td><td>7.7%</td></tr>
<tr><td>7</td><td>Arizona</td><td>39,746</td><td>3.4%</td><td>3</td><td>Florida</td><td>61,852</td><td>5.3%</td></tr>
<tr><td>31</td><td>Arkansas</td><td>11,707</td><td>1.0%</td><td>4</td><td>Pennsylvania</td><td>53,319</td><td>4.5%</td></tr>
<tr><td>1</td><td>California</td><td>214,828</td><td>18.3%</td><td>5</td><td>North Carolina</td><td>49,599</td><td>4.2%</td></tr>
<tr><td>12</td><td>Colorado</td><td>28,198</td><td>2.4%</td><td>6</td><td>Wisconsin</td><td>40,549</td><td>3.5%</td></tr>
<tr><td>34</td><td>Connecticut</td><td>8,235</td><td>0.7%</td><td>7</td><td>Arizona</td><td>39,746</td><td>3.4%</td></tr>
<tr><td>50</td><td>Delaware</td><td>215</td><td>0.0%</td><td>8</td><td>Michigan</td><td>35,534</td><td>3.0%</td></tr>
<tr><td>3</td><td>Florida</td><td>61,852</td><td>5.3%</td><td>9</td><td>Washington</td><td>34,952</td><td>3.0%</td></tr>
<tr><td>15</td><td>Georgia</td><td>25,421</td><td>2.2%</td><td>10</td><td>Missouri</td><td>34,004</td><td>2.9%</td></tr>
<tr><td>40</td><td>Hawaii</td><td>5,812</td><td>0.5%</td><td>11</td><td>Minnesota</td><td>29,832</td><td>2.5%</td></tr>
<tr><td>30</td><td>Idaho</td><td>11,850</td><td>1.0%</td><td>12</td><td>Colorado</td><td>28,198</td><td>2.4%</td></tr>
<tr><td>42</td><td>Illinois</td><td>4,909</td><td>0.4%</td><td>13</td><td>Virginia</td><td>27,732</td><td>2.4%</td></tr>
<tr><td>19</td><td>Indiana</td><td>23,475</td><td>2.0%</td><td>14</td><td>Tennessee</td><td>26,322</td><td>2.2%</td></tr>
<tr><td>26</td><td>Iowa</td><td>14,147</td><td>1.2%</td><td>15</td><td>Georgia</td><td>25,421</td><td>2.2%</td></tr>
<tr><td>28</td><td>Kansas</td><td>13,080</td><td>1.1%</td><td>16</td><td>New York</td><td>25,169</td><td>2.1%</td></tr>
<tr><td>49</td><td>Kentucky</td><td>2,363</td><td>0.2%</td><td>17</td><td>New Jersey</td><td>24,313</td><td>2.1%</td></tr>
<tr><td>35</td><td>Louisiana</td><td>7,977</td><td>0.7%</td><td>18</td><td>Maryland</td><td>23,714</td><td>2.0%</td></tr>
<tr><td>36</td><td>Maine</td><td>7,270</td><td>0.6%</td><td>19</td><td>Indiana</td><td>23,475</td><td>2.0%</td></tr>
<tr><td>18</td><td>Maryland</td><td>23,714</td><td>2.0%</td><td>20</td><td>Ohio</td><td>19,088</td><td>1.6%</td></tr>
<tr><td>29</td><td>Massachusetts</td><td>12,941</td><td>1.1%</td><td>21</td><td>Oklahoma</td><td>18,980</td><td>1.6%</td></tr>
<tr><td>8</td><td>Michigan</td><td>35,534</td><td>3.0%</td><td>22</td><td>Oregon</td><td>17,015</td><td>1.5%</td></tr>
<tr><td>11</td><td>Minnesota</td><td>29,832</td><td>2.5%</td><td>23</td><td>Alabama</td><td>14,991</td><td>1.3%</td></tr>
<tr><td>32</td><td>Mississippi</td><td>11,629</td><td>1.0%</td><td>24</td><td>South Carolina</td><td>14,742</td><td>1.3%</td></tr>
<tr><td>10</td><td>Missouri</td><td>34,004</td><td>2.9%</td><td>25</td><td>Nevada</td><td>14,445</td><td>1.2%</td></tr>
<tr><td>45</td><td>Montana</td><td>4,240</td><td>0.4%</td><td>26</td><td>Iowa</td><td>14,147</td><td>1.2%</td></tr>
<tr><td>27</td><td>Nebraska</td><td>13,692</td><td>1.2%</td><td>27</td><td>Nebraska</td><td>13,692</td><td>1.2%</td></tr>
<tr><td>25</td><td>Nevada</td><td>14,445</td><td>1.2%</td><td>28</td><td>Kansas</td><td>13,080</td><td>1.1%</td></tr>
<tr><td>43</td><td>New Hampshire</td><td>4,571</td><td>0.4%</td><td>29</td><td>Massachusetts</td><td>12,941</td><td>1.1%</td></tr>
<tr><td>17</td><td>New Jersey</td><td>24,313</td><td>2.1%</td><td>30</td><td>Idaho</td><td>11,850</td><td>1.0%</td></tr>
<tr><td>33</td><td>New Mexico</td><td>9,741</td><td>0.8%</td><td>31</td><td>Arkansas</td><td>11,707</td><td>1.0%</td></tr>
<tr><td>16</td><td>New York</td><td>25,169</td><td>2.1%</td><td>32</td><td>Mississippi</td><td>11,629</td><td>1.0%</td></tr>
<tr><td>5</td><td>North Carolina</td><td>49,599</td><td>4.2%</td><td>33</td><td>New Mexico</td><td>9,741</td><td>0.8%</td></tr>
<tr><td>46</td><td>North Dakota</td><td>4,003</td><td>0.3%</td><td>34</td><td>Connecticut</td><td>8,235</td><td>0.7%</td></tr>
<tr><td>20</td><td>Ohio</td><td>19,088</td><td>1.6%</td><td>35</td><td>Louisiana</td><td>7,977</td><td>0.7%</td></tr>
<tr><td>21</td><td>Oklahoma</td><td>18,980</td><td>1.6%</td><td>36</td><td>Maine</td><td>7,270</td><td>0.6%</td></tr>
<tr><td>22</td><td>Oregon</td><td>17,015</td><td>1.5%</td><td>37</td><td>Wyoming</td><td>7,159</td><td>0.6%</td></tr>
<tr><td>4</td><td>Pennsylvania</td><td>53,319</td><td>4.5%</td><td>38</td><td>Utah</td><td>6,894</td><td>0.6%</td></tr>
<tr><td>47</td><td>Rhode Island</td><td>2,778</td><td>0.2%</td><td>39</td><td>South Dakota</td><td>6,190</td><td>0.5%</td></tr>
<tr><td>24</td><td>South Carolina</td><td>14,742</td><td>1.3%</td><td>40</td><td>Hawaii</td><td>5,812</td><td>0.5%</td></tr>
<tr><td>39</td><td>South Dakota</td><td>6,190</td><td>0.5%</td><td>41</td><td>Alaska</td><td>5,538</td><td>0.5%</td></tr>
<tr><td>14</td><td>Tennessee</td><td>26,322</td><td>2.2%</td><td>42</td><td>Illinois</td><td>4,909</td><td>0.4%</td></tr>
<tr><td>2</td><td>Texas</td><td>90,066</td><td>7.7%</td><td>43</td><td>New Hampshire</td><td>4,571</td><td>0.4%</td></tr>
<tr><td>38</td><td>Utah</td><td>6,894</td><td>0.6%</td><td>44</td><td>West Virginia</td><td>4,429</td><td>0.4%</td></tr>
<tr><td>48</td><td>Vermont</td><td>2,647</td><td>0.2%</td><td>45</td><td>Montana</td><td>4,240</td><td>0.4%</td></tr>
<tr><td>13</td><td>Virginia</td><td>27,732</td><td>2.4%</td><td>46</td><td>North Dakota</td><td>4,003</td><td>0.3%</td></tr>
<tr><td>9</td><td>Washington</td><td>34,952</td><td>3.0%</td><td>47</td><td>Rhode Island</td><td>2,778</td><td>0.2%</td></tr>
<tr><td>44</td><td>West Virginia</td><td>4,429</td><td>0.4%</td><td>48</td><td>Vermont</td><td>2,647</td><td>0.2%</td></tr>
<tr><td>6</td><td>Wisconsin</td><td>40,549</td><td>3.5%</td><td>49</td><td>Kentucky</td><td>2,363</td><td>0.2%</td></tr>
<tr><td>37</td><td>Wyoming</td><td>7,159</td><td>0.6%</td><td>50</td><td>Delaware</td><td>215</td><td>0.0%</td></tr>
<tr><td></td><td></td><td></td><td></td><td></td><td>District of Columbia**</td><td>NA</td><td>NA</td></tr>
</table>

Source: Reported data from the Federal Bureau of Investigation
"Crime in the United States 2008" (Uniform Crime Reports, September 14, 2009, http://www.fbi.gov/ucr/ucr.htm)
*By law enforcement agencies submitting complete reports to the F.B.I. for 12 months in 2008. The F.B.I. estimates 1,483,396 reported and unreported arrests for driving under the influence occurred in 2008. Includes driving any vehicle while drunk or under the influence of liquor or narcotics. See important note at beginning of this chapter.
**Not available.

Reported Arrest Rate for Driving Under the Influence in 2008

National Rate = 470.3 Reported Arrests per 100,000 Population*

ALPHA ORDER

RANK	STATE	RATE
35	Alabama	397.3
5	Alaska	830.9
14	Arizona	619.6
26	Arkansas	487.0
17	California	587.7
13	Colorado	646.8
46	Connecticut	255.2
48	Delaware	24.6
38	Florida	338.1
32	Georgia	424.0
24	Hawaii	507.5
6	Idaho	825.7
NA	Illinois**	NA
25	Indiana	503.9
23	Iowa	511.5
10	Kansas	690.0
NA	Kentucky**	NA
40	Louisiana	322.7
19	Maine	553.2
31	Maryland	425.4
47	Massachusetts	222.4
33	Michigan	410.1
16	Minnesota	587.9
3	Mississippi	889.1
15	Missouri	613.5
28	Montana	454.6
4	Nebraska	837.9
18	Nevada	567.5
30	New Hampshire	442.7
41	New Jersey	291.0
12	New Mexico	673.7
44	New York	272.9
7	North Carolina	750.0
11	North Dakota	689.5
43	Ohio	278.0
21	Oklahoma	521.7
27	Oregon	466.2
29	Pennsylvania	443.6
45	Rhode Island	264.4
39	South Carolina	335.1
2	South Dakota	982.2
20	Tennessee	532.0
36	Texas	385.3
42	Utah	290.0
22	Vermont	519.2
37	Virginia	367.6
8	Washington	734.1
34	West Virginia	399.2
9	Wisconsin	731.9
1	Wyoming	1,355.8

RANK ORDER

RANK	STATE	RATE
1	Wyoming	1,355.8
2	South Dakota	982.2
3	Mississippi	889.1
4	Nebraska	837.9
5	Alaska	830.9
6	Idaho	825.7
7	North Carolina	750.0
8	Washington	734.1
9	Wisconsin	731.9
10	Kansas	690.0
11	North Dakota	689.5
12	New Mexico	673.7
13	Colorado	646.8
14	Arizona	619.6
15	Missouri	613.5
16	Minnesota	587.9
17	California	587.7
18	Nevada	567.5
19	Maine	553.2
20	Tennessee	532.0
21	Oklahoma	521.7
22	Vermont	519.2
23	Iowa	511.5
24	Hawaii	507.5
25	Indiana	503.9
26	Arkansas	487.0
27	Oregon	466.2
28	Montana	454.6
29	Pennsylvania	443.6
30	New Hampshire	442.7
31	Maryland	425.4
32	Georgia	424.0
33	Michigan	410.1
34	West Virginia	399.2
35	Alabama	397.3
36	Texas	385.3
37	Virginia	367.6
38	Florida	338.1
39	South Carolina	335.1
40	Louisiana	322.7
41	New Jersey	291.0
42	Utah	290.0
43	Ohio	278.0
44	New York	272.9
45	Rhode Island	264.4
46	Connecticut	255.2
47	Massachusetts	222.4
48	Delaware	24.6
NA	Illinois**	NA
NA	Kentucky**	NA
	District of Columbia**	NA

Source: CQ Press using reported data from the Federal Bureau of Investigation
   "Crime in the United States 2008" (Uniform Crime Reports, September 14, 2009, http://www.fbi.gov/ucr/ucr.htm)
*By law enforcement agencies submitting complete reports to the F.B.I. for 12 months in 2008. These rates based on population estimates for areas under the jurisdiction of those agencies reporting. Arrest rate based on the F.B.I. estimate of reported and unreported arrests for driving under the influence is 487.9 arrests per 100,000 population. See important note at beginning of this chapter. **Not available.

Reported Arrests for Drug Abuse Violations in 2008

National Total = 1,464,014 Reported Arrests*

ALPHA ORDER

RANK	STATE	ARRESTS	% of USA
27	Alabama	16,488	1.1%
48	Alaska	1,716	0.1%
13	Arizona	34,242	2.3%
31	Arkansas	11,513	0.8%
1	California	268,763	18.4%
25	Colorado	17,851	1.2%
28	Connecticut	16,132	1.1%
38	Delaware	5,895	0.4%
2	Florida	159,916	10.9%
11	Georgia	34,697	2.4%
46	Hawaii	2,022	0.1%
40	Idaho	5,514	0.4%
8	Illinois	45,612	3.1%
19	Indiana	22,671	1.5%
34	Iowa	8,497	0.6%
36	Kansas	6,854	0.5%
35	Kentucky	7,952	0.5%
24	Louisiana	17,959	1.2%
39	Maine	5,778	0.4%
4	Maryland	57,288	3.9%
21	Massachusetts	19,825	1.4%
15	Michigan	31,775	2.2%
23	Minnesota	18,196	1.2%
30	Mississippi	11,741	0.8%
10	Missouri	35,990	2.5%
49	Montana	1,620	0.1%
32	Nebraska	10,432	0.7%
29	Nevada	14,886	1.0%
43	New Hampshire	3,266	0.2%
7	New Jersey	52,749	3.6%
37	New Mexico	6,113	0.4%
6	New York	52,945	3.6%
9	North Carolina	36,571	2.5%
47	North Dakota	1,769	0.1%
16	Ohio	30,580	2.1%
20	Oklahoma	20,548	1.4%
26	Oregon	16,723	1.1%
5	Pennsylvania	56,228	3.8%
42	Rhode Island	3,791	0.3%
22	South Carolina	18,224	1.2%
45	South Dakota	2,395	0.2%
12	Tennessee	34,686	2.4%
3	Texas	136,897	9.4%
33	Utah	9,242	0.6%
50	Vermont	1,137	0.1%
14	Virginia	32,513	2.2%
18	Washington	23,440	1.6%
41	West Virginia	4,249	0.3%
17	Wisconsin	25,075	1.7%
44	Wyoming	2,969	0.2%

RANK ORDER

RANK	STATE	ARRESTS	% of USA
1	California	268,763	18.4%
2	Florida	159,916	10.9%
3	Texas	136,897	9.4%
4	Maryland	57,288	3.9%
5	Pennsylvania	56,228	3.8%
6	New York	52,945	3.6%
7	New Jersey	52,749	3.6%
8	Illinois	45,612	3.1%
9	North Carolina	36,571	2.5%
10	Missouri	35,990	2.5%
11	Georgia	34,697	2.4%
12	Tennessee	34,686	2.4%
13	Arizona	34,242	2.3%
14	Virginia	32,513	2.2%
15	Michigan	31,775	2.2%
16	Ohio	30,580	2.1%
17	Wisconsin	25,075	1.7%
18	Washington	23,440	1.6%
19	Indiana	22,671	1.5%
20	Oklahoma	20,548	1.4%
21	Massachusetts	19,825	1.4%
22	South Carolina	18,224	1.2%
23	Minnesota	18,196	1.2%
24	Louisiana	17,959	1.2%
25	Colorado	17,851	1.2%
26	Oregon	16,723	1.1%
27	Alabama	16,488	1.1%
28	Connecticut	16,132	1.1%
29	Nevada	14,886	1.0%
30	Mississippi	11,741	0.8%
31	Arkansas	11,513	0.8%
32	Nebraska	10,432	0.7%
33	Utah	9,242	0.6%
34	Iowa	8,497	0.6%
35	Kentucky	7,952	0.5%
36	Kansas	6,854	0.5%
37	New Mexico	6,113	0.4%
38	Delaware	5,895	0.4%
39	Maine	5,778	0.4%
40	Idaho	5,514	0.4%
41	West Virginia	4,249	0.3%
42	Rhode Island	3,791	0.3%
43	New Hampshire	3,266	0.2%
44	Wyoming	2,969	0.2%
45	South Dakota	2,395	0.2%
46	Hawaii	2,022	0.1%
47	North Dakota	1,769	0.1%
48	Alaska	1,716	0.1%
49	Montana	1,620	0.1%
50	Vermont	1,137	0.1%
	District of Columbia**	NA	NA

Source: Reported data from the Federal Bureau of Investigation
   "Crime in the United States 2008" (Uniform Crime Reports, September 14, 2009, http://www.fbi.gov/ucr/ucr.htm)
*By law enforcement agencies submitting complete reports to the F.B.I. for 12 months in 2008. The F.B.I. estimates 1,702,537 reported and unreported arrests for drug abuse violations occurred in 2008. Includes offenses relating to possession, sale, use, growing, and manufacturing of narcotic drugs. See important note at beginning of this chapter.
**Not available.

Reported Arrest Rate for Drug Abuse Violations in 2008

National Rate = 587.5 Reported Arrests per 100,000 Population*

ALPHA ORDER

RANK	STATE	RATE
28	Alabama	437.0
45	Alaska	257.5
18	Arizona	533.8
22	Arkansas	479.0
4	California	735.2
32	Colorado	409.5
19	Connecticut	499.9
7	Delaware	675.2
3	Florida	874.1
13	Georgia	578.7
47	Hawaii	176.6
34	Idaho	384.2
NA	Illinois**	NA
21	Indiana	486.7
43	Iowa	307.2
38	Kansas	361.5
NA	Kentucky**	NA
5	Louisiana	726.5
27	Maine	439.7
1	Maryland	1,027.7
41	Massachusetts	340.6
37	Michigan	366.7
40	Minnesota	358.6
2	Mississippi	897.6
8	Missouri	649.3
48	Montana	173.7
9	Nebraska	638.4
12	Nevada	584.8
42	New Hampshire	316.3
10	New Jersey	631.3
30	New Mexico	422.8
14	New York	574.0
17	North Carolina	553.0
44	North Dakota	304.7
26	Ohio	445.4
15	Oklahoma	564.8
24	Oregon	458.2
23	Pennsylvania	467.8
39	Rhode Island	360.8
31	South Carolina	414.3
36	South Dakota	380.0
6	Tennessee	701.0
11	Texas	585.6
33	Utah	388.8
46	Vermont	223.0
29	Virginia	431.0
20	Washington	492.3
35	West Virginia	383.0
25	Wisconsin	452.6
16	Wyoming	562.3

RANK ORDER

RANK	STATE	RATE
1	Maryland	1,027.7
2	Mississippi	897.6
3	Florida	874.1
4	California	735.2
5	Louisiana	726.5
6	Tennessee	701.0
7	Delaware	675.2
8	Missouri	649.3
9	Nebraska	638.4
10	New Jersey	631.3
11	Texas	585.6
12	Nevada	584.8
13	Georgia	578.7
14	New York	574.0
15	Oklahoma	564.8
16	Wyoming	562.3
17	North Carolina	553.0
18	Arizona	533.8
19	Connecticut	499.9
20	Washington	492.3
21	Indiana	486.7
22	Arkansas	479.0
23	Pennsylvania	467.8
24	Oregon	458.2
25	Wisconsin	452.6
26	Ohio	445.4
27	Maine	439.7
28	Alabama	437.0
29	Virginia	431.0
30	New Mexico	422.8
31	South Carolina	414.3
32	Colorado	409.5
33	Utah	388.8
34	Idaho	384.2
35	West Virginia	383.0
36	South Dakota	380.0
37	Michigan	366.7
38	Kansas	361.5
39	Rhode Island	360.8
40	Minnesota	358.6
41	Massachusetts	340.6
42	New Hampshire	316.3
43	Iowa	307.2
44	North Dakota	304.7
45	Alaska	257.5
46	Vermont	223.0
47	Hawaii	176.6
48	Montana	173.7
NA	Illinois**	NA
NA	Kentucky**	NA
	District of Columbia**	NA

Source: CQ Press using reported data from the Federal Bureau of Investigation
   "Crime in the United States 2008" (Uniform Crime Reports, September 14, 2009, http://www.fbi.gov/ucr/ucr.htm)
*By law enforcement agencies submitting complete reports to the F.B.I. for 12 months in 2008. These rates based on population estimates for areas under the jurisdiction of those agencies reporting. Arrest rate based on the F.B.I. estimate of reported and unreported arrests for drug abuse violations is 559.9 arrests per 100,000 population. See important note at beginning of this chapter. **Not available.

Reported Arrests for Sex Offenses in 2008

National Total = 64,246 Reported Arrests*

ALPHA ORDER

RANK	STATE	ARRESTS	% of USA	RANK	STATE	ARRESTS	% of USA
29	Alabama	582	0.9%	1	California	14,502	22.6%
41	Alaska	166	0.3%	2	Texas	4,059	6.3%
9	Arizona	1,773	2.8%	3	New York	3,887	6.0%
39	Arkansas	194	0.3%	4	Florida	3,452	5.4%
1	California	14,502	22.6%	5	Georgia	3,402	5.3%
22	Colorado	903	1.4%	6	Pennsylvania	2,779	4.3%
30	Connecticut	579	0.9%	7	Wisconsin	2,750	4.3%
38	Delaware	202	0.3%	8	Missouri	2,434	3.8%
4	Florida	3,452	5.4%	9	Arizona	1,773	2.8%
5	Georgia	3,402	5.3%	10	Nevada	1,594	2.5%
35	Hawaii	295	0.5%	11	New Jersey	1,527	2.4%
34	Idaho	314	0.5%	12	Minnesota	1,524	2.4%
19	Illinois	965	1.5%	13	Indiana	1,516	2.4%
13	Indiana	1,516	2.4%	14	North Carolina	1,362	2.1%
37	Iowa	237	0.4%	15	Maryland	1,343	2.1%
33	Kansas	325	0.5%	16	Oregon	1,334	2.1%
50	Kentucky	21	0.0%	17	Virginia	1,068	1.7%
27	Louisiana	596	0.9%	18	Washington	994	1.5%
36	Maine	275	0.4%	19	Illinois	965	1.5%
15	Maryland	1,343	2.1%	20	Ohio	964	1.5%
26	Massachusetts	696	1.1%	21	Michigan	962	1.5%
21	Michigan	962	1.5%	22	Colorado	903	1.4%
12	Minnesota	1,524	2.4%	23	Utah	811	1.3%
32	Mississippi	412	0.6%	24	Tennessee	731	1.1%
8	Missouri	2,434	3.8%	25	Oklahoma	720	1.1%
48	Montana	64	0.1%	26	Massachusetts	696	1.1%
28	Nebraska	595	0.9%	27	Louisiana	596	0.9%
10	Nevada	1,594	2.5%	28	Nebraska	595	0.9%
42	New Hampshire	152	0.2%	29	Alabama	582	0.9%
11	New Jersey	1,527	2.4%	30	Connecticut	579	0.9%
43	New Mexico	151	0.2%	31	South Carolina	442	0.7%
3	New York	3,887	6.0%	32	Mississippi	412	0.6%
14	North Carolina	1,362	2.1%	33	Kansas	325	0.5%
46	North Dakota	95	0.1%	34	Idaho	314	0.5%
20	Ohio	964	1.5%	35	Hawaii	295	0.5%
25	Oklahoma	720	1.1%	36	Maine	275	0.4%
16	Oregon	1,334	2.1%	37	Iowa	237	0.4%
6	Pennsylvania	2,779	4.3%	38	Delaware	202	0.3%
44	Rhode Island	122	0.2%	39	Arkansas	194	0.3%
31	South Carolina	442	0.7%	40	Wyoming	173	0.3%
47	South Dakota	77	0.1%	41	Alaska	166	0.3%
24	Tennessee	731	1.1%	42	New Hampshire	152	0.2%
2	Texas	4,059	6.3%	43	New Mexico	151	0.2%
23	Utah	811	1.3%	44	Rhode Island	122	0.2%
49	Vermont	23	0.0%	45	West Virginia	112	0.2%
17	Virginia	1,068	1.7%	46	North Dakota	95	0.1%
18	Washington	994	1.5%	47	South Dakota	77	0.1%
45	West Virginia	112	0.2%	48	Montana	64	0.1%
7	Wisconsin	2,750	4.3%	49	Vermont	23	0.0%
40	Wyoming	173	0.3%	50	Kentucky	21	0.0%
					District of Columbia**	NA	NA

Source: Reported data from the Federal Bureau of Investigation
"Crime in the United States 2008" (Uniform Crime Reports, September 14, 2009, http://www.fbi.gov/ucr/ucr.htm)
*By law enforcement agencies submitting complete reports to the F.B.I. for 12 months in 2008. The F.B.I. estimates 79,914 reported and unreported arrests for sex offenses occurred in 2008. Excludes forcible rape, prostitution, and commercialized vice. Includes statutory rape and offenses against chastity, common decency, morals, and the like. See important note at beginning of this chapter. **Not available.

Reported Arrest Rate for Sex Offenses in 2008

National Rate = 25.8 Reported Arrests per 100,000 Population*

ALPHA ORDER

RANK	STATE	RATE
33	Alabama	15.4
16	Alaska	24.9
14	Arizona	27.6
46	Arkansas	8.1
6	California	39.7
24	Colorado	20.7
29	Connecticut	17.9
19	Delaware	23.1
27	Florida	18.9
2	Georgia	56.7
15	Hawaii	25.8
21	Idaho	21.9
NA	Illinois**	NA
11	Indiana	32.5
45	Iowa	8.6
31	Kansas	17.1
NA	Kentucky**	NA
17	Louisiana	24.1
22	Maine	20.9
17	Maryland	24.1
39	Massachusetts	12.0
41	Michigan	11.1
13	Minnesota	30.0
12	Mississippi	31.5
4	Missouri	43.9
47	Montana	6.9
8	Nebraska	36.4
1	Nevada	62.6
35	New Hampshire	14.7
28	New Jersey	18.3
42	New Mexico	10.4
5	New York	42.1
25	North Carolina	20.6
32	North Dakota	16.4
37	Ohio	14.0
26	Oklahoma	19.8
7	Oregon	36.6
19	Pennsylvania	23.1
40	Rhode Island	11.6
44	South Carolina	10.0
38	South Dakota	12.2
34	Tennessee	14.8
30	Texas	17.4
9	Utah	34.1
48	Vermont	4.5
36	Virginia	14.2
22	Washington	20.9
43	West Virginia	10.1
3	Wisconsin	49.6
10	Wyoming	32.8

RANK ORDER

RANK	STATE	RATE
1	Nevada	62.6
2	Georgia	56.7
3	Wisconsin	49.6
4	Missouri	43.9
5	New York	42.1
6	California	39.7
7	Oregon	36.6
8	Nebraska	36.4
9	Utah	34.1
10	Wyoming	32.8
11	Indiana	32.5
12	Mississippi	31.5
13	Minnesota	30.0
14	Arizona	27.6
15	Hawaii	25.8
16	Alaska	24.9
17	Louisiana	24.1
17	Maryland	24.1
19	Delaware	23.1
19	Pennsylvania	23.1
21	Idaho	21.9
22	Maine	20.9
22	Washington	20.9
24	Colorado	20.7
25	North Carolina	20.6
26	Oklahoma	19.8
27	Florida	18.9
28	New Jersey	18.3
29	Connecticut	17.9
30	Texas	17.4
31	Kansas	17.1
32	North Dakota	16.4
33	Alabama	15.4
34	Tennessee	14.8
35	New Hampshire	14.7
36	Virginia	14.2
37	Ohio	14.0
38	South Dakota	12.2
39	Massachusetts	12.0
40	Rhode Island	11.6
41	Michigan	11.1
42	New Mexico	10.4
43	West Virginia	10.1
44	South Carolina	10.0
45	Iowa	8.6
46	Arkansas	8.1
47	Montana	6.9
48	Vermont	4.5
NA	Illinois**	NA
NA	Kentucky**	NA
	District of Columbia**	NA

Source: CQ Press using reported data from the Federal Bureau of Investigation
   "Crime in the United States 2008" (Uniform Crime Reports, September 14, 2009, http://www.fbi.gov/ucr/ucr.htm)
*By law enforcement agencies submitting complete reports to the F.B.I. for 12 months in 2008. These rates based on population estimates for areas under the jurisdiction of those agencies reporting. Arrest rate based on the F.B.I. estimate of reported and unreported arrests for sex offenses is 26.3 arrests per 100,000 population. See important note at beginning of this chapter.
**Not available.

Reported Arrests for Prostitution and Commercialized Vice in 2008

National Total = 64,843 Reported Arrests*

ALPHA ORDER

RANK	STATE	ARRESTS	% of USA
33	Alabama	260	0.4%
38	Alaska	159	0.2%
9	Arizona	1,602	2.5%
32	Arkansas	316	0.5%
1	California	13,385	20.6%
23	Colorado	618	1.0%
26	Connecticut	523	0.8%
40	Delaware	132	0.2%
3	Florida	6,059	9.3%
8	Georgia	1,848	2.8%
28	Hawaii	421	0.6%
46	Idaho	21	0.0%
5	Illinois	3,616	5.6%
15	Indiana	1,256	1.9%
41	Iowa	129	0.2%
34	Kansas	227	0.4%
25	Kentucky	539	0.8%
29	Louisiana	412	0.6%
45	Maine	26	0.0%
13	Maryland	1,337	2.1%
16	Massachusetts	1,229	1.9%
18	Michigan	761	1.2%
12	Minnesota	1,338	2.1%
42	Mississippi	119	0.2%
22	Missouri	635	1.0%
47	Montana	11	0.0%
37	Nebraska	212	0.3%
4	Nevada	4,659	7.2%
43	New Hampshire	56	0.1%
10	New Jersey	1,453	2.2%
35	New Mexico	219	0.3%
17	New York	824	1.3%
11	North Carolina	1,408	2.2%
50	North Dakota	3	0.0%
14	Ohio	1,266	2.0%
29	Oklahoma	412	0.6%
19	Oregon	752	1.2%
6	Pennsylvania	2,498	3.9%
36	Rhode Island	216	0.3%
31	South Carolina	388	0.6%
48	South Dakota	10	0.0%
7	Tennessee	2,111	3.3%
2	Texas	8,784	13.5%
27	Utah	463	0.7%
49	Vermont	6	0.0%
24	Virginia	558	0.9%
20	Washington	694	1.1%
39	West Virginia	150	0.2%
21	Wisconsin	687	1.1%
44	Wyoming	34	0.1%

RANK ORDER

RANK	STATE	ARRESTS	% of USA
1	California	13,385	20.6%
2	Texas	8,784	13.5%
3	Florida	6,059	9.3%
4	Nevada	4,659	7.2%
5	Illinois	3,616	5.6%
6	Pennsylvania	2,498	3.9%
7	Tennessee	2,111	3.3%
8	Georgia	1,848	2.8%
9	Arizona	1,602	2.5%
10	New Jersey	1,453	2.2%
11	North Carolina	1,408	2.2%
12	Minnesota	1,338	2.1%
13	Maryland	1,337	2.1%
14	Ohio	1,266	2.0%
15	Indiana	1,256	1.9%
16	Massachusetts	1,229	1.9%
17	New York	824	1.3%
18	Michigan	761	1.2%
19	Oregon	752	1.2%
20	Washington	694	1.1%
21	Wisconsin	687	1.1%
22	Missouri	635	1.0%
23	Colorado	618	1.0%
24	Virginia	558	0.9%
25	Kentucky	539	0.8%
26	Connecticut	523	0.8%
27	Utah	463	0.7%
28	Hawaii	421	0.6%
29	Louisiana	412	0.6%
29	Oklahoma	412	0.6%
31	South Carolina	388	0.6%
32	Arkansas	316	0.5%
33	Alabama	260	0.4%
34	Kansas	227	0.4%
35	New Mexico	219	0.3%
36	Rhode Island	216	0.3%
37	Nebraska	212	0.3%
38	Alaska	159	0.2%
39	West Virginia	150	0.2%
40	Delaware	132	0.2%
41	Iowa	129	0.2%
42	Mississippi	119	0.2%
43	New Hampshire	56	0.1%
44	Wyoming	34	0.1%
45	Maine	26	0.0%
46	Idaho	21	0.0%
47	Montana	11	0.0%
48	South Dakota	10	0.0%
49	Vermont	6	0.0%
50	North Dakota	3	0.0%
	District of Columbia**	NA	NA

Source: Reported data from the Federal Bureau of Investigation
"Crime in the United States 2008" (Uniform Crime Reports, September 14, 2009, http://www.fbi.gov/ucr/ucr.htm)
*By law enforcement agencies submitting complete reports to the F.B.I. for 12 months in 2008. The F.B.I. estimates 75,004 reported and unreported arrests for prostitution and commercialized vice occurred in 2008. Includes keeping a bawdy house and procuring or transporting women for immoral purposes. Attempts are included. See important note at beginning of this chapter.
**Not available.

Reported Arrest Rate for Prostitution and Commercialized Vice in 2008

National Rate = 26.0 Reported Arrests per 100,000 Population*

ALPHA ORDER

RANK	STATE	RATE
39	Alabama	6.9
12	Alaska	23.9
10	Arizona	25.0
28	Arkansas	13.1
5	California	36.6
26	Colorado	14.2
22	Connecticut	16.2
23	Delaware	15.1
6	Florida	33.1
7	Georgia	30.8
4	Hawaii	36.8
45	Idaho	1.5
NA	Illinois**	NA
8	Indiana	27.0
42	Iowa	4.7
31	Kansas	12.0
NA	Kentucky**	NA
21	Louisiana	16.7
43	Maine	2.0
11	Maryland	24.0
14	Massachusetts	21.1
36	Michigan	8.8
9	Minnesota	26.4
34	Mississippi	9.1
32	Missouri	11.5
46	Montana	1.2
29	Nebraska	13.0
1	Nevada	183.0
41	New Hampshire	5.4
20	New Jersey	17.4
23	New Mexico	15.1
35	New York	8.9
13	North Carolina	21.3
48	North Dakota	0.5
19	Ohio	18.4
33	Oklahoma	11.3
16	Oregon	20.6
15	Pennsylvania	20.8
16	Rhode Island	20.6
36	South Carolina	8.8
44	South Dakota	1.6
2	Tennessee	42.7
3	Texas	37.6
18	Utah	19.5
46	Vermont	1.2
38	Virginia	7.4
25	Washington	14.6
27	West Virginia	13.5
30	Wisconsin	12.4
40	Wyoming	6.4

RANK ORDER

RANK	STATE	RATE
1	Nevada	183.0
2	Tennessee	42.7
3	Texas	37.6
4	Hawaii	36.8
5	California	36.6
6	Florida	33.1
7	Georgia	30.8
8	Indiana	27.0
9	Minnesota	26.4
10	Arizona	25.0
11	Maryland	24.0
12	Alaska	23.9
13	North Carolina	21.3
14	Massachusetts	21.1
15	Pennsylvania	20.8
16	Oregon	20.6
16	Rhode Island	20.6
18	Utah	19.5
19	Ohio	18.4
20	New Jersey	17.4
21	Louisiana	16.7
22	Connecticut	16.2
23	Delaware	15.1
23	New Mexico	15.1
25	Washington	14.6
26	Colorado	14.2
27	West Virginia	13.5
28	Arkansas	13.1
29	Nebraska	13.0
30	Wisconsin	12.4
31	Kansas	12.0
32	Missouri	11.5
33	Oklahoma	11.3
34	Mississippi	9.1
35	New York	8.9
36	Michigan	8.8
36	South Carolina	8.8
38	Virginia	7.4
39	Alabama	6.9
40	Wyoming	6.4
41	New Hampshire	5.4
42	Iowa	4.7
43	Maine	2.0
44	South Dakota	1.6
45	Idaho	1.5
46	Montana	1.2
46	Vermont	1.2
48	North Dakota	0.5
NA	Illinois**	NA
NA	Kentucky**	NA
	District of Columbia**	NA

Source: CQ Press using reported data from the Federal Bureau of Investigation
    "Crime in the United States 2008" (Uniform Crime Reports, September 14, 2009, http://www.fbi.gov/ucr/ucr.htm)
*By law enforcement agencies submitting complete reports to the F.B.I. for 12 months in 2008. These rates based on population estimates for areas under the jurisdiction of those agencies reporting. Arrest rate based on the F.B.I. estimate of reported and unreported arrests for prostitution and commercialized vice is 24.7 arrests per 100,000 population. See important note at beginning of this chapter. **Not available.

Reported Arrests for Offenses Against Families and Children in 2008

National Total = 87,197 Reported Arrests*

ALPHA ORDER						RANK ORDER			
RANK	STATE	ARRESTS	% of USA			RANK	STATE	ARRESTS	% of USA
25	Alabama	1,055	1.2%			1	New Jersey	15,113	17.3%
37	Alaska	320	0.4%			2	Ohio	6,705	7.7%
7	Arizona	3,026	3.5%			3	North Carolina	6,534	7.5%
46	Arkansas	117	0.1%			4	Texas	4,939	5.7%
34	California	380	0.4%			5	Missouri	4,636	5.3%
8	Colorado	2,991	3.4%			6	Mississippi	3,606	4.1%
24	Connecticut	1,154	1.3%			7	Arizona	3,026	3.5%
42	Delaware	239	0.3%			8	Colorado	2,991	3.4%
NA	Florida**	NA	NA			9	Wisconsin	2,768	3.2%
10	Georgia	2,638	3.0%			10	Georgia	2,638	3.0%
49	Hawaii	47	0.1%			11	Michigan	2,610	3.0%
31	Idaho	622	0.7%			12	New York	2,472	2.8%
35	Illinois	362	0.4%			13	Maryland	2,220	2.5%
14	Indiana	1,790	2.1%			14	Indiana	1,790	2.1%
28	Iowa	870	1.0%			15	Tennessee	1,771	2.0%
41	Kansas	261	0.3%			16	Utah	1,667	1.9%
33	Kentucky	589	0.7%			17	Virginia	1,643	1.9%
22	Louisiana	1,186	1.4%			18	Nebraska	1,539	1.8%
47	Maine	93	0.1%			19	Nevada	1,491	1.7%
13	Maryland	2,220	2.5%			20	South Carolina	1,438	1.6%
21	Massachusetts	1,295	1.5%			21	Massachusetts	1,295	1.5%
11	Michigan	2,610	3.0%			22	Louisiana	1,186	1.4%
29	Minnesota	856	1.0%			23	Pennsylvania	1,155	1.3%
6	Mississippi	3,606	4.1%			24	Connecticut	1,154	1.3%
5	Missouri	4,636	5.3%			25	Alabama	1,055	1.2%
38	Montana	313	0.4%			26	Oklahoma	977	1.1%
18	Nebraska	1,539	1.8%			27	New Mexico	931	1.1%
19	Nevada	1,491	1.7%			28	Iowa	870	1.0%
43	New Hampshire	165	0.2%			29	Minnesota	856	1.0%
1	New Jersey	15,113	17.3%			30	Washington	691	0.8%
27	New Mexico	931	1.1%			31	Idaho	622	0.7%
12	New York	2,472	2.8%			32	Oregon	611	0.7%
3	North Carolina	6,534	7.5%			33	Kentucky	589	0.7%
44	North Dakota	164	0.2%			34	California	380	0.4%
2	Ohio	6,705	7.7%			35	Illinois	362	0.4%
26	Oklahoma	977	1.1%			36	South Dakota	342	0.4%
32	Oregon	611	0.7%			37	Alaska	320	0.4%
23	Pennsylvania	1,155	1.3%			38	Montana	313	0.4%
45	Rhode Island	159	0.2%			38	Vermont	313	0.4%
20	South Carolina	1,438	1.6%			40	Wyoming	267	0.3%
36	South Dakota	342	0.4%			41	Kansas	261	0.3%
15	Tennessee	1,771	2.0%			42	Delaware	239	0.3%
4	Texas	4,939	5.7%			43	New Hampshire	165	0.2%
16	Utah	1,667	1.9%			44	North Dakota	164	0.2%
38	Vermont	313	0.4%			45	Rhode Island	159	0.2%
17	Virginia	1,643	1.9%			46	Arkansas	117	0.1%
30	Washington	691	0.8%			47	Maine	93	0.1%
48	West Virginia	66	0.1%			48	West Virginia	66	0.1%
9	Wisconsin	2,768	3.2%			49	Hawaii	47	0.1%
40	Wyoming	267	0.3%			NA	Florida**	NA	NA
							District of Columbia**	NA	NA

Source: Reported data from the Federal Bureau of Investigation
   "Crime in the United States 2008" (Uniform Crime Reports, September 14, 2009, http://www.fbi.gov/ucr/ucr.htm)
*By law enforcement agencies submitting complete reports to the F.B.I. for 12 months in 2008. The F.B.I. estimates 118,419 reported and unreported arrests for offenses against families and children occurred in 2008. Includes nonsupport, neglect, desertion, or abuse of family and children. See important note at beginning of this chapter.
**Not available.

Reported Arrest Rate for Offenses Against Families and Children in 2008

National Rate = 37.8 Reported Arrests per 100,000 Population*

ALPHA ORDER

RANK	STATE	RATE
29	Alabama	28.0
15	Alaska	48.0
17	Arizona	47.2
45	Arkansas	4.9
47	California	1.0
8	Colorado	68.6
22	Connecticut	35.8
30	Delaware	27.4
NA	Florida**	NA
18	Georgia	44.0
46	Hawaii	4.1
19	Idaho	43.3
NA	Illinois**	NA
21	Indiana	38.4
26	Iowa	31.5
41	Kansas	13.8
NA	Kentucky**	NA
15	Louisiana	48.0
43	Maine	7.1
20	Maryland	39.8
33	Massachusetts	22.3
27	Michigan	30.1
36	Minnesota	16.9
1	Mississippi	275.7
6	Missouri	83.6
24	Montana	33.6
5	Nebraska	94.2
11	Nevada	58.6
38	New Hampshire	16.0
2	New Jersey	180.9
9	New Mexico	64.4
32	New York	26.8
3	North Carolina	98.8
28	North Dakota	28.2
4	Ohio	97.7
31	Oklahoma	26.9
37	Oregon	16.7
42	Pennsylvania	9.6
39	Rhode Island	15.1
25	South Carolina	32.7
12	South Dakota	54.3
22	Tennessee	35.8
35	Texas	21.1
7	Utah	70.1
10	Vermont	61.4
34	Virginia	21.8
40	Washington	14.5
44	West Virginia	5.9
14	Wisconsin	50.0
13	Wyoming	50.6

RANK ORDER

RANK	STATE	RATE
1	Mississippi	275.7
2	New Jersey	180.9
3	North Carolina	98.8
4	Ohio	97.7
5	Nebraska	94.2
6	Missouri	83.6
7	Utah	70.1
8	Colorado	68.6
9	New Mexico	64.4
10	Vermont	61.4
11	Nevada	58.6
12	South Dakota	54.3
13	Wyoming	50.6
14	Wisconsin	50.0
15	Alaska	48.0
15	Louisiana	48.0
17	Arizona	47.2
18	Georgia	44.0
19	Idaho	43.3
20	Maryland	39.8
21	Indiana	38.4
22	Connecticut	35.8
22	Tennessee	35.8
24	Montana	33.6
25	South Carolina	32.7
26	Iowa	31.5
27	Michigan	30.1
28	North Dakota	28.2
29	Alabama	28.0
30	Delaware	27.4
31	Oklahoma	26.9
32	New York	26.8
33	Massachusetts	22.3
34	Virginia	21.8
35	Texas	21.1
36	Minnesota	16.9
37	Oregon	16.7
38	New Hampshire	16.0
39	Rhode Island	15.1
40	Washington	14.5
41	Kansas	13.8
42	Pennsylvania	9.6
43	Maine	7.1
44	West Virginia	5.9
45	Arkansas	4.9
46	Hawaii	4.1
47	California	1.0
NA	Florida**	NA
NA	Illinois**	NA
NA	Kentucky**	NA
	District of Columbia**	NA

Source: CQ Press using reported data from the Federal Bureau of Investigation
   "Crime in the United States 2008" (Uniform Crime Reports, September 14, 2009, http://www.fbi.gov/ucr/ucr.htm)
*By law enforcement agencies submitting complete reports to the F.B.I. for 12 months in 2008. These rates based on population estimates for areas under the jurisdiction of those agencies reporting. Arrest rate based on the F.B.I. estimate of reported and unreported arrests for offenses against families and children is 38.9 arrests per 100,000 population. See important note at beginning of this chapter. **Not available.

Percent of Crimes Cleared in 2007

National Percent = 19.0% Cleared*

ALPHA ORDER

RANK	STATE	PERCENT
28	Alabama	18.0
1	Alaska	30.1
42	Arizona	15.1
23	Arkansas	19.0
38	California	16.8
26	Colorado	18.3
28	Connecticut	18.0
2	Delaware	28.0
NA	Florida**	NA
15	Georgia	21.1
NA	Hawaii**	NA
12	Idaho	21.9
NA	Illinois**	NA
28	Indiana	18.0
27	Iowa	18.2
45	Kansas	13.6
16	Kentucky	20.7
10	Louisiana	22.7
5	Maine	26.8
8	Maryland	23.5
33	Massachusetts	17.2
46	Michigan	13.4
13	Minnesota	21.8
28	Mississippi	18.0
14	Missouri	21.2
33	Montana	17.2
11	Nebraska	22.6
39	Nevada	16.7
36	New Hampshire	17.0
21	New Jersey	19.2
40	New Mexico	16.5
3	New York	27.3
7	North Carolina	23.9
19	North Dakota	19.5
43	Ohio	14.3
22	Oklahoma	19.1
24	Oregon	18.9
4	Pennsylvania	27.0
44	Rhode Island	13.9
17	South Carolina	20.6
46	South Dakota	13.4
20	Tennessee	19.3
33	Texas	17.2
18	Utah	19.7
32	Vermont	17.5
25	Virginia	18.5
36	Washington	17.0
41	West Virginia	16.0
6	Wisconsin	24.3
9	Wyoming	22.9

RANK ORDER

RANK	STATE	PERCENT
1	Alaska	30.1
2	Delaware	28.0
3	New York	27.3
4	Pennsylvania	27.0
5	Maine	26.8
6	Wisconsin	24.3
7	North Carolina	23.9
8	Maryland	23.5
9	Wyoming	22.9
10	Louisiana	22.7
11	Nebraska	22.6
12	Idaho	21.9
13	Minnesota	21.8
14	Missouri	21.2
15	Georgia	21.1
16	Kentucky	20.7
17	South Carolina	20.6
18	Utah	19.7
19	North Dakota	19.5
20	Tennessee	19.3
21	New Jersey	19.2
22	Oklahoma	19.1
23	Arkansas	19.0
24	Oregon	18.9
25	Virginia	18.5
26	Colorado	18.3
27	Iowa	18.2
28	Alabama	18.0
28	Connecticut	18.0
28	Indiana	18.0
28	Mississippi	18.0
32	Vermont	17.5
33	Massachusetts	17.2
33	Montana	17.2
33	Texas	17.2
36	New Hampshire	17.0
36	Washington	17.0
38	California	16.8
39	Nevada	16.7
40	New Mexico	16.5
41	West Virginia	16.0
42	Arizona	15.1
43	Ohio	14.3
44	Rhode Island	13.9
45	Kansas	13.6
46	Michigan	13.4
46	South Dakota	13.4
NA	Florida**	NA
NA	Hawaii**	NA
NA	Illinois**	NA
	District of Columbia**	NA

Source: Federal Bureau of Investigation (unpublished data)

*Includes murder, rape, robbery, aggravated assault, burglary, larceny and theft, and motor vehicle theft. A crime is considered cleared when at least one person is arrested, charged, and turned over to the court for prosecution. Clearances recorded in 2007 may be for crimes which occurred in prior years. Several crimes may be cleared by the arrest of one person while the arrest of many persons may clear only one crime.

**Not available.

Percent of Violent Crimes Cleared in 2007

National Percent = 43.7% Cleared*

ALPHA ORDER

RANK	STATE	PERCENT
42	Alabama	37.7
2	Alaska	60.8
39	Arizona	39.2
15	Arkansas	50.2
37	California	40.6
16	Colorado	49.4
28	Connecticut	45.1
5	Delaware	57.9
NA	Florida**	NA
38	Georgia	39.6
NA	Hawaii**	NA
3	Idaho	59.1
NA	Illinois**	NA
33	Indiana	42.5
7	Iowa	52.7
29	Kansas	45.0
19	Kentucky	48.0
17	Louisiana	49.3
4	Maine	58.8
7	Maryland	52.7
26	Massachusetts	45.6
47	Michigan	28.8
40	Minnesota	39.0
46	Mississippi	29.9
20	Missouri	47.8
31	Montana	44.5
6	Nebraska	53.8
44	Nevada	31.6
24	New Hampshire	46.0
35	New Jersey	41.5
13	New Mexico	50.5
13	New York	50.5
10	North Carolina	52.6
30	North Dakota	44.7
45	Ohio	30.4
21	Oklahoma	47.5
24	Oregon	46.0
7	Pennsylvania	52.7
34	Rhode Island	41.9
12	South Carolina	50.6
43	South Dakota	32.4
22	Tennessee	47.3
36	Texas	41.3
18	Utah	48.4
41	Vermont	38.8
32	Virginia	42.8
11	Washington	50.7
26	West Virginia	45.6
23	Wisconsin	46.1
1	Wyoming	64.5

RANK ORDER

RANK	STATE	PERCENT
1	Wyoming	64.5
2	Alaska	60.8
3	Idaho	59.1
4	Maine	58.8
5	Delaware	57.9
6	Nebraska	53.8
7	Iowa	52.7
7	Maryland	52.7
7	Pennsylvania	52.7
10	North Carolina	52.6
11	Washington	50.7
12	South Carolina	50.6
13	New Mexico	50.5
13	New York	50.5
15	Arkansas	50.2
16	Colorado	49.4
17	Louisiana	49.3
18	Utah	48.4
19	Kentucky	48.0
20	Missouri	47.8
21	Oklahoma	47.5
22	Tennessee	47.3
23	Wisconsin	46.1
24	New Hampshire	46.0
24	Oregon	46.0
26	Massachusetts	45.6
26	West Virginia	45.6
28	Connecticut	45.1
29	Kansas	45.0
30	North Dakota	44.7
31	Montana	44.5
32	Virginia	42.8
33	Indiana	42.5
34	Rhode Island	41.9
35	New Jersey	41.5
36	Texas	41.3
37	California	40.6
38	Georgia	39.6
39	Arizona	39.2
40	Minnesota	39.0
41	Vermont	38.8
42	Alabama	37.7
43	South Dakota	32.4
44	Nevada	31.6
45	Ohio	30.4
46	Mississippi	29.9
47	Michigan	28.8
NA	Florida**	NA
NA	Hawaii**	NA
NA	Illinois**	NA
	District of Columbia**	NA

Source: Federal Bureau of Investigation (unpublished data)
*Includes murder, rape, robbery, and aggravated assault. A crime is considered cleared when at least one person is arrested, charged, and turned over to the court for prosecution. Clearances recorded in 2007 may be for crimes which occurred in prior years. Several crimes may be cleared by the arrest of one person while the arrest of many persons may clear only one crime.
**Not available.

Percent of Murders Cleared in 2007

National Percent = 60.6% Cleared*

<table>
<tr><td colspan="3">ALPHA ORDER</td><td colspan="3">RANK ORDER</td></tr>
<tr><td>RANK</td><td>STATE</td><td>PERCENT</td><td>RANK</td><td>STATE</td><td>PERCENT</td></tr>
<tr><td>18</td><td>Alabama</td><td>68.9</td><td>1</td><td>Wyoming</td><td>100.0</td></tr>
<tr><td>8</td><td>Alaska</td><td>77.1</td><td>2</td><td>Maine</td><td>91.3</td></tr>
<tr><td>37</td><td>Arizona</td><td>55.3</td><td>3</td><td>North Dakota</td><td>85.7</td></tr>
<tr><td>17</td><td>Arkansas</td><td>69.3</td><td>4</td><td>Idaho</td><td>83.9</td></tr>
<tr><td>40</td><td>California</td><td>52.1</td><td>5</td><td>Washington</td><td>83.8</td></tr>
<tr><td>43</td><td>Colorado</td><td>51.0</td><td>6</td><td>Nebraska</td><td>80.0</td></tr>
<tr><td>39</td><td>Connecticut</td><td>52.3</td><td>7</td><td>South Carolina</td><td>79.0</td></tr>
<tr><td>33</td><td>Delaware</td><td>59.5</td><td>8</td><td>Alaska</td><td>77.1</td></tr>
<tr><td>NA</td><td>Florida**</td><td>NA</td><td>9</td><td>Utah</td><td>76.5</td></tr>
<tr><td>20</td><td>Georgia</td><td>67.9</td><td>10</td><td>Oklahoma</td><td>76.3</td></tr>
<tr><td>NA</td><td>Hawaii**</td><td>NA</td><td>11</td><td>Minnesota</td><td>75.0</td></tr>
<tr><td>4</td><td>Idaho</td><td>83.9</td><td>11</td><td>New Hampshire</td><td>75.0</td></tr>
<tr><td>NA</td><td>Illinois**</td><td>NA</td><td>13</td><td>North Carolina</td><td>74.8</td></tr>
<tr><td>27</td><td>Indiana</td><td>63.1</td><td>14</td><td>Iowa</td><td>72.2</td></tr>
<tr><td>14</td><td>Iowa</td><td>72.2</td><td>15</td><td>Texas</td><td>71.5</td></tr>
<tr><td>32</td><td>Kansas</td><td>59.7</td><td>16</td><td>Tennessee</td><td>70.9</td></tr>
<tr><td>35</td><td>Kentucky</td><td>58.9</td><td>17</td><td>Arkansas</td><td>69.3</td></tr>
<tr><td>42</td><td>Louisiana</td><td>51.3</td><td>18</td><td>Alabama</td><td>68.9</td></tr>
<tr><td>2</td><td>Maine</td><td>91.3</td><td>19</td><td>Oregon</td><td>68.6</td></tr>
<tr><td>29</td><td>Maryland</td><td>61.5</td><td>20</td><td>Georgia</td><td>67.9</td></tr>
<tr><td>44</td><td>Massachusetts</td><td>50.3</td><td>20</td><td>Wisconsin</td><td>67.9</td></tr>
<tr><td>46</td><td>Michigan</td><td>30.7</td><td>22</td><td>Nevada</td><td>67.4</td></tr>
<tr><td>11</td><td>Minnesota</td><td>75.0</td><td>23</td><td>New Mexico</td><td>65.2</td></tr>
<tr><td>26</td><td>Mississippi</td><td>63.8</td><td>24</td><td>Pennsylvania</td><td>64.3</td></tr>
<tr><td>28</td><td>Missouri</td><td>62.6</td><td>24</td><td>Vermont</td><td>64.3</td></tr>
<tr><td>38</td><td>Montana</td><td>55.0</td><td>26</td><td>Mississippi</td><td>63.8</td></tr>
<tr><td>6</td><td>Nebraska</td><td>80.0</td><td>27</td><td>Indiana</td><td>63.1</td></tr>
<tr><td>22</td><td>Nevada</td><td>67.4</td><td>28</td><td>Missouri</td><td>62.6</td></tr>
<tr><td>11</td><td>New Hampshire</td><td>75.0</td><td>29</td><td>Maryland</td><td>61.5</td></tr>
<tr><td>30</td><td>New Jersey</td><td>61.4</td><td>30</td><td>New Jersey</td><td>61.4</td></tr>
<tr><td>23</td><td>New Mexico</td><td>65.2</td><td>31</td><td>Virginia</td><td>59.8</td></tr>
<tr><td>34</td><td>New York</td><td>59.3</td><td>32</td><td>Kansas</td><td>59.7</td></tr>
<tr><td>13</td><td>North Carolina</td><td>74.8</td><td>33</td><td>Delaware</td><td>59.5</td></tr>
<tr><td>3</td><td>North Dakota</td><td>85.7</td><td>34</td><td>New York</td><td>59.3</td></tr>
<tr><td>45</td><td>Ohio</td><td>47.5</td><td>35</td><td>Kentucky</td><td>58.9</td></tr>
<tr><td>10</td><td>Oklahoma</td><td>76.3</td><td>36</td><td>West Virginia</td><td>58.7</td></tr>
<tr><td>19</td><td>Oregon</td><td>68.6</td><td>37</td><td>Arizona</td><td>55.3</td></tr>
<tr><td>24</td><td>Pennsylvania</td><td>64.3</td><td>38</td><td>Montana</td><td>55.0</td></tr>
<tr><td>41</td><td>Rhode Island</td><td>51.9</td><td>39</td><td>Connecticut</td><td>52.3</td></tr>
<tr><td>7</td><td>South Carolina</td><td>79.0</td><td>40</td><td>California</td><td>52.1</td></tr>
<tr><td>47</td><td>South Dakota</td><td>27.3</td><td>41</td><td>Rhode Island</td><td>51.9</td></tr>
<tr><td>16</td><td>Tennessee</td><td>70.9</td><td>42</td><td>Louisiana</td><td>51.3</td></tr>
<tr><td>15</td><td>Texas</td><td>71.5</td><td>43</td><td>Colorado</td><td>51.0</td></tr>
<tr><td>9</td><td>Utah</td><td>76.5</td><td>44</td><td>Massachusetts</td><td>50.3</td></tr>
<tr><td>24</td><td>Vermont</td><td>64.3</td><td>45</td><td>Ohio</td><td>47.5</td></tr>
<tr><td>31</td><td>Virginia</td><td>59.8</td><td>46</td><td>Michigan</td><td>30.7</td></tr>
<tr><td>5</td><td>Washington</td><td>83.8</td><td>47</td><td>South Dakota</td><td>27.3</td></tr>
<tr><td>36</td><td>West Virginia</td><td>58.7</td><td>NA</td><td>Florida**</td><td>NA</td></tr>
<tr><td>20</td><td>Wisconsin</td><td>67.9</td><td>NA</td><td>Hawaii**</td><td>NA</td></tr>
<tr><td>1</td><td>Wyoming</td><td>100.0</td><td>NA</td><td>Illinois**</td><td>NA</td></tr>
<tr><td></td><td></td><td></td><td></td><td>District of Columbia**</td><td>NA</td></tr>
</table>

Source: Federal Bureau of Investigation (unpublished data)

*Includes nonnegligent manslaughter. A crime is considered cleared when at least one person is arrested, charged, and turned over to the court for prosecution. Clearances recorded in 2007 may be for crimes which occurred in prior years. Several crimes may be cleared by the arrest of one person while the arrest of many persons may clear only one crime.

**Not available.

Percent of Rapes Cleared in 2007

National Percent = 39.2% Cleared*

ALPHA ORDER				RANK ORDER		
RANK	STATE	PERCENT		RANK	STATE	PERCENT
24	Alabama	37.8		1	Delaware	65.5
29	Alaska	33.3		2	Pennsylvania	60.2
37	Arizona	27.8		3	Wisconsin	58.6
17	Arkansas	41.2		4	Maryland	57.9
11	California	44.2		5	North Carolina	57.4
22	Colorado	38.9		6	Missouri	47.9
26	Connecticut	36.4		7	Kentucky	45.4
1	Delaware	65.5		8	Washington	45.3
NA	Florida**	NA		9	Vermont	44.6
14	Georgia	43.2		10	New York	44.3
NA	Hawaii**	NA		11	California	44.2
23	Idaho	37.9		12	Texas	43.6
NA	Illinois**	NA		13	Louisiana	43.4
27	Indiana	35.9		14	Georgia	43.2
43	Iowa	22.5		15	New Jersey	42.5
30	Kansas	32.7		16	Maine	42.3
7	Kentucky	45.4		17	Arkansas	41.2
13	Louisiana	43.4		17	Oklahoma	41.2
16	Maine	42.3		19	South Carolina	40.2
4	Maryland	57.9		20	New Mexico	39.6
35	Massachusetts	30.0		21	Virginia	39.1
42	Michigan	23.5		22	Colorado	38.9
45	Minnesota	20.3		23	Idaho	37.9
31	Mississippi	32.4		24	Alabama	37.8
6	Missouri	47.9		25	Wyoming	36.5
44	Montana	20.7		26	Connecticut	36.4
28	Nebraska	35.4		27	Indiana	35.9
40	Nevada	25.1		28	Nebraska	35.4
33	New Hampshire	30.6		29	Alaska	33.3
15	New Jersey	42.5		30	Kansas	32.7
20	New Mexico	39.6		31	Mississippi	32.4
10	New York	44.3		32	Rhode Island	32.2
5	North Carolina	57.4		33	New Hampshire	30.6
38	North Dakota	25.5		34	Utah	30.2
39	Ohio	25.3		35	Massachusetts	30.0
17	Oklahoma	41.2		36	Tennessee	29.8
41	Oregon	24.7		37	Arizona	27.8
2	Pennsylvania	60.2		38	North Dakota	25.5
32	Rhode Island	32.2		39	Ohio	25.3
19	South Carolina	40.2		40	Nevada	25.1
47	South Dakota	16.5		41	Oregon	24.7
36	Tennessee	29.8		42	Michigan	23.5
12	Texas	43.6		43	Iowa	22.5
34	Utah	30.2		44	Montana	20.7
9	Vermont	44.6		45	Minnesota	20.3
21	Virginia	39.1		46	West Virginia	18.3
8	Washington	45.3		47	South Dakota	16.5
46	West Virginia	18.3		NA	Florida**	NA
3	Wisconsin	58.6		NA	Hawaii**	NA
25	Wyoming	36.5		NA	Illinois**	NA
					District of Columbia**	NA

Source: Federal Bureau of Investigation (unpublished data)
*Forcible rape including attempts.   However, statutory rape without force and other sex offenses are excluded. A crime is considered cleared when at least one person is arrested, charged, and turned over to the court for prosecution. Clearances recorded in 2007 may be for crimes which occurred in prior years. Several crimes may be cleared by the arrest of one person while the arrest of many persons may clear only one crime.
**Not available.

Percent of Robberies Cleared in 2007

National Percent = 24.8% Cleared*

ALPHA ORDER

RANK ORDER

RANK	STATE	PERCENT		RANK	STATE	PERCENT
22	Alabama	27.1		1	Wyoming	45.1
17	Alaska	29.6		2	Maine	43.3
41	Arizona	20.3		3	New Hampshire	42.3
21	Arkansas	27.9		4	Vermont	38.1
31	California	24.4		5	Idaho	33.9
38	Colorado	21.7		6	North Dakota	33.8
24	Connecticut	26.0		7	Oklahoma	33.6
15	Delaware	30.0		8	North Carolina	33.2
NA	Florida**	NA		9	Utah	33.1
40	Georgia	20.6		10	Pennsylvania	31.4
NA	Hawaii**	NA		11	Kentucky	31.3
5	Idaho	33.9		11	Washington	31.3
NA	Illinois**	NA		13	Nebraska	31.0
29	Indiana	24.6		14	Oregon	30.7
20	Iowa	28.2		15	Delaware	30.0
37	Kansas	21.9		16	New York	29.9
11	Kentucky	31.3		17	Alaska	29.6
19	Louisiana	28.5		18	Maryland	28.6
2	Maine	43.3		19	Louisiana	28.5
18	Maryland	28.6		20	Iowa	28.2
34	Massachusetts	22.5		21	Arkansas	27.9
47	Michigan	14.7		22	Alabama	27.1
44	Minnesota	19.7		22	South Carolina	27.1
46	Mississippi	16.4		24	Connecticut	26.0
25	Missouri	25.9		25	Missouri	25.9
25	Montana	25.9		25	Montana	25.9
13	Nebraska	31.0		27	New Jersey	25.5
45	Nevada	18.1		28	Rhode Island	25.3
3	New Hampshire	42.3		29	Indiana	24.6
27	New Jersey	25.5		30	Texas	24.5
33	New Mexico	22.9		31	California	24.4
16	New York	29.9		32	Virginia	24.2
8	North Carolina	33.2		33	New Mexico	22.9
6	North Dakota	33.8		34	Massachusetts	22.5
43	Ohio	19.8		34	Tennessee	22.5
7	Oklahoma	33.6		36	Wisconsin	22.3
14	Oregon	30.7		37	Kansas	21.9
10	Pennsylvania	31.4		38	Colorado	21.7
28	Rhode Island	25.3		39	South Dakota	20.9
22	South Carolina	27.1		40	Georgia	20.6
39	South Dakota	20.9		41	Arizona	20.3
34	Tennessee	22.5		42	West Virginia	20.2
30	Texas	24.5		43	Ohio	19.8
9	Utah	33.1		44	Minnesota	19.7
4	Vermont	38.1		45	Nevada	18.1
32	Virginia	24.2		46	Mississippi	16.4
11	Washington	31.3		47	Michigan	14.7
42	West Virginia	20.2		NA	Florida**	NA
36	Wisconsin	22.3		NA	Hawaii**	NA
1	Wyoming	45.1		NA	Illinois**	NA
					District of Columbia**	NA

Source: Federal Bureau of Investigation (unpublished data)

*Robbery is the taking of anything of value by force or threat of force. Attempts are included. A crime is considered cleared when at least one person is arrested, charged, and turned over to the court for prosecution. Clearances recorded in 2007 may be for crimes which occurred in prior years. Several crimes may be cleared by the arrest of one person while the arrest of many persons may clear only one crime.

**Not available.

Percent of Aggravated Assaults Cleared in 2007

National Percent = 53.6% Cleared*

<table>
<tr><td colspan="3">ALPHA ORDER</td><td colspan="3">RANK ORDER</td></tr>
<tr><td>RANK</td><td>STATE</td><td>PERCENT</td><td>RANK</td><td>STATE</td><td>PERCENT</td></tr>
<tr><td>43</td><td>Alabama</td><td>42.8</td><td>1</td><td>Vermont</td><td>81.5</td></tr>
<tr><td>4</td><td>Alaska</td><td>70.1</td><td>2</td><td>Maine</td><td>72.6</td></tr>
<tr><td>40</td><td>Arizona</td><td>48.9</td><td>3</td><td>Delaware</td><td>70.5</td></tr>
<tr><td>21</td><td>Arkansas</td><td>56.6</td><td>4</td><td>Alaska</td><td>70.1</td></tr>
<tr><td>36</td><td>California</td><td>50.4</td><td>5</td><td>Wyoming</td><td>69.0</td></tr>
<tr><td>15</td><td>Colorado</td><td>59.7</td><td>6</td><td>Maryland</td><td>67.7</td></tr>
<tr><td>11</td><td>Connecticut</td><td>62.7</td><td>7</td><td>Pennsylvania</td><td>67.5</td></tr>
<tr><td>3</td><td>Delaware</td><td>70.5</td><td>8</td><td>Idaho</td><td>66.3</td></tr>
<tr><td>NA</td><td>Florida**</td><td>NA</td><td>9</td><td>Nebraska</td><td>64.4</td></tr>
<tr><td>37</td><td>Georgia</td><td>50.2</td><td>10</td><td>New York</td><td>63.7</td></tr>
<tr><td>NA</td><td>Hawaii**</td><td>NA</td><td>11</td><td>Connecticut</td><td>62.7</td></tr>
<tr><td>8</td><td>Idaho</td><td>66.3</td><td>12</td><td>North Carolina</td><td>62.0</td></tr>
<tr><td>NA</td><td>Illinois**</td><td>NA</td><td>13</td><td>Iowa</td><td>61.9</td></tr>
<tr><td>30</td><td>Indiana</td><td>54.1</td><td>14</td><td>Washington</td><td>61.6</td></tr>
<tr><td>13</td><td>Iowa</td><td>61.9</td><td>15</td><td>Colorado</td><td>59.7</td></tr>
<tr><td>38</td><td>Kansas</td><td>50.0</td><td>16</td><td>Wisconsin</td><td>59.4</td></tr>
<tr><td>17</td><td>Kentucky</td><td>59.1</td><td>17</td><td>Kentucky</td><td>59.1</td></tr>
<tr><td>24</td><td>Louisiana</td><td>55.6</td><td>18</td><td>New Mexico</td><td>58.0</td></tr>
<tr><td>2</td><td>Maine</td><td>72.6</td><td>18</td><td>Utah</td><td>58.0</td></tr>
<tr><td>6</td><td>Maryland</td><td>67.7</td><td>20</td><td>Tennessee</td><td>56.7</td></tr>
<tr><td>27</td><td>Massachusetts</td><td>55.0</td><td>21</td><td>Arkansas</td><td>56.6</td></tr>
<tr><td>47</td><td>Michigan</td><td>35.0</td><td>22</td><td>South Carolina</td><td>56.4</td></tr>
<tr><td>31</td><td>Minnesota</td><td>53.4</td><td>23</td><td>Oregon</td><td>56.2</td></tr>
<tr><td>44</td><td>Mississippi</td><td>41.0</td><td>24</td><td>Louisiana</td><td>55.6</td></tr>
<tr><td>26</td><td>Missouri</td><td>55.1</td><td>25</td><td>Virginia</td><td>55.2</td></tr>
<tr><td>39</td><td>Montana</td><td>49.1</td><td>26</td><td>Missouri</td><td>55.1</td></tr>
<tr><td>9</td><td>Nebraska</td><td>64.4</td><td>27</td><td>Massachusetts</td><td>55.0</td></tr>
<tr><td>45</td><td>Nevada</td><td>40.8</td><td>28</td><td>New Jersey</td><td>54.5</td></tr>
<tr><td>34</td><td>New Hampshire</td><td>52.3</td><td>29</td><td>West Virginia</td><td>54.2</td></tr>
<tr><td>28</td><td>New Jersey</td><td>54.5</td><td>30</td><td>Indiana</td><td>54.1</td></tr>
<tr><td>18</td><td>New Mexico</td><td>58.0</td><td>31</td><td>Minnesota</td><td>53.4</td></tr>
<tr><td>10</td><td>New York</td><td>63.7</td><td>32</td><td>North Dakota</td><td>52.7</td></tr>
<tr><td>12</td><td>North Carolina</td><td>62.0</td><td>33</td><td>Rhode Island</td><td>52.5</td></tr>
<tr><td>32</td><td>North Dakota</td><td>52.7</td><td>34</td><td>New Hampshire</td><td>52.3</td></tr>
<tr><td>42</td><td>Ohio</td><td>44.5</td><td>35</td><td>Oklahoma</td><td>51.2</td></tr>
<tr><td>35</td><td>Oklahoma</td><td>51.2</td><td>36</td><td>California</td><td>50.4</td></tr>
<tr><td>23</td><td>Oregon</td><td>56.2</td><td>37</td><td>Georgia</td><td>50.2</td></tr>
<tr><td>7</td><td>Pennsylvania</td><td>67.5</td><td>38</td><td>Kansas</td><td>50.0</td></tr>
<tr><td>33</td><td>Rhode Island</td><td>52.5</td><td>39</td><td>Montana</td><td>49.1</td></tr>
<tr><td>22</td><td>South Carolina</td><td>56.4</td><td>40</td><td>Arizona</td><td>48.9</td></tr>
<tr><td>46</td><td>South Dakota</td><td>40.6</td><td>40</td><td>Texas</td><td>48.9</td></tr>
<tr><td>20</td><td>Tennessee</td><td>56.7</td><td>42</td><td>Ohio</td><td>44.5</td></tr>
<tr><td>40</td><td>Texas</td><td>48.9</td><td>43</td><td>Alabama</td><td>42.8</td></tr>
<tr><td>18</td><td>Utah</td><td>58.0</td><td>44</td><td>Mississippi</td><td>41.0</td></tr>
<tr><td>1</td><td>Vermont</td><td>81.5</td><td>45</td><td>Nevada</td><td>40.8</td></tr>
<tr><td>25</td><td>Virginia</td><td>55.2</td><td>46</td><td>South Dakota</td><td>40.6</td></tr>
<tr><td>14</td><td>Washington</td><td>61.6</td><td>47</td><td>Michigan</td><td>35.0</td></tr>
<tr><td>29</td><td>West Virginia</td><td>54.2</td><td>NA</td><td>Florida**</td><td>NA</td></tr>
<tr><td>16</td><td>Wisconsin</td><td>59.4</td><td>NA</td><td>Hawaii**</td><td>NA</td></tr>
<tr><td>5</td><td>Wyoming</td><td>69.0</td><td>NA</td><td>Illinois**</td><td>NA</td></tr>
<tr><td></td><td></td><td></td><td colspan="2">District of Columbia**</td><td>NA</td></tr>
</table>

Source: Federal Bureau of Investigation (unpublished data)

*Aggravated assault is an attack for the purpose of inflicting severe bodily injury. A crime is considered cleared when at least one person is arrested, charged, and turned over to the court for prosecution. Clearances recorded in 2007 may be for crimes which occurred in prior years. Several crimes may be cleared by the arrest of one person while the arrest of many persons may clear only one crime.

**Not available.

Percent of Property Crimes Cleared in 2007

National Percent = 15.6% Cleared*

ALPHA ORDER				RANK ORDER		
RANK	STATE	PERCENT		RANK	STATE	PERCENT
22	Alabama	16.1		1	Maine	25.3
2	Alaska	24.1		2	Alaska	24.1
41	Arizona	12.2		2	New York	24.1
31	Arkansas	14.6		4	Pennsylvania	22.1
38	California	12.8		5	Delaware	22.0
29	Colorado	14.7		5	Wisconsin	22.0
25	Connecticut	15.2		7	North Carolina	20.6
5	Delaware	22.0		8	Minnesota	20.0
NA	Florida**	NA		8	Nebraska	20.0
11	Georgia	18.7		10	Wyoming	19.5
NA	Hawaii**	NA		11	Georgia	18.7
14	Idaho	18.0		12	Maryland	18.6
NA	Illinois**	NA		13	Louisiana	18.1
21	Indiana	16.2		14	Idaho	18.0
29	Iowa	14.7		15	Kentucky	17.9
47	Kansas	9.8		15	North Dakota	17.9
15	Kentucky	17.9		15	Utah	17.9
13	Louisiana	18.1		18	Missouri	17.4
1	Maine	25.3		19	Mississippi	16.9
12	Maryland	18.6		20	Oregon	16.8
44	Massachusetts	11.2		21	Indiana	16.2
46	Michigan	10.7		22	Alabama	16.1
8	Minnesota	20.0		23	New Jersey	15.8
19	Mississippi	16.9		23	Virginia	15.8
18	Missouri	17.4		25	Connecticut	15.2
33	Montana	14.5		25	South Carolina	15.2
8	Nebraska	20.0		27	Oklahoma	15.1
37	Nevada	14.0		28	New Hampshire	14.9
28	New Hampshire	14.9		29	Colorado	14.7
23	New Jersey	15.8		29	Iowa	14.7
45	New Mexico	11.0		31	Arkansas	14.6
2	New York	24.1		31	Washington	14.6
7	North Carolina	20.6		33	Montana	14.5
15	North Dakota	17.9		34	Vermont	14.4
40	Ohio	12.6		35	Tennessee	14.1
27	Oklahoma	15.1		35	Texas	14.1
20	Oregon	16.8		37	Nevada	14.0
4	Pennsylvania	22.1		38	California	12.8
42	Rhode Island	11.4		38	West Virginia	12.8
25	South Carolina	15.2		40	Ohio	12.6
43	South Dakota	11.3		41	Arizona	12.2
35	Tennessee	14.1		42	Rhode Island	11.4
35	Texas	14.1		43	South Dakota	11.3
15	Utah	17.9		44	Massachusetts	11.2
34	Vermont	14.4		45	New Mexico	11.0
23	Virginia	15.8		46	Michigan	10.7
31	Washington	14.6		47	Kansas	9.8
38	West Virginia	12.8		NA	Florida**	NA
5	Wisconsin	22.0		NA	Hawaii**	NA
10	Wyoming	19.5		NA	Illinois**	NA
					District of Columbia**	NA

Source: Federal Bureau of Investigation (unpublished data)

*Property crimes are offenses of burglary, larceny-theft, and motor vehicle theft. A crime is considered cleared when at least one person is arrested, charged, and turned over to the court for prosecution. Clearances recorded in 2007 may be for crimes which occurred in prior years. Several crimes may be cleared by the arrest of one person while the arrest of many persons may clear only one crime.

**Not available.

Percent of Burglaries Cleared in 2007

National Percent = 12.3% Cleared*

<table>
<thead>
<tr><th colspan="3">ALPHA ORDER</th><th colspan="3">RANK ORDER</th></tr>
<tr><th>RANK</th><th>STATE</th><th>PERCENT</th><th>RANK</th><th>STATE</th><th>PERCENT</th></tr>
</thead>
<tbody>
<tr><td>35</td><td>Alabama</td><td>10.3</td><td>1</td><td>Delaware</td><td>23.7</td></tr>
<tr><td>3</td><td>Alaska</td><td>19.1</td><td>2</td><td>Maine</td><td>20.7</td></tr>
<tr><td>45</td><td>Arizona</td><td>7.7</td><td>3</td><td>Alaska</td><td>19.1</td></tr>
<tr><td>34</td><td>Arkansas</td><td>10.5</td><td>4</td><td>Pennsylvania</td><td>19.0</td></tr>
<tr><td>25</td><td>California</td><td>12.2</td><td>5</td><td>Wyoming</td><td>18.5</td></tr>
<tr><td>39</td><td>Colorado</td><td>9.4</td><td>6</td><td>North Carolina</td><td>17.8</td></tr>
<tr><td>18</td><td>Connecticut</td><td>13.1</td><td>7</td><td>Maryland</td><td>17.4</td></tr>
<tr><td>1</td><td>Delaware</td><td>23.7</td><td>8</td><td>New York</td><td>16.6</td></tr>
<tr><td>NA</td><td>Florida**</td><td>NA</td><td>9</td><td>Virginia</td><td>15.9</td></tr>
<tr><td>17</td><td>Georgia</td><td>13.3</td><td>10</td><td>Missouri</td><td>15.5</td></tr>
<tr><td>NA</td><td>Hawaii**</td><td>NA</td><td>11</td><td>Louisiana</td><td>14.7</td></tr>
<tr><td>18</td><td>Idaho</td><td>13.1</td><td>12</td><td>Nebraska</td><td>14.4</td></tr>
<tr><td>NA</td><td>Illinois**</td><td>NA</td><td>13</td><td>Wisconsin</td><td>14.2</td></tr>
<tr><td>23</td><td>Indiana</td><td>12.4</td><td>14</td><td>New Jersey</td><td>14.1</td></tr>
<tr><td>37</td><td>Iowa</td><td>10.0</td><td>15</td><td>Oklahoma</td><td>14.0</td></tr>
<tr><td>47</td><td>Kansas</td><td>7.4</td><td>16</td><td>Kentucky</td><td>13.5</td></tr>
<tr><td>16</td><td>Kentucky</td><td>13.5</td><td>17</td><td>Georgia</td><td>13.3</td></tr>
<tr><td>11</td><td>Louisiana</td><td>14.7</td><td>18</td><td>Connecticut</td><td>13.1</td></tr>
<tr><td>2</td><td>Maine</td><td>20.7</td><td>18</td><td>Idaho</td><td>13.1</td></tr>
<tr><td>7</td><td>Maryland</td><td>17.4</td><td>18</td><td>North Dakota</td><td>13.1</td></tr>
<tr><td>38</td><td>Massachusetts</td><td>9.7</td><td>18</td><td>South Carolina</td><td>13.1</td></tr>
<tr><td>46</td><td>Michigan</td><td>7.6</td><td>22</td><td>Vermont</td><td>12.8</td></tr>
<tr><td>26</td><td>Minnesota</td><td>11.9</td><td>23</td><td>Indiana</td><td>12.4</td></tr>
<tr><td>30</td><td>Mississippi</td><td>11.0</td><td>24</td><td>Utah</td><td>12.3</td></tr>
<tr><td>10</td><td>Missouri</td><td>15.5</td><td>25</td><td>California</td><td>12.2</td></tr>
<tr><td>31</td><td>Montana</td><td>10.7</td><td>26</td><td>Minnesota</td><td>11.9</td></tr>
<tr><td>12</td><td>Nebraska</td><td>14.4</td><td>27</td><td>New Hampshire</td><td>11.7</td></tr>
<tr><td>40</td><td>Nevada</td><td>9.2</td><td>27</td><td>Rhode Island</td><td>11.7</td></tr>
<tr><td>27</td><td>New Hampshire</td><td>11.7</td><td>29</td><td>Washington</td><td>11.5</td></tr>
<tr><td>14</td><td>New Jersey</td><td>14.1</td><td>30</td><td>Mississippi</td><td>11.0</td></tr>
<tr><td>42</td><td>New Mexico</td><td>8.6</td><td>31</td><td>Montana</td><td>10.7</td></tr>
<tr><td>8</td><td>New York</td><td>16.6</td><td>31</td><td>Oregon</td><td>10.7</td></tr>
<tr><td>6</td><td>North Carolina</td><td>17.8</td><td>33</td><td>Texas</td><td>10.6</td></tr>
<tr><td>18</td><td>North Dakota</td><td>13.1</td><td>34</td><td>Arkansas</td><td>10.5</td></tr>
<tr><td>41</td><td>Ohio</td><td>9.0</td><td>35</td><td>Alabama</td><td>10.3</td></tr>
<tr><td>15</td><td>Oklahoma</td><td>14.0</td><td>35</td><td>Tennessee</td><td>10.3</td></tr>
<tr><td>31</td><td>Oregon</td><td>10.7</td><td>37</td><td>Iowa</td><td>10.0</td></tr>
<tr><td>4</td><td>Pennsylvania</td><td>19.0</td><td>38</td><td>Massachusetts</td><td>9.7</td></tr>
<tr><td>27</td><td>Rhode Island</td><td>11.7</td><td>39</td><td>Colorado</td><td>9.4</td></tr>
<tr><td>18</td><td>South Carolina</td><td>13.1</td><td>40</td><td>Nevada</td><td>9.2</td></tr>
<tr><td>44</td><td>South Dakota</td><td>8.2</td><td>41</td><td>Ohio</td><td>9.0</td></tr>
<tr><td>35</td><td>Tennessee</td><td>10.3</td><td>42</td><td>New Mexico</td><td>8.6</td></tr>
<tr><td>33</td><td>Texas</td><td>10.6</td><td>43</td><td>West Virginia</td><td>8.3</td></tr>
<tr><td>24</td><td>Utah</td><td>12.3</td><td>44</td><td>South Dakota</td><td>8.2</td></tr>
<tr><td>22</td><td>Vermont</td><td>12.8</td><td>45</td><td>Arizona</td><td>7.7</td></tr>
<tr><td>9</td><td>Virginia</td><td>15.9</td><td>46</td><td>Michigan</td><td>7.6</td></tr>
<tr><td>29</td><td>Washington</td><td>11.5</td><td>47</td><td>Kansas</td><td>7.4</td></tr>
<tr><td>43</td><td>West Virginia</td><td>8.3</td><td>NA</td><td>Florida**</td><td>NA</td></tr>
<tr><td>13</td><td>Wisconsin</td><td>14.2</td><td>NA</td><td>Hawaii**</td><td>NA</td></tr>
<tr><td>5</td><td>Wyoming</td><td>18.5</td><td>NA</td><td>Illinois**</td><td>NA</td></tr>
<tr><td></td><td></td><td></td><td></td><td>District of Columbia**</td><td>NA</td></tr>
</tbody>
</table>

Source: Federal Bureau of Investigation (unpublished data)

*Burglary is the unlawful entry of a structure to commit a felony or theft. Attempts are included. A crime is considered cleared when at least one person is arrested, charged, and turned over to the court for prosecution. Clearances recorded in 2007 may be for crimes which occurred in prior years. Several crimes may be cleared by the arrest of one person while the arrest of many persons may clear only one crime.

**Not available.

Percent of Larceny-Thefts Cleared in 2007

National Percent = 17.3% Cleared*

| | |

RANK	STATE	PERCENT		RANK	STATE	PERCENT
23	Alabama	17.9		1	Maine	26.2
3	Alaska	25.6		2	New York	26.0
37	Arizona	14.6		3	Alaska	25.6
28	Arkansas	16.4		4	Wisconsin	24.4
39	California	14.3		5	Pennsylvania	23.1
25	Colorado	17.0		6	Delaware	23.0
27	Connecticut	16.7		7	Minnesota	22.6
6	Delaware	23.0		8	North Carolina	21.9
NA	Florida**	NA		9	Nebraska	21.1
10	Georgia	20.8		10	Georgia	20.8
NA	Hawaii**	NA		11	Maryland	20.5
16	Idaho	19.4		12	Louisiana	20.1
NA	Illinois**	NA		13	Kentucky	19.9
24	Indiana	17.1		14	Utah	19.8
30	Iowa	16.0		15	Mississippi	19.5
47	Kansas	10.1		16	Idaho	19.4
13	Kentucky	19.9		16	Wyoming	19.4
12	Louisiana	20.1		18	Oregon	18.9
1	Maine	26.2		19	North Dakota	18.8
11	Maryland	20.5		20	Missouri	18.7
43	Massachusetts	12.3		20	Nevada	18.7
42	Michigan	12.7		22	New Jersey	18.1
7	Minnesota	22.6		23	Alabama	17.9
15	Mississippi	19.5		24	Indiana	17.1
20	Missouri	18.7		25	Colorado	17.0
36	Montana	14.8		26	Washington	16.9
9	Nebraska	21.1		27	Connecticut	16.7
20	Nevada	18.7		28	Arkansas	16.4
35	New Hampshire	15.2		29	South Carolina	16.2
22	New Jersey	18.1		30	Iowa	16.0
46	New Mexico	11.7		31	Virginia	15.7
2	New York	26.0		32	Tennessee	15.6
8	North Carolina	21.9		33	Oklahoma	15.4
19	North Dakota	18.8		33	Texas	15.4
38	Ohio	14.5		35	New Hampshire	15.2
33	Oklahoma	15.4		36	Montana	14.8
18	Oregon	18.9		37	Arizona	14.6
5	Pennsylvania	23.1		38	Ohio	14.5
44	Rhode Island	12.2		39	California	14.3
29	South Carolina	16.2		39	West Virginia	14.3
45	South Dakota	12.0		41	Vermont	14.1
32	Tennessee	15.6		42	Michigan	12.7
33	Texas	15.4		43	Massachusetts	12.3
14	Utah	19.8		44	Rhode Island	12.2
41	Vermont	14.1		45	South Dakota	12.0
31	Virginia	15.7		46	New Mexico	11.7
26	Washington	16.9		47	Kansas	10.1
39	West Virginia	14.3		NA	Florida**	NA
4	Wisconsin	24.4		NA	Hawaii**	NA
16	Wyoming	19.4		NA	Illinois**	NA
					District of Columbia**	NA

Source: Federal Bureau of Investigation (unpublished data)

*Larceny-theft is the unlawful taking of property without use of force, violence, or fraud. Attempts are included. Motor vehicle thefts are excluded. A crime is considered cleared when at least one person is arrested, charged, and turned over to the court for prosecution. Clearances recorded in 2007 may be for crimes which occurred in prior years. Several crimes may be cleared by the arrest of one person while the arrest of many persons may clear only one crime.

**Not available.

Percent of Motor Vehicle Thefts Cleared in 2007

National Percent = 12.3% Cleared*

<table>
<tr><td colspan="3">ALPHA ORDER</td><td colspan="3">RANK ORDER</td></tr>
<tr><td>RANK</td><td>STATE</td><td>PERCENT</td><td>RANK</td><td>STATE</td><td>PERCENT</td></tr>
<tr><td>12</td><td>Alabama</td><td>18.8</td><td>1</td><td>Maine</td><td>31.9</td></tr>
<tr><td>5</td><td>Alaska</td><td>22.1</td><td>2</td><td>Vermont</td><td>28.6</td></tr>
<tr><td>38</td><td>Arizona</td><td>9.9</td><td>3</td><td>Wyoming</td><td>24.7</td></tr>
<tr><td>22</td><td>Arkansas</td><td>15.5</td><td>4</td><td>New York</td><td>24.6</td></tr>
<tr><td>41</td><td>California</td><td>9.2</td><td>5</td><td>Alaska</td><td>22.1</td></tr>
<tr><td>36</td><td>Colorado</td><td>11.2</td><td>6</td><td>North Dakota</td><td>21.1</td></tr>
<tr><td>42</td><td>Connecticut</td><td>9.1</td><td>7</td><td>Pennsylvania</td><td>21.0</td></tr>
<tr><td>37</td><td>Delaware</td><td>10.6</td><td>8</td><td>New Hampshire</td><td>20.9</td></tr>
<tr><td>NA</td><td>Florida**</td><td>NA</td><td>8</td><td>North Carolina</td><td>20.9</td></tr>
<tr><td>14</td><td>Georgia</td><td>17.9</td><td>10</td><td>Nebraska</td><td>20.1</td></tr>
<tr><td>NA</td><td>Hawaii**</td><td>NA</td><td>11</td><td>Idaho</td><td>19.0</td></tr>
<tr><td>11</td><td>Idaho</td><td>19.0</td><td>12</td><td>Alabama</td><td>18.8</td></tr>
<tr><td>NA</td><td>Illinois**</td><td>NA</td><td>13</td><td>Wisconsin</td><td>18.1</td></tr>
<tr><td>15</td><td>Indiana</td><td>17.1</td><td>14</td><td>Georgia</td><td>17.9</td></tr>
<tr><td>21</td><td>Iowa</td><td>16.0</td><td>15</td><td>Indiana</td><td>17.1</td></tr>
<tr><td>27</td><td>Kansas</td><td>13.6</td><td>16</td><td>Montana</td><td>16.6</td></tr>
<tr><td>23</td><td>Kentucky</td><td>15.0</td><td>17</td><td>Virginia</td><td>16.4</td></tr>
<tr><td>24</td><td>Louisiana</td><td>14.4</td><td>18</td><td>Mississippi</td><td>16.3</td></tr>
<tr><td>1</td><td>Maine</td><td>31.9</td><td>19</td><td>Minnesota</td><td>16.2</td></tr>
<tr><td>35</td><td>Maryland</td><td>11.6</td><td>20</td><td>Oklahoma</td><td>16.1</td></tr>
<tr><td>44</td><td>Massachusetts</td><td>8.5</td><td>21</td><td>Iowa</td><td>16.0</td></tr>
<tr><td>45</td><td>Michigan</td><td>7.5</td><td>22</td><td>Arkansas</td><td>15.5</td></tr>
<tr><td>19</td><td>Minnesota</td><td>16.2</td><td>23</td><td>Kentucky</td><td>15.0</td></tr>
<tr><td>18</td><td>Mississippi</td><td>16.3</td><td>24</td><td>Louisiana</td><td>14.4</td></tr>
<tr><td>31</td><td>Missouri</td><td>13.2</td><td>25</td><td>Tennessee</td><td>14.3</td></tr>
<tr><td>16</td><td>Montana</td><td>16.6</td><td>26</td><td>West Virginia</td><td>14.2</td></tr>
<tr><td>10</td><td>Nebraska</td><td>20.1</td><td>27</td><td>Kansas</td><td>13.6</td></tr>
<tr><td>40</td><td>Nevada</td><td>9.5</td><td>27</td><td>South Dakota</td><td>13.6</td></tr>
<tr><td>8</td><td>New Hampshire</td><td>20.9</td><td>27</td><td>Texas</td><td>13.6</td></tr>
<tr><td>47</td><td>New Jersey</td><td>5.7</td><td>30</td><td>South Carolina</td><td>13.5</td></tr>
<tr><td>33</td><td>New Mexico</td><td>12.3</td><td>31</td><td>Missouri</td><td>13.2</td></tr>
<tr><td>4</td><td>New York</td><td>24.6</td><td>32</td><td>Oregon</td><td>12.5</td></tr>
<tr><td>8</td><td>North Carolina</td><td>20.9</td><td>33</td><td>New Mexico</td><td>12.3</td></tr>
<tr><td>6</td><td>North Dakota</td><td>21.1</td><td>34</td><td>Utah</td><td>12.2</td></tr>
<tr><td>39</td><td>Ohio</td><td>9.8</td><td>35</td><td>Maryland</td><td>11.6</td></tr>
<tr><td>20</td><td>Oklahoma</td><td>16.1</td><td>36</td><td>Colorado</td><td>11.2</td></tr>
<tr><td>32</td><td>Oregon</td><td>12.5</td><td>37</td><td>Delaware</td><td>10.6</td></tr>
<tr><td>7</td><td>Pennsylvania</td><td>21.0</td><td>38</td><td>Arizona</td><td>9.9</td></tr>
<tr><td>46</td><td>Rhode Island</td><td>7.3</td><td>39</td><td>Ohio</td><td>9.8</td></tr>
<tr><td>30</td><td>South Carolina</td><td>13.5</td><td>40</td><td>Nevada</td><td>9.5</td></tr>
<tr><td>27</td><td>South Dakota</td><td>13.6</td><td>41</td><td>California</td><td>9.2</td></tr>
<tr><td>25</td><td>Tennessee</td><td>14.3</td><td>42</td><td>Connecticut</td><td>9.1</td></tr>
<tr><td>27</td><td>Texas</td><td>13.6</td><td>43</td><td>Washington</td><td>8.6</td></tr>
<tr><td>34</td><td>Utah</td><td>12.2</td><td>44</td><td>Massachusetts</td><td>8.5</td></tr>
<tr><td>2</td><td>Vermont</td><td>28.6</td><td>45</td><td>Michigan</td><td>7.5</td></tr>
<tr><td>17</td><td>Virginia</td><td>16.4</td><td>46</td><td>Rhode Island</td><td>7.3</td></tr>
<tr><td>43</td><td>Washington</td><td>8.6</td><td>47</td><td>New Jersey</td><td>5.7</td></tr>
<tr><td>26</td><td>West Virginia</td><td>14.2</td><td>NA</td><td>Florida**</td><td>NA</td></tr>
<tr><td>13</td><td>Wisconsin</td><td>18.1</td><td>NA</td><td>Hawaii**</td><td>NA</td></tr>
<tr><td>3</td><td>Wyoming</td><td>24.7</td><td>NA</td><td>Illinois**</td><td>NA</td></tr>
<tr><td></td><td></td><td></td><td></td><td>District of Columbia**</td><td>NA</td></tr>
</table>

Source: Federal Bureau of Investigation (unpublished data)
*Motor vehicle theft includes the theft or attempted theft of a self-propelled vehicle. Excludes motorboats, construction equipment, airplanes, and farming equipment. A crime is considered cleared when at least one person is arrested, charged, and turned over to the court for prosecution. Clearances recorded in 2007 may be for crimes which occurred in prior years. Several crimes may be cleared by the arrest of one person while the arrest of many persons may clear only one crime.
**Not available.

II. CORRECTIONS

Prisoners in State Correctional Institutions: Year End 2008

National Total = 1,409,166 State Prisoners*

<table>
<tr><td colspan="4">ALPHA ORDER</td><td colspan="4">RANK ORDER</td></tr>
<tr><th>RANK</th><th>STATE</th><th>PRISONERS</th><th>% of USA</th><th>RANK</th><th>STATE</th><th>PRISONERS</th><th>% of USA</th></tr>
<tr><td>14</td><td>Alabama</td><td>30,508</td><td>2.2%</td><td>1</td><td>California</td><td>173,670</td><td>12.3%</td></tr>
<tr><td>41</td><td>Alaska</td><td>5,014</td><td>0.4%</td><td>2</td><td>Texas</td><td>172,506</td><td>12.2%</td></tr>
<tr><td>10</td><td>Arizona</td><td>39,589</td><td>2.8%</td><td>3</td><td>Florida</td><td>102,388</td><td>7.3%</td></tr>
<tr><td>28</td><td>Arkansas</td><td>14,716</td><td>1.0%</td><td>4</td><td>New York</td><td>60,347</td><td>4.3%</td></tr>
<tr><td>1</td><td>California</td><td>173,670</td><td>12.3%</td><td>5</td><td>Georgia</td><td>52,719</td><td>3.7%</td></tr>
<tr><td>23</td><td>Colorado</td><td>23,274</td><td>1.7%</td><td>6</td><td>Ohio</td><td>51,686</td><td>3.7%</td></tr>
<tr><td>26</td><td>Connecticut</td><td>20,661</td><td>1.5%</td><td>7</td><td>Pennsylvania</td><td>50,147</td><td>3.6%</td></tr>
<tr><td>36</td><td>Delaware</td><td>7,075</td><td>0.5%</td><td>8</td><td>Michigan</td><td>48,738</td><td>3.5%</td></tr>
<tr><td>3</td><td>Florida</td><td>102,388</td><td>7.3%</td><td>9</td><td>Illinois</td><td>45,474</td><td>3.2%</td></tr>
<tr><td>5</td><td>Georgia</td><td>52,719</td><td>3.7%</td><td>10</td><td>Arizona</td><td>39,589</td><td>2.8%</td></tr>
<tr><td>40</td><td>Hawaii</td><td>5,955</td><td>0.4%</td><td>11</td><td>North Carolina</td><td>39,482</td><td>2.8%</td></tr>
<tr><td>35</td><td>Idaho</td><td>7,290</td><td>0.5%</td><td>12</td><td>Louisiana</td><td>38,381</td><td>2.7%</td></tr>
<tr><td>9</td><td>Illinois</td><td>45,474</td><td>3.2%</td><td>13</td><td>Virginia</td><td>38,276</td><td>2.7%</td></tr>
<tr><td>16</td><td>Indiana</td><td>28,322</td><td>2.0%</td><td>14</td><td>Alabama</td><td>30,508</td><td>2.2%</td></tr>
<tr><td>33</td><td>Iowa</td><td>8,766</td><td>0.6%</td><td>15</td><td>Missouri</td><td>30,186</td><td>2.1%</td></tr>
<tr><td>34</td><td>Kansas</td><td>8,539</td><td>0.6%</td><td>16</td><td>Indiana</td><td>28,322</td><td>2.0%</td></tr>
<tr><td>25</td><td>Kentucky</td><td>21,706</td><td>1.5%</td><td>17</td><td>Tennessee</td><td>27,228</td><td>1.9%</td></tr>
<tr><td>12</td><td>Louisiana</td><td>38,381</td><td>2.7%</td><td>18</td><td>New Jersey</td><td>25,953</td><td>1.8%</td></tr>
<tr><td>47</td><td>Maine</td><td>2,195</td><td>0.2%</td><td>19</td><td>Oklahoma</td><td>25,864</td><td>1.8%</td></tr>
<tr><td>22</td><td>Maryland</td><td>23,324</td><td>1.7%</td><td>20</td><td>South Carolina</td><td>24,326</td><td>1.7%</td></tr>
<tr><td>31</td><td>Massachusetts</td><td>11,408</td><td>0.8%</td><td>21</td><td>Wisconsin</td><td>23,380</td><td>1.7%</td></tr>
<tr><td>8</td><td>Michigan</td><td>48,738</td><td>3.5%</td><td>22</td><td>Maryland</td><td>23,324</td><td>1.7%</td></tr>
<tr><td>32</td><td>Minnesota</td><td>9,406</td><td>0.7%</td><td>23</td><td>Colorado</td><td>23,274</td><td>1.7%</td></tr>
<tr><td>24</td><td>Mississippi</td><td>22,754</td><td>1.6%</td><td>24</td><td>Mississippi</td><td>22,754</td><td>1.6%</td></tr>
<tr><td>15</td><td>Missouri</td><td>30,186</td><td>2.1%</td><td>25</td><td>Kentucky</td><td>21,706</td><td>1.5%</td></tr>
<tr><td>44</td><td>Montana</td><td>3,607</td><td>0.3%</td><td>26</td><td>Connecticut</td><td>20,661</td><td>1.5%</td></tr>
<tr><td>42</td><td>Nebraska</td><td>4,520</td><td>0.3%</td><td>27</td><td>Washington</td><td>17,926</td><td>1.3%</td></tr>
<tr><td>30</td><td>Nevada</td><td>12,743</td><td>0.9%</td><td>28</td><td>Arkansas</td><td>14,716</td><td>1.0%</td></tr>
<tr><td>46</td><td>New Hampshire</td><td>2,904</td><td>0.2%</td><td>29</td><td>Oregon</td><td>14,167</td><td>1.0%</td></tr>
<tr><td>18</td><td>New Jersey</td><td>25,953</td><td>1.8%</td><td>30</td><td>Nevada</td><td>12,743</td><td>0.9%</td></tr>
<tr><td>38</td><td>New Mexico</td><td>6,402</td><td>0.5%</td><td>31</td><td>Massachusetts</td><td>11,408</td><td>0.8%</td></tr>
<tr><td>4</td><td>New York</td><td>60,347</td><td>4.3%</td><td>32</td><td>Minnesota</td><td>9,406</td><td>0.7%</td></tr>
<tr><td>11</td><td>North Carolina</td><td>39,482</td><td>2.8%</td><td>33</td><td>Iowa</td><td>8,766</td><td>0.6%</td></tr>
<tr><td>50</td><td>North Dakota</td><td>1,452</td><td>0.1%</td><td>34</td><td>Kansas</td><td>8,539</td><td>0.6%</td></tr>
<tr><td>6</td><td>Ohio</td><td>51,686</td><td>3.7%</td><td>35</td><td>Idaho</td><td>7,290</td><td>0.5%</td></tr>
<tr><td>19</td><td>Oklahoma</td><td>25,864</td><td>1.8%</td><td>36</td><td>Delaware</td><td>7,075</td><td>0.5%</td></tr>
<tr><td>29</td><td>Oregon</td><td>14,167</td><td>1.0%</td><td>37</td><td>Utah</td><td>6,546</td><td>0.5%</td></tr>
<tr><td>7</td><td>Pennsylvania</td><td>50,147</td><td>3.6%</td><td>38</td><td>New Mexico</td><td>6,402</td><td>0.5%</td></tr>
<tr><td>43</td><td>Rhode Island</td><td>4,045</td><td>0.3%</td><td>39</td><td>West Virginia</td><td>6,059</td><td>0.4%</td></tr>
<tr><td>20</td><td>South Carolina</td><td>24,326</td><td>1.7%</td><td>40</td><td>Hawaii</td><td>5,955</td><td>0.4%</td></tr>
<tr><td>45</td><td>South Dakota</td><td>3,342</td><td>0.2%</td><td>41</td><td>Alaska</td><td>5,014</td><td>0.4%</td></tr>
<tr><td>17</td><td>Tennessee</td><td>27,228</td><td>1.9%</td><td>42</td><td>Nebraska</td><td>4,520</td><td>0.3%</td></tr>
<tr><td>2</td><td>Texas</td><td>172,506</td><td>12.2%</td><td>43</td><td>Rhode Island</td><td>4,045</td><td>0.3%</td></tr>
<tr><td>37</td><td>Utah</td><td>6,546</td><td>0.5%</td><td>44</td><td>Montana</td><td>3,607</td><td>0.3%</td></tr>
<tr><td>48</td><td>Vermont</td><td>2,116</td><td>0.2%</td><td>45</td><td>South Dakota</td><td>3,342</td><td>0.2%</td></tr>
<tr><td>13</td><td>Virginia</td><td>38,276</td><td>2.7%</td><td>46</td><td>New Hampshire</td><td>2,904</td><td>0.2%</td></tr>
<tr><td>27</td><td>Washington</td><td>17,926</td><td>1.3%</td><td>47</td><td>Maine</td><td>2,195</td><td>0.2%</td></tr>
<tr><td>39</td><td>West Virginia</td><td>6,059</td><td>0.4%</td><td>48</td><td>Vermont</td><td>2,116</td><td>0.2%</td></tr>
<tr><td>21</td><td>Wisconsin</td><td>23,380</td><td>1.7%</td><td>49</td><td>Wyoming</td><td>2,084</td><td>0.1%</td></tr>
<tr><td>49</td><td>Wyoming</td><td>2,084</td><td>0.1%</td><td>50</td><td>North Dakota</td><td>1,452</td><td>0.1%</td></tr>
<tr><td></td><td></td><td></td><td></td><td></td><td>District of Columbia**</td><td>NA</td><td>NA</td></tr>
</table>

Source: U.S. Department of Justice, Bureau of Justice Statistics
  "Prisoners in 2008" (December 2009, NCJ 228417, http://bjs.ojp.usdoj.gov/)
*Advance figures as of December 31, 2008. Totals reflect all prisoners, including those sentenced to a year or less and those unsentenced. National total does not include 201,280 prisoners under federal jurisdiction. State and federal prisoners combined total 1,610,446.
**Responsibility for sentenced felons in D.C. was transferred to the Federal Bureau of Prisons in 2001.

Percent Change in Number of State Prisoners: 2007 to 2008

National Percent Change = 0.8% Increase*

RANK	STATE (ALPHA ORDER)	PERCENT CHANGE		RANK	STATE (RANK ORDER)	PERCENT CHANGE
7	Alabama	3.7		1	Pennsylvania	9.1
45	Alaska	(3.0)		2	Arizona	4.9
2	Arizona	4.9		3	Indiana	4.4
9	Arkansas	2.8		4	Florida	4.2
32	California	(0.4)		4	Montana	4.2
13	Colorado	1.9		6	North Carolina	4.0
38	Connecticut	(1.3)		7	Alabama	3.7
43	Delaware	(2.8)		7	Tennessee	3.7
4	Florida	4.2		9	Arkansas	2.8
43	Georgia	(2.8)		10	North Dakota	2.5
32	Hawaii	(0.4)		11	Louisiana	2.2
32	Idaho	(0.4)		11	Maine	2.2
21	Illinois	0.6		13	Colorado	1.9
3	Indiana	4.4		13	Ohio	1.9
24	Iowa	0.4		15	Oregon	1.6
42	Kansas	(1.8)		16	Mississippi	1.4
47	Kentucky	(3.3)		17	Missouri	1.1
11	Louisiana	2.2		18	South Dakota	0.9
11	Maine	2.2		18	Washington	0.9
35	Maryland	(0.5)		20	Rhode Island	0.7
31	Massachusetts	(0.2)		21	Illinois	0.6
45	Michigan	(3.0)		22	Utah	0.5
36	Minnesota	(0.7)		22	Virginia	0.5
16	Mississippi	1.4		24	Iowa	0.4
17	Missouri	1.1		24	South Carolina	0.4
4	Montana	4.2		24	Texas	0.4
27	Nebraska	0.3		27	Nebraska	0.3
NA	Nevada**	NA		28	Oklahoma	0.1
38	New Hampshire	(1.3)		29	West Virginia	0.0
47	New Jersey	(3.3)		29	Wyoming	0.0
37	New Mexico	(1.0)		31	Massachusetts	(0.2)
49	New York	(3.6)		32	California	(0.4)
6	North Carolina	4.0		32	Hawaii	(0.4)
10	North Dakota	2.5		32	Idaho	(0.4)
13	Ohio	1.9		35	Maryland	(0.5)
28	Oklahoma	0.1		36	Minnesota	(0.7)
15	Oregon	1.6		37	New Mexico	(1.0)
1	Pennsylvania	9.1		38	Connecticut	(1.3)
20	Rhode Island	0.7		38	New Hampshire	(1.3)
24	South Carolina	0.4		40	Vermont	(1.4)
18	South Dakota	0.9		41	Wisconsin	(1.5)
7	Tennessee	3.7		42	Kansas	(1.8)
24	Texas	0.4		43	Delaware	(2.8)
22	Utah	0.5		43	Georgia	(2.8)
40	Vermont	(1.4)		45	Alaska	(3.0)
22	Virginia	0.5		45	Michigan	(3.0)
18	Washington	0.9		47	Kentucky	(3.3)
29	West Virginia	0.0		47	New Jersey	(3.3)
41	Wisconsin	(1.5)		49	New York	(3.6)
29	Wyoming	0.0		NA	Nevada**	NA
					District of Columbia***	NA

Source: U.S. Department of Justice, Bureau of Justice Statistics
   "Prisoners in 2008" (December 2009, NCJ 228417, http://bjs.ojp.usdoj.gov/)
*From December 31, 2007 to December 31, 2008. Includes inmates sentenced to more than one year and those sentenced to a year or less or with no sentence. The percent change in number of prisoners under federal jurisdiction during the same period was an 0.8% increase. The combined state and federal increase was 0.8%. **Not available.
***Responsibility for sentenced felons in D.C. was transferred to the Federal Bureau of Prisons in 2001.

State Prisoners Sentenced to More than One Year in 2008

National Total = 1,357,703 State Prisoners*

<table>
<thead>
<tr><th colspan="4">ALPHA ORDER</th><th colspan="4">RANK ORDER</th></tr>
<tr><th>RANK</th><th>STATE</th><th>PRISONERS</th><th>% of USA</th><th>RANK</th><th>STATE</th><th>PRISONERS</th><th>% of USA</th></tr>
</thead>
<tbody>
<tr><td>15</td><td>Alabama</td><td>29,694</td><td>2.2%</td><td>1</td><td>California</td><td>172,583</td><td>12.7%</td></tr>
<tr><td>44</td><td>Alaska</td><td>2,966</td><td>0.2%</td><td>2</td><td>Texas</td><td>156,979</td><td>11.6%</td></tr>
<tr><td>12</td><td>Arizona</td><td>37,188</td><td>2.7%</td><td>3</td><td>Florida</td><td>102,388</td><td>7.5%</td></tr>
<tr><td>27</td><td>Arkansas</td><td>14,660</td><td>1.1%</td><td>4</td><td>New York</td><td>59,959</td><td>4.4%</td></tr>
<tr><td>1</td><td>California</td><td>172,583</td><td>12.7%</td><td>5</td><td>Georgia</td><td>52,705</td><td>3.9%</td></tr>
<tr><td>21</td><td>Colorado</td><td>23,274</td><td>1.7%</td><td>6</td><td>Ohio</td><td>51,686</td><td>3.8%</td></tr>
<tr><td>28</td><td>Connecticut</td><td>14,271</td><td>1.1%</td><td>7</td><td>Pennsylvania</td><td>48,962</td><td>3.6%</td></tr>
<tr><td>41</td><td>Delaware</td><td>4,067</td><td>0.3%</td><td>8</td><td>Michigan</td><td>48,738</td><td>3.6%</td></tr>
<tr><td>3</td><td>Florida</td><td>102,388</td><td>7.5%</td><td>9</td><td>Illinois</td><td>45,474</td><td>3.3%</td></tr>
<tr><td>5</td><td>Georgia</td><td>52,705</td><td>3.9%</td><td>10</td><td>Virginia</td><td>38,216</td><td>2.8%</td></tr>
<tr><td>40</td><td>Hawaii</td><td>4,304</td><td>0.3%</td><td>11</td><td>Louisiana</td><td>37,804</td><td>2.8%</td></tr>
<tr><td>35</td><td>Idaho</td><td>7,290</td><td>0.5%</td><td>12</td><td>Arizona</td><td>37,188</td><td>2.7%</td></tr>
<tr><td>9</td><td>Illinois</td><td>45,474</td><td>3.3%</td><td>13</td><td>North Carolina</td><td>34,229</td><td>2.5%</td></tr>
<tr><td>16</td><td>Indiana</td><td>28,301</td><td>2.1%</td><td>14</td><td>Missouri</td><td>30,175</td><td>2.2%</td></tr>
<tr><td>33</td><td>Iowa</td><td>8,766</td><td>0.6%</td><td>15</td><td>Alabama</td><td>29,694</td><td>2.2%</td></tr>
<tr><td>34</td><td>Kansas</td><td>8,539</td><td>0.6%</td><td>16</td><td>Indiana</td><td>28,301</td><td>2.1%</td></tr>
<tr><td>25</td><td>Kentucky</td><td>21,059</td><td>1.6%</td><td>17</td><td>Tennessee</td><td>27,228</td><td>2.0%</td></tr>
<tr><td>11</td><td>Louisiana</td><td>37,804</td><td>2.8%</td><td>18</td><td>New Jersey</td><td>25,953</td><td>1.9%</td></tr>
<tr><td>48</td><td>Maine</td><td>1,985</td><td>0.1%</td><td>19</td><td>Oklahoma</td><td>24,210</td><td>1.8%</td></tr>
<tr><td>22</td><td>Maryland</td><td>22,749</td><td>1.7%</td><td>20</td><td>South Carolina</td><td>23,456</td><td>1.7%</td></tr>
<tr><td>31</td><td>Massachusetts</td><td>10,166</td><td>0.7%</td><td>21</td><td>Colorado</td><td>23,274</td><td>1.7%</td></tr>
<tr><td>8</td><td>Michigan</td><td>48,738</td><td>3.6%</td><td>22</td><td>Maryland</td><td>22,749</td><td>1.7%</td></tr>
<tr><td>32</td><td>Minnesota</td><td>9,406</td><td>0.7%</td><td>23</td><td>Mississippi</td><td>21,698</td><td>1.6%</td></tr>
<tr><td>23</td><td>Mississippi</td><td>21,698</td><td>1.6%</td><td>24</td><td>Wisconsin</td><td>21,103</td><td>1.6%</td></tr>
<tr><td>14</td><td>Missouri</td><td>30,175</td><td>2.2%</td><td>25</td><td>Kentucky</td><td>21,059</td><td>1.6%</td></tr>
<tr><td>42</td><td>Montana</td><td>3,579</td><td>0.3%</td><td>26</td><td>Washington</td><td>17,926</td><td>1.3%</td></tr>
<tr><td>39</td><td>Nebraska</td><td>4,424</td><td>0.3%</td><td>27</td><td>Arkansas</td><td>14,660</td><td>1.1%</td></tr>
<tr><td>30</td><td>Nevada</td><td>12,743</td><td>0.9%</td><td>28</td><td>Connecticut</td><td>14,271</td><td>1.1%</td></tr>
<tr><td>45</td><td>New Hampshire</td><td>2,904</td><td>0.2%</td><td>29</td><td>Oregon</td><td>14,131</td><td>1.0%</td></tr>
<tr><td>18</td><td>New Jersey</td><td>25,953</td><td>1.9%</td><td>30</td><td>Nevada</td><td>12,743</td><td>0.9%</td></tr>
<tr><td>37</td><td>New Mexico</td><td>6,315</td><td>0.5%</td><td>31</td><td>Massachusetts</td><td>10,166</td><td>0.7%</td></tr>
<tr><td>4</td><td>New York</td><td>59,959</td><td>4.4%</td><td>32</td><td>Minnesota</td><td>9,406</td><td>0.7%</td></tr>
<tr><td>13</td><td>North Carolina</td><td>34,229</td><td>2.5%</td><td>33</td><td>Iowa</td><td>8,766</td><td>0.6%</td></tr>
<tr><td>50</td><td>North Dakota</td><td>1,452</td><td>0.1%</td><td>34</td><td>Kansas</td><td>8,539</td><td>0.6%</td></tr>
<tr><td>6</td><td>Ohio</td><td>51,686</td><td>3.8%</td><td>35</td><td>Idaho</td><td>7,290</td><td>0.5%</td></tr>
<tr><td>19</td><td>Oklahoma</td><td>24,210</td><td>1.8%</td><td>36</td><td>Utah</td><td>6,422</td><td>0.5%</td></tr>
<tr><td>29</td><td>Oregon</td><td>14,131</td><td>1.0%</td><td>37</td><td>New Mexico</td><td>6,315</td><td>0.5%</td></tr>
<tr><td>7</td><td>Pennsylvania</td><td>48,962</td><td>3.6%</td><td>38</td><td>West Virginia</td><td>6,019</td><td>0.4%</td></tr>
<tr><td>46</td><td>Rhode Island</td><td>2,522</td><td>0.2%</td><td>39</td><td>Nebraska</td><td>4,424</td><td>0.3%</td></tr>
<tr><td>20</td><td>South Carolina</td><td>23,456</td><td>1.7%</td><td>40</td><td>Hawaii</td><td>4,304</td><td>0.3%</td></tr>
<tr><td>43</td><td>South Dakota</td><td>3,333</td><td>0.2%</td><td>41</td><td>Delaware</td><td>4,067</td><td>0.3%</td></tr>
<tr><td>17</td><td>Tennessee</td><td>27,228</td><td>2.0%</td><td>42</td><td>Montana</td><td>3,579</td><td>0.3%</td></tr>
<tr><td>2</td><td>Texas</td><td>156,979</td><td>11.6%</td><td>43</td><td>South Dakota</td><td>3,333</td><td>0.2%</td></tr>
<tr><td>36</td><td>Utah</td><td>6,422</td><td>0.5%</td><td>44</td><td>Alaska</td><td>2,966</td><td>0.2%</td></tr>
<tr><td>49</td><td>Vermont</td><td>1,618</td><td>0.1%</td><td>45</td><td>New Hampshire</td><td>2,904</td><td>0.2%</td></tr>
<tr><td>10</td><td>Virginia</td><td>38,216</td><td>2.8%</td><td>46</td><td>Rhode Island</td><td>2,522</td><td>0.2%</td></tr>
<tr><td>26</td><td>Washington</td><td>17,926</td><td>1.3%</td><td>47</td><td>Wyoming</td><td>2,084</td><td>0.2%</td></tr>
<tr><td>38</td><td>West Virginia</td><td>6,019</td><td>0.4%</td><td>48</td><td>Maine</td><td>1,985</td><td>0.1%</td></tr>
<tr><td>24</td><td>Wisconsin</td><td>21,103</td><td>1.6%</td><td>49</td><td>Vermont</td><td>1,618</td><td>0.1%</td></tr>
<tr><td>47</td><td>Wyoming</td><td>2,084</td><td>0.2%</td><td>50</td><td>North Dakota</td><td>1,452</td><td>0.1%</td></tr>
<tr><td></td><td></td><td></td><td></td><td></td><td>District of Columbia**</td><td>NA</td><td>NA</td></tr>
</tbody>
</table>

Source: U.S. Department of Justice, Bureau of Justice Statistics
   "Prisoners in 2008" (December 2009, NCJ 228417, http://bjs.ojp.usdoj.gov/)
*Advance figures as of December 31, 2008. Does not include 182,333 prisoners under federal jurisdiction sentenced to more than one year. State and federal prisoners sentenced to more than one year total 1,540,036.
**Responsibility for sentenced felons in D.C. was transferred to the Federal Bureau of Prisons.

State Prisoner Imprisonment Rate in 2008

National Rate = 445 State Prisoners per 100,000 Population*

ALPHA ORDER

RANK	STATE	RATE
5	Alabama	634
23	Alaska	430
6	Arizona	567
10	Arkansas	511
17	California	467
17	Colorado	467
25	Connecticut	407
19	Delaware	463
7	Florida	557
8	Georgia	540
34	Hawaii	332
16	Idaho	474
33	Illinois	351
21	Indiana	442
40	Iowa	291
38	Kansas	303
12	Kentucky	492
1	Louisiana	853
50	Maine	151
26	Maryland	403
48	Massachusetts	218
14	Michigan	488
49	Minnesota	179
2	Mississippi	735
11	Missouri	509
31	Montana	368
43	Nebraska	247
15	Nevada	486
47	New Hampshire	220
39	New Jersey	298
36	New Mexico	316
37	New York	307
31	North Carolina	368
46	North Dakota	225
20	Ohio	449
3	Oklahoma	661
30	Oregon	371
27	Pennsylvania	393
44	Rhode Island	240
9	South Carolina	519
24	South Dakota	412
22	Tennessee	436
4	Texas	639
45	Utah	232
42	Vermont	260
13	Virginia	489
41	Washington	272
35	West Virginia	331
29	Wisconsin	374
28	Wyoming	387

RANK ORDER

RANK	STATE	RATE
1	Louisiana	853
2	Mississippi	735
3	Oklahoma	661
4	Texas	639
5	Alabama	634
6	Arizona	567
7	Florida	557
8	Georgia	540
9	South Carolina	519
10	Arkansas	511
11	Missouri	509
12	Kentucky	492
13	Virginia	489
14	Michigan	488
15	Nevada	486
16	Idaho	474
17	California	467
17	Colorado	467
19	Delaware	463
20	Ohio	449
21	Indiana	442
22	Tennessee	436
23	Alaska	430
24	South Dakota	412
25	Connecticut	407
26	Maryland	403
27	Pennsylvania	393
28	Wyoming	387
29	Wisconsin	374
30	Oregon	371
31	Montana	368
31	North Carolina	368
33	Illinois	351
34	Hawaii	332
35	West Virginia	331
36	New Mexico	316
37	New York	307
38	Kansas	303
39	New Jersey	298
40	Iowa	291
41	Washington	272
42	Vermont	260
43	Nebraska	247
44	Rhode Island	240
45	Utah	232
46	North Dakota	225
47	New Hampshire	220
48	Massachusetts	218
49	Minnesota	179
50	Maine	151
	District of Columbia**	NA

Source: U.S. Department of Justice, Bureau of Justice Statistics
"Prisoners in 2008" (December 2009, NCJ 228417, http://bjs.ojp.usdoj.gov/)
*As of December 31, 2008. Includes only inmates sentenced to more than one year. Does not include federal imprisonment rate of 60 prisoners per 100,000 population. State and federal combined imprisonment rate is 504 prisoners per 100,000 population.
**Responsibility for sentenced felons in D.C. was transferred to the Federal Bureau of Prisons in 2001.

Percent Change in State Prisoner Imprisonment Rate: 2007 to 2008

National Percent Change = 0.4% Decrease*

ALPHA ORDER

RANK	STATE	PERCENT CHANGE
5	Alabama	3.1
42	Alaska	(3.8)
7	Arizona	2.3
11	Arkansas	1.8
30	California	(0.8)
18	Colorado	0.4
29	Connecticut	(0.7)
43	Delaware	(3.9)
2	Florida	4.1
45	Georgia	(4.1)
35	Hawaii	(1.8)
37	Idaho	(1.9)
19	Illinois	0.3
3	Indiana	3.8
21	Iowa	0.0
39	Kansas	(2.9)
43	Kentucky	(3.9)
34	Louisiana	(1.4)
9	Maine	2.0
23	Maryland	(0.2)
49	Massachusetts	(12.4)
38	Michigan	(2.2)
33	Minnesota	(1.1)
20	Mississippi	0.1
16	Missouri	0.6
4	Montana	3.4
13	Nebraska	1.6
NA	Nevada**	NA
31	New Hampshire	(0.9)
41	New Jersey	(3.2)
15	New Mexico	1.0
47	New York	(4.7)
10	North Carolina	1.9
11	North Dakota	1.8
13	Ohio	1.6
27	Oklahoma	(0.6)
17	Oregon	0.5
1	Pennsylvania	7.7
8	Rhode Island	2.1
32	South Carolina	(1.0)
23	South Dakota	(0.2)
6	Tennessee	2.8
46	Texas	(4.5)
39	Utah	(2.9)
21	Vermont	0.0
23	Virginia	(0.2)
26	Washington	(0.4)
27	West Virginia	(0.6)
48	Wisconsin	(5.8)
35	Wyoming	(1.8)

RANK ORDER

RANK	STATE	PERCENT CHANGE
1	Pennsylvania	7.7
2	Florida	4.1
3	Indiana	3.8
4	Montana	3.4
5	Alabama	3.1
6	Tennessee	2.8
7	Arizona	2.3
8	Rhode Island	2.1
9	Maine	2.0
10	North Carolina	1.9
11	Arkansas	1.8
11	North Dakota	1.8
13	Nebraska	1.6
13	Ohio	1.6
15	New Mexico	1.0
16	Missouri	0.6
17	Oregon	0.5
18	Colorado	0.4
19	Illinois	0.3
20	Mississippi	0.1
21	Iowa	0.0
21	Vermont	0.0
23	Maryland	(0.2)
23	South Dakota	(0.2)
23	Virginia	(0.2)
26	Washington	(0.4)
27	Oklahoma	(0.6)
27	West Virginia	(0.6)
29	Connecticut	(0.7)
30	California	(0.8)
31	New Hampshire	(0.9)
32	South Carolina	(1.0)
33	Minnesota	(1.1)
34	Louisiana	(1.4)
35	Hawaii	(1.8)
35	Wyoming	(1.8)
37	Idaho	(1.9)
38	Michigan	(2.2)
39	Kansas	(2.9)
39	Utah	(2.9)
41	New Jersey	(3.2)
42	Alaska	(3.8)
43	Delaware	(3.9)
43	Kentucky	(3.9)
45	Georgia	(4.1)
46	Texas	(4.5)
47	New York	(4.7)
48	Wisconsin	(5.8)
49	Massachusetts	(12.4)
NA	Nevada**	NA
	District of Columbia***	NA

Source: CQ Press using data from U.S. Department of Justice, Bureau of Justice Statistics
   "Prisoners in 2008" (December 2009, NCJ 228417, http://bjs.ojp.usdoj.gov/)
*From December 31, 2007 to December 31, 2008. Includes only inmates sentenced to more than one year. The percent change in rate of prisoners under federal jurisdiction during the same period was a 1.7% increase. The combined state and federal decrease was -0.4%. **Not available.
***Responsibility for sentenced felons in D.C. was transferred to the Federal Bureau of Prisons in 2001.

State Prison Population as a Percent of Highest Capacity in 2008

National Percent = 97% of Highest Capacity*

ALPHA ORDER

RANK	STATE	PERCENT
20	Alabama	98
10	Alaska	111
43	Arizona	79
30	Arkansas	95
14	California	106
7	Colorado	120
NA	Connecticut**	NA
6	Delaware	123
37	Florida	88
15	Georgia	103
27	Hawaii	96
13	Idaho	108
2	Illinois	133
37	Indiana	88
48	Iowa	64
36	Kansas	92
33	Kentucky	93
8	Louisiana	114
12	Maine	109
24	Maryland	97
1	Massachusetts	140
24	Michigan	97
16	Minnesota	101
44	Mississippi	75
27	Missouri	96
33	Montana	93
9	Nebraska	113
40	Nevada	86
20	New Hampshire	98
27	New Jersey	96
49	New Mexico	48
19	New York	99
18	North Carolina	100
3	North Dakota	132
4	Ohio	127
31	Oklahoma	94
31	Oregon	94
16	Pennsylvania	101
37	Rhode Island	88
20	South Carolina	98
24	South Dakota	97
47	Tennessee	70
41	Texas	85
44	Utah	75
42	Vermont	80
33	Virginia	93
10	Washington	111
20	West Virginia	98
5	Wisconsin	125
44	Wyoming	75

RANK ORDER

RANK	STATE	PERCENT
1	Massachusetts	140
2	Illinois	133
3	North Dakota	132
4	Ohio	127
5	Wisconsin	125
6	Delaware	123
7	Colorado	120
8	Louisiana	114
9	Nebraska	113
10	Alaska	111
10	Washington	111
12	Maine	109
13	Idaho	108
14	California	106
15	Georgia	103
16	Minnesota	101
16	Pennsylvania	101
18	North Carolina	100
19	New York	99
20	Alabama	98
20	New Hampshire	98
20	South Carolina	98
20	West Virginia	98
24	Maryland	97
24	Michigan	97
24	South Dakota	97
27	Hawaii	96
27	Missouri	96
27	New Jersey	96
30	Arkansas	95
31	Oklahoma	94
31	Oregon	94
33	Kentucky	93
33	Montana	93
33	Virginia	93
36	Kansas	92
37	Florida	88
37	Indiana	88
37	Rhode Island	88
40	Nevada	86
41	Texas	85
42	Vermont	80
43	Arizona	79
44	Mississippi	75
44	Utah	75
44	Wyoming	75
47	Tennessee	70
48	Iowa	64
49	New Mexico	48
NA	Connecticut**	NA
	District of Columbia***	NA

Source: U.S. Department of Justice, Bureau of Justice Statistics
  "Prisoners in 2008" (December 2009, NCJ 228417, http://bjs.ojp.usdoj.gov/)
*As of December 31, 2008. Federal prison population is at 135% of highest rated capacity.
**Not available. ***Responsibility for sentenced felons in D.C. was transferred to the Federal Bureau of Prisons in 2001.

Percent of State Prisoners Held in Private Facilities in 2008

National Percent = 6.8% of State Prisoners*

ALPHA ORDER				RANK ORDER		
RANK	STATE	PERCENT		RANK	STATE	PERCENT
29	Alabama	0.3		1	New Mexico	45.8
6	Alaska	28.9		2	Montana	36.4
10	Arizona	21.1		3	Hawaii	35.4
31	Arkansas	0.0		4	Vermont	34.3
24	California	1.7		5	Idaho	29.0
8	Colorado	22.7		6	Alaska	28.9
31	Connecticut	0.0		7	Mississippi	24.2
31	Delaware	0.0		8	Colorado	22.7
18	Florida	8.9		9	Oklahoma	22.1
16	Georgia	9.7		10	Arizona	21.1
3	Hawaii	35.4		11	Wyoming	20.5
5	Idaho	29.0		12	Tennessee	18.9
NA	Illinois**	NA		13	Texas	11.6
17	Indiana	9.3		14	Kentucky	10.2
31	Iowa	0.0		14	New Jersey	10.2
31	Kansas	0.0		16	Georgia	9.7
14	Kentucky	10.2		17	Indiana	9.3
19	Louisiana	7.6		18	Florida	8.9
31	Maine	0.0		19	Louisiana	7.6
26	Maryland	0.8		20	Minnesota	6.5
31	Massachusetts	0.0		21	Washington	4.8
31	Michigan	0.0		22	Ohio	4.1
20	Minnesota	6.5		23	Virginia	4.0
7	Mississippi	24.2		24	California	1.7
31	Missouri	0.0		25	Pennsylvania	1.6
2	Montana	36.4		26	Maryland	0.8
31	Nebraska	0.0		27	North Carolina	0.5
31	Nevada	0.0		28	South Dakota	0.4
31	New Hampshire	0.0		29	Alabama	0.3
14	New Jersey	10.2		30	Wisconsin	0.1
1	New Mexico	45.8		31	Arkansas	0.0
31	New York	0.0		31	Connecticut	0.0
27	North Carolina	0.5		31	Delaware	0.0
31	North Dakota	0.0		31	Iowa	0.0
22	Ohio	4.1		31	Kansas	0.0
9	Oklahoma	22.1		31	Maine	0.0
31	Oregon	0.0		31	Massachusetts	0.0
25	Pennsylvania	1.6		31	Michigan	0.0
31	Rhode Island	0.0		31	Missouri	0.0
31	South Carolina	0.0		31	Nebraska	0.0
28	South Dakota	0.4		31	Nevada	0.0
12	Tennessee	18.9		31	New Hampshire	0.0
13	Texas	11.6		31	New York	0.0
31	Utah	0.0		31	North Dakota	0.0
4	Vermont	34.3		31	Oregon	0.0
23	Virginia	4.0		31	Rhode Island	0.0
21	Washington	4.8		31	South Carolina	0.0
31	West Virginia	0.0		31	Utah	0.0
30	Wisconsin	0.1		31	West Virginia	0.0
11	Wyoming	20.5		NA	Illinois**	NA
					District of Columbia***	NA

Source: U.S. Department of Justice, Bureau of Justice Statistics
"Prisoners in 2008" (December 2009, NCJ 228417, http://bjs.ojp.usdoj.gov/)

*As of December 31, 2008. Rate does not include federal prisoners. The federal prisoner percent is 16.5% of federal prisoners. The federal and state combined rate is 8.0%. **Not available.

***Responsibility for sentenced felons in D.C. was transferred to the Federal Bureau of Prisons in 2001.

Percent of State Prisoners Held in Local Jails in 2008

National Percent = 5.7% of State Prisoners*

ALPHA ORDER

RANK	STATE	PERCENT
14	Alabama	5.9
NA	Alaska**	NA
32	Arizona	0.1
9	Arkansas	10.5
24	California	1.6
31	Colorado	0.3
NA	Connecticut**	NA
NA	Delaware**	NA
29	Florida	1.1
10	Georgia	8.9
NA	Hawaii**	NA
16	Idaho	5.0
35	Illinois	0.0
13	Indiana	6.8
35	Iowa	0.0
35	Kansas	0.0
2	Kentucky	33.9
1	Louisiana	45.7
19	Maine	4.1
30	Maryland	0.6
24	Massachusetts	1.6
32	Michigan	0.1
15	Minnesota	5.8
4	Mississippi	21.4
35	Missouri	0.0
7	Montana	17.8
35	Nebraska	0.0
24	Nevada	1.6
24	New Hampshire	1.6
18	New Jersey	4.3
35	New Mexico	0.0
35	New York	0.0
35	North Carolina	0.0
17	North Dakota	4.9
35	Ohio	0.0
11	Oklahoma	8.3
32	Oregon	0.1
35	Pennsylvania	0.0
NA	Rhode Island**	NA
28	South Carolina	1.5
23	South Dakota	1.7
3	Tennessee	28.9
12	Texas	7.4
5	Utah	20.5
NA	Vermont**	NA
8	Virginia	15.8
21	Washington	2.4
6	West Virginia	19.2
20	Wisconsin	4.0
22	Wyoming	2.2

RANK ORDER

RANK	STATE	PERCENT
1	Louisiana	45.7
2	Kentucky	33.9
3	Tennessee	28.9
4	Mississippi	21.4
5	Utah	20.5
6	West Virginia	19.2
7	Montana	17.8
8	Virginia	15.8
9	Arkansas	10.5
10	Georgia	8.9
11	Oklahoma	8.3
12	Texas	7.4
13	Indiana	6.8
14	Alabama	5.9
15	Minnesota	5.8
16	Idaho	5.0
17	North Dakota	4.9
18	New Jersey	4.3
19	Maine	4.1
20	Wisconsin	4.0
21	Washington	2.4
22	Wyoming	2.2
23	South Dakota	1.7
24	California	1.6
24	Massachusetts	1.6
24	Nevada	1.6
24	New Hampshire	1.6
28	South Carolina	1.5
29	Florida	1.1
30	Maryland	0.6
31	Colorado	0.3
32	Arizona	0.1
32	Michigan	0.1
32	Oregon	0.1
35	Illinois	0.0
35	Iowa	0.0
35	Kansas	0.0
35	Missouri	0.0
35	Nebraska	0.0
35	New Mexico	0.0
35	New York	0.0
35	North Carolina	0.0
35	Ohio	0.0
35	Pennsylvania	0.0
NA	Alaska**	NA
NA	Connecticut**	NA
NA	Delaware**	NA
NA	Hawaii**	NA
NA	Rhode Island**	NA
NA	Vermont**	NA
	District of Columbia***	NA

Source: U.S. Department of Justice, Bureau of Justice Statistics
"Prisoners in 2008" (December 2009, NCJ 228417, http://bjs.ojp.usdoj.gov/)
*As of December 31, 2008. Rate does not include federal prisoners. The federal prisoner percent is 1.4% of federal prisoners.
 The federal and state combined rate is 5.2%.
**These states have an integrated system of prisons and jails.
***Responsibility for sentenced felons in D.C. was transferred to the Federal Bureau of Prisons in 2001.

Male Prisoners in State Correctional Institutions in 2008

National Total = 1,264,029 Male Prisoners*

ALPHA ORDER

RANK	STATE	PRISONERS	% of USA
15	Alabama	27,567	2.2%
44	Alaska	2,704	0.2%
12	Arizona	33,874	2.7%
27	Arkansas	13,606	1.1%
1	California	161,220	12.8%
22	Colorado	20,980	1.7%
28	Connecticut	13,468	1.1%
40	Delaware	3,862	0.3%
3	Florida	95,237	7.5%
5	Georgia	49,014	3.9%
41	Hawaii	3,829	0.3%
35	Idaho	6,532	0.5%
9	Illinois	42,753	3.4%
16	Indiana	25,808	2.0%
33	Iowa	8,017	0.6%
34	Kansas	7,970	0.6%
25	Kentucky	18,906	1.5%
10	Louisiana	35,324	2.8%
48	Maine	1,856	0.1%
20	Maryland	21,777	1.7%
31	Massachusetts	9,724	0.8%
7	Michigan	46,781	3.7%
32	Minnesota	8,778	0.7%
24	Mississippi	19,855	1.6%
14	Missouri	27,729	2.2%
42	Montana	3,218	0.3%
39	Nebraska	4,048	0.3%
30	Nevada	11,761	0.9%
45	New Hampshire	2,670	0.2%
18	New Jersey	24,654	2.0%
37	New Mexico	5,747	0.5%
4	New York	57,412	4.5%
13	North Carolina	32,218	2.5%
50	North Dakota	1,292	0.1%
6	Ohio	47,773	3.8%
21	Oklahoma	21,761	1.7%
29	Oregon	13,026	1.0%
8	Pennsylvania	46,261	3.7%
46	Rhode Island	2,418	0.2%
19	South Carolina	21,995	1.7%
43	South Dakota	2,979	0.2%
17	Tennessee	25,099	2.0%
2	Texas	146,262	11.6%
36	Utah	5,803	0.5%
49	Vermont	1,541	0.1%
11	Virginia	35,249	2.8%
26	Washington	16,522	1.3%
38	West Virginia	5,379	0.4%
23	Wisconsin	19,894	1.6%
47	Wyoming	1,876	0.1%

RANK ORDER

RANK	STATE	PRISONERS	% of USA
1	California	161,220	12.8%
2	Texas	146,262	11.6%
3	Florida	95,237	7.5%
4	New York	57,412	4.5%
5	Georgia	49,014	3.9%
6	Ohio	47,773	3.8%
7	Michigan	46,781	3.7%
8	Pennsylvania	46,261	3.7%
9	Illinois	42,753	3.4%
10	Louisiana	35,324	2.8%
11	Virginia	35,249	2.8%
12	Arizona	33,874	2.7%
13	North Carolina	32,218	2.5%
14	Missouri	27,729	2.2%
15	Alabama	27,567	2.2%
16	Indiana	25,808	2.0%
17	Tennessee	25,099	2.0%
18	New Jersey	24,654	2.0%
19	South Carolina	21,995	1.7%
20	Maryland	21,777	1.7%
21	Oklahoma	21,761	1.7%
22	Colorado	20,980	1.7%
23	Wisconsin	19,894	1.6%
24	Mississippi	19,855	1.6%
25	Kentucky	18,906	1.5%
26	Washington	16,522	1.3%
27	Arkansas	13,606	1.1%
28	Connecticut	13,468	1.1%
29	Oregon	13,026	1.0%
30	Nevada	11,761	0.9%
31	Massachusetts	9,724	0.8%
32	Minnesota	8,778	0.7%
33	Iowa	8,017	0.6%
34	Kansas	7,970	0.6%
35	Idaho	6,532	0.5%
36	Utah	5,803	0.5%
37	New Mexico	5,747	0.5%
38	West Virginia	5,379	0.4%
39	Nebraska	4,048	0.3%
40	Delaware	3,862	0.3%
41	Hawaii	3,829	0.3%
42	Montana	3,218	0.3%
43	South Dakota	2,979	0.2%
44	Alaska	2,704	0.2%
45	New Hampshire	2,670	0.2%
46	Rhode Island	2,418	0.2%
47	Wyoming	1,876	0.1%
48	Maine	1,856	0.1%
49	Vermont	1,541	0.1%
50	North Dakota	1,292	0.1%
	District of Columbia**	NA	NA

Source: U.S. Department of Justice, Bureau of Justice Statistics
"Prisoners in 2008" (December 2009, NCJ 228417, http://bjs.ojp.usdoj.gov/)
*As of December 31, 2008. Figure is for male prisoners sentenced to more than one year. National total does not include federal male inmates. There were 170,755 federal male prisoners. The combined federal and state male prisoner total was 1,434,784 prisoners.
**Responsibility for sentenced felons in D.C. was transferred to the Federal Bureau of Prisons.

Male State Prisoner Imprisonment Rate in 2008

National Rate = 840 Male State Prisoners per 100,000 Male Population*

ALPHA ORDER				RANK ORDER		
RANK	STATE	RATE		RANK	STATE	RATE
3	Alabama	1,215		1	Louisiana	1,642
26	Alaska	752		2	Mississippi	1,389
7	Arizona	1,031		3	Alabama	1,215
10	Arkansas	969		4	Oklahoma	1,203
17	California	872		5	Texas	1,191
20	Colorado	834		6	Florida	1,054
24	Connecticut	787		7	Arizona	1,031
14	Delaware	906		8	Georgia	1,021
6	Florida	1,054		9	South Carolina	1,000
8	Georgia	1,021		10	Arkansas	969
36	Hawaii	585		11	Missouri	957
19	Idaho	844		12	Michigan	951
32	Illinois	669		13	Virginia	918
22	Indiana	818		14	Delaware	906
40	Iowa	538		15	Kentucky	902
39	Kansas	570		16	Nevada	880
15	Kentucky	902		17	California	872
1	Louisiana	1,642		18	Ohio	851
50	Maine	289		19	Idaho	844
23	Maryland	796		20	Colorado	834
45	Massachusetts	434		21	Tennessee	824
12	Michigan	951		22	Indiana	818
49	Minnesota	336		23	Maryland	796
2	Mississippi	1,389		24	Connecticut	787
11	Missouri	957		25	Pennsylvania	762
33	Montana	660		26	Alaska	752
44	Nebraska	455		27	South Dakota	738
16	Nevada	880		28	Wisconsin	709
47	New Hampshire	410		29	North Carolina	707
38	New Jersey	578		30	Oregon	688
37	New Mexico	583		31	Wyoming	687
34	New York	605		32	Illinois	669
29	North Carolina	707		33	Montana	660
48	North Dakota	400		34	New York	605
18	Ohio	851		35	West Virginia	604
4	Oklahoma	1,203		36	Hawaii	585
30	Oregon	688		37	New Mexico	583
25	Pennsylvania	762		38	New Jersey	578
43	Rhode Island	475		39	Kansas	570
9	South Carolina	1,000		40	Iowa	538
27	South Dakota	738		41	Vermont	504
21	Tennessee	824		42	Washington	501
5	Texas	1,191		43	Rhode Island	475
46	Utah	415		44	Nebraska	455
41	Vermont	504		45	Massachusetts	434
13	Virginia	918		46	Utah	415
42	Washington	501		47	New Hampshire	410
35	West Virginia	604		48	North Dakota	400
28	Wisconsin	709		49	Minnesota	336
31	Wyoming	687		50	Maine	289
					District of Columbia**	NA

Source: U.S. Department of Justice, Bureau of Justice Statistics
    "Prisoners in 2008" (December 2009, NCJ 228417, http://bjs.ojp.usdoj.gov/)
*As of December 31, 2008. Rate is for male prisoners sentenced to more than one year. National rate does not include federal male inmates. Federal male imprisonment rate is 113 federal male prisoners per 100,000 male population. The combined federal and state male imprisonment rate is 952 male prisoners per 100,000 male population.
**Responsibility for sentenced felons in D.C. was transferred to the Federal Bureau of Prisons.

Female State Prisoner Imprisonment Rate in 2008

National Rate = 61 Female State Prisoners per 100,000 Female Population*

ALPHA ORDER

RANK	STATE	RATE
8	Alabama	88
12	Alaska	79
4	Arizona	101
21	Arkansas	72
26	California	62
7	Colorado	93
31	Connecticut	45
31	Delaware	45
15	Florida	76
18	Georgia	74
18	Hawaii	74
5	Idaho	99
39	Illinois	41
14	Indiana	77
30	Iowa	49
40	Kansas	40
6	Kentucky	98
3	Louisiana	109
48	Maine	19
43	Maryland	33
50	Massachusetts	13
41	Michigan	39
46	Minnesota	24
2	Mississippi	121
11	Missouri	81
18	Montana	74
36	Nebraska	42
15	Nevada	76
42	New Hampshire	35
44	New Jersey	29
28	New Mexico	56
45	New York	25
36	North Carolina	42
29	North Dakota	50
23	Ohio	66
1	Oklahoma	132
27	Oregon	58
36	Pennsylvania	42
48	Rhode Island	19
25	South Carolina	63
9	South Dakota	87
23	Tennessee	66
9	Texas	87
31	Utah	45
46	Vermont	24
17	Virginia	75
34	Washington	43
22	West Virginia	69
34	Wisconsin	43
12	Wyoming	79

RANK ORDER

RANK	STATE	RATE
1	Oklahoma	132
2	Mississippi	121
3	Louisiana	109
4	Arizona	101
5	Idaho	99
6	Kentucky	98
7	Colorado	93
8	Alabama	88
9	South Dakota	87
9	Texas	87
11	Missouri	81
12	Alaska	79
12	Wyoming	79
14	Indiana	77
15	Florida	76
15	Nevada	76
17	Virginia	75
18	Georgia	74
18	Hawaii	74
18	Montana	74
21	Arkansas	72
22	West Virginia	69
23	Ohio	66
23	Tennessee	66
25	South Carolina	63
26	California	62
27	Oregon	58
28	New Mexico	56
29	North Dakota	50
30	Iowa	49
31	Connecticut	45
31	Delaware	45
31	Utah	45
34	Washington	43
34	Wisconsin	43
36	Nebraska	42
36	North Carolina	42
36	Pennsylvania	42
39	Illinois	41
40	Kansas	40
41	Michigan	39
42	New Hampshire	35
43	Maryland	33
44	New Jersey	29
45	New York	25
46	Minnesota	24
46	Vermont	24
48	Maine	19
48	Rhode Island	19
50	Massachusetts	13
	District of Columbia**	NA

Source: U.S. Department of Justice, Bureau of Justice Statistics
"Prisoners in 2008" (December 2009, NCJ 228417, http://bjs.ojp.usdoj.gov/)
*As of December 31, 2008. Rate is for female prisoners sentenced to more than one year. National rate does not include federal female inmates. Federal female imprisonment rate is 7 federal female prisoners per 100,000 female population. The combined federal and state female imprisonment rate is 68 female prisoners per 100,000 female population.
**Responsibility for sentenced felons in D.C. was transferred to the Federal Bureau of Prisons.

Female Prisoners in State Correctional Institutions in 2008

National Total = 93,674 Female State Prisoners*

ALPHA ORDER

RANK	STATE	PRISONERS	% of USA
18	Alabama	2,127	2.3%
43	Alaska	262	0.3%
6	Arizona	3,314	3.5%
27	Arkansas	1,054	1.1%
1	California	11,363	12.1%
15	Colorado	2,294	2.4%
30	Connecticut	803	0.9%
46	Delaware	205	0.2%
3	Florida	7,151	7.6%
5	Georgia	3,691	3.9%
38	Hawaii	475	0.5%
31	Idaho	758	0.8%
8	Illinois	2,721	2.9%
11	Indiana	2,493	2.7%
32	Iowa	749	0.8%
36	Kansas	569	0.6%
16	Kentucky	2,153	2.3%
12	Louisiana	2,480	2.6%
48	Maine	129	0.1%
29	Maryland	972	1.0%
39	Massachusetts	442	0.5%
20	Michigan	1,957	2.1%
34	Minnesota	628	0.7%
21	Mississippi	1,843	2.0%
14	Missouri	2,446	2.6%
41	Montana	361	0.4%
40	Nebraska	376	0.4%
28	Nevada	982	1.0%
44	New Hampshire	234	0.2%
24	New Jersey	1,299	1.4%
37	New Mexico	568	0.6%
10	New York	2,547	2.7%
19	North Carolina	2,011	2.1%
47	North Dakota	160	0.2%
4	Ohio	3,913	4.2%
13	Oklahoma	2,449	2.6%
26	Oregon	1,105	1.2%
9	Pennsylvania	2,701	2.9%
49	Rhode Island	104	0.1%
22	South Carolina	1,461	1.6%
42	South Dakota	354	0.4%
17	Tennessee	2,129	2.3%
2	Texas	10,717	11.4%
35	Utah	619	0.7%
50	Vermont	77	0.1%
7	Virginia	2,967	3.2%
23	Washington	1,404	1.5%
33	West Virginia	640	0.7%
25	Wisconsin	1,209	1.3%
45	Wyoming	208	0.2%

RANK ORDER

RANK	STATE	PRISONERS	% of USA
1	California	11,363	12.1%
2	Texas	10,717	11.4%
3	Florida	7,151	7.6%
4	Ohio	3,913	4.2%
5	Georgia	3,691	3.9%
6	Arizona	3,314	3.5%
7	Virginia	2,967	3.2%
8	Illinois	2,721	2.9%
9	Pennsylvania	2,701	2.9%
10	New York	2,547	2.7%
11	Indiana	2,493	2.7%
12	Louisiana	2,480	2.6%
13	Oklahoma	2,449	2.6%
14	Missouri	2,446	2.6%
15	Colorado	2,294	2.4%
16	Kentucky	2,153	2.3%
17	Tennessee	2,129	2.3%
18	Alabama	2,127	2.3%
19	North Carolina	2,011	2.1%
20	Michigan	1,957	2.1%
21	Mississippi	1,843	2.0%
22	South Carolina	1,461	1.6%
23	Washington	1,404	1.5%
24	New Jersey	1,299	1.4%
25	Wisconsin	1,209	1.3%
26	Oregon	1,105	1.2%
27	Arkansas	1,054	1.1%
28	Nevada	982	1.0%
29	Maryland	972	1.0%
30	Connecticut	803	0.9%
31	Idaho	758	0.8%
32	Iowa	749	0.8%
33	West Virginia	640	0.7%
34	Minnesota	628	0.7%
35	Utah	619	0.7%
36	Kansas	569	0.6%
37	New Mexico	568	0.6%
38	Hawaii	475	0.5%
39	Massachusetts	442	0.5%
40	Nebraska	376	0.4%
41	Montana	361	0.4%
42	South Dakota	354	0.4%
43	Alaska	262	0.3%
44	New Hampshire	234	0.2%
45	Wyoming	208	0.2%
46	Delaware	205	0.2%
47	North Dakota	160	0.2%
48	Maine	129	0.1%
49	Rhode Island	104	0.1%
50	Vermont	77	0.1%
	District of Columbia**	NA	NA

Source: U.S. Department of Justice, Bureau of Justice Statistics
   "Prisoners in 2008" (December 2009, NCJ 228417, http://bjs.ojp.usdoj.gov/)
*As of December 31, 2008. Does not include 11,578 female prisoners under federal jurisdiction. State and federal female prisoners total 105,252.
**Responsibility for sentenced felons in D.C. was transferred to the Federal Bureau of Prisons.

Female Prisoners in State Correctional Institutions
as a Percent of All State Prisoners in 2008
National Percent = 6.9% of State Prisoners Are Female*

ALPHA ORDER

RANK	STATE	PERCENT
27	Alabama	7.2
14	Alaska	8.8
13	Arizona	8.9
27	Arkansas	7.2
34	California	6.6
10	Colorado	9.9
41	Connecticut	5.6
43	Delaware	5.0
29	Florida	7.0
29	Georgia	7.0
1	Hawaii	11.0
5	Idaho	10.4
38	Illinois	6.0
14	Indiana	8.8
16	Iowa	8.5
32	Kansas	6.7
6	Kentucky	10.2
34	Louisiana	6.6
36	Maine	6.5
46	Maryland	4.3
46	Massachusetts	4.3
50	Michigan	4.0
32	Minnesota	6.7
16	Mississippi	8.5
19	Missouri	8.1
7	Montana	10.1
16	Nebraska	8.5
25	Nevada	7.7
19	New Hampshire	8.1
43	New Jersey	5.0
12	New Mexico	9.0
48	New York	4.2
39	North Carolina	5.9
1	North Dakota	11.0
26	Ohio	7.6
7	Oklahoma	10.1
21	Oregon	7.8
42	Pennsylvania	5.5
49	Rhode Island	4.1
37	South Carolina	6.2
3	South Dakota	10.6
21	Tennessee	7.8
31	Texas	6.8
11	Utah	9.6
45	Vermont	4.8
21	Virginia	7.8
21	Washington	7.8
3	West Virginia	10.6
40	Wisconsin	5.7
9	Wyoming	10.0

RANK ORDER

RANK	STATE	PERCENT
1	Hawaii	11.0
1	North Dakota	11.0
3	South Dakota	10.6
3	West Virginia	10.6
5	Idaho	10.4
6	Kentucky	10.2
7	Montana	10.1
7	Oklahoma	10.1
9	Wyoming	10.0
10	Colorado	9.9
11	Utah	9.6
12	New Mexico	9.0
13	Arizona	8.9
14	Alaska	8.8
14	Indiana	8.8
16	Iowa	8.5
16	Mississippi	8.5
16	Nebraska	8.5
19	Missouri	8.1
19	New Hampshire	8.1
21	Oregon	7.8
21	Tennessee	7.8
21	Virginia	7.8
21	Washington	7.8
25	Nevada	7.7
26	Ohio	7.6
27	Alabama	7.2
27	Arkansas	7.2
29	Florida	7.0
29	Georgia	7.0
31	Texas	6.8
32	Kansas	6.7
32	Minnesota	6.7
34	California	6.6
34	Louisiana	6.6
36	Maine	6.5
37	South Carolina	6.2
38	Illinois	6.0
39	North Carolina	5.9
40	Wisconsin	5.7
41	Connecticut	5.6
42	Pennsylvania	5.5
43	Delaware	5.0
43	New Jersey	5.0
45	Vermont	4.8
46	Maryland	4.3
46	Massachusetts	4.3
48	New York	4.2
49	Rhode Island	4.1
50	Michigan	4.0
	District of Columbia**	NA

Source: CQ Press using data from U.S. Department of Justice, Bureau of Justice Statistics
"Prisoners in 2008" (December 2009, NCJ 228417, http://bjs.ojp.usdoj.gov/)

*As of December 31, 2008. Rate does not include federal female inmates. Federal female inmates constitute 6.3% of federal inmates. The federal and state combined rate is 6.8%.

**Responsibility for sentenced felons in D.C. was transferred to the Federal Bureau of Prisons.

Percent Change in Female State Prisoner Population: 2007 to 2008

National Percent Change = 0.6% Decrease*

ALPHA ORDER				RANK ORDER		
RANK	STATE	PERCENT CHANGE		RANK	STATE	PERCENT CHANGE
11	Alabama	4.8		1	Montana	21.1
34	Alaska	(3.7)		2	New Hampshire	18.8
8	Arizona	6.5		3	Pennsylvania	11.5
28	Arkansas	(1.1)		4	Tennessee	10.7
24	California	0.5		5	North Dakota	8.8
30	Colorado	(1.8)		6	Indiana	8.6
29	Connecticut	(1.6)		7	Maine	8.4
32	Delaware	(3.3)		8	Arizona	6.5
14	Florida	4.3		9	North Carolina	5.8
16	Georgia	4.1		10	New Mexico	5.4
38	Hawaii	(5.8)		11	Alabama	4.8
36	Idaho	(5.3)		12	Iowa	4.5
33	Illinois	(3.6)		13	Oregon	4.4
6	Indiana	8.6		14	Florida	4.3
12	Iowa	4.5		14	Minnesota	4.3
45	Kansas	(9.0)		16	Georgia	4.1
41	Kentucky	(7.3)		17	Nebraska	2.7
23	Louisiana	1.2		18	Ohio	2.4
7	Maine	8.4		19	Massachusetts	1.8
47	Maryland	(14.7)		20	Oklahoma	1.6
19	Massachusetts	1.8		21	West Virginia	1.4
39	Michigan	(5.9)		22	Virginia	1.3
14	Minnesota	4.3		23	Louisiana	1.2
26	Mississippi	0.4		24	California	0.5
31	Missouri	(2.9)		24	Utah	0.5
1	Montana	21.1		26	Mississippi	0.4
17	Nebraska	2.7		27	South Carolina	0.3
NA	Nevada**	NA		28	Arkansas	(1.1)
2	New Hampshire	18.8		29	Connecticut	(1.6)
42	New Jersey	(7.9)		30	Colorado	(1.8)
10	New Mexico	5.4		31	Missouri	(2.9)
37	New York	(5.4)		32	Delaware	(3.3)
9	North Carolina	5.8		33	Illinois	(3.6)
5	North Dakota	8.8		34	Alaska	(3.7)
18	Ohio	2.4		35	South Dakota	(4.1)
20	Oklahoma	1.6		36	Idaho	(5.3)
13	Oregon	4.4		37	New York	(5.4)
3	Pennsylvania	11.5		38	Hawaii	(5.8)
44	Rhode Island	(8.8)		39	Michigan	(5.9)
27	South Carolina	0.3		40	Washington	(6.9)
35	South Dakota	(4.1)		41	Kentucky	(7.3)
4	Tennessee	10.7		42	New Jersey	(7.9)
43	Texas	(8.4)		43	Texas	(8.4)
24	Utah	0.5		44	Rhode Island	(8.8)
49	Vermont	(23.0)		45	Kansas	(9.0)
22	Virginia	1.3		46	Wisconsin	(14.3)
40	Washington	(6.9)		47	Maryland	(14.7)
21	West Virginia	1.4		48	Wyoming	(15.4)
46	Wisconsin	(14.3)		49	Vermont	(23.0)
48	Wyoming	(15.4)		NA	Nevada**	NA
					District of Columbia***	NA

Source: U.S. Department of Justice, Bureau of Justice Statistics
   "Prisoners in 2008" (December 2009, NCJ 228417, http://bjs.ojp.usdoj.gov/)
*From December 31, 2007 to December 31, 2008. Does not include federal female inmates. The percent change in number of female prisoners under federal jurisdiction during the same period was a 0.4% increase. The combined state and federal decrease was -0.5%. **Not available.
***Responsibility for sentenced felons in D.C. was transferred to the Federal Bureau of Prisons.

Average Annual Percent Change in
Female State Prisoner Population: 2000 to 2007
National Average Percent Change = 3.0% Annual Increase*

ALPHA ORDER

RANK	STATE	PERCENT CHANGE
35	Alabama	1.8
1	Alaska	15.9
12	Arizona	8.2
26	Arkansas	4.8
39	California	0.9
11	Colorado	8.3
40	Connecticut	0.5
47	Delaware	(2.0)
14	Florida	7.6
30	Georgia	3.7
29	Hawaii	4.2
17	Idaho	7.2
44	Illinois	(0.1)
18	Indiana	6.8
33	Iowa	2.8
32	Kansas	3.1
5	Kentucky	11.8
37	Louisiana	1.4
6	Maine	9.8
38	Maryland	1.0
7	Massachusetts	9.6
45	Michigan	(0.3)
15	Minnesota	7.3
34	Mississippi	2.6
31	Missouri	3.4
46	Montana	(0.4)
24	Nebraska	5.2
NA	Nevada**	NA
15	New Hampshire	7.3
48	New Jersey	(2.2)
20	New Mexico	6.6
49	New York	(2.8)
27	North Carolina	4.6
2	North Dakota	15.4
28	Ohio	4.5
42	Oklahoma	0.1
9	Oregon	8.6
21	Pennsylvania	6.3
9	Rhode Island	8.6
36	South Carolina	1.6
8	South Dakota	9.1
25	Tennessee	5.0
42	Texas	0.1
13	Utah	7.9
3	Vermont	12.4
23	Virginia	5.7
22	Washington	5.9
4	West Virginia	11.9
40	Wisconsin	0.5
19	Wyoming	6.7

RANK ORDER

RANK	STATE	PERCENT CHANGE
1	Alaska	15.9
2	North Dakota	15.4
3	Vermont	12.4
4	West Virginia	11.9
5	Kentucky	11.8
6	Maine	9.8
7	Massachusetts	9.6
8	South Dakota	9.1
9	Oregon	8.6
9	Rhode Island	8.6
11	Colorado	8.3
12	Arizona	8.2
13	Utah	7.9
14	Florida	7.6
15	Minnesota	7.3
15	New Hampshire	7.3
17	Idaho	7.2
18	Indiana	6.8
19	Wyoming	6.7
20	New Mexico	6.6
21	Pennsylvania	6.3
22	Washington	5.9
23	Virginia	5.7
24	Nebraska	5.2
25	Tennessee	5.0
26	Arkansas	4.8
27	North Carolina	4.6
28	Ohio	4.5
29	Hawaii	4.2
30	Georgia	3.7
31	Missouri	3.4
32	Kansas	3.1
33	Iowa	2.8
34	Mississippi	2.6
35	Alabama	1.8
36	South Carolina	1.6
37	Louisiana	1.4
38	Maryland	1.0
39	California	0.9
40	Connecticut	0.5
40	Wisconsin	0.5
42	Oklahoma	0.1
42	Texas	0.1
44	Illinois	(0.1)
45	Michigan	(0.3)
46	Montana	(0.4)
47	Delaware	(2.0)
48	New Jersey	(2.2)
49	New York	(2.8)
NA	Nevada**	NA
	District of Columbia***	NA

Source: U.S. Department of Justice, Bureau of Justice Statistics
   "Prisoners in 2008" (December 2009, NCJ 228417, http://bjs.ojp.usdoj.gov/)
*National rate does not include federal female inmates. Federal female inmates increased by an average annual rate of 4.6%.
The combined federal and state female prison population grew at an annual average rate of 3.2%. **Not available.
***Responsibility for sentenced felons in D.C. was transferred to the Federal Bureau of Prisons.

White State Prisoner Incarceration Rate in 2005

National Rate = 412 White State Prisoners per 100,000 White Population*

ALPHA ORDER

RANK	STATE	RATE
9	Alabama	542
14	Alaska	500
6	Arizona	590
17	Arkansas	478
20	California	460
10	Colorado	525
44	Connecticut	211
27	Delaware	396
7	Florida	588
5	Georgia	623
21	Hawaii	453
2	Idaho	675
42	Illinois	223
19	Indiana	463
34	Iowa	309
22	Kansas	443
8	Kentucky	561
11	Louisiana	523
41	Maine	262
39	Maryland	288
45	Massachusetts	201
26	Michigan	412
43	Minnesota	212
12	Mississippi	503
15	Missouri	487
23	Montana	433
37	Nebraska	290
4	Nevada	627
38	New Hampshire	289
47	New Jersey	190
NA	New Mexico**	NA
48	New York	174
33	North Carolina	320
40	North Dakota	267
32	Ohio	344
1	Oklahoma	740
13	Oregon	502
35	Pennsylvania	305
46	Rhode Island	191
24	South Carolina	415
18	South Dakota	470
15	Tennessee	487
3	Texas	667
30	Utah	392
36	Vermont	304
27	Virginia	396
29	Washington	393
30	West Virginia	392
24	Wisconsin	415
NA	Wyoming**	NA

RANK ORDER

RANK	STATE	RATE
1	Oklahoma	740
2	Idaho	675
3	Texas	667
4	Nevada	627
5	Georgia	623
6	Arizona	590
7	Florida	588
8	Kentucky	561
9	Alabama	542
10	Colorado	525
11	Louisiana	523
12	Mississippi	503
13	Oregon	502
14	Alaska	500
15	Missouri	487
15	Tennessee	487
17	Arkansas	478
18	South Dakota	470
19	Indiana	463
20	California	460
21	Hawaii	453
22	Kansas	443
23	Montana	433
24	South Carolina	415
24	Wisconsin	415
26	Michigan	412
27	Delaware	396
27	Virginia	396
29	Washington	393
30	Utah	392
30	West Virginia	392
32	Ohio	344
33	North Carolina	320
34	Iowa	309
35	Pennsylvania	305
36	Vermont	304
37	Nebraska	290
38	New Hampshire	289
39	Maryland	288
40	North Dakota	267
41	Maine	262
42	Illinois	223
43	Minnesota	212
44	Connecticut	211
45	Massachusetts	201
46	Rhode Island	191
47	New Jersey	190
48	New York	174
NA	New Mexico**	NA
NA	Wyoming**	NA

District of Columbia*** 56

Source: U.S. Department of Justice, Bureau of Justice Statistics
  "Prison and Jail Inmates at Midyear 2005" (May 2006, NCJ 213133, http://www.ojp.usdoj.gov/bjs/abstract/pjim05.htm)
*As of June 30, 2005. "White" excludes Hispanics.
**Not available.
***The District of Columbia's figure excludes inmates sentenced to more than one year held by the Federal Bureau of Prisons.

Black State Prisoner Incarceration Rate in 2005

National Rate = 2,290 Black State Prisoners per 100,000 Black Population*

<table>
<tr><td colspan="3">ALPHA ORDER</td><td colspan="3">RANK ORDER</td></tr>
<tr><th>RANK</th><th>STATE</th><th>RATE</th><th>RANK</th><th>STATE</th><th>RATE</th></tr>
<tr><td>39</td><td>Alabama</td><td>1,916</td><td>1</td><td>South Dakota</td><td>4,710</td></tr>
<tr><td>33</td><td>Alaska</td><td>2,163</td><td>2</td><td>Wisconsin</td><td>4,416</td></tr>
<tr><td>8</td><td>Arizona</td><td>3,294</td><td>3</td><td>Iowa</td><td>4,200</td></tr>
<tr><td>41</td><td>Arkansas</td><td>1,846</td><td>4</td><td>Vermont</td><td>3,797</td></tr>
<tr><td>12</td><td>California</td><td>2,992</td><td>5</td><td>Utah</td><td>3,588</td></tr>
<tr><td>7</td><td>Colorado</td><td>3,491</td><td>6</td><td>Montana</td><td>3,569</td></tr>
<tr><td>22</td><td>Connecticut</td><td>2,532</td><td>7</td><td>Colorado</td><td>3,491</td></tr>
<tr><td>25</td><td>Delaware</td><td>2,517</td><td>8</td><td>Arizona</td><td>3,294</td></tr>
<tr><td>20</td><td>Florida</td><td>2,615</td><td>9</td><td>Oklahoma</td><td>3,252</td></tr>
<tr><td>34</td><td>Georgia</td><td>2,068</td><td>10</td><td>Texas</td><td>3,162</td></tr>
<tr><td>48</td><td>Hawaii</td><td>851</td><td>11</td><td>Kansas</td><td>3,096</td></tr>
<tr><td>15</td><td>Idaho</td><td>2,869</td><td>12</td><td>California</td><td>2,992</td></tr>
<tr><td>35</td><td>Illinois</td><td>2,020</td><td>13</td><td>Oregon</td><td>2,930</td></tr>
<tr><td>23</td><td>Indiana</td><td>2,526</td><td>14</td><td>Nevada</td><td>2,916</td></tr>
<tr><td>3</td><td>Iowa</td><td>4,200</td><td>15</td><td>Idaho</td><td>2,869</td></tr>
<tr><td>11</td><td>Kansas</td><td>3,096</td><td>16</td><td>Kentucky</td><td>2,793</td></tr>
<tr><td>16</td><td>Kentucky</td><td>2,793</td><td>17</td><td>Pennsylvania</td><td>2,792</td></tr>
<tr><td>26</td><td>Louisiana</td><td>2,452</td><td>18</td><td>North Dakota</td><td>2,683</td></tr>
<tr><td>37</td><td>Maine</td><td>1,992</td><td>19</td><td>New Hampshire</td><td>2,666</td></tr>
<tr><td>47</td><td>Maryland</td><td>1,579</td><td>20</td><td>Florida</td><td>2,615</td></tr>
<tr><td>45</td><td>Massachusetts</td><td>1,635</td><td>21</td><td>Missouri</td><td>2,556</td></tr>
<tr><td>30</td><td>Michigan</td><td>2,262</td><td>22</td><td>Connecticut</td><td>2,532</td></tr>
<tr><td>38</td><td>Minnesota</td><td>1,937</td><td>23</td><td>Indiana</td><td>2,526</td></tr>
<tr><td>43</td><td>Mississippi</td><td>1,742</td><td>24</td><td>Washington</td><td>2,522</td></tr>
<tr><td>21</td><td>Missouri</td><td>2,556</td><td>25</td><td>Delaware</td><td>2,517</td></tr>
<tr><td>6</td><td>Montana</td><td>3,569</td><td>26</td><td>Louisiana</td><td>2,452</td></tr>
<tr><td>27</td><td>Nebraska</td><td>2,418</td><td>27</td><td>Nebraska</td><td>2,418</td></tr>
<tr><td>14</td><td>Nevada</td><td>2,916</td><td>28</td><td>New Jersey</td><td>2,352</td></tr>
<tr><td>19</td><td>New Hampshire</td><td>2,666</td><td>29</td><td>Virginia</td><td>2,331</td></tr>
<tr><td>28</td><td>New Jersey</td><td>2,352</td><td>30</td><td>Michigan</td><td>2,262</td></tr>
<tr><td>NA</td><td>New Mexico**</td><td>NA</td><td>31</td><td>Ohio</td><td>2,196</td></tr>
<tr><td>46</td><td>New York</td><td>1,627</td><td>32</td><td>West Virginia</td><td>2,188</td></tr>
<tr><td>44</td><td>North Carolina</td><td>1,727</td><td>33</td><td>Alaska</td><td>2,163</td></tr>
<tr><td>18</td><td>North Dakota</td><td>2,683</td><td>34</td><td>Georgia</td><td>2,068</td></tr>
<tr><td>31</td><td>Ohio</td><td>2,196</td><td>35</td><td>Illinois</td><td>2,020</td></tr>
<tr><td>9</td><td>Oklahoma</td><td>3,252</td><td>36</td><td>Tennessee</td><td>2,006</td></tr>
<tr><td>13</td><td>Oregon</td><td>2,930</td><td>37</td><td>Maine</td><td>1,992</td></tr>
<tr><td>17</td><td>Pennsylvania</td><td>2,792</td><td>38</td><td>Minnesota</td><td>1,937</td></tr>
<tr><td>42</td><td>Rhode Island</td><td>1,838</td><td>39</td><td>Alabama</td><td>1,916</td></tr>
<tr><td>40</td><td>South Carolina</td><td>1,856</td><td>40</td><td>South Carolina</td><td>1,856</td></tr>
<tr><td>1</td><td>South Dakota</td><td>4,710</td><td>41</td><td>Arkansas</td><td>1,846</td></tr>
<tr><td>36</td><td>Tennessee</td><td>2,006</td><td>42</td><td>Rhode Island</td><td>1,838</td></tr>
<tr><td>10</td><td>Texas</td><td>3,162</td><td>43</td><td>Mississippi</td><td>1,742</td></tr>
<tr><td>5</td><td>Utah</td><td>3,588</td><td>44</td><td>North Carolina</td><td>1,727</td></tr>
<tr><td>4</td><td>Vermont</td><td>3,797</td><td>45</td><td>Massachusetts</td><td>1,635</td></tr>
<tr><td>29</td><td>Virginia</td><td>2,331</td><td>46</td><td>New York</td><td>1,627</td></tr>
<tr><td>24</td><td>Washington</td><td>2,522</td><td>47</td><td>Maryland</td><td>1,579</td></tr>
<tr><td>32</td><td>West Virginia</td><td>2,188</td><td>48</td><td>Hawaii</td><td>851</td></tr>
<tr><td>2</td><td>Wisconsin</td><td>4,416</td><td>NA</td><td>New Mexico**</td><td>NA</td></tr>
<tr><td>NA</td><td>Wyoming**</td><td>NA</td><td>NA</td><td>Wyoming**</td><td>NA</td></tr>
<tr><td></td><td></td><td></td><td colspan="2">District of Columbia***</td><td>1,065</td></tr>
</table>

Source: U.S. Department of Justice, Bureau of Justice Statistics
   "Prison and Jail Inmates at Midyear 2005" (May 2006, NCJ 213133, http://www.ojp.usdoj.gov/bjs/abstract/pjim05.htm)
*As of June 30, 2005. "Black" excludes Hispanics.
**Not available.
***The District of Columbia's figure excludes inmates sentenced to more than one year held by the Federal Bureau of Prisons.

Hispanic State Prisoner Incarceration Rate in 2005

National Rate = 742 Hispanic State Prisoners per 100,000 Hispanic Population*

ALPHA ORDER

RANK	STATE	RATE
NA	Alabama**	NA
35	Alaska	380
5	Arizona	1,075
36	Arkansas	288
13	California	782
7	Colorado	1,042
3	Connecticut	1,401
18	Delaware	683
34	Florida	382
26	Georgia	576
39	Hawaii	185
2	Idaho	1,654
32	Illinois	415
25	Indiana	579
15	Iowa	764
NA	Kansas**	NA
16	Kentucky	757
37	Louisiana	244
NA	Maine**	NA
NA	Maryland**	NA
4	Massachusetts	1,229
33	Michigan	397
NA	Minnesota**	NA
23	Mississippi	611
24	Missouri	587
9	Montana	846
17	Nebraska	739
21	Nevada	621
6	New Hampshire	1,063
20	New Jersey	630
NA	New Mexico**	NA
14	New York	778
NA	North Carolina**	NA
8	North Dakota	848
22	Ohio	613
11	Oklahoma	832
27	Oregon	573
1	Pennsylvania	1,714
19	Rhode Island	631
31	South Carolina	476
NA	South Dakota**	NA
28	Tennessee	561
12	Texas	830
10	Utah	838
NA	Vermont**	NA
30	Virginia	487
29	Washington	527
38	West Virginia	211
NA	Wisconsin**	NA
NA	Wyoming**	NA

RANK ORDER

RANK	STATE	RATE
1	Pennsylvania	1,714
2	Idaho	1,654
3	Connecticut	1,401
4	Massachusetts	1,229
5	Arizona	1,075
6	New Hampshire	1,063
7	Colorado	1,042
8	North Dakota	848
9	Montana	846
10	Utah	838
11	Oklahoma	832
12	Texas	830
13	California	782
14	New York	778
15	Iowa	764
16	Kentucky	757
17	Nebraska	739
18	Delaware	683
19	Rhode Island	631
20	New Jersey	630
21	Nevada	621
22	Ohio	613
23	Mississippi	611
24	Missouri	587
25	Indiana	579
26	Georgia	576
27	Oregon	573
28	Tennessee	561
29	Washington	527
30	Virginia	487
31	South Carolina	476
32	Illinois	415
33	Michigan	397
34	Florida	382
35	Alaska	380
36	Arkansas	288
37	Louisiana	244
38	West Virginia	211
39	Hawaii	185
NA	Alabama**	NA
NA	Kansas**	NA
NA	Maine**	NA
NA	Maryland**	NA
NA	Minnesota**	NA
NA	New Mexico**	NA
NA	North Carolina**	NA
NA	South Dakota**	NA
NA	Vermont**	NA
NA	Wisconsin**	NA
NA	Wyoming**	NA
	District of Columbia***	267

Source: U.S. Department of Justice, Bureau of Justice Statistics
   "Prison and Jail Inmates at Midyear 2005" (May 2006, NCJ 213133, http://www.ojp.usdoj.gov/bjs/abstract/pjim05.htm)
*As of June 30, 2005. "Hispanic" can be any race.
**Not available.
***The District of Columbia's figure excludes inmates sentenced to more than one year held by the Federal Bureau of Prisons.

Noncitizens Held in State Prisons in 2008

National Total = 65,729 Noncitizens*

ALPHA ORDER

RANK	STATE	NONCITIZENS	% of USA
33	Alabama	117	0.2%
41	Alaska	14	0.0%
5	Arizona	5,605	8.5%
31	Arkansas	174	0.3%
1	California	17,010	25.9%
11	Colorado	1,112	1.7%
15	Connecticut	742	1.1%
23	Delaware	360	0.5%
4	Florida	6,101	9.3%
7	Georgia	1,766	2.7%
35	Hawaii	99	0.2%
24	Idaho	324	0.5%
NA	Illinois**	NA	NA
19	Indiana	468	0.7%
30	Iowa	186	0.3%
26	Kansas	283	0.4%
36	Kentucky	83	0.1%
34	Louisiana	106	0.2%
40	Maine	16	0.0%
16	Maryland	686	1.0%
14	Massachusetts	914	1.4%
18	Michigan	615	0.9%
25	Minnesota	311	0.5%
NA	Mississippi**	NA	NA
20	Missouri	440	0.7%
42	Montana	13	0.0%
29	Nebraska	187	0.3%
6	Nevada	2,775	4.2%
NA	New Hampshire**	NA	NA
NA	New Jersey**	NA	NA
32	New Mexico	120	0.2%
3	New York	6,334	9.6%
9	North Carolina	1,687	2.6%
43	North Dakota	12	0.0%
17	Ohio	685	1.0%
22	Oklahoma	363	0.6%
8	Oregon	1,746	2.7%
13	Pennsylvania	1,008	1.5%
NA	Rhode Island**	NA	NA
21	South Carolina	376	0.6%
37	South Dakota	56	0.1%
28	Tennessee	250	0.4%
2	Texas	9,940	15.1%
27	Utah	263	0.4%
39	Vermont	22	0.0%
10	Virginia	1,223	1.9%
12	Washington	1,075	1.6%
44	West Virginia	8	0.0%
NA	Wisconsin**	NA	NA
38	Wyoming	54	0.1%

RANK ORDER

RANK	STATE	NONCITIZENS	% of USA
1	California	17,010	25.9%
2	Texas	9,940	15.1%
3	New York	6,334	9.6%
4	Florida	6,101	9.3%
5	Arizona	5,605	8.5%
6	Nevada	2,775	4.2%
7	Georgia	1,766	2.7%
8	Oregon	1,746	2.7%
9	North Carolina	1,687	2.6%
10	Virginia	1,223	1.9%
11	Colorado	1,112	1.7%
12	Washington	1,075	1.6%
13	Pennsylvania	1,008	1.5%
14	Massachusetts	914	1.4%
15	Connecticut	742	1.1%
16	Maryland	686	1.0%
17	Ohio	685	1.0%
18	Michigan	615	0.9%
19	Indiana	468	0.7%
20	Missouri	440	0.7%
21	South Carolina	376	0.6%
22	Oklahoma	363	0.6%
23	Delaware	360	0.5%
24	Idaho	324	0.5%
25	Minnesota	311	0.5%
26	Kansas	283	0.4%
27	Utah	263	0.4%
28	Tennessee	250	0.4%
29	Nebraska	187	0.3%
30	Iowa	186	0.3%
31	Arkansas	174	0.3%
32	New Mexico	120	0.2%
33	Alabama	117	0.2%
34	Louisiana	106	0.2%
35	Hawaii	99	0.2%
36	Kentucky	83	0.1%
37	South Dakota	56	0.1%
38	Wyoming	54	0.1%
39	Vermont	22	0.0%
40	Maine	16	0.0%
41	Alaska	14	0.0%
42	Montana	13	0.0%
43	North Dakota	12	0.0%
44	West Virginia	8	0.0%
NA	Illinois**	NA	NA
NA	Mississippi**	NA	NA
NA	New Hampshire**	NA	NA
NA	New Jersey**	NA	NA
NA	Rhode Island**	NA	NA
NA	Wisconsin**	NA	NA
	District of Columbia***	NA	NA

Source: U.S. Department of Justice, Bureau of Justice Statistics
   "Prison and Jail Inmates at Midyear 2008" (March 2009, NCJ 225619, http://bjs.ojp.usdoj.gov/)
*As of June 30, 2008. National total is for reporting states only. Does not include 28,995 noncitizens held in federal prisons.
**Not reported or not applicable.
***Responsibility for sentenced felons in D.C. was transferred to the Federal Bureau of Prisons.

Prisoners Under Sentence of Death as of January 1, 2009 (NAACP)

National Total = 3,241 State Prisoners*

ALPHA ORDER

RANK	STATE	PRISONERS	% of USA
5	Alabama	207	6.4%
NA	Alaska**	NA	NA
8	Arizona	129	4.0%
17	Arkansas	42	1.3%
1	California	678	20.9%
31	Colorado	3	0.1%
25	Connecticut	10	0.3%
20	Delaware	20	0.6%
2	Florida	402	12.4%
9	Georgia	109	3.4%
NA	Hawaii**	NA	NA
21	Idaho	18	0.6%
24	Illinois	15	0.5%
23	Indiana	17	0.5%
NA	Iowa**	NA	NA
25	Kansas	10	0.3%
18	Kentucky	36	1.1%
12	Louisiana	84	2.6%
NA	Maine**	NA	NA
30	Maryland	5	0.2%
NA	Massachusetts**	NA	NA
NA	Michigan**	NA	NA
NA	Minnesota**	NA	NA
15	Mississippi	61	1.9%
16	Missouri	52	1.6%
33	Montana	2	0.1%
25	Nebraska	10	0.3%
13	Nevada	79	2.4%
35	New Hampshire	1	0.0%
NA	New Jersey**	NA	NA
33	New Mexico	2	0.1%
37	New York	0	0.0%
7	North Carolina	167	5.2%
NA	North Dakota**	NA	NA
6	Ohio	181	5.6%
11	Oklahoma	86	2.7%
19	Oregon	35	1.1%
4	Pennsylvania	226	7.0%
NA	Rhode Island**	NA	NA
14	South Carolina	63	1.9%
31	South Dakota	3	0.1%
10	Tennessee	92	2.8%
3	Texas	358	11.0%
25	Utah	10	0.3%
NA	Vermont**	NA	NA
21	Virginia	18	0.6%
29	Washington	9	0.3%
NA	West Virginia**	NA	NA
NA	Wisconsin**	NA	NA
35	Wyoming	1	0.0%

RANK ORDER

RANK	STATE	PRISONERS	% of USA
1	California	678	20.9%
2	Florida	402	12.4%
3	Texas	358	11.0%
4	Pennsylvania	226	7.0%
5	Alabama	207	6.4%
6	Ohio	181	5.6%
7	North Carolina	167	5.2%
8	Arizona	129	4.0%
9	Georgia	109	3.4%
10	Tennessee	92	2.8%
11	Oklahoma	86	2.7%
12	Louisiana	84	2.6%
13	Nevada	79	2.4%
14	South Carolina	63	1.9%
15	Mississippi	61	1.9%
16	Missouri	52	1.6%
17	Arkansas	42	1.3%
18	Kentucky	36	1.1%
19	Oregon	35	1.1%
20	Delaware	20	0.6%
21	Idaho	18	0.6%
21	Virginia	18	0.6%
23	Indiana	17	0.5%
24	Illinois	15	0.5%
25	Connecticut	10	0.3%
25	Kansas	10	0.3%
25	Nebraska	10	0.3%
25	Utah	10	0.3%
29	Washington	9	0.3%
30	Maryland	5	0.2%
31	Colorado	3	0.1%
31	South Dakota	3	0.1%
33	Montana	2	0.1%
33	New Mexico	2	0.1%
35	New Hampshire	1	0.0%
35	Wyoming	1	0.0%
37	New York	0	0.0%
NA	Alaska**	NA	NA
NA	Hawaii**	NA	NA
NA	Iowa**	NA	NA
NA	Maine**	NA	NA
NA	Massachusetts**	NA	NA
NA	Michigan**	NA	NA
NA	Minnesota**	NA	NA
NA	New Jersey**	NA	NA
NA	North Dakota**	NA	NA
NA	Rhode Island**	NA	NA
NA	Vermont**	NA	NA
NA	West Virginia**	NA	NA
NA	Wisconsin**	NA	NA
	District of Columbia**	NA	NA

Source: NAACP Legal Defense and Educational Fund, Inc., Criminal Justice Project
"Death Row USA, Winter 2009" (http://www.naacpldf.org/content.aspx?article=1341)
*Total does not include 55 federal prisoners or nine military prisoners under sentence of death.
**No death penalty as of January 1, 2009.

Prisoners Under Sentence of Death in 2008

National Total = 3,156 State Prisoners*

<table>
<tr><td colspan="4"><u>ALPHA ORDER</u></td><td colspan="4"><u>RANK ORDER</u></td></tr>
<tr><th>RANK</th><th>STATE</th><th>PRISONERS</th><th>% of USA</th><th>RANK</th><th>STATE</th><th>PRISONERS</th><th>% of USA</th></tr>
<tr><td>5</td><td>Alabama</td><td>205</td><td>6.5%</td><td>1</td><td>California</td><td>669</td><td>21.2%</td></tr>
<tr><td>NA</td><td>Alaska**</td><td>NA</td><td>NA</td><td>2</td><td>Florida</td><td>390</td><td>12.4%</td></tr>
<tr><td>8</td><td>Arizona</td><td>119</td><td>3.8%</td><td>3</td><td>Texas</td><td>354</td><td>11.2%</td></tr>
<tr><td>17</td><td>Arkansas</td><td>41</td><td>1.3%</td><td>4</td><td>Pennsylvania</td><td>223</td><td>7.1%</td></tr>
<tr><td>1</td><td>California</td><td>669</td><td>21.2%</td><td>5</td><td>Alabama</td><td>205</td><td>6.5%</td></tr>
<tr><td>32</td><td>Colorado</td><td>2</td><td>0.1%</td><td>6</td><td>Ohio</td><td>172</td><td>5.4%</td></tr>
<tr><td>25</td><td>Connecticut</td><td>10</td><td>0.3%</td><td>7</td><td>North Carolina</td><td>161</td><td>5.1%</td></tr>
<tr><td>20</td><td>Delaware</td><td>20</td><td>0.6%</td><td>8</td><td>Arizona</td><td>119</td><td>3.8%</td></tr>
<tr><td>2</td><td>Florida</td><td>390</td><td>12.4%</td><td>9</td><td>Georgia</td><td>105</td><td>3.3%</td></tr>
<tr><td>9</td><td>Georgia</td><td>105</td><td>3.3%</td><td>10</td><td>Tennessee</td><td>87</td><td>2.8%</td></tr>
<tr><td>NA</td><td>Hawaii**</td><td>NA</td><td>NA</td><td>11</td><td>Oklahoma</td><td>85</td><td>2.7%</td></tr>
<tr><td>21</td><td>Idaho</td><td>17</td><td>0.5%</td><td>12</td><td>Louisiana</td><td>84</td><td>2.7%</td></tr>
<tr><td>22</td><td>Illinois</td><td>15</td><td>0.5%</td><td>13</td><td>Nevada</td><td>81</td><td>2.6%</td></tr>
<tr><td>24</td><td>Indiana</td><td>13</td><td>0.4%</td><td>14</td><td>Mississippi</td><td>60</td><td>1.9%</td></tr>
<tr><td>NA</td><td>Iowa**</td><td>NA</td><td>NA</td><td>15</td><td>South Carolina</td><td>58</td><td>1.8%</td></tr>
<tr><td>28</td><td>Kansas</td><td>8</td><td>0.3%</td><td>16</td><td>Missouri</td><td>50</td><td>1.6%</td></tr>
<tr><td>18</td><td>Kentucky</td><td>36</td><td>1.1%</td><td>17</td><td>Arkansas</td><td>41</td><td>1.3%</td></tr>
<tr><td>12</td><td>Louisiana</td><td>84</td><td>2.7%</td><td>18</td><td>Kentucky</td><td>36</td><td>1.1%</td></tr>
<tr><td>NA</td><td>Maine**</td><td>NA</td><td>NA</td><td>19</td><td>Oregon</td><td>35</td><td>1.1%</td></tr>
<tr><td>30</td><td>Maryland</td><td>5</td><td>0.2%</td><td>20</td><td>Delaware</td><td>20</td><td>0.6%</td></tr>
<tr><td>NA</td><td>Massachusetts**</td><td>NA</td><td>NA</td><td>21</td><td>Idaho</td><td>17</td><td>0.5%</td></tr>
<tr><td>NA</td><td>Michigan**</td><td>NA</td><td>NA</td><td>22</td><td>Illinois</td><td>15</td><td>0.5%</td></tr>
<tr><td>NA</td><td>Minnesota**</td><td>NA</td><td>NA</td><td>22</td><td>Virginia</td><td>15</td><td>0.5%</td></tr>
<tr><td>14</td><td>Mississippi</td><td>60</td><td>1.9%</td><td>24</td><td>Indiana</td><td>13</td><td>0.4%</td></tr>
<tr><td>16</td><td>Missouri</td><td>50</td><td>1.6%</td><td>25</td><td>Connecticut</td><td>10</td><td>0.3%</td></tr>
<tr><td>32</td><td>Montana</td><td>2</td><td>0.1%</td><td>25</td><td>Utah</td><td>10</td><td>0.3%</td></tr>
<tr><td>27</td><td>Nebraska</td><td>9</td><td>0.3%</td><td>27</td><td>Nebraska</td><td>9</td><td>0.3%</td></tr>
<tr><td>13</td><td>Nevada</td><td>81</td><td>2.6%</td><td>28</td><td>Kansas</td><td>8</td><td>0.3%</td></tr>
<tr><td>35</td><td>New Hampshire</td><td>1</td><td>0.0%</td><td>28</td><td>Washington</td><td>8</td><td>0.3%</td></tr>
<tr><td>NA</td><td>New Jersey**</td><td>NA</td><td>NA</td><td>30</td><td>Maryland</td><td>5</td><td>0.2%</td></tr>
<tr><td>32</td><td>New Mexico</td><td>2</td><td>0.1%</td><td>31</td><td>South Dakota</td><td>3</td><td>0.1%</td></tr>
<tr><td>37</td><td>New York</td><td>0</td><td>0.0%</td><td>32</td><td>Colorado</td><td>2</td><td>0.1%</td></tr>
<tr><td>7</td><td>North Carolina</td><td>161</td><td>5.1%</td><td>32</td><td>Montana</td><td>2</td><td>0.1%</td></tr>
<tr><td>NA</td><td>North Dakota**</td><td>NA</td><td>NA</td><td>32</td><td>New Mexico</td><td>2</td><td>0.1%</td></tr>
<tr><td>6</td><td>Ohio</td><td>172</td><td>5.4%</td><td>35</td><td>New Hampshire</td><td>1</td><td>0.0%</td></tr>
<tr><td>11</td><td>Oklahoma</td><td>85</td><td>2.7%</td><td>35</td><td>Wyoming</td><td>1</td><td>0.0%</td></tr>
<tr><td>19</td><td>Oregon</td><td>35</td><td>1.1%</td><td>37</td><td>New York</td><td>0</td><td>0.0%</td></tr>
<tr><td>4</td><td>Pennsylvania</td><td>223</td><td>7.1%</td><td>NA</td><td>Alaska**</td><td>NA</td><td>NA</td></tr>
<tr><td>NA</td><td>Rhode Island**</td><td>NA</td><td>NA</td><td>NA</td><td>Hawaii**</td><td>NA</td><td>NA</td></tr>
<tr><td>15</td><td>South Carolina</td><td>58</td><td>1.8%</td><td>NA</td><td>Iowa**</td><td>NA</td><td>NA</td></tr>
<tr><td>31</td><td>South Dakota</td><td>3</td><td>0.1%</td><td>NA</td><td>Maine**</td><td>NA</td><td>NA</td></tr>
<tr><td>10</td><td>Tennessee</td><td>87</td><td>2.8%</td><td>NA</td><td>Massachusetts**</td><td>NA</td><td>NA</td></tr>
<tr><td>3</td><td>Texas</td><td>354</td><td>11.2%</td><td>NA</td><td>Michigan**</td><td>NA</td><td>NA</td></tr>
<tr><td>25</td><td>Utah</td><td>10</td><td>0.3%</td><td>NA</td><td>Minnesota**</td><td>NA</td><td>NA</td></tr>
<tr><td>NA</td><td>Vermont**</td><td>NA</td><td>NA</td><td>NA</td><td>New Jersey**</td><td>NA</td><td>NA</td></tr>
<tr><td>22</td><td>Virginia</td><td>15</td><td>0.5%</td><td>NA</td><td>North Dakota**</td><td>NA</td><td>NA</td></tr>
<tr><td>28</td><td>Washington</td><td>8</td><td>0.3%</td><td>NA</td><td>Rhode Island**</td><td>NA</td><td>NA</td></tr>
<tr><td>NA</td><td>West Virginia**</td><td>NA</td><td>NA</td><td>NA</td><td>Vermont**</td><td>NA</td><td>NA</td></tr>
<tr><td>NA</td><td>Wisconsin**</td><td>NA</td><td>NA</td><td>NA</td><td>West Virginia**</td><td>NA</td><td>NA</td></tr>
<tr><td>35</td><td>Wyoming</td><td>1</td><td>0.0%</td><td>NA</td><td>Wisconsin**</td><td>NA</td><td>NA</td></tr>
<tr><td></td><td></td><td></td><td></td><td></td><td>District of Columbia**</td><td>NA</td><td>NA</td></tr>
</table>

Source: U.S. Department of Justice, Bureau of Justice Statistics
 "Capital Punishment 2008" (Bulletin, December 2009, NCJ 228662, http://bjs.ojp.usdoj.gov/)
*As of December 31, 2008. Does not include 51 federal prisoners under sentence of death. There were 37 executions in 2008.
**No death penalty as of December 31, 2008.

Male Prisoners Under Sentence of Death in 2008

National Total = 3,100 Male State Prisoners*

ALPHA ORDER

RANK	STATE	PRISONERS	% of USA
5	Alabama	201	6.5%
NA	Alaska**	NA	NA
8	Arizona	117	3.8%
17	Arkansas	41	1.3%
1	California	654	21.1%
32	Colorado	2	0.1%
25	Connecticut	10	0.3%
20	Delaware	20	0.6%
2	Florida	389	12.5%
9	Georgia	104	3.4%
NA	Hawaii**	NA	NA
21	Idaho	16	0.5%
22	Illinois	15	0.5%
24	Indiana	12	0.4%
NA	Iowa**	NA	NA
28	Kansas	8	0.3%
18	Kentucky	35	1.1%
12	Louisiana	82	2.6%
NA	Maine**	NA	NA
30	Maryland	5	0.2%
NA	Massachusetts**	NA	NA
NA	Michigan**	NA	NA
NA	Minnesota**	NA	NA
15	Mississippi	57	1.8%
16	Missouri	50	1.6%
32	Montana	2	0.1%
27	Nebraska	9	0.3%
13	Nevada	81	2.6%
35	New Hampshire	1	0.0%
NA	New Jersey**	NA	NA
32	New Mexico	2	0.1%
37	New York	0	0.0%
7	North Carolina	156	5.0%
NA	North Dakota**	NA	NA
6	Ohio	171	5.5%
11	Oklahoma	84	2.7%
18	Oregon	35	1.1%
4	Pennsylvania	218	7.0%
NA	Rhode Island**	NA	NA
14	South Carolina	58	1.9%
31	South Dakota	3	0.1%
10	Tennessee	85	2.7%
3	Texas	344	11.1%
25	Utah	10	0.3%
NA	Vermont**	NA	NA
23	Virginia	14	0.5%
28	Washington	8	0.3%
NA	West Virginia**	NA	NA
NA	Wisconsin**	NA	NA
35	Wyoming	1	0.0%

RANK ORDER

RANK	STATE	PRISONERS	% of USA
1	California	654	21.1%
2	Florida	389	12.5%
3	Texas	344	11.1%
4	Pennsylvania	218	7.0%
5	Alabama	201	6.5%
6	Ohio	171	5.5%
7	North Carolina	156	5.0%
8	Arizona	117	3.8%
9	Georgia	104	3.4%
10	Tennessee	85	2.7%
11	Oklahoma	84	2.7%
12	Louisiana	82	2.6%
13	Nevada	81	2.6%
14	South Carolina	58	1.9%
15	Mississippi	57	1.8%
16	Missouri	50	1.6%
17	Arkansas	41	1.3%
18	Kentucky	35	1.1%
18	Oregon	35	1.1%
20	Delaware	20	0.6%
21	Idaho	16	0.5%
22	Illinois	15	0.5%
23	Virginia	14	0.5%
24	Indiana	12	0.4%
25	Connecticut	10	0.3%
25	Utah	10	0.3%
27	Nebraska	9	0.3%
28	Kansas	8	0.3%
28	Washington	8	0.3%
30	Maryland	5	0.2%
31	South Dakota	3	0.1%
32	Colorado	2	0.1%
32	Montana	2	0.1%
32	New Mexico	2	0.1%
35	New Hampshire	1	0.0%
35	Wyoming	1	0.0%
37	New York	0	0.0%
NA	Alaska**	NA	NA
NA	Hawaii**	NA	NA
NA	Iowa**	NA	NA
NA	Maine**	NA	NA
NA	Massachusetts**	NA	NA
NA	Michigan**	NA	NA
NA	Minnesota**	NA	NA
NA	New Jersey**	NA	NA
NA	North Dakota**	NA	NA
NA	Rhode Island**	NA	NA
NA	Vermont**	NA	NA
NA	West Virginia**	NA	NA
NA	Wisconsin**	NA	NA
	District of Columbia**	NA	NA

Source: CQ Press using data from U.S. Department of Justice, Bureau of Justice Statistics
  "Capital Punishment 2008" (Bulletin, December 2009, NCJ 228662, http://bjs.ojp.usdoj.gov/)
*As of December 31, 2008. Does not include 49 male federal prisoners under sentence of death. There were 37 executions in 2008; all of the executed were male.
**No death penalty as of December 31, 2008.

Female Prisoners Under Sentence of Death in 2008

National Total = 56 Female State Prisoners*

ALPHA ORDER

ALPHA ORDER

RANK	STATE	PRISONERS	% of USA
5	Alabama	4	7.1%
NA	Alaska**	NA	NA
7	Arizona	2	3.6%
18	Arkansas	0	0.0%
1	California	15	26.8%
18	Colorado	0	0.0%
18	Connecticut	0	0.0%
18	Delaware	0	0.0%
10	Florida	1	1.8%
10	Georgia	1	1.8%
NA	Hawaii**	NA	NA
10	Idaho	1	1.8%
18	Illinois	0	0.0%
10	Indiana	1	1.8%
NA	Iowa**	NA	NA
18	Kansas	0	0.0%
10	Kentucky	1	1.8%
7	Louisiana	2	3.6%
NA	Maine**	NA	NA
18	Maryland	0	0.0%
NA	Massachusetts**	NA	NA
NA	Michigan**	NA	NA
NA	Minnesota**	NA	NA
6	Mississippi	3	5.4%
18	Missouri	0	0.0%
18	Montana	0	0.0%
18	Nebraska	0	0.0%
18	Nevada	0	0.0%
18	New Hampshire	0	0.0%
NA	New Jersey**	NA	NA
18	New Mexico	0	0.0%
18	New York	0	0.0%
3	North Carolina	5	8.9%
NA	North Dakota**	NA	NA
10	Ohio	1	1.8%
10	Oklahoma	1	1.8%
18	Oregon	0	0.0%
3	Pennsylvania	5	8.9%
NA	Rhode Island**	NA	NA
18	South Carolina	0	0.0%
18	South Dakota	0	0.0%
7	Tennessee	2	3.6%
2	Texas	10	17.9%
18	Utah	0	0.0%
NA	Vermont**	NA	NA
10	Virginia	1	1.8%
18	Washington	0	0.0%
NA	West Virginia**	NA	NA
NA	Wisconsin**	NA	NA
18	Wyoming	0	0.0%

RANK ORDER

RANK	STATE	PRISONERS	% of USA
1	California	15	26.8%
2	Texas	10	17.9%
3	North Carolina	5	8.9%
3	Pennsylvania	5	8.9%
5	Alabama	4	7.1%
6	Mississippi	3	5.4%
7	Arizona	2	3.6%
7	Louisiana	2	3.6%
7	Tennessee	2	3.6%
10	Florida	1	1.8%
10	Georgia	1	1.8%
10	Idaho	1	1.8%
10	Indiana	1	1.8%
10	Kentucky	1	1.8%
10	Ohio	1	1.8%
10	Oklahoma	1	1.8%
10	Virginia	1	1.8%
18	Arkansas	0	0.0%
18	Colorado	0	0.0%
18	Connecticut	0	0.0%
18	Delaware	0	0.0%
18	Illinois	0	0.0%
18	Kansas	0	0.0%
18	Maryland	0	0.0%
18	Missouri	0	0.0%
18	Montana	0	0.0%
18	Nebraska	0	0.0%
18	Nevada	0	0.0%
18	New Hampshire	0	0.0%
18	New Mexico	0	0.0%
18	New York	0	0.0%
18	Oregon	0	0.0%
18	South Carolina	0	0.0%
18	South Dakota	0	0.0%
18	Utah	0	0.0%
18	Washington	0	0.0%
18	Wyoming	0	0.0%
NA	Alaska**	NA	NA
NA	Hawaii**	NA	NA
NA	Iowa**	NA	NA
NA	Maine**	NA	NA
NA	Massachusetts**	NA	NA
NA	Michigan**	NA	NA
NA	Minnesota**	NA	NA
NA	New Jersey**	NA	NA
NA	North Dakota**	NA	NA
NA	Rhode Island**	NA	NA
NA	Vermont**	NA	NA
NA	West Virginia**	NA	NA
NA	Wisconsin**	NA	NA

District of Columbia** NA NA

Source: U.S. Department of Justice, Bureau of Justice Statistics
   "Capital Punishment 2008" (Bulletin, December 2009, NCJ 228662, http://bjs.ojp.usdoj.gov/)
*As of December 31, 2008. There was one federal female prisoner under sentence of death. There were 37 executions in 2008; none of the executed was female.
**No death penalty as of December 31, 2008.

Percent of Prisoners Under Sentence of Death Who Are Female: 2008

National Percent = 1.8% of State Death Sentence Prisoners*

ALPHA ORDER

RANK	STATE	PERCENT
12	Alabama	2.0
NA	Alaska**	NA
13	Arizona	1.7
18	Arkansas	0.0
10	California	2.2
18	Colorado	0.0
18	Connecticut	0.0
18	Delaware	0.0
17	Florida	0.3
15	Georgia	1.0
NA	Hawaii**	NA
3	Idaho	5.9
18	Illinois	0.0
1	Indiana	7.7
NA	Iowa**	NA
18	Kansas	0.0
6	Kentucky	2.8
8	Louisiana	2.4
NA	Maine**	NA
18	Maryland	0.0
NA	Massachusetts**	NA
NA	Michigan**	NA
NA	Minnesota**	NA
4	Mississippi	5.0
18	Missouri	0.0
18	Montana	0.0
18	Nebraska	0.0
18	Nevada	0.0
18	New Hampshire	0.0
NA	New Jersey**	NA
18	New Mexico	0.0
18	New York	0.0
5	North Carolina	3.1
NA	North Dakota**	NA
16	Ohio	0.6
14	Oklahoma	1.2
18	Oregon	0.0
10	Pennsylvania	2.2
NA	Rhode Island**	NA
18	South Carolina	0.0
18	South Dakota	0.0
9	Tennessee	2.3
6	Texas	2.8
18	Utah	0.0
NA	Vermont**	NA
2	Virginia	6.7
18	Washington	0.0
NA	West Virginia**	NA
NA	Wisconsin**	NA
18	Wyoming	0.0

RANK ORDER

RANK	STATE	PERCENT
1	Indiana	7.7
2	Virginia	6.7
3	Idaho	5.9
4	Mississippi	5.0
5	North Carolina	3.1
6	Kentucky	2.8
6	Texas	2.8
8	Louisiana	2.4
9	Tennessee	2.3
10	California	2.2
10	Pennsylvania	2.2
12	Alabama	2.0
13	Arizona	1.7
14	Oklahoma	1.2
15	Georgia	1.0
16	Ohio	0.6
17	Florida	0.3
18	Arkansas	0.0
18	Colorado	0.0
18	Connecticut	0.0
18	Delaware	0.0
18	Illinois	0.0
18	Kansas	0.0
18	Maryland	0.0
18	Missouri	0.0
18	Montana	0.0
18	Nebraska	0.0
18	Nevada	0.0
18	New Hampshire	0.0
18	New Mexico	0.0
18	New York	0.0
18	Oregon	0.0
18	South Carolina	0.0
18	South Dakota	0.0
18	Utah	0.0
18	Washington	0.0
18	Wyoming	0.0
NA	Alaska**	NA
NA	Hawaii**	NA
NA	Iowa**	NA
NA	Maine**	NA
NA	Massachusetts**	NA
NA	Michigan**	NA
NA	Minnesota**	NA
NA	New Jersey**	NA
NA	North Dakota**	NA
NA	Rhode Island**	NA
NA	Vermont**	NA
NA	West Virginia**	NA
NA	Wisconsin**	NA
	District of Columbia**	NA

Source: CQ Press using data from U.S. Department of Justice, Bureau of Justice Statistics
   "Capital Punishment 2008" (Bulletin, December 2009, NCJ 228662, http://bjs.ojp.usdoj.gov/)
*As of December 31, 2008. Does not include federal prisoners under sentence of death, 3.9% of whom are female. There were
37 executions in 2008; none of the executed was female.
**No death penalty as of December 31, 2008.

White Prisoners Under Sentence of Death in 2008

National Total = 1,775 White State Prisoners*

ALPHA ORDER					RANK ORDER			
RANK	STATE	PRISONERS	% of USA		RANK	STATE	PRISONERS	% of USA
4	Alabama	107	6.0%		1	California	397	22.4%
NA	Alaska**	NA	NA		2	Florida	255	14.4%
5	Arizona	102	5.7%		3	Texas	210	11.8%
20	Arkansas	16	0.9%		4	Alabama	107	6.0%
1	California	397	22.4%		5	Arizona	102	5.7%
35	Colorado	0	0.0%		6	Pennsylvania	81	4.6%
28	Connecticut	4	0.2%		7	Ohio	80	4.5%
21	Delaware	10	0.6%		8	North Carolina	66	3.7%
2	Florida	255	14.4%		9	Georgia	57	3.2%
9	Georgia	57	3.2%		10	Tennessee	49	2.8%
NA	Hawaii**	NA	NA		11	Nevada	48	2.7%
19	Idaho	17	1.0%		12	Oklahoma	45	2.5%
21	Illinois	10	0.6%		13	Oregon	31	1.7%
21	Indiana	10	0.6%		14	Kentucky	30	1.7%
NA	Iowa**	NA	NA		15	Louisiana	28	1.6%
28	Kansas	4	0.2%		15	Mississippi	28	1.6%
14	Kentucky	30	1.7%		15	Missouri	28	1.6%
15	Louisiana	28	1.6%		18	South Carolina	25	1.4%
NA	Maine**	NA	NA		19	Idaho	17	1.0%
33	Maryland	1	0.1%		20	Arkansas	16	0.9%
NA	Massachusetts**	NA	NA		21	Delaware	10	0.6%
NA	Michigan**	NA	NA		21	Illinois	10	0.6%
NA	Minnesota**	NA	NA		21	Indiana	10	0.6%
15	Mississippi	28	1.6%		24	Nebraska	8	0.5%
15	Missouri	28	1.6%		24	Utah	8	0.5%
31	Montana	2	0.1%		26	Virginia	7	0.4%
24	Nebraska	8	0.5%		27	Washington	5	0.3%
11	Nevada	48	2.7%		28	Connecticut	4	0.2%
35	New Hampshire	0	0.0%		28	Kansas	4	0.2%
NA	New Jersey**	NA	NA		30	South Dakota	3	0.2%
31	New Mexico	2	0.1%		31	Montana	2	0.1%
35	New York	0	0.0%		31	New Mexico	2	0.1%
8	North Carolina	66	3.7%		33	Maryland	1	0.1%
NA	North Dakota**	NA	NA		33	Wyoming	1	0.1%
7	Ohio	80	4.5%		35	Colorado	0	0.0%
12	Oklahoma	45	2.5%		35	New Hampshire	0	0.0%
13	Oregon	31	1.7%		35	New York	0	0.0%
6	Pennsylvania	81	4.6%		NA	Alaska**	NA	NA
NA	Rhode Island**	NA	NA		NA	Hawaii**	NA	NA
18	South Carolina	25	1.4%		NA	Iowa**	NA	NA
30	South Dakota	3	0.2%		NA	Maine**	NA	NA
10	Tennessee	49	2.8%		NA	Massachusetts**	NA	NA
3	Texas	210	11.8%		NA	Michigan**	NA	NA
24	Utah	8	0.5%		NA	Minnesota**	NA	NA
NA	Vermont**	NA	NA		NA	New Jersey**	NA	NA
26	Virginia	7	0.4%		NA	North Dakota**	NA	NA
27	Washington	5	0.3%		NA	Rhode Island**	NA	NA
NA	West Virginia**	NA	NA		NA	Vermont**	NA	NA
NA	Wisconsin**	NA	NA		NA	West Virginia**	NA	NA
33	Wyoming	1	0.1%		NA	Wisconsin**	NA	NA
					District of Columbia**		NA	NA

Source: U.S. Department of Justice, Bureau of Justice Statistics
"Capital Punishment 2008" (Bulletin, December 2009, NCJ 228662, http://bjs.ojp.usdoj.gov/)
*As of December 31, 2008. Does not include 23 white federal prisoners under sentence of death. There were 37 executions in 2008, 20 of which were white prisoners.
**No death penalty as of December 31, 2008.

Percent of Prisoners Under Sentence of Death Who Are White: 2008

National Percent = 56.2% of State Death Sentence Prisoners*

ALPHA ORDER

RANK	STATE	PERCENT
22	Alabama	52.2
NA	Alaska**	NA
8	Arizona	85.7
31	Arkansas	39.0
15	California	59.3
35	Colorado	0.0
30	Connecticut	40.0
23	Delaware	50.0
13	Florida	65.4
20	Georgia	54.3
NA	Hawaii**	NA
1	Idaho	100.0
12	Illinois	66.7
11	Indiana	76.9
NA	Iowa**	NA
23	Kansas	50.0
9	Kentucky	83.3
33	Louisiana	33.3
NA	Maine**	NA
34	Maryland	20.0
NA	Massachusetts**	NA
NA	Michigan**	NA
NA	Minnesota**	NA
25	Mississippi	46.7
19	Missouri	56.0
1	Montana	100.0
6	Nebraska	88.9
15	Nevada	59.3
35	New Hampshire	0.0
NA	New Jersey**	NA
1	New Mexico	100.0
35	New York	0.0
29	North Carolina	41.0
NA	North Dakota**	NA
27	Ohio	46.5
21	Oklahoma	52.9
7	Oregon	88.6
32	Pennsylvania	36.3
NA	Rhode Island**	NA
28	South Carolina	43.1
1	South Dakota	100.0
18	Tennessee	56.3
15	Texas	59.3
10	Utah	80.0
NA	Vermont**	NA
25	Virginia	46.7
14	Washington	62.5
NA	West Virginia**	NA
NA	Wisconsin**	NA
1	Wyoming	100.0

RANK ORDER

RANK	STATE	PERCENT
1	Idaho	100.0
1	Montana	100.0
1	New Mexico	100.0
1	South Dakota	100.0
1	Wyoming	100.0
6	Nebraska	88.9
7	Oregon	88.6
8	Arizona	85.7
9	Kentucky	83.3
10	Utah	80.0
11	Indiana	76.9
12	Illinois	66.7
13	Florida	65.4
14	Washington	62.5
15	California	59.3
15	Nevada	59.3
15	Texas	59.3
18	Tennessee	56.3
19	Missouri	56.0
20	Georgia	54.3
21	Oklahoma	52.9
22	Alabama	52.2
23	Delaware	50.0
23	Kansas	50.0
25	Mississippi	46.7
25	Virginia	46.7
27	Ohio	46.5
28	South Carolina	43.1
29	North Carolina	41.0
30	Connecticut	40.0
31	Arkansas	39.0
32	Pennsylvania	36.3
33	Louisiana	33.3
34	Maryland	20.0
35	Colorado	0.0
35	New Hampshire	0.0
35	New York	0.0
NA	Alaska**	NA
NA	Hawaii**	NA
NA	Iowa**	NA
NA	Maine**	NA
NA	Massachusetts**	NA
NA	Michigan**	NA
NA	Minnesota**	NA
NA	New Jersey**	NA
NA	North Dakota**	NA
NA	Rhode Island**	NA
NA	Vermont**	NA
NA	West Virginia**	NA
NA	Wisconsin**	NA
	District of Columbia**	NA

Source: CQ Press using data from U.S. Department of Justice, Bureau of Justice Statistics
   "Capital Punishment 2008" (Bulletin, December 2009, NCJ 228662, http://bjs.ojp.usdoj.gov/)
*As of December 31, 2008. Does not include federal prisoners under sentence of death, 45.1% of whom are white prisoners. Of the 37 executions in 2008, 54.1% were of white prisoners.
**No death penalty as of December 31, 2008.

Black Prisoners Under Sentence of Death in 2008

National Total = 1,311 Black State Prisoners*

ALPHA ORDER

RANK	STATE	PRISONERS	% of USA
5	Alabama	98	7.5%
NA	Alaska**	NA	NA
17	Arizona	13	1.0%
15	Arkansas	25	1.9%
1	California	243	18.5%
28	Colorado	2	0.2%
20	Connecticut	6	0.5%
18	Delaware	10	0.8%
3	Florida	135	10.3%
9	Georgia	47	3.6%
NA	Hawaii**	NA	NA
32	Idaho	0	0.0%
22	Illinois	5	0.4%
25	Indiana	3	0.2%
NA	Iowa**	NA	NA
23	Kansas	4	0.3%
20	Kentucky	6	0.5%
8	Louisiana	55	4.2%
NA	Maine**	NA	NA
23	Maryland	4	0.3%
NA	Massachusetts**	NA	NA
NA	Michigan**	NA	NA
NA	Minnesota**	NA	NA
14	Mississippi	31	2.4%
16	Missouri	22	1.7%
32	Montana	0	0.0%
29	Nebraska	1	0.1%
13	Nevada	32	2.4%
29	New Hampshire	1	0.1%
NA	New Jersey**	NA	NA
32	New Mexico	0	0.0%
32	New York	0	0.0%
7	North Carolina	86	6.6%
NA	North Dakota**	NA	NA
6	Ohio	89	6.8%
10	Oklahoma	36	2.7%
25	Oregon	3	0.2%
4	Pennsylvania	133	10.1%
NA	Rhode Island**	NA	NA
12	South Carolina	33	2.5%
32	South Dakota	0	0.0%
10	Tennessee	36	2.7%
2	Texas	140	10.7%
29	Utah	1	0.1%
NA	Vermont**	NA	NA
19	Virginia	8	0.6%
25	Washington	3	0.2%
NA	West Virginia**	NA	NA
NA	Wisconsin**	NA	NA
32	Wyoming	0	0.0%

RANK ORDER

RANK	STATE	PRISONERS	% of USA
1	California	243	18.5%
2	Texas	140	10.7%
3	Florida	135	10.3%
4	Pennsylvania	133	10.1%
5	Alabama	98	7.5%
6	Ohio	89	6.8%
7	North Carolina	86	6.6%
8	Louisiana	55	4.2%
9	Georgia	47	3.6%
10	Oklahoma	36	2.7%
10	Tennessee	36	2.7%
12	South Carolina	33	2.5%
13	Nevada	32	2.4%
14	Mississippi	31	2.4%
15	Arkansas	25	1.9%
16	Missouri	22	1.7%
17	Arizona	13	1.0%
18	Delaware	10	0.8%
19	Virginia	8	0.6%
20	Connecticut	6	0.5%
20	Kentucky	6	0.5%
22	Illinois	5	0.4%
23	Kansas	4	0.3%
23	Maryland	4	0.3%
25	Indiana	3	0.2%
25	Oregon	3	0.2%
25	Washington	3	0.2%
28	Colorado	2	0.2%
29	Nebraska	1	0.1%
29	New Hampshire	1	0.1%
29	Utah	1	0.1%
32	Idaho	0	0.0%
32	Montana	0	0.0%
32	New Mexico	0	0.0%
32	New York	0	0.0%
32	South Dakota	0	0.0%
32	Wyoming	0	0.0%
NA	Alaska**	NA	NA
NA	Hawaii**	NA	NA
NA	Iowa**	NA	NA
NA	Maine**	NA	NA
NA	Massachusetts**	NA	NA
NA	Michigan**	NA	NA
NA	Minnesota**	NA	NA
NA	New Jersey**	NA	NA
NA	North Dakota**	NA	NA
NA	Rhode Island**	NA	NA
NA	Vermont**	NA	NA
NA	West Virginia**	NA	NA
NA	Wisconsin**	NA	NA
	District of Columbia**	NA	NA

Source: U.S. Department of Justice, Bureau of Justice Statistics
   "Capital Punishment 2008" (Bulletin, December 2009, NCJ 228662, http://bjs.ojp.usdoj.gov/)
*As of December 31, 2008. Does not include 27 black federal prisoners under sentence of death. There were 37 executions in 2008, 17 of which were of black prisoners.
**No death penalty as of December 31, 2008.

Percent of Prisoners Under Sentence of Death Who Are Black: 2008

National Percent = 41.5% of State Death Sentence Prisoners*

ALPHA ORDER

RANK	STATE	PERCENT
15	Alabama	47.8
NA	Alaska**	NA
29	Arizona	10.9
5	Arkansas	61.0
23	California	36.3
1	Colorado	100.0
6	Connecticut	60.0
13	Delaware	50.0
24	Florida	34.6
16	Georgia	44.8
NA	Hawaii**	NA
32	Idaho	0.0
25	Illinois	33.3
26	Indiana	23.1
NA	Iowa**	NA
13	Kansas	50.0
27	Kentucky	16.7
4	Louisiana	65.5
NA	Maine**	NA
3	Maryland	80.0
NA	Massachusetts**	NA
NA	Michigan**	NA
NA	Minnesota**	NA
11	Mississippi	51.7
17	Missouri	44.0
32	Montana	0.0
28	Nebraska	11.1
20	Nevada	39.5
1	New Hampshire	100.0
NA	New Jersey**	NA
32	New Mexico	0.0
32	New York	0.0
9	North Carolina	53.4
NA	North Dakota**	NA
11	Ohio	51.7
18	Oklahoma	42.4
31	Oregon	8.6
7	Pennsylvania	59.6
NA	Rhode Island**	NA
8	South Carolina	56.9
32	South Dakota	0.0
19	Tennessee	41.4
20	Texas	39.5
30	Utah	10.0
NA	Vermont**	NA
10	Virginia	53.3
22	Washington	37.5
NA	West Virginia**	NA
NA	Wisconsin**	NA
32	Wyoming	0.0

RANK ORDER

RANK	STATE	PERCENT
1	Colorado	100.0
1	New Hampshire	100.0
3	Maryland	80.0
4	Louisiana	65.5
5	Arkansas	61.0
6	Connecticut	60.0
7	Pennsylvania	59.6
8	South Carolina	56.9
9	North Carolina	53.4
10	Virginia	53.3
11	Mississippi	51.7
11	Ohio	51.7
13	Delaware	50.0
13	Kansas	50.0
15	Alabama	47.8
16	Georgia	44.8
17	Missouri	44.0
18	Oklahoma	42.4
19	Tennessee	41.4
20	Nevada	39.5
20	Texas	39.5
22	Washington	37.5
23	California	36.3
24	Florida	34.6
25	Illinois	33.3
26	Indiana	23.1
27	Kentucky	16.7
28	Nebraska	11.1
29	Arizona	10.9
30	Utah	10.0
31	Oregon	8.6
32	Idaho	0.0
32	Montana	0.0
32	New Mexico	0.0
32	New York	0.0
32	South Dakota	0.0
32	Wyoming	0.0
NA	Alaska**	NA
NA	Hawaii**	NA
NA	Iowa**	NA
NA	Maine**	NA
NA	Massachusetts**	NA
NA	Michigan**	NA
NA	Minnesota**	NA
NA	New Jersey**	NA
NA	North Dakota**	NA
NA	Rhode Island**	NA
NA	Vermont**	NA
NA	West Virginia**	NA
NA	Wisconsin**	NA
	District of Columbia**	NA

Source: CQ Press using data from U.S. Department of Justice, Bureau of Justice Statistics
   "Capital Punishment 2008" (Bulletin, December 2009, NCJ 228662, http://bjs.ojp.usdoj.gov/)
*As of December 31, 2008. Does not include federal prisoners under sentence of death, 52.9% of whom are black prisoners. Of the 37 executions in 2008, 45.9% were of black prisoners.
**No death penalty as of December 31, 2008.

Hispanic Prisoners Under Sentence of Death in 2008

National Total = 369 Hispanic State Prisoners*

ALPHA ORDER

ALPHA ORDER

RANK	STATE	PRISONERS	% of USA
11	Alabama	2	0.5%
NA	Alaska**	NA	NA
5	Arizona	18	4.9%
25	Arkansas	0	0.0%
1	California	151	40.9%
25	Colorado	0	0.0%
18	Connecticut	1	0.3%
11	Delaware	2	0.5%
3	Florida	33	8.9%
11	Georgia	2	0.5%
NA	Hawaii**	NA	NA
18	Idaho	1	0.3%
11	Illinois	2	0.5%
18	Indiana	1	0.3%
NA	Iowa**	NA	NA
25	Kansas	0	0.0%
18	Kentucky	1	0.3%
11	Louisiana	2	0.5%
NA	Maine**	NA	NA
25	Maryland	0	0.0%
NA	Massachusetts**	NA	NA
NA	Michigan**	NA	NA
NA	Minnesota**	NA	NA
25	Mississippi	0	0.0%
25	Missouri	0	0.0%
25	Montana	0	0.0%
9	Nebraska	3	0.8%
6	Nevada	7	1.9%
25	New Hampshire	0	0.0%
NA	New Jersey**	NA	NA
18	New Mexico	1	0.3%
25	New York	0	0.0%
8	North Carolina	4	1.1%
NA	North Dakota**	NA	NA
7	Ohio	5	1.4%
11	Oklahoma	2	0.5%
11	Oregon	2	0.5%
4	Pennsylvania	21	5.7%
NA	Rhode Island**	NA	NA
18	South Carolina	1	0.3%
25	South Dakota	0	0.0%
18	Tennessee	1	0.3%
2	Texas	103	27.9%
9	Utah	3	0.8%
NA	Vermont**	NA	NA
25	Virginia	0	0.0%
25	Washington	0	0.0%
NA	West Virginia**	NA	NA
NA	Wisconsin**	NA	NA
25	Wyoming	0	0.0%

RANK ORDER

RANK	STATE	PRISONERS	% of USA
1	California	151	40.9%
2	Texas	103	27.9%
3	Florida	33	8.9%
4	Pennsylvania	21	5.7%
5	Arizona	18	4.9%
6	Nevada	7	1.9%
7	Ohio	5	1.4%
8	North Carolina	4	1.1%
9	Nebraska	3	0.8%
9	Utah	3	0.8%
11	Alabama	2	0.5%
11	Delaware	2	0.5%
11	Georgia	2	0.5%
11	Illinois	2	0.5%
11	Louisiana	2	0.5%
11	Oklahoma	2	0.5%
11	Oregon	2	0.5%
18	Connecticut	1	0.3%
18	Idaho	1	0.3%
18	Indiana	1	0.3%
18	Kentucky	1	0.3%
18	New Mexico	1	0.3%
18	South Carolina	1	0.3%
18	Tennessee	1	0.3%
25	Arkansas	0	0.0%
25	Colorado	0	0.0%
25	Kansas	0	0.0%
25	Maryland	0	0.0%
25	Mississippi	0	0.0%
25	Missouri	0	0.0%
25	Montana	0	0.0%
25	New Hampshire	0	0.0%
25	New York	0	0.0%
25	South Dakota	0	0.0%
25	Virginia	0	0.0%
25	Washington	0	0.0%
25	Wyoming	0	0.0%
NA	Alaska**	NA	NA
NA	Hawaii**	NA	NA
NA	Iowa**	NA	NA
NA	Maine**	NA	NA
NA	Massachusetts**	NA	NA
NA	Michigan**	NA	NA
NA	Minnesota**	NA	NA
NA	New Jersey**	NA	NA
NA	North Dakota**	NA	NA
NA	Rhode Island**	NA	NA
NA	Vermont**	NA	NA
NA	West Virginia**	NA	NA
NA	Wisconsin**	NA	NA
	District of Columbia**	NA	NA

Source: U.S. Department of Justice, Bureau of Justice Statistics
"Capital Punishment 2008" (Bulletin, December 2009, NCJ 228662, http://bjs.ojp.usdoj.gov/)
*As of December 31, 2008. Does not include four Hispanic federal prisoners under sentence of death. There were 37 executions in 2008, three of which were Hispanic prisoners. Hispanic can be of any race.
**No death penalty as of December 31, 2008.

Percent of Prisoners Under Sentence of Death Who Are Hispanic: 2008

National Percent = 11.7% of State Death Sentence Prisoners*

ALPHA ORDER

RANK	STATE	PERCENT
24	Alabama	1.0
NA	Alaska**	NA
6	Arizona	15.1
25	Arkansas	0.0
5	California	22.6
25	Colorado	0.0
8	Connecticut	10.0
8	Delaware	10.0
12	Florida	8.5
21	Georgia	1.9
NA	Hawaii**	NA
14	Idaho	5.9
7	Illinois	13.3
13	Indiana	7.7
NA	Iowa**	NA
25	Kansas	0.0
17	Kentucky	2.8
19	Louisiana	2.4
NA	Maine**	NA
25	Maryland	0.0
NA	Massachusetts**	NA
NA	Michigan**	NA
NA	Minnesota**	NA
25	Mississippi	0.0
25	Missouri	0.0
25	Montana	0.0
2	Nebraska	33.3
11	Nevada	8.6
25	New Hampshire	0.0
NA	New Jersey**	NA
1	New Mexico	50.0
25	New York	0.0
18	North Carolina	2.5
NA	North Dakota**	NA
16	Ohio	2.9
19	Oklahoma	2.4
15	Oregon	5.7
10	Pennsylvania	9.4
NA	Rhode Island**	NA
22	South Carolina	1.7
25	South Dakota	0.0
23	Tennessee	1.1
4	Texas	29.1
3	Utah	30.0
NA	Vermont**	NA
25	Virginia	0.0
25	Washington	0.0
NA	West Virginia**	NA
NA	Wisconsin**	NA
25	Wyoming	0.0

RANK ORDER

RANK	STATE	PERCENT
1	New Mexico	50.0
2	Nebraska	33.3
3	Utah	30.0
4	Texas	29.1
5	California	22.6
6	Arizona	15.1
7	Illinois	13.3
8	Connecticut	10.0
8	Delaware	10.0
10	Pennsylvania	9.4
11	Nevada	8.6
12	Florida	8.5
13	Indiana	7.7
14	Idaho	5.9
15	Oregon	5.7
16	Ohio	2.9
17	Kentucky	2.8
18	North Carolina	2.5
19	Louisiana	2.4
19	Oklahoma	2.4
21	Georgia	1.9
22	South Carolina	1.7
23	Tennessee	1.1
24	Alabama	1.0
25	Arkansas	0.0
25	Colorado	0.0
25	Kansas	0.0
25	Maryland	0.0
25	Mississippi	0.0
25	Missouri	0.0
25	Montana	0.0
25	New Hampshire	0.0
25	New York	0.0
25	South Dakota	0.0
25	Virginia	0.0
25	Washington	0.0
25	Wyoming	0.0
NA	Alaska**	NA
NA	Hawaii**	NA
NA	Iowa**	NA
NA	Maine**	NA
NA	Massachusetts**	NA
NA	Michigan**	NA
NA	Minnesota**	NA
NA	New Jersey**	NA
NA	North Dakota**	NA
NA	Rhode Island**	NA
NA	Vermont**	NA
NA	West Virginia**	NA
NA	Wisconsin**	NA
	District of Columbia**	NA

Source: CQ Press using data from U.S. Department of Justice, Bureau of Justice Statistics
 "Capital Punishment 2008" (Bulletin, December 2009, NCJ 228662, http://bjs.ojp.usdoj.gov/)
*As of December 31, 2008. Does not include federal prisoners under sentence of death, 7.8% of whom are Hispanic prisoners.
Of the 37 executions in 2008, 8.1% were of Hispanic prisoners. Hispanic can be of any race.
**No death penalty as of December 31, 2008.

Prisoners Executed in 2009

National Total = 52 Prisoners*

ALPHA ORDER

RANK	STATE	EXECUTIONS	% of USA
2	Alabama	6	11.5%
NA	Alaska**	NA	NA
12	Arizona	0	0.0%
12	Arkansas	0	0.0%
12	California	0	0.0%
12	Colorado	0	0.0%
12	Connecticut	0	0.0%
12	Delaware	0	0.0%
7	Florida	2	3.8%
4	Georgia	3	5.8%
NA	Hawaii**	NA	NA
12	Idaho	0	0.0%
12	Illinois	0	0.0%
10	Indiana	1	1.9%
NA	Iowa**	NA	NA
12	Kansas	0	0.0%
12	Kentucky	0	0.0%
12	Louisiana	0	0.0%
NA	Maine**	NA	NA
12	Maryland	0	0.0%
NA	Massachusetts**	NA	NA
NA	Michigan**	NA	NA
NA	Minnesota**	NA	NA
12	Mississippi	0	0.0%
10	Missouri	1	1.9%
12	Montana	0	0.0%
12	Nebraska	0	0.0%
12	Nevada	0	0.0%
12	New Hampshire	0	0.0%
NA	New Jersey**	NA	NA
12	New Mexico	0	0.0%
12	New York	0	0.0%
12	North Carolina	0	0.0%
NA	North Dakota**	NA	NA
3	Ohio	5	9.6%
4	Oklahoma	3	5.8%
12	Oregon	0	0.0%
12	Pennsylvania	0	0.0%
NA	Rhode Island**	NA	NA
7	South Carolina	2	3.8%
12	South Dakota	0	0.0%
7	Tennessee	2	3.8%
1	Texas	24	46.2%
12	Utah	0	0.0%
NA	Vermont**	NA	NA
4	Virginia	3	5.8%
12	Washington	0	0.0%
NA	West Virginia**	NA	NA
NA	Wisconsin**	NA	NA
12	Wyoming	0	0.0%

RANK ORDER

RANK	STATE	EXECUTIONS	% of USA
1	Texas	24	46.2%
2	Alabama	6	11.5%
3	Ohio	5	9.6%
4	Georgia	3	5.8%
4	Oklahoma	3	5.8%
4	Virginia	3	5.8%
7	Florida	2	3.8%
7	South Carolina	2	3.8%
7	Tennessee	2	3.8%
10	Indiana	1	1.9%
10	Missouri	1	1.9%
12	Arizona	0	0.0%
12	Arkansas	0	0.0%
12	California	0	0.0%
12	Colorado	0	0.0%
12	Connecticut	0	0.0%
12	Delaware	0	0.0%
12	Idaho	0	0.0%
12	Illinois	0	0.0%
12	Kansas	0	0.0%
12	Kentucky	0	0.0%
12	Louisiana	0	0.0%
12	Maryland	0	0.0%
12	Mississippi	0	0.0%
12	Montana	0	0.0%
12	Nebraska	0	0.0%
12	Nevada	0	0.0%
12	New Hampshire	0	0.0%
12	New Mexico	0	0.0%
12	New York	0	0.0%
12	North Carolina	0	0.0%
12	Oregon	0	0.0%
12	Pennsylvania	0	0.0%
12	South Dakota	0	0.0%
12	Utah	0	0.0%
12	Washington	0	0.0%
12	Wyoming	0	0.0%
NA	Alaska**	NA	NA
NA	Hawaii**	NA	NA
NA	Iowa**	NA	NA
NA	Maine**	NA	NA
NA	Massachusetts**	NA	NA
NA	Michigan**	NA	NA
NA	Minnesota**	NA	NA
NA	New Jersey**	NA	NA
NA	North Dakota**	NA	NA
NA	Rhode Island**	NA	NA
NA	Vermont**	NA	NA
NA	West Virginia**	NA	NA
NA	Wisconsin**	NA	NA
	District of Columbia**	NA	NA

Source: U.S. Department of Justice, Bureau of Justice Statistics
   "Capital Punishment 2008" (Bulletin, December 2009, NCJ 228662, http://bjs.ojp.usdoj.gov/)
*As of December 31, 2009.
**No death penalty as of December 31, 2008.

Prisoners Executed in 2008

National Total = 37 Prisoners*

ALPHA ORDER

RANK	STATE	EXECUTIONS	% of USA
10	Alabama	0	0.0%
NA	Alaska**	NA	NA
10	Arizona	0	0.0%
10	Arkansas	0	0.0%
10	California	0	0.0%
10	Colorado	0	0.0%
10	Connecticut	0	0.0%
10	Delaware	0	0.0%
5	Florida	2	5.4%
3	Georgia	3	8.1%
NA	Hawaii**	NA	NA
10	Idaho	0	0.0%
10	Illinois	0	0.0%
10	Indiana	0	0.0%
NA	Iowa**	NA	NA
10	Kansas	0	0.0%
9	Kentucky	1	2.7%
10	Louisiana	0	0.0%
NA	Maine**	NA	NA
10	Maryland	0	0.0%
NA	Massachusetts**	NA	NA
NA	Michigan**	NA	NA
NA	Minnesota**	NA	NA
5	Mississippi	2	5.4%
10	Missouri	0	0.0%
10	Montana	0	0.0%
10	Nebraska	0	0.0%
10	Nevada	0	0.0%
10	New Hampshire	0	0.0%
NA	New Jersey**	NA	NA
10	New Mexico	0	0.0%
10	New York	0	0.0%
10	North Carolina	0	0.0%
NA	North Dakota**	NA	NA
5	Ohio	2	5.4%
5	Oklahoma	2	5.4%
10	Oregon	0	0.0%
10	Pennsylvania	0	0.0%
NA	Rhode Island**	NA	NA
3	South Carolina	3	8.1%
10	South Dakota	0	0.0%
10	Tennessee	0	0.0%
1	Texas	18	48.6%
10	Utah	0	0.0%
NA	Vermont**	NA	NA
2	Virginia	4	10.8%
10	Washington	0	0.0%
NA	West Virginia**	NA	NA
NA	Wisconsin**	NA	NA
10	Wyoming	0	0.0%

RANK ORDER

RANK	STATE	EXECUTIONS	% of USA
1	Texas	18	48.6%
2	Virginia	4	10.8%
3	Georgia	3	8.1%
3	South Carolina	3	8.1%
5	Florida	2	5.4%
5	Mississippi	2	5.4%
5	Ohio	2	5.4%
5	Oklahoma	2	5.4%
9	Kentucky	1	2.7%
10	Alabama	0	0.0%
10	Arizona	0	0.0%
10	Arkansas	0	0.0%
10	California	0	0.0%
10	Colorado	0	0.0%
10	Connecticut	0	0.0%
10	Delaware	0	0.0%
10	Idaho	0	0.0%
10	Illinois	0	0.0%
10	Indiana	0	0.0%
10	Kansas	0	0.0%
10	Louisiana	0	0.0%
10	Maryland	0	0.0%
10	Missouri	0	0.0%
10	Montana	0	0.0%
10	Nebraska	0	0.0%
10	Nevada	0	0.0%
10	New Hampshire	0	0.0%
10	New Mexico	0	0.0%
10	New York	0	0.0%
10	North Carolina	0	0.0%
10	Oregon	0	0.0%
10	Pennsylvania	0	0.0%
10	South Dakota	0	0.0%
10	Tennessee	0	0.0%
10	Utah	0	0.0%
10	Washington	0	0.0%
10	Wyoming	0	0.0%
NA	Alaska**	NA	NA
NA	Hawaii**	NA	NA
NA	Iowa**	NA	NA
NA	Maine**	NA	NA
NA	Massachusetts**	NA	NA
NA	Michigan**	NA	NA
NA	Minnesota**	NA	NA
NA	New Jersey**	NA	NA
NA	North Dakota**	NA	NA
NA	Rhode Island**	NA	NA
NA	Vermont**	NA	NA
NA	West Virginia**	NA	NA
NA	Wisconsin**	NA	NA
	District of Columbia**	NA	NA

Source: U.S. Department of Justice, Bureau of Justice Statistics
  "Capital Punishment 2008" (Bulletin, December 2009, NCJ 228662, http://bjs.ojp.usdoj.gov/)
*There were no federal prisoners executed in 2008. All of the executions were by lethal injection except one, which was by electrocution.
**No death penalty as of December 31, 2008.

Percent of Prisoners Executed Who Were White: 2008

National Percent = 54.1% of State Prisoner Executions*

ALPHA ORDER				RANK ORDER		
RANK	STATE	PERCENT		RANK	STATE	PERCENT
10	Alabama	0.0		1	Kentucky	100.0
NA	Alaska**	NA		1	Mississippi	100.0
10	Arizona	0.0		1	Oklahoma	100.0
10	Arkansas	0.0		4	Georgia	66.7
10	California	0.0		5	Florida	50.0
10	Colorado	0.0		5	Ohio	50.0
10	Connecticut	0.0		5	Texas	50.0
10	Delaware	0.0		8	South Carolina	33.3
5	Florida	50.0		9	Virginia	25.0
4	Georgia	66.7		10	Alabama	0.0
NA	Hawaii**	NA		10	Arizona	0.0
10	Idaho	0.0		10	Arkansas	0.0
10	Illinois	0.0		10	California	0.0
10	Indiana	0.0		10	Colorado	0.0
NA	Iowa**	NA		10	Connecticut	0.0
10	Kansas	0.0		10	Delaware	0.0
1	Kentucky	100.0		10	Idaho	0.0
10	Louisiana	0.0		10	Illinois	0.0
NA	Maine**	NA		10	Indiana	0.0
10	Maryland	0.0		10	Kansas	0.0
NA	Massachusetts**	NA		10	Louisiana	0.0
NA	Michigan**	NA		10	Maryland	0.0
NA	Minnesota**	NA		10	Missouri	0.0
1	Mississippi	100.0		10	Montana	0.0
10	Missouri	0.0		10	Nebraska	0.0
10	Montana	0.0		10	Nevada	0.0
10	Nebraska	0.0		10	New Hampshire	0.0
10	Nevada	0.0		10	New Mexico	0.0
10	New Hampshire	0.0		10	New York	0.0
NA	New Jersey**	NA		10	North Carolina	0.0
10	New Mexico	0.0		10	Oregon	0.0
10	New York	0.0		10	Pennsylvania	0.0
10	North Carolina	0.0		10	South Dakota	0.0
NA	North Dakota**	NA		10	Tennessee	0.0
5	Ohio	50.0		10	Utah	0.0
1	Oklahoma	100.0		10	Washington	0.0
10	Oregon	0.0		10	Wyoming	0.0
10	Pennsylvania	0.0		NA	Alaska**	NA
NA	Rhode Island**	NA		NA	Hawaii**	NA
8	South Carolina	33.3		NA	Iowa**	NA
10	South Dakota	0.0		NA	Maine**	NA
10	Tennessee	0.0		NA	Massachusetts**	NA
5	Texas	50.0		NA	Michigan**	NA
10	Utah	0.0		NA	Minnesota**	NA
NA	Vermont**	NA		NA	New Jersey**	NA
9	Virginia	25.0		NA	North Dakota**	NA
10	Washington	0.0		NA	Rhode Island**	NA
NA	West Virginia**	NA		NA	Vermont**	NA
NA	Wisconsin**	NA		NA	West Virginia**	NA
10	Wyoming	0.0		NA	Wisconsin**	NA
				NA	District of Columbia**	NA

Source: CQ Press using data from U.S. Department of Justice, Bureau of Justice Statistics
   "Capital Punishment 2008" (Bulletin, December 2009, NCJ 228662, http://bjs.ojp.usdoj.gov/)
*There were no federal prisoners executed in 2008.
**No death penalty as of December 31, 2008.

Percent of Prisoners Executed Who Were Black: 2008

National Percent = 45.9% of State Prisoner Executions*

ALPHA ORDER				RANK ORDER		
RANK	STATE	PERCENT		RANK	STATE	PERCENT
7	Alabama	0.0		1	Virginia	75.0
NA	Alaska**	NA		2	South Carolina	66.7
7	Arizona	0.0		3	Florida	50.0
7	Arkansas	0.0		3	Ohio	50.0
7	California	0.0		3	Texas	50.0
7	Colorado	0.0		6	Georgia	33.3
7	Connecticut	0.0		7	Alabama	0.0
7	Delaware	0.0		7	Arizona	0.0
3	Florida	50.0		7	Arkansas	0.0
6	Georgia	33.3		7	California	0.0
NA	Hawaii**	NA		7	Colorado	0.0
7	Idaho	0.0		7	Connecticut	0.0
7	Illinois	0.0		7	Delaware	0.0
7	Indiana	0.0		7	Idaho	0.0
NA	Iowa**	NA		7	Illinois	0.0
7	Kansas	0.0		7	Indiana	0.0
7	Kentucky	0.0		7	Kansas	0.0
7	Louisiana	0.0		7	Kentucky	0.0
NA	Maine**	NA		7	Louisiana	0.0
7	Maryland	0.0		7	Maryland	0.0
NA	Massachusetts**	NA		7	Mississippi	0.0
NA	Michigan**	NA		7	Missouri	0.0
NA	Minnesota**	NA		7	Montana	0.0
7	Mississippi	0.0		7	Nebraska	0.0
7	Missouri	0.0		7	Nevada	0.0
7	Montana	0.0		7	New Hampshire	0.0
7	Nebraska	0.0		7	New Mexico	0.0
7	Nevada	0.0		7	New York	0.0
7	New Hampshire	0.0		7	North Carolina	0.0
NA	New Jersey**	NA		7	Oklahoma	0.0
7	New Mexico	0.0		7	Oregon	0.0
7	New York	0.0		7	Pennsylvania	0.0
7	North Carolina	0.0		7	South Dakota	0.0
NA	North Dakota**	NA		7	Tennessee	0.0
3	Ohio	50.0		7	Utah	0.0
7	Oklahoma	0.0		7	Washington	0.0
7	Oregon	0.0		7	Wyoming	0.0
7	Pennsylvania	0.0		NA	Alaska**	NA
NA	Rhode Island**	NA		NA	Hawaii**	NA
2	South Carolina	66.7		NA	Iowa**	NA
7	South Dakota	0.0		NA	Maine**	NA
7	Tennessee	0.0		NA	Massachusetts**	NA
3	Texas	50.0		NA	Michigan**	NA
7	Utah	0.0		NA	Minnesota**	NA
NA	Vermont**	NA		NA	New Jersey**	NA
1	Virginia	75.0		NA	North Dakota**	NA
7	Washington	0.0		NA	Rhode Island**	NA
NA	West Virginia**	NA		NA	Vermont**	NA
NA	Wisconsin**	NA		NA	West Virginia**	NA
7	Wyoming	0.0		NA	Wisconsin**	NA
					District of Columbia**	NA

Source: CQ Press using data from U.S. Department of Justice, Bureau of Justice Statistics
    "Capital Punishment 2008" (Bulletin, December 2009, NCJ 228662, http://bjs.ojp.usdoj.gov/)
*There were no federal prisoners executed in 2008.
**No death penalty as of December 31, 2008.

Prisoners Executed: 1930 to 2008

National Total = 4,995 Prisoners*

ALPHA ORDER

RANK	STATE	EXECUTIONS	% of USA
10	Alabama	173	3.5%
43	Alaska	0	0.0%
22	Arizona	61	1.2%
15	Arkansas	145	2.9%
5	California	305	6.1%
25	Colorado	48	1.0%
30	Connecticut	22	0.4%
29	Delaware	26	0.5%
6	Florida	236	4.7%
2	Georgia	409	8.2%
43	Hawaii	0	0.0%
39	Idaho	4	0.1%
18	Illinois	102	2.0%
23	Indiana	60	1.2%
33	Iowa	18	0.4%
34	Kansas	15	0.3%
17	Kentucky	106	2.1%
12	Louisiana	160	3.2%
43	Maine	0	0.0%
21	Maryland	73	1.5%
28	Massachusetts	27	0.5%
43	Michigan	0	0.0%
43	Minnesota	0	0.0%
11	Mississippi	164	3.3%
16	Missouri	128	2.6%
35	Montana	9	0.2%
38	Nebraska	7	0.1%
26	Nevada	41	0.8%
42	New Hampshire	1	0.0%
20	New Jersey	74	1.5%
35	New Mexico	9	0.2%
3	New York	329	6.6%
4	North Carolina	306	6.1%
43	North Dakota	0	0.0%
8	Ohio	200	4.0%
14	Oklahoma	148	3.0%
31	Oregon	21	0.4%
13	Pennsylvania	155	3.1%
43	Rhode Island	0	0.0%
7	South Carolina	202	4.0%
41	South Dakota	2	0.0%
19	Tennessee	97	1.9%
1	Texas	720	14.4%
32	Utah	19	0.4%
39	Vermont	4	0.1%
9	Virginia	194	3.9%
24	Washington	51	1.0%
27	West Virginia	40	0.8%
43	Wisconsin	0	0.0%
37	Wyoming	8	0.2%

RANK ORDER

RANK	STATE	EXECUTIONS	% of USA
1	Texas	720	14.4%
2	Georgia	409	8.2%
3	New York	329	6.6%
4	North Carolina	306	6.1%
5	California	305	6.1%
6	Florida	236	4.7%
7	South Carolina	202	4.0%
8	Ohio	200	4.0%
9	Virginia	194	3.9%
10	Alabama	173	3.5%
11	Mississippi	164	3.3%
12	Louisiana	160	3.2%
13	Pennsylvania	155	3.1%
14	Oklahoma	148	3.0%
15	Arkansas	145	2.9%
16	Missouri	128	2.6%
17	Kentucky	106	2.1%
18	Illinois	102	2.0%
19	Tennessee	97	1.9%
20	New Jersey	74	1.5%
21	Maryland	73	1.5%
22	Arizona	61	1.2%
23	Indiana	60	1.2%
24	Washington	51	1.0%
25	Colorado	48	1.0%
26	Nevada	41	0.8%
27	West Virginia	40	0.8%
28	Massachusetts	27	0.5%
29	Delaware	26	0.5%
30	Connecticut	22	0.4%
31	Oregon	21	0.4%
32	Utah	19	0.4%
33	Iowa	18	0.4%
34	Kansas	15	0.3%
35	Montana	9	0.2%
35	New Mexico	9	0.2%
37	Wyoming	8	0.2%
38	Nebraska	7	0.1%
39	Idaho	4	0.1%
39	Vermont	4	0.1%
41	South Dakota	2	0.0%
42	New Hampshire	1	0.0%
43	Alaska	0	0.0%
43	Hawaii	0	0.0%
43	Maine	0	0.0%
43	Michigan	0	0.0%
43	Minnesota	0	0.0%
43	North Dakota	0	0.0%
43	Rhode Island	0	0.0%
43	Wisconsin	0	0.0%
	District of Columbia	40	0.8%

Source: U.S. Department of Justice, Bureau of Justice Statistics
"Capital Punishment 2008" (Bulletin, December 2009, NCJ 228662, http://bjs.ojp.usdoj.gov/)
*Includes 36 executions by the federal government. Does not include 160 executions carried out under military authority from 1930 to 1961. There were no executions from 1968 to 1976.

Prisoners Executed: 1977 to 2008

National Total = 1,136 Prisoners*

ALPHA ORDER				RANK ORDER			
RANK	STATE	EXECUTIONS	% of USA	RANK	STATE	EXECUTIONS	% of USA
9	Alabama	38	3.3%	1	Texas	423	37.2%
35	Alaska	0	0.0%	2	Virginia	102	9.0%
13	Arizona	23	2.0%	3	Oklahoma	88	7.7%
11	Arkansas	27	2.4%	4	Florida	66	5.8%
16	California	13	1.1%	4	Missouri	66	5.8%
29	Colorado	1	0.1%	6	Georgia	43	3.8%
29	Connecticut	1	0.1%	6	North Carolina	43	3.8%
15	Delaware	14	1.2%	8	South Carolina	40	3.5%
4	Florida	66	5.8%	9	Alabama	38	3.3%
6	Georgia	43	3.8%	10	Ohio	28	2.5%
35	Hawaii	0	0.0%	11	Arkansas	27	2.4%
29	Idaho	1	0.1%	11	Louisiana	27	2.4%
17	Illinois	12	1.1%	13	Arizona	23	2.0%
14	Indiana	19	1.7%	14	Indiana	19	1.7%
35	Iowa	0	0.0%	15	Delaware	14	1.2%
35	Kansas	0	0.0%	16	California	13	1.1%
24	Kentucky	3	0.3%	17	Illinois	12	1.1%
11	Louisiana	27	2.4%	17	Nevada	12	1.1%
35	Maine	0	0.0%	19	Mississippi	10	0.9%
21	Maryland	5	0.4%	20	Utah	6	0.5%
35	Massachusetts	0	0.0%	21	Maryland	5	0.4%
35	Michigan	0	0.0%	22	Tennessee	4	0.4%
35	Minnesota	0	0.0%	22	Washington	4	0.4%
19	Mississippi	10	0.9%	24	Kentucky	3	0.3%
4	Missouri	66	5.8%	24	Montana	3	0.3%
24	Montana	3	0.3%	24	Nebraska	3	0.3%
24	Nebraska	3	0.3%	24	Pennsylvania	3	0.3%
17	Nevada	12	1.1%	28	Oregon	2	0.2%
35	New Hampshire	0	0.0%	29	Colorado	1	0.1%
35	New Jersey	0	0.0%	29	Connecticut	1	0.1%
29	New Mexico	1	0.1%	29	Idaho	1	0.1%
35	New York	0	0.0%	29	New Mexico	1	0.1%
6	North Carolina	43	3.8%	29	South Dakota	1	0.1%
35	North Dakota	0	0.0%	29	Wyoming	1	0.1%
10	Ohio	28	2.5%	35	Alaska	0	0.0%
3	Oklahoma	88	7.7%	35	Hawaii	0	0.0%
28	Oregon	2	0.2%	35	Iowa	0	0.0%
24	Pennsylvania	3	0.3%	35	Kansas	0	0.0%
35	Rhode Island	0	0.0%	35	Maine	0	0.0%
8	South Carolina	40	3.5%	35	Massachusetts	0	0.0%
29	South Dakota	1	0.1%	35	Michigan	0	0.0%
22	Tennessee	4	0.4%	35	Minnesota	0	0.0%
1	Texas	423	37.2%	35	New Hampshire	0	0.0%
20	Utah	6	0.5%	35	New Jersey	0	0.0%
35	Vermont	0	0.0%	35	New York	0	0.0%
2	Virginia	102	9.0%	35	North Dakota	0	0.0%
22	Washington	4	0.4%	35	Rhode Island	0	0.0%
35	West Virginia	0	0.0%	35	Vermont	0	0.0%
35	Wisconsin	0	0.0%	35	West Virginia	0	0.0%
29	Wyoming	1	0.1%	35	Wisconsin	0	0.0%
					District of Columbia	0	0.0%

Source: U.S. Department of Justice, Bureau of Justice Statistics
"Capital Punishment 2008" (Bulletin, December 2009, NCJ 228662, http://bjs.ojp.usdoj.gov/)
*As of December 31, 2008. Includes three executions by the federal government. All executions since 1977 have been for murder. The most common method of executions was lethal injection (966), followed by electrocution (154), lethal gas (11), hanging (3), and firing squad (2).

State Prisoner Deaths in 2007

National Total = 3,388 Deaths*

ALPHA ORDER					RANK ORDER			
RANK	STATE	DEATHS	% of USA		RANK	STATE	DEATHS	% of USA
21	Alabama	54	1.6%		1	Texas	435	12.8%
41	Alaska	10	0.3%		2	California	395	11.7%
18	Arizona	61	1.8%		3	Florida	249	7.3%
23	Arkansas	46	1.4%		4	Pennsylvania	150	4.4%
2	California	395	11.7%		5	New York	148	4.4%
26	Colorado	42	1.2%		6	Georgia	143	4.2%
31	Connecticut	27	0.8%		7	Ohio	123	3.6%
36	Delaware	15	0.4%		8	Michigan	117	3.5%
3	Florida	249	7.3%		9	Illinois	104	3.1%
6	Georgia	143	4.2%		10	Virginia	103	3.0%
38	Hawaii	13	0.4%		11	North Carolina	99	2.9%
37	Idaho	14	0.4%		12	Oklahoma	98	2.9%
9	Illinois	104	3.1%		13	Louisiana	82	2.4%
21	Indiana	54	1.6%		14	Missouri	78	2.3%
35	Iowa	17	0.5%		15	Mississippi	76	2.2%
33	Kansas	20	0.6%		16	Tennessee	73	2.2%
23	Kentucky	46	1.4%		17	South Carolina	72	2.1%
13	Louisiana	82	2.4%		18	Arizona	61	1.8%
48	Maine	1	0.0%		19	New Jersey	60	1.8%
20	Maryland	57	1.7%		20	Maryland	57	1.7%
27	Massachusetts	39	1.2%		21	Alabama	54	1.6%
8	Michigan	117	3.5%		21	Indiana	54	1.6%
38	Minnesota	13	0.4%		23	Arkansas	46	1.4%
15	Mississippi	76	2.2%		23	Kentucky	46	1.4%
14	Missouri	78	2.3%		25	Wisconsin	43	1.3%
47	Montana	5	0.1%		26	Colorado	42	1.2%
40	Nebraska	12	0.4%		27	Massachusetts	39	1.2%
27	Nevada	39	1.2%		27	Nevada	39	1.2%
46	New Hampshire	6	0.2%		27	Washington	39	1.2%
19	New Jersey	60	1.8%		30	Oregon	36	1.1%
32	New Mexico	22	0.6%		31	Connecticut	27	0.8%
5	New York	148	4.4%		32	New Mexico	22	0.6%
11	North Carolina	99	2.9%		33	Kansas	20	0.6%
50	North Dakota	0	0.0%		34	West Virginia	19	0.6%
7	Ohio	123	3.6%		35	Iowa	17	0.5%
12	Oklahoma	98	2.9%		36	Delaware	15	0.4%
30	Oregon	36	1.1%		37	Idaho	14	0.4%
4	Pennsylvania	150	4.4%		38	Hawaii	13	0.4%
42	Rhode Island	9	0.3%		38	Minnesota	13	0.4%
17	South Carolina	72	2.1%		40	Nebraska	12	0.4%
43	South Dakota	8	0.2%		41	Alaska	10	0.3%
16	Tennessee	73	2.2%		42	Rhode Island	9	0.3%
1	Texas	435	12.8%		43	South Dakota	8	0.2%
45	Utah	7	0.2%		43	Wyoming	8	0.2%
48	Vermont	1	0.0%		45	Utah	7	0.2%
10	Virginia	103	3.0%		46	New Hampshire	6	0.2%
27	Washington	39	1.2%		47	Montana	5	0.1%
34	West Virginia	19	0.6%		48	Maine	1	0.0%
25	Wisconsin	43	1.3%		48	Vermont	1	0.0%
43	Wyoming	8	0.2%		50	North Dakota	0	0.0%
					District of Columbia**		NA	NA

Source: U.S. Department of Justice, Bureau of Justice Statistics
   "HIV in Prisons, 2007-08" (December 2009, NCJ 228307, http://bjs.ojp.usdoj.gov/)
*Does not include deaths of federal prisoners.
**Not available.

Death Rate of State Prisoners in 2007

National Rate = 242 State Prisoner Deaths per 100,000 Inmates*

<table>
<tr><td colspan="3">ALPHA ORDER</td><td colspan="3">RANK ORDER</td></tr>
<tr><td>RANK</td><td>STATE</td><td>RATE</td><td>RANK</td><td>STATE</td><td>RATE</td></tr>
<tr><td>40</td><td>Alabama</td><td>184</td><td>1</td><td>Wyoming</td><td>384</td></tr>
<tr><td>38</td><td>Alaska</td><td>194</td><td>2</td><td>Oklahoma</td><td>379</td></tr>
<tr><td>43</td><td>Arizona</td><td>162</td><td>3</td><td>Massachusetts</td><td>341</td></tr>
<tr><td>7</td><td>Arkansas</td><td>321</td><td>4</td><td>New Mexico</td><td>340</td></tr>
<tr><td>27</td><td>California</td><td>227</td><td>5</td><td>Mississippi</td><td>339</td></tr>
<tr><td>40</td><td>Colorado</td><td>184</td><td>6</td><td>Pennsylvania</td><td>326</td></tr>
<tr><td>46</td><td>Connecticut</td><td>129</td><td>7</td><td>Arkansas</td><td>321</td></tr>
<tr><td>33</td><td>Delaware</td><td>206</td><td>8</td><td>West Virginia</td><td>314</td></tr>
<tr><td>18</td><td>Florida</td><td>254</td><td>9</td><td>South Carolina</td><td>297</td></tr>
<tr><td>14</td><td>Georgia</td><td>264</td><td>10</td><td>Nevada</td><td>291</td></tr>
<tr><td>32</td><td>Hawaii</td><td>217</td><td>11</td><td>Tennessee</td><td>278</td></tr>
<tr><td>39</td><td>Idaho</td><td>191</td><td>12</td><td>Virginia</td><td>271</td></tr>
<tr><td>25</td><td>Illinois</td><td>230</td><td>13</td><td>Nebraska</td><td>266</td></tr>
<tr><td>36</td><td>Indiana</td><td>199</td><td>14</td><td>Georgia</td><td>264</td></tr>
<tr><td>37</td><td>Iowa</td><td>195</td><td>15</td><td>Missouri</td><td>261</td></tr>
<tr><td>25</td><td>Kansas</td><td>230</td><td>15</td><td>North Carolina</td><td>261</td></tr>
<tr><td>34</td><td>Kentucky</td><td>205</td><td>17</td><td>Oregon</td><td>258</td></tr>
<tr><td>31</td><td>Louisiana</td><td>218</td><td>18</td><td>Florida</td><td>254</td></tr>
<tr><td>49</td><td>Maine</td><td>45</td><td>19</td><td>Texas</td><td>253</td></tr>
<tr><td>20</td><td>Maryland</td><td>243</td><td>20</td><td>Maryland</td><td>243</td></tr>
<tr><td>3</td><td>Massachusetts</td><td>341</td><td>21</td><td>Ohio</td><td>242</td></tr>
<tr><td>24</td><td>Michigan</td><td>233</td><td>21</td><td>South Dakota</td><td>242</td></tr>
<tr><td>45</td><td>Minnesota</td><td>137</td><td>23</td><td>New York</td><td>236</td></tr>
<tr><td>5</td><td>Mississippi</td><td>339</td><td>24</td><td>Michigan</td><td>233</td></tr>
<tr><td>15</td><td>Missouri</td><td>261</td><td>25</td><td>Illinois</td><td>230</td></tr>
<tr><td>44</td><td>Montana</td><td>144</td><td>25</td><td>Kansas</td><td>230</td></tr>
<tr><td>13</td><td>Nebraska</td><td>266</td><td>27</td><td>California</td><td>227</td></tr>
<tr><td>10</td><td>Nevada</td><td>291</td><td>28</td><td>New Jersey</td><td>224</td></tr>
<tr><td>35</td><td>New Hampshire</td><td>204</td><td>28</td><td>Rhode Island</td><td>224</td></tr>
<tr><td>28</td><td>New Jersey</td><td>224</td><td>30</td><td>Washington</td><td>219</td></tr>
<tr><td>4</td><td>New Mexico</td><td>340</td><td>31</td><td>Louisiana</td><td>218</td></tr>
<tr><td>23</td><td>New York</td><td>236</td><td>32</td><td>Hawaii</td><td>217</td></tr>
<tr><td>15</td><td>North Carolina</td><td>261</td><td>33</td><td>Delaware</td><td>206</td></tr>
<tr><td>50</td><td>North Dakota</td><td>0</td><td>34</td><td>Kentucky</td><td>205</td></tr>
<tr><td>21</td><td>Ohio</td><td>242</td><td>35</td><td>New Hampshire</td><td>204</td></tr>
<tr><td>2</td><td>Oklahoma</td><td>379</td><td>36</td><td>Indiana</td><td>199</td></tr>
<tr><td>17</td><td>Oregon</td><td>258</td><td>37</td><td>Iowa</td><td>195</td></tr>
<tr><td>6</td><td>Pennsylvania</td><td>326</td><td>38</td><td>Alaska</td><td>194</td></tr>
<tr><td>28</td><td>Rhode Island</td><td>224</td><td>39</td><td>Idaho</td><td>191</td></tr>
<tr><td>9</td><td>South Carolina</td><td>297</td><td>40</td><td>Alabama</td><td>184</td></tr>
<tr><td>21</td><td>South Dakota</td><td>242</td><td>40</td><td>Colorado</td><td>184</td></tr>
<tr><td>11</td><td>Tennessee</td><td>278</td><td>42</td><td>Wisconsin</td><td>181</td></tr>
<tr><td>19</td><td>Texas</td><td>253</td><td>43</td><td>Arizona</td><td>162</td></tr>
<tr><td>47</td><td>Utah</td><td>108</td><td>44</td><td>Montana</td><td>144</td></tr>
<tr><td>48</td><td>Vermont</td><td>47</td><td>45</td><td>Minnesota</td><td>137</td></tr>
<tr><td>12</td><td>Virginia</td><td>271</td><td>46</td><td>Connecticut</td><td>129</td></tr>
<tr><td>30</td><td>Washington</td><td>219</td><td>47</td><td>Utah</td><td>108</td></tr>
<tr><td>8</td><td>West Virginia</td><td>314</td><td>48</td><td>Vermont</td><td>47</td></tr>
<tr><td>42</td><td>Wisconsin</td><td>181</td><td>49</td><td>Maine</td><td>45</td></tr>
<tr><td>1</td><td>Wyoming</td><td>384</td><td>50</td><td>North Dakota</td><td>0</td></tr>
<tr><td></td><td></td><td></td><td></td><td>District of Columbia**</td><td>NA</td></tr>
</table>

Source: CQ Press using data from U.S. Department of Justice, Bureau of Justice Statistics
  "HIV in Prisons, 2007-08" (December 2009, NCJ 228307, http://bjs.ojp.usdoj.gov/)
*Does not include deaths of federal prisoners.
**Not available.

AIDS-Related Deaths of State Prisoners in 2007

National Total = 120 Deaths

ALPHA ORDER

RANK	STATE	DEATHS	% of USA
18	Alabama	2	1.7%
33	Alaska	0	0.0%
12	Arizona	3	2.5%
12	Arkansas	3	2.5%
12	California	3	2.5%
33	Colorado	0	0.0%
25	Connecticut	1	0.8%
33	Delaware	0	0.0%
1	Florida	14	11.7%
6	Georgia	6	5.0%
25	Hawaii	1	0.8%
33	Idaho	0	0.0%
6	Illinois	6	5.0%
18	Indiana	2	1.7%
33	Iowa	0	0.0%
33	Kansas	0	0.0%
18	Kentucky	2	1.7%
25	Louisiana	1	0.8%
33	Maine	0	0.0%
4	Maryland	8	6.7%
33	Massachusetts	0	0.0%
10	Michigan	4	3.3%
33	Minnesota	0	0.0%
18	Mississippi	2	1.7%
18	Missouri	2	1.7%
33	Montana	0	0.0%
33	Nebraska	0	0.0%
18	Nevada	2	1.7%
25	New Hampshire	1	0.8%
5	New Jersey	7	5.8%
33	New Mexico	0	0.0%
2	New York	11	9.2%
8	North Carolina	5	4.2%
33	North Dakota	0	0.0%
12	Ohio	3	2.5%
25	Oklahoma	1	0.8%
33	Oregon	0	0.0%
8	Pennsylvania	5	4.2%
25	Rhode Island	1	0.8%
10	South Carolina	4	3.3%
33	South Dakota	0	0.0%
12	Tennessee	3	2.5%
3	Texas	10	8.3%
33	Utah	0	0.0%
33	Vermont	0	0.0%
12	Virginia	3	2.5%
18	Washington	2	1.7%
25	West Virginia	1	0.8%
25	Wisconsin	1	0.8%
33	Wyoming	0	0.0%

RANK ORDER

RANK	STATE	DEATHS	% of USA
1	Florida	14	11.7%
2	New York	11	9.2%
3	Texas	10	8.3%
4	Maryland	8	6.7%
5	New Jersey	7	5.8%
6	Georgia	6	5.0%
6	Illinois	6	5.0%
8	North Carolina	5	4.2%
8	Pennsylvania	5	4.2%
10	Michigan	4	3.3%
10	South Carolina	4	3.3%
12	Arizona	3	2.5%
12	Arkansas	3	2.5%
12	California	3	2.5%
12	Ohio	3	2.5%
12	Tennessee	3	2.5%
12	Virginia	3	2.5%
18	Alabama	2	1.7%
18	Indiana	2	1.7%
18	Kentucky	2	1.7%
18	Mississippi	2	1.7%
18	Missouri	2	1.7%
18	Nevada	2	1.7%
18	Washington	2	1.7%
25	Connecticut	1	0.8%
25	Hawaii	1	0.8%
25	Louisiana	1	0.8%
25	New Hampshire	1	0.8%
25	Oklahoma	1	0.8%
25	Rhode Island	1	0.8%
25	West Virginia	1	0.8%
25	Wisconsin	1	0.8%
33	Alaska	0	0.0%
33	Colorado	0	0.0%
33	Delaware	0	0.0%
33	Idaho	0	0.0%
33	Iowa	0	0.0%
33	Kansas	0	0.0%
33	Maine	0	0.0%
33	Massachusetts	0	0.0%
33	Minnesota	0	0.0%
33	Montana	0	0.0%
33	Nebraska	0	0.0%
33	New Mexico	0	0.0%
33	North Dakota	0	0.0%
33	Oregon	0	0.0%
33	South Dakota	0	0.0%
33	Utah	0	0.0%
33	Vermont	0	0.0%
33	Wyoming	0	0.0%
	District of Columbia*	NA	NA

Source: U.S. Department of Justice, Bureau of Justice Statistics
  "HIV in Prisons, 2007-08" (December 2009, NCJ 228307, http://bjs.ojp.usdoj.gov/)
*Not available.

AIDS-Related Death Rate for State Prisoners in 2007

National Rate = 9 State Prisoner Deaths per 100,000 Inmates

ALPHA ORDER

RANK	STATE	RATE
21	Alabama	8
33	Alaska	0
21	Arizona	8
5	Arkansas	23
32	California	2
33	Colorado	0
28	Connecticut	5
33	Delaware	0
10	Florida	15
17	Georgia	11
7	Hawaii	18
33	Idaho	0
13	Illinois	13
21	Indiana	8
33	Iowa	0
33	Kansas	0
13	Kentucky	13
28	Louisiana	5
33	Maine	0
1	Maryland	35
33	Massachusetts	0
21	Michigan	8
33	Minnesota	0
16	Mississippi	12
25	Missouri	7
33	Montana	0
33	Nebraska	0
10	Nevada	15
2	New Hampshire	34
3	New Jersey	27
33	New Mexico	0
8	New York	17
13	North Carolina	13
33	North Dakota	0
26	Ohio	6
30	Oklahoma	4
33	Oregon	0
17	Pennsylvania	11
4	Rhode Island	26
8	South Carolina	17
33	South Dakota	0
10	Tennessee	15
26	Texas	6
33	Utah	0
33	Vermont	0
20	Virginia	9
17	Washington	11
6	West Virginia	22
30	Wisconsin	4
33	Wyoming	0

RANK ORDER

RANK	STATE	RATE
1	Maryland	35
2	New Hampshire	34
3	New Jersey	27
4	Rhode Island	26
5	Arkansas	23
6	West Virginia	22
7	Hawaii	18
8	New York	17
8	South Carolina	17
10	Florida	15
10	Nevada	15
10	Tennessee	15
13	Illinois	13
13	Kentucky	13
13	North Carolina	13
16	Mississippi	12
17	Georgia	11
17	Pennsylvania	11
17	Washington	11
20	Virginia	9
21	Alabama	8
21	Arizona	8
21	Indiana	8
21	Michigan	8
25	Missouri	7
26	Ohio	6
26	Texas	6
28	Connecticut	5
28	Louisiana	5
30	Oklahoma	4
30	Wisconsin	4
32	California	2
33	Alaska	0
33	Colorado	0
33	Delaware	0
33	Idaho	0
33	Iowa	0
33	Kansas	0
33	Maine	0
33	Massachusetts	0
33	Minnesota	0
33	Montana	0
33	Nebraska	0
33	New Mexico	0
33	North Dakota	0
33	Oregon	0
33	South Dakota	0
33	Utah	0
33	Vermont	0
33	Wyoming	0
	District of Columbia*	NA

Source: U.S. Department of Justice, Bureau of Justice Statistics
  "HIV in Prisons, 2007-08" (December 2009, NCJ 228307, http://bjs.ojp.usdoj.gov/)
*Not available.

AIDS-Related Deaths of State Prisoners
as a Percent of All Prison Deaths in 2007
National Percent = 3.5% of Deaths

ALPHA ORDER

RANK	STATE	PERCENT
19	Alabama	3.7
33	Alaska	0.0
15	Arizona	4.9
7	Arkansas	6.5
32	California	0.8
33	Colorado	0.0
19	Connecticut	3.7
33	Delaware	0.0
9	Florida	5.6
17	Georgia	4.2
5	Hawaii	7.7
33	Idaho	0.0
8	Illinois	5.8
19	Indiana	3.7
33	Iowa	0.0
33	Kansas	0.0
16	Kentucky	4.3
30	Louisiana	1.2
33	Maine	0.0
2	Maryland	14.0
33	Massachusetts	0.0
22	Michigan	3.4
33	Minnesota	0.0
25	Mississippi	2.6
25	Missouri	2.6
33	Montana	0.0
33	Nebraska	0.0
12	Nevada	5.1
1	New Hampshire	16.7
3	New Jersey	11.7
33	New Mexico	0.0
6	New York	7.4
12	North Carolina	5.1
33	North Dakota	0.0
27	Ohio	2.4
31	Oklahoma	1.0
33	Oregon	0.0
23	Pennsylvania	3.3
4	Rhode Island	11.1
9	South Carolina	5.6
33	South Dakota	0.0
18	Tennessee	4.1
28	Texas	2.3
33	Utah	0.0
33	Vermont	0.0
24	Virginia	2.9
12	Washington	5.1
11	West Virginia	5.3
28	Wisconsin	2.3
33	Wyoming	0.0

RANK ORDER

RANK	STATE	PERCENT
1	New Hampshire	16.7
2	Maryland	14.0
3	New Jersey	11.7
4	Rhode Island	11.1
5	Hawaii	7.7
6	New York	7.4
7	Arkansas	6.5
8	Illinois	5.8
9	Florida	5.6
9	South Carolina	5.6
11	West Virginia	5.3
12	Nevada	5.1
12	North Carolina	5.1
12	Washington	5.1
15	Arizona	4.9
16	Kentucky	4.3
17	Georgia	4.2
18	Tennessee	4.1
19	Alabama	3.7
19	Connecticut	3.7
19	Indiana	3.7
22	Michigan	3.4
23	Pennsylvania	3.3
24	Virginia	2.9
25	Mississippi	2.6
25	Missouri	2.6
27	Ohio	2.4
28	Texas	2.3
28	Wisconsin	2.3
30	Louisiana	1.2
31	Oklahoma	1.0
32	California	0.8
33	Alaska	0.0
33	Colorado	0.0
33	Delaware	0.0
33	Idaho	0.0
33	Iowa	0.0
33	Kansas	0.0
33	Maine	0.0
33	Massachusetts	0.0
33	Minnesota	0.0
33	Montana	0.0
33	Nebraska	0.0
33	New Mexico	0.0
33	North Dakota	0.0
33	Oregon	0.0
33	South Dakota	0.0
33	Utah	0.0
33	Vermont	0.0
33	Wyoming	0.0
	District of Columbia*	NA

Source: CQ Press using data from U.S. Department of Justice, Bureau of Justice Statistics
   "HIV in Prisons, 2007-08" (December 2009, NCJ 228307, http://bjs.ojp.usdoj.gov/)
*Not available.

State Prisoners Known to Be Positive for HIV Infection/AIDS in 2008

National Total = 20,606 Inmates*

<u>ALPHA ORDER</u>

RANK	STATE	PRISONERS	% of USA
18	Alabama	275	1.3%
44	Alaska	13	0.1%
22	Arizona	179	0.9%
28	Arkansas	118	0.6%
4	California	1,402	6.8%
23	Colorado	173	0.8%
16	Connecticut	380	1.8%
25	Delaware	132	0.6%
1	Florida	3,626	17.6%
5	Georgia	961	4.7%
40	Hawaii	23	0.1%
38	Idaho	28	0.1%
12	Illinois	457	2.2%
NA	Indiana**	NA	NA
35	Iowa	41	0.2%
33	Kansas	46	0.2%
27	Kentucky	131	0.6%
11	Louisiana	458	2.2%
46	Maine	9	0.0%
8	Maryland	588	2.9%
19	Massachusetts	264	1.3%
17	Michigan	341	1.7%
34	Minnesota	44	0.2%
20	Mississippi	246	1.2%
10	Missouri	461	2.2%
47	Montana	6	0.0%
41	Nebraska	16	0.1%
29	Nevada	116	0.6%
41	New Hampshire	16	0.1%
9	New Jersey	520	2.5%
37	New Mexico	33	0.2%
2	New York	3,500	17.0%
6	North Carolina	824	4.0%
47	North Dakota	6	0.0%
14	Ohio	414	2.0%
24	Oklahoma	139	0.7%
31	Oregon	55	0.3%
7	Pennsylvania	727	3.5%
32	Rhode Island	54	0.3%
15	South Carolina	409	2.0%
44	South Dakota	13	0.1%
21	Tennessee	188	0.9%
3	Texas	2,450	11.9%
36	Utah	36	0.2%
43	Vermont	14	0.1%
13	Virginia	433	2.1%
30	Washington	79	0.4%
39	West Virginia	25	0.1%
25	Wisconsin	132	0.6%
49	Wyoming	5	0.0%

<u>RANK ORDER</u>

RANK	STATE	PRISONERS	% of USA
1	Florida	3,626	17.6%
2	New York	3,500	17.0%
3	Texas	2,450	11.9%
4	California	1,402	6.8%
5	Georgia	961	4.7%
6	North Carolina	824	4.0%
7	Pennsylvania	727	3.5%
8	Maryland	588	2.9%
9	New Jersey	520	2.5%
10	Missouri	461	2.2%
11	Louisiana	458	2.2%
12	Illinois	457	2.2%
13	Virginia	433	2.1%
14	Ohio	414	2.0%
15	South Carolina	409	2.0%
16	Connecticut	380	1.8%
17	Michigan	341	1.7%
18	Alabama	275	1.3%
19	Massachusetts	264	1.3%
20	Mississippi	246	1.2%
21	Tennessee	188	0.9%
22	Arizona	179	0.9%
23	Colorado	173	0.8%
24	Oklahoma	139	0.7%
25	Delaware	132	0.6%
25	Wisconsin	132	0.6%
27	Kentucky	131	0.6%
28	Arkansas	118	0.6%
29	Nevada	116	0.6%
30	Washington	79	0.4%
31	Oregon	55	0.3%
32	Rhode Island	54	0.3%
33	Kansas	46	0.2%
34	Minnesota	44	0.2%
35	Iowa	41	0.2%
36	Utah	36	0.2%
37	New Mexico	33	0.2%
38	Idaho	28	0.1%
39	West Virginia	25	0.1%
40	Hawaii	23	0.1%
41	Nebraska	16	0.1%
41	New Hampshire	16	0.1%
43	Vermont	14	0.1%
44	Alaska	13	0.1%
44	South Dakota	13	0.1%
46	Maine	9	0.0%
47	Montana	6	0.0%
47	North Dakota	6	0.0%
49	Wyoming	5	0.0%
NA	Indiana**	NA	NA
	District of Columbia**	NA	NA

Source: U.S. Department of Justice, Bureau of Justice Statistics
   "HIV in Prisons, 2007-08" (December 2009, NCJ 228307, http://bjs.ojp.usdoj.gov/)
*As of December 31, 2008. Does not include 1,538 positive federal inmates.
**Not available. The District of Columbia prisoners are included in the federal figures.

State Prisoners Known to Be Positive for HIV Infection/AIDS as a Percent of Total Prison Population in 2008
National Percent = 1.6% of State Prisoners*

RANK	STATE	PERCENT
18	Alabama	1.1
47	Alaska	0.3
33	Arizona	0.5
21	Arkansas	0.9
24	California	0.8
26	Colorado	0.7
8	Connecticut	2.0
9	Delaware	1.9
2	Florida	3.6
10	Georgia	1.8
39	Hawaii	0.4
39	Idaho	0.4
19	Illinois	1.0
NA	Indiana**	NA
33	Iowa	0.5
33	Kansas	0.5
21	Kentucky	0.9
5	Louisiana	2.2
39	Maine	0.4
3	Maryland	2.5
4	Massachusetts	2.4
26	Michigan	0.7
33	Minnesota	0.5
15	Mississippi	1.4
13	Missouri	1.5
49	Montana	0.2
39	Nebraska	0.4
21	Nevada	0.9
30	New Hampshire	0.6
6	New Jersey	2.1
33	New Mexico	0.5
1	New York	5.8
6	North Carolina	2.1
39	North Dakota	0.4
24	Ohio	0.8
30	Oklahoma	0.6
39	Oregon	0.4
12	Pennsylvania	1.6
15	Rhode Island	1.4
11	South Carolina	1.7
39	South Dakota	0.4
19	Tennessee	1.0
13	Texas	1.5
26	Utah	0.7
26	Vermont	0.7
17	Virginia	1.3
39	Washington	0.4
33	West Virginia	0.5
30	Wisconsin	0.6
47	Wyoming	0.3

RANK	STATE	PERCENT
1	New York	5.8
2	Florida	3.6
3	Maryland	2.5
4	Massachusetts	2.4
5	Louisiana	2.2
6	New Jersey	2.1
6	North Carolina	2.1
8	Connecticut	2.0
9	Delaware	1.9
10	Georgia	1.8
11	South Carolina	1.7
12	Pennsylvania	1.6
13	Missouri	1.5
13	Texas	1.5
15	Mississippi	1.4
15	Rhode Island	1.4
17	Virginia	1.3
18	Alabama	1.1
19	Illinois	1.0
19	Tennessee	1.0
21	Arkansas	0.9
21	Kentucky	0.9
21	Nevada	0.9
24	California	0.8
24	Ohio	0.8
26	Colorado	0.7
26	Michigan	0.7
26	Utah	0.7
26	Vermont	0.7
30	New Hampshire	0.6
30	Oklahoma	0.6
30	Wisconsin	0.6
33	Arizona	0.5
33	Iowa	0.5
33	Kansas	0.5
33	Minnesota	0.5
33	New Mexico	0.5
33	West Virginia	0.5
39	Hawaii	0.4
39	Idaho	0.4
39	Maine	0.4
39	Nebraska	0.4
39	North Dakota	0.4
39	Oregon	0.4
39	South Dakota	0.4
39	Washington	0.4
47	Alaska	0.3
47	Wyoming	0.3
49	Montana	0.2
NA	Indiana**	NA
	District of Columbia**	NA

Source: U.S. Department of Justice, Bureau of Justice Statistics

"HIV in Prisons, 2007-08" (December 2009, NCJ 228307, http://bjs.ojp.usdoj.gov/)

*Federal rate is 0.8%. The combined state and federal rate is 1.5%.

**Not available.

Allegations of Sexual Violence in State Prisons: 2006

National Total = 4,516 Allegations*

ALPHA ORDER					RANK ORDER			
RANK	STATE		ALLEGATIONS	% of USA	RANK	STATE	ALLEGATIONS	% of USA
41	Alabama		9	0.2%	1	Texas	725	16.1%
49	Alaska		0	0.0%	2	Florida	463	10.3%
16	Arizona		73	1.6%	3	Michigan	415	9.2%
27	Arkansas		41	0.9%	4	New York	293	6.5%
7	California		166	3.7%	5	Georgia	259	5.7%
14	Colorado		95	2.1%	6	Ohio	211	4.7%
29	Connecticut		34	0.8%	7	California	166	3.7%
40	Delaware		10	0.2%	8	Louisiana	163	3.6%
2	Florida		463	10.3%	9	Missouri	158	3.5%
5	Georgia		259	5.7%	10	Iowa	141	3.1%
47	Hawaii		2	0.0%	11	Massachusetts	126	2.8%
22	Idaho		51	1.1%	12	Kansas	105	2.3%
18	Illinois		61	1.4%	13	Wisconsin	102	2.3%
15	Indiana		84	1.9%	14	Colorado	95	2.1%
10	Iowa		141	3.1%	15	Indiana	84	1.9%
12	Kansas		105	2.3%	16	Arizona	73	1.6%
35	Kentucky		23	0.5%	17	Washington	69	1.5%
8	Louisiana		163	3.6%	18	Illinois	61	1.4%
46	Maine		4	0.1%	19	Vermont	58	1.3%
29	Maryland		34	0.8%	19	Virginia	58	1.3%
11	Massachusetts		126	2.8%	21	Pennsylvania	55	1.2%
3	Michigan		415	9.2%	22	Idaho	51	1.1%
26	Minnesota		42	0.9%	23	Oregon	47	1.0%
44	Mississippi		6	0.1%	24	Tennessee	45	1.0%
9	Missouri		158	3.5%	25	Oklahoma	44	1.0%
36	Montana		20	0.4%	26	Minnesota	42	0.9%
34	Nebraska		29	0.6%	27	Arkansas	41	0.9%
31	Nevada		32	0.7%	28	Utah	38	0.8%
38	New Hampshire		13	0.3%	29	Connecticut	34	0.8%
45	New Jersey		5	0.1%	29	Maryland	34	0.8%
49	New Mexico		0	0.0%	31	Nevada	32	0.7%
4	New York		293	6.5%	32	North Carolina	31	0.7%
32	North Carolina		31	0.7%	32	Wyoming	31	0.7%
39	North Dakota		12	0.3%	34	Nebraska	29	0.6%
6	Ohio		211	4.7%	35	Kentucky	23	0.5%
25	Oklahoma		44	1.0%	36	Montana	20	0.4%
23	Oregon		47	1.0%	37	Rhode Island	14	0.3%
21	Pennsylvania		55	1.2%	38	New Hampshire	13	0.3%
37	Rhode Island		14	0.3%	39	North Dakota	12	0.3%
47	South Carolina		2	0.0%	40	Delaware	10	0.2%
41	South Dakota		9	0.2%	41	Alabama	9	0.2%
24	Tennessee		45	1.0%	41	South Dakota	9	0.2%
1	Texas		725	16.1%	43	West Virginia	8	0.2%
28	Utah		38	0.8%	44	Mississippi	6	0.1%
19	Vermont		58	1.3%	45	New Jersey	5	0.1%
19	Virginia		58	1.3%	46	Maine	4	0.1%
17	Washington		69	1.5%	47	Hawaii	2	0.0%
43	West Virginia		8	0.2%	47	South Carolina	2	0.0%
13	Wisconsin		102	2.3%	49	Alaska	0	0.0%
32	Wyoming		31	0.7%	49	New Mexico	0	0.0%
						District of Columbia**	NA	NA

Source: CQ Press using data from U.S. Department of Justice, Bureau of Justice Statistics
   "Sexual Violence Reported by Correctional Authorities, 2006" (August 2007, NCJ 218914, www.ojp.usdoj.gov/bjs/prisons.htm)
*As of December 31, 2006. Does not include 242 allegations in federal prisons. Includes all allegations of inmate-on-inmate as well as staff-on-inmate sexual violence. Includes allegations that are substantiated, unsubstantiated, unfounded, and where the investigation is ongoing. Inmate-on-inmate sexual violence includes nonconsensual sexual acts and abusive sexual contacts. Staff-on-inmate sexual violence includes sexual misconduct and sexual harassment with inmates. **Not available.

Rate of Allegations of Sexual Violence in State Prisons: 2006

National Rate = 3.7 Allegations per 1,000 Prisoners*

ALPHA ORDER

RANK	STATE	RATE
46	Alabama	0.4
49	Alaska	0.0
32	Arizona	2.4
27	Arkansas	3.2
42	California	1.0
15	Colorado	5.5
37	Connecticut	1.7
39	Delaware	1.4
13	Florida	5.6
13	Georgia	5.6
44	Hawaii	0.5
6	Idaho	10.8
40	Illinois	1.3
25	Indiana	3.7
3	Iowa	16.3
5	Kansas	11.7
36	Kentucky	1.8
8	Louisiana	9.4
33	Maine	2.0
38	Maryland	1.5
4	Massachusetts	11.8
10	Michigan	8.2
16	Minnesota	5.2
44	Mississippi	0.5
16	Missouri	5.2
7	Montana	10.2
12	Nebraska	6.4
29	Nevada	2.6
16	New Hampshire	5.2
47	New Jersey	0.2
49	New Mexico	0.0
21	New York	4.6
43	North Carolina	0.8
9	North Dakota	8.8
20	Ohio	4.7
29	Oklahoma	2.6
26	Oregon	3.6
40	Pennsylvania	1.3
24	Rhode Island	3.8
48	South Carolina	0.1
31	South Dakota	2.5
27	Tennessee	3.2
16	Texas	5.2
11	Utah	7.6
1	Vermont	34.6
33	Virginia	2.0
23	Washington	4.5
35	West Virginia	1.9
21	Wisconsin	4.6
2	Wyoming	25.2

RANK ORDER

RANK	STATE	RATE
1	Vermont	34.6
2	Wyoming	25.2
3	Iowa	16.3
4	Massachusetts	11.8
5	Kansas	11.7
6	Idaho	10.8
7	Montana	10.2
8	Louisiana	9.4
9	North Dakota	8.8
10	Michigan	8.2
11	Utah	7.6
12	Nebraska	6.4
13	Florida	5.6
13	Georgia	5.6
15	Colorado	5.5
16	Minnesota	5.2
16	Missouri	5.2
16	New Hampshire	5.2
16	Texas	5.2
20	Ohio	4.7
21	New York	4.6
21	Wisconsin	4.6
23	Washington	4.5
24	Rhode Island	3.8
25	Indiana	3.7
26	Oregon	3.6
27	Arkansas	3.2
27	Tennessee	3.2
29	Nevada	2.6
29	Oklahoma	2.6
31	South Dakota	2.5
32	Arizona	2.4
33	Maine	2.0
33	Virginia	2.0
35	West Virginia	1.9
36	Kentucky	1.8
37	Connecticut	1.7
38	Maryland	1.5
39	Delaware	1.4
40	Illinois	1.3
40	Pennsylvania	1.3
42	California	1.0
43	North Carolina	0.8
44	Hawaii	0.5
44	Mississippi	0.5
46	Alabama	0.4
47	New Jersey	0.2
48	South Carolina	0.1
49	Alaska	0.0
49	New Mexico	0.0
	District of Columbia**	NA

Source: CQ Press using data from U.S. Department of Justice, Bureau of Justice Statistics
"Sexual Violence Reported by Correctional Authorities, 2006" (August 2007, NCJ 218914, www.ojp.usdoj.gov/bjs/prisons.htm)
*As of December 31, 2006. Does not include 242 allegations in federal prisons. Includes all allegations of inmate-on-inmate as well as staff-on-inmate sexual violence. Includes allegations that are substantiated, unsubstantiated, unfounded, and where the investigation is ongoing. Inmate-on-inmate sexual violence includes nonconsensual sexual acts and abusive sexual contacts. Staff-on-inmate sexual violence includes sexual misconduct and sexual harassment with inmates. **Not available.

Adults Under State Community Supervision in 2008

National Total = 4,973,804 Adults*

ALPHA ORDER

RANK	STATE	ADULTS	% of USA		RANK	STATE	ADULTS	% of USA
25	Alabama	61,294	1.2%		1	Texas	530,001	10.7%
45	Alaska	8,440	0.2%		2	California	445,822	9.0%
18	Arizona	89,766	1.8%		3	Georgia	420,529	8.5%
29	Arkansas	51,077	1.0%		4	Florida	284,288	5.7%
2	California	445,822	9.0%		5	Ohio	280,081	5.6%
17	Colorado	100,566	2.0%		6	Pennsylvania	259,924	5.2%
26	Connecticut	58,878	1.2%		7	Michigan	198,114	4.0%
39	Delaware	17,767	0.4%		8	Massachusetts	187,493	3.8%
4	Florida	284,288	5.7%		9	Illinois	178,587	3.6%
3	Georgia	420,529	8.5%		10	New York	171,630	3.5%
37	Hawaii	21,001	0.4%		11	New Jersey	144,586	2.9%
28	Idaho	52,874	1.1%		12	Indiana	141,928	2.9%
9	Illinois	178,587	3.6%		13	Minnesota	132,708	2.7%
12	Indiana	141,928	2.9%		14	Washington	124,902	2.5%
33	Iowa	26,117	0.5%		15	North Carolina	112,676	2.3%
36	Kansas	21,221	0.4%		16	Maryland	109,580	2.2%
24	Kentucky	63,004	1.3%		17	Colorado	100,566	2.0%
22	Louisiana	64,589	1.3%		18	Arizona	89,766	1.8%
47	Maine	7,535	0.2%		19	Missouri	78,043	1.6%
16	Maryland	109,580	2.2%		20	Tennessee	68,633	1.4%
8	Massachusetts	187,493	3.8%		21	Wisconsin	66,784	1.3%
7	Michigan	198,114	4.0%		22	Louisiana	64,589	1.3%
13	Minnesota	132,708	2.7%		23	Oregon	64,083	1.3%
34	Mississippi	25,189	0.5%		24	Kentucky	63,004	1.3%
19	Missouri	78,043	1.6%		25	Alabama	61,294	1.2%
43	Montana	9,957	0.2%		26	Connecticut	58,878	1.2%
38	Nebraska	20,452	0.4%		27	Virginia	58,085	1.2%
40	Nevada	17,245	0.3%		28	Idaho	52,874	1.1%
48	New Hampshire	6,210	0.1%		29	Arkansas	51,077	1.0%
11	New Jersey	144,586	2.9%		30	South Carolina	43,201	0.9%
35	New Mexico	23,609	0.5%		31	Oklahoma	31,013	0.6%
10	New York	171,630	3.5%		32	Rhode Island	27,269	0.5%
15	North Carolina	112,676	2.3%		33	Iowa	26,117	0.5%
50	North Dakota	4,617	0.1%		34	Mississippi	25,189	0.5%
5	Ohio	280,081	5.6%		35	New Mexico	23,609	0.5%
31	Oklahoma	31,013	0.6%		36	Kansas	21,221	0.4%
23	Oregon	64,083	1.3%		37	Hawaii	21,001	0.4%
6	Pennsylvania	259,924	5.2%		38	Nebraska	20,452	0.4%
32	Rhode Island	27,269	0.5%		39	Delaware	17,767	0.4%
30	South Carolina	43,201	0.9%		40	Nevada	17,245	0.3%
44	South Dakota	8,866	0.2%		41	Utah	14,704	0.3%
20	Tennessee	68,633	1.4%		42	West Virginia	10,288	0.2%
1	Texas	530,001	10.7%		43	Montana	9,957	0.2%
41	Utah	14,704	0.3%		44	South Dakota	8,866	0.2%
46	Vermont	8,020	0.2%		45	Alaska	8,440	0.2%
27	Virginia	58,085	1.2%		46	Vermont	8,020	0.2%
14	Washington	124,902	2.5%		47	Maine	7,535	0.2%
42	West Virginia	10,288	0.2%		48	New Hampshire	6,210	0.1%
21	Wisconsin	66,784	1.3%		49	Wyoming	6,153	0.1%
49	Wyoming	6,153	0.1%		50	North Dakota	4,617	0.1%
						District of Columbia	14,405	0.3%

Source: U.S. Department of Justice, Bureau of Justice Statistics
   "Probation and Parole in the United States, 2008" (December 2009, NCJ 228230, http://bjs.ojp.usdoj.gov/)
*As of December 31, 2008. "Community supervision" includes probation and parole. National total does not include 121,377 adults under federal community supervision.

Rate of Adults Under State Community Supervision in 2008

National Rate = 2,201 Adults per 100,000 Adult Population*

ALPHA ORDER

RANK	STATE	RATE
26	Alabama	1,723
27	Alaska	1,653
23	Arizona	1,856
15	Arkansas	2,361
29	California	1,616
10	Colorado	2,667
16	Connecticut	2,181
11	Delaware	2,645
20	Florida	1,976
1	Georgia	5,846
19	Hawaii	2,078
2	Idaho	4,714
24	Illinois	1,828
8	Indiana	2,948
40	Iowa	1,136
43	Kansas	1,004
22	Kentucky	1,924
21	Louisiana	1,945
48	Maine	721
13	Maryland	2,543
3	Massachusetts	3,683
12	Michigan	2,600
4	Minnesota	3,329
39	Mississippi	1,154
25	Missouri	1,730
37	Montana	1,323
33	Nebraska	1,523
46	Nevada	884
50	New Hampshire	604
18	New Jersey	2,170
31	New Mexico	1,580
41	New York	1,134
30	North Carolina	1,599
45	North Dakota	922
6	Ohio	3,191
42	Oklahoma	1,127
17	Oregon	2,177
9	Pennsylvania	2,676
5	Rhode Island	3,313
38	South Carolina	1,254
35	South Dakota	1,453
36	Tennessee	1,440
7	Texas	2,979
47	Utah	770
28	Vermont	1,624
44	Virginia	971
14	Washington	2,473
49	West Virginia	719
32	Wisconsin	1,541
34	Wyoming	1,508

RANK ORDER

RANK	STATE	RATE
1	Georgia	5,846
2	Idaho	4,714
3	Massachusetts	3,683
4	Minnesota	3,329
5	Rhode Island	3,313
6	Ohio	3,191
7	Texas	2,979
8	Indiana	2,948
9	Pennsylvania	2,676
10	Colorado	2,667
11	Delaware	2,645
12	Michigan	2,600
13	Maryland	2,543
14	Washington	2,473
15	Arkansas	2,361
16	Connecticut	2,181
17	Oregon	2,177
18	New Jersey	2,170
19	Hawaii	2,078
20	Florida	1,976
21	Louisiana	1,945
22	Kentucky	1,924
23	Arizona	1,856
24	Illinois	1,828
25	Missouri	1,730
26	Alabama	1,723
27	Alaska	1,653
28	Vermont	1,624
29	California	1,616
30	North Carolina	1,599
31	New Mexico	1,580
32	Wisconsin	1,541
33	Nebraska	1,523
34	Wyoming	1,508
35	South Dakota	1,453
36	Tennessee	1,440
37	Montana	1,323
38	South Carolina	1,254
39	Mississippi	1,154
40	Iowa	1,136
41	New York	1,134
42	Oklahoma	1,127
43	Kansas	1,004
44	Virginia	971
45	North Dakota	922
46	Nevada	884
47	Utah	770
48	Maine	721
49	West Virginia	719
50	New Hampshire	604

District of Columbia   2,990

Source: U.S. Department of Justice, Bureau of Justice Statistics
"Probation and Parole in the United States, 2008" (December 2009, NCJ 228230, http://bjs.ojp.usdoj.gov/)
*As of December 31, 2008. "Community supervision" includes probation and parole. Federal rate is 52 adults under federal community supervision per 100,000 adult population.

Percent of Adults Under State Community Supervision in 2008

National Percent = 2.2% of Adults*

RANK	STATE	PERCENT
25	Alabama	1.7
25	Alaska	1.7
22	Arizona	1.9
15	Arkansas	2.4
28	California	1.6
9	Colorado	2.7
16	Connecticut	2.2
9	Delaware	2.7
20	Florida	2.0
1	Georgia	5.9
19	Hawaii	2.1
2	Idaho	4.8
24	Illinois	1.8
7	Indiana	3.0
40	Iowa	1.1
43	Kansas	1.0
22	Kentucky	1.9
20	Louisiana	2.0
48	Maine	0.7
12	Maryland	2.6
3	Massachusetts	3.7
12	Michigan	2.6
4	Minnesota	3.3
39	Mississippi	1.2
25	Missouri	1.7
37	Montana	1.3
32	Nebraska	1.5
45	Nevada	0.9
50	New Hampshire	0.6
16	New Jersey	2.2
28	New Mexico	1.6
40	New York	1.1
28	North Carolina	1.6
45	North Dakota	0.9
6	Ohio	3.2
40	Oklahoma	1.1
16	Oregon	2.2
9	Pennsylvania	2.7
4	Rhode Island	3.3
37	South Carolina	1.3
32	South Dakota	1.5
36	Tennessee	1.4
7	Texas	3.0
47	Utah	0.8
28	Vermont	1.6
43	Virginia	1.0
14	Washington	2.5
48	West Virginia	0.7
32	Wisconsin	1.5
32	Wyoming	1.5

RANK	STATE	PERCENT
1	Georgia	5.9
2	Idaho	4.8
3	Massachusetts	3.7
4	Minnesota	3.3
4	Rhode Island	3.3
6	Ohio	3.2
7	Indiana	3.0
7	Texas	3.0
9	Colorado	2.7
9	Delaware	2.7
9	Pennsylvania	2.7
12	Maryland	2.6
12	Michigan	2.6
14	Washington	2.5
15	Arkansas	2.4
16	Connecticut	2.2
16	New Jersey	2.2
16	Oregon	2.2
19	Hawaii	2.1
20	Florida	2.0
20	Louisiana	2.0
22	Arizona	1.9
22	Kentucky	1.9
24	Illinois	1.8
25	Alabama	1.7
25	Alaska	1.7
25	Missouri	1.7
28	California	1.6
28	New Mexico	1.6
28	North Carolina	1.6
28	Vermont	1.6
32	Nebraska	1.5
32	South Dakota	1.5
32	Wisconsin	1.5
32	Wyoming	1.5
36	Tennessee	1.4
37	Montana	1.3
37	South Carolina	1.3
39	Mississippi	1.2
40	Iowa	1.1
40	New York	1.1
40	Oklahoma	1.1
43	Kansas	1.0
43	Virginia	1.0
45	Nevada	0.9
45	North Dakota	0.9
47	Utah	0.8
48	Maine	0.7
48	West Virginia	0.7
50	New Hampshire	0.6

| | District of Columbia | 3.0 |

Source: CQ Press using data from U.S. Department of Justice, Bureau of Justice Statistics
"Probation and Parole in the United States, 2008" (December 2009, NCJ 228230, http://bjs.ojp.usdoj.gov/)
*As of December 31, 2008. Calculated using population 18 years old and older. "Community Supervision" includes probation and parole. National percent does not include adults under federal community supervision. The federal percent is 0.1% of the adult population.

Adults on State Probation in 2008

National Total = 4,248,169 Adults*

ALPHA ORDER

RANK	STATE	ADULTS	% of USA
23	Alabama	53,252	1.3%
46	Alaska	6,708	0.2%
18	Arizona	82,232	1.9%
30	Arkansas	31,169	0.7%
3	California	325,069	7.7%
17	Colorado	88,912	2.1%
21	Connecticut	56,550	1.3%
38	Delaware	17,216	0.4%
4	Florida	279,760	6.6%
2	Georgia	397,081	9.3%
37	Hawaii	19,097	0.4%
26	Idaho	49,513	1.2%
9	Illinois	144,904	3.4%
10	Indiana	131,291	3.1%
33	Iowa	22,958	0.5%
39	Kansas	16,263	0.4%
24	Kentucky	51,035	1.2%
29	Louisiana	40,025	0.9%
44	Maine	7,504	0.2%
16	Maryland	96,360	2.3%
7	Massachusetts	184,308	4.3%
8	Michigan	175,591	4.1%
12	Minnesota	127,627	3.0%
34	Mississippi	22,267	0.5%
20	Missouri	57,360	1.4%
42	Montana	9,072	0.2%
36	Nebraska	19,606	0.5%
40	Nevada	13,337	0.3%
49	New Hampshire	4,549	0.1%
11	New Jersey	128,737	3.0%
35	New Mexico	20,883	0.5%
13	New York	119,405	2.8%
15	North Carolina	109,678	2.6%
50	North Dakota	4,233	0.1%
5	Ohio	260,962	6.1%
31	Oklahoma	27,940	0.7%
27	Oregon	41,888	1.0%
6	Pennsylvania	186,973	4.4%
32	Rhode Island	26,754	0.6%
28	South Carolina	41,254	1.0%
47	South Dakota	6,146	0.1%
19	Tennessee	58,109	1.4%
1	Texas	427,080	10.1%
41	Utah	11,103	0.3%
45	Vermont	6,940	0.2%
22	Virginia	53,614	1.3%
14	Washington	113,134	2.7%
43	West Virginia	8,283	0.2%
25	Wisconsin	50,418	1.2%
48	Wyoming	5,438	0.1%

RANK ORDER

RANK	STATE	ADULTS	% of USA
1	Texas	427,080	10.1%
2	Georgia	397,081	9.3%
3	California	325,069	7.7%
4	Florida	279,760	6.6%
5	Ohio	260,962	6.1%
6	Pennsylvania	186,973	4.4%
7	Massachusetts	184,308	4.3%
8	Michigan	175,591	4.1%
9	Illinois	144,904	3.4%
10	Indiana	131,291	3.1%
11	New Jersey	128,737	3.0%
12	Minnesota	127,627	3.0%
13	New York	119,405	2.8%
14	Washington	113,134	2.7%
15	North Carolina	109,678	2.6%
16	Maryland	96,360	2.3%
17	Colorado	88,912	2.1%
18	Arizona	82,232	1.9%
19	Tennessee	58,109	1.4%
20	Missouri	57,360	1.4%
21	Connecticut	56,550	1.3%
22	Virginia	53,614	1.3%
23	Alabama	53,252	1.3%
24	Kentucky	51,035	1.2%
25	Wisconsin	50,418	1.2%
26	Idaho	49,513	1.2%
27	Oregon	41,888	1.0%
28	South Carolina	41,254	1.0%
29	Louisiana	40,025	0.9%
30	Arkansas	31,169	0.7%
31	Oklahoma	27,940	0.7%
32	Rhode Island	26,754	0.6%
33	Iowa	22,958	0.5%
34	Mississippi	22,267	0.5%
35	New Mexico	20,883	0.5%
36	Nebraska	19,606	0.5%
37	Hawaii	19,097	0.4%
38	Delaware	17,216	0.4%
39	Kansas	16,263	0.4%
40	Nevada	13,337	0.3%
41	Utah	11,103	0.3%
42	Montana	9,072	0.2%
43	West Virginia	8,283	0.2%
44	Maine	7,504	0.2%
45	Vermont	6,940	0.2%
46	Alaska	6,708	0.2%
47	South Dakota	6,146	0.1%
48	Wyoming	5,438	0.1%
49	New Hampshire	4,549	0.1%
50	North Dakota	4,233	0.1%
	District of Columbia	8,581	0.2%

Source: U.S. Department of Justice, Bureau of Justice Statistics
   "Probation and Parole in the United States, 2008" (December 2009, NCJ 228230, http://bjs.ojp.usdoj.gov/)
*As of December 31, 2008. Does not include 22,748 adults on federal probation.

Rate of Adults on State Probation in 2008

National Rate = 1,835 Adults on State Probation per 100,000 Adult Population*

ALPHA ORDER

RANK	STATE	RATE
22	Alabama	1,497
30	Alaska	1,314
19	Arizona	1,700
25	Arkansas	1,441
36	California	1,178
10	Colorado	2,358
14	Connecticut	2,094
8	Delaware	2,563
15	Florida	1,944
1	Georgia	5,520
18	Hawaii	1,890
2	Idaho	4,415
23	Illinois	1,483
7	Indiana	2,727
41	Iowa	998
45	Kansas	770
20	Kentucky	1,558
34	Louisiana	1,205
46	Maine	718
13	Maryland	2,236
3	Massachusetts	3,620
11	Michigan	2,304
5	Minnesota	3,202
38	Mississippi	1,020
31	Missouri	1,272
33	Montana	1,206
24	Nebraska	1,460
47	Nevada	684
50	New Hampshire	443
16	New Jersey	1,932
28	New Mexico	1,398
44	New York	789
21	North Carolina	1,557
43	North Dakota	845
6	Ohio	2,973
39	Oklahoma	1,016
26	Oregon	1,423
17	Pennsylvania	1,925
4	Rhode Island	3,251
35	South Carolina	1,198
40	South Dakota	1,007
32	Tennessee	1,219
9	Texas	2,401
48	Utah	582
27	Vermont	1,405
42	Virginia	896
12	Washington	2,240
49	West Virginia	579
37	Wisconsin	1,164
29	Wyoming	1,333

RANK ORDER

RANK	STATE	RATE
1	Georgia	5,520
2	Idaho	4,415
3	Massachusetts	3,620
4	Rhode Island	3,251
5	Minnesota	3,202
6	Ohio	2,973
7	Indiana	2,727
8	Delaware	2,563
9	Texas	2,401
10	Colorado	2,358
11	Michigan	2,304
12	Washington	2,240
13	Maryland	2,236
14	Connecticut	2,094
15	Florida	1,944
16	New Jersey	1,932
17	Pennsylvania	1,925
18	Hawaii	1,890
19	Arizona	1,700
20	Kentucky	1,558
21	North Carolina	1,557
22	Alabama	1,497
23	Illinois	1,483
24	Nebraska	1,460
25	Arkansas	1,441
26	Oregon	1,423
27	Vermont	1,405
28	New Mexico	1,398
29	Wyoming	1,333
30	Alaska	1,314
31	Missouri	1,272
32	Tennessee	1,219
33	Montana	1,206
34	Louisiana	1,205
35	South Carolina	1,198
36	California	1,178
37	Wisconsin	1,164
38	Mississippi	1,020
39	Oklahoma	1,016
40	South Dakota	1,007
41	Iowa	998
42	Virginia	896
43	North Dakota	845
44	New York	789
45	Kansas	770
46	Maine	718
47	Nevada	684
48	Utah	582
49	West Virginia	579
50	New Hampshire	443

District of Columbia   1,781

Source: U.S. Department of Justice, Bureau of Justice Statistics
    "Probation and Parole in the United States, 2008" (December 2009, NCJ 228230, http://bjs.ojp.usdoj.gov/)
*As of December 31, 2008. Federal rate is 10 adults on federal probation per 100,000 adult population.

Adults on State Parole in 2008

National Total = 729,540 Adults*

ALPHA ORDER

RANK	STATE	ADULTS	% of USA
21	Alabama	8,042	1.1%
41	Alaska	1,732	0.2%
22	Arizona	7,534	1.0%
11	Arkansas	19,908	2.7%
1	California	120,753	16.6%
18	Colorado	11,654	1.6%
37	Connecticut	2,328	0.3%
47	Delaware	551	0.1%
25	Florida	4,528	0.6%
7	Georgia	23,448	3.2%
40	Hawaii	1,904	0.3%
31	Idaho	3,361	0.5%
5	Illinois	33,683	4.6%
19	Indiana	10,637	1.5%
33	Iowa	3,159	0.4%
24	Kansas	4,958	0.7%
16	Kentucky	12,277	1.7%
6	Louisiana	24,636	3.4%
50	Maine	31	0.0%
15	Maryland	13,220	1.8%
32	Massachusetts	3,185	0.4%
8	Michigan	22,523	3.1%
23	Minnesota	5,081	0.7%
35	Mississippi	2,922	0.4%
10	Missouri	20,683	2.8%
44	Montana	885	0.1%
45	Nebraska	846	0.1%
27	Nevada	3,908	0.5%
42	New Hampshire	1,661	0.2%
14	New Jersey	15,849	2.2%
28	New Mexico	3,724	0.5%
4	New York	52,225	7.2%
30	North Carolina	3,409	0.5%
49	North Dakota	384	0.1%
12	Ohio	19,119	2.6%
34	Oklahoma	3,073	0.4%
9	Oregon	22,195	3.0%
3	Pennsylvania	72,951	10.0%
48	Rhode Island	515	0.1%
39	South Carolina	1,947	0.3%
36	South Dakota	2,720	0.4%
20	Tennessee	10,578	1.4%
2	Texas	102,921	14.1%
29	Utah	3,601	0.5%
43	Vermont	1,080	0.1%
26	Virginia	4,471	0.6%
17	Washington	11,768	1.6%
38	West Virginia	2,005	0.3%
13	Wisconsin	18,105	2.5%
46	Wyoming	727	0.1%

RANK ORDER

RANK	STATE	ADULTS	% of USA
1	California	120,753	16.6%
2	Texas	102,921	14.1%
3	Pennsylvania	72,951	10.0%
4	New York	52,225	7.2%
5	Illinois	33,683	4.6%
6	Louisiana	24,636	3.4%
7	Georgia	23,448	3.2%
8	Michigan	22,523	3.1%
9	Oregon	22,195	3.0%
10	Missouri	20,683	2.8%
11	Arkansas	19,908	2.7%
12	Ohio	19,119	2.6%
13	Wisconsin	18,105	2.5%
14	New Jersey	15,849	2.2%
15	Maryland	13,220	1.8%
16	Kentucky	12,277	1.7%
17	Washington	11,768	1.6%
18	Colorado	11,654	1.6%
19	Indiana	10,637	1.5%
20	Tennessee	10,578	1.4%
21	Alabama	8,042	1.1%
22	Arizona	7,534	1.0%
23	Minnesota	5,081	0.7%
24	Kansas	4,958	0.7%
25	Florida	4,528	0.6%
26	Virginia	4,471	0.6%
27	Nevada	3,908	0.5%
28	New Mexico	3,724	0.5%
29	Utah	3,601	0.5%
30	North Carolina	3,409	0.5%
31	Idaho	3,361	0.5%
32	Massachusetts	3,185	0.4%
33	Iowa	3,159	0.4%
34	Oklahoma	3,073	0.4%
35	Mississippi	2,922	0.4%
36	South Dakota	2,720	0.4%
37	Connecticut	2,328	0.3%
38	West Virginia	2,005	0.3%
39	South Carolina	1,947	0.3%
40	Hawaii	1,904	0.3%
41	Alaska	1,732	0.2%
42	New Hampshire	1,661	0.2%
43	Vermont	1,080	0.1%
44	Montana	885	0.1%
45	Nebraska	846	0.1%
46	Wyoming	727	0.1%
47	Delaware	551	0.1%
48	Rhode Island	515	0.1%
49	North Dakota	384	0.1%
50	Maine	31	0.0%
	District of Columbia	6,135	0.8%

Source: U.S. Department of Justice, Bureau of Justice Statistics
   "Probation and Parole in the United States, 2008" (December 2009, NCJ 228230, http://bjs.ojp.usdoj.gov/)
*As of December 31, 2008. Does not include 98,629 adults on federal parole.

Rate of Adults on State Parole in 2008

National Rate = 315 Adults on State Parole per 100,000 Adult Population*

ALPHA ORDER

RANK	STATE	RATE
23	Alabama	226
13	Alaska	339
33	Arizona	156
1	Arkansas	920
8	California	438
15	Colorado	309
40	Connecticut	86
41	Delaware	82
49	Florida	31
14	Georgia	326
30	Hawaii	188
17	Idaho	300
11	Illinois	345
25	Indiana	221
35	Iowa	137
21	Kansas	235
10	Kentucky	375
4	Louisiana	742
50	Maine	3
16	Maryland	307
44	Massachusetts	63
18	Michigan	296
37	Minnesota	127
36	Mississippi	134
6	Missouri	459
38	Montana	118
44	Nebraska	63
28	Nevada	200
32	New Hampshire	162
20	New Jersey	238
19	New Mexico	249
11	New York	345
48	North Carolina	48
42	North Dakota	77
27	Ohio	218
39	Oklahoma	112
2	Oregon	754
3	Pennsylvania	751
44	Rhode Island	63
47	South Carolina	57
7	South Dakota	446
24	Tennessee	222
5	Texas	579
29	Utah	189
26	Vermont	219
43	Virginia	75
22	Washington	233
34	West Virginia	140
9	Wisconsin	418
31	Wyoming	178

RANK ORDER

RANK	STATE	RATE
1	Arkansas	920
2	Oregon	754
3	Pennsylvania	751
4	Louisiana	742
5	Texas	579
6	Missouri	459
7	South Dakota	446
8	California	438
9	Wisconsin	418
10	Kentucky	375
11	Illinois	345
11	New York	345
13	Alaska	339
14	Georgia	326
15	Colorado	309
16	Maryland	307
17	Idaho	300
18	Michigan	296
19	New Mexico	249
20	New Jersey	238
21	Kansas	235
22	Washington	233
23	Alabama	226
24	Tennessee	222
25	Indiana	221
26	Vermont	219
27	Ohio	218
28	Nevada	200
29	Utah	189
30	Hawaii	188
31	Wyoming	178
32	New Hampshire	162
33	Arizona	156
34	West Virginia	140
35	Iowa	137
36	Mississippi	134
37	Minnesota	127
38	Montana	118
39	Oklahoma	112
40	Connecticut	86
41	Delaware	82
42	North Dakota	77
43	Virginia	75
44	Massachusetts	63
44	Nebraska	63
44	Rhode Island	63
47	South Carolina	57
48	North Carolina	48
49	Florida	31
50	Maine	3
	District of Columbia	1,274

Source: U.S. Department of Justice, Bureau of Justice Statistics
"Probation and Parole in the United States, 2008" (December 2009, NCJ 228230, http://bjs.ojp.usdoj.gov/)
*As of December 31, 2008. Federal rate is 43 adults on federal parole per 100,000 adult population.

Parolees Returned to Incarceration in 2008

Reporting States' Total = 178,180*

ALPHA ORDER

ALPHA ORDER

RANK	STATE	PAROLEES	% of USA
27	Alabama	882	0.5%
NA	Alaska**	NA	NA
16	Arizona	2,173	1.2%
11	Arkansas	3,402	1.9%
1	California	83,984	47.1%
6	Colorado	4,772	2.7%
24	Connecticut	1,001	0.6%
NA	Delaware**	NA	NA
22	Florida	1,520	0.9%
7	Georgia	3,937	2.2%
37	Hawaii	234	0.1%
30	Idaho	567	0.3%
3	Illinois	11,789	6.6%
28	Indiana	853	0.5%
29	Iowa	765	0.4%
23	Kansas	1,341	0.8%
14	Kentucky	2,584	1.5%
13	Louisiana	2,741	1.5%
44	Maine	0	0.0%
19	Maryland	1,641	0.9%
25	Massachusetts	900	0.5%
8	Michigan	3,928	2.2%
17	Minnesota	2,116	1.2%
41	Mississippi	172	0.1%
9	Missouri	3,724	2.1%
36	Montana	253	0.1%
34	Nebraska	255	0.1%
32	Nevada	519	0.3%
NA	New Hampshire**	NA	NA
18	New Jersey	1,848	1.0%
NA	New Mexico**	NA	NA
2	New York	12,358	6.9%
34	North Carolina	255	0.1%
38	North Dakota	187	0.1%
12	Ohio	3,052	1.7%
33	Oklahoma	265	0.1%
15	Oregon	2,541	1.4%
5	Pennsylvania	4,902	2.8%
42	Rhode Island	124	0.1%
39	South Carolina	176	0.1%
26	South Dakota	888	0.5%
21	Tennessee	1,604	0.9%
4	Texas	7,147	4.0%
20	Utah	1,619	0.9%
40	Vermont	174	0.1%
NA	Virginia**	NA	NA
NA	Washington**	NA	NA
31	West Virginia	550	0.3%
10	Wisconsin	3,664	2.1%
43	Wyoming	105	0.1%

RANK ORDER

RANK	STATE	PAROLEES	% of USA
1	California	83,984	47.1%
2	New York	12,358	6.9%
3	Illinois	11,789	6.6%
4	Texas	7,147	4.0%
5	Pennsylvania	4,902	2.8%
6	Colorado	4,772	2.7%
7	Georgia	3,937	2.2%
8	Michigan	3,928	2.2%
9	Missouri	3,724	2.1%
10	Wisconsin	3,664	2.1%
11	Arkansas	3,402	1.9%
12	Ohio	3,052	1.7%
13	Louisiana	2,741	1.5%
14	Kentucky	2,584	1.5%
15	Oregon	2,541	1.4%
16	Arizona	2,173	1.2%
17	Minnesota	2,116	1.2%
18	New Jersey	1,848	1.0%
19	Maryland	1,641	0.9%
20	Utah	1,619	0.9%
21	Tennessee	1,604	0.9%
22	Florida	1,520	0.9%
23	Kansas	1,341	0.8%
24	Connecticut	1,001	0.6%
25	Massachusetts	900	0.5%
26	South Dakota	888	0.5%
27	Alabama	882	0.5%
28	Indiana	853	0.5%
29	Iowa	765	0.4%
30	Idaho	567	0.3%
31	West Virginia	550	0.3%
32	Nevada	519	0.3%
33	Oklahoma	265	0.1%
34	Nebraska	255	0.1%
34	North Carolina	255	0.1%
36	Montana	253	0.1%
37	Hawaii	234	0.1%
38	North Dakota	187	0.1%
39	South Carolina	176	0.1%
40	Vermont	174	0.1%
41	Mississippi	172	0.1%
42	Rhode Island	124	0.1%
43	Wyoming	105	0.1%
44	Maine	0	0.0%
NA	Alaska**	NA	NA
NA	Delaware**	NA	NA
NA	New Hampshire**	NA	NA
NA	New Mexico**	NA	NA
NA	Virginia**	NA	NA
NA	Washington**	NA	NA
	District of Columbia	658	0.4%

Source: U.S. Department of Justice, Bureau of Justice Statistics
"Probation and Parole in the United States, 2008" (December 2009, NCJ 228230, http://bjs.ojp.usdoj.gov/)
*As of December 31, 2008. Does not include 9,595 federal parolees returned to incarceration. National total is only for those states reporting.
**Not available.

Percent of Parolees Returned to Incarceration in 2008

Reporting States' Percent = 14.5% Returned*

ALPHA ORDER

RANK	STATE	PERCENT
31	Alabama	8.2
NA	Alaska**	NA
26	Arizona	10.8
18	Arkansas	12.0
1	California	27.6
3	Colorado	23.1
4	Connecticut	22.0
NA	Delaware**	NA
17	Florida	12.8
23	Georgia	11.3
30	Hawaii	8.8
20	Idaho	11.6
7	Illinois	17.4
42	Indiana	4.0
15	Iowa	13.4
14	Kansas	13.7
15	Kentucky	13.4
35	Louisiana	7.2
44	Maine	0.0
33	Maryland	7.7
22	Massachusetts	11.5
18	Michigan	12.0
5	Minnesota	20.0
40	Mississippi	4.5
25	Missouri	10.9
11	Montana	15.5
13	Nebraska	14.1
37	Nevada	6.4
NA	New Hampshire**	NA
34	New Jersey	7.3
NA	New Mexico**	NA
10	New York	15.6
43	North Carolina	3.7
9	North Dakota	15.9
28	Ohio	10.7
38	Oklahoma	6.1
31	Oregon	8.2
41	Pennsylvania	4.1
20	Rhode Island	11.6
36	South Carolina	6.5
6	South Dakota	19.0
24	Tennessee	11.0
39	Texas	5.3
2	Utah	27.0
26	Vermont	10.8
NA	Virginia**	NA
NA	Washington**	NA
8	West Virginia	16.4
12	Wisconsin	14.5
29	Wyoming	10.0

RANK ORDER

RANK	STATE	PERCENT
1	California	27.6
2	Utah	27.0
3	Colorado	23.1
4	Connecticut	22.0
5	Minnesota	20.0
6	South Dakota	19.0
7	Illinois	17.4
8	West Virginia	16.4
9	North Dakota	15.9
10	New York	15.6
11	Montana	15.5
12	Wisconsin	14.5
13	Nebraska	14.1
14	Kansas	13.7
15	Iowa	13.4
15	Kentucky	13.4
17	Florida	12.8
18	Arkansas	12.0
18	Michigan	12.0
20	Idaho	11.6
20	Rhode Island	11.6
22	Massachusetts	11.5
23	Georgia	11.3
24	Tennessee	11.0
25	Missouri	10.9
26	Arizona	10.8
26	Vermont	10.8
28	Ohio	10.7
29	Wyoming	10.0
30	Hawaii	8.8
31	Alabama	8.2
31	Oregon	8.2
33	Maryland	7.7
34	New Jersey	7.3
35	Louisiana	7.2
36	South Carolina	6.5
37	Nevada	6.4
38	Oklahoma	6.1
39	Texas	5.3
40	Mississippi	4.5
41	Pennsylvania	4.1
42	Indiana	4.0
43	North Carolina	3.7
44	Maine	0.0
NA	Alaska**	NA
NA	Delaware**	NA
NA	New Hampshire**	NA
NA	New Mexico**	NA
NA	Virginia**	NA
NA	Washington**	NA

District of Columbia   8.4

Source: CQ Press using data from U.S. Department of Justice, Bureau of Justice Statistics
    "Probation and Parole in the United States, 2008" (December 2009, NCJ 228230, http://bjs.ojp.usdoj.gov/)
*As of December 31, 2008. Does not include federal parolees returned to incarceration. Federal return percent was 6.9%.
National figure is only for those states reporting.
**Not available.

State and Local Government Employees in Corrections in 2008

National Total = 747,549 Employees*

ALPHA ORDER

RANK	STATE	EMPLOYEES	% of USA
27	Alabama	8,452	1.1%
45	Alaska	1,886	0.3%
13	Arizona	16,431	2.2%
29	Arkansas	7,470	1.0%
1	California	94,697	12.7%
21	Colorado	11,058	1.5%
28	Connecticut	7,718	1.0%
40	Delaware	2,974	0.4%
4	Florida	46,574	6.2%
6	Georgia	30,438	4.1%
41	Hawaii	2,420	0.3%
39	Idaho	3,441	0.5%
11	Illinois	21,701	2.9%
19	Indiana	13,538	1.8%
36	Iowa	4,862	0.7%
30	Kansas	7,071	0.9%
26	Kentucky	8,731	1.2%
16	Louisiana	14,516	1.9%
42	Maine	2,089	0.3%
14	Maryland	15,806	2.1%
25	Massachusetts	8,864	1.2%
10	Michigan	22,010	2.9%
23	Minnesota	9,114	1.2%
34	Mississippi	5,423	0.7%
15	Missouri	15,505	2.1%
44	Montana	1,892	0.3%
37	Nebraska	4,400	0.6%
32	Nevada	6,710	0.9%
43	New Hampshire	2,025	0.3%
12	New Jersey	17,385	2.3%
33	New Mexico	6,193	0.8%
3	New York	60,543	8.1%
7	North Carolina	26,628	3.6%
50	North Dakota	1,067	0.1%
8	Ohio	26,094	3.5%
31	Oklahoma	6,889	0.9%
23	Oregon	9,114	1.2%
5	Pennsylvania	30,830	4.1%
46	Rhode Island	1,711	0.2%
22	South Carolina	10,831	1.4%
48	South Dakota	1,501	0.2%
20	Tennessee	13,254	1.8%
2	Texas	72,530	9.7%
35	Utah	5,359	0.7%
49	Vermont	1,189	0.2%
9	Virginia	23,986	3.2%
18	Washington	14,178	1.9%
38	West Virginia	3,575	0.5%
17	Wisconsin	14,362	1.9%
47	Wyoming	1,612	0.2%

RANK ORDER

RANK	STATE	EMPLOYEES	% of USA
1	California	94,697	12.7%
2	Texas	72,530	9.7%
3	New York	60,543	8.1%
4	Florida	46,574	6.2%
5	Pennsylvania	30,830	4.1%
6	Georgia	30,438	4.1%
7	North Carolina	26,628	3.6%
8	Ohio	26,094	3.5%
9	Virginia	23,986	3.2%
10	Michigan	22,010	2.9%
11	Illinois	21,701	2.9%
12	New Jersey	17,385	2.3%
13	Arizona	16,431	2.2%
14	Maryland	15,806	2.1%
15	Missouri	15,505	2.1%
16	Louisiana	14,516	1.9%
17	Wisconsin	14,362	1.9%
18	Washington	14,178	1.9%
19	Indiana	13,538	1.8%
20	Tennessee	13,254	1.8%
21	Colorado	11,058	1.5%
22	South Carolina	10,831	1.4%
23	Minnesota	9,114	1.2%
23	Oregon	9,114	1.2%
25	Massachusetts	8,864	1.2%
26	Kentucky	8,731	1.2%
27	Alabama	8,452	1.1%
28	Connecticut	7,718	1.0%
29	Arkansas	7,470	1.0%
30	Kansas	7,071	0.9%
31	Oklahoma	6,889	0.9%
32	Nevada	6,710	0.9%
33	New Mexico	6,193	0.8%
34	Mississippi	5,423	0.7%
35	Utah	5,359	0.7%
36	Iowa	4,862	0.7%
37	Nebraska	4,400	0.6%
38	West Virginia	3,575	0.5%
39	Idaho	3,441	0.5%
40	Delaware	2,974	0.4%
41	Hawaii	2,420	0.3%
42	Maine	2,089	0.3%
43	New Hampshire	2,025	0.3%
44	Montana	1,892	0.3%
45	Alaska	1,886	0.3%
46	Rhode Island	1,711	0.2%
47	Wyoming	1,612	0.2%
48	South Dakota	1,501	0.2%
49	Vermont	1,189	0.2%
50	North Dakota	1,067	0.1%
	District of Columbia	902	0.1%

Source: U.S. Bureau of the Census, Governments Division
"Government Employment and Payroll" (http://www.census.gov/govs/apes/index.html)
*Full-time equivalent as of March 2008.

State and Local Government Employees in Corrections as a Percent of All State and Local Government Employees in 2008
National Percent = 4.5% of Employees*

ALPHA ORDER

RANK	STATE	PERCENT
44	Alabama	2.9
31	Alaska	3.5
8	Arizona	5.1
19	Arkansas	4.5
8	California	5.1
20	Colorado	4.2
25	Connecticut	4.0
1	Delaware	5.9
8	Florida	5.1
3	Georgia	5.6
41	Hawaii	3.2
20	Idaho	4.2
35	Illinois	3.4
28	Indiana	3.8
47	Iowa	2.7
30	Kansas	3.6
31	Kentucky	3.5
8	Louisiana	5.1
47	Maine	2.7
4	Maryland	5.3
49	Massachusetts	2.6
18	Michigan	4.6
38	Minnesota	3.3
45	Mississippi	2.8
16	Missouri	4.7
35	Montana	3.4
28	Nebraska	3.8
1	Nevada	5.9
45	New Hampshire	2.8
35	New Jersey	3.4
14	New Mexico	4.8
13	New York	4.9
16	North Carolina	4.7
49	North Dakota	2.6
20	Ohio	4.2
41	Oklahoma	3.2
14	Oregon	4.8
7	Pennsylvania	5.2
38	Rhode Island	3.3
23	South Carolina	4.1
31	South Dakota	3.5
25	Tennessee	4.0
4	Texas	5.3
25	Utah	4.0
43	Vermont	3.0
4	Virginia	5.3
23	Washington	4.1
31	West Virginia	3.5
8	Wisconsin	5.1
38	Wyoming	3.3

RANK ORDER

RANK	STATE	PERCENT
1	Delaware	5.9
1	Nevada	5.9
3	Georgia	5.6
4	Maryland	5.3
4	Texas	5.3
4	Virginia	5.3
7	Pennsylvania	5.2
8	Arizona	5.1
8	California	5.1
8	Florida	5.1
8	Louisiana	5.1
8	Wisconsin	5.1
13	New York	4.9
14	New Mexico	4.8
14	Oregon	4.8
16	Missouri	4.7
16	North Carolina	4.7
18	Michigan	4.6
19	Arkansas	4.5
20	Colorado	4.2
20	Idaho	4.2
20	Ohio	4.2
23	South Carolina	4.1
23	Washington	4.1
25	Connecticut	4.0
25	Tennessee	4.0
25	Utah	4.0
28	Indiana	3.8
28	Nebraska	3.8
30	Kansas	3.6
31	Alaska	3.5
31	Kentucky	3.5
31	South Dakota	3.5
31	West Virginia	3.5
35	Illinois	3.4
35	Montana	3.4
35	New Jersey	3.4
38	Minnesota	3.3
38	Rhode Island	3.3
38	Wyoming	3.3
41	Hawaii	3.2
41	Oklahoma	3.2
43	Vermont	3.0
44	Alabama	2.9
45	Mississippi	2.8
45	New Hampshire	2.8
47	Iowa	2.7
47	Maine	2.7
49	Massachusetts	2.6
49	North Dakota	2.6
	District of Columbia	1.9

Source: CQ Press using data from U.S. Bureau of the Census, Governments Division
   "Government Employment and Payroll" (http://www.census.gov/govs/apes/index.html)
*Full-time equivalent as of March 2008.

Correctional Officers and Jailers in 2008

National Total = 428,040 Officers and Jailers*

ALPHA ORDER

RANK	STATE	OFFICERS	% of USA
24	Alabama	5,660	1.3%
42	Alaska	1,040	0.2%
11	Arizona	11,770	2.7%
28	Arkansas	4,750	1.1%
2	California	40,260	9.4%
18	Colorado	7,720	1.8%
30	Connecticut	4,390	1.0%
NA	Delaware**	NA	NA
NA	Florida**	NA	NA
4	Georgia	17,540	4.1%
36	Hawaii	1,760	0.4%
37	Idaho	1,560	0.4%
10	Illinois	12,430	2.9%
16	Indiana	8,670	2.0%
32	Iowa	3,130	0.7%
29	Kansas	4,680	1.1%
22	Kentucky	6,090	1.4%
13	Louisiana	11,020	2.6%
38	Maine	1,330	0.3%
14	Maryland	9,780	2.3%
26	Massachusetts	5,030	1.2%
12	Michigan	11,750	2.7%
27	Minnesota	4,980	1.2%
25	Mississippi	5,650	1.3%
17	Missouri	8,120	1.9%
39	Montana	1,320	0.3%
34	Nebraska	2,360	0.6%
33	Nevada	2,840	0.7%
41	New Hampshire	1,060	0.2%
9	New Jersey	13,140	3.1%
23	New Mexico	5,690	1.3%
3	New York	35,320	8.3%
5	North Carolina	16,500	3.9%
44	North Dakota	610	0.1%
8	Ohio	13,410	3.1%
21	Oklahoma	6,100	1.4%
31	Oregon	4,200	1.0%
6	Pennsylvania	16,030	3.7%
NA	Rhode Island**	NA	NA
20	South Carolina	7,560	1.8%
40	South Dakota	1,240	0.3%
15	Tennessee	9,510	2.2%
1	Texas	44,300	10.3%
35	Utah	2,300	0.5%
NA	Vermont**	NA	NA
7	Virginia	14,000	3.3%
NA	Washington**	NA	NA
NA	West Virginia**	NA	NA
19	Wisconsin	7,710	1.8%
43	Wyoming	830	0.2%

RANK ORDER

RANK	STATE	OFFICERS	% of USA
1	Texas	44,300	10.3%
2	California	40,260	9.4%
3	New York	35,320	8.3%
4	Georgia	17,540	4.1%
5	North Carolina	16,500	3.9%
6	Pennsylvania	16,030	3.7%
7	Virginia	14,000	3.3%
8	Ohio	13,410	3.1%
9	New Jersey	13,140	3.1%
10	Illinois	12,430	2.9%
11	Arizona	11,770	2.7%
12	Michigan	11,750	2.7%
13	Louisiana	11,020	2.6%
14	Maryland	9,780	2.3%
15	Tennessee	9,510	2.2%
16	Indiana	8,670	2.0%
17	Missouri	8,120	1.9%
18	Colorado	7,720	1.8%
19	Wisconsin	7,710	1.8%
20	South Carolina	7,560	1.8%
21	Oklahoma	6,100	1.4%
22	Kentucky	6,090	1.4%
23	New Mexico	5,690	1.3%
24	Alabama	5,660	1.3%
25	Mississippi	5,650	1.3%
26	Massachusetts	5,030	1.2%
27	Minnesota	4,980	1.2%
28	Arkansas	4,750	1.1%
29	Kansas	4,680	1.1%
30	Connecticut	4,390	1.0%
31	Oregon	4,200	1.0%
32	Iowa	3,130	0.7%
33	Nevada	2,840	0.7%
34	Nebraska	2,360	0.6%
35	Utah	2,300	0.5%
36	Hawaii	1,760	0.4%
37	Idaho	1,560	0.4%
38	Maine	1,330	0.3%
39	Montana	1,320	0.3%
40	South Dakota	1,240	0.3%
41	New Hampshire	1,060	0.2%
42	Alaska	1,040	0.2%
43	Wyoming	830	0.2%
44	North Dakota	610	0.1%
NA	Delaware**	NA	NA
NA	Florida**	NA	NA
NA	Rhode Island**	NA	NA
NA	Vermont**	NA	NA
NA	Washington**	NA	NA
NA	West Virginia**	NA	NA
	District of Columbia**	NA	NA

Source: U.S. Department of Labor, Bureau of Labor Statistics
    "Occupational Employment Statistics" (http://www.bls.gov/oes/)
*Occupational code 33-3012. As of May 2008. Does not include self-employed.
**Not available.

Rate of Correctional Officers and Jailers in 2008

National Rate = 141 Officers and Jailers per 100,000 Population*

ALPHA ORDER

RANK	STATE	RATE
30	Alabama	121
19	Alaska	152
5	Arizona	181
14	Arkansas	166
34	California	110
15	Colorado	156
29	Connecticut	125
NA	Delaware**	NA
NA	Florida**	NA
5	Georgia	181
22	Hawaii	137
37	Idaho	102
39	Illinois	96
25	Indiana	136
36	Iowa	104
12	Kansas	167
21	Kentucky	143
2	Louisiana	250
38	Maine	101
10	Maryland	174
44	Massachusetts	77
31	Michigan	117
40	Minnesota	95
3	Mississippi	192
22	Missouri	137
25	Montana	136
27	Nebraska	132
35	Nevada	109
43	New Hampshire	81
20	New Jersey	151
1	New Mexico	287
5	New York	181
9	North Carolina	179
40	North Dakota	95
31	Ohio	117
12	Oklahoma	167
33	Oregon	111
28	Pennsylvania	129
NA	Rhode Island**	NA
11	South Carolina	169
17	South Dakota	154
18	Tennessee	153
4	Texas	182
42	Utah	84
NA	Vermont**	NA
8	Virginia	180
NA	Washington**	NA
NA	West Virginia**	NA
22	Wisconsin	137
15	Wyoming	156

RANK ORDER

RANK	STATE	RATE
1	New Mexico	287
2	Louisiana	250
3	Mississippi	192
4	Texas	182
5	Arizona	181
5	Georgia	181
5	New York	181
8	Virginia	180
9	North Carolina	179
10	Maryland	174
11	South Carolina	169
12	Kansas	167
12	Oklahoma	167
14	Arkansas	166
15	Colorado	156
15	Wyoming	156
17	South Dakota	154
18	Tennessee	153
19	Alaska	152
20	New Jersey	151
21	Kentucky	143
22	Hawaii	137
22	Missouri	137
22	Wisconsin	137
25	Indiana	136
25	Montana	136
27	Nebraska	132
28	Pennsylvania	129
29	Connecticut	125
30	Alabama	121
31	Michigan	117
31	Ohio	117
33	Oregon	111
34	California	110
35	Nevada	109
36	Iowa	104
37	Idaho	102
38	Maine	101
39	Illinois	96
40	Minnesota	95
40	North Dakota	95
42	Utah	84
43	New Hampshire	81
44	Massachusetts	77
NA	Delaware**	NA
NA	Florida**	NA
NA	Rhode Island**	NA
NA	Vermont**	NA
NA	Washington**	NA
NA	West Virginia**	NA
	District of Columbia**	NA

Source: CQ Press using data from U.S. Department of Labor, Bureau of Labor Statistics
    "Occupational Employment Statistics" (http://www.bls.gov/oes/)
*Occupational code 33-3012. As of May 2008. Does not include self-employed.
**Not available.

Offenders in State Sex Offender Registries in 2008

National Total = 601,676 Offenders*

ALPHA ORDER

RANK	STATE	OFFENDERS	% of USA
20	Alabama	9,745	1.6%
33	Alaska	5,300	0.9%
13	Arizona	14,500	2.4%
23	Arkansas	8,099	1.3%
1	California	66,041	11.0%
19	Colorado	9,961	1.7%
35	Connecticut	4,769	0.8%
37	Delaware	3,461	0.6%
4	Florida	47,455	7.9%
11	Georgia	15,293	2.5%
42	Hawaii	2,500	0.4%
38	Idaho	3,072	0.5%
9	Illinois	19,695	3.3%
22	Indiana	9,486	1.6%
32	Iowa	5,499	0.9%
29	Kansas	5,911	1.0%
26	Kentucky	6,914	1.1%
24	Louisiana	7,937	1.3%
39	Maine	3,069	0.5%
30	Maryland	5,810	1.0%
12	Massachusetts	14,896	2.5%
3	Michigan	48,000	8.0%
6	Minnesota	20,336	3.4%
34	Mississippi	4,888	0.8%
25	Missouri	6,996	1.2%
47	Montana	1,746	0.3%
41	Nebraska	2,748	0.5%
28	Nevada	6,386	1.1%
45	New Hampshire	2,200	0.4%
16	New Jersey	12,000	2.0%
46	New Mexico	2,133	0.4%
5	New York	26,688	4.4%
15	North Carolina	12,167	2.0%
50	North Dakota	1,277	0.2%
10	Ohio	16,902	2.8%
31	Oklahoma	5,664	0.9%
14	Oregon	14,487	2.4%
21	Pennsylvania	9,730	1.6%
48	Rhode Island	1,659	0.3%
18	South Carolina	10,621	1.8%
43	South Dakota	2,467	0.4%
17	Tennessee	11,513	1.9%
2	Texas	52,574	8.7%
27	Utah	6,900	1.1%
44	Vermont	2,447	0.4%
36	Virginia	4,618	0.8%
8	Washington	20,016	3.3%
40	West Virginia	2,800	0.5%
7	Wisconsin	20,199	3.4%
49	Wyoming	1,355	0.2%

RANK ORDER

RANK	STATE	OFFENDERS	% of USA
1	California	66,041	11.0%
2	Texas	52,574	8.7%
3	Michigan	48,000	8.0%
4	Florida	47,455	7.9%
5	New York	26,688	4.4%
6	Minnesota	20,336	3.4%
7	Wisconsin	20,199	3.4%
8	Washington	20,016	3.3%
9	Illinois	19,695	3.3%
10	Ohio	16,902	2.8%
11	Georgia	15,293	2.5%
12	Massachusetts	14,896	2.5%
13	Arizona	14,500	2.4%
14	Oregon	14,487	2.4%
15	North Carolina	12,167	2.0%
16	New Jersey	12,000	2.0%
17	Tennessee	11,513	1.9%
18	South Carolina	10,621	1.8%
19	Colorado	9,961	1.7%
20	Alabama	9,745	1.6%
21	Pennsylvania	9,730	1.6%
22	Indiana	9,486	1.6%
23	Arkansas	8,099	1.3%
24	Louisiana	7,937	1.3%
25	Missouri	6,996	1.2%
26	Kentucky	6,914	1.1%
27	Utah	6,900	1.1%
28	Nevada	6,386	1.1%
29	Kansas	5,911	1.0%
30	Maryland	5,810	1.0%
31	Oklahoma	5,664	0.9%
32	Iowa	5,499	0.9%
33	Alaska	5,300	0.9%
34	Mississippi	4,888	0.8%
35	Connecticut	4,769	0.8%
36	Virginia	4,618	0.8%
37	Delaware	3,461	0.6%
38	Idaho	3,072	0.5%
39	Maine	3,069	0.5%
40	West Virginia	2,800	0.5%
41	Nebraska	2,748	0.5%
42	Hawaii	2,500	0.4%
43	South Dakota	2,467	0.4%
44	Vermont	2,447	0.4%
45	New Hampshire	2,200	0.4%
46	New Mexico	2,133	0.4%
47	Montana	1,746	0.3%
48	Rhode Island	1,659	0.3%
49	Wyoming	1,355	0.2%
50	North Dakota	1,277	0.2%
	District of Columbia	746	0.1%

Source: Parents for Megan's Law
"Megan's Law Report Card" (http://www.parentsformeganslaw.org/public/meganReportCard.html)
*Several factors in each state's authorizing legislation significantly influence the size of a state's registry. Among these factors are the number of different offenses requiring registration, the date that triggers the registration mandate, and the duration of the registration requirement.

III. DRUGS AND ALCOHOL

Methamphetamine Laboratory Seizures in 2008

National Total = 6,601 Laboratories*

RANK	STATE	LABORATORIES	% of USA
16	Alabama	127	1.9%
45	Alaska	0	0.0%
31	Arizona	10	0.2%
9	Arkansas	240	3.6%
5	California	346	5.2%
25	Colorado	33	0.5%
45	Connecticut	0	0.0%
45	Delaware	0	0.0%
17	Florida	125	1.9%
20	Georgia	78	1.2%
45	Hawaii	0	0.0%
33	Idaho	8	0.1%
7	Illinois	324	4.9%
2	Indiana	724	11.0%
11	Iowa	192	2.9%
13	Kansas	143	2.2%
4	Kentucky	416	6.3%
35	Louisiana	6	0.1%
45	Maine	0	0.0%
43	Maryland	1	0.0%
39	Massachusetts	3	0.0%
6	Michigan	329	5.0%
27	Minnesota	21	0.3%
8	Mississippi	296	4.5%
1	Missouri	1,471	22.3%
38	Montana	5	0.1%
22	Nebraska	57	0.9%
35	Nevada	6	0.1%
43	New Hampshire	1	0.0%
39	New Jersey	3	0.0%
21	New Mexico	61	0.9%
32	New York	9	0.1%
10	North Carolina	196	3.0%
26	North Dakota	27	0.4%
12	Ohio	162	2.5%
19	Oklahoma	102	1.5%
27	Oregon	21	0.3%
30	Pennsylvania	13	0.2%
45	Rhode Island	0	0.0%
23	South Carolina	46	0.7%
35	South Dakota	6	0.1%
3	Tennessee	533	8.1%
18	Texas	112	1.7%
34	Utah	7	0.1%
42	Vermont	2	0.0%
29	Virginia	19	0.3%
14	Washington	137	2.1%
24	West Virginia	43	0.7%
14	Wisconsin	137	2.1%
39	Wyoming	3	0.0%

RANK	STATE	LABORATORIES	% of USA
1	Missouri	1,471	22.3%
2	Indiana	724	11.0%
3	Tennessee	533	8.1%
4	Kentucky	416	6.3%
5	California	346	5.2%
6	Michigan	329	5.0%
7	Illinois	324	4.9%
8	Mississippi	296	4.5%
9	Arkansas	240	3.6%
10	North Carolina	196	3.0%
11	Iowa	192	2.9%
12	Ohio	162	2.5%
13	Kansas	143	2.2%
14	Washington	137	2.1%
14	Wisconsin	137	2.1%
16	Alabama	127	1.9%
17	Florida	125	1.9%
18	Texas	112	1.7%
19	Oklahoma	102	1.5%
20	Georgia	78	1.2%
21	New Mexico	61	0.9%
22	Nebraska	57	0.9%
23	South Carolina	46	0.7%
24	West Virginia	43	0.7%
25	Colorado	33	0.5%
26	North Dakota	27	0.4%
27	Minnesota	21	0.3%
27	Oregon	21	0.3%
29	Virginia	19	0.3%
30	Pennsylvania	13	0.2%
31	Arizona	10	0.2%
32	New York	9	0.1%
33	Idaho	8	0.1%
34	Utah	7	0.1%
35	Louisiana	6	0.1%
35	Nevada	6	0.1%
35	South Dakota	6	0.1%
38	Montana	5	0.1%
39	Massachusetts	3	0.0%
39	New Jersey	3	0.0%
39	Wyoming	3	0.0%
42	Vermont	2	0.0%
43	Maryland	1	0.0%
43	New Hampshire	1	0.0%
45	Alaska	0	0.0%
45	Connecticut	0	0.0%
45	Delaware	0	0.0%
45	Hawaii	0	0.0%
45	Maine	0	0.0%
45	Rhode Island	0	0.0%
	District of Columbia	0	0.0%

Source: Drug Enforcement Administration
 "State Fact Sheets 2008" (http://www.dea.gov/pubs/state_factsheets.html)
*Seizures by DEA, state, and local authorities.

Federal Methamphetamine Seizures in 2008

National Total = 4,154.5 Kilograms

<u>ALPHA ORDER</u>

RANK	STATE	KILOGRAMS	% of USA
34	Alabama	3.2	0.1%
39	Alaska	2.1	0.1%
3	Arizona	263.4	6.3%
13	Arkansas	28.2	0.7%
1	California	2,236.2	53.8%
14	Colorado	26.4	0.6%
43	Connecticut	0.0	0.0%
43	Delaware	0.0	0.0%
20	Florida	16.9	0.4%
7	Georgia	65.0	1.6%
8	Hawaii	54.4	1.3%
22	Idaho	11.6	0.3%
26	Illinois	8.3	0.2%
24	Indiana	9.7	0.2%
17	Iowa	21.0	0.5%
10	Kansas	39.6	1.0%
25	Kentucky	9.6	0.2%
23	Louisiana	10.1	0.2%
43	Maine	0.0	0.0%
33	Maryland	4.8	0.1%
36	Massachusetts	2.9	0.1%
31	Michigan	5.2	0.1%
15	Minnesota	25.4	0.6%
38	Mississippi	2.4	0.1%
21	Missouri	14.1	0.3%
37	Montana	2.7	0.1%
27	Nebraska	8.0	0.2%
9	Nevada	44.1	1.1%
43	New Hampshire	0.0	0.0%
6	New Jersey	74.6	1.8%
11	New Mexico	35.0	0.8%
28	New York	7.1	0.2%
19	North Carolina	19.2	0.5%
41	North Dakota	0.7	0.0%
40	Ohio	1.6	0.0%
17	Oklahoma	21.0	0.5%
12	Oregon	34.0	0.8%
30	Pennsylvania	5.7	0.1%
43	Rhode Island	0.0	0.0%
32	South Carolina	4.9	0.1%
29	South Dakota	6.3	0.2%
4	Tennessee	144.7	3.5%
2	Texas	783.6	18.9%
16	Utah	21.5	0.5%
43	Vermont	0.0	0.0%
34	Virginia	3.2	0.1%
5	Washington	75.2	1.8%
43	West Virginia	0.0	0.0%
43	Wisconsin	0.0	0.0%
42	Wyoming	0.3	0.0%

<u>RANK ORDER</u>

RANK	STATE	KILOGRAMS	% of USA
1	California	2,236.2	53.8%
2	Texas	783.6	18.9%
3	Arizona	263.4	6.3%
4	Tennessee	144.7	3.5%
5	Washington	75.2	1.8%
6	New Jersey	74.6	1.8%
7	Georgia	65.0	1.6%
8	Hawaii	54.4	1.3%
9	Nevada	44.1	1.1%
10	Kansas	39.6	1.0%
11	New Mexico	35.0	0.8%
12	Oregon	34.0	0.8%
13	Arkansas	28.2	0.7%
14	Colorado	26.4	0.6%
15	Minnesota	25.4	0.6%
16	Utah	21.5	0.5%
17	Iowa	21.0	0.5%
17	Oklahoma	21.0	0.5%
19	North Carolina	19.2	0.5%
20	Florida	16.9	0.4%
21	Missouri	14.1	0.3%
22	Idaho	11.6	0.3%
23	Louisiana	10.1	0.2%
24	Indiana	9.7	0.2%
25	Kentucky	9.6	0.2%
26	Illinois	8.3	0.2%
27	Nebraska	8.0	0.2%
28	New York	7.1	0.2%
29	South Dakota	6.3	0.2%
30	Pennsylvania	5.7	0.1%
31	Michigan	5.2	0.1%
32	South Carolina	4.9	0.1%
33	Maryland	4.8	0.1%
34	Alabama	3.2	0.1%
34	Virginia	3.2	0.1%
36	Massachusetts	2.9	0.1%
37	Montana	2.7	0.1%
38	Mississippi	2.4	0.1%
39	Alaska	2.1	0.1%
40	Ohio	1.6	0.0%
41	North Dakota	0.7	0.0%
42	Wyoming	0.3	0.0%
43	Connecticut	0.0	0.0%
43	Delaware	0.0	0.0%
43	Maine	0.0	0.0%
43	New Hampshire	0.0	0.0%
43	Rhode Island	0.0	0.0%
43	Vermont	0.0	0.0%
43	West Virginia	0.0	0.0%
43	Wisconsin	0.0	0.0%
	District of Columbia	0.6	0.0%

Source: Drug Enforcement Administration
"State Fact Sheets 2008" (http://www.dea.gov/pubs/state_factsheets.html)

Federal Marijuana Seizures in 2008

National Total = 1,428,848.7 Kilograms*

ALPHA ORDER				RANK ORDER			
RANK	STATE	KILOGRAMS	% of USA	RANK	STATE	KILOGRAMS	% of USA
15	Alabama	2,393.7	0.2%	1	Texas	570,793.1	39.9%
38	Alaska	179.4	0.0%	2	Arizona	351,992.4	24.6%
2	Arizona	351,992.4	24.6%	3	California	187,627.1	13.1%
28	Arkansas	868.0	0.1%	4	Oregon	70,214.2	4.9%
3	California	187,627.1	13.1%	5	Washington	70,186.2	4.9%
9	Colorado	24,089.2	1.7%	6	New Mexico	34,080.0	2.4%
37	Connecticut	210.2	0.0%	7	Florida	33,291.3	2.3%
47	Delaware	6.0	0.0%	8	Utah	32,275.5	2.3%
7	Florida	33,291.3	2.3%	9	Colorado	24,089.2	1.7%
16	Georgia	2,296.4	0.2%	10	Illinois	14,253.1	1.0%
44	Hawaii	24.8	0.0%	11	Kentucky	4,829.6	0.3%
49	Idaho	0.6	0.0%	12	South Carolina	3,973.5	0.3%
10	Illinois	14,253.1	1.0%	13	Michigan	3,472.1	0.2%
30	Indiana	846.8	0.1%	14	New York	2,820.7	0.2%
31	Iowa	646.0	0.0%	15	Alabama	2,393.7	0.2%
19	Kansas	1,553.6	0.1%	16	Georgia	2,296.4	0.2%
11	Kentucky	4,829.6	0.3%	17	Pennsylvania	2,282.1	0.2%
20	Louisiana	1,394.3	0.1%	18	North Carolina	1,805.7	0.1%
32	Maine	491.2	0.0%	19	Kansas	1,553.6	0.1%
22	Maryland	1,324.0	0.1%	20	Louisiana	1,394.3	0.1%
24	Massachusetts	988.6	0.1%	21	Nebraska	1,324.6	0.1%
13	Michigan	3,472.1	0.2%	22	Maryland	1,324.0	0.1%
42	Minnesota	37.1	0.0%	23	Tennessee	1,160.6	0.1%
29	Mississippi	867.9	0.1%	24	Massachusetts	988.6	0.1%
25	Missouri	949.8	0.1%	25	Missouri	949.8	0.1%
36	Montana	224.2	0.0%	26	New Jersey	946.8	0.1%
21	Nebraska	1,324.6	0.1%	27	Ohio	868.7	0.1%
39	Nevada	167.8	0.0%	28	Arkansas	868.0	0.1%
46	New Hampshire	6.2	0.0%	29	Mississippi	867.9	0.1%
26	New Jersey	946.8	0.1%	30	Indiana	846.8	0.1%
6	New Mexico	34,080.0	2.4%	31	Iowa	646.0	0.0%
14	New York	2,820.7	0.2%	32	Maine	491.2	0.0%
18	North Carolina	1,805.7	0.1%	33	Vermont	363.1	0.0%
35	North Dakota	259.8	0.0%	34	Oklahoma	321.9	0.0%
27	Ohio	868.7	0.1%	35	North Dakota	259.8	0.0%
34	Oklahoma	321.9	0.0%	36	Montana	224.2	0.0%
4	Oregon	70,214.2	4.9%	37	Connecticut	210.2	0.0%
17	Pennsylvania	2,282.1	0.2%	38	Alaska	179.4	0.0%
43	Rhode Island	25.9	0.0%	39	Nevada	167.8	0.0%
12	South Carolina	3,973.5	0.3%	40	Wisconsin	73.1	0.0%
48	South Dakota	3.0	0.0%	41	Virginia	44.7	0.0%
23	Tennessee	1,160.6	0.1%	42	Minnesota	37.1	0.0%
1	Texas	570,793.1	39.9%	43	Rhode Island	25.9	0.0%
8	Utah	32,275.5	2.3%	44	Hawaii	24.8	0.0%
33	Vermont	363.1	0.0%	45	West Virginia	17.5	0.0%
41	Virginia	44.7	0.0%	46	New Hampshire	6.2	0.0%
5	Washington	70,186.2	4.9%	47	Delaware	6.0	0.0%
45	West Virginia	17.5	0.0%	48	South Dakota	3.0	0.0%
40	Wisconsin	73.1	0.0%	49	Idaho	0.6	0.0%
50	Wyoming	0.2	0.0%	50	Wyoming	0.2	0.0%
					District of Columbia	6.4	0.0%

Source: Drug Enforcement Administration
   "State Fact Sheets 2008" (http://www.dea.gov/pubs/state_factsheets.html)

Federal Cocaine Seizures in 2008

National Total = 41,003.2 Kilograms

ALPHA ORDER

RANK	STATE	KILOGRAMS	% of USA
20	Alabama	214.7	0.5%
39	Alaska	13.7	0.0%
4	Arizona	1,905.8	4.6%
15	Arkansas	318.4	0.8%
3	California	8,508.5	20.8%
29	Colorado	52.6	0.1%
37	Connecticut	22.6	0.1%
35	Delaware	26.2	0.1%
2	Florida	9,371.3	22.9%
9	Georgia	1,016.1	2.5%
38	Hawaii	16.1	0.0%
42	Idaho	8.5	0.0%
8	Illinois	1,068.6	2.6%
32	Indiana	43.7	0.1%
34	Iowa	29.4	0.1%
26	Kansas	100.0	0.2%
14	Kentucky	353.9	0.9%
22	Louisiana	168.3	0.4%
47	Maine	1.4	0.0%
25	Maryland	108.1	0.3%
21	Massachusetts	211.9	0.5%
16	Michigan	306.5	0.7%
33	Minnesota	37.2	0.1%
18	Mississippi	232.4	0.6%
17	Missouri	257.9	0.6%
45	Montana	4.1	0.0%
31	Nebraska	47.1	0.1%
36	Nevada	24.6	0.1%
48	New Hampshire	1.3	0.0%
5	New Jersey	1,575.2	3.8%
10	New Mexico	602.7	1.5%
6	New York	1,481.1	3.6%
12	North Carolina	384.3	0.9%
50	North Dakota	0.2	0.0%
19	Ohio	219.8	0.5%
30	Oklahoma	51.6	0.1%
24	Oregon	123.3	0.3%
23	Pennsylvania	160.9	0.4%
41	Rhode Island	8.9	0.0%
13	South Carolina	373.8	0.9%
40	South Dakota	12.2	0.0%
7	Tennessee	1,375.1	3.4%
1	Texas	9,487.6	23.1%
28	Utah	61.8	0.2%
49	Vermont	0.7	0.0%
27	Virginia	84.7	0.2%
11	Washington	502.7	1.2%
44	West Virginia	4.3	0.0%
43	Wisconsin	8.1	0.0%
46	Wyoming	3.7	0.0%

RANK ORDER

RANK	STATE	KILOGRAMS	% of USA
1	Texas	9,487.6	23.1%
2	Florida	9,371.3	22.9%
3	California	8,508.5	20.8%
4	Arizona	1,905.8	4.6%
5	New Jersey	1,575.2	3.8%
6	New York	1,481.1	3.6%
7	Tennessee	1,375.1	3.4%
8	Illinois	1,068.6	2.6%
9	Georgia	1,016.1	2.5%
10	New Mexico	602.7	1.5%
11	Washington	502.7	1.2%
12	North Carolina	384.3	0.9%
13	South Carolina	373.8	0.9%
14	Kentucky	353.9	0.9%
15	Arkansas	318.4	0.8%
16	Michigan	306.5	0.7%
17	Missouri	257.9	0.6%
18	Mississippi	232.4	0.6%
19	Ohio	219.8	0.5%
20	Alabama	214.7	0.5%
21	Massachusetts	211.9	0.5%
22	Louisiana	168.3	0.4%
23	Pennsylvania	160.9	0.4%
24	Oregon	123.3	0.3%
25	Maryland	108.1	0.3%
26	Kansas	100.0	0.2%
27	Virginia	84.7	0.2%
28	Utah	61.8	0.2%
29	Colorado	52.6	0.1%
30	Oklahoma	51.6	0.1%
31	Nebraska	47.1	0.1%
32	Indiana	43.7	0.1%
33	Minnesota	37.2	0.1%
34	Iowa	29.4	0.1%
35	Delaware	26.2	0.1%
36	Nevada	24.6	0.1%
37	Connecticut	22.6	0.1%
38	Hawaii	16.1	0.0%
39	Alaska	13.7	0.0%
40	South Dakota	12.2	0.0%
41	Rhode Island	8.9	0.0%
42	Idaho	8.5	0.0%
43	Wisconsin	8.1	0.0%
44	West Virginia	4.3	0.0%
45	Montana	4.1	0.0%
46	Wyoming	3.7	0.0%
47	Maine	1.4	0.0%
48	New Hampshire	1.3	0.0%
49	Vermont	0.7	0.0%
50	North Dakota	0.2	0.0%
	District of Columbia	9.6	0.0%

Source: Drug Enforcement Administration
"State Fact Sheets 2008" (http://www.dea.gov/pubs/state_factsheets.html)

Federal Heroin Seizures in 2008

National Total = 1,728.3 Kilograms

ALPHA ORDER

RANK ORDER

RANK	STATE	KILOGRAMS	% of USA		RANK	STATE	KILOGRAMS	% of USA
36	Alabama	0.1	0.0%		1	California	377.6	21.8%
23	Alaska	6.4	0.4%		2	New York	279.3	16.2%
4	Arizona	152.8	8.8%		3	Florida	220.0	12.7%
38	Arkansas	0.0	0.0%		4	Arizona	152.8	8.8%
1	California	377.6	21.8%		5	Texas	141.6	8.2%
30	Colorado	3.2	0.2%		6	New Jersey	136.6	7.9%
24	Connecticut	6.3	0.4%		7	Illinois	118.2	6.8%
38	Delaware	0.0	0.0%		8	Tennessee	59.3	3.4%
3	Florida	220.0	12.7%		9	New Mexico	32.1	1.9%
29	Georgia	3.3	0.2%		10	Pennsylvania	25.2	1.5%
32	Hawaii	1.2	0.1%		11	Maryland	21.0	1.2%
38	Idaho	0.0	0.0%		12	Michigan	20.0	1.2%
7	Illinois	118.2	6.8%		13	North Carolina	14.6	0.8%
17	Indiana	11.4	0.7%		14	Ohio	13.1	0.8%
38	Iowa	0.0	0.0%		15	Louisiana	12.9	0.7%
16	Kansas	11.6	0.7%		16	Kansas	11.6	0.7%
20	Kentucky	7.5	0.4%		17	Indiana	11.4	0.7%
15	Louisiana	12.9	0.7%		18	Rhode Island	8.1	0.5%
38	Maine	0.0	0.0%		19	Massachusetts	7.6	0.4%
11	Maryland	21.0	1.2%		20	Kentucky	7.5	0.4%
19	Massachusetts	7.6	0.4%		21	Oklahoma	6.7	0.4%
12	Michigan	20.0	1.2%		21	Oregon	6.7	0.4%
34	Minnesota	0.7	0.0%		23	Alaska	6.4	0.4%
38	Mississippi	0.0	0.0%		24	Connecticut	6.3	0.4%
31	Missouri	1.6	0.1%		25	South Carolina	6.2	0.4%
38	Montana	0.0	0.0%		26	Washington	5.5	0.3%
38	Nebraska	0.0	0.0%		27	Utah	4.1	0.2%
28	Nevada	3.4	0.2%		28	Nevada	3.4	0.2%
38	New Hampshire	0.0	0.0%		29	Georgia	3.3	0.2%
6	New Jersey	136.6	7.9%		30	Colorado	3.2	0.2%
9	New Mexico	32.1	1.9%		31	Missouri	1.6	0.1%
2	New York	279.3	16.2%		32	Hawaii	1.2	0.1%
13	North Carolina	14.6	0.8%		32	Virginia	1.2	0.1%
38	North Dakota	0.0	0.0%		34	Minnesota	0.7	0.0%
14	Ohio	13.1	0.8%		35	Wisconsin	0.2	0.0%
21	Oklahoma	6.7	0.4%		36	Alabama	0.1	0.0%
21	Oregon	6.7	0.4%		36	West Virginia	0.1	0.0%
10	Pennsylvania	25.2	1.5%		38	Arkansas	0.0	0.0%
18	Rhode Island	8.1	0.5%		38	Delaware	0.0	0.0%
25	South Carolina	6.2	0.4%		38	Idaho	0.0	0.0%
38	South Dakota	0.0	0.0%		38	Iowa	0.0	0.0%
8	Tennessee	59.3	3.4%		38	Maine	0.0	0.0%
5	Texas	141.6	8.2%		38	Mississippi	0.0	0.0%
27	Utah	4.1	0.2%		38	Montana	0.0	0.0%
38	Vermont	0.0	0.0%		38	Nebraska	0.0	0.0%
32	Virginia	1.2	0.1%		38	New Hampshire	0.0	0.0%
26	Washington	5.5	0.3%		38	North Dakota	0.0	0.0%
36	West Virginia	0.1	0.0%		38	South Dakota	0.0	0.0%
35	Wisconsin	0.2	0.0%		38	Vermont	0.0	0.0%
38	Wyoming	0.0	0.0%		38	Wyoming	0.0	0.0%
						District of Columbia	0.9	0.1%

Source: Drug Enforcement Administration
"State Fact Sheets 2008" (http://www.dea.gov/pubs/state_factsheets.html)

Percent of Population Who Are Illicit Drug Users: 2007

National Percent = 8.1% of Population*

ALPHA ORDER

RANK	STATE	PERCENT
40	Alabama	7.0
4	Alaska	10.7
12	Arizona	9.1
19	Arkansas	8.6
12	California	9.1
3	Colorado	11.0
29	Connecticut	7.9
19	Delaware	8.6
31	Florida	7.7
32	Georgia	7.5
32	Hawaii	7.5
34	Idaho	7.4
37	Illinois	7.3
22	Indiana	8.4
50	Iowa	5.2
34	Kansas	7.4
27	Kentucky	8.1
24	Louisiana	8.2
10	Maine	9.6
40	Maryland	7.0
8	Massachusetts	9.8
12	Michigan	9.1
23	Minnesota	8.3
39	Mississippi	7.1
28	Missouri	8.0
5	Montana	10.3
43	Nebraska	6.7
16	Nevada	9.0
8	New Hampshire	9.8
47	New Jersey	6.5
10	New Mexico	9.6
12	New York	9.1
38	North Carolina	7.2
49	North Dakota	6.2
29	Ohio	7.9
21	Oklahoma	8.5
6	Oregon	10.2
40	Pennsylvania	7.0
1	Rhode Island	12.5
46	South Carolina	6.6
43	South Dakota	6.7
17	Tennessee	8.8
43	Texas	6.7
48	Utah	6.4
2	Vermont	11.5
24	Virginia	8.2
6	Washington	10.2
34	West Virginia	7.4
24	Wisconsin	8.2
18	Wyoming	8.7

RANK ORDER

RANK	STATE	PERCENT
1	Rhode Island	12.5
2	Vermont	11.5
3	Colorado	11.0
4	Alaska	10.7
5	Montana	10.3
6	Oregon	10.2
6	Washington	10.2
8	Massachusetts	9.8
8	New Hampshire	9.8
10	Maine	9.6
10	New Mexico	9.6
12	Arizona	9.1
12	California	9.1
12	Michigan	9.1
12	New York	9.1
16	Nevada	9.0
17	Tennessee	8.8
18	Wyoming	8.7
19	Arkansas	8.6
19	Delaware	8.6
21	Oklahoma	8.5
22	Indiana	8.4
23	Minnesota	8.3
24	Louisiana	8.2
24	Virginia	8.2
24	Wisconsin	8.2
27	Kentucky	8.1
28	Missouri	8.0
29	Connecticut	7.9
29	Ohio	7.9
31	Florida	7.7
32	Georgia	7.5
32	Hawaii	7.5
34	Idaho	7.4
34	Kansas	7.4
34	West Virginia	7.4
37	Illinois	7.3
38	North Carolina	7.2
39	Mississippi	7.1
40	Alabama	7.0
40	Maryland	7.0
40	Pennsylvania	7.0
43	Nebraska	6.7
43	South Dakota	6.7
43	Texas	6.7
46	South Carolina	6.6
47	New Jersey	6.5
48	Utah	6.4
49	North Dakota	6.2
50	Iowa	5.2

District of Columbia   12.1

Source: U.S. Department of Health and Human Services, Substance Abuse and Mental Health Services Administration "2006-2007 National Surveys on Drug Use and Health" (June 2009, http://www.oas.samhsa.gov/2k7state/toc.cfm)
*Population 12 years and older who used any illicit drug at least once within month of survey.

Percent of Population Who Are Marijuana Users: 2007

National Percent = 5.9% of Population*

ALPHA ORDER			RANK ORDER		
RANK	STATE	PERCENT	RANK	STATE	PERCENT
47	Alabama	4.5	1	Rhode Island	10.3
7	Alaska	8.1	2	Vermont	10.0
34	Arizona	5.3	3	Montana	8.7
24	Arkansas	5.8	4	Maine	8.3
16	California	6.6	5	Colorado	8.2
5	Colorado	8.2	5	New Hampshire	8.2
19	Connecticut	6.2	7	Alaska	8.1
18	Delaware	6.3	8	Massachusetts	7.9
29	Florida	5.5	9	Oregon	7.6
26	Georgia	5.7	10	Washington	7.4
34	Hawaii	5.3	11	Minnesota	7.3
31	Idaho	5.4	12	Michigan	7.0
31	Illinois	5.4	12	New Mexico	7.0
22	Indiana	6.0	14	New York	6.9
50	Iowa	3.8	14	Wyoming	6.9
28	Kansas	5.6	16	California	6.6
24	Kentucky	5.8	16	Virginia	6.6
31	Louisiana	5.4	18	Delaware	6.3
4	Maine	8.3	19	Connecticut	6.2
40	Maryland	5.1	20	Nevada	6.1
8	Massachusetts	7.9	20	Ohio	6.1
12	Michigan	7.0	22	Indiana	6.0
11	Minnesota	7.3	23	Wisconsin	5.9
46	Mississippi	4.6	24	Arkansas	5.8
29	Missouri	5.5	24	Kentucky	5.8
3	Montana	8.7	26	Georgia	5.7
40	Nebraska	5.1	26	Tennessee	5.7
20	Nevada	6.1	28	Kansas	5.6
5	New Hampshire	8.2	29	Florida	5.5
45	New Jersey	4.7	29	Missouri	5.5
12	New Mexico	7.0	31	Idaho	5.4
14	New York	6.9	31	Illinois	5.4
34	North Carolina	5.3	31	Louisiana	5.4
43	North Dakota	5.0	34	Arizona	5.3
20	Ohio	6.1	34	Hawaii	5.3
39	Oklahoma	5.2	34	North Carolina	5.3
9	Oregon	7.6	34	South Dakota	5.3
40	Pennsylvania	5.1	34	West Virginia	5.3
1	Rhode Island	10.3	39	Oklahoma	5.2
44	South Carolina	4.8	40	Maryland	5.1
34	South Dakota	5.3	40	Nebraska	5.1
26	Tennessee	5.7	40	Pennsylvania	5.1
48	Texas	4.3	43	North Dakota	5.0
49	Utah	4.2	44	South Carolina	4.8
2	Vermont	10.0	45	New Jersey	4.7
16	Virginia	6.6	46	Mississippi	4.6
10	Washington	7.4	47	Alabama	4.5
34	West Virginia	5.3	48	Texas	4.3
23	Wisconsin	5.9	49	Utah	4.2
14	Wyoming	6.9	50	Iowa	3.8
				District of Columbia	9.8

Source: U.S. Department of Health and Human Services, Substance Abuse and Mental Health Services Administration
"2006-2007 National Surveys on Drug Use and Health" (June 2009, http://www.oas.samhsa.gov/2k7state/toc.cfm)
*Population 12 years and older who used any marijuana at least once within month of survey.

Percent of Population Using Illicit Drugs Other Than Marijuana: 2007

National Percent = 3.8% of Population*

ALPHA ORDER

RANK ORDER

ALPHA ORDER				RANK ORDER		
RANK	STATE	PERCENT		RANK	STATE	PERCENT
19	Alabama	3.9		1	Arizona	5.5
19	Alaska	3.9		1	Rhode Island	5.5
1	Arizona	5.5		3	Tennessee	5.2
4	Arkansas	4.9		4	Arkansas	4.9
17	California	4.0		5	Louisiana	4.7
6	Colorado	4.6		6	Colorado	4.6
41	Connecticut	3.2		6	Oklahoma	4.6
27	Delaware	3.8		6	Washington	4.6
19	Florida	3.9		9	Missouri	4.2
38	Georgia	3.3		9	Oregon	4.2
47	Hawaii	2.8		9	West Virginia	4.2
36	Idaho	3.4		9	Wisconsin	4.2
38	Illinois	3.3		13	Indiana	4.1
13	Indiana	4.1		13	Massachusetts	4.1
48	Iowa	2.6		13	Nevada	4.1
28	Kansas	3.7		13	Vermont	4.1
19	Kentucky	3.9		17	California	4.0
5	Louisiana	4.7		17	Texas	4.0
38	Maine	3.3		19	Alabama	3.9
33	Maryland	3.5		19	Alaska	3.9
13	Massachusetts	4.1		19	Florida	3.9
19	Michigan	3.9		19	Kentucky	3.9
41	Minnesota	3.2		19	Michigan	3.9
28	Mississippi	3.7		19	Montana	3.9
9	Missouri	4.2		19	New Mexico	3.9
19	Montana	3.9		19	Wyoming	3.9
41	Nebraska	3.2		27	Delaware	3.8
13	Nevada	4.1		28	Kansas	3.7
33	New Hampshire	3.5		28	Mississippi	3.7
46	New Jersey	3.0		30	New York	3.6
19	New Mexico	3.9		30	North Carolina	3.6
30	New York	3.6		30	Virginia	3.6
30	North Carolina	3.6		33	Maryland	3.5
48	North Dakota	2.6		33	New Hampshire	3.5
33	Ohio	3.5		33	Ohio	3.5
6	Oklahoma	4.6		36	Idaho	3.4
9	Oregon	4.2		36	Utah	3.4
45	Pennsylvania	3.1		38	Georgia	3.3
1	Rhode Island	5.5		38	Illinois	3.3
41	South Carolina	3.2		38	Maine	3.3
48	South Dakota	2.6		41	Connecticut	3.2
3	Tennessee	5.2		41	Minnesota	3.2
17	Texas	4.0		41	Nebraska	3.2
36	Utah	3.4		41	South Carolina	3.2
13	Vermont	4.1		45	Pennsylvania	3.1
30	Virginia	3.6		46	New Jersey	3.0
6	Washington	4.6		47	Hawaii	2.8
9	West Virginia	4.2		48	Iowa	2.6
9	Wisconsin	4.2		48	North Dakota	2.6
19	Wyoming	3.9		48	South Dakota	2.6

District of Columbia   4.8

Source: U.S. Department of Health and Human Services, Substance Abuse and Mental Health Services Administration
"2006-2007 National Surveys on Drug Use and Health" (June 2009, http://www.oas.samhsa.gov/2k7state/toc.cfm)
*Population 12 years and older who used any illicit drug except marijuana at least once within month of survey.

Percent of Population Using Pain Medication for Nonmedical Reasons: 2007

National Percent = 5.1% of Population*

ALPHA ORDER

RANK	STATE	PERCENT
12	Alabama	6.0
24	Alaska	5.1
4	Arizona	6.5
1	Arkansas	7.3
20	California	5.4
18	Colorado	5.5
41	Connecticut	4.2
30	Delaware	4.8
33	Florida	4.7
22	Georgia	5.2
48	Hawaii	3.6
12	Idaho	6.0
39	Illinois	4.3
6	Indiana	6.2
46	Iowa	3.9
28	Kansas	4.9
6	Kentucky	6.2
6	Louisiana	6.2
37	Maine	4.6
39	Maryland	4.3
15	Massachusetts	5.7
15	Michigan	5.7
38	Minnesota	4.4
41	Mississippi	4.2
24	Missouri	5.1
18	Montana	5.5
47	Nebraska	3.7
6	Nevada	6.2
30	New Hampshire	4.8
48	New Jersey	3.6
10	New Mexico	6.1
43	New York	4.1
33	North Carolina	4.7
43	North Dakota	4.1
17	Ohio	5.6
2	Oklahoma	7.0
20	Oregon	5.4
45	Pennsylvania	4.0
10	Rhode Island	6.1
33	South Carolina	4.7
50	South Dakota	3.4
3	Tennessee	6.9
33	Texas	4.7
22	Utah	5.2
30	Vermont	4.8
24	Virginia	5.1
4	Washington	6.5
24	West Virginia	5.1
14	Wisconsin	5.8
28	Wyoming	4.9

RANK ORDER

RANK	STATE	PERCENT
1	Arkansas	7.3
2	Oklahoma	7.0
3	Tennessee	6.9
4	Arizona	6.5
4	Washington	6.5
6	Indiana	6.2
6	Kentucky	6.2
6	Louisiana	6.2
6	Nevada	6.2
10	New Mexico	6.1
10	Rhode Island	6.1
12	Alabama	6.0
12	Idaho	6.0
14	Wisconsin	5.8
15	Massachusetts	5.7
15	Michigan	5.7
17	Ohio	5.6
18	Colorado	5.5
18	Montana	5.5
20	California	5.4
20	Oregon	5.4
22	Georgia	5.2
22	Utah	5.2
24	Alaska	5.1
24	Missouri	5.1
24	Virginia	5.1
24	West Virginia	5.1
28	Kansas	4.9
28	Wyoming	4.9
30	Delaware	4.8
30	New Hampshire	4.8
30	Vermont	4.8
33	Florida	4.7
33	North Carolina	4.7
33	South Carolina	4.7
33	Texas	4.7
37	Maine	4.6
38	Minnesota	4.4
39	Illinois	4.3
39	Maryland	4.3
41	Connecticut	4.2
41	Mississippi	4.2
43	New York	4.1
43	North Dakota	4.1
45	Pennsylvania	4.0
46	Iowa	3.9
47	Nebraska	3.7
48	Hawaii	3.6
48	New Jersey	3.6
50	South Dakota	3.4

District of Columbia 4.0

Source: U.S. Department of Health and Human Services, Substance Abuse and Mental Health Services Administration
    "2006-2007 National Surveys on Drug Use and Health" (June 2009, http://www.oas.samhsa.gov/2k7state/toc.cfm)
*Percent of population 12 years and older using prescription-type pain relievers, tranquilizers, stimulants, and sedatives for nonmedical purposes within one year of survey.

Percent of Population Who Are Binge Drinkers: 2007

National Percent = 23.2% of Population*

RANK	STATE	PERCENT
47	Alabama	18.8
31	Alaska	22.7
27	Arizona	22.9
34	Arkansas	22.3
38	California	21.6
10	Colorado	26.2
17	Connecticut	25.1
24	Delaware	23.2
25	Florida	23.1
41	Georgia	21.1
27	Hawaii	22.9
45	Idaho	19.8
10	Illinois	26.2
34	Indiana	22.3
6	Iowa	27.5
14	Kansas	25.4
39	Kentucky	21.3
18	Louisiana	24.4
25	Maine	23.1
41	Maryland	21.1
9	Massachusetts	26.7
16	Michigan	25.2
2	Minnesota	28.8
49	Mississippi	18.7
19	Missouri	24.3
7	Montana	26.9
19	Nebraska	24.3
21	Nevada	24.2
12	New Hampshire	25.6
27	New Jersey	22.9
43	New Mexico	20.9
23	New York	23.3
44	North Carolina	20.4
1	North Dakota	32.0
15	Ohio	25.3
40	Oklahoma	21.2
37	Oregon	21.7
22	Pennsylvania	23.5
5	Rhode Island	27.9
36	South Carolina	21.9
4	South Dakota	28.3
46	Tennessee	19.2
30	Texas	22.8
50	Utah	15.6
12	Vermont	25.6
32	Virginia	22.6
33	Washington	22.5
47	West Virginia	18.8
2	Wisconsin	28.8
7	Wyoming	26.9

RANK	STATE	PERCENT
1	North Dakota	32.0
2	Minnesota	28.8
2	Wisconsin	28.8
4	South Dakota	28.3
5	Rhode Island	27.9
6	Iowa	27.5
7	Montana	26.9
7	Wyoming	26.9
9	Massachusetts	26.7
10	Colorado	26.2
10	Illinois	26.2
12	New Hampshire	25.6
12	Vermont	25.6
14	Kansas	25.4
15	Ohio	25.3
16	Michigan	25.2
17	Connecticut	25.1
18	Louisiana	24.4
19	Missouri	24.3
19	Nebraska	24.3
21	Nevada	24.2
22	Pennsylvania	23.5
23	New York	23.3
24	Delaware	23.2
25	Florida	23.1
25	Maine	23.1
27	Arizona	22.9
27	Hawaii	22.9
27	New Jersey	22.9
30	Texas	22.8
31	Alaska	22.7
32	Virginia	22.6
33	Washington	22.5
34	Arkansas	22.3
34	Indiana	22.3
36	South Carolina	21.9
37	Oregon	21.7
38	California	21.6
39	Kentucky	21.3
40	Oklahoma	21.2
41	Georgia	21.1
41	Maryland	21.1
43	New Mexico	20.9
44	North Carolina	20.4
45	Idaho	19.8
46	Tennessee	19.2
47	Alabama	18.8
47	West Virginia	18.8
49	Mississippi	18.7
50	Utah	15.6
	District of Columbia	28.6

Source: U.S. Department of Health and Human Services, Substance Abuse and Mental Health Services Administration
"2006-2007 National Surveys on Drug Use and Health" (June 2009, http://www.oas.samhsa.gov/2k7state/toc.cfm)
*Population 12 years and older who reported binge alcohol use at least once within month of survey. "Binge" alcohol use is defined as drinking five or more drinks on the same occasion on at least one day in the past 30 days. By "occasion" is meant at the same time or within a couple of hours of each other.

Percent of Population Reporting Illicit Drug Dependence or Abuse: 2007

National Percent = 2.8% of Population*

ALPHA ORDER

RANK	STATE	PERCENT
13	Alabama	3.0
2	Alaska	3.2
20	Arizona	2.9
2	Arkansas	3.2
33	California	2.7
2	Colorado	3.2
27	Connecticut	2.8
2	Delaware	3.2
33	Florida	2.7
9	Georgia	3.1
47	Hawaii	2.2
27	Idaho	2.8
33	Illinois	2.7
13	Indiana	3.0
49	Iowa	2.1
43	Kansas	2.3
13	Kentucky	3.0
9	Louisiana	3.1
13	Maine	3.0
13	Maryland	3.0
20	Massachusetts	2.9
20	Michigan	2.9
41	Minnesota	2.6
20	Mississippi	2.9
27	Missouri	2.8
9	Montana	3.1
43	Nebraska	2.3
33	Nevada	2.7
20	New Hampshire	2.9
43	New Jersey	2.3
2	New Mexico	3.2
9	New York	3.1
27	North Carolina	2.8
47	North Dakota	2.2
2	Ohio	3.2
33	Oklahoma	2.7
33	Oregon	2.7
43	Pennsylvania	2.3
1	Rhode Island	4.2
2	South Carolina	3.2
49	South Dakota	2.1
13	Tennessee	3.0
33	Texas	2.7
20	Utah	2.9
13	Vermont	3.0
27	Virginia	2.8
20	Washington	2.9
33	West Virginia	2.7
41	Wisconsin	2.6
27	Wyoming	2.8

RANK ORDER

RANK	STATE	PERCENT
1	Rhode Island	4.2
2	Alaska	3.2
2	Arkansas	3.2
2	Colorado	3.2
2	Delaware	3.2
2	New Mexico	3.2
2	Ohio	3.2
2	South Carolina	3.2
9	Georgia	3.1
9	Louisiana	3.1
9	Montana	3.1
9	New York	3.1
13	Alabama	3.0
13	Indiana	3.0
13	Kentucky	3.0
13	Maine	3.0
13	Maryland	3.0
13	Tennessee	3.0
13	Vermont	3.0
20	Arizona	2.9
20	Massachusetts	2.9
20	Michigan	2.9
20	Mississippi	2.9
20	New Hampshire	2.9
20	Utah	2.9
20	Washington	2.9
27	Connecticut	2.8
27	Idaho	2.8
27	Missouri	2.8
27	North Carolina	2.8
27	Virginia	2.8
27	Wyoming	2.8
33	California	2.7
33	Florida	2.7
33	Illinois	2.7
33	Nevada	2.7
33	Oklahoma	2.7
33	Oregon	2.7
33	Texas	2.7
33	West Virginia	2.7
41	Minnesota	2.6
41	Wisconsin	2.6
43	Kansas	2.3
43	Nebraska	2.3
43	New Jersey	2.3
43	Pennsylvania	2.3
47	Hawaii	2.2
47	North Dakota	2.2
49	Iowa	2.1
49	South Dakota	2.1

District of Columbia   4.5

Source: U.S. Department of Health and Human Services, Substance Abuse and Mental Health Services Administration
"2006-2007 National Surveys on Drug Use and Health" (June 2009, http://www.oas.samhsa.gov/2k7state/toc.cfm)
*Population 12 years and older reporting illicit drug dependence or abuse within one year of survey.

Percent of Population Needing But Not Receiving
Treatment for Illicit Drug Use: 2007
National Percent = 2.5% of Population*

<table>
<tr><td colspan="3">ALPHA ORDER</td><td colspan="3">RANK ORDER</td></tr>
<tr><td>RANK</td><td>STATE</td><td>PERCENT</td><td>RANK</td><td>STATE</td><td>PERCENT</td></tr>
<tr><td>26</td><td>Alabama</td><td>2.5</td><td>1</td><td>Rhode Island</td><td>3.7</td></tr>
<tr><td>7</td><td>Alaska</td><td>2.8</td><td>2</td><td>Arkansas</td><td>2.9</td></tr>
<tr><td>16</td><td>Arizona</td><td>2.6</td><td>2</td><td>Colorado</td><td>2.9</td></tr>
<tr><td>2</td><td>Arkansas</td><td>2.9</td><td>2</td><td>Delaware</td><td>2.9</td></tr>
<tr><td>16</td><td>California</td><td>2.6</td><td>2</td><td>Montana</td><td>2.9</td></tr>
<tr><td>2</td><td>Colorado</td><td>2.9</td><td>2</td><td>New Mexico</td><td>2.9</td></tr>
<tr><td>34</td><td>Connecticut</td><td>2.4</td><td>7</td><td>Alaska</td><td>2.8</td></tr>
<tr><td>2</td><td>Delaware</td><td>2.9</td><td>7</td><td>Georgia</td><td>2.8</td></tr>
<tr><td>16</td><td>Florida</td><td>2.6</td><td>7</td><td>Louisiana</td><td>2.8</td></tr>
<tr><td>7</td><td>Georgia</td><td>2.8</td><td>7</td><td>Maine</td><td>2.8</td></tr>
<tr><td>39</td><td>Hawaii</td><td>2.3</td><td>7</td><td>South Carolina</td><td>2.8</td></tr>
<tr><td>26</td><td>Idaho</td><td>2.5</td><td>12</td><td>New York</td><td>2.7</td></tr>
<tr><td>39</td><td>Illinois</td><td>2.3</td><td>12</td><td>Ohio</td><td>2.7</td></tr>
<tr><td>16</td><td>Indiana</td><td>2.6</td><td>12</td><td>Utah</td><td>2.7</td></tr>
<tr><td>47</td><td>Iowa</td><td>1.9</td><td>12</td><td>Vermont</td><td>2.7</td></tr>
<tr><td>47</td><td>Kansas</td><td>1.9</td><td>16</td><td>Arizona</td><td>2.6</td></tr>
<tr><td>26</td><td>Kentucky</td><td>2.5</td><td>16</td><td>California</td><td>2.6</td></tr>
<tr><td>7</td><td>Louisiana</td><td>2.8</td><td>16</td><td>Florida</td><td>2.6</td></tr>
<tr><td>7</td><td>Maine</td><td>2.8</td><td>16</td><td>Indiana</td><td>2.6</td></tr>
<tr><td>16</td><td>Maryland</td><td>2.6</td><td>16</td><td>Maryland</td><td>2.6</td></tr>
<tr><td>16</td><td>Massachusetts</td><td>2.6</td><td>16</td><td>Massachusetts</td><td>2.6</td></tr>
<tr><td>34</td><td>Michigan</td><td>2.4</td><td>16</td><td>New Hampshire</td><td>2.6</td></tr>
<tr><td>39</td><td>Minnesota</td><td>2.3</td><td>16</td><td>North Carolina</td><td>2.6</td></tr>
<tr><td>34</td><td>Mississippi</td><td>2.4</td><td>16</td><td>Tennessee</td><td>2.6</td></tr>
<tr><td>26</td><td>Missouri</td><td>2.5</td><td>16</td><td>Washington</td><td>2.6</td></tr>
<tr><td>2</td><td>Montana</td><td>2.9</td><td>26</td><td>Alabama</td><td>2.5</td></tr>
<tr><td>44</td><td>Nebraska</td><td>2.1</td><td>26</td><td>Idaho</td><td>2.5</td></tr>
<tr><td>26</td><td>Nevada</td><td>2.5</td><td>26</td><td>Kentucky</td><td>2.5</td></tr>
<tr><td>16</td><td>New Hampshire</td><td>2.6</td><td>26</td><td>Missouri</td><td>2.5</td></tr>
<tr><td>47</td><td>New Jersey</td><td>1.9</td><td>26</td><td>Nevada</td><td>2.5</td></tr>
<tr><td>2</td><td>New Mexico</td><td>2.9</td><td>26</td><td>Oklahoma</td><td>2.5</td></tr>
<tr><td>12</td><td>New York</td><td>2.7</td><td>26</td><td>Virginia</td><td>2.5</td></tr>
<tr><td>16</td><td>North Carolina</td><td>2.6</td><td>26</td><td>Wyoming</td><td>2.5</td></tr>
<tr><td>47</td><td>North Dakota</td><td>1.9</td><td>34</td><td>Connecticut</td><td>2.4</td></tr>
<tr><td>12</td><td>Ohio</td><td>2.7</td><td>34</td><td>Michigan</td><td>2.4</td></tr>
<tr><td>26</td><td>Oklahoma</td><td>2.5</td><td>34</td><td>Mississippi</td><td>2.4</td></tr>
<tr><td>34</td><td>Oregon</td><td>2.4</td><td>34</td><td>Oregon</td><td>2.4</td></tr>
<tr><td>45</td><td>Pennsylvania</td><td>2.0</td><td>34</td><td>Texas</td><td>2.4</td></tr>
<tr><td>1</td><td>Rhode Island</td><td>3.7</td><td>39</td><td>Hawaii</td><td>2.3</td></tr>
<tr><td>7</td><td>South Carolina</td><td>2.8</td><td>39</td><td>Illinois</td><td>2.3</td></tr>
<tr><td>45</td><td>South Dakota</td><td>2.0</td><td>39</td><td>Minnesota</td><td>2.3</td></tr>
<tr><td>16</td><td>Tennessee</td><td>2.6</td><td>39</td><td>West Virginia</td><td>2.3</td></tr>
<tr><td>34</td><td>Texas</td><td>2.4</td><td>43</td><td>Wisconsin</td><td>2.2</td></tr>
<tr><td>12</td><td>Utah</td><td>2.7</td><td>44</td><td>Nebraska</td><td>2.1</td></tr>
<tr><td>12</td><td>Vermont</td><td>2.7</td><td>45</td><td>Pennsylvania</td><td>2.0</td></tr>
<tr><td>26</td><td>Virginia</td><td>2.5</td><td>45</td><td>South Dakota</td><td>2.0</td></tr>
<tr><td>16</td><td>Washington</td><td>2.6</td><td>47</td><td>Iowa</td><td>1.9</td></tr>
<tr><td>39</td><td>West Virginia</td><td>2.3</td><td>47</td><td>Kansas</td><td>1.9</td></tr>
<tr><td>43</td><td>Wisconsin</td><td>2.2</td><td>47</td><td>New Jersey</td><td>1.9</td></tr>
<tr><td>26</td><td>Wyoming</td><td>2.5</td><td>47</td><td>North Dakota</td><td>1.9</td></tr>
<tr><td></td><td></td><td></td><td></td><td>District of Columbia</td><td>3.4</td></tr>
</table>

Source: U.S. Department of Health and Human Services, Substance Abuse and Mental Health Services Administration
"2006-2007 National Surveys on Drug Use and Health" (June 2009, http://www.oas.samhsa.gov/2k7state/toc.cfm)
*Percent of population 12 years and older needing but not receiving treatment within one year of survey.

Percent of Population Reporting Alcohol Dependence or Abuse: 2007

National Percent = 7.6% of Population*

ALPHA ORDER			RANK ORDER		
RANK	STATE	PERCENT	RANK	STATE	PERCENT
47	Alabama	6.3	1	North Dakota	10.0
25	Alaska	7.8	2	Colorado	9.6
32	Arizona	7.4	2	Montana	9.6
16	Arkansas	8.2	2	South Dakota	9.6
16	California	8.2	2	Wyoming	9.6
2	Colorado	9.6	6	Minnesota	9.4
13	Connecticut	8.5	7	Wisconsin	9.3
40	Delaware	6.7	8	Iowa	9.2
37	Florida	7.0	9	Massachusetts	9.0
39	Georgia	6.8	10	Hawaii	8.9
10	Hawaii	8.9	10	Nebraska	8.9
26	Idaho	7.7	12	Kansas	8.6
16	Illinois	8.2	13	Connecticut	8.5
34	Indiana	7.3	13	Rhode Island	8.5
8	Iowa	9.2	15	New Hampshire	8.3
12	Kansas	8.6	16	Arkansas	8.2
49	Kentucky	6.2	16	California	8.2
32	Louisiana	7.4	16	Illinois	8.2
30	Maine	7.5	16	Nevada	8.2
26	Maryland	7.7	16	Vermont	8.2
9	Massachusetts	9.0	21	Michigan	8.1
21	Michigan	8.1	21	Ohio	8.1
6	Minnesota	9.4	23	Missouri	8.0
47	Mississippi	6.3	23	New Mexico	8.0
23	Missouri	8.0	25	Alaska	7.8
2	Montana	9.6	26	Idaho	7.7
10	Nebraska	8.9	26	Maryland	7.7
16	Nevada	8.2	28	South Carolina	7.6
15	New Hampshire	8.3	28	Washington	7.6
44	New Jersey	6.5	30	Maine	7.5
23	New Mexico	8.0	30	Tennessee	7.5
41	New York	6.6	32	Arizona	7.4
45	North Carolina	6.4	32	Louisiana	7.4
1	North Dakota	10.0	34	Indiana	7.3
21	Ohio	8.1	34	Virginia	7.3
38	Oklahoma	6.9	36	Texas	7.2
41	Oregon	6.6	37	Florida	7.0
45	Pennsylvania	6.4	38	Oklahoma	6.9
13	Rhode Island	8.5	39	Georgia	6.8
28	South Carolina	7.6	40	Delaware	6.7
2	South Dakota	9.6	41	New York	6.6
30	Tennessee	7.5	41	Oregon	6.6
36	Texas	7.2	41	Utah	6.6
41	Utah	6.6	44	New Jersey	6.5
16	Vermont	8.2	45	North Carolina	6.4
34	Virginia	7.3	45	Pennsylvania	6.4
28	Washington	7.6	47	Alabama	6.3
50	West Virginia	6.1	47	Mississippi	6.3
7	Wisconsin	9.3	49	Kentucky	6.2
2	Wyoming	9.6	50	West Virginia	6.1

District of Columbia   10.1

Source: U.S. Department of Health and Human Services, Substance Abuse and Mental Health Services Administration
  "2006-2007 National Surveys on Drug Use and Health" (June 2009, http://www.oas.samhsa.gov/2k7state/toc.cfm)
*Population 12 years and older reporting alcohol dependence or abuse within one year of survey.

Percent of Population Needing But Not Receiving
Treatment for Alcohol Use: 2007
National Percent = 7.2% of Population*

ALPHA ORDER

RANK ORDER

RANK	STATE	PERCENT		RANK	STATE	PERCENT
47	Alabama	6.0		1	North Dakota	9.4
30	Alaska	7.1		2	Colorado	9.3
34	Arizona	7.0		3	Minnesota	9.1
15	Arkansas	7.8		3	South Dakota	9.1
15	California	7.8		3	Wyoming	9.1
2	Colorado	9.3		6	Montana	8.9
15	Connecticut	7.8		6	Wisconsin	8.9
40	Delaware	6.4		8	Iowa	8.8
36	Florida	6.7		8	Massachusetts	8.8
39	Georgia	6.5		10	Hawaii	8.7
10	Hawaii	8.7		11	Nebraska	8.3
25	Idaho	7.4		11	Rhode Island	8.3
15	Illinois	7.8		13	Kansas	8.1
36	Indiana	6.7		14	Nevada	7.9
8	Iowa	8.8		15	Arkansas	7.8
13	Kansas	8.1		15	California	7.8
50	Kentucky	5.8		15	Connecticut	7.8
28	Louisiana	7.2		15	Illinois	7.8
28	Maine	7.2		15	New Hampshire	7.8
27	Maryland	7.3		20	Michigan	7.7
8	Massachusetts	8.8		20	New Mexico	7.7
20	Michigan	7.7		20	Vermont	7.7
3	Minnesota	9.1		23	Missouri	7.6
47	Mississippi	6.0		24	Ohio	7.5
23	Missouri	7.6		25	Idaho	7.4
6	Montana	8.9		25	South Carolina	7.4
11	Nebraska	8.3		27	Maryland	7.3
14	Nevada	7.9		28	Louisiana	7.2
15	New Hampshire	7.8		28	Maine	7.2
43	New Jersey	6.2		30	Alaska	7.1
20	New Mexico	7.7		30	Tennessee	7.1
42	New York	6.3		30	Texas	7.1
43	North Carolina	6.2		30	Virginia	7.1
1	North Dakota	9.4		34	Arizona	7.0
24	Ohio	7.5		34	Washington	7.0
38	Oklahoma	6.6		36	Florida	6.7
40	Oregon	6.4		36	Indiana	6.7
46	Pennsylvania	6.1		38	Oklahoma	6.6
11	Rhode Island	8.3		39	Georgia	6.5
25	South Carolina	7.4		40	Delaware	6.4
3	South Dakota	9.1		40	Oregon	6.4
30	Tennessee	7.1		42	New York	6.3
30	Texas	7.1		43	New Jersey	6.2
43	Utah	6.2		43	North Carolina	6.2
20	Vermont	7.7		43	Utah	6.2
30	Virginia	7.1		46	Pennsylvania	6.1
34	Washington	7.0		47	Alabama	6.0
49	West Virginia	5.9		47	Mississippi	6.0
6	Wisconsin	8.9		49	West Virginia	5.9
3	Wyoming	9.1		50	Kentucky	5.8

	District of Columbia	9.7

Source: U.S. Department of Health and Human Services, Substance Abuse and Mental Health Services Administration
"2006-2007 National Surveys on Drug Use and Health" (June 2009, http://www.oas.samhsa.gov/2k7state/toc.cfm)
*Percent of population 12 years and older needing but not receiving treatment within one year of survey.

Substance Abuse Treatment Admissions in 2008

National Total = 1,898,998 Admissions*

ALPHA ORDER

RANK ORDER

RANK	STATE	ADMISSIONS	% of USA		RANK	STATE	ADMISSIONS	% of USA
NA	Alabama**	NA	NA		1	New York	313,759	16.5%
NA	Alaska**	NA	NA		2	California	197,289	10.4%
25	Arizona	21,372	1.1%		3	Ohio	99,239	5.2%
33	Arkansas	14,273	0.8%		4	Massachusetts	85,651	4.5%
2	California	197,289	10.4%		5	Colorado	78,818	4.2%
5	Colorado	78,818	4.2%		6	Pennsylvania	75,127	4.0%
15	Connecticut	45,982	2.4%		7	Illinois	70,959	3.7%
40	Delaware	7,964	0.4%		8	Maryland	65,783	3.5%
13	Florida	49,265	2.6%		9	New Jersey	65,333	3.4%
NA	Georgia**	NA	NA		10	Michigan	63,613	3.3%
41	Hawaii	7,237	0.4%		11	Oregon	50,716	2.7%
44	Idaho	5,688	0.3%		12	Minnesota	49,961	2.6%
7	Illinois	70,959	3.7%		13	Florida	49,265	2.6%
26	Indiana	19,113	1.0%		14	Missouri	49,067	2.6%
23	Iowa	23,301	1.2%		15	Connecticut	45,982	2.4%
28	Kansas	16,664	0.9%		16	Texas	45,775	2.4%
24	Kentucky	22,172	1.2%		17	Washington	39,651	2.1%
22	Louisiana	25,392	1.3%		18	North Carolina	38,402	2.0%
30	Maine	15,471	0.8%		19	Virginia	33,466	1.8%
8	Maryland	65,783	3.5%		20	South Carolina	30,368	1.6%
4	Massachusetts	85,651	4.5%		21	Wisconsin	29,116	1.5%
10	Michigan	63,613	3.3%		22	Louisiana	25,392	1.3%
12	Minnesota	49,961	2.6%		23	Iowa	23,301	1.2%
45	Mississippi	4,171	0.2%		24	Kentucky	22,172	1.2%
14	Missouri	49,067	2.6%		25	Arizona	21,372	1.1%
38	Montana	8,820	0.5%		26	Indiana	19,113	1.0%
29	Nebraska	16,265	0.9%		27	Oklahoma	17,847	0.9%
37	Nevada	9,700	0.5%		28	Kansas	16,664	0.9%
43	New Hampshire	6,136	0.3%		29	Nebraska	16,265	0.9%
9	New Jersey	65,333	3.4%		30	Maine	15,471	0.8%
35	New Mexico	10,904	0.6%		31	Utah	15,093	0.8%
1	New York	313,759	16.5%		32	South Dakota	15,045	0.8%
18	North Carolina	38,402	2.0%		33	Arkansas	14,273	0.8%
46	North Dakota	2,456	0.1%		34	Rhode Island	11,388	0.6%
3	Ohio	99,239	5.2%		35	New Mexico	10,904	0.6%
27	Oklahoma	17,847	0.9%		36	Tennessee	9,810	0.5%
11	Oregon	50,716	2.7%		37	Nevada	9,700	0.5%
6	Pennsylvania	75,127	4.0%		38	Montana	8,820	0.5%
34	Rhode Island	11,388	0.6%		39	Vermont	8,441	0.4%
20	South Carolina	30,368	1.6%		40	Delaware	7,964	0.4%
32	South Dakota	15,045	0.8%		41	Hawaii	7,237	0.4%
36	Tennessee	9,810	0.5%		42	West Virginia	6,935	0.4%
16	Texas	45,775	2.4%		43	New Hampshire	6,136	0.3%
31	Utah	15,093	0.8%		44	Idaho	5,688	0.3%
39	Vermont	8,441	0.4%		45	Mississippi	4,171	0.2%
19	Virginia	33,466	1.8%		46	North Dakota	2,456	0.1%
17	Washington	39,651	2.1%		NA	Alabama**	NA	NA
42	West Virginia	6,935	0.4%		NA	Alaska**	NA	NA
21	Wisconsin	29,116	1.5%		NA	Georgia**	NA	NA
NA	Wyoming**	NA	NA		NA	Wyoming**	NA	NA
					District of Columbia**		NA	NA

Source: U.S. Department of Health and Human Services, Substance Abuse & Mental Health Services Administration
   "Treatment Episode Data Set" (http://wwwdasis.samhsa.gov/webt/NewMapv1.htm)
*Preliminary figures as of December 28, 2009. National total is for reporting states only.
**Not available.

Female Admissions to Substance Abuse Treatment Programs as a Percent of All Admissions in 2008
National Percent = 34.1% of Admissions*

RANK	STATE	PERCENT
NA	Alabama**	NA
NA	Alaska**	NA
14	Arizona	35.7
33	Arkansas	32.1
13	California	35.8
46	Colorado	24.3
41	Connecticut	29.0
42	Delaware	27.6
5	Florida	38.3
NA	Georgia**	NA
15	Hawaii	35.4
5	Idaho	38.3
18	Illinois	34.7
29	Indiana	32.5
36	Iowa	31.1
24	Kansas	33.1
3	Kentucky	38.9
24	Louisiana	33.1
11	Maine	37.0
27	Maryland	32.6
38	Massachusetts	30.8
15	Michigan	35.4
23	Minnesota	33.2
8	Mississippi	38.1
39	Missouri	30.2
30	Montana	32.3
42	Nebraska	27.6
19	Nevada	34.6
4	New Hampshire	38.6
34	New Jersey	32.0
20	New Mexico	33.9
45	New York	24.9
31	North Carolina	32.2
12	North Dakota	36.0
10	Ohio	37.2
2	Oklahoma	40.2
22	Oregon	33.6
31	Pennsylvania	32.2
27	Rhode Island	32.6
26	South Carolina	32.8
44	South Dakota	26.9
20	Tennessee	33.9
1	Texas	41.7
36	Utah	31.1
7	Vermont	38.2
34	Virginia	32.0
9	Washington	37.6
15	West Virginia	35.4
40	Wisconsin	29.7
NA	Wyoming**	NA

RANK	STATE	PERCENT
1	Texas	41.7
2	Oklahoma	40.2
3	Kentucky	38.9
4	New Hampshire	38.6
5	Florida	38.3
5	Idaho	38.3
7	Vermont	38.2
8	Mississippi	38.1
9	Washington	37.6
10	Ohio	37.2
11	Maine	37.0
12	North Dakota	36.0
13	California	35.8
14	Arizona	35.7
15	Hawaii	35.4
15	Michigan	35.4
15	West Virginia	35.4
18	Illinois	34.7
19	Nevada	34.6
20	New Mexico	33.9
20	Tennessee	33.9
22	Oregon	33.6
23	Minnesota	33.2
24	Kansas	33.1
24	Louisiana	33.1
26	South Carolina	32.8
27	Maryland	32.6
27	Rhode Island	32.6
29	Indiana	32.5
30	Montana	32.3
31	North Carolina	32.2
31	Pennsylvania	32.2
33	Arkansas	32.1
34	New Jersey	32.0
34	Virginia	32.0
36	Iowa	31.1
36	Utah	31.1
38	Massachusetts	30.8
39	Missouri	30.2
40	Wisconsin	29.7
41	Connecticut	29.0
42	Delaware	27.6
42	Nebraska	27.6
44	South Dakota	26.9
45	New York	24.9
46	Colorado	24.3
NA	Alabama**	NA
NA	Alaska**	NA
NA	Georgia**	NA
NA	Wyoming**	NA
	District of Columbia**	NA

Source: U.S. Department of Health and Human Services, Substance Abuse & Mental Health Services Administration "Treatment Episode Data Set" (http://wwwdasis.samhsa.gov/webt/NewMapv1.htm)
*Preliminary figures as of December 28, 2009. National figure is a weighted average of reporting states.
**Not available.

White Admissions to Substance Abuse Treatment Programs as a Percent of All Admissions in 2008
National Percent = 63.2% of Admissions*

ALPHA ORDER

RANK	STATE	PERCENT
NA	Alabama**	NA
NA	Alaska**	NA
10	Arizona	81.1
17	Arkansas	76.9
42	California	48.7
7	Colorado	85.7
32	Connecticut	65.2
28	Delaware	68.1
23	Florida	72.9
NA	Georgia**	NA
46	Hawaii	29.8
9	Idaho	81.3
43	Illinois	48.2
13	Indiana	78.2
5	Iowa	88.5
24	Kansas	72.7
6	Kentucky	86.3
36	Louisiana	60.8
2	Maine	94.9
39	Maryland	54.3
11	Massachusetts	78.6
29	Michigan	67.4
19	Minnesota	75.2
38	Mississippi	56.4
26	Missouri	71.2
20	Montana	74.0
18	Nebraska	75.3
31	Nevada	65.4
1	New Hampshire	95.3
27	New Jersey	70.6
34	New Mexico	62.2
45	New York	45.5
35	North Carolina	61.9
22	North Dakota	73.7
40	Ohio	50.6
24	Oklahoma	72.7
14	Oregon	78.1
12	Pennsylvania	78.4
15	Rhode Island	77.8
33	South Carolina	63.9
41	South Dakota	48.9
21	Tennessee	73.9
44	Texas	45.9
16	Utah	77.5
3	Vermont	94.7
37	Virginia	59.3
30	Washington	67.0
4	West Virginia	89.9
8	Wisconsin	84.2
NA	Wyoming**	NA

RANK ORDER

RANK	STATE	PERCENT
1	New Hampshire	95.3
2	Maine	94.9
3	Vermont	94.7
4	West Virginia	89.9
5	Iowa	88.5
6	Kentucky	86.3
7	Colorado	85.7
8	Wisconsin	84.2
9	Idaho	81.3
10	Arizona	81.1
11	Massachusetts	78.6
12	Pennsylvania	78.4
13	Indiana	78.2
14	Oregon	78.1
15	Rhode Island	77.8
16	Utah	77.5
17	Arkansas	76.9
18	Nebraska	75.3
19	Minnesota	75.2
20	Montana	74.0
21	Tennessee	73.9
22	North Dakota	73.7
23	Florida	72.9
24	Kansas	72.7
24	Oklahoma	72.7
26	Missouri	71.2
27	New Jersey	70.6
28	Delaware	68.1
29	Michigan	67.4
30	Washington	67.0
31	Nevada	65.4
32	Connecticut	65.2
33	South Carolina	63.9
34	New Mexico	62.2
35	North Carolina	61.9
36	Louisiana	60.8
37	Virginia	59.3
38	Mississippi	56.4
39	Maryland	54.3
40	Ohio	50.6
41	South Dakota	48.9
42	California	48.7
43	Illinois	48.2
44	Texas	45.9
45	New York	45.5
46	Hawaii	29.8
NA	Alabama**	NA
NA	Alaska**	NA
NA	Georgia**	NA
NA	Wyoming**	NA
	District of Columbia**	NA

Source: U.S. Department of Health and Human Services, Substance Abuse & Mental Health Services Administration
   "Treatment Episode Data Set" (http://wwwdasis.samhsa.gov/webt/NewMapv1.htm)
*Preliminary figures as of December 28, 2009. National figure is a weighted average of reporting states.
**Not available.

Black Admissions to Substance Abuse Treatment Programs
as a Percent of All Admissions in 2008
National Percent = 20.4% of Admissions*

ALPHA ORDER

RANK ORDER

RANK	STATE	PERCENT		RANK	STATE	PERCENT
NA	Alabama**	NA		1	Illinois	44.1
NA	Alaska**	NA		2	Mississippi	42.0
33	Arizona	7.9		3	Maryland	41.0
15	Arkansas	19.3		4	Louisiana	37.3
20	California	16.2		5	North Carolina	34.3
34	Colorado	7.5		6	South Carolina	33.7
17	Connecticut	17.5		7	New York	33.1
8	Delaware	28.5		8	Delaware	28.5
14	Florida	22.0		9	Virginia	28.4
NA	Georgia**	NA		10	New Jersey	26.7
40	Hawaii	2.6		11	Michigan	26.0
45	Idaho	1.1		12	Missouri	25.2
1	Illinois	44.1		13	Tennessee	23.9
19	Indiana	16.3		14	Florida	22.0
32	Iowa	8.2		15	Arkansas	19.3
22	Kansas	15.1		16	Ohio	18.5
26	Kentucky	11.9		17	Connecticut	17.5
4	Louisiana	37.3		18	Texas	16.7
41	Maine	2.0		19	Indiana	16.3
3	Maryland	41.0		20	California	16.2
31	Massachusetts	8.3		21	Pennsylvania	16.0
11	Michigan	26.0		22	Kansas	15.1
27	Minnesota	11.1		23	Nevada	14.3
2	Mississippi	42.0		24	Oklahoma	13.6
12	Missouri	25.2		25	Wisconsin	12.5
46	Montana	0.8		26	Kentucky	11.9
28	Nebraska	9.9		27	Minnesota	11.1
23	Nevada	14.3		28	Nebraska	9.9
44	New Hampshire	1.5		29	Rhode Island	9.1
10	New Jersey	26.7		30	Washington	9.0
38	New Mexico	2.9		31	Massachusetts	8.3
7	New York	33.1		32	Iowa	8.2
5	North Carolina	34.3		33	Arizona	7.9
42	North Dakota	1.9		34	Colorado	7.5
16	Ohio	18.5		35	Oregon	4.4
24	Oklahoma	13.6		36	Utah	3.6
35	Oregon	4.4		36	West Virginia	3.6
21	Pennsylvania	16.0		38	New Mexico	2.9
29	Rhode Island	9.1		39	South Dakota	2.7
6	South Carolina	33.7		40	Hawaii	2.6
39	South Dakota	2.7		41	Maine	2.0
13	Tennessee	23.9		42	North Dakota	1.9
18	Texas	16.7		43	Vermont	1.8
36	Utah	3.6		44	New Hampshire	1.5
43	Vermont	1.8		45	Idaho	1.1
9	Virginia	28.4		46	Montana	0.8
30	Washington	9.0		NA	Alabama**	NA
36	West Virginia	3.6		NA	Alaska**	NA
25	Wisconsin	12.5		NA	Georgia**	NA
NA	Wyoming**	NA		NA	Wyoming**	NA
					District of Columbia**	NA

Source: U.S. Department of Health and Human Services, Substance Abuse & Mental Health Services Administration
"Treatment Episode Data Set" (http://wwwdasis.samhsa.gov/webt/NewMapv1.htm)
*Preliminary figures as of December 28, 2009. National figure is a weighted average of reporting states.
**Not available.

Hispanic Admissions to Substance Abuse Treatment Programs as a Percent of All Admissions in 2008
National Percent = 14.8% of Admissions*

ALPHA ORDER

RANK	STATE	PERCENT
NA	Alabama**	NA
NA	Alaska**	NA
4	Arizona	27.5
32	Arkansas	3.3
3	California	35.3
5	Colorado	26.9
7	Connecticut	18.5
22	Delaware	5.3
12	Florida	11.9
NA	Georgia**	NA
23	Hawaii	5.2
11	Idaho	14.0
18	Illinois	8.8
26	Indiana	4.7
25	Iowa	4.8
15	Kansas	10.0
45	Kentucky	0.8
38	Louisiana	1.8
41	Maine	1.7
28	Maryland	4.1
13	Massachusetts	11.8
32	Michigan	3.3
30	Minnesota	3.6
43	Mississippi	1.0
37	Missouri	1.9
30	Montana	3.6
20	Nebraska	7.1
8	Nevada	17.6
32	New Hampshire	3.3
10	New Jersey	14.2
1	New Mexico	44.7
6	New York	21.3
38	North Carolina	1.8
35	North Dakota	2.2
42	Ohio	1.3
24	Oklahoma	5.0
17	Oregon	9.3
21	Pennsylvania	5.7
16	Rhode Island	9.7
38	South Carolina	1.8
29	South Dakota	3.8
43	Tennessee	1.0
2	Texas	36.2
9	Utah	15.2
36	Vermont	2.1
19	Virginia	7.5
13	Washington	11.8
46	West Virginia	0.5
27	Wisconsin	4.3
NA	Wyoming**	NA

RANK ORDER

RANK	STATE	PERCENT
1	New Mexico	44.7
2	Texas	36.2
3	California	35.3
4	Arizona	27.5
5	Colorado	26.9
6	New York	21.3
7	Connecticut	18.5
8	Nevada	17.6
9	Utah	15.2
10	New Jersey	14.2
11	Idaho	14.0
12	Florida	11.9
13	Massachusetts	11.8
13	Washington	11.8
15	Kansas	10.0
16	Rhode Island	9.7
17	Oregon	9.3
18	Illinois	8.8
19	Virginia	7.5
20	Nebraska	7.1
21	Pennsylvania	5.7
22	Delaware	5.3
23	Hawaii	5.2
24	Oklahoma	5.0
25	Iowa	4.8
26	Indiana	4.7
27	Wisconsin	4.3
28	Maryland	4.1
29	South Dakota	3.8
30	Minnesota	3.6
30	Montana	3.6
32	Arkansas	3.3
32	Michigan	3.3
32	New Hampshire	3.3
35	North Dakota	2.2
36	Vermont	2.1
37	Missouri	1.9
38	Louisiana	1.8
38	North Carolina	1.8
38	South Carolina	1.8
41	Maine	1.7
42	Ohio	1.3
43	Mississippi	1.0
43	Tennessee	1.0
45	Kentucky	0.8
46	West Virginia	0.5
NA	Alabama**	NA
NA	Alaska**	NA
NA	Georgia**	NA
NA	Wyoming**	NA
	District of Columbia**	NA

Source: U.S. Department of Health and Human Services, Substance Abuse & Mental Health Services Administration
   "Treatment Episode Data Set" (http://wwwdasis.samhsa.gov/webt/NewMapv1.htm)
*Preliminary figures as of December 28, 2009. National figure is a weighted average of reporting states. Hispanic ethnic background can be of any race.
**Not available.

IV. FINANCE

Homeland Security Grants in 2010

National Total = $1,726,359,956*

<table>
<tr><td colspan="4">ALPHA ORDER</td><td colspan="4">RANK ORDER</td></tr>
<tr><th>RANK</th><th>STATE</th><th>GRANTS</th><th>% of USA</th><th>RANK</th><th>STATE</th><th>GRANTS</th><th>% of USA</th></tr>
<tr><td>30</td><td>Alabama</td><td>$11,293,846</td><td>0.7%</td><td>1</td><td>New York</td><td>$277,150,581</td><td>16.1%</td></tr>
<tr><td>36</td><td>Alaska</td><td>7,358,300</td><td>0.4%</td><td>2</td><td>California</td><td>268,685,401</td><td>15.6%</td></tr>
<tr><td>14</td><td>Arizona</td><td>30,086,524</td><td>1.7%</td><td>3</td><td>Texas</td><td>143,036,730</td><td>8.3%</td></tr>
<tr><td>39</td><td>Arkansas</td><td>7,093,544</td><td>0.4%</td><td>4</td><td>Illinois</td><td>87,934,150</td><td>5.1%</td></tr>
<tr><td>2</td><td>California</td><td>268,685,401</td><td>15.6%</td><td>5</td><td>Florida</td><td>71,139,501</td><td>4.1%</td></tr>
<tr><td>22</td><td>Colorado</td><td>19,209,759</td><td>1.1%</td><td>6</td><td>New Jersey</td><td>62,035,995</td><td>3.6%</td></tr>
<tr><td>25</td><td>Connecticut</td><td>14,954,871</td><td>0.9%</td><td>7</td><td>Pennsylvania</td><td>57,855,730</td><td>3.4%</td></tr>
<tr><td>46</td><td>Delaware</td><td>6,727,997</td><td>0.4%</td><td>8</td><td>Ohio</td><td>40,437,889</td><td>2.3%</td></tr>
<tr><td>5</td><td>Florida</td><td>71,139,501</td><td>4.1%</td><td>9</td><td>Massachusetts</td><td>35,713,314</td><td>2.1%</td></tr>
<tr><td>11</td><td>Georgia</td><td>33,716,473</td><td>2.0%</td><td>10</td><td>Michigan</td><td>34,075,707</td><td>2.0%</td></tr>
<tr><td>29</td><td>Hawaii</td><td>11,810,295</td><td>0.7%</td><td>11</td><td>Georgia</td><td>33,716,473</td><td>2.0%</td></tr>
<tr><td>43</td><td>Idaho</td><td>6,743,796</td><td>0.4%</td><td>12</td><td>Virginia</td><td>30,915,010</td><td>1.8%</td></tr>
<tr><td>4</td><td>Illinois</td><td>87,934,150</td><td>5.1%</td><td>13</td><td>Washington</td><td>30,615,761</td><td>1.8%</td></tr>
<tr><td>21</td><td>Indiana</td><td>19,314,399</td><td>1.1%</td><td>14</td><td>Arizona</td><td>30,086,524</td><td>1.7%</td></tr>
<tr><td>37</td><td>Iowa</td><td>7,097,117</td><td>0.4%</td><td>15</td><td>Missouri</td><td>28,169,120</td><td>1.6%</td></tr>
<tr><td>35</td><td>Kansas</td><td>7,409,670</td><td>0.4%</td><td>16</td><td>Maryland</td><td>27,342,383</td><td>1.6%</td></tr>
<tr><td>31</td><td>Kentucky</td><td>11,045,187</td><td>0.6%</td><td>17</td><td>Louisiana</td><td>23,694,494</td><td>1.4%</td></tr>
<tr><td>17</td><td>Louisiana</td><td>23,694,494</td><td>1.4%</td><td>18</td><td>North Carolina</td><td>21,273,139</td><td>1.2%</td></tr>
<tr><td>44</td><td>Maine</td><td>6,738,762</td><td>0.4%</td><td>19</td><td>Minnesota</td><td>19,907,805</td><td>1.2%</td></tr>
<tr><td>16</td><td>Maryland</td><td>27,342,383</td><td>1.6%</td><td>20</td><td>Tennessee</td><td>19,564,050</td><td>1.1%</td></tr>
<tr><td>9</td><td>Massachusetts</td><td>35,713,314</td><td>2.1%</td><td>21</td><td>Indiana</td><td>19,314,399</td><td>1.1%</td></tr>
<tr><td>10</td><td>Michigan</td><td>34,075,707</td><td>2.0%</td><td>22</td><td>Colorado</td><td>19,209,759</td><td>1.1%</td></tr>
<tr><td>19</td><td>Minnesota</td><td>19,907,805</td><td>1.2%</td><td>23</td><td>Nevada</td><td>16,492,596</td><td>1.0%</td></tr>
<tr><td>38</td><td>Mississippi</td><td>7,095,565</td><td>0.4%</td><td>24</td><td>Oregon</td><td>15,401,772</td><td>0.9%</td></tr>
<tr><td>15</td><td>Missouri</td><td>28,169,120</td><td>1.6%</td><td>25</td><td>Connecticut</td><td>14,954,871</td><td>0.9%</td></tr>
<tr><td>45</td><td>Montana</td><td>6,730,288</td><td>0.4%</td><td>26</td><td>Wisconsin</td><td>14,609,829</td><td>0.8%</td></tr>
<tr><td>34</td><td>Nebraska</td><td>8,398,024</td><td>0.5%</td><td>27</td><td>Oklahoma</td><td>13,999,310</td><td>0.8%</td></tr>
<tr><td>23</td><td>Nevada</td><td>16,492,596</td><td>1.0%</td><td>28</td><td>Rhode Island</td><td>11,814,031</td><td>0.7%</td></tr>
<tr><td>41</td><td>New Hampshire</td><td>7,056,165</td><td>0.4%</td><td>29</td><td>Hawaii</td><td>11,810,295</td><td>0.7%</td></tr>
<tr><td>6</td><td>New Jersey</td><td>62,035,995</td><td>3.6%</td><td>30</td><td>Alabama</td><td>11,293,846</td><td>0.7%</td></tr>
<tr><td>40</td><td>New Mexico</td><td>7,072,396</td><td>0.4%</td><td>31</td><td>Kentucky</td><td>11,045,187</td><td>0.6%</td></tr>
<tr><td>1</td><td>New York</td><td>277,150,581</td><td>16.1%</td><td>32</td><td>Utah</td><td>9,990,734</td><td>0.6%</td></tr>
<tr><td>18</td><td>North Carolina</td><td>21,273,139</td><td>1.2%</td><td>33</td><td>South Carolina</td><td>8,412,080</td><td>0.5%</td></tr>
<tr><td>48</td><td>North Dakota</td><td>6,722,374</td><td>0.4%</td><td>34</td><td>Nebraska</td><td>8,398,024</td><td>0.5%</td></tr>
<tr><td>8</td><td>Ohio</td><td>40,437,889</td><td>2.3%</td><td>35</td><td>Kansas</td><td>7,409,670</td><td>0.4%</td></tr>
<tr><td>27</td><td>Oklahoma</td><td>13,999,310</td><td>0.8%</td><td>36</td><td>Alaska</td><td>7,358,300</td><td>0.4%</td></tr>
<tr><td>24</td><td>Oregon</td><td>15,401,772</td><td>0.9%</td><td>37</td><td>Iowa</td><td>7,097,117</td><td>0.4%</td></tr>
<tr><td>7</td><td>Pennsylvania</td><td>57,855,730</td><td>3.4%</td><td>38</td><td>Mississippi</td><td>7,095,565</td><td>0.4%</td></tr>
<tr><td>28</td><td>Rhode Island</td><td>11,814,031</td><td>0.7%</td><td>39</td><td>Arkansas</td><td>7,093,544</td><td>0.4%</td></tr>
<tr><td>33</td><td>South Carolina</td><td>8,412,080</td><td>0.5%</td><td>40</td><td>New Mexico</td><td>7,072,396</td><td>0.4%</td></tr>
<tr><td>47</td><td>South Dakota</td><td>6,726,325</td><td>0.4%</td><td>41</td><td>New Hampshire</td><td>7,056,165</td><td>0.4%</td></tr>
<tr><td>20</td><td>Tennessee</td><td>19,564,050</td><td>1.1%</td><td>42</td><td>West Virginia</td><td>6,750,853</td><td>0.4%</td></tr>
<tr><td>3</td><td>Texas</td><td>143,036,730</td><td>8.3%</td><td>43</td><td>Idaho</td><td>6,743,796</td><td>0.4%</td></tr>
<tr><td>32</td><td>Utah</td><td>9,990,734</td><td>0.6%</td><td>44</td><td>Maine</td><td>6,738,762</td><td>0.4%</td></tr>
<tr><td>49</td><td>Vermont</td><td>6,721,884</td><td>0.4%</td><td>45</td><td>Montana</td><td>6,730,288</td><td>0.4%</td></tr>
<tr><td>12</td><td>Virginia</td><td>30,915,010</td><td>1.8%</td><td>46</td><td>Delaware</td><td>6,727,997</td><td>0.4%</td></tr>
<tr><td>13</td><td>Washington</td><td>30,615,761</td><td>1.8%</td><td>47</td><td>South Dakota</td><td>6,726,325</td><td>0.4%</td></tr>
<tr><td>42</td><td>West Virginia</td><td>6,750,853</td><td>0.4%</td><td>48</td><td>North Dakota</td><td>6,722,374</td><td>0.4%</td></tr>
<tr><td>26</td><td>Wisconsin</td><td>14,609,829</td><td>0.8%</td><td>49</td><td>Vermont</td><td>6,721,884</td><td>0.4%</td></tr>
<tr><td>50</td><td>Wyoming</td><td>6,719,732</td><td>0.4%</td><td>50</td><td>Wyoming</td><td>6,719,732</td><td>0.4%</td></tr>
<tr><td></td><td></td><td></td><td></td><td></td><td>District of Columbia</td><td>69,574,433</td><td>4.0%</td></tr>
</table>

Source: CQ Press using data from U.S. Department of Homeland Security
  "FY 2010 Preparedness Grant Programs Overview" (http://www.dhs.gov/xgovt/grants/)
*For fiscal year ending September 30. National total includes $15,924,265 in grants to U.S. territories. The Homeland Security Grant Program includes several sub-grant programs such as State Homeland Security, Urban Area Security Initiative, Law Enforcement Terrorism Prevention Program, and Emergency Management Performance.

Per Capita Homeland Security Grants in 2010

National Per Capita = $5.57*

ALPHA ORDER

RANK	STATE	PER CAPITA
46	Alabama	$2.40
5	Alaska	10.53
25	Arizona	4.56
45	Arkansas	2.45
10	California	7.27
31	Colorado	3.82
27	Connecticut	4.25
9	Delaware	7.60
30	Florida	3.84
38	Georgia	3.43
7	Hawaii	9.12
26	Idaho	4.36
13	Illinois	6.81
41	Indiana	3.01
48	Iowa	2.36
42	Kansas	2.63
44	Kentucky	2.56
18	Louisiana	5.27
19	Maine	5.11
20	Maryland	4.80
16	Massachusetts	5.42
39	Michigan	3.42
33	Minnesota	3.78
46	Mississippi	2.40
21	Missouri	4.70
12	Montana	6.90
22	Nebraska	4.67
14	Nevada	6.24
17	New Hampshire	5.33
11	New Jersey	7.12
36	New Mexico	3.52
1	New York	14.18
49	North Carolina	2.27
6	North Dakota	10.39
37	Ohio	3.50
32	Oklahoma	3.80
28	Oregon	4.03
23	Pennsylvania	4.59
3	Rhode Island	11.22
50	South Carolina	1.84
8	South Dakota	8.28
40	Tennessee	3.11
15	Texas	5.77
35	Utah	3.59
4	Vermont	10.81
29	Virginia	3.92
23	Washington	4.59
34	West Virginia	3.71
43	Wisconsin	2.58
2	Wyoming	12.35

RANK ORDER

RANK	STATE	PER CAPITA
1	New York	$14.18
2	Wyoming	12.35
3	Rhode Island	11.22
4	Vermont	10.81
5	Alaska	10.53
6	North Dakota	10.39
7	Hawaii	9.12
8	South Dakota	8.28
9	Delaware	7.60
10	California	7.27
11	New Jersey	7.12
12	Montana	6.90
13	Illinois	6.81
14	Nevada	6.24
15	Texas	5.77
16	Massachusetts	5.42
17	New Hampshire	5.33
18	Louisiana	5.27
19	Maine	5.11
20	Maryland	4.80
21	Missouri	4.70
22	Nebraska	4.67
23	Pennsylvania	4.59
23	Washington	4.59
25	Arizona	4.56
26	Idaho	4.36
27	Connecticut	4.25
28	Oregon	4.03
29	Virginia	3.92
30	Florida	3.84
31	Colorado	3.82
32	Oklahoma	3.80
33	Minnesota	3.78
34	West Virginia	3.71
35	Utah	3.59
36	New Mexico	3.52
37	Ohio	3.50
38	Georgia	3.43
39	Michigan	3.42
40	Tennessee	3.11
41	Indiana	3.01
42	Kansas	2.63
43	Wisconsin	2.58
44	Kentucky	2.56
45	Arkansas	2.45
46	Alabama	2.40
46	Mississippi	2.40
48	Iowa	2.36
49	North Carolina	2.27
50	South Carolina	1.84

District of Columbia 116.02

Source: CQ Press using data from U.S. Department of Homeland Security
   "FY 2010 Preparedness Grant Programs Overview" (http://www.dhs.gov/xgovt/grants/)
*For fiscal year ending September 30. National per capita does not include grants to U.S. territories. The Homeland Security Grant Program includes several sub-grant programs such as State Homeland Security, Urban Area Security Initiative, Law Enforcement Terrorism Prevention Program, and Emergency Management Performance.

Grants to Police Departments for Bulletproof Vests in 2009

National Total = $22,633,159*

ALPHA ORDER

RANK	STATE	GRANTS	% of USA
27	Alabama	$280,589	1.2%
48	Alaska	40,628	0.2%
14	Arizona	531,858	2.3%
29	Arkansas	257,740	1.1%
1	California	2,496,126	11.0%
21	Colorado	393,167	1.7%
33	Connecticut	199,228	0.9%
43	Delaware	93,935	0.4%
4	Florida	1,238,676	5.5%
13	Georgia	550,575	2.4%
49	Hawaii	30,705	0.1%
35	Idaho	169,217	0.7%
9	Illinois	824,101	3.6%
12	Indiana	564,558	2.5%
36	Iowa	146,267	0.6%
26	Kansas	300,162	1.3%
34	Kentucky	180,224	0.8%
28	Louisiana	277,248	1.2%
37	Maine	127,594	0.6%
22	Maryland	346,575	1.5%
8	Massachusetts	829,023	3.7%
11	Michigan	784,347	3.5%
17	Minnesota	457,392	2.0%
30	Mississippi	234,395	1.0%
20	Missouri	423,325	1.9%
38	Montana	124,238	0.5%
42	Nebraska	95,860	0.4%
45	Nevada	72,263	0.3%
44	New Hampshire	88,643	0.4%
6	New Jersey	940,670	4.2%
32	New Mexico	230,779	1.0%
2	New York	1,763,802	7.8%
10	North Carolina	823,026	3.6%
46	North Dakota	61,893	0.3%
5	Ohio	942,331	4.2%
25	Oklahoma	302,656	1.3%
24	Oregon	309,589	1.4%
7	Pennsylvania	888,103	3.9%
39	Rhode Island	109,475	0.5%
23	South Carolina	322,006	1.4%
47	South Dakota	47,292	0.2%
19	Tennessee	445,204	2.0%
3	Texas	1,413,617	6.2%
31	Utah	234,077	1.0%
50	Vermont	20,430	0.1%
18	Virginia	456,904	2.0%
16	Washington	457,605	2.0%
41	West Virginia	99,246	0.4%
15	Wisconsin	485,996	2.1%
40	Wyoming	102,317	0.5%

RANK ORDER

RANK	STATE	GRANTS	% of USA
1	California	$2,496,126	11.0%
2	New York	1,763,802	7.8%
3	Texas	1,413,617	6.2%
4	Florida	1,238,676	5.5%
5	Ohio	942,331	4.2%
6	New Jersey	940,670	4.2%
7	Pennsylvania	888,103	3.9%
8	Massachusetts	829,023	3.7%
9	Illinois	824,101	3.6%
10	North Carolina	823,026	3.6%
11	Michigan	784,347	3.5%
12	Indiana	564,558	2.5%
13	Georgia	550,575	2.4%
14	Arizona	531,858	2.3%
15	Wisconsin	485,996	2.1%
16	Washington	457,605	2.0%
17	Minnesota	457,392	2.0%
18	Virginia	456,904	2.0%
19	Tennessee	445,204	2.0%
20	Missouri	423,325	1.9%
21	Colorado	393,167	1.7%
22	Maryland	346,575	1.5%
23	South Carolina	322,006	1.4%
24	Oregon	309,589	1.4%
25	Oklahoma	302,656	1.3%
26	Kansas	300,162	1.3%
27	Alabama	280,589	1.2%
28	Louisiana	277,248	1.2%
29	Arkansas	257,740	1.1%
30	Mississippi	234,395	1.0%
31	Utah	234,077	1.0%
32	New Mexico	230,779	1.0%
33	Connecticut	199,228	0.9%
34	Kentucky	180,224	0.8%
35	Idaho	169,217	0.7%
36	Iowa	146,267	0.6%
37	Maine	127,594	0.6%
38	Montana	124,238	0.5%
39	Rhode Island	109,475	0.5%
40	Wyoming	102,317	0.5%
41	West Virginia	99,246	0.4%
42	Nebraska	95,860	0.4%
43	Delaware	93,935	0.4%
44	New Hampshire	88,643	0.4%
45	Nevada	72,263	0.3%
46	North Dakota	61,893	0.3%
47	South Dakota	47,292	0.2%
48	Alaska	40,628	0.2%
49	Hawaii	30,705	0.1%
50	Vermont	20,430	0.1%
	District of Columbia	17,482	0.1%

Source: U.S. Department of Justice, Office of Justice Programs
"Bulletproof Vest Partnership Program" (http://www.ojp.usdoj.gov/bvpbasi/)
*Does not include $87,445 in grants to U.S. territories.

State and Local Government Expenditures for Justice Activities in 2007

National Total = $190,965,276,000*

ALPHA ORDER

RANK	STATE	EXPENDITURES	% of USA
26	Alabama	$2,147,461,000	1.1%
43	Alaska	667,391,000	0.3%
12	Arizona	4,502,936,000	2.4%
36	Arkansas	1,133,794,000	0.6%
1	California	35,073,818,000	18.4%
18	Colorado	2,995,048,000	1.6%
25	Connecticut	2,190,794,000	1.1%
40	Delaware	730,995,000	0.4%
3	Florida	12,686,292,000	6.6%
10	Georgia	5,265,161,000	2.8%
38	Hawaii	783,506,000	0.4%
41	Idaho	722,015,000	0.4%
5	Illinois	7,255,374,000	3.8%
23	Indiana	2,532,485,000	1.3%
34	Iowa	1,323,929,000	0.7%
33	Kansas	1,334,155,000	0.7%
29	Kentucky	1,701,883,000	0.9%
21	Louisiana	2,840,232,000	1.5%
45	Maine	533,973,000	0.3%
14	Maryland	4,182,027,000	2.2%
15	Massachusetts	4,100,819,000	2.1%
9	Michigan	5,752,201,000	3.0%
19	Minnesota	2,877,235,000	1.5%
35	Mississippi	1,215,227,000	0.6%
22	Missouri	2,657,664,000	1.4%
46	Montana	515,205,000	0.3%
37	Nebraska	832,992,000	0.4%
27	Nevada	2,051,727,000	1.1%
44	New Hampshire	581,841,000	0.3%
7	New Jersey	6,466,829,000	3.4%
32	New Mexico	1,347,820,000	0.7%
2	New York	16,725,003,000	8.8%
13	North Carolina	4,383,306,000	2.3%
50	North Dakota	256,186,000	0.1%
8	Ohio	6,178,575,000	3.2%
30	Oklahoma	1,683,756,000	0.9%
24	Oregon	2,344,427,000	1.2%
6	Pennsylvania	7,192,227,000	3.8%
42	Rhode Island	674,029,000	0.4%
28	South Carolina	1,831,289,000	1.0%
48	South Dakota	339,689,000	0.2%
20	Tennessee	2,869,517,000	1.5%
4	Texas	12,046,114,000	6.3%
31	Utah	1,361,226,000	0.7%
49	Vermont	315,191,000	0.2%
11	Virginia	4,627,415,000	2.4%
16	Washington	3,722,587,000	1.9%
39	West Virginia	746,357,000	0.4%
17	Wisconsin	3,419,936,000	1.8%
47	Wyoming	437,743,000	0.2%

RANK ORDER

RANK	STATE	EXPENDITURES	% of USA
1	California	$35,073,818,000	18.4%
2	New York	16,725,003,000	8.8%
3	Florida	12,686,292,000	6.6%
4	Texas	12,046,114,000	6.3%
5	Illinois	7,255,374,000	3.8%
6	Pennsylvania	7,192,227,000	3.8%
7	New Jersey	6,466,829,000	3.4%
8	Ohio	6,178,575,000	3.2%
9	Michigan	5,752,201,000	3.0%
10	Georgia	5,265,161,000	2.8%
11	Virginia	4,627,415,000	2.4%
12	Arizona	4,502,936,000	2.4%
13	North Carolina	4,383,306,000	2.3%
14	Maryland	4,182,027,000	2.2%
15	Massachusetts	4,100,819,000	2.1%
16	Washington	3,722,587,000	1.9%
17	Wisconsin	3,419,936,000	1.8%
18	Colorado	2,995,048,000	1.6%
19	Minnesota	2,877,235,000	1.5%
20	Tennessee	2,869,517,000	1.5%
21	Louisiana	2,840,232,000	1.5%
22	Missouri	2,657,664,000	1.4%
23	Indiana	2,532,485,000	1.3%
24	Oregon	2,344,427,000	1.2%
25	Connecticut	2,190,794,000	1.1%
26	Alabama	2,147,461,000	1.1%
27	Nevada	2,051,727,000	1.1%
28	South Carolina	1,831,289,000	1.0%
29	Kentucky	1,701,883,000	0.9%
30	Oklahoma	1,683,756,000	0.9%
31	Utah	1,361,226,000	0.7%
32	New Mexico	1,347,820,000	0.7%
33	Kansas	1,334,155,000	0.7%
34	Iowa	1,323,929,000	0.7%
35	Mississippi	1,215,227,000	0.6%
36	Arkansas	1,133,794,000	0.6%
37	Nebraska	832,992,000	0.4%
38	Hawaii	783,506,000	0.4%
39	West Virginia	746,357,000	0.4%
40	Delaware	730,995,000	0.4%
41	Idaho	722,015,000	0.4%
42	Rhode Island	674,029,000	0.4%
43	Alaska	667,391,000	0.3%
44	New Hampshire	581,841,000	0.3%
45	Maine	533,973,000	0.3%
46	Montana	515,205,000	0.3%
47	Wyoming	437,743,000	0.2%
48	South Dakota	339,689,000	0.2%
49	Vermont	315,191,000	0.2%
50	North Dakota	256,186,000	0.1%
	District of Columbia	807,874,000	0.4%

Source: CQ Press using data from U.S. Bureau of the Census, Governments Division
"State and Local Government Finances 2006-2007" (http://www.census.gov/govs/estimate/index.html)
*Direct general expenditures. Includes police protection, corrections, and judicial and legal services.

Per Capita State and Local Government Expenditures for Justice Activities in 2007
National Per Capita = $634*

ALPHA ORDER

RANK	STATE	PER CAPITA
38	Alabama	$464
1	Alaska	980
9	Arizona	709
49	Arkansas	401
2	California	964
17	Colorado	618
15	Connecticut	628
4	Delaware	848
10	Florida	697
26	Georgia	553
18	Hawaii	613
33	Idaho	483
24	Illinois	566
50	Indiana	400
40	Iowa	444
34	Kansas	480
47	Kentucky	402
12	Louisiana	649
46	Maine	406
8	Maryland	744
14	Massachusetts	634
23	Michigan	572
25	Minnesota	555
43	Mississippi	416
39	Missouri	452
27	Montana	539
35	Nebraska	471
6	Nevada	803
41	New Hampshire	443
7	New Jersey	747
11	New Mexico	686
3	New York	861
32	North Carolina	485
47	North Dakota	402
28	Ohio	538
36	Oklahoma	467
15	Oregon	628
21	Pennsylvania	579
13	Rhode Island	640
43	South Carolina	416
42	South Dakota	427
36	Tennessee	467
31	Texas	505
29	Utah	510
30	Vermont	508
20	Virginia	601
22	Washington	577
45	West Virginia	412
19	Wisconsin	611
5	Wyoming	837

RANK ORDER

RANK	STATE	PER CAPITA
1	Alaska	$980
2	California	964
3	New York	861
4	Delaware	848
5	Wyoming	837
6	Nevada	803
7	New Jersey	747
8	Maryland	744
9	Arizona	709
10	Florida	697
11	New Mexico	686
12	Louisiana	649
13	Rhode Island	640
14	Massachusetts	634
15	Connecticut	628
15	Oregon	628
17	Colorado	618
18	Hawaii	613
19	Wisconsin	611
20	Virginia	601
21	Pennsylvania	579
22	Washington	577
23	Michigan	572
24	Illinois	566
25	Minnesota	555
26	Georgia	553
27	Montana	539
28	Ohio	538
29	Utah	510
30	Vermont	508
31	Texas	505
32	North Carolina	485
33	Idaho	483
34	Kansas	480
35	Nebraska	471
36	Oklahoma	467
36	Tennessee	467
38	Alabama	464
39	Missouri	452
40	Iowa	444
41	New Hampshire	443
42	South Dakota	427
43	Mississippi	416
43	South Carolina	416
45	West Virginia	412
46	Maine	406
47	Kentucky	402
47	North Dakota	402
49	Arkansas	401
50	Indiana	400

District of Columbia	1,374

Source: CQ Press using data from U.S. Bureau of the Census, Governments Division
"State and Local Government Finances 2006-2007" (http://www.census.gov/govs/estimate/index.html)
*Direct general expenditures. Includes police protection, corrections, and judicial and legal services.

State and Local Government Expenditures for Justice Activities
as a Percent of All Direct General Expenditures in 2007
National Percent = 8.4% of Direct General Expenditures*

ALPHA ORDER

RANK	STATE	PERCENT
35	Alabama	7.0
41	Alaska	6.4
2	Arizona	11.4
40	Arkansas	6.6
3	California	11.1
7	Colorado	8.9
25	Connecticut	7.6
6	Delaware	9.4
5	Florida	9.7
12	Georgia	8.3
32	Hawaii	7.2
18	Idaho	8.1
20	Illinois	8.0
45	Indiana	6.0
44	Iowa	6.1
34	Kansas	7.1
42	Kentucky	6.3
14	Louisiana	8.2
50	Maine	5.3
4	Maryland	9.8
25	Massachusetts	7.6
14	Michigan	8.2
35	Minnesota	7.0
48	Mississippi	5.5
30	Missouri	7.3
23	Montana	7.7
39	Nebraska	6.7
1	Nevada	11.9
37	New Hampshire	6.9
10	New Jersey	8.6
12	New Mexico	8.3
14	New York	8.2
28	North Carolina	7.4
49	North Dakota	5.4
30	Ohio	7.3
28	Oklahoma	7.4
7	Oregon	8.9
23	Pennsylvania	7.7
22	Rhode Island	7.8
47	South Carolina	5.9
38	South Dakota	6.8
20	Tennessee	8.0
14	Texas	8.2
18	Utah	8.1
45	Vermont	6.0
9	Virginia	8.7
27	Washington	7.5
42	West Virginia	6.3
11	Wisconsin	8.5
32	Wyoming	7.2

RANK ORDER

RANK	STATE	PERCENT
1	Nevada	11.9
2	Arizona	11.4
3	California	11.1
4	Maryland	9.8
5	Florida	9.7
6	Delaware	9.4
7	Colorado	8.9
7	Oregon	8.9
9	Virginia	8.7
10	New Jersey	8.6
11	Wisconsin	8.5
12	Georgia	8.3
12	New Mexico	8.3
14	Louisiana	8.2
14	Michigan	8.2
14	New York	8.2
14	Texas	8.2
18	Idaho	8.1
18	Utah	8.1
20	Illinois	8.0
20	Tennessee	8.0
22	Rhode Island	7.8
23	Montana	7.7
23	Pennsylvania	7.7
25	Connecticut	7.6
25	Massachusetts	7.6
27	Washington	7.5
28	North Carolina	7.4
28	Oklahoma	7.4
30	Missouri	7.3
30	Ohio	7.3
32	Hawaii	7.2
32	Wyoming	7.2
34	Kansas	7.1
35	Alabama	7.0
35	Minnesota	7.0
37	New Hampshire	6.9
38	South Dakota	6.8
39	Nebraska	6.7
40	Arkansas	6.6
41	Alaska	6.4
42	Kentucky	6.3
42	West Virginia	6.3
44	Iowa	6.1
45	Indiana	6.0
45	Vermont	6.0
47	South Carolina	5.9
48	Mississippi	5.5
49	North Dakota	5.4
50	Maine	5.3

District of Columbia — 9.5

Source: CQ Press using data from U.S. Bureau of the Census, Governments Division
"State and Local Government Finances 2006-2007" (http://www.census.gov/govs/estimate/index.html)
*Includes police protection, corrections, and judicial and legal services.

State Government Expenditures for Justice Activities in 2007

National Total = $74,325,805,000*

ALPHA ORDER

RANK	STATE	EXPENDITURES	% of USA
28	Alabama	$908,781,000	1.2%
36	Alaska	485,369,000	0.7%
17	Arizona	1,328,209,000	1.8%
33	Arkansas	528,527,000	0.7%
1	California	13,135,855,000	17.7%
19	Colorado	1,119,679,000	1.5%
15	Connecticut	1,441,403,000	1.9%
35	Delaware	508,256,000	0.7%
4	Florida	4,269,920,000	5.7%
12	Georgia	1,866,027,000	2.5%
40	Hawaii	443,987,000	0.6%
43	Idaho	315,113,000	0.4%
11	Illinois	1,939,380,000	2.6%
24	Indiana	972,608,000	1.3%
32	Iowa	563,679,000	0.8%
34	Kansas	522,225,000	0.7%
23	Kentucky	986,908,000	1.3%
27	Louisiana	918,817,000	1.2%
44	Maine	287,330,000	0.4%
10	Maryland	2,170,719,000	2.9%
7	Massachusetts	2,399,923,000	3.2%
9	Michigan	2,226,231,000	3.0%
20	Minnesota	1,091,097,000	1.5%
37	Mississippi	482,368,000	0.6%
21	Missouri	1,054,919,000	1.4%
45	Montana	259,941,000	0.3%
42	Nebraska	335,121,000	0.5%
38	Nevada	460,025,000	0.6%
46	New Hampshire	255,915,000	0.3%
6	New Jersey	2,771,748,000	3.7%
29	New Mexico	746,544,000	1.0%
2	New York	5,993,207,000	8.1%
8	North Carolina	2,301,138,000	3.1%
50	North Dakota	115,832,000	0.2%
14	Ohio	1,706,717,000	2.3%
26	Oklahoma	931,109,000	1.3%
22	Oregon	1,010,910,000	1.4%
5	Pennsylvania	2,867,867,000	3.9%
41	Rhode Island	352,011,000	0.5%
30	South Carolina	721,283,000	1.0%
49	South Dakota	168,847,000	0.2%
25	Tennessee	965,780,000	1.3%
3	Texas	4,395,842,000	5.9%
31	Utah	594,275,000	0.8%
47	Vermont	239,045,000	0.3%
13	Virginia	1,744,441,000	2.3%
16	Washington	1,438,935,000	1.9%
39	West Virginia	448,734,000	0.6%
18	Wisconsin	1,322,102,000	1.8%
48	Wyoming	211,106,000	0.3%

RANK ORDER

RANK	STATE	EXPENDITURES	% of USA
1	California	$13,135,855,000	17.7%
2	New York	5,993,207,000	8.1%
3	Texas	4,395,842,000	5.9%
4	Florida	4,269,920,000	5.7%
5	Pennsylvania	2,867,867,000	3.9%
6	New Jersey	2,771,748,000	3.7%
7	Massachusetts	2,399,923,000	3.2%
8	North Carolina	2,301,138,000	3.1%
9	Michigan	2,226,231,000	3.0%
10	Maryland	2,170,719,000	2.9%
11	Illinois	1,939,380,000	2.6%
12	Georgia	1,866,027,000	2.5%
13	Virginia	1,744,441,000	2.3%
14	Ohio	1,706,717,000	2.3%
15	Connecticut	1,441,403,000	1.9%
16	Washington	1,438,935,000	1.9%
17	Arizona	1,328,209,000	1.8%
18	Wisconsin	1,322,102,000	1.8%
19	Colorado	1,119,679,000	1.5%
20	Minnesota	1,091,097,000	1.5%
21	Missouri	1,054,919,000	1.4%
22	Oregon	1,010,910,000	1.4%
23	Kentucky	986,908,000	1.3%
24	Indiana	972,608,000	1.3%
25	Tennessee	965,780,000	1.3%
26	Oklahoma	931,109,000	1.3%
27	Louisiana	918,817,000	1.2%
28	Alabama	908,781,000	1.2%
29	New Mexico	746,544,000	1.0%
30	South Carolina	721,283,000	1.0%
31	Utah	594,275,000	0.8%
32	Iowa	563,679,000	0.8%
33	Arkansas	528,527,000	0.7%
34	Kansas	522,225,000	0.7%
35	Delaware	508,256,000	0.7%
36	Alaska	485,369,000	0.7%
37	Mississippi	482,368,000	0.6%
38	Nevada	460,025,000	0.6%
39	West Virginia	448,734,000	0.6%
40	Hawaii	443,987,000	0.6%
41	Rhode Island	352,011,000	0.5%
42	Nebraska	335,121,000	0.5%
43	Idaho	315,113,000	0.4%
44	Maine	287,330,000	0.4%
45	Montana	259,941,000	0.3%
46	New Hampshire	255,915,000	0.3%
47	Vermont	239,045,000	0.3%
48	Wyoming	211,106,000	0.3%
49	South Dakota	168,847,000	0.2%
50	North Dakota	115,832,000	0.2%
	District of Columbia**	NA	NA

Source: CQ Press using data from U.S. Bureau of the Census, Governments Division
"State and Local Government Finances 2006-2007" (http://www.census.gov/govs/estimate/index.html)
*Direct general expenditures. Includes police protection, corrections, and judicial and legal services.
**Not applicable.

Per Capita State Government Expenditures for Justice Activities in 2007

National Per Capita = $247*

ALPHA ORDER

RANK	STATE	PER CAPITA
34	Alabama	$196
1	Alaska	713
33	Arizona	209
40	Arkansas	187
9	California	361
22	Colorado	231
3	Connecticut	413
2	Delaware	590
20	Florida	235
34	Georgia	196
10	Hawaii	348
30	Idaho	211
49	Illinois	151
48	Indiana	154
37	Iowa	189
39	Kansas	188
21	Kentucky	233
32	Louisiana	210
28	Maine	218
5	Maryland	386
8	Massachusetts	371
27	Michigan	222
30	Minnesota	211
45	Mississippi	165
44	Missouri	179
14	Montana	272
37	Nebraska	189
43	Nevada	180
36	New Hampshire	195
12	New Jersey	320
7	New Mexico	380
13	New York	308
17	North Carolina	255
42	North Dakota	182
50	Ohio	149
16	Oklahoma	258
15	Oregon	271
22	Pennsylvania	231
11	Rhode Island	334
46	South Carolina	164
29	South Dakota	212
47	Tennessee	157
41	Texas	184
25	Utah	223
6	Vermont	385
24	Virginia	227
25	Washington	223
18	West Virginia	248
19	Wisconsin	236
4	Wyoming	403

RANK ORDER

RANK	STATE	PER CAPITA
1	Alaska	$713
2	Delaware	590
3	Connecticut	413
4	Wyoming	403
5	Maryland	386
6	Vermont	385
7	New Mexico	380
8	Massachusetts	371
9	California	361
10	Hawaii	348
11	Rhode Island	334
12	New Jersey	320
13	New York	308
14	Montana	272
15	Oregon	271
16	Oklahoma	258
17	North Carolina	255
18	West Virginia	248
19	Wisconsin	236
20	Florida	235
21	Kentucky	233
22	Colorado	231
22	Pennsylvania	231
24	Virginia	227
25	Utah	223
25	Washington	223
27	Michigan	222
28	Maine	218
29	South Dakota	212
30	Idaho	211
30	Minnesota	211
32	Louisiana	210
33	Arizona	209
34	Alabama	196
34	Georgia	196
36	New Hampshire	195
37	Iowa	189
37	Nebraska	189
39	Kansas	188
40	Arkansas	187
41	Texas	184
42	North Dakota	182
43	Nevada	180
44	Missouri	179
45	Mississippi	165
46	South Carolina	164
47	Tennessee	157
48	Indiana	154
49	Illinois	151
50	Ohio	149
	District of Columbia**	NA

Source: CQ Press using data from U.S. Bureau of the Census, Governments Division
   "State and Local Government Finances 2006-2007" (http://www.census.gov/govs/estimate/index.html)
*Direct general expenditures. Includes police protection, corrections, and judicial and legal services.
**Not applicable.

State Government Expenditures for Justice Activities as a Percent of All Direct General Expenditures in 2007
National Percent = 7.7% of Direct General Expenditures*

ALPHA ORDER

RANK	STATE	PERCENT
33	Alabama	6.2
24	Alaska	7.0
8	Arizona	8.5
40	Arkansas	5.6
1	California	12.4
5	Colorado	9.3
4	Connecticut	9.5
3	Delaware	10.1
5	Florida	9.3
26	Georgia	6.9
44	Hawaii	5.0
19	Idaho	7.5
42	Illinois	5.3
42	Indiana	5.3
39	Iowa	5.7
30	Kansas	6.4
37	Kentucky	6.0
45	Louisiana	4.9
46	Maine	4.8
2	Maryland	10.5
14	Massachusetts	8.0
17	Michigan	7.8
33	Minnesota	6.2
50	Mississippi	4.0
32	Missouri	6.3
24	Montana	7.0
38	Nebraska	5.9
11	Nevada	8.2
30	New Hampshire	6.4
12	New Jersey	8.1
15	New Mexico	7.9
12	New York	8.1
8	North Carolina	8.5
49	North Dakota	4.3
47	Ohio	4.7
15	Oklahoma	7.9
7	Oregon	8.7
27	Pennsylvania	6.6
23	Rhode Island	7.2
48	South Carolina	4.5
29	South Dakota	6.5
40	Tennessee	5.6
19	Texas	7.5
27	Utah	6.6
22	Vermont	7.3
19	Virginia	7.5
33	Washington	6.2
33	West Virginia	6.2
18	Wisconsin	7.7
8	Wyoming	8.5

RANK ORDER

RANK	STATE	PERCENT
1	California	12.4
2	Maryland	10.5
3	Delaware	10.1
4	Connecticut	9.5
5	Colorado	9.3
5	Florida	9.3
7	Oregon	8.7
8	Arizona	8.5
8	North Carolina	8.5
8	Wyoming	8.5
11	Nevada	8.2
12	New Jersey	8.1
12	New York	8.1
14	Massachusetts	8.0
15	New Mexico	7.9
15	Oklahoma	7.9
17	Michigan	7.8
18	Wisconsin	7.7
19	Idaho	7.5
19	Texas	7.5
19	Virginia	7.5
22	Vermont	7.3
23	Rhode Island	7.2
24	Alaska	7.0
24	Montana	7.0
26	Georgia	6.9
27	Pennsylvania	6.6
27	Utah	6.6
29	South Dakota	6.5
30	Kansas	6.4
30	New Hampshire	6.4
32	Missouri	6.3
33	Alabama	6.2
33	Minnesota	6.2
33	Washington	6.2
33	West Virginia	6.2
37	Kentucky	6.0
38	Nebraska	5.9
39	Iowa	5.7
40	Arkansas	5.6
40	Tennessee	5.6
42	Illinois	5.3
42	Indiana	5.3
44	Hawaii	5.0
45	Louisiana	4.9
46	Maine	4.8
47	Ohio	4.7
48	South Carolina	4.5
49	North Dakota	4.3
50	Mississippi	4.0
	District of Columbia**	NA

Source: CQ Press using data from U.S. Bureau of the Census, Governments Division
"State and Local Government Finances 2006-2007" (http://www.census.gov/govs/estimate/index.html)
*Includes police protection, corrections, and judicial and legal services.
**Not applicable.

Local Government Expenditures for Justice Activities in 2007

National Total = $116,639,471,000*

ALPHA ORDER

RANK	STATE	EXPENDITURES	% of USA
26	Alabama	$1,238,680,000	1.1%
47	Alaska	182,022,000	0.2%
11	Arizona	3,174,727,000	2.7%
35	Arkansas	605,267,000	0.5%
1	California	21,937,963,000	18.8%
19	Colorado	1,875,369,000	1.6%
32	Connecticut	749,391,000	0.6%
46	Delaware	222,739,000	0.2%
3	Florida	8,416,372,000	7.2%
10	Georgia	3,399,134,000	2.9%
39	Hawaii	339,519,000	0.3%
38	Idaho	406,902,000	0.3%
5	Illinois	5,315,994,000	4.6%
24	Indiana	1,559,877,000	1.3%
30	Iowa	760,250,000	0.7%
28	Kansas	811,930,000	0.7%
34	Kentucky	714,975,000	0.6%
17	Louisiana	1,921,415,000	1.6%
44	Maine	246,643,000	0.2%
16	Maryland	2,011,308,000	1.7%
21	Massachusetts	1,700,896,000	1.5%
9	Michigan	3,525,970,000	3.0%
20	Minnesota	1,786,138,000	1.5%
33	Mississippi	732,859,000	0.6%
22	Missouri	1,602,745,000	1.4%
43	Montana	255,264,000	0.2%
37	Nebraska	497,871,000	0.4%
23	Nevada	1,591,702,000	1.4%
40	New Hampshire	325,926,000	0.3%
8	New Jersey	3,695,081,000	3.2%
36	New Mexico	601,276,000	0.5%
2	New York	10,731,796,000	9.2%
15	North Carolina	2,082,168,000	1.8%
49	North Dakota	140,354,000	0.1%
6	Ohio	4,471,858,000	3.8%
31	Oklahoma	752,647,000	0.6%
25	Oregon	1,333,517,000	1.1%
7	Pennsylvania	4,324,360,000	3.7%
41	Rhode Island	322,018,000	0.3%
27	South Carolina	1,110,006,000	1.0%
48	South Dakota	170,842,000	0.1%
18	Tennessee	1,903,737,000	1.6%
4	Texas	7,650,272,000	6.6%
29	Utah	766,951,000	0.7%
50	Vermont	76,146,000	0.1%
12	Virginia	2,882,974,000	2.5%
13	Washington	2,283,652,000	2.0%
42	West Virginia	297,623,000	0.3%
14	Wisconsin	2,097,834,000	1.8%
45	Wyoming	226,637,000	0.2%

RANK ORDER

RANK	STATE	EXPENDITURES	% of USA
1	California	$21,937,963,000	18.8%
2	New York	10,731,796,000	9.2%
3	Florida	8,416,372,000	7.2%
4	Texas	7,650,272,000	6.6%
5	Illinois	5,315,994,000	4.6%
6	Ohio	4,471,858,000	3.8%
7	Pennsylvania	4,324,360,000	3.7%
8	New Jersey	3,695,081,000	3.2%
9	Michigan	3,525,970,000	3.0%
10	Georgia	3,399,134,000	2.9%
11	Arizona	3,174,727,000	2.7%
12	Virginia	2,882,974,000	2.5%
13	Washington	2,283,652,000	2.0%
14	Wisconsin	2,097,834,000	1.8%
15	North Carolina	2,082,168,000	1.8%
16	Maryland	2,011,308,000	1.7%
17	Louisiana	1,921,415,000	1.6%
18	Tennessee	1,903,737,000	1.6%
19	Colorado	1,875,369,000	1.6%
20	Minnesota	1,786,138,000	1.5%
21	Massachusetts	1,700,896,000	1.5%
22	Missouri	1,602,745,000	1.4%
23	Nevada	1,591,702,000	1.4%
24	Indiana	1,559,877,000	1.3%
25	Oregon	1,333,517,000	1.1%
26	Alabama	1,238,680,000	1.1%
27	South Carolina	1,110,006,000	1.0%
28	Kansas	811,930,000	0.7%
29	Utah	766,951,000	0.7%
30	Iowa	760,250,000	0.7%
31	Oklahoma	752,647,000	0.6%
32	Connecticut	749,391,000	0.6%
33	Mississippi	732,859,000	0.6%
34	Kentucky	714,975,000	0.6%
35	Arkansas	605,267,000	0.5%
36	New Mexico	601,276,000	0.5%
37	Nebraska	497,871,000	0.4%
38	Idaho	406,902,000	0.3%
39	Hawaii	339,519,000	0.3%
40	New Hampshire	325,926,000	0.3%
41	Rhode Island	322,018,000	0.3%
42	West Virginia	297,623,000	0.3%
43	Montana	255,264,000	0.2%
44	Maine	246,643,000	0.2%
45	Wyoming	226,637,000	0.2%
46	Delaware	222,739,000	0.2%
47	Alaska	182,022,000	0.2%
48	South Dakota	170,842,000	0.1%
49	North Dakota	140,354,000	0.1%
50	Vermont	76,146,000	0.1%
	District of Columbia	807,874,000	0.7%

Source: CQ Press using data from U.S. Bureau of the Census, Governments Division
"State and Local Government Finances 2006-2007" (http://www.census.gov/govs/estimate/index.html)
*Direct general expenditures. Includes police protection, corrections, and judicial and legal services.

Per Capita Local Government Expenditures for Justice Activities in 2007

National Per Capita = $387*

ALPHA ORDER

RANK	STATE	PER CAPITA
30	Alabama	$268
31	Alaska	267
4	Arizona	500
45	Arkansas	214
2	California	603
11	Colorado	387
43	Connecticut	215
35	Delaware	258
5	Florida	462
15	Georgia	357
33	Hawaii	266
29	Idaho	272
9	Illinois	414
40	Indiana	246
36	Iowa	255
25	Kansas	292
48	Kentucky	169
6	Louisiana	439
47	Maine	188
14	Maryland	358
34	Massachusetts	263
18	Michigan	351
20	Minnesota	345
38	Mississippi	251
28	Missouri	273
31	Montana	267
27	Nebraska	281
1	Nevada	623
39	New Hampshire	248
8	New Jersey	427
23	New Mexico	306
3	New York	552
41	North Carolina	230
42	North Dakota	220
10	Ohio	390
46	Oklahoma	209
15	Oregon	357
19	Pennsylvania	348
23	Rhode Island	306
37	South Carolina	252
43	South Dakota	215
22	Tennessee	310
21	Texas	321
26	Utah	287
50	Vermont	123
13	Virginia	374
17	Washington	354
49	West Virginia	164
12	Wisconsin	375
7	Wyoming	433

RANK ORDER

RANK	STATE	PER CAPITA
1	Nevada	$623
2	California	603
3	New York	552
4	Arizona	500
5	Florida	462
6	Louisiana	439
7	Wyoming	433
8	New Jersey	427
9	Illinois	414
10	Ohio	390
11	Colorado	387
12	Wisconsin	375
13	Virginia	374
14	Maryland	358
15	Georgia	357
15	Oregon	357
17	Washington	354
18	Michigan	351
19	Pennsylvania	348
20	Minnesota	345
21	Texas	321
22	Tennessee	310
23	New Mexico	306
23	Rhode Island	306
25	Kansas	292
26	Utah	287
27	Nebraska	281
28	Missouri	273
29	Idaho	272
30	Alabama	268
31	Alaska	267
31	Montana	267
33	Hawaii	266
34	Massachusetts	263
35	Delaware	258
36	Iowa	255
37	South Carolina	252
38	Mississippi	251
39	New Hampshire	248
40	Indiana	246
41	North Carolina	230
42	North Dakota	220
43	Connecticut	215
43	South Dakota	215
45	Arkansas	214
46	Oklahoma	209
47	Maine	188
48	Kentucky	169
49	West Virginia	164
50	Vermont	123

| | District of Columbia | 1,374 |

Source: CQ Press using data from U.S. Bureau of the Census, Governments Division
"State and Local Government Finances 2006-2007" (http://www.census.gov/govs/estimate/index.html)
*Direct general expenditures. Includes police protection, corrections, and judicial and legal services.

Local Government Expenditures for Justice Activities as a Percent of All Direct General Expenditures in 2007
National Percent = 9.0% of Direct General Expenditures*

ALPHA ORDER

RANK	STATE	PERCENT
30	Alabama	7.7
49	Alaska	5.3
3	Arizona	13.3
29	Arkansas	8.0
5	California	10.5
18	Colorado	8.7
48	Connecticut	5.5
26	Delaware	8.3
7	Florida	10.0
11	Georgia	9.3
1	Hawaii	16.2
21	Idaho	8.6
8	Illinois	9.9
42	Indiana	6.6
43	Iowa	6.5
31	Kansas	7.6
41	Kentucky	6.7
4	Louisiana	12.1
47	Maine	6.1
12	Maryland	9.2
37	Massachusetts	7.1
25	Michigan	8.5
31	Minnesota	7.6
37	Mississippi	7.1
28	Missouri	8.1
18	Montana	8.7
34	Nebraska	7.2
2	Nevada	13.7
34	New Hampshire	7.2
14	New Jersey	9.1
17	New Mexico	8.9
26	New York	8.3
43	North Carolina	6.5
39	North Dakota	6.9
12	Ohio	9.2
39	Oklahoma	6.9
14	Oregon	9.1
21	Pennsylvania	8.6
18	Rhode Island	8.7
33	South Carolina	7.3
34	South Dakota	7.2
6	Tennessee	10.1
21	Texas	8.6
8	Utah	9.9
50	Vermont	3.8
10	Virginia	9.6
21	Washington	8.6
45	West Virginia	6.4
16	Wisconsin	9.0
45	Wyoming	6.4

RANK ORDER

RANK	STATE	PERCENT
1	Hawaii	16.2
2	Nevada	13.7
3	Arizona	13.3
4	Louisiana	12.1
5	California	10.5
6	Tennessee	10.1
7	Florida	10.0
8	Illinois	9.9
8	Utah	9.9
10	Virginia	9.6
11	Georgia	9.3
12	Maryland	9.2
12	Ohio	9.2
14	New Jersey	9.1
14	Oregon	9.1
16	Wisconsin	9.0
17	New Mexico	8.9
18	Colorado	8.7
18	Montana	8.7
18	Rhode Island	8.7
21	Idaho	8.6
21	Pennsylvania	8.6
21	Texas	8.6
21	Washington	8.6
25	Michigan	8.5
26	Delaware	8.3
26	New York	8.3
28	Missouri	8.1
29	Arkansas	8.0
30	Alabama	7.7
31	Kansas	7.6
31	Minnesota	7.6
33	South Carolina	7.3
34	Nebraska	7.2
34	New Hampshire	7.2
34	South Dakota	7.2
37	Massachusetts	7.1
37	Mississippi	7.1
39	North Dakota	6.9
39	Oklahoma	6.9
41	Kentucky	6.7
42	Indiana	6.6
43	Iowa	6.5
43	North Carolina	6.5
45	West Virginia	6.4
45	Wyoming	6.4
47	Maine	6.1
48	Connecticut	5.5
49	Alaska	5.3
50	Vermont	3.8

District of Columbia — 9.5

Source: CQ Press using data from U.S. Bureau of the Census, Governments Division
"State and Local Government Finances 2006-2007" (http://www.census.gov/govs/estimate/index.html)
*Includes police protection, corrections, and judicial and legal services.

State and Local Government Expenditures for Police Protection in 2007

National Total = $84,096,751,000*

<table>
<tr><td colspan="4">ALPHA ORDER</td><td colspan="4">RANK ORDER</td></tr>
<tr><th>RANK</th><th>STATE</th><th>EXPENDITURES</th><th>% of USA</th><th>RANK</th><th>STATE</th><th>EXPENDITURES</th><th>% of USA</th></tr>
<tr><td>25</td><td>Alabama</td><td>$976,916,000</td><td>1.2%</td><td>1</td><td>California</td><td>$13,875,720,000</td><td>16.5%</td></tr>
<tr><td>44</td><td>Alaska</td><td>236,359,000</td><td>0.3%</td><td>2</td><td>New York</td><td>7,642,102,000</td><td>9.1%</td></tr>
<tr><td>11</td><td>Arizona</td><td>2,046,230,000</td><td>2.4%</td><td>3</td><td>Florida</td><td>6,287,670,000</td><td>7.5%</td></tr>
<tr><td>36</td><td>Arkansas</td><td>480,029,000</td><td>0.6%</td><td>4</td><td>Texas</td><td>5,245,805,000</td><td>6.2%</td></tr>
<tr><td>1</td><td>California</td><td>13,875,720,000</td><td>16.5%</td><td>5</td><td>Illinois</td><td>4,061,100,000</td><td>4.8%</td></tr>
<tr><td>21</td><td>Colorado</td><td>1,345,366,000</td><td>1.6%</td><td>6</td><td>New Jersey</td><td>3,057,957,000</td><td>3.6%</td></tr>
<tr><td>27</td><td>Connecticut</td><td>911,626,000</td><td>1.1%</td><td>7</td><td>Ohio</td><td>2,955,763,000</td><td>3.5%</td></tr>
<tr><td>39</td><td>Delaware</td><td>309,291,000</td><td>0.4%</td><td>8</td><td>Pennsylvania</td><td>2,669,195,000</td><td>3.2%</td></tr>
<tr><td>3</td><td>Florida</td><td>6,287,670,000</td><td>7.5%</td><td>9</td><td>Michigan</td><td>2,339,692,000</td><td>2.8%</td></tr>
<tr><td>10</td><td>Georgia</td><td>2,136,825,000</td><td>2.5%</td><td>10</td><td>Georgia</td><td>2,136,825,000</td><td>2.5%</td></tr>
<tr><td>40</td><td>Hawaii</td><td>305,291,000</td><td>0.4%</td><td>11</td><td>Arizona</td><td>2,046,230,000</td><td>2.4%</td></tr>
<tr><td>41</td><td>Idaho</td><td>299,721,000</td><td>0.4%</td><td>12</td><td>North Carolina</td><td>2,032,682,000</td><td>2.4%</td></tr>
<tr><td>5</td><td>Illinois</td><td>4,061,100,000</td><td>4.8%</td><td>13</td><td>Virginia</td><td>1,910,315,000</td><td>2.3%</td></tr>
<tr><td>23</td><td>Indiana</td><td>1,109,484,000</td><td>1.3%</td><td>14</td><td>Massachusetts</td><td>1,824,724,000</td><td>2.2%</td></tr>
<tr><td>33</td><td>Iowa</td><td>586,455,000</td><td>0.7%</td><td>15</td><td>Maryland</td><td>1,781,844,000</td><td>2.1%</td></tr>
<tr><td>30</td><td>Kansas</td><td>677,951,000</td><td>0.8%</td><td>16</td><td>Wisconsin</td><td>1,494,022,000</td><td>1.8%</td></tr>
<tr><td>31</td><td>Kentucky</td><td>628,609,000</td><td>0.7%</td><td>17</td><td>Washington</td><td>1,412,999,000</td><td>1.7%</td></tr>
<tr><td>22</td><td>Louisiana</td><td>1,211,657,000</td><td>1.4%</td><td>18</td><td>Minnesota</td><td>1,412,023,000</td><td>1.7%</td></tr>
<tr><td>45</td><td>Maine</td><td>231,648,000</td><td>0.3%</td><td>19</td><td>Missouri</td><td>1,400,558,000</td><td>1.7%</td></tr>
<tr><td>15</td><td>Maryland</td><td>1,781,844,000</td><td>2.1%</td><td>20</td><td>Tennessee</td><td>1,359,274,000</td><td>1.6%</td></tr>
<tr><td>14</td><td>Massachusetts</td><td>1,824,724,000</td><td>2.2%</td><td>21</td><td>Colorado</td><td>1,345,366,000</td><td>1.6%</td></tr>
<tr><td>9</td><td>Michigan</td><td>2,339,692,000</td><td>2.8%</td><td>22</td><td>Louisiana</td><td>1,211,657,000</td><td>1.4%</td></tr>
<tr><td>18</td><td>Minnesota</td><td>1,412,023,000</td><td>1.7%</td><td>23</td><td>Indiana</td><td>1,109,484,000</td><td>1.3%</td></tr>
<tr><td>35</td><td>Mississippi</td><td>572,710,000</td><td>0.7%</td><td>24</td><td>Nevada</td><td>984,690,000</td><td>1.2%</td></tr>
<tr><td>19</td><td>Missouri</td><td>1,400,558,000</td><td>1.7%</td><td>25</td><td>Alabama</td><td>976,916,000</td><td>1.2%</td></tr>
<tr><td>46</td><td>Montana</td><td>206,048,000</td><td>0.2%</td><td>26</td><td>Oregon</td><td>967,094,000</td><td>1.1%</td></tr>
<tr><td>37</td><td>Nebraska</td><td>357,455,000</td><td>0.4%</td><td>27</td><td>Connecticut</td><td>911,626,000</td><td>1.1%</td></tr>
<tr><td>24</td><td>Nevada</td><td>984,690,000</td><td>1.2%</td><td>28</td><td>South Carolina</td><td>901,023,000</td><td>1.1%</td></tr>
<tr><td>42</td><td>New Hampshire</td><td>295,732,000</td><td>0.4%</td><td>29</td><td>Oklahoma</td><td>719,148,000</td><td>0.9%</td></tr>
<tr><td>6</td><td>New Jersey</td><td>3,057,957,000</td><td>3.6%</td><td>30</td><td>Kansas</td><td>677,951,000</td><td>0.8%</td></tr>
<tr><td>32</td><td>New Mexico</td><td>597,627,000</td><td>0.7%</td><td>31</td><td>Kentucky</td><td>628,609,000</td><td>0.7%</td></tr>
<tr><td>2</td><td>New York</td><td>7,642,102,000</td><td>9.1%</td><td>32</td><td>New Mexico</td><td>597,627,000</td><td>0.7%</td></tr>
<tr><td>12</td><td>North Carolina</td><td>2,032,682,000</td><td>2.4%</td><td>33</td><td>Iowa</td><td>586,455,000</td><td>0.7%</td></tr>
<tr><td>50</td><td>North Dakota</td><td>105,716,000</td><td>0.1%</td><td>34</td><td>Utah</td><td>583,488,000</td><td>0.7%</td></tr>
<tr><td>7</td><td>Ohio</td><td>2,955,763,000</td><td>3.5%</td><td>35</td><td>Mississippi</td><td>572,710,000</td><td>0.7%</td></tr>
<tr><td>29</td><td>Oklahoma</td><td>719,148,000</td><td>0.9%</td><td>36</td><td>Arkansas</td><td>480,029,000</td><td>0.6%</td></tr>
<tr><td>26</td><td>Oregon</td><td>967,094,000</td><td>1.1%</td><td>37</td><td>Nebraska</td><td>357,455,000</td><td>0.4%</td></tr>
<tr><td>8</td><td>Pennsylvania</td><td>2,669,195,000</td><td>3.2%</td><td>38</td><td>Rhode Island</td><td>327,176,000</td><td>0.4%</td></tr>
<tr><td>38</td><td>Rhode Island</td><td>327,176,000</td><td>0.4%</td><td>39</td><td>Delaware</td><td>309,291,000</td><td>0.4%</td></tr>
<tr><td>28</td><td>South Carolina</td><td>901,023,000</td><td>1.1%</td><td>40</td><td>Hawaii</td><td>305,291,000</td><td>0.4%</td></tr>
<tr><td>49</td><td>South Dakota</td><td>136,968,000</td><td>0.2%</td><td>41</td><td>Idaho</td><td>299,721,000</td><td>0.4%</td></tr>
<tr><td>20</td><td>Tennessee</td><td>1,359,274,000</td><td>1.6%</td><td>42</td><td>New Hampshire</td><td>295,732,000</td><td>0.4%</td></tr>
<tr><td>4</td><td>Texas</td><td>5,245,805,000</td><td>6.2%</td><td>43</td><td>West Virginia</td><td>267,846,000</td><td>0.3%</td></tr>
<tr><td>34</td><td>Utah</td><td>583,488,000</td><td>0.7%</td><td>44</td><td>Alaska</td><td>236,359,000</td><td>0.3%</td></tr>
<tr><td>48</td><td>Vermont</td><td>141,411,000</td><td>0.2%</td><td>45</td><td>Maine</td><td>231,648,000</td><td>0.3%</td></tr>
<tr><td>13</td><td>Virginia</td><td>1,910,315,000</td><td>2.3%</td><td>46</td><td>Montana</td><td>206,048,000</td><td>0.2%</td></tr>
<tr><td>17</td><td>Washington</td><td>1,412,999,000</td><td>1.7%</td><td>47</td><td>Wyoming</td><td>175,324,000</td><td>0.2%</td></tr>
<tr><td>43</td><td>West Virginia</td><td>267,846,000</td><td>0.3%</td><td>48</td><td>Vermont</td><td>141,411,000</td><td>0.2%</td></tr>
<tr><td>16</td><td>Wisconsin</td><td>1,494,022,000</td><td>1.8%</td><td>49</td><td>South Dakota</td><td>136,968,000</td><td>0.2%</td></tr>
<tr><td>47</td><td>Wyoming</td><td>175,324,000</td><td>0.2%</td><td>50</td><td>North Dakota</td><td>105,716,000</td><td>0.1%</td></tr>
<tr><td></td><td></td><td></td><td></td><td></td><td>District of Columbia</td><td>500,392,000</td><td>0.6%</td></tr>
</table>

Source: U.S. Bureau of the Census, Governments Division
"State and Local Government Finances 2006-2007" (http://www.census.gov/govs/estimate/index.html)
*Direct general expenditures.

Per Capita State and Local Government Expenditures for Police Protection in 2007
National Per Capita = $279*

ALPHA ORDER

RANK	STATE	PER CAPITA
37	Alabama	$211
6	Alaska	347
9	Arizona	322
47	Arkansas	170
3	California	381
15	Colorado	278
19	Connecticut	261
4	Delaware	359
7	Florida	345
30	Georgia	224
24	Hawaii	239
40	Idaho	200
10	Illinois	317
45	Indiana	175
42	Iowa	197
23	Kansas	244
49	Kentucky	148
16	Louisiana	277
44	Maine	176
10	Maryland	317
14	Massachusetts	282
26	Michigan	233
17	Minnesota	272
43	Mississippi	196
25	Missouri	238
35	Montana	215
39	Nebraska	202
2	Nevada	385
28	New Hampshire	225
5	New Jersey	353
13	New Mexico	304
1	New York	393
28	North Carolina	225
48	North Dakota	166
21	Ohio	258
41	Oklahoma	199
20	Oregon	259
35	Pennsylvania	215
12	Rhode Island	311
38	South Carolina	205
46	South Dakota	172
31	Tennessee	221
32	Texas	220
33	Utah	219
27	Vermont	228
22	Virginia	248
33	Washington	219
49	West Virginia	148
18	Wisconsin	267
8	Wyoming	335

RANK ORDER

RANK	STATE	PER CAPITA
1	New York	$393
2	Nevada	385
3	California	381
4	Delaware	359
5	New Jersey	353
6	Alaska	347
7	Florida	345
8	Wyoming	335
9	Arizona	322
10	Illinois	317
10	Maryland	317
12	Rhode Island	311
13	New Mexico	304
14	Massachusetts	282
15	Colorado	278
16	Louisiana	277
17	Minnesota	272
18	Wisconsin	267
19	Connecticut	261
20	Oregon	259
21	Ohio	258
22	Virginia	248
23	Kansas	244
24	Hawaii	239
25	Missouri	238
26	Michigan	233
27	Vermont	228
28	New Hampshire	225
28	North Carolina	225
30	Georgia	224
31	Tennessee	221
32	Texas	220
33	Utah	219
33	Washington	219
35	Montana	215
35	Pennsylvania	215
37	Alabama	211
38	South Carolina	205
39	Nebraska	202
40	Idaho	200
41	Oklahoma	199
42	Iowa	197
43	Mississippi	196
44	Maine	176
45	Indiana	175
46	South Dakota	172
47	Arkansas	169
48	North Dakota	166
49	Kentucky	148
49	West Virginia	148
	District of Columbia	851

Source: CQ Press using data from U.S. Bureau of the Census, Governments Division
    "State and Local Government Finances 2006-2007" (http://www.census.gov/govs/estimate/index.html)
*Direct general expenditures.

State and Local Government Expenditures for Police Protection as a Percent of All Direct General Expenditures in 2007
National Percent = 3.7% of Direct General Expenditures

RANK	STATE	PERCENT
30	Alabama	3.2
46	Alaska	2.3
2	Arizona	5.2
38	Arkansas	2.8
5	California	4.4
8	Colorado	4.0
30	Connecticut	3.2
8	Delaware	4.0
3	Florida	4.8
24	Georgia	3.4
38	Hawaii	2.8
28	Idaho	3.3
4	Illinois	4.5
44	Indiana	2.6
41	Iowa	2.7
17	Kansas	3.6
46	Kentucky	2.3
20	Louisiana	3.5
46	Maine	2.3
6	Maryland	4.2
24	Massachusetts	3.4
28	Michigan	3.3
24	Minnesota	3.4
44	Mississippi	2.6
10	Missouri	3.8
33	Montana	3.1
34	Nebraska	2.9
1	Nevada	5.7
20	New Hampshire	3.5
7	New Jersey	4.1
13	New Mexico	3.7
13	New York	3.7
24	North Carolina	3.4
50	North Dakota	2.2
20	Ohio	3.5
30	Oklahoma	3.2
13	Oregon	3.7
34	Pennsylvania	2.9
10	Rhode Island	3.8
34	South Carolina	2.9
41	South Dakota	2.7
10	Tennessee	3.8
17	Texas	3.6
20	Utah	3.5
41	Vermont	2.7
17	Virginia	3.6
38	Washington	2.8
46	West Virginia	2.3
13	Wisconsin	3.7
34	Wyoming	2.9

RANK	STATE	PERCENT
1	Nevada	5.7
2	Arizona	5.2
3	Florida	4.8
4	Illinois	4.5
5	California	4.4
6	Maryland	4.2
7	New Jersey	4.1
8	Colorado	4.0
8	Delaware	4.0
10	Missouri	3.8
10	Rhode Island	3.8
10	Tennessee	3.8
13	New Mexico	3.7
13	New York	3.7
13	Oregon	3.7
13	Wisconsin	3.7
17	Kansas	3.6
17	Texas	3.6
17	Virginia	3.6
20	Louisiana	3.5
20	New Hampshire	3.5
20	Ohio	3.5
20	Utah	3.5
24	Georgia	3.4
24	Massachusetts	3.4
24	Minnesota	3.4
24	North Carolina	3.4
28	Idaho	3.3
28	Michigan	3.3
30	Alabama	3.2
30	Connecticut	3.2
30	Oklahoma	3.2
33	Montana	3.1
34	Nebraska	2.9
34	Pennsylvania	2.9
34	South Carolina	2.9
34	Wyoming	2.9
38	Arkansas	2.8
38	Hawaii	2.8
38	Washington	2.8
41	Iowa	2.7
41	South Dakota	2.7
41	Vermont	2.7
44	Indiana	2.6
44	Mississippi	2.6
46	Alaska	2.3
46	Kentucky	2.3
46	Maine	2.3
46	West Virginia	2.3
50	North Dakota	2.2
	District of Columbia	5.9

Source: CQ Press using data from U.S. Bureau of the Census, Governments Division
"State and Local Government Finances 2006-2007" (http://www.census.gov/govs/estimate/index.html)

State Government Expenditures for Police Protection in 2007

National Total = $11,383,131,000*

ALPHA ORDER

RANK	STATE	EXPENDITURES	% of USA
27	Alabama	$144,352,000	1.3%
37	Alaska	72,589,000	0.6%
15	Arizona	243,270,000	2.1%
39	Arkansas	70,621,000	0.6%
1	California	1,429,392,000	12.6%
31	Colorado	111,460,000	1.0%
20	Connecticut	205,351,000	1.8%
32	Delaware	102,672,000	0.9%
8	Florida	455,560,000	4.0%
13	Georgia	244,825,000	2.2%
50	Hawaii	13,411,000	0.1%
45	Idaho	45,085,000	0.4%
9	Illinois	403,897,000	3.5%
16	Indiana	229,518,000	2.0%
36	Iowa	86,250,000	0.8%
34	Kansas	94,301,000	0.8%
25	Kentucky	164,174,000	1.4%
19	Louisiana	210,567,000	1.8%
40	Maine	69,884,000	0.6%
10	Maryland	354,339,000	3.1%
7	Massachusetts	464,047,000	4.1%
12	Michigan	276,383,000	2.4%
14	Minnesota	244,684,000	2.1%
33	Mississippi	96,647,000	0.8%
21	Missouri	198,852,000	1.7%
47	Montana	34,002,000	0.3%
41	Nebraska	63,216,000	0.6%
35	Nevada	91,987,000	0.8%
44	New Hampshire	47,940,000	0.4%
5	New Jersey	491,836,000	4.3%
24	New Mexico	164,278,000	1.4%
2	New York	766,308,000	6.7%
6	North Carolina	490,556,000	4.3%
49	North Dakota	22,022,000	0.2%
18	Ohio	221,605,000	1.9%
26	Oklahoma	145,173,000	1.3%
23	Oregon	168,594,000	1.5%
3	Pennsylvania	713,481,000	6.3%
43	Rhode Island	60,048,000	0.5%
22	South Carolina	177,578,000	1.6%
48	South Dakota	28,066,000	0.2%
28	Tennessee	140,725,000	1.2%
4	Texas	605,724,000	5.3%
30	Utah	115,385,000	1.0%
38	Vermont	71,423,000	0.6%
11	Virginia	284,357,000	2.5%
17	Washington	226,609,000	2.0%
42	West Virginia	61,691,000	0.5%
29	Wisconsin	120,397,000	1.1%
46	Wyoming	37,999,000	0.3%

RANK ORDER

RANK	STATE	EXPENDITURES	% of USA
1	California	$1,429,392,000	12.6%
2	New York	766,308,000	6.7%
3	Pennsylvania	713,481,000	6.3%
4	Texas	605,724,000	5.3%
5	New Jersey	491,836,000	4.3%
6	North Carolina	490,556,000	4.3%
7	Massachusetts	464,047,000	4.1%
8	Florida	455,560,000	4.0%
9	Illinois	403,897,000	3.5%
10	Maryland	354,339,000	3.1%
11	Virginia	284,357,000	2.5%
12	Michigan	276,383,000	2.4%
13	Georgia	244,825,000	2.2%
14	Minnesota	244,684,000	2.1%
15	Arizona	243,270,000	2.1%
16	Indiana	229,518,000	2.0%
17	Washington	226,609,000	2.0%
18	Ohio	221,605,000	1.9%
19	Louisiana	210,567,000	1.8%
20	Connecticut	205,351,000	1.8%
21	Missouri	198,852,000	1.7%
22	South Carolina	177,578,000	1.6%
23	Oregon	168,594,000	1.5%
24	New Mexico	164,278,000	1.4%
25	Kentucky	164,174,000	1.4%
26	Oklahoma	145,173,000	1.3%
27	Alabama	144,352,000	1.3%
28	Tennessee	140,725,000	1.2%
29	Wisconsin	120,397,000	1.1%
30	Utah	115,385,000	1.0%
31	Colorado	111,460,000	1.0%
32	Delaware	102,672,000	0.9%
33	Mississippi	96,647,000	0.8%
34	Kansas	94,301,000	0.8%
35	Nevada	91,987,000	0.8%
36	Iowa	86,250,000	0.8%
37	Alaska	72,589,000	0.6%
38	Vermont	71,423,000	0.6%
39	Arkansas	70,621,000	0.6%
40	Maine	69,884,000	0.6%
41	Nebraska	63,216,000	0.6%
42	West Virginia	61,691,000	0.5%
43	Rhode Island	60,048,000	0.5%
44	New Hampshire	47,940,000	0.4%
45	Idaho	45,085,000	0.4%
46	Wyoming	37,999,000	0.3%
47	Montana	34,002,000	0.3%
48	South Dakota	28,066,000	0.2%
49	North Dakota	22,022,000	0.2%
50	Hawaii	13,411,000	0.1%
	District of Columbia**	NA	NA

Source: U.S. Bureau of the Census, Governments Division
  "State and Local Government Finances 2006-2007" (http://www.census.gov/govs/estimate/index.html)
*Direct general expenditures.
**Not applicable.

Per Capita State Government Expenditures for Police Protection in 2007

National Per Capita = $37.78*

ALPHA ORDER				RANK ORDER		
RANK	STATE	PER CAPITA		RANK	STATE	PER CAPITA
38	Alabama	$31.20		1	Delaware	$119.12
3	Alaska	106.57		2	Vermont	115.06
23	Arizona	38.29		3	Alaska	106.57
45	Arkansas	24.95		4	New Mexico	83.63
21	California	39.29		5	Wyoming	72.62
46	Colorado	23.02		6	Massachusetts	71.75
8	Connecticut	58.84		7	Maryland	63.06
1	Delaware	119.12		8	Connecticut	58.84
44	Florida	25.03		9	Pennsylvania	57.45
42	Georgia	25.71		10	Rhode Island	57.02
50	Hawaii	10.50		11	New Jersey	56.84
39	Idaho	30.13		12	North Carolina	54.26
37	Illinois	31.49		13	Maine	53.13
26	Indiana	36.23		14	Louisiana	48.15
40	Iowa	28.91		15	Minnesota	47.21
34	Kansas	33.95		16	Oregon	45.13
22	Kentucky	38.75		17	Utah	43.23
14	Louisiana	48.15		18	South Carolina	40.31
13	Maine	53.13		19	Oklahoma	40.24
7	Maryland	63.06		20	New York	39.44
6	Massachusetts	71.75		21	California	39.29
41	Michigan	27.50		22	Kentucky	38.75
15	Minnesota	47.21		23	Arizona	38.29
36	Mississippi	33.09		24	Virginia	36.94
35	Missouri	33.83		25	New Hampshire	36.53
29	Montana	35.54		26	Indiana	36.23
28	Nebraska	35.73		27	Nevada	36.01
27	Nevada	36.01		28	Nebraska	35.73
25	New Hampshire	36.53		29	Montana	35.54
11	New Jersey	56.84		30	South Dakota	35.27
4	New Mexico	83.63		31	Washington	35.14
20	New York	39.44		32	North Dakota	34.52
12	North Carolina	54.26		33	West Virginia	34.09
32	North Dakota	34.52		34	Kansas	33.95
49	Ohio	19.31		35	Missouri	33.83
19	Oklahoma	40.24		36	Mississippi	33.09
16	Oregon	45.13		37	Illinois	31.49
9	Pennsylvania	57.45		38	Alabama	31.20
10	Rhode Island	57.02		39	Idaho	30.13
18	South Carolina	40.31		40	Iowa	28.91
30	South Dakota	35.27		41	Michigan	27.50
47	Tennessee	22.89		42	Georgia	25.71
43	Texas	25.40		43	Texas	25.40
17	Utah	43.23		44	Florida	25.03
2	Vermont	115.06		45	Arkansas	24.95
24	Virginia	36.94		46	Colorado	23.02
31	Washington	35.14		47	Tennessee	22.89
33	West Virginia	34.09		48	Wisconsin	21.50
48	Wisconsin	21.50		49	Ohio	19.31
5	Wyoming	72.62		50	Hawaii	10.50
					District of Columbia**	NA

Source: CQ Press using data from U.S. Bureau of the Census, Governments Division
 "State and Local Government Finances 2006-2007" (http://www.census.gov/govs/estimate/index.html)
*Direct general expenditures.
**Not applicable.

State Government Expenditures for Police Protection as a Percent of All Direct General Expenditures in 2007
National Percent = 1.2% of Direct General Expenditures

RANK	STATE	PER CAPITA
32	Alabama	1.0
26	Alaska	1.1
8	Arizona	1.6
44	Arkansas	0.8
13	California	1.4
39	Colorado	0.9
13	Connecticut	1.4
2	Delaware	2.1
32	Florida	1.0
39	Georgia	0.9
50	Hawaii	0.2
26	Idaho	1.1
26	Illinois	1.1
16	Indiana	1.3
39	Iowa	0.9
19	Kansas	1.2
32	Kentucky	1.0
26	Louisiana	1.1
19	Maine	1.2
5	Maryland	1.7
8	Massachusetts	1.6
32	Michigan	1.0
13	Minnesota	1.4
44	Mississippi	0.8
19	Missouri	1.2
39	Montana	0.9
19	Nebraska	1.2
5	Nevada	1.7
19	New Hampshire	1.2
11	New Jersey	1.5
4	New Mexico	1.8
32	New York	1.0
3	North Carolina	1.9
44	North Dakota	0.8
49	Ohio	0.6
16	Oklahoma	1.3
11	Oregon	1.5
5	Pennsylvania	1.7
19	Rhode Island	1.2
26	South Carolina	1.1
26	South Dakota	1.1
44	Tennessee	0.8
32	Texas	1.0
16	Utah	1.3
1	Vermont	2.2
19	Virginia	1.2
32	Washington	1.0
39	West Virginia	0.9
48	Wisconsin	0.7
8	Wyoming	1.6

RANK	STATE	PER CAPITA
1	Vermont	2.2
2	Delaware	2.1
3	North Carolina	1.9
4	New Mexico	1.8
5	Maryland	1.7
5	Nevada	1.7
5	Pennsylvania	1.7
8	Arizona	1.6
8	Massachusetts	1.6
8	Wyoming	1.6
11	New Jersey	1.5
11	Oregon	1.5
13	California	1.4
13	Connecticut	1.4
13	Minnesota	1.4
16	Indiana	1.3
16	Oklahoma	1.3
16	Utah	1.3
19	Kansas	1.2
19	Maine	1.2
19	Missouri	1.2
19	Nebraska	1.2
19	New Hampshire	1.2
19	Rhode Island	1.2
19	Virginia	1.2
26	Alaska	1.1
26	Idaho	1.1
26	Illinois	1.1
26	Louisiana	1.1
26	South Carolina	1.1
26	South Dakota	1.1
32	Alabama	1.0
32	Florida	1.0
32	Kentucky	1.0
32	Michigan	1.0
32	New York	1.0
32	Texas	1.0
32	Washington	1.0
39	Colorado	0.9
39	Georgia	0.9
39	Iowa	0.9
39	Montana	0.9
39	West Virginia	0.9
44	Arkansas	0.8
44	Mississippi	0.8
44	North Dakota	0.8
44	Tennessee	0.8
48	Wisconsin	0.7
49	Ohio	0.6
50	Hawaii	0.2
	District of Columbia*	NA

Source: CQ Press using data from U.S. Bureau of the Census, Governments Division
"State and Local Government Finances 2006-2007" (http://www.census.gov/govs/estimate/index.html)
*Not applicable.

Local Government Expenditures for Police Protection in 2007

National Total = $72,713,620,000*

ALPHA ORDER

RANK	STATE	EXPENDITURES	% of USA
25	Alabama	$832,564,000	1.1%
45	Alaska	163,770,000	0.2%
11	Arizona	1,802,960,000	2.5%
36	Arkansas	409,408,000	0.6%
1	California	12,446,328,000	17.1%
17	Colorado	1,233,906,000	1.7%
28	Connecticut	706,275,000	1.0%
42	Delaware	206,619,000	0.3%
3	Florida	5,832,110,000	8.0%
10	Georgia	1,892,000,000	2.6%
38	Hawaii	291,880,000	0.4%
40	Idaho	254,636,000	0.4%
5	Illinois	3,657,203,000	5.0%
24	Indiana	879,966,000	1.2%
31	Iowa	500,205,000	0.7%
29	Kansas	583,650,000	0.8%
34	Kentucky	464,435,000	0.6%
22	Louisiana	1,001,090,000	1.4%
46	Maine	161,764,000	0.2%
14	Maryland	1,427,505,000	2.0%
16	Massachusetts	1,360,677,000	1.9%
8	Michigan	2,063,309,000	2.8%
21	Minnesota	1,167,339,000	1.6%
32	Mississippi	476,063,000	0.7%
19	Missouri	1,201,706,000	1.7%
44	Montana	172,046,000	0.2%
37	Nebraska	294,239,000	0.4%
23	Nevada	892,703,000	1.2%
41	New Hampshire	247,792,000	0.3%
7	New Jersey	2,566,121,000	3.5%
35	New Mexico	433,349,000	0.6%
2	New York	6,875,794,000	9.5%
13	North Carolina	1,542,126,000	2.1%
49	North Dakota	83,694,000	0.1%
6	Ohio	2,734,158,000	3.8%
30	Oklahoma	573,975,000	0.8%
26	Oregon	798,500,000	1.1%
9	Pennsylvania	1,955,714,000	2.7%
39	Rhode Island	267,128,000	0.4%
27	South Carolina	723,445,000	1.0%
48	South Dakota	108,902,000	0.1%
18	Tennessee	1,218,549,000	1.7%
4	Texas	4,640,081,000	6.4%
33	Utah	468,103,000	0.6%
50	Vermont	69,988,000	0.1%
12	Virginia	1,625,958,000	2.2%
20	Washington	1,186,390,000	1.6%
43	West Virginia	206,155,000	0.3%
15	Wisconsin	1,373,625,000	1.9%
47	Wyoming	137,325,000	0.2%

RANK ORDER

RANK	STATE	EXPENDITURES	% of USA
1	California	$12,446,328,000	17.1%
2	New York	6,875,794,000	9.5%
3	Florida	5,832,110,000	8.0%
4	Texas	4,640,081,000	6.4%
5	Illinois	3,657,203,000	5.0%
6	Ohio	2,734,158,000	3.8%
7	New Jersey	2,566,121,000	3.5%
8	Michigan	2,063,309,000	2.8%
9	Pennsylvania	1,955,714,000	2.7%
10	Georgia	1,892,000,000	2.6%
11	Arizona	1,802,960,000	2.5%
12	Virginia	1,625,958,000	2.2%
13	North Carolina	1,542,126,000	2.1%
14	Maryland	1,427,505,000	2.0%
15	Wisconsin	1,373,625,000	1.9%
16	Massachusetts	1,360,677,000	1.9%
17	Colorado	1,233,906,000	1.7%
18	Tennessee	1,218,549,000	1.7%
19	Missouri	1,201,706,000	1.7%
20	Washington	1,186,390,000	1.6%
21	Minnesota	1,167,339,000	1.6%
22	Louisiana	1,001,090,000	1.4%
23	Nevada	892,703,000	1.2%
24	Indiana	879,966,000	1.2%
25	Alabama	832,564,000	1.1%
26	Oregon	798,500,000	1.1%
27	South Carolina	723,445,000	1.0%
28	Connecticut	706,275,000	1.0%
29	Kansas	583,650,000	0.8%
30	Oklahoma	573,975,000	0.8%
31	Iowa	500,205,000	0.7%
32	Mississippi	476,063,000	0.7%
33	Utah	468,103,000	0.6%
34	Kentucky	464,435,000	0.6%
35	New Mexico	433,349,000	0.6%
36	Arkansas	409,408,000	0.6%
37	Nebraska	294,239,000	0.4%
38	Hawaii	291,880,000	0.4%
39	Rhode Island	267,128,000	0.4%
40	Idaho	254,636,000	0.4%
41	New Hampshire	247,792,000	0.3%
42	Delaware	206,619,000	0.3%
43	West Virginia	206,155,000	0.3%
44	Montana	172,046,000	0.2%
45	Alaska	163,770,000	0.2%
46	Maine	161,764,000	0.2%
47	Wyoming	137,325,000	0.2%
48	South Dakota	108,902,000	0.1%
49	North Dakota	83,694,000	0.1%
50	Vermont	69,988,000	0.1%
	District of Columbia	500,392,000	0.7%

Source: U.S. Bureau of the Census, Governments Division
   "State and Local Government Finances 2006-2007" (http://www.census.gov/govs/estimate/index.html)
*Direct general expenditures.

Per Capita Local Government Expenditures for Police Protection in 2007

National Per Capita = $241*

RANK	STATE	PER CAPITA
32	Alabama	$180
13	Alaska	240
7	Arizona	284
43	Arkansas	145
3	California	342
9	Colorado	255
26	Connecticut	202
13	Delaware	240
4	Florida	320
27	Georgia	199
16	Hawaii	229
36	Idaho	170
6	Illinois	285
44	Indiana	139
37	Iowa	168
22	Kansas	210
50	Kentucky	110
16	Louisiana	229
47	Maine	123
10	Maryland	254
22	Massachusetts	210
24	Michigan	205
18	Minnesota	225
40	Mississippi	163
25	Missouri	204
32	Montana	180
38	Nebraska	166
2	Nevada	349
30	New Hampshire	189
5	New Jersey	297
19	New Mexico	221
1	New York	354
35	North Carolina	171
46	North Dakota	131
15	Ohio	238
41	Oklahoma	159
20	Oregon	214
42	Pennsylvania	157
10	Rhode Island	254
39	South Carolina	164
45	South Dakota	137
28	Tennessee	198
29	Texas	195
34	Utah	175
49	Vermont	113
21	Virginia	211
31	Washington	184
48	West Virginia	114
12	Wisconsin	245
8	Wyoming	262

RANK	STATE	PER CAPITA
1	New York	$354
2	Nevada	349
3	California	342
4	Florida	320
5	New Jersey	297
6	Illinois	285
7	Arizona	284
8	Wyoming	262
9	Colorado	255
10	Maryland	254
10	Rhode Island	254
12	Wisconsin	245
13	Alaska	240
13	Delaware	240
15	Ohio	238
16	Hawaii	229
16	Louisiana	229
18	Minnesota	225
19	New Mexico	221
20	Oregon	214
21	Virginia	211
22	Kansas	210
22	Massachusetts	210
24	Michigan	205
25	Missouri	204
26	Connecticut	202
27	Georgia	199
28	Tennessee	198
29	Texas	195
30	New Hampshire	189
31	Washington	184
32	Alabama	180
32	Montana	180
34	Utah	175
35	North Carolina	171
36	Idaho	170
37	Iowa	168
38	Nebraska	166
39	South Carolina	164
40	Mississippi	163
41	Oklahoma	159
42	Pennsylvania	157
43	Arkansas	145
44	Indiana	139
45	South Dakota	137
46	North Dakota	131
47	Maine	123
48	West Virginia	114
49	Vermont	113
50	Kentucky	110

| | District of Columbia | 851 |

Source: CQ Press using data from U.S. Bureau of the Census, Governments Division
   "State and Local Government Finances 2006-2007" (http://www.census.gov/govs/estimate/index.html)
*Direct general expenditures.

Local Government Expenditures for Police Protection as a Percent of All Direct General Expenditures in 2007
National Percent = 5.6% of Direct General Expenditures

<table>
<tr><td colspan="3">ALPHA ORDER</td><td colspan="3">RANK ORDER</td></tr>
<tr><td>RANK</td><td>STATE</td><td>PERCENT</td><td>RANK</td><td>STATE</td><td>PERCENT</td></tr>
<tr><td>28</td><td>Alabama</td><td>5.2</td><td>1</td><td>Hawaii</td><td>13.9</td></tr>
<tr><td>35</td><td>Alaska</td><td>4.8</td><td>2</td><td>Delaware</td><td>7.7</td></tr>
<tr><td>4</td><td>Arizona</td><td>7.6</td><td>2</td><td>Nevada</td><td>7.7</td></tr>
<tr><td>23</td><td>Arkansas</td><td>5.4</td><td>4</td><td>Arizona</td><td>7.6</td></tr>
<tr><td>15</td><td>California</td><td>5.9</td><td>5</td><td>Rhode Island</td><td>7.2</td></tr>
<tr><td>18</td><td>Colorado</td><td>5.7</td><td>6</td><td>Florida</td><td>6.9</td></tr>
<tr><td>32</td><td>Connecticut</td><td>5.1</td><td>7</td><td>Illinois</td><td>6.8</td></tr>
<tr><td>2</td><td>Delaware</td><td>7.7</td><td>8</td><td>Maryland</td><td>6.5</td></tr>
<tr><td>6</td><td>Florida</td><td>6.9</td><td>8</td><td>Tennessee</td><td>6.5</td></tr>
<tr><td>28</td><td>Georgia</td><td>5.2</td><td>10</td><td>New Mexico</td><td>6.4</td></tr>
<tr><td>1</td><td>Hawaii</td><td>13.9</td><td>11</td><td>Louisiana</td><td>6.3</td></tr>
<tr><td>23</td><td>Idaho</td><td>5.4</td><td>11</td><td>New Jersey</td><td>6.3</td></tr>
<tr><td>7</td><td>Illinois</td><td>6.8</td><td>13</td><td>Missouri</td><td>6.1</td></tr>
<tr><td>49</td><td>Indiana</td><td>3.7</td><td>14</td><td>Utah</td><td>6.0</td></tr>
<tr><td>42</td><td>Iowa</td><td>4.3</td><td>15</td><td>California</td><td>5.9</td></tr>
<tr><td>21</td><td>Kansas</td><td>5.5</td><td>15</td><td>Montana</td><td>5.9</td></tr>
<tr><td>42</td><td>Kentucky</td><td>4.3</td><td>15</td><td>Wisconsin</td><td>5.9</td></tr>
<tr><td>11</td><td>Louisiana</td><td>6.3</td><td>18</td><td>Colorado</td><td>5.7</td></tr>
<tr><td>46</td><td>Maine</td><td>4.0</td><td>18</td><td>Massachusetts</td><td>5.7</td></tr>
<tr><td>8</td><td>Maryland</td><td>6.5</td><td>20</td><td>Ohio</td><td>5.6</td></tr>
<tr><td>18</td><td>Massachusetts</td><td>5.7</td><td>21</td><td>Kansas</td><td>5.5</td></tr>
<tr><td>33</td><td>Michigan</td><td>5.0</td><td>21</td><td>New Hampshire</td><td>5.5</td></tr>
<tr><td>33</td><td>Minnesota</td><td>5.0</td><td>23</td><td>Arkansas</td><td>5.4</td></tr>
<tr><td>38</td><td>Mississippi</td><td>4.6</td><td>23</td><td>Idaho</td><td>5.4</td></tr>
<tr><td>13</td><td>Missouri</td><td>6.1</td><td>23</td><td>Oregon</td><td>5.4</td></tr>
<tr><td>15</td><td>Montana</td><td>5.9</td><td>23</td><td>Virginia</td><td>5.4</td></tr>
<tr><td>42</td><td>Nebraska</td><td>4.3</td><td>27</td><td>New York</td><td>5.3</td></tr>
<tr><td>2</td><td>Nevada</td><td>7.7</td><td>28</td><td>Alabama</td><td>5.2</td></tr>
<tr><td>21</td><td>New Hampshire</td><td>5.5</td><td>28</td><td>Georgia</td><td>5.2</td></tr>
<tr><td>11</td><td>New Jersey</td><td>6.3</td><td>28</td><td>Oklahoma</td><td>5.2</td></tr>
<tr><td>10</td><td>New Mexico</td><td>6.4</td><td>28</td><td>Texas</td><td>5.2</td></tr>
<tr><td>27</td><td>New York</td><td>5.3</td><td>32</td><td>Connecticut</td><td>5.1</td></tr>
<tr><td>35</td><td>North Carolina</td><td>4.8</td><td>33</td><td>Michigan</td><td>5.0</td></tr>
<tr><td>45</td><td>North Dakota</td><td>4.1</td><td>33</td><td>Minnesota</td><td>5.0</td></tr>
<tr><td>20</td><td>Ohio</td><td>5.6</td><td>35</td><td>Alaska</td><td>4.8</td></tr>
<tr><td>28</td><td>Oklahoma</td><td>5.2</td><td>35</td><td>North Carolina</td><td>4.8</td></tr>
<tr><td>23</td><td>Oregon</td><td>5.4</td><td>35</td><td>South Carolina</td><td>4.8</td></tr>
<tr><td>47</td><td>Pennsylvania</td><td>3.9</td><td>38</td><td>Mississippi</td><td>4.6</td></tr>
<tr><td>5</td><td>Rhode Island</td><td>7.2</td><td>38</td><td>South Dakota</td><td>4.6</td></tr>
<tr><td>35</td><td>South Carolina</td><td>4.8</td><td>40</td><td>Washington</td><td>4.5</td></tr>
<tr><td>38</td><td>South Dakota</td><td>4.6</td><td>41</td><td>West Virginia</td><td>4.4</td></tr>
<tr><td>8</td><td>Tennessee</td><td>6.5</td><td>42</td><td>Iowa</td><td>4.3</td></tr>
<tr><td>28</td><td>Texas</td><td>5.2</td><td>42</td><td>Kentucky</td><td>4.3</td></tr>
<tr><td>14</td><td>Utah</td><td>6.0</td><td>42</td><td>Nebraska</td><td>4.3</td></tr>
<tr><td>50</td><td>Vermont</td><td>3.5</td><td>45</td><td>North Dakota</td><td>4.1</td></tr>
<tr><td>23</td><td>Virginia</td><td>5.4</td><td>46</td><td>Maine</td><td>4.0</td></tr>
<tr><td>40</td><td>Washington</td><td>4.5</td><td>47</td><td>Pennsylvania</td><td>3.9</td></tr>
<tr><td>41</td><td>West Virginia</td><td>4.4</td><td>47</td><td>Wyoming</td><td>3.9</td></tr>
<tr><td>15</td><td>Wisconsin</td><td>5.9</td><td>49</td><td>Indiana</td><td>3.7</td></tr>
<tr><td>47</td><td>Wyoming</td><td>3.9</td><td>50</td><td>Vermont</td><td>3.5</td></tr>
<tr><td></td><td></td><td></td><td></td><td>District of Columbia</td><td>5.9</td></tr>
</table>

Source: CQ Press using data from U.S. Bureau of the Census, Governments Division
"State and Local Government Finances 2006-2007" (http://www.census.gov/govs/estimate/index.html)

State and Local Government Expenditures for Corrections in 2007

National Total = $68,102,050,000*

ALPHA ORDER

RANK	STATE	EXPENDITURES	% of USA
25	Alabama	$769,125,000	1.1%
41	Alaska	240,596,000	0.4%
15	Arizona	1,545,176,000	2.3%
33	Arkansas	448,168,000	0.7%
1	California	12,625,215,000	18.5%
18	Colorado	1,176,162,000	1.7%
29	Connecticut	660,036,000	1.0%
40	Delaware	265,937,000	0.4%
4	Florida	4,229,602,000	6.2%
7	Georgia	2,209,743,000	3.2%
44	Hawaii	197,273,000	0.3%
39	Idaho	269,671,000	0.4%
10	Illinois	1,866,530,000	2.7%
21	Indiana	974,616,000	1.4%
34	Iowa	436,375,000	0.6%
36	Kansas	382,998,000	0.6%
30	Kentucky	657,081,000	1.0%
19	Louisiana	1,070,261,000	1.6%
43	Maine	198,479,000	0.3%
12	Maryland	1,661,182,000	2.4%
17	Massachusetts	1,285,168,000	1.9%
6	Michigan	2,370,719,000	3.5%
23	Minnesota	839,502,000	1.2%
35	Mississippi	431,104,000	0.6%
24	Missouri	800,980,000	1.2%
45	Montana	181,273,000	0.3%
37	Nebraska	325,930,000	0.5%
27	Nevada	661,730,000	1.0%
47	New Hampshire	163,587,000	0.2%
8	New Jersey	2,029,435,000	3.0%
32	New Mexico	468,560,000	0.7%
2	New York	5,660,855,000	8.3%
11	North Carolina	1,743,448,000	2.6%
50	North Dakota	89,224,000	0.1%
13	Ohio	1,628,288,000	2.4%
26	Oklahoma	666,865,000	1.0%
20	Oregon	990,308,000	1.5%
5	Pennsylvania	3,048,721,000	4.5%
42	Rhode Island	220,383,000	0.3%
28	South Carolina	661,641,000	1.0%
48	South Dakota	139,807,000	0.2%
22	Tennessee	949,403,000	1.4%
3	Texas	4,711,843,000	6.9%
31	Utah	476,429,000	0.7%
49	Vermont	113,549,000	0.2%
9	Virginia	1,942,540,000	2.9%
14	Washington	1,580,901,000	2.3%
38	West Virginia	272,636,000	0.4%
16	Wisconsin	1,365,799,000	2.0%
46	Wyoming	171,491,000	0.3%

RANK ORDER

RANK	STATE	EXPENDITURES	% of USA
1	California	$12,625,215,000	18.5%
2	New York	5,660,855,000	8.3%
3	Texas	4,711,843,000	6.9%
4	Florida	4,229,602,000	6.2%
5	Pennsylvania	3,048,721,000	4.5%
6	Michigan	2,370,719,000	3.5%
7	Georgia	2,209,743,000	3.2%
8	New Jersey	2,029,435,000	3.0%
9	Virginia	1,942,540,000	2.9%
10	Illinois	1,866,530,000	2.7%
11	North Carolina	1,743,448,000	2.6%
12	Maryland	1,661,182,000	2.4%
13	Ohio	1,628,288,000	2.4%
14	Washington	1,580,901,000	2.3%
15	Arizona	1,545,176,000	2.3%
16	Wisconsin	1,365,799,000	2.0%
17	Massachusetts	1,285,168,000	1.9%
18	Colorado	1,176,162,000	1.7%
19	Louisiana	1,070,261,000	1.6%
20	Oregon	990,308,000	1.5%
21	Indiana	974,616,000	1.4%
22	Tennessee	949,403,000	1.4%
23	Minnesota	839,502,000	1.2%
24	Missouri	800,980,000	1.2%
25	Alabama	769,125,000	1.1%
26	Oklahoma	666,865,000	1.0%
27	Nevada	661,730,000	1.0%
28	South Carolina	661,641,000	1.0%
29	Connecticut	660,036,000	1.0%
30	Kentucky	657,081,000	1.0%
31	Utah	476,429,000	0.7%
32	New Mexico	468,560,000	0.7%
33	Arkansas	448,168,000	0.7%
34	Iowa	436,375,000	0.6%
35	Mississippi	431,104,000	0.6%
36	Kansas	382,998,000	0.6%
37	Nebraska	325,930,000	0.5%
38	West Virginia	272,636,000	0.4%
39	Idaho	269,671,000	0.4%
40	Delaware	265,937,000	0.4%
41	Alaska	240,596,000	0.4%
42	Rhode Island	220,383,000	0.3%
43	Maine	198,479,000	0.3%
44	Hawaii	197,273,000	0.3%
45	Montana	181,273,000	0.3%
46	Wyoming	171,491,000	0.3%
47	New Hampshire	163,587,000	0.2%
48	South Dakota	139,807,000	0.2%
49	Vermont	113,549,000	0.2%
50	North Dakota	89,224,000	0.1%
	District of Columbia	225,705,000	0.3%

Source: U.S. Bureau of the Census, Governments Division
"State and Local Government Finances 2006-2007" (http://www.census.gov/govs/estimate/index.html)
*Direct general expenditures.

Per Capita State and Local Government Expenditures for Corrections in 2007

National Per Capita = $226*

ALPHA ORDER				RANK ORDER		
RANK	STATE	PER CAPITA		RANK	STATE	PER CAPITA
33	Alabama	$166		1	Alaska	$353
1	Alaska	353		2	California	347
14	Arizona	243		3	Wyoming	328
35	Arkansas	158		4	Delaware	309
2	California	347		5	Maryland	296
14	Colorado	243		6	New York	291
25	Connecticut	189		7	Oregon	265
4	Delaware	309		8	Nevada	259
19	Florida	232		9	Virginia	252
19	Georgia	232		10	Louisiana	245
37	Hawaii	154		10	Pennsylvania	245
30	Idaho	180		10	Washington	245
44	Illinois	146		13	Wisconsin	244
37	Indiana	154		14	Arizona	243
44	Iowa	146		14	Colorado	243
48	Kansas	138		16	New Mexico	239
36	Kentucky	155		17	Michigan	236
10	Louisiana	245		18	New Jersey	235
40	Maine	151		19	Florida	232
5	Maryland	296		19	Georgia	232
22	Massachusetts	199		21	Rhode Island	209
17	Michigan	236		22	Massachusetts	199
34	Minnesota	162		23	Texas	198
43	Mississippi	148		24	North Carolina	193
49	Missouri	136		25	Connecticut	189
25	Montana	189		25	Montana	189
28	Nebraska	184		27	Oklahoma	185
8	Nevada	259		28	Nebraska	184
50	New Hampshire	125		29	Vermont	183
18	New Jersey	235		30	Idaho	180
16	New Mexico	239		31	Utah	179
6	New York	291		32	South Dakota	176
24	North Carolina	193		33	Alabama	166
47	North Dakota	140		34	Minnesota	162
46	Ohio	142		35	Arkansas	158
27	Oklahoma	185		36	Kentucky	155
7	Oregon	265		37	Hawaii	154
10	Pennsylvania	245		37	Indiana	154
21	Rhode Island	209		37	Tennessee	154
42	South Carolina	150		40	Maine	151
32	South Dakota	176		40	West Virginia	151
37	Tennessee	154		42	South Carolina	150
23	Texas	198		43	Mississippi	148
31	Utah	179		44	Illinois	146
29	Vermont	183		44	Iowa	146
9	Virginia	252		46	Ohio	142
10	Washington	245		47	North Dakota	140
40	West Virginia	151		48	Kansas	138
13	Wisconsin	244		49	Missouri	136
3	Wyoming	328		50	New Hampshire	125
					District of Columbia	384

Source: CQ Press using data from U.S. Bureau of the Census, Governments Division
"State and Local Government Finances 2006-2007" (http://www.census.gov/govs/estimate/index.html)
*Direct general expenditures.

State and Local Government Expenditures for Corrections as a Percent of All Direct General Expenditures in 2007
National Percent = 3.0% of Direct General Expenditures

ALPHA ORDER

RANK	STATE	PERCENT
31	Alabama	2.5
34	Alaska	2.3
2	Arizona	3.9
27	Arkansas	2.6
1	California	4.0
7	Colorado	3.5
34	Connecticut	2.3
9	Delaware	3.4
13	Florida	3.2
7	Georgia	3.5
50	Hawaii	1.8
17	Idaho	3.0
40	Illinois	2.1
34	Indiana	2.3
43	Iowa	2.0
43	Kansas	2.0
32	Kentucky	2.4
16	Louisiana	3.1
43	Maine	2.0
2	Maryland	3.9
32	Massachusetts	2.4
9	Michigan	3.4
40	Minnesota	2.1
46	Mississippi	1.9
38	Missouri	2.2
25	Montana	2.7
27	Nebraska	2.6
4	Nevada	3.8
46	New Hampshire	1.9
25	New Jersey	2.7
18	New Mexico	2.9
21	New York	2.8
18	North Carolina	2.9
46	North Dakota	1.9
46	Ohio	1.9
18	Oklahoma	2.9
4	Oregon	3.8
12	Pennsylvania	3.3
27	Rhode Island	2.6
40	South Carolina	2.1
21	South Dakota	2.8
27	Tennessee	2.6
13	Texas	3.2
21	Utah	2.8
38	Vermont	2.2
6	Virginia	3.7
13	Washington	3.2
34	West Virginia	2.3
9	Wisconsin	3.4
21	Wyoming	2.8

RANK ORDER

RANK	STATE	PERCENT
1	California	4.0
2	Arizona	3.9
2	Maryland	3.9
4	Nevada	3.8
4	Oregon	3.8
6	Virginia	3.7
7	Colorado	3.5
7	Georgia	3.5
9	Delaware	3.4
9	Michigan	3.4
9	Wisconsin	3.4
12	Pennsylvania	3.3
13	Florida	3.2
13	Texas	3.2
13	Washington	3.2
16	Louisiana	3.1
17	Idaho	3.0
18	New Mexico	2.9
18	North Carolina	2.9
18	Oklahoma	2.9
21	New York	2.8
21	South Dakota	2.8
21	Utah	2.8
21	Wyoming	2.8
25	Montana	2.7
25	New Jersey	2.7
27	Arkansas	2.6
27	Nebraska	2.6
27	Rhode Island	2.6
27	Tennessee	2.6
31	Alabama	2.5
32	Kentucky	2.4
32	Massachusetts	2.4
34	Alaska	2.3
34	Connecticut	2.3
34	Indiana	2.3
34	West Virginia	2.3
38	Missouri	2.2
38	Vermont	2.2
40	Illinois	2.1
40	Minnesota	2.1
40	South Carolina	2.1
43	Iowa	2.0
43	Kansas	2.0
43	Maine	2.0
46	Mississippi	1.9
46	New Hampshire	1.9
46	North Dakota	1.9
46	Ohio	1.9
50	Hawaii	1.8

District of Columbia 2.7

Source: CQ Press using data from U.S. Bureau of the Census, Governments Division
"State and Local Government Finances 2006-2007" (http://www.census.gov/govs/estimate/index.html)

State Government Expenditures for Corrections in 2007

National Total = $44,021,189,000*

ALPHA ORDER

RANK	STATE	EXPENDITURES	% of USA
26	Alabama	$487,175,000	1.1%
38	Alaska	237,144,000	0.5%
17	Arizona	898,226,000	2.0%
31	Arkansas	331,214,000	0.8%
1	California	7,786,971,000	17.7%
18	Colorado	747,689,000	1.7%
19	Connecticut	659,966,000	1.5%
36	Delaware	265,937,000	0.6%
4	Florida	2,542,387,000	5.8%
8	Georgia	1,422,381,000	3.2%
42	Hawaii	197,273,000	0.4%
41	Idaho	201,857,000	0.5%
11	Illinois	1,198,667,000	2.7%
21	Indiana	603,969,000	1.4%
37	Iowa	255,707,000	0.6%
35	Kansas	271,551,000	0.6%
29	Kentucky	451,475,000	1.0%
25	Louisiana	521,879,000	1.2%
45	Maine	130,051,000	0.3%
9	Maryland	1,347,424,000	3.1%
15	Massachusetts	1,010,277,000	2.3%
5	Michigan	1,766,440,000	4.0%
27	Minnesota	469,256,000	1.1%
33	Mississippi	301,308,000	0.7%
20	Missouri	625,123,000	1.4%
44	Montana	146,574,000	0.3%
40	Nebraska	212,510,000	0.5%
34	Nevada	292,821,000	0.7%
48	New Hampshire	109,320,000	0.2%
7	New Jersey	1,423,034,000	3.2%
30	New Mexico	341,179,000	0.8%
3	New York	3,016,304,000	6.9%
10	North Carolina	1,267,815,000	2.9%
50	North Dakota	53,596,000	0.1%
12	Ohio	1,176,364,000	2.7%
24	Oklahoma	568,943,000	1.3%
22	Oregon	597,477,000	1.4%
6	Pennsylvania	1,665,077,000	3.8%
43	Rhode Island	178,364,000	0.4%
28	South Carolina	465,885,000	1.1%
49	South Dakota	102,081,000	0.2%
23	Tennessee	594,538,000	1.4%
2	Texas	3,177,347,000	7.2%
32	Utah	310,334,000	0.7%
47	Vermont	113,487,000	0.3%
13	Virginia	1,106,136,000	2.5%
14	Washington	1,089,670,000	2.5%
39	West Virginia	233,280,000	0.5%
16	Wisconsin	930,537,000	2.1%
46	Wyoming	117,169,000	0.3%

RANK ORDER

RANK	STATE	EXPENDITURES	% of USA
1	California	$7,786,971,000	17.7%
2	Texas	3,177,347,000	7.2%
3	New York	3,016,304,000	6.9%
4	Florida	2,542,387,000	5.8%
5	Michigan	1,766,440,000	4.0%
6	Pennsylvania	1,665,077,000	3.8%
7	New Jersey	1,423,034,000	3.2%
8	Georgia	1,422,381,000	3.2%
9	Maryland	1,347,424,000	3.1%
10	North Carolina	1,267,815,000	2.9%
11	Illinois	1,198,667,000	2.7%
12	Ohio	1,176,364,000	2.7%
13	Virginia	1,106,136,000	2.5%
14	Washington	1,089,670,000	2.5%
15	Massachusetts	1,010,277,000	2.3%
16	Wisconsin	930,537,000	2.1%
17	Arizona	898,226,000	2.0%
18	Colorado	747,689,000	1.7%
19	Connecticut	659,966,000	1.5%
20	Missouri	625,123,000	1.4%
21	Indiana	603,969,000	1.4%
22	Oregon	597,477,000	1.4%
23	Tennessee	594,538,000	1.4%
24	Oklahoma	568,943,000	1.3%
25	Louisiana	521,879,000	1.2%
26	Alabama	487,175,000	1.1%
27	Minnesota	469,256,000	1.1%
28	South Carolina	465,885,000	1.1%
29	Kentucky	451,475,000	1.0%
30	New Mexico	341,179,000	0.8%
31	Arkansas	331,214,000	0.8%
32	Utah	310,334,000	0.7%
33	Mississippi	301,308,000	0.7%
34	Nevada	292,821,000	0.7%
35	Kansas	271,551,000	0.6%
36	Delaware	265,937,000	0.6%
37	Iowa	255,707,000	0.6%
38	Alaska	237,144,000	0.5%
39	West Virginia	233,280,000	0.5%
40	Nebraska	212,510,000	0.5%
41	Idaho	201,857,000	0.5%
42	Hawaii	197,273,000	0.4%
43	Rhode Island	178,364,000	0.4%
44	Montana	146,574,000	0.3%
45	Maine	130,051,000	0.3%
46	Wyoming	117,169,000	0.3%
47	Vermont	113,487,000	0.3%
48	New Hampshire	109,320,000	0.2%
49	South Dakota	102,081,000	0.2%
50	North Dakota	53,596,000	0.1%
	District of Columbia**	NA	NA

Source: U.S. Bureau of the Census, Governments Division
    "State and Local Government Finances 2006-2007" (http://www.census.gov/govs/estimate/index.html)
*Direct general expenditures.
**Not applicable.

Per Capita State Government Expenditures for Corrections in 2007

National Per Capita = $146*

ALPHA ORDER

RANK	STATE	PER CAPITA
39	Alabama	$105
1	Alaska	348
23	Arizona	141
33	Arkansas	117
5	California	214
18	Colorado	154
6	Connecticut	189
2	Delaware	309
24	Florida	140
21	Georgia	149
18	Hawaii	154
26	Idaho	135
46	Illinois	93
45	Indiana	95
48	Iowa	86
43	Kansas	98
36	Kentucky	107
32	Louisiana	119
42	Maine	99
3	Maryland	240
16	Massachusetts	156
8	Michigan	176
47	Minnesota	91
40	Mississippi	103
37	Missouri	106
20	Montana	153
31	Nebraska	120
35	Nevada	115
50	New Hampshire	83
13	New Jersey	164
9	New Mexico	174
17	New York	155
24	North Carolina	140
49	North Dakota	84
41	Ohio	102
15	Oklahoma	158
14	Oregon	160
27	Pennsylvania	134
10	Rhode Island	169
37	South Carolina	106
30	South Dakota	128
44	Tennessee	97
28	Texas	133
34	Utah	116
7	Vermont	183
22	Virginia	144
10	Washington	169
29	West Virginia	129
12	Wisconsin	166
4	Wyoming	224

RANK ORDER

RANK	STATE	PER CAPITA
1	Alaska	$348
2	Delaware	309
3	Maryland	240
4	Wyoming	224
5	California	214
6	Connecticut	189
7	Vermont	183
8	Michigan	176
9	New Mexico	174
10	Rhode Island	169
10	Washington	169
12	Wisconsin	166
13	New Jersey	164
14	Oregon	160
15	Oklahoma	158
16	Massachusetts	156
17	New York	155
18	Colorado	154
18	Hawaii	154
20	Montana	153
21	Georgia	149
22	Virginia	144
23	Arizona	141
24	Florida	140
24	North Carolina	140
26	Idaho	135
27	Pennsylvania	134
28	Texas	133
29	West Virginia	129
30	South Dakota	128
31	Nebraska	120
32	Louisiana	119
33	Arkansas	117
34	Utah	116
35	Nevada	115
36	Kentucky	107
37	Missouri	106
37	South Carolina	106
39	Alabama	105
40	Mississippi	103
41	Ohio	102
42	Maine	99
43	Kansas	98
44	Tennessee	97
45	Indiana	95
46	Illinois	93
47	Minnesota	91
48	Iowa	86
49	North Dakota	84
50	New Hampshire	83
	District of Columbia**	NA

Source: CQ Press using data from U.S. Bureau of the Census, Governments Division
"State and Local Government Finances 2006-2007" (http://www.census.gov/govs/estimate/index.html)
*Direct general expenditures.
**Not applicable.

State Government Expenditures for Corrections as a Percent of All Direct General Expenditures in 2007
National Percent = 4.6% of Direct General Expenditures

ALPHA ORDER

RANK	STATE	PERCENT
35	Alabama	3.3
32	Alaska	3.4
5	Arizona	5.7
29	Arkansas	3.5
1	California	7.3
3	Colorado	6.2
19	Connecticut	4.3
9	Delaware	5.3
6	Florida	5.5
10	Georgia	5.2
48	Hawaii	2.2
13	Idaho	4.8
35	Illinois	3.3
35	Indiana	3.3
46	Iowa	2.6
35	Kansas	3.3
42	Kentucky	2.8
42	Louisiana	2.8
48	Maine	2.2
2	Maryland	6.5
32	Massachusetts	3.4
3	Michigan	6.2
45	Minnesota	2.7
47	Mississippi	2.5
26	Missouri	3.7
22	Montana	3.9
24	Nebraska	3.8
10	Nevada	5.2
42	New Hampshire	2.8
20	New Jersey	4.2
27	New Mexico	3.6
21	New York	4.1
16	North Carolina	4.7
50	North Dakota	2.0
39	Ohio	3.2
13	Oklahoma	4.8
12	Oregon	5.1
24	Pennsylvania	3.8
27	Rhode Island	3.6
41	South Carolina	2.9
22	South Dakota	3.9
29	Tennessee	3.5
8	Texas	5.4
32	Utah	3.4
29	Vermont	3.5
13	Virginia	4.8
16	Washington	4.7
39	West Virginia	3.2
6	Wisconsin	5.5
16	Wyoming	4.7

RANK ORDER

RANK	STATE	PERCENT
1	California	7.3
2	Maryland	6.5
3	Colorado	6.2
3	Michigan	6.2
5	Arizona	5.7
6	Florida	5.5
6	Wisconsin	5.5
8	Texas	5.4
9	Delaware	5.3
10	Georgia	5.2
10	Nevada	5.2
12	Oregon	5.1
13	Idaho	4.8
13	Oklahoma	4.8
13	Virginia	4.8
16	North Carolina	4.7
16	Washington	4.7
16	Wyoming	4.7
19	Connecticut	4.3
20	New Jersey	4.2
21	New York	4.1
22	Montana	3.9
22	South Dakota	3.9
24	Nebraska	3.8
24	Pennsylvania	3.8
26	Missouri	3.7
27	New Mexico	3.6
27	Rhode Island	3.6
29	Arkansas	3.5
29	Tennessee	3.5
29	Vermont	3.5
32	Alaska	3.4
32	Massachusetts	3.4
32	Utah	3.4
35	Alabama	3.3
35	Illinois	3.3
35	Indiana	3.3
35	Kansas	3.3
39	Ohio	3.2
39	West Virginia	3.2
41	South Carolina	2.9
42	Kentucky	2.8
42	Louisiana	2.8
42	New Hampshire	2.8
45	Minnesota	2.7
46	Iowa	2.6
47	Mississippi	2.5
48	Hawaii	2.2
48	Maine	2.2
50	North Dakota	2.0
	District of Columbia*	NA

Source: CQ Press using data from U.S. Bureau of the Census, Governments Division
"State and Local Government Finances 2006-2007" (http://www.census.gov/govs/estimate/index.html)
*Not applicable.

Local Government Expenditures for Corrections in 2007

National Total = $24,080,861,000*

ALPHA ORDER

RANK	STATE	EXPENDITURES	% of USA
24	Alabama	$281,950,000	1.2%
46	Alaska	3,452,000	0.0%
9	Arizona	646,950,000	2.7%
33	Arkansas	116,954,000	0.5%
1	California	4,838,244,000	20.1%
17	Colorado	428,473,000	1.8%
47	Connecticut	70,000	0.0%
49	Delaware	0	0.0%
3	Florida	1,687,215,000	7.0%
7	Georgia	787,362,000	3.3%
49	Hawaii	0	0.0%
38	Idaho	67,814,000	0.3%
8	Illinois	667,863,000	2.8%
19	Indiana	370,647,000	1.5%
28	Iowa	180,668,000	0.8%
35	Kansas	111,447,000	0.5%
26	Kentucky	205,606,000	0.9%
12	Louisiana	548,382,000	2.3%
37	Maine	68,428,000	0.3%
23	Maryland	313,758,000	1.3%
25	Massachusetts	274,891,000	1.1%
11	Michigan	604,279,000	2.5%
20	Minnesota	370,246,000	1.5%
31	Mississippi	129,796,000	0.5%
29	Missouri	175,857,000	0.7%
45	Montana	34,699,000	0.1%
34	Nebraska	113,420,000	0.5%
21	Nevada	368,909,000	1.5%
40	New Hampshire	54,267,000	0.2%
10	New Jersey	606,401,000	2.5%
32	New Mexico	127,381,000	0.5%
2	New York	2,644,551,000	11.0%
14	North Carolina	475,633,000	2.0%
44	North Dakota	35,628,000	0.1%
15	Ohio	451,924,000	1.9%
36	Oklahoma	97,922,000	0.4%
18	Oregon	392,831,000	1.6%
5	Pennsylvania	1,383,644,000	5.7%
41	Rhode Island	42,019,000	0.2%
27	South Carolina	195,756,000	0.8%
43	South Dakota	37,726,000	0.2%
22	Tennessee	354,865,000	1.5%
4	Texas	1,534,496,000	6.4%
30	Utah	166,095,000	0.7%
48	Vermont	62,000	0.0%
6	Virginia	836,404,000	3.5%
13	Washington	491,231,000	2.0%
42	West Virginia	39,356,000	0.2%
16	Wisconsin	435,262,000	1.8%
39	Wyoming	54,322,000	0.2%

RANK ORDER

RANK	STATE	EXPENDITURES	% of USA
1	California	$4,838,244,000	20.1%
2	New York	2,644,551,000	11.0%
3	Florida	1,687,215,000	7.0%
4	Texas	1,534,496,000	6.4%
5	Pennsylvania	1,383,644,000	5.7%
6	Virginia	836,404,000	3.5%
7	Georgia	787,362,000	3.3%
8	Illinois	667,863,000	2.8%
9	Arizona	646,950,000	2.7%
10	New Jersey	606,401,000	2.5%
11	Michigan	604,279,000	2.5%
12	Louisiana	548,382,000	2.3%
13	Washington	491,231,000	2.0%
14	North Carolina	475,633,000	2.0%
15	Ohio	451,924,000	1.9%
16	Wisconsin	435,262,000	1.8%
17	Colorado	428,473,000	1.8%
18	Oregon	392,831,000	1.6%
19	Indiana	370,647,000	1.5%
20	Minnesota	370,246,000	1.5%
21	Nevada	368,909,000	1.5%
22	Tennessee	354,865,000	1.5%
23	Maryland	313,758,000	1.3%
24	Alabama	281,950,000	1.2%
25	Massachusetts	274,891,000	1.1%
26	Kentucky	205,606,000	0.9%
27	South Carolina	195,756,000	0.8%
28	Iowa	180,668,000	0.8%
29	Missouri	175,857,000	0.7%
30	Utah	166,095,000	0.7%
31	Mississippi	129,796,000	0.5%
32	New Mexico	127,381,000	0.5%
33	Arkansas	116,954,000	0.5%
34	Nebraska	113,420,000	0.5%
35	Kansas	111,447,000	0.5%
36	Oklahoma	97,922,000	0.4%
37	Maine	68,428,000	0.3%
38	Idaho	67,814,000	0.3%
39	Wyoming	54,322,000	0.2%
40	New Hampshire	54,267,000	0.2%
41	Rhode Island	42,019,000	0.2%
42	West Virginia	39,356,000	0.2%
43	South Dakota	37,726,000	0.2%
44	North Dakota	35,628,000	0.1%
45	Montana	34,699,000	0.1%
46	Alaska	3,452,000	0.0%
47	Connecticut	70,000	0.0%
48	Vermont	62,000	0.0%
49	Delaware	0	0.0%
49	Hawaii	0	0.0%
	District of Columbia	225,705,000	0.9%

Source: U.S. Bureau of the Census, Governments Division
   "State and Local Government Finances 2006-2007" (http://www.census.gov/govs/estimate/index.html)
*Direct general expenditures.

Per Capita Local Government Expenditures for Corrections in 2007

National Per Capita = $79.93*

ALPHA ORDER

RANK	STATE	PER CAPITA
21	Alabama	$60.94
46	Alaska	5.07
9	Arizona	101.83
38	Arkansas	41.32
3	California	133.00
11	Colorado	88.48
48	Connecticut	0.02
49	Delaware	0.00
10	Florida	92.71
12	Georgia	82.68
49	Hawaii	0.00
33	Idaho	45.33
29	Illinois	52.07
24	Indiana	58.50
22	Iowa	60.56
39	Kansas	40.13
31	Kentucky	48.53
4	Louisiana	125.39
30	Maine	52.02
27	Maryland	55.84
36	Massachusetts	42.50
23	Michigan	60.13
15	Minnesota	71.44
34	Mississippi	44.44
43	Missouri	29.92
42	Montana	36.27
19	Nebraska	64.10
1	Nevada	144.42
37	New Hampshire	41.35
16	New Jersey	70.08
17	New Mexico	64.84
2	New York	136.11
28	North Carolina	52.60
26	North Dakota	55.85
41	Ohio	39.37
44	Oklahoma	27.14
7	Oregon	105.16
5	Pennsylvania	111.41
40	Rhode Island	39.90
34	South Carolina	44.44
32	South Dakota	47.41
25	Tennessee	57.71
18	Texas	64.36
20	Utah	62.23
47	Vermont	0.10
6	Virginia	108.64
14	Washington	76.17
45	West Virginia	21.75
13	Wisconsin	77.74
8	Wyoming	103.82

RANK ORDER

RANK	STATE	PER CAPITA
1	Nevada	$144.42
2	New York	136.11
3	California	133.00
4	Louisiana	125.39
5	Pennsylvania	111.41
6	Virginia	108.64
7	Oregon	105.16
8	Wyoming	103.82
9	Arizona	101.83
10	Florida	92.71
11	Colorado	88.48
12	Georgia	82.68
13	Wisconsin	77.74
14	Washington	76.17
15	Minnesota	71.44
16	New Jersey	70.08
17	New Mexico	64.84
18	Texas	64.36
19	Nebraska	64.10
20	Utah	62.23
21	Alabama	60.94
22	Iowa	60.56
23	Michigan	60.13
24	Indiana	58.50
25	Tennessee	57.71
26	North Dakota	55.85
27	Maryland	55.84
28	North Carolina	52.60
29	Illinois	52.07
30	Maine	52.02
31	Kentucky	48.53
32	South Dakota	47.41
33	Idaho	45.33
34	Mississippi	44.44
34	South Carolina	44.44
36	Massachusetts	42.50
37	New Hampshire	41.35
38	Arkansas	41.32
39	Kansas	40.13
40	Rhode Island	39.90
41	Ohio	39.37
42	Montana	36.27
43	Missouri	29.92
44	Oklahoma	27.14
45	West Virginia	21.75
46	Alaska	5.07
47	Vermont	0.10
48	Connecticut	0.02
49	Delaware	0.00
49	Hawaii	0.00

District of Columbia   383.94

Source: CQ Press using data from U.S. Bureau of the Census, Governments Division
"State and Local Government Finances 2006-2007" (http://www.census.gov/govs/estimate/index.html)
*Direct general expenditures.

Local Government Expenditures for Corrections as a Percent of All Direct General Expenditures in 2007
National Percent = 1.9% of Direct General Expenditures

ALPHA ORDER

RANK	STATE	PERCENT
18	Alabama	1.7
46	Alaska	0.1
5	Arizona	2.7
26	Arkansas	1.5
7	California	2.3
10	Colorado	2.0
47	Connecticut	0.0
47	Delaware	0.0
10	Florida	2.0
8	Georgia	2.2
47	Hawaii	0.0
32	Idaho	1.4
36	Illinois	1.2
22	Indiana	1.6
26	Iowa	1.5
41	Kansas	1.0
13	Kentucky	1.9
1	Louisiana	3.5
18	Maine	1.7
32	Maryland	1.4
39	Massachusetts	1.1
26	Michigan	1.5
22	Minnesota	1.6
34	Mississippi	1.3
42	Missouri	0.9
36	Montana	1.2
22	Nebraska	1.6
2	Nevada	3.2
36	New Hampshire	1.2
26	New Jersey	1.5
13	New Mexico	1.9
10	New York	2.0
26	North Carolina	1.5
18	North Dakota	1.7
42	Ohio	0.9
42	Oklahoma	0.9
5	Oregon	2.7
3	Pennsylvania	2.8
39	Rhode Island	1.1
34	South Carolina	1.3
22	South Dakota	1.6
13	Tennessee	1.9
18	Texas	1.7
9	Utah	2.1
47	Vermont	0.0
3	Virginia	2.8
17	Washington	1.8
45	West Virginia	0.8
13	Wisconsin	1.9
26	Wyoming	1.5

RANK ORDER

RANK	STATE	PERCENT
1	Louisiana	3.5
2	Nevada	3.2
3	Pennsylvania	2.8
3	Virginia	2.8
5	Arizona	2.7
5	Oregon	2.7
7	California	2.3
8	Georgia	2.2
9	Utah	2.1
10	Colorado	2.0
10	Florida	2.0
10	New York	2.0
13	Kentucky	1.9
13	New Mexico	1.9
13	Tennessee	1.9
13	Wisconsin	1.9
17	Washington	1.8
18	Alabama	1.7
18	Maine	1.7
18	North Dakota	1.7
18	Texas	1.7
22	Indiana	1.6
22	Minnesota	1.6
22	Nebraska	1.6
22	South Dakota	1.6
26	Arkansas	1.5
26	Iowa	1.5
26	Michigan	1.5
26	New Jersey	1.5
26	North Carolina	1.5
26	Wyoming	1.5
32	Idaho	1.4
32	Maryland	1.4
34	Mississippi	1.3
34	South Carolina	1.3
36	Illinois	1.2
36	Montana	1.2
36	New Hampshire	1.2
39	Massachusetts	1.1
39	Rhode Island	1.1
41	Kansas	1.0
42	Missouri	0.9
42	Ohio	0.9
42	Oklahoma	0.9
45	West Virginia	0.8
46	Alaska	0.1
47	Connecticut	0.0
47	Delaware	0.0
47	Hawaii	0.0
47	Vermont	0.0

District of Columbia 2.7

Source: CQ Press using data from U.S. Bureau of the Census, Governments Division
"State and Local Government Finances 2006-2007" (http://www.census.gov/govs/estimate/index.html)

State and Local Government Expenditures for Judicial and Legal Services in 2007
National Total = $38,766,475,000*

ALPHA ORDER

RANK	STATE	EXPENDITURES	% of USA
27	Alabama	$401,420,000	1.0%
39	Alaska	190,436,000	0.5%
12	Arizona	911,530,000	2.4%
38	Arkansas	205,597,000	0.5%
1	California	8,572,883,000	22.1%
22	Colorado	473,520,000	1.2%
17	Connecticut	619,132,000	1.6%
40	Delaware	155,767,000	0.4%
3	Florida	2,169,020,000	5.6%
11	Georgia	918,593,000	2.4%
33	Hawaii	280,942,000	0.7%
41	Idaho	152,623,000	0.4%
8	Illinois	1,327,744,000	3.4%
24	Indiana	448,385,000	1.2%
30	Iowa	301,099,000	0.8%
34	Kansas	273,206,000	0.7%
25	Kentucky	416,193,000	1.1%
21	Louisiana	558,314,000	1.4%
46	Maine	103,846,000	0.3%
14	Maryland	739,001,000	1.9%
10	Massachusetts	990,927,000	2.6%
9	Michigan	1,041,790,000	2.7%
16	Minnesota	625,710,000	1.6%
36	Mississippi	211,413,000	0.5%
23	Missouri	456,126,000	1.2%
43	Montana	127,884,000	0.3%
42	Nebraska	149,607,000	0.4%
26	Nevada	405,307,000	1.0%
45	New Hampshire	122,522,000	0.3%
7	New Jersey	1,379,437,000	3.6%
32	New Mexico	281,633,000	0.7%
2	New York	3,422,046,000	8.8%
18	North Carolina	607,176,000	1.6%
49	North Dakota	61,246,000	0.2%
5	Ohio	1,594,524,000	4.1%
31	Oklahoma	297,743,000	0.8%
28	Oregon	387,025,000	1.0%
6	Pennsylvania	1,474,311,000	3.8%
44	Rhode Island	126,470,000	0.3%
35	South Carolina	268,625,000	0.7%
48	South Dakota	62,914,000	0.2%
19	Tennessee	560,840,000	1.4%
4	Texas	2,088,466,000	5.4%
29	Utah	301,309,000	0.8%
50	Vermont	60,231,000	0.2%
13	Virginia	774,560,000	2.0%
15	Washington	728,687,000	1.9%
37	West Virginia	205,875,000	0.5%
20	Wisconsin	560,115,000	1.4%
47	Wyoming	90,928,000	0.2%

RANK ORDER

RANK	STATE	EXPENDITURES	% of USA
1	California	$8,572,883,000	22.1%
2	New York	3,422,046,000	8.8%
3	Florida	2,169,020,000	5.6%
4	Texas	2,088,466,000	5.4%
5	Ohio	1,594,524,000	4.1%
6	Pennsylvania	1,474,311,000	3.8%
7	New Jersey	1,379,437,000	3.6%
8	Illinois	1,327,744,000	3.4%
9	Michigan	1,041,790,000	2.7%
10	Massachusetts	990,927,000	2.6%
11	Georgia	918,593,000	2.4%
12	Arizona	911,530,000	2.4%
13	Virginia	774,560,000	2.0%
14	Maryland	739,001,000	1.9%
15	Washington	728,687,000	1.9%
16	Minnesota	625,710,000	1.6%
17	Connecticut	619,132,000	1.6%
18	North Carolina	607,176,000	1.6%
19	Tennessee	560,840,000	1.4%
20	Wisconsin	560,115,000	1.4%
21	Louisiana	558,314,000	1.4%
22	Colorado	473,520,000	1.2%
23	Missouri	456,126,000	1.2%
24	Indiana	448,385,000	1.2%
25	Kentucky	416,193,000	1.1%
26	Nevada	405,307,000	1.0%
27	Alabama	401,420,000	1.0%
28	Oregon	387,025,000	1.0%
29	Utah	301,309,000	0.8%
30	Iowa	301,099,000	0.8%
31	Oklahoma	297,743,000	0.8%
32	New Mexico	281,633,000	0.7%
33	Hawaii	280,942,000	0.7%
34	Kansas	273,206,000	0.7%
35	South Carolina	268,625,000	0.7%
36	Mississippi	211,413,000	0.5%
37	West Virginia	205,875,000	0.5%
38	Arkansas	205,597,000	0.5%
39	Alaska	190,436,000	0.5%
40	Delaware	155,767,000	0.4%
41	Idaho	152,623,000	0.4%
42	Nebraska	149,607,000	0.4%
43	Montana	127,884,000	0.3%
44	Rhode Island	126,470,000	0.3%
45	New Hampshire	122,522,000	0.3%
46	Maine	103,846,000	0.3%
47	Wyoming	90,928,000	0.2%
48	South Dakota	62,914,000	0.2%
49	North Dakota	61,246,000	0.2%
50	Vermont	60,231,000	0.2%
	District of Columbia	81,777,000	0.2%

Source: U.S. Bureau of the Census, Governments Division
"State and Local Government Finances 2006-2007" (http://www.census.gov/govs/estimate/index.html)
*Direct general expenditures. Includes courts, prosecution and legal services, and public defense.

Per Capita State and Local Government Expenditures for Judicial and Legal Services in 2007
National Per Capita = $129*

ALPHA ORDER

RANK	STATE	PER CAPITA
40	Alabama	$87
1	Alaska	280
11	Arizona	143
46	Arkansas	73
2	California	236
31	Colorado	98
5	Connecticut	177
4	Delaware	181
19	Florida	119
35	Georgia	96
3	Hawaii	220
27	Idaho	102
24	Illinois	104
48	Indiana	71
28	Iowa	101
31	Kansas	98
31	Kentucky	98
16	Louisiana	128
43	Maine	79
15	Maryland	132
10	Massachusetts	153
24	Michigan	104
17	Minnesota	121
47	Mississippi	72
45	Missouri	78
14	Montana	134
41	Nebraska	85
8	Nevada	159
37	New Hampshire	93
8	New Jersey	159
11	New Mexico	143
6	New York	176
49	North Carolina	67
35	North Dakota	96
13	Ohio	139
42	Oklahoma	83
24	Oregon	104
19	Pennsylvania	119
18	Rhode Island	120
50	South Carolina	61
43	South Dakota	79
38	Tennessee	91
39	Texas	88
22	Utah	113
34	Vermont	97
28	Virginia	101
22	Washington	113
21	West Virginia	114
30	Wisconsin	100
7	Wyoming	174

RANK ORDER

RANK	STATE	PER CAPITA
1	Alaska	$280
2	California	236
3	Hawaii	220
4	Delaware	181
5	Connecticut	177
6	New York	176
7	Wyoming	174
8	Nevada	159
8	New Jersey	159
10	Massachusetts	153
11	Arizona	143
11	New Mexico	143
13	Ohio	139
14	Montana	134
15	Maryland	132
16	Louisiana	128
17	Minnesota	121
18	Rhode Island	120
19	Florida	119
19	Pennsylvania	119
21	West Virginia	114
22	Utah	113
22	Washington	113
24	Illinois	104
24	Michigan	104
24	Oregon	104
27	Idaho	102
28	Iowa	101
28	Virginia	101
30	Wisconsin	100
31	Colorado	98
31	Kansas	98
31	Kentucky	98
34	Vermont	97
35	Georgia	96
35	North Dakota	96
37	New Hampshire	93
38	Tennessee	91
39	Texas	88
40	Alabama	87
41	Nebraska	85
42	Oklahoma	83
43	Maine	79
43	South Dakota	79
45	Missouri	78
46	Arkansas	73
47	Mississippi	72
48	Indiana	71
49	North Carolina	67
50	South Carolina	61
	District of Columbia	139

Source: CQ Press using data from U.S. Bureau of the Census, Governments Division
   "State and Local Government Finances 2006-2007" (http://www.census.gov/govs/estimate/index.html)
*Direct general expenditures. Includes courts, prosecution and legal services, and public defense.

State and Local Government Expenditures for Judicial and Legal Services as a Percent of All Direct General Expenditures in 2007
National Percent = 1.7% of Direct General Expenditures*

ALPHA ORDER

RANK	STATE	PERCENT
38	Alabama	1.3
9	Alaska	1.8
4	Arizona	2.3
42	Arkansas	1.2
1	California	2.7
32	Colorado	1.4
5	Connecticut	2.1
6	Delaware	2.0
13	Florida	1.7
32	Georgia	1.4
2	Hawaii	2.6
13	Idaho	1.7
22	Illinois	1.5
45	Indiana	1.1
32	Iowa	1.4
22	Kansas	1.5
22	Kentucky	1.5
19	Louisiana	1.6
47	Maine	1.0
13	Maryland	1.7
9	Massachusetts	1.8
22	Michigan	1.5
22	Minnesota	1.5
49	Mississippi	0.9
42	Missouri	1.2
7	Montana	1.9
42	Nebraska	1.2
3	Nevada	2.4
32	New Hampshire	1.4
9	New Jersey	1.8
13	New Mexico	1.7
13	New York	1.7
47	North Carolina	1.0
38	North Dakota	1.3
7	Ohio	1.9
38	Oklahoma	1.3
22	Oregon	1.5
19	Pennsylvania	1.6
22	Rhode Island	1.5
49	South Carolina	0.9
38	South Dakota	1.3
19	Tennessee	1.6
32	Texas	1.4
9	Utah	1.8
45	Vermont	1.1
22	Virginia	1.5
22	Washington	1.5
13	West Virginia	1.7
32	Wisconsin	1.4
22	Wyoming	1.5

RANK ORDER

RANK	STATE	PERCENT
1	California	2.7
2	Hawaii	2.6
3	Nevada	2.4
4	Arizona	2.3
5	Connecticut	2.1
6	Delaware	2.0
7	Montana	1.9
7	Ohio	1.9
9	Alaska	1.8
9	Massachusetts	1.8
9	New Jersey	1.8
9	Utah	1.8
13	Florida	1.7
13	Idaho	1.7
13	Maryland	1.7
13	New Mexico	1.7
13	New York	1.7
13	West Virginia	1.7
19	Louisiana	1.6
19	Pennsylvania	1.6
19	Tennessee	1.6
22	Illinois	1.5
22	Kansas	1.5
22	Kentucky	1.5
22	Michigan	1.5
22	Minnesota	1.5
22	Oregon	1.5
22	Rhode Island	1.5
22	Virginia	1.5
22	Washington	1.5
22	Wyoming	1.5
32	Colorado	1.4
32	Georgia	1.4
32	Iowa	1.4
32	New Hampshire	1.4
32	Texas	1.4
32	Wisconsin	1.4
38	Alabama	1.3
38	North Dakota	1.3
38	Oklahoma	1.3
38	South Dakota	1.3
42	Arkansas	1.2
42	Missouri	1.2
42	Nebraska	1.2
45	Indiana	1.1
45	Vermont	1.1
47	Maine	1.0
47	North Carolina	1.0
49	Mississippi	0.9
49	South Carolina	0.9
	District of Columbia	1.0

Source: CQ Press using data from U.S. Bureau of the Census, Governments Division
"State and Local Government Finances 2006-2007" (http://www.census.gov/govs/estimate/index.html)
*Includes courts, prosecution and legal services, and public defense.

State Government Expenditures for Judicial and Legal Services in 2007

National Total = $18,921,485,000*

ALPHA ORDER

RANK	STATE	EXPENDITURES	% of USA
16	Alabama	$277,254,000	1.5%
30	Alaska	175,636,000	0.9%
27	Arizona	186,713,000	1.0%
36	Arkansas	126,692,000	0.7%
1	California	3,919,492,000	20.7%
18	Colorado	260,530,000	1.4%
7	Connecticut	576,086,000	3.0%
34	Delaware	139,647,000	0.7%
3	Florida	1,271,973,000	6.7%
26	Georgia	198,821,000	1.1%
21	Hawaii	233,303,000	1.2%
45	Idaho	68,171,000	0.4%
14	Illinois	336,816,000	1.8%
35	Indiana	139,121,000	0.7%
24	Iowa	221,722,000	1.2%
32	Kansas	156,373,000	0.8%
12	Kentucky	371,259,000	2.0%
28	Louisiana	186,371,000	1.0%
40	Maine	87,395,000	0.5%
10	Maryland	468,956,000	2.5%
4	Massachusetts	925,599,000	4.9%
29	Michigan	183,408,000	1.0%
11	Minnesota	377,157,000	2.0%
41	Mississippi	84,413,000	0.4%
22	Missouri	230,944,000	1.2%
42	Montana	79,365,000	0.4%
46	Nebraska	59,395,000	0.3%
44	Nevada	75,217,000	0.4%
39	New Hampshire	98,655,000	0.5%
5	New Jersey	856,878,000	4.5%
20	New Mexico	241,087,000	1.3%
2	New York	2,210,595,000	11.7%
8	North Carolina	542,767,000	2.9%
49	North Dakota	40,214,000	0.2%
15	Ohio	308,748,000	1.6%
25	Oklahoma	216,993,000	1.1%
19	Oregon	244,839,000	1.3%
9	Pennsylvania	489,309,000	2.6%
38	Rhode Island	113,599,000	0.6%
43	South Carolina	77,820,000	0.4%
50	South Dakota	38,700,000	0.2%
23	Tennessee	230,517,000	1.2%
6	Texas	612,771,000	3.2%
31	Utah	168,556,000	0.9%
48	Vermont	54,135,000	0.3%
13	Virginia	353,948,000	1.9%
37	Washington	122,656,000	0.6%
33	West Virginia	153,763,000	0.8%
17	Wisconsin	271,168,000	1.4%
47	Wyoming	55,938,000	0.3%

RANK ORDER

RANK	STATE	EXPENDITURES	% of USA
1	California	$3,919,492,000	20.7%
2	New York	2,210,595,000	11.7%
3	Florida	1,271,973,000	6.7%
4	Massachusetts	925,599,000	4.9%
5	New Jersey	856,878,000	4.5%
6	Texas	612,771,000	3.2%
7	Connecticut	576,086,000	3.0%
8	North Carolina	542,767,000	2.9%
9	Pennsylvania	489,309,000	2.6%
10	Maryland	468,956,000	2.5%
11	Minnesota	377,157,000	2.0%
12	Kentucky	371,259,000	2.0%
13	Virginia	353,948,000	1.9%
14	Illinois	336,816,000	1.8%
15	Ohio	308,748,000	1.6%
16	Alabama	277,254,000	1.5%
17	Wisconsin	271,168,000	1.4%
18	Colorado	260,530,000	1.4%
19	Oregon	244,839,000	1.3%
20	New Mexico	241,087,000	1.3%
21	Hawaii	233,303,000	1.2%
22	Missouri	230,944,000	1.2%
23	Tennessee	230,517,000	1.2%
24	Iowa	221,722,000	1.2%
25	Oklahoma	216,993,000	1.1%
26	Georgia	198,821,000	1.1%
27	Arizona	186,713,000	1.0%
28	Louisiana	186,371,000	1.0%
29	Michigan	183,408,000	1.0%
30	Alaska	175,636,000	0.9%
31	Utah	168,556,000	0.9%
32	Kansas	156,373,000	0.8%
33	West Virginia	153,763,000	0.8%
34	Delaware	139,647,000	0.7%
35	Indiana	139,121,000	0.7%
36	Arkansas	126,692,000	0.7%
37	Washington	122,656,000	0.6%
38	Rhode Island	113,599,000	0.6%
39	New Hampshire	98,655,000	0.5%
40	Maine	87,395,000	0.5%
41	Mississippi	84,413,000	0.4%
42	Montana	79,365,000	0.4%
43	South Carolina	77,820,000	0.4%
44	Nevada	75,217,000	0.4%
45	Idaho	68,171,000	0.4%
46	Nebraska	59,395,000	0.3%
47	Wyoming	55,938,000	0.3%
48	Vermont	54,135,000	0.3%
49	North Dakota	40,214,000	0.2%
50	South Dakota	38,700,000	0.2%
	District of Columbia**	NA	NA

Source: U.S. Bureau of the Census, Governments Division
"State and Local Government Finances 2006-2007" (http://www.census.gov/govs/estimate/index.html)
*Direct general expenditures. Includes courts, prosecution and legal services, and public defense.
**Not applicable.

Per Capita State Government Expenditures for Judicial and Legal Services in 2007
National Per Capita = $62.80*

ALPHA ORDER				RANK ORDER		
RANK	**STATE**	**PER CAPITA**		**RANK**	**STATE**	**PER CAPITA**
27	Alabama	$59.93		1	Alaska	$257.87
1	Alaska	257.87		2	Hawaii	182.65
41	Arizona	29.39		3	Connecticut	165.07
34	Arkansas	44.76		4	Delaware	162.01
9	California	107.74		5	Massachusetts	143.11
29	Colorado	53.80		6	New Mexico	122.73
3	Connecticut	165.07		7	New York	113.78
4	Delaware	162.01		8	Rhode Island	107.87
20	Florida	69.89		9	California	107.74
47	Georgia	20.88		10	Wyoming	106.90
2	Hawaii	182.65		11	New Jersey	99.03
33	Idaho	45.56		12	Kentucky	87.64
44	Illinois	26.26		13	Vermont	87.21
46	Indiana	21.96		14	West Virginia	84.96
18	Iowa	74.32		15	Maryland	83.46
28	Kansas	56.30		16	Montana	82.96
12	Kentucky	87.64		17	New Hampshire	75.18
35	Louisiana	42.62		18	Iowa	74.32
21	Maine	66.44		19	Minnesota	72.78
15	Maryland	83.46		20	Florida	69.89
5	Massachusetts	143.11		21	Maine	66.44
49	Michigan	18.25		22	Oregon	65.54
19	Minnesota	72.78		23	Utah	63.16
42	Mississippi	28.90		24	North Dakota	63.04
37	Missouri	39.29		25	Oklahoma	60.14
16	Montana	82.96		26	North Carolina	60.03
39	Nebraska	33.57		27	Alabama	59.93
40	Nevada	29.45		28	Kansas	56.30
17	New Hampshire	75.18		29	Colorado	53.80
11	New Jersey	99.03		30	South Dakota	48.64
6	New Mexico	122.73		31	Wisconsin	48.43
7	New York	113.78		32	Virginia	45.97
26	North Carolina	60.03		33	Idaho	45.56
24	North Dakota	63.04		34	Arkansas	44.76
43	Ohio	26.90		35	Louisiana	42.62
25	Oklahoma	60.14		36	Pennsylvania	39.40
22	Oregon	65.54		37	Missouri	39.29
36	Pennsylvania	39.40		38	Tennessee	37.49
8	Rhode Island	107.87		39	Nebraska	33.57
50	South Carolina	17.67		40	Nevada	29.45
30	South Dakota	48.64		41	Arizona	29.39
38	Tennessee	37.49		42	Mississippi	28.90
45	Texas	25.70		43	Ohio	26.90
23	Utah	63.16		44	Illinois	26.26
13	Vermont	87.21		45	Texas	25.70
32	Virginia	45.97		46	Indiana	21.96
48	Washington	19.02		47	Georgia	20.88
14	West Virginia	84.96		48	Washington	19.02
31	Wisconsin	48.43		49	Michigan	18.25
10	Wyoming	106.90		50	South Carolina	17.67

District of Columbia**   NA

Source: CQ Press using data from U.S. Bureau of the Census, Governments Division
"State and Local Government Finances 2006-2007" (http://www.census.gov/govs/estimate/index.html)
*Direct general expenditures. Includes courts, prosecution and legal services, and public defense.
**Not applicable.

State Government Expenditures for Judicial and Legal Services as a Percent of All Direct General Expenditures in 2007
National Percent = 2.0% of Direct General Expenditures*

ALPHA ORDER

RANK	STATE	PERCENT
23	Alabama	1.9
8	Alaska	2.5
38	Arizona	1.2
35	Arkansas	1.3
2	California	3.7
15	Colorado	2.2
1	Connecticut	3.8
5	Delaware	2.8
5	Florida	2.8
46	Georgia	0.7
7	Hawaii	2.6
28	Idaho	1.6
43	Illinois	0.9
45	Indiana	0.8
15	Iowa	2.2
23	Kansas	1.9
12	Kentucky	2.3
41	Louisiana	1.0
30	Maine	1.5
12	Maryland	2.3
3	Massachusetts	3.1
48	Michigan	0.6
15	Minnesota	2.2
46	Mississippi	0.7
34	Missouri	1.4
19	Montana	2.1
39	Nebraska	1.1
35	Nevada	1.3
8	New Hampshire	2.5
8	New Jersey	2.5
8	New Mexico	2.5
4	New York	3.0
22	North Carolina	2.0
30	North Dakota	1.5
43	Ohio	0.9
26	Oklahoma	1.8
19	Oregon	2.1
39	Pennsylvania	1.1
12	Rhode Island	2.3
49	South Carolina	0.5
30	South Dakota	1.5
35	Tennessee	1.3
41	Texas	1.0
23	Utah	1.9
27	Vermont	1.7
30	Virginia	1.5
49	Washington	0.5
19	West Virginia	2.1
28	Wisconsin	1.6
15	Wyoming	2.2

RANK ORDER

RANK	STATE	PERCENT
1	Connecticut	3.8
2	California	3.7
3	Massachusetts	3.1
4	New York	3.0
5	Delaware	2.8
5	Florida	2.8
7	Hawaii	2.6
8	Alaska	2.5
8	New Hampshire	2.5
8	New Jersey	2.5
8	New Mexico	2.5
12	Kentucky	2.3
12	Maryland	2.3
12	Rhode Island	2.3
15	Colorado	2.2
15	Iowa	2.2
15	Minnesota	2.2
15	Wyoming	2.2
19	Montana	2.1
19	Oregon	2.1
19	West Virginia	2.1
22	North Carolina	2.0
23	Alabama	1.9
23	Kansas	1.9
23	Utah	1.9
26	Oklahoma	1.8
27	Vermont	1.7
28	Idaho	1.6
28	Wisconsin	1.6
30	Maine	1.5
30	North Dakota	1.5
30	South Dakota	1.5
30	Virginia	1.5
34	Missouri	1.4
35	Arkansas	1.3
35	Nevada	1.3
35	Tennessee	1.3
38	Arizona	1.2
39	Nebraska	1.1
39	Pennsylvania	1.1
41	Louisiana	1.0
41	Texas	1.0
43	Illinois	0.9
43	Ohio	0.9
45	Indiana	0.8
46	Georgia	0.7
46	Mississippi	0.7
48	Michigan	0.6
49	South Carolina	0.5
49	Washington	0.5
	District of Columbia**	NA

Source: CQ Press using data from U.S. Bureau of the Census, Governments Division
"State and Local Government Finances 2006-2007" (http://www.census.gov/govs/estimate/index.html)
*Includes courts, prosecution and legal services, and public defense.
**Not applicable.

Local Government Expenditures for Judicial and Legal Services in 2007

National Total = $19,844,990,000*

ALPHA ORDER

RANK	STATE	EXPENDITURES	% of USA
27	Alabama	$124,166,000	0.6%
48	Alaska	14,800,000	0.1%
9	Arizona	724,817,000	3.7%
33	Arkansas	78,905,000	0.4%
1	California	4,653,391,000	23.4%
22	Colorado	212,990,000	1.1%
40	Connecticut	43,046,000	0.2%
47	Delaware	16,120,000	0.1%
7	Florida	897,047,000	4.5%
10	Georgia	719,772,000	3.6%
38	Hawaii	47,639,000	0.2%
30	Idaho	84,452,000	0.4%
5	Illinois	990,928,000	5.0%
17	Indiana	309,264,000	1.6%
32	Iowa	79,377,000	0.4%
28	Kansas	116,833,000	0.6%
39	Kentucky	44,934,000	0.2%
14	Louisiana	371,943,000	1.9%
46	Maine	16,451,000	0.1%
19	Maryland	270,045,000	1.4%
34	Massachusetts	65,328,000	0.3%
8	Michigan	858,382,000	4.3%
20	Minnesota	248,553,000	1.3%
26	Mississippi	127,000,000	0.6%
21	Missouri	225,182,000	1.1%
37	Montana	48,519,000	0.2%
29	Nebraska	90,212,000	0.5%
16	Nevada	330,090,000	1.7%
44	New Hampshire	23,867,000	0.1%
12	New Jersey	522,559,000	2.6%
41	New Mexico	40,546,000	0.2%
4	New York	1,211,451,000	6.1%
35	North Carolina	64,409,000	0.3%
45	North Dakota	21,032,000	0.1%
3	Ohio	1,285,776,000	6.5%
31	Oklahoma	80,750,000	0.4%
24	Oregon	142,186,000	0.7%
6	Pennsylvania	985,002,000	5.0%
49	Rhode Island	12,871,000	0.1%
23	South Carolina	190,805,000	1.0%
43	South Dakota	24,214,000	0.1%
15	Tennessee	330,323,000	1.7%
2	Texas	1,475,695,000	7.4%
25	Utah	132,753,000	0.7%
50	Vermont	6,096,000	0.0%
13	Virginia	420,612,000	2.1%
11	Washington	606,031,000	3.1%
36	West Virginia	52,112,000	0.3%
18	Wisconsin	288,947,000	1.5%
42	Wyoming	34,990,000	0.2%

RANK ORDER

RANK	STATE	EXPENDITURES	% of USA
1	California	$4,653,391,000	23.4%
2	Texas	1,475,695,000	7.4%
3	Ohio	1,285,776,000	6.5%
4	New York	1,211,451,000	6.1%
5	Illinois	990,928,000	5.0%
6	Pennsylvania	985,002,000	5.0%
7	Florida	897,047,000	4.5%
8	Michigan	858,382,000	4.3%
9	Arizona	724,817,000	3.7%
10	Georgia	719,772,000	3.6%
11	Washington	606,031,000	3.1%
12	New Jersey	522,559,000	2.6%
13	Virginia	420,612,000	2.1%
14	Louisiana	371,943,000	1.9%
15	Tennessee	330,323,000	1.7%
16	Nevada	330,090,000	1.7%
17	Indiana	309,264,000	1.6%
18	Wisconsin	288,947,000	1.5%
19	Maryland	270,045,000	1.4%
20	Minnesota	248,553,000	1.3%
21	Missouri	225,182,000	1.1%
22	Colorado	212,990,000	1.1%
23	South Carolina	190,805,000	1.0%
24	Oregon	142,186,000	0.7%
25	Utah	132,753,000	0.7%
26	Mississippi	127,000,000	0.6%
27	Alabama	124,166,000	0.6%
28	Kansas	116,833,000	0.6%
29	Nebraska	90,212,000	0.5%
30	Idaho	84,452,000	0.4%
31	Oklahoma	80,750,000	0.4%
32	Iowa	79,377,000	0.4%
33	Arkansas	78,905,000	0.4%
34	Massachusetts	65,328,000	0.3%
35	North Carolina	64,409,000	0.3%
36	West Virginia	52,112,000	0.3%
37	Montana	48,519,000	0.2%
38	Hawaii	47,639,000	0.2%
39	Kentucky	44,934,000	0.2%
40	Connecticut	43,046,000	0.2%
41	New Mexico	40,546,000	0.2%
42	Wyoming	34,990,000	0.2%
43	South Dakota	24,214,000	0.1%
44	New Hampshire	23,867,000	0.1%
45	North Dakota	21,032,000	0.1%
46	Maine	16,451,000	0.1%
47	Delaware	16,120,000	0.1%
48	Alaska	14,800,000	0.1%
49	Rhode Island	12,871,000	0.1%
50	Vermont	6,096,000	0.0%
	District of Columbia	81,777,000	0.4%

Source: U.S. Bureau of the Census, Governments Division
"State and Local Government Finances 2006-2007" (http://www.census.gov/govs/estimate/index.html)
*Direct general expenditures. Includes courts, prosecution and legal services, and public defense.

Per Capita Local Government Expenditures for Judicial and Legal Services in 2007
National Per Capita = $65.87*

ALPHA ORDER

RANK	STATE	PER CAPITA
37	Alabama	$26.84
40	Alaska	21.73
3	Arizona	114.08
36	Arkansas	27.88
2	California	127.92
26	Colorado	43.98
45	Connecticut	12.33
42	Delaware	18.70
22	Florida	49.29
10	Georgia	75.58
32	Hawaii	37.30
15	Idaho	56.45
9	Illinois	77.26
23	Indiana	48.81
38	Iowa	26.61
29	Kansas	42.07
47	Kentucky	10.61
7	Louisiana	85.05
44	Maine	12.51
24	Maryland	48.06
48	Massachusetts	10.10
6	Michigan	85.41
25	Minnesota	47.96
27	Mississippi	43.48
30	Missouri	38.31
20	Montana	50.72
19	Nebraska	50.98
1	Nevada	129.23
43	New Hampshire	18.19
14	New Jersey	60.39
41	New Mexico	20.64
12	New York	62.35
50	North Carolina	7.12
33	North Dakota	32.97
4	Ohio	112.02
39	Oklahoma	22.38
31	Oregon	38.06
8	Pennsylvania	79.31
46	Rhode Island	12.22
28	South Carolina	43.32
34	South Dakota	30.43
17	Tennessee	53.72
13	Texas	61.89
21	Utah	49.74
49	Vermont	9.82
16	Virginia	54.63
5	Washington	93.97
35	West Virginia	28.79
18	Wisconsin	51.61
11	Wyoming	66.87

RANK ORDER

RANK	STATE	PER CAPITA
1	Nevada	$129.23
2	California	127.92
3	Arizona	114.08
4	Ohio	112.02
5	Washington	93.97
6	Michigan	85.41
7	Louisiana	85.05
8	Pennsylvania	79.31
9	Illinois	77.26
10	Georgia	75.58
11	Wyoming	66.87
12	New York	62.35
13	Texas	61.89
14	New Jersey	60.39
15	Idaho	56.45
16	Virginia	54.63
17	Tennessee	53.72
18	Wisconsin	51.61
19	Nebraska	50.98
20	Montana	50.72
21	Utah	49.74
22	Florida	49.29
23	Indiana	48.81
24	Maryland	48.06
25	Minnesota	47.96
26	Colorado	43.98
27	Mississippi	43.48
28	South Carolina	43.32
29	Kansas	42.07
30	Missouri	38.31
31	Oregon	38.06
32	Hawaii	37.30
33	North Dakota	32.97
34	South Dakota	30.43
35	West Virginia	28.79
36	Arkansas	27.88
37	Alabama	26.84
38	Iowa	26.61
39	Oklahoma	22.38
40	Alaska	21.73
41	New Mexico	20.64
42	Delaware	18.70
43	New Hampshire	18.19
44	Maine	12.51
45	Connecticut	12.33
46	Rhode Island	12.22
47	Kentucky	10.61
48	Massachusetts	10.10
49	Vermont	9.82
50	North Carolina	7.12

District of Columbia   139.11

Source: CQ Press using data from U.S. Bureau of the Census, Governments Division
"State and Local Government Finances 2006-2007" (http://www.census.gov/govs/estimate/index.html)
*Direct general expenditures. Includes courts, prosecution and legal services, and public defense.

Local Government Expenditures for Judicial and Legal Services as a Percent of All Direct General Expenditures in 2007
National Percent = 1.5% of Direct General Expenditures*

ALPHA ORDER

RANK	STATE	PERCENT
37	Alabama	0.8
43	Alaska	0.4
1	Arizona	3.0
30	Arkansas	1.0
7	California	2.2
30	Colorado	1.0
46	Connecticut	0.3
40	Delaware	0.6
25	Florida	1.1
9	Georgia	2.0
5	Hawaii	2.3
11	Idaho	1.8
11	Illinois	1.8
18	Indiana	1.3
38	Iowa	0.7
25	Kansas	1.1
43	Kentucky	0.4
4	Louisiana	2.4
43	Maine	0.4
22	Maryland	1.2
46	Massachusetts	0.3
8	Michigan	2.1
25	Minnesota	1.1
22	Mississippi	1.2
25	Missouri	1.1
14	Montana	1.7
18	Nebraska	1.3
2	Nevada	2.8
42	New Hampshire	0.5
18	New Jersey	1.3
40	New Mexico	0.6
36	New York	0.9
50	North Carolina	0.2
30	North Dakota	1.0
3	Ohio	2.6
38	Oklahoma	0.7
30	Oregon	1.0
9	Pennsylvania	2.0
46	Rhode Island	0.3
18	South Carolina	1.3
30	South Dakota	1.0
11	Tennessee	1.8
14	Texas	1.7
14	Utah	1.7
46	Vermont	0.3
17	Virginia	1.4
5	Washington	2.3
25	West Virginia	1.1
22	Wisconsin	1.2
30	Wyoming	1.0

RANK ORDER

RANK	STATE	PERCENT
1	Arizona	3.0
2	Nevada	2.8
3	Ohio	2.6
4	Louisiana	2.4
5	Hawaii	2.3
5	Washington	2.3
7	California	2.2
8	Michigan	2.1
9	Georgia	2.0
9	Pennsylvania	2.0
11	Idaho	1.8
11	Illinois	1.8
11	Tennessee	1.8
14	Montana	1.7
14	Texas	1.7
14	Utah	1.7
17	Virginia	1.4
18	Indiana	1.3
18	Nebraska	1.3
18	New Jersey	1.3
18	South Carolina	1.3
22	Maryland	1.2
22	Mississippi	1.2
22	Wisconsin	1.2
25	Florida	1.1
25	Kansas	1.1
25	Minnesota	1.1
25	Missouri	1.1
25	West Virginia	1.1
30	Arkansas	1.0
30	Colorado	1.0
30	North Dakota	1.0
30	Oregon	1.0
30	South Dakota	1.0
30	Wyoming	1.0
36	New York	0.9
37	Alabama	0.8
38	Iowa	0.7
38	Oklahoma	0.7
40	Delaware	0.6
40	New Mexico	0.6
42	New Hampshire	0.5
43	Alaska	0.4
43	Kentucky	0.4
43	Maine	0.4
46	Connecticut	0.3
46	Massachusetts	0.3
46	Rhode Island	0.3
46	Vermont	0.3
50	North Carolina	0.2

| | District of Columbia | 1.0 |

Source: CQ Press using data from U.S. Bureau of the Census, Governments Division
 "State and Local Government Finances 2006-2007" (http://www.census.gov/govs/estimate/index.html)
*Includes courts, prosecution and legal services, and public defense.

State and Local Government Judicial and Legal Payroll in 2008

National Total = $23,736,889,044*

ALPHA ORDER

RANK	STATE	PAYROLL	% of USA
28	Alabama	$236,606,160	1.0%
42	Alaska	89,339,700	0.4%
12	Arizona	608,254,548	2.6%
37	Arkansas	108,797,688	0.5%
1	California	3,849,348,192	16.2%
18	Colorado	393,667,260	1.7%
22	Connecticut	294,218,112	1.2%
39	Delaware	98,118,156	0.4%
3	Florida	1,661,486,004	7.0%
9	Georgia	696,235,344	2.9%
33	Hawaii	176,689,608	0.7%
40	Idaho	95,872,320	0.4%
7	Illinois	913,390,044	3.8%
19	Indiana	354,628,308	1.5%
30	Iowa	187,911,996	0.8%
32	Kansas	178,014,180	0.7%
24	Kentucky	261,181,788	1.1%
27	Louisiana	250,444,956	1.1%
47	Maine	50,006,388	0.2%
14	Maryland	493,719,600	2.1%
11	Massachusetts	618,685,704	2.6%
10	Michigan	647,171,352	2.7%
17	Minnesota	397,133,016	1.7%
36	Mississippi	116,445,660	0.5%
23	Missouri	284,202,780	1.2%
44	Montana	69,066,012	0.3%
41	Nebraska	95,095,812	0.4%
25	Nevada	258,813,852	1.1%
45	New Hampshire	63,848,652	0.3%
4	New Jersey	1,375,669,368	5.8%
34	New Mexico	169,547,880	0.7%
2	New York	2,261,493,660	9.5%
16	North Carolina	400,742,472	1.7%
49	North Dakota	37,582,644	0.2%
6	Ohio	951,337,260	4.0%
29	Oklahoma	197,136,432	0.8%
26	Oregon	251,399,340	1.1%
8	Pennsylvania	782,489,844	3.3%
43	Rhode Island	80,860,128	0.3%
31	South Carolina	184,354,128	0.8%
48	South Dakota	40,043,868	0.2%
20	Tennessee	351,746,232	1.5%
5	Texas	1,296,740,736	5.5%
35	Utah	156,445,428	0.7%
50	Vermont	36,052,068	0.2%
15	Virginia	490,701,972	2.1%
13	Washington	501,615,012	2.1%
38	West Virginia	102,706,320	0.4%
21	Wisconsin	321,490,380	1.4%
46	Wyoming	50,501,616	0.2%

RANK ORDER

RANK	STATE	PAYROLL	% of USA
1	California	$3,849,348,192	16.2%
2	New York	2,261,493,660	9.5%
3	Florida	1,661,486,004	7.0%
4	New Jersey	1,375,669,368	5.8%
5	Texas	1,296,740,736	5.5%
6	Ohio	951,337,260	4.0%
7	Illinois	913,390,044	3.8%
8	Pennsylvania	782,489,844	3.3%
9	Georgia	696,235,344	2.9%
10	Michigan	647,171,352	2.7%
11	Massachusetts	618,685,704	2.6%
12	Arizona	608,254,548	2.6%
13	Washington	501,615,012	2.1%
14	Maryland	493,719,600	2.1%
15	Virginia	490,701,972	2.1%
16	North Carolina	400,742,472	1.7%
17	Minnesota	397,133,016	1.7%
18	Colorado	393,667,260	1.7%
19	Indiana	354,628,308	1.5%
20	Tennessee	351,746,232	1.5%
21	Wisconsin	321,490,380	1.4%
22	Connecticut	294,218,112	1.2%
23	Missouri	284,202,780	1.2%
24	Kentucky	261,181,788	1.1%
25	Nevada	258,813,852	1.1%
26	Oregon	251,399,340	1.1%
27	Louisiana	250,444,956	1.1%
28	Alabama	236,606,160	1.0%
29	Oklahoma	197,136,432	0.8%
30	Iowa	187,911,996	0.8%
31	South Carolina	184,354,128	0.8%
32	Kansas	178,014,180	0.7%
33	Hawaii	176,689,608	0.7%
34	New Mexico	169,547,880	0.7%
35	Utah	156,445,428	0.7%
36	Mississippi	116,445,660	0.5%
37	Arkansas	108,797,688	0.5%
38	West Virginia	102,706,320	0.4%
39	Delaware	98,118,156	0.4%
40	Idaho	95,872,320	0.4%
41	Nebraska	95,095,812	0.4%
42	Alaska	89,339,700	0.4%
43	Rhode Island	80,860,128	0.3%
44	Montana	69,066,012	0.3%
45	New Hampshire	63,848,652	0.3%
46	Wyoming	50,501,616	0.2%
47	Maine	50,006,388	0.2%
48	South Dakota	40,043,868	0.2%
49	North Dakota	37,582,644	0.2%
50	Vermont	36,052,068	0.2%
	District of Columbia	147,839,064	0.6%

Source: CQ Press using data from U.S. Bureau of the Census, Governments Division
"Government Employment and Payroll" (http://www.census.gov/govs/apes/index.html)
*Twelve times the March 2008 total payroll. Includes court and court-related activities (except probation and parole, which are part of corrections), court activities of sheriffs' offices, prosecuting attorneys' and public defenders' offices, legal departments, and attorneys providing government-wide legal service.

State and Local Government Police Protection Payroll in 2008

National Total = $56,391,256,848*

ALPHA ORDER

RANK	STATE	PAYROLL	% of USA
26	Alabama	$558,074,352	1.0%
45	Alaska	119,496,636	0.2%
10	Arizona	1,418,813,976	2.5%
34	Arkansas	304,562,436	0.5%
1	California	9,275,738,988	16.4%
17	Colorado	917,530,536	1.6%
23	Connecticut	722,630,460	1.3%
42	Delaware	162,451,464	0.3%
3	Florida	4,012,809,336	7.1%
14	Georgia	1,179,531,540	2.1%
37	Hawaii	248,194,152	0.4%
40	Idaho	198,377,724	0.4%
6	Illinois	2,615,189,712	4.6%
21	Indiana	801,030,960	1.4%
32	Iowa	362,525,904	0.6%
30	Kansas	455,127,888	0.8%
31	Kentucky	454,801,932	0.8%
22	Louisiana	753,954,096	1.3%
43	Maine	153,799,800	0.3%
15	Maryland	1,168,448,472	2.1%
9	Massachusetts	1,752,924,804	3.1%
11	Michigan	1,279,390,572	2.3%
24	Minnesota	694,976,688	1.2%
33	Mississippi	315,162,636	0.6%
20	Missouri	827,476,932	1.5%
46	Montana	109,995,564	0.2%
38	Nebraska	231,775,320	0.4%
25	Nevada	657,686,424	1.2%
39	New Hampshire	211,458,072	0.4%
5	New Jersey	2,831,648,700	5.0%
35	New Mexico	299,788,344	0.5%
2	New York	5,851,250,832	10.4%
13	North Carolina	1,209,610,020	2.1%
50	North Dakota	62,792,772	0.1%
8	Ohio	1,801,586,868	3.2%
29	Oklahoma	487,832,268	0.9%
27	Oregon	557,393,028	1.0%
7	Pennsylvania	1,993,332,672	3.5%
41	Rhode Island	196,342,824	0.3%
28	South Carolina	535,508,088	0.9%
48	South Dakota	84,457,332	0.1%
19	Tennessee	845,285,676	1.5%
4	Texas	3,492,037,164	6.2%
36	Utah	295,463,676	0.5%
49	Vermont	81,375,144	0.1%
12	Virginia	1,276,243,656	2.3%
16	Washington	1,057,379,208	1.9%
44	West Virginia	145,608,252	0.3%
18	Wisconsin	908,359,632	1.6%
47	Wyoming	101,561,244	0.2%

RANK ORDER

RANK	STATE	PAYROLL	% of USA
1	California	$9,275,738,988	16.4%
2	New York	5,851,250,832	10.4%
3	Florida	4,012,809,336	7.1%
4	Texas	3,492,037,164	6.2%
5	New Jersey	2,831,648,700	5.0%
6	Illinois	2,615,189,712	4.6%
7	Pennsylvania	1,993,332,672	3.5%
8	Ohio	1,801,586,868	3.2%
9	Massachusetts	1,752,924,804	3.1%
10	Arizona	1,418,813,976	2.5%
11	Michigan	1,279,390,572	2.3%
12	Virginia	1,276,243,656	2.3%
13	North Carolina	1,209,610,020	2.1%
14	Georgia	1,179,531,540	2.1%
15	Maryland	1,168,448,472	2.1%
16	Washington	1,057,379,208	1.9%
17	Colorado	917,530,536	1.6%
18	Wisconsin	908,359,632	1.6%
19	Tennessee	845,285,676	1.5%
20	Missouri	827,476,932	1.5%
21	Indiana	801,030,960	1.4%
22	Louisiana	753,954,096	1.3%
23	Connecticut	722,630,460	1.3%
24	Minnesota	694,976,688	1.2%
25	Nevada	657,686,424	1.2%
26	Alabama	558,074,352	1.0%
27	Oregon	557,393,028	1.0%
28	South Carolina	535,508,088	0.9%
29	Oklahoma	487,832,268	0.9%
30	Kansas	455,127,888	0.8%
31	Kentucky	454,801,932	0.8%
32	Iowa	362,525,904	0.6%
33	Mississippi	315,162,636	0.6%
34	Arkansas	304,562,436	0.5%
35	New Mexico	299,788,344	0.5%
36	Utah	295,463,676	0.5%
37	Hawaii	248,194,152	0.4%
38	Nebraska	231,775,320	0.4%
39	New Hampshire	211,458,072	0.4%
40	Idaho	198,377,724	0.4%
41	Rhode Island	196,342,824	0.3%
42	Delaware	162,451,464	0.3%
43	Maine	153,799,800	0.3%
44	West Virginia	145,608,252	0.3%
45	Alaska	119,496,636	0.2%
46	Montana	109,995,564	0.2%
47	Wyoming	101,561,244	0.2%
48	South Dakota	84,457,332	0.1%
49	Vermont	81,375,144	0.1%
50	North Dakota	62,792,772	0.1%
	District of Columbia	312,462,072	0.6%

Source: CQ Press using data from U.S. Bureau of the Census, Governments Division
   "Government Employment and Payroll" (http://www.census.gov/govs/apes/index.html)
*Twelve times the March 2008 total payroll. Includes all activities concerned with the enforcement of law and order, including coroners' offices, police training academies, investigation bureaus, and local jails.

State and Local Government Corrections Payroll in 2008

National Total = $35,807,086,656*

ALPHA ORDER

ALPHA ORDER

RANK ORDER

RANK	STATE	PAYROLL	% of USA		RANK	STATE	PAYROLL	% of USA
28	Alabama	$297,903,324	0.8%		1	California	$6,838,946,856	19.1%
41	Alaska	103,521,468	0.3%		2	New York	3,412,469,088	9.5%
15	Arizona	736,154,496	2.1%		3	Texas	2,510,850,264	7.0%
34	Arkansas	222,824,700	0.6%		4	Florida	2,025,845,700	5.7%
1	California	6,838,946,856	19.1%		5	Pennsylvania	1,421,236,776	4.0%
17	Colorado	575,274,684	1.6%		6	Ohio	1,195,351,836	3.3%
21	Connecticut	487,867,032	1.4%		7	Illinois	1,191,841,548	3.3%
39	Delaware	137,829,072	0.4%		8	Michigan	1,154,229,276	3.2%
4	Florida	2,025,845,700	5.7%		9	New Jersey	1,152,646,344	3.2%
10	Georgia	1,041,727,800	2.9%		10	Georgia	1,041,727,800	2.9%
40	Hawaii	125,616,456	0.4%		11	North Carolina	1,016,923,560	2.8%
38	Idaho	143,979,492	0.4%		12	Virginia	947,042,316	2.6%
7	Illinois	1,191,841,548	3.3%		13	Maryland	821,112,300	2.3%
20	Indiana	507,492,924	1.4%		14	Washington	747,655,728	2.1%
33	Iowa	235,824,924	0.7%		15	Arizona	736,154,496	2.1%
30	Kansas	265,880,052	0.7%		16	Wisconsin	701,480,640	2.0%
29	Kentucky	267,872,976	0.7%		17	Colorado	575,274,684	1.6%
18	Louisiana	570,647,328	1.6%		18	Louisiana	570,647,328	1.6%
45	Maine	95,651,736	0.3%		19	Massachusetts	515,168,964	1.4%
13	Maryland	821,112,300	2.3%		20	Indiana	507,492,924	1.4%
19	Massachusetts	515,168,964	1.4%		21	Connecticut	487,867,032	1.4%
8	Michigan	1,154,229,276	3.2%		22	Missouri	477,627,576	1.3%
23	Minnesota	471,332,220	1.3%		23	Minnesota	471,332,220	1.3%
36	Mississippi	162,904,452	0.5%		24	Tennessee	459,555,636	1.3%
22	Missouri	477,627,576	1.3%		25	Oregon	442,252,092	1.2%
46	Montana	72,928,476	0.2%		26	Nevada	410,076,108	1.1%
37	Nebraska	161,017,896	0.4%		27	South Carolina	376,269,192	1.1%
26	Nevada	410,076,108	1.1%		28	Alabama	297,903,324	0.8%
43	New Hampshire	102,205,968	0.3%		29	Kentucky	267,872,976	0.7%
9	New Jersey	1,152,646,344	3.2%		30	Kansas	265,880,052	0.7%
31	New Mexico	257,836,680	0.7%		31	New Mexico	257,836,680	0.7%
2	New York	3,412,469,088	9.5%		32	Oklahoma	254,689,704	0.7%
11	North Carolina	1,016,923,560	2.8%		33	Iowa	235,824,924	0.7%
50	North Dakota	39,130,380	0.1%		34	Arkansas	222,824,700	0.6%
6	Ohio	1,195,351,836	3.3%		35	Utah	219,425,016	0.6%
32	Oklahoma	254,689,704	0.7%		36	Mississippi	162,904,452	0.5%
25	Oregon	442,252,092	1.2%		37	Nebraska	161,017,896	0.4%
5	Pennsylvania	1,421,236,776	4.0%		38	Idaho	143,979,492	0.4%
42	Rhode Island	103,366,836	0.3%		39	Delaware	137,829,072	0.4%
27	South Carolina	376,269,192	1.1%		40	Hawaii	125,616,456	0.4%
49	South Dakota	51,966,216	0.1%		41	Alaska	103,521,468	0.3%
24	Tennessee	459,555,636	1.3%		42	Rhode Island	103,366,836	0.3%
3	Texas	2,510,850,264	7.0%		43	New Hampshire	102,205,968	0.3%
35	Utah	219,425,016	0.6%		44	West Virginia	100,453,464	0.3%
48	Vermont	57,683,088	0.2%		45	Maine	95,651,736	0.3%
12	Virginia	947,042,316	2.6%		46	Montana	72,928,476	0.2%
14	Washington	747,655,728	2.1%		47	Wyoming	64,238,544	0.2%
44	West Virginia	100,453,464	0.3%		48	Vermont	57,683,088	0.2%
16	Wisconsin	701,480,640	2.0%		49	South Dakota	51,966,216	0.1%
47	Wyoming	64,238,544	0.2%		50	North Dakota	39,130,380	0.1%
						District of Columbia	53,257,452	0.1%

Source: CQ Press using data from U.S. Bureau of the Census, Governments Division
"Government Employment and Payroll" (http://www.census.gov/govs/apes/index.html)
*Twelve times the March 2008 total payroll. Includes all activities pertaining to the confinement and correction of adults and minors accused or convicted of criminal offenses. Includes any pardon, probation, or parole activity.

Average Annual Wages of Correctional Officers and Jailers in 2008

National Average = $41,340*

ALPHA ORDER				RANK ORDER		
RANK	**STATE**	**SALARY**		**RANK**	**STATE**	**SALARY**
28	Alabama	$32,570		1	California	$63,230
7	Alaska	48,130		2	New Jersey	62,240
24	Arizona	37,130		3	Massachusetts	54,850
39	Arkansas	29,740		4	Nevada	54,820
1	California	63,230		5	New York	53,530
13	Colorado	44,130		6	Illinois	51,490
10	Connecticut	45,630		7	Alaska	48,130
NA	Delaware**	NA		8	Washington	47,880
NA	Florida**	NA		9	Hawaii	46,390
42	Georgia	29,020		10	Connecticut	45,630
9	Hawaii	46,390		11	Oregon	45,010
26	Idaho	33,430		12	Michigan	44,220
6	Illinois	51,490		13	Colorado	44,130
35	Indiana	30,770		14	Pennsylvania	43,980
19	Iowa	39,960		15	Maryland	43,890
25	Kansas	33,730		16	Minnesota	42,240
39	Kentucky	29,740		17	Wisconsin	41,880
30	Louisiana	31,280		18	Ohio	40,070
27	Maine	33,390		19	Iowa	39,960
15	Maryland	43,890		20	Virginia	38,710
3	Massachusetts	54,850		21	Utah	38,400
12	Michigan	44,220		22	New Hampshire	37,880
16	Minnesota	42,240		23	Wyoming	37,640
45	Mississippi	25,440		24	Arizona	37,130
41	Missouri	29,170		25	Kansas	33,730
37	Montana	30,300		26	Idaho	33,430
34	Nebraska	30,900		27	Maine	33,390
4	Nevada	54,820		28	Alabama	32,570
22	New Hampshire	37,880		29	North Carolina	31,590
2	New Jersey	62,240		30	Louisiana	31,280
44	New Mexico	27,780		31	South Dakota	31,180
5	New York	53,530		32	South Carolina	31,060
29	North Carolina	31,590		33	Tennessee	30,990
36	North Dakota	30,370		34	Nebraska	30,900
18	Ohio	40,070		35	Indiana	30,770
43	Oklahoma	27,970		36	North Dakota	30,370
11	Oregon	45,010		37	Montana	30,300
14	Pennsylvania	43,980		38	Texas	29,870
NA	Rhode Island**	NA		39	Arkansas	29,740
32	South Carolina	31,060		39	Kentucky	29,740
31	South Dakota	31,180		41	Missouri	29,170
33	Tennessee	30,990		42	Georgia	29,020
38	Texas	29,870		43	Oklahoma	27,970
21	Utah	38,400		44	New Mexico	27,780
NA	Vermont**	NA		45	Mississippi	25,440
20	Virginia	38,710		NA	Delaware**	NA
8	Washington	47,880		NA	Florida**	NA
NA	West Virginia**	NA		NA	Rhode Island**	NA
17	Wisconsin	41,880		NA	Vermont**	NA
23	Wyoming	37,640		NA	West Virginia**	NA
					District of Columbia**	NA

Source: U.S. Department of Labor, Bureau of Labor Statistics
   "Occupational Employment Statistics" (http://www.bls.gov/oes/)
*Occupational code 33-3012. As of May 2008. Does not include self-employed.
**Not available.

Average Annual Wages of Police and Sheriff Patrol Officers in 2008

National Average = $52,810*

ALPHA ORDER

RANK	STATE	SALARY
45	Alabama	$37,620
6	Alaska	59,580
15	Arizona	53,020
47	Arkansas	36,030
2	California	74,660
7	Colorado	58,550
9	Connecticut	56,800
11	Delaware	55,740
19	Florida	51,320
40	Georgia	38,340
22	Hawaii	49,710
25	Idaho	46,300
3	Illinois	62,680
29	Indiana	44,970
28	Iowa	45,070
32	Kansas	41,510
39	Kentucky	38,590
49	Louisiana	34,290
42	Maine	38,210
10	Maryland	55,990
13	Massachusetts	54,750
20	Michigan	51,260
16	Minnesota	52,410
50	Mississippi	30,460
34	Missouri	41,150
33	Montana	41,310
31	Nebraska	44,020
5	Nevada	61,760
26	New Hampshire	45,590
1	New Jersey	75,400
37	New Mexico	40,730
8	New York	57,020
38	North Carolina	40,310
36	North Dakota	40,780
21	Ohio	49,890
41	Oklahoma	38,280
12	Oregon	55,320
14	Pennsylvania	54,080
18	Rhode Island	51,440
46	South Carolina	37,180
43	South Dakota	38,010
44	Tennessee	37,990
24	Texas	48,010
30	Utah	44,340
35	Vermont	40,860
23	Virginia	48,970
4	Washington	62,670
48	West Virginia	35,060
17	Wisconsin	51,660
27	Wyoming	45,200

RANK ORDER

RANK	STATE	SALARY
1	New Jersey	$75,400
2	California	74,660
3	Illinois	62,680
4	Washington	62,670
5	Nevada	61,760
6	Alaska	59,580
7	Colorado	58,550
8	New York	57,020
9	Connecticut	56,800
10	Maryland	55,990
11	Delaware	55,740
12	Oregon	55,320
13	Massachusetts	54,750
14	Pennsylvania	54,080
15	Arizona	53,020
16	Minnesota	52,410
17	Wisconsin	51,660
18	Rhode Island	51,440
19	Florida	51,320
20	Michigan	51,260
21	Ohio	49,890
22	Hawaii	49,710
23	Virginia	48,970
24	Texas	48,010
25	Idaho	46,300
26	New Hampshire	45,590
27	Wyoming	45,200
28	Iowa	45,070
29	Indiana	44,970
30	Utah	44,340
31	Nebraska	44,020
32	Kansas	41,510
33	Montana	41,310
34	Missouri	41,150
35	Vermont	40,860
36	North Dakota	40,780
37	New Mexico	40,730
38	North Carolina	40,310
39	Kentucky	38,590
40	Georgia	38,340
41	Oklahoma	38,280
42	Maine	38,210
43	South Dakota	38,010
44	Tennessee	37,990
45	Alabama	37,620
46	South Carolina	37,180
47	Arkansas	36,030
48	West Virginia	35,060
49	Louisiana	34,290
50	Mississippi	30,460
	District of Columbia	64,400

Source: U.S. Department of Labor, Bureau of Labor Statistics
"Occupational Employment Statistics" (http://www.bls.gov/oes/)
*Occupational code 33-3051. As of May 2008. Does not include self-employed.

Average Annual Wages of Detectives and Criminal Investigators in 2008

National Average = $63,840*

ALPHA ORDER			RANK ORDER		
RANK	STATE	SALARY	RANK	STATE	SALARY
44	Alabama	$50,060	1	New Jersey	$83,520
5	Alaska	73,550	2	Delaware	78,810
35	Arizona	55,450	3	California	76,930
50	Arkansas	44,650	4	Massachusetts	74,280
3	California	76,930	5	Alaska	73,550
11	Colorado	70,840	6	Washington	73,450
12	Connecticut	70,640	7	Maryland	73,380
2	Delaware	78,810	8	Hawaii	73,170
23	Florida	62,030	9	Virginia	73,080
39	Georgia	53,100	10	Illinois	72,380
8	Hawaii	73,170	11	Colorado	70,840
32	Idaho	56,370	12	Connecticut	70,640
10	Illinois	72,380	13	Nevada	68,510
42	Indiana	51,250	14	Michigan	67,770
21	Iowa	62,380	15	Pennsylvania	67,250
34	Kansas	55,480	16	New York	67,030
36	Kentucky	54,710	17	Oregon	65,450
47	Louisiana	48,660	18	Minnesota	65,210
31	Maine	56,550	19	Rhode Island	65,110
7	Maryland	73,380	20	Wisconsin	62,460
4	Massachusetts	74,280	21	Iowa	62,380
14	Michigan	67,770	22	Vermont	62,130
18	Minnesota	65,210	23	Florida	62,030
45	Mississippi	49,290	24	New Hampshire	61,640
41	Missouri	51,310	25	Ohio	61,420
27	Montana	59,880	26	Utah	60,570
30	Nebraska	58,050	27	Montana	59,880
13	Nevada	68,510	28	Wyoming	59,350
24	New Hampshire	61,640	29	North Dakota	58,190
1	New Jersey	83,520	30	Nebraska	58,050
40	New Mexico	52,600	31	Maine	56,550
16	New York	67,030	32	Idaho	56,370
46	North Carolina	48,790	33	Texas	55,900
29	North Dakota	58,190	34	Kansas	55,480
25	Ohio	61,420	35	Arizona	55,450
48	Oklahoma	47,230	36	Kentucky	54,710
17	Oregon	65,450	37	South Dakota	53,590
15	Pennsylvania	67,250	38	Tennessee	53,110
19	Rhode Island	65,110	39	Georgia	53,100
43	South Carolina	50,200	40	New Mexico	52,600
37	South Dakota	53,590	41	Missouri	51,310
38	Tennessee	53,110	42	Indiana	51,250
33	Texas	55,900	43	South Carolina	50,200
26	Utah	60,570	44	Alabama	50,060
22	Vermont	62,130	45	Mississippi	49,290
9	Virginia	73,080	46	North Carolina	48,790
6	Washington	73,450	47	Louisiana	48,660
49	West Virginia	47,080	48	Oklahoma	47,230
20	Wisconsin	62,460	49	West Virginia	47,080
28	Wyoming	59,350	50	Arkansas	44,650
				District of Columbia	87,870

Source: U.S. Department of Labor, Bureau of Labor Statistics
"Occupational Employment Statistics" (http://www.bls.gov/oes/)
*Occupational code 33-3021. As of May 2008. Does not include self-employed.

Average Annual Wages of Private Detectives and Investigators in 2008

National Average = $46,480*

ALPHA ORDER

RANK	STATE	SALARY
27	Alabama	$41,720
4	Alaska	54,900
10	Arizona	48,300
15	Arkansas	45,290
3	California	56,620
31	Colorado	40,910
30	Connecticut	40,930
9	Delaware	48,350
23	Florida	42,870
38	Georgia	34,820
12	Hawaii	46,780
13	Idaho	46,030
22	Illinois	43,730
25	Indiana	42,460
14	Iowa	45,560
42	Kansas	32,340
40	Kentucky	34,260
37	Louisiana	35,260
33	Maine	39,820
28	Maryland	41,280
39	Massachusetts	34,510
19	Michigan	44,430
17	Minnesota	44,580
17	Mississippi	44,580
32	Missouri	40,110
NA	Montana**	NA
NA	Nebraska**	NA
6	Nevada	52,070
34	New Hampshire	38,090
2	New Jersey	63,050
43	New Mexico	32,120
5	New York	52,140
20	North Carolina	44,080
45	North Dakota	24,550
24	Ohio	42,710
29	Oklahoma	41,210
21	Oregon	43,760
26	Pennsylvania	41,980
8	Rhode Island	48,670
16	South Carolina	44,800
44	South Dakota	25,920
36	Tennessee	37,120
11	Texas	47,640
35	Utah	37,340
NA	Vermont**	NA
1	Virginia	65,140
7	Washington	50,980
NA	West Virginia**	NA
41	Wisconsin	33,200
NA	Wyoming**	NA

RANK ORDER

RANK	STATE	SALARY
1	Virginia	$65,140
2	New Jersey	63,050
3	California	56,620
4	Alaska	54,900
5	New York	52,140
6	Nevada	52,070
7	Washington	50,980
8	Rhode Island	48,670
9	Delaware	48,350
10	Arizona	48,300
11	Texas	47,640
12	Hawaii	46,780
13	Idaho	46,030
14	Iowa	45,560
15	Arkansas	45,290
16	South Carolina	44,800
17	Minnesota	44,580
17	Mississippi	44,580
19	Michigan	44,430
20	North Carolina	44,080
21	Oregon	43,760
22	Illinois	43,730
23	Florida	42,870
24	Ohio	42,710
25	Indiana	42,460
26	Pennsylvania	41,980
27	Alabama	41,720
28	Maryland	41,280
29	Oklahoma	41,210
30	Connecticut	40,930
31	Colorado	40,910
32	Missouri	40,110
33	Maine	39,820
34	New Hampshire	38,090
35	Utah	37,340
36	Tennessee	37,120
37	Louisiana	35,260
38	Georgia	34,820
39	Massachusetts	34,510
40	Kentucky	34,260
41	Wisconsin	33,200
42	Kansas	32,340
43	New Mexico	32,120
44	South Dakota	25,920
45	North Dakota	24,550
NA	Montana**	NA
NA	Nebraska**	NA
NA	Vermont**	NA
NA	West Virginia**	NA
NA	Wyoming**	NA
	District of Columbia**	NA

Source: U.S. Department of Labor, Bureau of Labor Statistics
    "Occupational Employment Statistics" (http://www.bls.gov/oes/)
*Occupational code 33-9021. As of May 2008. Does not include self-employed.
**Not available.

Average Annual Wages of Security Guards in 2008

National Average = $25,840*

ALPHA ORDER				RANK ORDER		
RANK	**STATE**	**SALARY**		**RANK**	**STATE**	**SALARY**
49	Alabama	$20,770		1	Alaska	$36,500
1	Alaska	36,500		2	Washington	32,290
39	Arizona	24,120		3	Maryland	30,430
44	Arkansas	22,700		4	Vermont	30,120
17	California	25,950		5	Virginia	28,970
15	Colorado	26,140		6	Connecticut	28,770
6	Connecticut	28,770		7	New York	28,250
38	Delaware	24,610		8	New Jersey	28,060
46	Florida	22,580		9	Idaho	27,830
42	Georgia	23,760		10	New Hampshire	27,810
24	Hawaii	25,700		11	Massachusetts	27,580
9	Idaho	27,830		12	Minnesota	27,020
18	Illinois	25,940		13	Missouri	26,940
34	Indiana	24,900		14	South Carolina	26,330
21	Iowa	25,870		15	Colorado	26,140
28	Kansas	25,230		16	Nevada	26,080
39	Kentucky	24,120		17	California	25,950
43	Louisiana	23,050		18	Illinois	25,940
33	Maine	24,920		18	Utah	25,940
3	Maryland	30,430		20	Pennsylvania	25,880
11	Massachusetts	27,580		21	Iowa	25,870
26	Michigan	25,390		22	North Dakota	25,840
12	Minnesota	27,020		23	Rhode Island	25,830
50	Mississippi	20,340		24	Hawaii	25,700
13	Missouri	26,940		25	Oklahoma	25,460
37	Montana	24,680		26	Michigan	25,390
31	Nebraska	24,940		27	Oregon	25,320
16	Nevada	26,080		28	Kansas	25,230
10	New Hampshire	27,810		29	Wisconsin	25,030
8	New Jersey	28,060		30	New Mexico	24,980
30	New Mexico	24,980		31	Nebraska	24,940
7	New York	28,250		32	Ohio	24,930
41	North Carolina	23,850		33	Maine	24,920
22	North Dakota	25,840		34	Indiana	24,900
32	Ohio	24,930		35	Wyoming	24,840
25	Oklahoma	25,460		36	Texas	24,830
27	Oregon	25,320		37	Montana	24,680
20	Pennsylvania	25,880		38	Delaware	24,610
23	Rhode Island	25,830		39	Arizona	24,120
14	South Carolina	26,330		39	Kentucky	24,120
47	South Dakota	22,250		41	North Carolina	23,850
45	Tennessee	22,590		42	Georgia	23,760
36	Texas	24,830		43	Louisiana	23,050
18	Utah	25,940		44	Arkansas	22,700
4	Vermont	30,120		45	Tennessee	22,590
5	Virginia	28,970		46	Florida	22,580
2	Washington	32,290		47	South Dakota	22,250
48	West Virginia	21,280		48	West Virginia	21,280
29	Wisconsin	25,030		49	Alabama	20,770
35	Wyoming	24,840		50	Mississippi	20,340

District of Columbia   33,140

Source: U.S. Department of Labor, Bureau of Labor Statistics
"Occupational Employment Statistics" (http://www.bls.gov/oes/)
*Occupational code 33-9032. As of May 2008. Does not include self-employed.

Base Salary for Justices of States' Highest Courts in 2009

National Average = $150,042

ALPHA ORDER				RANK ORDER		
RANK	STATE	SALARY		RANK	STATE	SALARY
7	Alabama	$180,005		1	California	$218,237
8	Alaska	179,520		2	Illinois	196,322
19	Arizona	155,000		3	Pennsylvania	186,450
30	Arkansas	139,821		4	New Jersey	185,482
1	California	218,237		5	Delaware	185,050
31	Colorado	139,660		6	Virginia	183,839
14	Connecticut	162,520		7	Alabama	180,005
5	Delaware	185,050		8	Alaska	179,520
16	Florida	161,200		9	Nevada	170,000
10	Georgia	167,210		10	Georgia	167,210
18	Hawaii	159,072		11	Michigan	164,610
46	Idaho	119,506		12	Washington	164,221
2	Illinois	196,322		13	Iowa	163,200
21	Indiana	151,328		14	Connecticut	162,520
13	Iowa	163,200		15	Maryland	162,352
37	Kansas	135,905		16	Florida	161,200
39	Kentucky	134,160		17	Tennessee	159,288
36	Louisiana	136,967		18	Hawaii	159,072
45	Maine	119,594		19	Arizona	155,000
15	Maryland	162,352		20	Rhode Island	152,403
25	Massachusetts	145,984		21	Indiana	151,328
11	Michigan	164,610		22	New York	151,200
26	Minnesota	145,981		23	Texas	150,000
49	Mississippi	112,530		24	New Hampshire	146,917
35	Missouri	137,034		25	Massachusetts	145,984
50	Montana	106,185		26	Minnesota	145,981
38	Nebraska	135,881		27	Utah	145,350
9	Nevada	170,000		28	Ohio	141,600
24	New Hampshire	146,917		29	Wisconsin	141,566
4	New Jersey	185,482		30	Arkansas	139,821
43	New Mexico	123,691		31	Colorado	139,660
22	New York	151,200		32	Oklahoma	137,655
33	North Carolina	137,249		33	North Carolina	137,249
48	North Dakota	118,121		34	South Carolina	137,171
28	Ohio	141,600		35	Missouri	137,034
32	Oklahoma	137,655		36	Louisiana	136,967
42	Oregon	125,688		37	Kansas	135,905
3	Pennsylvania	186,450		38	Nebraska	135,881
20	Rhode Island	152,403		39	Kentucky	134,160
34	South Carolina	137,171		40	Vermont	129,245
47	South Dakota	118,173		41	Wyoming	126,500
17	Tennessee	159,288		42	Oregon	125,688
23	Texas	150,000		43	New Mexico	123,691
27	Utah	145,350		44	West Virginia	121,000
40	Vermont	129,245		45	Maine	119,594
6	Virginia	183,839		46	Idaho	119,506
12	Washington	164,221		47	South Dakota	118,173
44	West Virginia	121,000		48	North Dakota	118,121
29	Wisconsin	141,566		49	Mississippi	112,530
41	Wyoming	126,500		50	Montana	106,185
					District of Columbia	184,500

Source: National Center for State Courts
"Survey of Judicial Salaries-January 2009" (Volume 34, Number 1)
(http://www.ncsconline.org/D_KIS/Salary_Survey/Index.html)

Base Salary for Judges of Intermediate Appellate Courts in 2009

National Average = $145,445

ALPHA ORDER

RANK	STATE	SALARY
3	Alabama	$178,878
6	Alaska	169,608
14	Arizona	150,000
23	Arkansas	135,515
1	California	204,599
25	Colorado	134,128
12	Connecticut	152,637
NA	Delaware*	NA
11	Florida	153,140
8	Georgia	166,186
17	Hawaii	147,288
37	Idaho	118,506
2	Illinois	184,775
18	Indiana	147,103
16	Iowa	147,900
30	Kansas	131,518
34	Kentucky	128,760
32	Louisiana	130,194
NA	Maine*	NA
15	Maryland	149,552
24	Massachusetts	135,087
13	Michigan	151,441
22	Minnesota	137,552
39	Mississippi	105,050
35	Missouri	128,207
NA	Montana*	NA
33	Nebraska	129,087
NA	Nevada*	NA
NA	New Hampshire*	NA
5	New Jersey	175,534
38	New Mexico	117,506
19	New York	144,000
29	North Carolina	131,531
NA	North Dakota*	NA
28	Ohio	132,000
31	Oklahoma	130,410
36	Oregon	122,820
4	Pennsylvania	175,923
NA	Rhode Island*	NA
26	South Carolina	133,741
NA	South Dakota*	NA
10	Tennessee	153,984
20	Texas	141,250
21	Utah	138,750
NA	Vermont*	NA
7	Virginia	168,322
9	Washington	156,328
NA	West Virginia*	NA
27	Wisconsin	133,552
NA	Wyoming*	NA

RANK ORDER

RANK	STATE	SALARY
1	California	$204,599
2	Illinois	184,775
3	Alabama	178,878
4	Pennsylvania	175,923
5	New Jersey	175,534
6	Alaska	169,608
7	Virginia	168,322
8	Georgia	166,186
9	Washington	156,328
10	Tennessee	153,984
11	Florida	153,140
12	Connecticut	152,637
13	Michigan	151,441
14	Arizona	150,000
15	Maryland	149,552
16	Iowa	147,900
17	Hawaii	147,288
18	Indiana	147,103
19	New York	144,000
20	Texas	141,250
21	Utah	138,750
22	Minnesota	137,552
23	Arkansas	135,515
24	Massachusetts	135,087
25	Colorado	134,128
26	South Carolina	133,741
27	Wisconsin	133,552
28	Ohio	132,000
29	North Carolina	131,531
30	Kansas	131,518
31	Oklahoma	130,410
32	Louisiana	130,194
33	Nebraska	129,087
34	Kentucky	128,760
35	Missouri	128,207
36	Oregon	122,820
37	Idaho	118,506
38	New Mexico	117,506
39	Mississippi	105,050
NA	Delaware*	NA
NA	Maine*	NA
NA	Montana*	NA
NA	Nevada*	NA
NA	New Hampshire*	NA
NA	North Dakota*	NA
NA	Rhode Island*	NA
NA	South Dakota*	NA
NA	Vermont*	NA
NA	West Virginia*	NA
NA	Wyoming*	NA
	District of Columbia*	NA

Source: National Center for State Courts
   "Survey of Judicial Salaries-January 2009" (Volume 34, Number 1)
   (http://www.ncsconline.org/D_KIS/Salary_Survey/Index.html)
*No intermediate court.

Base Salary for Judges of General Trial Courts in 2008

National Average = $134,207

ALPHA ORDER

RANK	STATE	SALARY
21	Alabama	$134,943
4	Alaska	165,996
13	Arizona	145,000
24	Arkansas	131,206
1	California	178,789
28	Colorado	128,598
11	Connecticut	146,780
3	Delaware	168,850
12	Florida	145,080
40	Georgia	120,252
14	Hawaii	143,292
45	Idaho	112,043
2	Illinois	169,555
31	Indiana	125,647
17	Iowa	137,700
41	Kansas	120,037
35	Kentucky	123,384
34	Louisiana	124,085
44	Maine	112,145
15	Maryland	140,352
26	Massachusetts	129,694
16	Michigan	139,919
27	Minnesota	129,124
49	Mississippi	104,170
38	Missouri	120,484
50	Montana	99,234
30	Nebraska	125,690
7	Nevada	160,000
19	New Hampshire	137,084
5	New Jersey	165,000
46	New Mexico	111,631
20	New York	136,700
32	North Carolina	124,382
48	North Dakota	108,236
37	Ohio	121,350
33	Oklahoma	124,373
43	Oregon	114,468
6	Pennsylvania	161,850
18	Rhode Island	137,212
25	South Carolina	130,312
47	South Dakota	110,377
10	Tennessee	148,668
22	Texas	132,500
23	Utah	132,150
36	Vermont	122,867
8	Virginia	158,134
9	Washington	148,832
42	West Virginia	116,000
29	Wisconsin	125,992
39	Wyoming	120,400

RANK ORDER

RANK	STATE	SALARY
1	California	$178,789
2	Illinois	169,555
3	Delaware	168,850
4	Alaska	165,996
5	New Jersey	165,000
6	Pennsylvania	161,850
7	Nevada	160,000
8	Virginia	158,134
9	Washington	148,832
10	Tennessee	148,668
11	Connecticut	146,780
12	Florida	145,080
13	Arizona	145,000
14	Hawaii	143,292
15	Maryland	140,352
16	Michigan	139,919
17	Iowa	137,700
18	Rhode Island	137,212
19	New Hampshire	137,084
20	New York	136,700
21	Alabama	134,943
22	Texas	132,500
23	Utah	132,150
24	Arkansas	131,206
25	South Carolina	130,312
26	Massachusetts	129,694
27	Minnesota	129,124
28	Colorado	128,598
29	Wisconsin	125,992
30	Nebraska	125,690
31	Indiana	125,647
32	North Carolina	124,382
33	Oklahoma	124,373
34	Louisiana	124,085
35	Kentucky	123,384
36	Vermont	122,867
37	Ohio	121,350
38	Missouri	120,484
39	Wyoming	120,400
40	Georgia	120,252
41	Kansas	120,037
42	West Virginia	116,000
43	Oregon	114,468
44	Maine	112,145
45	Idaho	112,043
46	New Mexico	111,631
47	South Dakota	110,377
48	North Dakota	108,236
49	Mississippi	104,170
50	Montana	99,234
	District of Columbia	174,000

Source: National Center for State Courts
"Survey of Judicial Salaries-January 2009" (Volume 34, Number 1)
(http://www.ncsconline.org/D_KIS/Salary_Survey/Index.html)

V. JUVENILES

Important Note Regarding Juvenile Arrest Rates

The juvenile arrest rates shown on pages 185 to 238 were calculated by the editors as follows:

    The state arrest numbers reported by the FBI are only from those law enforcement agencies that submitted complete arrests reports for 12 months in 2008. Included in the FBI report are population totals of these reporting jurisdictions by state. Using these FBI population figures, we first determined what percentage the FBI numbers represented of each state's total resident population. Next, using 2008 Census state estimates for 10- to 17-year-olds, we multiplied the percentages derived from the FBI population figures into the Census Bureau's total juvenile population counts. The resulting juvenile population is the base that was used to determine juvenile arrests per 100,000 juvenile population. The national rate was calculated in the same manner.

    Reports from law enforcement agencies in Illinois, Kentucky, and the District of Columbia were insufficient to calculate rates. Reports from New York and Mississippi represented less than half of their state population. Rates for these states should be interpreted with caution.

Reported Arrests of Juveniles in 2008

National Total = 1,741,379 Reported Arrests*

<u>ALPHA ORDER</u>

RANK	STATE	ARRESTS	% of USA
34	Alabama	12,832	0.7%
47	Alaska	3,951	0.2%
6	Arizona	53,826	3.1%
33	Arkansas	13,209	0.8%
1	California	227,754	13.1%
11	Colorado	43,398	2.5%
27	Connecticut	19,458	1.1%
40	Delaware	7,199	0.4%
3	Florida	118,296	6.8%
16	Georgia	38,807	2.2%
35	Hawaii	12,029	0.7%
32	Idaho	14,863	0.9%
20	Illinois	33,161	1.9%
17	Indiana	38,675	2.2%
26	Iowa	20,893	1.2%
36	Kansas	11,183	0.6%
48	Kentucky	3,671	0.2%
28	Louisiana	19,068	1.1%
41	Maine	6,990	0.4%
8	Maryland	47,175	2.7%
30	Massachusetts	17,974	1.0%
18	Michigan	36,027	2.1%
9	Minnesota	45,954	2.6%
37	Mississippi	10,347	0.6%
10	Missouri	45,321	2.6%
39	Montana	7,251	0.4%
31	Nebraska	15,375	0.9%
23	Nevada	24,656	1.4%
42	New Hampshire	6,906	0.4%
7	New Jersey	51,527	3.0%
38	New Mexico	9,587	0.6%
14	New York	40,142	2.3%
13	North Carolina	40,840	2.3%
44	North Dakota	6,719	0.4%
15	Ohio	38,975	2.2%
25	Oklahoma	21,697	1.2%
22	Oregon	28,909	1.7%
4	Pennsylvania	102,605	5.9%
46	Rhode Island	5,576	0.3%
29	South Carolina	18,306	1.1%
45	South Dakota	5,793	0.3%
19	Tennessee	35,507	2.0%
2	Texas	171,536	9.9%
24	Utah	24,576	1.4%
50	Vermont	1,403	0.1%
12	Virginia	40,940	2.4%
21	Washington	30,669	1.8%
49	West Virginia	2,317	0.1%
5	Wisconsin	100,121	5.7%
43	Wyoming	6,861	0.4%

<u>RANK ORDER</u>

RANK	STATE	ARRESTS	% of USA
1	California	227,754	13.1%
2	Texas	171,536	9.9%
3	Florida	118,296	6.8%
4	Pennsylvania	102,605	5.9%
5	Wisconsin	100,121	5.7%
6	Arizona	53,826	3.1%
7	New Jersey	51,527	3.0%
8	Maryland	47,175	2.7%
9	Minnesota	45,954	2.6%
10	Missouri	45,321	2.6%
11	Colorado	43,398	2.5%
12	Virginia	40,940	2.4%
13	North Carolina	40,840	2.3%
14	New York	40,142	2.3%
15	Ohio	38,975	2.2%
16	Georgia	38,807	2.2%
17	Indiana	38,675	2.2%
18	Michigan	36,027	2.1%
19	Tennessee	35,507	2.0%
20	Illinois	33,161	1.9%
21	Washington	30,669	1.8%
22	Oregon	28,909	1.7%
23	Nevada	24,656	1.4%
24	Utah	24,576	1.4%
25	Oklahoma	21,697	1.2%
26	Iowa	20,893	1.2%
27	Connecticut	19,458	1.1%
28	Louisiana	19,068	1.1%
29	South Carolina	18,306	1.1%
30	Massachusetts	17,974	1.0%
31	Nebraska	15,375	0.9%
32	Idaho	14,863	0.9%
33	Arkansas	13,209	0.8%
34	Alabama	12,832	0.7%
35	Hawaii	12,029	0.7%
36	Kansas	11,183	0.6%
37	Mississippi	10,347	0.6%
38	New Mexico	9,587	0.6%
39	Montana	7,251	0.4%
40	Delaware	7,199	0.4%
41	Maine	6,990	0.4%
42	New Hampshire	6,906	0.4%
43	Wyoming	6,861	0.4%
44	North Dakota	6,719	0.4%
45	South Dakota	5,793	0.3%
46	Rhode Island	5,576	0.3%
47	Alaska	3,951	0.2%
48	Kentucky	3,671	0.2%
49	West Virginia	2,317	0.1%
50	Vermont	1,403	0.1%

District of Columbia** NA NA

Source: Reported data from the Federal Bureau of Investigation
"Crime in the United States 2008" (Uniform Crime Reports, September 14, 2009, http://www.fbi.gov/ucr/ucr.htm)
*Arrests of youths 17 years and younger by law enforcement agencies submitting complete reports to the F.B.I. for 12 months in 2008. See important note at beginning of this chapter.
**Not available.

Reported Juvenile Arrest Rate in 2008

National Rate = 6,470.5 Reported Arrests per 100,000 Juvenile Population*

ALPHA ORDER

RANK ORDER

RANK	STATE	RATE		RANK	STATE	RATE
45	Alabama	3,149.1		1	Wisconsin	17,047.8
41	Alaska	5,066.8		2	Wyoming	12,375.3
17	Arizona	7,559.5		3	North Dakota	11,572.7
40	Arkansas	5,088.1		4	Hawaii	11,056.7
34	California	5,513.6		5	Colorado	9,571.7
5	Colorado	9,571.7		6	Idaho	8,927.9
33	Connecticut	5,532.3		7	Nevada	8,805.6
13	Delaware	7,928.2		8	Nebraska	8,631.6
24	Florida	6,666.2		9	South Dakota	8,511.2
30	Georgia	5,728.3		10	Minnesota	8,464.2
4	Hawaii	11,056.7		11	Utah	8,338.5
6	Idaho	8,927.9		12	Pennsylvania	8,207.6
NA	Illinois**	NA		13	Delaware	7,928.2
18	Indiana	7,479.3		14	Maryland	7,836.1
20	Iowa	7,126.5		15	Oregon	7,690.2
35	Kansas	5,411.8		16	Missouri	7,570.8
NA	Kentucky**	NA		17	Arizona	7,559.5
21	Louisiana	6,887.2		18	Indiana	7,479.3
36	Maine	5,318.9		19	Montana	7,475.8
14	Maryland	7,836.1		20	Iowa	7,126.5
46	Massachusetts	3,057.8		21	Louisiana	6,887.2
44	Michigan	3,712.4		22	Mississippi	6,878.6
10	Minnesota	8,464.2		23	Tennessee	6,769.8
22	Mississippi	6,878.6		24	Florida	6,666.2
16	Missouri	7,570.8		25	Texas	6,325.8
19	Montana	7,475.8		26	New Hampshire	6,250.9
8	Nebraska	8,631.6		27	New Mexico	6,082.8
7	Nevada	8,805.6		28	Washington	6,076.8
26	New Hampshire	6,250.9		29	North Carolina	5,881.7
31	New Jersey	5,710.3		30	Georgia	5,728.3
27	New Mexico	6,082.8		31	New Jersey	5,710.3
42	New York	4,184.6		32	Oklahoma	5,573.7
29	North Carolina	5,881.7		33	Connecticut	5,532.3
3	North Dakota	11,572.7		34	California	5,513.6
38	Ohio	5,207.7		35	Kansas	5,411.8
32	Oklahoma	5,573.7		36	Maine	5,318.9
15	Oregon	7,690.2		37	Virginia	5,269.1
12	Pennsylvania	8,207.6		38	Ohio	5,207.7
39	Rhode Island	5,202.5		39	Rhode Island	5,202.5
43	South Carolina	3,963.0		40	Arkansas	5,088.1
9	South Dakota	8,511.2		41	Alaska	5,066.8
23	Tennessee	6,769.8		42	New York	4,184.6
25	Texas	6,325.8		43	South Carolina	3,963.0
11	Utah	8,338.5		44	Michigan	3,712.4
47	Vermont	2,725.0		45	Alabama	3,149.1
37	Virginia	5,269.1		46	Massachusetts	3,057.8
28	Washington	6,076.8		47	Vermont	2,725.0
48	West Virginia	2,153.2		48	West Virginia	2,153.2
1	Wisconsin	17,047.8		NA	Illinois**	NA
2	Wyoming	12,375.3		NA	Kentucky**	NA
					District of Columbia**	NA

Source: CQ Press using reported data from the Federal Bureau of Investigation
   "Crime in the United States 2008" (Uniform Crime Reports, September 14, 2009, http://www.fbi.gov/ucr/ucr.htm)
*By law enforcement agencies submitting complete reports to the F.B.I. for 12 months in 2008. Arrests of youths 17 years and younger divided into population of 10 to 17 year olds. See important note at beginning of this chapter.
**Not available.

Reported Arrests of Juveniles as a Percent of All Arrests in 2008

National Percent = 14.7% of Reported Arrests*

ALPHA ORDER				RANK ORDER		
RANK	STATE	PERCENT		RANK	STATE	PERCENT
49	Alabama	6.0		1	Wisconsin	24.3
42	Alaska	10.3		2	North Dakota	24.1
18	Arizona	16.1		3	Hawaii	22.8
48	Arkansas	9.5		4	Minnesota	22.5
26	California	14.7		5	Montana	22.4
10	Colorado	19.6		6	Utah	21.6
20	Connecticut	15.8		7	Pennsylvania	21.2
16	Delaware	16.9		8	South Dakota	20.9
42	Florida	10.3		9	Idaho	20.7
27	Georgia	14.4		10	Colorado	19.6
3	Hawaii	22.8		10	Oregon	19.6
9	Idaho	20.7		12	Illinois	19.2
12	Illinois	19.2		13	Iowa	17.9
14	Indiana	17.5		14	Indiana	17.5
13	Iowa	17.9		15	Nebraska	17.2
28	Kansas	13.9		16	Delaware	16.9
45	Kentucky	10.2		17	Wyoming	16.7
29	Louisiana	13.6		18	Arizona	16.1
37	Maine	12.3		19	Rhode Island	15.9
22	Maryland	15.7		20	Connecticut	15.8
39	Massachusetts	12.0		20	New Hampshire	15.8
35	Michigan	13.0		22	Maryland	15.7
4	Minnesota	22.5		23	Ohio	15.6
47	Mississippi	9.6		24	Texas	15.0
29	Missouri	13.6		25	Nevada	14.8
5	Montana	22.4		26	California	14.7
15	Nebraska	17.2		27	Georgia	14.4
25	Nevada	14.8		28	Kansas	13.9
20	New Hampshire	15.8		29	Louisiana	13.6
34	New Jersey	13.3		29	Missouri	13.6
38	New Mexico	12.2		31	New York	13.4
31	New York	13.4		31	Oklahoma	13.4
46	North Carolina	9.9		31	Washington	13.4
2	North Dakota	24.1		34	New Jersey	13.3
23	Ohio	15.6		35	Michigan	13.0
31	Oklahoma	13.4		36	Virginia	12.4
10	Oregon	19.6		37	Maine	12.3
7	Pennsylvania	21.2		38	New Mexico	12.2
19	Rhode Island	15.9		39	Massachusetts	12.0
42	South Carolina	10.3		40	Tennessee	11.5
8	South Dakota	20.9		41	Vermont	10.4
40	Tennessee	11.5		42	Alaska	10.3
24	Texas	15.0		42	Florida	10.3
6	Utah	21.6		42	South Carolina	10.3
41	Vermont	10.4		45	Kentucky	10.2
36	Virginia	12.4		46	North Carolina	9.9
31	Washington	13.4		47	Mississippi	9.6
50	West Virginia	5.6		48	Arkansas	9.5
1	Wisconsin	24.3		49	Alabama	6.0
17	Wyoming	16.7		50	West Virginia	5.6

District of Columbia**   NA

Source: CQ Press using reported data from the Federal Bureau of Investigation
    "Crime in the United States 2008" (Uniform Crime Reports, September 14, 2009, http://www.fbi.gov/ucr/ucr.htm)
*Arrests of youths 17 years and younger by law enforcement agencies submitting complete reports to the F.B.I. for 12 months in 2008.
**Not available.

Reported Arrests of Juveniles for Crime Index Offenses in 2008

National Total = 459,034 Reported Arrests*

RANK	STATE	ARRESTS	% of USA
31	Alabama	4,492	1.0%
43	Alaska	1,500	0.3%
10	Arizona	12,684	2.8%
32	Arkansas	4,264	0.9%
1	California	64,965	14.2%
19	Colorado	9,299	2.0%
29	Connecticut	5,279	1.2%
39	Delaware	2,194	0.5%
2	Florida	45,074	9.8%
14	Georgia	11,006	2.4%
41	Hawaii	1,819	0.4%
34	Idaho	3,169	0.7%
17	Illinois	9,581	2.1%
15	Indiana	10,461	2.3%
24	Iowa	6,019	1.3%
36	Kansas	2,629	0.6%
42	Kentucky	1,793	0.4%
26	Louisiana	5,985	1.3%
38	Maine	2,211	0.5%
6	Maryland	16,120	3.5%
28	Massachusetts	5,375	1.2%
11	Michigan	12,569	2.7%
12	Minnesota	11,397	2.5%
37	Mississippi	2,450	0.5%
9	Missouri	13,216	2.9%
40	Montana	1,891	0.4%
33	Nebraska	3,817	0.8%
27	Nevada	5,747	1.3%
48	New Hampshire	946	0.2%
13	New Jersey	11,287	2.5%
35	New Mexico	2,873	0.6%
7	New York	13,443	2.9%
8	North Carolina	13,321	2.9%
45	North Dakota	1,297	0.3%
18	Ohio	9,325	2.0%
25	Oklahoma	6,006	1.3%
21	Oregon	7,899	1.7%
4	Pennsylvania	19,107	4.2%
44	Rhode Island	1,377	0.3%
30	South Carolina	4,531	1.0%
46	South Dakota	1,175	0.3%
20	Tennessee	8,720	1.9%
3	Texas	36,928	8.0%
23	Utah	6,637	1.4%
50	Vermont	340	0.1%
22	Virginia	7,848	1.7%
16	Washington	10,112	2.2%
49	West Virginia	697	0.2%
5	Wisconsin	16,909	3.7%
47	Wyoming	1,170	0.3%

RANK	STATE	ARRESTS	% of USA
1	California	64,965	14.2%
2	Florida	45,074	9.8%
3	Texas	36,928	8.0%
4	Pennsylvania	19,107	4.2%
5	Wisconsin	16,909	3.7%
6	Maryland	16,120	3.5%
7	New York	13,443	2.9%
8	North Carolina	13,321	2.9%
9	Missouri	13,216	2.9%
10	Arizona	12,684	2.8%
11	Michigan	12,569	2.7%
12	Minnesota	11,397	2.5%
13	New Jersey	11,287	2.5%
14	Georgia	11,006	2.4%
15	Indiana	10,461	2.3%
16	Washington	10,112	2.2%
17	Illinois	9,581	2.1%
18	Ohio	9,325	2.0%
19	Colorado	9,299	2.0%
20	Tennessee	8,720	1.9%
21	Oregon	7,899	1.7%
22	Virginia	7,848	1.7%
23	Utah	6,637	1.4%
24	Iowa	6,019	1.3%
25	Oklahoma	6,006	1.3%
26	Louisiana	5,985	1.3%
27	Nevada	5,747	1.3%
28	Massachusetts	5,375	1.2%
29	Connecticut	5,279	1.2%
30	South Carolina	4,531	1.0%
31	Alabama	4,492	1.0%
32	Arkansas	4,264	0.9%
33	Nebraska	3,817	0.8%
34	Idaho	3,169	0.7%
35	New Mexico	2,873	0.6%
36	Kansas	2,629	0.6%
37	Mississippi	2,450	0.5%
38	Maine	2,211	0.5%
39	Delaware	2,194	0.5%
40	Montana	1,891	0.4%
41	Hawaii	1,819	0.4%
42	Kentucky	1,793	0.4%
43	Alaska	1,500	0.3%
44	Rhode Island	1,377	0.3%
45	North Dakota	1,297	0.3%
46	South Dakota	1,175	0.3%
47	Wyoming	1,170	0.3%
48	New Hampshire	946	0.2%
49	West Virginia	697	0.2%
50	Vermont	340	0.1%
	District of Columbia**	NA	NA

Source: CQ Press using reported data from the Federal Bureau of Investigation
"Crime in the United States 2008" (Uniform Crime Reports, September 14, 2009, http://www.fbi.gov/ucr/ucr.htm)
*Arrests of youths 17 years and younger by law enforcement agencies submitting complete reports to the F.B.I. for 12 months in 2008. Crime index offenses consist of murder, forcible rape, robbery, aggravated assault, burglary, larceny-theft, motor vehicle theft, and arson. See important note at beginning of this chapter.
**Not available.

Reported Juvenile Arrest Rate for Crime Index Offenses in 2008

National Rate = 1,705.7 Reported Arrests per 100,000 Juvenile Population*

ALPHA ORDER

RANK	STATE	RATE
42	Alabama	1,102.4
19	Alaska	1,923.6
23	Arizona	1,781.4
28	Arkansas	1,642.5
31	California	1,572.7
15	Colorado	2,051.0
34	Connecticut	1,500.9
4	Delaware	2,416.2
3	Florida	2,540.0
30	Georgia	1,624.6
26	Hawaii	1,672.0
21	Idaho	1,903.6
NA	Illinois**	NA
16	Indiana	2,023.0
13	Iowa	2,053.1
39	Kansas	1,272.3
NA	Kentucky**	NA
8	Louisiana	2,161.7
25	Maine	1,682.4
2	Maryland	2,677.7
45	Massachusetts	914.4
37	Michigan	1,295.2
12	Minnesota	2,099.2
29	Mississippi	1,628.8
7	Missouri	2,207.7
18	Montana	1,949.6
9	Nebraska	2,142.9
14	Nevada	2,052.5
46	New Hampshire	856.3
40	New Jersey	1,250.8
22	New Mexico	1,822.9
35	New York	1,401.4
20	North Carolina	1,918.5
6	North Dakota	2,233.9
41	Ohio	1,246.0
32	Oklahoma	1,542.9
11	Oregon	2,101.3
33	Pennsylvania	1,528.4
38	Rhode Island	1,284.8
44	South Carolina	980.9
24	South Dakota	1,726.3
27	Tennessee	1,662.6
36	Texas	1,361.8
5	Utah	2,251.9
47	Vermont	660.4
43	Virginia	1,010.1
17	Washington	2,003.6
48	West Virginia	647.7
1	Wisconsin	2,879.1
10	Wyoming	2,110.4

RANK ORDER

RANK	STATE	RATE
1	Wisconsin	2,879.1
2	Maryland	2,677.7
3	Florida	2,540.0
4	Delaware	2,416.2
5	Utah	2,251.9
6	North Dakota	2,233.9
7	Missouri	2,207.7
8	Louisiana	2,161.7
9	Nebraska	2,142.9
10	Wyoming	2,110.4
11	Oregon	2,101.3
12	Minnesota	2,099.2
13	Iowa	2,053.1
14	Nevada	2,052.5
15	Colorado	2,051.0
16	Indiana	2,023.0
17	Washington	2,003.6
18	Montana	1,949.6
19	Alaska	1,923.6
20	North Carolina	1,918.5
21	Idaho	1,903.6
22	New Mexico	1,822.9
23	Arizona	1,781.4
24	South Dakota	1,726.3
25	Maine	1,682.4
26	Hawaii	1,672.0
27	Tennessee	1,662.6
28	Arkansas	1,642.5
29	Mississippi	1,628.8
30	Georgia	1,624.6
31	California	1,572.7
32	Oklahoma	1,542.9
33	Pennsylvania	1,528.4
34	Connecticut	1,500.9
35	New York	1,401.4
36	Texas	1,361.8
37	Michigan	1,295.2
38	Rhode Island	1,284.8
39	Kansas	1,272.3
40	New Jersey	1,250.8
41	Ohio	1,246.0
42	Alabama	1,102.4
43	Virginia	1,010.1
44	South Carolina	980.9
45	Massachusetts	914.4
46	New Hampshire	856.3
47	Vermont	660.4
48	West Virginia	647.7
NA	Illinois**	NA
NA	Kentucky**	NA
	District of Columbia**	NA

Source: CQ Press using reported data from the Federal Bureau of Investigation
"Crime in the United States 2008" (Uniform Crime Reports, September 14, 2009, http://www.fbi.gov/ucr/ucr.htm)
*By law enforcement agencies submitting complete reports to the F.B.I. for 12 months in 2008. Arrests of youths 17 years and younger divided into population of 10 to 17 year olds. See important note at beginning of this chapter. Crime index offenses consist of murder, forcible rape, robbery, aggravated assault, burglary, larceny-theft, motor vehicle theft, and arson.
**Not available.

Reported Arrests of Juveniles for Crime Index Offenses
as a Percent of All Such Arrests in 2008
National Percent = 23.4% of Reported Crime Index Offense Arrests*

ALPHA ORDER

RANK	STATE	PERCENT
49	Alabama	14.5
25	Alaska	24.1
22	Arizona	24.8
39	Arkansas	21.1
37	California	22.0
15	Colorado	29.4
29	Connecticut	22.9
31	Delaware	22.6
34	Florida	22.2
32	Georgia	22.5
12	Hawaii	31.1
2	Idaho	37.6
13	Illinois	29.9
17	Indiana	26.9
6	Iowa	33.1
16	Kansas	27.2
39	Kentucky	21.1
41	Louisiana	20.7
24	Maine	24.4
11	Maryland	31.5
45	Massachusetts	17.4
18	Michigan	26.4
8	Minnesota	32.7
43	Mississippi	18.8
29	Missouri	22.9
4	Montana	34.6
7	Nebraska	33.0
26	Nevada	23.9
21	New Hampshire	25.0
27	New Jersey	23.2
28	New Mexico	23.0
38	New York	21.6
46	North Carolina	16.8
1	North Dakota	38.3
35	Ohio	22.1
19	Oklahoma	26.1
23	Oregon	24.6
35	Pennsylvania	22.1
14	Rhode Island	29.7
44	South Carolina	17.8
3	South Dakota	36.2
47	Tennessee	16.4
33	Texas	22.4
9	Utah	32.0
48	Vermont	15.7
42	Virginia	19.4
20	Washington	25.7
50	West Virginia	11.0
5	Wisconsin	33.5
10	Wyoming	31.6

RANK ORDER

RANK	STATE	PERCENT
1	North Dakota	38.3
2	Idaho	37.6
3	South Dakota	36.2
4	Montana	34.6
5	Wisconsin	33.5
6	Iowa	33.1
7	Nebraska	33.0
8	Minnesota	32.7
9	Utah	32.0
10	Wyoming	31.6
11	Maryland	31.5
12	Hawaii	31.1
13	Illinois	29.9
14	Rhode Island	29.7
15	Colorado	29.4
16	Kansas	27.2
17	Indiana	26.9
18	Michigan	26.4
19	Oklahoma	26.1
20	Washington	25.7
21	New Hampshire	25.0
22	Arizona	24.8
23	Oregon	24.6
24	Maine	24.4
25	Alaska	24.1
26	Nevada	23.9
27	New Jersey	23.2
28	New Mexico	23.0
29	Connecticut	22.9
29	Missouri	22.9
31	Delaware	22.6
32	Georgia	22.5
33	Texas	22.4
34	Florida	22.2
35	Ohio	22.1
35	Pennsylvania	22.1
37	California	22.0
38	New York	21.6
39	Arkansas	21.1
39	Kentucky	21.1
41	Louisiana	20.7
42	Virginia	19.4
43	Mississippi	18.8
44	South Carolina	17.8
45	Massachusetts	17.4
46	North Carolina	16.8
47	Tennessee	16.4
48	Vermont	15.7
49	Alabama	14.5
50	West Virginia	11.0

District of Columbia**   NA

Source: CQ Press using reported data from the Federal Bureau of Investigation
   "Crime in the United States 2008" (Uniform Crime Reports, September 14, 2009, http://www.fbi.gov/ucr/ucr.htm)
*Arrests of youths 17 years and younger by law enforcement agencies submitting complete reports to the F.B.I. for 12 months in 2008. Crime index offenses consist of murder, forcible rape, robbery, aggravated assault, burglary, larceny-theft, motor vehicle theft, and arson.
**Not available.

Reported Arrests of Juveniles for Violent Crime in 2008

National Total = 82,343 Reported Arrests*

ALPHA ORDER

RANK	STATE	ARRESTS	% of USA
30	Alabama	719	0.9%
41	Alaska	212	0.3%
17	Arizona	1,619	2.0%
32	Arkansas	468	0.6%
1	California	17,172	20.9%
25	Colorado	902	1.1%
21	Connecticut	1,186	1.4%
31	Delaware	574	0.7%
2	Florida	8,373	10.2%
12	Georgia	1,890	2.3%
36	Hawaii	288	0.3%
39	Idaho	227	0.3%
6	Illinois	3,503	4.3%
18	Indiana	1,498	1.8%
28	Iowa	743	0.9%
35	Kansas	336	0.4%
37	Kentucky	279	0.3%
13	Louisiana	1,666	2.0%
45	Maine	86	0.1%
5	Maryland	3,657	4.4%
11	Massachusetts	1,964	2.4%
9	Michigan	2,187	2.7%
22	Minnesota	1,135	1.4%
40	Mississippi	218	0.3%
16	Missouri	1,642	2.0%
43	Montana	109	0.1%
38	Nebraska	247	0.3%
24	Nevada	939	1.1%
44	New Hampshire	93	0.1%
7	New Jersey	2,980	3.6%
33	New Mexico	440	0.5%
8	New York	2,497	3.0%
10	North Carolina	2,119	2.6%
48	North Dakota	68	0.1%
20	Ohio	1,196	1.5%
27	Oklahoma	790	1.0%
29	Oregon	720	0.9%
3	Pennsylvania	5,309	6.4%
42	Rhode Island	200	0.2%
26	South Carolina	893	1.1%
49	South Dakota	54	0.1%
14	Tennessee	1,663	2.0%
4	Texas	4,900	6.0%
34	Utah	359	0.4%
50	Vermont	47	0.1%
23	Virginia	1,105	1.3%
19	Washington	1,247	1.5%
46	West Virginia	77	0.1%
15	Wisconsin	1,644	2.0%
47	Wyoming	73	0.1%

RANK ORDER

RANK	STATE	ARRESTS	% of USA
1	California	17,172	20.9%
2	Florida	8,373	10.2%
3	Pennsylvania	5,309	6.4%
4	Texas	4,900	6.0%
5	Maryland	3,657	4.4%
6	Illinois	3,503	4.3%
7	New Jersey	2,980	3.6%
8	New York	2,497	3.0%
9	Michigan	2,187	2.7%
10	North Carolina	2,119	2.6%
11	Massachusetts	1,964	2.4%
12	Georgia	1,890	2.3%
13	Louisiana	1,666	2.0%
14	Tennessee	1,663	2.0%
15	Wisconsin	1,644	2.0%
16	Missouri	1,642	2.0%
17	Arizona	1,619	2.0%
18	Indiana	1,498	1.8%
19	Washington	1,247	1.5%
20	Ohio	1,196	1.5%
21	Connecticut	1,186	1.4%
22	Minnesota	1,135	1.4%
23	Virginia	1,105	1.3%
24	Nevada	939	1.1%
25	Colorado	902	1.1%
26	South Carolina	893	1.1%
27	Oklahoma	790	1.0%
28	Iowa	743	0.9%
29	Oregon	720	0.9%
30	Alabama	719	0.9%
31	Delaware	574	0.7%
32	Arkansas	468	0.6%
33	New Mexico	440	0.5%
34	Utah	359	0.4%
35	Kansas	336	0.4%
36	Hawaii	288	0.3%
37	Kentucky	279	0.3%
38	Nebraska	247	0.3%
39	Idaho	227	0.3%
40	Mississippi	218	0.3%
41	Alaska	212	0.3%
42	Rhode Island	200	0.2%
43	Montana	109	0.1%
44	New Hampshire	93	0.1%
45	Maine	86	0.1%
46	West Virginia	77	0.1%
47	Wyoming	73	0.1%
48	North Dakota	68	0.1%
49	South Dakota	54	0.1%
50	Vermont	47	0.1%
	District of Columbia**	NA	NA

Source: Reported data from the Federal Bureau of Investigation
   "Crime in the United States 2008" (Uniform Crime Reports, September 14, 2009, http://www.fbi.gov/ucr/ucr.htm)
*Arrests of youths 17 years and younger by law enforcement agencies submitting complete reports to the F.B.I. for 12 months in 2008. Violent crimes are offenses of murder, forcible rape, robbery, and aggravated assault. See important note at beginning of this chapter.
**Not available.

Reported Juvenile Arrest Rate for Violent Crime in 2008

National Rate = 306.0 Reported Arrests per 100,000 Juvenile Population*

ALPHA ORDER

RANK	STATE	RATE
33	Alabama	176.4
18	Alaska	271.9
23	Arizona	227.4
32	Arkansas	180.3
6	California	415.7
27	Colorado	198.9
7	Connecticut	337.2
1	Delaware	632.1
4	Florida	471.8
16	Georgia	279.0
19	Hawaii	264.7
39	Idaho	136.4
NA	Illinois**	NA
13	Indiana	289.7
21	Iowa	253.4
34	Kansas	162.6
NA	Kentucky**	NA
3	Louisiana	601.7
48	Maine	65.4
2	Maryland	607.5
9	Massachusetts	334.1
24	Michigan	225.4
25	Minnesota	209.1
36	Mississippi	144.9
17	Missouri	274.3
43	Montana	112.4
38	Nebraska	138.7
8	Nevada	335.4
45	New Hampshire	84.2
10	New Jersey	330.2
15	New Mexico	279.2
20	New York	260.3
12	North Carolina	305.2
42	North Dakota	117.1
35	Ohio	159.8
26	Oklahoma	202.9
29	Oregon	191.5
5	Pennsylvania	424.7
30	Rhode Island	186.6
28	South Carolina	193.3
46	South Dakota	79.3
11	Tennessee	317.1
31	Texas	180.7
41	Utah	121.8
44	Vermont	91.3
37	Virginia	142.2
22	Washington	247.1
47	West Virginia	71.6
14	Wisconsin	279.9
40	Wyoming	131.7

RANK ORDER

RANK	STATE	RATE
1	Delaware	632.1
2	Maryland	607.5
3	Louisiana	601.7
4	Florida	471.8
5	Pennsylvania	424.7
6	California	415.7
7	Connecticut	337.2
8	Nevada	335.4
9	Massachusetts	334.1
10	New Jersey	330.2
11	Tennessee	317.1
12	North Carolina	305.2
13	Indiana	289.7
14	Wisconsin	279.9
15	New Mexico	279.2
16	Georgia	279.0
17	Missouri	274.3
18	Alaska	271.9
19	Hawaii	264.7
20	New York	260.3
21	Iowa	253.4
22	Washington	247.1
23	Arizona	227.4
24	Michigan	225.4
25	Minnesota	209.1
26	Oklahoma	202.9
27	Colorado	198.9
28	South Carolina	193.3
29	Oregon	191.5
30	Rhode Island	186.6
31	Texas	180.7
32	Arkansas	180.3
33	Alabama	176.4
34	Kansas	162.6
35	Ohio	159.8
36	Mississippi	144.9
37	Virginia	142.2
38	Nebraska	138.7
39	Idaho	136.4
40	Wyoming	131.7
41	Utah	121.8
42	North Dakota	117.1
43	Montana	112.4
44	Vermont	91.3
45	New Hampshire	84.2
46	South Dakota	79.3
47	West Virginia	71.6
48	Maine	65.4
NA	Illinois**	NA
NA	Kentucky**	NA
	District of Columbia**	NA

Source: CQ Press using reported data from the Federal Bureau of Investigation
    "Crime in the United States 2008" (Uniform Crime Reports, September 14, 2009, http://www.fbi.gov/ucr/ucr.htm)
*By law enforcement agencies submitting complete reports to the F.B.I. for 12 months in 2008. Arrests of youths 17 years and younger divided into population of 10 to 17 year olds. See important note at beginning of this chapter. Violent crimes are offenses of murder, forcible rape, robbery, and aggravated assault.
**Not available.

Reported Arrests of Juveniles for Violent Crime
as a Percent of All Such Arrests in 2008
National Percent = 16.1% of Reported Violent Crime Arrests*

ALPHA ORDER

RANK ORDER

RANK	STATE	PERCENT		RANK	STATE	PERCENT
46	Alabama	11.0		1	Illinois	40.2
48	Alaska	10.0		2	Maryland	28.1
19	Arizona	17.5		3	Rhode Island	22.8
49	Arkansas	9.9		4	Hawaii	21.8
32	California	13.7		5	New Jersey	21.4
29	Colorado	14.5		6	Pennsylvania	20.6
9	Connecticut	20.0		7	Wisconsin	20.4
10	Delaware	19.5		8	Minnesota	20.2
22	Florida	15.9		9	Connecticut	20.0
21	Georgia	16.5		10	Delaware	19.5
4	Hawaii	21.8		11	New York	18.7
22	Idaho	15.9		12	Louisiana	18.0
1	Illinois	40.2		12	Washington	18.0
14	Indiana	17.9		14	Indiana	17.9
15	Iowa	17.6		15	Iowa	17.6
33	Kansas	13.5		15	Michigan	17.6
25	Kentucky	15.4		15	Ohio	17.6
12	Louisiana	18.0		15	Utah	17.6
41	Maine	11.7		19	Arizona	17.5
2	Maryland	28.1		20	North Dakota	16.7
24	Massachusetts	15.7		21	Georgia	16.5
15	Michigan	17.6		22	Florida	15.9
8	Minnesota	20.2		22	Idaho	15.9
44	Mississippi	11.2		24	Massachusetts	15.7
35	Missouri	13.1		25	Kentucky	15.4
36	Montana	12.8		26	New Hampshire	14.9
38	Nebraska	12.6		26	Oregon	14.9
30	Nevada	14.4		28	Virginia	14.8
26	New Hampshire	14.9		29	Colorado	14.5
5	New Jersey	21.4		30	Nevada	14.4
37	New Mexico	12.7		31	Texas	14.3
11	New York	18.7		32	California	13.7
44	North Carolina	11.2		33	Kansas	13.5
20	North Dakota	16.7		34	Oklahoma	13.3
15	Ohio	17.6		35	Missouri	13.1
34	Oklahoma	13.3		36	Montana	12.8
26	Oregon	14.9		37	New Mexico	12.7
6	Pennsylvania	20.6		38	Nebraska	12.6
3	Rhode Island	22.8		39	South Carolina	12.3
39	South Carolina	12.3		40	Tennessee	12.2
42	South Dakota	11.6		41	Maine	11.7
40	Tennessee	12.2		42	South Dakota	11.6
31	Texas	14.3		43	Wyoming	11.5
15	Utah	17.6		44	Mississippi	11.2
47	Vermont	10.3		44	North Carolina	11.2
28	Virginia	14.8		46	Alabama	11.0
12	Washington	18.0		47	Vermont	10.3
50	West Virginia	6.0		48	Alaska	10.0
7	Wisconsin	20.4		49	Arkansas	9.9
43	Wyoming	11.5		50	West Virginia	6.0

District of Columbia**   NA

Source: CQ Press using reported data from the Federal Bureau of Investigation
    "Crime in the United States 2008" (Uniform Crime Reports, September 14, 2009, http://www.fbi.gov/ucr/ucr.htm)
*Arrests of youths 17 years and younger by law enforcement agencies submitting complete reports to the F.B.I. for 12 months in 2008. Violent crimes are offenses of murder, forcible rape, robbery, and aggravated assault.
**Not available.

Reported Arrests of Juveniles for Murder in 2008

National Total = 1,055 Reported Arrests*

RANK	STATE	ARRESTS	% of USA
15	Alabama	21	2.0%
43	Alaska	0	0.0%
12	Arizona	29	2.7%
39	Arkansas	2	0.2%
1	California	224	21.2%
34	Colorado	5	0.5%
24	Connecticut	12	1.1%
37	Delaware	4	0.4%
2	Florida	81	7.7%
7	Georgia	37	3.5%
43	Hawaii	0	0.0%
38	Idaho	3	0.3%
5	Illinois	54	5.1%
18	Indiana	18	1.7%
30	Iowa	6	0.6%
34	Kansas	5	0.5%
30	Kentucky	6	0.6%
21	Louisiana	15	1.4%
43	Maine	0	0.0%
10	Maryland	31	2.9%
28	Massachusetts	8	0.8%
24	Michigan	12	1.1%
24	Minnesota	12	1.1%
22	Mississippi	14	1.3%
8	Missouri	35	3.3%
40	Montana	1	0.1%
34	Nebraska	5	0.5%
27	Nevada	11	1.0%
43	New Hampshire	0	0.0%
14	New Jersey	26	2.5%
30	New Mexico	6	0.6%
9	New York	34	3.2%
6	North Carolina	49	4.6%
43	North Dakota	0	0.0%
20	Ohio	16	1.5%
17	Oklahoma	19	1.8%
23	Oregon	13	1.2%
4	Pennsylvania	56	5.3%
43	Rhode Island	0	0.0%
13	South Carolina	27	2.6%
43	South Dakota	0	0.0%
18	Tennessee	18	1.7%
3	Texas	73	6.9%
30	Utah	6	0.6%
40	Vermont	1	0.1%
16	Virginia	20	1.9%
28	Washington	8	0.8%
43	West Virginia	0	0.0%
10	Wisconsin	31	2.9%
40	Wyoming	1	0.1%

RANK	STATE	ARRESTS	% of USA
1	California	224	21.2%
2	Florida	81	7.7%
3	Texas	73	6.9%
4	Pennsylvania	56	5.3%
5	Illinois	54	5.1%
6	North Carolina	49	4.6%
7	Georgia	37	3.5%
8	Missouri	35	3.3%
9	New York	34	3.2%
10	Maryland	31	2.9%
10	Wisconsin	31	2.9%
12	Arizona	29	2.7%
13	South Carolina	27	2.6%
14	New Jersey	26	2.5%
15	Alabama	21	2.0%
16	Virginia	20	1.9%
17	Oklahoma	19	1.8%
18	Indiana	18	1.7%
18	Tennessee	18	1.7%
20	Ohio	16	1.5%
21	Louisiana	15	1.4%
22	Mississippi	14	1.3%
23	Oregon	13	1.2%
24	Connecticut	12	1.1%
24	Michigan	12	1.1%
24	Minnesota	12	1.1%
27	Nevada	11	1.0%
28	Massachusetts	8	0.8%
28	Washington	8	0.8%
30	Iowa	6	0.6%
30	Kentucky	6	0.6%
30	New Mexico	6	0.6%
30	Utah	6	0.6%
34	Colorado	5	0.5%
34	Kansas	5	0.5%
34	Nebraska	5	0.5%
37	Delaware	4	0.4%
38	Idaho	3	0.3%
39	Arkansas	2	0.2%
40	Montana	1	0.1%
40	Vermont	1	0.1%
40	Wyoming	1	0.1%
43	Alaska	0	0.0%
43	Hawaii	0	0.0%
43	Maine	0	0.0%
43	New Hampshire	0	0.0%
43	North Dakota	0	0.0%
43	Rhode Island	0	0.0%
43	South Dakota	0	0.0%
43	West Virginia	0	0.0%
	District of Columbia**	NA	NA

Source: Reported data from the Federal Bureau of Investigation
"Crime in the United States 2008" (Uniform Crime Reports, September 14, 2009, http://www.fbi.gov/ucr/ucr.htm)
*Arrests of youths 17 years and younger by law enforcement agencies submitting complete reports to the F.B.I. for 12 months in 2008. Includes nonnegligent manslaughter. See important note at beginning of this chapter.
**Not available.

Reported Juvenile Arrest Rate for Murder in 2008

National Rate = 3.9 Reported Arrests per 100,000 Juvenile Population*

ALPHA ORDER

RANK	STATE	RATE
9	Alabama	5.2
41	Alaska	0.0
15	Arizona	4.1
40	Arkansas	0.8
6	California	5.4
38	Colorado	1.1
21	Connecticut	3.4
14	Delaware	4.4
12	Florida	4.6
5	Georgia	5.5
41	Hawaii	0.0
33	Idaho	1.8
NA	Illinois**	NA
18	Indiana	3.5
30	Iowa	2.0
27	Kansas	2.4
NA	Kentucky**	NA
6	Louisiana	5.4
41	Maine	0.0
10	Maryland	5.1
36	Massachusetts	1.4
37	Michigan	1.2
28	Minnesota	2.2
1	Mississippi	9.3
3	Missouri	5.8
39	Montana	1.0
24	Nebraska	2.8
16	Nevada	3.9
41	New Hampshire	0.0
23	New Jersey	2.9
17	New Mexico	3.8
18	New York	3.5
2	North Carolina	7.1
41	North Dakota	0.0
29	Ohio	2.1
11	Oklahoma	4.9
18	Oregon	3.5
13	Pennsylvania	4.5
41	Rhode Island	0.0
3	South Carolina	5.8
41	South Dakota	0.0
21	Tennessee	3.4
25	Texas	2.7
30	Utah	2.0
32	Vermont	1.9
26	Virginia	2.6
35	Washington	1.6
41	West Virginia	0.0
8	Wisconsin	5.3
33	Wyoming	1.8

RANK ORDER

RANK	STATE	RATE
1	Mississippi	9.3
2	North Carolina	7.1
3	Missouri	5.8
3	South Carolina	5.8
5	Georgia	5.5
6	California	5.4
6	Louisiana	5.4
8	Wisconsin	5.3
9	Alabama	5.2
10	Maryland	5.1
11	Oklahoma	4.9
12	Florida	4.6
13	Pennsylvania	4.5
14	Delaware	4.4
15	Arizona	4.1
16	Nevada	3.9
17	New Mexico	3.8
18	Indiana	3.5
18	New York	3.5
18	Oregon	3.5
21	Connecticut	3.4
21	Tennessee	3.4
23	New Jersey	2.9
24	Nebraska	2.8
25	Texas	2.7
26	Virginia	2.6
27	Kansas	2.4
28	Minnesota	2.2
29	Ohio	2.1
30	Iowa	2.0
30	Utah	2.0
32	Vermont	1.9
33	Idaho	1.8
33	Wyoming	1.8
35	Washington	1.6
36	Massachusetts	1.4
37	Michigan	1.2
38	Colorado	1.1
39	Montana	1.0
40	Arkansas	0.8
41	Alaska	0.0
41	Hawaii	0.0
41	Maine	0.0
41	New Hampshire	0.0
41	North Dakota	0.0
41	Rhode Island	0.0
41	South Dakota	0.0
41	West Virginia	0.0
NA	Illinois**	NA
NA	Kentucky**	NA
	District of Columbia**	NA

Source: CQ Press using reported data from the Federal Bureau of Investigation
  "Crime in the United States 2008" (Uniform Crime Reports, September 14, 2009, http://www.fbi.gov/ucr/ucr.htm)
*By law enforcement agencies submitting complete reports to the F.B.I. for 12 months in 2008. Includes nonnegligent manslaughter. Arrests of youths 17 years and younger divided into population of 10 to 17 year olds. See important note at beginning of this chapter.
**Not available.

Reported Arrests of Juveniles for Murder
as a Percent of All Such Arrests in 2008
National Percent = 9.8% of Reported Murder Arrests*

ALPHA ORDER

RANK	STATE	PERCENT
37	Alabama	6.7
43	Alaska	0.0
24	Arizona	9.4
42	Arkansas	1.7
10	California	12.1
41	Colorado	3.2
15	Connecticut	10.9
7	Delaware	12.5
26	Florida	9.2
13	Georgia	11.6
43	Hawaii	0.0
1	Idaho	21.4
3	Illinois	14.8
37	Indiana	6.7
11	Iowa	12.0
18	Kansas	10.6
15	Kentucky	10.9
33	Louisiana	8.2
43	Maine	0.0
21	Maryland	10.1
19	Massachusetts	10.4
29	Michigan	8.5
17	Minnesota	10.8
19	Mississippi	10.4
22	Missouri	9.8
27	Montana	9.1
13	Nebraska	11.6
35	Nevada	7.5
43	New Hampshire	0.0
24	New Jersey	9.4
29	New Mexico	8.5
7	New York	12.5
29	North Carolina	8.5
43	North Dakota	0.0
28	Ohio	8.6
12	Oklahoma	11.9
4	Oregon	13.7
23	Pennsylvania	9.7
43	Rhode Island	0.0
5	South Carolina	13.6
43	South Dakota	0.0
40	Tennessee	5.9
29	Texas	8.5
6	Utah	12.8
7	Vermont	12.5
39	Virginia	6.5
34	Washington	7.7
43	West Virginia	0.0
2	Wisconsin	15.9
36	Wyoming	7.1

RANK ORDER

RANK	STATE	PERCENT
1	Idaho	21.4
2	Wisconsin	15.9
3	Illinois	14.8
4	Oregon	13.7
5	South Carolina	13.6
6	Utah	12.8
7	Delaware	12.5
7	New York	12.5
7	Vermont	12.5
10	California	12.1
11	Iowa	12.0
12	Oklahoma	11.9
13	Georgia	11.6
13	Nebraska	11.6
15	Connecticut	10.9
15	Kentucky	10.9
17	Minnesota	10.8
18	Kansas	10.6
19	Massachusetts	10.4
19	Mississippi	10.4
21	Maryland	10.1
22	Missouri	9.8
23	Pennsylvania	9.7
24	Arizona	9.4
24	New Jersey	9.4
26	Florida	9.2
27	Montana	9.1
28	Ohio	8.6
29	Michigan	8.5
29	New Mexico	8.5
29	North Carolina	8.5
29	Texas	8.5
33	Louisiana	8.2
34	Washington	7.7
35	Nevada	7.5
36	Wyoming	7.1
37	Alabama	6.7
37	Indiana	6.7
39	Virginia	6.5
40	Tennessee	5.9
41	Colorado	3.2
42	Arkansas	1.7
43	Alaska	0.0
43	Hawaii	0.0
43	Maine	0.0
43	New Hampshire	0.0
43	North Dakota	0.0
43	Rhode Island	0.0
43	South Dakota	0.0
43	West Virginia	0.0

District of Columbia**	NA

Source: CQ Press using reported data from the Federal Bureau of Investigation
"Crime in the United States 2008" (Uniform Crime Reports, September 14, 2009, http://www.fbi.gov/ucr/ucr.htm)
*Arrests of youths 17 years and younger by law enforcement agencies submitting complete reports to the F.B.I. for 12 months in 2008. Includes nonnegligent manslaughter.
**Not available.

Reported Arrests of Juveniles for Rape in 2008

National Total = 2,747 Reported Arrests*

<u>ALPHA ORDER</u>

RANK	STATE	ARRESTS	% of USA
31	Alabama	26	0.9%
49	Alaska	2	0.1%
30	Arizona	28	1.0%
35	Arkansas	16	0.6%
3	California	235	8.6%
15	Colorado	58	2.1%
20	Connecticut	48	1.7%
31	Delaware	26	0.9%
2	Florida	242	8.8%
10	Georgia	63	2.3%
44	Hawaii	8	0.3%
33	Idaho	18	0.7%
9	Illinois	74	2.7%
16	Indiana	52	1.9%
29	Iowa	29	1.1%
23	Kansas	40	1.5%
47	Kentucky	5	0.2%
25	Louisiana	35	1.3%
41	Maine	10	0.4%
16	Maryland	52	1.9%
27	Massachusetts	31	1.1%
7	Michigan	114	4.1%
38	Minnesota	13	0.5%
38	Mississippi	13	0.5%
11	Missouri	62	2.3%
48	Montana	4	0.1%
33	Nebraska	18	0.7%
27	Nevada	31	1.1%
41	New Hampshire	10	0.4%
12	New Jersey	61	2.2%
40	New Mexico	12	0.4%
12	New York	61	2.2%
22	North Carolina	43	1.6%
36	North Dakota	15	0.5%
8	Ohio	92	3.3%
23	Oklahoma	40	1.5%
25	Oregon	35	1.3%
4	Pennsylvania	212	7.7%
37	Rhode Island	14	0.5%
21	South Carolina	45	1.6%
45	South Dakota	7	0.3%
14	Tennessee	60	2.2%
1	Texas	294	10.7%
16	Utah	52	1.9%
43	Vermont	9	0.3%
16	Virginia	52	1.9%
6	Washington	115	4.2%
49	West Virginia	2	0.1%
5	Wisconsin	156	5.7%
45	Wyoming	7	0.3%

<u>RANK ORDER</u>

RANK	STATE	ARRESTS	% of USA
1	Texas	294	10.7%
2	Florida	242	8.8%
3	California	235	8.6%
4	Pennsylvania	212	7.7%
5	Wisconsin	156	5.7%
6	Washington	115	4.2%
7	Michigan	114	4.1%
8	Ohio	92	3.3%
9	Illinois	74	2.7%
10	Georgia	63	2.3%
11	Missouri	62	2.3%
12	New Jersey	61	2.2%
12	New York	61	2.2%
14	Tennessee	60	2.2%
15	Colorado	58	2.1%
16	Indiana	52	1.9%
16	Maryland	52	1.9%
16	Utah	52	1.9%
16	Virginia	52	1.9%
20	Connecticut	48	1.7%
21	South Carolina	45	1.6%
22	North Carolina	43	1.6%
23	Kansas	40	1.5%
23	Oklahoma	40	1.5%
25	Louisiana	35	1.3%
25	Oregon	35	1.3%
27	Massachusetts	31	1.1%
27	Nevada	31	1.1%
29	Iowa	29	1.1%
30	Arizona	28	1.0%
31	Alabama	26	0.9%
31	Delaware	26	0.9%
33	Idaho	18	0.7%
33	Nebraska	18	0.7%
35	Arkansas	16	0.6%
36	North Dakota	15	0.5%
37	Rhode Island	14	0.5%
38	Minnesota	13	0.5%
38	Mississippi	13	0.5%
40	New Mexico	12	0.4%
41	Maine	10	0.4%
41	New Hampshire	10	0.4%
43	Vermont	9	0.3%
44	Hawaii	8	0.3%
45	South Dakota	7	0.3%
45	Wyoming	7	0.3%
47	Kentucky	5	0.2%
48	Montana	4	0.1%
49	Alaska	2	0.1%
49	West Virginia	2	0.1%
	District of Columbia**	NA	NA

Source: Reported data from the Federal Bureau of Investigation
"Crime in the United States 2008" (Uniform Crime Reports, September 14, 2009, http://www.fbi.gov/ucr/ucr.htm)
*Arrests of youths 17 years and younger by law enforcement agencies submitting complete reports to the F.B.I. for 12 months in 2008. Forcible rape is the carnal knowledge of a female forcibly and against her will. Assaults or attempts to commit rape by force or threat of force are included. However, statutory rape without force and other sex offenses are excluded. See important note at beginning of this chapter. **Not available.

Reported Juvenile Arrest Rate for Rape in 2008

National Rate = 10.2 Reported Arrests per 100,000 Juvenile Population*

ALPHA ORDER

RANK	STATE	RATE
38	Alabama	6.4
46	Alaska	2.6
45	Arizona	3.9
40	Arkansas	6.2
42	California	5.7
12	Colorado	12.8
9	Connecticut	13.6
1	Delaware	28.6
9	Florida	13.6
28	Georgia	9.3
35	Hawaii	7.4
19	Idaho	10.8
NA	Illinois**	NA
24	Indiana	10.1
26	Iowa	9.9
5	Kansas	19.4
NA	Kentucky**	NA
13	Louisiana	12.6
33	Maine	7.6
31	Maryland	8.6
43	Massachusetts	5.3
16	Michigan	11.7
47	Minnesota	2.4
31	Mississippi	8.6
21	Missouri	10.4
44	Montana	4.1
24	Nebraska	10.1
18	Nevada	11.1
30	New Hampshire	9.1
36	New Jersey	6.8
33	New Mexico	7.6
38	New York	6.4
40	North Carolina	6.2
3	North Dakota	25.8
15	Ohio	12.3
22	Oklahoma	10.3
28	Oregon	9.3
8	Pennsylvania	17.0
11	Rhode Island	13.1
27	South Carolina	9.7
22	South Dakota	10.3
17	Tennessee	11.4
19	Texas	10.8
6	Utah	17.6
7	Vermont	17.5
37	Virginia	6.7
4	Washington	22.8
48	West Virginia	1.9
2	Wisconsin	26.6
13	Wyoming	12.6

RANK ORDER

RANK	STATE	RATE
1	Delaware	28.6
2	Wisconsin	26.6
3	North Dakota	25.8
4	Washington	22.8
5	Kansas	19.4
6	Utah	17.6
7	Vermont	17.5
8	Pennsylvania	17.0
9	Connecticut	13.6
9	Florida	13.6
11	Rhode Island	13.1
12	Colorado	12.8
13	Louisiana	12.6
13	Wyoming	12.6
15	Ohio	12.3
16	Michigan	11.7
17	Tennessee	11.4
18	Nevada	11.1
19	Idaho	10.8
19	Texas	10.8
21	Missouri	10.4
22	Oklahoma	10.3
22	South Dakota	10.3
24	Indiana	10.1
24	Nebraska	10.1
26	Iowa	9.9
27	South Carolina	9.7
28	Georgia	9.3
28	Oregon	9.3
30	New Hampshire	9.1
31	Maryland	8.6
31	Mississippi	8.6
33	Maine	7.6
33	New Mexico	7.6
35	Hawaii	7.4
36	New Jersey	6.8
37	Virginia	6.7
38	Alabama	6.4
38	New York	6.4
40	Arkansas	6.2
40	North Carolina	6.2
42	California	5.7
43	Massachusetts	5.3
44	Montana	4.1
45	Arizona	3.9
46	Alaska	2.6
47	Minnesota	2.4
48	West Virginia	1.9
NA	Illinois**	NA
NA	Kentucky**	NA
	District of Columbia**	NA

Source: CQ Press using reported data from the Federal Bureau of Investigation
    "Crime in the United States 2008" (Uniform Crime Reports, September 14, 2009, http://www.fbi.gov/ucr/ucr.htm)
*By law enforcement agencies submitting complete reports to the F.B.I. for 12 months in 2008. Arrests of youths 17 years and younger divided into population of 10 to 17 year olds. See important note at beginning of this chapter. Forcible rape is the carnal knowledge of a female forcibly and against her will. Assaults or attempts to commit rape by force or threat of force are included. **Not available.

Reported Arrests of Juveniles for Rape
as a Percent of All Such Arrests in 2008
National Percent = 14.7% of Reported Rape Arrests*

ALPHA ORDER

RANK	STATE	PERCENT
48	Alabama	7.3
50	Alaska	3.7
23	Arizona	15.1
45	Arkansas	8.2
39	California	11.3
32	Colorado	12.8
9	Connecticut	19.7
12	Delaware	18.8
29	Florida	13.7
7	Georgia	20.1
47	Hawaii	7.8
14	Idaho	17.6
17	Illinois	16.4
8	Indiana	19.8
3	Iowa	26.9
6	Kansas	21.9
22	Kentucky	15.2
24	Louisiana	14.7
28	Maine	13.9
31	Maryland	12.9
42	Massachusetts	10.0
9	Michigan	19.7
36	Minnesota	12.3
46	Mississippi	7.9
39	Missouri	11.3
19	Montana	16.0
36	Nebraska	12.3
38	Nevada	11.8
25	New Hampshire	14.5
17	New Jersey	16.4
43	New Mexico	9.3
41	New York	11.2
44	North Carolina	8.3
1	North Dakota	33.3
11	Ohio	18.9
33	Oklahoma	12.7
33	Oregon	12.7
13	Pennsylvania	18.2
4	Rhode Island	24.1
20	South Carolina	15.6
30	South Dakota	13.2
15	Tennessee	17.4
25	Texas	14.5
2	Utah	28.7
33	Vermont	12.7
27	Virginia	14.1
16	Washington	17.0
49	West Virginia	5.0
5	Wisconsin	22.0
20	Wyoming	15.6

RANK ORDER

RANK	STATE	PERCENT
1	North Dakota	33.3
2	Utah	28.7
3	Iowa	26.9
4	Rhode Island	24.1
5	Wisconsin	22.0
6	Kansas	21.9
7	Georgia	20.1
8	Indiana	19.8
9	Connecticut	19.7
9	Michigan	19.7
11	Ohio	18.9
12	Delaware	18.8
13	Pennsylvania	18.2
14	Idaho	17.6
15	Tennessee	17.4
16	Washington	17.0
17	Illinois	16.4
17	New Jersey	16.4
19	Montana	16.0
20	South Carolina	15.6
20	Wyoming	15.6
22	Kentucky	15.2
23	Arizona	15.1
24	Louisiana	14.7
25	New Hampshire	14.5
25	Texas	14.5
27	Virginia	14.1
28	Maine	13.9
29	Florida	13.7
30	South Dakota	13.2
31	Maryland	12.9
32	Colorado	12.8
33	Oklahoma	12.7
33	Oregon	12.7
33	Vermont	12.7
36	Minnesota	12.3
36	Nebraska	12.3
38	Nevada	11.8
39	California	11.3
39	Missouri	11.3
41	New York	11.2
42	Massachusetts	10.0
43	New Mexico	9.3
44	North Carolina	8.3
45	Arkansas	8.2
46	Mississippi	7.9
47	Hawaii	7.8
48	Alabama	7.3
49	West Virginia	5.0
50	Alaska	3.7

District of Columbia**	NA

Source: CQ Press using reported data from the Federal Bureau of Investigation
"Crime in the United States 2008" (Uniform Crime Reports, September 14, 2009, http://www.fbi.gov/ucr/ucr.htm)
*Arrests of youths 17 years and younger by law enforcement agencies submitting complete reports to the F.B.I. for 12 months in 2008. Forcible rape is the carnal knowledge of a female forcibly and against her will. Assaults or attempts to commit rape by force or threat of force are included. However, statutory rape without force and other sex offenses are excluded.
**Not available.

Reported Arrests of Juveniles for Robbery in 2008

National Total = 30,482 Reported Arrests*

ALPHA ORDER

RANK	STATE	ARRESTS	% of USA
23	Alabama	351	1.2%
41	Alaska	44	0.1%
18	Arizona	457	1.5%
34	Arkansas	96	0.3%
1	California	6,879	22.6%
27	Colorado	232	0.8%
24	Connecticut	299	1.0%
30	Delaware	194	0.6%
2	Florida	2,960	9.7%
11	Georgia	724	2.4%
31	Hawaii	157	0.5%
44	Idaho	18	0.1%
6	Illinois	1,529	5.0%
21	Indiana	385	1.3%
35	Iowa	94	0.3%
40	Kansas	52	0.2%
32	Kentucky	146	0.5%
25	Louisiana	264	0.9%
43	Maine	24	0.1%
4	Maryland	1,947	6.4%
16	Massachusetts	529	1.7%
10	Michigan	772	2.5%
20	Minnesota	402	1.3%
33	Mississippi	107	0.4%
14	Missouri	543	1.8%
47	Montana	6	0.0%
37	Nebraska	75	0.2%
22	Nevada	369	1.2%
42	New Hampshire	31	0.1%
7	New Jersey	1,461	4.8%
39	New Mexico	55	0.2%
8	New York	1,045	3.4%
9	North Carolina	864	2.8%
48	North Dakota	4	0.0%
13	Ohio	600	2.0%
29	Oklahoma	201	0.7%
28	Oregon	212	0.7%
3	Pennsylvania	2,028	6.7%
36	Rhode Island	88	0.3%
26	South Carolina	252	0.8%
49	South Dakota	2	0.0%
15	Tennessee	535	1.8%
5	Texas	1,729	5.7%
38	Utah	68	0.2%
50	Vermont	1	0.0%
17	Virginia	506	1.7%
19	Washington	452	1.5%
45	West Virginia	16	0.1%
12	Wisconsin	646	2.1%
46	Wyoming	12	0.0%

RANK ORDER

RANK	STATE	ARRESTS	% of USA
1	California	6,879	22.6%
2	Florida	2,960	9.7%
3	Pennsylvania	2,028	6.7%
4	Maryland	1,947	6.4%
5	Texas	1,729	5.7%
6	Illinois	1,529	5.0%
7	New Jersey	1,461	4.8%
8	New York	1,045	3.4%
9	North Carolina	864	2.8%
10	Michigan	772	2.5%
11	Georgia	724	2.4%
12	Wisconsin	646	2.1%
13	Ohio	600	2.0%
14	Missouri	543	1.8%
15	Tennessee	535	1.8%
16	Massachusetts	529	1.7%
17	Virginia	506	1.7%
18	Arizona	457	1.5%
19	Washington	452	1.5%
20	Minnesota	402	1.3%
21	Indiana	385	1.3%
22	Nevada	369	1.2%
23	Alabama	351	1.2%
24	Connecticut	299	1.0%
25	Louisiana	264	0.9%
26	South Carolina	252	0.8%
27	Colorado	232	0.8%
28	Oregon	212	0.7%
29	Oklahoma	201	0.7%
30	Delaware	194	0.6%
31	Hawaii	157	0.5%
32	Kentucky	146	0.5%
33	Mississippi	107	0.4%
34	Arkansas	96	0.3%
35	Iowa	94	0.3%
36	Rhode Island	88	0.3%
37	Nebraska	75	0.2%
38	Utah	68	0.2%
39	New Mexico	55	0.2%
40	Kansas	52	0.2%
41	Alaska	44	0.1%
42	New Hampshire	31	0.1%
43	Maine	24	0.1%
44	Idaho	18	0.1%
45	West Virginia	16	0.1%
46	Wyoming	12	0.0%
47	Montana	6	0.0%
48	North Dakota	4	0.0%
49	South Dakota	2	0.0%
50	Vermont	1	0.0%
	District of Columbia**	NA	NA

Source: Reported data from the Federal Bureau of Investigation
"Crime in the United States 2008" (Uniform Crime Reports, September 14, 2009, http://www.fbi.gov/ucr/ucr.htm)
*Arrests of youths 17 years and younger by law enforcement agencies submitting complete reports to the F.B.I. for 12 months in 2008. Robbery is the taking or attempting to take anything of value by force or threat of force. See important note at beginning of this chapter.
**Not available.

Reported Juvenile Arrest Rate for Robbery in 2008

National Rate = 113.3 Reported Arrests per 100,000 Juvenile Population*

ALPHA ORDER

RANK	STATE	RATE
18	Alabama	86.1
29	Alaska	56.4
27	Arizona	64.2
35	Arkansas	37.0
4	California	166.5
33	Colorado	51.2
19	Connecticut	85.0
2	Delaware	213.7
3	Florida	166.8
12	Georgia	106.9
7	Hawaii	144.3
44	Idaho	10.8
NA	Illinois**	NA
23	Indiana	74.5
37	Iowa	32.1
39	Kansas	25.2
NA	Kentucky**	NA
14	Louisiana	95.4
42	Maine	18.3
1	Maryland	323.4
16	Massachusetts	90.0
22	Michigan	79.6
24	Minnesota	74.0
25	Mississippi	71.1
15	Missouri	90.7
46	Montana	6.2
34	Nebraska	42.1
8	Nevada	131.8
38	New Hampshire	28.1
6	New Jersey	161.9
36	New Mexico	34.9
11	New York	108.9
9	North Carolina	124.4
45	North Dakota	6.9
21	Ohio	80.2
32	Oklahoma	51.6
29	Oregon	56.4
5	Pennsylvania	162.2
20	Rhode Island	82.1
31	South Carolina	54.6
47	South Dakota	2.9
13	Tennessee	102.0
28	Texas	63.8
40	Utah	23.1
48	Vermont	1.9
26	Virginia	65.1
17	Washington	89.6
43	West Virginia	14.9
10	Wisconsin	110.0
41	Wyoming	21.6

RANK ORDER

RANK	STATE	RATE
1	Maryland	323.4
2	Delaware	213.7
3	Florida	166.8
4	California	166.5
5	Pennsylvania	162.2
6	New Jersey	161.9
7	Hawaii	144.3
8	Nevada	131.8
9	North Carolina	124.4
10	Wisconsin	110.0
11	New York	108.9
12	Georgia	106.9
13	Tennessee	102.0
14	Louisiana	95.4
15	Missouri	90.7
16	Massachusetts	90.0
17	Washington	89.6
18	Alabama	86.1
19	Connecticut	85.0
20	Rhode Island	82.1
21	Ohio	80.2
22	Michigan	79.6
23	Indiana	74.5
24	Minnesota	74.0
25	Mississippi	71.1
26	Virginia	65.1
27	Arizona	64.2
28	Texas	63.8
29	Alaska	56.4
29	Oregon	56.4
31	South Carolina	54.6
32	Oklahoma	51.6
33	Colorado	51.2
34	Nebraska	42.1
35	Arkansas	37.0
36	New Mexico	34.9
37	Iowa	32.1
38	New Hampshire	28.1
39	Kansas	25.2
40	Utah	23.1
41	Wyoming	21.6
42	Maine	18.3
43	West Virginia	14.9
44	Idaho	10.8
45	North Dakota	6.9
46	Montana	6.2
47	South Dakota	2.9
48	Vermont	1.9
NA	Illinois**	NA
NA	Kentucky**	NA
	District of Columbia**	NA

Source: CQ Press using reported data from the Federal Bureau of Investigation
"Crime in the United States 2008" (Uniform Crime Reports, September 14, 2009, http://www.fbi.gov/ucr/ucr.htm)
*By law enforcement agencies submitting complete reports to the F.B.I. for 12 months in 2008. Arrests of youths 17 years and younger divided into population of 10 to 17 year olds. See important note at beginning of this chapter. Robbery is the taking or attempting to take anything of value by force or threat of force.
**Not available.

Reported Arrests of Juveniles for Robbery
as a Percent of All Such Arrests in 2008
National Percent = 27.1% of Reported Robbery Arrests*

ALPHA ORDER

RANK	STATE	PERCENT
40	Alabama	17.1
41	Alaska	16.0
26	Arizona	22.4
43	Arkansas	15.4
11	California	30.7
17	Colorado	25.1
22	Connecticut	24.0
14	Delaware	27.2
18	Florida	24.9
19	Georgia	24.5
3	Hawaii	39.9
35	Idaho	18.6
1	Illinois	52.3
31	Indiana	19.9
23	Iowa	23.3
36	Kansas	18.2
20	Kentucky	24.4
16	Louisiana	25.5
46	Maine	13.0
2	Maryland	43.8
15	Massachusetts	25.6
9	Michigan	31.0
8	Minnesota	31.3
34	Mississippi	18.7
26	Missouri	22.4
47	Montana	12.8
33	Nebraska	18.9
30	Nevada	20.1
29	New Hampshire	20.7
6	New Jersey	33.4
45	New Mexico	13.2
10	New York	30.8
32	North Carolina	19.8
41	North Dakota	16.0
25	Ohio	22.9
21	Oklahoma	24.2
39	Oregon	17.9
13	Pennsylvania	27.4
5	Rhode Island	34.0
36	South Carolina	18.2
49	South Dakota	6.5
36	Tennessee	18.2
28	Texas	21.1
44	Utah	13.7
50	Vermont	4.8
24	Virginia	23.1
12	Washington	27.6
48	West Virginia	11.2
7	Wisconsin	32.6
4	Wyoming	34.3

RANK ORDER

RANK	STATE	PERCENT
1	Illinois	52.3
2	Maryland	43.8
3	Hawaii	39.9
4	Wyoming	34.3
5	Rhode Island	34.0
6	New Jersey	33.4
7	Wisconsin	32.6
8	Minnesota	31.3
9	Michigan	31.0
10	New York	30.8
11	California	30.7
12	Washington	27.6
13	Pennsylvania	27.4
14	Delaware	27.2
15	Massachusetts	25.6
16	Louisiana	25.5
17	Colorado	25.1
18	Florida	24.9
19	Georgia	24.5
20	Kentucky	24.4
21	Oklahoma	24.2
22	Connecticut	24.0
23	Iowa	23.3
24	Virginia	23.1
25	Ohio	22.9
26	Arizona	22.4
26	Missouri	22.4
28	Texas	21.1
29	New Hampshire	20.7
30	Nevada	20.1
31	Indiana	19.9
32	North Carolina	19.8
33	Nebraska	18.9
34	Mississippi	18.7
35	Idaho	18.6
36	Kansas	18.2
36	South Carolina	18.2
36	Tennessee	18.2
39	Oregon	17.9
40	Alabama	17.1
41	Alaska	16.0
41	North Dakota	16.0
43	Arkansas	15.4
44	Utah	13.7
45	New Mexico	13.2
46	Maine	13.0
47	Montana	12.8
48	West Virginia	11.2
49	South Dakota	6.5
50	Vermont	4.8
	District of Columbia**	NA

Source: CQ Press using reported data from the Federal Bureau of Investigation
"Crime in the United States 2008" (Uniform Crime Reports, September 14, 2009, http://www.fbi.gov/ucr/ucr.htm)
*Arrests of youths 17 years and younger by law enforcement agencies submitting complete reports to the F.B.I. for 12 months in 2008. Robbery is the taking or attempting to take anything of value by force or threat of force.
**Not available.

Reported Arrests of Juveniles for Aggravated Assault in 2008

National Total = 48,059 Reported Arrests*

<table>
<tr><td colspan="4">ALPHA ORDER</td><td colspan="4">RANK ORDER</td></tr>
<tr><th>RANK</th><th>STATE</th><th>ARRESTS</th><th>% of USA</th><th>RANK</th><th>STATE</th><th>ARRESTS</th><th>% of USA</th></tr>
<tr><td>33</td><td>Alabama</td><td>321</td><td>0.7%</td><td>1</td><td>California</td><td>9,834</td><td>20.5%</td></tr>
<tr><td>37</td><td>Alaska</td><td>166</td><td>0.3%</td><td>2</td><td>Florida</td><td>5,090</td><td>10.6%</td></tr>
<tr><td>13</td><td>Arizona</td><td>1,105</td><td>2.3%</td><td>3</td><td>Pennsylvania</td><td>3,013</td><td>6.3%</td></tr>
<tr><td>31</td><td>Arkansas</td><td>354</td><td>0.7%</td><td>4</td><td>Texas</td><td>2,804</td><td>5.8%</td></tr>
<tr><td>1</td><td>California</td><td>9,834</td><td>20.5%</td><td>5</td><td>Illinois</td><td>1,846</td><td>3.8%</td></tr>
<tr><td>23</td><td>Colorado</td><td>607</td><td>1.3%</td><td>6</td><td>Maryland</td><td>1,627</td><td>3.4%</td></tr>
<tr><td>18</td><td>Connecticut</td><td>827</td><td>1.7%</td><td>7</td><td>New Jersey</td><td>1,432</td><td>3.0%</td></tr>
<tr><td>32</td><td>Delaware</td><td>350</td><td>0.7%</td><td>8</td><td>Massachusetts</td><td>1,396</td><td>2.9%</td></tr>
<tr><td>2</td><td>Florida</td><td>5,090</td><td>10.6%</td><td>9</td><td>New York</td><td>1,357</td><td>2.8%</td></tr>
<tr><td>14</td><td>Georgia</td><td>1,066</td><td>2.2%</td><td>10</td><td>Louisiana</td><td>1,352</td><td>2.8%</td></tr>
<tr><td>39</td><td>Hawaii</td><td>123</td><td>0.3%</td><td>11</td><td>Michigan</td><td>1,289</td><td>2.7%</td></tr>
<tr><td>36</td><td>Idaho</td><td>188</td><td>0.4%</td><td>12</td><td>North Carolina</td><td>1,163</td><td>2.4%</td></tr>
<tr><td>5</td><td>Illinois</td><td>1,846</td><td>3.8%</td><td>13</td><td>Arizona</td><td>1,105</td><td>2.3%</td></tr>
<tr><td>16</td><td>Indiana</td><td>1,043</td><td>2.2%</td><td>14</td><td>Georgia</td><td>1,066</td><td>2.2%</td></tr>
<tr><td>22</td><td>Iowa</td><td>614</td><td>1.3%</td><td>15</td><td>Tennessee</td><td>1,050</td><td>2.2%</td></tr>
<tr><td>34</td><td>Kansas</td><td>239</td><td>0.5%</td><td>16</td><td>Indiana</td><td>1,043</td><td>2.2%</td></tr>
<tr><td>40</td><td>Kentucky</td><td>122</td><td>0.3%</td><td>17</td><td>Missouri</td><td>1,002</td><td>2.1%</td></tr>
<tr><td>10</td><td>Louisiana</td><td>1,352</td><td>2.8%</td><td>18</td><td>Connecticut</td><td>827</td><td>1.7%</td></tr>
<tr><td>46</td><td>Maine</td><td>52</td><td>0.1%</td><td>19</td><td>Wisconsin</td><td>811</td><td>1.7%</td></tr>
<tr><td>6</td><td>Maryland</td><td>1,627</td><td>3.4%</td><td>20</td><td>Minnesota</td><td>708</td><td>1.5%</td></tr>
<tr><td>8</td><td>Massachusetts</td><td>1,396</td><td>2.9%</td><td>21</td><td>Washington</td><td>672</td><td>1.4%</td></tr>
<tr><td>11</td><td>Michigan</td><td>1,289</td><td>2.7%</td><td>22</td><td>Iowa</td><td>614</td><td>1.3%</td></tr>
<tr><td>20</td><td>Minnesota</td><td>708</td><td>1.5%</td><td>23</td><td>Colorado</td><td>607</td><td>1.3%</td></tr>
<tr><td>43</td><td>Mississippi</td><td>84</td><td>0.2%</td><td>24</td><td>South Carolina</td><td>569</td><td>1.2%</td></tr>
<tr><td>17</td><td>Missouri</td><td>1,002</td><td>2.1%</td><td>25</td><td>Oklahoma</td><td>530</td><td>1.1%</td></tr>
<tr><td>41</td><td>Montana</td><td>98</td><td>0.2%</td><td>26</td><td>Nevada</td><td>528</td><td>1.1%</td></tr>
<tr><td>38</td><td>Nebraska</td><td>149</td><td>0.3%</td><td>27</td><td>Virginia</td><td>527</td><td>1.1%</td></tr>
<tr><td>26</td><td>Nevada</td><td>528</td><td>1.1%</td><td>28</td><td>Ohio</td><td>488</td><td>1.0%</td></tr>
<tr><td>46</td><td>New Hampshire</td><td>52</td><td>0.1%</td><td>29</td><td>Oregon</td><td>460</td><td>1.0%</td></tr>
<tr><td>7</td><td>New Jersey</td><td>1,432</td><td>3.0%</td><td>30</td><td>New Mexico</td><td>367</td><td>0.8%</td></tr>
<tr><td>30</td><td>New Mexico</td><td>367</td><td>0.8%</td><td>31</td><td>Arkansas</td><td>354</td><td>0.7%</td></tr>
<tr><td>9</td><td>New York</td><td>1,357</td><td>2.8%</td><td>32</td><td>Delaware</td><td>350</td><td>0.7%</td></tr>
<tr><td>12</td><td>North Carolina</td><td>1,163</td><td>2.4%</td><td>33</td><td>Alabama</td><td>321</td><td>0.7%</td></tr>
<tr><td>48</td><td>North Dakota</td><td>49</td><td>0.1%</td><td>34</td><td>Kansas</td><td>239</td><td>0.5%</td></tr>
<tr><td>28</td><td>Ohio</td><td>488</td><td>1.0%</td><td>35</td><td>Utah</td><td>233</td><td>0.5%</td></tr>
<tr><td>25</td><td>Oklahoma</td><td>530</td><td>1.1%</td><td>36</td><td>Idaho</td><td>188</td><td>0.4%</td></tr>
<tr><td>29</td><td>Oregon</td><td>460</td><td>1.0%</td><td>37</td><td>Alaska</td><td>166</td><td>0.3%</td></tr>
<tr><td>3</td><td>Pennsylvania</td><td>3,013</td><td>6.3%</td><td>38</td><td>Nebraska</td><td>149</td><td>0.3%</td></tr>
<tr><td>41</td><td>Rhode Island</td><td>98</td><td>0.2%</td><td>39</td><td>Hawaii</td><td>123</td><td>0.3%</td></tr>
<tr><td>24</td><td>South Carolina</td><td>569</td><td>1.2%</td><td>40</td><td>Kentucky</td><td>122</td><td>0.3%</td></tr>
<tr><td>49</td><td>South Dakota</td><td>45</td><td>0.1%</td><td>41</td><td>Montana</td><td>98</td><td>0.2%</td></tr>
<tr><td>15</td><td>Tennessee</td><td>1,050</td><td>2.2%</td><td>41</td><td>Rhode Island</td><td>98</td><td>0.2%</td></tr>
<tr><td>4</td><td>Texas</td><td>2,804</td><td>5.8%</td><td>43</td><td>Mississippi</td><td>84</td><td>0.2%</td></tr>
<tr><td>35</td><td>Utah</td><td>233</td><td>0.5%</td><td>44</td><td>West Virginia</td><td>59</td><td>0.1%</td></tr>
<tr><td>50</td><td>Vermont</td><td>36</td><td>0.1%</td><td>45</td><td>Wyoming</td><td>53</td><td>0.1%</td></tr>
<tr><td>27</td><td>Virginia</td><td>527</td><td>1.1%</td><td>46</td><td>Maine</td><td>52</td><td>0.1%</td></tr>
<tr><td>21</td><td>Washington</td><td>672</td><td>1.4%</td><td>46</td><td>New Hampshire</td><td>52</td><td>0.1%</td></tr>
<tr><td>44</td><td>West Virginia</td><td>59</td><td>0.1%</td><td>48</td><td>North Dakota</td><td>49</td><td>0.1%</td></tr>
<tr><td>19</td><td>Wisconsin</td><td>811</td><td>1.7%</td><td>49</td><td>South Dakota</td><td>45</td><td>0.1%</td></tr>
<tr><td>45</td><td>Wyoming</td><td>53</td><td>0.1%</td><td>50</td><td>Vermont</td><td>36</td><td>0.1%</td></tr>
<tr><td></td><td></td><td></td><td></td><td></td><td>District of Columbia**</td><td>NA</td><td>NA</td></tr>
</table>

Source: Reported data from the Federal Bureau of Investigation
   "Crime in the United States 2008" (Uniform Crime Reports, September 14, 2009, http://www.fbi.gov/ucr/ucr.htm)
*Arrests of youths 17 years and younger by law enforcement agencies submitting complete reports to the F.B.I. for 12 months in 2008. Aggravated assault is an attack for the purpose of inflicting severe bodily injury. See important note at beginning of this chapter.
**Not available.

Reported Juvenile Arrest Rate for Aggravated Assault in 2008

National Rate = 178.6 Reported Arrests per 100,000 Juvenile Population*

ALPHA ORDER

RANK	STATE	RATE
40	Alabama	78.8
10	Alaska	212.9
19	Arizona	155.2
22	Arkansas	136.4
6	California	238.1
24	Colorado	133.9
8	Connecticut	235.1
2	Delaware	385.5
3	Florida	286.8
18	Georgia	157.4
31	Hawaii	113.1
32	Idaho	112.9
NA	Illinois**	NA
12	Indiana	201.7
11	Iowa	209.4
30	Kansas	115.7
NA	Kentucky**	NA
1	Louisiana	488.3
48	Maine	39.6
4	Maryland	270.3
7	Massachusetts	237.5
26	Michigan	132.8
27	Minnesota	130.4
45	Mississippi	55.8
16	Missouri	167.4
34	Montana	101.0
38	Nebraska	83.6
14	Nevada	188.6
47	New Hampshire	47.1
17	New Jersey	158.7
9	New Mexico	232.9
20	New York	141.5
15	North Carolina	167.5
37	North Dakota	84.4
44	Ohio	65.2
23	Oklahoma	136.2
29	Oregon	122.4
5	Pennsylvania	241.0
36	Rhode Island	91.4
28	South Carolina	123.2
43	South Dakota	66.1
13	Tennessee	200.2
33	Texas	103.4
39	Utah	79.1
41	Vermont	69.9
42	Virginia	67.8
25	Washington	133.2
46	West Virginia	54.8
21	Wisconsin	138.1
35	Wyoming	95.6

RANK ORDER

RANK	STATE	RATE
1	Louisiana	488.3
2	Delaware	385.5
3	Florida	286.8
4	Maryland	270.3
5	Pennsylvania	241.0
6	California	238.1
7	Massachusetts	237.5
8	Connecticut	235.1
9	New Mexico	232.9
10	Alaska	212.9
11	Iowa	209.4
12	Indiana	201.7
13	Tennessee	200.2
14	Nevada	188.6
15	North Carolina	167.5
16	Missouri	167.4
17	New Jersey	158.7
18	Georgia	157.4
19	Arizona	155.2
20	New York	141.5
21	Wisconsin	138.1
22	Arkansas	136.4
23	Oklahoma	136.2
24	Colorado	133.9
25	Washington	133.2
26	Michigan	132.8
27	Minnesota	130.4
28	South Carolina	123.2
29	Oregon	122.4
30	Kansas	115.7
31	Hawaii	113.1
32	Idaho	112.9
33	Texas	103.4
34	Montana	101.0
35	Wyoming	95.6
36	Rhode Island	91.4
37	North Dakota	84.4
38	Nebraska	83.6
39	Utah	79.1
40	Alabama	78.8
41	Vermont	69.9
42	Virginia	67.8
43	South Dakota	66.1
44	Ohio	65.2
45	Mississippi	55.8
46	West Virginia	54.8
47	New Hampshire	47.1
48	Maine	39.6
NA	Illinois**	NA
NA	Kentucky**	NA
	District of Columbia**	NA

Source: CQ Press using reported data from the Federal Bureau of Investigation

"Crime in the United States 2008" (Uniform Crime Reports, September 14, 2009, http://www.fbi.gov/ucr/ucr.htm)

*By law enforcement agencies submitting complete reports to the F.B.I. for 12 months in 2008. Arrests of youths 17 years and younger divided into population of 10 to 17 year olds. See important note at beginning of this chapter. Aggravated assault is an attack for the purpose of inflicting severe bodily injury.

**Not available.

Reported Arrests of Juveniles for Aggravated Assault as a Percent of All Such Arrests in 2008
National Percent = 13.1% of Reported Aggravated Assault Arrests*

ALPHA ORDER

RANK	STATE	PERCENT
48	Alabama	8.4
45	Alaska	9.4
12	Arizona	16.5
46	Arkansas	9.3
43	California	9.9
26	Colorado	13.0
3	Connecticut	19.1
10	Delaware	17.0
25	Florida	13.3
24	Georgia	13.5
16	Hawaii	15.3
15	Idaho	15.5
1	Illinois	37.1
6	Indiana	17.7
11	Iowa	16.7
32	Kansas	12.1
38	Kentucky	10.8
8	Louisiana	17.4
36	Maine	11.0
2	Maryland	20.7
22	Massachusetts	13.9
20	Michigan	14.0
9	Minnesota	17.2
49	Mississippi	7.8
37	Missouri	10.9
29	Montana	12.7
38	Nebraska	10.8
30	Nevada	12.4
26	New Hampshire	13.0
13	New Jersey	16.0
28	New Mexico	12.9
17	New York	14.9
47	North Carolina	8.7
19	North Dakota	14.6
22	Ohio	13.9
35	Oklahoma	11.4
20	Oregon	14.0
4	Pennsylvania	18.1
5	Rhode Island	17.9
40	South Carolina	10.5
31	South Dakota	12.2
40	Tennessee	10.5
32	Texas	12.1
7	Utah	17.6
42	Vermont	10.1
34	Virginia	11.5
18	Washington	14.8
50	West Virginia	5.5
14	Wisconsin	15.7
44	Wyoming	9.8

RANK ORDER

RANK	STATE	PERCENT
1	Illinois	37.1
2	Maryland	20.7
3	Connecticut	19.1
4	Pennsylvania	18.1
5	Rhode Island	17.9
6	Indiana	17.7
7	Utah	17.6
8	Louisiana	17.4
9	Minnesota	17.2
10	Delaware	17.0
11	Iowa	16.7
12	Arizona	16.5
13	New Jersey	16.0
14	Wisconsin	15.7
15	Idaho	15.5
16	Hawaii	15.3
17	New York	14.9
18	Washington	14.8
19	North Dakota	14.6
20	Michigan	14.0
20	Oregon	14.0
22	Massachusetts	13.9
22	Ohio	13.9
24	Georgia	13.5
25	Florida	13.3
26	Colorado	13.0
26	New Hampshire	13.0
28	New Mexico	12.9
29	Montana	12.7
30	Nevada	12.4
31	South Dakota	12.2
32	Kansas	12.1
32	Texas	12.1
34	Virginia	11.5
35	Oklahoma	11.4
36	Maine	11.0
37	Missouri	10.9
38	Kentucky	10.8
38	Nebraska	10.8
40	South Carolina	10.5
40	Tennessee	10.5
42	Vermont	10.1
43	California	9.9
44	Wyoming	9.8
45	Alaska	9.4
46	Arkansas	9.3
47	North Carolina	8.7
48	Alabama	8.4
49	Mississippi	7.8
50	West Virginia	5.5

District of Columbia** — NA

Source: CQ Press using reported data from the Federal Bureau of Investigation
"Crime in the United States 2008" (Uniform Crime Reports, September 14, 2009, http://www.fbi.gov/ucr/ucr.htm)
*Arrests of youths 17 years and younger by law enforcement agencies submitting complete reports to the F.B.I. for 12 months in 2008. Aggravated assault is an attack for the purpose of inflicting severe bodily injury.
**Not available.

Reported Arrests of Juveniles for Property Crime in 2008

National Total = 376,691 Reported Arrests*

ALPHA ORDER

RANK	STATE	ARRESTS	% of USA
30	Alabama	3,773	1.0%
43	Alaska	1,288	0.3%
9	Arizona	11,065	2.9%
29	Arkansas	3,796	1.0%
1	California	47,793	12.7%
16	Colorado	8,397	2.2%
28	Connecticut	4,093	1.1%
40	Delaware	1,620	0.4%
2	Florida	36,701	9.7%
13	Georgia	9,116	2.4%
41	Hawaii	1,531	0.4%
34	Idaho	2,942	0.8%
23	Illinois	6,078	1.6%
14	Indiana	8,963	2.4%
24	Iowa	5,276	1.4%
36	Kansas	2,293	0.6%
42	Kentucky	1,514	0.4%
27	Louisiana	4,319	1.1%
38	Maine	2,125	0.6%
6	Maryland	12,463	3.3%
33	Massachusetts	3,411	0.9%
11	Michigan	10,382	2.8%
12	Minnesota	10,262	2.7%
37	Mississippi	2,232	0.6%
7	Missouri	11,574	3.1%
39	Montana	1,782	0.5%
32	Nebraska	3,570	0.9%
26	Nevada	4,808	1.3%
48	New Hampshire	853	0.2%
17	New Jersey	8,307	2.2%
35	New Mexico	2,433	0.6%
10	New York	10,946	2.9%
8	North Carolina	11,202	3.0%
44	North Dakota	1,229	0.3%
18	Ohio	8,129	2.2%
25	Oklahoma	5,216	1.4%
19	Oregon	7,179	1.9%
5	Pennsylvania	13,798	3.7%
45	Rhode Island	1,177	0.3%
31	South Carolina	3,638	1.0%
46	South Dakota	1,121	0.3%
20	Tennessee	7,057	1.9%
3	Texas	32,028	8.5%
22	Utah	6,278	1.7%
50	Vermont	293	0.1%
21	Virginia	6,743	1.8%
15	Washington	8,865	2.4%
49	West Virginia	620	0.2%
4	Wisconsin	15,265	4.1%
47	Wyoming	1,097	0.3%

RANK ORDER

RANK	STATE	ARRESTS	% of USA
1	California	47,793	12.7%
2	Florida	36,701	9.7%
3	Texas	32,028	8.5%
4	Wisconsin	15,265	4.1%
5	Pennsylvania	13,798	3.7%
6	Maryland	12,463	3.3%
7	Missouri	11,574	3.1%
8	North Carolina	11,202	3.0%
9	Arizona	11,065	2.9%
10	New York	10,946	2.9%
11	Michigan	10,382	2.8%
12	Minnesota	10,262	2.7%
13	Georgia	9,116	2.4%
14	Indiana	8,963	2.4%
15	Washington	8,865	2.4%
16	Colorado	8,397	2.2%
17	New Jersey	8,307	2.2%
18	Ohio	8,129	2.2%
19	Oregon	7,179	1.9%
20	Tennessee	7,057	1.9%
21	Virginia	6,743	1.8%
22	Utah	6,278	1.7%
23	Illinois	6,078	1.6%
24	Iowa	5,276	1.4%
25	Oklahoma	5,216	1.4%
26	Nevada	4,808	1.3%
27	Louisiana	4,319	1.1%
28	Connecticut	4,093	1.1%
29	Arkansas	3,796	1.0%
30	Alabama	3,773	1.0%
31	South Carolina	3,638	1.0%
32	Nebraska	3,570	0.9%
33	Massachusetts	3,411	0.9%
34	Idaho	2,942	0.8%
35	New Mexico	2,433	0.6%
36	Kansas	2,293	0.6%
37	Mississippi	2,232	0.6%
38	Maine	2,125	0.6%
39	Montana	1,782	0.5%
40	Delaware	1,620	0.4%
41	Hawaii	1,531	0.4%
42	Kentucky	1,514	0.4%
43	Alaska	1,288	0.3%
44	North Dakota	1,229	0.3%
45	Rhode Island	1,177	0.3%
46	South Dakota	1,121	0.3%
47	Wyoming	1,097	0.3%
48	New Hampshire	853	0.2%
49	West Virginia	620	0.2%
50	Vermont	293	0.1%
	District of Columbia**	NA	NA

Source: Reported data from the Federal Bureau of Investigation
"Crime in the United States 2008" (Uniform Crime Reports, September 14, 2009, http://www.fbi.gov/ucr/ucr.htm)
*Arrests of youths 17 years and younger by law enforcement agencies submitting complete reports to the F.B.I. for 12 months in 2008. Property crimes are offenses of burglary, larceny-theft, motor vehicle theft, and arson. See important note at beginning of this chapter.
**Not available.

Reported Juvenile Arrest Rate for Property Crime in 2008

National Rate = 1,399.7 Reported Arrests per 100,000 Juvenile Population*

ALPHA ORDER

RANK	STATE	RATE
41	Alabama	925.9
19	Alaska	1,651.7
24	Arizona	1,554.0
27	Arkansas	1,462.2
34	California	1,157.0
11	Colorado	1,852.0
33	Connecticut	1,163.7
14	Delaware	1,784.1
5	Florida	2,068.2
29	Georgia	1,345.6
28	Hawaii	1,407.2
15	Idaho	1,767.2
NA	Illinois**	NA
17	Indiana	1,733.3
13	Iowa	1,799.6
36	Kansas	1,109.7
NA	Kentucky**	NA
23	Louisiana	1,560.0
21	Maine	1,617.0
4	Maryland	2,070.2
46	Massachusetts	580.3
40	Michigan	1,069.8
10	Minnesota	1,890.1
26	Mississippi	1,483.8
8	Missouri	1,933.4
12	Montana	1,837.2
6	Nebraska	2,004.2
18	Nevada	1,717.1
45	New Hampshire	772.1
42	New Jersey	920.6
25	New Mexico	1,543.7
35	New York	1,141.1
22	North Carolina	1,613.3
3	North Dakota	2,116.8
39	Ohio	1,086.2
31	Oklahoma	1,339.9
9	Oregon	1,909.7
37	Pennsylvania	1,103.7
38	Rhode Island	1,098.2
44	South Carolina	787.6
20	South Dakota	1,647.0
30	Tennessee	1,345.5
32	Texas	1,181.1
2	Utah	2,130.1
48	Vermont	569.1
43	Virginia	867.8
16	Washington	1,756.5
47	West Virginia	576.2
1	Wisconsin	2,599.2
7	Wyoming	1,978.7

RANK ORDER

RANK	STATE	RATE
1	Wisconsin	2,599.2
2	Utah	2,130.1
3	North Dakota	2,116.8
4	Maryland	2,070.2
5	Florida	2,068.2
6	Nebraska	2,004.2
7	Wyoming	1,978.7
8	Missouri	1,933.4
9	Oregon	1,909.7
10	Minnesota	1,890.1
11	Colorado	1,852.0
12	Montana	1,837.2
13	Iowa	1,799.6
14	Delaware	1,784.1
15	Idaho	1,767.2
16	Washington	1,756.5
17	Indiana	1,733.3
18	Nevada	1,717.1
19	Alaska	1,651.7
20	South Dakota	1,647.0
21	Maine	1,617.0
22	North Carolina	1,613.3
23	Louisiana	1,560.0
24	Arizona	1,554.0
25	New Mexico	1,543.7
26	Mississippi	1,483.8
27	Arkansas	1,462.2
28	Hawaii	1,407.2
29	Georgia	1,345.6
30	Tennessee	1,345.5
31	Oklahoma	1,339.9
32	Texas	1,181.1
33	Connecticut	1,163.7
34	California	1,157.0
35	New York	1,141.1
36	Kansas	1,109.7
37	Pennsylvania	1,103.7
38	Rhode Island	1,098.2
39	Ohio	1,086.2
40	Michigan	1,069.8
41	Alabama	925.9
42	New Jersey	920.6
43	Virginia	867.8
44	South Carolina	787.6
45	New Hampshire	772.1
46	Massachusetts	580.3
47	West Virginia	576.2
48	Vermont	569.1
NA	Illinois**	NA
NA	Kentucky**	NA
	District of Columbia**	NA

Source: CQ Press using reported data from the Federal Bureau of Investigation
"Crime in the United States 2008" (Uniform Crime Reports, September 14, 2009, http://www.fbi.gov/ucr/ucr.htm)
*By law enforcement agencies submitting complete reports to the F.B.I. for 12 months in 2008. Arrests of youths 17 years and younger divided into population of 10 to 17 year olds. See important note at beginning of this chapter. Property crimes are offenses of burglary, larceny-theft, motor vehicle theft, and arson.
**Not available.

Reported Arrests of Juveniles for Property Crime
as a Percent of All Such Arrests in 2008
National Percent = 25.9% of Reported Property Crime Arrests*

ALPHA ORDER

RANK	STATE	PERCENT
49	Alabama	15.4
15	Alaska	31.4
25	Arizona	26.4
30	Arkansas	24.6
20	California	28.0
12	Colorado	33.0
36	Connecticut	23.9
34	Delaware	24.0
31	Florida	24.5
33	Georgia	24.4
10	Hawaii	33.8
1	Idaho	42.0
27	Illinois	26.0
19	Indiana	29.4
5	Iowa	37.8
14	Kansas	31.9
39	Kentucky	22.6
41	Louisiana	21.9
29	Maine	25.5
13	Maryland	32.7
45	Massachusetts	18.5
18	Michigan	29.5
9	Minnesota	35.1
43	Mississippi	20.1
28	Missouri	25.6
4	Montana	38.6
6	Nebraska	37.2
21	Nevada	27.4
23	New Hampshire	27.0
34	New Jersey	24.0
23	New Mexico	27.0
40	New York	22.4
45	North Carolina	18.5
2	North Dakota	41.3
37	Ohio	22.9
17	Oklahoma	30.6
25	Oregon	26.4
38	Pennsylvania	22.7
16	Rhode Island	31.3
44	South Carolina	20.0
3	South Dakota	40.3
47	Tennessee	17.8
31	Texas	24.5
11	Utah	33.5
48	Vermont	17.1
42	Virginia	20.4
21	Washington	27.4
50	West Virginia	12.3
7	Wisconsin	36.0
8	Wyoming	35.7

RANK ORDER

RANK	STATE	PERCENT
1	Idaho	42.0
2	North Dakota	41.3
3	South Dakota	40.3
4	Montana	38.6
5	Iowa	37.8
6	Nebraska	37.2
7	Wisconsin	36.0
8	Wyoming	35.7
9	Minnesota	35.1
10	Hawaii	33.8
11	Utah	33.5
12	Colorado	33.0
13	Maryland	32.7
14	Kansas	31.9
15	Alaska	31.4
16	Rhode Island	31.3
17	Oklahoma	30.6
18	Michigan	29.5
19	Indiana	29.4
20	California	28.0
21	Nevada	27.4
21	Washington	27.4
23	New Hampshire	27.0
23	New Mexico	27.0
25	Arizona	26.4
25	Oregon	26.4
27	Illinois	26.0
28	Missouri	25.6
29	Maine	25.5
30	Arkansas	24.6
31	Florida	24.5
31	Texas	24.5
33	Georgia	24.4
34	Delaware	24.0
34	New Jersey	24.0
36	Connecticut	23.9
37	Ohio	22.9
38	Pennsylvania	22.7
39	Kentucky	22.6
40	New York	22.4
41	Louisiana	21.9
42	Virginia	20.4
43	Mississippi	20.1
44	South Carolina	20.0
45	Massachusetts	18.5
45	North Carolina	18.5
47	Tennessee	17.8
48	Vermont	17.1
49	Alabama	15.4
50	West Virginia	12.3

District of Columbia**   NA

Source: CQ Press using reported data from the Federal Bureau of Investigation
    "Crime in the United States 2008" (Uniform Crime Reports, September 14, 2009, http://www.fbi.gov/ucr/ucr.htm)
*Arrests of youths 17 years and younger by law enforcement agencies submitting complete reports to the F.B.I. for 12 months
in 2008. Property crimes are offenses of burglary, larceny-theft, motor vehicle theft, and arson.
**Not available.

Reported Arrests of Juveniles for Burglary in 2008

National Total = 74,171 Reported Arrests*

ALPHA ORDER

RANK	STATE	ARRESTS	% of USA
29	Alabama	760	1.0%
43	Alaska	145	0.2%
12	Arizona	1,523	2.1%
26	Arkansas	856	1.2%
1	California	15,658	21.1%
22	Colorado	1,002	1.4%
31	Connecticut	666	0.9%
38	Delaware	300	0.4%
2	Florida	9,753	13.1%
8	Georgia	2,188	2.9%
42	Hawaii	185	0.2%
34	Idaho	381	0.5%
19	Illinois	1,087	1.5%
17	Indiana	1,276	1.7%
30	Iowa	724	1.0%
39	Kansas	291	0.4%
37	Kentucky	313	0.4%
20	Louisiana	1,036	1.4%
35	Maine	372	0.5%
6	Maryland	2,318	3.1%
28	Massachusetts	761	1.0%
10	Michigan	1,729	2.3%
24	Minnesota	972	1.3%
32	Mississippi	561	0.8%
9	Missouri	1,799	2.4%
44	Montana	138	0.2%
36	Nebraska	331	0.4%
23	Nevada	1,000	1.3%
45	New Hampshire	134	0.2%
14	New Jersey	1,503	2.0%
40	New Mexico	259	0.3%
7	New York	2,273	3.1%
4	North Carolina	3,023	4.1%
47	North Dakota	100	0.1%
15	Ohio	1,479	2.0%
21	Oklahoma	1,024	1.4%
27	Oregon	813	1.1%
5	Pennsylvania	2,319	3.1%
41	Rhode Island	240	0.3%
25	South Carolina	858	1.2%
46	South Dakota	105	0.1%
16	Tennessee	1,404	1.9%
3	Texas	5,599	7.5%
33	Utah	396	0.5%
50	Vermont	60	0.1%
18	Virginia	1,154	1.6%
13	Washington	1,515	2.0%
49	West Virginia	70	0.1%
11	Wisconsin	1,628	2.2%
48	Wyoming	90	0.1%

RANK ORDER

RANK	STATE	ARRESTS	% of USA
1	California	15,658	21.1%
2	Florida	9,753	13.1%
3	Texas	5,599	7.5%
4	North Carolina	3,023	4.1%
5	Pennsylvania	2,319	3.1%
6	Maryland	2,318	3.1%
7	New York	2,273	3.1%
8	Georgia	2,188	2.9%
9	Missouri	1,799	2.4%
10	Michigan	1,729	2.3%
11	Wisconsin	1,628	2.2%
12	Arizona	1,523	2.1%
13	Washington	1,515	2.0%
14	New Jersey	1,503	2.0%
15	Ohio	1,479	2.0%
16	Tennessee	1,404	1.9%
17	Indiana	1,276	1.7%
18	Virginia	1,154	1.6%
19	Illinois	1,087	1.5%
20	Louisiana	1,036	1.4%
21	Oklahoma	1,024	1.4%
22	Colorado	1,002	1.4%
23	Nevada	1,000	1.3%
24	Minnesota	972	1.3%
25	South Carolina	858	1.2%
26	Arkansas	856	1.2%
27	Oregon	813	1.1%
28	Massachusetts	761	1.0%
29	Alabama	760	1.0%
30	Iowa	724	1.0%
31	Connecticut	666	0.9%
32	Mississippi	561	0.8%
33	Utah	396	0.5%
34	Idaho	381	0.5%
35	Maine	372	0.5%
36	Nebraska	331	0.4%
37	Kentucky	313	0.4%
38	Delaware	300	0.4%
39	Kansas	291	0.4%
40	New Mexico	259	0.3%
41	Rhode Island	240	0.3%
42	Hawaii	185	0.2%
43	Alaska	145	0.2%
44	Montana	138	0.2%
45	New Hampshire	134	0.2%
46	South Dakota	105	0.1%
47	North Dakota	100	0.1%
48	Wyoming	90	0.1%
49	West Virginia	70	0.1%
50	Vermont	60	0.1%
	District of Columbia**	NA	NA

Source: Reported data from the Federal Bureau of Investigation
  "Crime in the United States 2008" (Uniform Crime Reports, September 14, 2009, http://www.fbi.gov/ucr/ucr.htm)
*Arrests of youths 17 years and younger by law enforcement agencies submitting complete reports to the F.B.I. for 12 months in 2008. Burglary is the unlawful entry of a structure to commit a felony or theft. Attempts are included. See important note at beginning of this chapter.
**Not available.

Reported Juvenile Arrest Rate for Burglary in 2008

National Rate = 275.6 Reported Arrests per 100,000 Juvenile Population*

ALPHA ORDER

RANK	STATE	RATE
28	Alabama	186.5
29	Alaska	185.9
24	Arizona	213.9
9	Arkansas	329.7
4	California	379.1
22	Colorado	221.0
27	Connecticut	189.4
8	Delaware	330.4
1	Florida	549.6
10	Georgia	323.0
36	Hawaii	170.0
20	Idaho	228.9
NA	Illinois**	NA
18	Indiana	246.8
17	Iowa	247.0
43	Kansas	140.8
NA	Kentucky**	NA
5	Louisiana	374.2
13	Maine	283.1
3	Maryland	385.0
45	Massachusetts	129.5
34	Michigan	178.2
33	Minnesota	179.0
6	Mississippi	373.0
11	Missouri	300.5
42	Montana	142.3
30	Nebraska	185.8
7	Nevada	357.1
46	New Hampshire	121.3
37	New Jersey	166.6
38	New Mexico	164.3
19	New York	237.0
2	North Carolina	435.4
35	North Dakota	172.2
26	Ohio	197.6
16	Oklahoma	263.1
23	Oregon	216.3
32	Pennsylvania	185.5
21	Rhode Island	223.9
31	South Carolina	185.7
40	South Dakota	154.3
15	Tennessee	267.7
25	Texas	206.5
44	Utah	134.4
47	Vermont	116.5
41	Virginia	148.5
12	Washington	300.2
48	West Virginia	65.1
14	Wisconsin	277.2
39	Wyoming	162.3

RANK ORDER

RANK	STATE	RATE
1	Florida	549.6
2	North Carolina	435.4
3	Maryland	385.0
4	California	379.1
5	Louisiana	374.2
6	Mississippi	373.0
7	Nevada	357.1
8	Delaware	330.4
9	Arkansas	329.7
10	Georgia	323.0
11	Missouri	300.5
12	Washington	300.2
13	Maine	283.1
14	Wisconsin	277.2
15	Tennessee	267.7
16	Oklahoma	263.1
17	Iowa	247.0
18	Indiana	246.8
19	New York	237.0
20	Idaho	228.9
21	Rhode Island	223.9
22	Colorado	221.0
23	Oregon	216.3
24	Arizona	213.9
25	Texas	206.5
26	Ohio	197.6
27	Connecticut	189.4
28	Alabama	186.5
29	Alaska	185.9
30	Nebraska	185.8
31	South Carolina	185.7
32	Pennsylvania	185.5
33	Minnesota	179.0
34	Michigan	178.2
35	North Dakota	172.2
36	Hawaii	170.0
37	New Jersey	166.6
38	New Mexico	164.3
39	Wyoming	162.3
40	South Dakota	154.3
41	Virginia	148.5
42	Montana	142.3
43	Kansas	140.8
44	Utah	134.4
45	Massachusetts	129.5
46	New Hampshire	121.3
47	Vermont	116.5
48	West Virginia	65.1
NA	Illinois**	NA
NA	Kentucky**	NA
	District of Columbia**	NA

Source: CQ Press using reported data from the Federal Bureau of Investigation
    "Crime in the United States 2008" (Uniform Crime Reports, September 14, 2009, http://www.fbi.gov/ucr/ucr.htm)
*By law enforcement agencies submitting complete reports to the F.B.I. for 12 months in 2008. Arrests of youths 17 years and younger divided into population of 10 to 17 year olds. See important note at beginning of this chapter. Burglary is the unlawful entry of a structure to commit a felony or theft. Attempts are included.
**Not available.

Reported Arrests of Juveniles for Burglary
as a Percent of All Such Arrests in 2008
National Percent = 27.7% of Reported Burglary Arrests*

ALPHA ORDER

RANK	STATE	PERCENT
49	Alabama	18.5
12	Alaska	31.7
19	Arizona	29.9
24	Arkansas	28.6
28	California	27.8
9	Colorado	33.5
41	Connecticut	23.4
32	Delaware	27.2
14	Florida	31.0
10	Georgia	32.9
17	Hawaii	30.8
1	Idaho	40.6
4	Illinois	37.6
26	Indiana	28.5
3	Iowa	38.0
30	Kansas	27.6
35	Kentucky	25.7
33	Louisiana	27.0
31	Maine	27.5
13	Maryland	31.3
47	Massachusetts	20.4
29	Michigan	27.7
23	Minnesota	28.7
37	Mississippi	25.0
36	Missouri	25.4
2	Montana	38.3
6	Nebraska	36.5
24	Nevada	28.6
18	New Hampshire	30.7
41	New Jersey	23.4
45	New Mexico	21.3
22	New York	28.8
46	North Carolina	20.9
7	North Dakota	35.6
40	Ohio	23.8
10	Oklahoma	32.9
21	Oregon	28.9
44	Pennsylvania	22.5
15	Rhode Island	30.9
39	South Carolina	24.2
5	South Dakota	37.4
43	Tennessee	22.6
27	Texas	28.4
20	Utah	29.5
48	Vermont	20.0
37	Virginia	25.0
15	Washington	30.9
50	West Virginia	12.0
8	Wisconsin	34.9
34	Wyoming	26.9

RANK ORDER

RANK	STATE	PERCENT
1	Idaho	40.6
2	Montana	38.3
3	Iowa	38.0
4	Illinois	37.6
5	South Dakota	37.4
6	Nebraska	36.5
7	North Dakota	35.6
8	Wisconsin	34.9
9	Colorado	33.5
10	Georgia	32.9
10	Oklahoma	32.9
12	Alaska	31.7
13	Maryland	31.3
14	Florida	31.0
15	Rhode Island	30.9
15	Washington	30.9
17	Hawaii	30.8
18	New Hampshire	30.7
19	Arizona	29.9
20	Utah	29.5
21	Oregon	28.9
22	New York	28.8
23	Minnesota	28.7
24	Arkansas	28.6
24	Nevada	28.6
26	Indiana	28.5
27	Texas	28.4
28	California	27.8
29	Michigan	27.7
30	Kansas	27.6
31	Maine	27.5
32	Delaware	27.2
33	Louisiana	27.0
34	Wyoming	26.9
35	Kentucky	25.7
36	Missouri	25.4
37	Mississippi	25.0
37	Virginia	25.0
39	South Carolina	24.2
40	Ohio	23.8
41	Connecticut	23.4
41	New Jersey	23.4
43	Tennessee	22.6
44	Pennsylvania	22.5
45	New Mexico	21.3
46	North Carolina	20.9
47	Massachusetts	20.4
48	Vermont	20.0
49	Alabama	18.5
50	West Virginia	12.0

District of Columbia** — NA

Source: CQ Press using reported data from the Federal Bureau of Investigation
"Crime in the United States 2008" (Uniform Crime Reports, September 14, 2009, http://www.fbi.gov/ucr/ucr.htm)
*Arrests of youths 17 years and younger by law enforcement agencies submitting complete reports to the F.B.I. for 12 months in 2008. Burglary is the unlawful entry of a structure to commit a felony or theft. Attempts are included.
**Not available.

Reported Arrests of Juveniles for Larceny-Theft in 2008

National Total = 276,140 Reported Arrests*

ALPHA ORDER

RANK	STATE	ARRESTS	% of USA
30	Alabama	2,844	1.0%
43	Alaska	1,055	0.4%
8	Arizona	8,769	3.2%
31	Arkansas	2,843	1.0%
1	California	27,836	10.1%
14	Colorado	6,866	2.5%
27	Connecticut	3,179	1.2%
40	Delaware	1,246	0.5%
3	Florida	24,657	8.9%
17	Georgia	6,246	2.3%
41	Hawaii	1,225	0.4%
34	Idaho	2,411	0.9%
26	Illinois	3,345	1.2%
13	Indiana	6,902	2.5%
23	Iowa	4,239	1.5%
36	Kansas	1,882	0.7%
42	Kentucky	1,122	0.4%
29	Louisiana	3,045	1.1%
37	Maine	1,632	0.6%
9	Maryland	8,415	3.0%
33	Massachusetts	2,469	0.9%
12	Michigan	7,676	2.8%
7	Minnesota	8,824	3.2%
38	Mississippi	1,535	0.6%
6	Missouri	8,861	3.2%
39	Montana	1,503	0.5%
28	Nebraska	3,063	1.1%
25	Nevada	3,435	1.2%
48	New Hampshire	671	0.2%
16	New Jersey	6,335	2.3%
35	New Mexico	2,056	0.7%
10	New York	8,056	2.9%
11	North Carolina	7,767	2.8%
44	North Dakota	1,036	0.4%
18	Ohio	6,204	2.2%
24	Oklahoma	3,909	1.4%
19	Oregon	5,925	2.1%
5	Pennsylvania	10,329	3.7%
47	Rhode Island	865	0.3%
32	South Carolina	2,621	0.9%
46	South Dakota	929	0.3%
22	Tennessee	5,141	1.9%
2	Texas	25,055	9.1%
20	Utah	5,666	2.1%
50	Vermont	202	0.1%
21	Virginia	5,198	1.9%
15	Washington	6,814	2.5%
49	West Virginia	517	0.2%
4	Wisconsin	12,744	4.6%
45	Wyoming	944	0.3%

RANK ORDER

RANK	STATE	ARRESTS	% of USA
1	California	27,836	10.1%
2	Texas	25,055	9.1%
3	Florida	24,657	8.9%
4	Wisconsin	12,744	4.6%
5	Pennsylvania	10,329	3.7%
6	Missouri	8,861	3.2%
7	Minnesota	8,824	3.2%
8	Arizona	8,769	3.2%
9	Maryland	8,415	3.0%
10	New York	8,056	2.9%
11	North Carolina	7,767	2.8%
12	Michigan	7,676	2.8%
13	Indiana	6,902	2.5%
14	Colorado	6,866	2.5%
15	Washington	6,814	2.5%
16	New Jersey	6,335	2.3%
17	Georgia	6,246	2.3%
18	Ohio	6,204	2.2%
19	Oregon	5,925	2.1%
20	Utah	5,666	2.1%
21	Virginia	5,198	1.9%
22	Tennessee	5,141	1.9%
23	Iowa	4,239	1.5%
24	Oklahoma	3,909	1.4%
25	Nevada	3,435	1.2%
26	Illinois	3,345	1.2%
27	Connecticut	3,179	1.2%
28	Nebraska	3,063	1.1%
29	Louisiana	3,045	1.1%
30	Alabama	2,844	1.0%
31	Arkansas	2,843	1.0%
32	South Carolina	2,621	0.9%
33	Massachusetts	2,469	0.9%
34	Idaho	2,411	0.9%
35	New Mexico	2,056	0.7%
36	Kansas	1,882	0.7%
37	Maine	1,632	0.6%
38	Mississippi	1,535	0.6%
39	Montana	1,503	0.5%
40	Delaware	1,246	0.5%
41	Hawaii	1,225	0.4%
42	Kentucky	1,122	0.4%
43	Alaska	1,055	0.4%
44	North Dakota	1,036	0.4%
45	Wyoming	944	0.3%
46	South Dakota	929	0.3%
47	Rhode Island	865	0.3%
48	New Hampshire	671	0.2%
49	West Virginia	517	0.2%
50	Vermont	202	0.1%
	District of Columbia**	NA	NA

Source: Reported data from the Federal Bureau of Investigation
"Crime in the United States 2008" (Uniform Crime Reports, September 14, 2009, http://www.fbi.gov/ucr/ucr.htm)
*Arrests of youths 17 years and younger by law enforcement agencies submitting complete reports to the F.B.I. for 12 months in 2008. Larceny-theft is the unlawful taking of property without use of force, violence, or fraud. Attempts are included. Motor vehicle thefts are excluded. See important note at beginning of this chapter.
**Not available.

Reported Juvenile Arrest Rate for Larceny-Theft in 2008

National Rate = 1,026.1 Reported Arrests per 100,000 Juvenile Population*

ALPHA ORDER

RANK	STATE	RATE
41	Alabama	697.9
17	Alaska	1,352.9
22	Arizona	1,231.5
27	Arkansas	1,095.1
42	California	673.9
9	Colorado	1,514.3
34	Connecticut	903.9
15	Delaware	1,372.2
14	Florida	1,389.5
32	Georgia	922.0
24	Hawaii	1,126.0
11	Idaho	1,448.2
NA	Illinois**	NA
19	Indiana	1,334.8
12	Iowa	1,445.9
33	Kansas	910.8
NA	Kentucky**	NA
26	Louisiana	1,099.8
21	Maine	1,241.8
13	Maryland	1,397.8
47	Massachusetts	420.0
39	Michigan	791.0
6	Minnesota	1,625.3
28	Mississippi	1,020.5
10	Missouri	1,480.2
8	Montana	1,549.6
4	Nebraska	1,719.6
23	Nevada	1,226.8
44	New Hampshire	607.3
40	New Jersey	702.1
20	New Mexico	1,304.5
35	New York	839.8
25	North Carolina	1,118.6
3	North Dakota	1,784.4
36	Ohio	828.9
29	Oklahoma	1,004.2
7	Oregon	1,576.1
37	Pennsylvania	826.2
38	Rhode Island	807.1
45	South Carolina	567.4
16	South Dakota	1,364.9
30	Tennessee	980.2
31	Texas	924.0
2	Utah	1,922.5
48	Vermont	392.3
43	Virginia	669.0
18	Washington	1,350.1
46	West Virginia	480.5
1	Wisconsin	2,169.9
5	Wyoming	1,702.7

RANK ORDER

RANK	STATE	RATE
1	Wisconsin	2,169.9
2	Utah	1,922.5
3	North Dakota	1,784.4
4	Nebraska	1,719.6
5	Wyoming	1,702.7
6	Minnesota	1,625.3
7	Oregon	1,576.1
8	Montana	1,549.6
9	Colorado	1,514.3
10	Missouri	1,480.2
11	Idaho	1,448.2
12	Iowa	1,445.9
13	Maryland	1,397.8
14	Florida	1,389.5
15	Delaware	1,372.2
16	South Dakota	1,364.9
17	Alaska	1,352.9
18	Washington	1,350.1
19	Indiana	1,334.8
20	New Mexico	1,304.5
21	Maine	1,241.8
22	Arizona	1,231.5
23	Nevada	1,226.8
24	Hawaii	1,126.0
25	North Carolina	1,118.6
26	Louisiana	1,099.8
27	Arkansas	1,095.1
28	Mississippi	1,020.5
29	Oklahoma	1,004.2
30	Tennessee	980.2
31	Texas	924.0
32	Georgia	922.0
33	Kansas	910.8
34	Connecticut	903.9
35	New York	839.8
36	Ohio	828.9
37	Pennsylvania	826.2
38	Rhode Island	807.1
39	Michigan	791.0
40	New Jersey	702.1
41	Alabama	697.9
42	California	673.9
43	Virginia	669.0
44	New Hampshire	607.3
45	South Carolina	567.4
46	West Virginia	480.5
47	Massachusetts	420.0
48	Vermont	392.3
NA	Illinois**	NA
NA	Kentucky**	NA
	District of Columbia**	NA

Source: CQ Press using reported data from the Federal Bureau of Investigation
     "Crime in the United States 2008" (Uniform Crime Reports, September 14, 2009, http://www.fbi.gov/ucr/ucr.htm)
*By law enforcement agencies submitting complete reports to the F.B.I. for 12 months in 2008. Arrests of youths 17 years and younger divided into population of 10 to 17 year olds. See important note at beginning of this chapter. Larceny-theft is the unlawful taking of property without use of force, violence, or fraud. Attempts are included. Motor vehicle thefts are excluded.
**Not available.

Reported Arrests of Juveniles for Larceny-Theft
as a Percent of All Such Arrests in 2008
National Percent = 25.3% of Reported Larceny and Theft Arrests*

RANK	STATE	PERCENT
49	Alabama	14.8
14	Alaska	31.6
25	Arizona	25.8
30	Arkansas	23.8
19	California	29.2
13	Colorado	32.8
31	Connecticut	23.6
33	Delaware	23.1
34	Florida	22.6
37	Georgia	21.9
10	Hawaii	35.3
1	Idaho	41.6
39	Illinois	21.1
20	Indiana	28.9
5	Iowa	37.4
12	Kansas	33.1
38	Kentucky	21.3
41	Louisiana	20.6
28	Maine	24.8
15	Maryland	31.3
45	Massachusetts	17.8
18	Michigan	29.9
7	Minnesota	36.5
44	Mississippi	18.5
27	Missouri	25.7
4	Montana	37.8
6	Nebraska	37.2
22	Nevada	27.0
25	New Hampshire	25.8
32	New Jersey	23.5
21	New Mexico	28.0
40	New York	20.9
46	North Carolina	17.6
2	North Dakota	41.5
36	Ohio	22.2
17	Oklahoma	30.0
24	Oregon	26.2
35	Pennsylvania	22.3
16	Rhode Island	31.0
43	South Carolina	19.1
3	South Dakota	39.7
47	Tennessee	16.6
29	Texas	24.0
11	Utah	33.7
48	Vermont	15.4
42	Virginia	19.2
23	Washington	26.4
50	West Virginia	12.1
9	Wisconsin	35.7
8	Wyoming	36.4

RANK	STATE	PERCENT
1	Idaho	41.6
2	North Dakota	41.5
3	South Dakota	39.7
4	Montana	37.8
5	Iowa	37.4
6	Nebraska	37.2
7	Minnesota	36.5
8	Wyoming	36.4
9	Wisconsin	35.7
10	Hawaii	35.3
11	Utah	33.7
12	Kansas	33.1
13	Colorado	32.8
14	Alaska	31.6
15	Maryland	31.3
16	Rhode Island	31.0
17	Oklahoma	30.0
18	Michigan	29.9
19	California	29.2
20	Indiana	28.9
21	New Mexico	28.0
22	Nevada	27.0
23	Washington	26.4
24	Oregon	26.2
25	Arizona	25.8
25	New Hampshire	25.8
27	Missouri	25.7
28	Maine	24.8
29	Texas	24.0
30	Arkansas	23.8
31	Connecticut	23.6
32	New Jersey	23.5
33	Delaware	23.1
34	Florida	22.6
35	Pennsylvania	22.3
36	Ohio	22.2
37	Georgia	21.9
38	Kentucky	21.3
39	Illinois	21.1
40	New York	20.9
41	Louisiana	20.6
42	Virginia	19.2
43	South Carolina	19.1
44	Mississippi	18.5
45	Massachusetts	17.8
46	North Carolina	17.6
47	Tennessee	16.6
48	Vermont	15.4
49	Alabama	14.8
50	West Virginia	12.1

District of Columbia**   NA

Source: CQ Press using reported data from the Federal Bureau of Investigation
"Crime in the United States 2008" (Uniform Crime Reports, September 14, 2009, http://www.fbi.gov/ucr/ucr.htm)
*Arrests of youths 17 years and younger by law enforcement agencies submitting complete reports to the F.B.I. for 12 months in 2008. Larceny-theft is the unlawful taking of property without use of force, violence, or fraud. Attempts are included. Motor vehicle thefts are excluded.
**Not available.

Reported Arrests of Juveniles for Motor Vehicle Theft in 2008

National Total = 21,215 Reported Arrests*

ALPHA ORDER

RANK	STATE	ARRESTS	% of USA
29	Alabama	137	0.6%
42	Alaska	63	0.3%
12	Arizona	613	2.9%
40	Arkansas	77	0.4%
1	California	3,477	16.4%
16	Colorado	398	1.9%
26	Connecticut	199	0.9%
46	Delaware	37	0.2%
2	Florida	2,147	10.1%
11	Georgia	624	2.9%
33	Hawaii	109	0.5%
39	Idaho	78	0.4%
3	Illinois	1,619	7.6%
10	Indiana	673	3.2%
23	Iowa	228	1.1%
38	Kansas	80	0.4%
45	Kentucky	44	0.2%
25	Louisiana	207	1.0%
36	Maine	93	0.4%
4	Maryland	1,405	6.6%
30	Massachusetts	131	0.6%
7	Michigan	845	4.0%
17	Minnesota	368	1.7%
35	Mississippi	101	0.5%
8	Missouri	767	3.6%
34	Montana	108	0.5%
31	Nebraska	129	0.6%
21	Nevada	254	1.2%
50	New Hampshire	22	0.1%
22	New Jersey	233	1.1%
41	New Mexico	73	0.3%
13	New York	464	2.2%
19	North Carolina	303	1.4%
37	North Dakota	86	0.4%
18	Ohio	335	1.6%
27	Oklahoma	159	0.7%
20	Oregon	261	1.2%
6	Pennsylvania	849	4.0%
46	Rhode Island	37	0.2%
32	South Carolina	116	0.5%
43	South Dakota	56	0.3%
14	Tennessee	434	2.0%
5	Texas	1,113	5.2%
28	Utah	153	0.7%
49	Vermont	23	0.1%
24	Virginia	221	1.0%
15	Washington	401	1.9%
48	West Virginia	28	0.1%
8	Wisconsin	767	3.6%
44	Wyoming	51	0.2%

RANK ORDER

RANK	STATE	ARRESTS	% of USA
1	California	3,477	16.4%
2	Florida	2,147	10.1%
3	Illinois	1,619	7.6%
4	Maryland	1,405	6.6%
5	Texas	1,113	5.2%
6	Pennsylvania	849	4.0%
7	Michigan	845	4.0%
8	Missouri	767	3.6%
8	Wisconsin	767	3.6%
10	Indiana	673	3.2%
11	Georgia	624	2.9%
12	Arizona	613	2.9%
13	New York	464	2.2%
14	Tennessee	434	2.0%
15	Washington	401	1.9%
16	Colorado	398	1.9%
17	Minnesota	368	1.7%
18	Ohio	335	1.6%
19	North Carolina	303	1.4%
20	Oregon	261	1.2%
21	Nevada	254	1.2%
22	New Jersey	233	1.1%
23	Iowa	228	1.1%
24	Virginia	221	1.0%
25	Louisiana	207	1.0%
26	Connecticut	199	0.9%
27	Oklahoma	159	0.7%
28	Utah	153	0.7%
29	Alabama	137	0.6%
30	Massachusetts	131	0.6%
31	Nebraska	129	0.6%
32	South Carolina	116	0.5%
33	Hawaii	109	0.5%
34	Montana	108	0.5%
35	Mississippi	101	0.5%
36	Maine	93	0.4%
37	North Dakota	86	0.4%
38	Kansas	80	0.4%
39	Idaho	78	0.4%
40	Arkansas	77	0.4%
41	New Mexico	73	0.3%
42	Alaska	63	0.3%
43	South Dakota	56	0.3%
44	Wyoming	51	0.2%
45	Kentucky	44	0.2%
46	Delaware	37	0.2%
46	Rhode Island	37	0.2%
48	West Virginia	28	0.1%
49	Vermont	23	0.1%
50	New Hampshire	22	0.1%
	District of Columbia**	NA	NA

Source: Reported data from the Federal Bureau of Investigation

"Crime in the United States 2008" (Uniform Crime Reports, September 14, 2009, http://www.fbi.gov/ucr/ucr.htm)

*Arrests of youths 17 years and younger by law enforcement agencies submitting complete reports to the F.B.I. for 12 months in 2008. Motor vehicle theft includes the theft or attempted theft of a self-propelled vehicle. Excludes motorboats, construction equipment, airplanes, and farming equipment. See important note at beginning of this chapter.

**Not available.

Reported Juvenile Arrest Rate for Motor Vehicle Theft in 2008

National Rate = 78.8 Reported Arrests per 100,000 Juvenile Population*

ALPHA ORDER

RANK	STATE	RATE
41	Alabama	33.6
18	Alaska	80.8
14	Arizona	86.1
42	Arkansas	29.7
15	California	84.2
12	Colorado	87.8
28	Connecticut	56.6
38	Delaware	40.7
6	Florida	121.0
9	Georgia	92.1
8	Hawaii	100.2
31	Idaho	46.9
NA	Illinois**	NA
4	Indiana	130.1
20	Iowa	77.8
39	Kansas	38.7
NA	Kentucky**	NA
21	Louisiana	74.8
23	Maine	70.8
1	Maryland	233.4
47	Massachusetts	22.3
13	Michigan	87.1
26	Minnesota	67.8
27	Mississippi	67.1
5	Missouri	128.1
7	Montana	111.3
22	Nebraska	72.4
11	Nevada	90.7
48	New Hampshire	19.9
45	New Jersey	25.8
32	New Mexico	46.3
30	New York	48.4
35	North Carolina	43.6
2	North Dakota	148.1
33	Ohio	44.8
37	Oklahoma	40.8
24	Oregon	69.4
25	Pennsylvania	67.9
40	Rhode Island	34.5
46	South Carolina	25.1
17	South Dakota	82.3
16	Tennessee	82.7
36	Texas	41.0
29	Utah	51.9
34	Vermont	44.7
43	Virginia	28.4
19	Washington	79.5
44	West Virginia	26.0
3	Wisconsin	130.6
10	Wyoming	92.0

RANK ORDER

RANK	STATE	RATE
1	Maryland	233.4
2	North Dakota	148.1
3	Wisconsin	130.6
4	Indiana	130.1
5	Missouri	128.1
6	Florida	121.0
7	Montana	111.3
8	Hawaii	100.2
9	Georgia	92.1
10	Wyoming	92.0
11	Nevada	90.7
12	Colorado	87.8
13	Michigan	87.1
14	Arizona	86.1
15	California	84.2
16	Tennessee	82.7
17	South Dakota	82.3
18	Alaska	80.8
19	Washington	79.5
20	Iowa	77.8
21	Louisiana	74.8
22	Nebraska	72.4
23	Maine	70.8
24	Oregon	69.4
25	Pennsylvania	67.9
26	Minnesota	67.8
27	Mississippi	67.1
28	Connecticut	56.6
29	Utah	51.9
30	New York	48.4
31	Idaho	46.9
32	New Mexico	46.3
33	Ohio	44.8
34	Vermont	44.7
35	North Carolina	43.6
36	Texas	41.0
37	Oklahoma	40.8
38	Delaware	40.7
39	Kansas	38.7
40	Rhode Island	34.5
41	Alabama	33.6
42	Arkansas	29.7
43	Virginia	28.4
44	West Virginia	26.0
45	New Jersey	25.8
46	South Carolina	25.1
47	Massachusetts	22.3
48	New Hampshire	19.9
NA	Illinois**	NA
NA	Kentucky**	NA
	District of Columbia**	NA

Source: CQ Press using reported data from the Federal Bureau of Investigation
"Crime in the United States 2008" (Uniform Crime Reports, September 14, 2009, http://www.fbi.gov/ucr/ucr.htm)
*By law enforcement agencies submitting complete reports to the F.B.I. for 12 months in 2008. Arrests of youths 17 years and younger divided into population of 10 to 17 year olds. See important note at beginning of this chapter. Motor vehicle theft includes the theft or attempted theft of a self-propelled vehicle. Excludes motorboats, construction equipment, airplanes, and farming equipment. **Not available.

Reported Arrests of Juveniles for Motor Vehicle Theft
as a Percent of All Such Arrests in 2008
National Percent = 25.2% of Reported Motor Vehicle Theft Arrests*

ALPHA ORDER

RANK ORDER

RANK	STATE	PERCENT
50	Alabama	12.8
31	Alaska	23.5
30	Arizona	23.6
45	Arkansas	18.5
41	California	20.2
14	Colorado	30.7
20	Connecticut	28.0
36	Delaware	21.6
29	Florida	23.7
15	Georgia	29.8
25	Hawaii	25.7
6	Idaho	42.2
9	Illinois	35.9
11	Indiana	34.2
7	Iowa	41.2
37	Kansas	21.5
16	Kentucky	29.3
35	Louisiana	22.5
19	Maine	28.2
5	Maryland	42.7
45	Massachusetts	18.5
17	Michigan	28.9
27	Minnesota	24.9
40	Mississippi	20.8
33	Missouri	22.9
3	Montana	47.6
10	Nebraska	34.5
34	Nevada	22.7
24	New Hampshire	25.9
26	New Jersey	25.4
39	New Mexico	20.9
32	New York	23.3
42	North Carolina	20.1
1	North Dakota	49.1
13	Ohio	31.0
21	Oklahoma	26.9
47	Oregon	18.0
28	Pennsylvania	24.4
22	Rhode Island	26.8
49	South Carolina	15.0
2	South Dakota	48.7
43	Tennessee	18.7
43	Texas	18.7
12	Utah	33.3
23	Vermont	26.4
38	Virginia	21.0
18	Washington	28.4
48	West Virginia	15.6
4	Wisconsin	46.1
8	Wyoming	40.8

RANK	STATE	PERCENT
1	North Dakota	49.1
2	South Dakota	48.7
3	Montana	47.6
4	Wisconsin	46.1
5	Maryland	42.7
6	Idaho	42.2
7	Iowa	41.2
8	Wyoming	40.8
9	Illinois	35.9
10	Nebraska	34.5
11	Indiana	34.2
12	Utah	33.3
13	Ohio	31.0
14	Colorado	30.7
15	Georgia	29.8
16	Kentucky	29.3
17	Michigan	28.9
18	Washington	28.4
19	Maine	28.2
20	Connecticut	28.0
21	Oklahoma	26.9
22	Rhode Island	26.8
23	Vermont	26.4
24	New Hampshire	25.9
25	Hawaii	25.7
26	New Jersey	25.4
27	Minnesota	24.9
28	Pennsylvania	24.4
29	Florida	23.7
30	Arizona	23.6
31	Alaska	23.5
32	New York	23.3
33	Missouri	22.9
34	Nevada	22.7
35	Louisiana	22.5
36	Delaware	21.6
37	Kansas	21.5
38	Virginia	21.0
39	New Mexico	20.9
40	Mississippi	20.8
41	California	20.2
42	North Carolina	20.1
43	Tennessee	18.7
43	Texas	18.7
45	Arkansas	18.5
45	Massachusetts	18.5
47	Oregon	18.0
48	West Virginia	15.6
49	South Carolina	15.0
50	Alabama	12.8

District of Columbia**   NA

Source: CQ Press using reported data from the Federal Bureau of Investigation
   "Crime in the United States 2008" (Uniform Crime Reports, September 14, 2009, http://www.fbi.gov/ucr/ucr.htm)
*Arrests of youths 17 years and younger by law enforcement agencies submitting complete reports to the F.B.I. for 12 months in 2008. Motor vehicle theft includes the theft or attempted theft of a self-propelled vehicle. Excludes motorboats, construction equipment, airplanes, and farming equipment.
**Not available.

Reported Arrests of Juveniles for Arson in 2008

National Total = 5,165 Reported Arrests*

ALPHA ORDER

RANK	STATE	ARRESTS	% of USA
38	Alabama	32	0.6%
44	Alaska	25	0.5%
8	Arizona	160	3.1%
45	Arkansas	20	0.4%
1	California	822	15.9%
14	Colorado	131	2.5%
28	Connecticut	49	0.9%
33	Delaware	37	0.7%
11	Florida	144	2.8%
26	Georgia	58	1.1%
46	Hawaii	12	0.2%
24	Idaho	72	1.4%
42	Illinois	27	0.5%
18	Indiana	112	2.2%
22	Iowa	85	1.6%
32	Kansas	40	0.8%
34	Kentucky	35	0.7%
39	Louisiana	31	0.6%
41	Maine	28	0.5%
2	Maryland	325	6.3%
27	Massachusetts	50	1.0%
13	Michigan	132	2.6%
21	Minnesota	98	1.9%
34	Mississippi	35	0.7%
10	Missouri	147	2.8%
37	Montana	33	0.6%
29	Nebraska	47	0.9%
17	Nevada	119	2.3%
43	New Hampshire	26	0.5%
5	New Jersey	236	4.6%
30	New Mexico	45	0.9%
9	New York	153	3.0%
20	North Carolina	109	2.1%
49	North Dakota	7	0.1%
19	Ohio	111	2.1%
16	Oklahoma	124	2.4%
6	Oregon	180	3.5%
3	Pennsylvania	301	5.8%
34	Rhode Island	35	0.7%
31	South Carolina	43	0.8%
39	South Dakota	31	0.6%
23	Tennessee	78	1.5%
4	Texas	261	5.1%
25	Utah	63	1.2%
48	Vermont	8	0.2%
7	Virginia	170	3.3%
12	Washington	135	2.6%
50	West Virginia	5	0.1%
15	Wisconsin	126	2.4%
46	Wyoming	12	0.2%

RANK ORDER

RANK	STATE	ARRESTS	% of USA
1	California	822	15.9%
2	Maryland	325	6.3%
3	Pennsylvania	301	5.8%
4	Texas	261	5.1%
5	New Jersey	236	4.6%
6	Oregon	180	3.5%
7	Virginia	170	3.3%
8	Arizona	160	3.1%
9	New York	153	3.0%
10	Missouri	147	2.8%
11	Florida	144	2.8%
12	Washington	135	2.6%
13	Michigan	132	2.6%
14	Colorado	131	2.5%
15	Wisconsin	126	2.4%
16	Oklahoma	124	2.4%
17	Nevada	119	2.3%
18	Indiana	112	2.2%
19	Ohio	111	2.1%
20	North Carolina	109	2.1%
21	Minnesota	98	1.9%
22	Iowa	85	1.6%
23	Tennessee	78	1.5%
24	Idaho	72	1.4%
25	Utah	63	1.2%
26	Georgia	58	1.1%
27	Massachusetts	50	1.0%
28	Connecticut	49	0.9%
29	Nebraska	47	0.9%
30	New Mexico	45	0.9%
31	South Carolina	43	0.8%
32	Kansas	40	0.8%
33	Delaware	37	0.7%
34	Kentucky	35	0.7%
34	Mississippi	35	0.7%
34	Rhode Island	35	0.7%
37	Montana	33	0.6%
38	Alabama	32	0.6%
39	Louisiana	31	0.6%
39	South Dakota	31	0.6%
41	Maine	28	0.5%
42	Illinois	27	0.5%
43	New Hampshire	26	0.5%
44	Alaska	25	0.5%
45	Arkansas	20	0.4%
46	Hawaii	12	0.2%
46	Wyoming	12	0.2%
48	Vermont	8	0.2%
49	North Dakota	7	0.1%
50	West Virginia	5	0.1%
	District of Columbia**	NA	NA

Source: Reported data from the Federal Bureau of Investigation
"Crime in the United States 2008" (Uniform Crime Reports, September 14, 2009, http://www.fbi.gov/ucr/ucr.htm)
*Arrests of youths 17 years and younger by law enforcement agencies submitting complete reports to the F.B.I. for 12 months in 2008. Arson is the willful burning of or attempt to burn a building, vehicle, or another's personal property. See important note at beginning of this chapter.
**Not available.

Reported Juvenile Arrest Rate for Arson in 2008

National Rate = 19.2 Reported Arrests per 100,000 Juvenile Population*

ALPHA ORDER

RANK ORDER

RANK	STATE	RATE		RANK	STATE	RATE
46	Alabama	7.9		1	Maryland	54.0
9	Alaska	32.1		2	Oregon	47.9
21	Arizona	22.5		3	South Dakota	45.5
47	Arkansas	7.7		4	Idaho	43.2
28	California	19.9		5	Nevada	42.5
12	Colorado	28.9		6	Delaware	40.7
36	Connecticut	13.9		7	Montana	34.0
6	Delaware	40.7		8	Rhode Island	32.7
45	Florida	8.1		9	Alaska	32.1
43	Georgia	8.6		10	Oklahoma	31.9
40	Hawaii	11.0		11	Iowa	29.0
4	Idaho	43.2		12	Colorado	28.9
NA	Illinois**	NA		13	New Mexico	28.6
23	Indiana	21.7		14	Washington	26.7
11	Iowa	29.0		15	Nebraska	26.4
29	Kansas	19.4		16	New Jersey	26.2
NA	Kentucky**	NA		17	Missouri	24.6
39	Louisiana	11.2		18	Pennsylvania	24.1
27	Maine	21.3		19	New Hampshire	23.5
1	Maryland	54.0		20	Mississippi	23.3
44	Massachusetts	8.5		21	Arizona	22.5
37	Michigan	13.6		22	Virginia	21.9
30	Minnesota	18.1		23	Indiana	21.7
20	Mississippi	23.3		24	Wyoming	21.6
17	Missouri	24.6		25	Wisconsin	21.5
7	Montana	34.0		26	Utah	21.4
15	Nebraska	26.4		27	Maine	21.3
5	Nevada	42.5		28	California	19.9
19	New Hampshire	23.5		29	Kansas	19.4
16	New Jersey	26.2		30	Minnesota	18.1
13	New Mexico	28.6		31	New York	15.9
31	New York	15.9		32	North Carolina	15.7
32	North Carolina	15.7		33	Vermont	15.5
38	North Dakota	12.1		34	Tennessee	14.9
35	Ohio	14.8		35	Ohio	14.8
10	Oklahoma	31.9		36	Connecticut	13.9
2	Oregon	47.9		37	Michigan	13.6
18	Pennsylvania	24.1		38	North Dakota	12.1
8	Rhode Island	32.7		39	Louisiana	11.2
42	South Carolina	9.3		40	Hawaii	11.0
3	South Dakota	45.5		41	Texas	9.6
34	Tennessee	14.9		42	South Carolina	9.3
41	Texas	9.6		43	Georgia	8.6
26	Utah	21.4		44	Massachusetts	8.5
33	Vermont	15.5		45	Florida	8.1
22	Virginia	21.9		46	Alabama	7.9
14	Washington	26.7		47	Arkansas	7.7
48	West Virginia	4.6		48	West Virginia	4.6
25	Wisconsin	21.5		NA	Illinois**	NA
24	Wyoming	21.6		NA	Kentucky**	NA
					District of Columbia**	NA

Source: CQ Press using reported data from the Federal Bureau of Investigation
  "Crime in the United States 2008" (Uniform Crime Reports, September 14, 2009, http://www.fbi.gov/ucr/ucr.htm)
*By law enforcement agencies submitting complete reports to the F.B.I. for 12 months in 2008. Arrests of youths 17 years and younger divided into population of 10 to 17 year olds. See important note at beginning of this chapter. Arson is the willful burning of or attempt to burn a building, vehicle, or another's personal property.
**Not available.

Reported Arrests of Juveniles for Arson
as a Percent of All Such Arrests in 2008
National Percent = 46.3% of Reported Arson Arrests*

ALPHA ORDER

RANK	STATE	PERCENT
48	Alabama	25.2
17	Alaska	54.3
5	Arizona	61.1
43	Arkansas	32.8
14	California	55.3
9	Colorado	58.0
32	Connecticut	41.5
19	Delaware	52.9
35	Florida	37.9
46	Georgia	30.5
33	Hawaii	38.7
1	Idaho	85.7
37	Illinois	36.0
21	Indiana	51.6
6	Iowa	60.3
24	Kansas	48.2
12	Kentucky	56.5
49	Louisiana	18.2
27	Maine	44.4
11	Maryland	57.5
36	Massachusetts	37.6
30	Michigan	44.0
21	Minnesota	51.6
40	Mississippi	34.7
34	Missouri	38.1
10	Montana	57.9
6	Nebraska	60.3
18	Nevada	54.1
14	New Hampshire	55.3
8	New Jersey	59.4
28	New Mexico	44.1
39	New York	35.2
41	North Carolina	34.5
44	North Dakota	31.8
25	Ohio	46.1
26	Oklahoma	44.6
20	Oregon	52.3
28	Pennsylvania	44.1
2	Rhode Island	74.5
42	South Carolina	33.6
3	South Dakota	70.5
47	Tennessee	29.2
38	Texas	35.7
4	Utah	61.8
31	Vermont	42.1
13	Virginia	55.6
23	Washington	48.9
50	West Virginia	14.7
45	Wisconsin	31.6
16	Wyoming	54.5

RANK ORDER

RANK	STATE	PERCENT
1	Idaho	85.7
2	Rhode Island	74.5
3	South Dakota	70.5
4	Utah	61.8
5	Arizona	61.1
6	Iowa	60.3
6	Nebraska	60.3
8	New Jersey	59.4
9	Colorado	58.0
10	Montana	57.9
11	Maryland	57.5
12	Kentucky	56.5
13	Virginia	55.6
14	California	55.3
14	New Hampshire	55.3
16	Wyoming	54.5
17	Alaska	54.3
18	Nevada	54.1
19	Delaware	52.9
20	Oregon	52.3
21	Indiana	51.6
21	Minnesota	51.6
23	Washington	48.9
24	Kansas	48.2
25	Ohio	46.1
26	Oklahoma	44.6
27	Maine	44.4
28	New Mexico	44.1
28	Pennsylvania	44.1
30	Michigan	44.0
31	Vermont	42.1
32	Connecticut	41.5
33	Hawaii	38.7
34	Missouri	38.1
35	Florida	37.9
36	Massachusetts	37.6
37	Illinois	36.0
38	Texas	35.7
39	New York	35.2
40	Mississippi	34.7
41	North Carolina	34.5
42	South Carolina	33.6
43	Arkansas	32.8
44	North Dakota	31.8
45	Wisconsin	31.6
46	Georgia	30.5
47	Tennessee	29.2
48	Alabama	25.2
49	Louisiana	18.2
50	West Virginia	14.7
	District of Columbia**	NA

Source: CQ Press using reported data from the Federal Bureau of Investigation
   "Crime in the United States 2008" (Uniform Crime Reports, September 14, 2009, http://www.fbi.gov/ucr/ucr.htm)
*Arrests of youths 17 years and younger by law enforcement agencies submitting complete reports to the F.B.I. for 12 months in 2008. Arson is the willful burning of or attempt to burn a building, vehicle, or another's personal property.
**Not available.

Reported Arrests of Juveniles for Weapons Violations in 2008

National Total = 32,656 Reported Arrests*

ALPHA ORDER

RANK	STATE	ARRESTS	% of USA
32	Alabama	190	0.6%
45	Alaska	33	0.1%
20	Arizona	538	1.6%
35	Arkansas	162	0.5%
1	California	8,131	24.9%
19	Colorado	556	1.7%
27	Connecticut	316	1.0%
36	Delaware	154	0.5%
2	Florida	1,852	5.7%
9	Georgia	1,344	4.1%
47	Hawaii	24	0.1%
34	Idaho	168	0.5%
10	Illinois	1,098	3.4%
28	Indiana	297	0.9%
36	Iowa	154	0.5%
39	Kansas	122	0.4%
40	Kentucky	58	0.2%
26	Louisiana	321	1.0%
42	Maine	46	0.1%
8	Maryland	1,357	4.2%
29	Massachusetts	265	0.8%
11	Michigan	824	2.5%
12	Minnesota	787	2.4%
33	Mississippi	187	0.6%
13	Missouri	728	2.2%
48	Montana	20	0.1%
31	Nebraska	198	0.6%
21	Nevada	444	1.4%
50	New Hampshire	13	0.0%
5	New Jersey	1,422	4.4%
30	New Mexico	211	0.6%
17	New York	575	1.8%
7	North Carolina	1,370	4.2%
44	North Dakota	41	0.1%
16	Ohio	592	1.8%
25	Oklahoma	323	1.0%
24	Oregon	328	1.0%
4	Pennsylvania	1,481	4.5%
38	Rhode Island	138	0.4%
22	South Carolina	438	1.3%
41	South Dakota	57	0.2%
15	Tennessee	604	1.8%
3	Texas	1,641	5.0%
23	Utah	355	1.1%
49	Vermont	15	0.0%
18	Virginia	558	1.7%
14	Washington	634	1.9%
46	West Virginia	27	0.1%
6	Wisconsin	1,402	4.3%
42	Wyoming	46	0.1%

RANK ORDER

RANK	STATE	ARRESTS	% of USA
1	California	8,131	24.9%
2	Florida	1,852	5.7%
3	Texas	1,641	5.0%
4	Pennsylvania	1,481	4.5%
5	New Jersey	1,422	4.4%
6	Wisconsin	1,402	4.3%
7	North Carolina	1,370	4.2%
8	Maryland	1,357	4.2%
9	Georgia	1,344	4.1%
10	Illinois	1,098	3.4%
11	Michigan	824	2.5%
12	Minnesota	787	2.4%
13	Missouri	728	2.2%
14	Washington	634	1.9%
15	Tennessee	604	1.8%
16	Ohio	592	1.8%
17	New York	575	1.8%
18	Virginia	558	1.7%
19	Colorado	556	1.7%
20	Arizona	538	1.6%
21	Nevada	444	1.4%
22	South Carolina	438	1.3%
23	Utah	355	1.1%
24	Oregon	328	1.0%
25	Oklahoma	323	1.0%
26	Louisiana	321	1.0%
27	Connecticut	316	1.0%
28	Indiana	297	0.9%
29	Massachusetts	265	0.8%
30	New Mexico	211	0.6%
31	Nebraska	198	0.6%
32	Alabama	190	0.6%
33	Mississippi	187	0.6%
34	Idaho	168	0.5%
35	Arkansas	162	0.5%
36	Delaware	154	0.5%
36	Iowa	154	0.5%
38	Rhode Island	138	0.4%
39	Kansas	122	0.4%
40	Kentucky	58	0.2%
41	South Dakota	57	0.2%
42	Maine	46	0.1%
42	Wyoming	46	0.1%
44	North Dakota	41	0.1%
45	Alaska	33	0.1%
46	West Virginia	27	0.1%
47	Hawaii	24	0.1%
48	Montana	20	0.1%
49	Vermont	15	0.0%
50	New Hampshire	13	0.0%
	District of Columbia**	NA	NA

Source: Reported data from the Federal Bureau of Investigation
"Crime in the United States 2008" (Uniform Crime Reports, September 14, 2009, http://www.fbi.gov/ucr/ucr.htm)
*Arrests of youths 17 years and younger by law enforcement agencies submitting complete reports to the F.B.I. for 12 months in 2008. Weapons violations include illegal carrying and possession. See important note at beginning of this chapter.
**Not available.

Reported Juvenile Arrest Rate for Weapons Violations in 2008

National Rate = 121.3 Reported Arrests per 100,000 Juvenile Population*

ALPHA ORDER

RANK	STATE	RATE
40	Alabama	46.6
42	Alaska	42.3
31	Arizona	75.6
34	Arkansas	62.4
5	California	196.8
14	Colorado	122.6
24	Connecticut	89.8
6	Delaware	169.6
21	Florida	104.4
3	Georgia	198.4
46	Hawaii	22.1
22	Idaho	100.9
NA	Illinois**	NA
38	Indiana	57.4
39	Iowa	52.5
37	Kansas	59.0
NA	Kentucky**	NA
18	Louisiana	115.9
43	Maine	35.0
2	Maryland	225.4
41	Massachusetts	45.1
26	Michigan	84.9
9	Minnesota	145.0
13	Mississippi	124.3
15	Missouri	121.6
47	Montana	20.6
20	Nebraska	111.2
7	Nevada	158.6
48	New Hampshire	11.8
8	New Jersey	157.6
10	New Mexico	133.9
36	New York	59.9
4	North Carolina	197.3
33	North Dakota	70.6
30	Ohio	79.1
28	Oklahoma	83.0
25	Oregon	87.3
17	Pennsylvania	118.5
11	Rhode Island	128.8
23	South Carolina	94.8
27	South Dakota	83.7
19	Tennessee	115.2
35	Texas	60.5
16	Utah	120.5
44	Vermont	29.1
32	Virginia	71.8
12	Washington	125.6
45	West Virginia	25.1
1	Wisconsin	238.7
28	Wyoming	83.0

RANK ORDER

RANK	STATE	RATE
1	Wisconsin	238.7
2	Maryland	225.4
3	Georgia	198.4
4	North Carolina	197.3
5	California	196.8
6	Delaware	169.6
7	Nevada	158.6
8	New Jersey	157.6
9	Minnesota	145.0
10	New Mexico	133.9
11	Rhode Island	128.8
12	Washington	125.6
13	Mississippi	124.3
14	Colorado	122.6
15	Missouri	121.6
16	Utah	120.5
17	Pennsylvania	118.5
18	Louisiana	115.9
19	Tennessee	115.2
20	Nebraska	111.2
21	Florida	104.4
22	Idaho	100.9
23	South Carolina	94.8
24	Connecticut	89.8
25	Oregon	87.3
26	Michigan	84.9
27	South Dakota	83.7
28	Oklahoma	83.0
28	Wyoming	83.0
30	Ohio	79.1
31	Arizona	75.6
32	Virginia	71.8
33	North Dakota	70.6
34	Arkansas	62.4
35	Texas	60.5
36	New York	59.9
37	Kansas	59.0
38	Indiana	57.4
39	Iowa	52.5
40	Alabama	46.6
41	Massachusetts	45.1
42	Alaska	42.3
43	Maine	35.0
44	Vermont	29.1
45	West Virginia	25.1
46	Hawaii	22.1
47	Montana	20.6
48	New Hampshire	11.8
NA	Illinois**	NA
NA	Kentucky**	NA
	District of Columbia**	NA

Source: CQ Press using reported data from the Federal Bureau of Investigation
"Crime in the United States 2008" (Uniform Crime Reports, September 14, 2009, http://www.fbi.gov/ucr/ucr.htm)
*By law enforcement agencies submitting complete reports to the F.B.I. for 12 months in 2008. Arrests of youths 17 years and younger divided into population of 10 to 17 year olds. See important note at beginning of this chapter. Weapons violations include illegal carrying and possession.
**Not available.

Reported Arrests of Juveniles for Weapons Violations
as a Percent of All Such Arrests in 2008
National Percent = 22.3% of Reported Weapons Violations Arrests*

ALPHA ORDER

RANK	STATE	PERCENT
45	Alabama	12.3
49	Alaska	9.6
41	Arizona	14.6
46	Arkansas	12.2
19	California	25.6
15	Colorado	27.1
22	Connecticut	22.6
8	Delaware	32.3
21	Florida	22.9
14	Georgia	27.2
47	Hawaii	12.1
16	Idaho	26.9
17	Illinois	26.7
38	Indiana	15.5
10	Iowa	29.7
36	Kansas	16.7
50	Kentucky	9.5
30	Louisiana	18.4
44	Maine	12.9
9	Maryland	31.4
26	Massachusetts	18.9
34	Michigan	17.8
4	Minnesota	34.7
28	Mississippi	18.6
32	Missouri	17.9
37	Montana	16.5
32	Nebraska	17.9
24	Nevada	21.6
40	New Hampshire	14.8
12	New Jersey	28.1
5	New Mexico	34.1
35	New York	17.0
30	North Carolina	18.4
20	North Dakota	24.7
25	Ohio	19.7
39	Oklahoma	15.2
29	Oregon	18.5
7	Pennsylvania	32.4
3	Rhode Island	35.3
18	South Carolina	26.0
2	South Dakota	44.2
27	Tennessee	18.7
42	Texas	14.1
11	Utah	29.6
1	Vermont	83.3
43	Virginia	13.8
23	Washington	22.0
48	West Virginia	10.1
12	Wisconsin	28.1
6	Wyoming	33.8

RANK ORDER

RANK	STATE	PERCENT
1	Vermont	83.3
2	South Dakota	44.2
3	Rhode Island	35.3
4	Minnesota	34.7
5	New Mexico	34.1
6	Wyoming	33.8
7	Pennsylvania	32.4
8	Delaware	32.3
9	Maryland	31.4
10	Iowa	29.7
11	Utah	29.6
12	New Jersey	28.1
12	Wisconsin	28.1
14	Georgia	27.2
15	Colorado	27.1
16	Idaho	26.9
17	Illinois	26.7
18	South Carolina	26.0
19	California	25.6
20	North Dakota	24.7
21	Florida	22.9
22	Connecticut	22.6
23	Washington	22.0
24	Nevada	21.6
25	Ohio	19.7
26	Massachusetts	18.9
27	Tennessee	18.7
28	Mississippi	18.6
29	Oregon	18.5
30	Louisiana	18.4
30	North Carolina	18.4
32	Missouri	17.9
32	Nebraska	17.9
34	Michigan	17.8
35	New York	17.0
36	Kansas	16.7
37	Montana	16.5
38	Indiana	15.5
39	Oklahoma	15.2
40	New Hampshire	14.8
41	Arizona	14.6
42	Texas	14.1
43	Virginia	13.8
44	Maine	12.9
45	Alabama	12.3
46	Arkansas	12.2
47	Hawaii	12.1
48	West Virginia	10.1
49	Alaska	9.6
50	Kentucky	9.5
	District of Columbia**	NA

Source: CQ Press using reported data from the Federal Bureau of Investigation
"Crime in the United States 2008" (Uniform Crime Reports, September 14, 2009, http://www.fbi.gov/ucr/ucr.htm)
*Arrests of youths 17 years and younger by law enforcement agencies submitting complete reports to the F.B.I. for 12 months in 2008. Weapons violations include illegal carrying and possession.
**Not available.

Reported Arrests of Juveniles for Driving Under the Influence in 2008

National Total = 12,499 Reported Arrests*

ALPHA ORDER

RANK	STATE	ARRESTS	% of USA
36	Alabama	93	0.7%
38	Alaska	89	0.7%
4	Arizona	561	4.5%
27	Arkansas	147	1.2%
1	California	1,468	11.7%
11	Colorado	435	3.5%
39	Connecticut	86	0.7%
50	Delaware	0	0.0%
8	Florida	498	4.0%
21	Georgia	205	1.6%
41	Hawaii	70	0.6%
20	Idaho	209	1.7%
45	Illinois	32	0.3%
24	Indiana	167	1.3%
17	Iowa	226	1.8%
15	Kansas	245	2.0%
49	Kentucky	8	0.1%
42	Louisiana	69	0.6%
34	Maine	95	0.8%
19	Maryland	214	1.7%
32	Massachusetts	101	0.8%
10	Michigan	482	3.9%
6	Minnesota	530	4.2%
28	Mississippi	137	1.1%
12	Missouri	425	3.4%
44	Montana	63	0.5%
14	Nebraska	281	2.2%
29	Nevada	124	1.0%
40	New Hampshire	76	0.6%
13	New Jersey	342	2.7%
30	New Mexico	112	0.9%
18	New York	216	1.7%
7	North Carolina	517	4.1%
43	North Dakota	67	0.5%
26	Ohio	158	1.3%
16	Oklahoma	233	1.9%
25	Oregon	161	1.3%
5	Pennsylvania	559	4.5%
47	Rhode Island	25	0.2%
35	South Carolina	94	0.8%
31	South Dakota	107	0.9%
22	Tennessee	204	1.6%
2	Texas	1,082	8.7%
33	Utah	98	0.8%
48	Vermont	24	0.2%
23	Virginia	183	1.5%
9	Washington	488	3.9%
46	West Virginia	29	0.2%
3	Wisconsin	573	4.6%
37	Wyoming	91	0.7%

RANK ORDER

RANK	STATE	ARRESTS	% of USA
1	California	1,468	11.7%
2	Texas	1,082	8.7%
3	Wisconsin	573	4.6%
4	Arizona	561	4.5%
5	Pennsylvania	559	4.5%
6	Minnesota	530	4.2%
7	North Carolina	517	4.1%
8	Florida	498	4.0%
9	Washington	488	3.9%
10	Michigan	482	3.9%
11	Colorado	435	3.5%
12	Missouri	425	3.4%
13	New Jersey	342	2.7%
14	Nebraska	281	2.2%
15	Kansas	245	2.0%
16	Oklahoma	233	1.9%
17	Iowa	226	1.8%
18	New York	216	1.7%
19	Maryland	214	1.7%
20	Idaho	209	1.7%
21	Georgia	205	1.6%
22	Tennessee	204	1.6%
23	Virginia	183	1.5%
24	Indiana	167	1.3%
25	Oregon	161	1.3%
26	Ohio	158	1.3%
27	Arkansas	147	1.2%
28	Mississippi	137	1.1%
29	Nevada	124	1.0%
30	New Mexico	112	0.9%
31	South Dakota	107	0.9%
32	Massachusetts	101	0.8%
33	Utah	98	0.8%
34	Maine	95	0.8%
35	South Carolina	94	0.8%
36	Alabama	93	0.7%
37	Wyoming	91	0.7%
38	Alaska	89	0.7%
39	Connecticut	86	0.7%
40	New Hampshire	76	0.6%
41	Hawaii	70	0.6%
42	Louisiana	69	0.6%
43	North Dakota	67	0.5%
44	Montana	63	0.5%
45	Illinois	32	0.3%
46	West Virginia	29	0.2%
47	Rhode Island	25	0.2%
48	Vermont	24	0.2%
49	Kentucky	8	0.1%
50	Delaware	0	0.0%
	District of Columbia**	NA	NA

Source: Reported data from the Federal Bureau of Investigation
   "Crime in the United States 2008" (Uniform Crime Reports, September 14, 2009, http://www.fbi.gov/ucr/ucr.htm)
*Arrests of youths 17 years and younger by law enforcement agencies submitting complete reports to the F.B.I. for 12 months in 2008. Includes driving any vehicle while drunk or under the influence of liquor or narcotics. See important note at beginning of this chapter.
**Not available.

Reported Juvenile Arrest Rate for Driving Under the Influence in 2008

National Rate = 46.4 Reported Arrests per 100,000 Juvenile Population*

ALPHA ORDER

RANK	STATE	RATE
43	Alabama	22.8
7	Alaska	114.1
13	Arizona	78.8
23	Arkansas	56.6
32	California	35.5
11	Colorado	95.9
40	Connecticut	24.5
48	Delaware	0.0
37	Florida	28.1
36	Georgia	30.3
21	Hawaii	64.3
4	Idaho	125.5
NA	Illinois**	NA
35	Indiana	32.3
14	Iowa	77.1
5	Kansas	118.6
NA	Kentucky**	NA
39	Louisiana	24.9
16	Maine	72.3
32	Maryland	35.5
47	Massachusetts	17.2
24	Michigan	49.7
8	Minnesota	97.6
12	Mississippi	91.1
18	Missouri	71.0
20	Montana	65.0
2	Nebraska	157.8
27	Nevada	44.3
19	New Hampshire	68.8
31	New Jersey	37.9
17	New Mexico	71.1
44	New York	22.5
15	North Carolina	74.5
6	North Dakota	115.4
45	Ohio	21.1
22	Oklahoma	59.9
28	Oregon	42.8
26	Pennsylvania	44.7
42	Rhode Island	23.3
46	South Carolina	20.3
3	South Dakota	157.2
30	Tennessee	38.9
29	Texas	39.9
34	Utah	33.3
25	Vermont	46.6
41	Virginia	23.6
10	Washington	96.7
38	West Virginia	27.0
8	Wisconsin	97.6
1	Wyoming	164.1

RANK ORDER

RANK	STATE	RATE
1	Wyoming	164.1
2	Nebraska	157.8
3	South Dakota	157.2
4	Idaho	125.5
5	Kansas	118.6
6	North Dakota	115.4
7	Alaska	114.1
8	Minnesota	97.6
8	Wisconsin	97.6
10	Washington	96.7
11	Colorado	95.9
12	Mississippi	91.1
13	Arizona	78.8
14	Iowa	77.1
15	North Carolina	74.5
16	Maine	72.3
17	New Mexico	71.1
18	Missouri	71.0
19	New Hampshire	68.8
20	Montana	65.0
21	Hawaii	64.3
22	Oklahoma	59.9
23	Arkansas	56.6
24	Michigan	49.7
25	Vermont	46.6
26	Pennsylvania	44.7
27	Nevada	44.3
28	Oregon	42.8
29	Texas	39.9
30	Tennessee	38.9
31	New Jersey	37.9
32	California	35.5
32	Maryland	35.5
34	Utah	33.3
35	Indiana	32.3
36	Georgia	30.3
37	Florida	28.1
38	West Virginia	27.0
39	Louisiana	24.9
40	Connecticut	24.5
41	Virginia	23.6
42	Rhode Island	23.3
43	Alabama	22.8
44	New York	22.5
45	Ohio	21.1
46	South Carolina	20.3
47	Massachusetts	17.2
48	Delaware	0.0
NA	Illinois**	NA
NA	Kentucky**	NA
	District of Columbia**	NA

Source: CQ Press using reported data from the Federal Bureau of Investigation
   "Crime in the United States 2008" (Uniform Crime Reports, September 14, 2009, http://www.fbi.gov/ucr/ucr.htm)
*By law enforcement agencies submitting complete reports to the F.B.I. for 12 months in 2008. Arrests of youths 17 years and younger divided into population of 10 to 17 year olds. See important note at beginning of this chapter. Includes driving any vehicle while drunk or under the influence of liquor or narcotics.
**Not available.

Reported Arrests of Juveniles for Driving Under the Influence as a Percent of All Such Arrests in 2008

National Percent = 1.1% of Reported Driving Under the Influence Arrests*

ALPHA ORDER

RANK	STATE	PERCENT
47	Alabama	0.6
8	Alaska	1.6
12	Arizona	1.4
18	Arkansas	1.3
42	California	0.7
10	Colorado	1.5
27	Connecticut	1.0
50	Delaware	0.0
37	Florida	0.8
37	Georgia	0.8
21	Hawaii	1.2
3	Idaho	1.8
42	Illinois	0.7
42	Indiana	0.7
8	Iowa	1.6
2	Kansas	1.9
49	Kentucky	0.3
30	Louisiana	0.9
18	Maine	1.3
30	Maryland	0.9
37	Massachusetts	0.8
12	Michigan	1.4
3	Minnesota	1.8
21	Mississippi	1.2
21	Missouri	1.2
10	Montana	1.5
1	Nebraska	2.1
30	Nevada	0.9
5	New Hampshire	1.7
12	New Jersey	1.4
26	New Mexico	1.1
30	New York	0.9
27	North Carolina	1.0
5	North Dakota	1.7
37	Ohio	0.8
21	Oklahoma	1.2
30	Oregon	0.9
27	Pennsylvania	1.0
30	Rhode Island	0.9
47	South Carolina	0.6
5	South Dakota	1.7
37	Tennessee	0.8
21	Texas	1.2
12	Utah	1.4
30	Vermont	0.9
42	Virginia	0.7
12	Washington	1.4
42	West Virginia	0.7
12	Wisconsin	1.4
18	Wyoming	1.3

RANK ORDER

RANK	STATE	PERCENT
1	Nebraska	2.1
2	Kansas	1.9
3	Idaho	1.8
3	Minnesota	1.8
5	New Hampshire	1.7
5	North Dakota	1.7
5	South Dakota	1.7
8	Alaska	1.6
8	Iowa	1.6
10	Colorado	1.5
10	Montana	1.5
12	Arizona	1.4
12	Michigan	1.4
12	New Jersey	1.4
12	Utah	1.4
12	Washington	1.4
12	Wisconsin	1.4
18	Arkansas	1.3
18	Maine	1.3
18	Wyoming	1.3
21	Hawaii	1.2
21	Mississippi	1.2
21	Missouri	1.2
21	Oklahoma	1.2
21	Texas	1.2
26	New Mexico	1.1
27	Connecticut	1.0
27	North Carolina	1.0
27	Pennsylvania	1.0
30	Louisiana	0.9
30	Maryland	0.9
30	Nevada	0.9
30	New York	0.9
30	Oregon	0.9
30	Rhode Island	0.9
30	Vermont	0.9
37	Florida	0.8
37	Georgia	0.8
37	Massachusetts	0.8
37	Ohio	0.8
37	Tennessee	0.8
42	California	0.7
42	Illinois	0.7
42	Indiana	0.7
42	Virginia	0.7
42	West Virginia	0.7
47	Alabama	0.6
47	South Carolina	0.6
49	Kentucky	0.3
50	Delaware	0.0
	District of Columbia**	NA

Source: CQ Press using reported data from the Federal Bureau of Investigation
   "Crime in the United States 2008" (Uniform Crime Reports, September 14, 2009, http://www.fbi.gov/ucr/ucr.htm)
*Arrests of youths 17 years and younger by law enforcement agencies submitting complete reports to the F.B.I. for 12 months in 2008. Includes driving any vehicle while drunk or under the influence of liquor or narcotics.
**Not available.

Reported Arrests of Juveniles for Drug Abuse Violations in 2008

National Total = 150,969 Reported Arrests*

ALPHA ORDER

RANK	STATE	ARRESTS	% of USA
32	Alabama	987	0.7%
48	Alaska	265	0.2%
8	Arizona	5,413	3.6%
34	Arkansas	948	0.6%
1	California	21,661	14.3%
11	Colorado	3,456	2.3%
28	Connecticut	1,604	1.1%
37	Delaware	705	0.5%
3	Florida	13,011	8.6%
15	Georgia	3,157	2.1%
44	Hawaii	409	0.3%
36	Idaho	781	0.5%
5	Illinois	6,055	4.0%
21	Indiana	2,380	1.6%
31	Iowa	1,165	0.8%
33	Kansas	976	0.6%
41	Kentucky	506	0.3%
29	Louisiana	1,600	1.1%
40	Maine	561	0.4%
4	Maryland	7,648	5.1%
23	Massachusetts	2,115	1.4%
13	Michigan	3,278	2.2%
17	Minnesota	2,785	1.8%
38	Mississippi	683	0.5%
12	Missouri	3,398	2.3%
46	Montana	297	0.2%
30	Nebraska	1,166	0.8%
26	Nevada	1,723	1.1%
39	New Hampshire	642	0.4%
7	New Jersey	5,766	3.8%
35	New Mexico	919	0.6%
9	New York	5,141	3.4%
14	North Carolina	3,174	2.1%
47	North Dakota	278	0.2%
19	Ohio	2,691	1.8%
24	Oklahoma	1,873	1.2%
22	Oregon	2,303	1.5%
5	Pennsylvania	6,055	4.0%
43	Rhode Island	426	0.3%
25	South Carolina	1,800	1.2%
45	South Dakota	403	0.3%
16	Tennessee	3,004	2.0%
2	Texas	15,326	10.2%
27	Utah	1,663	1.1%
50	Vermont	141	0.1%
18	Virginia	2,736	1.8%
20	Washington	2,555	1.7%
49	West Virginia	219	0.1%
10	Wisconsin	4,597	3.0%
42	Wyoming	505	0.3%

RANK ORDER

RANK	STATE	ARRESTS	% of USA
1	California	21,661	14.3%
2	Texas	15,326	10.2%
3	Florida	13,011	8.6%
4	Maryland	7,648	5.1%
5	Illinois	6,055	4.0%
5	Pennsylvania	6,055	4.0%
7	New Jersey	5,766	3.8%
8	Arizona	5,413	3.6%
9	New York	5,141	3.4%
10	Wisconsin	4,597	3.0%
11	Colorado	3,456	2.3%
12	Missouri	3,398	2.3%
13	Michigan	3,278	2.2%
14	North Carolina	3,174	2.1%
15	Georgia	3,157	2.1%
16	Tennessee	3,004	2.0%
17	Minnesota	2,785	1.8%
18	Virginia	2,736	1.8%
19	Ohio	2,691	1.8%
20	Washington	2,555	1.7%
21	Indiana	2,380	1.6%
22	Oregon	2,303	1.5%
23	Massachusetts	2,115	1.4%
24	Oklahoma	1,873	1.2%
25	South Carolina	1,800	1.2%
26	Nevada	1,723	1.1%
27	Utah	1,663	1.1%
28	Connecticut	1,604	1.1%
29	Louisiana	1,600	1.1%
30	Nebraska	1,166	0.8%
31	Iowa	1,165	0.8%
32	Alabama	987	0.7%
33	Kansas	976	0.6%
34	Arkansas	948	0.6%
35	New Mexico	919	0.6%
36	Idaho	781	0.5%
37	Delaware	705	0.5%
38	Mississippi	683	0.5%
39	New Hampshire	642	0.4%
40	Maine	561	0.4%
41	Kentucky	506	0.3%
42	Wyoming	505	0.3%
43	Rhode Island	426	0.3%
44	Hawaii	409	0.3%
45	South Dakota	403	0.3%
46	Montana	297	0.2%
47	North Dakota	278	0.2%
48	Alaska	265	0.2%
49	West Virginia	219	0.1%
50	Vermont	141	0.1%
	District of Columbia**	NA	NA

Source: Reported data from the Federal Bureau of Investigation
   "Crime in the United States 2008" (Uniform Crime Reports, September 14, 2009, http://www.fbi.gov/ucr/ucr.htm)
*Arrests of youths 17 years and younger by law enforcement agencies submitting complete reports to the F.B.I. for 12 months in 2008. Includes offenses relating to possession, sale, use, growing, and manufacturing of narcotic drugs. See important note at beginning of this chapter.
**Not available.

Reported Juvenile Arrest Rate for Drug Abuse Violations in 2008

National Rate = 561.0 Reported Arrests per 100,000 Juvenile Population*

ALPHA ORDER

RANK	STATE	RATE
47	Alabama	242.2
43	Alaska	339.8
6	Arizona	760.2
39	Arkansas	365.2
21	California	524.4
5	Colorado	762.2
32	Connecticut	456.1
4	Delaware	776.4
7	Florida	733.2
29	Georgia	466.0
38	Hawaii	375.9
28	Idaho	469.1
NA	Illinois**	NA
30	Indiana	460.3
36	Iowa	397.4
27	Kansas	472.3
NA	Kentucky**	NA
15	Louisiana	577.9
34	Maine	426.9
1	Maryland	1,270.4
40	Massachusetts	359.8
44	Michigan	337.8
22	Minnesota	513.0
33	Mississippi	454.1
17	Missouri	567.6
45	Montana	306.2
8	Nebraska	654.6
10	Nevada	615.3
14	New Hampshire	581.1
9	New Jersey	639.0
13	New Mexico	583.1
20	New York	535.9
31	North Carolina	457.1
26	North Dakota	478.8
41	Ohio	359.6
25	Oklahoma	481.2
11	Oregon	612.6
24	Pennsylvania	484.4
35	Rhode Island	397.5
37	South Carolina	389.7
12	South Dakota	592.1
16	Tennessee	572.7
18	Texas	565.2
19	Utah	564.2
46	Vermont	273.9
42	Virginia	352.1
23	Washington	506.3
48	West Virginia	203.5
3	Wisconsin	782.7
2	Wyoming	910.9

RANK ORDER

RANK	STATE	RATE
1	Maryland	1,270.4
2	Wyoming	910.9
3	Wisconsin	782.7
4	Delaware	776.4
5	Colorado	762.2
6	Arizona	760.2
7	Florida	733.2
8	Nebraska	654.6
9	New Jersey	639.0
10	Nevada	615.3
11	Oregon	612.6
12	South Dakota	592.1
13	New Mexico	583.1
14	New Hampshire	581.1
15	Louisiana	577.9
16	Tennessee	572.7
17	Missouri	567.6
18	Texas	565.2
19	Utah	564.2
20	New York	535.9
21	California	524.4
22	Minnesota	513.0
23	Washington	506.3
24	Pennsylvania	484.4
25	Oklahoma	481.2
26	North Dakota	478.8
27	Kansas	472.3
28	Idaho	469.1
29	Georgia	466.0
30	Indiana	460.3
31	North Carolina	457.1
32	Connecticut	456.1
33	Mississippi	454.1
34	Maine	426.9
35	Rhode Island	397.5
36	Iowa	397.4
37	South Carolina	389.7
38	Hawaii	375.9
39	Arkansas	365.2
40	Massachusetts	359.8
41	Ohio	359.6
42	Virginia	352.1
43	Alaska	339.8
44	Michigan	337.8
45	Montana	306.2
46	Vermont	273.9
47	Alabama	242.2
48	West Virginia	203.5
NA	Illinois**	NA
NA	Kentucky**	NA
	District of Columbia**	NA

Source: CQ Press using reported data from the Federal Bureau of Investigation
   "Crime in the United States 2008" (Uniform Crime Reports, September 14, 2009, http://www.fbi.gov/ucr/ucr.htm)
*By law enforcement agencies submitting complete reports to the F.B.I. for 12 months in 2008. Arrests of youths 17 years and younger divided into population of 10 to 17 year olds. See important note at beginning of this chapter. Includes offenses relating to possession, sale, use, growing, and manufacturing of narcotic drugs.
**Not available.

Reported Arrests of Juveniles for Drug Abuse Violations
as a Percent of All Such Arrests in 2008
National Percent = 10.3% of Reported Drug Abuse Violations Arrests*

ALPHA ORDER

RANK ORDER

RANK	STATE	PERCENT
48	Alabama	6.0
11	Alaska	15.4
9	Arizona	15.8
44	Arkansas	8.2
45	California	8.1
3	Colorado	19.4
32	Connecticut	9.9
21	Delaware	12.0
45	Florida	8.1
37	Georgia	9.1
1	Hawaii	20.2
14	Idaho	14.2
19	Illinois	13.3
30	Indiana	10.5
17	Iowa	13.7
14	Kansas	14.2
47	Kentucky	6.4
39	Louisiana	8.9
34	Maine	9.7
18	Maryland	13.4
29	Massachusetts	10.7
31	Michigan	10.3
12	Minnesota	15.3
49	Mississippi	5.8
36	Missouri	9.4
4	Montana	18.3
23	Nebraska	11.2
22	Nevada	11.6
2	New Hampshire	19.7
26	New Jersey	10.9
13	New Mexico	15.0
34	New York	9.7
41	North Carolina	8.7
10	North Dakota	15.7
40	Ohio	8.8
37	Oklahoma	9.1
16	Oregon	13.8
28	Pennsylvania	10.8
23	Rhode Island	11.2
32	South Carolina	9.9
8	South Dakota	16.8
41	Tennessee	8.7
23	Texas	11.2
6	Utah	18.0
20	Vermont	12.4
43	Virginia	8.4
26	Washington	10.9
50	West Virginia	5.2
4	Wisconsin	18.3
7	Wyoming	17.0

RANK	STATE	PERCENT
1	Hawaii	20.2
2	New Hampshire	19.7
3	Colorado	19.4
4	Montana	18.3
4	Wisconsin	18.3
6	Utah	18.0
7	Wyoming	17.0
8	South Dakota	16.8
9	Arizona	15.8
10	North Dakota	15.7
11	Alaska	15.4
12	Minnesota	15.3
13	New Mexico	15.0
14	Idaho	14.2
14	Kansas	14.2
16	Oregon	13.8
17	Iowa	13.7
18	Maryland	13.4
19	Illinois	13.3
20	Vermont	12.4
21	Delaware	12.0
22	Nevada	11.6
23	Nebraska	11.2
23	Rhode Island	11.2
23	Texas	11.2
26	New Jersey	10.9
26	Washington	10.9
28	Pennsylvania	10.8
29	Massachusetts	10.7
30	Indiana	10.5
31	Michigan	10.3
32	Connecticut	9.9
32	South Carolina	9.9
34	Maine	9.7
34	New York	9.7
36	Missouri	9.4
37	Georgia	9.1
37	Oklahoma	9.1
39	Louisiana	8.9
40	Ohio	8.8
41	North Carolina	8.7
41	Tennessee	8.7
43	Virginia	8.4
44	Arkansas	8.2
45	California	8.1
45	Florida	8.1
47	Kentucky	6.4
48	Alabama	6.0
49	Mississippi	5.8
50	West Virginia	5.2

District of Columbia**   NA

Source: CQ Press using reported data from the Federal Bureau of Investigation
    "Crime in the United States 2008" (Uniform Crime Reports, September 14, 2009, http://www.fbi.gov/ucr/ucr.htm)
*Arrests of youths 17 years and younger by law enforcement agencies submitting complete reports to the F.B.I. for 12 months in 2008. Includes offenses relating to possession, sale, use, growing, and manufacturing of narcotic drugs.
**Not available.

Reported Arrests of Juveniles for Sex Offenses in 2008

National Total = 11,339 Reported Arrests*

ALPHA ORDER

RANK	STATE	ARRESTS	% of USA
43	Alabama	26	0.2%
38	Alaska	42	0.4%
10	Arizona	307	2.7%
39	Arkansas	38	0.3%
1	California	2,184	19.3%
16	Colorado	225	2.0%
23	Connecticut	140	1.2%
37	Delaware	45	0.4%
9	Florida	310	2.7%
6	Georgia	545	4.8%
34	Hawaii	68	0.6%
28	Idaho	89	0.8%
31	Illinois	84	0.7%
14	Indiana	247	2.2%
32	Iowa	78	0.7%
29	Kansas	87	0.8%
49	Kentucky	3	0.0%
25	Louisiana	122	1.1%
35	Maine	51	0.4%
13	Maryland	292	2.6%
29	Massachusetts	87	0.8%
15	Michigan	237	2.1%
11	Minnesota	302	2.7%
36	Mississippi	47	0.4%
7	Missouri	432	3.8%
45	Montana	20	0.2%
24	Nebraska	123	1.1%
21	Nevada	153	1.3%
41	New Hampshire	31	0.3%
11	New Jersey	302	2.7%
47	New Mexico	14	0.1%
3	New York	736	6.5%
26	North Carolina	121	1.1%
43	North Dakota	26	0.2%
17	Ohio	217	1.9%
33	Oklahoma	69	0.6%
20	Oregon	180	1.6%
5	Pennsylvania	550	4.9%
40	Rhode Island	34	0.3%
27	South Carolina	93	0.8%
42	South Dakota	30	0.3%
22	Tennessee	151	1.3%
4	Texas	676	6.0%
8	Utah	314	2.8%
50	Vermont	2	0.0%
18	Virginia	209	1.8%
19	Washington	183	1.6%
48	West Virginia	12	0.1%
2	Wisconsin	986	8.7%
46	Wyoming	19	0.2%

RANK ORDER

RANK	STATE	ARRESTS	% of USA
1	California	2,184	19.3%
2	Wisconsin	986	8.7%
3	New York	736	6.5%
4	Texas	676	6.0%
5	Pennsylvania	550	4.9%
6	Georgia	545	4.8%
7	Missouri	432	3.8%
8	Utah	314	2.8%
9	Florida	310	2.7%
10	Arizona	307	2.7%
11	Minnesota	302	2.7%
11	New Jersey	302	2.7%
13	Maryland	292	2.6%
14	Indiana	247	2.2%
15	Michigan	237	2.1%
16	Colorado	225	2.0%
17	Ohio	217	1.9%
18	Virginia	209	1.8%
19	Washington	183	1.6%
20	Oregon	180	1.6%
21	Nevada	153	1.3%
22	Tennessee	151	1.3%
23	Connecticut	140	1.2%
24	Nebraska	123	1.1%
25	Louisiana	122	1.1%
26	North Carolina	121	1.1%
27	South Carolina	93	0.8%
28	Idaho	89	0.8%
29	Kansas	87	0.8%
29	Massachusetts	87	0.8%
31	Illinois	84	0.7%
32	Iowa	78	0.7%
33	Oklahoma	69	0.6%
34	Hawaii	68	0.6%
35	Maine	51	0.4%
36	Mississippi	47	0.4%
37	Delaware	45	0.4%
38	Alaska	42	0.4%
39	Arkansas	38	0.3%
40	Rhode Island	34	0.3%
41	New Hampshire	31	0.3%
42	South Dakota	30	0.3%
43	Alabama	26	0.2%
43	North Dakota	26	0.2%
45	Montana	20	0.2%
46	Wyoming	19	0.2%
47	New Mexico	14	0.1%
48	West Virginia	12	0.1%
49	Kentucky	3	0.0%
50	Vermont	2	0.0%
	District of Columbia**	NA	NA

Source: Reported data from the Federal Bureau of Investigation
"Crime in the United States 2008" (Uniform Crime Reports, September 14, 2009, http://www.fbi.gov/ucr/ucr.htm)
*Arrests of youths 17 years and younger by law enforcement agencies submitting complete reports to the F.B.I. for 12 months in 2008. Excludes forcible rape, prostitution, and commercialized vice. Includes statutory rape and offenses against chastity, common decency, morals, and the like. See important note at beginning of this chapter.
**Not available.

Reported Juvenile Arrest Rate for Sex Offenses in 2008

National Rate = 42.1 Reported Arrests per 100,000 Juvenile Population*

ALPHA ORDER

RANK	STATE	RATE
47	Alabama	6.4
10	Alaska	53.9
22	Arizona	43.1
44	Arkansas	14.6
12	California	52.9
13	Colorado	49.6
24	Connecticut	39.8
13	Delaware	49.6
41	Florida	17.5
3	Georgia	80.4
7	Hawaii	62.5
11	Idaho	53.5
NA	Illinois**	NA
17	Indiana	47.8
35	Iowa	26.6
23	Kansas	42.1
NA	Kentucky**	NA
19	Louisiana	44.1
25	Maine	38.8
15	Maryland	48.5
43	Massachusetts	14.8
37	Michigan	24.4
8	Minnesota	55.6
30	Mississippi	31.2
5	Missouri	72.2
38	Montana	20.6
6	Nebraska	69.1
9	Nevada	54.6
33	New Hampshire	28.1
28	New Jersey	33.5
46	New Mexico	8.9
4	New York	76.7
42	North Carolina	17.4
18	North Dakota	44.8
31	Ohio	29.0
40	Oklahoma	17.7
16	Oregon	47.9
21	Pennsylvania	44.0
29	Rhode Island	31.7
39	South Carolina	20.1
19	South Dakota	44.1
32	Tennessee	28.8
36	Texas	24.9
2	Utah	106.5
48	Vermont	3.9
34	Virginia	26.9
26	Washington	36.3
45	West Virginia	11.2
1	Wisconsin	167.9
27	Wyoming	34.3

RANK ORDER

RANK	STATE	RATE
1	Wisconsin	167.9
2	Utah	106.5
3	Georgia	80.4
4	New York	76.7
5	Missouri	72.2
6	Nebraska	69.1
7	Hawaii	62.5
8	Minnesota	55.6
9	Nevada	54.6
10	Alaska	53.9
11	Idaho	53.5
12	California	52.9
13	Colorado	49.6
13	Delaware	49.6
15	Maryland	48.5
16	Oregon	47.9
17	Indiana	47.8
18	North Dakota	44.8
19	Louisiana	44.1
19	South Dakota	44.1
21	Pennsylvania	44.0
22	Arizona	43.1
23	Kansas	42.1
24	Connecticut	39.8
25	Maine	38.8
26	Washington	36.3
27	Wyoming	34.3
28	New Jersey	33.5
29	Rhode Island	31.7
30	Mississippi	31.2
31	Ohio	29.0
32	Tennessee	28.8
33	New Hampshire	28.1
34	Virginia	26.9
35	Iowa	26.6
36	Texas	24.9
37	Michigan	24.4
38	Montana	20.6
39	South Carolina	20.1
40	Oklahoma	17.7
41	Florida	17.5
42	North Carolina	17.4
43	Massachusetts	14.8
44	Arkansas	14.6
45	West Virginia	11.2
46	New Mexico	8.9
47	Alabama	6.4
48	Vermont	3.9
NA	Illinois**	NA
NA	Kentucky**	NA
	District of Columbia**	NA

Source: CQ Press using reported data from the Federal Bureau of Investigation
   "Crime in the United States 2008" (Uniform Crime Reports, September 14, 2009, http://www.fbi.gov/ucr/ucr.htm)
*By law enforcement agencies submitting complete reports to the F.B.I. for 12 months in 2008. Arrests of youths 17 years and younger divided into population of 10 to 17 year olds. See important note at beginning of this chapter. Excludes forcible rape, prostitution, and commercialized vice. Includes statutory rape and offenses against chastity, common decency, morals, and the like. **Not available.

Reported Arrests of Juveniles for Sex Offenses
as a Percent of All Such Arrests in 2008
National Percent = 17.6% of Reported Sex Offense Arrests*

ALPHA ORDER

RANK	STATE	PERCENT
50	Alabama	4.5
10	Alaska	25.3
32	Arizona	17.3
26	Arkansas	19.6
36	California	15.1
11	Colorado	24.9
13	Connecticut	24.2
16	Delaware	22.3
46	Florida	9.0
35	Georgia	16.0
14	Hawaii	23.1
6	Idaho	28.3
48	Illinois	8.7
34	Indiana	16.3
4	Iowa	32.9
9	Kansas	26.8
37	Kentucky	14.3
21	Louisiana	20.5
29	Maine	18.5
17	Maryland	21.7
39	Massachusetts	12.5
12	Michigan	24.6
23	Minnesota	19.8
40	Mississippi	11.4
31	Missouri	17.7
5	Montana	31.3
19	Nebraska	20.7
43	Nevada	9.6
22	New Hampshire	20.4
23	New Jersey	19.8
45	New Mexico	9.3
28	New York	18.9
47	North Carolina	8.9
8	North Dakota	27.4
15	Ohio	22.5
43	Oklahoma	9.6
38	Oregon	13.5
23	Pennsylvania	19.8
7	Rhode Island	27.9
18	South Carolina	21.0
1	South Dakota	39.0
19	Tennessee	20.7
33	Texas	16.7
2	Utah	38.7
48	Vermont	8.7
26	Virginia	19.6
30	Washington	18.4
42	West Virginia	10.7
3	Wisconsin	35.9
41	Wyoming	11.0

RANK ORDER

RANK	STATE	PERCENT
1	South Dakota	39.0
2	Utah	38.7
3	Wisconsin	35.9
4	Iowa	32.9
5	Montana	31.3
6	Idaho	28.3
7	Rhode Island	27.9
8	North Dakota	27.4
9	Kansas	26.8
10	Alaska	25.3
11	Colorado	24.9
12	Michigan	24.6
13	Connecticut	24.2
14	Hawaii	23.1
15	Ohio	22.5
16	Delaware	22.3
17	Maryland	21.7
18	South Carolina	21.0
19	Nebraska	20.7
19	Tennessee	20.7
21	Louisiana	20.5
22	New Hampshire	20.4
23	Minnesota	19.8
23	New Jersey	19.8
23	Pennsylvania	19.8
26	Arkansas	19.6
26	Virginia	19.6
28	New York	18.9
29	Maine	18.5
30	Washington	18.4
31	Missouri	17.7
32	Arizona	17.3
33	Texas	16.7
34	Indiana	16.3
35	Georgia	16.0
36	California	15.1
37	Kentucky	14.3
38	Oregon	13.5
39	Massachusetts	12.5
40	Mississippi	11.4
41	Wyoming	11.0
42	West Virginia	10.7
43	Nevada	9.6
43	Oklahoma	9.6
45	New Mexico	9.3
46	Florida	9.0
47	North Carolina	8.9
48	Illinois	8.7
48	Vermont	8.7
50	Alabama	4.5
	District of Columbia**	NA

Source: CQ Press using reported data from the Federal Bureau of Investigation
   "Crime in the United States 2008" (Uniform Crime Reports, September 14, 2009, http://www.fbi.gov/ucr/ucr.htm)
*Arrests of youths 17 years and younger by law enforcement agencies submitting complete reports to the F.B.I. for 12 months in 2008. Excludes forcible rape, prostitution, and commercialized vice. Includes statutory rape and offenses against chastity, common decency, morals, and the like.
**Not available.

Reported Arrests of Juveniles for Prostitution and Commercialized Vice in 2008

National Total = 1,211 Reported Arrests*

ALPHA ORDER					RANK ORDER			
RANK	STATE	ARRESTS	% of USA		RANK	STATE	ARRESTS	% of USA
41	Alabama	0	0.0%		1	California	487	40.2%
28	Alaska	2	0.2%		2	Texas	139	11.5%
10	Arizona	27	2.2%		3	Nevada	63	5.2%
28	Arkansas	2	0.2%		4	Washington	54	4.5%
1	California	487	40.2%		5	Florida	53	4.4%
13	Colorado	24	2.0%		6	Minnesota	45	3.7%
25	Connecticut	4	0.3%		7	Illinois	37	3.1%
34	Delaware	1	0.1%		8	Georgia	31	2.6%
5	Florida	53	4.4%		9	New Jersey	30	2.5%
8	Georgia	31	2.6%		10	Arizona	27	2.2%
19	Hawaii	11	0.9%		10	Wisconsin	27	2.2%
28	Idaho	2	0.2%		12	Tennessee	26	2.1%
7	Illinois	37	3.1%		13	Colorado	24	2.0%
28	Indiana	2	0.2%		14	Oregon	23	1.9%
28	Iowa	2	0.2%		14	Utah	23	1.9%
34	Kansas	1	0.1%		16	Michigan	16	1.3%
41	Kentucky	0	0.0%		17	Maryland	12	1.0%
25	Louisiana	4	0.3%		17	North Carolina	12	1.0%
41	Maine	0	0.0%		19	Hawaii	11	0.9%
17	Maryland	12	1.0%		19	Pennsylvania	11	0.9%
23	Massachusetts	6	0.5%		21	New York	10	0.8%
16	Michigan	16	1.3%		22	Missouri	8	0.7%
6	Minnesota	45	3.7%		23	Massachusetts	6	0.5%
34	Mississippi	1	0.1%		24	Ohio	5	0.4%
22	Missouri	8	0.7%		25	Connecticut	4	0.3%
41	Montana	0	0.0%		25	Louisiana	4	0.3%
34	Nebraska	1	0.1%		25	Virginia	4	0.3%
3	Nevada	63	5.2%		28	Alaska	2	0.2%
41	New Hampshire	0	0.0%		28	Arkansas	2	0.2%
9	New Jersey	30	2.5%		28	Idaho	2	0.2%
28	New Mexico	2	0.2%		28	Indiana	2	0.2%
21	New York	10	0.8%		28	Iowa	2	0.2%
17	North Carolina	12	1.0%		28	New Mexico	2	0.2%
41	North Dakota	0	0.0%		34	Delaware	1	0.1%
24	Ohio	5	0.4%		34	Kansas	1	0.1%
34	Oklahoma	1	0.1%		34	Mississippi	1	0.1%
14	Oregon	23	1.9%		34	Nebraska	1	0.1%
19	Pennsylvania	11	0.9%		34	Oklahoma	1	0.1%
41	Rhode Island	0	0.0%		34	South Carolina	1	0.1%
34	South Carolina	1	0.1%		34	West Virginia	1	0.1%
41	South Dakota	0	0.0%		41	Alabama	0	0.0%
12	Tennessee	26	2.1%		41	Kentucky	0	0.0%
2	Texas	139	11.5%		41	Maine	0	0.0%
14	Utah	23	1.9%		41	Montana	0	0.0%
41	Vermont	0	0.0%		41	New Hampshire	0	0.0%
25	Virginia	4	0.3%		41	North Dakota	0	0.0%
4	Washington	54	4.5%		41	Rhode Island	0	0.0%
34	West Virginia	1	0.1%		41	South Dakota	0	0.0%
10	Wisconsin	27	2.2%		41	Vermont	0	0.0%
41	Wyoming	0	0.0%		41	Wyoming	0	0.0%
					District of Columbia**		NA	NA

Source: Reported data from the Federal Bureau of Investigation
"Crime in the United States 2008" (Uniform Crime Reports, September 14, 2009, http://www.fbi.gov/ucr/ucr.htm)
*Arrests of youths 17 years and younger by law enforcement agencies submitting complete reports to the F.B.I. for 12 months in 2008. Includes keeping a bawdy house or procuring or transporting women for immoral purposes. Attempts are included. See important note at beginning of this chapter.
**Not available.

Reported Juvenile Arrest Rate for Prostitution and Commercialized Vice in 2008

National Rate = 4.5 Reported Arrests per 100,000 Juvenile Population*

ALPHA ORDER

RANK	STATE	RATE
40	Alabama	0.0
16	Alaska	2.6
13	Arizona	3.8
30	Arkansas	0.8
2	California	11.8
8	Colorado	5.3
24	Connecticut	1.1
24	Delaware	1.1
15	Florida	3.0
11	Georgia	4.6
4	Hawaii	10.1
23	Idaho	1.2
NA	Illinois**	NA
37	Indiana	0.4
31	Iowa	0.7
35	Kansas	0.5
NA	Kentucky**	NA
20	Louisiana	1.4
40	Maine	0.0
17	Maryland	2.0
26	Massachusetts	1.0
19	Michigan	1.6
5	Minnesota	8.3
31	Mississippi	0.7
21	Missouri	1.3
40	Montana	0.0
34	Nebraska	0.6
1	Nevada	22.5
40	New Hampshire	0.0
14	New Jersey	3.3
21	New Mexico	1.3
26	New York	1.0
18	North Carolina	1.7
40	North Dakota	0.0
31	Ohio	0.7
38	Oklahoma	0.3
7	Oregon	6.1
28	Pennsylvania	0.9
40	Rhode Island	0.0
39	South Carolina	0.2
40	South Dakota	0.0
10	Tennessee	5.0
9	Texas	5.1
6	Utah	7.8
40	Vermont	0.0
35	Virginia	0.5
3	Washington	10.7
28	West Virginia	0.9
11	Wisconsin	4.6
40	Wyoming	0.0

RANK ORDER

RANK	STATE	RATE
1	Nevada	22.5
2	California	11.8
3	Washington	10.7
4	Hawaii	10.1
5	Minnesota	8.3
6	Utah	7.8
7	Oregon	6.1
8	Colorado	5.3
9	Texas	5.1
10	Tennessee	5.0
11	Georgia	4.6
11	Wisconsin	4.6
13	Arizona	3.8
14	New Jersey	3.3
15	Florida	3.0
16	Alaska	2.6
17	Maryland	2.0
18	North Carolina	1.7
19	Michigan	1.6
20	Louisiana	1.4
21	Missouri	1.3
21	New Mexico	1.3
23	Idaho	1.2
24	Connecticut	1.1
24	Delaware	1.1
26	Massachusetts	1.0
26	New York	1.0
28	Pennsylvania	0.9
28	West Virginia	0.9
30	Arkansas	0.8
31	Iowa	0.7
31	Mississippi	0.7
31	Ohio	0.7
34	Nebraska	0.6
35	Kansas	0.5
35	Virginia	0.5
37	Indiana	0.4
38	Oklahoma	0.3
39	South Carolina	0.2
40	Alabama	0.0
40	Maine	0.0
40	Montana	0.0
40	New Hampshire	0.0
40	North Dakota	0.0
40	Rhode Island	0.0
40	South Dakota	0.0
40	Vermont	0.0
40	Wyoming	0.0
NA	Illinois**	NA
NA	Kentucky**	NA
	District of Columbia**	NA

Source: CQ Press using reported data from the Federal Bureau of Investigation
   "Crime in the United States 2008" (Uniform Crime Reports, September 14, 2009, http://www.fbi.gov/ucr/ucr.htm)
*By law enforcement agencies submitting complete reports to the F.B.I. for 12 months in 2008. Arrests of youths 17 years and younger divided into population of 10 to 17 year olds. See important note at beginning of this chapter. Includes keeping a bawdy house or procuring or transporting women for immoral purposes. Attempts are included.
**Not available.

Reported Arrests of Juveniles for Prostitution and Commercialized Vice as a Percent of All Such Arrests in 2008
National Percent = 1.9% of Reported Prostitution/Commercialized Vice Arrests*

ALPHA ORDER

RANK	STATE	PERCENT
41	Alabama	0.0
17	Alaska	1.3
12	Arizona	1.7
32	Arkansas	0.6
6	California	3.6
4	Colorado	3.9
27	Connecticut	0.8
27	Delaware	0.8
23	Florida	0.9
12	Georgia	1.7
9	Hawaii	2.6
1	Idaho	9.5
21	Illinois	1.0
39	Indiana	0.2
14	Iowa	1.6
35	Kansas	0.4
41	Kentucky	0.0
21	Louisiana	1.0
41	Maine	0.0
23	Maryland	0.9
33	Massachusetts	0.5
10	Michigan	2.1
7	Minnesota	3.4
27	Mississippi	0.8
17	Missouri	1.3
41	Montana	0.0
33	Nebraska	0.5
16	Nevada	1.4
41	New Hampshire	0.0
10	New Jersey	2.1
23	New Mexico	0.9
19	New York	1.2
23	North Carolina	0.9
41	North Dakota	0.0
35	Ohio	0.4
39	Oklahoma	0.2
8	Oregon	3.1
35	Pennsylvania	0.4
41	Rhode Island	0.0
38	South Carolina	0.3
41	South Dakota	0.0
19	Tennessee	1.2
14	Texas	1.6
3	Utah	5.0
41	Vermont	0.0
30	Virginia	0.7
2	Washington	7.8
30	West Virginia	0.7
4	Wisconsin	3.9
41	Wyoming	0.0

RANK ORDER

RANK	STATE	PERCENT
1	Idaho	9.5
2	Washington	7.8
3	Utah	5.0
4	Colorado	3.9
4	Wisconsin	3.9
6	California	3.6
7	Minnesota	3.4
8	Oregon	3.1
9	Hawaii	2.6
10	Michigan	2.1
10	New Jersey	2.1
12	Arizona	1.7
12	Georgia	1.7
14	Iowa	1.6
14	Texas	1.6
16	Nevada	1.4
17	Alaska	1.3
17	Missouri	1.3
19	New York	1.2
19	Tennessee	1.2
21	Illinois	1.0
21	Louisiana	1.0
23	Florida	0.9
23	Maryland	0.9
23	New Mexico	0.9
23	North Carolina	0.9
27	Connecticut	0.8
27	Delaware	0.8
27	Mississippi	0.8
30	Virginia	0.7
30	West Virginia	0.7
32	Arkansas	0.6
33	Massachusetts	0.5
33	Nebraska	0.5
35	Kansas	0.4
35	Ohio	0.4
35	Pennsylvania	0.4
38	South Carolina	0.3
39	Indiana	0.2
39	Oklahoma	0.2
41	Alabama	0.0
41	Kentucky	0.0
41	Maine	0.0
41	Montana	0.0
41	New Hampshire	0.0
41	North Dakota	0.0
41	Rhode Island	0.0
41	South Dakota	0.0
41	Vermont	0.0
41	Wyoming	0.0

District of Columbia**   NA

Source: CQ Press using reported data from the Federal Bureau of Investigation
"Crime in the United States 2008" (Uniform Crime Reports, September 14, 2009, http://www.fbi.gov/ucr/ucr.htm)
*Arrests of youths 17 years and younger by law enforcement agencies submitting complete reports to the F.B.I. for 12 months in 2008. Includes keeping a bawdy house or procuring or transporting women for immoral purposes. Attempts are included.
**Not available.

Reported Arrests of Juveniles for
Offenses Against Families and Children in 2008
National Total = 4,378 Reported Arrests*

ALPHA ORDER

RANK	STATE	ARRESTS	% of USA
32	Alabama	15	0.3%
45	Alaska	2	0.0%
5	Arizona	284	6.5%
45	Arkansas	2	0.0%
36	California	10	0.2%
20	Colorado	77	1.8%
19	Connecticut	87	2.0%
44	Delaware	3	0.1%
NA	Florida**	NA	NA
8	Georgia	184	4.2%
45	Hawaii	2	0.0%
30	Idaho	22	0.5%
39	Illinois	8	0.2%
2	Indiana	346	7.9%
34	Iowa	12	0.3%
29	Kansas	26	0.6%
48	Kentucky	1	0.0%
10	Louisiana	135	3.1%
48	Maine	1	0.0%
25	Maryland	38	0.9%
14	Massachusetts	103	2.4%
35	Michigan	11	0.3%
26	Minnesota	37	0.8%
4	Mississippi	293	6.7%
17	Missouri	90	2.1%
21	Montana	50	1.1%
26	Nebraska	37	0.8%
39	Nevada	8	0.2%
39	New Hampshire	8	0.2%
9	New Jersey	152	3.5%
43	New Mexico	4	0.1%
3	New York	319	7.3%
15	North Carolina	101	2.3%
18	North Dakota	88	2.0%
1	Ohio	690	15.8%
13	Oklahoma	118	2.7%
36	Oregon	10	0.2%
23	Pennsylvania	49	1.1%
16	Rhode Island	95	2.2%
7	South Carolina	205	4.7%
11	South Dakota	129	2.9%
21	Tennessee	50	1.1%
24	Texas	44	1.0%
12	Utah	127	2.9%
36	Vermont	10	0.2%
30	Virginia	22	0.5%
32	Washington	15	0.3%
42	West Virginia	6	0.1%
6	Wisconsin	223	5.1%
28	Wyoming	29	0.7%

RANK ORDER

RANK	STATE	ARRESTS	% of USA
1	Ohio	690	15.8%
2	Indiana	346	7.9%
3	New York	319	7.3%
4	Mississippi	293	6.7%
5	Arizona	284	6.5%
6	Wisconsin	223	5.1%
7	South Carolina	205	4.7%
8	Georgia	184	4.2%
9	New Jersey	152	3.5%
10	Louisiana	135	3.1%
11	South Dakota	129	2.9%
12	Utah	127	2.9%
13	Oklahoma	118	2.7%
14	Massachusetts	103	2.4%
15	North Carolina	101	2.3%
16	Rhode Island	95	2.2%
17	Missouri	90	2.1%
18	North Dakota	88	2.0%
19	Connecticut	87	2.0%
20	Colorado	77	1.8%
21	Montana	50	1.1%
21	Tennessee	50	1.1%
23	Pennsylvania	49	1.1%
24	Texas	44	1.0%
25	Maryland	38	0.9%
26	Minnesota	37	0.8%
26	Nebraska	37	0.8%
28	Wyoming	29	0.7%
29	Kansas	26	0.6%
30	Idaho	22	0.5%
30	Virginia	22	0.5%
32	Alabama	15	0.3%
32	Washington	15	0.3%
34	Iowa	12	0.3%
35	Michigan	11	0.3%
36	California	10	0.2%
36	Oregon	10	0.2%
36	Vermont	10	0.2%
39	Illinois	8	0.2%
39	Nevada	8	0.2%
39	New Hampshire	8	0.2%
42	West Virginia	6	0.1%
43	New Mexico	4	0.1%
44	Delaware	3	0.1%
45	Alaska	2	0.0%
45	Arkansas	2	0.0%
45	Hawaii	2	0.0%
48	Kentucky	1	0.0%
48	Maine	1	0.0%
NA	Florida**	NA	NA
	District of Columbia**	NA	NA

Source: Reported data from the Federal Bureau of Investigation
"Crime in the United States 2008" (Uniform Crime Reports, September 14, 2009, http://www.fbi.gov/ucr/ucr.htm)
*Arrests of youths 17 years and younger by law enforcement agencies submitting complete reports to the F.B.I. for 12 months in 2008. Includes nonsupport, neglect, desertion, or abuse of family and children. See important note at beginning of this chapter.
**Not available.

Reported Juvenile Arrest Rate for
Offenses Against Families and Children in 2008
National Rate = 17.5 Reported Arrests per 100,000 Juvenile Population*

ALPHA ORDER

RANK	STATE	RATE
34	Alabama	3.7
40	Alaska	2.6
12	Arizona	39.9
47	Arkansas	0.8
49	California	0.2
21	Colorado	17.0
17	Connecticut	24.7
35	Delaware	3.3
NA	Florida**	NA
16	Georgia	27.2
43	Hawaii	1.8
25	Idaho	13.2
42	Illinois	2.4
6	Indiana	66.9
32	Iowa	4.1
26	Kansas	12.6
45	Kentucky	1.4
9	Louisiana	48.8
47	Maine	0.8
30	Maryland	6.3
20	Massachusetts	17.5
46	Michigan	1.1
29	Minnesota	6.8
1	Mississippi	194.8
23	Missouri	15.0
8	Montana	51.6
18	Nebraska	20.8
37	Nevada	2.9
28	New Hampshire	7.2
22	New Jersey	16.8
41	New Mexico	2.5
14	New York	33.3
24	North Carolina	14.5
3	North Dakota	151.6
4	Ohio	92.2
15	Oklahoma	30.3
39	Oregon	2.7
33	Pennsylvania	3.9
5	Rhode Island	88.6
10	South Carolina	44.4
2	South Dakota	189.5
27	Tennessee	9.5
44	Texas	1.6
11	Utah	43.1
19	Vermont	19.4
38	Virginia	2.8
36	Washington	3.0
31	West Virginia	5.6
13	Wisconsin	38.0
7	Wyoming	52.3

RANK ORDER

RANK	STATE	RATE
1	Mississippi	194.8
2	South Dakota	189.5
3	North Dakota	151.6
4	Ohio	92.2
5	Rhode Island	88.6
6	Indiana	66.9
7	Wyoming	52.3
8	Montana	51.6
9	Louisiana	48.8
10	South Carolina	44.4
11	Utah	43.1
12	Arizona	39.9
13	Wisconsin	38.0
14	New York	33.3
15	Oklahoma	30.3
16	Georgia	27.2
17	Connecticut	24.7
18	Nebraska	20.8
19	Vermont	19.4
20	Massachusetts	17.5
21	Colorado	17.0
22	New Jersey	16.8
23	Missouri	15.0
24	North Carolina	14.5
25	Idaho	13.2
26	Kansas	12.6
27	Tennessee	9.5
28	New Hampshire	7.2
29	Minnesota	6.8
30	Maryland	6.3
31	West Virginia	5.6
32	Iowa	4.1
33	Pennsylvania	3.9
34	Alabama	3.7
35	Delaware	3.3
36	Washington	3.0
37	Nevada	2.9
38	Virginia	2.8
39	Oregon	2.7
40	Alaska	2.6
41	New Mexico	2.5
42	Illinois	2.4
43	Hawaii	1.8
44	Texas	1.6
45	Kentucky	1.4
46	Michigan	1.1
47	Arkansas	0.8
47	Maine	0.8
49	California	0.2
NA	Florida**	NA
	District of Columbia**	NA

Source: CQ Press using reported data from the Federal Bureau of Investigation
   "Crime in the United States 2008" (Uniform Crime Reports, September 14, 2009, http://www.fbi.gov/ucr/ucr.htm)
*By law enforcement agencies submitting complete reports to the F.B.I. for 12 months in 2008. Arrests of youths 17 years and younger divided into population of 10 to 17 year olds. See important note at beginning of this chapter. Includes nonsupport, neglect, desertion, or abuse of family and children.
**Not available.

Reported Arrests of Juveniles for Offenses Against Families and Children as a Percent of All Such Arrests in 2008

National Percent = 5.0% of Offenses Against Families and Children Arrests*

ALPHA ORDER

RANK	STATE	PERCENT
38	Alabama	1.4
45	Alaska	0.6
13	Arizona	9.4
34	Arkansas	1.7
28	California	2.6
28	Colorado	2.6
19	Connecticut	7.5
40	Delaware	1.3
NA	Florida**	NA
20	Georgia	7.0
22	Hawaii	4.3
25	Idaho	3.5
31	Illinois	2.2
4	Indiana	19.3
38	Iowa	1.4
12	Kansas	10.0
49	Kentucky	0.2
9	Louisiana	11.4
42	Maine	1.1
34	Maryland	1.7
17	Massachusetts	8.0
47	Michigan	0.4
22	Minnesota	4.3
15	Mississippi	8.1
33	Missouri	1.9
5	Montana	16.0
30	Nebraska	2.4
46	Nevada	0.5
21	New Hampshire	4.8
43	New Jersey	1.0
47	New Mexico	0.4
7	New York	12.9
37	North Carolina	1.5
2	North Dakota	53.7
11	Ohio	10.3
8	Oklahoma	12.1
36	Oregon	1.6
24	Pennsylvania	4.2
1	Rhode Island	59.7
6	South Carolina	14.3
3	South Dakota	37.7
27	Tennessee	2.8
44	Texas	0.9
18	Utah	7.6
26	Vermont	3.2
40	Virginia	1.3
31	Washington	2.2
14	West Virginia	9.1
15	Wisconsin	8.1
10	Wyoming	10.9

RANK ORDER

RANK	STATE	PERCENT
1	Rhode Island	59.7
2	North Dakota	53.7
3	South Dakota	37.7
4	Indiana	19.3
5	Montana	16.0
6	South Carolina	14.3
7	New York	12.9
8	Oklahoma	12.1
9	Louisiana	11.4
10	Wyoming	10.9
11	Ohio	10.3
12	Kansas	10.0
13	Arizona	9.4
14	West Virginia	9.1
15	Mississippi	8.1
15	Wisconsin	8.1
17	Massachusetts	8.0
18	Utah	7.6
19	Connecticut	7.5
20	Georgia	7.0
21	New Hampshire	4.8
22	Hawaii	4.3
22	Minnesota	4.3
24	Pennsylvania	4.2
25	Idaho	3.5
26	Vermont	3.2
27	Tennessee	2.8
28	California	2.6
28	Colorado	2.6
30	Nebraska	2.4
31	Illinois	2.2
31	Washington	2.2
33	Missouri	1.9
34	Arkansas	1.7
34	Maryland	1.7
36	Oregon	1.6
37	North Carolina	1.5
38	Alabama	1.4
38	Iowa	1.4
40	Delaware	1.3
40	Virginia	1.3
42	Maine	1.1
43	New Jersey	1.0
44	Texas	0.9
45	Alaska	0.6
46	Nevada	0.5
47	Michigan	0.4
47	New Mexico	0.4
49	Kentucky	0.2
NA	Florida**	NA
	District of Columbia**	NA

Source: CQ Press using reported data from the Federal Bureau of Investigation
"Crime in the United States 2008" (Uniform Crime Reports, September 14, 2009, http://www.fbi.gov/ucr/ucr.htm)
*Arrests of youths 17 years and younger by law enforcement agencies submitting complete reports to the F.B.I. for 12 months in 2008. Includes nonsupport, neglect, desertion, or abuse of family and children.
**Not available.

Inmates Under Age 18 Held in State Prisons in 2008

National Total = 3,650 Prisoners*

ALPHA ORDER

RANK	STATE	PRISONERS	% of USA
9	Alabama	123	3.4%
30	Alaska	10	0.3%
7	Arizona	156	4.3%
25	Arkansas	17	0.5%
41	California	0	0.0%
19	Colorado	37	1.0%
2	Connecticut	375	10.3%
22	Delaware	25	0.7%
3	Florida	301	8.2%
1	Georgia	1,113	30.5%
41	Hawaii	0	0.0%
41	Idaho	0	0.0%
NA	Illinois**	NA	NA
13	Indiana	63	1.7%
26	Iowa	16	0.4%
36	Kansas	4	0.1%
41	Kentucky	0	0.0%
20	Louisiana	26	0.7%
41	Maine	0	0.0%
14	Maryland	61	1.7%
38	Massachusetts	3	0.1%
8	Michigan	140	3.8%
29	Minnesota	13	0.4%
18	Mississippi	39	1.1%
20	Missouri	26	0.7%
32	Montana	8	0.2%
27	Nebraska	15	0.4%
10	Nevada	118	3.2%
41	New Hampshire	0	0.0%
24	New Jersey	19	0.5%
40	New Mexico	1	0.0%
4	New York	206	5.6%
5	North Carolina	186	5.1%
41	North Dakota	0	0.0%
12	Ohio	75	2.1%
35	Oklahoma	7	0.2%
32	Oregon	8	0.2%
15	Pennsylvania	55	1.5%
30	Rhode Island	10	0.3%
11	South Carolina	96	2.6%
41	South Dakota	0	0.0%
28	Tennessee	14	0.4%
6	Texas	157	4.3%
23	Utah	21	0.6%
32	Vermont	8	0.2%
17	Virginia	45	1.2%
38	Washington	3	0.1%
41	West Virginia	0	0.0%
16	Wisconsin	46	1.3%
36	Wyoming	4	0.1%

RANK ORDER

RANK	STATE	PRISONERS	% of USA
1	Georgia	1,113	30.5%
2	Connecticut	375	10.3%
3	Florida	301	8.2%
4	New York	206	5.6%
5	North Carolina	186	5.1%
6	Texas	157	4.3%
7	Arizona	156	4.3%
8	Michigan	140	3.8%
9	Alabama	123	3.4%
10	Nevada	118	3.2%
11	South Carolina	96	2.6%
12	Ohio	75	2.1%
13	Indiana	63	1.7%
14	Maryland	61	1.7%
15	Pennsylvania	55	1.5%
16	Wisconsin	46	1.3%
17	Virginia	45	1.2%
18	Mississippi	39	1.1%
19	Colorado	37	1.0%
20	Louisiana	26	0.7%
20	Missouri	26	0.7%
22	Delaware	25	0.7%
23	Utah	21	0.6%
24	New Jersey	19	0.5%
25	Arkansas	17	0.5%
26	Iowa	16	0.4%
27	Nebraska	15	0.4%
28	Tennessee	14	0.4%
29	Minnesota	13	0.4%
30	Alaska	10	0.3%
30	Rhode Island	10	0.3%
32	Montana	8	0.2%
32	Oregon	8	0.2%
32	Vermont	8	0.2%
35	Oklahoma	7	0.2%
36	Kansas	4	0.1%
36	Wyoming	4	0.1%
38	Massachusetts	3	0.1%
38	Washington	3	0.1%
40	New Mexico	1	0.0%
41	California	0	0.0%
41	Hawaii	0	0.0%
41	Idaho	0	0.0%
41	Kentucky	0	0.0%
41	Maine	0	0.0%
41	New Hampshire	0	0.0%
41	North Dakota	0	0.0%
41	South Dakota	0	0.0%
41	West Virginia	0	0.0%
NA	Illinois**	NA	NA
	District of Columbia**	NA	NA

Source: U.S. Department of Justice, Bureau of Justice Statistics
"Prison and Jail Inmates at Midyear 2008" (March 2009, NCJ 225619, http://bjs.ojp.usdoj.gov/)
*As of June 30, 2008.
**Not available. Responsibility for sentenced felons in D.C. was transferred to the Federal Bureau of Prisons.

Juveniles in Residential Custody in 2006

National Total = 92,854 Juveniles*

ALPHA ORDER

RANK	STATE	JUVENILES	% of USA
13	Alabama	1,752	1.9%
41	Alaska	363	0.4%
14	Arizona	1,737	1.9%
33	Arkansas	813	0.9%
1	California	15,240	16.4%
12	Colorado	2,034	2.2%
38	Connecticut	498	0.5%
44	Delaware	303	0.3%
3	Florida	7,302	7.9%
8	Georgia	2,631	2.8%
49	Hawaii	123	0.1%
37	Idaho	522	0.6%
8	Illinois	2,631	2.8%
10	Indiana	2,616	2.8%
27	Iowa	1,062	1.1%
28	Kansas	1,053	1.1%
23	Kentucky	1,242	1.3%
24	Louisiana	1,200	1.3%
47	Maine	210	0.2%
26	Maryland	1,104	1.2%
25	Massachusetts	1,164	1.3%
7	Michigan	2,760	3.0%
16	Minnesota	1,623	1.7%
40	Mississippi	444	0.5%
21	Missouri	1,293	1.4%
45	Montana	243	0.3%
34	Nebraska	735	0.8%
31	Nevada	885	1.0%
48	New Hampshire	189	0.2%
15	New Jersey	1,704	1.8%
39	New Mexico	471	0.5%
5	New York	4,197	4.5%
29	North Carolina	1,029	1.1%
46	North Dakota	240	0.3%
6	Ohio	4,149	4.5%
30	Oklahoma	924	1.0%
22	Oregon	1,254	1.4%
4	Pennsylvania	4,323	4.7%
42	Rhode Island	348	0.4%
20	South Carolina	1,320	1.4%
35	South Dakota	597	0.6%
18	Tennessee	1,419	1.5%
2	Texas	8,247	8.9%
32	Utah	864	0.9%
50	Vermont	54	0.1%
11	Virginia	2,310	2.5%
17	Washington	1,455	1.6%
36	West Virginia	579	0.6%
19	Wisconsin	1,347	1.5%
43	Wyoming	315	0.3%

RANK ORDER

RANK	STATE	JUVENILES	% of USA
1	California	15,240	16.4%
2	Texas	8,247	8.9%
3	Florida	7,302	7.9%
4	Pennsylvania	4,323	4.7%
5	New York	4,197	4.5%
6	Ohio	4,149	4.5%
7	Michigan	2,760	3.0%
8	Georgia	2,631	2.8%
8	Illinois	2,631	2.8%
10	Indiana	2,616	2.8%
11	Virginia	2,310	2.5%
12	Colorado	2,034	2.2%
13	Alabama	1,752	1.9%
14	Arizona	1,737	1.9%
15	New Jersey	1,704	1.8%
16	Minnesota	1,623	1.7%
17	Washington	1,455	1.6%
18	Tennessee	1,419	1.5%
19	Wisconsin	1,347	1.5%
20	South Carolina	1,320	1.4%
21	Missouri	1,293	1.4%
22	Oregon	1,254	1.4%
23	Kentucky	1,242	1.3%
24	Louisiana	1,200	1.3%
25	Massachusetts	1,164	1.3%
26	Maryland	1,104	1.2%
27	Iowa	1,062	1.1%
28	Kansas	1,053	1.1%
29	North Carolina	1,029	1.1%
30	Oklahoma	924	1.0%
31	Nevada	885	1.0%
32	Utah	864	0.9%
33	Arkansas	813	0.9%
34	Nebraska	735	0.8%
35	South Dakota	597	0.6%
36	West Virginia	579	0.6%
37	Idaho	522	0.6%
38	Connecticut	498	0.5%
39	New Mexico	471	0.5%
40	Mississippi	444	0.5%
41	Alaska	363	0.4%
42	Rhode Island	348	0.4%
43	Wyoming	315	0.3%
44	Delaware	303	0.3%
45	Montana	243	0.3%
46	North Dakota	240	0.3%
47	Maine	210	0.2%
48	New Hampshire	189	0.2%
49	Hawaii	123	0.1%
50	Vermont	54	0.1%
	District of Columbia	339	0.4%

Source: U.S. Department of Justice, Office of Juvenile Justice and Delinquency Prevention
    "Census of Juveniles in Residential Placement Databook" (http://www.ojjdp.ncjrs.gov/ojstatbb/cjrp/)
*Based on state of offense. Includes 1,467 juveniles not shown by state and 132 juveniles in tribal facilities.

Rate of Juveniles in Residential Custody: 2006

National Rate = 295 Juveniles per 100,000 Juvenile Population*

ALPHA ORDER

RANK	STATE	RATE
10	Alabama	342
3	Alaska	430
33	Arizona	246
31	Arkansas	261
9	California	351
4	Colorado	397
44	Connecticut	170
13	Delaware	327
4	Florida	397
26	Georgia	276
49	Hawaii	92
22	Idaho	297
38	Illinois	206
7	Indiana	364
14	Iowa	323
11	Kansas	335
27	Kentucky	273
25	Louisiana	279
45	Maine	152
43	Maryland	174
41	Massachusetts	198
29	Michigan	268
24	Minnesota	280
48	Mississippi	128
36	Missouri	227
34	Montana	235
6	Nebraska	368
19	Nevada	317
46	New Hampshire	148
42	New Jersey	176
40	New Mexico	204
28	New York	270
47	North Carolina	144
8	North Dakota	355
15	Ohio	322
35	Oklahoma	232
18	Oregon	319
16	Pennsylvania	321
21	Rhode Island	308
19	South Carolina	317
1	South Dakota	672
37	Tennessee	216
11	Texas	335
30	Utah	267
50	Vermont	81
23	Virginia	283
38	Washington	206
17	West Virginia	320
32	Wisconsin	251
2	Wyoming	559

RANK ORDER

RANK	STATE	RATE
1	South Dakota	672
2	Wyoming	559
3	Alaska	430
4	Colorado	397
4	Florida	397
6	Nebraska	368
7	Indiana	364
8	North Dakota	355
9	California	351
10	Alabama	342
11	Kansas	335
11	Texas	335
13	Delaware	327
14	Iowa	323
15	Ohio	322
16	Pennsylvania	321
17	West Virginia	320
18	Oregon	319
19	Nevada	317
19	South Carolina	317
21	Rhode Island	308
22	Idaho	297
23	Virginia	283
24	Minnesota	280
25	Louisiana	279
26	Georgia	276
27	Kentucky	273
28	New York	270
29	Michigan	268
30	Utah	267
31	Arkansas	261
32	Wisconsin	251
33	Arizona	246
34	Montana	235
35	Oklahoma	232
36	Missouri	227
37	Tennessee	216
38	Illinois	206
38	Washington	206
40	New Mexico	204
41	Massachusetts	198
42	New Jersey	176
43	Maryland	174
44	Connecticut	170
45	Maine	152
46	New Hampshire	148
47	North Carolina	144
48	Mississippi	128
49	Hawaii	92
50	Vermont	81
	District of Columbia	671

Source: U.S. Department of Justice, Office of Juvenile Justice and Delinquency Prevention
"Census of Juveniles in Residential Placement Databook" (http://www.ojjdp.ncjrs.gov/ojstatbb/cjrp/)
*"Juvenile" includes youths age 10 through the upper age of jurisdiction in each state. Based on state of offense. National rate
Includes juveniles not shown by state and juveniles in tribal facilities.

Percent of Juveniles in Residential Custody Who Are Female: 2006

National Percent = 15.0%*

ALPHA ORDER				RANK ORDER		
RANK	STATE	PERCENT		RANK	STATE	PERCENT
8	Alabama	21.9		1	Hawaii	34.1
12	Alaska	20.7		2	Nebraska	33.1
15	Arizona	20.0		3	Iowa	32.8
16	Arkansas	19.6		4	Wyoming	29.5
39	California	12.2		5	South Dakota	27.1
34	Colorado	13.3		6	Montana	24.7
7	Connecticut	22.9		7	Connecticut	22.9
48	Delaware	8.9		8	Alabama	21.9
31	Florida	13.9		9	Indiana	21.6
28	Georgia	14.6		10	Kentucky	21.3
1	Hawaii	34.1		11	New York	20.9
12	Idaho	20.7		12	Alaska	20.7
36	Illinois	12.7		12	Idaho	20.7
9	Indiana	21.6		14	Mississippi	20.3
3	Iowa	32.8		15	Arizona	20.0
44	Kansas	10.8		16	Arkansas	19.6
10	Kentucky	21.3		17	Michigan	19.3
25	Louisiana	15.8		18	Utah	19.1
42	Maine	11.4		19	New Hampshire	19.0
49	Maryland	8.4		20	North Carolina	17.8
41	Massachusetts	11.9		21	Nevada	16.9
17	Michigan	19.3		22	Minnesota	16.5
22	Minnesota	16.5		23	North Dakota	16.3
14	Mississippi	20.3		24	Washington	15.9
29	Missouri	14.2		25	Louisiana	15.8
6	Montana	24.7		26	New Mexico	15.3
2	Nebraska	33.1		27	West Virginia	15.0
21	Nevada	16.9		28	Georgia	14.6
19	New Hampshire	19.0		29	Missouri	14.2
46	New Jersey	10.4		30	Wisconsin	14.0
26	New Mexico	15.3		31	Florida	13.9
11	New York	20.9		32	Ohio	13.4
20	North Carolina	17.8		32	Texas	13.4
23	North Dakota	16.3		34	Colorado	13.3
32	Ohio	13.4		35	Virginia	13.0
40	Oklahoma	12.0		36	Illinois	12.7
38	Oregon	12.4		36	South Carolina	12.7
45	Pennsylvania	10.7		38	Oregon	12.4
47	Rhode Island	10.3		39	California	12.2
36	South Carolina	12.7		40	Oklahoma	12.0
5	South Dakota	27.1		41	Massachusetts	11.9
42	Tennessee	11.4		42	Maine	11.4
32	Texas	13.4		42	Tennessee	11.4
18	Utah	19.1		44	Kansas	10.8
50	Vermont	5.6		45	Pennsylvania	10.7
35	Virginia	13.0		46	New Jersey	10.4
24	Washington	15.9		47	Rhode Island	10.3
27	West Virginia	15.0		48	Delaware	8.9
30	Wisconsin	14.0		49	Maryland	8.4
4	Wyoming	29.5		50	Vermont	5.6

	District of Columbia	8.8

Source: CQ Press using data from U.S. Department of Justice, Office of Juvenile Justice and Delinquency Prevention
   "Census of Juveniles in Residential Placement Databook" (http://www.ojjdp.ncjrs.gov/ojstatbb/cjrp/)
*Based on state of offense. Includes juveniles not shown by state and juveniles in tribal facilities.

Rate of White Juveniles in Residential Custody: 2006

National Rate = 170 White Juveniles per 100,000 White Juvenile Population*

ALPHA ORDER

RANK	STATE	RATE
14	Alabama	213
9	Alaska	257
21	Arizona	183
22	Arkansas	172
24	California	163
5	Colorado	284
48	Connecticut	56
41	Delaware	103
3	Florida	288
37	Georgia	124
50	Hawaii	18
4	Idaho	286
40	Illinois	114
7	Indiana	278
10	Iowa	253
15	Kansas	208
16	Kentucky	204
35	Louisiana	129
30	Maine	146
44	Maryland	74
42	Massachusetts	95
25	Michigan	162
28	Minnesota	151
47	Mississippi	61
34	Missouri	134
20	Montana	184
13	Nebraska	236
11	Nevada	247
38	New Hampshire	123
49	New Jersey	46
43	New Mexico	83
39	New York	118
44	North Carolina	74
12	North Dakota	240
19	Ohio	188
29	Oklahoma	149
6	Oregon	281
33	Pennsylvania	136
27	Rhode Island	160
26	South Carolina	161
2	South Dakota	371
32	Tennessee	140
18	Texas	196
17	Utah	197
46	Vermont	71
36	Virginia	127
23	Washington	164
8	West Virginia	277
31	Wisconsin	141
1	Wyoming	416

RANK ORDER

RANK	STATE	RATE
1	Wyoming	416
2	South Dakota	371
3	Florida	288
4	Idaho	286
5	Colorado	284
6	Oregon	281
7	Indiana	278
8	West Virginia	277
9	Alaska	257
10	Iowa	253
11	Nevada	247
12	North Dakota	240
13	Nebraska	236
14	Alabama	213
15	Kansas	208
16	Kentucky	204
17	Utah	197
18	Texas	196
19	Ohio	188
20	Montana	184
21	Arizona	183
22	Arkansas	172
23	Washington	164
24	California	163
25	Michigan	162
26	South Carolina	161
27	Rhode Island	160
28	Minnesota	151
29	Oklahoma	149
30	Maine	146
31	Wisconsin	141
32	Tennessee	140
33	Pennsylvania	136
34	Missouri	134
35	Louisiana	129
36	Virginia	127
37	Georgia	124
38	New Hampshire	123
39	New York	118
40	Illinois	114
41	Delaware	103
42	Massachusetts	95
43	New Mexico	83
44	Maryland	74
44	North Carolina	74
46	Vermont	71
47	Mississippi	61
48	Connecticut	56
49	New Jersey	46
50	Hawaii	18

District of Columbia — 197

Source: U.S. Department of Justice, Office of Juvenile Justice and Delinquency Prevention
    "Census of Juveniles in Residential Placement Databook" (http://www.ojjdp.ncjrs.gov/ojstatbb/cjrp/)
*"Juvenile" includes youths age 10 through the upper age of jurisdiction in each state. Based on state of offense. National rate
Includes juveniles not shown by state and juveniles in tribal facilities.

Percent of Juveniles in Residential Custody Who Are White: 2006

National Percent = 35%*

<table>
<tr><td colspan="3">ALPHA ORDER</td><td colspan="3">RANK ORDER</td></tr>
<tr><th>RANK</th><th>STATE</th><th>PERCENT</th><th>RANK</th><th>STATE</th><th>PERCENT</th></tr>
<tr><td>27</td><td>Alabama</td><td>40</td><td>1</td><td>Maine</td><td>91</td></tr>
<tr><td>31</td><td>Alaska</td><td>37</td><td>2</td><td>Vermont</td><td>83</td></tr>
<tr><td>32</td><td>Arizona</td><td>36</td><td>3</td><td>West Virginia</td><td>81</td></tr>
<tr><td>17</td><td>Arkansas</td><td>47</td><td>4</td><td>Idaho</td><td>80</td></tr>
<tr><td>47</td><td>California</td><td>16</td><td>5</td><td>New Hampshire</td><td>78</td></tr>
<tr><td>17</td><td>Colorado</td><td>47</td><td>6</td><td>Iowa</td><td>69</td></tr>
<tr><td>44</td><td>Connecticut</td><td>23</td><td>7</td><td>Oregon</td><td>68</td></tr>
<tr><td>46</td><td>Delaware</td><td>20</td><td>8</td><td>Montana</td><td>67</td></tr>
<tr><td>29</td><td>Florida</td><td>39</td><td>9</td><td>Kentucky</td><td>65</td></tr>
<tr><td>40</td><td>Georgia</td><td>24</td><td>10</td><td>Wyoming</td><td>64</td></tr>
<tr><td>50</td><td>Hawaii</td><td>5</td><td>11</td><td>Indiana</td><td>62</td></tr>
<tr><td>4</td><td>Idaho</td><td>80</td><td>12</td><td>Utah</td><td>60</td></tr>
<tr><td>35</td><td>Illinois</td><td>32</td><td>13</td><td>North Dakota</td><td>59</td></tr>
<tr><td>11</td><td>Indiana</td><td>62</td><td>14</td><td>Washington</td><td>58</td></tr>
<tr><td>6</td><td>Iowa</td><td>69</td><td>15</td><td>Nebraska</td><td>52</td></tr>
<tr><td>16</td><td>Kansas</td><td>48</td><td>16</td><td>Kansas</td><td>48</td></tr>
<tr><td>9</td><td>Kentucky</td><td>65</td><td>17</td><td>Arkansas</td><td>47</td></tr>
<tr><td>39</td><td>Louisiana</td><td>26</td><td>17</td><td>Colorado</td><td>47</td></tr>
<tr><td>1</td><td>Maine</td><td>91</td><td>17</td><td>Missouri</td><td>47</td></tr>
<tr><td>44</td><td>Maryland</td><td>23</td><td>17</td><td>Tennessee</td><td>47</td></tr>
<tr><td>32</td><td>Massachusetts</td><td>36</td><td>21</td><td>Ohio</td><td>46</td></tr>
<tr><td>23</td><td>Michigan</td><td>44</td><td>22</td><td>Wisconsin</td><td>45</td></tr>
<tr><td>23</td><td>Minnesota</td><td>44</td><td>23</td><td>Michigan</td><td>44</td></tr>
<tr><td>40</td><td>Mississippi</td><td>24</td><td>23</td><td>Minnesota</td><td>44</td></tr>
<tr><td>17</td><td>Missouri</td><td>47</td><td>23</td><td>South Dakota</td><td>44</td></tr>
<tr><td>8</td><td>Montana</td><td>67</td><td>26</td><td>Oklahoma</td><td>43</td></tr>
<tr><td>15</td><td>Nebraska</td><td>52</td><td>27</td><td>Alabama</td><td>40</td></tr>
<tr><td>27</td><td>Nevada</td><td>40</td><td>27</td><td>Nevada</td><td>40</td></tr>
<tr><td>5</td><td>New Hampshire</td><td>78</td><td>29</td><td>Florida</td><td>39</td></tr>
<tr><td>47</td><td>New Jersey</td><td>16</td><td>30</td><td>Rhode Island</td><td>38</td></tr>
<tr><td>49</td><td>New Mexico</td><td>13</td><td>31</td><td>Alaska</td><td>37</td></tr>
<tr><td>40</td><td>New York</td><td>24</td><td>32</td><td>Arizona</td><td>36</td></tr>
<tr><td>35</td><td>North Carolina</td><td>32</td><td>32</td><td>Massachusetts</td><td>36</td></tr>
<tr><td>13</td><td>North Dakota</td><td>59</td><td>34</td><td>Pennsylvania</td><td>33</td></tr>
<tr><td>21</td><td>Ohio</td><td>46</td><td>35</td><td>Illinois</td><td>32</td></tr>
<tr><td>26</td><td>Oklahoma</td><td>43</td><td>35</td><td>North Carolina</td><td>32</td></tr>
<tr><td>7</td><td>Oregon</td><td>68</td><td>37</td><td>South Carolina</td><td>30</td></tr>
<tr><td>34</td><td>Pennsylvania</td><td>33</td><td>38</td><td>Virginia</td><td>29</td></tr>
<tr><td>30</td><td>Rhode Island</td><td>38</td><td>39</td><td>Louisiana</td><td>26</td></tr>
<tr><td>37</td><td>South Carolina</td><td>30</td><td>40</td><td>Georgia</td><td>24</td></tr>
<tr><td>23</td><td>South Dakota</td><td>44</td><td>40</td><td>Mississippi</td><td>24</td></tr>
<tr><td>17</td><td>Tennessee</td><td>47</td><td>40</td><td>New York</td><td>24</td></tr>
<tr><td>40</td><td>Texas</td><td>24</td><td>40</td><td>Texas</td><td>24</td></tr>
<tr><td>12</td><td>Utah</td><td>60</td><td>44</td><td>Connecticut</td><td>23</td></tr>
<tr><td>2</td><td>Vermont</td><td>83</td><td>44</td><td>Maryland</td><td>23</td></tr>
<tr><td>38</td><td>Virginia</td><td>29</td><td>46</td><td>Delaware</td><td>20</td></tr>
<tr><td>14</td><td>Washington</td><td>58</td><td>47</td><td>California</td><td>16</td></tr>
<tr><td>3</td><td>West Virginia</td><td>81</td><td>47</td><td>New Jersey</td><td>16</td></tr>
<tr><td>22</td><td>Wisconsin</td><td>45</td><td>49</td><td>New Mexico</td><td>13</td></tr>
<tr><td>10</td><td>Wyoming</td><td>64</td><td>50</td><td>Hawaii</td><td>5</td></tr>
<tr><td></td><td></td><td></td><td></td><td>District of Columbia</td><td>4</td></tr>
</table>

Source: U.S. Department of Justice, Office of Juvenile Justice and Delinquency Prevention
   "Census of Juveniles in Residential Placement Databook" (http://www.ojjdp.ncjrs.gov/ojstatbb/cjrp/)
*Based on state of offense. Includes juveniles not shown by state and juveniles in tribal facilities.

Rate of Black Juveniles in Residential Custody: 2006

National Rate = 767 Black Juveniles per 100,000 Black Juvenile Population*

ALPHA ORDER

RANK	STATE	RATE
35	Alabama	610
20	Alaska	902
32	Arizona	658
37	Arkansas	595
8	California	1,268
9	Colorado	1,234
34	Connecticut	618
22	Delaware	893
18	Florida	972
39	Georgia	544
50	Hawaii	65
44	Idaho	382
41	Illinois	500
19	Indiana	945
4	Iowa	1,525
11	Kansas	1,230
23	Kentucky	865
40	Louisiana	521
43	Maine	447
46	Maryland	364
28	Massachusetts	706
33	Michigan	654
7	Minnesota	1,364
49	Mississippi	213
30	Missouri	701
16	Montana	1,038
6	Nebraska	1,471
20	Nevada	902
10	New Hampshire	1,233
29	New Jersey	705
38	New Mexico	550
26	New York	754
48	North Carolina	315
47	North Dakota	318
17	Ohio	989
25	Oklahoma	756
15	Oregon	1,104
12	Pennsylvania	1,229
5	Rhode Island	1,501
36	South Carolina	605
2	South Dakota	3,049
42	Tennessee	483
24	Texas	843
3	Utah	1,981
45	Vermont	381
27	Virginia	741
31	Washington	698
14	West Virginia	1,205
13	Wisconsin	1,206
1	Wyoming	4,138

RANK ORDER

RANK	STATE	RATE
1	Wyoming	4,138
2	South Dakota	3,049
3	Utah	1,981
4	Iowa	1,525
5	Rhode Island	1,501
6	Nebraska	1,471
7	Minnesota	1,364
8	California	1,268
9	Colorado	1,234
10	New Hampshire	1,233
11	Kansas	1,230
12	Pennsylvania	1,229
13	Wisconsin	1,206
14	West Virginia	1,205
15	Oregon	1,104
16	Montana	1,038
17	Ohio	989
18	Florida	972
19	Indiana	945
20	Alaska	902
20	Nevada	902
22	Delaware	893
23	Kentucky	865
24	Texas	843
25	Oklahoma	756
26	New York	754
27	Virginia	741
28	Massachusetts	706
29	New Jersey	705
30	Missouri	701
31	Washington	698
32	Arizona	658
33	Michigan	654
34	Connecticut	618
35	Alabama	610
36	South Carolina	605
37	Arkansas	595
38	New Mexico	550
39	Georgia	544
40	Louisiana	521
41	Illinois	500
42	Tennessee	483
43	Maine	447
44	Idaho	382
45	Vermont	381
46	Maryland	364
47	North Dakota	318
48	North Carolina	315
49	Mississippi	213
50	Hawaii	65

District of Columbia	789

Source: U.S. Department of Justice, Office of Juvenile Justice and Delinquency Prevention
"Census of Juveniles in Residential Placement Databook" (http://www.ojjdp.ncjrs.gov/ojstatbb/cjrp/)
*"Juvenile" includes youths age 10 through the upper age of jurisdiction in each state. Based on state of offense. National rate
Includes juveniles not shown by state and juveniles in tribal facilities.

Percent of Juveniles in Residential Custody Who Are Black: 2006

National Percent = 40%*

ALPHA ORDER

RANK	STATE	PERCENT
10	Alabama	58
38	Alaska	11
37	Arizona	12
17	Arkansas	47
30	California	28
35	Colorado	16
21	Connecticut	44
3	Delaware	72
12	Florida	52
4	Georgia	71
48	Hawaii	2
49	Idaho	1
17	Illinois	47
26	Indiana	31
33	Iowa	19
28	Kansas	29
26	Kentucky	31
2	Louisiana	73
46	Maine	4
4	Maryland	71
28	Massachusetts	29
17	Michigan	47
24	Minnesota	33
1	Mississippi	76
16	Missouri	48
46	Montana	4
32	Nebraska	25
30	Nevada	28
38	New Hampshire	11
7	New Jersey	66
44	New Mexico	6
12	New York	52
9	North Carolina	59
49	North Dakota	1
14	Ohio	49
23	Oklahoma	34
40	Oregon	10
11	Pennsylvania	54
22	Rhode Island	35
6	South Carolina	69
43	South Dakota	8
14	Tennessee	49
24	Texas	33
40	Utah	10
44	Vermont	6
8	Virginia	63
34	Washington	18
35	West Virginia	16
20	Wisconsin	45
40	Wyoming	10

RANK ORDER

RANK	STATE	PERCENT
1	Mississippi	76
2	Louisiana	73
3	Delaware	72
4	Georgia	71
4	Maryland	71
6	South Carolina	69
7	New Jersey	66
8	Virginia	63
9	North Carolina	59
10	Alabama	58
11	Pennsylvania	54
12	Florida	52
12	New York	52
14	Ohio	49
14	Tennessee	49
16	Missouri	48
17	Arkansas	47
17	Illinois	47
17	Michigan	47
20	Wisconsin	45
21	Connecticut	44
22	Rhode Island	35
23	Oklahoma	34
24	Minnesota	33
24	Texas	33
26	Indiana	31
26	Kentucky	31
28	Kansas	29
28	Massachusetts	29
30	California	28
30	Nevada	28
32	Nebraska	25
33	Iowa	19
34	Washington	18
35	Colorado	16
35	West Virginia	16
37	Arizona	12
38	Alaska	11
38	New Hampshire	11
40	Oregon	10
40	Utah	10
40	Wyoming	10
43	South Dakota	8
44	New Mexico	6
44	Vermont	6
46	Maine	4
46	Montana	4
48	Hawaii	2
49	Idaho	1
49	North Dakota	1

District of Columbia	91

Source: U.S. Department of Justice, Office of Juvenile Justice and Delinquency Prevention
"Census of Juveniles in Residential Placement Databook" (http://www.ojjdp.ncjrs.gov/ojstatbb/cjrp/)
*Based on state of offense. Includes juveniles not shown by state and juveniles in tribal facilities.

Rate of Hispanic Juveniles in Residential Custody: 2006

National Rate = 326 Hispanic Juveniles per 100,000 Hispanic Juvenile Population

ALPHA ORDER

RANK	STATE	RATE
37	Alabama	195
38	Alaska	178
25	Arizona	282
35	Arkansas	196
11	California	396
7	Colorado	544
15	Connecticut	337
22	Delaware	285
42	Florida	140
40	Georgia	173
46	Hawaii	108
20	Idaho	305
35	Illinois	196
14	Indiana	356
13	Iowa	361
6	Kansas	553
33	Kentucky	203
48	Louisiana	71
49	Maine	0
45	Maryland	116
9	Massachusetts	474
31	Michigan	214
27	Minnesota	274
49	Mississippi	0
34	Missouri	199
17	Montana	333
4	Nebraska	565
28	Nevada	261
10	New Hampshire	399
39	New Jersey	176
22	New Mexico	285
21	New York	290
44	North Carolina	121
12	North Dakota	387
29	Ohio	252
32	Oklahoma	207
19	Oregon	316
5	Pennsylvania	560
18	Rhode Island	327
47	South Carolina	100
1	South Dakota	1,139
41	Tennessee	147
16	Texas	335
8	Utah	513
3	Vermont	613
26	Virginia	275
29	Washington	252
24	West Virginia	283
43	Wisconsin	135
2	Wyoming	945

RANK ORDER

RANK	STATE	RATE
1	South Dakota	1,139
2	Wyoming	945
3	Vermont	613
4	Nebraska	565
5	Pennsylvania	560
6	Kansas	553
7	Colorado	544
8	Utah	513
9	Massachusetts	474
10	New Hampshire	399
11	California	396
12	North Dakota	387
13	Iowa	361
14	Indiana	356
15	Connecticut	337
16	Texas	335
17	Montana	333
18	Rhode Island	327
19	Oregon	316
20	Idaho	305
21	New York	290
22	Delaware	285
22	New Mexico	285
24	West Virginia	283
25	Arizona	282
26	Virginia	275
27	Minnesota	274
28	Nevada	261
29	Ohio	252
29	Washington	252
31	Michigan	214
32	Oklahoma	207
33	Kentucky	203
34	Missouri	199
35	Arkansas	196
35	Illinois	196
37	Alabama	195
38	Alaska	178
39	New Jersey	176
40	Georgia	173
41	Tennessee	147
42	Florida	140
43	Wisconsin	135
44	North Carolina	121
45	Maryland	116
46	Hawaii	108
47	South Carolina	100
48	Louisiana	71
49	Maine	0
49	Mississippi	0
	District of Columbia	274

Source: U.S. Department of Justice, Office of Juvenile Justice and Delinquency Prevention
"Census of Juveniles in Residential Placement Databook" (http://www.ojjdp.ncjrs.gov/ojstatbb/cjrp/)
*"Juvenile" includes youths age 10 through the upper age of jurisdiction in each state. Based on state of offense. National rate
Includes juveniles not shown by state and juveniles in tribal facilities.

Percent of Juveniles in Residential Custody Who Are Hispanic: 2006

National Percent = 20%*

ALPHA ORDER

RANK	STATE	PERCENT
41	Alabama	2
41	Alaska	2
3	Arizona	44
31	Arkansas	5
2	California	51
5	Colorado	34
6	Connecticut	29
26	Delaware	7
23	Florida	8
31	Georgia	5
20	Hawaii	12
19	Idaho	13
12	Illinois	17
28	Indiana	6
28	Iowa	6
11	Kansas	19
41	Kentucky	2
46	Louisiana	1
49	Maine	0
36	Maryland	4
7	Massachusetts	27
36	Michigan	4
31	Minnesota	5
49	Mississippi	0
38	Missouri	3
31	Montana	5
15	Nebraska	15
8	Nevada	26
23	New Hampshire	8
12	New Jersey	17
1	New Mexico	72
10	New York	21
28	North Carolina	6
38	North Dakota	3
41	Ohio	2
23	Oklahoma	8
18	Oregon	14
22	Pennsylvania	10
12	Rhode Island	17
46	South Carolina	1
31	South Dakota	5
41	Tennessee	2
4	Texas	42
9	Utah	25
21	Vermont	11
26	Virginia	7
15	Washington	15
46	West Virginia	1
38	Wisconsin	3
15	Wyoming	15

RANK ORDER

RANK	STATE	PERCENT
1	New Mexico	72
2	California	51
3	Arizona	44
4	Texas	42
5	Colorado	34
6	Connecticut	29
7	Massachusetts	27
8	Nevada	26
9	Utah	25
10	New York	21
11	Kansas	19
12	Illinois	17
12	New Jersey	17
12	Rhode Island	17
15	Nebraska	15
15	Washington	15
15	Wyoming	15
18	Oregon	14
19	Idaho	13
20	Hawaii	12
21	Vermont	11
22	Pennsylvania	10
23	Florida	8
23	New Hampshire	8
23	Oklahoma	8
26	Delaware	7
26	Virginia	7
28	Indiana	6
28	Iowa	6
28	North Carolina	6
31	Arkansas	5
31	Georgia	5
31	Minnesota	5
31	Montana	5
31	South Dakota	5
36	Maryland	4
36	Michigan	4
38	Missouri	3
38	North Dakota	3
38	Wisconsin	3
41	Alabama	2
41	Alaska	2
41	Kentucky	2
41	Ohio	2
41	Tennessee	2
46	Louisiana	1
46	South Carolina	1
46	West Virginia	1
49	Maine	0
49	Mississippi	0
	District of Columbia	4

Source: U.S. Department of Justice, Office of Juvenile Justice and Delinquency Prevention
"Census of Juveniles in Residential Placement Databook" (http://www.ojjdp.ncjrs.gov/ojstatbb/cjrp/)
*Based on state of offense. Includes juveniles not shown by state and juveniles in tribal facilities.

Public High School Dropout Rate in 2006

National Rate = 3.9%*

<table>
<tr><td colspan="3">ALPHA ORDER</td><td colspan="3">RANK ORDER</td></tr>
<tr><td>RANK</td><td>STATE</td><td>RATE</td><td>RANK</td><td>STATE</td><td>RATE</td></tr>
<tr><td>41</td><td>Alabama</td><td>2.5</td><td>1</td><td>Louisiana</td><td>8.4</td></tr>
<tr><td>2</td><td>Alaska</td><td>8.0</td><td>2</td><td>Alaska</td><td>8.0</td></tr>
<tr><td>5</td><td>Arizona</td><td>7.6</td><td>3</td><td>Colorado</td><td>7.8</td></tr>
<tr><td>32</td><td>Arkansas</td><td>3.1</td><td>4</td><td>Nevada</td><td>7.7</td></tr>
<tr><td>24</td><td>California</td><td>3.7</td><td>5</td><td>Arizona</td><td>7.6</td></tr>
<tr><td>3</td><td>Colorado</td><td>7.8</td><td>6</td><td>Wyoming</td><td>5.7</td></tr>
<tr><td>46</td><td>Connecticut</td><td>2.0</td><td>7</td><td>Washington</td><td>5.6</td></tr>
<tr><td>8</td><td>Delaware</td><td>5.5</td><td>8</td><td>Delaware</td><td>5.5</td></tr>
<tr><td>17</td><td>Florida</td><td>4.1</td><td>8</td><td>New Mexico</td><td>5.5</td></tr>
<tr><td>11</td><td>Georgia</td><td>5.2</td><td>10</td><td>Maine</td><td>5.4</td></tr>
<tr><td>12</td><td>Hawaii</td><td>4.7</td><td>11</td><td>Georgia</td><td>5.2</td></tr>
<tr><td>39</td><td>Idaho</td><td>2.7</td><td>12</td><td>Hawaii</td><td>4.7</td></tr>
<tr><td>21</td><td>Illinois</td><td>4.0</td><td>13</td><td>Oregon</td><td>4.6</td></tr>
<tr><td>35</td><td>Indiana</td><td>2.9</td><td>14</td><td>New York</td><td>4.4</td></tr>
<tr><td>43</td><td>Iowa</td><td>2.2</td><td>14</td><td>South Dakota</td><td>4.4</td></tr>
<tr><td>42</td><td>Kansas</td><td>2.4</td><td>16</td><td>Texas</td><td>4.3</td></tr>
<tr><td>29</td><td>Kentucky</td><td>3.3</td><td>17</td><td>Florida</td><td>4.1</td></tr>
<tr><td>1</td><td>Louisiana</td><td>8.4</td><td>17</td><td>Missouri</td><td>4.1</td></tr>
<tr><td>10</td><td>Maine</td><td>5.4</td><td>17</td><td>Ohio</td><td>4.1</td></tr>
<tr><td>22</td><td>Maryland</td><td>3.9</td><td>17</td><td>Rhode Island</td><td>4.1</td></tr>
<tr><td>28</td><td>Massachusetts</td><td>3.4</td><td>21</td><td>Illinois</td><td>4.0</td></tr>
<tr><td>27</td><td>Michigan</td><td>3.5</td><td>22</td><td>Maryland</td><td>3.9</td></tr>
<tr><td>32</td><td>Minnesota</td><td>3.1</td><td>22</td><td>West Virginia</td><td>3.9</td></tr>
<tr><td>34</td><td>Mississippi</td><td>3.0</td><td>24</td><td>California</td><td>3.7</td></tr>
<tr><td>17</td><td>Missouri</td><td>4.1</td><td>24</td><td>Montana</td><td>3.7</td></tr>
<tr><td>24</td><td>Montana</td><td>3.7</td><td>26</td><td>Oklahoma</td><td>3.6</td></tr>
<tr><td>36</td><td>Nebraska</td><td>2.8</td><td>27</td><td>Michigan</td><td>3.5</td></tr>
<tr><td>4</td><td>Nevada</td><td>7.7</td><td>28</td><td>Massachusetts</td><td>3.4</td></tr>
<tr><td>31</td><td>New Hampshire</td><td>3.2</td><td>29</td><td>Kentucky</td><td>3.3</td></tr>
<tr><td>47</td><td>New Jersey</td><td>1.7</td><td>29</td><td>Utah</td><td>3.3</td></tr>
<tr><td>8</td><td>New Mexico</td><td>5.5</td><td>31</td><td>New Hampshire</td><td>3.2</td></tr>
<tr><td>14</td><td>New York</td><td>4.4</td><td>32</td><td>Arkansas</td><td>3.1</td></tr>
<tr><td>NA</td><td>North Carolina**</td><td>NA</td><td>32</td><td>Minnesota</td><td>3.1</td></tr>
<tr><td>45</td><td>North Dakota</td><td>2.1</td><td>34</td><td>Mississippi</td><td>3.0</td></tr>
<tr><td>17</td><td>Ohio</td><td>4.1</td><td>35</td><td>Indiana</td><td>2.9</td></tr>
<tr><td>26</td><td>Oklahoma</td><td>3.6</td><td>36</td><td>Nebraska</td><td>2.8</td></tr>
<tr><td>13</td><td>Oregon</td><td>4.6</td><td>36</td><td>Pennsylvania</td><td>2.8</td></tr>
<tr><td>36</td><td>Pennsylvania</td><td>2.8</td><td>36</td><td>Tennessee</td><td>2.8</td></tr>
<tr><td>17</td><td>Rhode Island</td><td>4.1</td><td>39</td><td>Idaho</td><td>2.7</td></tr>
<tr><td>NA</td><td>South Carolina**</td><td>NA</td><td>39</td><td>Virginia</td><td>2.7</td></tr>
<tr><td>14</td><td>South Dakota</td><td>4.4</td><td>41</td><td>Alabama</td><td>2.5</td></tr>
<tr><td>36</td><td>Tennessee</td><td>2.8</td><td>42</td><td>Kansas</td><td>2.4</td></tr>
<tr><td>16</td><td>Texas</td><td>4.3</td><td>43</td><td>Iowa</td><td>2.2</td></tr>
<tr><td>29</td><td>Utah</td><td>3.3</td><td>43</td><td>Wisconsin</td><td>2.2</td></tr>
<tr><td>NA</td><td>Vermont**</td><td>NA</td><td>45</td><td>North Dakota</td><td>2.1</td></tr>
<tr><td>39</td><td>Virginia</td><td>2.7</td><td>46</td><td>Connecticut</td><td>2.0</td></tr>
<tr><td>7</td><td>Washington</td><td>5.6</td><td>47</td><td>New Jersey</td><td>1.7</td></tr>
<tr><td>22</td><td>West Virginia</td><td>3.9</td><td>NA</td><td>North Carolina**</td><td>NA</td></tr>
<tr><td>43</td><td>Wisconsin</td><td>2.2</td><td>NA</td><td>South Carolina**</td><td>NA</td></tr>
<tr><td>6</td><td>Wyoming</td><td>5.7</td><td>NA</td><td>Vermont**</td><td>NA</td></tr>
<tr><td></td><td></td><td></td><td></td><td>District of Columbia**</td><td>NA</td></tr>
</table>

Source: U.S. Department of Education, National Center for Education Statistics
"Public School Graduates and Dropouts from the Common Core of Data: School Year 2005-06" (NCES 2008353rev)
(http://nces.ed.gov/pubs2008/2008353rev.pdf)
*"Event" dropout rates showing the number of 9th-12th grade dropouts divided by the number of students enrolled at the beginning of the school year in those grades. National rate is for reporting states.
**Not available.

Percent of High School Students Who Carried a Weapon on School Property in 2007
National Percent = 5.9%*

ALPHA ORDER

RANK	STATE	PERCENT
NA	Alabama**	NA
7	Alaska	8.4
10	Arizona	7.0
13	Arkansas	6.8
NA	California**	NA
NA	Colorado**	NA
22	Connecticut	5.5
23	Delaware	5.4
20	Florida	5.6
24	Georgia	5.3
37	Hawaii	3.7
6	Idaho	8.9
37	Illinois	3.7
11	Indiana	6.9
35	Iowa	4.4
19	Kansas	5.7
8	Kentucky	8.0
NA	Louisiana**	NA
28	Maine	4.9
17	Maryland	5.9
25	Massachusetts	5.0
25	Michigan	5.0
NA	Minnesota**	NA
30	Mississippi	4.8
34	Missouri	4.6
2	Montana	9.7
NA	Nebraska**	NA
32	Nevada	4.7
18	New Hampshire	5.8
NA	New Jersey**	NA
4	New Mexico	9.3
32	New York	4.7
13	North Carolina	6.8
25	North Dakota	5.0
36	Ohio	4.1
5	Oklahoma	9.0
NA	Oregon**	NA
NA	Pennsylvania**	NA
28	Rhode Island	4.9
30	South Carolina	4.8
16	South Dakota	6.3
20	Tennessee	5.6
13	Texas	6.8
9	Utah	7.5
3	Vermont	9.6
NA	Virginia**	NA
NA	Washington**	NA
11	West Virginia	6.9
39	Wisconsin	3.6
1	Wyoming	11.4

RANK ORDER

RANK	STATE	PERCENT
1	Wyoming	11.4
2	Montana	9.7
3	Vermont	9.6
4	New Mexico	9.3
5	Oklahoma	9.0
6	Idaho	8.9
7	Alaska	8.4
8	Kentucky	8.0
9	Utah	7.5
10	Arizona	7.0
11	Indiana	6.9
11	West Virginia	6.9
13	Arkansas	6.8
13	North Carolina	6.8
13	Texas	6.8
16	South Dakota	6.3
17	Maryland	5.9
18	New Hampshire	5.8
19	Kansas	5.7
20	Florida	5.6
20	Tennessee	5.6
22	Connecticut	5.5
23	Delaware	5.4
24	Georgia	5.3
25	Massachusetts	5.0
25	Michigan	5.0
25	North Dakota	5.0
28	Maine	4.9
28	Rhode Island	4.9
30	Mississippi	4.8
30	South Carolina	4.8
32	Nevada	4.7
32	New York	4.7
34	Missouri	4.6
35	Iowa	4.4
36	Ohio	4.1
37	Hawaii	3.7
37	Illinois	3.7
39	Wisconsin	3.6
NA	Alabama**	NA
NA	California**	NA
NA	Colorado**	NA
NA	Louisiana**	NA
NA	Minnesota**	NA
NA	Nebraska**	NA
NA	New Jersey**	NA
NA	Oregon**	NA
NA	Pennsylvania**	NA
NA	Virginia**	NA
NA	Washington**	NA
	District of Columbia**	NA

Source: U.S. Department of Health and Human Services, Centers for Disease Control and Prevention
"Youth Risk Behavior Surveillance--U.S., 2007" (http://www.cdc.gov/HealthyYouth/yrbs/)
*Weapons include guns, knives, clubs, or other instruments. National percent includes nonreporting states.
**Not available.

Percent of High School Students Who Were Threatened or Injured with a Weapon on School Property in 2007
National Percent = 7.8%*

ALPHA ORDER

RANK	STATE	PERCENT
NA	Alabama**	NA
23	Alaska	7.7
2	Arizona	11.2
10	Arkansas	9.1
NA	California**	NA
NA	Colorado**	NA
23	Connecticut	7.7
36	Delaware	5.6
12	Florida	8.6
19	Georgia	8.1
33	Hawaii	6.4
3	Idaho	10.2
21	Illinois	7.8
7	Indiana	9.6
28	Iowa	7.1
12	Kansas	8.6
14	Kentucky	8.3
NA	Louisiana**	NA
31	Maine	6.8
7	Maryland	9.6
38	Massachusetts	5.3
19	Michigan	8.1
NA	Minnesota**	NA
14	Mississippi	8.3
9	Missouri	9.3
29	Montana	7.0
NA	Nebraska**	NA
21	Nevada	7.8
25	New Hampshire	7.3
NA	New Jersey**	NA
4	New Mexico	10.1
25	New York	7.3
32	North Carolina	6.6
39	North Dakota	5.2
14	Ohio	8.3
29	Oklahoma	7.0
NA	Oregon**	NA
NA	Pennsylvania**	NA
14	Rhode Island	8.3
5	South Carolina	9.8
35	South Dakota	5.9
25	Tennessee	7.3
11	Texas	8.7
1	Utah	11.4
34	Vermont	6.2
NA	Virginia**	NA
NA	Washington**	NA
6	West Virginia	9.7
36	Wisconsin	5.6
14	Wyoming	8.3

RANK ORDER

RANK	STATE	PERCENT
1	Utah	11.4
2	Arizona	11.2
3	Idaho	10.2
4	New Mexico	10.1
5	South Carolina	9.8
6	West Virginia	9.7
7	Indiana	9.6
7	Maryland	9.6
9	Missouri	9.3
10	Arkansas	9.1
11	Texas	8.7
12	Florida	8.6
12	Kansas	8.6
14	Kentucky	8.3
14	Mississippi	8.3
14	Ohio	8.3
14	Rhode Island	8.3
14	Wyoming	8.3
19	Georgia	8.1
19	Michigan	8.1
21	Illinois	7.8
21	Nevada	7.8
23	Alaska	7.7
23	Connecticut	7.7
25	New Hampshire	7.3
25	New York	7.3
25	Tennessee	7.3
28	Iowa	7.1
29	Montana	7.0
29	Oklahoma	7.0
31	Maine	6.8
32	North Carolina	6.6
33	Hawaii	6.4
34	Vermont	6.2
35	South Dakota	5.9
36	Delaware	5.6
36	Wisconsin	5.6
38	Massachusetts	5.3
39	North Dakota	5.2
NA	Alabama**	NA
NA	California**	NA
NA	Colorado**	NA
NA	Louisiana**	NA
NA	Minnesota**	NA
NA	Nebraska**	NA
NA	New Jersey**	NA
NA	Oregon**	NA
NA	Pennsylvania**	NA
NA	Virginia**	NA
NA	Washington**	NA
	District of Columbia**	NA

Source: U.S. Department of Health and Human Services, Centers for Disease Control and Prevention
"Youth Risk Behavior Surveillance--U.S., 2007" (http://www.cdc.gov/HealthyYouth/yrbs/)
*One or more times during the 12 months preceding the survey. National percent includes nonreporting states.
**Not available.

Percent of Public School Teachers Who Reported Being Threatened With Injury by a Student in 2008
National Percent = 8.1% of Teachers*

ALPHA ORDER

RANK	STATE	PERCENT
35	Alabama	6.8
23	Alaska	7.8
36	Arizona	6.6
44	Arkansas	5.7
18	California	8.6
34	Colorado	6.9
31	Connecticut	7.2
3	Delaware	11.7
4	Florida	11.4
43	Georgia	5.8
26	Hawaii	7.6
42	Idaho	5.9
20	Illinois	8.2
8	Indiana	10.2
36	Iowa	6.6
44	Kansas	5.7
9	Kentucky	9.9
7	Louisiana	10.4
12	Maine	9.5
2	Maryland	12.7
10	Massachusetts	9.7
41	Michigan	6.0
30	Minnesota	7.3
5	Mississippi	10.7
15	Missouri	8.7
39	Montana	6.4
31	Nebraska	7.2
13	Nevada	9.3
38	New Hampshire	6.5
48	New Jersey	4.7
1	New Mexico	12.8
6	New York	10.5
11	North Carolina	9.6
50	North Dakota	3.2
15	Ohio	8.7
29	Oklahoma	7.4
40	Oregon	6.3
49	Pennsylvania	4.6
15	Rhode Island	8.7
19	South Carolina	8.5
24	South Dakota	7.7
24	Tennessee	7.7
26	Texas	7.6
44	Utah	5.7
26	Vermont	7.6
20	Virginia	8.2
33	Washington	7.0
22	West Virginia	8.0
14	Wisconsin	9.0
47	Wyoming	5.4

RANK ORDER

RANK	STATE	PERCENT
1	New Mexico	12.8
2	Maryland	12.7
3	Delaware	11.7
4	Florida	11.4
5	Mississippi	10.7
6	New York	10.5
7	Louisiana	10.4
8	Indiana	10.2
9	Kentucky	9.9
10	Massachusetts	9.7
11	North Carolina	9.6
12	Maine	9.5
13	Nevada	9.3
14	Wisconsin	9.0
15	Missouri	8.7
15	Ohio	8.7
15	Rhode Island	8.7
18	California	8.6
19	South Carolina	8.5
20	Illinois	8.2
20	Virginia	8.2
22	West Virginia	8.0
23	Alaska	7.8
24	South Dakota	7.7
24	Tennessee	7.7
26	Hawaii	7.6
26	Texas	7.6
26	Vermont	7.6
29	Oklahoma	7.4
30	Minnesota	7.3
31	Connecticut	7.2
31	Nebraska	7.2
33	Washington	7.0
34	Colorado	6.9
35	Alabama	6.8
36	Arizona	6.6
36	Iowa	6.6
38	New Hampshire	6.5
39	Montana	6.4
40	Oregon	6.3
41	Michigan	6.0
42	Idaho	5.9
43	Georgia	5.8
44	Arkansas	5.7
44	Kansas	5.7
44	Utah	5.7
47	Wyoming	5.4
48	New Jersey	4.7
49	Pennsylvania	4.6
50	North Dakota	3.2

District of Columbia   16.9

Source: U.S. Department of Justice, Bureau of Justice Statistics
"Indicators of School Crime and Safety: 2009" (December 2009, NCJ 228478, http://bjs.ojp.usdoj.gov/)
*For school year 2007-2008.

Percent of Public School Teachers Who Reported Being Physically Attacked by a Student in 2008
National Percent = 4.3% of Teachers*

ALPHA ORDER

RANK	STATE	PERCENT
39	Alabama	3.2
2	Alaska**	6.7
12	Arizona	5.0
28	Arkansas	3.9
35	California	3.6
14	Colorado	4.7
37	Connecticut**	3.3
9	Delaware	5.4
24	Florida	4.0
24	Georgia	4.0
21	Hawaii**	4.1
43	Idaho**	2.9
28	Illinois	3.9
14	Indiana	4.7
40	Iowa	3.1
12	Kansas	5.0
8	Kentucky	5.8
24	Louisiana**	4.0
11	Maine	5.2
1	Maryland	8.4
21	Massachusetts	4.1
36	Michigan**	3.5
3	Minnesota	6.6
43	Mississippi	2.9
10	Missouri	5.3
24	Montana	4.0
18	Nebraska	4.2
37	Nevada**	3.3
46	New Hampshire**	2.2
48	New Jersey**	1.8
17	New Mexico**	4.3
5	New York	6.4
7	North Carolina**	5.9
49	North Dakota**	1.7
46	Ohio**	2.2
40	Oklahoma	3.1
28	Oregon**	3.9
33	Pennsylvania	3.8
NA	Rhode Island***	NA
43	South Carolina**	2.9
16	South Dakota	4.5
28	Tennessee	3.9
18	Texas	4.2
33	Utah	3.8
18	Vermont**	4.2
6	Virginia	6.0
21	Washington	4.1
28	West Virginia	3.9
3	Wisconsin	6.6
42	Wyoming	3.0

RANK ORDER

RANK	STATE	PERCENT
1	Maryland	8.4
2	Alaska**	6.7
3	Minnesota	6.6
3	Wisconsin	6.6
5	New York	6.4
6	Virginia	6.0
7	North Carolina**	5.9
8	Kentucky	5.8
9	Delaware	5.4
10	Missouri	5.3
11	Maine	5.2
12	Arizona	5.0
12	Kansas	5.0
14	Colorado	4.7
14	Indiana	4.7
16	South Dakota	4.5
17	New Mexico**	4.3
18	Nebraska	4.2
18	Texas	4.2
18	Vermont**	4.2
21	Hawaii**	4.1
21	Massachusetts	4.1
21	Washington	4.1
24	Florida	4.0
24	Georgia	4.0
24	Louisiana**	4.0
24	Montana	4.0
28	Arkansas	3.9
28	Illinois	3.9
28	Oregon**	3.9
28	Tennessee	3.9
28	West Virginia	3.9
33	Pennsylvania	3.8
33	Utah	3.8
35	California	3.6
36	Michigan**	3.5
37	Connecticut**	3.3
37	Nevada**	3.3
39	Alabama	3.2
40	Iowa	3.1
40	Oklahoma	3.1
42	Wyoming	3.0
43	Idaho**	2.9
43	Mississippi	2.9
43	South Carolina**	2.9
46	New Hampshire**	2.2
46	Ohio**	2.2
48	New Jersey**	1.8
49	North Dakota**	1.7
NA	Rhode Island***	NA

District of Columbia — 7.1

Source: U.S. Department of Justice, Bureau of Justice Statistics
    "Indicators of School Crime and Safety: 2009" (December 2009, NCJ 228478, http://bjs.ojp.usdoj.gov/)
*For school year 2007-2008.
**Data from these states should be interpreted with caution.
***Not available.

Percent of High School Students Who Drink Alcohol: 2007

National Percent = 44.7%*

ALPHA ORDER				RANK ORDER		
RANK	STATE	PERCENT		RANK	STATE	PERCENT
NA	Alabama**	NA		1	Wisconsin	48.9
31	Alaska	39.7		2	Texas	48.3
8	Arizona	45.6		3	Montana	46.5
27	Arkansas	42.2		4	Massachusetts	46.2
NA	California**	NA		5	North Dakota	46.1
NA	Colorado**	NA		6	Connecticut	46.0
6	Connecticut	46.0		7	Ohio	45.7
9	Delaware	45.2		8	Arizona	45.6
26	Florida	42.3		9	Delaware	45.2
33	Georgia	37.7		10	New Hampshire	44.8
38	Hawaii	29.1		11	South Dakota	44.5
23	Idaho	42.5		12	Missouri	44.4
14	Illinois	43.7		13	Indiana	43.9
13	Indiana	43.9		14	Illinois	43.7
28	Iowa	41.0		14	New York	43.7
24	Kansas	42.4		16	West Virginia	43.5
29	Kentucky	40.6		17	New Mexico	43.2
NA	Louisiana**	NA		18	Oklahoma	43.1
32	Maine	39.3		19	Maryland	42.9
19	Maryland	42.9		19	Rhode Island	42.9
4	Massachusetts	46.2		21	Michigan	42.8
21	Michigan	42.8		22	Vermont	42.6
NA	Minnesota**	NA		23	Idaho	42.5
29	Mississippi	40.6		24	Kansas	42.4
12	Missouri	44.4		24	Wyoming	42.4
3	Montana	46.5		26	Florida	42.3
NA	Nebraska**	NA		27	Arkansas	42.2
35	Nevada	37.0		28	Iowa	41.0
10	New Hampshire	44.8		29	Kentucky	40.6
NA	New Jersey**	NA		29	Mississippi	40.6
17	New Mexico	43.2		31	Alaska	39.7
14	New York	43.7		32	Maine	39.3
33	North Carolina	37.7		33	Georgia	37.7
5	North Dakota	46.1		33	North Carolina	37.7
7	Ohio	45.7		35	Nevada	37.0
18	Oklahoma	43.1		36	South Carolina	36.8
NA	Oregon**	NA		37	Tennessee	36.7
NA	Pennsylvania**	NA		38	Hawaii	29.1
19	Rhode Island	42.9		39	Utah	17.0
36	South Carolina	36.8		NA	Alabama**	NA
11	South Dakota	44.5		NA	California**	NA
37	Tennessee	36.7		NA	Colorado**	NA
2	Texas	48.3		NA	Louisiana**	NA
39	Utah	17.0		NA	Minnesota**	NA
22	Vermont	42.6		NA	Nebraska**	NA
NA	Virginia**	NA		NA	New Jersey**	NA
NA	Washington**	NA		NA	Oregon**	NA
16	West Virginia	43.5		NA	Pennsylvania**	NA
1	Wisconsin	48.9		NA	Virginia**	NA
24	Wyoming	42.4		NA	Washington**	NA
					District of Columbia**	NA

Source: U.S. Department of Health and Human Services, Centers for Disease Control and Prevention
    "Youth Risk Behavior Surveillance--U.S., 2007" (http://www.cdc.gov/HealthyYouth/yrbs/)
*Drank alcohol on one or more of the 30 days preceding the survey. National percent includes nonreporting states.
**Not available.

Percent of High School Students Who Use Marijuana: 2007

National Percent = 19.7%*

ALPHA ORDER

RANK	STATE	PERCENT
NA	Alabama**	NA
12	Alaska	20.5
9	Arizona	22.0
30	Arkansas	16.4
NA	California**	NA
NA	Colorado**	NA
6	Connecticut	23.2
1	Delaware	25.1
21	Florida	18.9
15	Georgia	19.6
33	Hawaii	15.7
26	Idaho	17.9
13	Illinois	20.3
21	Indiana	18.9
38	Iowa	11.5
35	Kansas	15.3
30	Kentucky	16.4
NA	Louisiana**	NA
9	Maine	22.0
16	Maryland	19.4
3	Massachusetts	24.6
25	Michigan	18.0
NA	Minnesota**	NA
29	Mississippi	16.7
20	Missouri	19.0
11	Montana	21.0
NA	Nebraska**	NA
34	Nevada	15.5
8	New Hampshire	22.9
NA	New Jersey**	NA
2	New Mexico	25.0
23	New York	18.6
19	North Carolina	19.1
36	North Dakota	14.8
27	Ohio	17.7
32	Oklahoma	15.9
NA	Oregon**	NA
NA	Pennsylvania**	NA
6	Rhode Island	23.2
23	South Carolina	18.6
27	South Dakota	17.7
16	Tennessee	19.4
18	Texas	19.3
39	Utah	8.7
4	Vermont	24.1
NA	Virginia**	NA
NA	Washington**	NA
5	West Virginia	23.5
13	Wisconsin	20.3
37	Wyoming	14.4

RANK ORDER

RANK	STATE	PERCENT
1	Delaware	25.1
2	New Mexico	25.0
3	Massachusetts	24.6
4	Vermont	24.1
5	West Virginia	23.5
6	Connecticut	23.2
6	Rhode Island	23.2
8	New Hampshire	22.9
9	Arizona	22.0
9	Maine	22.0
11	Montana	21.0
12	Alaska	20.5
13	Illinois	20.3
13	Wisconsin	20.3
15	Georgia	19.6
16	Maryland	19.4
16	Tennessee	19.4
18	Texas	19.3
19	North Carolina	19.1
20	Missouri	19.0
21	Florida	18.9
21	Indiana	18.9
23	New York	18.6
23	South Carolina	18.6
25	Michigan	18.0
26	Idaho	17.9
27	Ohio	17.7
27	South Dakota	17.7
29	Mississippi	16.7
30	Arkansas	16.4
30	Kentucky	16.4
32	Oklahoma	15.9
33	Hawaii	15.7
34	Nevada	15.5
35	Kansas	15.3
36	North Dakota	14.8
37	Wyoming	14.4
38	Iowa	11.5
39	Utah	8.7
NA	Alabama**	NA
NA	California**	NA
NA	Colorado**	NA
NA	Louisiana**	NA
NA	Minnesota**	NA
NA	Nebraska**	NA
NA	New Jersey**	NA
NA	Oregon**	NA
NA	Pennsylvania**	NA
NA	Virginia**	NA
NA	Washington**	NA
	District of Columbia**	NA

Source: U.S. Department of Health and Human Services, Centers for Disease Control and Prevention
"Youth Risk Behavior Surveillance--U.S., 2007" (http://www.cdc.gov/HealthyYouth/yrbs/)
*Used marijuana one or more times in the 30 days preceding the survey. National percent includes nonreporting states.
**Not available.

Admissions of Juveniles to Substance Abuse Treatment Programs
as a Percent of All Admissions in 2008
National Percent = 9.2% of Admissions*

ALPHA ORDER				RANK ORDER		
RANK	STATE	PERCENT		RANK	STATE	PERCENT
NA	Alabama**	NA		1	Hawaii	34.7
NA	Alaska**	NA		2	Florida	21.1
44	Arizona	0.3		2	Idaho	21.1
29	Arkansas	5.4		4	South Carolina	16.1
9	California	12.8		5	Washington	14.9
39	Colorado	3.2		6	Texas	13.9
42	Connecticut	1.4		7	Kansas	13.7
NA	Delaware**	NA		8	Tennessee	13.6
2	Florida	21.1		9	California	12.8
NA	Georgia**	NA		10	North Dakota	12.7
1	Hawaii	34.7		11	South Dakota	12.3
2	Idaho	21.1		12	Nevada	11.9
13	Illinois	10.9		13	Illinois	10.9
36	Indiana	3.9		14	Iowa	10.4
14	Iowa	10.4		15	Oklahoma	10.2
7	Kansas	13.7		16	Montana	9.9
34	Kentucky	4.3		17	Ohio	9.7
24	Louisiana	7.0		17	Oregon	9.7
34	Maine	4.3		19	Utah	8.8
23	Maryland	7.5		20	Minnesota	8.3
41	Massachusetts	1.8		21	Vermont	8.0
33	Michigan	4.7		22	Virginia	7.8
20	Minnesota	8.3		23	Maryland	7.5
31	Mississippi	5.2		24	Louisiana	7.0
26	Missouri	6.1		25	Pennsylvania	6.5
16	Montana	9.9		26	Missouri	6.1
43	Nebraska	1.0		27	Rhode Island	5.7
12	Nevada	11.9		28	West Virginia	5.5
29	New Hampshire	5.4		29	Arkansas	5.4
32	New Jersey	5.1		29	New Hampshire	5.4
44	New Mexico	0.3		31	Mississippi	5.2
37	New York	3.8		32	New Jersey	5.1
38	North Carolina	3.5		33	Michigan	4.7
10	North Dakota	12.7		34	Kentucky	4.3
17	Ohio	9.7		34	Maine	4.3
15	Oklahoma	10.2		36	Indiana	3.9
17	Oregon	9.7		37	New York	3.8
25	Pennsylvania	6.5		38	North Carolina	3.5
27	Rhode Island	5.7		39	Colorado	3.2
4	South Carolina	16.1		40	Wisconsin	2.4
11	South Dakota	12.3		41	Massachusetts	1.8
8	Tennessee	13.6		42	Connecticut	1.4
6	Texas	13.9		43	Nebraska	1.0
19	Utah	8.8		44	Arizona	0.3
21	Vermont	8.0		44	New Mexico	0.3
22	Virginia	7.8		NA	Alabama**	NA
5	Washington	14.9		NA	Alaska**	NA
28	West Virginia	5.5		NA	Delaware**	NA
40	Wisconsin	2.4		NA	Georgia**	NA
NA	Wyoming**	NA		NA	Wyoming**	NA
					District of Columbia**	NA

Source: U.S. Department of Health and Human Services, Substance Abuse & Mental Health Services Administration
    "Treatment Episode Data Set" (http://wwwdasis.samhsa.gov/webt/NewMapv1.htm)
*Preliminary figures as of December 28, 2009. National figure is a weighted average of reporting states. Admissions of those 17 or younger.
**Not available.

Victims of Child Abuse and Neglect in 2007

National Total = 742,661 Children*

ALPHA ORDER

RANK	STATE	CHILDREN	% of USA
22	Alabama	9,247	1.2%
38	Alaska	3,138	0.4%
36	Arizona	4,025	0.5%
20	Arkansas	9,847	1.3%
1	California	88,319	11.9%
18	Colorado	10,588	1.4%
19	Connecticut	9,875	1.3%
40	Delaware	2,116	0.3%
4	Florida	53,484	7.2%
7	Georgia	35,729	4.8%
41	Hawaii	2,075	0.3%
43	Idaho	1,582	0.2%
8	Illinois	31,058	4.2%
11	Indiana	18,380	2.5%
13	Iowa	14,051	1.9%
39	Kansas	2,272	0.3%
10	Kentucky	18,778	2.5%
21	Louisiana	9,468	1.3%
34	Maine	4,118	0.6%
NA	Maryland**	NA	NA
6	Massachusetts	37,690	5.1%
NA	Michigan**	NA	NA
29	Minnesota	6,847	0.9%
27	Mississippi	7,002	0.9%
25	Missouri	7,235	1.0%
42	Montana	1,886	0.3%
35	Nebraska	4,108	0.6%
32	Nevada	5,417	0.7%
46	New Hampshire	912	0.1%
24	New Jersey	7,543	1.0%
31	New Mexico	6,065	0.8%
2	New York	83,502	11.2%
9	North Carolina	25,976	3.5%
45	North Dakota	1,288	0.2%
5	Ohio	38,484	5.2%
15	Oklahoma	13,179	1.8%
17	Oregon	11,552	1.6%
33	Pennsylvania	4,177	0.6%
37	Rhode Island	3,857	0.5%
16	South Carolina	12,762	1.7%
44	South Dakota	1,485	0.2%
12	Tennessee	16,059	2.2%
3	Texas	71,111	9.6%
14	Utah	13,611	1.8%
47	Vermont	872	0.1%
30	Virginia	6,413	0.9%
28	Washington	6,984	0.9%
26	West Virginia	7,109	1.0%
23	Wisconsin	7,856	1.1%
48	Wyoming	772	0.1%

RANK ORDER

RANK	STATE	CHILDREN	% of USA
1	California	88,319	11.9%
2	New York	83,502	11.2%
3	Texas	71,111	9.6%
4	Florida	53,484	7.2%
5	Ohio	38,484	5.2%
6	Massachusetts	37,690	5.1%
7	Georgia	35,729	4.8%
8	Illinois	31,058	4.2%
9	North Carolina	25,976	3.5%
10	Kentucky	18,778	2.5%
11	Indiana	18,380	2.5%
12	Tennessee	16,059	2.2%
13	Iowa	14,051	1.9%
14	Utah	13,611	1.8%
15	Oklahoma	13,179	1.8%
16	South Carolina	12,762	1.7%
17	Oregon	11,552	1.6%
18	Colorado	10,588	1.4%
19	Connecticut	9,875	1.3%
20	Arkansas	9,847	1.3%
21	Louisiana	9,468	1.3%
22	Alabama	9,247	1.2%
23	Wisconsin	7,856	1.1%
24	New Jersey	7,543	1.0%
25	Missouri	7,235	1.0%
26	West Virginia	7,109	1.0%
27	Mississippi	7,002	0.9%
28	Washington	6,984	0.9%
29	Minnesota	6,847	0.9%
30	Virginia	6,413	0.9%
31	New Mexico	6,065	0.8%
32	Nevada	5,417	0.7%
33	Pennsylvania	4,177	0.6%
34	Maine	4,118	0.6%
35	Nebraska	4,108	0.6%
36	Arizona	4,025	0.5%
37	Rhode Island	3,857	0.5%
38	Alaska	3,138	0.4%
39	Kansas	2,272	0.3%
40	Delaware	2,116	0.3%
41	Hawaii	2,075	0.3%
42	Montana	1,886	0.3%
43	Idaho	1,582	0.2%
44	South Dakota	1,485	0.2%
45	North Dakota	1,288	0.2%
46	New Hampshire	912	0.1%
47	Vermont	872	0.1%
48	Wyoming	772	0.1%
NA	Maryland**	NA	NA
NA	Michigan**	NA	NA
	District of Columbia	2,757	0.4%

Source: U.S. Department of Health and Human Services, Children's Bureau
  "Child Maltreatment 2007" (http://www.acf.hhs.gov/programs/cb/pubs/cm07/index.htm)
*Does not include 10,696 victims in Puerto Rico. State-substantiated or indicated incidents. Some children may be counted twice if they were victims of multiple types of abuse. Fifty-nine percent of maltreated children suffered neglect, 10.8% physical abuse, 7.6% sexual abuse, and the remainder suffered emotional maltreatment, medical neglect, or other forms of maltreatment.
**Not available.

Rate of Child Abuse and Neglect in 2007

National Rate = 10.6 Abused Children per 1,000 Population Under 18*

<u>ALPHA ORDER</u>

RANK	STATE	RATE
32	Alabama	8.2
6	Alaska	17.2
47	Arizona	2.4
11	Arkansas	14.1
25	California	9.4
29	Colorado	8.9
17	Connecticut	12.0
23	Delaware	10.3
15	Florida	13.2
11	Georgia	14.1
35	Hawaii	7.3
42	Idaho	3.9
24	Illinois	9.7
20	Indiana	11.6
2	Iowa	19.8
45	Kansas	3.3
4	Kentucky	18.7
30	Louisiana	8.8
9	Maine	14.7
NA	Maryland**	NA
1	Massachusetts	26.3
NA	Michigan**	NA
39	Minnesota	5.4
27	Mississippi	9.1
40	Missouri	5.1
31	Montana	8.6
26	Nebraska	9.2
32	Nevada	8.2
46	New Hampshire	3.1
43	New Jersey	3.7
16	New Mexico	12.1
3	New York	18.9
19	North Carolina	11.7
28	North Dakota	9.0
13	Ohio	14.0
9	Oklahoma	14.7
14	Oregon	13.4
48	Pennsylvania	1.5
8	Rhode Island	16.5
17	South Carolina	12.0
34	South Dakota	7.5
21	Tennessee	10.9
22	Texas	10.7
7	Utah	16.7
36	Vermont	6.6
44	Virginia	3.5
41	Washington	4.5
5	West Virginia	18.4
38	Wisconsin	5.9
37	Wyoming	6.2

<u>RANK ORDER</u>

RANK	STATE	RATE
1	Massachusetts	26.3
2	Iowa	19.8
3	New York	18.9
4	Kentucky	18.7
5	West Virginia	18.4
6	Alaska	17.2
7	Utah	16.7
8	Rhode Island	16.5
9	Maine	14.7
9	Oklahoma	14.7
11	Arkansas	14.1
11	Georgia	14.1
13	Ohio	14.0
14	Oregon	13.4
15	Florida	13.2
16	New Mexico	12.1
17	Connecticut	12.0
17	South Carolina	12.0
19	North Carolina	11.7
20	Indiana	11.6
21	Tennessee	10.9
22	Texas	10.7
23	Delaware	10.3
24	Illinois	9.7
25	California	9.4
26	Nebraska	9.2
27	Mississippi	9.1
28	North Dakota	9.0
29	Colorado	8.9
30	Louisiana	8.8
31	Montana	8.6
32	Alabama	8.2
32	Nevada	8.2
34	South Dakota	7.5
35	Hawaii	7.3
36	Vermont	6.6
37	Wyoming	6.2
38	Wisconsin	5.9
39	Minnesota	5.4
40	Missouri	5.1
41	Washington	4.5
42	Idaho	3.9
43	New Jersey	3.7
44	Virginia	3.5
45	Kansas	3.3
46	New Hampshire	3.1
47	Arizona	2.4
48	Pennsylvania	1.5
NA	Maryland**	NA
NA	Michigan**	NA
	District of Columbia	24.2

Source: U.S. Department of Health and Human Services, Children's Bureau
   "Child Maltreatment 2007" (http://www.acf.hhs.gov/programs/cb/pubs/cm07/index.htm)
*State-substantiated or indicated incidents.
**Not available.

Physically Abused Children in 2007

National Total = 78,846 Children*

ALPHA ORDER

RANK	STATE	CHILDREN	% of USA
7	Alabama	3,148	4.0%
40	Alaska	216	0.3%
25	Arizona	1,108	1.4%
24	Arkansas	1,135	1.4%
3	California	6,835	8.7%
20	Colorado	1,272	1.6%
34	Connecticut	336	0.4%
36	Delaware	317	0.4%
6	Florida	3,488	4.4%
8	Georgia	2,873	3.6%
45	Hawaii	58	0.1%
39	Idaho	225	0.3%
4	Illinois	4,264	5.4%
19	Indiana	1,361	1.7%
16	Iowa	1,401	1.8%
35	Kansas	332	0.4%
14	Kentucky	1,530	1.9%
13	Louisiana	1,540	2.0%
41	Maine	210	0.3%
NA	Maryland**	NA	NA
11	Massachusetts	2,394	3.0%
NA	Michigan**	NA	NA
29	Minnesota	861	1.1%
23	Mississippi	1,149	1.5%
15	Missouri	1,462	1.9%
42	Montana	118	0.1%
37	Nebraska	289	0.4%
31	Nevada	506	0.6%
44	New Hampshire	114	0.1%
12	New Jersey	1,802	2.3%
32	New Mexico	505	0.6%
21	New York	1,231	1.6%
9	North Carolina	2,536	3.2%
NA	North Dakota**	NA	NA
2	Ohio	9,233	11.7%
30	Oklahoma	735	0.9%
NA	Oregon**	NA	NA
18	Pennsylvania	1,382	1.8%
38	Rhode Island	248	0.3%
10	South Carolina	2,500	3.2%
43	South Dakota	117	0.1%
5	Tennessee	3,974	5.0%
1	Texas	9,817	12.5%
26	Utah	1,091	1.4%
33	Vermont	390	0.5%
17	Virginia	1,388	1.8%
27	Washington	979	1.2%
22	West Virginia	1,166	1.5%
28	Wisconsin	910	1.2%
46	Wyoming	54	0.1%

RANK ORDER

RANK	STATE	CHILDREN	% of USA
1	Texas	9,817	12.5%
2	Ohio	9,233	11.7%
3	California	6,835	8.7%
4	Illinois	4,264	5.4%
5	Tennessee	3,974	5.0%
6	Florida	3,488	4.4%
7	Alabama	3,148	4.0%
8	Georgia	2,873	3.6%
9	North Carolina	2,536	3.2%
10	South Carolina	2,500	3.2%
11	Massachusetts	2,394	3.0%
12	New Jersey	1,802	2.3%
13	Louisiana	1,540	2.0%
14	Kentucky	1,530	1.9%
15	Missouri	1,462	1.9%
16	Iowa	1,401	1.8%
17	Virginia	1,388	1.8%
18	Pennsylvania	1,382	1.8%
19	Indiana	1,361	1.7%
20	Colorado	1,272	1.6%
21	New York	1,231	1.6%
22	West Virginia	1,166	1.5%
23	Mississippi	1,149	1.5%
24	Arkansas	1,135	1.4%
25	Arizona	1,108	1.4%
26	Utah	1,091	1.4%
27	Washington	979	1.2%
28	Wisconsin	910	1.2%
29	Minnesota	861	1.1%
30	Oklahoma	735	0.9%
31	Nevada	506	0.6%
32	New Mexico	505	0.6%
33	Vermont	390	0.5%
34	Connecticut	336	0.4%
35	Kansas	332	0.4%
36	Delaware	317	0.4%
37	Nebraska	289	0.4%
38	Rhode Island	248	0.3%
39	Idaho	225	0.3%
40	Alaska	216	0.3%
41	Maine	210	0.3%
42	Montana	118	0.1%
43	South Dakota	117	0.1%
44	New Hampshire	114	0.1%
45	Hawaii	58	0.1%
46	Wyoming	54	0.1%
NA	Maryland**	NA	NA
NA	Michigan**	NA	NA
NA	North Dakota**	NA	NA
NA	Oregon**	NA	NA
	District of Columbia	246	0.3%

Source: U.S. Department of Health and Human Services, Children's Bureau
"Child Maltreatment 2007" (http://www.acf.hhs.gov/programs/cb/pubs/cm07/index.htm)
*Does not include 1,020 victims in Puerto Rico. State-substantiated or indicated incidents. Some children may be counted twice if they were victims of multiple types of abuse. Fifty-nine percent of maltreated children suffered neglect, 10.8% physical abuse, 7.6% sexual abuse, and the remainder suffered emotional maltreatment, medical neglect, or other forms of maltreatment.
**Not available.

Rate of Physically Abused Children in 2007

National Rate = 1.1 Physically Abused Children per 1,000 Population Under 18*

ALPHA ORDER

RANK	STATE	RATE
4	Alabama	2.8
17	Alaska	1.2
31	Arizona	0.7
9	Arkansas	1.6
31	California	0.7
18	Colorado	1.1
42	Connecticut	0.4
10	Delaware	1.5
24	Florida	0.9
18	Georgia	1.1
46	Hawaii	0.2
35	Idaho	0.6
15	Illinois	1.3
24	Indiana	0.9
7	Iowa	2.0
39	Kansas	0.5
10	Kentucky	1.5
14	Louisiana	1.4
27	Maine	0.8
NA	Maryland**	NA
8	Massachusetts	1.7
NA	Michigan**	NA
31	Minnesota	0.7
10	Mississippi	1.5
22	Missouri	1.0
39	Montana	0.5
35	Nebraska	0.6
27	Nevada	0.8
42	New Hampshire	0.4
24	New Jersey	0.9
22	New Mexico	1.0
45	New York	0.3
18	North Carolina	1.1
NA	North Dakota**	NA
1	Ohio	3.4
27	Oklahoma	0.8
NA	Oregon**	NA
39	Pennsylvania	0.5
18	Rhode Island	1.1
6	South Carolina	2.4
35	South Dakota	0.6
5	Tennessee	2.7
10	Texas	1.5
15	Utah	1.3
2	Vermont	3.0
27	Virginia	0.8
35	Washington	0.6
2	West Virginia	3.0
31	Wisconsin	0.7
42	Wyoming	0.4

RANK ORDER

RANK	STATE	RATE
1	Ohio	3.4
2	Vermont	3.0
2	West Virginia	3.0
4	Alabama	2.8
5	Tennessee	2.7
6	South Carolina	2.4
7	Iowa	2.0
8	Massachusetts	1.7
9	Arkansas	1.6
10	Delaware	1.5
10	Kentucky	1.5
10	Mississippi	1.5
10	Texas	1.5
14	Louisiana	1.4
15	Illinois	1.3
15	Utah	1.3
17	Alaska	1.2
18	Colorado	1.1
18	Georgia	1.1
18	North Carolina	1.1
18	Rhode Island	1.1
22	Missouri	1.0
22	New Mexico	1.0
24	Florida	0.9
24	Indiana	0.9
24	New Jersey	0.9
27	Maine	0.8
27	Nevada	0.8
27	Oklahoma	0.8
27	Virginia	0.8
31	Arizona	0.7
31	California	0.7
31	Minnesota	0.7
31	Wisconsin	0.7
35	Idaho	0.6
35	Nebraska	0.6
35	South Dakota	0.6
35	Washington	0.6
39	Kansas	0.5
39	Montana	0.5
39	Pennsylvania	0.5
42	Connecticut	0.4
42	New Hampshire	0.4
42	Wyoming	0.4
45	New York	0.3
46	Hawaii	0.2
NA	Maryland**	NA
NA	Michigan**	NA
NA	North Dakota**	NA
NA	Oregon**	NA
	District of Columbia	2.2

Source: CQ Press using data from U.S. Department of Health and Human Services, Children's Bureau
"Child Maltreatment 2007" (http://www.acf.hhs.gov/programs/cb/pubs/cm07/index.htm)
*Does not include victims in Puerto Rico. State-substantiated or indicated incidents. Some children may be counted twice if they were victims of multiple types of abuse. Fifty-nine percent of maltreated children suffered neglect, 10.8% physical abuse, 7.6% sexual abuse, and the remainder suffered emotional maltreatment, medical neglect, or other forms of maltreatment.
**Not available.

Sexually Abused Children in 2007

National Total = 56,263 Children*

ALPHA ORDER

RANK	STATE	CHILDREN	% of USA
9	Alabama	2,100	3.7%
42	Alaska	85	0.2%
32	Arizona	268	0.5%
10	Arkansas	1,961	3.5%
2	California	5,348	9.5%
17	Colorado	824	1.5%
31	Connecticut	301	0.5%
38	Delaware	127	0.2%
13	Florida	1,792	3.2%
15	Georgia	1,080	1.9%
46	Hawaii	36	0.1%
44	Idaho	67	0.1%
4	Illinois	4,484	8.0%
6	Indiana	2,861	5.1%
24	Iowa	554	1.0%
22	Kansas	583	1.0%
20	Kentucky	746	1.3%
28	Louisiana	383	0.7%
36	Maine	184	0.3%
NA	Maryland**	NA	NA
25	Massachusetts	545	1.0%
NA	Michigan**	NA	NA
18	Minnesota	772	1.4%
19	Mississippi	765	1.4%
14	Missouri	1,640	2.9%
41	Montana	106	0.2%
33	Nebraska	236	0.4%
35	Nevada	200	0.4%
40	New Hampshire	115	0.2%
21	New Jersey	683	1.2%
39	New Mexico	126	0.2%
23	New York	576	1.0%
11	North Carolina	1,950	3.5%
NA	North Dakota**	NA	NA
1	Ohio	6,352	11.3%
29	Oklahoma	334	0.6%
NA	Oregon**	NA	NA
7	Pennsylvania	2,503	4.4%
37	Rhode Island	155	0.3%
26	South Carolina	484	0.9%
45	South Dakota	42	0.1%
5	Tennessee	3,676	6.5%
3	Texas	5,205	9.3%
8	Utah	2,147	3.8%
27	Vermont	408	0.7%
16	Virginia	867	1.5%
30	Washington	314	0.6%
34	West Virginia	224	0.4%
12	Wisconsin	1,902	3.4%
43	Wyoming	71	0.1%

RANK ORDER

RANK	STATE	CHILDREN	% of USA
1	Ohio	6,352	11.3%
2	California	5,348	9.5%
3	Texas	5,205	9.3%
4	Illinois	4,484	8.0%
5	Tennessee	3,676	6.5%
6	Indiana	2,861	5.1%
7	Pennsylvania	2,503	4.4%
8	Utah	2,147	3.8%
9	Alabama	2,100	3.7%
10	Arkansas	1,961	3.5%
11	North Carolina	1,950	3.5%
12	Wisconsin	1,902	3.4%
13	Florida	1,792	3.2%
14	Missouri	1,640	2.9%
15	Georgia	1,080	1.9%
16	Virginia	867	1.5%
17	Colorado	824	1.5%
18	Minnesota	772	1.4%
19	Mississippi	765	1.4%
20	Kentucky	746	1.3%
21	New Jersey	683	1.2%
22	Kansas	583	1.0%
23	New York	576	1.0%
24	Iowa	554	1.0%
25	Massachusetts	545	1.0%
26	South Carolina	484	0.9%
27	Vermont	408	0.7%
28	Louisiana	383	0.7%
29	Oklahoma	334	0.6%
30	Washington	314	0.6%
31	Connecticut	301	0.5%
32	Arizona	268	0.5%
33	Nebraska	236	0.4%
34	West Virginia	224	0.4%
35	Nevada	200	0.4%
36	Maine	184	0.3%
37	Rhode Island	155	0.3%
38	Delaware	127	0.2%
39	New Mexico	126	0.2%
40	New Hampshire	115	0.2%
41	Montana	106	0.2%
42	Alaska	85	0.2%
43	Wyoming	71	0.1%
44	Idaho	67	0.1%
45	South Dakota	42	0.1%
46	Hawaii	36	0.1%
NA	Maryland**	NA	NA
NA	Michigan**	NA	NA
NA	North Dakota**	NA	NA
NA	Oregon**	NA	NA
	District of Columbia	81	0.1%

Source: U.S. Department of Health and Human Services, Children's Bureau
"Child Maltreatment 2007" (http://www.acf.hhs.gov/programs/cb/pubs/cm07/index.htm)
*Does not include 197 victims in Puerto Rico. State-substantiated or indicated incidents. Some children may be counted twice if they were victims of multiple types of abuse. Fifty-nine percent of maltreated children suffered neglect, 10.8% physical abuse, 7.6% sexual abuse, and the remainder suffered emotional maltreatment, medical neglect, or other forms of maltreatment.
**Not available.

Rate of Sexually Abused Children in 2007

National Rate = 1.1 Sexually Abused Children per 1,000 Population Under 18*

ALPHA ORDER

RANK	STATE	RATE
6	Alabama	1.9
26	Alaska	0.5
41	Arizona	0.2
2	Arkansas	2.8
21	California	0.6
17	Colorado	0.7
31	Connecticut	0.4
21	Delaware	0.6
31	Florida	0.4
31	Georgia	0.4
45	Hawaii	0.1
41	Idaho	0.2
8	Illinois	1.4
7	Indiana	1.8
14	Iowa	0.8
14	Kansas	0.8
17	Kentucky	0.7
31	Louisiana	0.4
17	Maine	0.7
NA	Maryland**	NA
31	Massachusetts	0.4
NA	Michigan**	NA
21	Minnesota	0.6
11	Mississippi	1.0
10	Missouri	1.2
26	Montana	0.5
26	Nebraska	0.5
38	Nevada	0.3
31	New Hampshire	0.4
38	New Jersey	0.3
38	New Mexico	0.3
45	New York	0.1
12	North Carolina	0.9
NA	North Dakota**	NA
5	Ohio	2.3
31	Oklahoma	0.4
NA	Oregon**	NA
12	Pennsylvania	0.9
17	Rhode Island	0.7
26	South Carolina	0.5
41	South Dakota	0.2
4	Tennessee	2.5
14	Texas	0.8
3	Utah	2.6
1	Vermont	3.1
26	Virginia	0.5
41	Washington	0.2
21	West Virginia	0.6
8	Wisconsin	1.4
21	Wyoming	0.6

RANK ORDER

RANK	STATE	RATE
1	Vermont	3.1
2	Arkansas	2.8
3	Utah	2.6
4	Tennessee	2.5
5	Ohio	2.3
6	Alabama	1.9
7	Indiana	1.8
8	Illinois	1.4
8	Wisconsin	1.4
10	Missouri	1.2
11	Mississippi	1.0
12	North Carolina	0.9
12	Pennsylvania	0.9
14	Iowa	0.8
14	Kansas	0.8
14	Texas	0.8
17	Colorado	0.7
17	Kentucky	0.7
17	Maine	0.7
17	Rhode Island	0.7
21	California	0.6
21	Delaware	0.6
21	Minnesota	0.6
21	West Virginia	0.6
21	Wyoming	0.6
26	Alaska	0.5
26	Montana	0.5
26	Nebraska	0.5
26	South Carolina	0.5
26	Virginia	0.5
31	Connecticut	0.4
31	Florida	0.4
31	Georgia	0.4
31	Louisiana	0.4
31	Massachusetts	0.4
31	New Hampshire	0.4
31	Oklahoma	0.4
38	Nevada	0.3
38	New Jersey	0.3
38	New Mexico	0.3
41	Arizona	0.2
41	Idaho	0.2
41	South Dakota	0.2
41	Washington	0.2
45	Hawaii	0.1
45	New York	0.1
NA	Maryland**	NA
NA	Michigan**	NA
NA	North Dakota**	NA
NA	Oregon**	NA
	District of Columbia	0.7

Source: CQ Press using data from U.S. Department of Health and Human Services, Children's Bureau
"Child Maltreatment 2007" (http://www.acf.hhs.gov/programs/cb/pubs/cm07/index.htm)
*Does not include victims in Puerto Rico. State-substantiated or indicated incidents. Some children may be counted twice if they were victims of multiple types of abuse. Fifty-nine percent of maltreated children suffered neglect, 10.8% physical abuse, 7.6% sexual abuse, and the remainder suffered emotional maltreatment, medical neglect, or other forms of maltreatment.
**Not available.

Emotionally Abused Children in 2007

National Total = 30,008 Children*

RANK	STATE	CHILDREN	% of USA
32	Alabama	20	0.1%
9	Alaska	541	1.8%
30	Arizona	30	0.1%
23	Arkansas	56	0.2%
1	California	10,805	36.0%
16	Colorado	220	0.7%
20	Connecticut	107	0.4%
11	Delaware	472	1.6%
13	Florida	261	0.9%
3	Georgia	4,544	15.1%
42	Hawaii	3	0.0%
44	Idaho	1	0.0%
38	Illinois	9	0.0%
NA	Indiana**	NA	NA
22	Iowa	64	0.2%
15	Kansas	226	0.8%
24	Kentucky	52	0.2%
31	Louisiana	25	0.1%
7	Maine	755	2.5%
NA	Maryland**	NA	NA
38	Massachusetts	9	0.0%
NA	Michigan**	NA	NA
34	Minnesota	16	0.1%
10	Mississippi	527	1.8%
18	Missouri	128	0.4%
14	Montana	260	0.9%
37	Nebraska	10	0.0%
17	Nevada	178	0.6%
35	New Hampshire	11	0.0%
41	New Jersey	6	0.0%
8	New Mexico	640	2.1%
29	New York	37	0.1%
19	North Carolina	110	0.4%
NA	North Dakota**	NA	NA
4	Ohio	2,400	8.0%
6	Oklahoma	868	2.9%
NA	Oregon**	NA	NA
28	Pennsylvania	38	0.1%
43	Rhode Island	2	0.0%
21	South Carolina	79	0.3%
38	South Dakota	9	0.0%
27	Tennessee	39	0.1%
12	Texas	325	1.1%
2	Utah	4,905	16.3%
35	Vermont	11	0.0%
26	Virginia	40	0.1%
NA	Washington**	NA	NA
5	West Virginia	1,083	3.6%
33	Wisconsin	17	0.1%
25	Wyoming	44	0.1%

RANK	STATE	CHILDREN	% of USA
1	California	10,805	36.0%
2	Utah	4,905	16.3%
3	Georgia	4,544	15.1%
4	Ohio	2,400	8.0%
5	West Virginia	1,083	3.6%
6	Oklahoma	868	2.9%
7	Maine	755	2.5%
8	New Mexico	640	2.1%
9	Alaska	541	1.8%
10	Mississippi	527	1.8%
11	Delaware	472	1.6%
12	Texas	325	1.1%
13	Florida	261	0.9%
14	Montana	260	0.9%
15	Kansas	226	0.8%
16	Colorado	220	0.7%
17	Nevada	178	0.6%
18	Missouri	128	0.4%
19	North Carolina	110	0.4%
20	Connecticut	107	0.4%
21	South Carolina	79	0.3%
22	Iowa	64	0.2%
23	Arkansas	56	0.2%
24	Kentucky	52	0.2%
25	Wyoming	44	0.1%
26	Virginia	40	0.1%
27	Tennessee	39	0.1%
28	Pennsylvania	38	0.1%
29	New York	37	0.1%
30	Arizona	30	0.1%
31	Louisiana	25	0.1%
32	Alabama	20	0.1%
33	Wisconsin	17	0.1%
34	Minnesota	16	0.1%
35	New Hampshire	11	0.0%
35	Vermont	11	0.0%
37	Nebraska	10	0.0%
38	Illinois	9	0.0%
38	Massachusetts	9	0.0%
38	South Dakota	9	0.0%
41	New Jersey	6	0.0%
42	Hawaii	3	0.0%
43	Rhode Island	2	0.0%
44	Idaho	1	0.0%
NA	Indiana**	NA	NA
NA	Maryland**	NA	NA
NA	Michigan**	NA	NA
NA	North Dakota**	NA	NA
NA	Oregon**	NA	NA
NA	Washington**	NA	NA
	District of Columbia	25	0.1%

Source: U.S. Department of Health and Human Services, Children's Bureau
"Child Maltreatment 2007" (http://www.acf.hhs.gov/programs/cb/pubs/cm07/index.htm)
*Does not include 1,358 victims in Puerto Rico. State-substantiated or indicated incidents. Some children may be counted twice if they were victims of multiple types of abuse. Fifty-nine percent of maltreated children suffered neglect, 10.8% physical abuse, 7.6% sexual abuse, and the remainder suffered emotional maltreatment, medical neglect, or other forms of maltreatment.
**Not available.

Rate of Emotionally Abused Children in 2007

National Rate = 0.4 Emotionally Abused Children per 1,000 Population*

ALPHA ORDER

RANK	STATE	RATE
25	Alabama	0.0
2	Alaska	3.0
25	Arizona	0.0
17	Arkansas	0.1
8	California	1.2
16	Colorado	0.2
17	Connecticut	0.1
5	Delaware	2.3
17	Florida	0.1
6	Georgia	1.8
25	Hawaii	0.0
25	Idaho	0.0
25	Illinois	0.0
NA	Indiana**	NA
17	Iowa	0.1
14	Kansas	0.3
17	Kentucky	0.1
25	Louisiana	0.0
4	Maine	2.7
NA	Maryland**	NA
25	Massachusetts	0.0
NA	Michigan**	NA
25	Minnesota	0.0
12	Mississippi	0.7
17	Missouri	0.1
8	Montana	1.2
25	Nebraska	0.0
14	Nevada	0.3
25	New Hampshire	0.0
25	New Jersey	0.0
7	New Mexico	1.3
25	New York	0.0
25	North Carolina	0.0
NA	North Dakota**	NA
11	Ohio	0.9
10	Oklahoma	1.0
NA	Oregon**	NA
25	Pennsylvania	0.0
25	Rhode Island	0.0
17	South Carolina	0.1
25	South Dakota	0.0
25	Tennessee	0.0
25	Texas	0.0
1	Utah	6.0
17	Vermont	0.1
25	Virginia	0.0
NA	Washington**	NA
3	West Virginia	2.8
25	Wisconsin	0.0
13	Wyoming	0.4

RANK ORDER

RANK	STATE	RATE
1	Utah	6.0
2	Alaska	3.0
3	West Virginia	2.8
4	Maine	2.7
5	Delaware	2.3
6	Georgia	1.8
7	New Mexico	1.3
8	California	1.2
8	Montana	1.2
10	Oklahoma	1.0
11	Ohio	0.9
12	Mississippi	0.7
13	Wyoming	0.4
14	Kansas	0.3
14	Nevada	0.3
16	Colorado	0.2
17	Arkansas	0.1
17	Connecticut	0.1
17	Florida	0.1
17	Iowa	0.1
17	Kentucky	0.1
17	Missouri	0.1
17	South Carolina	0.1
17	Vermont	0.1
25	Alabama	0.0
25	Arizona	0.0
25	Hawaii	0.0
25	Idaho	0.0
25	Illinois	0.0
25	Louisiana	0.0
25	Massachusetts	0.0
25	Minnesota	0.0
25	Nebraska	0.0
25	New Hampshire	0.0
25	New Jersey	0.0
25	New York	0.0
25	North Carolina	0.0
25	Pennsylvania	0.0
25	Rhode Island	0.0
25	South Dakota	0.0
25	Tennessee	0.0
25	Texas	0.0
25	Virginia	0.0
25	Wisconsin	0.0
NA	Indiana**	NA
NA	Maryland**	NA
NA	Michigan**	NA
NA	North Dakota**	NA
NA	Oregon**	NA
NA	Washington**	NA
	District of Columbia	0.2

Source: CQ Press using data from U.S. Department of Health and Human Services, Children's Bureau
"Child Maltreatment 2007" (http://www.acf.hhs.gov/programs/cb/pubs/cm07/index.htm)
*Does not include victims in Puerto Rico. State-substantiated or indicated incidents. Some children may be counted twice if they were victims of multiple types of abuse. Fifty-nine percent of maltreated children suffered neglect, 10.8% physical abuse, 7.6% sexual abuse, and the remainder suffered emotional maltreatment, medical neglect, or other forms of maltreatment.
**Not available.

Neglected Children in 2007

National Total = 432,814 Children*

ALPHA ORDER				RANK ORDER			
RANK	STATE	CHILDREN	% of USA	RANK	STATE	CHILDREN	% of USA
27	Alabama	3,257	0.8%	1	California	56,827	13.1%
36	Alaska	1,704	0.4%	2	New York	47,880	11.1%
32	Arizona	2,465	0.6%	3	Texas	46,806	10.8%
19	Arkansas	5,439	1.3%	4	Massachusetts	32,131	7.4%
1	California	56,827	13.1%	5	Georgia	21,687	5.0%
16	Colorado	6,890	1.6%	6	North Carolina	20,389	4.7%
13	Connecticut	8,188	1.9%	7	Ohio	19,428	4.5%
40	Delaware	816	0.2%	8	Florida	19,280	4.5%
8	Florida	19,280	4.5%	9	Illinois	17,897	4.1%
5	Georgia	21,687	5.0%	10	Kentucky	15,957	3.7%
45	Hawaii	58	0.0%	11	Indiana	12,302	2.8%
39	Idaho	1,094	0.3%	12	Iowa	10,322	2.4%
9	Illinois	17,897	4.1%	13	Connecticut	8,188	1.9%
11	Indiana	12,302	2.8%	14	South Carolina	7,701	1.8%
12	Iowa	10,322	2.4%	15	Oklahoma	7,664	1.8%
43	Kansas	413	0.1%	16	Colorado	6,890	1.6%
10	Kentucky	15,957	3.7%	17	Tennessee	6,604	1.5%
18	Louisiana	6,441	1.5%	18	Louisiana	6,441	1.5%
35	Maine	1,814	0.4%	19	Arkansas	5,439	1.3%
NA	Maryland**	NA	NA	20	Washington	5,329	1.2%
4	Massachusetts	32,131	7.4%	21	New Jersey	4,853	1.1%
NA	Michigan**	NA	NA	22	Minnesota	4,721	1.1%
22	Minnesota	4,721	1.1%	23	Mississippi	3,896	0.9%
23	Mississippi	3,896	0.9%	24	New Mexico	3,895	0.9%
31	Missouri	2,866	0.7%	25	Virginia	3,645	0.8%
38	Montana	1,097	0.3%	26	Nevada	3,582	0.8%
29	Nebraska	3,083	0.7%	27	Alabama	3,257	0.8%
26	Nevada	3,582	0.8%	28	Rhode Island	3,176	0.7%
41	New Hampshire	556	0.1%	29	Nebraska	3,083	0.7%
21	New Jersey	4,853	1.1%	30	West Virginia	3,005	0.7%
24	New Mexico	3,895	0.9%	31	Missouri	2,866	0.7%
2	New York	47,880	11.1%	32	Arizona	2,465	0.6%
6	North Carolina	20,389	4.7%	33	Wisconsin	2,432	0.6%
NA	North Dakota**	NA	NA	34	Utah	2,076	0.5%
7	Ohio	19,428	4.5%	35	Maine	1,814	0.4%
15	Oklahoma	7,664	1.8%	36	Alaska	1,704	0.4%
NA	Oregon**	NA	NA	37	South Dakota	1,235	0.3%
44	Pennsylvania	93	0.0%	38	Montana	1,097	0.3%
28	Rhode Island	3,176	0.7%	39	Idaho	1,094	0.3%
14	South Carolina	7,701	1.8%	40	Delaware	816	0.2%
37	South Dakota	1,235	0.3%	41	New Hampshire	556	0.1%
17	Tennessee	6,604	1.5%	42	Wyoming	548	0.1%
3	Texas	46,806	10.8%	43	Kansas	413	0.1%
34	Utah	2,076	0.5%	44	Pennsylvania	93	0.0%
46	Vermont	14	0.0%	45	Hawaii	58	0.0%
25	Virginia	3,645	0.8%	46	Vermont	14	0.0%
20	Washington	5,329	1.2%	NA	Maryland**	NA	NA
30	West Virginia	3,005	0.7%	NA	Michigan**	NA	NA
33	Wisconsin	2,432	0.6%	NA	North Dakota**	NA	NA
42	Wyoming	548	0.1%	NA	Oregon**	NA	NA
					District of Columbia	1,258	0.3%

Source: U.S. Department of Health and Human Services, Children's Bureau
"Child Maltreatment 2007" (http://www.acf.hhs.gov/programs/cb/pubs/cm07/index.htm)
*Does not include 4,130 victims in Puerto Rico. State-substantiated or indicated incidents. Some children may be counted twice if they were victims of multiple types of abuse. Fifty-nine percent of maltreated children suffered neglect, 10.8% physical abuse, 7.6% sexual abuse, and the remainder suffered emotional maltreatment, medical neglect, or other forms of maltreatment.
**Not available.

Rate of Neglected Children in 2007

National Rate = 6.2 Neglected Children per 1,000 Population Under 18*

ALPHA ORDER

RANK	STATE	RATE
34	Alabama	2.9
7	Alaska	9.4
42	Arizona	1.5
11	Arkansas	7.8
21	California	6.1
23	Colorado	5.8
6	Connecticut	10.0
31	Delaware	4.0
28	Florida	4.8
9	Georgia	8.6
44	Hawaii	0.2
35	Idaho	2.7
24	Illinois	5.6
11	Indiana	7.8
3	Iowa	14.5
43	Kansas	0.6
2	Kentucky	15.9
22	Louisiana	6.0
19	Maine	6.5
NA	Maryland**	NA
1	Massachusetts	22.4
NA	Michigan**	NA
32	Minnesota	3.7
26	Mississippi	5.1
38	Missouri	2.0
27	Montana	5.0
18	Nebraska	6.9
25	Nevada	5.4
40	New Hampshire	1.9
37	New Jersey	2.4
11	New Mexico	7.8
5	New York	10.8
8	North Carolina	9.2
NA	North Dakota**	NA
16	Ohio	7.1
10	Oklahoma	8.5
NA	Oregon**	NA
46	Pennsylvania	0.0
4	Rhode Island	13.6
15	South Carolina	7.3
20	South Dakota	6.3
29	Tennessee	4.5
16	Texas	7.1
36	Utah	2.5
45	Vermont	0.1
38	Virginia	2.0
33	Washington	3.5
11	West Virginia	7.8
41	Wisconsin	1.8
30	Wyoming	4.4

RANK ORDER

RANK	STATE	RATE
1	Massachusetts	22.4
2	Kentucky	15.9
3	Iowa	14.5
4	Rhode Island	13.6
5	New York	10.8
6	Connecticut	10.0
7	Alaska	9.4
8	North Carolina	9.2
9	Georgia	8.6
10	Oklahoma	8.5
11	Arkansas	7.8
11	Indiana	7.8
11	New Mexico	7.8
11	West Virginia	7.8
15	South Carolina	7.3
16	Ohio	7.1
16	Texas	7.1
18	Nebraska	6.9
19	Maine	6.5
20	South Dakota	6.3
21	California	6.1
22	Louisiana	6.0
23	Colorado	5.8
24	Illinois	5.6
25	Nevada	5.4
26	Mississippi	5.1
27	Montana	5.0
28	Florida	4.8
29	Tennessee	4.5
30	Wyoming	4.4
31	Delaware	4.0
32	Minnesota	3.7
33	Washington	3.5
34	Alabama	2.9
35	Idaho	2.7
36	Utah	2.5
37	New Jersey	2.4
38	Missouri	2.0
38	Virginia	2.0
40	New Hampshire	1.9
41	Wisconsin	1.8
42	Arizona	1.5
43	Kansas	0.6
44	Hawaii	0.2
45	Vermont	0.1
46	Pennsylvania	0.0
NA	Maryland**	NA
NA	Michigan**	NA
NA	North Dakota**	NA
NA	Oregon**	NA

District of Columbia 11.1

Source: CQ Press using data from U.S. Department of Health and Human Services, Children's Bureau
"Child Maltreatment 2007" (http://www.acf.hhs.gov/programs/cb/pubs/cm07/index.htm)
*Does not include victims in Puerto Rico. State-substantiated or indicated incidents. Some children may be counted twice if they were victims of multiple types of abuse. Fifty-nine percent of maltreated children suffered neglect, 10.8% physical abuse, 7.6% sexual abuse, and the remainder suffered emotional maltreatment, medical neglect, or other forms of maltreatment.
**Not available.

Child Abuse and Neglect Fatalities in 2007

National Total = 1,760 Fatalities*

RANK	STATE	FATALITIES	% of USA
20	Alabama	23	1.3%
36	Alaska	4	0.2%
16	Arizona	28	1.6%
23	Arkansas	20	1.1%
2	California	184	10.5%
16	Colorado	28	1.6%
36	Connecticut	4	0.2%
45	Delaware	0	0.0%
3	Florida	153	8.7%
7	Georgia	61	3.5%
36	Hawaii	4	0.2%
41	Idaho	1	0.1%
6	Illinois	74	4.2%
8	Indiana	53	3.0%
34	Iowa	5	0.3%
31	Kansas	10	0.6%
12	Kentucky	41	2.3%
18	Louisiana	27	1.5%
41	Maine	1	0.1%
NA	Maryland**	NA	NA
NA	Massachusetts**	NA	NA
NA	Michigan**	NA	NA
26	Minnesota	17	1.0%
24	Mississippi	19	1.1%
9	Missouri	50	2.8%
41	Montana	1	0.1%
27	Nebraska	16	0.9%
22	Nevada	21	1.2%
34	New Hampshire	5	0.3%
13	New Jersey	33	1.9%
33	New Mexico	7	0.4%
4	New York	96	5.5%
NA	North Carolina**	NA	NA
41	North Dakota	1	0.1%
5	Ohio	90	5.1%
14	Oklahoma	31	1.8%
28	Oregon	12	0.7%
10	Pennsylvania	47	2.7%
45	Rhode Island	0	0.0%
24	South Carolina	19	1.1%
32	South Dakota	8	0.5%
11	Tennessee	44	2.5%
1	Texas	228	13.0%
30	Utah	11	0.6%
39	Vermont	3	0.2%
14	Virginia	31	1.8%
18	Washington	27	1.5%
28	West Virginia	12	0.7%
21	Wisconsin	22	1.3%
40	Wyoming	2	0.1%

RANK	STATE	FATALITIES	% of USA
1	Texas	228	13.0%
2	California	184	10.5%
3	Florida	153	8.7%
4	New York	96	5.5%
5	Ohio	90	5.1%
6	Illinois	74	4.2%
7	Georgia	61	3.5%
8	Indiana	53	3.0%
9	Missouri	50	2.8%
10	Pennsylvania	47	2.7%
11	Tennessee	44	2.5%
12	Kentucky	41	2.3%
13	New Jersey	33	1.9%
14	Oklahoma	31	1.8%
14	Virginia	31	1.8%
16	Arizona	28	1.6%
16	Colorado	28	1.6%
18	Louisiana	27	1.5%
18	Washington	27	1.5%
20	Alabama	23	1.3%
21	Wisconsin	22	1.3%
22	Nevada	21	1.2%
23	Arkansas	20	1.1%
24	Mississippi	19	1.1%
24	South Carolina	19	1.1%
26	Minnesota	17	1.0%
27	Nebraska	16	0.9%
28	Oregon	12	0.7%
28	West Virginia	12	0.7%
30	Utah	11	0.6%
31	Kansas	10	0.6%
32	South Dakota	8	0.5%
33	New Mexico	7	0.4%
34	Iowa	5	0.3%
34	New Hampshire	5	0.3%
36	Alaska	4	0.2%
36	Connecticut	4	0.2%
36	Hawaii	4	0.2%
39	Vermont	3	0.2%
40	Wyoming	2	0.1%
41	Idaho	1	0.1%
41	Maine	1	0.1%
41	Montana	1	0.1%
41	North Dakota	1	0.1%
45	Delaware	0	0.0%
45	Rhode Island	0	0.0%
NA	Maryland**	NA	NA
NA	Massachusetts**	NA	NA
NA	Michigan**	NA	NA
NA	North Carolina**	NA	NA
	District of Columbia	2	0.1%

Source: U.S. Department of Health and Human Services, Children's Bureau
"Child Maltreatment 2007" (http://www.acf.hhs.gov/programs/cb/pubs/cm07/index.htm)
*National total includes estimates for states not shown. The three main categories of maltreatment related to fatalities were neglect (34.1%), combinations of maltreatments (35.2%), and physical abuse (26.4%).
**Not available.

Rate of Child Abuse and Neglect Fatalities in 2006

National Rate = 2.35 Fatalities per 100,000 Population Under 18*

ALPHA ORDER

RANK	STATE	RATE
22	Alabama	2.05
20	Alaska	2.20
28	Arizona	1.68
13	Arkansas	2.85
23	California	1.96
17	Colorado	2.35
41	Connecticut	0.49
45	Delaware	0.00
3	Florida	3.78
16	Georgia	2.41
34	Hawaii	1.40
44	Idaho	0.25
18	Illinois	2.31
8	Indiana	3.34
39	Iowa	0.70
33	Kansas	1.44
1	Kentucky	4.08
14	Louisiana	2.50
43	Maine	0.36
NA	Maryland**	NA
NA	Massachusetts**	NA
NA	Michigan**	NA
37	Minnesota	1.35
15	Mississippi	2.47
5	Missouri	3.51
42	Montana	0.46
4	Nebraska	3.59
10	Nevada	3.18
28	New Hampshire	1.68
31	New Jersey	1.60
34	New Mexico	1.40
21	New York	2.18
NA	North Carolina**	NA
39	North Dakota	0.70
9	Ohio	3.27
6	Oklahoma	3.45
36	Oregon	1.39
27	Pennsylvania	1.69
45	Rhode Island	0.00
24	South Carolina	1.79
2	South Dakota	4.06
12	Tennessee	2.99
7	Texas	3.44
37	Utah	1.35
19	Vermont	2.28
26	Virginia	1.70
25	Washington	1.76
11	West Virginia	3.10
30	Wisconsin	1.67
31	Wyoming	1.60

RANK ORDER

RANK	STATE	RATE
1	Kentucky	4.08
2	South Dakota	4.06
3	Florida	3.78
4	Nebraska	3.59
5	Missouri	3.51
6	Oklahoma	3.45
7	Texas	3.44
8	Indiana	3.34
9	Ohio	3.27
10	Nevada	3.18
11	West Virginia	3.10
12	Tennessee	2.99
13	Arkansas	2.85
14	Louisiana	2.50
15	Mississippi	2.47
16	Georgia	2.41
17	Colorado	2.35
18	Illinois	2.31
19	Vermont	2.28
20	Alaska	2.20
21	New York	2.18
22	Alabama	2.05
23	California	1.96
24	South Carolina	1.79
25	Washington	1.76
26	Virginia	1.70
27	Pennsylvania	1.69
28	Arizona	1.68
28	New Hampshire	1.68
30	Wisconsin	1.67
31	New Jersey	1.60
31	Wyoming	1.60
33	Kansas	1.44
34	Hawaii	1.40
34	New Mexico	1.40
36	Oregon	1.39
37	Minnesota	1.35
37	Utah	1.35
39	Iowa	0.70
39	North Dakota	0.70
41	Connecticut	0.49
42	Montana	0.46
43	Maine	0.36
44	Idaho	0.25
45	Delaware	0.00
45	Rhode Island	0.00
NA	Maryland**	NA
NA	Massachusetts**	NA
NA	Michigan**	NA
NA	North Carolina**	NA
	District of Columbia	1.76

Source: U.S. Department of Health and Human Services, Children's Bureau
"Child Maltreatment 2007" (http://www.acf.hhs.gov/programs/cb/pubs/cm07/index.htm)
*National rate is weighted and includes estimates for states not shown. The three main categories of maltreatment related to fatalities were neglect (34.1%), combinations of maltreatments (35.2%), and physical abuse (26.4%).
**Not available.

VI. LAW ENFORCEMENT

Federal Law Enforcement Officers in 2004

National Total = 104,884 Officers*

ALPHA ORDER

RANK	STATE	OFFICERS	% of USA
27	Alabama	779	0.7%
41	Alaska	399	0.4%
5	Arizona	5,143	4.9%
34	Arkansas	555	0.5%
2	California	13,365	12.7%
14	Colorado	1,554	1.5%
39	Connecticut	461	0.4%
49	Delaware	112	0.1%
4	Florida	6,627	6.3%
9	Georgia	2,500	2.4%
30	Hawaii	677	0.6%
43	Idaho	338	0.3%
8	Illinois	2,988	2.8%
29	Indiana	699	0.7%
46	Iowa	219	0.2%
32	Kansas	594	0.6%
17	Kentucky	1,411	1.3%
16	Louisiana	1,430	1.4%
35	Maine	548	0.5%
13	Maryland	1,558	1.5%
15	Massachusetts	1,437	1.4%
11	Michigan	2,260	2.2%
23	Minnesota	1,067	1.0%
33	Mississippi	574	0.5%
21	Missouri	1,208	1.2%
31	Montana	629	0.6%
44	Nebraska	292	0.3%
36	Nevada	499	0.5%
49	New Hampshire	112	0.1%
10	New Jersey	2,453	2.3%
19	New Mexico	1,281	1.2%
3	New York	8,159	7.8%
18	North Carolina	1,344	1.3%
37	North Dakota	498	0.5%
20	Ohio	1,249	1.2%
26	Oklahoma	825	0.8%
28	Oregon	737	0.7%
7	Pennsylvania	3,436	3.3%
48	Rhode Island	151	0.1%
24	South Carolina	959	0.9%
45	South Dakota	264	0.3%
22	Tennessee	1,201	1.1%
1	Texas	14,633	14.0%
42	Utah	362	0.3%
40	Vermont	434	0.4%
6	Virginia	4,086	3.9%
12	Washington	2,042	1.9%
25	West Virginia	844	0.8%
38	Wisconsin	478	0.5%
47	Wyoming	215	0.2%

RANK ORDER

RANK	STATE	OFFICERS	% of USA
1	Texas	14,633	14.0%
2	California	13,365	12.7%
3	New York	8,159	7.8%
4	Florida	6,627	6.3%
5	Arizona	5,143	4.9%
6	Virginia	4,086	3.9%
7	Pennsylvania	3,436	3.3%
8	Illinois	2,988	2.8%
9	Georgia	2,500	2.4%
10	New Jersey	2,453	2.3%
11	Michigan	2,260	2.2%
12	Washington	2,042	1.9%
13	Maryland	1,558	1.5%
14	Colorado	1,554	1.5%
15	Massachusetts	1,437	1.4%
16	Louisiana	1,430	1.4%
17	Kentucky	1,411	1.3%
18	North Carolina	1,344	1.3%
19	New Mexico	1,281	1.2%
20	Ohio	1,249	1.2%
21	Missouri	1,208	1.2%
22	Tennessee	1,201	1.1%
23	Minnesota	1,067	1.0%
24	South Carolina	959	0.9%
25	West Virginia	844	0.8%
26	Oklahoma	825	0.8%
27	Alabama	779	0.7%
28	Oregon	737	0.7%
29	Indiana	699	0.7%
30	Hawaii	677	0.6%
31	Montana	629	0.6%
32	Kansas	594	0.6%
33	Mississippi	574	0.5%
34	Arkansas	555	0.5%
35	Maine	548	0.5%
36	Nevada	499	0.5%
37	North Dakota	498	0.5%
38	Wisconsin	478	0.5%
39	Connecticut	461	0.4%
40	Vermont	434	0.4%
41	Alaska	399	0.4%
42	Utah	362	0.3%
43	Idaho	338	0.3%
44	Nebraska	292	0.3%
45	South Dakota	264	0.3%
46	Iowa	219	0.2%
47	Wyoming	215	0.2%
48	Rhode Island	151	0.1%
49	Delaware	112	0.1%
49	New Hampshire	112	0.1%
	District of Columbia	9,201	8.8%

Source: U.S. Department of Justice, Bureau of Justice Statistics
"Federal Law Enforcement Officers, 2004" (July 2006, NCJ 212750, http://www.ojp.usdoj.gov/bjs/fedle.htm)
*Full-time officers authorized to carry firearms and make arrests. Includes F.B.I.; Customs Service; Immigration and Naturalization Service; I.R.S.; Postal Inspection; Drug Enforcement Administration; Secret Service; National Park Service; Bureau of Alcohol, Tobacco, Firearms and Explosives; Capitol Police; U.S. Courts; Federal Bureau of Prisons; Tennessee Valley Authority; and U.S. Forest Service.

Rate of Federal Law Enforcement Officers in 2004

National Rate = 36 Officers per 100,000 Population*

ALPHA ORDER			RANK ORDER		
RANK	STATE	RATE	RANK	STATE	RATE
39	Alabama	17	1	Arizona	90
7	Alaska	61	2	North Dakota	78
1	Arizona	90	3	Vermont	70
36	Arkansas	20	4	Montana	68
15	California	37	5	New Mexico	67
16	Colorado	34	6	Texas	65
45	Connecticut	13	7	Alaska	61
43	Delaware	14	8	Virginia	55
14	Florida	38	9	Hawaii	54
21	Georgia	28	10	West Virginia	46
9	Hawaii	54	11	Maine	42
25	Idaho	24	11	New York	42
25	Illinois	24	11	Wyoming	42
46	Indiana	11	14	Florida	38
50	Iowa	7	15	California	37
29	Kansas	22	16	Colorado	34
16	Kentucky	34	16	Kentucky	34
20	Louisiana	32	16	South Dakota	34
11	Maine	42	19	Washington	33
21	Maryland	28	20	Louisiana	32
29	Massachusetts	22	21	Georgia	28
29	Michigan	22	21	Maryland	28
32	Minnesota	21	21	New Jersey	28
36	Mississippi	20	21	Pennsylvania	28
32	Missouri	21	25	Idaho	24
4	Montana	68	25	Illinois	24
39	Nebraska	17	27	Oklahoma	23
32	Nevada	21	27	South Carolina	23
48	New Hampshire	9	29	Kansas	22
21	New Jersey	28	29	Massachusetts	22
5	New Mexico	67	29	Michigan	22
11	New York	42	32	Minnesota	21
41	North Carolina	16	32	Missouri	21
2	North Dakota	78	32	Nevada	21
46	Ohio	11	32	Oregon	21
27	Oklahoma	23	36	Arkansas	20
32	Oregon	21	36	Mississippi	20
21	Pennsylvania	28	36	Tennessee	20
43	Rhode Island	14	39	Alabama	17
27	South Carolina	23	39	Nebraska	17
16	South Dakota	34	41	North Carolina	16
36	Tennessee	20	42	Utah	15
6	Texas	65	43	Delaware	14
42	Utah	15	43	Rhode Island	14
3	Vermont	70	45	Connecticut	13
8	Virginia	55	46	Indiana	11
19	Washington	33	46	Ohio	11
10	West Virginia	46	48	New Hampshire	9
48	Wisconsin	9	48	Wisconsin	9
11	Wyoming	42	50	Iowa	7
				District of Columbia	1,662

Source: U.S. Department of Justice, Bureau of Justice Statistics
  "Federal Law Enforcement Officers, 2004" (July 2006, NCJ 212750, http://www.ojp.usdoj.gov/bjs/fedle.htm)
*Full-time officers authorized to carry firearms and make arrests.   Includes F.B.I.; Customs Service; Immigration and Naturalization Service; I.R.S.; Postal Inspection; Drug Enforcement Administration; Secret Service; National Park Service; Bureau of Alcohol, Tobacco, Firearms and Explosives; Capitol Police; U.S. Courts; Federal Bureau of Prisons; Tennessee Valley Authority; and U.S. Forest Service.

State and Local Justice System Employees in 2008

National Total = 2,128,846 Employees*

ALPHA ORDER

RANK	STATE	EMPLOYEES	% of USA
24	Alabama	27,240	1.3%
46	Alaska	5,104	0.2%
13	Arizona	49,733	2.3%
32	Arkansas	18,990	0.9%
1	California	255,827	12.0%
22	Colorado	31,998	1.5%
27	Connecticut	23,655	1.1%
42	Delaware	7,281	0.3%
4	Florida	150,905	7.1%
9	Georgia	72,110	3.4%
39	Hawaii	9,556	0.4%
40	Idaho	9,526	0.4%
5	Illinois	84,558	4.0%
19	Indiana	39,884	1.9%
35	Iowa	15,061	0.7%
30	Kansas	20,445	1.0%
26	Kentucky	25,435	1.2%
18	Louisiana	39,987	1.9%
44	Maine	6,313	0.3%
16	Maryland	41,427	1.9%
14	Massachusetts	45,274	2.1%
12	Michigan	56,184	2.6%
25	Minnesota	27,074	1.3%
33	Mississippi	17,470	0.8%
15	Missouri	41,588	2.0%
45	Montana	6,026	0.3%
37	Nebraska	11,151	0.5%
31	Nevada	19,293	0.9%
41	New Hampshire	7,369	0.3%
8	New Jersey	75,181	3.5%
34	New Mexico	16,108	0.8%
2	New York	181,056	8.5%
10	North Carolina	61,263	2.9%
50	North Dakota	3,317	0.2%
7	Ohio	80,780	3.8%
29	Oklahoma	22,524	1.1%
28	Oregon	23,094	1.1%
6	Pennsylvania	83,192	3.9%
43	Rhode Island	6,471	0.3%
23	South Carolina	28,803	1.4%
48	South Dakota	4,387	0.2%
17	Tennessee	40,231	1.9%
3	Texas	165,399	7.8%
36	Utah	14,530	0.7%
49	Vermont	3,370	0.2%
11	Virginia	57,251	2.7%
20	Washington	37,954	1.8%
38	West Virginia	9,700	0.5%
21	Wisconsin	36,345	1.7%
47	Wyoming	4,670	0.2%

RANK ORDER

RANK	STATE	EMPLOYEES	% of USA
1	California	255,827	12.0%
2	New York	181,056	8.5%
3	Texas	165,399	7.8%
4	Florida	150,905	7.1%
5	Illinois	84,558	4.0%
6	Pennsylvania	83,192	3.9%
7	Ohio	80,780	3.8%
8	New Jersey	75,181	3.5%
9	Georgia	72,110	3.4%
10	North Carolina	61,263	2.9%
11	Virginia	57,251	2.7%
12	Michigan	56,184	2.6%
13	Arizona	49,733	2.3%
14	Massachusetts	45,274	2.1%
15	Missouri	41,588	2.0%
16	Maryland	41,427	1.9%
17	Tennessee	40,231	1.9%
18	Louisiana	39,987	1.9%
19	Indiana	39,884	1.9%
20	Washington	37,954	1.8%
21	Wisconsin	36,345	1.7%
22	Colorado	31,998	1.5%
23	South Carolina	28,803	1.4%
24	Alabama	27,240	1.3%
25	Minnesota	27,074	1.3%
26	Kentucky	25,435	1.2%
27	Connecticut	23,655	1.1%
28	Oregon	23,094	1.1%
29	Oklahoma	22,524	1.1%
30	Kansas	20,445	1.0%
31	Nevada	19,293	0.9%
32	Arkansas	18,990	0.9%
33	Mississippi	17,470	0.8%
34	New Mexico	16,108	0.8%
35	Iowa	15,061	0.7%
36	Utah	14,530	0.7%
37	Nebraska	11,151	0.5%
38	West Virginia	9,700	0.5%
39	Hawaii	9,556	0.4%
40	Idaho	9,526	0.4%
41	New Hampshire	7,369	0.3%
42	Delaware	7,281	0.3%
43	Rhode Island	6,471	0.3%
44	Maine	6,313	0.3%
45	Montana	6,026	0.3%
46	Alaska	5,104	0.2%
47	Wyoming	4,670	0.2%
48	South Dakota	4,387	0.2%
49	Vermont	3,370	0.2%
50	North Dakota	3,317	0.2%
	District of Columbia	6,756	0.3%

Source: CQ Press using data from U.S. Bureau of the Census, Governments Division
"Government Employment and Payroll" (http://www.census.gov/govs/apes/index.html)
*Full-time equivalent as of March 2008. Includes police, courts, prosecution, public defense, and corrections.

Rate of State and Local Justice System Employment in 2008

National Rate = 70.0 Employees Per 10,000 Population*

ALPHA ORDER

RANK	STATE	RATE
39	Alabama	58.4
9	Alaska	74.4
8	Arizona	76.5
23	Arkansas	66.5
19	California	69.6
26	Colorado	64.8
21	Connecticut	67.6
5	Delaware	83.4
6	Florida	82.3
9	Georgia	74.4
11	Hawaii	74.2
30	Idaho	62.5
25	Illinois	65.5
30	Indiana	62.5
49	Iowa	50.2
15	Kansas	73.0
37	Kentucky	59.6
2	Louisiana	90.7
50	Maine	48.0
14	Maryland	73.5
18	Massachusetts	69.7
41	Michigan	56.2
47	Minnesota	51.9
38	Mississippi	59.4
16	Missouri	70.3
33	Montana	62.3
30	Nebraska	62.5
11	Nevada	74.2
42	New Hampshire	56.0
4	New Jersey	86.6
7	New Mexico	81.2
1	New York	92.9
24	North Carolina	66.4
48	North Dakota	51.7
16	Ohio	70.3
34	Oklahoma	61.8
36	Oregon	60.9
22	Pennsylvania	66.8
35	Rhode Island	61.6
29	South Carolina	64.3
43	South Dakota	54.6
27	Tennessee	64.7
20	Texas	68.0
46	Utah	53.1
44	Vermont	54.2
13	Virginia	73.7
40	Washington	58.0
45	West Virginia	53.5
28	Wisconsin	64.6
3	Wyoming	87.7

RANK ORDER

RANK	STATE	RATE
1	New York	92.9
2	Louisiana	90.7
3	Wyoming	87.7
4	New Jersey	86.6
5	Delaware	83.4
6	Florida	82.3
7	New Mexico	81.2
8	Arizona	76.5
9	Alaska	74.4
9	Georgia	74.4
11	Hawaii	74.2
11	Nevada	74.2
13	Virginia	73.7
14	Maryland	73.5
15	Kansas	73.0
16	Missouri	70.3
16	Ohio	70.3
18	Massachusetts	69.7
19	California	69.6
20	Texas	68.0
21	Connecticut	67.6
22	Pennsylvania	66.8
23	Arkansas	66.5
24	North Carolina	66.4
25	Illinois	65.5
26	Colorado	64.8
27	Tennessee	64.7
28	Wisconsin	64.6
29	South Carolina	64.3
30	Idaho	62.5
30	Indiana	62.5
30	Nebraska	62.5
33	Montana	62.3
34	Oklahoma	61.8
35	Rhode Island	61.6
36	Oregon	60.9
37	Kentucky	59.6
38	Mississippi	59.4
39	Alabama	58.4
40	Washington	58.0
41	Michigan	56.2
42	New Hampshire	56.0
43	South Dakota	54.6
44	Vermont	54.2
45	West Virginia	53.5
46	Utah	53.1
47	Minnesota	51.9
48	North Dakota	51.7
49	Iowa	50.2
50	Maine	48.0

District of Columbia   114.2

Source: CQ Press using data from U.S. Bureau of the Census, Governments Division
"Government Employment and Payroll" (http://www.census.gov/govs/apes/index.html)
*Full-time equivalent as of March 2008. Includes police, courts, prosecution, public defense, and corrections.

State and Local Judicial and Legal Employment in 2008

National Total = 429,207 Employees*

ALPHA ORDER

RANK	STATE	EMPLOYEES	% of USA
25	Alabama	5,144	1.2%
43	Alaska	1,482	0.3%
11	Arizona	11,450	2.7%
35	Arkansas	3,184	0.7%
1	California	50,294	11.7%
22	Colorado	6,522	1.5%
26	Connecticut	5,050	1.2%
41	Delaware	1,811	0.4%
2	Florida	34,824	8.1%
9	Georgia	13,981	3.3%
33	Hawaii	3,285	0.8%
40	Idaho	1,854	0.4%
8	Illinois	16,062	3.7%
15	Indiana	8,308	1.9%
34	Iowa	3,246	0.8%
30	Kansas	3,823	0.9%
21	Kentucky	6,546	1.5%
20	Louisiana	6,938	1.6%
46	Maine	1,002	0.2%
16	Maryland	8,225	1.9%
12	Massachusetts	10,435	2.4%
10	Michigan	11,791	2.7%
23	Minnesota	6,402	1.5%
37	Mississippi	2,776	0.6%
17	Missouri	7,489	1.7%
42	Montana	1,561	0.4%
39	Nebraska	2,025	0.5%
32	Nevada	3,732	0.9%
45	New Hampshire	1,286	0.3%
5	New Jersey	21,600	5.0%
31	New Mexico	3,792	0.9%
3	New York	33,644	7.8%
18	North Carolina	7,455	1.7%
49	North Dakota	808	0.2%
6	Ohio	21,594	5.0%
29	Oklahoma	4,316	1.0%
27	Oregon	4,820	1.1%
7	Pennsylvania	18,057	4.2%
44	Rhode Island	1,341	0.3%
28	South Carolina	4,428	1.0%
48	South Dakota	910	0.2%
19	Tennessee	7,124	1.7%
4	Texas	26,487	6.2%
36	Utah	2,983	0.7%
50	Vermont	676	0.2%
13	Virginia	9,150	2.1%
14	Washington	8,370	2.0%
38	West Virginia	2,342	0.5%
24	Wisconsin	5,670	1.3%
47	Wyoming	968	0.2%

RANK ORDER

RANK	STATE	EMPLOYEES	% of USA
1	California	50,294	11.7%
2	Florida	34,824	8.1%
3	New York	33,644	7.8%
4	Texas	26,487	6.2%
5	New Jersey	21,600	5.0%
6	Ohio	21,594	5.0%
7	Pennsylvania	18,057	4.2%
8	Illinois	16,062	3.7%
9	Georgia	13,981	3.3%
10	Michigan	11,791	2.7%
11	Arizona	11,450	2.7%
12	Massachusetts	10,435	2.4%
13	Virginia	9,150	2.1%
14	Washington	8,370	2.0%
15	Indiana	8,308	1.9%
16	Maryland	8,225	1.9%
17	Missouri	7,489	1.7%
18	North Carolina	7,455	1.7%
19	Tennessee	7,124	1.7%
20	Louisiana	6,938	1.6%
21	Kentucky	6,546	1.5%
22	Colorado	6,522	1.5%
23	Minnesota	6,402	1.5%
24	Wisconsin	5,670	1.3%
25	Alabama	5,144	1.2%
26	Connecticut	5,050	1.2%
27	Oregon	4,820	1.1%
28	South Carolina	4,428	1.0%
29	Oklahoma	4,316	1.0%
30	Kansas	3,823	0.9%
31	New Mexico	3,792	0.9%
32	Nevada	3,732	0.9%
33	Hawaii	3,285	0.8%
34	Iowa	3,246	0.8%
35	Arkansas	3,184	0.7%
36	Utah	2,983	0.7%
37	Mississippi	2,776	0.6%
38	West Virginia	2,342	0.5%
39	Nebraska	2,025	0.5%
40	Idaho	1,854	0.4%
41	Delaware	1,811	0.4%
42	Montana	1,561	0.4%
43	Alaska	1,482	0.3%
44	Rhode Island	1,341	0.3%
45	New Hampshire	1,286	0.3%
46	Maine	1,002	0.2%
47	Wyoming	968	0.2%
48	South Dakota	910	0.2%
49	North Dakota	808	0.2%
50	Vermont	676	0.2%
	District of Columbia	2,144	0.5%

Source: U.S. Bureau of the Census, Governments Division
"Government Employment and Payroll" (http://www.census.gov/govs/apes/index.html)
*Full-time equivalent as of March 2008. Includes courts, prosecution, and public defense.

Rate of State and Local Judicial and Legal Employment in 2008

National Rate = 14.1 Employees Per 10,000 Population*

ALPHA ORDER

RANK	STATE	RATE
40	Alabama	11.0
3	Alaska	21.6
9	Arizona	17.6
39	Arkansas	11.2
20	California	13.7
22	Colorado	13.2
17	Connecticut	14.4
4	Delaware	20.7
6	Florida	19.0
17	Georgia	14.4
1	Hawaii	25.5
32	Idaho	12.2
30	Illinois	12.4
23	Indiana	13.0
44	Iowa	10.8
21	Kansas	13.6
14	Kentucky	15.3
13	Louisiana	15.7
50	Maine	7.6
15	Maryland	14.6
11	Massachusetts	16.1
33	Michigan	11.8
31	Minnesota	12.3
48	Mississippi	9.4
27	Missouri	12.7
11	Montana	16.1
37	Nebraska	11.4
17	Nevada	14.4
47	New Hampshire	9.8
2	New Jersey	24.9
5	New Mexico	19.1
10	New York	17.3
49	North Carolina	8.1
29	North Dakota	12.6
7	Ohio	18.8
33	Oklahoma	11.8
27	Oregon	12.7
16	Pennsylvania	14.5
25	Rhode Island	12.8
46	South Carolina	9.9
38	South Dakota	11.3
36	Tennessee	11.5
41	Texas	10.9
41	Utah	10.9
41	Vermont	10.9
33	Virginia	11.8
25	Washington	12.8
24	West Virginia	12.9
45	Wisconsin	10.1
8	Wyoming	18.2

RANK ORDER

RANK	STATE	RATE
1	Hawaii	25.5
2	New Jersey	24.9
3	Alaska	21.6
4	Delaware	20.7
5	New Mexico	19.1
6	Florida	19.0
7	Ohio	18.8
8	Wyoming	18.2
9	Arizona	17.6
10	New York	17.3
11	Massachusetts	16.1
11	Montana	16.1
13	Louisiana	15.7
14	Kentucky	15.3
15	Maryland	14.6
16	Pennsylvania	14.5
17	Connecticut	14.4
17	Georgia	14.4
17	Nevada	14.4
20	California	13.7
21	Kansas	13.6
22	Colorado	13.2
23	Indiana	13.0
24	West Virginia	12.9
25	Rhode Island	12.8
25	Washington	12.8
27	Missouri	12.7
27	Oregon	12.7
29	North Dakota	12.6
30	Illinois	12.4
31	Minnesota	12.3
32	Idaho	12.2
33	Michigan	11.8
33	Oklahoma	11.8
33	Virginia	11.8
36	Tennessee	11.5
37	Nebraska	11.4
38	South Dakota	11.3
39	Arkansas	11.2
40	Alabama	11.0
41	Texas	10.9
41	Utah	10.9
41	Vermont	10.9
44	Iowa	10.8
45	Wisconsin	10.1
46	South Carolina	9.9
47	New Hampshire	9.8
48	Mississippi	9.4
49	North Carolina	8.1
50	Maine	7.6
	District of Columbia	36.2

Source: CQ Press using data from U.S. Bureau of the Census, Governments Division
   "Government Employment and Payroll" (http://www.census.gov/govs/apes/index.html)
*Full-time equivalent as of March 2008. Includes courts, prosecution, and public defense.

State and Local Police Officers in 2008

National Total = 707,723 Officers*

<table>
<tr><td colspan="4">ALPHA ORDER</td><td colspan="4">RANK ORDER</td></tr>
<tr><th>RANK</th><th>STATE</th><th>EMPLOYEES</th><th>% of USA</th><th>RANK</th><th>STATE</th><th>EMPLOYEES</th><th>% of USA</th></tr>
<tr><td>24</td><td>Alabama</td><td>10,254</td><td>1.4%</td><td>1</td><td>California</td><td>75,093</td><td>10.6%</td></tr>
<tr><td>49</td><td>Alaska</td><td>1,094</td><td>0.2%</td><td>2</td><td>New York</td><td>73,504</td><td>10.4%</td></tr>
<tr><td>14</td><td>Arizona</td><td>15,910</td><td>2.2%</td><td>3</td><td>Texas</td><td>48,280</td><td>6.8%</td></tr>
<tr><td>31</td><td>Arkansas</td><td>6,293</td><td>0.9%</td><td>4</td><td>Florida</td><td>44,083</td><td>6.2%</td></tr>
<tr><td>1</td><td>California</td><td>75,093</td><td>10.6%</td><td>5</td><td>Illinois</td><td>36,315</td><td>5.1%</td></tr>
<tr><td>23</td><td>Colorado</td><td>10,476</td><td>1.5%</td><td>6</td><td>New Jersey</td><td>27,810</td><td>3.9%</td></tr>
<tr><td>26</td><td>Connecticut</td><td>8,394</td><td>1.2%</td><td>7</td><td>Pennsylvania</td><td>27,549</td><td>3.9%</td></tr>
<tr><td>44</td><td>Delaware</td><td>1,797</td><td>0.3%</td><td>8</td><td>Ohio</td><td>25,109</td><td>3.5%</td></tr>
<tr><td>4</td><td>Florida</td><td>44,083</td><td>6.2%</td><td>9</td><td>Massachusetts</td><td>21,916</td><td>3.1%</td></tr>
<tr><td>10</td><td>Georgia</td><td>21,643</td><td>3.1%</td><td>10</td><td>Georgia</td><td>21,643</td><td>3.1%</td></tr>
<tr><td>39</td><td>Hawaii</td><td>2,991</td><td>0.4%</td><td>11</td><td>North Carolina</td><td>21,434</td><td>3.0%</td></tr>
<tr><td>40</td><td>Idaho</td><td>2,985</td><td>0.4%</td><td>12</td><td>Virginia</td><td>18,491</td><td>2.6%</td></tr>
<tr><td>5</td><td>Illinois</td><td>36,315</td><td>5.1%</td><td>13</td><td>Michigan</td><td>17,879</td><td>2.5%</td></tr>
<tr><td>19</td><td>Indiana</td><td>12,572</td><td>1.8%</td><td>14</td><td>Arizona</td><td>15,910</td><td>2.2%</td></tr>
<tr><td>34</td><td>Iowa</td><td>5,177</td><td>0.7%</td><td>15</td><td>Tennessee</td><td>14,749</td><td>2.1%</td></tr>
<tr><td>30</td><td>Kansas</td><td>6,595</td><td>0.9%</td><td>16</td><td>Louisiana</td><td>14,061</td><td>2.0%</td></tr>
<tr><td>27</td><td>Kentucky</td><td>7,448</td><td>1.1%</td><td>17</td><td>Missouri</td><td>13,282</td><td>1.9%</td></tr>
<tr><td>16</td><td>Louisiana</td><td>14,061</td><td>2.0%</td><td>18</td><td>Maryland</td><td>12,602</td><td>1.8%</td></tr>
<tr><td>43</td><td>Maine</td><td>2,499</td><td>0.4%</td><td>19</td><td>Indiana</td><td>12,572</td><td>1.8%</td></tr>
<tr><td>18</td><td>Maryland</td><td>12,602</td><td>1.8%</td><td>20</td><td>Wisconsin</td><td>12,356</td><td>1.7%</td></tr>
<tr><td>9</td><td>Massachusetts</td><td>21,916</td><td>3.1%</td><td>21</td><td>Washington</td><td>10,962</td><td>1.5%</td></tr>
<tr><td>13</td><td>Michigan</td><td>17,879</td><td>2.5%</td><td>22</td><td>South Carolina</td><td>10,943</td><td>1.5%</td></tr>
<tr><td>25</td><td>Minnesota</td><td>8,600</td><td>1.2%</td><td>23</td><td>Colorado</td><td>10,476</td><td>1.5%</td></tr>
<tr><td>29</td><td>Mississippi</td><td>6,607</td><td>0.9%</td><td>24</td><td>Alabama</td><td>10,254</td><td>1.4%</td></tr>
<tr><td>17</td><td>Missouri</td><td>13,282</td><td>1.9%</td><td>25</td><td>Minnesota</td><td>8,600</td><td>1.2%</td></tr>
<tr><td>45</td><td>Montana</td><td>1,690</td><td>0.2%</td><td>26</td><td>Connecticut</td><td>8,394</td><td>1.2%</td></tr>
<tr><td>37</td><td>Nebraska</td><td>3,504</td><td>0.5%</td><td>27</td><td>Kentucky</td><td>7,448</td><td>1.1%</td></tr>
<tr><td>33</td><td>Nevada</td><td>5,753</td><td>0.8%</td><td>28</td><td>Oklahoma</td><td>7,405</td><td>1.0%</td></tr>
<tr><td>38</td><td>New Hampshire</td><td>3,042</td><td>0.4%</td><td>29</td><td>Mississippi</td><td>6,607</td><td>0.9%</td></tr>
<tr><td>6</td><td>New Jersey</td><td>27,810</td><td>3.9%</td><td>30</td><td>Kansas</td><td>6,595</td><td>0.9%</td></tr>
<tr><td>35</td><td>New Mexico</td><td>4,467</td><td>0.6%</td><td>31</td><td>Arkansas</td><td>6,293</td><td>0.9%</td></tr>
<tr><td>2</td><td>New York</td><td>73,504</td><td>10.4%</td><td>32</td><td>Oregon</td><td>5,988</td><td>0.8%</td></tr>
<tr><td>11</td><td>North Carolina</td><td>21,434</td><td>3.0%</td><td>33</td><td>Nevada</td><td>5,753</td><td>0.8%</td></tr>
<tr><td>48</td><td>North Dakota</td><td>1,166</td><td>0.2%</td><td>34</td><td>Iowa</td><td>5,177</td><td>0.7%</td></tr>
<tr><td>8</td><td>Ohio</td><td>25,109</td><td>3.5%</td><td>35</td><td>New Mexico</td><td>4,467</td><td>0.6%</td></tr>
<tr><td>28</td><td>Oklahoma</td><td>7,405</td><td>1.0%</td><td>36</td><td>Utah</td><td>4,247</td><td>0.6%</td></tr>
<tr><td>32</td><td>Oregon</td><td>5,988</td><td>0.8%</td><td>37</td><td>Nebraska</td><td>3,504</td><td>0.5%</td></tr>
<tr><td>7</td><td>Pennsylvania</td><td>27,549</td><td>3.9%</td><td>38</td><td>New Hampshire</td><td>3,042</td><td>0.4%</td></tr>
<tr><td>42</td><td>Rhode Island</td><td>2,744</td><td>0.4%</td><td>39</td><td>Hawaii</td><td>2,991</td><td>0.4%</td></tr>
<tr><td>22</td><td>South Carolina</td><td>10,943</td><td>1.5%</td><td>40</td><td>Idaho</td><td>2,985</td><td>0.4%</td></tr>
<tr><td>46</td><td>South Dakota</td><td>1,521</td><td>0.2%</td><td>41</td><td>West Virginia</td><td>2,918</td><td>0.4%</td></tr>
<tr><td>15</td><td>Tennessee</td><td>14,749</td><td>2.1%</td><td>42</td><td>Rhode Island</td><td>2,744</td><td>0.4%</td></tr>
<tr><td>3</td><td>Texas</td><td>48,280</td><td>6.8%</td><td>43</td><td>Maine</td><td>2,499</td><td>0.4%</td></tr>
<tr><td>36</td><td>Utah</td><td>4,247</td><td>0.6%</td><td>44</td><td>Delaware</td><td>1,797</td><td>0.3%</td></tr>
<tr><td>50</td><td>Vermont</td><td>993</td><td>0.1%</td><td>45</td><td>Montana</td><td>1,690</td><td>0.2%</td></tr>
<tr><td>12</td><td>Virginia</td><td>18,491</td><td>2.6%</td><td>46</td><td>South Dakota</td><td>1,521</td><td>0.2%</td></tr>
<tr><td>21</td><td>Washington</td><td>10,962</td><td>1.5%</td><td>47</td><td>Wyoming</td><td>1,462</td><td>0.2%</td></tr>
<tr><td>41</td><td>West Virginia</td><td>2,918</td><td>0.4%</td><td>48</td><td>North Dakota</td><td>1,166</td><td>0.2%</td></tr>
<tr><td>20</td><td>Wisconsin</td><td>12,356</td><td>1.7%</td><td>49</td><td>Alaska</td><td>1,094</td><td>0.2%</td></tr>
<tr><td>47</td><td>Wyoming</td><td>1,462</td><td>0.2%</td><td>50</td><td>Vermont</td><td>993</td><td>0.1%</td></tr>
<tr><td></td><td></td><td></td><td></td><td></td><td>District of Columbia</td><td>3,070</td><td>0.4%</td></tr>
</table>

Source: U.S. Bureau of the Census, Governments Division
   "Government Employment and Payroll" (http://www.census.gov/govs/apes/index.html)
*Full-time equivalent as of March 2008. Does not include employees of police departments who are not officers.

Rate of State and Local Police Officers in 2008

National Rate = 23.3 Officers Per 10,000 Population*

RANK	STATE	RATE
25	Alabama	22.0
48	Alaska	15.9
8	Arizona	24.5
25	Arkansas	22.0
31	California	20.4
29	Colorado	21.2
11	Connecticut	24.0
30	Delaware	20.6
10	Florida	24.1
22	Georgia	22.3
15	Hawaii	23.2
35	Idaho	19.6
5	Illinois	28.1
34	Indiana	19.7
43	Iowa	17.2
14	Kansas	23.5
42	Kentucky	17.4
4	Louisiana	31.9
37	Maine	19.0
21	Maryland	22.4
2	Massachusetts	33.7
40	Michigan	17.9
45	Minnesota	16.5
18	Mississippi	22.5
18	Missouri	22.5
41	Montana	17.5
35	Nebraska	19.6
23	Nevada	22.1
17	New Hampshire	23.1
3	New Jersey	32.0
18	New Mexico	22.5
1	New York	37.7
15	North Carolina	23.2
39	North Dakota	18.2
28	Ohio	21.9
32	Oklahoma	20.3
49	Oregon	15.8
23	Pennsylvania	22.1
7	Rhode Island	26.1
9	South Carolina	24.4
38	South Dakota	18.9
13	Tennessee	23.7
33	Texas	19.8
50	Utah	15.5
47	Vermont	16.0
12	Virginia	23.8
44	Washington	16.7
46	West Virginia	16.1
25	Wisconsin	22.0
6	Wyoming	27.4

RANK	STATE	RATE
1	New York	37.7
2	Massachusetts	33.7
3	New Jersey	32.0
4	Louisiana	31.9
5	Illinois	28.1
6	Wyoming	27.4
7	Rhode Island	26.1
8	Arizona	24.5
9	South Carolina	24.4
10	Florida	24.1
11	Connecticut	24.0
12	Virginia	23.8
13	Tennessee	23.7
14	Kansas	23.5
15	Hawaii	23.2
15	North Carolina	23.2
17	New Hampshire	23.1
18	Mississippi	22.5
18	Missouri	22.5
18	New Mexico	22.5
21	Maryland	22.4
22	Georgia	22.3
23	Nevada	22.1
23	Pennsylvania	22.1
25	Alabama	22.0
25	Arkansas	22.0
25	Wisconsin	22.0
28	Ohio	21.9
29	Colorado	21.2
30	Delaware	20.6
31	California	20.4
32	Oklahoma	20.3
33	Texas	19.8
34	Indiana	19.7
35	Idaho	19.6
35	Nebraska	19.6
37	Maine	19.0
38	South Dakota	18.9
39	North Dakota	18.2
40	Michigan	17.9
41	Montana	17.5
42	Kentucky	17.4
43	Iowa	17.2
44	Washington	16.7
45	Minnesota	16.5
46	West Virginia	16.1
47	Vermont	16.0
48	Alaska	15.9
49	Oregon	15.8
50	Utah	15.5
	District of Columbia	51.9

Source: CQ Press using data from U.S. Bureau of the Census, Governments Division
"Government Employment and Payroll" (http://www.census.gov/govs/apes/index.html)
*Full-time equivalent as of March 2008. Does not include employees of police departments who are not officers.

Law Enforcement Agencies in 2004

National Total = 17,876 Agencies*

ALPHA ORDER

ALPHA ORDER

RANK	STATE	AGENCIES	% of USA
16	Alabama	414	2.3%
47	Alaska	64	0.4%
37	Arizona	138	0.8%
24	Arkansas	355	2.0%
11	California	517	2.9%
29	Colorado	248	1.4%
43	Connecticut	118	0.7%
49	Delaware	49	0.3%
19	Florida	384	2.1%
7	Georgia	560	3.1%
50	Hawaii	7	0.0%
41	Idaho	121	0.7%
3	Illinois	898	5.0%
13	Indiana	495	2.8%
17	Iowa	407	2.3%
22	Kansas	365	2.0%
18	Kentucky	390	2.2%
23	Louisiana	356	2.0%
37	Maine	138	0.8%
36	Maryland	140	0.8%
21	Massachusetts	367	2.1%
6	Michigan	568	3.2%
15	Minnesota	457	2.6%
25	Mississippi	341	1.9%
5	Missouri	583	3.3%
40	Montana	124	0.7%
30	Nebraska	245	1.4%
45	Nevada	70	0.4%
32	New Hampshire	215	1.2%
8	New Jersey	546	3.1%
35	New Mexico	144	0.8%
9	New York	543	3.0%
12	North Carolina	497	2.8%
41	North Dakota	121	0.7%
4	Ohio	823	4.6%
14	Oklahoma	464	2.6%
33	Oregon	180	1.0%
2	Pennsylvania	1,149	6.4%
48	Rhode Island	51	0.3%
27	South Carolina	268	1.5%
34	South Dakota	167	0.9%
20	Tennessee	370	2.1%
1	Texas	1,775	9.9%
39	Utah	134	0.7%
46	Vermont	68	0.4%
26	Virginia	334	1.9%
28	Washington	261	1.5%
31	West Virginia	229	1.3%
10	Wisconsin	526	2.9%
44	Wyoming	87	0.5%

RANK ORDER

RANK	STATE	AGENCIES	% of USA
1	Texas	1,775	9.9%
2	Pennsylvania	1,149	6.4%
3	Illinois	898	5.0%
4	Ohio	823	4.6%
5	Missouri	583	3.3%
6	Michigan	568	3.2%
7	Georgia	560	3.1%
8	New Jersey	546	3.1%
9	New York	543	3.0%
10	Wisconsin	526	2.9%
11	California	517	2.9%
12	North Carolina	497	2.8%
13	Indiana	495	2.8%
14	Oklahoma	464	2.6%
15	Minnesota	457	2.6%
16	Alabama	414	2.3%
17	Iowa	407	2.3%
18	Kentucky	390	2.2%
19	Florida	384	2.1%
20	Tennessee	370	2.1%
21	Massachusetts	367	2.1%
22	Kansas	365	2.0%
23	Louisiana	356	2.0%
24	Arkansas	355	2.0%
25	Mississippi	341	1.9%
26	Virginia	334	1.9%
27	South Carolina	268	1.5%
28	Washington	261	1.5%
29	Colorado	248	1.4%
30	Nebraska	245	1.4%
31	West Virginia	229	1.3%
32	New Hampshire	215	1.2%
33	Oregon	180	1.0%
34	South Dakota	167	0.9%
35	New Mexico	144	0.8%
36	Maryland	140	0.8%
37	Arizona	138	0.8%
37	Maine	138	0.8%
39	Utah	134	0.7%
40	Montana	124	0.7%
41	Idaho	121	0.7%
41	North Dakota	121	0.7%
43	Connecticut	118	0.7%
44	Wyoming	87	0.5%
45	Nevada	70	0.4%
46	Vermont	68	0.4%
47	Alaska	64	0.4%
48	Rhode Island	51	0.3%
49	Delaware	49	0.3%
50	Hawaii	7	0.0%
	District of Columbia	5	0.0%

Source: U.S. Department of Justice, Bureau of Justice Statistics
"Census of State and Local Law Enforcement Agencies, 2004" (June 2007, NCJ212749, www.ojp.usdoj.gov/bjs/sandlle.htm)
*Includes state and local police, sheriffs' departments, and special police agencies.

Population per Law Enforcement Agency in 2004

National Rate = 16,426 Population per Agency*

<table>
<tr><td colspan="3">ALPHA ORDER</td><td colspan="3">RANK ORDER</td></tr>
<tr><td>RANK</td><td>STATE</td><td>RATE</td><td>RANK</td><td>STATE</td><td>RATE</td></tr>
<tr><td>31</td><td>Alabama</td><td>10,912</td><td>1</td><td>Hawaii</td><td>179,900</td></tr>
<tr><td>35</td><td>Alaska</td><td>10,263</td><td>2</td><td>California</td><td>69,325</td></tr>
<tr><td>4</td><td>Arizona</td><td>41,635</td><td>3</td><td>Florida</td><td>45,226</td></tr>
<tr><td>41</td><td>Arkansas</td><td>7,738</td><td>4</td><td>Arizona</td><td>41,635</td></tr>
<tr><td>2</td><td>California</td><td>69,325</td><td>5</td><td>Maryland</td><td>39,666</td></tr>
<tr><td>13</td><td>Colorado</td><td>18,542</td><td>6</td><td>New York</td><td>35,528</td></tr>
<tr><td>8</td><td>Connecticut</td><td>29,609</td><td>7</td><td>Nevada</td><td>33,321</td></tr>
<tr><td>18</td><td>Delaware</td><td>16,914</td><td>8</td><td>Connecticut</td><td>29,609</td></tr>
<tr><td>3</td><td>Florida</td><td>45,226</td><td>9</td><td>Washington</td><td>23,776</td></tr>
<tr><td>19</td><td>Georgia</td><td>15,956</td><td>10</td><td>Virginia</td><td>22,373</td></tr>
<tr><td>1</td><td>Hawaii</td><td>179,900</td><td>11</td><td>Rhode Island</td><td>21,155</td></tr>
<tr><td>29</td><td>Idaho</td><td>11,525</td><td>12</td><td>Oregon</td><td>19,940</td></tr>
<tr><td>23</td><td>Illinois</td><td>14,158</td><td>13</td><td>Colorado</td><td>18,542</td></tr>
<tr><td>28</td><td>Indiana</td><td>12,572</td><td>14</td><td>Utah</td><td>18,071</td></tr>
<tr><td>45</td><td>Iowa</td><td>7,257</td><td>15</td><td>Michigan</td><td>17,770</td></tr>
<tr><td>43</td><td>Kansas</td><td>7,502</td><td>16</td><td>Massachusetts</td><td>17,537</td></tr>
<tr><td>33</td><td>Kentucky</td><td>10,616</td><td>17</td><td>North Carolina</td><td>17,165</td></tr>
<tr><td>27</td><td>Louisiana</td><td>12,628</td><td>18</td><td>Delaware</td><td>16,914</td></tr>
<tr><td>37</td><td>Maine</td><td>9,521</td><td>19</td><td>Georgia</td><td>15,956</td></tr>
<tr><td>5</td><td>Maryland</td><td>39,666</td><td>20</td><td>Tennessee</td><td>15,907</td></tr>
<tr><td>16</td><td>Massachusetts</td><td>17,537</td><td>21</td><td>New Jersey</td><td>15,890</td></tr>
<tr><td>15</td><td>Michigan</td><td>17,770</td><td>22</td><td>South Carolina</td><td>15,652</td></tr>
<tr><td>30</td><td>Minnesota</td><td>11,147</td><td>23</td><td>Illinois</td><td>14,158</td></tr>
<tr><td>39</td><td>Mississippi</td><td>8,483</td><td>24</td><td>Ohio</td><td>13,926</td></tr>
<tr><td>36</td><td>Missouri</td><td>9,868</td><td>25</td><td>New Mexico</td><td>13,199</td></tr>
<tr><td>44</td><td>Montana</td><td>7,471</td><td>26</td><td>Texas</td><td>12,686</td></tr>
<tr><td>46</td><td>Nebraska</td><td>7,131</td><td>27</td><td>Louisiana</td><td>12,628</td></tr>
<tr><td>7</td><td>Nevada</td><td>33,321</td><td>28</td><td>Indiana</td><td>12,572</td></tr>
<tr><td>47</td><td>New Hampshire</td><td>6,037</td><td>29</td><td>Idaho</td><td>11,525</td></tr>
<tr><td>21</td><td>New Jersey</td><td>15,890</td><td>30</td><td>Minnesota</td><td>11,147</td></tr>
<tr><td>25</td><td>New Mexico</td><td>13,199</td><td>31</td><td>Alabama</td><td>10,912</td></tr>
<tr><td>6</td><td>New York</td><td>35,528</td><td>32</td><td>Pennsylvania</td><td>10,772</td></tr>
<tr><td>17</td><td>North Carolina</td><td>17,165</td><td>33</td><td>Kentucky</td><td>10,616</td></tr>
<tr><td>49</td><td>North Dakota</td><td>5,255</td><td>34</td><td>Wisconsin</td><td>10,454</td></tr>
<tr><td>24</td><td>Ohio</td><td>13,926</td><td>35</td><td>Alaska</td><td>10,263</td></tr>
<tr><td>42</td><td>Oklahoma</td><td>7,592</td><td>36</td><td>Missouri</td><td>9,868</td></tr>
<tr><td>12</td><td>Oregon</td><td>19,940</td><td>37</td><td>Maine</td><td>9,521</td></tr>
<tr><td>32</td><td>Pennsylvania</td><td>10,772</td><td>38</td><td>Vermont</td><td>9,129</td></tr>
<tr><td>11</td><td>Rhode Island</td><td>21,155</td><td>39</td><td>Mississippi</td><td>8,483</td></tr>
<tr><td>22</td><td>South Carolina</td><td>15,652</td><td>40</td><td>West Virginia</td><td>7,908</td></tr>
<tr><td>50</td><td>South Dakota</td><td>4,612</td><td>41</td><td>Arkansas</td><td>7,738</td></tr>
<tr><td>20</td><td>Tennessee</td><td>15,907</td><td>42</td><td>Oklahoma</td><td>7,592</td></tr>
<tr><td>26</td><td>Texas</td><td>12,686</td><td>43</td><td>Kansas</td><td>7,502</td></tr>
<tr><td>14</td><td>Utah</td><td>18,071</td><td>44</td><td>Montana</td><td>7,471</td></tr>
<tr><td>38</td><td>Vermont</td><td>9,129</td><td>45</td><td>Iowa</td><td>7,257</td></tr>
<tr><td>10</td><td>Virginia</td><td>22,373</td><td>46</td><td>Nebraska</td><td>7,131</td></tr>
<tr><td>9</td><td>Washington</td><td>23,776</td><td>47</td><td>New Hampshire</td><td>6,037</td></tr>
<tr><td>40</td><td>West Virginia</td><td>7,908</td><td>48</td><td>Wyoming</td><td>5,811</td></tr>
<tr><td>34</td><td>Wisconsin</td><td>10,454</td><td>49</td><td>North Dakota</td><td>5,255</td></tr>
<tr><td>48</td><td>Wyoming</td><td>5,811</td><td>50</td><td>South Dakota</td><td>4,612</td></tr>
<tr><td></td><td></td><td></td><td></td><td>District of Columbia</td><td>115,944</td></tr>
</table>

Source: CQ Press using data from U.S. Department of Justice, Bureau of Justice Statistics
"Census of State and Local Law Enforcement Agencies, 2004" (June 2007, NCJ 212749, www.ojp.usdoj.gov/bjs/sandlle.htm)
*Includes state and local police, sheriffs' departments, and special police agencies.

Law Enforcement Agencies per 1,000 Square Miles in 2004

National Rate = 4.7 Agencies per 1,000 Square Miles*

RANK	STATE	RATE
21	Alabama	7.9
50	Alaska	0.1
44	Arizona	1.2
27	Arkansas	6.7
36	California	3.2
38	Colorado	2.4
6	Connecticut	21.3
7	Delaware	19.7
31	Florida	5.8
15	Georgia	9.4
48	Hawaii	0.6
43	Idaho	1.4
9	Illinois	15.5
10	Indiana	13.6
23	Iowa	7.2
33	Kansas	4.4
13	Kentucky	9.7
26	Louisiana	6.9
34	Maine	3.9
11	Maryland	11.3
2	Massachusetts	34.8
30	Michigan	5.9
32	Minnesota	5.3
25	Mississippi	7.0
18	Missouri	8.4
47	Montana	0.8
36	Nebraska	3.2
48	Nevada	0.6
5	New Hampshire	23.0
1	New Jersey	62.6
44	New Mexico	1.2
12	New York	10.0
16	North Carolina	9.2
41	North Dakota	1.7
8	Ohio	18.4
28	Oklahoma	6.6
40	Oregon	1.8
4	Pennsylvania	24.9
3	Rhode Island	33.0
18	South Carolina	8.4
39	South Dakota	2.2
17	Tennessee	8.8
28	Texas	6.6
42	Utah	1.6
24	Vermont	7.1
22	Virginia	7.8
35	Washington	3.7
14	West Virginia	9.5
20	Wisconsin	8.0
46	Wyoming	0.9

RANK	STATE	RATE
1	New Jersey	62.6
2	Massachusetts	34.8
3	Rhode Island	33.0
4	Pennsylvania	24.9
5	New Hampshire	23.0
6	Connecticut	21.3
7	Delaware	19.7
8	Ohio	18.4
9	Illinois	15.5
10	Indiana	13.6
11	Maryland	11.3
12	New York	10.0
13	Kentucky	9.7
14	West Virginia	9.5
15	Georgia	9.4
16	North Carolina	9.2
17	Tennessee	8.8
18	Missouri	8.4
18	South Carolina	8.4
20	Wisconsin	8.0
21	Alabama	7.9
22	Virginia	7.8
23	Iowa	7.2
24	Vermont	7.1
25	Mississippi	7.0
26	Louisiana	6.9
27	Arkansas	6.7
28	Oklahoma	6.6
28	Texas	6.6
30	Michigan	5.9
31	Florida	5.8
32	Minnesota	5.3
33	Kansas	4.4
34	Maine	3.9
35	Washington	3.7
36	California	3.2
36	Nebraska	3.2
38	Colorado	2.4
39	South Dakota	2.2
40	Oregon	1.8
41	North Dakota	1.7
42	Utah	1.6
43	Idaho	1.4
44	Arizona	1.2
44	New Mexico	1.2
46	Wyoming	0.9
47	Montana	0.8
48	Hawaii	0.6
48	Nevada	0.6
50	Alaska	0.1
	District of Columbia**	NA

Source: CQ Press using data from U.S. Department of Justice, Bureau of Justice Statistics
"Census of State and Local Law Enforcement Agencies, 2004" (June 2007, NCJ 212749, www.ojp.usdoj.gov/bjs/sandlle.htm)
*Includes state and local police, sheriffs' departments, and special police agencies.
**The District of Columbia has five agencies for its 68 square miles.

Full-Time Sworn Officers in Law Enforcement Agencies in 2004

National Total = 731,903 Officers*

ALPHA ORDER

RANK	STATE	OFFICERS	% of USA
22	Alabama	10,920	1.5%
48	Alaska	1,409	0.2%
19	Arizona	12,659	1.7%
32	Arkansas	6,333	0.9%
1	California	75,622	10.3%
21	Colorado	11,086	1.5%
26	Connecticut	8,008	1.1%
44	Delaware	1,982	0.3%
4	Florida	45,267	6.2%
9	Georgia	23,499	3.2%
40	Hawaii	3,002	0.4%
41	Idaho	2,964	0.4%
5	Illinois	39,714	5.4%
20	Indiana	12,083	1.7%
34	Iowa	5,424	0.7%
29	Kansas	7,141	1.0%
28	Kentucky	7,655	1.0%
14	Louisiana	17,996	2.5%
43	Maine	2,571	0.4%
16	Maryland	15,144	2.1%
13	Massachusetts	18,174	2.5%
12	Michigan	20,762	2.8%
25	Minnesota	9,018	1.2%
30	Mississippi	7,013	1.0%
17	Missouri	14,073	1.9%
45	Montana	1,912	0.3%
37	Nebraska	3,786	0.5%
33	Nevada	5,976	0.8%
42	New Hampshire	2,805	0.4%
6	New Jersey	31,812	4.3%
35	New Mexico	4,894	0.7%
2	New York	66,037	9.0%
11	North Carolina	20,973	2.9%
49	North Dakota	1,307	0.2%
8	Ohio	25,856	3.5%
27	Oklahoma	8,007	1.1%
31	Oregon	6,338	0.9%
7	Pennsylvania	26,629	3.6%
39	Rhode Island	3,071	0.4%
24	South Carolina	10,762	1.5%
47	South Dakota	1,621	0.2%
15	Tennessee	15,248	2.1%
3	Texas	54,780	7.5%
36	Utah	4,573	0.6%
50	Vermont	1,156	0.2%
10	Virginia	21,655	3.0%
23	Washington	10,822	1.5%
38	West Virginia	3,207	0.4%
18	Wisconsin	13,072	1.8%
46	Wyoming	1,662	0.2%

RANK ORDER

RANK	STATE	OFFICERS	% of USA
1	California	75,622	10.3%
2	New York	66,037	9.0%
3	Texas	54,780	7.5%
4	Florida	45,267	6.2%
5	Illinois	39,714	5.4%
6	New Jersey	31,812	4.3%
7	Pennsylvania	26,629	3.6%
8	Ohio	25,856	3.5%
9	Georgia	23,499	3.2%
10	Virginia	21,655	3.0%
11	North Carolina	20,973	2.9%
12	Michigan	20,762	2.8%
13	Massachusetts	18,174	2.5%
14	Louisiana	17,996	2.5%
15	Tennessee	15,248	2.1%
16	Maryland	15,144	2.1%
17	Missouri	14,073	1.9%
18	Wisconsin	13,072	1.8%
19	Arizona	12,659	1.7%
20	Indiana	12,083	1.7%
21	Colorado	11,086	1.5%
22	Alabama	10,920	1.5%
23	Washington	10,822	1.5%
24	South Carolina	10,762	1.5%
25	Minnesota	9,018	1.2%
26	Connecticut	8,008	1.1%
27	Oklahoma	8,007	1.1%
28	Kentucky	7,655	1.0%
29	Kansas	7,141	1.0%
30	Mississippi	7,013	1.0%
31	Oregon	6,338	0.9%
32	Arkansas	6,333	0.9%
33	Nevada	5,976	0.8%
34	Iowa	5,424	0.7%
35	New Mexico	4,894	0.7%
36	Utah	4,573	0.6%
37	Nebraska	3,786	0.5%
38	West Virginia	3,207	0.4%
39	Rhode Island	3,071	0.4%
40	Hawaii	3,002	0.4%
41	Idaho	2,964	0.4%
42	New Hampshire	2,805	0.4%
43	Maine	2,571	0.4%
44	Delaware	1,982	0.3%
45	Montana	1,912	0.3%
46	Wyoming	1,662	0.2%
47	South Dakota	1,621	0.2%
48	Alaska	1,409	0.2%
49	North Dakota	1,307	0.2%
50	Vermont	1,156	0.2%
	District of Columbia	4,423	0.6%

Source: U.S. Department of Justice, Bureau of Justice Statistics
    "Census of State and Local Law Enforcement Agencies, 2004" (June 2007, NCJ 212749, www.ojp.usdoj.gov/bjs/sandlle.htm)
*Includes state and local police, sheriffs' departments, and special police agencies.

Rate of Full-Time Sworn Officers in Law Enforcement Agencies in 2004

National Rate = 249 Officers per 100,000 Population*

ALPHA ORDER

RANK	STATE	RATE
21	Alabama	241
33	Alaska	215
30	Arizona	220
26	Arkansas	230
36	California	211
21	Colorado	241
27	Connecticut	229
23	Delaware	239
11	Florida	262
10	Georgia	266
24	Hawaii	238
35	Idaho	213
5	Illinois	312
42	Indiana	194
46	Iowa	184
12	Kansas	261
45	Kentucky	185
1	Louisiana	399
41	Maine	195
9	Maryland	272
8	Massachusetts	283
40	Michigan	205
47	Minnesota	177
20	Mississippi	242
18	Missouri	245
38	Montana	206
31	Nebraska	217
15	Nevada	256
32	New Hampshire	216
2	New Jersey	366
14	New Mexico	257
3	New York	344
17	North Carolina	246
38	North Dakota	206
29	Ohio	226
28	Oklahoma	227
49	Oregon	176
33	Pennsylvania	215
7	Rhode Island	284
15	South Carolina	256
37	South Dakota	210
13	Tennessee	258
19	Texas	244
43	Utah	191
44	Vermont	186
6	Virginia	290
50	Washington	174
47	West Virginia	177
25	Wisconsin	237
4	Wyoming	328

RANK ORDER

RANK	STATE	RATE
1	Louisiana	399
2	New Jersey	366
3	New York	344
4	Wyoming	328
5	Illinois	312
6	Virginia	290
7	Rhode Island	284
8	Massachusetts	283
9	Maryland	272
10	Georgia	266
11	Florida	262
12	Kansas	261
13	Tennessee	258
14	New Mexico	257
15	Nevada	256
15	South Carolina	256
17	North Carolina	246
18	Missouri	245
19	Texas	244
20	Mississippi	242
21	Alabama	241
21	Colorado	241
23	Delaware	239
24	Hawaii	238
25	Wisconsin	237
26	Arkansas	230
27	Connecticut	229
28	Oklahoma	227
29	Ohio	226
30	Arizona	220
31	Nebraska	217
32	New Hampshire	216
33	Alaska	215
33	Pennsylvania	215
35	Idaho	213
36	California	211
37	South Dakota	210
38	Montana	206
38	North Dakota	206
40	Michigan	205
41	Maine	195
42	Indiana	194
43	Utah	191
44	Vermont	186
45	Kentucky	185
46	Iowa	184
47	Minnesota	177
47	West Virginia	177
49	Oregon	176
50	Washington	174
	District of Columbia	799

Source: CQ Press using data from U.S. Department of Justice, Bureau of Justice Statistics
"Census of State and Local Law Enforcement Agencies, 2004" (June 2007, NCJ 212749, www.ojp.usdoj.gov/bjs/sandlle.htm)
*Includes state and local police, sheriffs' departments, and special police agencies.

Percent of Full-Time Law Enforcement Agency Employees
Who Are Sworn Officers: 2004
National Percent = 68.0% of Employees*

RANK	STATE	PERCENT
29	Alabama	65.7
42	Alaska	61.9
48	Arizona	57.9
31	Arkansas	65.4
39	California	62.9
28	Colorado	66.6
3	Connecticut	81.4
19	Delaware	70.8
46	Florida	58.9
26	Georgia	67.7
9	Hawaii	75.0
45	Idaho	60.3
5	Illinois	76.2
39	Indiana	62.9
25	Iowa	67.8
32	Kansas	65.2
8	Kentucky	75.4
16	Louisiana	71.8
35	Maine	63.8
14	Maryland	72.0
10	Massachusetts	74.8
13	Michigan	73.1
37	Minnesota	63.5
44	Mississippi	60.5
21	Missouri	70.1
47	Montana	58.7
23	Nebraska	68.7
38	Nevada	63.4
7	New Hampshire	75.7
5	New Jersey	76.2
24	New Mexico	67.9
22	New York	69.5
18	North Carolina	71.3
11	North Dakota	73.9
29	Ohio	65.7
33	Oklahoma	64.4
43	Oregon	61.4
1	Pennsylvania	82.0
2	Rhode Island	81.5
15	South Carolina	71.9
39	South Dakota	62.9
34	Tennessee	64.3
36	Texas	63.6
49	Utah	57.7
17	Vermont	71.4
4	Virginia	78.2
27	Washington	66.9
12	West Virginia	73.7
20	Wisconsin	70.2
50	Wyoming	54.8

RANK	STATE	PERCENT
1	Pennsylvania	82.0
2	Rhode Island	81.5
3	Connecticut	81.4
4	Virginia	78.2
5	Illinois	76.2
5	New Jersey	76.2
7	New Hampshire	75.7
8	Kentucky	75.4
9	Hawaii	75.0
10	Massachusetts	74.8
11	North Dakota	73.9
12	West Virginia	73.7
13	Michigan	73.1
14	Maryland	72.0
15	South Carolina	71.9
16	Louisiana	71.8
17	Vermont	71.4
18	North Carolina	71.3
19	Delaware	70.8
20	Wisconsin	70.2
21	Missouri	70.1
22	New York	69.5
23	Nebraska	68.7
24	New Mexico	67.9
25	Iowa	67.8
26	Georgia	67.7
27	Washington	66.9
28	Colorado	66.6
29	Alabama	65.7
29	Ohio	65.7
31	Arkansas	65.4
32	Kansas	65.2
33	Oklahoma	64.4
34	Tennessee	64.3
35	Maine	63.8
36	Texas	63.6
37	Minnesota	63.5
38	Nevada	63.4
39	California	62.9
39	Indiana	62.9
39	South Dakota	62.9
42	Alaska	61.9
43	Oregon	61.4
44	Mississippi	60.5
45	Idaho	60.3
46	Florida	58.9
47	Montana	58.7
48	Arizona	57.9
49	Utah	57.7
50	Wyoming	54.8

| | District of Columbia | 83.6 |

Source: CQ Press using data from U.S. Department of Justice, Bureau of Justice Statistics
"Census of State and Local Law Enforcement Agencies, 2004" (June 2007, NCJ 212749, www.ojp.usdoj.gov/bjs/sandlle.htm)
*Includes state and local police, sheriffs' departments, and special police agencies.

Full-Time Sworn Law Enforcement Officers per 1,000 Square Miles in 2004

National Rate = 284 Officers per 1,000 Square Miles*

<table>
<tr><td colspan="3">ALPHA ORDER</td><td colspan="3">RANK ORDER</td></tr>
<tr><td>RANK</td><td>STATE</td><td>RATE</td><td>RANK</td><td>STATE</td><td>RATE</td></tr>
<tr><td>23</td><td>Alabama</td><td>317</td><td>1</td><td>New Jersey</td><td>4,787</td></tr>
<tr><td>50</td><td>Alaska</td><td>3</td><td>2</td><td>Rhode Island</td><td>2,438</td></tr>
<tr><td>30</td><td>Arizona</td><td>192</td><td>3</td><td>Massachusetts</td><td>2,301</td></tr>
<tr><td>31</td><td>Arkansas</td><td>182</td><td>4</td><td>Connecticut</td><td>1,775</td></tr>
<tr><td>11</td><td>California</td><td>734</td><td>5</td><td>New York</td><td>1,741</td></tr>
<tr><td>36</td><td>Colorado</td><td>160</td><td>6</td><td>Maryland</td><td>1,696</td></tr>
<tr><td>4</td><td>Connecticut</td><td>1,775</td><td>7</td><td>Florida</td><td>1,168</td></tr>
<tr><td>8</td><td>Delaware</td><td>1,124</td><td>8</td><td>Delaware</td><td>1,124</td></tr>
<tr><td>7</td><td>Florida</td><td>1,168</td><td>9</td><td>Illinois</td><td>900</td></tr>
<tr><td>14</td><td>Georgia</td><td>584</td><td>10</td><td>Ohio</td><td>878</td></tr>
<tr><td>21</td><td>Hawaii</td><td>366</td><td>11</td><td>California</td><td>734</td></tr>
<tr><td>44</td><td>Idaho</td><td>59</td><td>12</td><td>Pennsylvania</td><td>705</td></tr>
<tr><td>9</td><td>Illinois</td><td>900</td><td>13</td><td>Virginia</td><td>647</td></tr>
<tr><td>17</td><td>Indiana</td><td>527</td><td>14</td><td>Georgia</td><td>584</td></tr>
<tr><td>37</td><td>Iowa</td><td>142</td><td>15</td><td>Tennessee</td><td>563</td></tr>
<tr><td>38</td><td>Kansas</td><td>133</td><td>16</td><td>North Carolina</td><td>547</td></tr>
<tr><td>27</td><td>Kentucky</td><td>251</td><td>17</td><td>Indiana</td><td>527</td></tr>
<tr><td>18</td><td>Louisiana</td><td>483</td><td>18</td><td>Louisiana</td><td>483</td></tr>
<tr><td>39</td><td>Maine</td><td>114</td><td>19</td><td>South Carolina</td><td>468</td></tr>
<tr><td>6</td><td>Maryland</td><td>1,696</td><td>20</td><td>New Hampshire</td><td>396</td></tr>
<tr><td>3</td><td>Massachusetts</td><td>2,301</td><td>21</td><td>Hawaii</td><td>366</td></tr>
<tr><td>24</td><td>Michigan</td><td>294</td><td>22</td><td>Texas</td><td>321</td></tr>
<tr><td>35</td><td>Minnesota</td><td>163</td><td>23</td><td>Alabama</td><td>317</td></tr>
<tr><td>28</td><td>Mississippi</td><td>239</td><td>24</td><td>Michigan</td><td>294</td></tr>
<tr><td>25</td><td>Missouri</td><td>288</td><td>25</td><td>Missouri</td><td>288</td></tr>
<tr><td>49</td><td>Montana</td><td>22</td><td>26</td><td>Wisconsin</td><td>284</td></tr>
<tr><td>43</td><td>Nebraska</td><td>71</td><td>27</td><td>Kentucky</td><td>251</td></tr>
<tr><td>42</td><td>Nevada</td><td>85</td><td>28</td><td>Mississippi</td><td>239</td></tr>
<tr><td>20</td><td>New Hampshire</td><td>396</td><td>29</td><td>Washington</td><td>227</td></tr>
<tr><td>1</td><td>New Jersey</td><td>4,787</td><td>30</td><td>Arizona</td><td>192</td></tr>
<tr><td>44</td><td>New Mexico</td><td>59</td><td>31</td><td>Arkansas</td><td>182</td></tr>
<tr><td>5</td><td>New York</td><td>1,741</td><td>32</td><td>West Virginia</td><td>180</td></tr>
<tr><td>16</td><td>North Carolina</td><td>547</td><td>33</td><td>Oklahoma</td><td>178</td></tr>
<tr><td>48</td><td>North Dakota</td><td>25</td><td>34</td><td>Vermont</td><td>168</td></tr>
<tr><td>10</td><td>Ohio</td><td>878</td><td>35</td><td>Minnesota</td><td>163</td></tr>
<tr><td>33</td><td>Oklahoma</td><td>178</td><td>36</td><td>Colorado</td><td>160</td></tr>
<tr><td>40</td><td>Oregon</td><td>105</td><td>37</td><td>Iowa</td><td>142</td></tr>
<tr><td>12</td><td>Pennsylvania</td><td>705</td><td>38</td><td>Kansas</td><td>133</td></tr>
<tr><td>2</td><td>Rhode Island</td><td>2,438</td><td>39</td><td>Maine</td><td>114</td></tr>
<tr><td>19</td><td>South Carolina</td><td>468</td><td>40</td><td>Oregon</td><td>105</td></tr>
<tr><td>46</td><td>South Dakota</td><td>33</td><td>41</td><td>Utah</td><td>93</td></tr>
<tr><td>15</td><td>Tennessee</td><td>563</td><td>42</td><td>Nevada</td><td>85</td></tr>
<tr><td>22</td><td>Texas</td><td>321</td><td>43</td><td>Nebraska</td><td>71</td></tr>
<tr><td>41</td><td>Utah</td><td>93</td><td>44</td><td>Idaho</td><td>59</td></tr>
<tr><td>34</td><td>Vermont</td><td>168</td><td>44</td><td>New Mexico</td><td>59</td></tr>
<tr><td>13</td><td>Virginia</td><td>647</td><td>46</td><td>South Dakota</td><td>33</td></tr>
<tr><td>29</td><td>Washington</td><td>227</td><td>47</td><td>Wyoming</td><td>31</td></tr>
<tr><td>32</td><td>West Virginia</td><td>180</td><td>48</td><td>North Dakota</td><td>25</td></tr>
<tr><td>26</td><td>Wisconsin</td><td>284</td><td>49</td><td>Montana</td><td>22</td></tr>
<tr><td>47</td><td>Wyoming</td><td>31</td><td>50</td><td>Alaska</td><td>3</td></tr>
<tr><td></td><td></td><td></td><td></td><td>District of Columbia**</td><td>NA</td></tr>
</table>

Source: CQ Press using data from U.S. Department of Justice, Bureau of Justice Statistics
"Census of State and Local Law Enforcement Agencies, 2004" (June 2007, NCJ 212749, www.ojp.usdoj.gov/bjs/sandlle.htm)
*Includes state and local police, sheriffs' departments, and special police agencies.
**The District of Columbia has 4,423 sworn officers for its 68 square miles.

State Government Law Enforcement Officers in 2008

National Total = 71,653 Officers*

ALPHA ORDER

RANK	STATE	OFFICERS	% of USA
25	Alabama	934	1.3%
39	Alaska	344	0.5%
20	Arizona	1,275	1.8%
32	Arkansas	589	0.8%
1	California	8,222	11.5%
29	Colorado	765	1.1%
21	Connecticut	1,270	1.8%
24	Delaware	1,050	1.5%
6	Florida	3,002	4.2%
19	Georgia	1,281	1.8%
48	Hawaii	0	0.0%
43	Idaho	268	0.4%
10	Illinois	2,432	3.4%
17	Indiana	1,417	2.0%
30	Iowa	669	0.9%
28	Kansas	843	1.2%
22	Kentucky	1,175	1.6%
18	Louisiana	1,321	1.8%
39	Maine	344	0.5%
8	Maryland	2,479	3.5%
7	Massachusetts	2,620	3.7%
14	Michigan	1,830	2.6%
36	Minnesota	529	0.7%
NA	Mississippi**	NA	NA
16	Missouri	1,583	2.2%
44	Montana	231	0.3%
37	Nebraska	496	0.7%
34	Nevada	548	0.8%
38	New Hampshire	391	0.5%
4	New Jersey	4,461	6.2%
35	New Mexico	540	0.8%
2	New York	5,216	7.3%
9	North Carolina	2,463	3.4%
47	North Dakota	138	0.2%
12	Ohio	1,989	2.8%
27	Oklahoma	853	1.2%
33	Oregon	581	0.8%
3	Pennsylvania	4,681	6.5%
42	Rhode Island	276	0.4%
13	South Carolina	1,958	2.7%
46	South Dakota	193	0.3%
15	Tennessee	1,602	2.2%
5	Texas	3,506	4.9%
31	Utah	605	0.8%
41	Vermont	339	0.5%
11	Virginia	2,187	3.1%
23	Washington	1,080	1.5%
NA	West Virginia**	NA	NA
26	Wisconsin	877	1.2%
45	Wyoming	200	0.3%

RANK ORDER

RANK	STATE	OFFICERS	% of USA
1	California	8,222	11.5%
2	New York	5,216	7.3%
3	Pennsylvania	4,681	6.5%
4	New Jersey	4,461	6.2%
5	Texas	3,506	4.9%
6	Florida	3,002	4.2%
7	Massachusetts	2,620	3.7%
8	Maryland	2,479	3.5%
9	North Carolina	2,463	3.4%
10	Illinois	2,432	3.4%
11	Virginia	2,187	3.1%
12	Ohio	1,989	2.8%
13	South Carolina	1,958	2.7%
14	Michigan	1,830	2.6%
15	Tennessee	1,602	2.2%
16	Missouri	1,583	2.2%
17	Indiana	1,417	2.0%
18	Louisiana	1,321	1.8%
19	Georgia	1,281	1.8%
20	Arizona	1,275	1.8%
21	Connecticut	1,270	1.8%
22	Kentucky	1,175	1.6%
23	Washington	1,080	1.5%
24	Delaware	1,050	1.5%
25	Alabama	934	1.3%
26	Wisconsin	877	1.2%
27	Oklahoma	853	1.2%
28	Kansas	843	1.2%
29	Colorado	765	1.1%
30	Iowa	669	0.9%
31	Utah	605	0.8%
32	Arkansas	589	0.8%
33	Oregon	581	0.8%
34	Nevada	548	0.8%
35	New Mexico	540	0.8%
36	Minnesota	529	0.7%
37	Nebraska	496	0.7%
38	New Hampshire	391	0.5%
39	Alaska	344	0.5%
39	Maine	344	0.5%
41	Vermont	339	0.5%
42	Rhode Island	276	0.4%
43	Idaho	268	0.4%
44	Montana	231	0.3%
45	Wyoming	200	0.3%
46	South Dakota	193	0.3%
47	North Dakota	138	0.2%
48	Hawaii	0	0.0%
NA	Mississippi**	NA	NA
NA	West Virginia**	NA	NA
	District of Columbia	0	0.0%

Source: CQ Press using reported data from the Federal Bureau of Investigation
"Crime in the United States 2008" (Uniform Crime Reports, September 14, 2009, http://www.fbi.gov/ucr/ucr.htm)
*Includes state police agencies and other agencies with law enforcement powers. Hawaii and the District of Columbia do not have state police agencies.
**Not available.

Percent of State Government Law Enforcement Officers Who Are Female in 2007
National Percent = 7.8% of Officers*

ALPHA ORDER

RANK	STATE	PERCENT
44	Alabama	2.8
36	Alaska	4.4
31	Arizona	5.5
38	Arkansas	4.2
6	California	10.5
22	Colorado	6.8
22	Connecticut	6.8
1	Delaware	15.6
2	Florida	11.7
26	Georgia	6.2
NA	Hawaii**	NA
39	Idaho	4.1
9	Illinois	10.4
29	Indiana	5.7
25	Iowa	6.6
42	Kansas	3.6
43	Kentucky	3.3
39	Louisiana	4.1
21	Maine	7.0
10	Maryland	10.1
18	Massachusetts	8.0
3	Michigan	11.5
11	Minnesota	9.3
NA	Mississippi**	NA
35	Missouri	4.5
33	Montana	5.2
30	Nebraska	5.6
16	Nevada	8.4
6	New Hampshire	10.5
27	New Jersey	5.8
44	New Mexico	2.8
13	New York	8.6
12	North Carolina	9.0
37	North Dakota	4.3
15	Ohio	8.5
47	Oklahoma	2.2
6	Oregon	10.5
34	Pennsylvania	4.7
20	Rhode Island	7.6
13	South Carolina	8.6
46	South Dakota	2.6
3	Tennessee	11.5
27	Texas	5.8
32	Utah	5.3
17	Vermont	8.3
24	Virginia	6.7
19	Washington	7.8
NA	West Virginia**	NA
5	Wisconsin	11.4
41	Wyoming	4.0

RANK ORDER

RANK	STATE	PERCENT
1	Delaware	15.6
2	Florida	11.7
3	Michigan	11.5
3	Tennessee	11.5
5	Wisconsin	11.4
6	California	10.5
6	New Hampshire	10.5
6	Oregon	10.5
9	Illinois	10.4
10	Maryland	10.1
11	Minnesota	9.3
12	North Carolina	9.0
13	New York	8.6
13	South Carolina	8.6
15	Ohio	8.5
16	Nevada	8.4
17	Vermont	8.3
18	Massachusetts	8.0
19	Washington	7.8
20	Rhode Island	7.6
21	Maine	7.0
22	Colorado	6.8
22	Connecticut	6.8
24	Virginia	6.7
25	Iowa	6.6
26	Georgia	6.2
27	New Jersey	5.8
27	Texas	5.8
29	Indiana	5.7
30	Nebraska	5.6
31	Arizona	5.5
32	Utah	5.3
33	Montana	5.2
34	Pennsylvania	4.7
35	Missouri	4.5
36	Alaska	4.4
37	North Dakota	4.3
38	Arkansas	4.2
39	Idaho	4.1
39	Louisiana	4.1
41	Wyoming	4.0
42	Kansas	3.6
43	Kentucky	3.3
44	Alabama	2.8
44	New Mexico	2.8
46	South Dakota	2.6
47	Oklahoma	2.2
NA	Hawaii**	NA
NA	Mississippi**	NA
NA	West Virginia**	NA
	District of Columbia**	NA

Source: CQ Press using reported data from the Federal Bureau of Investigation
"Crime in the United States 2008" (Uniform Crime Reports, September 14, 2009, http://www.fbi.gov/ucr/ucr.htm)
*Includes state police agencies and other agencies with law enforcement powers.
**Hawaii and the District of Columbia do not have state police agencies. Figures for Mississippi and West Virginia are not available.

Full-Time Sworn Officers in State Police Departments in 2004

National Total = 58,190 Officers*

ALPHA ORDER

RANK	STATE	OFFICERS	% of USA
25	Alabama	681	1.2%
40	Alaska	380	0.7%
16	Arizona	1,125	1.9%
36	Arkansas	508	0.9%
1	California	7,085	12.2%
25	Colorado	681	1.2%
15	Connecticut	1,152	2.0%
27	Delaware	642	1.1%
10	Florida	1,654	2.8%
22	Georgia	856	1.5%
50	Hawaii*	0	0.0%
44	Idaho	288	0.5%
7	Illinois	2,008	3.5%
14	Indiana	1,158	2.0%
39	Iowa	389	0.7%
32	Kansas	541	0.9%
21	Kentucky	936	1.6%
18	Louisiana	1,063	1.8%
41	Maine	338	0.6%
11	Maryland	1,596	2.7%
6	Massachusetts	2,200	3.8%
9	Michigan	1,862	3.2%
31	Minnesota	544	0.9%
34	Mississippi	535	0.9%
17	Missouri	1,097	1.9%
45	Montana	206	0.4%
37	Nebraska	503	0.9%
38	Nevada	421	0.7%
43	New Hampshire	289	0.5%
5	New Jersey	2,768	4.8%
30	New Mexico	566	1.0%
2	New York	4,667	8.0%
12	North Carolina	1,517	2.6%
49	North Dakota	135	0.2%
13	Ohio	1,502	2.6%
23	Oklahoma	808	1.4%
29	Oregon	621	1.1%
3	Pennsylvania	4,200	7.2%
46	Rhode Island	190	0.3%
24	South Carolina	785	1.3%
48	South Dakota	154	0.3%
20	Tennessee	972	1.7%
4	Texas	3,437	5.9%
33	Utah	538	0.9%
42	Vermont	325	0.6%
8	Virginia	1,869	3.2%
19	Washington	1,059	1.8%
28	West Virginia	641	1.1%
35	Wisconsin	510	0.9%
47	Wyoming	188	0.3%

RANK ORDER

RANK	STATE	OFFICERS	% of USA
1	California	7,085	12.2%
2	New York	4,667	8.0%
3	Pennsylvania	4,200	7.2%
4	Texas	3,437	5.9%
5	New Jersey	2,768	4.8%
6	Massachusetts	2,200	3.8%
7	Illinois	2,008	3.5%
8	Virginia	1,869	3.2%
9	Michigan	1,862	3.2%
10	Florida	1,654	2.8%
11	Maryland	1,596	2.7%
12	North Carolina	1,517	2.6%
13	Ohio	1,502	2.6%
14	Indiana	1,158	2.0%
15	Connecticut	1,152	2.0%
16	Arizona	1,125	1.9%
17	Missouri	1,097	1.9%
18	Louisiana	1,063	1.8%
19	Washington	1,059	1.8%
20	Tennessee	972	1.7%
21	Kentucky	936	1.6%
22	Georgia	856	1.5%
23	Oklahoma	808	1.4%
24	South Carolina	785	1.3%
25	Alabama	681	1.2%
25	Colorado	681	1.2%
27	Delaware	642	1.1%
28	West Virginia	641	1.1%
29	Oregon	621	1.1%
30	New Mexico	566	1.0%
31	Minnesota	544	0.9%
32	Kansas	541	0.9%
33	Utah	538	0.9%
34	Mississippi	535	0.9%
35	Wisconsin	510	0.9%
36	Arkansas	508	0.9%
37	Nebraska	503	0.9%
38	Nevada	421	0.7%
39	Iowa	389	0.7%
40	Alaska	380	0.7%
41	Maine	338	0.6%
42	Vermont	325	0.6%
43	New Hampshire	289	0.5%
44	Idaho	288	0.5%
45	Montana	206	0.4%
46	Rhode Island	190	0.3%
47	Wyoming	188	0.3%
48	South Dakota	154	0.3%
49	North Dakota	135	0.2%
50	Hawaii*	0	0.0%
	District of Columbia*	0	0.0%

Source: U.S. Department of Justice, Bureau of Justice Statistics
"Census of State and Local Law Enforcement Agencies, 2004" (June 2007, NCJ 212749, www.ojp.usdoj.gov/bjs/sandlle.htm)
*All states except Hawaii and the District of Columbia have a state police department.

Rate of Full-Time Sworn Officers in State Police Departments in 2004

National Rate = 20 Officers per 100,000 Population*

ALPHA ORDER

RANK	STATE	RATE
41	Alabama	15
2	Alaska	58
24	Arizona	20
31	Arkansas	18
24	California	20
41	Colorado	15
8	Connecticut	33
1	Delaware	77
47	Florida	10
47	Georgia	10
50	Hawaii*	0
22	Idaho	21
39	Illinois	16
28	Indiana	19
44	Iowa	13
24	Kansas	20
17	Kentucky	23
15	Louisiana	24
13	Maine	26
11	Maryland	29
6	Massachusetts	34
31	Michigan	18
46	Minnesota	11
31	Mississippi	18
28	Missouri	19
20	Montana	22
11	Nebraska	29
31	Nevada	18
20	New Hampshire	22
9	New Jersey	32
10	New Mexico	30
15	New York	24
31	North Carolina	18
22	North Dakota	21
44	Ohio	13
17	Oklahoma	23
37	Oregon	17
6	Pennsylvania	34
31	Rhode Island	18
28	South Carolina	19
24	South Dakota	20
39	Tennessee	16
41	Texas	15
17	Utah	23
3	Vermont	52
14	Virginia	25
37	Washington	17
5	West Virginia	35
49	Wisconsin	9
4	Wyoming	37

RANK ORDER

RANK	STATE	RATE
1	Delaware	77
2	Alaska	58
3	Vermont	52
4	Wyoming	37
5	West Virginia	35
6	Massachusetts	34
6	Pennsylvania	34
8	Connecticut	33
9	New Jersey	32
10	New Mexico	30
11	Maryland	29
11	Nebraska	29
13	Maine	26
14	Virginia	25
15	Louisiana	24
15	New York	24
17	Kentucky	23
17	Oklahoma	23
17	Utah	23
20	Montana	22
20	New Hampshire	22
22	Idaho	21
22	North Dakota	21
24	Arizona	20
24	California	20
24	Kansas	20
24	South Dakota	20
28	Indiana	19
28	Missouri	19
28	South Carolina	19
31	Arkansas	18
31	Michigan	18
31	Mississippi	18
31	Nevada	18
31	North Carolina	18
31	Rhode Island	18
37	Oregon	17
37	Washington	17
39	Illinois	16
39	Tennessee	16
41	Alabama	15
41	Colorado	15
41	Texas	15
44	Iowa	13
44	Ohio	13
46	Minnesota	11
47	Florida	10
47	Georgia	10
49	Wisconsin	9
50	Hawaii*	0
	District of Columbia*	0

Source: U.S. Department of Justice, Bureau of Justice Statistics
"Census of State and Local Law Enforcement Agencies, 2004" (June 2007, NCJ 212749, www.ojp.usdoj.gov/bjs/sandlle.htm)
*All states except Hawaii and the District of Columbia have a state police department.

Percent of Full-Time State Police Department Employees
Who Are Sworn Officers: 2004
National Percent = 65.2% of Employees*

<table>
<tr><td colspan="3">ALPHA ORDER</td><td colspan="3">RANK ORDER</td></tr>
<tr><td>RANK</td><td>STATE</td><td>PERCENT</td><td>RANK</td><td>STATE</td><td>PERCENT</td></tr>
<tr><td>43</td><td>Alabama</td><td>53.7</td><td>1</td><td>North Carolina</td><td>87.7</td></tr>
<tr><td>34</td><td>Alaska</td><td>59.0</td><td>2</td><td>New York</td><td>83.8</td></tr>
<tr><td>39</td><td>Arizona</td><td>56.1</td><td>3</td><td>Massachusetts</td><td>83.4</td></tr>
<tr><td>35</td><td>Arkansas</td><td>58.9</td><td>4</td><td>Rhode Island</td><td>81.5</td></tr>
<tr><td>15</td><td>California</td><td>71.5</td><td>5</td><td>South Carolina</td><td>81.3</td></tr>
<tr><td>13</td><td>Colorado</td><td>72.8</td><td>6</td><td>New Mexico</td><td>80.4</td></tr>
<tr><td>20</td><td>Connecticut</td><td>69.7</td><td>7</td><td>Iowa</td><td>80.2</td></tr>
<tr><td>10</td><td>Delaware</td><td>75.8</td><td>8</td><td>Florida</td><td>76.6</td></tr>
<tr><td>8</td><td>Florida</td><td>76.6</td><td>9</td><td>Nevada</td><td>76.3</td></tr>
<tr><td>23</td><td>Georgia</td><td>67.5</td><td>10</td><td>Delaware</td><td>75.8</td></tr>
<tr><td>NA</td><td>Hawaii**</td><td>NA</td><td>11</td><td>Montana</td><td>75.2</td></tr>
<tr><td>33</td><td>Idaho</td><td>59.3</td><td>12</td><td>Virginia</td><td>74.0</td></tr>
<tr><td>38</td><td>Illinois</td><td>56.5</td><td>13</td><td>Colorado</td><td>72.8</td></tr>
<tr><td>28</td><td>Indiana</td><td>64.4</td><td>14</td><td>Pennsylvania</td><td>71.6</td></tr>
<tr><td>7</td><td>Iowa</td><td>80.2</td><td>15</td><td>California</td><td>71.5</td></tr>
<tr><td>28</td><td>Kansas</td><td>64.4</td><td>15</td><td>Wisconsin</td><td>71.5</td></tr>
<tr><td>42</td><td>Kentucky</td><td>54.6</td><td>17</td><td>Nebraska</td><td>70.3</td></tr>
<tr><td>21</td><td>Louisiana</td><td>68.7</td><td>17</td><td>New Hampshire</td><td>70.3</td></tr>
<tr><td>30</td><td>Maine</td><td>64.0</td><td>17</td><td>North Dakota</td><td>70.3</td></tr>
<tr><td>26</td><td>Maryland</td><td>65.7</td><td>20</td><td>Connecticut</td><td>69.7</td></tr>
<tr><td>3</td><td>Massachusetts</td><td>83.4</td><td>21</td><td>Louisiana</td><td>68.7</td></tr>
<tr><td>22</td><td>Michigan</td><td>68.4</td><td>22</td><td>Michigan</td><td>68.4</td></tr>
<tr><td>25</td><td>Minnesota</td><td>66.3</td><td>23</td><td>Georgia</td><td>67.5</td></tr>
<tr><td>46</td><td>Mississippi</td><td>51.9</td><td>24</td><td>South Dakota</td><td>67.2</td></tr>
<tr><td>47</td><td>Missouri</td><td>48.8</td><td>25</td><td>Minnesota</td><td>66.3</td></tr>
<tr><td>11</td><td>Montana</td><td>75.2</td><td>26</td><td>Maryland</td><td>65.7</td></tr>
<tr><td>17</td><td>Nebraska</td><td>70.3</td><td>27</td><td>West Virginia</td><td>64.5</td></tr>
<tr><td>9</td><td>Nevada</td><td>76.3</td><td>28</td><td>Indiana</td><td>64.4</td></tr>
<tr><td>17</td><td>New Hampshire</td><td>70.3</td><td>28</td><td>Kansas</td><td>64.4</td></tr>
<tr><td>31</td><td>New Jersey</td><td>63.8</td><td>30</td><td>Maine</td><td>64.0</td></tr>
<tr><td>6</td><td>New Mexico</td><td>80.4</td><td>31</td><td>New Jersey</td><td>63.8</td></tr>
<tr><td>2</td><td>New York</td><td>83.8</td><td>32</td><td>Vermont</td><td>59.6</td></tr>
<tr><td>1</td><td>North Carolina</td><td>87.7</td><td>33</td><td>Idaho</td><td>59.3</td></tr>
<tr><td>17</td><td>North Dakota</td><td>70.3</td><td>34</td><td>Alaska</td><td>59.0</td></tr>
<tr><td>36</td><td>Ohio</td><td>57.5</td><td>35</td><td>Arkansas</td><td>58.9</td></tr>
<tr><td>37</td><td>Oklahoma</td><td>56.6</td><td>36</td><td>Ohio</td><td>57.5</td></tr>
<tr><td>41</td><td>Oregon</td><td>54.7</td><td>37</td><td>Oklahoma</td><td>56.6</td></tr>
<tr><td>14</td><td>Pennsylvania</td><td>71.6</td><td>38</td><td>Illinois</td><td>56.5</td></tr>
<tr><td>4</td><td>Rhode Island</td><td>81.5</td><td>39</td><td>Arizona</td><td>56.1</td></tr>
<tr><td>5</td><td>South Carolina</td><td>81.3</td><td>40</td><td>Wyoming</td><td>55.5</td></tr>
<tr><td>24</td><td>South Dakota</td><td>67.2</td><td>41</td><td>Oregon</td><td>54.7</td></tr>
<tr><td>45</td><td>Tennessee</td><td>52.0</td><td>42</td><td>Kentucky</td><td>54.6</td></tr>
<tr><td>49</td><td>Texas</td><td>45.2</td><td>43</td><td>Alabama</td><td>53.7</td></tr>
<tr><td>44</td><td>Utah</td><td>52.8</td><td>44</td><td>Utah</td><td>52.8</td></tr>
<tr><td>32</td><td>Vermont</td><td>59.6</td><td>45</td><td>Tennessee</td><td>52.0</td></tr>
<tr><td>12</td><td>Virginia</td><td>74.0</td><td>46</td><td>Mississippi</td><td>51.9</td></tr>
<tr><td>48</td><td>Washington</td><td>46.1</td><td>47</td><td>Missouri</td><td>48.8</td></tr>
<tr><td>27</td><td>West Virginia</td><td>64.5</td><td>48</td><td>Washington</td><td>46.1</td></tr>
<tr><td>15</td><td>Wisconsin</td><td>71.5</td><td>49</td><td>Texas</td><td>45.2</td></tr>
<tr><td>40</td><td>Wyoming</td><td>55.5</td><td>NA</td><td>Hawaii**</td><td>NA</td></tr>
<tr><td></td><td></td><td></td><td></td><td>District of Columbia**</td><td>NA</td></tr>
</table>

Source: CQ Press using data from U.S. Department of Justice, Bureau of Justice Statistics
"Census of State and Local Law Enforcement Agencies, 2004" (June 2007, NCJ 212749, www.ojp.usdoj.gov/bjs/sandlle.htm)
*All states except Hawaii and the District of Columbia have a state police department.
**Not applicable.

Local Police Departments in 2004

National Total = 12,766 Departments*

ALPHA ORDER

RANK	STATE	DEPARTMENTS	% of USA
17	Alabama	317	2.5%
44	Alaska	56	0.4%
36	Arizona	96	0.8%
21	Arkansas	255	2.0%
15	California	338	2.6%
30	Colorado	166	1.3%
35	Connecticut	106	0.8%
49	Delaware	36	0.3%
19	Florida	280	2.2%
12	Georgia	356	2.8%
50	Hawaii	4	0.0%
41	Idaho	74	0.6%
3	Illinois	726	5.7%
10	Indiana	376	2.9%
18	Iowa	299	2.3%
24	Kansas	238	1.9%
23	Kentucky	252	2.0%
20	Louisiana	260	2.0%
34	Maine	113	0.9%
40	Maryland	81	0.6%
16	Massachusetts	324	2.5%
6	Michigan	455	3.6%
13	Minnesota	355	2.8%
25	Mississippi	225	1.8%
7	Missouri	440	3.4%
42	Montana	59	0.5%
32	Nebraska	144	1.1%
48	Nevada	37	0.3%
27	New Hampshire	196	1.5%
5	New Jersey	481	3.8%
39	New Mexico	90	0.7%
9	New York	422	3.3%
11	North Carolina	358	2.8%
42	North Dakota	59	0.5%
4	Ohio	688	5.4%
14	Oklahoma	353	2.8%
33	Oregon	135	1.1%
1	Pennsylvania	994	7.8%
47	Rhode Island	39	0.3%
28	South Carolina	192	1.5%
37	South Dakota	93	0.7%
22	Tennessee	254	2.0%
2	Texas	784	6.1%
38	Utah	91	0.7%
46	Vermont	49	0.4%
29	Virginia	172	1.3%
26	Washington	204	1.6%
31	West Virginia	158	1.2%
8	Wisconsin	430	3.4%
45	Wyoming	55	0.4%

RANK ORDER

RANK	STATE	DEPARTMENTS	% of USA
1	Pennsylvania	994	7.8%
2	Texas	784	6.1%
3	Illinois	726	5.7%
4	Ohio	688	5.4%
5	New Jersey	481	3.8%
6	Michigan	455	3.6%
7	Missouri	440	3.4%
8	Wisconsin	430	3.4%
9	New York	422	3.3%
10	Indiana	376	2.9%
11	North Carolina	358	2.8%
12	Georgia	356	2.8%
13	Minnesota	355	2.8%
14	Oklahoma	353	2.8%
15	California	338	2.6%
16	Massachusetts	324	2.5%
17	Alabama	317	2.5%
18	Iowa	299	2.3%
19	Florida	280	2.2%
20	Louisiana	260	2.0%
21	Arkansas	255	2.0%
22	Tennessee	254	2.0%
23	Kentucky	252	2.0%
24	Kansas	238	1.9%
25	Mississippi	225	1.8%
26	Washington	204	1.6%
27	New Hampshire	196	1.5%
28	South Carolina	192	1.5%
29	Virginia	172	1.3%
30	Colorado	166	1.3%
31	West Virginia	158	1.2%
32	Nebraska	144	1.1%
33	Oregon	135	1.1%
34	Maine	113	0.9%
35	Connecticut	106	0.8%
36	Arizona	96	0.8%
37	South Dakota	93	0.7%
38	Utah	91	0.7%
39	New Mexico	90	0.7%
40	Maryland	81	0.6%
41	Idaho	74	0.6%
42	Montana	59	0.5%
42	North Dakota	59	0.5%
44	Alaska	56	0.4%
45	Wyoming	55	0.4%
46	Vermont	49	0.4%
47	Rhode Island	39	0.3%
48	Nevada	37	0.3%
49	Delaware	36	0.3%
50	Hawaii	4	0.0%
	District of Columbia	1	0.0%

Source: U.S. Department of Justice, Bureau of Justice Statistics
"Census of State and Local Law Enforcement Agencies, 2004" (June 2007, NCJ 212749, www.ojp.usdoj.gov/bjs/sandlle.htm)
*Includes consolidated police-sheriffs' departments.

Full-Time Officers in Local Police Departments in 2004

National Total = 446,974 Officers*

<table>
<tr><td colspan="4">ALPHA ORDER</td><td colspan="4">RANK ORDER</td></tr>
<tr><th>RANK</th><th>STATE</th><th>OFFICERS</th><th>% of USA</th><th>RANK</th><th>STATE</th><th>OFFICERS</th><th>% of USA</th></tr>
<tr><td>20</td><td>Alabama</td><td>7,140</td><td>1.6%</td><td>1</td><td>New York</td><td>54,039</td><td>12.1%</td></tr>
<tr><td>46</td><td>Alaska</td><td>818</td><td>0.2%</td><td>2</td><td>California</td><td>38,264</td><td>8.6%</td></tr>
<tr><td>16</td><td>Arizona</td><td>8,962</td><td>2.0%</td><td>3</td><td>Texas</td><td>32,408</td><td>7.3%</td></tr>
<tr><td>32</td><td>Arkansas</td><td>3,674</td><td>0.8%</td><td>4</td><td>Illinois</td><td>27,548</td><td>6.2%</td></tr>
<tr><td>2</td><td>California</td><td>38,264</td><td>8.6%</td><td>5</td><td>Florida</td><td>21,832</td><td>4.9%</td></tr>
<tr><td>23</td><td>Colorado</td><td>6,375</td><td>1.4%</td><td>6</td><td>New Jersey</td><td>21,543</td><td>4.8%</td></tr>
<tr><td>21</td><td>Connecticut</td><td>6,614</td><td>1.5%</td><td>7</td><td>Pennsylvania</td><td>18,951</td><td>4.2%</td></tr>
<tr><td>44</td><td>Delaware</td><td>1,083</td><td>0.2%</td><td>8</td><td>Ohio</td><td>16,667</td><td>3.7%</td></tr>
<tr><td>5</td><td>Florida</td><td>21,832</td><td>4.9%</td><td>9</td><td>Massachusetts</td><td>13,330</td><td>3.0%</td></tr>
<tr><td>11</td><td>Georgia</td><td>12,138</td><td>2.7%</td><td>10</td><td>Michigan</td><td>13,126</td><td>2.9%</td></tr>
<tr><td>36</td><td>Hawaii</td><td>2,618</td><td>0.6%</td><td>11</td><td>Georgia</td><td>12,138</td><td>2.7%</td></tr>
<tr><td>43</td><td>Idaho</td><td>1,387</td><td>0.3%</td><td>12</td><td>North Carolina</td><td>11,056</td><td>2.5%</td></tr>
<tr><td>4</td><td>Illinois</td><td>27,548</td><td>6.2%</td><td>13</td><td>Virginia</td><td>10,302</td><td>2.3%</td></tr>
<tr><td>19</td><td>Indiana</td><td>7,424</td><td>1.7%</td><td>14</td><td>Maryland</td><td>9,902</td><td>2.2%</td></tr>
<tr><td>34</td><td>Iowa</td><td>3,191</td><td>0.7%</td><td>15</td><td>Missouri</td><td>9,588</td><td>2.1%</td></tr>
<tr><td>29</td><td>Kansas</td><td>4,089</td><td>0.9%</td><td>16</td><td>Arizona</td><td>8,962</td><td>2.0%</td></tr>
<tr><td>28</td><td>Kentucky</td><td>4,691</td><td>1.0%</td><td>17</td><td>Tennessee</td><td>8,680</td><td>1.9%</td></tr>
<tr><td>22</td><td>Louisiana</td><td>6,434</td><td>1.4%</td><td>18</td><td>Wisconsin</td><td>7,782</td><td>1.7%</td></tr>
<tr><td>41</td><td>Maine</td><td>1,574</td><td>0.4%</td><td>19</td><td>Indiana</td><td>7,424</td><td>1.7%</td></tr>
<tr><td>14</td><td>Maryland</td><td>9,902</td><td>2.2%</td><td>20</td><td>Alabama</td><td>7,140</td><td>1.6%</td></tr>
<tr><td>9</td><td>Massachusetts</td><td>13,330</td><td>3.0%</td><td>21</td><td>Connecticut</td><td>6,614</td><td>1.5%</td></tr>
<tr><td>10</td><td>Michigan</td><td>13,126</td><td>2.9%</td><td>22</td><td>Louisiana</td><td>6,434</td><td>1.4%</td></tr>
<tr><td>25</td><td>Minnesota</td><td>5,489</td><td>1.2%</td><td>23</td><td>Colorado</td><td>6,375</td><td>1.4%</td></tr>
<tr><td>31</td><td>Mississippi</td><td>3,829</td><td>0.9%</td><td>24</td><td>Washington</td><td>6,174</td><td>1.4%</td></tr>
<tr><td>15</td><td>Missouri</td><td>9,588</td><td>2.1%</td><td>25</td><td>Minnesota</td><td>5,489</td><td>1.2%</td></tr>
<tr><td>47</td><td>Montana</td><td>811</td><td>0.2%</td><td>26</td><td>Oklahoma</td><td>5,253</td><td>1.2%</td></tr>
<tr><td>40</td><td>Nebraska</td><td>2,160</td><td>0.5%</td><td>27</td><td>South Carolina</td><td>4,752</td><td>1.1%</td></tr>
<tr><td>30</td><td>Nevada</td><td>3,908</td><td>0.9%</td><td>28</td><td>Kentucky</td><td>4,691</td><td>1.0%</td></tr>
<tr><td>38</td><td>New Hampshire</td><td>2,240</td><td>0.5%</td><td>29</td><td>Kansas</td><td>4,089</td><td>0.9%</td></tr>
<tr><td>6</td><td>New Jersey</td><td>21,543</td><td>4.8%</td><td>30</td><td>Nevada</td><td>3,908</td><td>0.9%</td></tr>
<tr><td>35</td><td>New Mexico</td><td>2,752</td><td>0.6%</td><td>31</td><td>Mississippi</td><td>3,829</td><td>0.9%</td></tr>
<tr><td>1</td><td>New York</td><td>54,039</td><td>12.1%</td><td>32</td><td>Arkansas</td><td>3,674</td><td>0.8%</td></tr>
<tr><td>12</td><td>North Carolina</td><td>11,056</td><td>2.5%</td><td>33</td><td>Oregon</td><td>3,647</td><td>0.8%</td></tr>
<tr><td>49</td><td>North Dakota</td><td>624</td><td>0.1%</td><td>34</td><td>Iowa</td><td>3,191</td><td>0.7%</td></tr>
<tr><td>8</td><td>Ohio</td><td>16,667</td><td>3.7%</td><td>35</td><td>New Mexico</td><td>2,752</td><td>0.6%</td></tr>
<tr><td>26</td><td>Oklahoma</td><td>5,253</td><td>1.2%</td><td>36</td><td>Hawaii</td><td>2,618</td><td>0.6%</td></tr>
<tr><td>33</td><td>Oregon</td><td>3,647</td><td>0.8%</td><td>37</td><td>Utah</td><td>2,446</td><td>0.5%</td></tr>
<tr><td>7</td><td>Pennsylvania</td><td>18,951</td><td>4.2%</td><td>38</td><td>New Hampshire</td><td>2,240</td><td>0.5%</td></tr>
<tr><td>39</td><td>Rhode Island</td><td>2,221</td><td>0.5%</td><td>39</td><td>Rhode Island</td><td>2,221</td><td>0.5%</td></tr>
<tr><td>27</td><td>South Carolina</td><td>4,752</td><td>1.1%</td><td>40</td><td>Nebraska</td><td>2,160</td><td>0.5%</td></tr>
<tr><td>45</td><td>South Dakota</td><td>915</td><td>0.2%</td><td>41</td><td>Maine</td><td>1,574</td><td>0.4%</td></tr>
<tr><td>17</td><td>Tennessee</td><td>8,680</td><td>1.9%</td><td>42</td><td>West Virginia</td><td>1,399</td><td>0.3%</td></tr>
<tr><td>3</td><td>Texas</td><td>32,408</td><td>7.3%</td><td>43</td><td>Idaho</td><td>1,387</td><td>0.3%</td></tr>
<tr><td>37</td><td>Utah</td><td>2,446</td><td>0.5%</td><td>44</td><td>Delaware</td><td>1,083</td><td>0.2%</td></tr>
<tr><td>50</td><td>Vermont</td><td>616</td><td>0.1%</td><td>45</td><td>South Dakota</td><td>915</td><td>0.2%</td></tr>
<tr><td>13</td><td>Virginia</td><td>10,302</td><td>2.3%</td><td>46</td><td>Alaska</td><td>818</td><td>0.2%</td></tr>
<tr><td>24</td><td>Washington</td><td>6,174</td><td>1.4%</td><td>47</td><td>Montana</td><td>811</td><td>0.2%</td></tr>
<tr><td>42</td><td>West Virginia</td><td>1,399</td><td>0.3%</td><td>48</td><td>Wyoming</td><td>708</td><td>0.2%</td></tr>
<tr><td>18</td><td>Wisconsin</td><td>7,782</td><td>1.7%</td><td>49</td><td>North Dakota</td><td>624</td><td>0.1%</td></tr>
<tr><td>48</td><td>Wyoming</td><td>708</td><td>0.2%</td><td>50</td><td>Vermont</td><td>616</td><td>0.1%</td></tr>
<tr><td></td><td></td><td></td><td></td><td></td><td>District of Columbia</td><td>3,800</td><td>0.9%</td></tr>
</table>

Source: U.S. Department of Justice, Bureau of Justice Statistics
   "Census of State and Local Law Enforcement Agencies, 2004" (June 2007, NCJ 212749, www.ojp.usdoj.gov/bjs/sandlle.htm)
*Includes consolidated police-sheriffs' departments.

Rate of Full-Time Sworn Officers in Local Police Departments in 2004

National Rate = 152 Officers per 100,000 Population*

<table>
<tr><td colspan="3">ALPHA ORDER</td><td colspan="3">RANK ORDER</td></tr>
<tr><td>RANK</td><td>STATE</td><td>RATE</td><td>RANK</td><td>STATE</td><td>RATE</td></tr>
<tr><td>12</td><td>Alabama</td><td>158</td><td>1</td><td>New York</td><td>281</td></tr>
<tr><td>32</td><td>Alaska</td><td>125</td><td>2</td><td>New Jersey</td><td>248</td></tr>
<tr><td>13</td><td>Arizona</td><td>156</td><td>3</td><td>Illinois</td><td>217</td></tr>
<tr><td>27</td><td>Arkansas</td><td>133</td><td>4</td><td>Massachusetts</td><td>208</td></tr>
<tr><td>42</td><td>California</td><td>107</td><td>5</td><td>Hawaii</td><td>207</td></tr>
<tr><td>24</td><td>Colorado</td><td>139</td><td>6</td><td>Rhode Island</td><td>206</td></tr>
<tr><td>7</td><td>Connecticut</td><td>189</td><td>7</td><td>Connecticut</td><td>189</td></tr>
<tr><td>29</td><td>Delaware</td><td>130</td><td>8</td><td>Maryland</td><td>178</td></tr>
<tr><td>32</td><td>Florida</td><td>125</td><td>9</td><td>New Hampshire</td><td>172</td></tr>
<tr><td>26</td><td>Georgia</td><td>137</td><td>10</td><td>Missouri</td><td>167</td></tr>
<tr><td>5</td><td>Hawaii</td><td>207</td><td>10</td><td>Nevada</td><td>167</td></tr>
<tr><td>45</td><td>Idaho</td><td>100</td><td>12</td><td>Alabama</td><td>158</td></tr>
<tr><td>3</td><td>Illinois</td><td>217</td><td>13</td><td>Arizona</td><td>156</td></tr>
<tr><td>35</td><td>Indiana</td><td>119</td><td>14</td><td>Pennsylvania</td><td>153</td></tr>
<tr><td>40</td><td>Iowa</td><td>108</td><td>15</td><td>Kansas</td><td>149</td></tr>
<tr><td>15</td><td>Kansas</td><td>149</td><td>15</td><td>Oklahoma</td><td>149</td></tr>
<tr><td>38</td><td>Kentucky</td><td>113</td><td>17</td><td>Tennessee</td><td>147</td></tr>
<tr><td>21</td><td>Louisiana</td><td>142</td><td>18</td><td>New Mexico</td><td>145</td></tr>
<tr><td>35</td><td>Maine</td><td>119</td><td>18</td><td>Ohio</td><td>145</td></tr>
<tr><td>8</td><td>Maryland</td><td>178</td><td>20</td><td>Texas</td><td>144</td></tr>
<tr><td>4</td><td>Massachusetts</td><td>208</td><td>21</td><td>Louisiana</td><td>142</td></tr>
<tr><td>29</td><td>Michigan</td><td>130</td><td>22</td><td>Wisconsin</td><td>141</td></tr>
<tr><td>40</td><td>Minnesota</td><td>108</td><td>23</td><td>Wyoming</td><td>140</td></tr>
<tr><td>28</td><td>Mississippi</td><td>132</td><td>24</td><td>Colorado</td><td>139</td></tr>
<tr><td>10</td><td>Missouri</td><td>167</td><td>25</td><td>Virginia</td><td>138</td></tr>
<tr><td>49</td><td>Montana</td><td>87</td><td>26</td><td>Georgia</td><td>137</td></tr>
<tr><td>34</td><td>Nebraska</td><td>124</td><td>27</td><td>Arkansas</td><td>133</td></tr>
<tr><td>10</td><td>Nevada</td><td>167</td><td>28</td><td>Mississippi</td><td>132</td></tr>
<tr><td>9</td><td>New Hampshire</td><td>172</td><td>29</td><td>Delaware</td><td>130</td></tr>
<tr><td>2</td><td>New Jersey</td><td>248</td><td>29</td><td>Michigan</td><td>130</td></tr>
<tr><td>18</td><td>New Mexico</td><td>145</td><td>31</td><td>North Carolina</td><td>129</td></tr>
<tr><td>1</td><td>New York</td><td>281</td><td>32</td><td>Alaska</td><td>125</td></tr>
<tr><td>31</td><td>North Carolina</td><td>129</td><td>32</td><td>Florida</td><td>125</td></tr>
<tr><td>48</td><td>North Dakota</td><td>98</td><td>34</td><td>Nebraska</td><td>124</td></tr>
<tr><td>18</td><td>Ohio</td><td>145</td><td>35</td><td>Indiana</td><td>119</td></tr>
<tr><td>15</td><td>Oklahoma</td><td>149</td><td>35</td><td>Maine</td><td>119</td></tr>
<tr><td>44</td><td>Oregon</td><td>101</td><td>35</td><td>South Dakota</td><td>119</td></tr>
<tr><td>14</td><td>Pennsylvania</td><td>153</td><td>38</td><td>Kentucky</td><td>113</td></tr>
<tr><td>6</td><td>Rhode Island</td><td>206</td><td>38</td><td>South Carolina</td><td>113</td></tr>
<tr><td>38</td><td>South Carolina</td><td>113</td><td>40</td><td>Iowa</td><td>108</td></tr>
<tr><td>35</td><td>South Dakota</td><td>119</td><td>40</td><td>Minnesota</td><td>108</td></tr>
<tr><td>17</td><td>Tennessee</td><td>147</td><td>42</td><td>California</td><td>107</td></tr>
<tr><td>20</td><td>Texas</td><td>144</td><td>43</td><td>Utah</td><td>102</td></tr>
<tr><td>43</td><td>Utah</td><td>102</td><td>44</td><td>Oregon</td><td>101</td></tr>
<tr><td>47</td><td>Vermont</td><td>99</td><td>45</td><td>Idaho</td><td>100</td></tr>
<tr><td>25</td><td>Virginia</td><td>138</td><td>45</td><td>Washington</td><td>100</td></tr>
<tr><td>45</td><td>Washington</td><td>100</td><td>47</td><td>Vermont</td><td>99</td></tr>
<tr><td>50</td><td>West Virginia</td><td>77</td><td>48</td><td>North Dakota</td><td>98</td></tr>
<tr><td>22</td><td>Wisconsin</td><td>141</td><td>49</td><td>Montana</td><td>87</td></tr>
<tr><td>23</td><td>Wyoming</td><td>140</td><td>50</td><td>West Virginia</td><td>77</td></tr>
<tr><td></td><td></td><td></td><td></td><td>District of Columbia</td><td>687</td></tr>
</table>

Source: U.S. Department of Justice, Bureau of Justice Statistics
   "Census of State and Local Law Enforcement Agencies, 2004" (June 2007, NCJ 212749, www.ojp.usdoj.gov/bjs/sandlle.htm)
*Includes consolidated police-sheriffs' departments.

Percent of Full-Time Local Police Department Employees
Who Are Sworn Officers: 2004
National Percent = 78.0% of Employees*

ALPHA ORDER

RANK	STATE	PERCENT
38	Alabama	75.0
50	Alaska	62.7
44	Arizona	72.0
32	Arkansas	77.2
46	California	71.7
40	Colorado	74.0
4	Connecticut	84.1
45	Delaware	71.8
47	Florida	71.6
11	Georgia	81.9
41	Hawaii	73.6
29	Idaho	77.4
9	Illinois	82.1
18	Indiana	79.8
9	Iowa	82.1
31	Kansas	77.3
16	Kentucky	80.1
16	Louisiana	80.1
33	Maine	76.7
5	Maryland	83.6
3	Massachusetts	85.5
6	Michigan	83.4
14	Minnesota	80.6
26	Mississippi	77.6
34	Missouri	76.5
25	Montana	78.1
21	Nebraska	79.5
49	Nevada	67.3
26	New Hampshire	77.6
8	New Jersey	82.4
48	New Mexico	69.4
39	New York	74.5
13	North Carolina	81.5
7	North Dakota	83.2
12	Ohio	81.7
37	Oklahoma	75.6
35	Oregon	75.9
1	Pennsylvania	87.8
22	Rhode Island	79.2
19	South Carolina	79.7
43	South Dakota	72.1
20	Tennessee	79.6
23	Texas	78.6
29	Utah	77.4
24	Vermont	78.4
26	Virginia	77.6
36	Washington	75.7
2	West Virginia	85.6
14	Wisconsin	80.6
42	Wyoming	72.2

RANK ORDER

RANK	STATE	PERCENT
1	Pennsylvania	87.8
2	West Virginia	85.6
3	Massachusetts	85.5
4	Connecticut	84.1
5	Maryland	83.6
6	Michigan	83.4
7	North Dakota	83.2
8	New Jersey	82.4
9	Illinois	82.1
9	Iowa	82.1
11	Georgia	81.9
12	Ohio	81.7
13	North Carolina	81.5
14	Minnesota	80.6
14	Wisconsin	80.6
16	Kentucky	80.1
16	Louisiana	80.1
18	Indiana	79.8
19	South Carolina	79.7
20	Tennessee	79.6
21	Nebraska	79.5
22	Rhode Island	79.2
23	Texas	78.6
24	Vermont	78.4
25	Montana	78.1
26	Mississippi	77.6
26	New Hampshire	77.6
26	Virginia	77.6
29	Idaho	77.4
29	Utah	77.4
31	Kansas	77.3
32	Arkansas	77.2
33	Maine	76.7
34	Missouri	76.5
35	Oregon	75.9
36	Washington	75.7
37	Oklahoma	75.6
38	Alabama	75.0
39	New York	74.5
40	Colorado	74.0
41	Hawaii	73.6
42	Wyoming	72.2
43	South Dakota	72.1
44	Arizona	72.0
45	Delaware	71.8
46	California	71.7
47	Florida	71.6
48	New Mexico	69.4
49	Nevada	67.3
50	Alaska	62.7

District of Columbia 86.1

Source: CQ Press using data from U.S. Department of Justice, Bureau of Justice Statistics
    "Census of State and Local Law Enforcement Agencies, 2004" (June 2007, NCJ 212749, www.ojp.usdoj.gov/bjs/sandlle.htm)
*Includes consolidated police-sheriffs' departments.

Sheriffs' Departments in 2004

National Total = 3,067 Departments*

ALPHA ORDER

RANK	STATE	DEPARTMENTS	% of USA
20	Alabama	67	2.2%
48	Alaska	0	0.0%
42	Arizona	15	0.5%
18	Arkansas	75	2.4%
26	California	58	1.9%
25	Colorado	62	2.0%
48	Connecticut	0	0.0%
47	Delaware	2	0.1%
23	Florida	65	2.1%
2	Georgia	159	5.2%
48	Hawaii	0	0.0%
32	Idaho	44	1.4%
7	Illinois	102	3.3%
12	Indiana	92	3.0%
9	Iowa	99	3.2%
6	Kansas	104	3.4%
4	Kentucky	119	3.9%
23	Louisiana	65	2.1%
40	Maine	16	0.5%
37	Maryland	24	0.8%
44	Massachusetts	12	0.4%
15	Michigan	83	2.7%
14	Minnesota	87	2.8%
16	Mississippi	82	2.7%
5	Missouri	113	3.7%
28	Montana	55	1.8%
11	Nebraska	93	3.0%
40	Nevada	16	0.5%
45	New Hampshire	10	0.3%
39	New Jersey	21	0.7%
35	New Mexico	33	1.1%
27	New York	57	1.9%
8	North Carolina	100	3.3%
30	North Dakota	53	1.7%
13	Ohio	88	2.9%
17	Oklahoma	77	2.5%
34	Oregon	36	1.2%
21	Pennsylvania	66	2.2%
46	Rhode Island	4	0.1%
31	South Carolina	46	1.5%
21	South Dakota	66	2.2%
10	Tennessee	94	3.1%
1	Texas	253	8.2%
36	Utah	29	0.9%
43	Vermont	14	0.5%
3	Virginia	122	4.0%
33	Washington	39	1.3%
28	West Virginia	55	1.8%
19	Wisconsin	72	2.3%
38	Wyoming	23	0.7%

RANK ORDER

RANK	STATE	DEPARTMENTS	% of USA
1	Texas	253	8.2%
2	Georgia	159	5.2%
3	Virginia	122	4.0%
4	Kentucky	119	3.9%
5	Missouri	113	3.7%
6	Kansas	104	3.4%
7	Illinois	102	3.3%
8	North Carolina	100	3.3%
9	Iowa	99	3.2%
10	Tennessee	94	3.1%
11	Nebraska	93	3.0%
12	Indiana	92	3.0%
13	Ohio	88	2.9%
14	Minnesota	87	2.8%
15	Michigan	83	2.7%
16	Mississippi	82	2.7%
17	Oklahoma	77	2.5%
18	Arkansas	75	2.4%
19	Wisconsin	72	2.3%
20	Alabama	67	2.2%
21	Pennsylvania	66	2.2%
21	South Dakota	66	2.2%
23	Florida	65	2.1%
23	Louisiana	65	2.1%
25	Colorado	62	2.0%
26	California	58	1.9%
27	New York	57	1.9%
28	Montana	55	1.8%
28	West Virginia	55	1.8%
30	North Dakota	53	1.7%
31	South Carolina	46	1.5%
32	Idaho	44	1.4%
33	Washington	39	1.3%
34	Oregon	36	1.2%
35	New Mexico	33	1.1%
36	Utah	29	0.9%
37	Maryland	24	0.8%
38	Wyoming	23	0.7%
39	New Jersey	21	0.7%
40	Maine	16	0.5%
40	Nevada	16	0.5%
42	Arizona	15	0.5%
43	Vermont	14	0.5%
44	Massachusetts	12	0.4%
45	New Hampshire	10	0.3%
46	Rhode Island	4	0.1%
47	Delaware	2	0.1%
48	Alaska	0	0.0%
48	Connecticut	0	0.0%
48	Hawaii	0	0.0%
	District of Columbia	0	0.0%

Source: U.S. Department of Justice, Bureau of Justice Statistics
"Census of State and Local Law Enforcement Agencies, 2004" (June 2007, NCJ 212749, www.ojp.usdoj.gov/bjs/sandlle.htm)
*Sheriffs' departments generally operate at the county level.

Full-Time Officers in Sheriffs' Departments in 2004

National Total = 175,018 Officers*

ALPHA ORDER

RANK	STATE	OFFICERS	% of USA
21	Alabama	2,423	1.4%
48	Alaska	0	0.0%
22	Arizona	2,028	1.2%
31	Arkansas	1,454	0.8%
1	California	25,768	14.7%
16	Colorado	3,391	1.9%
48	Connecticut	0	0.0%
47	Delaware	15	0.0%
2	Florida	18,802	10.7%
6	Georgia	8,860	5.1%
48	Hawaii	0	0.0%
34	Idaho	1,155	0.7%
5	Illinois	8,881	5.1%
18	Indiana	2,735	1.6%
30	Iowa	1,516	0.9%
23	Kansas	1,975	1.1%
29	Kentucky	1,543	0.9%
4	Louisiana	9,643	5.5%
44	Maine	375	0.2%
25	Maryland	1,924	1.1%
26	Massachusetts	1,914	1.1%
10	Michigan	4,911	2.8%
20	Minnesota	2,458	1.4%
27	Mississippi	1,626	0.9%
19	Missouri	2,546	1.5%
39	Montana	679	0.4%
37	Nebraska	993	0.6%
36	Nevada	1,012	0.6%
45	New Hampshire	147	0.1%
15	New Jersey	3,631	2.1%
35	New Mexico	1,090	0.6%
12	New York	4,216	2.4%
8	North Carolina	6,869	3.9%
42	North Dakota	433	0.2%
9	Ohio	5,745	3.3%
33	Oklahoma	1,201	0.7%
24	Oregon	1,945	1.1%
28	Pennsylvania	1,578	0.9%
41	Rhode Island	437	0.2%
14	South Carolina	4,027	2.3%
43	South Dakota	387	0.2%
11	Tennessee	4,665	2.7%
3	Texas	11,836	6.8%
32	Utah	1,325	0.8%
46	Vermont	132	0.1%
7	Virginia	8,169	4.7%
17	Washington	2,939	1.7%
38	West Virginia	914	0.5%
13	Wisconsin	4,108	2.3%
40	Wyoming	597	0.3%

RANK ORDER

RANK	STATE	OFFICERS	% of USA
1	California	25,768	14.7%
2	Florida	18,802	10.7%
3	Texas	11,836	6.8%
4	Louisiana	9,643	5.5%
5	Illinois	8,881	5.1%
6	Georgia	8,860	5.1%
7	Virginia	8,169	4.7%
8	North Carolina	6,869	3.9%
9	Ohio	5,745	3.3%
10	Michigan	4,911	2.8%
11	Tennessee	4,665	2.7%
12	New York	4,216	2.4%
13	Wisconsin	4,108	2.3%
14	South Carolina	4,027	2.3%
15	New Jersey	3,631	2.1%
16	Colorado	3,391	1.9%
17	Washington	2,939	1.7%
18	Indiana	2,735	1.6%
19	Missouri	2,546	1.5%
20	Minnesota	2,458	1.4%
21	Alabama	2,423	1.4%
22	Arizona	2,028	1.2%
23	Kansas	1,975	1.1%
24	Oregon	1,945	1.1%
25	Maryland	1,924	1.1%
26	Massachusetts	1,914	1.1%
27	Mississippi	1,626	0.9%
28	Pennsylvania	1,578	0.9%
29	Kentucky	1,543	0.9%
30	Iowa	1,516	0.9%
31	Arkansas	1,454	0.8%
32	Utah	1,325	0.8%
33	Oklahoma	1,201	0.7%
34	Idaho	1,155	0.7%
35	New Mexico	1,090	0.6%
36	Nevada	1,012	0.6%
37	Nebraska	993	0.6%
38	West Virginia	914	0.5%
39	Montana	679	0.4%
40	Wyoming	597	0.3%
41	Rhode Island	437	0.2%
42	North Dakota	433	0.2%
43	South Dakota	387	0.2%
44	Maine	375	0.2%
45	New Hampshire	147	0.1%
46	Vermont	132	0.1%
47	Delaware	15	0.0%
48	Alaska	0	0.0%
48	Connecticut	0	0.0%
48	Hawaii	0	0.0%
	District of Columbia	0	0.0%

Source: U.S. Department of Justice, Bureau of Justice Statistics
"Census of State and Local Law Enforcement Agencies, 2004" (June 2007, NCJ 212749, www.ojp.usdoj.gov/bjs/sandlle.htm)
*Sheriffs' departments generally operate at the county level.

Rate of Full-Time Sworn Officers in Sheriffs' Departments in 2004

National Rate = 60 Officers per 100,000 Population*

<table>
<tr><td colspan="3">ALPHA ORDER</td><td colspan="3">RANK ORDER</td></tr>
<tr><td>RANK</td><td>STATE</td><td>RATE</td><td>RANK</td><td>STATE</td><td>RATE</td></tr>
<tr><td>22</td><td>Alabama</td><td>53</td><td>1</td><td>Louisiana</td><td>214</td></tr>
<tr><td>48</td><td>Alaska</td><td>0</td><td>2</td><td>Wyoming</td><td>118</td></tr>
<tr><td>38</td><td>Arizona</td><td>35</td><td>3</td><td>Virginia</td><td>110</td></tr>
<tr><td>22</td><td>Arkansas</td><td>53</td><td>4</td><td>Florida</td><td>108</td></tr>
<tr><td>13</td><td>California</td><td>72</td><td>5</td><td>Georgia</td><td>100</td></tr>
<tr><td>11</td><td>Colorado</td><td>74</td><td>6</td><td>South Carolina</td><td>96</td></tr>
<tr><td>48</td><td>Connecticut</td><td>0</td><td>7</td><td>Idaho</td><td>83</td></tr>
<tr><td>47</td><td>Delaware</td><td>2</td><td>8</td><td>North Carolina</td><td>80</td></tr>
<tr><td>4</td><td>Florida</td><td>108</td><td>9</td><td>Tennessee</td><td>79</td></tr>
<tr><td>5</td><td>Georgia</td><td>100</td><td>10</td><td>Wisconsin</td><td>75</td></tr>
<tr><td>48</td><td>Hawaii</td><td>0</td><td>11</td><td>Colorado</td><td>74</td></tr>
<tr><td>7</td><td>Idaho</td><td>83</td><td>12</td><td>Montana</td><td>73</td></tr>
<tr><td>15</td><td>Illinois</td><td>70</td><td>13</td><td>California</td><td>72</td></tr>
<tr><td>32</td><td>Indiana</td><td>44</td><td>13</td><td>Kansas</td><td>72</td></tr>
<tr><td>25</td><td>Iowa</td><td>51</td><td>15</td><td>Illinois</td><td>70</td></tr>
<tr><td>13</td><td>Kansas</td><td>72</td><td>16</td><td>North Dakota</td><td>68</td></tr>
<tr><td>37</td><td>Kentucky</td><td>37</td><td>17</td><td>Nebraska</td><td>57</td></tr>
<tr><td>1</td><td>Louisiana</td><td>214</td><td>17</td><td>New Mexico</td><td>57</td></tr>
<tr><td>42</td><td>Maine</td><td>28</td><td>19</td><td>Mississippi</td><td>56</td></tr>
<tr><td>38</td><td>Maryland</td><td>35</td><td>20</td><td>Utah</td><td>55</td></tr>
<tr><td>41</td><td>Massachusetts</td><td>30</td><td>21</td><td>Oregon</td><td>54</td></tr>
<tr><td>29</td><td>Michigan</td><td>49</td><td>22</td><td>Alabama</td><td>53</td></tr>
<tr><td>30</td><td>Minnesota</td><td>48</td><td>22</td><td>Arkansas</td><td>53</td></tr>
<tr><td>19</td><td>Mississippi</td><td>56</td><td>22</td><td>Texas</td><td>53</td></tr>
<tr><td>32</td><td>Missouri</td><td>44</td><td>25</td><td>Iowa</td><td>51</td></tr>
<tr><td>12</td><td>Montana</td><td>73</td><td>26</td><td>Ohio</td><td>50</td></tr>
<tr><td>17</td><td>Nebraska</td><td>57</td><td>26</td><td>South Dakota</td><td>50</td></tr>
<tr><td>34</td><td>Nevada</td><td>43</td><td>26</td><td>West Virginia</td><td>50</td></tr>
<tr><td>46</td><td>New Hampshire</td><td>11</td><td>29</td><td>Michigan</td><td>49</td></tr>
<tr><td>35</td><td>New Jersey</td><td>42</td><td>30</td><td>Minnesota</td><td>48</td></tr>
<tr><td>17</td><td>New Mexico</td><td>57</td><td>31</td><td>Washington</td><td>47</td></tr>
<tr><td>43</td><td>New York</td><td>22</td><td>32</td><td>Indiana</td><td>44</td></tr>
<tr><td>8</td><td>North Carolina</td><td>80</td><td>32</td><td>Missouri</td><td>44</td></tr>
<tr><td>16</td><td>North Dakota</td><td>68</td><td>34</td><td>Nevada</td><td>43</td></tr>
<tr><td>26</td><td>Ohio</td><td>50</td><td>35</td><td>New Jersey</td><td>42</td></tr>
<tr><td>40</td><td>Oklahoma</td><td>34</td><td>36</td><td>Rhode Island</td><td>40</td></tr>
<tr><td>21</td><td>Oregon</td><td>54</td><td>37</td><td>Kentucky</td><td>37</td></tr>
<tr><td>45</td><td>Pennsylvania</td><td>13</td><td>38</td><td>Arizona</td><td>35</td></tr>
<tr><td>36</td><td>Rhode Island</td><td>40</td><td>38</td><td>Maryland</td><td>35</td></tr>
<tr><td>6</td><td>South Carolina</td><td>96</td><td>40</td><td>Oklahoma</td><td>34</td></tr>
<tr><td>26</td><td>South Dakota</td><td>50</td><td>41</td><td>Massachusetts</td><td>30</td></tr>
<tr><td>9</td><td>Tennessee</td><td>79</td><td>42</td><td>Maine</td><td>28</td></tr>
<tr><td>22</td><td>Texas</td><td>53</td><td>43</td><td>New York</td><td>22</td></tr>
<tr><td>20</td><td>Utah</td><td>55</td><td>44</td><td>Vermont</td><td>21</td></tr>
<tr><td>44</td><td>Vermont</td><td>21</td><td>45</td><td>Pennsylvania</td><td>13</td></tr>
<tr><td>3</td><td>Virginia</td><td>110</td><td>46</td><td>New Hampshire</td><td>11</td></tr>
<tr><td>31</td><td>Washington</td><td>47</td><td>47</td><td>Delaware</td><td>2</td></tr>
<tr><td>26</td><td>West Virginia</td><td>50</td><td>48</td><td>Alaska</td><td>0</td></tr>
<tr><td>10</td><td>Wisconsin</td><td>75</td><td>48</td><td>Connecticut</td><td>0</td></tr>
<tr><td>2</td><td>Wyoming</td><td>118</td><td>48</td><td>Hawaii</td><td>0</td></tr>
<tr><td></td><td></td><td></td><td></td><td>District of Columbia</td><td>0</td></tr>
</table>

Source: U.S. Department of Justice, Bureau of Justice Statistics
"Census of State and Local Law Enforcement Agencies, 2004" (June 2007, NCJ 212749, www.ojp.usdoj.gov/bjs/sandlle.htm)
*Sheriffs' departments generally operate at the county level.

Percent of Full-Time Sheriffs' Department Employees
Who Are Sworn Officers: 2004
National Percent = 53.6% of Employees*

ALPHA ORDER

RANK	STATE	PERCENT
29	Alabama	49.6
NA	Alaska**	NA
47	Arizona	33.2
37	Arkansas	44.7
19	California	56.4
19	Colorado	56.4
NA	Connecticut**	NA
28	Delaware	50.0
32	Florida	48.3
17	Georgia	57.7
NA	Hawaii**	NA
33	Idaho	46.2
9	Illinois	66.7
44	Indiana	38.4
31	Iowa	48.4
26	Kansas	52.6
5	Kentucky	79.2
8	Louisiana	67.6
45	Maine	34.1
24	Maryland	54.2
42	Massachusetts	40.7
22	Michigan	56.3
39	Minnesota	44.5
41	Mississippi	41.8
15	Missouri	60.5
38	Montana	44.6
19	Nebraska	56.4
11	Nevada	65.6
13	New Hampshire	62.8
7	New Jersey	69.4
2	New Mexico	84.1
46	New York	33.3
18	North Carolina	56.8
10	North Dakota	66.1
25	Ohio	53.4
39	Oklahoma	44.5
33	Oregon	46.2
4	Pennsylvania	80.3
1	Rhode Island	97.5
14	South Carolina	62.7
35	South Dakota	46.0
30	Tennessee	48.9
36	Texas	44.9
43	Utah	39.5
6	Vermont	70.6
3	Virginia	83.3
16	Washington	59.5
12	West Virginia	63.6
23	Wisconsin	55.4
27	Wyoming	50.4

RANK ORDER

RANK	STATE	PERCENT
1	Rhode Island	97.5
2	New Mexico	84.1
3	Virginia	83.3
4	Pennsylvania	80.3
5	Kentucky	79.2
6	Vermont	70.6
7	New Jersey	69.4
8	Louisiana	67.6
9	Illinois	66.7
10	North Dakota	66.1
11	Nevada	65.6
12	West Virginia	63.6
13	New Hampshire	62.8
14	South Carolina	62.7
15	Missouri	60.5
16	Washington	59.5
17	Georgia	57.7
18	North Carolina	56.8
19	California	56.4
19	Colorado	56.4
19	Nebraska	56.4
22	Michigan	56.3
23	Wisconsin	55.4
24	Maryland	54.2
25	Ohio	53.4
26	Kansas	52.6
27	Wyoming	50.4
28	Delaware	50.0
29	Alabama	49.6
30	Tennessee	48.9
31	Iowa	48.4
32	Florida	48.3
33	Idaho	46.2
33	Oregon	46.2
35	South Dakota	46.0
36	Texas	44.9
37	Arkansas	44.7
38	Montana	44.6
39	Minnesota	44.5
39	Oklahoma	44.5
41	Mississippi	41.8
42	Massachusetts	40.7
43	Utah	39.5
44	Indiana	38.4
45	Maine	34.1
46	New York	33.3
47	Arizona	33.2
NA	Alaska**	NA
NA	Connecticut**	NA
NA	Hawaii**	NA
	District of Columbia**	NA

Source: CQ Press using data from U.S. Department of Justice, Bureau of Justice Statistics
  "Census of State and Local Law Enforcement Agencies, 2004" (June 2007, NCJ 212749, www.ojp.usdoj.gov/bjs/sandlle.htm)
*Sheriffs' departments generally operate at the county level.
**Not applicable.

Law Enforcement Officers Feloniously Killed in 2008

National Total = 41 Officers

RANK	STATE	OFFICERS	% of USA
20	Alabama	0	0.0%
20	Alaska	0	0.0%
8	Arizona	2	4.9%
20	Arkansas	0	0.0%
1	California	3	7.3%
20	Colorado	0	0.0%
20	Connecticut	0	0.0%
20	Delaware	0	0.0%
1	Florida	3	7.3%
8	Georgia	2	4.9%
20	Hawaii	0	0.0%
20	Idaho	0	0.0%
1	Illinois	3	7.3%
20	Indiana	0	0.0%
20	Iowa	0	0.0%
20	Kansas	0	0.0%
16	Kentucky	1	2.4%
8	Louisiana	2	4.9%
20	Maine	0	0.0%
16	Maryland	1	2.4%
20	Massachusetts	0	0.0%
16	Michigan	1	2.4%
20	Minnesota	0	0.0%
20	Mississippi	0	0.0%
1	Missouri	3	7.3%
20	Montana	0	0.0%
20	Nebraska	0	0.0%
20	Nevada	0	0.0%
20	New Hampshire	0	0.0%
20	New Jersey	0	0.0%
20	New Mexico	0	0.0%
20	New York	0	0.0%
8	North Carolina	2	4.9%
20	North Dakota	0	0.0%
8	Ohio	2	4.9%
20	Oklahoma	0	0.0%
8	Oregon	2	4.9%
1	Pennsylvania	3	7.3%
20	Rhode Island	0	0.0%
8	South Carolina	2	4.9%
20	South Dakota	0	0.0%
16	Tennessee	1	2.4%
1	Texas	3	7.3%
20	Utah	0	0.0%
20	Vermont	0	0.0%
1	Virginia	3	7.3%
8	Washington	2	4.9%
20	West Virginia	0	0.0%
20	Wisconsin	0	0.0%
20	Wyoming	0	0.0%

RANK	STATE	OFFICERS	% of USA
1	California	3	7.3%
1	Florida	3	7.3%
1	Illinois	3	7.3%
1	Missouri	3	7.3%
1	Pennsylvania	3	7.3%
1	Texas	3	7.3%
1	Virginia	3	7.3%
8	Arizona	2	4.9%
8	Georgia	2	4.9%
8	Louisiana	2	4.9%
8	North Carolina	2	4.9%
8	Ohio	2	4.9%
8	Oregon	2	4.9%
8	South Carolina	2	4.9%
8	Washington	2	4.9%
16	Kentucky	1	2.4%
16	Maryland	1	2.4%
16	Michigan	1	2.4%
16	Tennessee	1	2.4%
20	Alabama	0	0.0%
20	Alaska	0	0.0%
20	Arkansas	0	0.0%
20	Colorado	0	0.0%
20	Connecticut	0	0.0%
20	Delaware	0	0.0%
20	Hawaii	0	0.0%
20	Idaho	0	0.0%
20	Indiana	0	0.0%
20	Iowa	0	0.0%
20	Kansas	0	0.0%
20	Maine	0	0.0%
20	Massachusetts	0	0.0%
20	Minnesota	0	0.0%
20	Mississippi	0	0.0%
20	Montana	0	0.0%
20	Nebraska	0	0.0%
20	Nevada	0	0.0%
20	New Hampshire	0	0.0%
20	New Jersey	0	0.0%
20	New Mexico	0	0.0%
20	New York	0	0.0%
20	North Dakota	0	0.0%
20	Oklahoma	0	0.0%
20	Rhode Island	0	0.0%
20	South Dakota	0	0.0%
20	Utah	0	0.0%
20	Vermont	0	0.0%
20	West Virginia	0	0.0%
20	Wisconsin	0	0.0%
20	Wyoming	0	0.0%
	District of Columbia	0	0.0%

Source: Reported data from the Federal Bureau of Investigation
  "Law Enforcement Officers Killed and Assaulted 2008" (http://www.fbi.gov/ucr/killed/2008/table_01.html)

Law Enforcement Officers Feloniously Killed: 1999 to 2008

National Total = 509 Officers*

ALPHA ORDER

RANK	STATE	OFFICERS	% of USA
16	Alabama	14	2.8%
28	Alaska	4	0.8%
11	Arizona	16	3.1%
28	Arkansas	4	0.8%
2	California	46	9.0%
28	Colorado	4	0.8%
37	Connecticut	2	0.4%
44	Delaware	0	0.0%
5	Florida	22	4.3%
3	Georgia	25	4.9%
33	Hawaii	3	0.6%
33	Idaho	3	0.6%
9	Illinois	18	3.5%
16	Indiana	14	2.8%
44	Iowa	0	0.0%
26	Kansas	6	1.2%
22	Kentucky	9	1.8%
3	Louisiana	25	4.9%
44	Maine	0	0.0%
16	Maryland	14	2.8%
33	Massachusetts	3	0.6%
9	Michigan	18	3.5%
28	Minnesota	4	0.8%
20	Mississippi	12	2.4%
16	Missouri	14	2.8%
41	Montana	1	0.2%
41	Nebraska	1	0.2%
37	Nevada	2	0.4%
37	New Hampshire	2	0.4%
23	New Jersey	7	1.4%
23	New Mexico	7	1.4%
14	New York	15	2.9%
6	North Carolina	20	3.9%
44	North Dakota	0	0.0%
14	Ohio	15	2.9%
26	Oklahoma	6	1.2%
33	Oregon	3	0.6%
11	Pennsylvania	16	3.1%
41	Rhode Island	1	0.2%
8	South Carolina	19	3.7%
44	South Dakota	0	0.0%
11	Tennessee	16	3.1%
1	Texas	52	10.2%
28	Utah	4	0.8%
44	Vermont	0	0.0%
6	Virginia	20	3.9%
21	Washington	10	2.0%
37	West Virginia	2	0.4%
23	Wisconsin	7	1.4%
44	Wyoming	0	0.0%

RANK ORDER

RANK	STATE	OFFICERS	% of USA
1	Texas	52	10.2%
2	California	46	9.0%
3	Georgia	25	4.9%
3	Louisiana	25	4.9%
5	Florida	22	4.3%
6	North Carolina	20	3.9%
6	Virginia	20	3.9%
8	South Carolina	19	3.7%
9	Illinois	18	3.5%
9	Michigan	18	3.5%
11	Arizona	16	3.1%
11	Pennsylvania	16	3.1%
11	Tennessee	16	3.1%
14	New York	15	2.9%
14	Ohio	15	2.9%
16	Alabama	14	2.8%
16	Indiana	14	2.8%
16	Maryland	14	2.8%
16	Missouri	14	2.8%
20	Mississippi	12	2.4%
21	Washington	10	2.0%
22	Kentucky	9	1.8%
23	New Jersey	7	1.4%
23	New Mexico	7	1.4%
23	Wisconsin	7	1.4%
26	Kansas	6	1.2%
26	Oklahoma	6	1.2%
28	Alaska	4	0.8%
28	Arkansas	4	0.8%
28	Colorado	4	0.8%
28	Minnesota	4	0.8%
28	Utah	4	0.8%
33	Hawaii	3	0.6%
33	Idaho	3	0.6%
33	Massachusetts	3	0.6%
33	Oregon	3	0.6%
37	Connecticut	2	0.4%
37	Nevada	2	0.4%
37	New Hampshire	2	0.4%
37	West Virginia	2	0.4%
41	Montana	1	0.2%
41	Nebraska	1	0.2%
41	Rhode Island	1	0.2%
44	Delaware	0	0.0%
44	Iowa	0	0.0%
44	Maine	0	0.0%
44	North Dakota	0	0.0%
44	South Dakota	0	0.0%
44	Vermont	0	0.0%
44	Wyoming	0	0.0%
	District of Columbia	3	0.6%

Source: Reported data from the Federal Bureau of Investigation
   "Law Enforcement Officers Killed and Assaulted 2008" (http://www.fbi.gov/ucr/killed/2008/table_01.html)
*Total does not include 21 officers killed in U.S. territories (20 officers killed in Puerto Rico and 1 in the U.S. Virgin Islands).
Total also does not include the 72 deaths that resulted from the events of September 11, 2001.

Law Enforcement Officers Accidentally Killed in 2008

National Total = 68 Officers*

ALPHA ORDER

RANK	STATE	OFFICERS	% of USA
9	Alabama	2	3.1%
26	Alaska	0	0.0%
9	Arizona	2	3.1%
9	Arkansas	2	3.1%
1	California	11	16.9%
26	Colorado	0	0.0%
16	Connecticut	1	1.5%
26	Delaware	0	0.0%
4	Florida	4	6.2%
5	Georgia	3	4.6%
26	Hawaii	0	0.0%
26	Idaho	0	0.0%
26	Illinois	0	0.0%
9	Indiana	2	3.1%
26	Iowa	0	0.0%
26	Kansas	0	0.0%
26	Kentucky	0	0.0%
26	Louisiana	0	0.0%
26	Maine	0	0.0%
5	Maryland	3	4.6%
26	Massachusetts	0	0.0%
26	Michigan	0	0.0%
26	Minnesota	0	0.0%
16	Mississippi	1	1.5%
26	Missouri	0	0.0%
16	Montana	1	1.5%
26	Nebraska	0	0.0%
16	Nevada	1	1.5%
26	New Hampshire	0	0.0%
9	New Jersey	2	3.1%
16	New Mexico	1	1.5%
5	New York	3	4.6%
9	North Carolina	2	3.1%
26	North Dakota	0	0.0%
9	Ohio	2	3.1%
5	Oklahoma	3	4.6%
26	Oregon	0	0.0%
3	Pennsylvania	5	7.7%
26	Rhode Island	0	0.0%
16	South Carolina	1	1.5%
26	South Dakota	0	0.0%
16	Tennessee	1	1.5%
2	Texas	9	13.8%
16	Utah	1	1.5%
26	Vermont	0	0.0%
16	Virginia	1	1.5%
26	Washington	0	0.0%
26	West Virginia	0	0.0%
16	Wisconsin	1	1.5%
26	Wyoming	0	0.0%

RANK ORDER

RANK	STATE	OFFICERS	% of USA
1	California	11	16.9%
2	Texas	9	13.8%
3	Pennsylvania	5	7.7%
4	Florida	4	6.2%
5	Georgia	3	4.6%
5	Maryland	3	4.6%
5	New York	3	4.6%
5	Oklahoma	3	4.6%
9	Alabama	2	3.1%
9	Arizona	2	3.1%
9	Arkansas	2	3.1%
9	Indiana	2	3.1%
9	New Jersey	2	3.1%
9	North Carolina	2	3.1%
9	Ohio	2	3.1%
16	Connecticut	1	1.5%
16	Mississippi	1	1.5%
16	Montana	1	1.5%
16	Nevada	1	1.5%
16	New Mexico	1	1.5%
16	South Carolina	1	1.5%
16	Tennessee	1	1.5%
16	Utah	1	1.5%
16	Virginia	1	1.5%
16	Wisconsin	1	1.5%
26	Alaska	0	0.0%
26	Colorado	0	0.0%
26	Delaware	0	0.0%
26	Hawaii	0	0.0%
26	Idaho	0	0.0%
26	Illinois	0	0.0%
26	Iowa	0	0.0%
26	Kansas	0	0.0%
26	Kentucky	0	0.0%
26	Louisiana	0	0.0%
26	Maine	0	0.0%
26	Massachusetts	0	0.0%
26	Michigan	0	0.0%
26	Minnesota	0	0.0%
26	Missouri	0	0.0%
26	Nebraska	0	0.0%
26	New Hampshire	0	0.0%
26	North Dakota	0	0.0%
26	Oregon	0	0.0%
26	Rhode Island	0	0.0%
26	South Dakota	0	0.0%
26	Vermont	0	0.0%
26	Washington	0	0.0%
26	West Virginia	0	0.0%
26	Wyoming	0	0.0%
	District of Columbia	0	0.0%

Source: Reported data from the Federal Bureau of Investigation
"Law Enforcement Officers Killed and Assaulted 2008" (http://www.fbi.gov/ucr/killed/2008/table_01.html)
*Total does not include two officers killed in Puerto Rico and one officer killed in the U.S. Virgin Islands.

Law Enforcement Officers Accidentally Killed: 1999 to 2008

National Total = 727 Officers*

ALPHA ORDER

RANK	STATE	OFFICERS	% of USA
14	Alabama	18	2.5%
39	Alaska	2	0.3%
10	Arizona	22	3.0%
24	Arkansas	10	1.4%
2	California	78	10.7%
27	Colorado	9	1.2%
37	Connecticut	4	0.6%
39	Delaware	2	0.3%
3	Florida	47	6.5%
6	Georgia	28	3.9%
32	Hawaii	6	0.8%
46	Idaho	1	0.1%
8	Illinois	23	3.2%
12	Indiana	20	2.8%
39	Iowa	2	0.3%
35	Kansas	5	0.7%
32	Kentucky	6	0.8%
7	Louisiana	25	3.4%
46	Maine	1	0.1%
16	Maryland	17	2.3%
24	Massachusetts	10	1.4%
16	Michigan	17	2.3%
29	Minnesota	7	1.0%
21	Mississippi	13	1.8%
10	Missouri	22	3.0%
32	Montana	6	0.8%
39	Nebraska	2	0.3%
35	Nevada	5	0.7%
49	New Hampshire	0	0.0%
16	New Jersey	17	2.3%
22	New Mexico	12	1.7%
8	New York	23	3.2%
5	North Carolina	30	4.1%
49	North Dakota	0	0.0%
20	Ohio	15	2.1%
22	Oklahoma	12	1.7%
28	Oregon	8	1.1%
13	Pennsylvania	19	2.6%
39	Rhode Island	2	0.3%
14	South Carolina	18	2.5%
39	South Dakota	2	0.3%
4	Tennessee	31	4.3%
1	Texas	81	11.1%
29	Utah	7	1.0%
39	Vermont	2	0.3%
19	Virginia	16	2.2%
24	Washington	10	1.4%
37	West Virginia	4	0.6%
29	Wisconsin	7	1.0%
46	Wyoming	1	0.1%

RANK ORDER

RANK	STATE	OFFICERS	% of USA
1	Texas	81	11.1%
2	California	78	10.7%
3	Florida	47	6.5%
4	Tennessee	31	4.3%
5	North Carolina	30	4.1%
6	Georgia	28	3.9%
7	Louisiana	25	3.4%
8	Illinois	23	3.2%
8	New York	23	3.2%
10	Arizona	22	3.0%
10	Missouri	22	3.0%
12	Indiana	20	2.8%
13	Pennsylvania	19	2.6%
14	Alabama	18	2.5%
14	South Carolina	18	2.5%
16	Maryland	17	2.3%
16	Michigan	17	2.3%
16	New Jersey	17	2.3%
19	Virginia	16	2.2%
20	Ohio	15	2.1%
21	Mississippi	13	1.8%
22	New Mexico	12	1.7%
22	Oklahoma	12	1.7%
24	Arkansas	10	1.4%
24	Massachusetts	10	1.4%
24	Washington	10	1.4%
27	Colorado	9	1.2%
28	Oregon	8	1.1%
29	Minnesota	7	1.0%
29	Utah	7	1.0%
29	Wisconsin	7	1.0%
32	Hawaii	6	0.8%
32	Kentucky	6	0.8%
32	Montana	6	0.8%
35	Kansas	5	0.7%
35	Nevada	5	0.7%
37	Connecticut	4	0.6%
37	West Virginia	4	0.6%
39	Alaska	2	0.3%
39	Delaware	2	0.3%
39	Iowa	2	0.3%
39	Nebraska	2	0.3%
39	Rhode Island	2	0.3%
39	South Dakota	2	0.3%
39	Vermont	2	0.3%
46	Idaho	1	0.1%
46	Maine	1	0.1%
46	Wyoming	1	0.1%
49	New Hampshire	0	0.0%
49	North Dakota	0	0.0%
	District of Columbia	2	0.3%

Source: Reported data from the Federal Bureau of Investigation
"Law Enforcement Officers Killed and Assaulted 2008" (http://www.fbi.gov/ucr/killed/2008/table_01.html)
*Total does not include 19 officers killed in U.S. territories.

Law Enforcement Officers Assaulted in 2008

National Total = 58,792 Officers*

<table>
<tr><td colspan="4">ALPHA ORDER</td><td colspan="4">RANK ORDER</td></tr>
<tr><th>RANK</th><th>STATE</th><th>OFFICERS</th><th>% of USA</th><th>RANK</th><th>STATE</th><th>OFFICERS</th><th>% of USA</th></tr>
<tr><td>36</td><td>Alabama</td><td>259</td><td>0.4%</td><td>1</td><td>Florida</td><td>8,049</td><td>13.7%</td></tr>
<tr><td>34</td><td>Alaska</td><td>287</td><td>0.5%</td><td>2</td><td>California</td><td>7,639</td><td>13.0%</td></tr>
<tr><td>9</td><td>Arizona</td><td>2,118</td><td>3.6%</td><td>3</td><td>Texas</td><td>4,808</td><td>8.2%</td></tr>
<tr><td>33</td><td>Arkansas</td><td>302</td><td>0.5%</td><td>4</td><td>Maryland</td><td>3,844</td><td>6.5%</td></tr>
<tr><td>2</td><td>California</td><td>7,639</td><td>13.0%</td><td>5</td><td>Pennsylvania</td><td>3,348</td><td>5.7%</td></tr>
<tr><td>19</td><td>Colorado</td><td>810</td><td>1.4%</td><td>6</td><td>New Jersey</td><td>2,378</td><td>4.0%</td></tr>
<tr><td>21</td><td>Connecticut</td><td>757</td><td>1.3%</td><td>7</td><td>Missouri</td><td>2,159</td><td>3.7%</td></tr>
<tr><td>26</td><td>Delaware</td><td>644</td><td>1.1%</td><td>8</td><td>North Carolina</td><td>2,120</td><td>3.6%</td></tr>
<tr><td>1</td><td>Florida</td><td>8,049</td><td>13.7%</td><td>9</td><td>Arizona</td><td>2,118</td><td>3.6%</td></tr>
<tr><td>16</td><td>Georgia</td><td>866</td><td>1.5%</td><td>10</td><td>Tennessee</td><td>1,979</td><td>3.4%</td></tr>
<tr><td>32</td><td>Hawaii</td><td>312</td><td>0.5%</td><td>11</td><td>Louisiana</td><td>1,693</td><td>2.9%</td></tr>
<tr><td>37</td><td>Idaho</td><td>252</td><td>0.4%</td><td>12</td><td>Indiana</td><td>1,306</td><td>2.2%</td></tr>
<tr><td>NA</td><td>Illinois**</td><td>NA</td><td>NA</td><td>13</td><td>Virginia</td><td>1,277</td><td>2.2%</td></tr>
<tr><td>12</td><td>Indiana</td><td>1,306</td><td>2.2%</td><td>14</td><td>Wisconsin</td><td>1,125</td><td>1.9%</td></tr>
<tr><td>29</td><td>Iowa</td><td>469</td><td>0.8%</td><td>15</td><td>Oklahoma</td><td>904</td><td>1.5%</td></tr>
<tr><td>23</td><td>Kansas</td><td>717</td><td>1.2%</td><td>16</td><td>Georgia</td><td>866</td><td>1.5%</td></tr>
<tr><td>27</td><td>Kentucky</td><td>591</td><td>1.0%</td><td>17</td><td>Washington</td><td>862</td><td>1.5%</td></tr>
<tr><td>11</td><td>Louisiana</td><td>1,693</td><td>2.9%</td><td>18</td><td>South Carolina</td><td>830</td><td>1.4%</td></tr>
<tr><td>40</td><td>Maine</td><td>230</td><td>0.4%</td><td>19</td><td>Colorado</td><td>810</td><td>1.4%</td></tr>
<tr><td>4</td><td>Maryland</td><td>3,844</td><td>6.5%</td><td>20</td><td>New York</td><td>772</td><td>1.3%</td></tr>
<tr><td>45</td><td>Massachusetts</td><td>85</td><td>0.1%</td><td>21</td><td>Connecticut</td><td>757</td><td>1.3%</td></tr>
<tr><td>NA</td><td>Michigan**</td><td>NA</td><td>NA</td><td>22</td><td>New Mexico</td><td>741</td><td>1.3%</td></tr>
<tr><td>41</td><td>Minnesota</td><td>198</td><td>0.3%</td><td>23</td><td>Kansas</td><td>717</td><td>1.2%</td></tr>
<tr><td>42</td><td>Mississippi</td><td>186</td><td>0.3%</td><td>24</td><td>Nevada</td><td>699</td><td>1.2%</td></tr>
<tr><td>7</td><td>Missouri</td><td>2,159</td><td>3.7%</td><td>25</td><td>Utah</td><td>683</td><td>1.2%</td></tr>
<tr><td>38</td><td>Montana</td><td>247</td><td>0.4%</td><td>26</td><td>Delaware</td><td>644</td><td>1.1%</td></tr>
<tr><td>39</td><td>Nebraska</td><td>244</td><td>0.4%</td><td>27</td><td>Kentucky</td><td>591</td><td>1.0%</td></tr>
<tr><td>24</td><td>Nevada</td><td>699</td><td>1.2%</td><td>28</td><td>Ohio</td><td>506</td><td>0.9%</td></tr>
<tr><td>35</td><td>New Hampshire</td><td>275</td><td>0.5%</td><td>29</td><td>Iowa</td><td>469</td><td>0.8%</td></tr>
<tr><td>6</td><td>New Jersey</td><td>2,378</td><td>4.0%</td><td>30</td><td>Rhode Island</td><td>378</td><td>0.6%</td></tr>
<tr><td>22</td><td>New Mexico</td><td>741</td><td>1.3%</td><td>31</td><td>Oregon</td><td>377</td><td>0.6%</td></tr>
<tr><td>20</td><td>New York</td><td>772</td><td>1.3%</td><td>32</td><td>Hawaii</td><td>312</td><td>0.5%</td></tr>
<tr><td>8</td><td>North Carolina</td><td>2,120</td><td>3.6%</td><td>33</td><td>Arkansas</td><td>302</td><td>0.5%</td></tr>
<tr><td>46</td><td>North Dakota</td><td>76</td><td>0.1%</td><td>34</td><td>Alaska</td><td>287</td><td>0.5%</td></tr>
<tr><td>28</td><td>Ohio</td><td>506</td><td>0.9%</td><td>35</td><td>New Hampshire</td><td>275</td><td>0.5%</td></tr>
<tr><td>15</td><td>Oklahoma</td><td>904</td><td>1.5%</td><td>36</td><td>Alabama</td><td>259</td><td>0.4%</td></tr>
<tr><td>31</td><td>Oregon</td><td>377</td><td>0.6%</td><td>37</td><td>Idaho</td><td>252</td><td>0.4%</td></tr>
<tr><td>5</td><td>Pennsylvania</td><td>3,348</td><td>5.7%</td><td>38</td><td>Montana</td><td>247</td><td>0.4%</td></tr>
<tr><td>30</td><td>Rhode Island</td><td>378</td><td>0.6%</td><td>39</td><td>Nebraska</td><td>244</td><td>0.4%</td></tr>
<tr><td>18</td><td>South Carolina</td><td>830</td><td>1.4%</td><td>40</td><td>Maine</td><td>230</td><td>0.4%</td></tr>
<tr><td>43</td><td>South Dakota</td><td>161</td><td>0.3%</td><td>41</td><td>Minnesota</td><td>198</td><td>0.3%</td></tr>
<tr><td>10</td><td>Tennessee</td><td>1,979</td><td>3.4%</td><td>42</td><td>Mississippi</td><td>186</td><td>0.3%</td></tr>
<tr><td>3</td><td>Texas</td><td>4,808</td><td>8.2%</td><td>43</td><td>South Dakota</td><td>161</td><td>0.3%</td></tr>
<tr><td>25</td><td>Utah</td><td>683</td><td>1.2%</td><td>44</td><td>Wyoming</td><td>89</td><td>0.2%</td></tr>
<tr><td>47</td><td>Vermont</td><td>37</td><td>0.1%</td><td>45</td><td>Massachusetts</td><td>85</td><td>0.1%</td></tr>
<tr><td>13</td><td>Virginia</td><td>1,277</td><td>2.2%</td><td>46</td><td>North Dakota</td><td>76</td><td>0.1%</td></tr>
<tr><td>17</td><td>Washington</td><td>862</td><td>1.5%</td><td>47</td><td>Vermont</td><td>37</td><td>0.1%</td></tr>
<tr><td>NA</td><td>West Virginia**</td><td>NA</td><td>NA</td><td>NA</td><td>Illinois**</td><td>NA</td><td>NA</td></tr>
<tr><td>14</td><td>Wisconsin</td><td>1,125</td><td>1.9%</td><td>NA</td><td>Michigan**</td><td>NA</td><td>NA</td></tr>
<tr><td>44</td><td>Wyoming</td><td>89</td><td>0.2%</td><td>NA</td><td>West Virginia**</td><td>NA</td><td>NA</td></tr>
<tr><td></td><td></td><td></td><td></td><td></td><td>District of Columbia</td><td>103</td><td>0.2%</td></tr>
</table>

Source: Reported data from the Federal Bureau of Investigation
"Law Enforcement Officers Killed and Assaulted 2008" (http://www.fbi.gov/ucr/killed/2008/table_01.html)
*Figures based on reporting agencies for each state. Assaulted includes by firearm, knife, other dangerous weapons, or personal weapons (e.g. fists).
**Not available.

Rate of Law Enforcement Officers Assaulted in 2008

National Rate = 25.9 Officers Assaulted per 100,000 Population*

ALPHA ORDER

RANK	STATE	RATE
46	Alabama	5.8
8	Alaska	42.6
14	Arizona	33.4
40	Arkansas	11.6
23	California	24.1
31	Colorado	17.6
25	Connecticut	21.6
1	Delaware	73.9
7	Florida	44.0
41	Georgia	11.4
17	Hawaii	27.2
34	Idaho	16.7
NA	Illinois**	NA
16	Indiana	27.8
36	Iowa	15.8
4	Kansas	61.7
5	Kentucky	59.3
3	Louisiana	65.3
32	Maine	17.5
2	Maryland	70.5
44	Massachusetts	10.0
NA	Michigan**	NA
47	Minnesota	4.3
42	Mississippi	11.1
10	Missouri	37.2
20	Montana	26.8
26	Nebraska	20.2
18	Nevada	26.9
9	New Hampshire	37.4
15	New Jersey	28.3
6	New Mexico	45.5
45	New York	8.4
18	North Carolina	26.9
39	North Dakota	12.4
29	Ohio	18.8
21	Oklahoma	26.0
43	Oregon	10.4
11	Pennsylvania	36.7
12	Rhode Island	36.0
30	South Carolina	18.5
24	South Dakota	23.5
13	Tennessee	33.7
28	Texas	19.9
22	Utah	25.4
38	Vermont	13.8
35	Virginia	16.5
37	Washington	14.1
NA	West Virginia**	NA
26	Wisconsin	20.2
33	Wyoming	16.9

RANK ORDER

RANK	STATE	RATE
1	Delaware	73.9
2	Maryland	70.5
3	Louisiana	65.3
4	Kansas	61.7
5	Kentucky	59.3
6	New Mexico	45.5
7	Florida	44.0
8	Alaska	42.6
9	New Hampshire	37.4
10	Missouri	37.2
11	Pennsylvania	36.7
12	Rhode Island	36.0
13	Tennessee	33.7
14	Arizona	33.4
15	New Jersey	28.3
16	Indiana	27.8
17	Hawaii	27.2
18	Nevada	26.9
18	North Carolina	26.9
20	Montana	26.8
21	Oklahoma	26.0
22	Utah	25.4
23	California	24.1
24	South Dakota	23.5
25	Connecticut	21.6
26	Nebraska	20.2
26	Wisconsin	20.2
28	Texas	19.9
29	Ohio	18.8
30	South Carolina	18.5
31	Colorado	17.6
32	Maine	17.5
33	Wyoming	16.9
34	Idaho	16.7
35	Virginia	16.5
36	Iowa	15.8
37	Washington	14.1
38	Vermont	13.8
39	North Dakota	12.4
40	Arkansas	11.6
41	Georgia	11.4
42	Mississippi	11.1
43	Oregon	10.4
44	Massachusetts	10.0
45	New York	8.4
46	Alabama	5.8
47	Minnesota	4.3
NA	Illinois**	NA
NA	Michigan**	NA
NA	West Virginia**	NA
	District of Columbia**	NA

Source: CQ Press using reported data from the Federal Bureau of Investigation
"Law Enforcement Officers Killed and Assaulted 2008" (http://www.fbi.gov/ucr/killed/2008/table_01.html)
*Figures based on reporting agencies and the population for those agencies for each state. Assaulted includes by firearm, knife, other dangerous weapons, or personal weapons (e.g. fists).
**Not available.

Percent of Law Enforcement Officers Assaulted in 2008

National Percent = 11.3% of Officers Assaulted*

RANK	STATE	PERCENT
47	Alabama	2.4
5	Alaska	23.6
12	Arizona	16.6
40	Arkansas	5.9
27	California	9.5
36	Colorado	7.3
30	Connecticut	8.8
2	Delaware	28.0
8	Florida	18.8
42	Georgia	4.8
22	Hawaii	11.7
27	Idaho	9.5
NA	Illinois**	NA
14	Indiana	16.4
24	Iowa	10.4
4	Kansas	26.8
1	Kentucky	30.7
7	Louisiana	19.4
21	Maine	11.9
3	Maryland	27.2
45	Massachusetts	2.7
NA	Michigan**	NA
46	Minnesota	2.6
41	Mississippi	4.9
15	Missouri	15.1
10	Montana	17.8
25	Nebraska	9.6
19	Nevada	13.4
9	New Hampshire	18.7
25	New Jersey	9.6
6	New Mexico	22.2
44	New York	3.2
23	North Carolina	11.2
36	North Dakota	7.3
32	Ohio	8.6
18	Oklahoma	13.6
36	Oregon	7.3
11	Pennsylvania	16.9
16	Rhode Island	14.6
36	South Carolina	7.3
17	South Dakota	14.0
20	Tennessee	13.2
29	Texas	9.2
12	Utah	16.6
43	Vermont	3.9
34	Virginia	7.8
33	Washington	8.5
NA	West Virginia**	NA
31	Wisconsin	8.7
35	Wyoming	7.5

RANK	STATE	PERCENT
1	Kentucky	30.7
2	Delaware	28.0
3	Maryland	27.2
4	Kansas	26.8
5	Alaska	23.6
6	New Mexico	22.2
7	Louisiana	19.4
8	Florida	18.8
9	New Hampshire	18.7
10	Montana	17.8
11	Pennsylvania	16.9
12	Arizona	16.6
12	Utah	16.6
14	Indiana	16.4
15	Missouri	15.1
16	Rhode Island	14.6
17	South Dakota	14.0
18	Oklahoma	13.6
19	Nevada	13.4
20	Tennessee	13.2
21	Maine	11.9
22	Hawaii	11.7
23	North Carolina	11.2
24	Iowa	10.4
25	Nebraska	9.6
25	New Jersey	9.6
27	California	9.5
27	Idaho	9.5
29	Texas	9.2
30	Connecticut	8.8
31	Wisconsin	8.7
32	Ohio	8.6
33	Washington	8.5
34	Virginia	7.8
35	Wyoming	7.5
36	Colorado	7.3
36	North Dakota	7.3
36	Oregon	7.3
36	South Carolina	7.3
40	Arkansas	5.9
41	Mississippi	4.9
42	Georgia	4.8
43	Vermont	3.9
44	New York	3.2
45	Massachusetts	2.7
46	Minnesota	2.6
47	Alabama	2.4
NA	Illinois**	NA
NA	Michigan**	NA
NA	West Virginia**	NA

District of Columbia 24.2

Source: CQ Press using reported data from the Federal Bureau of Investigation
"Law Enforcement Officers Killed and Assaulted 2008" (http://www.fbi.gov/ucr/killed/2008/table_01.html)
*Figures based on reporting agencies and the number of officers for those agencies for each state. Assaulted includes by firearm, knife, other dangerous weapons, or personal weapons (e.g. fists).
**Not available.

Detectives and Criminal Investigators in 2008

National Total = 104,480 Detectives and Investigators*

ALPHA ORDER

RANK	STATE	EMPLOYEES	% of USA
22	Alabama	1,310	1.3%
50	Alaska	110	0.1%
5	Arizona	5,110	4.9%
32	Arkansas	610	0.6%
2	California	11,880	11.4%
16	Colorado	1,710	1.6%
28	Connecticut	1,030	1.0%
46	Delaware	230	0.2%
4	Florida	7,000	6.7%
6	Georgia	4,170	4.0%
35	Hawaii	490	0.5%
40	Idaho	350	0.3%
10	Illinois	2,920	2.8%
25	Indiana	1,200	1.1%
36	Iowa	430	0.4%
30	Kansas	880	0.8%
33	Kentucky	590	0.6%
14	Louisiana	1,910	1.8%
37	Maine	410	0.4%
22	Maryland	1,310	1.3%
21	Massachusetts	1,440	1.4%
13	Michigan	1,990	1.9%
27	Minnesota	1,110	1.1%
26	Mississippi	1,120	1.1%
15	Missouri	1,830	1.8%
38	Montana	400	0.4%
43	Nebraska	330	0.3%
33	Nevada	590	0.6%
43	New Hampshire	330	0.3%
7	New Jersey	3,460	3.3%
19	New Mexico	1,550	1.5%
3	New York	9,310	8.9%
11	North Carolina	2,820	2.7%
47	North Dakota	220	0.2%
12	Ohio	2,700	2.6%
24	Oklahoma	1,220	1.2%
31	Oregon	640	0.6%
9	Pennsylvania	3,100	3.0%
40	Rhode Island	350	0.3%
29	South Carolina	970	0.9%
45	South Dakota	240	0.2%
18	Tennessee	1,560	1.5%
1	Texas	12,970	12.4%
40	Utah	350	0.3%
47	Vermont	220	0.2%
8	Virginia	3,450	3.3%
20	Washington	1,530	1.5%
39	West Virginia	370	0.4%
17	Wisconsin	1,700	1.6%
47	Wyoming	220	0.2%

RANK ORDER

RANK	STATE	EMPLOYEES	% of USA
1	Texas	12,970	12.4%
2	California	11,880	11.4%
3	New York	9,310	8.9%
4	Florida	7,000	6.7%
5	Arizona	5,110	4.9%
6	Georgia	4,170	4.0%
7	New Jersey	3,460	3.3%
8	Virginia	3,450	3.3%
9	Pennsylvania	3,100	3.0%
10	Illinois	2,920	2.8%
11	North Carolina	2,820	2.7%
12	Ohio	2,700	2.6%
13	Michigan	1,990	1.9%
14	Louisiana	1,910	1.8%
15	Missouri	1,830	1.8%
16	Colorado	1,710	1.6%
17	Wisconsin	1,700	1.6%
18	Tennessee	1,560	1.5%
19	New Mexico	1,550	1.5%
20	Washington	1,530	1.5%
21	Massachusetts	1,440	1.4%
22	Alabama	1,310	1.3%
22	Maryland	1,310	1.3%
24	Oklahoma	1,220	1.2%
25	Indiana	1,200	1.1%
26	Mississippi	1,120	1.1%
27	Minnesota	1,110	1.1%
28	Connecticut	1,030	1.0%
29	South Carolina	970	0.9%
30	Kansas	880	0.8%
31	Oregon	640	0.6%
32	Arkansas	610	0.6%
33	Kentucky	590	0.6%
33	Nevada	590	0.6%
35	Hawaii	490	0.5%
36	Iowa	430	0.4%
37	Maine	410	0.4%
38	Montana	400	0.4%
39	West Virginia	370	0.4%
40	Idaho	350	0.3%
40	Rhode Island	350	0.3%
40	Utah	350	0.3%
43	Nebraska	330	0.3%
43	New Hampshire	330	0.3%
45	South Dakota	240	0.2%
46	Delaware	230	0.2%
47	North Dakota	220	0.2%
47	Vermont	220	0.2%
47	Wyoming	220	0.2%
50	Alaska	110	0.1%
	District of Columbia	2,770	2.7%

Source: U.S. Department of Labor, Bureau of Labor Statistics
   "Occupational Employment Statistics" (http://www.bls.gov/oes/)
*Occupational code 33-3021. As of May 2008. Does not include self-employed.

Rate of Detectives and Criminal Investigators in 2008

National Rate = 34 Detectives and Investigators per 100,000 Population*

ALPHA ORDER

RANK	STATE	RATE
27	Alabama	28
47	Alaska	16
1	Arizona	79
40	Arkansas	21
19	California	32
14	Colorado	35
26	Connecticut	29
28	Delaware	26
11	Florida	38
6	Georgia	43
11	Hawaii	38
33	Idaho	23
33	Illinois	23
44	Indiana	19
48	Iowa	14
20	Kansas	31
48	Kentucky	14
6	Louisiana	43
20	Maine	31
33	Maryland	23
38	Massachusetts	22
42	Michigan	20
40	Minnesota	21
11	Mississippi	38
20	Missouri	31
8	Montana	41
44	Nebraska	19
33	Nevada	23
29	New Hampshire	25
10	New Jersey	40
2	New Mexico	78
4	New York	48
20	North Carolina	31
16	North Dakota	34
32	Ohio	24
17	Oklahoma	33
46	Oregon	17
29	Pennsylvania	25
17	Rhode Island	33
38	South Carolina	22
24	South Dakota	30
29	Tennessee	25
3	Texas	53
50	Utah	13
14	Vermont	35
5	Virginia	44
33	Washington	23
42	West Virginia	20
24	Wisconsin	30
8	Wyoming	41

RANK ORDER

RANK	STATE	RATE
1	Arizona	79
2	New Mexico	78
3	Texas	53
4	New York	48
5	Virginia	44
6	Georgia	43
6	Louisiana	43
8	Montana	41
8	Wyoming	41
10	New Jersey	40
11	Florida	38
11	Hawaii	38
11	Mississippi	38
14	Colorado	35
14	Vermont	35
16	North Dakota	34
17	Oklahoma	33
17	Rhode Island	33
19	California	32
20	Kansas	31
20	Maine	31
20	Missouri	31
20	North Carolina	31
24	South Dakota	30
24	Wisconsin	30
26	Connecticut	29
27	Alabama	28
28	Delaware	26
29	New Hampshire	25
29	Pennsylvania	25
29	Tennessee	25
32	Ohio	24
33	Idaho	23
33	Illinois	23
33	Maryland	23
33	Nevada	23
33	Washington	23
38	Massachusetts	22
38	South Carolina	22
40	Arkansas	21
40	Minnesota	21
42	Michigan	20
42	West Virginia	20
44	Indiana	19
44	Nebraska	19
46	Oregon	17
47	Alaska	16
48	Iowa	14
48	Kentucky	14
50	Utah	13

District of Columbia	468

Source: CQ Press using data from U.S. Department of Labor, Bureau of Labor Statistics
"Occupational Employment Statistics" (http://www.bls.gov/oes/)
*Occupational code 33-3021. As of May 2008. Does not include self-employed.

Private Detectives and Investigators in 2008

National Total = 35,380 Private Detectives and Investigators*

ALPHA ORDER

RANK	STATE	EMPLOYEES	% of USA
18	Alabama	440	1.2%
31	Alaska	90	0.3%
17	Arizona	530	1.5%
32	Arkansas	80	0.2%
1	California	5,420	15.1%
12	Colorado	690	1.9%
23	Connecticut	260	0.7%
37	Delaware	40	0.1%
2	Florida	3,280	9.2%
NA	Georgia**	NA	NA
36	Hawaii	50	0.1%
37	Idaho	40	0.1%
5	Illinois	2,380	6.6%
21	Indiana	370	1.0%
32	Iowa	80	0.2%
NA	Kansas**	NA	NA
26	Kentucky	150	0.4%
22	Louisiana	310	0.9%
NA	Maine**	NA	NA
NA	Maryland**	NA	NA
11	Massachusetts	770	2.1%
14	Michigan	610	1.7%
NA	Minnesota**	NA	NA
27	Mississippi	140	0.4%
7	Missouri	1,060	3.0%
37	Montana	40	0.1%
NA	Nebraska**	NA	NA
25	Nevada	170	0.5%
NA	New Hampshire**	NA	NA
10	New Jersey	860	2.4%
30	New Mexico	100	0.3%
6	New York	1,390	3.9%
13	North Carolina	660	1.8%
NA	North Dakota**	NA	NA
9	Ohio	990	2.8%
20	Oklahoma	390	1.1%
24	Oregon	190	0.5%
3	Pennsylvania	2,720	7.6%
34	Rhode Island	60	0.2%
28	South Carolina	120	0.3%
28	South Dakota	120	0.3%
14	Tennessee	610	1.7%
4	Texas	2,470	6.9%
34	Utah	60	0.2%
NA	Vermont**	NA	NA
7	Virginia	1,060	3.0%
18	Washington	440	1.2%
NA	West Virginia**	NA	NA
16	Wisconsin	570	1.6%
NA	Wyoming**	NA	NA

RANK ORDER

RANK	STATE	EMPLOYEES	% of USA
1	California	5,420	15.1%
2	Florida	3,280	9.2%
3	Pennsylvania	2,720	7.6%
4	Texas	2,470	6.9%
5	Illinois	2,380	6.6%
6	New York	1,390	3.9%
7	Missouri	1,060	3.0%
7	Virginia	1,060	3.0%
9	Ohio	990	2.8%
10	New Jersey	860	2.4%
11	Massachusetts	770	2.1%
12	Colorado	690	1.9%
13	North Carolina	660	1.8%
14	Michigan	610	1.7%
14	Tennessee	610	1.7%
16	Wisconsin	570	1.6%
17	Arizona	530	1.5%
18	Alabama	440	1.2%
18	Washington	440	1.2%
20	Oklahoma	390	1.1%
21	Indiana	370	1.0%
22	Louisiana	310	0.9%
23	Connecticut	260	0.7%
24	Oregon	190	0.5%
25	Nevada	170	0.5%
26	Kentucky	150	0.4%
27	Mississippi	140	0.4%
28	South Carolina	120	0.3%
28	South Dakota	120	0.3%
30	New Mexico	100	0.3%
31	Alaska	90	0.3%
32	Arkansas	80	0.2%
32	Iowa	80	0.2%
34	Rhode Island	60	0.2%
34	Utah	60	0.2%
36	Hawaii	50	0.1%
37	Delaware	40	0.1%
37	Idaho	40	0.1%
37	Montana	40	0.1%
NA	Georgia**	NA	NA
NA	Kansas**	NA	NA
NA	Maine**	NA	NA
NA	Maryland**	NA	NA
NA	Minnesota**	NA	NA
NA	Nebraska**	NA	NA
NA	New Hampshire**	NA	NA
NA	North Dakota**	NA	NA
NA	Vermont**	NA	NA
NA	West Virginia**	NA	NA
NA	Wyoming**	NA	NA
	District of Columbia**	NA	NA

Source: U.S. Department of Labor, Bureau of Labor Statistics
    "Occupational Employment Statistics" (http://www.bls.gov/oes/)
*Occupational code 33-9021. As of May 2008. Does not include self-employed.
**Not available.

Rate of Private Detectives and Investigators in 2008

National Rate = 12 Private Detectives and Investigators per 100,000 Population*

ALPHA ORDER

RANK	STATE	RATE
16	Alabama	9
9	Alaska	13
18	Arizona	8
35	Arkansas	3
5	California	15
7	Colorado	14
19	Connecticut	7
28	Delaware	5
2	Florida	18
NA	Georgia**	NA
32	Hawaii	4
35	Idaho	3
2	Illinois	18
25	Indiana	6
35	Iowa	3
NA	Kansas**	NA
32	Kentucky	4
19	Louisiana	7
NA	Maine**	NA
NA	Maryland**	NA
10	Massachusetts	12
25	Michigan	6
NA	Minnesota**	NA
28	Mississippi	5
2	Missouri	18
32	Montana	4
NA	Nebraska**	NA
19	Nevada	7
NA	New Hampshire**	NA
12	New Jersey	10
28	New Mexico	5
19	New York	7
19	North Carolina	7
NA	North Dakota**	NA
16	Ohio	9
11	Oklahoma	11
28	Oregon	5
1	Pennsylvania	22
25	Rhode Island	6
35	South Carolina	3
5	South Dakota	15
12	Tennessee	10
12	Texas	10
39	Utah	2
NA	Vermont**	NA
7	Virginia	14
19	Washington	7
NA	West Virginia**	NA
12	Wisconsin	10
NA	Wyoming**	NA

RANK ORDER

RANK	STATE	RATE
1	Pennsylvania	22
2	Florida	18
2	Illinois	18
2	Missouri	18
5	California	15
5	South Dakota	15
7	Colorado	14
7	Virginia	14
9	Alaska	13
10	Massachusetts	12
11	Oklahoma	11
12	New Jersey	10
12	Tennessee	10
12	Texas	10
12	Wisconsin	10
16	Alabama	9
16	Ohio	9
18	Arizona	8
19	Connecticut	7
19	Louisiana	7
19	Nevada	7
19	New York	7
19	North Carolina	7
19	Washington	7
25	Indiana	6
25	Michigan	6
25	Rhode Island	6
28	Delaware	5
28	Mississippi	5
28	New Mexico	5
28	Oregon	5
32	Hawaii	4
32	Kentucky	4
32	Montana	4
35	Arkansas	3
35	Idaho	3
35	Iowa	3
35	South Carolina	3
39	Utah	2
NA	Georgia**	NA
NA	Kansas**	NA
NA	Maine**	NA
NA	Maryland**	NA
NA	Minnesota**	NA
NA	Nebraska**	NA
NA	New Hampshire**	NA
NA	North Dakota**	NA
NA	Vermont**	NA
NA	West Virginia**	NA
NA	Wyoming**	NA
	District of Columbia**	NA

Source: CQ Press using data from U.S. Department of Labor, Bureau of Labor Statistics
"Occupational Employment Statistics" (http://www.bls.gov/oes/)
*Occupational code 33-9021. As of May 2008. Does not include self-employed.
**Not available.

Security Guards in 2008

National Total = 1,046,760 Guards*

ALPHA ORDER					RANK ORDER			
RANK	STATE		EMPLOYEES	% of USA	RANK	STATE	EMPLOYEES	% of USA
22	Alabama		14,000	1.3%	1	California	138,800	13.3%
43	Alaska		2,370	0.2%	2	New York	100,210	9.6%
11	Arizona		25,000	2.4%	3	Florida	79,520	7.6%
34	Arkansas		6,600	0.6%	4	Texas	78,740	7.5%
1	California		138,800	13.3%	5	Illinois	46,330	4.4%
23	Colorado		13,780	1.3%	6	New Jersey	40,390	3.9%
25	Connecticut		12,630	1.2%	7	Pennsylvania	38,270	3.7%
40	Delaware		3,600	0.3%	8	Ohio	32,060	3.1%
3	Florida		79,520	7.6%	9	Virginia	30,250	2.9%
10	Georgia		28,750	2.7%	10	Georgia	28,750	2.7%
29	Hawaii		10,700	1.0%	11	Arizona	25,000	2.4%
42	Idaho		2,560	0.2%	12	North Carolina	24,580	2.3%
5	Illinois		46,330	4.4%	13	Michigan	24,170	2.3%
18	Indiana		18,560	1.8%	14	Maryland	24,030	2.3%
34	Iowa		6,600	0.6%	15	Tennessee	23,450	2.2%
37	Kansas		5,660	0.5%	16	Massachusetts	21,320	2.0%
27	Kentucky		11,970	1.1%	17	Nevada	20,130	1.9%
20	Louisiana		16,600	1.6%	18	Indiana	18,560	1.8%
45	Maine		2,020	0.2%	19	Missouri	17,740	1.7%
14	Maryland		24,030	2.3%	20	Louisiana	16,600	1.6%
16	Massachusetts		21,320	2.0%	21	Washington	15,210	1.5%
13	Michigan		24,170	2.3%	22	Alabama	14,000	1.3%
26	Minnesota		12,380	1.2%	23	Colorado	13,780	1.3%
30	Mississippi		10,090	1.0%	24	South Carolina	13,230	1.3%
19	Missouri		17,740	1.7%	25	Connecticut	12,630	1.2%
46	Montana		1,710	0.2%	26	Minnesota	12,380	1.2%
39	Nebraska		4,040	0.4%	27	Kentucky	11,970	1.1%
17	Nevada		20,130	1.9%	28	Wisconsin	10,930	1.0%
44	New Hampshire		2,310	0.2%	29	Hawaii	10,700	1.0%
6	New Jersey		40,390	3.9%	30	Mississippi	10,090	1.0%
33	New Mexico		7,280	0.7%	31	Oklahoma	9,490	0.9%
2	New York		100,210	9.6%	32	Oregon	7,570	0.7%
12	North Carolina		24,580	2.3%	33	New Mexico	7,280	0.7%
47	North Dakota		1,310	0.1%	34	Arkansas	6,600	0.6%
8	Ohio		32,060	3.1%	34	Iowa	6,600	0.6%
31	Oklahoma		9,490	0.9%	36	Utah	5,880	0.6%
32	Oregon		7,570	0.7%	37	Kansas	5,660	0.5%
7	Pennsylvania		38,270	3.7%	38	West Virginia	5,440	0.5%
41	Rhode Island		3,170	0.3%	39	Nebraska	4,040	0.4%
24	South Carolina		13,230	1.3%	40	Delaware	3,600	0.3%
48	South Dakota		1,220	0.1%	41	Rhode Island	3,170	0.3%
15	Tennessee		23,450	2.2%	42	Idaho	2,560	0.2%
4	Texas		78,740	7.5%	43	Alaska	2,370	0.2%
36	Utah		5,880	0.6%	44	New Hampshire	2,310	0.2%
49	Vermont		1,030	0.1%	45	Maine	2,020	0.2%
9	Virginia		30,250	2.9%	46	Montana	1,710	0.2%
21	Washington		15,210	1.5%	47	North Dakota	1,310	0.1%
38	West Virginia		5,440	0.5%	48	South Dakota	1,220	0.1%
28	Wisconsin		10,930	1.0%	49	Vermont	1,030	0.1%
50	Wyoming		850	0.1%	50	Wyoming	850	0.1%
						District of Columbia	12,230	1.2%

Source: U.S. Department of Labor, Bureau of Labor Statistics
   "Occupational Employment Statistics" (http://www.bls.gov/oes/)
*Occupational code 33-9032. As of May 2008. Does not include self-employed.

Rate of Security Guards in 2008

National Rate = 344 Guards per 100,000 Population*

ALPHA ORDER				RANK ORDER		
RANK	STATE	RATE		RANK	STATE	RATE
22	Alabama	300		1	Hawaii	831
16	Alaska	345		2	Nevada	774
9	Arizona	385		3	New York	514
36	Arkansas	231		4	New Jersey	465
10	California	378		5	Florida	434
29	Colorado	279		6	Maryland	427
14	Connecticut	361		7	Delaware	412
7	Delaware	412		8	Virginia	389
5	Florida	434		9	Arizona	385
25	Georgia	297		10	California	378
1	Hawaii	831		11	Tennessee	377
46	Idaho	168		12	Louisiana	376
15	Illinois	359		13	New Mexico	367
27	Indiana	291		14	Connecticut	361
38	Iowa	220		15	Illinois	359
41	Kansas	202		16	Alaska	345
28	Kentucky	280		17	Mississippi	343
12	Louisiana	376		18	Massachusetts	328
49	Maine	153		19	Texas	324
6	Maryland	427		20	Pennsylvania	307
18	Massachusetts	328		21	Rhode Island	302
33	Michigan	242		22	Alabama	300
34	Minnesota	237		22	Missouri	300
17	Mississippi	343		22	West Virginia	300
22	Missouri	300		25	Georgia	297
44	Montana	177		26	South Carolina	295
37	Nebraska	227		27	Indiana	291
2	Nevada	774		28	Kentucky	280
45	New Hampshire	176		29	Colorado	279
4	New Jersey	465		29	Ohio	279
13	New Mexico	367		31	North Carolina	267
3	New York	514		32	Oklahoma	261
31	North Carolina	267		33	Michigan	242
40	North Dakota	204		34	Minnesota	237
29	Ohio	279		35	Washington	232
32	Oklahoma	261		36	Arkansas	231
42	Oregon	200		37	Nebraska	227
20	Pennsylvania	307		38	Iowa	220
21	Rhode Island	302		39	Utah	215
26	South Carolina	295		40	North Dakota	204
50	South Dakota	152		41	Kansas	202
11	Tennessee	377		42	Oregon	200
19	Texas	324		43	Wisconsin	194
39	Utah	215		44	Montana	177
47	Vermont	166		45	New Hampshire	176
8	Virginia	389		46	Idaho	168
35	Washington	232		47	Vermont	166
22	West Virginia	300		48	Wyoming	160
43	Wisconsin	194		49	Maine	153
48	Wyoming	160		50	South Dakota	152
					District of Columbia	2,066

Source: CQ Press using data from U.S. Department of Labor, Bureau of Labor Statistics
   "Occupational Employment Statistics" (http://www.bls.gov/oes/)
*Occupational code 33-9032. As of May 2008. Does not include self-employed.

U.S. District Court Judges in 2008

National Total = 678 Judges*

ALPHA ORDER					RANK ORDER			

RANK	STATE	JUDGES	% of USA		RANK	STATE	JUDGES	% of USA
13	Alabama	14	2.1%		1	California	61	9.0%
40	Alaska	3	0.4%		2	New York	52	7.7%
16	Arizona	13	1.9%		2	Texas	52	7.7%
26	Arkansas	8	1.2%		4	Pennsylvania	38	5.6%
1	California	61	9.0%		5	Florida	37	5.4%
29	Colorado	7	1.0%		6	Illinois	30	4.4%
26	Connecticut	8	1.2%		7	Louisiana	22	3.2%
38	Delaware	4	0.6%		8	Ohio	20	2.9%
5	Florida	37	5.4%		9	Michigan	19	2.8%
10	Georgia	18	2.7%		10	Georgia	18	2.7%
38	Hawaii	4	0.6%		11	New Jersey	17	2.5%
48	Idaho	2	0.3%		12	Virginia	15	2.2%
6	Illinois	30	4.4%		13	Alabama	14	2.1%
21	Indiana	10	1.5%		13	Missouri	14	2.1%
36	Iowa	5	0.7%		13	Tennessee	14	2.1%
34	Kansas	6	0.9%		16	Arizona	13	1.9%
21	Kentucky	10	1.5%		16	Massachusetts	13	1.9%
7	Louisiana	22	3.2%		16	North Carolina	13	1.9%
40	Maine	3	0.4%		19	Oklahoma	11	1.6%
21	Maryland	10	1.5%		19	Washington	11	1.6%
16	Massachusetts	13	1.9%		21	Indiana	10	1.5%
9	Michigan	19	2.8%		21	Kentucky	10	1.5%
29	Minnesota	7	1.0%		21	Maryland	10	1.5%
25	Mississippi	9	1.3%		21	South Carolina	10	1.5%
13	Missouri	14	2.1%		25	Mississippi	9	1.3%
40	Montana	3	0.4%		26	Arkansas	8	1.2%
40	Nebraska	3	0.4%		26	Connecticut	8	1.2%
29	Nevada	7	1.0%		26	West Virginia	8	1.2%
40	New Hampshire	3	0.4%		29	Colorado	7	1.0%
11	New Jersey	17	2.5%		29	Minnesota	7	1.0%
29	New Mexico	7	1.0%		29	Nevada	7	1.0%
2	New York	52	7.7%		29	New Mexico	7	1.0%
16	North Carolina	13	1.9%		29	Wisconsin	7	1.0%
48	North Dakota	2	0.3%		34	Kansas	6	0.9%
8	Ohio	20	2.9%		34	Oregon	6	0.9%
19	Oklahoma	11	1.6%		36	Iowa	5	0.7%
34	Oregon	6	0.9%		36	Utah	5	0.7%
4	Pennsylvania	38	5.6%		38	Delaware	4	0.6%
40	Rhode Island	3	0.4%		38	Hawaii	4	0.6%
21	South Carolina	10	1.5%		40	Alaska	3	0.4%
40	South Dakota	3	0.4%		40	Maine	3	0.4%
13	Tennessee	14	2.1%		40	Montana	3	0.4%
2	Texas	52	7.7%		40	Nebraska	3	0.4%
36	Utah	5	0.7%		40	New Hampshire	3	0.4%
48	Vermont	2	0.3%		40	Rhode Island	3	0.4%
12	Virginia	15	2.2%		40	South Dakota	3	0.4%
19	Washington	11	1.6%		40	Wyoming	3	0.4%
26	West Virginia	8	1.2%		48	Idaho	2	0.3%
29	Wisconsin	7	1.0%		48	North Dakota	2	0.3%
40	Wyoming	3	0.4%		48	Vermont	2	0.3%
						District of Columbia	15	2.2%

Source: Administrative Office of the United States Courts
  "2008 Federal Court Management Statistics" (http://www.uscourts.gov/fcmstat/index.html)
*Total includes 11 judgeships in U.S. territories.

Population per U.S. District Court Judge in 2008

National Rate = 456,334 People per U.S. District Judge*

<table>
<tr><td colspan="3">ALPHA ORDER</td><td colspan="3">RANK ORDER</td></tr>
<tr><td>RANK</td><td>STATE</td><td>RATE</td><td>RANK</td><td>STATE</td><td>RATE</td></tr>
<tr><td>36</td><td>Alabama</td><td>334,105</td><td>1</td><td>Wisconsin</td><td>803,944</td></tr>
<tr><td>46</td><td>Alaska</td><td>229,375</td><td>2</td><td>Idaho</td><td>763,753</td></tr>
<tr><td>20</td><td>Arizona</td><td>499,952</td><td>3</td><td>Minnesota</td><td>747,224</td></tr>
<tr><td>34</td><td>Arkansas</td><td>358,471</td><td>4</td><td>North Carolina</td><td>711,318</td></tr>
<tr><td>8</td><td>California</td><td>599,678</td><td>5</td><td>Colorado</td><td>705,030</td></tr>
<tr><td>5</td><td>Colorado</td><td>705,030</td><td>6</td><td>Indiana</td><td>638,831</td></tr>
<tr><td>28</td><td>Connecticut</td><td>437,867</td><td>7</td><td>Oregon</td><td>630,499</td></tr>
<tr><td>48</td><td>Delaware</td><td>219,053</td><td>8</td><td>California</td><td>599,678</td></tr>
<tr><td>21</td><td>Florida</td><td>497,943</td><td>9</td><td>Iowa</td><td>598,797</td></tr>
<tr><td>15</td><td>Georgia</td><td>538,769</td><td>10</td><td>Washington</td><td>596,916</td></tr>
<tr><td>41</td><td>Hawaii</td><td>321,870</td><td>11</td><td>Nebraska</td><td>593,983</td></tr>
<tr><td>2</td><td>Idaho</td><td>763,753</td><td>12</td><td>Ohio</td><td>576,404</td></tr>
<tr><td>30</td><td>Illinois</td><td>428,098</td><td>13</td><td>Maryland</td><td>565,866</td></tr>
<tr><td>6</td><td>Indiana</td><td>638,831</td><td>14</td><td>Utah</td><td>545,469</td></tr>
<tr><td>9</td><td>Iowa</td><td>598,797</td><td>15</td><td>Georgia</td><td>538,769</td></tr>
<tr><td>23</td><td>Kansas</td><td>466,229</td><td>16</td><td>Michigan</td><td>526,447</td></tr>
<tr><td>29</td><td>Kentucky</td><td>428,793</td><td>17</td><td>Virginia</td><td>519,695</td></tr>
<tr><td>49</td><td>Louisiana</td><td>202,342</td><td>18</td><td>New Jersey</td><td>509,612</td></tr>
<tr><td>27</td><td>Maine</td><td>439,897</td><td>19</td><td>Massachusetts</td><td>503,353</td></tr>
<tr><td>13</td><td>Maryland</td><td>565,866</td><td>20</td><td>Arizona</td><td>499,952</td></tr>
<tr><td>19</td><td>Massachusetts</td><td>503,353</td><td>21</td><td>Florida</td><td>497,943</td></tr>
<tr><td>16</td><td>Michigan</td><td>526,447</td><td>22</td><td>Texas</td><td>467,390</td></tr>
<tr><td>3</td><td>Minnesota</td><td>747,224</td><td>23</td><td>Kansas</td><td>466,229</td></tr>
<tr><td>39</td><td>Mississippi</td><td>326,690</td><td>24</td><td>South Carolina</td><td>450,328</td></tr>
<tr><td>31</td><td>Missouri</td><td>425,453</td><td>25</td><td>Tennessee</td><td>445,747</td></tr>
<tr><td>40</td><td>Montana</td><td>322,678</td><td>26</td><td>New Hampshire</td><td>440,624</td></tr>
<tr><td>11</td><td>Nebraska</td><td>593,983</td><td>27</td><td>Maine</td><td>439,897</td></tr>
<tr><td>33</td><td>Nevada</td><td>373,682</td><td>28</td><td>Connecticut</td><td>437,867</td></tr>
<tr><td>26</td><td>New Hampshire</td><td>440,624</td><td>29</td><td>Kentucky</td><td>428,793</td></tr>
<tr><td>18</td><td>New Jersey</td><td>509,612</td><td>30</td><td>Illinois</td><td>428,098</td></tr>
<tr><td>44</td><td>New Mexico</td><td>283,823</td><td>31</td><td>Missouri</td><td>425,453</td></tr>
<tr><td>32</td><td>New York</td><td>374,381</td><td>32</td><td>New York</td><td>374,381</td></tr>
<tr><td>4</td><td>North Carolina</td><td>711,318</td><td>33</td><td>Nevada</td><td>373,682</td></tr>
<tr><td>42</td><td>North Dakota</td><td>320,711</td><td>34</td><td>Arkansas</td><td>358,471</td></tr>
<tr><td>12</td><td>Ohio</td><td>576,404</td><td>35</td><td>Rhode Island</td><td>351,167</td></tr>
<tr><td>37</td><td>Oklahoma</td><td>331,275</td><td>36</td><td>Alabama</td><td>334,105</td></tr>
<tr><td>7</td><td>Oregon</td><td>630,499</td><td>37</td><td>Oklahoma</td><td>331,275</td></tr>
<tr><td>38</td><td>Pennsylvania</td><td>330,694</td><td>38</td><td>Pennsylvania</td><td>330,694</td></tr>
<tr><td>35</td><td>Rhode Island</td><td>351,167</td><td>39</td><td>Mississippi</td><td>326,690</td></tr>
<tr><td>24</td><td>South Carolina</td><td>450,328</td><td>40</td><td>Montana</td><td>322,678</td></tr>
<tr><td>45</td><td>South Dakota</td><td>268,177</td><td>41</td><td>Hawaii</td><td>321,870</td></tr>
<tr><td>25</td><td>Tennessee</td><td>445,747</td><td>42</td><td>North Dakota</td><td>320,711</td></tr>
<tr><td>22</td><td>Texas</td><td>467,390</td><td>43</td><td>Vermont</td><td>310,525</td></tr>
<tr><td>14</td><td>Utah</td><td>545,469</td><td>44</td><td>New Mexico</td><td>283,823</td></tr>
<tr><td>43</td><td>Vermont</td><td>310,525</td><td>45</td><td>South Dakota</td><td>268,177</td></tr>
<tr><td>17</td><td>Virginia</td><td>519,695</td><td>46</td><td>Alaska</td><td>229,375</td></tr>
<tr><td>10</td><td>Washington</td><td>596,916</td><td>47</td><td>West Virginia</td><td>226,859</td></tr>
<tr><td>47</td><td>West Virginia</td><td>226,859</td><td>48</td><td>Delaware</td><td>219,053</td></tr>
<tr><td>1</td><td>Wisconsin</td><td>803,944</td><td>49</td><td>Louisiana</td><td>202,342</td></tr>
<tr><td>50</td><td>Wyoming</td><td>177,660</td><td>50</td><td>Wyoming</td><td>177,660</td></tr>
<tr><td></td><td></td><td></td><td></td><td>District of Columbia</td><td>39,338</td></tr>
</table>

Source: CQ Press using data from Administrative Office of the United States Courts
"2008 Federal Court Management Statistics" (http://www.uscourts.gov/fcmstat/index.html)
*National rate does not include judgeships or population in U.S. territories.

Authorized Wiretaps in 2008

National Total = 1,505 Wiretaps*

ALPHA ORDER

RANK	STATE	WIRETAPS	% of USA
NA	Alabama**	NA	NA
23	Alaska	0	0.0%
10	Arizona	22	1.5%
NA	Arkansas**	NA	NA
2	California	418	27.8%
5	Colorado	77	5.1%
23	Connecticut	0	0.0%
23	Delaware	0	0.0%
4	Florida	102	6.8%
8	Georgia	44	2.9%
21	Hawaii	1	0.1%
23	Idaho	0	0.0%
12	Illinois	18	1.2%
19	Indiana	2	0.1%
23	Iowa	0	0.0%
17	Kansas	3	0.2%
NA	Kentucky**	NA	NA
23	Louisiana	0	0.0%
23	Maine	0	0.0%
5	Maryland	77	5.1%
15	Massachusetts	5	0.3%
NA	Michigan**	NA	NA
23	Minnesota	0	0.0%
23	Mississippi	0	0.0%
23	Missouri	0	0.0%
NA	Montana**	NA	NA
23	Nebraska	0	0.0%
7	Nevada	48	3.2%
23	New Hampshire	0	0.0%
3	New Jersey	175	11.6%
23	New Mexico	0	0.0%
1	New York	433	28.8%
23	North Carolina	0	0.0%
23	North Dakota	0	0.0%
14	Ohio	6	0.4%
17	Oklahoma	3	0.2%
16	Oregon	4	0.3%
11	Pennsylvania	21	1.4%
23	Rhode Island	0	0.0%
23	South Carolina	0	0.0%
23	South Dakota	0	0.0%
9	Tennessee	34	2.3%
19	Texas	2	0.1%
23	Utah	0	0.0%
NA	Vermont**	NA	NA
23	Virginia	0	0.0%
23	Washington	0	0.0%
23	West Virginia	0	0.0%
13	Wisconsin	9	0.6%
21	Wyoming	1	0.1%

RANK ORDER

RANK	STATE	WIRETAPS	% of USA
1	New York	433	28.8%
2	California	418	27.8%
3	New Jersey	175	11.6%
4	Florida	102	6.8%
5	Colorado	77	5.1%
5	Maryland	77	5.1%
7	Nevada	48	3.2%
8	Georgia	44	2.9%
9	Tennessee	34	2.3%
10	Arizona	22	1.5%
11	Pennsylvania	21	1.4%
12	Illinois	18	1.2%
13	Wisconsin	9	0.6%
14	Ohio	6	0.4%
15	Massachusetts	5	0.3%
16	Oregon	4	0.3%
17	Kansas	3	0.2%
17	Oklahoma	3	0.2%
19	Indiana	2	0.1%
19	Texas	2	0.1%
21	Hawaii	1	0.1%
21	Wyoming	1	0.1%
23	Alaska	0	0.0%
23	Connecticut	0	0.0%
23	Delaware	0	0.0%
23	Idaho	0	0.0%
23	Iowa	0	0.0%
23	Louisiana	0	0.0%
23	Maine	0	0.0%
23	Minnesota	0	0.0%
23	Mississippi	0	0.0%
23	Missouri	0	0.0%
23	Nebraska	0	0.0%
23	New Hampshire	0	0.0%
23	New Mexico	0	0.0%
23	North Carolina	0	0.0%
23	North Dakota	0	0.0%
23	Rhode Island	0	0.0%
23	South Carolina	0	0.0%
23	South Dakota	0	0.0%
23	Utah	0	0.0%
23	Virginia	0	0.0%
23	Washington	0	0.0%
23	West Virginia	0	0.0%
NA	Alabama**	NA	NA
NA	Arkansas**	NA	NA
NA	Kentucky**	NA	NA
NA	Michigan**	NA	NA
NA	Montana**	NA	NA
NA	Vermont**	NA	NA
	District of Columbia	0	0.0%

Source: Administrative Office of the United States Courts
"2008 Wiretap Report" (2009) (www.uscourts.gov/wiretap08/contents.html)
*Total does not include 386 wiretaps authorized under federal statute.
**No state statute authorizing wiretaps.

VII. OFFENSES

Crimes in 2008

National Total = 11,149,927 Crimes*

ALPHA ORDER

RANK	STATE	CRIMES	% of USA
20	Alabama	211,454	1.9%
46	Alaska	24,598	0.2%
11	Arizona	307,979	2.8%
28	Arkansas	123,882	1.1%
1	California	1,265,920	11.4%
25	Colorado	157,671	1.4%
33	Connecticut	96,514	0.9%
40	Delaware	37,444	0.3%
3	Florida	885,199	7.9%
6	Georgia	435,319	3.9%
39	Hawaii	49,516	0.4%
41	Idaho	35,502	0.3%
5	Illinois	446,135	4.0%
15	Indiana	233,998	2.1%
36	Iowa	81,209	0.7%
31	Kansas	106,140	1.0%
29	Kentucky	122,960	1.1%
21	Louisiana	197,574	1.8%
42	Maine	33,832	0.3%
16	Maryland	233,558	2.1%
22	Massachusetts	185,133	1.7%
10	Michigan	343,751	3.1%
24	Minnesota	162,527	1.5%
34	Mississippi	94,781	0.9%
14	Missouri	246,404	2.2%
45	Montana	27,679	0.2%
37	Nebraska	56,754	0.5%
30	Nevada	108,477	1.0%
44	New Hampshire	29,595	0.3%
17	New Jersey	227,477	2.0%
35	New Mexico	90,468	0.8%
4	New York	466,118	4.2%
8	North Carolina	416,060	3.7%
50	North Dakota	13,220	0.1%
7	Ohio	431,859	3.9%
26	Oklahoma	144,568	1.3%
27	Oregon	134,144	1.2%
9	Pennsylvania	351,068	3.1%
43	Rhode Island	32,470	0.3%
18	South Carolina	222,374	2.0%
49	South Dakota	14,854	0.1%
12	Tennessee	296,142	2.7%
2	Texas	1,093,134	9.8%
32	Utah	97,943	0.9%
47	Vermont	16,615	0.1%
19	Virginia	215,516	1.9%
13	Washington	267,839	2.4%
38	West Virginia	51,575	0.5%
23	Wisconsin	170,548	1.5%
48	Wyoming	15,710	0.1%

RANK ORDER

RANK	STATE	CRIMES	% of USA
1	California	1,265,920	11.4%
2	Texas	1,093,134	9.8%
3	Florida	885,199	7.9%
4	New York	466,118	4.2%
5	Illinois	446,135	4.0%
6	Georgia	435,319	3.9%
7	Ohio	431,859	3.9%
8	North Carolina	416,060	3.7%
9	Pennsylvania	351,068	3.1%
10	Michigan	343,751	3.1%
11	Arizona	307,979	2.8%
12	Tennessee	296,142	2.7%
13	Washington	267,839	2.4%
14	Missouri	246,404	2.2%
15	Indiana	233,998	2.1%
16	Maryland	233,558	2.1%
17	New Jersey	227,477	2.0%
18	South Carolina	222,374	2.0%
19	Virginia	215,516	1.9%
20	Alabama	211,454	1.9%
21	Louisiana	197,574	1.8%
22	Massachusetts	185,133	1.7%
23	Wisconsin	170,548	1.5%
24	Minnesota	162,527	1.5%
25	Colorado	157,671	1.4%
26	Oklahoma	144,568	1.3%
27	Oregon	134,144	1.2%
28	Arkansas	123,882	1.1%
29	Kentucky	122,960	1.1%
30	Nevada	108,477	1.0%
31	Kansas	106,140	1.0%
32	Utah	97,943	0.9%
33	Connecticut	96,514	0.9%
34	Mississippi	94,781	0.9%
35	New Mexico	90,468	0.8%
36	Iowa	81,209	0.7%
37	Nebraska	56,754	0.5%
38	West Virginia	51,575	0.5%
39	Hawaii	49,516	0.4%
40	Delaware	37,444	0.3%
41	Idaho	35,502	0.3%
42	Maine	33,832	0.3%
43	Rhode Island	32,470	0.3%
44	New Hampshire	29,595	0.3%
45	Montana	27,679	0.2%
46	Alaska	24,598	0.2%
47	Vermont	16,615	0.1%
48	Wyoming	15,710	0.1%
49	South Dakota	14,854	0.1%
50	North Dakota	13,220	0.1%
	District of Columbia	38,720	0.3%

Source: CQ Press using reported data from the Federal Bureau of Investigation
"Crime in the United States 2008" (Uniform Crime Reports, September 14, 2009, http://www.fbi.gov/ucr/ucr.htm)
*Includes murder, rape, robbery, aggravated assault, burglary, larceny-theft, and motor vehicle theft.

Average Time Between Crimes in 2008

National Rate = A Crime Occurs Every 2.8 Seconds*

ALPHA ORDER

RANK	STATE	MINUTES.SECONDS
31	Alabama	2.29
5	Alaska	21.26
40	Arizona	1.43
23	Arkansas	4.15
50	California	0.25
26	Colorado	3.20
18	Connecticut	5.28
11	Delaware	14.05
48	Florida	0.36
44	Georgia	1.13
12	Hawaii	10.38
10	Idaho	14.51
46	Illinois	1.11
36	Indiana	2.15
15	Iowa	6.29
20	Kansas	4.58
22	Kentucky	4.17
30	Louisiana	2.40
9	Maine	15.35
35	Maryland	2.16
29	Massachusetts	2.51
41	Michigan	1.32
27	Minnesota	3.14
17	Mississippi	5.34
37	Missouri	2.08
6	Montana	19.02
14	Nebraska	9.17
21	Nevada	4.52
7	New Hampshire	17.49
34	New Jersey	2.19
16	New Mexico	5.50
47	New York	1.08
43	North Carolina	1.16
1	North Dakota	39.52
44	Ohio	1.13
25	Oklahoma	3.39
24	Oregon	3.56
42	Pennsylvania	1.30
8	Rhode Island	16.14
33	South Carolina	2.22
2	South Dakota	35.29
39	Tennessee	1.47
49	Texas	0.29
19	Utah	5.23
4	Vermont	31.43
32	Virginia	2.27
38	Washington	1.58
13	West Virginia	10.13
28	Wisconsin	3.05
3	Wyoming	33.33

RANK ORDER

RANK	STATE	MINUTES.SECONDS
1	North Dakota	39.52
2	South Dakota	35.29
3	Wyoming	33.33
4	Vermont	31.43
5	Alaska	21.26
6	Montana	19.02
7	New Hampshire	17.49
8	Rhode Island	16.14
9	Maine	15.35
10	Idaho	14.51
11	Delaware	14.05
12	Hawaii	10.38
13	West Virginia	10.13
14	Nebraska	9.17
15	Iowa	6.29
16	New Mexico	5.50
17	Mississippi	5.34
18	Connecticut	5.28
19	Utah	5.23
20	Kansas	4.58
21	Nevada	4.52
22	Kentucky	4.17
23	Arkansas	4.15
24	Oregon	3.56
25	Oklahoma	3.39
26	Colorado	3.20
27	Minnesota	3.14
28	Wisconsin	3.05
29	Massachusetts	2.51
30	Louisiana	2.40
31	Alabama	2.29
32	Virginia	2.27
33	South Carolina	2.22
34	New Jersey	2.19
35	Maryland	2.16
36	Indiana	2.15
37	Missouri	2.08
38	Washington	1.58
39	Tennessee	1.47
40	Arizona	1.43
41	Michigan	1.32
42	Pennsylvania	1.30
43	North Carolina	1.16
44	Georgia	1.13
44	Ohio	1.13
46	Illinois	1.11
47	New York	1.08
48	Florida	0.36
49	Texas	0.29
50	California	0.25
	District of Columbia	13.37

Source: CQ Press using reported data from the Federal Bureau of Investigation
"Crime in the United States 2008" (Uniform Crime Reports, September 14, 2009, http://www.fbi.gov/ucr/ucr.htm)
*Includes murder, rape, robbery, aggravated assault, burglary, larceny-theft, and motor vehicle theft.

Crimes per Square Mile in 2008

National Rate = 2.9 Crimes per Square Mile*

ALPHA ORDER

RANK	STATE	RATE
21	Alabama	4.0
50	Alaska	0.0
28	Arizona	2.7
30	Arkansas	2.3
10	California	7.7
36	Colorado	1.5
5	Connecticut	17.4
6	Delaware	15.0
7	Florida	13.5
14	Georgia	7.3
19	Hawaii	4.5
45	Idaho	0.4
10	Illinois	7.7
17	Indiana	6.4
37	Iowa	1.4
39	Kansas	1.3
27	Kentucky	3.0
22	Louisiana	3.8
41	Maine	1.0
3	Maryland	18.8
4	Massachusetts	17.5
24	Michigan	3.6
34	Minnesota	1.9
33	Mississippi	2.0
25	Missouri	3.5
46	Montana	0.2
43	Nebraska	0.7
41	Nevada	1.0
26	New Hampshire	3.2
1	New Jersey	26.1
43	New Mexico	0.7
9	New York	8.5
10	North Carolina	7.7
46	North Dakota	0.2
8	Ohio	9.6
31	Oklahoma	2.1
37	Oregon	1.4
13	Pennsylvania	7.6
2	Rhode Island	21.0
16	South Carolina	6.9
46	South Dakota	0.2
15	Tennessee	7.0
20	Texas	4.1
40	Utah	1.2
35	Vermont	1.7
18	Virginia	5.0
22	Washington	3.8
31	West Virginia	2.1
29	Wisconsin	2.6
46	Wyoming	0.2

RANK ORDER

RANK	STATE	RATE
1	New Jersey	26.1
2	Rhode Island	21.0
3	Maryland	18.8
4	Massachusetts	17.5
5	Connecticut	17.4
6	Delaware	15.0
7	Florida	13.5
8	Ohio	9.6
9	New York	8.5
10	California	7.7
10	Illinois	7.7
10	North Carolina	7.7
13	Pennsylvania	7.6
14	Georgia	7.3
15	Tennessee	7.0
16	South Carolina	6.9
17	Indiana	6.4
18	Virginia	5.0
19	Hawaii	4.5
20	Texas	4.1
21	Alabama	4.0
22	Louisiana	3.8
22	Washington	3.8
24	Michigan	3.6
25	Missouri	3.5
26	New Hampshire	3.2
27	Kentucky	3.0
28	Arizona	2.7
29	Wisconsin	2.6
30	Arkansas	2.3
31	Oklahoma	2.1
31	West Virginia	2.1
33	Mississippi	2.0
34	Minnesota	1.9
35	Vermont	1.7
36	Colorado	1.5
37	Iowa	1.4
37	Oregon	1.4
39	Kansas	1.3
40	Utah	1.2
41	Maine	1.0
41	Nevada	1.0
43	Nebraska	0.7
43	New Mexico	0.7
45	Idaho	0.4
46	Montana	0.2
46	North Dakota	0.2
46	South Dakota	0.2
46	Wyoming	0.2
50	Alaska	0.0

District of Columbia	569.4

Source: CQ Press using reported data from the Federal Bureau of Investigation
    "Crime in the United States 2008" (Uniform Crime Reports, September 14, 2009, http://www.fbi.gov/ucr/ucr.htm)
*Includes murder, rape, robbery, aggravated assault, burglary, larceny-theft, and motor vehicle theft. "Square miles" includes total land and water area.

Percent Change in Number of Crimes: 2007 to 2008

National Percent Change = 0.9% Decrease*

ALPHA ORDER

RANK	STATE	PERCENT CHANGE
8	Alabama	3.4
49	Alaska	(10.9)
26	Arizona	(0.8)
32	Arkansas	(2.5)
33	California	(2.6)
36	Colorado	(3.3)
6	Connecticut	3.8
4	Delaware	6.7
20	Florida	0.8
6	Georgia	3.8
50	Hawaii	(14.2)
38	Idaho	(4.8)
22	Illinois	0.1
29	Indiana	(1.1)
44	Iowa	(6.6)
47	Kansas	(7.5)
9	Kentucky	3.0
37	Louisiana	(4.2)
19	Maine	0.9
12	Maryland	2.1
14	Massachusetts	1.7
40	Michigan	(5.2)
42	Minnesota	(6.0)
46	Mississippi	(7.0)
30	Missouri	(1.2)
41	Montana	(5.3)
48	Nebraska	(7.7)
44	Nevada	(6.6)
1	New Hampshire	10.8
9	New Jersey	3.0
5	New Mexico	4.6
18	New York	1.0
20	North Carolina	0.8
14	North Dakota	1.7
27	Ohio	(0.9)
24	Oklahoma	(0.7)
43	Oregon	(6.1)
14	Pennsylvania	1.7
3	Rhode Island	7.7
23	South Carolina	(0.3)
11	South Dakota	2.4
24	Tennessee	(0.7)
31	Texas	(1.3)
27	Utah	(0.9)
2	Vermont	9.3
12	Virginia	2.1
39	Washington	(5.1)
17	West Virginia	1.6
34	Wisconsin	(2.7)
35	Wyoming	(3.2)

RANK ORDER

RANK	STATE	PERCENT CHANGE
1	New Hampshire	10.8
2	Vermont	9.3
3	Rhode Island	7.7
4	Delaware	6.7
5	New Mexico	4.6
6	Connecticut	3.8
6	Georgia	3.8
8	Alabama	3.4
9	Kentucky	3.0
9	New Jersey	3.0
11	South Dakota	2.4
12	Maryland	2.1
12	Virginia	2.1
14	Massachusetts	1.7
14	North Dakota	1.7
14	Pennsylvania	1.7
17	West Virginia	1.6
18	New York	1.0
19	Maine	0.9
20	Florida	0.8
20	North Carolina	0.8
22	Illinois	0.1
23	South Carolina	(0.3)
24	Oklahoma	(0.7)
24	Tennessee	(0.7)
26	Arizona	(0.8)
27	Ohio	(0.9)
27	Utah	(0.9)
29	Indiana	(1.1)
30	Missouri	(1.2)
31	Texas	(1.3)
32	Arkansas	(2.5)
33	California	(2.6)
34	Wisconsin	(2.7)
35	Wyoming	(3.2)
36	Colorado	(3.3)
37	Louisiana	(4.2)
38	Idaho	(4.8)
39	Washington	(5.1)
40	Michigan	(5.2)
41	Montana	(5.3)
42	Minnesota	(6.0)
43	Oregon	(6.1)
44	Iowa	(6.6)
44	Nevada	(6.6)
46	Mississippi	(7.0)
47	Kansas	(7.5)
48	Nebraska	(7.7)
49	Alaska	(10.9)
50	Hawaii	(14.2)

District of Columbia   4.0

Source: CQ Press using reported data from the Federal Bureau of Investigation
"Crime in the United States 2008" (Uniform Crime Reports, September 14, 2009, http://www.fbi.gov/ucr/ucr.htm)
*Includes murder, rape, robbery, aggravated assault, burglary, larceny-theft, and motor vehicle theft.

Crime Rate in 2008

National Rate = 3,667.0 Crimes per 100,000 Population*

ALPHA ORDER

RANK	STATE	RATE
6	Alabama	4,535.7
22	Alaska	3,584.2
4	Arizona	4,738.0
11	Arkansas	4,338.5
26	California	3,444.1
29	Colorado	3,192.1
41	Connecticut	2,756.5
12	Delaware	4,288.7
2	Florida	4,829.7
8	Georgia	4,494.4
18	Hawaii	3,843.8
47	Idaho	2,329.8
25	Illinois	3,458.0
21	Indiana	3,669.6
42	Iowa	2,704.7
19	Kansas	3,787.8
35	Kentucky	2,880.1
10	Louisiana	4,479.3
45	Maine	2,569.9
15	Maryland	4,145.8
37	Massachusetts	2,849.1
27	Michigan	3,436.3
31	Minnesota	3,113.4
28	Mississippi	3,225.3
14	Missouri	4,168.1
36	Montana	2,861.1
30	Nebraska	3,182.3
13	Nevada	4,172.0
48	New Hampshire	2,249.1
44	New Jersey	2,619.9
5	New Mexico	4,559.1
46	New York	2,391.6
7	North Carolina	4,511.4
49	North Dakota	2,060.9
20	Ohio	3,759.9
17	Oklahoma	3,969.1
24	Oregon	3,539.4
39	Pennsylvania	2,820.2
32	Rhode Island	3,090.0
1	South Carolina	4,963.9
50	South Dakota	1,847.0
3	Tennessee	4,765.0
9	Texas	4,493.5
23	Utah	3,579.2
43	Vermont	2,674.4
40	Virginia	2,774.0
16	Washington	4,089.6
38	West Virginia	2,842.4
33	Wisconsin	3,030.4
34	Wyoming	2,949.3

RANK ORDER

RANK	STATE	RATE
1	South Carolina	4,963.9
2	Florida	4,829.7
3	Tennessee	4,765.0
4	Arizona	4,738.0
5	New Mexico	4,559.1
6	Alabama	4,535.7
7	North Carolina	4,511.4
8	Georgia	4,494.4
9	Texas	4,493.5
10	Louisiana	4,479.3
11	Arkansas	4,338.5
12	Delaware	4,288.7
13	Nevada	4,172.0
14	Missouri	4,168.1
15	Maryland	4,145.8
16	Washington	4,089.6
17	Oklahoma	3,969.1
18	Hawaii	3,843.8
19	Kansas	3,787.8
20	Ohio	3,759.9
21	Indiana	3,669.6
22	Alaska	3,584.2
23	Utah	3,579.2
24	Oregon	3,539.4
25	Illinois	3,458.0
26	California	3,444.1
27	Michigan	3,436.3
28	Mississippi	3,225.3
29	Colorado	3,192.1
30	Nebraska	3,182.3
31	Minnesota	3,113.4
32	Rhode Island	3,090.0
33	Wisconsin	3,030.4
34	Wyoming	2,949.3
35	Kentucky	2,880.1
36	Montana	2,861.1
37	Massachusetts	2,849.1
38	West Virginia	2,842.4
39	Pennsylvania	2,820.2
40	Virginia	2,774.0
41	Connecticut	2,756.5
42	Iowa	2,704.7
43	Vermont	2,674.4
44	New Jersey	2,619.9
45	Maine	2,569.9
46	New York	2,391.6
47	Idaho	2,329.8
48	New Hampshire	2,249.1
49	North Dakota	2,060.9
50	South Dakota	1,847.0

District of Columbia	6,542.3

Source: CQ Press using reported data from the Federal Bureau of Investigation
    "Crime in the United States 2008" (Uniform Crime Reports, September 14, 2009, http://www.fbi.gov/ucr/ucr.htm)
*Includes murder, rape, robbery, aggravated assault, burglary, larceny-theft, and motor vehicle theft.

Percent Change in Crime Rate: 2007 to 2008

National Percent Change = 1.7% Decrease*

ALPHA ORDER			RANK ORDER		
RANK	STATE	PERCENT CHANGE	RANK	STATE	PERCENT CHANGE
8	Alabama	2.6	1	New Hampshire	10.8
49	Alaska	(11.3)	2	Vermont	9.3
32	Arizona	(3.2)	3	Rhode Island	8.4
32	Arkansas	(3.2)	4	Delaware	5.7
30	California	(3.1)	5	New Mexico	3.9
36	Colorado	(4.8)	6	Connecticut	3.8
6	Connecticut	3.8	7	New Jersey	3.0
4	Delaware	5.7	8	Alabama	2.6
19	Florida	0.4	9	Kentucky	2.4
10	Georgia	2.3	10	Georgia	2.3
50	Hawaii	(14.5)	11	Maryland	1.8
38	Idaho	(6.3)	12	Pennsylvania	1.5
21	Illinois	(0.3)	12	West Virginia	1.5
25	Indiana	(1.6)	14	North Dakota	1.4
43	Iowa	(7.1)	14	South Dakota	1.4
48	Kansas	(8.3)	14	Virginia	1.4
9	Kentucky	2.4	17	Maine	0.9
42	Louisiana	(6.8)	17	Massachusetts	0.9
17	Maine	0.9	19	Florida	0.4
11	Maryland	1.8	20	New York	0.0
17	Massachusetts	0.9	21	Illinois	(0.3)
35	Michigan	(4.6)	22	North Carolina	(0.9)
41	Minnesota	(6.4)	23	Ohio	(1.0)
45	Mississippi	(7.6)	24	Oklahoma	(1.4)
27	Missouri	(1.8)	25	Indiana	(1.6)
38	Montana	(6.3)	25	Tennessee	(1.6)
47	Nebraska	(8.1)	27	Missouri	(1.8)
46	Nevada	(7.9)	28	South Carolina	(1.9)
1	New Hampshire	10.8	29	Texas	(3.0)
7	New Jersey	3.0	30	California	(3.1)
5	New Mexico	3.9	30	Wisconsin	(3.1)
20	New York	0.0	32	Arizona	(3.2)
22	North Carolina	(0.9)	32	Arkansas	(3.2)
14	North Dakota	1.4	34	Utah	(4.2)
23	Ohio	(1.0)	35	Michigan	(4.6)
24	Oklahoma	(1.4)	36	Colorado	(4.8)
44	Oregon	(7.2)	37	Wyoming	(5.0)
12	Pennsylvania	1.5	38	Idaho	(6.3)
3	Rhode Island	8.4	38	Montana	(6.3)
28	South Carolina	(1.9)	38	Washington	(6.3)
14	South Dakota	1.4	41	Minnesota	(6.4)
25	Tennessee	(1.6)	42	Louisiana	(6.8)
29	Texas	(3.0)	43	Iowa	(7.1)
34	Utah	(4.2)	44	Oregon	(7.2)
2	Vermont	9.3	45	Mississippi	(7.6)
14	Virginia	1.4	46	Nevada	(7.9)
38	Washington	(6.3)	47	Nebraska	(8.1)
12	West Virginia	1.5	48	Kansas	(8.3)
30	Wisconsin	(3.1)	49	Alaska	(11.3)
37	Wyoming	(5.0)	50	Hawaii	(14.5)

District of Columbia   3.4

Source: CQ Press using reported data from the Federal Bureau of Investigation
"Crime in the United States 2008" (Uniform Crime Reports, September 14, 2009, http://www.fbi.gov/ucr/ucr.htm)
*Includes murder, rape, robbery, aggravated assault, burglary, larceny-theft, and motor vehicle theft.

Violent Crimes in 2008

National Total = 1,382,012 Violent Crimes*

ALPHA ORDER

RANK	STATE	CRIMES	% of USA
21	Alabama	21,111	1.5%
40	Alaska	4,474	0.3%
16	Arizona	29,059	2.1%
27	Arkansas	14,374	1.0%
1	California	185,173	13.4%
25	Colorado	16,946	1.2%
32	Connecticut	10,427	0.8%
36	Delaware	6,141	0.4%
2	Florida	126,265	9.1%
8	Georgia	46,384	3.4%
41	Hawaii	3,512	0.3%
42	Idaho	3,483	0.3%
5	Illinois	67,780	4.9%
20	Indiana	21,283	1.5%
34	Iowa	8,520	0.6%
31	Kansas	11,505	0.8%
30	Kentucky	12,646	0.9%
17	Louisiana	28,944	2.1%
47	Maine	1,547	0.1%
12	Maryland	35,393	2.6%
15	Massachusetts	29,174	2.1%
7	Michigan	50,166	3.6%
28	Minnesota	13,717	1.0%
35	Mississippi	8,373	0.6%
14	Missouri	29,819	2.2%
44	Montana	2,497	0.2%
38	Nebraska	5,416	0.4%
24	Nevada	18,837	1.4%
45	New Hampshire	2,069	0.1%
18	New Jersey	28,351	2.1%
29	New Mexico	12,896	0.9%
4	New York	77,585	5.6%
10	North Carolina	43,099	3.1%
49	North Dakota	1,068	0.1%
11	Ohio	39,997	2.9%
23	Oklahoma	19,184	1.4%
33	Oregon	9,747	0.7%
6	Pennsylvania	51,036	3.7%
43	Rhode Island	2,621	0.2%
13	South Carolina	32,691	2.4%
46	South Dakota	1,620	0.1%
9	Tennessee	44,897	3.2%
3	Texas	123,564	8.9%
37	Utah	6,070	0.4%
50	Vermont	844	0.1%
22	Virginia	19,882	1.4%
19	Washington	21,691	1.6%
39	West Virginia	4,968	0.4%
26	Wisconsin	15,421	1.1%
48	Wyoming	1,236	0.1%

RANK ORDER

RANK	STATE	CRIMES	% of USA
1	California	185,173	13.4%
2	Florida	126,265	9.1%
3	Texas	123,564	8.9%
4	New York	77,585	5.6%
5	Illinois	67,780	4.9%
6	Pennsylvania	51,036	3.7%
7	Michigan	50,166	3.6%
8	Georgia	46,384	3.4%
9	Tennessee	44,897	3.2%
10	North Carolina	43,099	3.1%
11	Ohio	39,997	2.9%
12	Maryland	35,393	2.6%
13	South Carolina	32,691	2.4%
14	Missouri	29,819	2.2%
15	Massachusetts	29,174	2.1%
16	Arizona	29,059	2.1%
17	Louisiana	28,944	2.1%
18	New Jersey	28,351	2.1%
19	Washington	21,691	1.6%
20	Indiana	21,283	1.5%
21	Alabama	21,111	1.5%
22	Virginia	19,882	1.4%
23	Oklahoma	19,184	1.4%
24	Nevada	18,837	1.4%
25	Colorado	16,946	1.2%
26	Wisconsin	15,421	1.1%
27	Arkansas	14,374	1.0%
28	Minnesota	13,717	1.0%
29	New Mexico	12,896	0.9%
30	Kentucky	12,646	0.9%
31	Kansas	11,505	0.8%
32	Connecticut	10,427	0.8%
33	Oregon	9,747	0.7%
34	Iowa	8,520	0.6%
35	Mississippi	8,373	0.6%
36	Delaware	6,141	0.4%
37	Utah	6,070	0.4%
38	Nebraska	5,416	0.4%
39	West Virginia	4,968	0.4%
40	Alaska	4,474	0.3%
41	Hawaii	3,512	0.3%
42	Idaho	3,483	0.3%
43	Rhode Island	2,621	0.2%
44	Montana	2,497	0.2%
45	New Hampshire	2,069	0.1%
46	South Dakota	1,620	0.1%
47	Maine	1,547	0.1%
48	Wyoming	1,236	0.1%
49	North Dakota	1,068	0.1%
50	Vermont	844	0.1%
	District of Columbia	8,509	0.6%

Source: Reported data from the Federal Bureau of Investigation
"Crime in the United States 2008" (Uniform Crime Reports, September 14, 2009, http://www.fbi.gov/ucr/ucr.htm)
*Violent crimes are offenses of murder, forcible rape, robbery, and aggravated assault.

Average Time Between Violent Crimes in 2008

National Rate = A Violent Crime Occurs Every 22.8 Seconds*

ALPHA ORDER				RANK ORDER		
RANK	STATE	HOURS.MINUTES		RANK	STATE	HOURS.MINUTES
30	Alabama	0.25		1	Vermont	10.25
11	Alaska	1.58		2	North Dakota	8.13
34	Arizona	0.18		3	Wyoming	7.07
24	Arkansas	0.37		4	Maine	5.41
50	California	0.03		5	South Dakota	5.25
26	Colorado	0.31		6	New Hampshire	4.15
19	Connecticut	0.50		7	Montana	3.31
15	Delaware	1.26		8	Rhode Island	3.21
48	Florida	0.04		9	Idaho	2.31
43	Georgia	0.11		10	Hawaii	2.30
10	Hawaii	2.30		11	Alaska	1.58
9	Idaho	2.31		12	West Virginia	1.46
46	Illinois	0.08		13	Nebraska	1.37
30	Indiana	0.25		14	Utah	1.27
17	Iowa	1.02		15	Delaware	1.26
20	Kansas	0.46		16	Mississippi	1.03
21	Kentucky	0.41		17	Iowa	1.02
34	Louisiana	0.18		18	Oregon	0.54
4	Maine	5.41		19	Connecticut	0.50
39	Maryland	0.15		20	Kansas	0.46
34	Massachusetts	0.18		21	Kentucky	0.41
43	Michigan	0.11		21	New Mexico	0.41
23	Minnesota	0.38		23	Minnesota	0.38
16	Mississippi	1.03		24	Arkansas	0.37
37	Missouri	0.17		25	Wisconsin	0.34
7	Montana	3.31		26	Colorado	0.31
13	Nebraska	1.37		27	Nevada	0.28
27	Nevada	0.28		27	Oklahoma	0.28
6	New Hampshire	4.15		29	Virginia	0.26
33	New Jersey	0.19		30	Alabama	0.25
21	New Mexico	0.41		30	Indiana	0.25
47	New York	0.07		30	Washington	0.25
41	North Carolina	0.12		33	New Jersey	0.19
2	North Dakota	8.13		34	Arizona	0.18
40	Ohio	0.13		34	Louisiana	0.18
27	Oklahoma	0.28		34	Massachusetts	0.18
18	Oregon	0.54		37	Missouri	0.17
45	Pennsylvania	0.10		38	South Carolina	0.16
8	Rhode Island	3.21		39	Maryland	0.15
38	South Carolina	0.16		40	Ohio	0.13
5	South Dakota	5.25		41	North Carolina	0.12
41	Tennessee	0.12		41	Tennessee	0.12
48	Texas	0.04		43	Georgia	0.11
14	Utah	1.27		43	Michigan	0.11
1	Vermont	10.25		45	Pennsylvania	0.10
29	Virginia	0.26		46	Illinois	0.08
30	Washington	0.25		47	New York	0.07
12	West Virginia	1.46		48	Florida	0.04
25	Wisconsin	0.34		48	Texas	0.04
3	Wyoming	7.07		50	California	0.03
					District of Columbia	1.02

Source: CQ Press using reported data from the Federal Bureau of Investigation
"Crime in the United States 2008" (Uniform Crime Reports, September 14, 2009, http://www.fbi.gov/ucr/ucr.htm)
*Violent crimes are offenses of murder, forcible rape, robbery, and aggravated assault.

Violent Crimes per Square Mile in 2008

National Rate = 0.36 Violent Crimes per Square Mile*

ALPHA ORDER

RANK	STATE	RATE
23	Alabama	0.40
49	Alaska	0.01
29	Arizona	0.25
27	Arkansas	0.27
10	California	1.13
35	Colorado	0.16
6	Connecticut	1.88
4	Delaware	2.47
5	Florida	1.92
16	Georgia	0.78
24	Hawaii	0.32
44	Idaho	0.04
9	Illinois	1.17
17	Indiana	0.58
37	Iowa	0.15
38	Kansas	0.14
25	Kentucky	0.31
18	Louisiana	0.56
44	Maine	0.04
2	Maryland	2.85
3	Massachusetts	2.76
19	Michigan	0.52
35	Minnesota	0.16
33	Mississippi	0.17
22	Missouri	0.43
46	Montana	0.02
42	Nebraska	0.07
33	Nevada	0.17
31	New Hampshire	0.22
1	New Jersey	3.25
39	New Mexico	0.11
8	New York	1.42
15	North Carolina	0.80
46	North Dakota	0.02
14	Ohio	0.89
27	Oklahoma	0.27
40	Oregon	0.10
11	Pennsylvania	1.11
7	Rhode Island	1.70
13	South Carolina	1.02
46	South Dakota	0.02
12	Tennessee	1.07
20	Texas	0.46
42	Utah	0.07
41	Vermont	0.09
20	Virginia	0.46
26	Washington	0.30
32	West Virginia	0.21
30	Wisconsin	0.24
49	Wyoming	0.01

RANK ORDER

RANK	STATE	RATE
1	New Jersey	3.25
2	Maryland	2.85
3	Massachusetts	2.76
4	Delaware	2.47
5	Florida	1.92
6	Connecticut	1.88
7	Rhode Island	1.70
8	New York	1.42
9	Illinois	1.17
10	California	1.13
11	Pennsylvania	1.11
12	Tennessee	1.07
13	South Carolina	1.02
14	Ohio	0.89
15	North Carolina	0.80
16	Georgia	0.78
17	Indiana	0.58
18	Louisiana	0.56
19	Michigan	0.52
20	Texas	0.46
20	Virginia	0.46
22	Missouri	0.43
23	Alabama	0.40
24	Hawaii	0.32
25	Kentucky	0.31
26	Washington	0.30
27	Arkansas	0.27
27	Oklahoma	0.27
29	Arizona	0.25
30	Wisconsin	0.24
31	New Hampshire	0.22
32	West Virginia	0.21
33	Mississippi	0.17
33	Nevada	0.17
35	Colorado	0.16
35	Minnesota	0.16
37	Iowa	0.15
38	Kansas	0.14
39	New Mexico	0.11
40	Oregon	0.10
41	Vermont	0.09
42	Nebraska	0.07
42	Utah	0.07
44	Idaho	0.04
44	Maine	0.04
46	Montana	0.02
46	North Dakota	0.02
46	South Dakota	0.02
49	Alaska	0.01
49	Wyoming	0.01

District of Columbia   125.13

Source: CQ Press using reported data from the Federal Bureau of Investigation
   "Crime in the United States 2008" (Uniform Crime Reports, September 14, 2009, http://www.fbi.gov/ucr/ucr.htm)
*Violent crimes are offenses of murder, forcible rape, robbery, and aggravated assault. "Square miles" includes total land and water area.

Percent Change in Number of Violent Crimes: 2007 to 2008

National Percent Change = 1.9% Decrease*

ALPHA ORDER

RANK	STATE	PERCENT CHANGE
11	Alabama	1.8
24	Alaska	(1.0)
42	Arizona	(5.0)
39	Arkansas	(4.2)
36	California	(3.1)
20	Colorado	0.2
3	Connecticut	16.3
9	Delaware	3.0
40	Florida	(4.3)
29	Georgia	(1.5)
19	Hawaii	0.3
35	Idaho	(3.0)
25	Illinois	(1.1)
17	Indiana	0.6
37	Iowa	(3.2)
47	Kansas	(8.4)
14	Kentucky	1.1
46	Louisiana	(7.6)
22	Maine	(0.5)
31	Maryland	(1.9)
8	Massachusetts	4.8
45	Michigan	(7.1)
48	Minnesota	(8.6)
29	Mississippi	(1.5)
18	Missouri	0.5
49	Montana	(9.3)
15	Nebraska	0.9
32	Nevada	(2.2)
4	New Hampshire	14.5
23	New Jersey	(0.9)
27	New Mexico	(1.4)
34	New York	(2.9)
10	North Carolina	2.0
2	North Dakota	17.2
12	Ohio	1.6
7	Oklahoma	6.2
50	Oregon	(9.6)
27	Pennsylvania	(1.4)
6	Rhode Island	9.0
44	South Carolina	(5.9)
1	South Dakota	20.3
37	Tennessee	(3.2)
13	Texas	1.2
33	Utah	(2.3)
5	Vermont	9.3
41	Virginia	(4.4)
16	Washington	0.7
21	West Virginia	(0.4)
43	Wisconsin	(5.4)
26	Wyoming	(1.2)

RANK ORDER

RANK	STATE	PERCENT CHANGE
1	South Dakota	20.3
2	North Dakota	17.2
3	Connecticut	16.3
4	New Hampshire	14.5
5	Vermont	9.3
6	Rhode Island	9.0
7	Oklahoma	6.2
8	Massachusetts	4.8
9	Delaware	3.0
10	North Carolina	2.0
11	Alabama	1.8
12	Ohio	1.6
13	Texas	1.2
14	Kentucky	1.1
15	Nebraska	0.9
16	Washington	0.7
17	Indiana	0.6
18	Missouri	0.5
19	Hawaii	0.3
20	Colorado	0.2
21	West Virginia	(0.4)
22	Maine	(0.5)
23	New Jersey	(0.9)
24	Alaska	(1.0)
25	Illinois	(1.1)
26	Wyoming	(1.2)
27	New Mexico	(1.4)
27	Pennsylvania	(1.4)
29	Georgia	(1.5)
29	Mississippi	(1.5)
31	Maryland	(1.9)
32	Nevada	(2.2)
33	Utah	(2.3)
34	New York	(2.9)
35	Idaho	(3.0)
36	California	(3.1)
37	Iowa	(3.2)
37	Tennessee	(3.2)
39	Arkansas	(4.2)
40	Florida	(4.3)
41	Virginia	(4.4)
42	Arizona	(5.0)
43	Wisconsin	(5.4)
44	South Carolina	(5.9)
45	Michigan	(7.1)
46	Louisiana	(7.6)
47	Kansas	(8.4)
48	Minnesota	(8.6)
49	Montana	(9.3)
50	Oregon	(9.6)

District of Columbia   2.3

Source: Reported data from the Federal Bureau of Investigation
"Crime in the United States 2008" (Uniform Crime Reports, September 14, 2009, http://www.fbi.gov/ucr/ucr.htm)
*Violent crimes are offenses of murder, forcible rape, robbery, and aggravated assault.

Violent Crime Rate in 2008

National Rate = 454.5 Violent Crimes per 100,000 Population*

ALPHA ORDER

RANK	STATE	RATE
19	Alabama	452.8
7	Alaska	651.9
21	Arizona	447.0
15	Arkansas	503.4
14	California	503.8
26	Colorado	343.1
31	Connecticut	297.8
4	Delaware	703.4
5	Florida	688.9
17	Georgia	478.9
37	Hawaii	272.6
44	Idaho	228.6
11	Illinois	525.4
27	Indiana	333.8
34	Iowa	283.8
22	Kansas	410.6
32	Kentucky	296.2
6	Louisiana	656.2
50	Maine	117.5
9	Maryland	628.2
20	Massachusetts	449.0
16	Michigan	501.5
38	Minnesota	262.8
33	Mississippi	284.9
13	Missouri	504.4
39	Montana	258.1
30	Nebraska	303.7
2	Nevada	724.5
48	New Hampshire	157.2
29	New Jersey	326.5
8	New Mexico	649.9
24	New York	398.1
18	North Carolina	467.3
47	North Dakota	166.5
25	Ohio	348.2
10	Oklahoma	526.7
40	Oregon	257.2
23	Pennsylvania	410.0
42	Rhode Island	249.4
1	South Carolina	729.7
46	South Dakota	201.4
3	Tennessee	722.4
12	Texas	507.9
45	Utah	221.8
49	Vermont	135.9
41	Virginia	255.9
28	Washington	331.2
36	West Virginia	273.8
35	Wisconsin	274.0
43	Wyoming	232.0

RANK ORDER

RANK	STATE	RATE
1	South Carolina	729.7
2	Nevada	724.5
3	Tennessee	722.4
4	Delaware	703.4
5	Florida	688.9
6	Louisiana	656.2
7	Alaska	651.9
8	New Mexico	649.9
9	Maryland	628.2
10	Oklahoma	526.7
11	Illinois	525.4
12	Texas	507.9
13	Missouri	504.4
14	California	503.8
15	Arkansas	503.4
16	Michigan	501.5
17	Georgia	478.9
18	North Carolina	467.3
19	Alabama	452.8
20	Massachusetts	449.0
21	Arizona	447.0
22	Kansas	410.6
23	Pennsylvania	410.0
24	New York	398.1
25	Ohio	348.2
26	Colorado	343.1
27	Indiana	333.8
28	Washington	331.2
29	New Jersey	326.5
30	Nebraska	303.7
31	Connecticut	297.8
32	Kentucky	296.2
33	Mississippi	284.9
34	Iowa	283.8
35	Wisconsin	274.0
36	West Virginia	273.8
37	Hawaii	272.6
38	Minnesota	262.8
39	Montana	258.1
40	Oregon	257.2
41	Virginia	255.9
42	Rhode Island	249.4
43	Wyoming	232.0
44	Idaho	228.6
45	Utah	221.8
46	South Dakota	201.4
47	North Dakota	166.5
48	New Hampshire	157.2
49	Vermont	135.9
50	Maine	117.5

District of Columbia   1,437.7

Source: Reported data from the Federal Bureau of Investigation
"Crime in the United States 2008" (Uniform Crime Reports, September 14, 2009, http://www.fbi.gov/ucr/ucr.htm)
*Violent crimes are offenses of murder, forcible rape, robbery, and aggravated assault.

Percent Change in Violent Crime Rate: 2007 to 2008

National Percent Change = 2.7% Decrease*

RANK	STATE	PERCENT CHANGE
11	Alabama	1.1
24	Alaska	(1.4)
44	Arizona	(7.4)
39	Arkansas	(4.9)
33	California	(3.6)
23	Colorado	(1.3)
3	Connecticut	16.3
9	Delaware	2.1
38	Florida	(4.7)
30	Georgia	(2.9)
16	Hawaii	(0.1)
37	Idaho	(4.5)
25	Illinois	(1.5)
15	Indiana	0.1
34	Iowa	(3.7)
47	Kansas	(9.3)
12	Kentucky	0.4
48	Louisiana	(10.0)
18	Maine	(0.4)
27	Maryland	(2.1)
8	Massachusetts	4.0
43	Michigan	(6.4)
46	Minnesota	(9.0)
28	Mississippi	(2.2)
16	Missouri	(0.1)
49	Montana	(10.2)
12	Nebraska	0.4
32	Nevada	(3.5)
4	New Hampshire	14.5
22	New Jersey	(0.8)
28	New Mexico	(2.2)
35	New York	(3.9)
14	North Carolina	0.2
2	North Dakota	16.9
10	Ohio	1.5
7	Oklahoma	5.4
50	Oregon	(10.6)
26	Pennsylvania	(1.6)
5	Rhode Island	9.8
44	South Carolina	(7.4)
1	South Dakota	19.1
36	Tennessee	(4.1)
19	Texas	(0.5)
41	Utah	(5.5)
6	Vermont	9.3
40	Virginia	(5.1)
21	Washington	(0.6)
19	West Virginia	(0.5)
42	Wisconsin	(5.8)
31	Wyoming	(3.0)

RANK	STATE	PERCENT CHANGE
1	South Dakota	19.1
2	North Dakota	16.9
3	Connecticut	16.3
4	New Hampshire	14.5
5	Rhode Island	9.8
6	Vermont	9.3
7	Oklahoma	5.4
8	Massachusetts	4.0
9	Delaware	2.1
10	Ohio	1.5
11	Alabama	1.1
12	Kentucky	0.4
12	Nebraska	0.4
14	North Carolina	0.2
15	Indiana	0.1
16	Hawaii	(0.1)
16	Missouri	(0.1)
18	Maine	(0.4)
19	Texas	(0.5)
19	West Virginia	(0.5)
21	Washington	(0.6)
22	New Jersey	(0.8)
23	Colorado	(1.3)
24	Alaska	(1.4)
25	Illinois	(1.5)
26	Pennsylvania	(1.6)
27	Maryland	(2.1)
28	Mississippi	(2.2)
28	New Mexico	(2.2)
30	Georgia	(2.9)
31	Wyoming	(3.0)
32	Nevada	(3.5)
33	California	(3.6)
34	Iowa	(3.7)
35	New York	(3.9)
36	Tennessee	(4.1)
37	Idaho	(4.5)
38	Florida	(4.7)
39	Arkansas	(4.9)
40	Virginia	(5.1)
41	Utah	(5.5)
42	Wisconsin	(5.8)
43	Michigan	(6.4)
44	Arizona	(7.4)
44	South Carolina	(7.4)
46	Minnesota	(9.0)
47	Kansas	(9.3)
48	Louisiana	(10.0)
49	Montana	(10.2)
50	Oregon	(10.6)

	District of Columbia	1.7

Source: Reported data from the Federal Bureau of Investigation
    "Crime in the United States 2008" (Uniform Crime Reports, September 14, 2009, http://www.fbi.gov/ucr/ucr.htm)
*Violent crimes are offenses of murder, forcible rape, robbery, and aggravated assault.

Violent Crimes With Firearms in 2008

National Total = 326,792 Violent Crimes*

ALPHA ORDER

RANK	STATE	CRIMES	% of USA
18	Alabama	4,745	1.5%
38	Alaska	715	0.2%
9	Arizona	10,118	3.1%
22	Arkansas	3,705	1.1%
1	California	42,660	13.1%
25	Colorado	3,306	1.0%
32	Connecticut	1,613	0.5%
31	Delaware	1,842	0.6%
NA	Florida**	NA	NA
4	Georgia	15,588	4.8%
42	Hawaii	302	0.1%
40	Idaho	433	0.1%
NA	Illinois**	NA	NA
16	Indiana	5,728	1.8%
36	Iowa	908	0.3%
29	Kansas	2,360	0.7%
26	Kentucky	2,835	0.9%
12	Louisiana	7,610	2.3%
45	Maine	123	0.0%
13	Maryland	6,619	2.0%
23	Massachusetts	3,564	1.1%
5	Michigan	14,588	4.5%
28	Minnesota	2,602	0.8%
30	Mississippi	2,318	0.7%
10	Missouri	10,038	3.1%
41	Montana	304	0.1%
34	Nebraska	1,127	0.3%
20	Nevada	4,722	1.4%
43	New Hampshire	245	0.1%
15	New Jersey	6,412	2.0%
27	New Mexico	2,780	0.9%
17	New York	5,496	1.7%
6	North Carolina	14,308	4.4%
48	North Dakota	24	0.0%
8	Ohio	10,863	3.3%
21	Oklahoma	4,356	1.3%
33	Oregon	1,338	0.4%
7	Pennsylvania	13,650	4.2%
39	Rhode Island	537	0.2%
11	South Carolina	9,210	2.8%
44	South Dakota	150	0.0%
3	Tennessee	16,037	4.9%
2	Texas	36,479	11.2%
35	Utah	1,069	0.3%
47	Vermont	90	0.0%
14	Virginia	6,552	2.0%
24	Washington	3,396	1.0%
37	West Virginia	758	0.2%
19	Wisconsin	4,734	1.4%
45	Wyoming	123	0.0%

RANK ORDER

RANK	STATE	CRIMES	% of USA
1	California	42,660	13.1%
2	Texas	36,479	11.2%
3	Tennessee	16,037	4.9%
4	Georgia	15,588	4.8%
5	Michigan	14,588	4.5%
6	North Carolina	14,308	4.4%
7	Pennsylvania	13,650	4.2%
8	Ohio	10,863	3.3%
9	Arizona	10,118	3.1%
10	Missouri	10,038	3.1%
11	South Carolina	9,210	2.8%
12	Louisiana	7,610	2.3%
13	Maryland	6,619	2.0%
14	Virginia	6,552	2.0%
15	New Jersey	6,412	2.0%
16	Indiana	5,728	1.8%
17	New York	5,496	1.7%
18	Alabama	4,745	1.5%
19	Wisconsin	4,734	1.4%
20	Nevada	4,722	1.4%
21	Oklahoma	4,356	1.3%
22	Arkansas	3,705	1.1%
23	Massachusetts	3,564	1.1%
24	Washington	3,396	1.0%
25	Colorado	3,306	1.0%
26	Kentucky	2,835	0.9%
27	New Mexico	2,780	0.9%
28	Minnesota	2,602	0.8%
29	Kansas	2,360	0.7%
30	Mississippi	2,318	0.7%
31	Delaware	1,842	0.6%
32	Connecticut	1,613	0.5%
33	Oregon	1,338	0.4%
34	Nebraska	1,127	0.3%
35	Utah	1,069	0.3%
36	Iowa	908	0.3%
37	West Virginia	758	0.2%
38	Alaska	715	0.2%
39	Rhode Island	537	0.2%
40	Idaho	433	0.1%
41	Montana	304	0.1%
42	Hawaii	302	0.1%
43	New Hampshire	245	0.1%
44	South Dakota	150	0.0%
45	Maine	123	0.0%
45	Wyoming	123	0.0%
47	Vermont	90	0.0%
48	North Dakota	24	0.0%
NA	Florida**	NA	NA
NA	Illinois**	NA	NA
	District of Columbia**	NA	NA

Source: CQ Press using reported data from the Federal Bureau of Investigation
   "Crime in the United States 2008" (Uniform Crime Reports, September 14, 2009, http://www.fbi.gov/ucr/ucr.htm)
*Includes murder, robbery, and aggravated assault. Does not include rape. National total reflects only those violent crimes for which the type of weapon was known and reported. There were an additional 182,773 violent crimes (excluding rape) for which the type of weapon was not reported to the F.B.I.
**Not available.

Violent Crime Rate With Firearms in 2008

National Rate = 125.6 Violent Crimes per 100,000 Population*

ALPHA ORDER

RANK	STATE	RATE
13	Alabama	146.7
23	Alaska	106.1
11	Arizona	157.7
14	Arkansas	142.0
19	California	116.6
29	Colorado	71.3
36	Connecticut	47.8
5	Delaware	211.0
NA	Florida**	NA
4	Georgia	214.6
42	Hawaii	26.4
41	Idaho	30.0
NA	Illinois**	NA
21	Indiana	113.5
40	Iowa	32.8
22	Kansas	106.4
26	Kentucky	79.7
3	Louisiana	216.4
47	Maine	9.3
16	Maryland	132.4
31	Massachusetts	61.2
10	Michigan	167.6
33	Minnesota	52.5
15	Mississippi	139.0
8	Missouri	173.4
39	Montana	32.9
30	Nebraska	68.8
7	Nevada	181.6
43	New Hampshire	23.7
27	New Jersey	75.2
9	New Mexico	173.1
34	New York	51.2
6	North Carolina	192.0
48	North Dakota	4.1
18	Ohio	127.3
17	Oklahoma	127.4
38	Oregon	36.7
20	Pennsylvania	114.8
35	Rhode Island	51.1
2	South Carolina	239.3
45	South Dakota	23.0
1	Tennessee	274.3
12	Texas	150.2
37	Utah	39.8
46	Vermont	14.9
24	Virginia	85.1
32	Washington	55.4
28	West Virginia	72.5
25	Wisconsin	84.7
44	Wyoming	23.3

RANK ORDER

RANK	STATE	RATE
1	Tennessee	274.3
2	South Carolina	239.3
3	Louisiana	216.4
4	Georgia	214.6
5	Delaware	211.0
6	North Carolina	192.0
7	Nevada	181.6
8	Missouri	173.4
9	New Mexico	173.1
10	Michigan	167.6
11	Arizona	157.7
12	Texas	150.2
13	Alabama	146.7
14	Arkansas	142.0
15	Mississippi	139.0
16	Maryland	132.4
17	Oklahoma	127.4
18	Ohio	127.3
19	California	116.6
20	Pennsylvania	114.8
21	Indiana	113.5
22	Kansas	106.4
23	Alaska	106.1
24	Virginia	85.1
25	Wisconsin	84.7
26	Kentucky	79.7
27	New Jersey	75.2
28	West Virginia	72.5
29	Colorado	71.3
30	Nebraska	68.8
31	Massachusetts	61.2
32	Washington	55.4
33	Minnesota	52.5
34	New York	51.2
35	Rhode Island	51.1
36	Connecticut	47.8
37	Utah	39.8
38	Oregon	36.7
39	Montana	32.9
40	Iowa	32.8
41	Idaho	30.0
42	Hawaii	26.4
43	New Hampshire	23.7
44	Wyoming	23.3
45	South Dakota	23.0
46	Vermont	14.9
47	Maine	9.3
48	North Dakota	4.1
NA	Florida**	NA
NA	Illinois**	NA
	District of Columbia**	NA

Source: CQ Press using reported data from the Federal Bureau of Investigation
"Crime in the United States 2008" (Uniform Crime Reports, September 14, 2009, http://www.fbi.gov/ucr/ucr.htm)
*Based only on population of reporting jurisdictions. Includes murder, robbery, and aggravated assault. Does not include rape.
National rate reflects only those violent crimes for which the type of weapon was known and reported.
**Not available.

Percent of Violent Crimes Involving Firearms in 2008

National Percent = 29.4% of Violent Crimes*

ALPHA ORDER

RANK	STATE	PERCENT
4	Alabama	40.9
36	Alaska	18.0
6	Arizona	37.4
17	Arkansas	29.7
26	California	24.3
29	Colorado	23.9
33	Connecticut	20.6
14	Delaware	31.9
NA	Florida**	NA
2	Georgia	43.4
47	Hawaii	10.4
38	Idaho	16.4
NA	Illinois**	NA
15	Indiana	31.6
44	Iowa	12.2
20	Kansas	28.8
19	Kentucky	29.2
9	Louisiana	34.2
46	Maine	10.5
22	Maryland	27.0
41	Massachusetts	14.0
11	Michigan	33.7
31	Minnesota	22.4
1	Mississippi	47.6
8	Missouri	36.2
40	Montana	14.3
27	Nebraska	24.2
23	Nevada	26.6
37	New Hampshire	17.7
25	New Jersey	24.5
21	New Mexico	28.2
34	New York	20.2
3	North Carolina	41.0
48	North Dakota	3.0
10	Ohio	34.1
24	Oklahoma	25.4
39	Oregon	15.8
18	Pennsylvania	29.4
30	Rhode Island	22.9
12	South Carolina	33.4
42	South Dakota	13.9
5	Tennessee	38.7
15	Texas	31.6
32	Utah	20.8
43	Vermont	12.6
7	Virginia	36.6
35	Washington	18.6
27	West Virginia	24.2
13	Wisconsin	33.1
45	Wyoming	11.8

RANK ORDER

RANK	STATE	PERCENT
1	Mississippi	47.6
2	Georgia	43.4
3	North Carolina	41.0
4	Alabama	40.9
5	Tennessee	38.7
6	Arizona	37.4
7	Virginia	36.6
8	Missouri	36.2
9	Louisiana	34.2
10	Ohio	34.1
11	Michigan	33.7
12	South Carolina	33.4
13	Wisconsin	33.1
14	Delaware	31.9
15	Indiana	31.6
15	Texas	31.6
17	Arkansas	29.7
18	Pennsylvania	29.4
19	Kentucky	29.2
20	Kansas	28.8
21	New Mexico	28.2
22	Maryland	27.0
23	Nevada	26.6
24	Oklahoma	25.4
25	New Jersey	24.5
26	California	24.3
27	Nebraska	24.2
27	West Virginia	24.2
29	Colorado	23.9
30	Rhode Island	22.9
31	Minnesota	22.4
32	Utah	20.8
33	Connecticut	20.6
34	New York	20.2
35	Washington	18.6
36	Alaska	18.0
37	New Hampshire	17.7
38	Idaho	16.4
39	Oregon	15.8
40	Montana	14.3
41	Massachusetts	14.0
42	South Dakota	13.9
43	Vermont	12.6
44	Iowa	12.2
45	Wyoming	11.8
46	Maine	10.5
47	Hawaii	10.4
48	North Dakota	3.0
NA	Florida**	NA
NA	Illinois**	NA
	District of Columbia**	NA

Source: CQ Press using reported data from the Federal Bureau of Investigation
"Crime in the United States 2008" (Uniform Crime Reports, September 14, 2009, http://www.fbi.gov/ucr/ucr.htm)
*Includes murder, robbery, and aggravated assault. Does not include rape. National percent reflects only those violent crimes for which the type of weapon was known and reported. There were an additional 182,773 violent crimes (excluding rape) for which the type of weapon was not reported to the F.B.I.
**Not available.

Murders in 2008

National Total = 16,272 Murders*

ALPHA ORDER

RANK	STATE	MURDERS	% of USA
18	Alabama	353	2.2%
42	Alaska	28	0.2%
15	Arizona	407	2.5%
27	Arkansas	162	1.0%
1	California	2,142	13.2%
28	Colorado	157	1.0%
31	Connecticut	123	0.8%
38	Delaware	57	0.4%
3	Florida	1,168	7.2%
7	Georgia	636	3.9%
44	Hawaii	25	0.2%
45	Idaho	23	0.1%
5	Illinois	790	4.9%
19	Indiana	327	2.0%
35	Iowa	76	0.5%
32	Kansas	113	0.7%
23	Kentucky	198	1.2%
11	Louisiana	527	3.2%
40	Maine	31	0.2%
12	Maryland	493	3.0%
25	Massachusetts	167	1.0%
10	Michigan	542	3.3%
33	Minnesota	109	0.7%
21	Mississippi	237	1.5%
13	Missouri	455	2.8%
45	Montana	23	0.1%
36	Nebraska	68	0.4%
26	Nevada	163	1.0%
48	New Hampshire	13	0.1%
16	New Jersey	376	2.3%
30	New Mexico	142	0.9%
4	New York	836	5.1%
8	North Carolina	604	3.7%
50	North Dakota	3	0.0%
9	Ohio	543	3.3%
22	Oklahoma	212	1.3%
34	Oregon	82	0.5%
6	Pennsylvania	701	4.3%
41	Rhode Island	29	0.2%
20	South Carolina	305	1.9%
43	South Dakota	26	0.2%
14	Tennessee	408	2.5%
2	Texas	1,374	8.4%
39	Utah	39	0.2%
47	Vermont	17	0.1%
17	Virginia	368	2.3%
24	Washington	192	1.2%
37	West Virginia	60	0.4%
29	Wisconsin	146	0.9%
49	Wyoming	10	0.1%

RANK ORDER

RANK	STATE	MURDERS	% of USA
1	California	2,142	13.2%
2	Texas	1,374	8.4%
3	Florida	1,168	7.2%
4	New York	836	5.1%
5	Illinois	790	4.9%
6	Pennsylvania	701	4.3%
7	Georgia	636	3.9%
8	North Carolina	604	3.7%
9	Ohio	543	3.3%
10	Michigan	542	3.3%
11	Louisiana	527	3.2%
12	Maryland	493	3.0%
13	Missouri	455	2.8%
14	Tennessee	408	2.5%
15	Arizona	407	2.5%
16	New Jersey	376	2.3%
17	Virginia	368	2.3%
18	Alabama	353	2.2%
19	Indiana	327	2.0%
20	South Carolina	305	1.9%
21	Mississippi	237	1.5%
22	Oklahoma	212	1.3%
23	Kentucky	198	1.2%
24	Washington	192	1.2%
25	Massachusetts	167	1.0%
26	Nevada	163	1.0%
27	Arkansas	162	1.0%
28	Colorado	157	1.0%
29	Wisconsin	146	0.9%
30	New Mexico	142	0.9%
31	Connecticut	123	0.8%
32	Kansas	113	0.7%
33	Minnesota	109	0.7%
34	Oregon	82	0.5%
35	Iowa	76	0.5%
36	Nebraska	68	0.4%
37	West Virginia	60	0.4%
38	Delaware	57	0.4%
39	Utah	39	0.2%
40	Maine	31	0.2%
41	Rhode Island	29	0.2%
42	Alaska	28	0.2%
43	South Dakota	26	0.2%
44	Hawaii	25	0.2%
45	Idaho	23	0.1%
45	Montana	23	0.1%
47	Vermont	17	0.1%
48	New Hampshire	13	0.1%
49	Wyoming	10	0.1%
50	North Dakota	3	0.0%
	District of Columbia	186	1.1%

Source: Reported data from the Federal Bureau of Investigation
   "Crime in the United States 2008" (Uniform Crime Reports, September 14, 2009, http://www.fbi.gov/ucr/ucr.htm)
*Includes nonnegligent manslaughter.

Average Time Between Murders in 2008

National Rate = A Murder Occurs Every 32.3 Minutes*

ALPHA ORDER

RANK	STATE	HOURS.MINUTES
33	Alabama	24.53
9	Alaska	313.43
36	Arizona	21.35
24	Arkansas	54.13
50	California	4.06
23	Colorado	55.57
20	Connecticut	71.25
13	Delaware	154.07
48	Florida	7.31
44	Georgia	13.49
7	Hawaii	351.22
5	Idaho	381.55
46	Illinois	11.07
32	Indiana	26.52
16	Iowa	115.35
19	Kansas	77.44
28	Kentucky	44.22
40	Louisiana	16.40
11	Maine	283.21
39	Maryland	17.49
26	Massachusetts	52.36
41	Michigan	16.13
18	Minnesota	80.35
30	Mississippi	37.04
38	Missouri	19.19
5	Montana	381.55
15	Nebraska	129.11
25	Nevada	53.53
3	New Hampshire	675.41
35	New Jersey	23.22
21	New Mexico	61.52
47	New York	10.31
43	North Carolina	14.32
1	North Dakota	2,928.00
42	Ohio	16.11
29	Oklahoma	41.26
17	Oregon	107.07
45	Pennsylvania	12.32
10	Rhode Island	302.54
31	South Carolina	28.48
8	South Dakota	337.51
37	Tennessee	21.32
49	Texas	6.23
12	Utah	225.14
4	Vermont	516.43
34	Virginia	23.52
27	Washington	45.45
14	West Virginia	146.24
22	Wisconsin	60.10
2	Wyoming	878.24

RANK ORDER

RANK	STATE	HOURS.MINUTES
1	North Dakota	2,928.00
2	Wyoming	878.24
3	New Hampshire	675.41
4	Vermont	516.43
5	Idaho	381.55
5	Montana	381.55
7	Hawaii	351.22
8	South Dakota	337.51
9	Alaska	313.43
10	Rhode Island	302.54
11	Maine	283.21
12	Utah	225.14
13	Delaware	154.07
14	West Virginia	146.24
15	Nebraska	129.11
16	Iowa	115.35
17	Oregon	107.07
18	Minnesota	80.35
19	Kansas	77.44
20	Connecticut	71.25
21	New Mexico	61.52
22	Wisconsin	60.10
23	Colorado	55.57
24	Arkansas	54.13
25	Nevada	53.53
26	Massachusetts	52.36
27	Washington	45.45
28	Kentucky	44.22
29	Oklahoma	41.26
30	Mississippi	37.04
31	South Carolina	28.48
32	Indiana	26.52
33	Alabama	24.53
34	Virginia	23.52
35	New Jersey	23.22
36	Arizona	21.35
37	Tennessee	21.32
38	Missouri	19.19
39	Maryland	17.49
40	Louisiana	16.40
41	Michigan	16.13
42	Ohio	16.11
43	North Carolina	14.32
44	Georgia	13.49
45	Pennsylvania	12.32
46	Illinois	11.07
47	New York	10.31
48	Florida	7.31
49	Texas	6.23
50	California	4.06
	District of Columbia	47.14

Source: CQ Press using reported data from the Federal Bureau of Investigation
"Crime in the United States 2008" (Uniform Crime Reports, September 14, 2009, http://www.fbi.gov/ucr/ucr.htm)
*Includes nonnegligent manslaughter.

Percent Change in Number of Murders: 2007 to 2008

National Percent Change = 3.9% Decrease*

RANK	STATE	PERCENT CHANGE		RANK	STATE	PERCENT CHANGE
41	Alabama	(14.3)		1	Iowa	105.4
47	Alaska	(36.4)		2	Montana	64.3
37	Arizona	(13.0)		3	Delaware	54.1
43	Arkansas	(15.2)		4	South Dakota	52.9
28	California	(5.2)		5	Rhode Island	52.6
20	Colorado	2.6		6	Maine	47.6
9	Connecticut	16.0		7	Vermont	41.7
3	Delaware	54.1		8	Missouri	18.2
23	Florida	(2.7)		9	Connecticut	16.0
35	Georgia	(11.4)		10	Mississippi	13.9
11	Hawaii	13.6		11	Hawaii	13.6
49	Idaho	(53.1)		12	Oregon	12.3
16	Illinois	5.1		13	Washington	11.0
31	Indiana	(8.1)		14	Kansas	5.6
1	Iowa	105.4		15	Ohio	5.2
14	Kansas	5.6		16	Illinois	5.1
24	Kentucky	(2.9)		17	New York	4.4
38	Louisiana	(13.3)		18	North Carolina	3.2
6	Maine	47.6		19	Tennessee	2.8
34	Maryland	(10.8)		20	Colorado	2.6
32	Massachusetts	(9.2)		21	Nebraska	0.0
44	Michigan	(19.8)		22	New Jersey	(1.1)
29	Minnesota	(6.0)		23	Florida	(2.7)
10	Mississippi	13.9		24	Kentucky	(2.9)
8	Missouri	18.2		25	Pennsylvania	(3.0)
2	Montana	64.3		26	Texas	(3.2)
21	Nebraska	0.0		27	Oklahoma	(4.5)
42	Nevada	(15.1)		28	California	(5.2)
38	New Hampshire	(13.3)		29	Minnesota	(6.0)
22	New Jersey	(1.1)		30	West Virginia	(6.3)
36	New Mexico	(12.3)		31	Indiana	(8.1)
17	New York	4.4		32	Massachusetts	(9.2)
18	North Carolina	3.2		33	Virginia	(9.4)
50	North Dakota	(75.0)		34	Maryland	(10.8)
15	Ohio	5.2		35	Georgia	(11.4)
27	Oklahoma	(4.5)		36	New Mexico	(12.3)
12	Oregon	12.3		37	Arizona	(13.0)
25	Pennsylvania	(3.0)		38	Louisiana	(13.3)
5	Rhode Island	52.6		38	New Hampshire	(13.3)
40	South Carolina	(13.4)		40	South Carolina	(13.4)
4	South Dakota	52.9		41	Alabama	(14.3)
19	Tennessee	2.8		42	Nevada	(15.1)
26	Texas	(3.2)		43	Arkansas	(15.2)
46	Utah	(32.8)		44	Michigan	(19.8)
7	Vermont	41.7		45	Wisconsin	(20.2)
33	Virginia	(9.4)		46	Utah	(32.8)
13	Washington	11.0		47	Alaska	(36.4)
30	West Virginia	(6.3)		48	Wyoming	(37.5)
45	Wisconsin	(20.2)		49	Idaho	(53.1)
48	Wyoming	(37.5)		50	North Dakota	(75.0)
					District of Columbia	2.8

ALPHA ORDER — RANK ORDER

Source: Reported data from the Federal Bureau of Investigation
"Crime in the United States 2008" (Uniform Crime Reports, September 14, 2009, http://www.fbi.gov/ucr/ucr.htm)
*Includes nonnegligent manslaughter.

Murder Rate in 2008

National Rate = 5.4 Murders per 100,000 Population*

ALPHA ORDER

RANK	STATE	RATE
5	Alabama	7.6
28	Alaska	4.1
13	Arizona	6.3
18	Arkansas	5.7
16	California	5.8
33	Colorado	3.2
31	Connecticut	3.5
10	Delaware	6.5
12	Florida	6.4
8	Georgia	6.6
45	Hawaii	1.9
47	Idaho	1.5
15	Illinois	6.1
22	Indiana	5.1
40	Iowa	2.5
29	Kansas	4.0
25	Kentucky	4.6
1	Louisiana	11.9
41	Maine	2.4
2	Maryland	8.8
38	Massachusetts	2.6
21	Michigan	5.4
44	Minnesota	2.1
3	Mississippi	8.1
4	Missouri	7.7
41	Montana	2.4
30	Nebraska	3.8
13	Nevada	6.3
49	New Hampshire	1.0
26	New Jersey	4.3
6	New Mexico	7.2
26	New York	4.3
10	North Carolina	6.5
50	North Dakota	0.5
23	Ohio	4.7
16	Oklahoma	5.8
43	Oregon	2.2
19	Pennsylvania	5.6
36	Rhode Island	2.8
7	South Carolina	6.8
33	South Dakota	3.2
8	Tennessee	6.6
19	Texas	5.6
48	Utah	1.4
37	Vermont	2.7
23	Virginia	4.7
35	Washington	2.9
32	West Virginia	3.3
38	Wisconsin	2.6
45	Wyoming	1.9

RANK ORDER

RANK	STATE	RATE
1	Louisiana	11.9
2	Maryland	8.8
3	Mississippi	8.1
4	Missouri	7.7
5	Alabama	7.6
6	New Mexico	7.2
7	South Carolina	6.8
8	Georgia	6.6
8	Tennessee	6.6
10	Delaware	6.5
10	North Carolina	6.5
12	Florida	6.4
13	Arizona	6.3
13	Nevada	6.3
15	Illinois	6.1
16	California	5.8
16	Oklahoma	5.8
18	Arkansas	5.7
19	Pennsylvania	5.6
19	Texas	5.6
21	Michigan	5.4
22	Indiana	5.1
23	Ohio	4.7
23	Virginia	4.7
25	Kentucky	4.6
26	New Jersey	4.3
26	New York	4.3
28	Alaska	4.1
29	Kansas	4.0
30	Nebraska	3.8
31	Connecticut	3.5
32	West Virginia	3.3
33	Colorado	3.2
33	South Dakota	3.2
35	Washington	2.9
36	Rhode Island	2.8
37	Vermont	2.7
38	Massachusetts	2.6
38	Wisconsin	2.6
40	Iowa	2.5
41	Maine	2.4
41	Montana	2.4
43	Oregon	2.2
44	Minnesota	2.1
45	Hawaii	1.9
45	Wyoming	1.9
47	Idaho	1.5
48	Utah	1.4
49	New Hampshire	1.0
50	North Dakota	0.5
	District of Columbia	31.4

Source: Reported data from the Federal Bureau of Investigation
  "Crime in the United States 2008" (Uniform Crime Reports, September 14, 2009, http://www.fbi.gov/ucr/ucr.htm)
*Includes nonnegligent manslaughter.

Percent Change in Murder Rate: 2007 to 2008

National Percent Change = 4.7% Decrease*

ALPHA ORDER			RANK ORDER		
RANK	STATE	PERCENT CHANGE	RANK	STATE	PERCENT CHANGE
39	Alabama	(14.9)	1	Iowa	104.4
47	Alaska	(36.6)	2	Montana	62.7
40	Arizona	(15.2)	3	Rhode Island	53.7
42	Arkansas	(15.8)	4	Delaware	52.6
28	California	(5.7)	5	South Dakota	51.4
20	Colorado	1.0	6	Maine	47.7
9	Connecticut	16.1	7	Vermont	41.7
4	Delaware	52.6	8	Missouri	17.5
23	Florida	(3.2)	9	Connecticut	16.1
35	Georgia	(12.7)	10	Hawaii	13.2
10	Hawaii	13.2	10	Mississippi	13.2
49	Idaho	(53.8)	12	Oregon	11.1
15	Illinois	4.7	13	Washington	9.6
31	Indiana	(8.6)	14	Ohio	5.1
1	Iowa	104.4	15	Illinois	4.7
16	Kansas	4.6	16	Kansas	4.6
25	Kentucky	(3.6)	17	New York	3.3
41	Louisiana	(15.6)	18	Tennessee	1.8
6	Maine	47.7	19	North Carolina	1.4
34	Maryland	(11.1)	20	Colorado	1.0
32	Massachusetts	(9.9)	21	Nebraska	(0.5)
44	Michigan	(19.3)	22	New Jersey	(1.0)
29	Minnesota	(6.4)	23	Florida	(3.2)
10	Mississippi	13.2	23	Pennsylvania	(3.2)
8	Missouri	17.5	25	Kentucky	(3.6)
2	Montana	62.7	26	Texas	(4.9)
21	Nebraska	(0.5)	27	Oklahoma	(5.2)
43	Nevada	(16.2)	28	California	(5.7)
37	New Hampshire	(13.3)	29	Minnesota	(6.4)
22	New Jersey	(1.0)	29	West Virginia	(6.4)
36	New Mexico	(13.0)	31	Indiana	(8.6)
17	New York	3.3	32	Massachusetts	(9.9)
19	North Carolina	1.4	33	Virginia	(10.0)
50	North Dakota	(75.1)	34	Maryland	(11.1)
14	Ohio	5.1	35	Georgia	(12.7)
27	Oklahoma	(5.2)	36	New Mexico	(13.0)
12	Oregon	11.1	37	New Hampshire	(13.3)
23	Pennsylvania	(3.2)	38	South Carolina	(14.7)
3	Rhode Island	53.7	39	Alabama	(14.9)
38	South Carolina	(14.7)	40	Arizona	(15.2)
5	South Dakota	51.4	41	Louisiana	(15.6)
18	Tennessee	1.8	42	Arkansas	(15.8)
26	Texas	(4.9)	43	Nevada	(16.2)
46	Utah	(35.0)	44	Michigan	(19.3)
7	Vermont	41.7	45	Wisconsin	(20.6)
33	Virginia	(10.0)	46	Utah	(35.0)
13	Washington	9.6	47	Alaska	(36.6)
29	West Virginia	(6.4)	48	Wyoming	(38.7)
45	Wisconsin	(20.6)	49	Idaho	(53.8)
48	Wyoming	(38.7)	50	North Dakota	(75.1)

District of Columbia   2.1

Source: Reported data from the Federal Bureau of Investigation
"Crime in the United States 2008" (Uniform Crime Reports, September 14, 2009, http://www.fbi.gov/ucr/ucr.htm)
*Includes nonnegligent manslaughter.

Murders With Firearms in 2008

National Total = 9,484 Murders*

ALPHA ORDER | | | | RANK ORDER

RANK	STATE	MURDERS	% of USA		RANK	STATE	MURDERS	% of USA
14	Alabama	262	2.8%		1	California	1,487	15.7%
40	Alaska	13	0.1%		2	Texas	895	9.4%
13	Arizona	290	3.1%		3	Pennsylvania	521	5.5%
23	Arkansas	110	1.2%		4	New York	475	5.0%
1	California	1,487	15.7%		5	Georgia	435	4.6%
28	Colorado	86	0.9%		6	Illinois*	421	4.4%
30	Connecticut	71	0.7%		7	Michigan	375	4.0%
34	Delaware	44	0.5%		8	North Carolina	362	3.8%
NA	Florida**	NA	NA		9	Maryland	353	3.7%
5	Georgia	435	4.6%		10	Missouri	349	3.7%
42	Hawaii	11	0.1%		11	Louisiana	309	3.3%
39	Idaho	14	0.1%		12	Ohio	293	3.1%
6	Illinois*	421	4.4%		13	Arizona	290	3.1%
18	Indiana	220	2.3%		14	Alabama	262	2.8%
36	Iowa	25	0.3%		15	Tennessee	240	2.5%
31	Kansas	61	0.6%		15	Virginia	240	2.5%
22	Kentucky	121	1.3%		17	New Jersey	236	2.5%
11	Louisiana	309	3.3%		18	Indiana	220	2.3%
42	Maine	11	0.1%		19	South Carolina	206	2.2%
9	Maryland	353	3.7%		20	Mississippi	142	1.5%
26	Massachusetts	89	0.9%		21	Oklahoma	128	1.3%
7	Michigan	375	4.0%		22	Kentucky	121	1.3%
32	Minnesota	54	0.6%		23	Arkansas	110	1.2%
20	Mississippi	142	1.5%		23	Washington	110	1.2%
10	Missouri	349	3.7%		25	Nevada	93	1.0%
42	Montana	11	0.1%		26	Massachusetts	89	0.9%
45	Nebraska	9	0.1%		27	New Mexico	88	0.9%
25	Nevada	93	1.0%		28	Colorado	86	0.9%
48	New Hampshire	2	0.0%		29	Wisconsin	80	0.8%
17	New Jersey	236	2.5%		30	Connecticut	71	0.7%
27	New Mexico	88	0.9%		31	Kansas	61	0.6%
4	New York	475	5.0%		32	Minnesota	54	0.6%
8	North Carolina	362	3.8%		33	Oregon	47	0.5%
49	North Dakota	0	0.0%		34	Delaware	44	0.5%
12	Ohio	293	3.1%		35	West Virginia	33	0.3%
21	Oklahoma	128	1.3%		36	Iowa	25	0.3%
33	Oregon	47	0.5%		37	Utah	19	0.2%
3	Pennsylvania	521	5.5%		38	Rhode Island	18	0.2%
38	Rhode Island	18	0.2%		39	Idaho	14	0.1%
19	South Carolina	206	2.2%		40	Alaska	13	0.1%
40	South Dakota	13	0.1%		40	South Dakota	13	0.1%
15	Tennessee	240	2.5%		42	Hawaii	11	0.1%
2	Texas	895	9.4%		42	Maine	11	0.1%
37	Utah	19	0.2%		42	Montana	11	0.1%
46	Vermont	8	0.1%		45	Nebraska	9	0.1%
15	Virginia	240	2.5%		46	Vermont	8	0.1%
23	Washington	110	1.2%		47	Wyoming	4	0.0%
35	West Virginia	33	0.3%		48	New Hampshire	2	0.0%
29	Wisconsin	80	0.8%		49	North Dakota	0	0.0%
47	Wyoming	4	0.0%		NA	Florida**	NA	NA
						District of Columbia**	NA	NA

Source: Reported data from the Federal Bureau of Investigation
"Crime in the United States 2008" (Uniform Crime Reports, September 14, 2009, http://www.fbi.gov/ucr/ucr.htm)
*Of the 14,180 murders in 2008 for which supplemental data were received by the F.B.I. There were an additional 2,092 murders for which the type of murder weapon was not reported to the F.B.I. Includes nonnegligent manslaughter. Numbers are for reporting jurisdictions only. Illinois's figure is for Chicago and Rockford only.
**Not available.

Murder Rate With Firearms in 2008

National Rate = 3.9 Murders per 100,000 Population*

ALPHA ORDER				RANK ORDER		
RANK	STATE	RATE		RANK	STATE	RATE
4	Alabama	8.1		1	Illinois*	14.1
31	Alaska	1.9		2	Louisiana	8.8
12	Arizona	4.5		3	Mississippi	8.5
17	Arkansas	4.2		4	Alabama	8.1
18	California	4.1		5	Maryland	7.1
31	Colorado	1.9		6	Georgia	6.0
29	Connecticut	2.1		6	Missouri	6.0
10	Delaware	5.0		8	New Mexico	5.5
NA	Florida**	NA		9	South Carolina	5.4
6	Georgia	6.0		10	Delaware	5.0
41	Hawaii	1.0		11	North Carolina	4.9
41	Idaho	1.0		12	Arizona	4.5
1	Illinois*	14.1		13	Indiana	4.4
13	Indiana	4.4		13	New York	4.4
43	Iowa	0.9		13	Pennsylvania	4.4
28	Kansas	2.7		16	Michigan	4.3
23	Kentucky	3.4		17	Arkansas	4.2
2	Louisiana	8.8		18	California	4.1
44	Maine	0.8		18	Tennessee	4.1
5	Maryland	7.1		20	Oklahoma	3.7
35	Massachusetts	1.5		20	Texas	3.7
16	Michigan	4.3		22	Nevada	3.6
40	Minnesota	1.1		23	Kentucky	3.4
3	Mississippi	8.5		23	Ohio	3.4
6	Missouri	6.0		25	West Virginia	3.2
39	Montana	1.2		26	Virginia	3.1
47	Nebraska	0.5		27	New Jersey	2.8
22	Nevada	3.6		28	Kansas	2.7
48	New Hampshire	0.2		29	Connecticut	2.1
27	New Jersey	2.8		30	South Dakota	2.0
8	New Mexico	5.5		31	Alaska	1.9
13	New York	4.4		31	Colorado	1.9
11	North Carolina	4.9		33	Washington	1.8
49	North Dakota	0.0		34	Rhode Island	1.7
23	Ohio	3.4		35	Massachusetts	1.5
20	Oklahoma	3.7		36	Wisconsin	1.4
37	Oregon	1.3		37	Oregon	1.3
13	Pennsylvania	4.4		37	Vermont	1.3
34	Rhode Island	1.7		39	Montana	1.2
9	South Carolina	5.4		40	Minnesota	1.1
30	South Dakota	2.0		41	Hawaii	1.0
18	Tennessee	4.1		41	Idaho	1.0
20	Texas	3.7		43	Iowa	0.9
46	Utah	0.7		44	Maine	0.8
37	Vermont	1.3		44	Wyoming	0.8
26	Virginia	3.1		46	Utah	0.7
33	Washington	1.8		47	Nebraska	0.5
25	West Virginia	3.2		48	New Hampshire	0.2
36	Wisconsin	1.4		49	North Dakota	0.0
44	Wyoming	0.8		NA	Florida**	NA
					District of Columbia**	NA

Source: CQ Press using reported data from the Federal Bureau of Investigation
 "Crime in the United States 2008" (Uniform Crime Reports, September 14, 2009, http://www.fbi.gov/ucr/ucr.htm)
*Of the 14,180 murders in 2008 for which supplemental data were received by the F.B.I. There were an additional 2,092 murders for which the type of murder weapon was not reported to the F.B.I. Includes nonnegligent manslaughter. National and state rates based on population for reporting jurisdictions only. Illinois's rate is for Chicago and Rockford only.
**Not available.

Percent of Murders Involving Firearms in 2008

National Percent = 66.9% of Murders*

ALPHA ORDER

RANK ORDER

RANK	STATE	PERCENT		RANK	STATE	PERCENT
3	Alabama	77.5		1	Illinois*	79.4
39	Alaska	48.1		2	Louisiana	79.2
9	Arizona	71.6		3	Alabama	77.5
12	Arkansas	70.1		4	Delaware	77.2
14	California	69.4		4	Mississippi	77.2
33	Colorado	57.0		6	Missouri	76.7
21	Connecticut	63.4		7	Pennsylvania	74.4
4	Delaware	77.2		8	Indiana	71.9
NA	Florida**	NA		9	Arizona	71.6
11	Georgia	70.8		9	Maryland	71.6
43	Hawaii	44.0		11	Georgia	70.8
25	Idaho	60.9		12	Arkansas	70.1
1	Illinois*	79.4		13	Michigan	70.0
8	Indiana	71.9		14	California	69.4
47	Iowa	33.8		15	South Carolina	67.8
35	Kansas	55.5		16	Kentucky	66.5
16	Kentucky	66.5		17	New Mexico	65.7
2	Louisiana	79.2		18	Virginia	65.6
46	Maine	35.5		19	Texas	65.2
9	Maryland	71.6		20	Ohio	63.7
37	Massachusetts	54.3		21	Connecticut	63.4
13	Michigan	70.0		22	New Jersey	62.8
38	Minnesota	50.9		23	Rhode Island	62.1
4	Mississippi	77.2		24	North Carolina	61.8
6	Missouri	76.7		25	Idaho	60.9
40	Montana	47.8		26	Oklahoma	60.4
44	Nebraska	40.9		27	West Virginia	60.0
32	Nevada	57.1		28	South Dakota	59.1
48	New Hampshire	16.7		29	Tennessee	58.8
22	New Jersey	62.8		30	Washington	57.9
17	New Mexico	65.7		31	Oregon	57.3
34	New York	56.9		32	Nevada	57.1
24	North Carolina	61.8		33	Colorado	57.0
49	North Dakota	0.0		34	New York	56.9
20	Ohio	63.7		35	Kansas	55.5
26	Oklahoma	60.4		36	Wisconsin	54.8
31	Oregon	57.3		37	Massachusetts	54.3
7	Pennsylvania	74.4		38	Minnesota	50.9
23	Rhode Island	62.1		39	Alaska	48.1
15	South Carolina	67.8		40	Montana	47.8
28	South Dakota	59.1		41	Vermont	47.1
29	Tennessee	58.8		42	Utah	46.3
19	Texas	65.2		43	Hawaii	44.0
42	Utah	46.3		44	Nebraska	40.9
41	Vermont	47.1		45	Wyoming	40.0
18	Virginia	65.6		46	Maine	35.5
30	Washington	57.9		47	Iowa	33.8
27	West Virginia	60.0		48	New Hampshire	16.7
36	Wisconsin	54.8		49	North Dakota	0.0
45	Wyoming	40.0		NA	Florida**	NA
					District of Columbia**	NA

Source: CQ Press using reported data from the Federal Bureau of Investigation
"Crime in the United States 2008" (Uniform Crime Reports, September 14, 2009, http://www.fbi.gov/ucr/ucr.htm)
*Of the 14,180 murders in 2008 for which supplemental data were received by the F.B.I. There were an additional 2,092 murders for which the type of murder weapon was not reported to the F.B.I. Includes nonnegligent manslaughter. National and state percents based on reporting jurisdictions only. Illinois's percent is for Chicago and Rockford only.
**Not available.

Murders With Handguns in 2008

National Total = 6,755 Murders*

ALPHA ORDER

RANK	STATE	MURDERS	% of USA
9	Alabama	241	3.6%
38	Alaska	9	0.1%
8	Arizona	243	3.6%
25	Arkansas	65	1.0%
1	California	1,156	17.1%
30	Colorado	50	0.7%
31	Connecticut	46	0.7%
33	Delaware	29	0.4%
NA	Florida**	NA	NA
5	Georgia	371	5.5%
41	Hawaii	7	0.1%
38	Idaho	9	0.1%
3	Illinois*	412	6.1%
16	Indiana	134	2.0%
37	Iowa	13	0.2%
32	Kansas	41	0.6%
23	Kentucky	78	1.2%
9	Louisiana	241	3.6%
42	Maine	6	0.1%
6	Maryland	328	4.9%
27	Massachusetts	59	0.9%
15	Michigan	165	2.4%
28	Minnesota	51	0.8%
19	Mississippi	115	1.7%
13	Missouri	172	2.5%
43	Montana	5	0.1%
47	Nebraska	1	0.0%
26	Nevada	60	0.9%
47	New Hampshire	1	0.0%
11	New Jersey	202	3.0%
24	New Mexico	70	1.0%
20	New York	107	1.6%
7	North Carolina	261	3.9%
49	North Dakota	0	0.0%
12	Ohio	175	2.6%
21	Oklahoma	106	1.6%
34	Oregon	24	0.4%
4	Pennsylvania	398	5.9%
38	Rhode Island	9	0.1%
17	South Carolina	125	1.9%
44	South Dakota	4	0.1%
14	Tennessee	170	2.5%
2	Texas	706	10.5%
35	Utah	16	0.2%
44	Vermont	4	0.1%
18	Virginia	121	1.8%
22	Washington	82	1.2%
36	West Virginia	14	0.2%
28	Wisconsin	51	0.8%
46	Wyoming	2	0.0%

RANK ORDER

RANK	STATE	MURDERS	% of USA
1	California	1,156	17.1%
2	Texas	706	10.5%
3	Illinois*	412	6.1%
4	Pennsylvania	398	5.9%
5	Georgia	371	5.5%
6	Maryland	328	4.9%
7	North Carolina	261	3.9%
8	Arizona	243	3.6%
9	Alabama	241	3.6%
9	Louisiana	241	3.6%
11	New Jersey	202	3.0%
12	Ohio	175	2.6%
13	Missouri	172	2.5%
14	Tennessee	170	2.5%
15	Michigan	165	2.4%
16	Indiana	134	2.0%
17	South Carolina	125	1.9%
18	Virginia	121	1.8%
19	Mississippi	115	1.7%
20	New York	107	1.6%
21	Oklahoma	106	1.6%
22	Washington	82	1.2%
23	Kentucky	78	1.2%
24	New Mexico	70	1.0%
25	Arkansas	65	1.0%
26	Nevada	60	0.9%
27	Massachusetts	59	0.9%
28	Minnesota	51	0.8%
28	Wisconsin	51	0.8%
30	Colorado	50	0.7%
31	Connecticut	46	0.7%
32	Kansas	41	0.6%
33	Delaware	29	0.4%
34	Oregon	24	0.4%
35	Utah	16	0.2%
36	West Virginia	14	0.2%
37	Iowa	13	0.2%
38	Alaska	9	0.1%
38	Idaho	9	0.1%
38	Rhode Island	9	0.1%
41	Hawaii	7	0.1%
42	Maine	6	0.1%
43	Montana	5	0.1%
44	South Dakota	4	0.1%
44	Vermont	4	0.1%
46	Wyoming	2	0.0%
47	Nebraska	1	0.0%
47	New Hampshire	1	0.0%
49	North Dakota	0	0.0%
NA	Florida**	NA	NA
	District of Columbia**	NA	NA

Source: Reported data from the Federal Bureau of Investigation
   "Crime in the United States 2008" (Uniform Crime Reports, September 14, 2009, http://www.fbi.gov/ucr/ucr.htm)
*Of the 14,180 murders in 2008 for which supplemental data were received by the F.B.I. There were an additional 2,092 murders for which the type of murder weapon was not reported to the F.B.I. There were also 1,910 murders that were reported as murders by "firearms, type unknown." Murder includes nonnegligent manslaughter. Numbers are for reporting jurisdictions only. Illinois's figure is for Chicago and Rockford only. **Not available.

Murder Rate With Handguns in 2008

National Rate = 2.8 Murders per 100,000 Population*

RANK	STATE (ALPHA ORDER)	RATE		RANK	STATE (RANK ORDER)	RATE
2	Alabama	7.5		1	Illinois*	13.8
28	Alaska	1.3		2	Alabama	7.5
8	Arizona	3.8		3	Louisiana	6.9
19	Arkansas	2.5		3	Mississippi	6.9
12	California	3.2		5	Maryland	6.6
31	Colorado	1.1		6	Georgia	5.1
27	Connecticut	1.4		7	New Mexico	4.4
10	Delaware	3.3		8	Arizona	3.8
NA	Florida**	NA		9	North Carolina	3.5
6	Georgia	5.1		10	Delaware	3.3
39	Hawaii	0.6		10	Pennsylvania	3.3
39	Idaho	0.6		12	California	3.2
1	Illinois*	13.8		12	South Carolina	3.2
18	Indiana	2.7		14	Oklahoma	3.1
43	Iowa	0.5		15	Missouri	3.0
25	Kansas	1.8		16	Tennessee	2.9
22	Kentucky	2.2		16	Texas	2.9
3	Louisiana	6.9		18	Indiana	2.7
43	Maine	0.5		19	Arkansas	2.5
5	Maryland	6.6		20	New Jersey	2.4
32	Massachusetts	1.0		21	Nevada	2.3
24	Michigan	1.9		22	Kentucky	2.2
32	Minnesota	1.0		23	Ohio	2.1
3	Mississippi	6.9		24	Michigan	1.9
15	Missouri	3.0		25	Kansas	1.8
43	Montana	0.5		26	Virginia	1.6
47	Nebraska	0.1		27	Connecticut	1.4
21	Nevada	2.3		28	Alaska	1.3
47	New Hampshire	0.1		28	Washington	1.3
20	New Jersey	2.4		28	West Virginia	1.3
7	New Mexico	4.4		31	Colorado	1.1
32	New York	1.0		32	Massachusetts	1.0
9	North Carolina	3.5		32	Minnesota	1.0
49	North Dakota	0.0		32	New York	1.0
23	Ohio	2.1		35	Rhode Island	0.9
14	Oklahoma	3.1		35	Wisconsin	0.9
37	Oregon	0.7		37	Oregon	0.7
10	Pennsylvania	3.3		37	Vermont	0.7
35	Rhode Island	0.9		39	Hawaii	0.6
12	South Carolina	3.2		39	Idaho	0.6
39	South Dakota	0.6		39	South Dakota	0.6
16	Tennessee	2.9		39	Utah	0.6
16	Texas	2.9		43	Iowa	0.5
39	Utah	0.6		43	Maine	0.5
37	Vermont	0.7		43	Montana	0.5
26	Virginia	1.6		46	Wyoming	0.4
28	Washington	1.3		47	Nebraska	0.1
28	West Virginia	1.3		47	New Hampshire	0.1
35	Wisconsin	0.9		49	North Dakota	0.0
46	Wyoming	0.4		NA	Florida**	NA
					District of Columbia**	NA

Source: CQ Press using reported data from the Federal Bureau of Investigation
  "Crime in the United States 2008" (Uniform Crime Reports, September 14, 2009, http://www.fbi.gov/ucr/ucr.htm)
*Of the 14,180 murders in 2008 for which supplemental data were received by the F.B.I. There were an additional 2,092 murders for which the type of murder weapon was not reported to the F.B.I. There were also 1,910 murders that were reported as murders by "firearms, type unknown." Murder includes nonnegligent manslaughter. Numbers are for reporting jurisdictions only. Illinois's figure is for Chicago and Rockford only. **Not available.

Percent of Murders Involving Handguns in 2008

National Percent = 47.6% of Murders*

<table>
<tr><th colspan="3">ALPHA ORDER</th><th colspan="3">RANK ORDER</th></tr>
<tr><th>RANK</th><th>STATE</th><th>PERCENT</th><th>RANK</th><th>STATE</th><th>PERCENT</th></tr>
<tr><td>2</td><td>Alabama</td><td>71.3</td><td>1</td><td>Illinois*</td><td>77.7</td></tr>
<tr><td>32</td><td>Alaska</td><td>33.3</td><td>2</td><td>Alabama</td><td>71.3</td></tr>
<tr><td>7</td><td>Arizona</td><td>60.0</td><td>3</td><td>Maryland</td><td>66.5</td></tr>
<tr><td>21</td><td>Arkansas</td><td>41.4</td><td>4</td><td>Mississippi</td><td>62.5</td></tr>
<tr><td>9</td><td>California</td><td>54.0</td><td>5</td><td>Louisiana</td><td>61.8</td></tr>
<tr><td>33</td><td>Colorado</td><td>33.1</td><td>6</td><td>Georgia</td><td>60.4</td></tr>
<tr><td>22</td><td>Connecticut</td><td>41.1</td><td>7</td><td>Arizona</td><td>60.0</td></tr>
<tr><td>13</td><td>Delaware</td><td>50.9</td><td>8</td><td>Pennsylvania</td><td>56.9</td></tr>
<tr><td>NA</td><td>Florida**</td><td>NA</td><td>9</td><td>California</td><td>54.0</td></tr>
<tr><td>6</td><td>Georgia</td><td>60.4</td><td>10</td><td>New Jersey</td><td>53.7</td></tr>
<tr><td>38</td><td>Hawaii</td><td>28.0</td><td>11</td><td>New Mexico</td><td>52.2</td></tr>
<tr><td>24</td><td>Idaho</td><td>39.1</td><td>12</td><td>Texas</td><td>51.5</td></tr>
<tr><td>1</td><td>Illinois*</td><td>77.7</td><td>13</td><td>Delaware</td><td>50.9</td></tr>
<tr><td>17</td><td>Indiana</td><td>43.8</td><td>14</td><td>Oklahoma</td><td>50.0</td></tr>
<tr><td>45</td><td>Iowa</td><td>17.6</td><td>15</td><td>Minnesota</td><td>48.1</td></tr>
<tr><td>28</td><td>Kansas</td><td>37.3</td><td>16</td><td>North Carolina</td><td>44.5</td></tr>
<tr><td>19</td><td>Kentucky</td><td>42.9</td><td>17</td><td>Indiana</td><td>43.8</td></tr>
<tr><td>5</td><td>Louisiana</td><td>61.8</td><td>18</td><td>Washington</td><td>43.2</td></tr>
<tr><td>43</td><td>Maine</td><td>19.4</td><td>19</td><td>Kentucky</td><td>42.9</td></tr>
<tr><td>3</td><td>Maryland</td><td>66.5</td><td>20</td><td>Tennessee</td><td>41.7</td></tr>
<tr><td>30</td><td>Massachusetts</td><td>36.0</td><td>21</td><td>Arkansas</td><td>41.4</td></tr>
<tr><td>36</td><td>Michigan</td><td>30.8</td><td>22</td><td>Connecticut</td><td>41.1</td></tr>
<tr><td>15</td><td>Minnesota</td><td>48.1</td><td>22</td><td>South Carolina</td><td>41.1</td></tr>
<tr><td>4</td><td>Mississippi</td><td>62.5</td><td>24</td><td>Idaho</td><td>39.1</td></tr>
<tr><td>27</td><td>Missouri</td><td>37.8</td><td>25</td><td>Utah</td><td>39.0</td></tr>
<tr><td>41</td><td>Montana</td><td>21.7</td><td>26</td><td>Ohio</td><td>38.0</td></tr>
<tr><td>48</td><td>Nebraska</td><td>4.5</td><td>27</td><td>Missouri</td><td>37.8</td></tr>
<tr><td>29</td><td>Nevada</td><td>36.8</td><td>28</td><td>Kansas</td><td>37.3</td></tr>
<tr><td>47</td><td>New Hampshire</td><td>8.3</td><td>29</td><td>Nevada</td><td>36.8</td></tr>
<tr><td>10</td><td>New Jersey</td><td>53.7</td><td>30</td><td>Massachusetts</td><td>36.0</td></tr>
<tr><td>11</td><td>New Mexico</td><td>52.2</td><td>31</td><td>Wisconsin</td><td>34.9</td></tr>
<tr><td>46</td><td>New York</td><td>12.8</td><td>32</td><td>Alaska</td><td>33.3</td></tr>
<tr><td>16</td><td>North Carolina</td><td>44.5</td><td>33</td><td>Colorado</td><td>33.1</td></tr>
<tr><td>49</td><td>North Dakota</td><td>0.0</td><td>33</td><td>Virginia</td><td>33.1</td></tr>
<tr><td>26</td><td>Ohio</td><td>38.0</td><td>35</td><td>Rhode Island</td><td>31.0</td></tr>
<tr><td>14</td><td>Oklahoma</td><td>50.0</td><td>36</td><td>Michigan</td><td>30.8</td></tr>
<tr><td>37</td><td>Oregon</td><td>29.3</td><td>37</td><td>Oregon</td><td>29.3</td></tr>
<tr><td>8</td><td>Pennsylvania</td><td>56.9</td><td>38</td><td>Hawaii</td><td>28.0</td></tr>
<tr><td>35</td><td>Rhode Island</td><td>31.0</td><td>39</td><td>West Virginia</td><td>25.5</td></tr>
<tr><td>22</td><td>South Carolina</td><td>41.1</td><td>40</td><td>Vermont</td><td>23.5</td></tr>
<tr><td>44</td><td>South Dakota</td><td>18.2</td><td>41</td><td>Montana</td><td>21.7</td></tr>
<tr><td>20</td><td>Tennessee</td><td>41.7</td><td>42</td><td>Wyoming</td><td>20.0</td></tr>
<tr><td>12</td><td>Texas</td><td>51.5</td><td>43</td><td>Maine</td><td>19.4</td></tr>
<tr><td>25</td><td>Utah</td><td>39.0</td><td>44</td><td>South Dakota</td><td>18.2</td></tr>
<tr><td>40</td><td>Vermont</td><td>23.5</td><td>45</td><td>Iowa</td><td>17.6</td></tr>
<tr><td>33</td><td>Virginia</td><td>33.1</td><td>46</td><td>New York</td><td>12.8</td></tr>
<tr><td>18</td><td>Washington</td><td>43.2</td><td>47</td><td>New Hampshire</td><td>8.3</td></tr>
<tr><td>39</td><td>West Virginia</td><td>25.5</td><td>48</td><td>Nebraska</td><td>4.5</td></tr>
<tr><td>31</td><td>Wisconsin</td><td>34.9</td><td>49</td><td>North Dakota</td><td>0.0</td></tr>
<tr><td>42</td><td>Wyoming</td><td>20.0</td><td>NA</td><td>Florida**</td><td>NA</td></tr>
<tr><td></td><td></td><td></td><td></td><td>District of Columbia**</td><td>NA</td></tr>
</table>

Source: CQ Press using reported data from the Federal Bureau of Investigation
    "Crime in the United States 2008" (Uniform Crime Reports, September 14, 2009, http://www.fbi.gov/ucr/ucr.htm)
*Of the 14,180 murders in 2008 for which supplemental data were received by the F.B.I. There were an additional 2,092 murders for which the type of murder weapon was not reported to the F.B.I. There were also 1,910 murders that were reported as murders by "firearms, type unknown." Murder includes nonnegligent manslaughter. Numbers are for reporting jurisdictions only. Illinois's figure is for Chicago and Rockford only. **Not available.

Murders With Rifles in 2008

National Total = 375 Murders*

RANK	STATE	MURDERS	% of USA
34	Alabama	1	0.3%
34	Alaska	1	0.3%
9	Arizona	15	4.0%
34	Arkansas	1	0.3%
2	California	48	12.8%
22	Colorado	3	0.8%
34	Connecticut	1	0.3%
44	Delaware	0	0.0%
NA	Florida**	NA	NA
5	Georgia	20	5.3%
34	Hawaii	1	0.3%
26	Idaho	2	0.5%
22	Illinois*	3	0.8%
7	Indiana	16	4.3%
26	Iowa	2	0.5%
26	Kansas	2	0.5%
15	Kentucky	8	2.1%
5	Louisiana	20	5.3%
26	Maine	2	0.5%
19	Maryland	4	1.1%
26	Massachusetts	2	0.5%
7	Michigan	16	4.3%
34	Minnesota	1	0.3%
19	Mississippi	4	1.1%
3	Missouri	25	6.7%
22	Montana	3	0.8%
34	Nebraska	1	0.3%
34	Nevada	1	0.3%
34	New Hampshire	1	0.3%
34	New Jersey	1	0.3%
19	New Mexico	4	1.1%
11	New York	12	3.2%
4	North Carolina	22	5.9%
44	North Dakota	0	0.0%
18	Ohio	5	1.3%
17	Oklahoma	6	1.6%
26	Oregon	2	0.5%
9	Pennsylvania	15	4.0%
44	Rhode Island	0	0.0%
14	South Carolina	9	2.4%
44	South Dakota	0	0.0%
13	Tennessee	11	2.9%
1	Texas	58	15.5%
44	Utah	0	0.0%
22	Vermont	3	0.8%
11	Virginia	12	3.2%
26	Washington	2	0.5%
26	West Virginia	2	0.5%
16	Wisconsin	7	1.9%
44	Wyoming	0	0.0%

RANK	STATE	MURDERS	% of USA
1	Texas	58	15.5%
2	California	48	12.8%
3	Missouri	25	6.7%
4	North Carolina	22	5.9%
5	Georgia	20	5.3%
5	Louisiana	20	5.3%
7	Indiana	16	4.3%
7	Michigan	16	4.3%
9	Arizona	15	4.0%
9	Pennsylvania	15	4.0%
11	New York	12	3.2%
11	Virginia	12	3.2%
13	Tennessee	11	2.9%
14	South Carolina	9	2.4%
15	Kentucky	8	2.1%
16	Wisconsin	7	1.9%
17	Oklahoma	6	1.6%
18	Ohio	5	1.3%
19	Maryland	4	1.1%
19	Mississippi	4	1.1%
19	New Mexico	4	1.1%
22	Colorado	3	0.8%
22	Illinois*	3	0.8%
22	Montana	3	0.8%
22	Vermont	3	0.8%
26	Idaho	2	0.5%
26	Iowa	2	0.5%
26	Kansas	2	0.5%
26	Maine	2	0.5%
26	Massachusetts	2	0.5%
26	Oregon	2	0.5%
26	Washington	2	0.5%
26	West Virginia	2	0.5%
34	Alabama	1	0.3%
34	Alaska	1	0.3%
34	Arkansas	1	0.3%
34	Connecticut	1	0.3%
34	Hawaii	1	0.3%
34	Minnesota	1	0.3%
34	Nebraska	1	0.3%
34	Nevada	1	0.3%
34	New Hampshire	1	0.3%
34	New Jersey	1	0.3%
44	Delaware	0	0.0%
44	North Dakota	0	0.0%
44	Rhode Island	0	0.0%
44	South Dakota	0	0.0%
44	Utah	0	0.0%
44	Wyoming	0	0.0%
NA	Florida**	NA	NA
	District of Columbia**	NA	NA

Source: Reported data from the Federal Bureau of Investigation
"Crime in the United States 2008" (Uniform Crime Reports, September 14, 2009, http://www.fbi.gov/ucr/ucr.htm)
*Of the 14,180 murders in 2008 for which supplemental data were received by the F.B.I. There were an additional 2,092 murders for which the type of murder weapon was not reported to the F.B.I. There were also 1,910 murders that were reported as murders by "firearms, type unknown." Murder includes nonnegligent manslaughter. Numbers are for reporting jurisdictions only. Illinois's figure is for Chicago and Rockford only. **Not available.

Percent of Murders Involving Rifles in 2008

National Percent = 2.6% of Murders*

ALPHA ORDER

RANK	STATE	PERCENT
42	Alabama	0.3
15	Alaska	3.7
15	Arizona	3.7
39	Arkansas	0.6
27	California	2.2
30	Colorado	2.0
36	Connecticut	0.9
44	Delaware	0.0
NA	Florida**	NA
18	Georgia	3.3
13	Hawaii	4.0
3	Idaho	8.7
39	Illinois*	0.6
7	Indiana	5.2
24	Iowa	2.7
31	Kansas	1.8
11	Kentucky	4.4
8	Louisiana	5.1
5	Maine	6.5
38	Maryland	0.8
33	Massachusetts	1.2
20	Michigan	3.0
36	Minnesota	0.9
27	Mississippi	2.2
6	Missouri	5.5
2	Montana	13.0
10	Nebraska	4.5
39	Nevada	0.6
4	New Hampshire	8.3
42	New Jersey	0.3
20	New Mexico	3.0
32	New York	1.4
14	North Carolina	3.8
44	North Dakota	0.0
34	Ohio	1.1
23	Oklahoma	2.8
26	Oregon	2.4
29	Pennsylvania	2.1
44	Rhode Island	0.0
20	South Carolina	3.0
44	South Dakota	0.0
24	Tennessee	2.7
12	Texas	4.2
44	Utah	0.0
1	Vermont	17.6
18	Virginia	3.3
34	Washington	1.1
17	West Virginia	3.6
9	Wisconsin	4.8
44	Wyoming	0.0

RANK ORDER

RANK	STATE	PERCENT
1	Vermont	17.6
2	Montana	13.0
3	Idaho	8.7
4	New Hampshire	8.3
5	Maine	6.5
6	Missouri	5.5
7	Indiana	5.2
8	Louisiana	5.1
9	Wisconsin	4.8
10	Nebraska	4.5
11	Kentucky	4.4
12	Texas	4.2
13	Hawaii	4.0
14	North Carolina	3.8
15	Alaska	3.7
15	Arizona	3.7
17	West Virginia	3.6
18	Georgia	3.3
18	Virginia	3.3
20	Michigan	3.0
20	New Mexico	3.0
20	South Carolina	3.0
23	Oklahoma	2.8
24	Iowa	2.7
24	Tennessee	2.7
26	Oregon	2.4
27	California	2.2
27	Mississippi	2.2
29	Pennsylvania	2.1
30	Colorado	2.0
31	Kansas	1.8
32	New York	1.4
33	Massachusetts	1.2
34	Ohio	1.1
34	Washington	1.1
36	Connecticut	0.9
36	Minnesota	0.9
38	Maryland	0.8
39	Arkansas	0.6
39	Illinois*	0.6
39	Nevada	0.6
42	Alabama	0.3
42	New Jersey	0.3
44	Delaware	0.0
44	North Dakota	0.0
44	Rhode Island	0.0
44	South Dakota	0.0
44	Utah	0.0
44	Wyoming	0.0
NA	Florida**	NA
	District of Columbia**	NA

Source: CQ Press using reported data from the Federal Bureau of Investigation
   "Crime in the United States 2008" (Uniform Crime Reports, September 14, 2009, http://www.fbi.gov/ucr/ucr.htm)
*Of the 14,180 murders in 2008 for which supplemental data were received by the F.B.I. There were an additional 2,092 murders for which the type of murder weapon was not reported to the F.B.I. There were also 1,910 murders that were reported as murders by "firearms, type unknown." Murder includes nonnegligent manslaughter. Numbers are for reporting jurisdictions only. Illinois's figure is for Chicago and Rockford only. **Not available.

Murders With Shotguns in 2008

National Total = 444 Murders*

ALPHA ORDER

RANK	STATE	MURDERS	% of USA
4	Alabama	20	4.5%
27	Alaska	3	0.7%
8	Arizona	16	3.6%
20	Arkansas	9	2.0%
1	California	64	14.4%
32	Colorado	2	0.5%
41	Connecticut	0	0.0%
32	Delaware	2	0.5%
NA	Florida**	NA	NA
11	Georgia	13	2.9%
32	Hawaii	2	0.5%
27	Idaho	3	0.7%
39	Illinois*	1	0.2%
25	Indiana	4	0.9%
25	Iowa	4	0.9%
27	Kansas	3	0.7%
11	Kentucky	13	2.9%
15	Louisiana	12	2.7%
41	Maine	0	0.0%
11	Maryland	13	2.9%
41	Massachusetts	0	0.0%
21	Michigan	8	1.8%
32	Minnesota	2	0.5%
16	Mississippi	11	2.5%
10	Missouri	15	3.4%
39	Montana	1	0.2%
32	Nebraska	2	0.5%
23	Nevada	6	1.4%
41	New Hampshire	0	0.0%
27	New Jersey	3	0.7%
22	New Mexico	7	1.6%
4	New York	20	4.5%
3	North Carolina	25	5.6%
41	North Dakota	0	0.0%
24	Ohio	5	1.1%
17	Oklahoma	10	2.3%
32	Oregon	2	0.5%
8	Pennsylvania	16	3.6%
41	Rhode Island	0	0.0%
7	South Carolina	18	4.1%
32	South Dakota	2	0.5%
6	Tennessee	19	4.3%
2	Texas	52	11.7%
41	Utah	0	0.0%
41	Vermont	0	0.0%
11	Virginia	13	2.9%
17	Washington	10	2.3%
17	West Virginia	10	2.3%
27	Wisconsin	3	0.7%
41	Wyoming	0	0.0%

RANK ORDER

RANK	STATE	MURDERS	% of USA
1	California	64	14.4%
2	Texas	52	11.7%
3	North Carolina	25	5.6%
4	Alabama	20	4.5%
4	New York	20	4.5%
6	Tennessee	19	4.3%
7	South Carolina	18	4.1%
8	Arizona	16	3.6%
8	Pennsylvania	16	3.6%
10	Missouri	15	3.4%
11	Georgia	13	2.9%
11	Kentucky	13	2.9%
11	Maryland	13	2.9%
11	Virginia	13	2.9%
15	Louisiana	12	2.7%
16	Mississippi	11	2.5%
17	Oklahoma	10	2.3%
17	Washington	10	2.3%
17	West Virginia	10	2.3%
20	Arkansas	9	2.0%
21	Michigan	8	1.8%
22	New Mexico	7	1.6%
23	Nevada	6	1.4%
24	Ohio	5	1.1%
25	Indiana	4	0.9%
25	Iowa	4	0.9%
27	Alaska	3	0.7%
27	Idaho	3	0.7%
27	Kansas	3	0.7%
27	New Jersey	3	0.7%
27	Wisconsin	3	0.7%
32	Colorado	2	0.5%
32	Delaware	2	0.5%
32	Hawaii	2	0.5%
32	Minnesota	2	0.5%
32	Nebraska	2	0.5%
32	Oregon	2	0.5%
32	South Dakota	2	0.5%
39	Illinois*	1	0.2%
39	Montana	1	0.2%
41	Connecticut	0	0.0%
41	Maine	0	0.0%
41	Massachusetts	0	0.0%
41	New Hampshire	0	0.0%
41	North Dakota	0	0.0%
41	Rhode Island	0	0.0%
41	Utah	0	0.0%
41	Vermont	0	0.0%
41	Wyoming	0	0.0%
NA	Florida**	NA	NA
	District of Columbia**	NA	NA

Source: Reported data from the Federal Bureau of Investigation
"Crime in the United States 2008" (Uniform Crime Reports, September 14, 2009, http://www.fbi.gov/ucr/ucr.htm)
*Of the 14,180 murders in 2008 for which supplemental data were received by the F.B.I. There were an additional 2,092 murders for which the type of murder weapon was not reported to the F.B.I. There were also 1,910 murders that were reported as murders by "firearms, type unknown." Murder includes nonnegligent manslaughter. Numbers are for reporting jurisdictions only. Illinois's figure is for Chicago and Rockford only. **Not available.

Percent of Murders Involving Shotguns in 2008

National Percent = 3.1% of Murders*

ALPHA ORDER

RANK	STATE	PERCENT
9	Alabama	5.9
3	Alaska	11.1
19	Arizona	4.0
11	Arkansas	5.7
26	California	3.0
36	Colorado	1.3
41	Connecticut	0.0
23	Delaware	3.5
NA	Florida**	NA
32	Georgia	2.1
6	Hawaii	8.0
2	Idaho	13.0
40	Illinois*	0.2
36	Indiana	1.3
12	Iowa	5.4
27	Kansas	2.7
7	Kentucky	7.1
25	Louisiana	3.1
41	Maine	0.0
28	Maryland	2.6
41	Massachusetts	0.0
35	Michigan	1.5
34	Minnesota	1.9
8	Mississippi	6.0
24	Missouri	3.3
17	Montana	4.3
4	Nebraska	9.1
21	Nevada	3.7
41	New Hampshire	0.0
39	New Jersey	0.8
14	New Mexico	5.2
29	New York	2.4
17	North Carolina	4.3
41	North Dakota	0.0
38	Ohio	1.1
15	Oklahoma	4.7
29	Oregon	2.4
31	Pennsylvania	2.3
41	Rhode Island	0.0
9	South Carolina	5.9
4	South Dakota	9.1
15	Tennessee	4.7
20	Texas	3.8
41	Utah	0.0
41	Vermont	0.0
22	Virginia	3.6
13	Washington	5.3
1	West Virginia	18.2
32	Wisconsin	2.1
41	Wyoming	0.0

RANK ORDER

RANK	STATE	PERCENT
1	West Virginia	18.2
2	Idaho	13.0
3	Alaska	11.1
4	Nebraska	9.1
4	South Dakota	9.1
6	Hawaii	8.0
7	Kentucky	7.1
8	Mississippi	6.0
9	Alabama	5.9
9	South Carolina	5.9
11	Arkansas	5.7
12	Iowa	5.4
13	Washington	5.3
14	New Mexico	5.2
15	Oklahoma	4.7
15	Tennessee	4.7
17	Montana	4.3
17	North Carolina	4.3
19	Arizona	4.0
20	Texas	3.8
21	Nevada	3.7
22	Virginia	3.6
23	Delaware	3.5
24	Missouri	3.3
25	Louisiana	3.1
26	California	3.0
27	Kansas	2.7
28	Maryland	2.6
29	New York	2.4
29	Oregon	2.4
31	Pennsylvania	2.3
32	Georgia	2.1
32	Wisconsin	2.1
34	Minnesota	1.9
35	Michigan	1.5
36	Colorado	1.3
36	Indiana	1.3
38	Ohio	1.1
39	New Jersey	0.8
40	Illinois*	0.2
41	Connecticut	0.0
41	Maine	0.0
41	Massachusetts	0.0
41	New Hampshire	0.0
41	North Dakota	0.0
41	Rhode Island	0.0
41	Utah	0.0
41	Vermont	0.0
41	Wyoming	0.0
NA	Florida**	NA
	District of Columbia**	NA

Source: CQ Press using reported data from the Federal Bureau of Investigation
   "Crime in the United States 2008" (Uniform Crime Reports, September 14, 2009, http://www.fbi.gov/ucr/ucr.htm)
*Of the 14,180 murders in 2008 for which supplemental data were received by the F.B.I. There were an additional 2,092 murders for which the type of murder weapon was not reported to the F.B.I. There were also 1,910 murders that were reported as murders by "firearms, type unknown." Murder includes nonnegligent manslaughter. Numbers are for reporting jurisdictions only. Illinois's figure is for Chicago and Rockford only. **Not available.

Murders With Knives or Cutting Instruments in 2008

National Total = 1,897 Murders*

ALPHA ORDER

RANK	STATE	MURDERS	% of USA
27	Alabama	24	1.3%
46	Alaska	1	0.1%
13	Arizona	45	2.4%
30	Arkansas	17	0.9%
1	California	294	15.5%
20	Colorado	31	1.6%
23	Connecticut	27	1.4%
38	Delaware	6	0.3%
NA	Florida**	NA	NA
4	Georgia	73	3.8%
36	Hawaii	8	0.4%
48	Idaho	0	0.0%
12	Illinois*	48	2.5%
22	Indiana	28	1.5%
31	Iowa	16	0.8%
33	Kansas	15	0.8%
25	Kentucky	25	1.3%
17	Louisiana	33	1.7%
35	Maine	10	0.5%
7	Maryland	61	3.2%
11	Massachusetts	49	2.6%
15	Michigan	40	2.1%
28	Minnesota	22	1.2%
33	Mississippi	15	0.8%
14	Missouri	41	2.2%
41	Montana	4	0.2%
41	Nebraska	4	0.2%
23	Nevada	27	1.4%
43	New Hampshire	3	0.2%
5	New Jersey	67	3.5%
28	New Mexico	22	1.2%
3	New York	184	9.7%
8	North Carolina	54	2.8%
45	North Dakota	2	0.1%
16	Ohio	38	2.0%
17	Oklahoma	33	1.7%
31	Oregon	16	0.8%
6	Pennsylvania	66	3.5%
38	Rhode Island	6	0.3%
20	South Carolina	31	1.6%
46	South Dakota	1	0.1%
10	Tennessee	53	2.8%
2	Texas	230	12.1%
36	Utah	8	0.4%
48	Vermont	0	0.0%
8	Virginia	54	2.8%
19	Washington	32	1.7%
40	West Virginia	5	0.3%
25	Wisconsin	25	1.3%
43	Wyoming	3	0.2%

RANK ORDER

RANK	STATE	MURDERS	% of USA
1	California	294	15.5%
2	Texas	230	12.1%
3	New York	184	9.7%
4	Georgia	73	3.8%
5	New Jersey	67	3.5%
6	Pennsylvania	66	3.5%
7	Maryland	61	3.2%
8	North Carolina	54	2.8%
8	Virginia	54	2.8%
10	Tennessee	53	2.8%
11	Massachusetts	49	2.6%
12	Illinois*	48	2.5%
13	Arizona	45	2.4%
14	Missouri	41	2.2%
15	Michigan	40	2.1%
16	Ohio	38	2.0%
17	Louisiana	33	1.7%
17	Oklahoma	33	1.7%
19	Washington	32	1.7%
20	Colorado	31	1.6%
20	South Carolina	31	1.6%
22	Indiana	28	1.5%
23	Connecticut	27	1.4%
23	Nevada	27	1.4%
25	Kentucky	25	1.3%
25	Wisconsin	25	1.3%
27	Alabama	24	1.3%
28	Minnesota	22	1.2%
28	New Mexico	22	1.2%
30	Arkansas	17	0.9%
31	Iowa	16	0.8%
31	Oregon	16	0.8%
33	Kansas	15	0.8%
33	Mississippi	15	0.8%
35	Maine	10	0.5%
36	Hawaii	8	0.4%
36	Utah	8	0.4%
38	Delaware	6	0.3%
38	Rhode Island	6	0.3%
40	West Virginia	5	0.3%
41	Montana	4	0.2%
41	Nebraska	4	0.2%
43	New Hampshire	3	0.2%
43	Wyoming	3	0.2%
45	North Dakota	2	0.1%
46	Alaska	1	0.1%
46	South Dakota	1	0.1%
48	Idaho	0	0.0%
48	Vermont	0	0.0%
NA	Florida**	NA	NA
	District of Columbia**	NA	NA

Source: Reported data from the Federal Bureau of Investigation
"Crime in the United States 2008" (Uniform Crime Reports, September 14, 2009, http://www.fbi.gov/ucr/ucr.htm)
*Of the 14,180 murders in 2008 for which supplemental data were received by the F.B.I. There were an additional 2,092 murders for which the type of murder weapon was not reported to the F.B.I. There were also 1,910 murders that were reported as murders by "firearms, type unknown." Murder includes nonnegligent manslaughter. Numbers are for reporting jurisdictions only. Illinois's figure is for Chicago and Rockford only. **Not available.

Percent of Murders Involving Knives or Cutting Instruments in 2008

National Percent = 13.4% of Murders*

ALPHA ORDER

RANK	STATE	PERCENT
45	Alabama	7.1
47	Alaska	3.7
31	Arizona	11.1
32	Arkansas	10.8
25	California	13.7
12	Colorado	20.5
7	Connecticut	24.1
33	Delaware	10.5
NA	Florida**	NA
30	Georgia	11.9
3	Hawaii	32.0
48	Idaho	0.0
38	Illinois*	9.1
36	Indiana	9.2
9	Iowa	21.6
27	Kansas	13.6
25	Kentucky	13.7
41	Louisiana	8.5
2	Maine	32.3
29	Maryland	12.4
5	Massachusetts	29.9
44	Michigan	7.5
10	Minnesota	20.8
43	Mississippi	8.2
40	Missouri	9.0
17	Montana	17.4
15	Nebraska	18.2
21	Nevada	16.6
6	New Hampshire	25.0
16	New Jersey	17.8
22	New Mexico	16.4
8	New York	22.0
36	North Carolina	9.2
1	North Dakota	66.7
42	Ohio	8.3
23	Oklahoma	15.6
13	Oregon	19.5
35	Pennsylvania	9.4
11	Rhode Island	20.7
34	South Carolina	10.2
46	South Dakota	4.5
28	Tennessee	13.0
19	Texas	16.8
13	Utah	19.5
48	Vermont	0.0
24	Virginia	14.8
19	Washington	16.8
38	West Virginia	9.1
18	Wisconsin	17.1
4	Wyoming	30.0

RANK ORDER

RANK	STATE	PERCENT
1	North Dakota	66.7
2	Maine	32.3
3	Hawaii	32.0
4	Wyoming	30.0
5	Massachusetts	29.9
6	New Hampshire	25.0
7	Connecticut	24.1
8	New York	22.0
9	Iowa	21.6
10	Minnesota	20.8
11	Rhode Island	20.7
12	Colorado	20.5
13	Oregon	19.5
13	Utah	19.5
15	Nebraska	18.2
16	New Jersey	17.8
17	Montana	17.4
18	Wisconsin	17.1
19	Texas	16.8
19	Washington	16.8
21	Nevada	16.6
22	New Mexico	16.4
23	Oklahoma	15.6
24	Virginia	14.8
25	California	13.7
25	Kentucky	13.7
27	Kansas	13.6
28	Tennessee	13.0
29	Maryland	12.4
30	Georgia	11.9
31	Arizona	11.1
32	Arkansas	10.8
33	Delaware	10.5
34	South Carolina	10.2
35	Pennsylvania	9.4
36	Indiana	9.2
36	North Carolina	9.2
38	Illinois*	9.1
38	West Virginia	9.1
40	Missouri	9.0
41	Louisiana	8.5
42	Ohio	8.3
43	Mississippi	8.2
44	Michigan	7.5
45	Alabama	7.1
46	South Dakota	4.5
47	Alaska	3.7
48	Idaho	0.0
48	Vermont	0.0
NA	Florida**	NA

District of Columbia**   NA

Source: CQ Press using reported data from the Federal Bureau of Investigation
"Crime in the United States 2008" (Uniform Crime Reports, September 14, 2009, http://www.fbi.gov/ucr/ucr.htm)
*Of the 14,180 murders in 2008 for which supplemental data were received by the F.B.I. There were an additional 2,092 murders for which the type of murder weapon was not reported to the F.B.I. There were also 1,910 murders that were reported as murders by "firearms, type unknown." Murder includes nonnegligent manslaughter. Numbers are for reporting jurisdictions only. Illinois's figure is for Chicago and Rockford only. **Not available.

Murders by Hands, Fists, or Feet in 2008

National Total = 861 Murders*

ALPHA ORDER

RANK ORDER

RANK	STATE	MURDERS	% of USA
17	Alabama	17	2.0%
30	Alaska	7	0.8%
10	Arizona	25	2.9%
36	Arkansas	5	0.6%
1	California	120	13.9%
17	Colorado	17	2.0%
39	Connecticut	3	0.3%
42	Delaware	2	0.2%
NA	Florida**	NA	NA
27	Georgia	8	0.9%
32	Hawaii	6	0.7%
32	Idaho	6	0.7%
23	Illinois*	11	1.3%
15	Indiana	19	2.2%
21	Iowa	13	1.5%
17	Kansas	17	2.0%
26	Kentucky	9	1.0%
20	Louisiana	14	1.6%
32	Maine	6	0.7%
7	Maryland	28	3.3%
39	Massachusetts	3	0.3%
8	Michigan	27	3.1%
27	Minnesota	8	0.9%
30	Mississippi	7	0.8%
22	Missouri	12	1.4%
37	Montana	4	0.5%
44	Nebraska	1	0.1%
27	Nevada	8	0.9%
49	New Hampshire	0	0.0%
5	New Jersey	34	3.9%
23	New Mexico	11	1.3%
6	New York	29	3.4%
3	North Carolina	68	7.9%
44	North Dakota	1	0.1%
4	Ohio	39	4.5%
13	Oklahoma	23	2.7%
44	Oregon	1	0.1%
8	Pennsylvania	27	3.1%
44	Rhode Island	1	0.1%
11	South Carolina	24	2.8%
44	South Dakota	1	0.1%
11	Tennessee	24	2.8%
2	Texas	107	12.4%
32	Utah	6	0.7%
39	Vermont	3	0.3%
23	Virginia	11	1.3%
13	Washington	23	2.7%
37	West Virginia	4	0.5%
15	Wisconsin	19	2.2%
42	Wyoming	2	0.2%

RANK	STATE	MURDERS	% of USA
1	California	120	13.9%
2	Texas	107	12.4%
3	North Carolina	68	7.9%
4	Ohio	39	4.5%
5	New Jersey	34	3.9%
6	New York	29	3.4%
7	Maryland	28	3.3%
8	Michigan	27	3.1%
8	Pennsylvania	27	3.1%
10	Arizona	25	2.9%
11	South Carolina	24	2.8%
11	Tennessee	24	2.8%
13	Oklahoma	23	2.7%
13	Washington	23	2.7%
15	Indiana	19	2.2%
15	Wisconsin	19	2.2%
17	Alabama	17	2.0%
17	Colorado	17	2.0%
17	Kansas	17	2.0%
20	Louisiana	14	1.6%
21	Iowa	13	1.5%
22	Missouri	12	1.4%
23	Illinois*	11	1.3%
23	New Mexico	11	1.3%
23	Virginia	11	1.3%
26	Kentucky	9	1.0%
27	Georgia	8	0.9%
27	Minnesota	8	0.9%
27	Nevada	8	0.9%
30	Alaska	7	0.8%
30	Mississippi	7	0.8%
32	Hawaii	6	0.7%
32	Idaho	6	0.7%
32	Maine	6	0.7%
32	Utah	6	0.7%
36	Arkansas	5	0.6%
37	Montana	4	0.5%
37	West Virginia	4	0.5%
39	Connecticut	3	0.3%
39	Massachusetts	3	0.3%
39	Vermont	3	0.3%
42	Delaware	2	0.2%
42	Wyoming	2	0.2%
44	Nebraska	1	0.1%
44	North Dakota	1	0.1%
44	Oregon	1	0.1%
44	Rhode Island	1	0.1%
44	South Dakota	1	0.1%
49	New Hampshire	0	0.0%
NA	Florida**	NA	NA
	District of Columbia**	NA	NA

Source: Reported data from the Federal Bureau of Investigation
"Crime in the United States 2008" (Uniform Crime Reports, September 14, 2009, http://www.fbi.gov/ucr/ucr.htm)
*Of the 14,180 murders in 2008 for which supplemental data were received by the F.B.I. There were an additional 2,092 murders for which the type of murder weapon was not reported to the F.B.I. There were also 1,910 murders that were reported as murders by "firearms, type unknown." Murder includes nonnegligent manslaughter. Numbers are for reporting jurisdictions only. Illinois's figure is for Chicago and Rockford only. **Not available.

Percent of Murders Involving Hands, Fists, or Feet in 2008

National Percent = 6.1% of Murders*

ALPHA ORDER

RANK	STATE	PERCENT
29	Alabama	5.0
3	Alaska	25.9
24	Arizona	6.2
41	Arkansas	3.2
28	California	5.6
15	Colorado	11.3
43	Connecticut	2.7
38	Delaware	3.5
NA	Florida**	NA
47	Georgia	1.3
4	Hawaii	24.0
2	Idaho	26.1
45	Illinois*	2.1
24	Indiana	6.2
7	Iowa	17.6
10	Kansas	15.5
31	Kentucky	4.9
37	Louisiana	3.6
6	Maine	19.4
27	Maryland	5.7
46	Massachusetts	1.8
29	Michigan	5.0
22	Minnesota	7.5
36	Mississippi	3.8
44	Missouri	2.6
9	Montana	17.4
33	Nebraska	4.5
31	Nevada	4.9
49	New Hampshire	0.0
17	New Jersey	9.0
19	New Mexico	8.2
38	New York	3.5
14	North Carolina	11.6
1	North Dakota	33.3
18	Ohio	8.5
16	Oklahoma	10.8
48	Oregon	1.2
35	Pennsylvania	3.9
40	Rhode Island	3.4
20	South Carolina	7.9
33	South Dakota	4.5
26	Tennessee	5.9
21	Texas	7.8
11	Utah	14.6
7	Vermont	17.6
42	Virginia	3.0
13	Washington	12.1
23	West Virginia	7.3
12	Wisconsin	13.0
5	Wyoming	20.0

RANK ORDER

RANK	STATE	PERCENT
1	North Dakota	33.3
2	Idaho	26.1
3	Alaska	25.9
4	Hawaii	24.0
5	Wyoming	20.0
6	Maine	19.4
7	Iowa	17.6
7	Vermont	17.6
9	Montana	17.4
10	Kansas	15.5
11	Utah	14.6
12	Wisconsin	13.0
13	Washington	12.1
14	North Carolina	11.6
15	Colorado	11.3
16	Oklahoma	10.8
17	New Jersey	9.0
18	Ohio	8.5
19	New Mexico	8.2
20	South Carolina	7.9
21	Texas	7.8
22	Minnesota	7.5
23	West Virginia	7.3
24	Arizona	6.2
24	Indiana	6.2
26	Tennessee	5.9
27	Maryland	5.7
28	California	5.6
29	Alabama	5.0
29	Michigan	5.0
31	Kentucky	4.9
31	Nevada	4.9
33	Nebraska	4.5
33	South Dakota	4.5
35	Pennsylvania	3.9
36	Mississippi	3.8
37	Louisiana	3.6
38	Delaware	3.5
38	New York	3.5
40	Rhode Island	3.4
41	Arkansas	3.2
42	Virginia	3.0
43	Connecticut	2.7
44	Missouri	2.6
45	Illinois*	2.1
46	Massachusetts	1.8
47	Georgia	1.3
48	Oregon	1.2
49	New Hampshire	0.0
NA	Florida**	NA
	District of Columbia**	NA

Source: CQ Press using reported data from the Federal Bureau of Investigation
"Crime in the United States 2008" (Uniform Crime Reports, September 14, 2009, http://www.fbi.gov/ucr/ucr.htm)
*Of the 14,180 murders in 2008 for which supplemental data were received by the F.B.I. There were an additional 2,092 murders for which the type of murder weapon was not reported to the F.B.I. There were also 1,910 murders that were reported as murders by "firearms, type unknown." Murder includes nonnegligent manslaughter. Numbers are for reporting jurisdictions only. Illinois's figure is for Chicago and Rockford only. **Not available.

Rapes in 2008

National Total = 89,000 Rapes*

ALPHA ORDER

RANK	STATE	RAPES	% of USA
20	Alabama	1,617	1.8%
39	Alaska	441	0.5%
18	Arizona	1,673	1.9%
24	Arkansas	1,395	1.6%
1	California	8,903	10.0%
12	Colorado	2,098	2.4%
36	Connecticut	674	0.8%
43	Delaware	366	0.4%
3	Florida	5,972	6.7%
11	Georgia	2,195	2.5%
44	Hawaii	365	0.4%
38	Idaho	551	0.6%
6	Illinois	4,118	4.6%
17	Indiana	1,720	1.9%
35	Iowa	888	1.0%
26	Kansas	1,190	1.3%
23	Kentucky	1,408	1.6%
25	Louisiana	1,232	1.4%
42	Maine	375	0.4%
29	Maryland	1,127	1.3%
16	Massachusetts	1,736	2.0%
4	Michigan	4,502	5.1%
14	Minnesota	1,805	2.0%
34	Mississippi	890	1.0%
21	Missouri	1,615	1.8%
46	Montana	294	0.3%
37	Nebraska	583	0.7%
32	Nevada	1,102	1.2%
41	New Hampshire	391	0.4%
30	New Jersey	1,122	1.3%
28	New Mexico	1,139	1.3%
8	New York	2,801	3.1%
10	North Carolina	2,284	2.6%
48	North Dakota	232	0.3%
5	Ohio	4,419	5.0%
22	Oklahoma	1,466	1.6%
27	Oregon	1,156	1.3%
7	Pennsylvania	3,478	3.9%
47	Rhode Island	277	0.3%
19	South Carolina	1,638	1.8%
40	South Dakota	432	0.5%
13	Tennessee	2,062	2.3%
2	Texas	8,014	9.0%
33	Utah	893	1.0%
50	Vermont	127	0.1%
15	Virginia	1,758	2.0%
9	Washington	2,628	3.0%
45	West Virginia	362	0.4%
31	Wisconsin	1,120	1.3%
49	Wyoming	180	0.2%

RANK ORDER

RANK	STATE	RAPES	% of USA
1	California	8,903	10.0%
2	Texas	8,014	9.0%
3	Florida	5,972	6.7%
4	Michigan	4,502	5.1%
5	Ohio	4,419	5.0%
6	Illinois	4,118	4.6%
7	Pennsylvania	3,478	3.9%
8	New York	2,801	3.1%
9	Washington	2,628	3.0%
10	North Carolina	2,284	2.6%
11	Georgia	2,195	2.5%
12	Colorado	2,098	2.4%
13	Tennessee	2,062	2.3%
14	Minnesota	1,805	2.0%
15	Virginia	1,758	2.0%
16	Massachusetts	1,736	2.0%
17	Indiana	1,720	1.9%
18	Arizona	1,673	1.9%
19	South Carolina	1,638	1.8%
20	Alabama	1,617	1.8%
21	Missouri	1,615	1.8%
22	Oklahoma	1,466	1.6%
23	Kentucky	1,408	1.6%
24	Arkansas	1,395	1.6%
25	Louisiana	1,232	1.4%
26	Kansas	1,190	1.3%
27	Oregon	1,156	1.3%
28	New Mexico	1,139	1.3%
29	Maryland	1,127	1.3%
30	New Jersey	1,122	1.3%
31	Wisconsin	1,120	1.3%
32	Nevada	1,102	1.2%
33	Utah	893	1.0%
34	Mississippi	890	1.0%
35	Iowa	888	1.0%
36	Connecticut	674	0.8%
37	Nebraska	583	0.7%
38	Idaho	551	0.6%
39	Alaska	441	0.5%
40	South Dakota	432	0.5%
41	New Hampshire	391	0.4%
42	Maine	375	0.4%
43	Delaware	366	0.4%
44	Hawaii	365	0.4%
45	West Virginia	362	0.4%
46	Montana	294	0.3%
47	Rhode Island	277	0.3%
48	North Dakota	232	0.3%
49	Wyoming	180	0.2%
50	Vermont	127	0.1%
	District of Columbia	186	0.2%

Source: Reported data from the Federal Bureau of Investigation
   "Crime in the United States 2008" (Uniform Crime Reports, September 14, 2009, http://www.fbi.gov/ucr/ucr.htm)
*Forcible rape is the carnal knowledge of a female forcibly and against her will. Assaults or attempts to commit rape by force or threat of force are included. However, statutory rape without force and other sex offenses are excluded.

Average Time Between Rapes in 2008

National Rate = A Rape Occurs Every 5.9 Minutes*

ALPHA ORDER

RANK	STATE	HOURS.MINUTES
30	Alabama	5.26
12	Alaska	19.55
33	Arizona	5.15
27	Arkansas	6.18
50	California	0.59
39	Colorado	4.11
15	Connecticut	13.02
8	Delaware	24.00
48	Florida	1.28
40	Georgia	4.00
7	Hawaii	24.04
13	Idaho	15.56
45	Illinois	2.08
34	Indiana	5.07
16	Iowa	9.53
25	Kansas	7.23
28	Kentucky	6.14
26	Louisiana	7.08
9	Maine	23.25
22	Maryland	7.47
35	Massachusetts	5.04
47	Michigan	1.57
37	Minnesota	4.52
17	Mississippi	9.52
30	Missouri	5.26
5	Montana	29.53
14	Nebraska	15.04
19	Nevada	7.58
10	New Hampshire	22.28
20	New Jersey	7.50
23	New Mexico	7.43
43	New York	3.08
41	North Carolina	3.51
3	North Dakota	37.52
46	Ohio	1.59
29	Oklahoma	5.59
24	Oregon	7.36
44	Pennsylvania	2.32
4	Rhode Island	31.43
32	South Carolina	5.22
11	South Dakota	20.20
38	Tennessee	4.16
49	Texas	1.06
18	Utah	9.50
1	Vermont	69.10
36	Virginia	5.00
42	Washington	3.20
6	West Virginia	24.16
20	Wisconsin	7.50
2	Wyoming	48.48

RANK ORDER

RANK	STATE	HOURS.MINUTES
1	Vermont	69.10
2	Wyoming	48.48
3	North Dakota	37.52
4	Rhode Island	31.43
5	Montana	29.53
6	West Virginia	24.16
7	Hawaii	24.04
8	Delaware	24.00
9	Maine	23.25
10	New Hampshire	22.28
11	South Dakota	20.20
12	Alaska	19.55
13	Idaho	15.56
14	Nebraska	15.04
15	Connecticut	13.02
16	Iowa	9.53
17	Mississippi	9.52
18	Utah	9.50
19	Nevada	7.58
20	New Jersey	7.50
20	Wisconsin	7.50
22	Maryland	7.47
23	New Mexico	7.43
24	Oregon	7.36
25	Kansas	7.23
26	Louisiana	7.08
27	Arkansas	6.18
28	Kentucky	6.14
29	Oklahoma	5.59
30	Alabama	5.26
30	Missouri	5.26
32	South Carolina	5.22
33	Arizona	5.15
34	Indiana	5.07
35	Massachusetts	5.04
36	Virginia	5.00
37	Minnesota	4.52
38	Tennessee	4.16
39	Colorado	4.11
40	Georgia	4.00
41	North Carolina	3.51
42	Washington	3.20
43	New York	3.08
44	Pennsylvania	2.32
45	Illinois	2.08
46	Ohio	1.59
47	Michigan	1.57
48	Florida	1.28
49	Texas	1.06
50	California	0.59
	District of Columbia	47.14

Source: CQ Press using reported data from the Federal Bureau of Investigation
   "Crime in the United States 2008" (Uniform Crime Reports, September 14, 2009, http://www.fbi.gov/ucr/ucr.htm)
*Forcible rape is the carnal knowledge of a female forcibly and against her will. Assaults or attempts to commit rape by force or threat of force are included. However, statutory rape without force and other sex offenses are excluded.

Percent Change in Number of Rapes: 2007 to 2008

National Percent Change = 1.6% Decrease*

ALPHA ORDER

RANK	STATE	PERCENT CHANGE
14	Alabama	4.7
50	Alaska	(16.6)
47	Arizona	(9.9)
8	Arkansas	10.0
26	California	(1.2)
13	Colorado	5.0
16	Connecticut	2.4
9	Delaware	8.9
32	Florida	(2.9)
19	Georgia	0.8
5	Hawaii	12.0
39	Idaho	(4.7)
23	Illinois	0.4
27	Indiana	(1.3)
30	Iowa	(1.8)
33	Kansas	(3.3)
17	Kentucky	2.0
48	Louisiana	(11.6)
35	Maine	(4.1)
38	Maryland	(4.4)
12	Massachusetts	6.2
28	Michigan	(1.7)
34	Minnesota	(3.6)
49	Mississippi	(14.4)
42	Missouri	(5.8)
18	Montana	1.4
6	Nebraska	10.6
22	Nevada	0.5
2	New Hampshire	17.4
11	New Jersey	6.9
7	New Mexico	10.4
37	New York	(4.3)
36	North Carolina	(4.2)
4	North Dakota	12.1
25	Ohio	(0.7)
44	Oklahoma	(6.0)
45	Oregon	(7.9)
19	Pennsylvania	0.8
10	Rhode Island	8.2
42	South Carolina	(5.8)
1	South Dakota	40.3
41	Tennessee	(5.2)
40	Texas	(5.0)
28	Utah	(1.7)
15	Vermont	3.3
21	Virginia	0.7
24	Washington	0.0
31	West Virginia	(1.9)
46	Wisconsin	(8.4)
3	Wyoming	12.5

RANK ORDER

RANK	STATE	PERCENT CHANGE
1	South Dakota	40.3
2	New Hampshire	17.4
3	Wyoming	12.5
4	North Dakota	12.1
5	Hawaii	12.0
6	Nebraska	10.6
7	New Mexico	10.4
8	Arkansas	10.0
9	Delaware	8.9
10	Rhode Island	8.2
11	New Jersey	6.9
12	Massachusetts	6.2
13	Colorado	5.0
14	Alabama	4.7
15	Vermont	3.3
16	Connecticut	2.4
17	Kentucky	2.0
18	Montana	1.4
19	Georgia	0.8
19	Pennsylvania	0.8
21	Virginia	0.7
22	Nevada	0.5
23	Illinois	0.4
24	Washington	0.0
25	Ohio	(0.7)
26	California	(1.2)
27	Indiana	(1.3)
28	Michigan	(1.7)
28	Utah	(1.7)
30	Iowa	(1.8)
31	West Virginia	(1.9)
32	Florida	(2.9)
33	Kansas	(3.3)
34	Minnesota	(3.6)
35	Maine	(4.1)
36	North Carolina	(4.2)
37	New York	(4.3)
38	Maryland	(4.4)
39	Idaho	(4.7)
40	Texas	(5.0)
41	Tennessee	(5.2)
42	Missouri	(5.8)
42	South Carolina	(5.8)
44	Oklahoma	(6.0)
45	Oregon	(7.9)
46	Wisconsin	(8.4)
47	Arizona	(9.9)
48	Louisiana	(11.6)
49	Mississippi	(14.4)
50	Alaska	(16.6)

District of Columbia   (3.1)

Source: Reported data from the Federal Bureau of Investigation
"Crime in the United States 2008" (Uniform Crime Reports, September 14, 2009, http://www.fbi.gov/ucr/ucr.htm)
*Forcible rape is the carnal knowledge of a female forcibly and against her will. Assaults or attempts to commit rape by force or threat of force are included. However, statutory rape without force and other sex offenses are excluded.

Rape Rate in 2008

National Rate = 29.3 Rapes per 100,000 Population*

ALPHA ORDER

RANK	STATE	RATE
16	Alabama	34.7
1	Alaska	64.3
39	Arizona	25.7
4	Arkansas	48.9
41	California	24.2
6	Colorado	42.5
48	Connecticut	19.3
9	Delaware	41.9
23	Florida	32.6
42	Georgia	22.7
32	Hawaii	28.3
14	Idaho	36.2
25	Illinois	31.9
36	Indiana	27.0
30	Iowa	29.6
6	Kansas	42.5
20	Kentucky	33.0
33	Louisiana	27.9
31	Maine	28.5
45	Maryland	20.0
37	Massachusetts	26.7
5	Michigan	45.0
17	Minnesota	34.6
28	Mississippi	30.3
35	Missouri	27.3
27	Montana	30.4
22	Nebraska	32.7
8	Nevada	42.4
29	New Hampshire	29.7
50	New Jersey	12.9
2	New Mexico	57.4
49	New York	14.4
40	North Carolina	24.8
14	North Dakota	36.2
12	Ohio	38.5
10	Oklahoma	40.2
26	Oregon	30.5
33	Pennsylvania	27.9
38	Rhode Island	26.4
13	South Carolina	36.6
3	South Dakota	53.7
19	Tennessee	33.2
21	Texas	32.9
23	Utah	32.6
44	Vermont	20.4
43	Virginia	22.6
11	Washington	40.1
45	West Virginia	20.0
47	Wisconsin	19.9
18	Wyoming	33.8

RANK ORDER

RANK	STATE	RATE
1	Alaska	64.3
2	New Mexico	57.4
3	South Dakota	53.7
4	Arkansas	48.9
5	Michigan	45.0
6	Colorado	42.5
6	Kansas	42.5
8	Nevada	42.4
9	Delaware	41.9
10	Oklahoma	40.2
11	Washington	40.1
12	Ohio	38.5
13	South Carolina	36.6
14	Idaho	36.2
14	North Dakota	36.2
16	Alabama	34.7
17	Minnesota	34.6
18	Wyoming	33.8
19	Tennessee	33.2
20	Kentucky	33.0
21	Texas	32.9
22	Nebraska	32.7
23	Florida	32.6
23	Utah	32.6
25	Illinois	31.9
26	Oregon	30.5
27	Montana	30.4
28	Mississippi	30.3
29	New Hampshire	29.7
30	Iowa	29.6
31	Maine	28.5
32	Hawaii	28.3
33	Louisiana	27.9
33	Pennsylvania	27.9
35	Missouri	27.3
36	Indiana	27.0
37	Massachusetts	26.7
38	Rhode Island	26.4
39	Arizona	25.7
40	North Carolina	24.8
41	California	24.2
42	Georgia	22.7
43	Virginia	22.6
44	Vermont	20.4
45	Maryland	20.0
45	West Virginia	20.0
47	Wisconsin	19.9
48	Connecticut	19.3
49	New York	14.4
50	New Jersey	12.9

	District of Columbia	31.4

Source: Reported data from the Federal Bureau of Investigation
"Crime in the United States 2008" (Uniform Crime Reports, September 14, 2009, http://www.fbi.gov/ucr/ucr.htm)
*Forcible rape is the carnal knowledge of a female forcibly and against her will. Assaults or attempts to commit rape by force or threat of force are included. However, statutory rape without force and other sex offenses are excluded.

Percent Change in Rape Rate: 2007 to 2008

National Percent Change = 2.4% Decrease*

ALPHA ORDER

RANK	STATE	PERCENT CHANGE
13	Alabama	3.9
50	Alaska	(17.0)
47	Arizona	(12.1)
8	Arkansas	9.2
27	California	(1.8)
14	Colorado	3.3
16	Connecticut	2.5
10	Delaware	7.9
31	Florida	(3.3)
22	Georgia	(0.7)
4	Hawaii	11.5
40	Idaho	(6.2)
20	Illinois	0.0
27	Indiana	(1.8)
30	Iowa	(2.2)
34	Kansas	(4.2)
17	Kentucky	1.3
48	Louisiana	(13.9)
32	Maine	(4.0)
35	Maryland	(4.7)
12	Massachusetts	5.5
25	Michigan	(1.0)
33	Minnesota	(4.1)
49	Mississippi	(15.0)
41	Missouri	(6.3)
19	Montana	0.4
6	Nebraska	10.1
23	Nevada	(0.8)
2	New Hampshire	17.4
11	New Jersey	6.9
7	New Mexico	9.6
37	New York	(5.2)
38	North Carolina	(5.9)
3	North Dakota	11.8
24	Ohio	(0.9)
42	Oklahoma	(6.6)
45	Oregon	(8.9)
18	Pennsylvania	0.7
9	Rhode Island	8.9
44	South Carolina	(7.3)
1	South Dakota	38.9
39	Tennessee	(6.0)
43	Texas	(6.7)
36	Utah	(4.9)
15	Vermont	3.2
20	Virginia	0.0
26	Washington	(1.3)
29	West Virginia	(2.0)
45	Wisconsin	(8.9)
5	Wyoming	10.4

RANK ORDER

RANK	STATE	PERCENT CHANGE
1	South Dakota	38.9
2	New Hampshire	17.4
3	North Dakota	11.8
4	Hawaii	11.5
5	Wyoming	10.4
6	Nebraska	10.1
7	New Mexico	9.6
8	Arkansas	9.2
9	Rhode Island	8.9
10	Delaware	7.9
11	New Jersey	6.9
12	Massachusetts	5.5
13	Alabama	3.9
14	Colorado	3.3
15	Vermont	3.2
16	Connecticut	2.5
17	Kentucky	1.3
18	Pennsylvania	0.7
19	Montana	0.4
20	Illinois	0.0
20	Virginia	0.0
22	Georgia	(0.7)
23	Nevada	(0.8)
24	Ohio	(0.9)
25	Michigan	(1.0)
26	Washington	(1.3)
27	California	(1.8)
27	Indiana	(1.8)
29	West Virginia	(2.0)
30	Iowa	(2.2)
31	Florida	(3.3)
32	Maine	(4.0)
33	Minnesota	(4.1)
34	Kansas	(4.2)
35	Maryland	(4.7)
36	Utah	(4.9)
37	New York	(5.2)
38	North Carolina	(5.9)
39	Tennessee	(6.0)
40	Idaho	(6.2)
41	Missouri	(6.3)
42	Oklahoma	(6.6)
43	Texas	(6.7)
44	South Carolina	(7.3)
45	Oregon	(8.9)
45	Wisconsin	(8.9)
47	Arizona	(12.1)
48	Louisiana	(13.9)
49	Mississippi	(15.0)
50	Alaska	(17.0)

District of Columbia (3.7)

Source: Reported data from the Federal Bureau of Investigation
"Crime in the United States 2008" (Uniform Crime Reports, September 14, 2009, http://www.fbi.gov/ucr/ucr.htm)
*Forcible rape is the carnal knowledge of a female forcibly and against her will. Assaults or attempts to commit rape by force or threat of force are included. However, statutory rape without force and other sex offenses are excluded.

Rape Rate per 100,000 Female Population in 2008

National Rate = 57.7 Rapes per 100,000 Female Population*

ALPHA ORDER

RANK	STATE	RATE
18	Alabama	67.3
1	Alaska	134.2
38	Arizona	51.6
4	Arkansas	95.8
40	California	48.5
7	Colorado	85.7
48	Connecticut	37.6
9	Delaware	81.4
24	Florida	64.1
42	Georgia	44.6
31	Hawaii	57.1
13	Idaho	72.8
25	Illinois	63.0
36	Indiana	53.2
30	Iowa	58.4
8	Kansas	84.4
23	Kentucky	64.6
34	Louisiana	54.3
32	Maine	55.6
47	Maryland	38.8
37	Massachusetts	51.9
5	Michigan	88.6
16	Minnesota	68.9
28	Mississippi	58.8
35	Missouri	53.4
26	Montana	60.9
21	Nebraska	64.8
6	Nevada	86.4
29	New Hampshire	58.6
50	New Jersey	25.3
2	New Mexico	113.2
49	New York	27.9
40	North Carolina	48.5
14	North Dakota	72.6
12	Ohio	75.1
11	Oklahoma	79.5
27	Oregon	60.6
33	Pennsylvania	54.4
39	Rhode Island	51.1
15	South Carolina	71.3
3	South Dakota	107.1
22	Tennessee	64.7
20	Texas	65.8
19	Utah	65.9
44	Vermont	40.2
43	Virginia	44.5
10	Washington	80.1
46	West Virginia	39.1
45	Wisconsin	39.6
17	Wyoming	68.6

RANK ORDER

RANK	STATE	RATE
1	Alaska	134.2
2	New Mexico	113.2
3	South Dakota	107.1
4	Arkansas	95.8
5	Michigan	88.6
6	Nevada	86.4
7	Colorado	85.7
8	Kansas	84.4
9	Delaware	81.4
10	Washington	80.1
11	Oklahoma	79.5
12	Ohio	75.1
13	Idaho	72.8
14	North Dakota	72.6
15	South Carolina	71.3
16	Minnesota	68.9
17	Wyoming	68.6
18	Alabama	67.3
19	Utah	65.9
20	Texas	65.8
21	Nebraska	64.8
22	Tennessee	64.7
23	Kentucky	64.6
24	Florida	64.1
25	Illinois	63.0
26	Montana	60.9
27	Oregon	60.6
28	Mississippi	58.8
29	New Hampshire	58.6
30	Iowa	58.4
31	Hawaii	57.1
32	Maine	55.6
33	Pennsylvania	54.4
34	Louisiana	54.3
35	Missouri	53.4
36	Indiana	53.2
37	Massachusetts	51.9
38	Arizona	51.6
39	Rhode Island	51.1
40	California	48.5
40	North Carolina	48.5
42	Georgia	44.6
43	Virginia	44.5
44	Vermont	40.2
45	Wisconsin	39.6
46	West Virginia	39.1
47	Maryland	38.8
48	Connecticut	37.6
49	New York	27.9
50	New Jersey	25.3

District of Columbia	59.6

Source: CQ Press using reported data from the Federal Bureau of Investigation
   "Crime in the United States 2008" (Uniform Crime Reports, September 14, 2009, http://www.fbi.gov/ucr/ucr.htm)
*Forcible rape is the carnal knowledge of a female forcibly and against her will. Assaults or attempts to commit rape by force or threat of force are included. However, statutory rape without force and other sex offenses are excluded. Calculated with 2008 female population.

Robberies in 2008

National Total = 441,855 Robberies*

ALPHA ORDER

ALPHA ORDER

RANK	STATE	ROBBERIES	% of USA
18	Alabama	7,346	1.7%
42	Alaska	645	0.1%
14	Arizona	9,697	2.2%
31	Arkansas	2,735	0.6%
1	California	69,385	15.7%
29	Colorado	3,365	0.8%
27	Connecticut	3,907	0.9%
34	Delaware	1,838	0.4%
3	Florida	36,273	8.2%
8	Georgia	17,357	3.9%
39	Hawaii	1,086	0.2%
45	Idaho	241	0.1%
5	Illinois	24,054	5.4%
15	Indiana	7,532	1.7%
38	Iowa	1,248	0.3%
35	Kansas	1,684	0.4%
26	Kentucky	4,004	0.9%
23	Louisiana	5,994	1.4%
44	Maine	333	0.1%
10	Maryland	13,203	3.0%
19	Massachusetts	7,069	1.6%
11	Michigan	12,964	2.9%
25	Minnesota	4,177	0.9%
30	Mississippi	3,016	0.7%
17	Missouri	7,390	1.7%
46	Montana	172	0.0%
37	Nebraska	1,299	0.3%
21	Nevada	6,473	1.5%
43	New Hampshire	419	0.1%
12	New Jersey	12,701	2.9%
33	New Mexico	2,172	0.5%
4	New York	31,778	7.2%
9	North Carolina	14,334	3.2%
50	North Dakota	72	0.0%
7	Ohio	18,719	4.2%
28	Oklahoma	3,683	0.8%
32	Oregon	2,641	0.6%
6	Pennsylvania	18,873	4.3%
41	Rhode Island	879	0.2%
20	South Carolina	6,599	1.5%
47	South Dakota	120	0.0%
13	Tennessee	10,800	2.4%
2	Texas	37,753	8.5%
36	Utah	1,421	0.3%
48	Vermont	89	0.0%
16	Virginia	7,437	1.7%
22	Washington	6,347	1.4%
40	West Virginia	889	0.2%
24	Wisconsin	5,126	1.2%
49	Wyoming	86	0.0%

RANK ORDER

RANK	STATE	ROBBERIES	% of USA
1	California	69,385	15.7%
2	Texas	37,753	8.5%
3	Florida	36,273	8.2%
4	New York	31,778	7.2%
5	Illinois	24,054	5.4%
6	Pennsylvania	18,873	4.3%
7	Ohio	18,719	4.2%
8	Georgia	17,357	3.9%
9	North Carolina	14,334	3.2%
10	Maryland	13,203	3.0%
11	Michigan	12,964	2.9%
12	New Jersey	12,701	2.9%
13	Tennessee	10,800	2.4%
14	Arizona	9,697	2.2%
15	Indiana	7,532	1.7%
16	Virginia	7,437	1.7%
17	Missouri	7,390	1.7%
18	Alabama	7,346	1.7%
19	Massachusetts	7,069	1.6%
20	South Carolina	6,599	1.5%
21	Nevada	6,473	1.5%
22	Washington	6,347	1.4%
23	Louisiana	5,994	1.4%
24	Wisconsin	5,126	1.2%
25	Minnesota	4,177	0.9%
26	Kentucky	4,004	0.9%
27	Connecticut	3,907	0.9%
28	Oklahoma	3,683	0.8%
29	Colorado	3,365	0.8%
30	Mississippi	3,016	0.7%
31	Arkansas	2,735	0.6%
32	Oregon	2,641	0.6%
33	New Mexico	2,172	0.5%
34	Delaware	1,838	0.4%
35	Kansas	1,684	0.4%
36	Utah	1,421	0.3%
37	Nebraska	1,299	0.3%
38	Iowa	1,248	0.3%
39	Hawaii	1,086	0.2%
40	West Virginia	889	0.2%
41	Rhode Island	879	0.2%
42	Alaska	645	0.1%
43	New Hampshire	419	0.1%
44	Maine	333	0.1%
45	Idaho	241	0.1%
46	Montana	172	0.0%
47	South Dakota	120	0.0%
48	Vermont	89	0.0%
49	Wyoming	86	0.0%
50	North Dakota	72	0.0%
	District of Columbia	4,430	1.0%

Source: Reported data from the Federal Bureau of Investigation
"Crime in the United States 2008" (Uniform Crime Reports, September 14, 2009, http://www.fbi.gov/ucr/ucr.htm)
*Robbery is the taking or attempting to take anything of value by force or threat of force.

Average Time Between Robberies in 2008

National Rate = A Robbery Occurs Every 1.2 Minutes*

ALPHA ORDER

RANK	STATE	HOURS.MINUTES
33	Alabama	1.12
9	Alaska	13.37
37	Arizona	0.55
20	Arkansas	3.13
50	California	0.08
22	Colorado	2.37
24	Connecticut	2.15
17	Delaware	4.47
48	Florida	0.14
43	Georgia	0.31
12	Hawaii	8.05
6	Idaho	36.27
46	Illinois	0.22
36	Indiana	1.10
13	Iowa	7.02
16	Kansas	5.13
25	Kentucky	2.11
28	Louisiana	1.28
7	Maine	26.23
41	Maryland	0.40
32	Massachusetts	1.14
39	Michigan	0.41
26	Minnesota	2.06
21	Mississippi	2.55
34	Missouri	1.11
5	Montana	51.04
14	Nebraska	6.46
30	Nevada	1.22
8	New Hampshire	20.58
39	New Jersey	0.41
18	New Mexico	4.02
47	New York	0.17
42	North Carolina	0.37
1	North Dakota	122.00
44	Ohio	0.28
23	Oklahoma	2.23
19	Oregon	3.20
44	Pennsylvania	0.28
10	Rhode Island	9.59
31	South Carolina	1.20
4	South Dakota	73.12
38	Tennessee	0.49
48	Texas	0.14
15	Utah	6.11
3	Vermont	98.42
34	Virginia	1.11
29	Washington	1.23
11	West Virginia	9.53
27	Wisconsin	1.43
2	Wyoming	102.08

RANK ORDER

RANK	STATE	HOURS.MINUTES
1	North Dakota	122.00
2	Wyoming	102.08
3	Vermont	98.42
4	South Dakota	73.12
5	Montana	51.04
6	Idaho	36.27
7	Maine	26.23
8	New Hampshire	20.58
9	Alaska	13.37
10	Rhode Island	9.59
11	West Virginia	9.53
12	Hawaii	8.05
13	Iowa	7.02
14	Nebraska	6.46
15	Utah	6.11
16	Kansas	5.13
17	Delaware	4.47
18	New Mexico	4.02
19	Oregon	3.20
20	Arkansas	3.13
21	Mississippi	2.55
22	Colorado	2.37
23	Oklahoma	2.23
24	Connecticut	2.15
25	Kentucky	2.11
26	Minnesota	2.06
27	Wisconsin	1.43
28	Louisiana	1.28
29	Washington	1.23
30	Nevada	1.22
31	South Carolina	1.20
32	Massachusetts	1.14
33	Alabama	1.12
34	Missouri	1.11
34	Virginia	1.11
36	Indiana	1.10
37	Arizona	0.55
38	Tennessee	0.49
39	Michigan	0.41
39	New Jersey	0.41
41	Maryland	0.40
42	North Carolina	0.37
43	Georgia	0.31
44	Ohio	0.28
44	Pennsylvania	0.28
46	Illinois	0.22
47	New York	0.17
48	Florida	0.14
48	Texas	0.14
50	California	0.08
	District of Columbia	1.59

Source: CQ Press using reported data from the Federal Bureau of Investigation
"Crime in the United States 2008" (Uniform Crime Reports, September 14, 2009, http://www.fbi.gov/ucr/ucr.htm)
*Robbery is the taking or attempting to take anything of value by force or threat of force.

Percent Change in Number of Robberies: 2007 to 2008

National Percent Change = 0.7% Decrease*

ALPHA ORDER

RANK	STATE	PERCENT CHANGE
27	Alabama	(0.7)
4	Alaska	10.6
23	Arizona	0.8
47	Arkansas	(9.6)
29	California	(1.6)
33	Colorado	(2.5)
6	Connecticut	8.3
7	Delaware	7.7
41	Florida	(4.9)
24	Georgia	0.1
31	Hawaii	(1.7)
15	Idaho	3.4
13	Illinois	4.1
39	Indiana	(4.3)
42	Iowa	(5.0)
50	Kansas	(16.5)
29	Kentucky	(1.6)
28	Louisiana	(1.5)
40	Maine	(4.6)
26	Maryland	(0.4)
22	Massachusetts	0.9
38	Michigan	(3.4)
49	Minnesota	(12.4)
10	Mississippi	5.2
16	Missouri	3.1
48	Montana	(9.9)
1	Nebraska	17.2
45	Nevada	(6.6)
36	New Hampshire	(3.0)
21	New Jersey	1.2
43	New Mexico	(6.4)
20	New York	2.2
9	North Carolina	5.8
17	North Dakota	2.9
18	Ohio	2.5
5	Oklahoma	9.2
46	Oregon	(7.7)
36	Pennsylvania	(3.0)
2	Rhode Island	17.0
14	South Carolina	4.0
8	South Dakota	7.1
32	Tennessee	(2.0)
34	Texas	(2.6)
24	Utah	0.1
3	Vermont	11.3
35	Virginia	(2.8)
11	Washington	4.9
12	West Virginia	4.3
43	Wisconsin	(6.4)
19	Wyoming	2.4

RANK ORDER

RANK	STATE	PERCENT CHANGE
1	Nebraska	17.2
2	Rhode Island	17.0
3	Vermont	11.3
4	Alaska	10.6
5	Oklahoma	9.2
6	Connecticut	8.3
7	Delaware	7.7
8	South Dakota	7.1
9	North Carolina	5.8
10	Mississippi	5.2
11	Washington	4.9
12	West Virginia	4.3
13	Illinois	4.1
14	South Carolina	4.0
15	Idaho	3.4
16	Missouri	3.1
17	North Dakota	2.9
18	Ohio	2.5
19	Wyoming	2.4
20	New York	2.2
21	New Jersey	1.2
22	Massachusetts	0.9
23	Arizona	0.8
24	Georgia	0.1
24	Utah	0.1
26	Maryland	(0.4)
27	Alabama	(0.7)
28	Louisiana	(1.5)
29	California	(1.6)
29	Kentucky	(1.6)
31	Hawaii	(1.7)
32	Tennessee	(2.0)
33	Colorado	(2.5)
34	Texas	(2.6)
35	Virginia	(2.8)
36	New Hampshire	(3.0)
36	Pennsylvania	(3.0)
38	Michigan	(3.4)
39	Indiana	(4.3)
40	Maine	(4.6)
41	Florida	(4.9)
42	Iowa	(5.0)
43	New Mexico	(6.4)
43	Wisconsin	(6.4)
45	Nevada	(6.6)
46	Oregon	(7.7)
47	Arkansas	(9.6)
48	Montana	(9.9)
49	Minnesota	(12.4)
50	Kansas	(16.5)

	District of Columbia	4.0

Source: Reported data from the Federal Bureau of Investigation
"Crime in the United States 2008" (Uniform Crime Reports, September 14, 2009, http://www.fbi.gov/ucr/ucr.htm)
*Robbery is the taking or attempting to take anything of value by force or threat of force.

Robbery Rate in 2008

National Rate = 145.3 Robberies per 100,000 Population*

ALPHA ORDER			RANK ORDER		
RANK	STATE	RATE	RANK	STATE	RATE
11	Alabama	157.6	1	Nevada	248.9
30	Alaska	94.0	2	Maryland	234.4
15	Arizona	149.2	3	Delaware	210.5
28	Arkansas	95.8	4	Florida	197.9
5	California	188.8	5	California	188.8
38	Colorado	68.1	6	Illinois	186.4
22	Connecticut	111.6	7	Georgia	179.2
3	Delaware	210.5	8	Tennessee	173.8
4	Florida	197.9	9	New York	163.0
7	Georgia	179.2	9	Ohio	163.0
33	Hawaii	84.3	11	Alabama	157.6
47	Idaho	15.8	12	North Carolina	155.4
6	Illinois	186.4	13	Texas	155.2
21	Indiana	118.1	14	Pennsylvania	151.6
42	Iowa	41.6	15	Arizona	149.2
39	Kansas	60.1	16	South Carolina	147.3
31	Kentucky	93.8	17	New Jersey	146.3
18	Louisiana	135.9	18	Louisiana	135.9
44	Maine	25.3	19	Michigan	129.6
2	Maryland	234.4	20	Missouri	125.0
24	Massachusetts	108.8	21	Indiana	118.1
19	Michigan	129.6	22	Connecticut	111.6
35	Minnesota	80.0	23	New Mexico	109.5
25	Mississippi	102.6	24	Massachusetts	108.8
20	Missouri	125.0	25	Mississippi	102.6
45	Montana	17.8	26	Oklahoma	101.1
36	Nebraska	72.8	27	Washington	96.9
1	Nevada	248.9	28	Arkansas	95.8
43	New Hampshire	31.8	29	Virginia	95.7
17	New Jersey	146.3	30	Alaska	94.0
23	New Mexico	109.5	31	Kentucky	93.8
9	New York	163.0	32	Wisconsin	91.1
12	North Carolina	155.4	33	Hawaii	84.3
50	North Dakota	11.2	34	Rhode Island	83.7
9	Ohio	163.0	35	Minnesota	80.0
26	Oklahoma	101.1	36	Nebraska	72.8
37	Oregon	69.7	37	Oregon	69.7
14	Pennsylvania	151.6	38	Colorado	68.1
34	Rhode Island	83.7	39	Kansas	60.1
16	South Carolina	147.3	40	Utah	51.9
48	South Dakota	14.9	41	West Virginia	49.0
8	Tennessee	173.8	42	Iowa	41.6
13	Texas	155.2	43	New Hampshire	31.8
40	Utah	51.9	44	Maine	25.3
49	Vermont	14.3	45	Montana	17.8
29	Virginia	95.7	46	Wyoming	16.1
27	Washington	96.9	47	Idaho	15.8
41	West Virginia	49.0	48	South Dakota	14.9
32	Wisconsin	91.1	49	Vermont	14.3
46	Wyoming	16.1	50	North Dakota	11.2
				District of Columbia	748.5

Source: Reported data from the Federal Bureau of Investigation
   "Crime in the United States 2008" (Uniform Crime Reports, September 14, 2009, http://www.fbi.gov/ucr/ucr.htm)
*Robbery is the taking or attempting to take anything of value by force or threat of force.

Percent Change in Robbery Rate: 2007 to 2008

National Percent Change = 1.5% Decrease*

ALPHA ORDER

RANK	STATE	PERCENT CHANGE
24	Alabama	(1.4)
4	Alaska	10.2
26	Arizona	(1.7)
47	Arkansas	(10.2)
28	California	(2.2)
36	Colorado	(4.1)
6	Connecticut	8.3
7	Delaware	6.7
41	Florida	(5.3)
24	Georgia	(1.4)
27	Hawaii	(2.1)
18	Idaho	1.8
12	Illinois	3.7
40	Indiana	(4.8)
42	Iowa	(5.4)
50	Kansas	(17.2)
28	Kentucky	(2.2)
36	Louisiana	(4.1)
39	Maine	(4.5)
23	Maryland	(0.7)
22	Massachusetts	0.2
30	Michigan	(2.7)
49	Minnesota	(12.8)
9	Mississippi	4.5
14	Missouri	2.6
48	Montana	(10.8)
2	Nebraska	16.7
45	Nevada	(7.9)
32	New Hampshire	(3.0)
19	New Jersey	1.2
44	New Mexico	(7.1)
19	New York	1.2
11	North Carolina	4.0
14	North Dakota	2.6
16	Ohio	2.3
5	Oklahoma	8.4
46	Oregon	(8.8)
33	Pennsylvania	(3.1)
1	Rhode Island	17.8
16	South Carolina	2.3
8	South Dakota	6.1
31	Tennessee	(2.9)
38	Texas	(4.3)
34	Utah	(3.3)
3	Vermont	11.2
35	Virginia	(3.5)
13	Washington	3.6
10	West Virginia	4.2
43	Wisconsin	(6.8)
21	Wyoming	0.5

RANK ORDER

RANK	STATE	PERCENT CHANGE
1	Rhode Island	17.8
2	Nebraska	16.7
3	Vermont	11.2
4	Alaska	10.2
5	Oklahoma	8.4
6	Connecticut	8.3
7	Delaware	6.7
8	South Dakota	6.1
9	Mississippi	4.5
10	West Virginia	4.2
11	North Carolina	4.0
12	Illinois	3.7
13	Washington	3.6
14	Missouri	2.6
14	North Dakota	2.6
16	Ohio	2.3
16	South Carolina	2.3
18	Idaho	1.8
19	New Jersey	1.2
19	New York	1.2
21	Wyoming	0.5
22	Massachusetts	0.2
23	Maryland	(0.7)
24	Alabama	(1.4)
24	Georgia	(1.4)
26	Arizona	(1.7)
27	Hawaii	(2.1)
28	California	(2.2)
28	Kentucky	(2.2)
30	Michigan	(2.7)
31	Tennessee	(2.9)
32	New Hampshire	(3.0)
33	Pennsylvania	(3.1)
34	Utah	(3.3)
35	Virginia	(3.5)
36	Colorado	(4.1)
36	Louisiana	(4.1)
38	Texas	(4.3)
39	Maine	(4.5)
40	Indiana	(4.8)
41	Florida	(5.3)
42	Iowa	(5.4)
43	Wisconsin	(6.8)
44	New Mexico	(7.1)
45	Nevada	(7.9)
46	Oregon	(8.8)
47	Arkansas	(10.2)
48	Montana	(10.8)
49	Minnesota	(12.8)
50	Kansas	(17.2)

District of Columbia	3.3

Source: Reported data from the Federal Bureau of Investigation
   "Crime in the United States 2008" (Uniform Crime Reports, September 14, 2009, http://www.fbi.gov/ucr/ucr.htm)
*Robbery is the taking or attempting to take anything of value by force or threat of force.

Robberies With Firearms in 2008

National Total = 163,163 Robberies*

<table>
<tr><td colspan="4">ALPHA ORDER</td><td colspan="4">RANK ORDER</td></tr>
<tr><td>RANK</td><td>STATE</td><td>ROBBERIES</td><td>% of USA</td><td>RANK</td><td>STATE</td><td>ROBBERIES</td><td>% of USA</td></tr>
<tr><td>21</td><td>Alabama</td><td>2,225</td><td>1.4%</td><td>1</td><td>California</td><td>22,047</td><td>13.5%</td></tr>
<tr><td>39</td><td>Alaska</td><td>167</td><td>0.1%</td><td>2</td><td>Texas</td><td>17,962</td><td>11.0%</td></tr>
<tr><td>10</td><td>Arizona</td><td>4,986</td><td>3.1%</td><td>3</td><td>Florida</td><td>16,915</td><td>10.4%</td></tr>
<tr><td>28</td><td>Arkansas</td><td>1,279</td><td>0.8%</td><td>4</td><td>Georgia</td><td>9,677</td><td>5.9%</td></tr>
<tr><td>1</td><td>California</td><td>22,047</td><td>13.5%</td><td>5</td><td>Pennsylvania</td><td>7,781</td><td>4.8%</td></tr>
<tr><td>29</td><td>Colorado</td><td>1,191</td><td>0.7%</td><td>6</td><td>North Carolina</td><td>7,288</td><td>4.5%</td></tr>
<tr><td>30</td><td>Connecticut</td><td>994</td><td>0.6%</td><td>7</td><td>Ohio</td><td>7,200</td><td>4.4%</td></tr>
<tr><td>32</td><td>Delaware</td><td>827</td><td>0.5%</td><td>8</td><td>Tennessee</td><td>6,416</td><td>3.9%</td></tr>
<tr><td>3</td><td>Florida</td><td>16,915</td><td>10.4%</td><td>9</td><td>Michigan</td><td>6,295</td><td>3.9%</td></tr>
<tr><td>4</td><td>Georgia</td><td>9,677</td><td>5.9%</td><td>10</td><td>Arizona</td><td>4,986</td><td>3.1%</td></tr>
<tr><td>41</td><td>Hawaii</td><td>109</td><td>0.1%</td><td>11</td><td>Maryland</td><td>4,243</td><td>2.6%</td></tr>
<tr><td>43</td><td>Idaho</td><td>64</td><td>0.0%</td><td>12</td><td>Virginia</td><td>4,166</td><td>2.6%</td></tr>
<tr><td>NA</td><td>Illinois**</td><td>NA</td><td>NA</td><td>13</td><td>New Jersey</td><td>4,113</td><td>2.5%</td></tr>
<tr><td>15</td><td>Indiana</td><td>3,773</td><td>2.3%</td><td>14</td><td>Missouri</td><td>3,785</td><td>2.3%</td></tr>
<tr><td>37</td><td>Iowa</td><td>295</td><td>0.2%</td><td>15</td><td>Indiana</td><td>3,773</td><td>2.3%</td></tr>
<tr><td>35</td><td>Kansas</td><td>513</td><td>0.3%</td><td>16</td><td>South Carolina</td><td>3,402</td><td>2.1%</td></tr>
<tr><td>24</td><td>Kentucky</td><td>1,490</td><td>0.9%</td><td>17</td><td>Louisiana</td><td>2,966</td><td>1.8%</td></tr>
<tr><td>17</td><td>Louisiana</td><td>2,966</td><td>1.8%</td><td>18</td><td>New York</td><td>2,831</td><td>1.7%</td></tr>
<tr><td>44</td><td>Maine</td><td>53</td><td>0.0%</td><td>19</td><td>Nevada</td><td>2,693</td><td>1.7%</td></tr>
<tr><td>11</td><td>Maryland</td><td>4,243</td><td>2.6%</td><td>20</td><td>Wisconsin</td><td>2,651</td><td>1.6%</td></tr>
<tr><td>23</td><td>Massachusetts</td><td>1,616</td><td>1.0%</td><td>21</td><td>Alabama</td><td>2,225</td><td>1.4%</td></tr>
<tr><td>9</td><td>Michigan</td><td>6,295</td><td>3.9%</td><td>22</td><td>Oklahoma</td><td>1,764</td><td>1.1%</td></tr>
<tr><td>26</td><td>Minnesota</td><td>1,322</td><td>0.8%</td><td>23</td><td>Massachusetts</td><td>1,616</td><td>1.0%</td></tr>
<tr><td>27</td><td>Mississippi</td><td>1,316</td><td>0.8%</td><td>24</td><td>Kentucky</td><td>1,490</td><td>0.9%</td></tr>
<tr><td>14</td><td>Missouri</td><td>3,785</td><td>2.3%</td><td>25</td><td>Washington</td><td>1,481</td><td>0.9%</td></tr>
<tr><td>45</td><td>Montana</td><td>29</td><td>0.0%</td><td>26</td><td>Minnesota</td><td>1,322</td><td>0.8%</td></tr>
<tr><td>33</td><td>Nebraska</td><td>619</td><td>0.4%</td><td>27</td><td>Mississippi</td><td>1,316</td><td>0.8%</td></tr>
<tr><td>19</td><td>Nevada</td><td>2,693</td><td>1.7%</td><td>28</td><td>Arkansas</td><td>1,279</td><td>0.8%</td></tr>
<tr><td>42</td><td>New Hampshire</td><td>76</td><td>0.0%</td><td>29</td><td>Colorado</td><td>1,191</td><td>0.7%</td></tr>
<tr><td>13</td><td>New Jersey</td><td>4,113</td><td>2.5%</td><td>30</td><td>Connecticut</td><td>994</td><td>0.6%</td></tr>
<tr><td>31</td><td>New Mexico</td><td>950</td><td>0.6%</td><td>31</td><td>New Mexico</td><td>950</td><td>0.6%</td></tr>
<tr><td>18</td><td>New York</td><td>2,831</td><td>1.7%</td><td>32</td><td>Delaware</td><td>827</td><td>0.5%</td></tr>
<tr><td>6</td><td>North Carolina</td><td>7,288</td><td>4.5%</td><td>33</td><td>Nebraska</td><td>619</td><td>0.4%</td></tr>
<tr><td>49</td><td>North Dakota</td><td>9</td><td>0.0%</td><td>34</td><td>Oregon</td><td>611</td><td>0.4%</td></tr>
<tr><td>7</td><td>Ohio</td><td>7,200</td><td>4.4%</td><td>35</td><td>Kansas</td><td>513</td><td>0.3%</td></tr>
<tr><td>22</td><td>Oklahoma</td><td>1,764</td><td>1.1%</td><td>36</td><td>Utah</td><td>450</td><td>0.3%</td></tr>
<tr><td>34</td><td>Oregon</td><td>611</td><td>0.4%</td><td>37</td><td>Iowa</td><td>295</td><td>0.2%</td></tr>
<tr><td>5</td><td>Pennsylvania</td><td>7,781</td><td>4.8%</td><td>38</td><td>Rhode Island</td><td>215</td><td>0.1%</td></tr>
<tr><td>38</td><td>Rhode Island</td><td>215</td><td>0.1%</td><td>39</td><td>Alaska</td><td>167</td><td>0.1%</td></tr>
<tr><td>16</td><td>South Carolina</td><td>3,402</td><td>2.1%</td><td>40</td><td>West Virginia</td><td>166</td><td>0.1%</td></tr>
<tr><td>46</td><td>South Dakota</td><td>25</td><td>0.0%</td><td>41</td><td>Hawaii</td><td>109</td><td>0.1%</td></tr>
<tr><td>8</td><td>Tennessee</td><td>6,416</td><td>3.9%</td><td>42</td><td>New Hampshire</td><td>76</td><td>0.0%</td></tr>
<tr><td>2</td><td>Texas</td><td>17,962</td><td>11.0%</td><td>43</td><td>Idaho</td><td>64</td><td>0.0%</td></tr>
<tr><td>36</td><td>Utah</td><td>450</td><td>0.3%</td><td>44</td><td>Maine</td><td>53</td><td>0.0%</td></tr>
<tr><td>48</td><td>Vermont</td><td>22</td><td>0.0%</td><td>45</td><td>Montana</td><td>29</td><td>0.0%</td></tr>
<tr><td>12</td><td>Virginia</td><td>4,166</td><td>2.6%</td><td>46</td><td>South Dakota</td><td>25</td><td>0.0%</td></tr>
<tr><td>25</td><td>Washington</td><td>1,481</td><td>0.9%</td><td>47</td><td>Wyoming</td><td>23</td><td>0.0%</td></tr>
<tr><td>40</td><td>West Virginia</td><td>166</td><td>0.1%</td><td>48</td><td>Vermont</td><td>22</td><td>0.0%</td></tr>
<tr><td>20</td><td>Wisconsin</td><td>2,651</td><td>1.6%</td><td>49</td><td>North Dakota</td><td>9</td><td>0.0%</td></tr>
<tr><td>47</td><td>Wyoming</td><td>23</td><td>0.0%</td><td>NA</td><td>Illinois**</td><td>NA</td><td>NA</td></tr>
<tr><td></td><td></td><td></td><td></td><td></td><td>District of Columbia</td><td>1,811</td><td>1.1%</td></tr>
</table>

Source: Reported data from the Federal Bureau of Investigation
  "Crime in the United States 2008" (Uniform Crime Reports, September 14, 2009, http://www.fbi.gov/ucr/ucr.htm)
*Of the 375,484 robberies in 2008 for which supplemental data were received by the F.B.I. There were an additional 66,371 robberies for which the type of weapon was not reported to the F.B.I. Robbery is the taking or attempting to take anything of value by force or threat of force. Numbers are for reporting jurisdictions only.
**Not available.

Robbery Rate With Firearms in 2008

National Rate = 62.7 Robberies per 100,000 Population*

ALPHA ORDER

RANK	STATE	RATE
16	Alabama	68.8
33	Alaska	24.8
12	Arizona	77.7
23	Arkansas	49.0
19	California	60.3
32	Colorado	25.7
28	Connecticut	29.4
5	Delaware	94.7
6	Florida	92.5
1	Georgia	133.2
41	Hawaii	9.5
43	Idaho	4.4
NA	Illinois**	NA
13	Indiana	74.8
40	Iowa	10.7
35	Kansas	23.1
26	Kentucky	41.9
10	Louisiana	84.3
45	Maine	4.0
8	Maryland	84.9
29	Massachusetts	27.8
15	Michigan	72.3
30	Minnesota	26.7
11	Mississippi	78.9
17	Missouri	65.4
48	Montana	3.1
27	Nebraska	37.8
3	Nevada	103.6
42	New Hampshire	7.4
24	New Jersey	48.3
20	New Mexico	59.1
31	New York	26.4
4	North Carolina	97.8
49	North Dakota	1.6
9	Ohio	84.4
22	Oklahoma	51.6
37	Oregon	16.7
17	Pennsylvania	65.4
36	Rhode Island	20.5
7	South Carolina	88.4
46	South Dakota	3.8
2	Tennessee	109.8
14	Texas	73.9
37	Utah	16.7
47	Vermont	3.6
21	Virginia	54.1
34	Washington	24.2
39	West Virginia	15.9
25	Wisconsin	47.4
43	Wyoming	4.4

RANK ORDER

RANK	STATE	RATE
1	Georgia	133.2
2	Tennessee	109.8
3	Nevada	103.6
4	North Carolina	97.8
5	Delaware	94.7
6	Florida	92.5
7	South Carolina	88.4
8	Maryland	84.9
9	Ohio	84.4
10	Louisiana	84.3
11	Mississippi	78.9
12	Arizona	77.7
13	Indiana	74.8
14	Texas	73.9
15	Michigan	72.3
16	Alabama	68.8
17	Missouri	65.4
17	Pennsylvania	65.4
19	California	60.3
20	New Mexico	59.1
21	Virginia	54.1
22	Oklahoma	51.6
23	Arkansas	49.0
24	New Jersey	48.3
25	Wisconsin	47.4
26	Kentucky	41.9
27	Nebraska	37.8
28	Connecticut	29.4
29	Massachusetts	27.8
30	Minnesota	26.7
31	New York	26.4
32	Colorado	25.7
33	Alaska	24.8
34	Washington	24.2
35	Kansas	23.1
36	Rhode Island	20.5
37	Oregon	16.7
37	Utah	16.7
39	West Virginia	15.9
40	Iowa	10.7
41	Hawaii	9.5
42	New Hampshire	7.4
43	Idaho	4.4
43	Wyoming	4.4
45	Maine	4.0
46	South Dakota	3.8
47	Vermont	3.6
48	Montana	3.1
49	North Dakota	1.6
NA	Illinois**	NA

District of Columbia 306.0

Source: CQ Press using reported data from the Federal Bureau of Investigation
"Crime in the United States 2008" (Uniform Crime Reports, September 14, 2009, http://www.fbi.gov/ucr/ucr.htm)
*Based only on population of reporting jurisdictions. Robbery is the taking or attempting to take anything of value by force or threat of force. National rate reflects only those robberies for which the type of weapon was known and reported.
**Not available.

Percent of Robberies Involving Firearms in 2008

National Percent = 43.5% of Robberies*

<table>
<tr><td colspan="3">ALPHA ORDER</td><td colspan="3">RANK ORDER</td></tr>
<tr><td>RANK</td><td>STATE</td><td>PERCENT</td><td>RANK</td><td>STATE</td><td>PERCENT</td></tr>
<tr><td>2</td><td>Alabama</td><td>61.5</td><td>1</td><td>Georgia</td><td>64.2</td></tr>
<tr><td>37</td><td>Alaska</td><td>26.0</td><td>2</td><td>Alabama</td><td>61.5</td></tr>
<tr><td>10</td><td>Arizona</td><td>51.7</td><td>3</td><td>Tennessee</td><td>60.2</td></tr>
<tr><td>16</td><td>Arkansas</td><td>48.1</td><td>4</td><td>Mississippi</td><td>59.9</td></tr>
<tr><td>31</td><td>California</td><td>31.8</td><td>5</td><td>Louisiana</td><td>56.8</td></tr>
<tr><td>27</td><td>Colorado</td><td>37.8</td><td>6</td><td>North Carolina</td><td>56.7</td></tr>
<tr><td>31</td><td>Connecticut</td><td>31.8</td><td>6</td><td>South Carolina</td><td>56.7</td></tr>
<tr><td>21</td><td>Delaware</td><td>45.0</td><td>8</td><td>Virginia</td><td>56.4</td></tr>
<tr><td>19</td><td>Florida</td><td>46.7</td><td>9</td><td>Indiana</td><td>52.5</td></tr>
<tr><td>1</td><td>Georgia</td><td>64.2</td><td>10</td><td>Arizona</td><td>51.7</td></tr>
<tr><td>49</td><td>Hawaii</td><td>10.7</td><td>10</td><td>Wisconsin</td><td>51.7</td></tr>
<tr><td>34</td><td>Idaho</td><td>29.8</td><td>12</td><td>Missouri</td><td>51.5</td></tr>
<tr><td>NA</td><td>Illinois**</td><td>NA</td><td>13</td><td>Michigan</td><td>50.5</td></tr>
<tr><td>9</td><td>Indiana</td><td>52.5</td><td>14</td><td>Oklahoma</td><td>48.5</td></tr>
<tr><td>42</td><td>Iowa</td><td>23.9</td><td>15</td><td>Nebraska</td><td>48.2</td></tr>
<tr><td>26</td><td>Kansas</td><td>39.9</td><td>16</td><td>Arkansas</td><td>48.1</td></tr>
<tr><td>25</td><td>Kentucky</td><td>41.3</td><td>17</td><td>Texas</td><td>47.6</td></tr>
<tr><td>5</td><td>Louisiana</td><td>56.8</td><td>18</td><td>New Mexico</td><td>46.8</td></tr>
<tr><td>47</td><td>Maine</td><td>15.9</td><td>19</td><td>Florida</td><td>46.7</td></tr>
<tr><td>20</td><td>Maryland</td><td>46.2</td><td>20</td><td>Maryland</td><td>46.2</td></tr>
<tr><td>38</td><td>Massachusetts</td><td>24.9</td><td>21</td><td>Delaware</td><td>45.0</td></tr>
<tr><td>13</td><td>Michigan</td><td>50.5</td><td>22</td><td>Ohio</td><td>41.8</td></tr>
<tr><td>29</td><td>Minnesota</td><td>31.9</td><td>22</td><td>Pennsylvania</td><td>41.8</td></tr>
<tr><td>4</td><td>Mississippi</td><td>59.9</td><td>24</td><td>Nevada</td><td>41.6</td></tr>
<tr><td>12</td><td>Missouri</td><td>51.5</td><td>25</td><td>Kentucky</td><td>41.3</td></tr>
<tr><td>46</td><td>Montana</td><td>17.3</td><td>26</td><td>Kansas</td><td>39.9</td></tr>
<tr><td>15</td><td>Nebraska</td><td>48.2</td><td>27</td><td>Colorado</td><td>37.8</td></tr>
<tr><td>24</td><td>Nevada</td><td>41.6</td><td>28</td><td>New Jersey</td><td>33.5</td></tr>
<tr><td>45</td><td>New Hampshire</td><td>21.5</td><td>29</td><td>Minnesota</td><td>31.9</td></tr>
<tr><td>28</td><td>New Jersey</td><td>33.5</td><td>29</td><td>West Virginia</td><td>31.9</td></tr>
<tr><td>18</td><td>New Mexico</td><td>46.8</td><td>31</td><td>California</td><td>31.8</td></tr>
<tr><td>35</td><td>New York</td><td>29.7</td><td>31</td><td>Connecticut</td><td>31.8</td></tr>
<tr><td>6</td><td>North Carolina</td><td>56.7</td><td>31</td><td>Utah</td><td>31.8</td></tr>
<tr><td>48</td><td>North Dakota</td><td>12.9</td><td>34</td><td>Idaho</td><td>29.8</td></tr>
<tr><td>22</td><td>Ohio</td><td>41.8</td><td>35</td><td>New York</td><td>29.7</td></tr>
<tr><td>14</td><td>Oklahoma</td><td>48.5</td><td>36</td><td>Wyoming</td><td>27.1</td></tr>
<tr><td>43</td><td>Oregon</td><td>23.3</td><td>37</td><td>Alaska</td><td>26.0</td></tr>
<tr><td>22</td><td>Pennsylvania</td><td>41.8</td><td>38</td><td>Massachusetts</td><td>24.9</td></tr>
<tr><td>40</td><td>Rhode Island</td><td>24.5</td><td>39</td><td>Vermont</td><td>24.7</td></tr>
<tr><td>6</td><td>South Carolina</td><td>56.7</td><td>40</td><td>Rhode Island</td><td>24.5</td></tr>
<tr><td>44</td><td>South Dakota</td><td>21.6</td><td>41</td><td>Washington</td><td>24.2</td></tr>
<tr><td>3</td><td>Tennessee</td><td>60.2</td><td>42</td><td>Iowa</td><td>23.9</td></tr>
<tr><td>17</td><td>Texas</td><td>47.6</td><td>43</td><td>Oregon</td><td>23.3</td></tr>
<tr><td>31</td><td>Utah</td><td>31.8</td><td>44</td><td>South Dakota</td><td>21.6</td></tr>
<tr><td>39</td><td>Vermont</td><td>24.7</td><td>45</td><td>New Hampshire</td><td>21.5</td></tr>
<tr><td>8</td><td>Virginia</td><td>56.4</td><td>46</td><td>Montana</td><td>17.3</td></tr>
<tr><td>41</td><td>Washington</td><td>24.2</td><td>47</td><td>Maine</td><td>15.9</td></tr>
<tr><td>29</td><td>West Virginia</td><td>31.9</td><td>48</td><td>North Dakota</td><td>12.9</td></tr>
<tr><td>10</td><td>Wisconsin</td><td>51.7</td><td>49</td><td>Hawaii</td><td>10.7</td></tr>
<tr><td>36</td><td>Wyoming</td><td>27.1</td><td>NA</td><td>Illinois**</td><td>NA</td></tr>
<tr><td></td><td></td><td></td><td></td><td>District of Columbia</td><td>40.9</td></tr>
</table>

Source: CQ Press using reported data from the Federal Bureau of Investigation
"Crime in the United States 2008" (Uniform Crime Reports, September 14, 2009, http://www.fbi.gov/ucr/ucr.htm)
*Of the 375,484 robberies in 2008 for which supplemental data were received by the F.B.I. There were an additional 66,371 robberies for which the type of weapon was not reported to the F.B.I. Robbery is the taking or attempting to take anything of value by force or threat of force. Numbers are for reporting jurisdictions only.
**Not available.

Robberies With Knives or Cutting Instruments in 2008

National Total = 28,754 Robberies*

ALPHA ORDER

RANK	STATE	ROBBERIES	% of USA
30	Alabama	191	0.7%
40	Alaska	60	0.2%
9	Arizona	840	2.9%
31	Arkansas	164	0.6%
1	California	6,245	21.7%
23	Colorado	306	1.1%
22	Connecticut	313	1.1%
35	Delaware	116	0.4%
3	Florida	2,267	7.9%
13	Georgia	616	2.1%
39	Hawaii	94	0.3%
44	Idaho	32	0.1%
NA	Illinois**	NA	NA
20	Indiana	415	1.4%
37	Iowa	109	0.4%
34	Kansas	118	0.4%
26	Kentucky	267	0.9%
28	Louisiana	264	0.9%
43	Maine	43	0.1%
10	Maryland	833	2.9%
5	Massachusetts	1,255	4.4%
15	Michigan	592	2.1%
27	Minnesota	265	0.9%
33	Mississippi	124	0.4%
18	Missouri	418	1.5%
47	Montana	14	0.0%
38	Nebraska	95	0.3%
14	Nevada	593	2.1%
41	New Hampshire	48	0.2%
6	New Jersey	1,022	3.6%
29	New Mexico	247	0.9%
7	New York	959	3.3%
8	North Carolina	894	3.1%
49	North Dakota	10	0.0%
11	Ohio	719	2.5%
25	Oklahoma	286	1.0%
24	Oregon	300	1.0%
4	Pennsylvania	1,282	4.5%
35	Rhode Island	116	0.4%
19	South Carolina	417	1.5%
45	South Dakota	19	0.1%
12	Tennessee	697	2.4%
2	Texas	3,218	11.2%
32	Utah	152	0.5%
45	Vermont	19	0.1%
17	Virginia	489	1.7%
16	Washington	551	1.9%
42	West Virginia	46	0.2%
21	Wisconsin	330	1.1%
48	Wyoming	13	0.0%

RANK ORDER

RANK	STATE	ROBBERIES	% of USA
1	California	6,245	21.7%
2	Texas	3,218	11.2%
3	Florida	2,267	7.9%
4	Pennsylvania	1,282	4.5%
5	Massachusetts	1,255	4.4%
6	New Jersey	1,022	3.6%
7	New York	959	3.3%
8	North Carolina	894	3.1%
9	Arizona	840	2.9%
10	Maryland	833	2.9%
11	Ohio	719	2.5%
12	Tennessee	697	2.4%
13	Georgia	616	2.1%
14	Nevada	593	2.1%
15	Michigan	592	2.1%
16	Washington	551	1.9%
17	Virginia	489	1.7%
18	Missouri	418	1.5%
19	South Carolina	417	1.5%
20	Indiana	415	1.4%
21	Wisconsin	330	1.1%
22	Connecticut	313	1.1%
23	Colorado	306	1.1%
24	Oregon	300	1.0%
25	Oklahoma	286	1.0%
26	Kentucky	267	0.9%
27	Minnesota	265	0.9%
28	Louisiana	264	0.9%
29	New Mexico	247	0.9%
30	Alabama	191	0.7%
31	Arkansas	164	0.6%
32	Utah	152	0.5%
33	Mississippi	124	0.4%
34	Kansas	118	0.4%
35	Delaware	116	0.4%
35	Rhode Island	116	0.4%
37	Iowa	109	0.4%
38	Nebraska	95	0.3%
39	Hawaii	94	0.3%
40	Alaska	60	0.2%
41	New Hampshire	48	0.2%
42	West Virginia	46	0.2%
43	Maine	43	0.1%
44	Idaho	32	0.1%
45	South Dakota	19	0.1%
45	Vermont	19	0.1%
47	Montana	14	0.0%
48	Wyoming	13	0.0%
49	North Dakota	10	0.0%
NA	Illinois**	NA	NA
	District of Columbia	234	0.8%

Source: Reported data from the Federal Bureau of Investigation
   "Crime in the United States 2008" (Uniform Crime Reports, September 14, 2009, http://www.fbi.gov/ucr/ucr.htm)
*Of the 375,484 robberies in 2008 for which supplemental data were received by the F.B.I. There were an additional 66,371 robberies for which the type of weapon was not reported to the F.B.I. Robbery is the taking or attempting to take anything of value by force or threat of force. Numbers are for reporting jurisdictions only.
**Not available.

Percent of Robberies Involving Knives or Cutting Instruments in 2008

National Percent = 7.7% of Robberies*

ALPHA ORDER				RANK ORDER		
RANK	STATE	PERCENT		RANK	STATE	PERCENT
45	Alabama	5.3		1	Vermont	21.3
16	Alaska	9.3		2	Massachusetts	19.3
25	Arizona	8.7		3	South Dakota	16.4
41	Arkansas	6.2		4	Wyoming	15.3
21	California	9.0		5	Idaho	14.9
15	Colorado	9.7		6	North Dakota	14.3
14	Connecticut	10.0		7	New Hampshire	13.6
39	Delaware	6.3		8	Rhode Island	13.2
39	Florida	6.3		9	Maine	12.9
49	Georgia	4.1		10	New Mexico	12.2
17	Hawaii	9.2		11	Oregon	11.5
5	Idaho	14.9		12	Utah	10.7
NA	Illinois**	NA		13	New York	10.1
42	Indiana	5.8		14	Connecticut	10.0
23	Iowa	8.8		15	Colorado	9.7
17	Kansas	9.2		16	Alaska	9.3
30	Kentucky	7.4		17	Hawaii	9.2
46	Louisiana	5.1		17	Kansas	9.2
9	Maine	12.9		17	Nevada	9.2
20	Maryland	9.1		20	Maryland	9.1
2	Massachusetts	19.3		21	California	9.0
47	Michigan	4.8		21	Washington	9.0
37	Minnesota	6.4		23	Iowa	8.8
44	Mississippi	5.6		23	West Virginia	8.8
43	Missouri	5.7		25	Arizona	8.7
27	Montana	8.3		26	Texas	8.5
30	Nebraska	7.4		27	Montana	8.3
17	Nevada	9.2		27	New Jersey	8.3
7	New Hampshire	13.6		29	Oklahoma	7.9
27	New Jersey	8.3		30	Kentucky	7.4
10	New Mexico	12.2		30	Nebraska	7.4
13	New York	10.1		32	North Carolina	7.0
32	North Carolina	7.0		32	South Carolina	7.0
6	North Dakota	14.3		34	Pennsylvania	6.9
48	Ohio	4.2		35	Virginia	6.6
29	Oklahoma	7.9		36	Tennessee	6.5
11	Oregon	11.5		37	Minnesota	6.4
34	Pennsylvania	6.9		37	Wisconsin	6.4
8	Rhode Island	13.2		39	Delaware	6.3
32	South Carolina	7.0		39	Florida	6.3
3	South Dakota	16.4		41	Arkansas	6.2
36	Tennessee	6.5		42	Indiana	5.8
26	Texas	8.5		43	Missouri	5.7
12	Utah	10.7		44	Mississippi	5.6
1	Vermont	21.3		45	Alabama	5.3
35	Virginia	6.6		46	Louisiana	5.1
21	Washington	9.0		47	Michigan	4.8
23	West Virginia	8.8		48	Ohio	4.2
37	Wisconsin	6.4		49	Georgia	4.1
4	Wyoming	15.3		NA	Illinois**	NA
					District of Columbia	5.3

Source: CQ Press using reported data from the Federal Bureau of Investigation
   "Crime in the United States 2008" (Uniform Crime Reports, September 14, 2009, http://www.fbi.gov/ucr/ucr.htm)
*Of the 375,484 robberies in 2008 for which supplemental data were received by the F.B.I. There were an additional 66,371 robberies for which the type of weapon was not reported to the F.B.I. Robbery is the taking or attempting to take anything of value by force or threat of force. Numbers are for reporting jurisdictions only.
**Not available.

Robberies With Blunt Objects and Other Dangerous Weapons in 2008

National Total = 32,693 Robberies*

ALPHA ORDER

RANK	STATE	ROBBERIES	% of USA
30	Alabama	196	0.6%
41	Alaska	71	0.2%
11	Arizona	840	2.6%
31	Arkansas	172	0.5%
1	California	6,415	19.6%
24	Colorado	353	1.1%
25	Connecticut	336	1.0%
36	Delaware	141	0.4%
3	Florida	3,075	9.4%
8	Georgia	1,061	3.2%
40	Hawaii	80	0.2%
45	Idaho	29	0.1%
NA	Illinois**	NA	NA
20	Indiana	531	1.6%
32	Iowa	160	0.5%
33	Kansas	157	0.5%
19	Kentucky	553	1.7%
26	Louisiana	331	1.0%
44	Maine	34	0.1%
22	Maryland	478	1.5%
12	Massachusetts	798	2.4%
7	Michigan	1,095	3.3%
15	Minnesota	635	1.9%
29	Mississippi	222	0.7%
17	Missouri	589	1.8%
43	Montana	39	0.1%
38	Nebraska	98	0.3%
18	Nevada	557	1.7%
42	New Hampshire	45	0.1%
13	New Jersey	778	2.4%
35	New Mexico	156	0.5%
6	New York	1,186	3.6%
9	North Carolina	1,059	3.2%
48	North Dakota	11	0.0%
4	Ohio	1,575	4.8%
28	Oklahoma	261	0.8%
27	Oregon	267	0.8%
5	Pennsylvania	1,218	3.7%
37	Rhode Island	108	0.3%
21	South Carolina	490	1.5%
46	South Dakota	15	0.0%
10	Tennessee	852	2.6%
2	Texas	3,398	10.4%
33	Utah	157	0.5%
47	Vermont	13	0.0%
14	Virginia	664	2.0%
16	Washington	611	1.9%
39	West Virginia	90	0.3%
23	Wisconsin	453	1.4%
49	Wyoming	8	0.0%

RANK ORDER

RANK	STATE	ROBBERIES	% of USA
1	California	6,415	19.6%
2	Texas	3,398	10.4%
3	Florida	3,075	9.4%
4	Ohio	1,575	4.8%
5	Pennsylvania	1,218	3.7%
6	New York	1,186	3.6%
7	Michigan	1,095	3.3%
8	Georgia	1,061	3.2%
9	North Carolina	1,059	3.2%
10	Tennessee	852	2.6%
11	Arizona	840	2.6%
12	Massachusetts	798	2.4%
13	New Jersey	778	2.4%
14	Virginia	664	2.0%
15	Minnesota	635	1.9%
16	Washington	611	1.9%
17	Missouri	589	1.8%
18	Nevada	557	1.7%
19	Kentucky	553	1.7%
20	Indiana	531	1.6%
21	South Carolina	490	1.5%
22	Maryland	478	1.5%
23	Wisconsin	453	1.4%
24	Colorado	353	1.1%
25	Connecticut	336	1.0%
26	Louisiana	331	1.0%
27	Oregon	267	0.8%
28	Oklahoma	261	0.8%
29	Mississippi	222	0.7%
30	Alabama	196	0.6%
31	Arkansas	172	0.5%
32	Iowa	160	0.5%
33	Kansas	157	0.5%
33	Utah	157	0.5%
35	New Mexico	156	0.5%
36	Delaware	141	0.4%
37	Rhode Island	108	0.3%
38	Nebraska	98	0.3%
39	West Virginia	90	0.3%
40	Hawaii	80	0.2%
41	Alaska	71	0.2%
42	New Hampshire	45	0.1%
43	Montana	39	0.1%
44	Maine	34	0.1%
45	Idaho	29	0.1%
46	South Dakota	15	0.0%
47	Vermont	13	0.0%
48	North Dakota	11	0.0%
49	Wyoming	8	0.0%
NA	Illinois**	NA	NA
	District of Columbia	181	0.6%

Source: Reported data from the Federal Bureau of Investigation
"Crime in the United States 2008" (Uniform Crime Reports, September 14, 2009, http://www.fbi.gov/ucr/ucr.htm)
*Of the 375,484 robberies in 2008 for which supplemental data were received by the F.B.I. There were an additional 66,371 robberies for which the type of weapon was not reported to the F.B.I. Robbery is the taking or attempting to take anything of value by force or threat of force. Numbers are for reporting jurisdictions only.
**Not available.

Percent of Robberies Involving Blunt Objects and Other Dangerous Weapons in 2008
National Percent = 8.7% of Robberies*

ALPHA ORDER

RANK	STATE	PERCENT
48	Alabama	5.4
16	Alaska	11.1
30	Arizona	8.7
44	Arkansas	6.5
24	California	9.3
15	Colorado	11.2
18	Connecticut	10.7
38	Delaware	7.7
32	Florida	8.5
43	Georgia	7.0
37	Hawaii	7.8
7	Idaho	13.5
NA	Illinois**	NA
41	Indiana	7.4
8	Iowa	13.0
14	Kansas	12.2
4	Kentucky	15.3
46	Louisiana	6.3
19	Maine	10.2
49	Maryland	5.2
12	Massachusetts	12.3
28	Michigan	8.8
4	Minnesota	15.3
21	Mississippi	10.1
35	Missouri	8.0
1	Montana	23.2
40	Nebraska	7.6
31	Nevada	8.6
10	New Hampshire	12.7
46	New Jersey	6.3
38	New Mexico	7.7
11	New York	12.5
33	North Carolina	8.2
3	North Dakota	15.7
25	Ohio	9.1
42	Oklahoma	7.2
19	Oregon	10.2
44	Pennsylvania	6.5
12	Rhode Island	12.3
33	South Carolina	8.2
9	South Dakota	12.9
35	Tennessee	8.0
26	Texas	9.0
16	Utah	11.1
6	Vermont	14.6
26	Virginia	9.0
22	Washington	10.0
2	West Virginia	17.3
28	Wisconsin	8.8
23	Wyoming	9.4

RANK ORDER

RANK	STATE	PERCENT
1	Montana	23.2
2	West Virginia	17.3
3	North Dakota	15.7
4	Kentucky	15.3
4	Minnesota	15.3
6	Vermont	14.6
7	Idaho	13.5
8	Iowa	13.0
9	South Dakota	12.9
10	New Hampshire	12.7
11	New York	12.5
12	Massachusetts	12.3
12	Rhode Island	12.3
14	Kansas	12.2
15	Colorado	11.2
16	Alaska	11.1
16	Utah	11.1
18	Connecticut	10.7
19	Maine	10.2
19	Oregon	10.2
21	Mississippi	10.1
22	Washington	10.0
23	Wyoming	9.4
24	California	9.3
25	Ohio	9.1
26	Texas	9.0
26	Virginia	9.0
28	Michigan	8.8
28	Wisconsin	8.8
30	Arizona	8.7
31	Nevada	8.6
32	Florida	8.5
33	North Carolina	8.2
33	South Carolina	8.2
35	Missouri	8.0
35	Tennessee	8.0
37	Hawaii	7.8
38	Delaware	7.7
38	New Mexico	7.7
40	Nebraska	7.6
41	Indiana	7.4
42	Oklahoma	7.2
43	Georgia	7.0
44	Arkansas	6.5
44	Pennsylvania	6.5
46	Louisiana	6.3
46	New Jersey	6.3
48	Alabama	5.4
49	Maryland	5.2
NA	Illinois**	NA

District of Columbia   4.1

Source: CQ Press using reported data from the Federal Bureau of Investigation
"Crime in the United States 2008" (Uniform Crime Reports, September 14, 2009, http://www.fbi.gov/ucr/ucr.htm)
*Of the 375,484 robberies in 2008 for which supplemental data were received by the F.B.I. There were an additional 66,371 robberies for which the type of weapon was not reported to the F.B.I. Robbery is the taking or attempting to take anything of value by force or threat of force. Numbers are for reporting jurisdictions only.
**Not available.

Robberies Committed With Hands, Fists, or Feet in 2008

National Total = 150,874 Robberies*

RANK	STATE	ROBBERIES	% of USA
30	Alabama	1,006	0.7%
40	Alaska	344	0.2%
13	Arizona	2,979	2.0%
29	Arkansas	1,045	0.7%
1	California	34,580	22.9%
27	Colorado	1,298	0.9%
24	Connecticut	1,486	1.0%
31	Delaware	754	0.5%
2	Florida	13,967	9.3%
9	Georgia	3,715	2.5%
32	Hawaii	738	0.5%
44	Idaho	90	0.1%
NA	Illinois**	NA	NA
18	Indiana	2,467	1.6%
34	Iowa	670	0.4%
37	Kansas	498	0.3%
28	Kentucky	1,294	0.9%
23	Louisiana	1,660	1.1%
42	Maine	203	0.1%
10	Maryland	3,621	2.4%
14	Massachusetts	2,820	1.9%
8	Michigan	4,477	3.0%
20	Minnesota	1,920	1.3%
36	Mississippi	536	0.4%
17	Missouri	2,555	1.7%
45	Montana	86	0.1%
38	Nebraska	473	0.3%
16	Nevada	2,630	1.7%
43	New Hampshire	184	0.1%
6	New Jersey	6,369	4.2%
33	New Mexico	678	0.4%
7	New York	4,548	3.0%
10	North Carolina	3,621	2.4%
48	North Dakota	40	0.0%
5	Ohio	7,748	5.1%
26	Oklahoma	1,328	0.9%
25	Oregon	1,440	1.0%
4	Pennsylvania	8,355	5.5%
39	Rhode Island	440	0.3%
21	South Carolina	1,691	1.1%
46	South Dakota	57	0.0%
15	Tennessee	2,701	1.8%
3	Texas	13,140	8.7%
35	Utah	656	0.4%
49	Vermont	35	0.0%
19	Virginia	2,071	1.4%
12	Washington	3,473	2.3%
41	West Virginia	219	0.1%
22	Wisconsin	1,690	1.1%
47	Wyoming	41	0.0%

RANK	STATE	ROBBERIES	% of USA
1	California	34,580	22.9%
2	Florida	13,967	9.3%
3	Texas	13,140	8.7%
4	Pennsylvania	8,355	5.5%
5	Ohio	7,748	5.1%
6	New Jersey	6,369	4.2%
7	New York	4,548	3.0%
8	Michigan	4,477	3.0%
9	Georgia	3,715	2.5%
10	Maryland	3,621	2.4%
10	North Carolina	3,621	2.4%
12	Washington	3,473	2.3%
13	Arizona	2,979	2.0%
14	Massachusetts	2,820	1.9%
15	Tennessee	2,701	1.8%
16	Nevada	2,630	1.7%
17	Missouri	2,555	1.7%
18	Indiana	2,467	1.6%
19	Virginia	2,071	1.4%
20	Minnesota	1,920	1.3%
21	South Carolina	1,691	1.1%
22	Wisconsin	1,690	1.1%
23	Louisiana	1,660	1.1%
24	Connecticut	1,486	1.0%
25	Oregon	1,440	1.0%
26	Oklahoma	1,328	0.9%
27	Colorado	1,298	0.9%
28	Kentucky	1,294	0.9%
29	Arkansas	1,045	0.7%
30	Alabama	1,006	0.7%
31	Delaware	754	0.5%
32	Hawaii	738	0.5%
33	New Mexico	678	0.4%
34	Iowa	670	0.4%
35	Utah	656	0.4%
36	Mississippi	536	0.4%
37	Kansas	498	0.3%
38	Nebraska	473	0.3%
39	Rhode Island	440	0.3%
40	Alaska	344	0.2%
41	West Virginia	219	0.1%
42	Maine	203	0.1%
43	New Hampshire	184	0.1%
44	Idaho	90	0.1%
45	Montana	86	0.1%
46	South Dakota	57	0.0%
47	Wyoming	41	0.0%
48	North Dakota	40	0.0%
49	Vermont	35	0.0%
NA	Illinois**	NA	NA
	District of Columbia	2,204	1.5%

Source: Reported data from the Federal Bureau of Investigation
   "Crime in the United States 2008" (Uniform Crime Reports, September 14, 2009, http://www.fbi.gov/ucr/ucr.htm)
*Also called strong-armed robberies. Of the 375,484 robberies in 2008 for which supplemental data were received by the F.B.I.
There were an additional 66,371 robberies for which the type of weapon was not reported to the F.B.I. Robbery is the taking or
attempting to take anything of value by force or threat of force. Numbers are for reporting jurisdictions only.
**Not available.

Percent of Robberies Committed With Hands, Fists, or Feet in 2008

National Percent = 40.2% of Robberies*

ALPHA ORDER				RANK ORDER		
RANK	STATE	PERCENT		RANK	STATE	PERCENT
46	Alabama	27.8		1	Hawaii	72.3
7	Alaska	53.6		2	Maine	61.0
42	Arizona	30.9		3	North Dakota	57.1
28	Arkansas	39.3		4	Washington	56.8
12	California	49.9		5	Oregon	55.0
24	Colorado	41.2		6	Iowa	54.3
16	Connecticut	47.5		7	Alaska	53.6
25	Delaware	41.0		8	New Hampshire	52.1
31	Florida	38.6		9	New Jersey	51.9
48	Georgia	24.7		10	Montana	51.2
1	Hawaii	72.3		11	Rhode Island	50.1
23	Idaho	41.9		12	California	49.9
NA	Illinois**	NA		13	South Dakota	49.1
38	Indiana	34.3		14	Wyoming	48.2
6	Iowa	54.3		15	New York	47.8
30	Kansas	38.7		16	Connecticut	47.5
34	Kentucky	35.9		17	Minnesota	46.4
41	Louisiana	31.8		17	Utah	46.4
2	Maine	61.0		19	Ohio	44.9
27	Maryland	39.5		20	Pennsylvania	44.8
21	Massachusetts	43.5		21	Massachusetts	43.5
34	Michigan	35.9		22	West Virginia	42.0
17	Minnesota	46.4		23	Idaho	41.9
49	Mississippi	24.4		24	Colorado	41.2
36	Missouri	34.8		25	Delaware	41.0
10	Montana	51.2		26	Nevada	40.6
32	Nebraska	36.8		27	Maryland	39.5
26	Nevada	40.6		28	Arkansas	39.3
8	New Hampshire	52.1		28	Vermont	39.3
9	New Jersey	51.9		30	Kansas	38.7
39	New Mexico	33.4		31	Florida	38.6
15	New York	47.8		32	Nebraska	36.8
43	North Carolina	28.2		33	Oklahoma	36.5
3	North Dakota	57.1		34	Kentucky	35.9
19	Ohio	44.9		34	Michigan	35.9
33	Oklahoma	36.5		36	Missouri	34.8
5	Oregon	55.0		36	Texas	34.8
20	Pennsylvania	44.8		38	Indiana	34.3
11	Rhode Island	50.1		39	New Mexico	33.4
43	South Carolina	28.2		40	Wisconsin	33.0
13	South Dakota	49.1		41	Louisiana	31.8
47	Tennessee	25.3		42	Arizona	30.9
36	Texas	34.8		43	North Carolina	28.2
17	Utah	46.4		43	South Carolina	28.2
28	Vermont	39.3		45	Virginia	28.0
45	Virginia	28.0		46	Alabama	27.8
4	Washington	56.8		47	Tennessee	25.3
22	West Virginia	42.0		48	Georgia	24.7
40	Wisconsin	33.0		49	Mississippi	24.4
14	Wyoming	48.2		NA	Illinois**	NA
					District of Columbia	49.8

Source: CQ Press using reported data from the Federal Bureau of Investigation
   "Crime in the United States 2008" (Uniform Crime Reports, September 14, 2009, http://www.fbi.gov/ucr/ucr.htm)
*Also called strong-armed robberies. Of the 375,484 robberies in 2008 for which supplemental data were received by the F.B.I.
There were an additional 66,371 robberies for which the type of weapon was not reported to the F.B.I. Robbery is the taking or
attempting to take anything of value by force or threat of force. Numbers are for reporting jurisdictions only.
**Not available.

Bank Robberies in 2008

National Total = 6,690 Robberies*

ALPHA ORDER

RANK	STATE	ROBBERIES	% of USA
22	Alabama	97	1.4%
42	Alaska	15	0.2%
10	Arizona	236	3.5%
33	Arkansas	38	0.6%
1	California	912	13.6%
17	Colorado	133	2.0%
26	Connecticut	79	1.2%
40	Delaware	16	0.2%
4	Florida	355	5.3%
11	Georgia	204	3.0%
39	Hawaii	18	0.3%
42	Idaho	15	0.2%
5	Illinois	318	4.8%
18	Indiana	113	1.7%
35	Iowa	32	0.5%
37	Kansas	27	0.4%
31	Kentucky	57	0.9%
32	Louisiana	41	0.6%
44	Maine	10	0.1%
14	Maryland	155	2.3%
7	Massachusetts	286	4.3%
9	Michigan	253	3.8%
30	Minnesota	58	0.9%
28	Mississippi	72	1.1%
23	Missouri	96	1.4%
48	Montana	2	0.0%
36	Nebraska	29	0.4%
27	Nevada	76	1.1%
38	New Hampshire	19	0.3%
13	New Jersey	194	2.9%
25	New Mexico	82	1.2%
2	New York	499	7.5%
11	North Carolina	204	3.0%
46	North Dakota	4	0.1%
8	Ohio	277	4.1%
34	Oklahoma	34	0.5%
16	Oregon	154	2.3%
6	Pennsylvania	314	4.7%
44	Rhode Island	10	0.1%
20	South Carolina	108	1.6%
46	South Dakota	4	0.1%
24	Tennessee	90	1.3%
3	Texas	481	7.2%
29	Utah	59	0.9%
48	Vermont	2	0.0%
21	Virginia	101	1.5%
14	Washington	155	2.3%
40	West Virginia	16	0.2%
19	Wisconsin	109	1.6%
50	Wyoming	0	0.0%

RANK ORDER

RANK	STATE	ROBBERIES	% of USA
1	California	912	13.6%
2	New York	499	7.5%
3	Texas	481	7.2%
4	Florida	355	5.3%
5	Illinois	318	4.8%
6	Pennsylvania	314	4.7%
7	Massachusetts	286	4.3%
8	Ohio	277	4.1%
9	Michigan	253	3.8%
10	Arizona	236	3.5%
11	Georgia	204	3.0%
11	North Carolina	204	3.0%
13	New Jersey	194	2.9%
14	Maryland	155	2.3%
14	Washington	155	2.3%
16	Oregon	154	2.3%
17	Colorado	133	2.0%
18	Indiana	113	1.7%
19	Wisconsin	109	1.6%
20	South Carolina	108	1.6%
21	Virginia	101	1.5%
22	Alabama	97	1.4%
23	Missouri	96	1.4%
24	Tennessee	90	1.3%
25	New Mexico	82	1.2%
26	Connecticut	79	1.2%
27	Nevada	76	1.1%
28	Mississippi	72	1.1%
29	Utah	59	0.9%
30	Minnesota	58	0.9%
31	Kentucky	57	0.9%
32	Louisiana	41	0.6%
33	Arkansas	38	0.6%
34	Oklahoma	34	0.5%
35	Iowa	32	0.5%
36	Nebraska	29	0.4%
37	Kansas	27	0.4%
38	New Hampshire	19	0.3%
39	Hawaii	18	0.3%
40	Delaware	16	0.2%
40	West Virginia	16	0.2%
42	Alaska	15	0.2%
42	Idaho	15	0.2%
44	Maine	10	0.1%
44	Rhode Island	10	0.1%
46	North Dakota	4	0.1%
46	South Dakota	4	0.1%
48	Montana	2	0.0%
48	Vermont	2	0.0%
50	Wyoming	0	0.0%
	District of Columbia	31	0.5%

Source: Reported data from the Federal Bureau of Investigation
"Bank Crime Statistics, Federally Insured Financial Institutions, January 1, 2008 - December 31, 2008"
(http://www.fbi.gov/publications/bcs/bcs2008/bank_crime_2008final.htm)
*Does not include 10 robberies in U.S. territories. In addition, there were 121 bank burglaries and 28 bank larcenies. During these 6,849 bank crimes, 2 people were killed, 123 were injured, and 105 were taken hostage. Loot valued at $61,914,663 was taken in 6,225 cases. Of this, $8,940,477 was recovered.

Aggravated Assaults in 2008

National Total = 834,885 Aggravated Assaults*

ALPHA ORDER

RANK	STATE	ASSAULTS	% of USA
21	Alabama	11,795	1.4%
40	Alaska	3,360	0.4%
16	Arizona	17,282	2.1%
26	Arkansas	10,082	1.2%
1	California	104,743	12.5%
23	Colorado	11,326	1.4%
34	Connecticut	5,723	0.7%
36	Delaware	3,880	0.5%
2	Florida	82,852	9.9%
9	Georgia	26,196	3.1%
42	Hawaii	2,036	0.2%
41	Idaho	2,668	0.3%
5	Illinois	38,818	4.6%
22	Indiana	11,704	1.4%
32	Iowa	6,308	0.8%
29	Kansas	8,518	1.0%
31	Kentucky	7,036	0.8%
12	Louisiana	21,191	2.5%
48	Maine	808	0.1%
13	Maryland	20,570	2.5%
15	Massachusetts	20,202	2.4%
6	Michigan	32,158	3.9%
30	Minnesota	7,626	0.9%
35	Mississippi	4,230	0.5%
14	Missouri	20,359	2.4%
43	Montana	2,008	0.2%
39	Nebraska	3,466	0.4%
24	Nevada	11,099	1.3%
45	New Hampshire	1,246	0.1%
18	New Jersey	14,152	1.7%
27	New Mexico	9,443	1.1%
4	New York	42,170	5.1%
10	North Carolina	25,877	3.1%
49	North Dakota	761	0.1%
17	Ohio	16,316	2.0%
19	Oklahoma	13,823	1.7%
33	Oregon	5,868	0.7%
8	Pennsylvania	27,984	3.4%
44	Rhode Island	1,436	0.2%
11	South Carolina	24,149	2.9%
46	South Dakota	1,042	0.1%
7	Tennessee	31,627	3.8%
3	Texas	76,423	9.2%
37	Utah	3,717	0.4%
50	Vermont	611	0.1%
25	Virginia	10,319	1.2%
20	Washington	12,524	1.5%
38	West Virginia	3,657	0.4%
28	Wisconsin	9,029	1.1%
47	Wyoming	960	0.1%

RANK ORDER

RANK	STATE	ASSAULTS	% of USA
1	California	104,743	12.5%
2	Florida	82,852	9.9%
3	Texas	76,423	9.2%
4	New York	42,170	5.1%
5	Illinois	38,818	4.6%
6	Michigan	32,158	3.9%
7	Tennessee	31,627	3.8%
8	Pennsylvania	27,984	3.4%
9	Georgia	26,196	3.1%
10	North Carolina	25,877	3.1%
11	South Carolina	24,149	2.9%
12	Louisiana	21,191	2.5%
13	Maryland	20,570	2.5%
14	Missouri	20,359	2.4%
15	Massachusetts	20,202	2.4%
16	Arizona	17,282	2.1%
17	Ohio	16,316	2.0%
18	New Jersey	14,152	1.7%
19	Oklahoma	13,823	1.7%
20	Washington	12,524	1.5%
21	Alabama	11,795	1.4%
22	Indiana	11,704	1.4%
23	Colorado	11,326	1.4%
24	Nevada	11,099	1.3%
25	Virginia	10,319	1.2%
26	Arkansas	10,082	1.2%
27	New Mexico	9,443	1.1%
28	Wisconsin	9,029	1.1%
29	Kansas	8,518	1.0%
30	Minnesota	7,626	0.9%
31	Kentucky	7,036	0.8%
32	Iowa	6,308	0.8%
33	Oregon	5,868	0.7%
34	Connecticut	5,723	0.7%
35	Mississippi	4,230	0.5%
36	Delaware	3,880	0.5%
37	Utah	3,717	0.4%
38	West Virginia	3,657	0.4%
39	Nebraska	3,466	0.4%
40	Alaska	3,360	0.4%
41	Idaho	2,668	0.3%
42	Hawaii	2,036	0.2%
43	Montana	2,008	0.2%
44	Rhode Island	1,436	0.2%
45	New Hampshire	1,246	0.1%
46	South Dakota	1,042	0.1%
47	Wyoming	960	0.1%
48	Maine	808	0.1%
49	North Dakota	761	0.1%
50	Vermont	611	0.1%
	District of Columbia	3,707	0.4%

Source: Reported data from the Federal Bureau of Investigation
"Crime in the United States 2008" (Uniform Crime Reports, September 14, 2009, http://www.fbi.gov/ucr/ucr.htm)
*Aggravated assault is an attack for the purpose of inflicting severe bodily injury.

Average Time Between Aggravated Assaults in 2008

National Rate = An Aggravated Assault Occurs Every 37.8 Seconds*

ALPHA ORDER

RANK	STATE	HOURS.MINUTES
30	Alabama	0.44
11	Alaska	2.37
35	Arizona	0.31
25	Arkansas	0.52
50	California	0.05
27	Colorado	0.47
17	Connecticut	1.32
15	Delaware	2.16
48	Florida	0.07
41	Georgia	0.20
9	Hawaii	4.19
10	Idaho	3.17
46	Illinois	0.14
29	Indiana	0.45
19	Iowa	1.23
22	Kansas	1.02
20	Kentucky	1.15
39	Louisiana	0.25
3	Maine	10.52
36	Maryland	0.26
36	Massachusetts	0.26
45	Michigan	0.16
21	Minnesota	1.09
16	Mississippi	2.05
36	Missouri	0.26
8	Montana	4.22
12	Nebraska	2.32
27	Nevada	0.47
6	New Hampshire	7.03
33	New Jersey	0.37
24	New Mexico	0.56
47	New York	0.13
41	North Carolina	0.20
2	North Dakota	11.32
34	Ohio	0.32
32	Oklahoma	0.38
18	Oregon	1.30
43	Pennsylvania	0.19
7	Rhode Island	6.07
40	South Carolina	0.22
5	South Dakota	8.26
44	Tennessee	0.17
48	Texas	0.07
14	Utah	2.22
1	Vermont	14.23
26	Virginia	0.51
31	Washington	0.42
13	West Virginia	2.24
23	Wisconsin	0.58
4	Wyoming	9.09

RANK ORDER

RANK	STATE	HOURS.MINUTES
1	Vermont	14.23
2	North Dakota	11.32
3	Maine	10.52
4	Wyoming	9.09
5	South Dakota	8.26
6	New Hampshire	7.03
7	Rhode Island	6.07
8	Montana	4.22
9	Hawaii	4.19
10	Idaho	3.17
11	Alaska	2.37
12	Nebraska	2.32
13	West Virginia	2.24
14	Utah	2.22
15	Delaware	2.16
16	Mississippi	2.05
17	Connecticut	1.32
18	Oregon	1.30
19	Iowa	1.23
20	Kentucky	1.15
21	Minnesota	1.09
22	Kansas	1.02
23	Wisconsin	0.58
24	New Mexico	0.56
25	Arkansas	0.52
26	Virginia	0.51
27	Colorado	0.47
27	Nevada	0.47
29	Indiana	0.45
30	Alabama	0.44
31	Washington	0.42
32	Oklahoma	0.38
33	New Jersey	0.37
34	Ohio	0.32
35	Arizona	0.31
36	Maryland	0.26
36	Massachusetts	0.26
36	Missouri	0.26
39	Louisiana	0.25
40	South Carolina	0.22
41	Georgia	0.20
41	North Carolina	0.20
43	Pennsylvania	0.19
44	Tennessee	0.17
45	Michigan	0.16
46	Illinois	0.14
47	New York	0.13
48	Florida	0.07
48	Texas	0.07
50	California	0.05

District of Columbia   2.22

Source: CQ Press using reported data from the Federal Bureau of Investigation
"Crime in the United States 2008" (Uniform Crime Reports, September 14, 2009, http://www.fbi.gov/ucr/ucr.htm)
*Aggravated assault is an attack for the purpose of inflicting severe bodily injury.

Percent Change in Number of Aggravated Assaults: 2007 to 2008

National Percent Change = 2.5% Decrease*

ALPHA ORDER				RANK ORDER		
RANK	STATE	PERCENT CHANGE		RANK	STATE	PERCENT CHANGE
11	Alabama	3.7		1	Connecticut	24.6
19	Alaska	(0.1)		2	North Dakota	22.3
43	Arizona	(7.4)		3	New Hampshire	21.3
38	Arkansas	(4.2)		4	South Dakota	14.5
35	California	(4.1)		5	Vermont	9.7
17	Colorado	0.2		6	Oklahoma	7.0
1	Connecticut	24.6		7	Massachusetts	6.3
18	Delaware	0.0		8	Indiana	4.5
35	Florida	(4.1)		9	Rhode Island	4.2
27	Georgia	(2.4)		10	Texas	4.1
21	Hawaii	(0.6)		11	Alabama	3.7
26	Idaho	(2.2)		12	Kentucky	2.6
39	Illinois	(4.3)		13	Maine	1.9
8	Indiana	4.5		14	Ohio	1.1
34	Iowa	(3.7)		15	Nevada	0.6
44	Kansas	(7.5)		16	North Carolina	0.5
12	Kentucky	2.6		17	Colorado	0.2
47	Louisiana	(8.8)		18	Delaware	0.0
13	Maine	1.9		19	Alaska	(0.1)
27	Maryland	(2.4)		20	Missouri	(0.3)
7	Massachusetts	6.3		21	Hawaii	(0.6)
48	Michigan	(8.9)		21	Pennsylvania	(0.6)
44	Minnesota	(7.5)		23	West Virginia	(1.2)
33	Mississippi	(3.6)		24	New Mexico	(1.3)
20	Missouri	(0.3)		24	Washington	(1.3)
50	Montana	(11.1)		26	Idaho	(2.2)
40	Nebraska	(5.4)		27	Georgia	(2.4)
15	Nevada	0.6		27	Maryland	(2.4)
3	New Hampshire	21.3		29	Utah	(2.8)
31	New Jersey	(3.2)		30	Wyoming	(3.1)
24	New Mexico	(1.3)		31	New Jersey	(3.2)
42	New York	(6.5)		32	Tennessee	(3.5)
16	North Carolina	0.5		33	Mississippi	(3.6)
2	North Dakota	22.3		34	Iowa	(3.7)
14	Ohio	1.1		35	California	(4.1)
6	Oklahoma	7.0		35	Florida	(4.1)
49	Oregon	(10.9)		35	Wisconsin	(4.1)
21	Pennsylvania	(0.6)		38	Arkansas	(4.2)
9	Rhode Island	4.2		39	Illinois	(4.3)
46	South Carolina	(8.2)		40	Nebraska	(5.4)
4	South Dakota	14.5		41	Virginia	(6.2)
32	Tennessee	(3.5)		42	New York	(6.5)
10	Texas	4.1		43	Arizona	(7.4)
29	Utah	(2.8)		44	Kansas	(7.5)
5	Vermont	9.7		44	Minnesota	(7.5)
41	Virginia	(6.2)		46	South Carolina	(8.2)
24	Washington	(1.3)		47	Louisiana	(8.8)
23	West Virginia	(1.2)		48	Michigan	(8.9)
35	Wisconsin	(4.1)		49	Oregon	(10.9)
30	Wyoming	(3.1)		50	Montana	(11.1)
					District of Columbia	0.6

Source: Reported data from the Federal Bureau of Investigation
"Crime in the United States 2008" (Uniform Crime Reports, September 14, 2009, http://www.fbi.gov/ucr/ucr.htm)
*Aggravated assault is an attack for the purpose of inflicting severe bodily injury.

Aggravated Assault Rate in 2008

National Rate = 274.6 Aggravated Assaults per 100,000 Population*

ALPHA ORDER

RANK	STATE	RATE
22	Alabama	253.0
3	Alaska	489.6
21	Arizona	265.9
11	Arkansas	353.1
18	California	285.0
23	Colorado	229.3
35	Connecticut	163.5
7	Delaware	444.4
6	Florida	452.0
20	Georgia	270.5
38	Hawaii	158.1
33	Idaho	175.1
17	Illinois	300.9
31	Indiana	183.5
26	Iowa	210.1
16	Kansas	304.0
34	Kentucky	164.8
4	Louisiana	480.4
50	Maine	61.4
10	Maryland	365.1
15	Massachusetts	310.9
13	Michigan	321.5
40	Minnesota	146.1
41	Mississippi	143.9
12	Missouri	344.4
27	Montana	207.6
29	Nebraska	194.3
8	Nevada	426.9
49	New Hampshire	94.7
36	New Jersey	163.0
5	New Mexico	475.9
25	New York	216.4
19	North Carolina	280.6
47	North Dakota	118.6
42	Ohio	142.1
9	Oklahoma	379.5
39	Oregon	154.8
24	Pennsylvania	224.8
43	Rhode Island	136.7
1	South Carolina	539.1
46	South Dakota	129.6
2	Tennessee	508.9
14	Texas	314.1
44	Utah	135.8
48	Vermont	98.3
45	Virginia	132.8
30	Washington	191.2
28	West Virginia	201.5
37	Wisconsin	160.4
32	Wyoming	180.2

RANK ORDER

RANK	STATE	RATE
1	South Carolina	539.1
2	Tennessee	508.9
3	Alaska	489.6
4	Louisiana	480.4
5	New Mexico	475.9
6	Florida	452.0
7	Delaware	444.4
8	Nevada	426.9
9	Oklahoma	379.5
10	Maryland	365.1
11	Arkansas	353.1
12	Missouri	344.4
13	Michigan	321.5
14	Texas	314.1
15	Massachusetts	310.9
16	Kansas	304.0
17	Illinois	300.9
18	California	285.0
19	North Carolina	280.6
20	Georgia	270.5
21	Arizona	265.9
22	Alabama	253.0
23	Colorado	229.3
24	Pennsylvania	224.8
25	New York	216.4
26	Iowa	210.1
27	Montana	207.6
28	West Virginia	201.5
29	Nebraska	194.3
30	Washington	191.2
31	Indiana	183.5
32	Wyoming	180.2
33	Idaho	175.1
34	Kentucky	164.8
35	Connecticut	163.5
36	New Jersey	163.0
37	Wisconsin	160.4
38	Hawaii	158.1
39	Oregon	154.8
40	Minnesota	146.1
41	Mississippi	143.9
42	Ohio	142.1
43	Rhode Island	136.7
44	Utah	135.8
45	Virginia	132.8
46	South Dakota	129.6
47	North Dakota	118.6
48	Vermont	98.3
49	New Hampshire	94.7
50	Maine	61.4

District of Columbia   626.4

Source: Reported data from the Federal Bureau of Investigation
"Crime in the United States 2008" (Uniform Crime Reports, September 14, 2009, http://www.fbi.gov/ucr/ucr.htm)
*Aggravated assault is an attack for the purpose of inflicting severe bodily injury.

Percent Change in Aggravated Assault Rate: 2007 to 2008

National Percent Change = 3.2% Decrease*

ALPHA ORDER			RANK ORDER		
RANK	STATE	PERCENT CHANGE	RANK	STATE	PERCENT CHANGE
10	Alabama	2.9	1	Connecticut	24.6
15	Alaska	(0.5)	2	North Dakota	22.0
46	Arizona	(9.7)	3	New Hampshire	21.3
37	Arkansas	(4.9)	4	South Dakota	13.4
34	California	(4.6)	5	Vermont	9.7
23	Colorado	(1.4)	6	Oklahoma	6.3
1	Connecticut	24.6	7	Massachusetts	5.5
19	Delaware	(1.0)	8	Rhode Island	4.9
33	Florida	(4.5)	9	Indiana	4.0
28	Georgia	(3.8)	10	Alabama	2.9
19	Hawaii	(1.0)	11	Texas	2.3
28	Idaho	(3.8)	12	Kentucky	1.9
36	Illinois	(4.7)	12	Maine	1.9
9	Indiana	4.0	14	Ohio	1.0
30	Iowa	(4.2)	15	Alaska	(0.5)
45	Kansas	(8.4)	16	Pennsylvania	(0.7)
12	Kentucky	1.9	17	Missouri	(0.8)
48	Louisiana	(11.2)	17	Nevada	(0.8)
12	Maine	1.9	19	Delaware	(1.0)
26	Maryland	(2.6)	19	Hawaii	(1.0)
7	Massachusetts	5.5	21	North Carolina	(1.2)
44	Michigan	(8.3)	22	West Virginia	(1.3)
43	Minnesota	(7.9)	23	Colorado	(1.4)
31	Mississippi	(4.3)	24	New Mexico	(2.0)
17	Missouri	(0.8)	25	Washington	(2.5)
50	Montana	(12.0)	26	Maryland	(2.6)
39	Nebraska	(5.9)	27	New Jersey	(3.2)
17	Nevada	(0.8)	28	Georgia	(3.8)
3	New Hampshire	21.3	28	Idaho	(3.8)
27	New Jersey	(3.2)	30	Iowa	(4.2)
24	New Mexico	(2.0)	31	Mississippi	(4.3)
42	New York	(7.4)	32	Tennessee	(4.4)
21	North Carolina	(1.2)	33	Florida	(4.5)
2	North Dakota	22.0	34	California	(4.6)
14	Ohio	1.0	34	Wisconsin	(4.6)
6	Oklahoma	6.3	36	Illinois	(4.7)
49	Oregon	(11.9)	37	Arkansas	(4.9)
16	Pennsylvania	(0.7)	37	Wyoming	(4.9)
8	Rhode Island	4.9	39	Nebraska	(5.9)
46	South Carolina	(9.7)	40	Utah	(6.0)
4	South Dakota	13.4	41	Virginia	(6.8)
32	Tennessee	(4.4)	42	New York	(7.4)
11	Texas	2.3	43	Minnesota	(7.9)
40	Utah	(6.0)	44	Michigan	(8.3)
5	Vermont	9.7	45	Kansas	(8.4)
41	Virginia	(6.8)	46	Arizona	(9.7)
25	Washington	(2.5)	46	South Carolina	(9.7)
22	West Virginia	(1.3)	48	Louisiana	(11.2)
34	Wisconsin	(4.6)	49	Oregon	(11.9)
37	Wyoming	(4.9)	50	Montana	(12.0)
				District of Columbia	0.0

Source: Reported data from the Federal Bureau of Investigation
"Crime in the United States 2008" (Uniform Crime Reports, September 14, 2009, http://www.fbi.gov/ucr/ucr.htm)
*Aggravated assault is an attack for the purpose of inflicting severe bodily injury.

Aggravated Assaults With Firearms in 2008

National Total = 154,145 Aggravated Assaults*

ALPHA ORDER

ALPHA ORDER

RANK	STATE	ASSAULTS	% of USA
16	Alabama	2,258	1.5%
38	Alaska	535	0.3%
11	Arizona	4,842	3.1%
15	Arkansas	2,316	1.5%
1	California	19,126	12.4%
20	Colorado	2,029	1.3%
37	Connecticut	548	0.4%
31	Delaware	971	0.6%
3	Florida	16,697	10.8%
9	Georgia	5,476	3.6%
43	Hawaii	182	0.1%
40	Idaho	355	0.2%
NA	Illinois**	NA	NA
28	Indiana	1,735	1.1%
35	Iowa	588	0.4%
26	Kansas	1,786	1.2%
30	Kentucky	1,224	0.8%
12	Louisiana	4,335	2.8%
48	Maine	59	0.0%
21	Maryland	2,023	1.3%
24	Massachusetts	1,859	1.2%
5	Michigan	7,918	5.1%
29	Minnesota	1,226	0.8%
32	Mississippi	860	0.6%
7	Missouri	5,904	3.8%
42	Montana	264	0.2%
39	Nebraska	499	0.3%
23	Nevada	1,936	1.3%
44	New Hampshire	167	0.1%
19	New Jersey	2,063	1.3%
27	New Mexico	1,742	1.1%
17	New York	2,190	1.4%
6	North Carolina	6,658	4.3%
49	North Dakota	15	0.0%
13	Ohio	3,370	2.2%
14	Oklahoma	2,464	1.6%
33	Oregon	680	0.4%
10	Pennsylvania	5,348	3.5%
41	Rhode Island	304	0.2%
8	South Carolina	5,602	3.6%
45	South Dakota	112	0.1%
4	Tennessee	9,381	6.1%
2	Texas	17,622	11.4%
34	Utah	600	0.4%
47	Vermont	60	0.0%
18	Virginia	2,146	1.4%
25	Washington	1,805	1.2%
36	West Virginia	559	0.4%
22	Wisconsin	2,003	1.3%
46	Wyoming	96	0.1%

RANK ORDER

RANK	STATE	ASSAULTS	% of USA
1	California	19,126	12.4%
2	Texas	17,622	11.4%
3	Florida	16,697	10.8%
4	Tennessee	9,381	6.1%
5	Michigan	7,918	5.1%
6	North Carolina	6,658	4.3%
7	Missouri	5,904	3.8%
8	South Carolina	5,602	3.6%
9	Georgia	5,476	3.6%
10	Pennsylvania	5,348	3.5%
11	Arizona	4,842	3.1%
12	Louisiana	4,335	2.8%
13	Ohio	3,370	2.2%
14	Oklahoma	2,464	1.6%
15	Arkansas	2,316	1.5%
16	Alabama	2,258	1.5%
17	New York	2,190	1.4%
18	Virginia	2,146	1.4%
19	New Jersey	2,063	1.3%
20	Colorado	2,029	1.3%
21	Maryland	2,023	1.3%
22	Wisconsin	2,003	1.3%
23	Nevada	1,936	1.3%
24	Massachusetts	1,859	1.2%
25	Washington	1,805	1.2%
26	Kansas	1,786	1.2%
27	New Mexico	1,742	1.1%
28	Indiana	1,735	1.1%
29	Minnesota	1,226	0.8%
30	Kentucky	1,224	0.8%
31	Delaware	971	0.6%
32	Mississippi	860	0.6%
33	Oregon	680	0.4%
34	Utah	600	0.4%
35	Iowa	588	0.4%
36	West Virginia	559	0.4%
37	Connecticut	548	0.4%
38	Alaska	535	0.3%
39	Nebraska	499	0.3%
40	Idaho	355	0.2%
41	Rhode Island	304	0.2%
42	Montana	264	0.2%
43	Hawaii	182	0.1%
44	New Hampshire	167	0.1%
45	South Dakota	112	0.1%
46	Wyoming	96	0.1%
47	Vermont	60	0.0%
48	Maine	59	0.0%
49	North Dakota	15	0.0%
NA	Illinois**	NA	NA
	District of Columbia	847	0.5%

Source: Reported data from the Federal Bureau of Investigation
"Crime in the United States 2008" (Uniform Crime Reports, September 14, 2009, http://www.fbi.gov/ucr/ucr.htm)
*Of the 720,575 aggravated assaults in 2008 for which supplemental data were received by the F.B.I. There were an additional 114,310 aggravated assaults for which the type of weapon was not reported to the F.B.I. Aggravated assault is an attack for the purpose of inflicting severe bodily injury. Numbers are for reporting jurisdictions only.
**Not available.

Aggravated Assault Rate With Firearms in 2008

National Rate = 59.2 Aggravated Assaults per 100,000 Population*

ALPHA ORDER

RANK	STATE	RATE
18	Alabama	69.8
12	Alaska	79.4
13	Arizona	75.5
10	Arkansas	88.7
20	California	52.3
23	Colorado	43.8
44	Connecticut	16.2
4	Delaware	111.2
7	Florida	91.3
14	Georgia	75.4
46	Hawaii	15.9
36	Idaho	24.6
NA	Illinois**	NA
27	Indiana	34.4
39	Iowa	21.3
11	Kansas	80.5
27	Kentucky	34.4
3	Louisiana	123.3
48	Maine	4.5
24	Maryland	40.5
29	Massachusetts	31.9
8	Michigan	91.0
35	Minnesota	24.7
21	Mississippi	51.6
6	Missouri	102.0
33	Montana	28.6
30	Nebraska	30.5
15	Nevada	74.5
44	New Hampshire	16.2
37	New Jersey	24.2
5	New Mexico	108.5
40	New York	20.4
9	North Carolina	89.3
49	North Dakota	2.6
25	Ohio	39.5
17	Oklahoma	72.1
41	Oregon	18.6
22	Pennsylvania	45.0
32	Rhode Island	28.9
2	South Carolina	145.5
43	South Dakota	17.2
1	Tennessee	160.5
16	Texas	72.5
38	Utah	22.3
47	Vermont	9.9
34	Virginia	27.9
31	Washington	29.5
19	West Virginia	53.4
26	Wisconsin	35.8
42	Wyoming	18.2

RANK ORDER

RANK	STATE	RATE
1	Tennessee	160.5
2	South Carolina	145.5
3	Louisiana	123.3
4	Delaware	111.2
5	New Mexico	108.5
6	Missouri	102.0
7	Florida	91.3
8	Michigan	91.0
9	North Carolina	89.3
10	Arkansas	88.7
11	Kansas	80.5
12	Alaska	79.4
13	Arizona	75.5
14	Georgia	75.4
15	Nevada	74.5
16	Texas	72.5
17	Oklahoma	72.1
18	Alabama	69.8
19	West Virginia	53.4
20	California	52.3
21	Mississippi	51.6
22	Pennsylvania	45.0
23	Colorado	43.8
24	Maryland	40.5
25	Ohio	39.5
26	Wisconsin	35.8
27	Indiana	34.4
27	Kentucky	34.4
29	Massachusetts	31.9
30	Nebraska	30.5
31	Washington	29.5
32	Rhode Island	28.9
33	Montana	28.6
34	Virginia	27.9
35	Minnesota	24.7
36	Idaho	24.6
37	New Jersey	24.2
38	Utah	22.3
39	Iowa	21.3
40	New York	20.4
41	Oregon	18.6
42	Wyoming	18.2
43	South Dakota	17.2
44	Connecticut	16.2
44	New Hampshire	16.2
46	Hawaii	15.9
47	Vermont	9.9
48	Maine	4.5
49	North Dakota	2.6
NA	Illinois**	NA
	District of Columbia	143.1

Source: CQ Press using reported data from the Federal Bureau of Investigation
   "Crime in the United States 2008" (Uniform Crime Reports, September 14, 2009, http://www.fbi.gov/ucr/ucr.htm)
*Based only on population of reporting jurisdictions. Aggravated assault is an attack for the purpose of inflicting severe bodily injury. National rate reflects only those assaults for which the type of weapon was known and reported.
**Not available.

Percent of Aggravated Assaults Involving Firearms in 2008

National Percent = 21.4% of Aggravated Assaults*

<table>
<tr><td colspan="3">ALPHA ORDER</td><td colspan="3">RANK ORDER</td></tr>
<tr><td>RANK</td><td>STATE</td><td>PERCENT</td><td>RANK</td><td>STATE</td><td>PERCENT</td></tr>
<tr><td>5</td><td>Alabama</td><td>29.5</td><td>1</td><td>Mississippi</td><td>34.6</td></tr>
<tr><td>32</td><td>Alaska</td><td>16.2</td><td>2</td><td>North Carolina</td><td>31.1</td></tr>
<tr><td>6</td><td>Arizona</td><td>28.5</td><td>3</td><td>Tennessee</td><td>30.9</td></tr>
<tr><td>13</td><td>Arkansas</td><td>24.0</td><td>4</td><td>Missouri</td><td>29.6</td></tr>
<tr><td>26</td><td>California</td><td>18.4</td><td>5</td><td>Alabama</td><td>29.5</td></tr>
<tr><td>24</td><td>Colorado</td><td>19.3</td><td>6</td><td>Arizona</td><td>28.5</td></tr>
<tr><td>40</td><td>Connecticut</td><td>11.9</td><td>7</td><td>Georgia</td><td>27.1</td></tr>
<tr><td>12</td><td>Delaware</td><td>25.0</td><td>8</td><td>Kansas</td><td>26.3</td></tr>
<tr><td>22</td><td>Florida</td><td>20.2</td><td>8</td><td>South Carolina</td><td>26.3</td></tr>
<tr><td>7</td><td>Georgia</td><td>27.1</td><td>10</td><td>Michigan</td><td>26.2</td></tr>
<tr><td>44</td><td>Hawaii</td><td>9.9</td><td>11</td><td>Louisiana</td><td>26.0</td></tr>
<tr><td>36</td><td>Idaho</td><td>14.8</td><td>12</td><td>Delaware</td><td>25.0</td></tr>
<tr><td>NA</td><td>Illinois**</td><td>NA</td><td>13</td><td>Arkansas</td><td>24.0</td></tr>
<tr><td>29</td><td>Indiana</td><td>16.3</td><td>14</td><td>Ohio</td><td>23.8</td></tr>
<tr><td>47</td><td>Iowa</td><td>9.6</td><td>15</td><td>Texas</td><td>23.1</td></tr>
<tr><td>8</td><td>Kansas</td><td>26.3</td><td>16</td><td>New Mexico</td><td>22.7</td></tr>
<tr><td>21</td><td>Kentucky</td><td>20.7</td><td>17</td><td>Wisconsin</td><td>22.2</td></tr>
<tr><td>11</td><td>Louisiana</td><td>26.0</td><td>18</td><td>West Virginia</td><td>21.8</td></tr>
<tr><td>48</td><td>Maine</td><td>7.3</td><td>19</td><td>Rhode Island</td><td>21.2</td></tr>
<tr><td>37</td><td>Maryland</td><td>13.6</td><td>19</td><td>Virginia</td><td>21.2</td></tr>
<tr><td>44</td><td>Massachusetts</td><td>9.9</td><td>21</td><td>Kentucky</td><td>20.7</td></tr>
<tr><td>10</td><td>Michigan</td><td>26.2</td><td>22</td><td>Florida</td><td>20.2</td></tr>
<tr><td>28</td><td>Minnesota</td><td>16.6</td><td>23</td><td>Pennsylvania</td><td>19.7</td></tr>
<tr><td>1</td><td>Mississippi</td><td>34.6</td><td>24</td><td>Colorado</td><td>19.3</td></tr>
<tr><td>4</td><td>Missouri</td><td>29.6</td><td>25</td><td>Oklahoma</td><td>18.5</td></tr>
<tr><td>37</td><td>Montana</td><td>13.6</td><td>26</td><td>California</td><td>18.4</td></tr>
<tr><td>35</td><td>Nebraska</td><td>14.9</td><td>27</td><td>Nevada</td><td>17.4</td></tr>
<tr><td>27</td><td>Nevada</td><td>17.4</td><td>28</td><td>Minnesota</td><td>16.6</td></tr>
<tr><td>29</td><td>New Hampshire</td><td>16.3</td><td>29</td><td>Indiana</td><td>16.3</td></tr>
<tr><td>33</td><td>New Jersey</td><td>15.2</td><td>29</td><td>New Hampshire</td><td>16.3</td></tr>
<tr><td>16</td><td>New Mexico</td><td>22.7</td><td>29</td><td>Utah</td><td>16.3</td></tr>
<tr><td>39</td><td>New York</td><td>13.0</td><td>32</td><td>Alaska</td><td>16.2</td></tr>
<tr><td>2</td><td>North Carolina</td><td>31.1</td><td>33</td><td>New Jersey</td><td>15.2</td></tr>
<tr><td>49</td><td>North Dakota</td><td>2.0</td><td>34</td><td>Washington</td><td>15.1</td></tr>
<tr><td>14</td><td>Ohio</td><td>23.8</td><td>35</td><td>Nebraska</td><td>14.9</td></tr>
<tr><td>25</td><td>Oklahoma</td><td>18.5</td><td>36</td><td>Idaho</td><td>14.8</td></tr>
<tr><td>42</td><td>Oregon</td><td>11.8</td><td>37</td><td>Maryland</td><td>13.6</td></tr>
<tr><td>23</td><td>Pennsylvania</td><td>19.7</td><td>37</td><td>Montana</td><td>13.6</td></tr>
<tr><td>19</td><td>Rhode Island</td><td>21.2</td><td>39</td><td>New York</td><td>13.0</td></tr>
<tr><td>8</td><td>South Carolina</td><td>26.3</td><td>40</td><td>Connecticut</td><td>11.9</td></tr>
<tr><td>40</td><td>South Dakota</td><td>11.9</td><td>40</td><td>South Dakota</td><td>11.9</td></tr>
<tr><td>3</td><td>Tennessee</td><td>30.9</td><td>42</td><td>Oregon</td><td>11.8</td></tr>
<tr><td>15</td><td>Texas</td><td>23.1</td><td>43</td><td>Wyoming</td><td>10.1</td></tr>
<tr><td>29</td><td>Utah</td><td>16.3</td><td>44</td><td>Hawaii</td><td>9.9</td></tr>
<tr><td>44</td><td>Vermont</td><td>9.9</td><td>44</td><td>Massachusetts</td><td>9.9</td></tr>
<tr><td>19</td><td>Virginia</td><td>21.2</td><td>44</td><td>Vermont</td><td>9.9</td></tr>
<tr><td>34</td><td>Washington</td><td>15.1</td><td>47</td><td>Iowa</td><td>9.6</td></tr>
<tr><td>18</td><td>West Virginia</td><td>21.8</td><td>48</td><td>Maine</td><td>7.3</td></tr>
<tr><td>17</td><td>Wisconsin</td><td>22.2</td><td>49</td><td>North Dakota</td><td>2.0</td></tr>
<tr><td>43</td><td>Wyoming</td><td>10.1</td><td>NA</td><td>Illinois**</td><td>NA</td></tr>
<tr><td></td><td></td><td></td><td></td><td>District of Columbia</td><td>22.8</td></tr>
</table>

Source: CQ Press using reported data from the Federal Bureau of Investigation
  "Crime in the United States 2008" (Uniform Crime Reports, September 14, 2009, http://www.fbi.gov/ucr/ucr.htm)
*Of the 720,575 aggravated assaults in 2008 for which supplemental data were received by the F.B.I. There were an additional 114,310 aggravated assaults for which the type of weapon was not reported to the F.B.I. Aggravated assault is an attack for the purpose of inflicting severe bodily injury. Numbers are for reporting jurisdictions only.
**Not available.

Aggravated Assaults With Knives or Cutting Instruments in 2008

National Total = 136,025 Aggravated Assaults*

ALPHA ORDER

RANK	STATE	ASSAULTS	% of USA
28	Alabama	1,107	0.8%
36	Alaska	679	0.5%
15	Arizona	2,954	2.2%
24	Arkansas	1,605	1.2%
2	California	16,601	12.2%
18	Colorado	2,486	1.8%
32	Connecticut	1,017	0.7%
35	Delaware	864	0.6%
3	Florida	14,597	10.7%
11	Georgia	3,650	2.7%
41	Hawaii	413	0.3%
39	Idaho	466	0.3%
NA	Illinois**	NA	NA
25	Indiana	1,486	1.1%
31	Iowa	1,025	0.8%
26	Kansas	1,367	1.0%
34	Kentucky	885	0.7%
17	Louisiana	2,593	1.9%
46	Maine	206	0.2%
12	Maryland	3,433	2.5%
7	Massachusetts	4,357	3.2%
5	Michigan	5,855	4.3%
23	Minnesota	1,641	1.2%
38	Mississippi	497	0.4%
16	Missouri	2,719	2.0%
45	Montana	272	0.2%
37	Nebraska	598	0.4%
22	Nevada	2,144	1.6%
44	New Hampshire	343	0.3%
13	New Jersey	3,062	2.3%
27	New Mexico	1,333	1.0%
6	New York	4,646	3.4%
8	North Carolina	4,221	3.1%
49	North Dakota	92	0.1%
14	Ohio	2,963	2.2%
21	Oklahoma	2,149	1.6%
30	Oregon	1,030	0.8%
9	Pennsylvania	4,098	3.0%
40	Rhode Island	452	0.3%
10	South Carolina	3,887	2.9%
43	South Dakota	345	0.3%
4	Tennessee	6,539	4.8%
1	Texas	16,875	12.4%
29	Utah	1,036	0.8%
48	Vermont	134	0.1%
19	Virginia	2,311	1.7%
20	Washington	2,171	1.6%
42	West Virginia	403	0.3%
33	Wisconsin	926	0.7%
47	Wyoming	173	0.1%

RANK ORDER

RANK	STATE	ASSAULTS	% of USA
1	Texas	16,875	12.4%
2	California	16,601	12.2%
3	Florida	14,597	10.7%
4	Tennessee	6,539	4.8%
5	Michigan	5,855	4.3%
6	New York	4,646	3.4%
7	Massachusetts	4,357	3.2%
8	North Carolina	4,221	3.1%
9	Pennsylvania	4,098	3.0%
10	South Carolina	3,887	2.9%
11	Georgia	3,650	2.7%
12	Maryland	3,433	2.5%
13	New Jersey	3,062	2.3%
14	Ohio	2,963	2.2%
15	Arizona	2,954	2.2%
16	Missouri	2,719	2.0%
17	Louisiana	2,593	1.9%
18	Colorado	2,486	1.8%
19	Virginia	2,311	1.7%
20	Washington	2,171	1.6%
21	Oklahoma	2,149	1.6%
22	Nevada	2,144	1.6%
23	Minnesota	1,641	1.2%
24	Arkansas	1,605	1.2%
25	Indiana	1,486	1.1%
26	Kansas	1,367	1.0%
27	New Mexico	1,333	1.0%
28	Alabama	1,107	0.8%
29	Utah	1,036	0.8%
30	Oregon	1,030	0.8%
31	Iowa	1,025	0.8%
32	Connecticut	1,017	0.7%
33	Wisconsin	926	0.7%
34	Kentucky	885	0.7%
35	Delaware	864	0.6%
36	Alaska	679	0.5%
37	Nebraska	598	0.4%
38	Mississippi	497	0.4%
39	Idaho	466	0.3%
40	Rhode Island	452	0.3%
41	Hawaii	413	0.3%
42	West Virginia	403	0.3%
43	South Dakota	345	0.3%
44	New Hampshire	343	0.3%
45	Montana	272	0.2%
46	Maine	206	0.2%
47	Wyoming	173	0.1%
48	Vermont	134	0.1%
49	North Dakota	92	0.1%
NA	Illinois**	NA	NA
	District of Columbia	1,086	0.8%

Source: Reported data from the Federal Bureau of Investigation
    "Crime in the United States 2008" (Uniform Crime Reports, September 14, 2009, http://www.fbi.gov/ucr/ucr.htm)
*Of the 720,575 aggravated assaults in 2008 for which supplemental data were received by the F.B.I. There were an additional 114,310 aggravated assaults for which the type of weapon was not reported to the F.B.I. Aggravated assault is an attack for the purpose of inflicting severe bodily injury. Numbers are for reporting jurisdictions only.
**Not available.

Percent of Aggravated Assaults Involving Knives or Cutting Instruments in 2008

National Percent = 18.9% of Aggravated Assaults*

ALPHA ORDER

RANK	STATE	PERCENT
44	Alabama	14.5
20	Alaska	20.5
34	Arizona	17.4
37	Arkansas	16.6
39	California	16.0
7	Colorado	23.6
15	Connecticut	22.1
13	Delaware	22.3
33	Florida	17.7
30	Georgia	18.1
12	Hawaii	22.4
24	Idaho	19.4
NA	Illinois**	NA
46	Indiana	13.9
36	Iowa	16.7
21	Kansas	20.1
43	Kentucky	15.0
41	Louisiana	15.6
6	Maine	25.5
9	Maryland	23.1
8	Massachusetts	23.3
24	Michigan	19.4
13	Minnesota	22.3
22	Mississippi	20.0
47	Missouri	13.6
45	Montana	14.0
32	Nebraska	17.8
26	Nevada	19.3
2	New Hampshire	33.5
11	New Jersey	22.6
34	New Mexico	17.4
5	New York	27.7
23	North Carolina	19.7
48	North Dakota	12.5
19	Ohio	21.0
38	Oklahoma	16.2
31	Oregon	17.9
42	Pennsylvania	15.1
3	Rhode Island	31.5
27	South Carolina	18.3
1	South Dakota	36.6
18	Tennessee	21.5
15	Texas	22.1
4	Utah	28.2
17	Vermont	22.0
10	Virginia	22.8
28	Washington	18.2
40	West Virginia	15.7
49	Wisconsin	10.3
28	Wyoming	18.2

RANK ORDER

RANK	STATE	PERCENT
1	South Dakota	36.6
2	New Hampshire	33.5
3	Rhode Island	31.5
4	Utah	28.2
5	New York	27.7
6	Maine	25.5
7	Colorado	23.6
8	Massachusetts	23.3
9	Maryland	23.1
10	Virginia	22.8
11	New Jersey	22.6
12	Hawaii	22.4
13	Delaware	22.3
13	Minnesota	22.3
15	Connecticut	22.1
15	Texas	22.1
17	Vermont	22.0
18	Tennessee	21.5
19	Ohio	21.0
20	Alaska	20.5
21	Kansas	20.1
22	Mississippi	20.0
23	North Carolina	19.7
24	Idaho	19.4
24	Michigan	19.4
26	Nevada	19.3
27	South Carolina	18.3
28	Washington	18.2
28	Wyoming	18.2
30	Georgia	18.1
31	Oregon	17.9
32	Nebraska	17.8
33	Florida	17.7
34	Arizona	17.4
34	New Mexico	17.4
36	Iowa	16.7
37	Arkansas	16.6
38	Oklahoma	16.2
39	California	16.0
40	West Virginia	15.7
41	Louisiana	15.6
42	Pennsylvania	15.1
43	Kentucky	15.0
44	Alabama	14.5
45	Montana	14.0
46	Indiana	13.9
47	Missouri	13.6
48	North Dakota	12.5
49	Wisconsin	10.3
NA	Illinois**	NA

District of Columbia 29.3

Source: CQ Press using reported data from the Federal Bureau of Investigation
"Crime in the United States 2008" (Uniform Crime Reports, September 14, 2009, http://www.fbi.gov/ucr/ucr.htm)
*Of the 720,575 aggravated assaults in 2008 for which supplemental data were received by the F.B.I. There were an additional 114,310 aggravated assaults for which the type of weapon was not reported to the F.B.I. Aggravated assault is an attack for the purpose of inflicting severe bodily injury. Numbers are for reporting jurisdictions only.
**Not available.

Aggravated Assaults With Blunt Objects and Other Dangerous Weapons in 2008

National Total = 241,311 Aggravated Assaults*

ALPHA ORDER

RANK	STATE	ASSAULTS	% of USA
31	Alabama	1,672	0.7%
37	Alaska	895	0.4%
14	Arizona	5,141	2.1%
27	Arkansas	2,168	0.9%
1	California	37,917	15.7%
23	Colorado	2,767	1.1%
33	Connecticut	1,597	0.7%
32	Delaware	1,624	0.7%
2	Florida	32,236	13.4%
11	Georgia	5,251	2.2%
41	Hawaii	602	0.2%
38	Idaho	773	0.3%
NA	Illinois**	NA	NA
22	Indiana	3,367	1.4%
35	Iowa	1,433	0.6%
26	Kansas	2,265	0.9%
24	Kentucky	2,371	1.0%
18	Louisiana	4,368	1.8%
47	Maine	210	0.1%
13	Maryland	5,168	2.1%
6	Massachusetts	9,863	4.1%
5	Michigan	10,603	4.4%
28	Minnesota	2,023	0.8%
40	Mississippi	620	0.3%
10	Missouri	5,384	2.2%
42	Montana	588	0.2%
34	Nebraska	1,516	0.6%
12	Nevada	5,214	2.2%
46	New Hampshire	277	0.1%
19	New Jersey	4,183	1.7%
25	New Mexico	2,278	0.9%
16	New York	4,921	2.0%
9	North Carolina	5,795	2.4%
48	North Dakota	145	0.1%
17	Ohio	4,436	1.8%
15	Oklahoma	4,940	2.0%
29	Oregon	1,971	0.8%
7	Pennsylvania	6,787	2.8%
43	Rhode Island	497	0.2%
8	South Carolina	5,819	2.4%
44	South Dakota	325	0.1%
4	Tennessee	11,196	4.6%
3	Texas	26,750	11.1%
36	Utah	1,307	0.5%
49	Vermont	143	0.1%
21	Virginia	3,451	1.4%
20	Washington	3,848	1.6%
39	West Virginia	736	0.3%
30	Wisconsin	1,916	0.8%
45	Wyoming	284	0.1%

RANK ORDER

RANK	STATE	ASSAULTS	% of USA
1	California	37,917	15.7%
2	Florida	32,236	13.4%
3	Texas	26,750	11.1%
4	Tennessee	11,196	4.6%
5	Michigan	10,603	4.4%
6	Massachusetts	9,863	4.1%
7	Pennsylvania	6,787	2.8%
8	South Carolina	5,819	2.4%
9	North Carolina	5,795	2.4%
10	Missouri	5,384	2.2%
11	Georgia	5,251	2.2%
12	Nevada	5,214	2.2%
13	Maryland	5,168	2.1%
14	Arizona	5,141	2.1%
15	Oklahoma	4,940	2.0%
16	New York	4,921	2.0%
17	Ohio	4,436	1.8%
18	Louisiana	4,368	1.8%
19	New Jersey	4,183	1.7%
20	Washington	3,848	1.6%
21	Virginia	3,451	1.4%
22	Indiana	3,367	1.4%
23	Colorado	2,767	1.1%
24	Kentucky	2,371	1.0%
25	New Mexico	2,278	0.9%
26	Kansas	2,265	0.9%
27	Arkansas	2,168	0.9%
28	Minnesota	2,023	0.8%
29	Oregon	1,971	0.8%
30	Wisconsin	1,916	0.8%
31	Alabama	1,672	0.7%
32	Delaware	1,624	0.7%
33	Connecticut	1,597	0.7%
34	Nebraska	1,516	0.6%
35	Iowa	1,433	0.6%
36	Utah	1,307	0.5%
37	Alaska	895	0.4%
38	Idaho	773	0.3%
39	West Virginia	736	0.3%
40	Mississippi	620	0.3%
41	Hawaii	602	0.2%
42	Montana	588	0.2%
43	Rhode Island	497	0.2%
44	South Dakota	325	0.1%
45	Wyoming	284	0.1%
46	New Hampshire	277	0.1%
47	Maine	210	0.1%
48	North Dakota	145	0.1%
49	Vermont	143	0.1%
NA	Illinois**	NA	NA
	District of Columbia	1,310	0.5%

Source: Reported data from the Federal Bureau of Investigation
   "Crime in the United States 2008" (Uniform Crime Reports, September 14, 2009, http://www.fbi.gov/ucr/ucr.htm)
*Of the 720,575 aggravated assaults in 2008 for which supplemental data were received by the F.B.I. There were an additional 114,310 aggravated assaults for which the type of weapon was not reported to the F.B.I. Aggravated assault is an attack for the purpose of inflicting severe bodily injury. Numbers are for reporting jurisdictions only.
**Not available.

Percent of Aggravated Assaults Involving Blunt Objects and Other Dangerous Weapons in 2008
National Percent = 33.5% of Aggravated Assaults*

ALPHA ORDER

RANK	STATE	PERCENT
47	Alabama	21.8
34	Alaska	27.1
26	Arizona	30.3
46	Arkansas	22.5
9	California	36.5
38	Colorado	26.3
13	Connecticut	34.8
4	Delaware	41.9
6	Florida	39.0
40	Georgia	26.0
20	Hawaii	32.6
21	Idaho	32.2
NA	Illinois**	NA
23	Indiana	31.6
45	Iowa	23.4
19	Kansas	33.3
5	Kentucky	40.1
39	Louisiana	26.2
40	Maine	26.0
14	Maryland	34.7
1	Massachusetts	52.6
11	Michigan	35.1
32	Minnesota	27.4
43	Mississippi	24.9
37	Missouri	27.0
26	Montana	30.3
3	Nebraska	45.2
2	Nevada	47.0
34	New Hampshire	27.1
25	New Jersey	30.8
29	New Mexico	29.7
30	New York	29.3
34	North Carolina	27.1
49	North Dakota	19.8
24	Ohio	31.4
7	Oklahoma	37.2
17	Oregon	34.2
42	Pennsylvania	25.0
15	Rhode Island	34.6
33	South Carolina	27.3
16	South Dakota	34.5
8	Tennessee	36.8
11	Texas	35.1
10	Utah	35.6
44	Vermont	23.5
18	Virginia	34.0
21	Washington	32.2
31	West Virginia	28.8
48	Wisconsin	21.3
28	Wyoming	29.9

RANK ORDER

RANK	STATE	PERCENT
1	Massachusetts	52.6
2	Nevada	47.0
3	Nebraska	45.2
4	Delaware	41.9
5	Kentucky	40.1
6	Florida	39.0
7	Oklahoma	37.2
8	Tennessee	36.8
9	California	36.5
10	Utah	35.6
11	Michigan	35.1
11	Texas	35.1
13	Connecticut	34.8
14	Maryland	34.7
15	Rhode Island	34.6
16	South Dakota	34.5
17	Oregon	34.2
18	Virginia	34.0
19	Kansas	33.3
20	Hawaii	32.6
21	Idaho	32.2
21	Washington	32.2
23	Indiana	31.6
24	Ohio	31.4
25	New Jersey	30.8
26	Arizona	30.3
26	Montana	30.3
28	Wyoming	29.9
29	New Mexico	29.7
30	New York	29.3
31	West Virginia	28.8
32	Minnesota	27.4
33	South Carolina	27.3
34	Alaska	27.1
34	New Hampshire	27.1
34	North Carolina	27.1
37	Missouri	27.0
38	Colorado	26.3
39	Louisiana	26.2
40	Georgia	26.0
40	Maine	26.0
42	Pennsylvania	25.0
43	Mississippi	24.9
44	Vermont	23.5
45	Iowa	23.4
46	Arkansas	22.5
47	Alabama	21.8
48	Wisconsin	21.3
49	North Dakota	19.8
NA	Illinois**	NA

District of Columbia 35.3

Source: CQ Press using reported data from the Federal Bureau of Investigation
"Crime in the United States 2008" (Uniform Crime Reports, September 14, 2009, http://www.fbi.gov/ucr/ucr.htm)
*Of the 720,575 aggravated assaults in 2008 for which supplemental data were received by the F.B.I. There were an additional 114,310 aggravated assaults for which the type of weapon was not reported to the F.B.I. Aggravated assault is an attack for the purpose of inflicting severe bodily injury. Numbers are for reporting jurisdictions only.
**Not available.

Aggravated Assaults Committed With Hands, Fists, or Feet in 2008

National Total = 189,094 Aggravated Assaults*

<table>
<tr><td colspan="4">ALPHA ORDER</td><td colspan="4">RANK ORDER</td></tr>
<tr><td>RANK</td><td>STATE</td><td>ASSAULTS</td><td>% of USA</td><td>RANK</td><td>STATE</td><td>ASSAULTS</td><td>% of USA</td></tr>
<tr><td>25</td><td>Alabama</td><td>2,622</td><td>1.4%</td><td>1</td><td>California</td><td>30,248</td><td>16.0%</td></tr>
<tr><td>34</td><td>Alaska</td><td>1,198</td><td>0.6%</td><td>2</td><td>Florida</td><td>19,151</td><td>10.1%</td></tr>
<tr><td>17</td><td>Arizona</td><td>4,037</td><td>2.1%</td><td>3</td><td>Texas</td><td>15,032</td><td>7.9%</td></tr>
<tr><td>19</td><td>Arkansas</td><td>3,552</td><td>1.9%</td><td>4</td><td>Pennsylvania</td><td>10,908</td><td>5.8%</td></tr>
<tr><td>1</td><td>California</td><td>30,248</td><td>16.0%</td><td>5</td><td>South Carolina</td><td>5,976</td><td>3.2%</td></tr>
<tr><td>22</td><td>Colorado</td><td>3,248</td><td>1.7%</td><td>6</td><td>Missouri</td><td>5,946</td><td>3.1%</td></tr>
<tr><td>31</td><td>Connecticut</td><td>1,433</td><td>0.8%</td><td>7</td><td>Michigan</td><td>5,856</td><td>3.1%</td></tr>
<tr><td>43</td><td>Delaware</td><td>421</td><td>0.2%</td><td>8</td><td>Georgia</td><td>5,829</td><td>3.1%</td></tr>
<tr><td>2</td><td>Florida</td><td>19,151</td><td>10.1%</td><td>9</td><td>Louisiana</td><td>5,347</td><td>2.8%</td></tr>
<tr><td>8</td><td>Georgia</td><td>5,829</td><td>3.1%</td><td>10</td><td>New York</td><td>5,044</td><td>2.7%</td></tr>
<tr><td>40</td><td>Hawaii</td><td>649</td><td>0.3%</td><td>11</td><td>North Carolina</td><td>4,734</td><td>2.5%</td></tr>
<tr><td>37</td><td>Idaho</td><td>809</td><td>0.4%</td><td>12</td><td>Maryland</td><td>4,257</td><td>2.3%</td></tr>
<tr><td>NA</td><td>Illinois**</td><td>NA</td><td>NA</td><td>13</td><td>New Jersey</td><td>4,253</td><td>2.2%</td></tr>
<tr><td>16</td><td>Indiana</td><td>4,067</td><td>2.2%</td><td>14</td><td>Wisconsin</td><td>4,167</td><td>2.2%</td></tr>
<tr><td>23</td><td>Iowa</td><td>3,079</td><td>1.6%</td><td>15</td><td>Washington</td><td>4,123</td><td>2.2%</td></tr>
<tr><td>33</td><td>Kansas</td><td>1,383</td><td>0.7%</td><td>16</td><td>Indiana</td><td>4,067</td><td>2.2%</td></tr>
<tr><td>31</td><td>Kentucky</td><td>1,433</td><td>0.8%</td><td>17</td><td>Arizona</td><td>4,037</td><td>2.1%</td></tr>
<tr><td>9</td><td>Louisiana</td><td>5,347</td><td>2.8%</td><td>18</td><td>Oklahoma</td><td>3,740</td><td>2.0%</td></tr>
<tr><td>45</td><td>Maine</td><td>333</td><td>0.2%</td><td>19</td><td>Arkansas</td><td>3,552</td><td>1.9%</td></tr>
<tr><td>12</td><td>Maryland</td><td>4,257</td><td>2.3%</td><td>20</td><td>Ohio</td><td>3,362</td><td>1.8%</td></tr>
<tr><td>24</td><td>Massachusetts</td><td>2,660</td><td>1.4%</td><td>21</td><td>Tennessee</td><td>3,291</td><td>1.7%</td></tr>
<tr><td>7</td><td>Michigan</td><td>5,856</td><td>3.1%</td><td>22</td><td>Colorado</td><td>3,248</td><td>1.7%</td></tr>
<tr><td>26</td><td>Minnesota</td><td>2,482</td><td>1.3%</td><td>23</td><td>Iowa</td><td>3,079</td><td>1.6%</td></tr>
<tr><td>41</td><td>Mississippi</td><td>512</td><td>0.3%</td><td>24</td><td>Massachusetts</td><td>2,660</td><td>1.4%</td></tr>
<tr><td>6</td><td>Missouri</td><td>5,946</td><td>3.1%</td><td>25</td><td>Alabama</td><td>2,622</td><td>1.4%</td></tr>
<tr><td>36</td><td>Montana</td><td>815</td><td>0.4%</td><td>26</td><td>Minnesota</td><td>2,482</td><td>1.3%</td></tr>
<tr><td>38</td><td>Nebraska</td><td>740</td><td>0.4%</td><td>27</td><td>New Mexico</td><td>2,323</td><td>1.2%</td></tr>
<tr><td>30</td><td>Nevada</td><td>1,805</td><td>1.0%</td><td>28</td><td>Virginia</td><td>2,231</td><td>1.2%</td></tr>
<tr><td>47</td><td>New Hampshire</td><td>236</td><td>0.1%</td><td>29</td><td>Oregon</td><td>2,085</td><td>1.1%</td></tr>
<tr><td>13</td><td>New Jersey</td><td>4,253</td><td>2.2%</td><td>30</td><td>Nevada</td><td>1,805</td><td>1.0%</td></tr>
<tr><td>27</td><td>New Mexico</td><td>2,323</td><td>1.2%</td><td>31</td><td>Connecticut</td><td>1,433</td><td>0.8%</td></tr>
<tr><td>10</td><td>New York</td><td>5,044</td><td>2.7%</td><td>31</td><td>Kentucky</td><td>1,433</td><td>0.8%</td></tr>
<tr><td>11</td><td>North Carolina</td><td>4,734</td><td>2.5%</td><td>33</td><td>Kansas</td><td>1,383</td><td>0.7%</td></tr>
<tr><td>42</td><td>North Dakota</td><td>482</td><td>0.3%</td><td>34</td><td>Alaska</td><td>1,198</td><td>0.6%</td></tr>
<tr><td>20</td><td>Ohio</td><td>3,362</td><td>1.8%</td><td>35</td><td>West Virginia</td><td>862</td><td>0.5%</td></tr>
<tr><td>18</td><td>Oklahoma</td><td>3,740</td><td>2.0%</td><td>36</td><td>Montana</td><td>815</td><td>0.4%</td></tr>
<tr><td>29</td><td>Oregon</td><td>2,085</td><td>1.1%</td><td>37</td><td>Idaho</td><td>809</td><td>0.4%</td></tr>
<tr><td>4</td><td>Pennsylvania</td><td>10,908</td><td>5.8%</td><td>38</td><td>Nebraska</td><td>740</td><td>0.4%</td></tr>
<tr><td>48</td><td>Rhode Island</td><td>183</td><td>0.1%</td><td>39</td><td>Utah</td><td>729</td><td>0.4%</td></tr>
<tr><td>5</td><td>South Carolina</td><td>5,976</td><td>3.2%</td><td>40</td><td>Hawaii</td><td>649</td><td>0.3%</td></tr>
<tr><td>49</td><td>South Dakota</td><td>160</td><td>0.1%</td><td>41</td><td>Mississippi</td><td>512</td><td>0.3%</td></tr>
<tr><td>21</td><td>Tennessee</td><td>3,291</td><td>1.7%</td><td>42</td><td>North Dakota</td><td>482</td><td>0.3%</td></tr>
<tr><td>3</td><td>Texas</td><td>15,032</td><td>7.9%</td><td>43</td><td>Delaware</td><td>421</td><td>0.2%</td></tr>
<tr><td>39</td><td>Utah</td><td>729</td><td>0.4%</td><td>44</td><td>Wyoming</td><td>396</td><td>0.2%</td></tr>
<tr><td>46</td><td>Vermont</td><td>272</td><td>0.1%</td><td>45</td><td>Maine</td><td>333</td><td>0.2%</td></tr>
<tr><td>28</td><td>Virginia</td><td>2,231</td><td>1.2%</td><td>46</td><td>Vermont</td><td>272</td><td>0.1%</td></tr>
<tr><td>15</td><td>Washington</td><td>4,123</td><td>2.2%</td><td>47</td><td>New Hampshire</td><td>236</td><td>0.1%</td></tr>
<tr><td>35</td><td>West Virginia</td><td>862</td><td>0.5%</td><td>48</td><td>Rhode Island</td><td>183</td><td>0.1%</td></tr>
<tr><td>14</td><td>Wisconsin</td><td>4,167</td><td>2.2%</td><td>49</td><td>South Dakota</td><td>160</td><td>0.1%</td></tr>
<tr><td>44</td><td>Wyoming</td><td>396</td><td>0.2%</td><td>NA</td><td>Illinois**</td><td>NA</td><td>NA</td></tr>
<tr><td></td><td></td><td></td><td></td><td></td><td>District of Columbia</td><td>464</td><td>0.2%</td></tr>
</table>

Source: Reported data from the Federal Bureau of Investigation
   "Crime in the United States 2008" (Uniform Crime Reports, September 14, 2009, http://www.fbi.gov/ucr/ucr.htm)
*Of the 720,575 aggravated assaults in 2008 for which supplemental data were received by the F.B.I. There were an additional 114,310 aggravated assaults for which the type of weapon was not reported to the F.B.I. Aggravated assault is an attack for the purpose of inflicting severe bodily injury. Numbers are for reporting jurisdictions only.
**Not available.

Percent of Aggravated Assaults Committed With Hands, Fists, or Feet in 2008

National Percent = 26.2% of Aggravated Assaults*

<table>
<tr><td colspan="3">ALPHA ORDER</td><td colspan="3">RANK ORDER</td></tr>
<tr><th>RANK</th><th>STATE</th><th>PERCENT</th><th>RANK</th><th>STATE</th><th>PERCENT</th></tr>
<tr><td>15</td><td>Alabama</td><td>34.2</td><td>1</td><td>North Dakota</td><td>65.7</td></tr>
<tr><td>11</td><td>Alaska</td><td>36.2</td><td>2</td><td>Iowa</td><td>50.3</td></tr>
<tr><td>32</td><td>Arizona</td><td>23.8</td><td>3</td><td>Wisconsin</td><td>46.2</td></tr>
<tr><td>10</td><td>Arkansas</td><td>36.8</td><td>4</td><td>Vermont</td><td>44.7</td></tr>
<tr><td>26</td><td>California</td><td>29.1</td><td>5</td><td>Montana</td><td>42.0</td></tr>
<tr><td>22</td><td>Colorado</td><td>30.8</td><td>6</td><td>Wyoming</td><td>41.7</td></tr>
<tr><td>21</td><td>Connecticut</td><td>31.2</td><td>7</td><td>Maine</td><td>41.2</td></tr>
<tr><td>48</td><td>Delaware</td><td>10.9</td><td>8</td><td>Pennsylvania</td><td>40.2</td></tr>
<tr><td>34</td><td>Florida</td><td>23.2</td><td>9</td><td>Indiana</td><td>38.2</td></tr>
<tr><td>27</td><td>Georgia</td><td>28.8</td><td>10</td><td>Arkansas</td><td>36.8</td></tr>
<tr><td>13</td><td>Hawaii</td><td>35.2</td><td>11</td><td>Alaska</td><td>36.2</td></tr>
<tr><td>16</td><td>Idaho</td><td>33.7</td><td>11</td><td>Oregon</td><td>36.2</td></tr>
<tr><td>NA</td><td>Illinois**</td><td>NA</td><td>13</td><td>Hawaii</td><td>35.2</td></tr>
<tr><td>9</td><td>Indiana</td><td>38.2</td><td>14</td><td>Washington</td><td>34.5</td></tr>
<tr><td>2</td><td>Iowa</td><td>50.3</td><td>15</td><td>Alabama</td><td>34.2</td></tr>
<tr><td>40</td><td>Kansas</td><td>20.3</td><td>16</td><td>Idaho</td><td>33.7</td></tr>
<tr><td>31</td><td>Kentucky</td><td>24.2</td><td>16</td><td>Minnesota</td><td>33.7</td></tr>
<tr><td>19</td><td>Louisiana</td><td>32.1</td><td>16</td><td>West Virginia</td><td>33.7</td></tr>
<tr><td>7</td><td>Maine</td><td>41.2</td><td>19</td><td>Louisiana</td><td>32.1</td></tr>
<tr><td>28</td><td>Maryland</td><td>28.6</td><td>20</td><td>New Jersey</td><td>31.4</td></tr>
<tr><td>46</td><td>Massachusetts</td><td>14.2</td><td>21</td><td>Connecticut</td><td>31.2</td></tr>
<tr><td>43</td><td>Michigan</td><td>19.4</td><td>22</td><td>Colorado</td><td>30.8</td></tr>
<tr><td>16</td><td>Minnesota</td><td>33.7</td><td>23</td><td>New Mexico</td><td>30.3</td></tr>
<tr><td>39</td><td>Mississippi</td><td>20.6</td><td>24</td><td>New York</td><td>30.0</td></tr>
<tr><td>25</td><td>Missouri</td><td>29.8</td><td>25</td><td>Missouri</td><td>29.8</td></tr>
<tr><td>5</td><td>Montana</td><td>42.0</td><td>26</td><td>California</td><td>29.1</td></tr>
<tr><td>36</td><td>Nebraska</td><td>22.1</td><td>27</td><td>Georgia</td><td>28.8</td></tr>
<tr><td>45</td><td>Nevada</td><td>16.3</td><td>28</td><td>Maryland</td><td>28.6</td></tr>
<tr><td>35</td><td>New Hampshire</td><td>23.1</td><td>29</td><td>Oklahoma</td><td>28.1</td></tr>
<tr><td>20</td><td>New Jersey</td><td>31.4</td><td>29</td><td>South Carolina</td><td>28.1</td></tr>
<tr><td>23</td><td>New Mexico</td><td>30.3</td><td>31</td><td>Kentucky</td><td>24.2</td></tr>
<tr><td>24</td><td>New York</td><td>30.0</td><td>32</td><td>Arizona</td><td>23.8</td></tr>
<tr><td>36</td><td>North Carolina</td><td>22.1</td><td>32</td><td>Ohio</td><td>23.8</td></tr>
<tr><td>1</td><td>North Dakota</td><td>65.7</td><td>34</td><td>Florida</td><td>23.2</td></tr>
<tr><td>32</td><td>Ohio</td><td>23.8</td><td>35</td><td>New Hampshire</td><td>23.1</td></tr>
<tr><td>29</td><td>Oklahoma</td><td>28.1</td><td>36</td><td>Nebraska</td><td>22.1</td></tr>
<tr><td>11</td><td>Oregon</td><td>36.2</td><td>36</td><td>North Carolina</td><td>22.1</td></tr>
<tr><td>8</td><td>Pennsylvania</td><td>40.2</td><td>38</td><td>Virginia</td><td>22.0</td></tr>
<tr><td>47</td><td>Rhode Island</td><td>12.7</td><td>39</td><td>Mississippi</td><td>20.6</td></tr>
<tr><td>29</td><td>South Carolina</td><td>28.1</td><td>40</td><td>Kansas</td><td>20.3</td></tr>
<tr><td>44</td><td>South Dakota</td><td>17.0</td><td>41</td><td>Utah</td><td>19.9</td></tr>
<tr><td>49</td><td>Tennessee</td><td>10.8</td><td>42</td><td>Texas</td><td>19.7</td></tr>
<tr><td>42</td><td>Texas</td><td>19.7</td><td>43</td><td>Michigan</td><td>19.4</td></tr>
<tr><td>41</td><td>Utah</td><td>19.9</td><td>44</td><td>South Dakota</td><td>17.0</td></tr>
<tr><td>4</td><td>Vermont</td><td>44.7</td><td>45</td><td>Nevada</td><td>16.3</td></tr>
<tr><td>38</td><td>Virginia</td><td>22.0</td><td>46</td><td>Massachusetts</td><td>14.2</td></tr>
<tr><td>14</td><td>Washington</td><td>34.5</td><td>47</td><td>Rhode Island</td><td>12.7</td></tr>
<tr><td>16</td><td>West Virginia</td><td>33.7</td><td>48</td><td>Delaware</td><td>10.9</td></tr>
<tr><td>3</td><td>Wisconsin</td><td>46.2</td><td>49</td><td>Tennessee</td><td>10.8</td></tr>
<tr><td>6</td><td>Wyoming</td><td>41.7</td><td>NA</td><td>Illinois**</td><td>NA</td></tr>
<tr><td></td><td></td><td></td><td></td><td>District of Columbia</td><td>12.5</td></tr>
</table>

Source: CQ Press using reported data from the Federal Bureau of Investigation

"Crime in the United States 2008" (Uniform Crime Reports, September 14, 2009, http://www.fbi.gov/ucr/ucr.htm)

*Of the 720,575 aggravated assaults in 2008 for which supplemental data were received by the F.B.I. There were an additional 114,310 aggravated assaults for which the type of weapon was not reported to the F.B.I. Aggravated assault is an attack for the purpose of inflicting severe bodily injury. Numbers are for reporting jurisdictions only.

**Not available.

Property Crimes in 2008

National Total = 9,767,915 Property Crimes*

ALPHA ORDER

RANK	STATE	CRIMES	% of USA
19	Alabama	190,343	1.9%
46	Alaska	20,124	0.2%
11	Arizona	278,920	2.9%
29	Arkansas	109,508	1.1%
1	California	1,080,747	11.1%
25	Colorado	140,725	1.4%
34	Connecticut	86,087	0.9%
42	Delaware	31,303	0.3%
3	Florida	758,934	7.8%
5	Georgia	388,935	4.0%
39	Hawaii	46,004	0.5%
41	Idaho	32,019	0.3%
7	Illinois	378,355	3.9%
15	Indiana	212,715	2.2%
36	Iowa	72,689	0.7%
30	Kansas	94,635	1.0%
28	Kentucky	110,314	1.1%
21	Louisiana	168,630	1.7%
40	Maine	32,285	0.3%
17	Maryland	198,165	2.0%
22	Massachusetts	155,959	1.6%
10	Michigan	293,585	3.0%
24	Minnesota	148,810	1.5%
33	Mississippi	86,408	0.9%
14	Missouri	216,585	2.2%
45	Montana	25,182	0.3%
37	Nebraska	51,338	0.5%
32	Nevada	89,640	0.9%
44	New Hampshire	27,526	0.3%
16	New Jersey	199,126	2.0%
35	New Mexico	77,572	0.8%
6	New York	388,533	4.0%
8	North Carolina	372,961	3.8%
50	North Dakota	12,152	0.1%
4	Ohio	391,862	4.0%
26	Oklahoma	125,384	1.3%
27	Oregon	124,397	1.3%
9	Pennsylvania	300,032	3.1%
43	Rhode Island	29,849	0.3%
20	South Carolina	189,683	1.9%
49	South Dakota	13,234	0.1%
12	Tennessee	251,245	2.6%
2	Texas	969,570	9.9%
31	Utah	91,873	0.9%
47	Vermont	15,771	0.2%
18	Virginia	195,634	2.0%
13	Washington	246,148	2.5%
38	West Virginia	46,607	0.5%
23	Wisconsin	155,127	1.6%
48	Wyoming	14,474	0.1%

RANK ORDER

RANK	STATE	CRIMES	% of USA
1	California	1,080,747	11.1%
2	Texas	969,570	9.9%
3	Florida	758,934	7.8%
4	Ohio	391,862	4.0%
5	Georgia	388,935	4.0%
6	New York	388,533	4.0%
7	Illinois	378,355	3.9%
8	North Carolina	372,961	3.8%
9	Pennsylvania	300,032	3.1%
10	Michigan	293,585	3.0%
11	Arizona	278,920	2.9%
12	Tennessee	251,245	2.6%
13	Washington	246,148	2.5%
14	Missouri	216,585	2.2%
15	Indiana	212,715	2.2%
16	New Jersey	199,126	2.0%
17	Maryland	198,165	2.0%
18	Virginia	195,634	2.0%
19	Alabama	190,343	1.9%
20	South Carolina	189,683	1.9%
21	Louisiana	168,630	1.7%
22	Massachusetts	155,959	1.6%
23	Wisconsin	155,127	1.6%
24	Minnesota	148,810	1.5%
25	Colorado	140,725	1.4%
26	Oklahoma	125,384	1.3%
27	Oregon	124,397	1.3%
28	Kentucky	110,314	1.1%
29	Arkansas	109,508	1.1%
30	Kansas	94,635	1.0%
31	Utah	91,873	0.9%
32	Nevada	89,640	0.9%
33	Mississippi	86,408	0.9%
34	Connecticut	86,087	0.9%
35	New Mexico	77,572	0.8%
36	Iowa	72,689	0.7%
37	Nebraska	51,338	0.5%
38	West Virginia	46,607	0.5%
39	Hawaii	46,004	0.5%
40	Maine	32,285	0.3%
41	Idaho	32,019	0.3%
42	Delaware	31,303	0.3%
43	Rhode Island	29,849	0.3%
44	New Hampshire	27,526	0.3%
45	Montana	25,182	0.3%
46	Alaska	20,124	0.2%
47	Vermont	15,771	0.2%
48	Wyoming	14,474	0.1%
49	South Dakota	13,234	0.1%
50	North Dakota	12,152	0.1%
	District of Columbia	30,211	0.3%

Source: Reported data from the Federal Bureau of Investigation
"Crime in the United States 2008" (Uniform Crime Reports, September 14, 2009, http://www.fbi.gov/ucr/ucr.htm)
*Property crimes are offenses of burglary, larceny-theft, and motor vehicle theft.

Average Time Between Property Crimes in 2008

National Rate = A Property Crime Occurs Every 3.2 Seconds*

ALPHA ORDER

RANK	STATE	MINUTES.SECONDS
32	Alabama	2.46
5	Alaska	26.11
40	Arizona	1.53
22	Arkansas	4.49
50	California	0.29
26	Colorado	3.45
17	Connecticut	6.07
9	Delaware	16.50
48	Florida	0.41
45	Georgia	1.22
12	Hawaii	11.28
10	Idaho	16.28
44	Illinois	1.23
36	Indiana	2.29
15	Iowa	7.15
21	Kansas	5.34
23	Kentucky	4.47
30	Louisiana	3.08
11	Maine	16.19
34	Maryland	2.40
29	Massachusetts	3.23
41	Michigan	1.48
27	Minnesota	3.32
18	Mississippi	6.06
37	Missouri	2.26
6	Montana	20.56
14	Nebraska	10.16
19	Nevada	5.53
7	New Hampshire	19.09
35	New Jersey	2.39
16	New Mexico	6.47
45	New York	1.22
43	North Carolina	1.25
1	North Dakota	43.22
47	Ohio	1.21
25	Oklahoma	4.12
24	Oregon	4.14
42	Pennsylvania	1.46
8	Rhode Island	17.40
31	South Carolina	2.47
2	South Dakota	39.49
39	Tennessee	2.06
49	Texas	0.32
20	Utah	5.44
4	Vermont	33.25
33	Virginia	2.41
38	Washington	2.08
13	West Virginia	11.19
28	Wisconsin	3.24
3	Wyoming	36.25

RANK ORDER

RANK	STATE	MINUTES.SECONDS
1	North Dakota	43.22
2	South Dakota	39.49
3	Wyoming	36.25
4	Vermont	33.25
5	Alaska	26.11
6	Montana	20.56
7	New Hampshire	19.09
8	Rhode Island	17.40
9	Delaware	16.50
10	Idaho	16.28
11	Maine	16.19
12	Hawaii	11.28
13	West Virginia	11.19
14	Nebraska	10.16
15	Iowa	7.15
16	New Mexico	6.47
17	Connecticut	6.07
18	Mississippi	6.06
19	Nevada	5.53
20	Utah	5.44
21	Kansas	5.34
22	Arkansas	4.49
23	Kentucky	4.47
24	Oregon	4.14
25	Oklahoma	4.12
26	Colorado	3.45
27	Minnesota	3.32
28	Wisconsin	3.24
29	Massachusetts	3.23
30	Louisiana	3.08
31	South Carolina	2.47
32	Alabama	2.46
33	Virginia	2.41
34	Maryland	2.40
35	New Jersey	2.39
36	Indiana	2.29
37	Missouri	2.26
38	Washington	2.08
39	Tennessee	2.06
40	Arizona	1.53
41	Michigan	1.48
42	Pennsylvania	1.46
43	North Carolina	1.25
44	Illinois	1.23
45	Georgia	1.22
45	New York	1.22
47	Ohio	1.21
48	Florida	0.41
49	Texas	0.32
50	California	0.29

District of Columbia 17.27

Source: CQ Press using reported data from the Federal Bureau of Investigation
"Crime in the United States 2008" (Uniform Crime Reports, September 14, 2009, http://www.fbi.gov/ucr/ucr.htm)
*Property crimes are offenses of burglary, larceny-theft, and motor vehicle theft.

Property Crimes per Square Mile in 2008

National Rate = 2.6 Property Crimes per Square Mile*

ALPHA ORDER

RANK	STATE	RATE
20	Alabama	3.6
50	Alaska	0.0
28	Arizona	2.4
30	Arkansas	2.1
11	California	6.6
36	Colorado	1.4
4	Connecticut	15.5
6	Delaware	12.6
7	Florida	11.5
12	Georgia	6.5
19	Hawaii	4.2
45	Idaho	0.4
12	Illinois	6.5
17	Indiana	5.8
37	Iowa	1.3
39	Kansas	1.2
27	Kentucky	2.7
23	Louisiana	3.3
41	Maine	0.9
3	Maryland	16.0
5	Massachusetts	14.8
25	Michigan	3.0
34	Minnesota	1.7
32	Mississippi	1.8
24	Missouri	3.1
46	Montana	0.2
43	Nebraska	0.7
42	Nevada	0.8
26	New Hampshire	2.9
1	New Jersey	22.8
44	New Mexico	0.6
9	New York	7.1
10	North Carolina	6.9
46	North Dakota	0.2
8	Ohio	8.7
32	Oklahoma	1.8
37	Oregon	1.3
12	Pennsylvania	6.5
2	Rhode Island	19.3
16	South Carolina	5.9
46	South Dakota	0.2
15	Tennessee	6.0
20	Texas	3.6
40	Utah	1.1
35	Vermont	1.6
18	Virginia	4.6
22	Washington	3.5
31	West Virginia	1.9
28	Wisconsin	2.4
49	Wyoming	0.1

RANK ORDER

RANK	STATE	RATE
1	New Jersey	22.8
2	Rhode Island	19.3
3	Maryland	16.0
4	Connecticut	15.5
5	Massachusetts	14.8
6	Delaware	12.6
7	Florida	11.5
8	Ohio	8.7
9	New York	7.1
10	North Carolina	6.9
11	California	6.6
12	Georgia	6.5
12	Illinois	6.5
12	Pennsylvania	6.5
15	Tennessee	6.0
16	South Carolina	5.9
17	Indiana	5.8
18	Virginia	4.6
19	Hawaii	4.2
20	Alabama	3.6
20	Texas	3.6
22	Washington	3.5
23	Louisiana	3.3
24	Missouri	3.1
25	Michigan	3.0
26	New Hampshire	2.9
27	Kentucky	2.7
28	Arizona	2.4
28	Wisconsin	2.4
30	Arkansas	2.1
31	West Virginia	1.9
32	Mississippi	1.8
32	Oklahoma	1.8
34	Minnesota	1.7
35	Vermont	1.6
36	Colorado	1.4
37	Iowa	1.3
37	Oregon	1.3
39	Kansas	1.2
40	Utah	1.1
41	Maine	0.9
42	Nevada	0.8
43	Nebraska	0.7
44	New Mexico	0.6
45	Idaho	0.4
46	Montana	0.2
46	North Dakota	0.2
46	South Dakota	0.2
49	Wyoming	0.1
50	Alaska	0.0

District of Columbia   444.3

Source: CQ Press using reported data from the Federal Bureau of Investigation
  "Crime in the United States 2008" (Uniform Crime Reports, September 14, 2009, http://www.fbi.gov/ucr/ucr.htm)
*Property crimes are offenses of burglary, larceny-theft, and motor vehicle theft. "Square miles" includes total land and water area.

Percent Change in Number of Property Crimes: 2007 to 2008

National Percent Change = 0.8% Decrease*

ALPHA ORDER			RANK ORDER		
RANK	STATE	PERCENT CHANGE	RANK	STATE	PERCENT CHANGE
7	Alabama	3.6	1	New Hampshire	10.6
49	Alaska	(12.9)	2	Vermont	9.3
25	Arizona	(0.3)	3	Rhode Island	7.6
32	Arkansas	(2.3)	4	Delaware	7.4
34	California	(2.5)	5	New Mexico	5.7
37	Colorado	(3.7)	6	Georgia	4.5
12	Connecticut	2.4	7	Alabama	3.6
4	Delaware	7.4	7	New Jersey	3.6
16	Florida	1.7	9	Kentucky	3.3
6	Georgia	4.5	10	Virginia	2.9
50	Hawaii	(15.2)	11	Maryland	2.8
38	Idaho	(4.9)	12	Connecticut	2.4
23	Illinois	0.3	13	Pennsylvania	2.2
28	Indiana	(1.3)	14	West Virginia	1.9
44	Iowa	(7.0)	15	New York	1.8
45	Kansas	(7.3)	16	Florida	1.7
9	Kentucky	3.3	17	Massachusetts	1.1
36	Louisiana	(3.6)	18	Maine	0.9
18	Maine	0.9	19	North Carolina	0.7
11	Maryland	2.8	19	South Carolina	0.7
17	Massachusetts	1.1	21	South Dakota	0.6
38	Michigan	(4.9)	22	North Dakota	0.5
42	Minnesota	(5.7)	23	Illinois	0.3
46	Mississippi	(7.5)	24	Tennessee	(0.2)
29	Missouri	(1.4)	25	Arizona	(0.3)
38	Montana	(4.9)	26	Utah	(0.8)
48	Nebraska	(8.5)	27	Ohio	(1.1)
46	Nevada	(7.5)	28	Indiana	(1.3)
1	New Hampshire	10.6	29	Missouri	(1.4)
7	New Jersey	3.6	30	Texas	(1.6)
5	New Mexico	5.7	31	Oklahoma	(1.7)
15	New York	1.8	32	Arkansas	(2.3)
19	North Carolina	0.7	33	Wisconsin	(2.4)
22	North Dakota	0.5	34	California	(2.5)
27	Ohio	(1.1)	35	Wyoming	(3.4)
31	Oklahoma	(1.7)	36	Louisiana	(3.6)
43	Oregon	(5.9)	37	Colorado	(3.7)
13	Pennsylvania	2.2	38	Idaho	(4.9)
3	Rhode Island	7.6	38	Michigan	(4.9)
19	South Carolina	0.7	38	Montana	(4.9)
21	South Dakota	0.6	41	Washington	(5.6)
24	Tennessee	(0.2)	42	Minnesota	(5.7)
30	Texas	(1.6)	43	Oregon	(5.9)
26	Utah	(0.8)	44	Iowa	(7.0)
2	Vermont	9.3	45	Kansas	(7.3)
10	Virginia	2.9	46	Mississippi	(7.5)
41	Washington	(5.6)	46	Nevada	(7.5)
14	West Virginia	1.9	48	Nebraska	(8.5)
33	Wisconsin	(2.4)	49	Alaska	(12.9)
35	Wyoming	(3.4)	50	Hawaii	(15.2)

District of Columbia   4.5

Source: Reported data from the Federal Bureau of Investigation
"Crime in the United States 2008" (Uniform Crime Reports, September 14, 2009, http://www.fbi.gov/ucr/ucr.htm)
*Property crimes are offenses of burglary, larceny-theft, and motor vehicle theft.

Property Crime Rate in 2008

National Rate = 3,212.5 Property Crimes per 100,000 Population*

ALPHA ORDER

RANK	STATE	RATE
4	Alabama	4,082.9
28	Alaska	2,932.3
1	Arizona	4,291.0
10	Arkansas	3,835.1
25	California	2,940.3
31	Colorado	2,849.0
40	Connecticut	2,458.7
14	Delaware	3,585.3
3	Florida	4,140.8
7	Georgia	4,015.5
15	Hawaii	3,571.2
46	Idaho	2,101.2
27	Illinois	2,932.6
22	Indiana	3,335.8
42	Iowa	2,420.9
20	Kansas	3,377.2
36	Kentucky	2,583.9
11	Louisiana	3,823.1
41	Maine	2,452.4
16	Maryland	3,517.6
44	Massachusetts	2,400.1
26	Michigan	2,934.8
30	Minnesota	2,850.6
24	Mississippi	2,940.4
13	Missouri	3,663.7
35	Montana	2,603.0
29	Nebraska	2,878.6
17	Nevada	3,447.5
47	New Hampshire	2,091.9
45	New Jersey	2,293.4
9	New Mexico	3,909.2
48	New York	1,993.5
5	North Carolina	4,044.1
49	North Dakota	1,894.4
19	Ohio	3,411.7
18	Oklahoma	3,442.4
23	Oregon	3,282.2
43	Pennsylvania	2,410.2
32	Rhode Island	2,840.6
2	South Carolina	4,234.2
50	South Dakota	1,645.6
6	Tennessee	4,042.6
8	Texas	3,985.6
21	Utah	3,357.4
38	Vermont	2,538.5
39	Virginia	2,518.1
12	Washington	3,758.4
37	West Virginia	2,568.6
33	Wisconsin	2,756.4
34	Wyoming	2,717.3

RANK ORDER

RANK	STATE	RATE
1	Arizona	4,291.0
2	South Carolina	4,234.2
3	Florida	4,140.8
4	Alabama	4,082.9
5	North Carolina	4,044.1
6	Tennessee	4,042.6
7	Georgia	4,015.5
8	Texas	3,985.6
9	New Mexico	3,909.2
10	Arkansas	3,835.1
11	Louisiana	3,823.1
12	Washington	3,758.4
13	Missouri	3,663.7
14	Delaware	3,585.3
15	Hawaii	3,571.2
16	Maryland	3,517.6
17	Nevada	3,447.5
18	Oklahoma	3,442.4
19	Ohio	3,411.7
20	Kansas	3,377.2
21	Utah	3,357.4
22	Indiana	3,335.8
23	Oregon	3,282.2
24	Mississippi	2,940.4
25	California	2,940.3
26	Michigan	2,934.8
27	Illinois	2,932.6
28	Alaska	2,932.3
29	Nebraska	2,878.6
30	Minnesota	2,850.6
31	Colorado	2,849.0
32	Rhode Island	2,840.6
33	Wisconsin	2,756.4
34	Wyoming	2,717.3
35	Montana	2,603.0
36	Kentucky	2,583.9
37	West Virginia	2,568.6
38	Vermont	2,538.5
39	Virginia	2,518.1
40	Connecticut	2,458.7
41	Maine	2,452.4
42	Iowa	2,420.9
43	Pennsylvania	2,410.2
44	Massachusetts	2,400.1
45	New Jersey	2,293.4
46	Idaho	2,101.2
47	New Hampshire	2,091.9
48	New York	1,993.5
49	North Dakota	1,894.4
50	South Dakota	1,645.6

District of Columbia — 5,104.6

Source: Reported data from the Federal Bureau of Investigation
   "Crime in the United States 2008" (Uniform Crime Reports, September 14, 2009, http://www.fbi.gov/ucr/ucr.htm)
*Property crimes are offenses of burglary, larceny-theft, and motor vehicle theft.

Percent Change in Property Crime Rate: 2007 to 2008

National Percent Change = 1.6% Decrease*

<u>ALPHA ORDER</u>

RANK	STATE	PERCENT CHANGE
8	Alabama	2.8
49	Alaska	(13.2)
29	Arizona	(2.8)
31	Arkansas	(3.0)
32	California	(3.1)
36	Colorado	(5.2)
10	Connecticut	2.5
4	Delaware	6.4
15	Florida	1.3
7	Georgia	2.9
50	Hawaii	(15.5)
41	Idaho	(6.5)
20	Illinois	(0.1)
26	Indiana	(1.8)
44	Iowa	(7.4)
46	Kansas	(8.2)
9	Kentucky	2.6
40	Louisiana	(6.2)
16	Maine	1.0
10	Maryland	2.5
18	Massachusetts	0.4
35	Michigan	(4.3)
39	Minnesota	(6.1)
45	Mississippi	(8.1)
27	Missouri	(2.0)
38	Montana	(5.9)
48	Nebraska	(8.9)
47	Nevada	(8.7)
1	New Hampshire	10.6
6	New Jersey	3.6
5	New Mexico	4.9
17	New York	0.8
23	North Carolina	(1.1)
19	North Dakota	0.3
25	Ohio	(1.3)
28	Oklahoma	(2.4)
43	Oregon	(6.9)
12	Pennsylvania	2.1
3	Rhode Island	8.3
22	South Carolina	(0.9)
21	South Dakota	(0.4)
23	Tennessee	(1.1)
33	Texas	(3.3)
34	Utah	(4.1)
2	Vermont	9.3
12	Virginia	2.1
42	Washington	(6.8)
14	West Virginia	1.7
30	Wisconsin	(2.9)
36	Wyoming	(5.2)

<u>RANK ORDER</u>

RANK	STATE	PERCENT CHANGE
1	New Hampshire	10.6
2	Vermont	9.3
3	Rhode Island	8.3
4	Delaware	6.4
5	New Mexico	4.9
6	New Jersey	3.6
7	Georgia	2.9
8	Alabama	2.8
9	Kentucky	2.6
10	Connecticut	2.5
10	Maryland	2.5
12	Pennsylvania	2.1
12	Virginia	2.1
14	West Virginia	1.7
15	Florida	1.3
16	Maine	1.0
17	New York	0.8
18	Massachusetts	0.4
19	North Dakota	0.3
20	Illinois	(0.1)
21	South Dakota	(0.4)
22	South Carolina	(0.9)
23	North Carolina	(1.1)
23	Tennessee	(1.1)
25	Ohio	(1.3)
26	Indiana	(1.8)
27	Missouri	(2.0)
28	Oklahoma	(2.4)
29	Arizona	(2.8)
30	Wisconsin	(2.9)
31	Arkansas	(3.0)
32	California	(3.1)
33	Texas	(3.3)
34	Utah	(4.1)
35	Michigan	(4.3)
36	Colorado	(5.2)
36	Wyoming	(5.2)
38	Montana	(5.9)
39	Minnesota	(6.1)
40	Louisiana	(6.2)
41	Idaho	(6.5)
42	Washington	(6.8)
43	Oregon	(6.9)
44	Iowa	(7.4)
45	Mississippi	(8.1)
46	Kansas	(8.2)
47	Nevada	(8.7)
48	Nebraska	(8.9)
49	Alaska	(13.2)
50	Hawaii	(15.5)

District of Columbia   3.9

Source: Reported data from the Federal Bureau of Investigation
"Crime in the United States 2008" (Uniform Crime Reports, September 14, 2009, http://www.fbi.gov/ucr/ucr.htm)
*Property crimes are offenses of burglary, larceny-theft, and motor vehicle theft.

Burglaries in 2008

National Total = 2,222,196 Burglaries*

ALPHA ORDER

ALPHA ORDER | RANK ORDER

RANK	STATE	BURGLARIES	% of USA	RANK	STATE	BURGLARIES	% of USA
14	Alabama	50,408	2.3%	1	California	237,835	10.7%
47	Alaska	3,240	0.1%	2	Texas	230,123	10.4%
12	Arizona	56,481	2.5%	3	Florida	188,467	8.5%
23	Arkansas	33,694	1.5%	4	North Carolina	111,602	5.0%
1	California	237,835	10.7%	5	Ohio	102,544	4.6%
26	Colorado	28,256	1.3%	6	Georgia	100,629	4.5%
35	Connecticut	15,011	0.7%	7	Illinois	78,968	3.6%
40	Delaware	6,760	0.3%	8	Michigan	74,176	3.3%
3	Florida	188,467	8.5%	9	New York	65,735	3.0%
6	Georgia	100,629	4.5%	10	Tennessee	65,006	2.9%
38	Hawaii	9,379	0.4%	11	Pennsylvania	58,620	2.6%
41	Idaho	6,701	0.3%	12	Arizona	56,481	2.5%
7	Illinois	78,968	3.6%	13	Washington	52,478	2.4%
15	Indiana	48,645	2.2%	14	Alabama	50,408	2.3%
34	Iowa	16,450	0.7%	15	Indiana	48,645	2.2%
33	Kansas	19,612	0.9%	16	South Carolina	45,967	2.1%
25	Kentucky	28,839	1.3%	17	Missouri	45,788	2.1%
18	Louisiana	43,320	1.9%	18	Louisiana	43,320	1.9%
42	Maine	6,522	0.3%	19	New Jersey	40,401	1.8%
20	Maryland	38,849	1.7%	20	Maryland	38,849	1.7%
21	Massachusetts	36,094	1.6%	21	Massachusetts	36,094	1.6%
8	Michigan	74,176	3.3%	22	Oklahoma	35,081	1.6%
28	Minnesota	26,410	1.2%	23	Arkansas	33,694	1.5%
29	Mississippi	26,024	1.2%	24	Virginia	31,993	1.4%
17	Missouri	45,788	2.1%	25	Kentucky	28,839	1.3%
46	Montana	3,332	0.1%	26	Colorado	28,256	1.3%
39	Nebraska	8,775	0.4%	27	Wisconsin	27,479	1.2%
30	Nevada	24,156	1.1%	28	Minnesota	26,410	1.2%
44	New Hampshire	4,286	0.2%	29	Mississippi	26,024	1.2%
19	New Jersey	40,401	1.8%	30	Nevada	24,156	1.1%
31	New Mexico	21,713	1.0%	31	New Mexico	21,713	1.0%
9	New York	65,735	3.0%	32	Oregon	20,879	0.9%
4	North Carolina	111,602	5.0%	33	Kansas	19,612	0.9%
50	North Dakota	2,106	0.1%	34	Iowa	16,450	0.7%
5	Ohio	102,544	4.6%	35	Connecticut	15,011	0.7%
22	Oklahoma	35,081	1.6%	36	Utah	14,682	0.7%
32	Oregon	20,879	0.9%	37	West Virginia	11,066	0.5%
11	Pennsylvania	58,620	2.6%	38	Hawaii	9,379	0.4%
43	Rhode Island	5,750	0.3%	39	Nebraska	8,775	0.4%
16	South Carolina	45,967	2.1%	40	Delaware	6,760	0.3%
48	South Dakota	2,430	0.1%	41	Idaho	6,701	0.3%
10	Tennessee	65,006	2.9%	42	Maine	6,522	0.3%
2	Texas	230,123	10.4%	43	Rhode Island	5,750	0.3%
36	Utah	14,682	0.7%	44	New Hampshire	4,286	0.2%
45	Vermont	3,462	0.2%	45	Vermont	3,462	0.2%
24	Virginia	31,993	1.4%	46	Montana	3,332	0.1%
13	Washington	52,478	2.4%	47	Alaska	3,240	0.1%
37	West Virginia	11,066	0.5%	48	South Dakota	2,430	0.1%
27	Wisconsin	27,479	1.2%	49	Wyoming	2,184	0.1%
49	Wyoming	2,184	0.1%	50	North Dakota	2,106	0.1%
					District of Columbia	3,788	0.2%

Source: Reported data from the Federal Bureau of Investigation
"Crime in the United States 2008" (Uniform Crime Reports, September 14, 2009, http://www.fbi.gov/ucr/ucr.htm)
*Burglary is the unlawful entry of a structure to commit a felony or theft. Attempts are included.

Average Time Between Burglaries in 2008

National Rate = A Burglary Occurs Every 14.2 Seconds*

ALPHA ORDER

RANK	STATE	HOURS.MINUTES
37	Alabama	0.10
4	Alaska	2.43
37	Arizona	0.10
27	Arkansas	0.16
49	California	0.02
24	Colorado	0.19
16	Connecticut	0.35
11	Delaware	1.18
48	Florida	0.03
45	Georgia	0.05
13	Hawaii	0.56
10	Idaho	1.19
43	Illinois	0.07
34	Indiana	0.11
17	Iowa	0.32
18	Kansas	0.27
26	Kentucky	0.18
33	Louisiana	0.12
9	Maine	1.21
30	Maryland	0.14
30	Massachusetts	0.14
43	Michigan	0.07
22	Minnesota	0.20
22	Mississippi	0.20
34	Missouri	0.11
5	Montana	2.38
12	Nebraska	1.00
21	Nevada	0.22
7	New Hampshire	2.03
32	New Jersey	0.13
20	New Mexico	0.24
41	New York	0.08
45	North Carolina	0.05
1	North Dakota	4.10
45	Ohio	0.05
29	Oklahoma	0.15
19	Oregon	0.25
40	Pennsylvania	0.09
8	Rhode Island	1.32
34	South Carolina	0.11
3	South Dakota	3.37
41	Tennessee	0.08
49	Texas	0.02
15	Utah	0.36
6	Vermont	2.32
27	Virginia	0.16
37	Washington	0.10
14	West Virginia	0.47
24	Wisconsin	0.19
2	Wyoming	4.01

RANK ORDER

RANK	STATE	HOURS.MINUTES
1	North Dakota	4.10
2	Wyoming	4.01
3	South Dakota	3.37
4	Alaska	2.43
5	Montana	2.38
6	Vermont	2.32
7	New Hampshire	2.03
8	Rhode Island	1.32
9	Maine	1.21
10	Idaho	1.19
11	Delaware	1.18
12	Nebraska	1.00
13	Hawaii	0.56
14	West Virginia	0.47
15	Utah	0.36
16	Connecticut	0.35
17	Iowa	0.32
18	Kansas	0.27
19	Oregon	0.25
20	New Mexico	0.24
21	Nevada	0.22
22	Minnesota	0.20
22	Mississippi	0.20
24	Colorado	0.19
24	Wisconsin	0.19
26	Kentucky	0.18
27	Arkansas	0.16
27	Virginia	0.16
29	Oklahoma	0.15
30	Maryland	0.14
30	Massachusetts	0.14
32	New Jersey	0.13
33	Louisiana	0.12
34	Indiana	0.11
34	Missouri	0.11
34	South Carolina	0.11
37	Alabama	0.10
37	Arizona	0.10
37	Washington	0.10
40	Pennsylvania	0.09
41	New York	0.08
41	Tennessee	0.08
43	Illinois	0.07
43	Michigan	0.07
45	Georgia	0.05
45	North Carolina	0.05
45	Ohio	0.05
48	Florida	0.03
49	California	0.02
49	Texas	0.02

District of Columbia — 2.19

Source: Reported data from the Federal Bureau of Investigation
"Crime in the United States 2008" (Uniform Crime Reports, September 14, 2009, http://www.fbi.gov/ucr/ucr.htm)
*Burglary is the unlawful entry of a structure to commit a felony or theft. Attempts are included.

Percent Change in Number of Burglaries: 2007 to 2008

National Percent Change = 2.0% Increase*

ALPHA ORDER

RANK	STATE	PERCENT CHANGE
3	Alabama	11.2
49	Alaska	(12.0)
35	Arizona	(2.3)
11	Arkansas	5.1
29	California	0.3
33	Colorado	(1.7)
31	Connecticut	(1.0)
8	Delaware	6.6
18	Florida	3.6
4	Georgia	11.0
19	Hawaii	3.1
43	Idaho	(4.0)
13	Illinois	4.6
17	Indiana	3.7
39	Iowa	(2.9)
42	Kansas	(3.2)
15	Kentucky	4.2
39	Louisiana	(2.9)
35	Maine	(2.3)
12	Maryland	4.7
26	Massachusetts	1.2
33	Michigan	(1.7)
48	Minnesota	(11.0)
45	Mississippi	(6.9)
9	Missouri	5.4
5	Montana	10.1
41	Nebraska	(3.0)
38	Nevada	(2.8)
50	New Hampshire	(14.0)
7	New Jersey	7.8
1	New Mexico	14.3
25	New York	1.4
21	North Carolina	2.6
37	North Dakota	(2.7)
16	Ohio	4.1
20	Oklahoma	2.8
47	Oregon	(8.5)
13	Pennsylvania	4.6
6	Rhode Island	9.8
24	South Carolina	1.7
23	South Dakota	2.2
10	Tennessee	5.3
28	Texas	0.8
44	Utah	(5.5)
2	Vermont	11.5
27	Virginia	1.0
30	Washington	(0.4)
22	West Virginia	2.3
32	Wisconsin	(1.3)
46	Wyoming	(7.0)

RANK ORDER

RANK	STATE	PERCENT CHANGE
1	New Mexico	14.3
2	Vermont	11.5
3	Alabama	11.2
4	Georgia	11.0
5	Montana	10.1
6	Rhode Island	9.8
7	New Jersey	7.8
8	Delaware	6.6
9	Missouri	5.4
10	Tennessee	5.3
11	Arkansas	5.1
12	Maryland	4.7
13	Illinois	4.6
13	Pennsylvania	4.6
15	Kentucky	4.2
16	Ohio	4.1
17	Indiana	3.7
18	Florida	3.6
19	Hawaii	3.1
20	Oklahoma	2.8
21	North Carolina	2.6
22	West Virginia	2.3
23	South Dakota	2.2
24	South Carolina	1.7
25	New York	1.4
26	Massachusetts	1.2
27	Virginia	1.0
28	Texas	0.8
29	California	0.3
30	Washington	(0.4)
31	Connecticut	(1.0)
32	Wisconsin	(1.3)
33	Colorado	(1.7)
33	Michigan	(1.7)
35	Arizona	(2.3)
35	Maine	(2.3)
37	North Dakota	(2.7)
38	Nevada	(2.8)
39	Iowa	(2.9)
39	Louisiana	(2.9)
41	Nebraska	(3.0)
42	Kansas	(3.2)
43	Idaho	(4.0)
44	Utah	(5.5)
45	Mississippi	(6.9)
46	Wyoming	(7.0)
47	Oregon	(8.5)
48	Minnesota	(11.0)
49	Alaska	(12.0)
50	New Hampshire	(14.0)

District of Columbia   (3.5)

Source: Reported data from the Federal Bureau of Investigation
"Crime in the United States 2008" (Uniform Crime Reports, September 14, 2009, http://www.fbi.gov/ucr/ucr.htm)
*Burglary is the unlawful entry of a structure to commit a felony or theft. Attempts are included.

Burglary Rate in 2008

National Rate = 730.8 Burglaries per 100,000 Population*

ALPHA ORDER

RANK	STATE	RATE
4	Alabama	1,081.3
39	Alaska	472.1
15	Arizona	868.9
2	Arkansas	1,180.0
25	California	647.1
28	Colorado	572.0
43	Connecticut	428.7
18	Delaware	774.3
7	Florida	1,028.3
6	Georgia	1,038.9
21	Hawaii	728.1
42	Idaho	439.8
26	Illinois	612.1
19	Indiana	762.8
32	Iowa	547.9
22	Kansas	699.9
24	Kentucky	675.5
9	Louisiana	982.1
36	Maine	495.4
23	Maryland	689.6
30	Massachusetts	555.5
20	Michigan	741.5
35	Minnesota	505.9
14	Mississippi	885.6
17	Missouri	774.5
46	Montana	344.4
37	Nebraska	492.0
12	Nevada	929.0
49	New Hampshire	325.7
41	New Jersey	465.3
3	New Mexico	1,094.2
47	New York	337.3
1	North Carolina	1,210.1
48	North Dakota	328.3
13	Ohio	892.8
10	Oklahoma	963.1
31	Oregon	550.9
40	Pennsylvania	470.9
33	Rhode Island	547.2
8	South Carolina	1,026.1
50	South Dakota	302.2
5	Tennessee	1,046.0
11	Texas	946.0
34	Utah	536.5
29	Vermont	557.2
44	Virginia	411.8
16	Washington	801.3
27	West Virginia	609.9
38	Wisconsin	488.3
45	Wyoming	410.0

RANK ORDER

RANK	STATE	RATE
1	North Carolina	1,210.1
2	Arkansas	1,180.0
3	New Mexico	1,094.2
4	Alabama	1,081.3
5	Tennessee	1,046.0
6	Georgia	1,038.9
7	Florida	1,028.3
8	South Carolina	1,026.1
9	Louisiana	982.1
10	Oklahoma	963.1
11	Texas	946.0
12	Nevada	929.0
13	Ohio	892.8
14	Mississippi	885.6
15	Arizona	868.9
16	Washington	801.3
17	Missouri	774.5
18	Delaware	774.3
19	Indiana	762.8
20	Michigan	741.5
21	Hawaii	728.1
22	Kansas	699.9
23	Maryland	689.6
24	Kentucky	675.5
25	California	647.1
26	Illinois	612.1
27	West Virginia	609.9
28	Colorado	572.0
29	Vermont	557.2
30	Massachusetts	555.5
31	Oregon	550.9
32	Iowa	547.9
33	Rhode Island	547.2
34	Utah	536.5
35	Minnesota	505.9
36	Maine	495.4
37	Nebraska	492.0
38	Wisconsin	488.3
39	Alaska	472.1
40	Pennsylvania	470.9
41	New Jersey	465.3
42	Idaho	439.8
43	Connecticut	428.7
44	Virginia	411.8
45	Wyoming	410.0
46	Montana	344.4
47	New York	337.3
48	North Dakota	328.3
49	New Hampshire	325.7
50	South Dakota	302.2
	District of Columbia	640.0

Source: Reported data from the Federal Bureau of Investigation
"Crime in the United States 2008" (Uniform Crime Reports, September 14, 2009, http://www.fbi.gov/ucr/ucr.htm)
*Burglary is the unlawful entry of a structure to commit a felony or theft. Attempts are included.

Percent Change in Burglary Rate: 2007 to 2008

National Percent Change = 1.2% Increase*

ALPHA ORDER

RANK	STATE	PERCENT CHANGE
4	Alabama	10.4
49	Alaska	(12.4)
41	Arizona	(4.7)
12	Arkansas	4.3
28	California	(0.2)
36	Colorado	(3.3)
29	Connecticut	(1.0)
8	Delaware	5.6
17	Florida	3.2
5	Georgia	9.3
19	Hawaii	2.7
42	Idaho	(5.5)
14	Illinois	4.2
17	Indiana	3.2
37	Iowa	(3.4)
39	Kansas	(4.1)
16	Kentucky	3.5
42	Louisiana	(5.5)
34	Maine	(2.3)
11	Maryland	4.4
24	Massachusetts	0.5
29	Michigan	(1.0)
48	Minnesota	(11.4)
44	Mississippi	(7.5)
9	Missouri	4.8
6	Montana	9.0
38	Nebraska	(3.5)
39	Nevada	(4.1)
50	New Hampshire	(14.0)
7	New Jersey	7.8
1	New Mexico	13.5
25	New York	0.4
23	North Carolina	0.8
35	North Dakota	(2.9)
15	Ohio	3.9
21	Oklahoma	2.1
47	Oregon	(9.5)
10	Pennsylvania	4.5
3	Rhode Island	10.6
27	South Carolina	0.0
22	South Dakota	1.2
12	Tennessee	4.3
29	Texas	(1.0)
45	Utah	(8.7)
2	Vermont	11.5
26	Virginia	0.2
32	Washington	(1.7)
20	West Virginia	2.2
33	Wisconsin	(1.8)
45	Wyoming	(8.7)

RANK ORDER

RANK	STATE	PERCENT CHANGE
1	New Mexico	13.5
2	Vermont	11.5
3	Rhode Island	10.6
4	Alabama	10.4
5	Georgia	9.3
6	Montana	9.0
7	New Jersey	7.8
8	Delaware	5.6
9	Missouri	4.8
10	Pennsylvania	4.5
11	Maryland	4.4
12	Arkansas	4.3
12	Tennessee	4.3
14	Illinois	4.2
15	Ohio	3.9
16	Kentucky	3.5
17	Florida	3.2
17	Indiana	3.2
19	Hawaii	2.7
20	West Virginia	2.2
21	Oklahoma	2.1
22	South Dakota	1.2
23	North Carolina	0.8
24	Massachusetts	0.5
25	New York	0.4
26	Virginia	0.2
27	South Carolina	0.0
28	California	(0.2)
29	Connecticut	(1.0)
29	Michigan	(1.0)
29	Texas	(1.0)
32	Washington	(1.7)
33	Wisconsin	(1.8)
34	Maine	(2.3)
35	North Dakota	(2.9)
36	Colorado	(3.3)
37	Iowa	(3.4)
38	Nebraska	(3.5)
39	Kansas	(4.1)
39	Nevada	(4.1)
41	Arizona	(4.7)
42	Idaho	(5.5)
42	Louisiana	(5.5)
44	Mississippi	(7.5)
45	Utah	(8.7)
45	Wyoming	(8.7)
47	Oregon	(9.5)
48	Minnesota	(11.4)
49	Alaska	(12.4)
50	New Hampshire	(14.0)

District of Columbia — (4.1)

Source: Reported data from the Federal Bureau of Investigation
"Crime in the United States 2008" (Uniform Crime Reports, September 14, 2009, http://www.fbi.gov/ucr/ucr.htm)
*Burglary is the unlawful entry of a structure to commit a felony or theft. Attempts are included.

Larceny-Thefts in 2008

National Total = 6,588,873 Larceny-Thefts*

ALPHA ORDER

RANK	STATE	THEFTS	% of USA
19	Alabama	126,477	1.9%
46	Alaska	15,246	0.2%
10	Arizona	185,221	2.8%
30	Arkansas	69,303	1.1%
2	California	650,385	9.9%
25	Colorado	98,950	1.5%
32	Connecticut	62,113	0.9%
42	Delaware	22,002	0.3%
3	Florida	506,958	7.7%
7	Georgia	248,678	3.8%
39	Hawaii	31,492	0.5%
41	Idaho	23,650	0.4%
5	Illinois	266,815	4.0%
16	Indiana	146,615	2.2%
34	Iowa	51,907	0.8%
31	Kansas	67,628	1.0%
28	Kentucky	73,808	1.1%
23	Louisiana	111,567	1.7%
40	Maine	24,587	0.4%
18	Maryland	133,983	2.0%
24	Massachusetts	107,128	1.6%
11	Michigan	183,168	2.8%
22	Minnesota	112,322	1.7%
33	Mississippi	54,032	0.8%
15	Missouri	150,032	2.3%
45	Montana	20,277	0.3%
37	Nebraska	38,375	0.6%
35	Nevada	49,581	0.8%
43	New Hampshire	21,853	0.3%
17	New Jersey	138,545	2.1%
36	New Mexico	47,855	0.7%
4	New York	297,684	4.5%
8	North Carolina	234,616	3.6%
50	North Dakota	9,164	0.1%
6	Ohio	260,786	4.0%
27	Oklahoma	79,422	1.2%
26	Oregon	92,187	1.4%
9	Pennsylvania	218,941	3.3%
44	Rhode Island	20,899	0.3%
20	South Carolina	126,064	1.9%
49	South Dakota	10,004	0.2%
12	Tennessee	167,015	2.5%
1	Texas	654,097	9.9%
29	Utah	69,996	1.1%
47	Vermont	11,724	0.2%
14	Virginia	150,382	2.3%
13	Washington	165,339	2.5%
38	West Virginia	32,337	0.5%
21	Wisconsin	116,128	1.8%
48	Wyoming	11,577	0.2%

RANK ORDER

RANK	STATE	THEFTS	% of USA
1	Texas	654,097	9.9%
2	California	650,385	9.9%
3	Florida	506,958	7.7%
4	New York	297,684	4.5%
5	Illinois	266,815	4.0%
6	Ohio	260,786	4.0%
7	Georgia	248,678	3.8%
8	North Carolina	234,616	3.6%
9	Pennsylvania	218,941	3.3%
10	Arizona	185,221	2.8%
11	Michigan	183,168	2.8%
12	Tennessee	167,015	2.5%
13	Washington	165,339	2.5%
14	Virginia	150,382	2.3%
15	Missouri	150,032	2.3%
16	Indiana	146,615	2.2%
17	New Jersey	138,545	2.1%
18	Maryland	133,983	2.0%
19	Alabama	126,477	1.9%
20	South Carolina	126,064	1.9%
21	Wisconsin	116,128	1.8%
22	Minnesota	112,322	1.7%
23	Louisiana	111,567	1.7%
24	Massachusetts	107,128	1.6%
25	Colorado	98,950	1.5%
26	Oregon	92,187	1.4%
27	Oklahoma	79,422	1.2%
28	Kentucky	73,808	1.1%
29	Utah	69,996	1.1%
30	Arkansas	69,303	1.1%
31	Kansas	67,628	1.0%
32	Connecticut	62,113	0.9%
33	Mississippi	54,032	0.8%
34	Iowa	51,907	0.8%
35	Nevada	49,581	0.8%
36	New Mexico	47,855	0.7%
37	Nebraska	38,375	0.6%
38	West Virginia	32,337	0.5%
39	Hawaii	31,492	0.5%
40	Maine	24,587	0.4%
41	Idaho	23,650	0.4%
42	Delaware	22,002	0.3%
43	New Hampshire	21,853	0.3%
44	Rhode Island	20,899	0.3%
45	Montana	20,277	0.3%
46	Alaska	15,246	0.2%
47	Vermont	11,724	0.2%
48	Wyoming	11,577	0.2%
49	South Dakota	10,004	0.2%
50	North Dakota	9,164	0.1%
	District of Columbia	19,958	0.3%

Source: Reported data from the Federal Bureau of Investigation
"Crime in the United States 2008" (Uniform Crime Reports, September 14, 2009, http://www.fbi.gov/ucr/ucr.htm)
*Larceny-theft is the unlawful taking of property without use of force, violence, or fraud. Attempts are included. Motor vehicle thefts are excluded.

Average Time Between Larceny-Thefts in 2008

National Rate = A Larceny-Theft Occurs Every 4.8 Seconds*

RANK	STATE	MINUTES.SECONDS
32	Alabama	4.10
5	Alaska	34.34
41	Arizona	2.51
21	Arkansas	7.36
49	California	0.49
26	Colorado	5.20
19	Connecticut	8.29
9	Delaware	23.57
48	Florida	1.02
44	Georgia	2.07
12	Hawaii	16.44
10	Idaho	22.17
46	Illinois	1.59
35	Indiana	3.35
17	Iowa	10.09
20	Kansas	7.47
23	Kentucky	7.08
28	Louisiana	4.43
11	Maine	21.26
33	Maryland	3.56
27	Massachusetts	4.55
40	Michigan	2.53
29	Minnesota	4.41
18	Mississippi	9.45
36	Missouri	3.31
6	Montana	25.59
14	Nebraska	13.44
16	Nevada	10.38
8	New Hampshire	24.07
34	New Jersey	3.48
15	New Mexico	11.01
47	New York	1.46
43	North Carolina	2.15
1	North Dakota	57.31
45	Ohio	2.01
24	Oklahoma	6.38
25	Oregon	5.43
42	Pennsylvania	2.25
7	Rhode Island	25.13
31	South Carolina	4.11
2	South Dakota	52.41
39	Tennessee	3.10
49	Texas	0.49
22	Utah	7.32
4	Vermont	44.57
37	Virginia	3.30
38	Washington	3.11
13	West Virginia	16.18
30	Wisconsin	4.32
3	Wyoming	45.31

RANK	STATE	MINUTES.SECONDS
1	North Dakota	57.31
2	South Dakota	52.41
3	Wyoming	45.31
4	Vermont	44.57
5	Alaska	34.34
6	Montana	25.59
7	Rhode Island	25.13
8	New Hampshire	24.07
9	Delaware	23.57
10	Idaho	22.17
11	Maine	21.26
12	Hawaii	16.44
13	West Virginia	16.18
14	Nebraska	13.44
15	New Mexico	11.01
16	Nevada	10.38
17	Iowa	10.09
18	Mississippi	9.45
19	Connecticut	8.29
20	Kansas	7.47
21	Arkansas	7.36
22	Utah	7.32
23	Kentucky	7.08
24	Oklahoma	6.38
25	Oregon	5.43
26	Colorado	5.20
27	Massachusetts	4.55
28	Louisiana	4.43
29	Minnesota	4.41
30	Wisconsin	4.32
31	South Carolina	4.11
32	Alabama	4.10
33	Maryland	3.56
34	New Jersey	3.48
35	Indiana	3.35
36	Missouri	3.31
37	Virginia	3.30
38	Washington	3.11
39	Tennessee	3.10
40	Michigan	2.53
41	Arizona	2.51
42	Pennsylvania	2.25
43	North Carolina	2.15
44	Georgia	2.07
45	Ohio	2.01
46	Illinois	1.59
47	New York	1.46
48	Florida	1.02
49	California	0.49
49	Texas	0.49
	District of Columbia	26.25

Source: CQ Press using reported data from the Federal Bureau of Investigation
  "Crime in the United States 2008" (Uniform Crime Reports, September 14, 2009, http://www.fbi.gov/ucr/ucr.htm)
*Larceny-theft is the unlawful taking of property without use of force, violence, or fraud. Attempts are included. Motor vehicle thefts are excluded.

Percent Change in Number of Larceny-Thefts: 2007 to 2008

National Percent Change = 0.3% Increase*

<table>
<tr><td colspan="3">ALPHA ORDER</td><td colspan="3">RANK ORDER</td></tr>
<tr><td>RANK</td><td>STATE</td><td>PERCENT CHANGE</td><td>RANK</td><td>STATE</td><td>PERCENT CHANGE</td></tr>
<tr><td>20</td><td>Alabama</td><td>1.8</td><td>1</td><td>New Hampshire</td><td>17.4</td></tr>
<tr><td>49</td><td>Alaska</td><td>(10.3)</td><td>2</td><td>Vermont</td><td>9.7</td></tr>
<tr><td>5</td><td>Arizona</td><td>6.7</td><td>3</td><td>Rhode Island</td><td>8.4</td></tr>
<tr><td>43</td><td>Arkansas</td><td>(5.0)</td><td>4</td><td>Delaware</td><td>7.4</td></tr>
<tr><td>24</td><td>California</td><td>(0.3)</td><td>5</td><td>Arizona</td><td>6.7</td></tr>
<tr><td>33</td><td>Colorado</td><td>(1.6)</td><td>6</td><td>New Mexico</td><td>5.3</td></tr>
<tr><td>11</td><td>Connecticut</td><td>4.0</td><td>7</td><td>Maryland</td><td>5.2</td></tr>
<tr><td>4</td><td>Delaware</td><td>7.4</td><td>8</td><td>Kentucky</td><td>4.8</td></tr>
<tr><td>15</td><td>Florida</td><td>3.3</td><td>9</td><td>New Jersey</td><td>4.3</td></tr>
<tr><td>11</td><td>Georgia</td><td>4.0</td><td>10</td><td>Virginia</td><td>4.1</td></tr>
<tr><td>50</td><td>Hawaii</td><td>(18.0)</td><td>11</td><td>Connecticut</td><td>4.0</td></tr>
<tr><td>41</td><td>Idaho</td><td>(3.4)</td><td>11</td><td>Georgia</td><td>4.0</td></tr>
<tr><td>26</td><td>Illinois</td><td>(0.4)</td><td>13</td><td>Pennsylvania</td><td>3.7</td></tr>
<tr><td>33</td><td>Indiana</td><td>(1.6)</td><td>14</td><td>Massachusetts</td><td>3.4</td></tr>
<tr><td>47</td><td>Iowa</td><td>(7.8)</td><td>15</td><td>Florida</td><td>3.3</td></tr>
<tr><td>46</td><td>Kansas</td><td>(7.7)</td><td>16</td><td>New York</td><td>3.0</td></tr>
<tr><td>8</td><td>Kentucky</td><td>4.8</td><td>17</td><td>West Virginia</td><td>2.8</td></tr>
<tr><td>40</td><td>Louisiana</td><td>(3.2)</td><td>18</td><td>Utah</td><td>2.6</td></tr>
<tr><td>19</td><td>Maine</td><td>2.2</td><td>19</td><td>Maine</td><td>2.2</td></tr>
<tr><td>7</td><td>Maryland</td><td>5.2</td><td>20</td><td>Alabama</td><td>1.8</td></tr>
<tr><td>14</td><td>Massachusetts</td><td>3.4</td><td>21</td><td>North Dakota</td><td>1.7</td></tr>
<tr><td>42</td><td>Michigan</td><td>(4.2)</td><td>22</td><td>North Carolina</td><td>0.4</td></tr>
<tr><td>38</td><td>Minnesota</td><td>(2.9)</td><td>23</td><td>South Carolina</td><td>0.0</td></tr>
<tr><td>45</td><td>Mississippi</td><td>(7.0)</td><td>24</td><td>California</td><td>(0.3)</td></tr>
<tr><td>33</td><td>Missouri</td><td>(1.6)</td><td>24</td><td>Nevada</td><td>(0.3)</td></tr>
<tr><td>44</td><td>Montana</td><td>(6.6)</td><td>26</td><td>Illinois</td><td>(0.4)</td></tr>
<tr><td>48</td><td>Nebraska</td><td>(8.3)</td><td>26</td><td>South Dakota</td><td>(0.4)</td></tr>
<tr><td>24</td><td>Nevada</td><td>(0.3)</td><td>28</td><td>Oklahoma</td><td>(0.7)</td></tr>
<tr><td>1</td><td>New Hampshire</td><td>17.4</td><td>29</td><td>Tennessee</td><td>(0.8)</td></tr>
<tr><td>9</td><td>New Jersey</td><td>4.3</td><td>30</td><td>Ohio</td><td>(1.2)</td></tr>
<tr><td>6</td><td>New Mexico</td><td>5.3</td><td>31</td><td>Texas</td><td>(1.3)</td></tr>
<tr><td>16</td><td>New York</td><td>3.0</td><td>31</td><td>Wisconsin</td><td>(1.3)</td></tr>
<tr><td>22</td><td>North Carolina</td><td>0.4</td><td>33</td><td>Colorado</td><td>(1.6)</td></tr>
<tr><td>21</td><td>North Dakota</td><td>1.7</td><td>33</td><td>Indiana</td><td>(1.6)</td></tr>
<tr><td>30</td><td>Ohio</td><td>(1.2)</td><td>33</td><td>Missouri</td><td>(1.6)</td></tr>
<tr><td>28</td><td>Oklahoma</td><td>(0.7)</td><td>36</td><td>Wyoming</td><td>(2.2)</td></tr>
<tr><td>37</td><td>Oregon</td><td>(2.7)</td><td>37</td><td>Oregon</td><td>(2.7)</td></tr>
<tr><td>13</td><td>Pennsylvania</td><td>3.7</td><td>38</td><td>Minnesota</td><td>(2.9)</td></tr>
<tr><td>3</td><td>Rhode Island</td><td>8.4</td><td>39</td><td>Washington</td><td>(3.0)</td></tr>
<tr><td>23</td><td>South Carolina</td><td>0.0</td><td>40</td><td>Louisiana</td><td>(3.2)</td></tr>
<tr><td>26</td><td>South Dakota</td><td>(0.4)</td><td>41</td><td>Idaho</td><td>(3.4)</td></tr>
<tr><td>29</td><td>Tennessee</td><td>(0.8)</td><td>42</td><td>Michigan</td><td>(4.2)</td></tr>
<tr><td>31</td><td>Texas</td><td>(1.3)</td><td>43</td><td>Arkansas</td><td>(5.0)</td></tr>
<tr><td>18</td><td>Utah</td><td>2.6</td><td>44</td><td>Montana</td><td>(6.6)</td></tr>
<tr><td>2</td><td>Vermont</td><td>9.7</td><td>45</td><td>Mississippi</td><td>(7.0)</td></tr>
<tr><td>10</td><td>Virginia</td><td>4.1</td><td>46</td><td>Kansas</td><td>(7.7)</td></tr>
<tr><td>39</td><td>Washington</td><td>(3.0)</td><td>47</td><td>Iowa</td><td>(7.8)</td></tr>
<tr><td>17</td><td>West Virginia</td><td>2.8</td><td>48</td><td>Nebraska</td><td>(8.3)</td></tr>
<tr><td>31</td><td>Wisconsin</td><td>(1.3)</td><td>49</td><td>Alaska</td><td>(10.3)</td></tr>
<tr><td>36</td><td>Wyoming</td><td>(2.2)</td><td>50</td><td>Hawaii</td><td>(18.0)</td></tr>
<tr><td></td><td></td><td></td><td></td><td>District of Columbia</td><td>14.8</td></tr>
</table>

Source: Reported data from the Federal Bureau of Investigation
   "Crime in the United States 2008" (Uniform Crime Reports, September 14, 2009, http://www.fbi.gov/ucr/ucr.htm)
*Larceny-theft is the unlawful taking of property without use of force, violence, or fraud. Attempts are included. Motor vehicle thefts are excluded.

Larceny-Theft Rate in 2008

National Rate = 2,167.0 Larceny-Thefts per 100,000 Population*

ALPHA ORDER

RANK	STATE	RATE
4	Alabama	2,713.0
22	Alaska	2,221.5
1	Arizona	2,849.5
16	Arkansas	2,427.1
40	California	1,769.4
30	Colorado	2,003.3
39	Connecticut	1,774.0
13	Delaware	2,520.0
3	Florida	2,766.0
7	Georgia	2,567.5
14	Hawaii	2,444.7
47	Idaho	1,552.0
28	Illinois	2,068.1
20	Indiana	2,299.2
42	Iowa	1,728.8
17	Kansas	2,413.4
42	Kentucky	1,728.8
11	Louisiana	2,529.4
35	Maine	1,867.7
19	Maryland	2,378.3
45	Massachusetts	1,648.6
37	Michigan	1,831.1
26	Minnesota	2,151.6
36	Mississippi	1,838.7
10	Missouri	2,537.9
27	Montana	2,095.9
25	Nebraska	2,151.8
33	Nevada	1,906.8
44	New Hampshire	1,660.8
46	New Jersey	1,595.7
18	New Mexico	2,411.6
48	New York	1,527.3
9	North Carolina	2,544.0
49	North Dakota	1,428.6
21	Ohio	2,270.5
23	Oklahoma	2,180.5
15	Oregon	2,432.3
41	Pennsylvania	1,758.8
31	Rhode Island	1,988.9
2	South Carolina	2,814.1
50	South Dakota	1,244.0
6	Tennessee	2,687.3
5	Texas	2,688.8
8	Utah	2,557.9
34	Vermont	1,887.1
32	Virginia	1,935.6
12	Washington	2,524.6
38	West Virginia	1,782.2
29	Wisconsin	2,063.4
24	Wyoming	2,173.4

RANK ORDER

RANK	STATE	RATE
1	Arizona	2,849.5
2	South Carolina	2,814.1
3	Florida	2,766.0
4	Alabama	2,713.0
5	Texas	2,688.8
6	Tennessee	2,687.3
7	Georgia	2,567.5
8	Utah	2,557.9
9	North Carolina	2,544.0
10	Missouri	2,537.9
11	Louisiana	2,529.4
12	Washington	2,524.6
13	Delaware	2,520.0
14	Hawaii	2,444.7
15	Oregon	2,432.3
16	Arkansas	2,427.1
17	Kansas	2,413.4
18	New Mexico	2,411.6
19	Maryland	2,378.3
20	Indiana	2,299.2
21	Ohio	2,270.5
22	Alaska	2,221.5
23	Oklahoma	2,180.5
24	Wyoming	2,173.4
25	Nebraska	2,151.8
26	Minnesota	2,151.6
27	Montana	2,095.9
28	Illinois	2,068.1
29	Wisconsin	2,063.4
30	Colorado	2,003.3
31	Rhode Island	1,988.9
32	Virginia	1,935.6
33	Nevada	1,906.8
34	Vermont	1,887.1
35	Maine	1,867.7
36	Mississippi	1,838.7
37	Michigan	1,831.1
38	West Virginia	1,782.2
39	Connecticut	1,774.0
40	California	1,769.4
41	Pennsylvania	1,758.8
42	Iowa	1,728.8
42	Kentucky	1,728.8
44	New Hampshire	1,660.8
45	Massachusetts	1,648.6
46	New Jersey	1,595.7
47	Idaho	1,552.0
48	New York	1,527.3
49	North Dakota	1,428.6
50	South Dakota	1,244.0

District of Columbia — 3,372.2

Source: Reported data from the Federal Bureau of Investigation
"Crime in the United States 2008" (Uniform Crime Reports, September 14, 2009, http://www.fbi.gov/ucr/ucr.htm)
*Larceny-theft is the unlawful taking of property without use of force, violence, or fraud. Attempts are included. Motor vehicle thefts are excluded.

Percent Change in Larceny-Theft Rate: 2007 to 2008

National Percent Change = 0.5% Decrease*

ALPHA ORDER				RANK ORDER		
RANK	STATE	PERCENT CHANGE		RANK	STATE	PERCENT CHANGE
20	Alabama	1.1		1	New Hampshire	17.4
49	Alaska	(10.7)		2	Vermont	9.7
8	Arizona	4.1		3	Rhode Island	9.1
42	Arkansas	(5.7)		4	Delaware	6.4
21	California	(0.8)		5	Maryland	5.0
35	Colorado	(3.2)		6	New Mexico	4.5
10	Connecticut	4.0		7	New Jersey	4.4
4	Delaware	6.4		8	Arizona	4.1
13	Florida	2.8		8	Kentucky	4.1
16	Georgia	2.5		10	Connecticut	4.0
50	Hawaii	(18.3)		11	Pennsylvania	3.6
41	Idaho	(4.9)		12	Virginia	3.3
21	Illinois	(0.8)		13	Florida	2.8
32	Indiana	(2.1)		14	West Virginia	2.7
46	Iowa	(8.3)		15	Massachusetts	2.6
47	Kansas	(8.6)		16	Georgia	2.5
8	Kentucky	4.1		17	Maine	2.3
42	Louisiana	(5.7)		18	New York	2.0
17	Maine	2.3		19	North Dakota	1.4
5	Maryland	5.0		20	Alabama	1.1
15	Massachusetts	2.6		21	California	(0.8)
37	Michigan	(3.5)		21	Illinois	(0.8)
36	Minnesota	(3.3)		21	Utah	(0.8)
45	Mississippi	(7.6)		24	North Carolina	(1.3)
33	Missouri	(2.2)		25	Ohio	(1.4)
44	Montana	(7.5)		25	Oklahoma	(1.4)
48	Nebraska	(8.8)		25	South Dakota	(1.4)
29	Nevada	(1.7)		28	South Carolina	(1.6)
1	New Hampshire	17.4		29	Nevada	(1.7)
7	New Jersey	4.4		29	Tennessee	(1.7)
6	New Mexico	4.5		31	Wisconsin	(1.8)
18	New York	2.0		32	Indiana	(2.1)
24	North Carolina	(1.3)		33	Missouri	(2.2)
19	North Dakota	1.4		34	Texas	(3.0)
25	Ohio	(1.4)		35	Colorado	(3.2)
25	Oklahoma	(1.4)		36	Minnesota	(3.3)
38	Oregon	(3.8)		37	Michigan	(3.5)
11	Pennsylvania	3.6		38	Oregon	(3.8)
3	Rhode Island	9.1		39	Wyoming	(4.0)
28	South Carolina	(1.6)		40	Washington	(4.2)
25	South Dakota	(1.4)		41	Idaho	(4.9)
29	Tennessee	(1.7)		42	Arkansas	(5.7)
34	Texas	(3.0)		42	Louisiana	(5.7)
21	Utah	(0.8)		44	Montana	(7.5)
2	Vermont	9.7		45	Mississippi	(7.6)
12	Virginia	3.3		46	Iowa	(8.3)
40	Washington	(4.2)		47	Kansas	(8.6)
14	West Virginia	2.7		48	Nebraska	(8.8)
31	Wisconsin	(1.8)		49	Alaska	(10.7)
39	Wyoming	(4.0)		50	Hawaii	(18.3)
					District of Columbia	14.1

Source: Reported data from the Federal Bureau of Investigation
   "Crime in the United States 2008" (Uniform Crime Reports, September 14, 2009, http://www.fbi.gov/ucr/ucr.htm)
*Larceny-theft is the unlawful taking of property without use of force, violence, or fraud. Attempts are included. Motor vehicle thefts are excluded.

Motor Vehicle Thefts in 2008

National Total = 956,846 Motor Vehicle Thefts*

ALPHA ORDER

RANK	STATE	THEFTS	% of USA
22	Alabama	13,458	1.4%
43	Alaska	1,638	0.2%
5	Arizona	37,218	3.9%
34	Arkansas	6,511	0.7%
1	California	192,527	20.1%
21	Colorado	13,519	1.4%
29	Connecticut	8,963	0.9%
41	Delaware	2,541	0.3%
3	Florida	63,509	6.6%
4	Georgia	39,628	4.1%
36	Hawaii	5,133	0.5%
42	Idaho	1,668	0.2%
7	Illinois	32,572	3.4%
18	Indiana	17,455	1.8%
37	Iowa	4,332	0.5%
32	Kansas	7,395	0.8%
31	Kentucky	7,667	0.8%
20	Louisiana	13,743	1.4%
46	Maine	1,176	0.1%
11	Maryland	25,333	2.6%
24	Massachusetts	12,737	1.3%
6	Michigan	36,241	3.8%
28	Minnesota	10,078	1.1%
35	Mississippi	6,352	0.7%
14	Missouri	20,765	2.2%
44	Montana	1,573	0.2%
38	Nebraska	4,188	0.4%
19	Nevada	15,903	1.7%
45	New Hampshire	1,387	0.1%
15	New Jersey	20,180	2.1%
30	New Mexico	8,004	0.8%
12	New York	25,114	2.6%
10	North Carolina	26,743	2.8%
47	North Dakota	882	0.1%
8	Ohio	28,532	3.0%
27	Oklahoma	10,881	1.1%
26	Oregon	11,331	1.2%
13	Pennsylvania	22,471	2.3%
40	Rhode Island	3,200	0.3%
17	South Carolina	17,652	1.8%
48	South Dakota	800	0.1%
16	Tennessee	19,224	2.0%
2	Texas	85,350	8.9%
33	Utah	7,195	0.8%
50	Vermont	585	0.1%
23	Virginia	13,259	1.4%
9	Washington	28,331	3.0%
39	West Virginia	3,204	0.3%
25	Wisconsin	11,520	1.2%
49	Wyoming	713	0.1%

RANK ORDER

RANK	STATE	THEFTS	% of USA
1	California	192,527	20.1%
2	Texas	85,350	8.9%
3	Florida	63,509	6.6%
4	Georgia	39,628	4.1%
5	Arizona	37,218	3.9%
6	Michigan	36,241	3.8%
7	Illinois	32,572	3.4%
8	Ohio	28,532	3.0%
9	Washington	28,331	3.0%
10	North Carolina	26,743	2.8%
11	Maryland	25,333	2.6%
12	New York	25,114	2.6%
13	Pennsylvania	22,471	2.3%
14	Missouri	20,765	2.2%
15	New Jersey	20,180	2.1%
16	Tennessee	19,224	2.0%
17	South Carolina	17,652	1.8%
18	Indiana	17,455	1.8%
19	Nevada	15,903	1.7%
20	Louisiana	13,743	1.4%
21	Colorado	13,519	1.4%
22	Alabama	13,458	1.4%
23	Virginia	13,259	1.4%
24	Massachusetts	12,737	1.3%
25	Wisconsin	11,520	1.2%
26	Oregon	11,331	1.2%
27	Oklahoma	10,881	1.1%
28	Minnesota	10,078	1.1%
29	Connecticut	8,963	0.9%
30	New Mexico	8,004	0.8%
31	Kentucky	7,667	0.8%
32	Kansas	7,395	0.8%
33	Utah	7,195	0.8%
34	Arkansas	6,511	0.7%
35	Mississippi	6,352	0.7%
36	Hawaii	5,133	0.5%
37	Iowa	4,332	0.5%
38	Nebraska	4,188	0.4%
39	West Virginia	3,204	0.3%
40	Rhode Island	3,200	0.3%
41	Delaware	2,541	0.3%
42	Idaho	1,668	0.2%
43	Alaska	1,638	0.2%
44	Montana	1,573	0.2%
45	New Hampshire	1,387	0.1%
46	Maine	1,176	0.1%
47	North Dakota	882	0.1%
48	South Dakota	800	0.1%
49	Wyoming	713	0.1%
50	Vermont	585	0.1%
	District of Columbia	6,465	0.7%

Source: Reported data from the Federal Bureau of Investigation
"Crime in the United States 2008" (Uniform Crime Reports, September 14, 2009, http://www.fbi.gov/ucr/ucr.htm)
*Includes the theft or attempted theft of a self-propelled vehicle. Excludes motorboats, construction equipment, airplanes, and farming equipment.

Average Time Between Motor Vehicle Thefts in 2008

National Rate = A Motor Vehicle Theft Occurs Every 33.0 Seconds*

<table>
<tr><td colspan="3">ALPHA ORDER</td><td colspan="3">RANK ORDER</td></tr>
<tr><th>RANK</th><th>STATE</th><th>HOURS.MINUTES</th><th>RANK</th><th>STATE</th><th>HOURS.MINUTES</th></tr>
<tr><td>29</td><td>Alabama</td><td>0.39</td><td>1</td><td>Vermont</td><td>15.01</td></tr>
<tr><td>8</td><td>Alaska</td><td>5.22</td><td>2</td><td>Wyoming</td><td>12.19</td></tr>
<tr><td>45</td><td>Arizona</td><td>0.14</td><td>3</td><td>South Dakota</td><td>10.59</td></tr>
<tr><td>17</td><td>Arkansas</td><td>1.21</td><td>4</td><td>North Dakota</td><td>9.58</td></tr>
<tr><td>50</td><td>California</td><td>0.03</td><td>5</td><td>Maine</td><td>7.28</td></tr>
<tr><td>29</td><td>Colorado</td><td>0.39</td><td>6</td><td>New Hampshire</td><td>6.20</td></tr>
<tr><td>22</td><td>Connecticut</td><td>0.59</td><td>7</td><td>Montana</td><td>5.35</td></tr>
<tr><td>10</td><td>Delaware</td><td>3.28</td><td>8</td><td>Alaska</td><td>5.22</td></tr>
<tr><td>48</td><td>Florida</td><td>0.08</td><td>9</td><td>Idaho</td><td>5.16</td></tr>
<tr><td>47</td><td>Georgia</td><td>0.13</td><td>10</td><td>Delaware</td><td>3.28</td></tr>
<tr><td>15</td><td>Hawaii</td><td>1.43</td><td>11</td><td>Rhode Island</td><td>2.44</td></tr>
<tr><td>9</td><td>Idaho</td><td>5.16</td><td>11</td><td>West Virginia</td><td>2.44</td></tr>
<tr><td>44</td><td>Illinois</td><td>0.16</td><td>13</td><td>Nebraska</td><td>2.06</td></tr>
<tr><td>33</td><td>Indiana</td><td>0.30</td><td>14</td><td>Iowa</td><td>2.02</td></tr>
<tr><td>14</td><td>Iowa</td><td>2.02</td><td>15</td><td>Hawaii</td><td>1.43</td></tr>
<tr><td>19</td><td>Kansas</td><td>1.11</td><td>16</td><td>Mississippi</td><td>1.23</td></tr>
<tr><td>20</td><td>Kentucky</td><td>1.09</td><td>17</td><td>Arkansas</td><td>1.21</td></tr>
<tr><td>31</td><td>Louisiana</td><td>0.38</td><td>18</td><td>Utah</td><td>1.13</td></tr>
<tr><td>5</td><td>Maine</td><td>7.28</td><td>19</td><td>Kansas</td><td>1.11</td></tr>
<tr><td>39</td><td>Maryland</td><td>0.21</td><td>20</td><td>Kentucky</td><td>1.09</td></tr>
<tr><td>27</td><td>Massachusetts</td><td>0.41</td><td>21</td><td>New Mexico</td><td>1.06</td></tr>
<tr><td>45</td><td>Michigan</td><td>0.14</td><td>22</td><td>Connecticut</td><td>0.59</td></tr>
<tr><td>23</td><td>Minnesota</td><td>0.52</td><td>23</td><td>Minnesota</td><td>0.52</td></tr>
<tr><td>16</td><td>Mississippi</td><td>1.23</td><td>24</td><td>Oklahoma</td><td>0.49</td></tr>
<tr><td>37</td><td>Missouri</td><td>0.25</td><td>25</td><td>Oregon</td><td>0.47</td></tr>
<tr><td>7</td><td>Montana</td><td>5.35</td><td>26</td><td>Wisconsin</td><td>0.46</td></tr>
<tr><td>13</td><td>Nebraska</td><td>2.06</td><td>27</td><td>Massachusetts</td><td>0.41</td></tr>
<tr><td>32</td><td>Nevada</td><td>0.33</td><td>28</td><td>Virginia</td><td>0.40</td></tr>
<tr><td>6</td><td>New Hampshire</td><td>6.20</td><td>29</td><td>Alabama</td><td>0.39</td></tr>
<tr><td>36</td><td>New Jersey</td><td>0.26</td><td>29</td><td>Colorado</td><td>0.39</td></tr>
<tr><td>21</td><td>New Mexico</td><td>1.06</td><td>31</td><td>Louisiana</td><td>0.38</td></tr>
<tr><td>39</td><td>New York</td><td>0.21</td><td>32</td><td>Nevada</td><td>0.33</td></tr>
<tr><td>41</td><td>North Carolina</td><td>0.20</td><td>33</td><td>Indiana</td><td>0.30</td></tr>
<tr><td>4</td><td>North Dakota</td><td>9.58</td><td>33</td><td>South Carolina</td><td>0.30</td></tr>
<tr><td>42</td><td>Ohio</td><td>0.19</td><td>35</td><td>Tennessee</td><td>0.28</td></tr>
<tr><td>24</td><td>Oklahoma</td><td>0.49</td><td>36</td><td>New Jersey</td><td>0.26</td></tr>
<tr><td>25</td><td>Oregon</td><td>0.47</td><td>37</td><td>Missouri</td><td>0.25</td></tr>
<tr><td>38</td><td>Pennsylvania</td><td>0.23</td><td>38</td><td>Pennsylvania</td><td>0.23</td></tr>
<tr><td>11</td><td>Rhode Island</td><td>2.44</td><td>39</td><td>Maryland</td><td>0.21</td></tr>
<tr><td>33</td><td>South Carolina</td><td>0.30</td><td>39</td><td>New York</td><td>0.21</td></tr>
<tr><td>3</td><td>South Dakota</td><td>10.59</td><td>41</td><td>North Carolina</td><td>0.20</td></tr>
<tr><td>35</td><td>Tennessee</td><td>0.28</td><td>42</td><td>Ohio</td><td>0.19</td></tr>
<tr><td>49</td><td>Texas</td><td>0.06</td><td>42</td><td>Washington</td><td>0.19</td></tr>
<tr><td>18</td><td>Utah</td><td>1.13</td><td>44</td><td>Illinois</td><td>0.16</td></tr>
<tr><td>1</td><td>Vermont</td><td>15.01</td><td>45</td><td>Arizona</td><td>0.14</td></tr>
<tr><td>28</td><td>Virginia</td><td>0.40</td><td>45</td><td>Michigan</td><td>0.14</td></tr>
<tr><td>42</td><td>Washington</td><td>0.19</td><td>47</td><td>Georgia</td><td>0.13</td></tr>
<tr><td>11</td><td>West Virginia</td><td>2.44</td><td>48</td><td>Florida</td><td>0.08</td></tr>
<tr><td>26</td><td>Wisconsin</td><td>0.46</td><td>49</td><td>Texas</td><td>0.06</td></tr>
<tr><td>2</td><td>Wyoming</td><td>12.19</td><td>50</td><td>California</td><td>0.03</td></tr>
<tr><td></td><td></td><td></td><td></td><td>District of Columbia</td><td>1.22</td></tr>
</table>

Source: CQ Press using reported data from the Federal Bureau of Investigation
"Crime in the United States 2008" (Uniform Crime Reports, September 14, 2009, http://www.fbi.gov/ucr/ucr.htm)
*Includes the theft or attempted theft of a self-propelled vehicle. Excludes motorboats, construction equipment, airplanes, and farming equipment.

Percent Change in Number of Motor Vehicle Thefts: 2007 to 2008

National Percent Change = 12.7% Decrease*

ALPHA ORDER				RANK ORDER		
RANK	STATE	PERCENT CHANGE		RANK	STATE	PERCENT CHANGE
10	Alabama	(5.4)		1	Delaware	9.7
50	Alaska	(32.3)		2	South Dakota	8.8
45	Arizona	(23.1)		3	New Hampshire	6.8
14	Arkansas	(7.1)		4	South Carolina	3.7
29	California	(12.2)		5	Rhode Island	(0.8)
41	Colorado	(19.5)		6	Connecticut	(2.2)
6	Connecticut	(2.2)		7	North Dakota	(3.5)
1	Delaware	9.7		8	Illinois	(3.9)
32	Florida	(13.8)		9	North Carolina	(4.4)
13	Georgia	(7.0)		10	Alabama	(5.4)
46	Hawaii	(23.6)		11	Virginia	(5.7)
48	Idaho	(25.1)		12	Maine	(6.6)
8	Illinois	(3.9)		13	Georgia	(7.0)
24	Indiana	(10.7)		14	Arkansas	(7.1)
27	Iowa	(11.3)		15	New Jersey	(8.1)
31	Kansas	(13.7)		16	West Virginia	(8.2)
28	Kentucky	(11.6)		17	Vermont	(8.7)
19	Louisiana	(9.5)		18	Texas	(9.1)
12	Maine	(6.6)		19	Louisiana	(9.5)
25	Maryland	(10.8)		20	Montana	(10.4)
36	Massachusetts	(15.0)		20	New York	(10.4)
34	Michigan	(14.0)		20	Wyoming	(10.4)
41	Minnesota	(19.5)		23	New Mexico	(10.5)
33	Mississippi	(13.9)		24	Indiana	(10.7)
30	Missouri	(12.7)		25	Maryland	(10.8)
20	Montana	(10.4)		26	Tennessee	(11.2)
41	Nebraska	(19.5)		27	Iowa	(11.3)
49	Nevada	(28.8)		28	Kentucky	(11.6)
3	New Hampshire	6.8		29	California	(12.2)
15	New Jersey	(8.1)		30	Missouri	(12.7)
23	New Mexico	(10.5)		31	Kansas	(13.7)
20	New York	(10.4)		32	Florida	(13.8)
9	North Carolina	(4.4)		33	Mississippi	(13.9)
7	North Dakota	(3.5)		34	Michigan	(14.0)
38	Ohio	(15.5)		35	Wisconsin	(14.2)
40	Oklahoma	(19.2)		36	Massachusetts	(15.0)
44	Oregon	(22.1)		37	Pennsylvania	(15.1)
37	Pennsylvania	(15.1)		38	Ohio	(15.5)
5	Rhode Island	(0.8)		39	Utah	(18.3)
4	South Carolina	3.7		40	Oklahoma	(19.2)
2	South Dakota	8.8		41	Colorado	(19.5)
26	Tennessee	(11.2)		41	Minnesota	(19.5)
18	Texas	(9.1)		41	Nebraska	(19.5)
39	Utah	(18.3)		44	Oregon	(22.1)
17	Vermont	(8.7)		45	Arizona	(23.1)
11	Virginia	(5.7)		46	Hawaii	(23.6)
47	Washington	(24.7)		47	Washington	(24.7)
16	West Virginia	(8.2)		48	Idaho	(25.1)
35	Wisconsin	(14.2)		49	Nevada	(28.8)
20	Wyoming	(10.4)		50	Alaska	(32.3)
					District of Columbia	(14.9)

Source: Reported data from the Federal Bureau of Investigation
   "Crime in the United States 2008" (Uniform Crime Reports, September 14, 2009, http://www.fbi.gov/ucr/ucr.htm)
*Includes the theft or attempted theft of a self-propelled vehicle. Excludes motorboats, construction equipment, airplanes, and farming equipment.

Motor Vehicle Theft Rate in 2008

National Rate = 314.7 Motor Vehicle Thefts per 100,000 Population*

ALPHA ORDER				RANK ORDER		
RANK	STATE	RATE		RANK	STATE	RATE
21	Alabama	288.7		1	Nevada	611.6
29	Alaska	238.7		2	Arizona	572.6
2	Arizona	572.6		3	California	523.8
32	Arkansas	228.0		4	Maryland	449.7
3	California	523.8		5	Washington	432.6
22	Colorado	273.7		6	Georgia	409.1
26	Connecticut	256.0		7	New Mexico	403.4
19	Delaware	291.0		8	Hawaii	398.5
13	Florida	346.5		9	South Carolina	394.0
6	Georgia	409.1		10	Michigan	362.3
8	Hawaii	398.5		11	Missouri	351.3
46	Idaho	109.5		12	Texas	350.8
27	Illinois	252.5		13	Florida	346.5
22	Indiana	273.7		14	Louisiana	311.6
42	Iowa	144.3		15	Tennessee	309.3
24	Kansas	263.9		16	Rhode Island	304.5
38	Kentucky	179.6		17	Oregon	299.0
14	Louisiana	311.6		18	Oklahoma	298.7
50	Maine	89.3		19	Delaware	291.0
4	Maryland	449.7		20	North Carolina	290.0
35	Massachusetts	196.0		21	Alabama	288.7
10	Michigan	362.3		22	Colorado	273.7
36	Minnesota	193.1		22	Indiana	273.7
33	Mississippi	216.2		24	Kansas	263.9
11	Missouri	351.3		25	Utah	262.9
41	Montana	162.6		26	Connecticut	256.0
30	Nebraska	234.8		27	Illinois	252.5
1	Nevada	611.6		28	Ohio	248.4
47	New Hampshire	105.4		29	Alaska	238.7
31	New Jersey	232.4		30	Nebraska	234.8
7	New Mexico	403.4		31	New Jersey	232.4
45	New York	128.9		32	Arkansas	228.0
20	North Carolina	290.0		33	Mississippi	216.2
43	North Dakota	137.5		34	Wisconsin	204.7
28	Ohio	248.4		35	Massachusetts	196.0
18	Oklahoma	298.7		36	Minnesota	193.1
17	Oregon	299.0		37	Pennsylvania	180.5
37	Pennsylvania	180.5		38	Kentucky	179.6
16	Rhode Island	304.5		39	West Virginia	176.6
9	South Carolina	394.0		40	Virginia	170.7
48	South Dakota	99.5		41	Montana	162.6
15	Tennessee	309.3		42	Iowa	144.3
12	Texas	350.8		43	North Dakota	137.5
25	Utah	262.9		44	Wyoming	133.9
49	Vermont	94.2		45	New York	128.9
40	Virginia	170.7		46	Idaho	109.5
5	Washington	432.6		47	New Hampshire	105.4
39	West Virginia	176.6		48	South Dakota	99.5
34	Wisconsin	204.7		49	Vermont	94.2
44	Wyoming	133.9		50	Maine	89.3
				District of Columbia		1,092.4

Source: Reported data from the Federal Bureau of Investigation
"Crime in the United States 2008" (Uniform Crime Reports, September 14, 2009, http://www.fbi.gov/ucr/ucr.htm)
*Includes the theft or attempted theft of a self-propelled vehicle. Excludes motorboats, construction equipment, airplanes, and farming equipment.

Percent Change in Motor Vehicle Theft Rate: 2007 to 2008

National Percent Change = 13.4% Decrease*

<table>
<tr><td colspan="3">ALPHA ORDER</td><td colspan="3">RANK ORDER</td></tr>
<tr><th>RANK</th><th>STATE</th><th>PERCENT CHANGE</th><th>RANK</th><th>STATE</th><th>PERCENT CHANGE</th></tr>
<tr><td>10</td><td>Alabama</td><td>(6.1)</td><td>1</td><td>Delaware</td><td>8.7</td></tr>
<tr><td>50</td><td>Alaska</td><td>(32.5)</td><td>2</td><td>South Dakota</td><td>7.8</td></tr>
<tr><td>46</td><td>Arizona</td><td>(25.0)</td><td>3</td><td>New Hampshire</td><td>6.8</td></tr>
<tr><td>13</td><td>Arkansas</td><td>(7.8)</td><td>4</td><td>South Carolina</td><td>2.0</td></tr>
<tr><td>29</td><td>California</td><td>(12.7)</td><td>5</td><td>Rhode Island</td><td>(0.1)</td></tr>
<tr><td>42</td><td>Colorado</td><td>(20.8)</td><td>6</td><td>Connecticut</td><td>(2.2)</td></tr>
<tr><td>6</td><td>Connecticut</td><td>(2.2)</td><td>7</td><td>North Dakota</td><td>(3.8)</td></tr>
<tr><td>1</td><td>Delaware</td><td>8.7</td><td>8</td><td>Illinois</td><td>(4.2)</td></tr>
<tr><td>32</td><td>Florida</td><td>(14.1)</td><td>9</td><td>North Carolina</td><td>(6.0)</td></tr>
<tr><td>15</td><td>Georgia</td><td>(8.3)</td><td>10</td><td>Alabama</td><td>(6.1)</td></tr>
<tr><td>45</td><td>Hawaii</td><td>(23.8)</td><td>11</td><td>Virginia</td><td>(6.3)</td></tr>
<tr><td>48</td><td>Idaho</td><td>(26.3)</td><td>12</td><td>Maine</td><td>(6.5)</td></tr>
<tr><td>8</td><td>Illinois</td><td>(4.2)</td><td>13</td><td>Arkansas</td><td>(7.8)</td></tr>
<tr><td>21</td><td>Indiana</td><td>(11.2)</td><td>14</td><td>New Jersey</td><td>(8.0)</td></tr>
<tr><td>24</td><td>Iowa</td><td>(11.7)</td><td>15</td><td>Georgia</td><td>(8.3)</td></tr>
<tr><td>33</td><td>Kansas</td><td>(14.5)</td><td>16</td><td>West Virginia</td><td>(8.4)</td></tr>
<tr><td>28</td><td>Kentucky</td><td>(12.2)</td><td>17</td><td>Vermont</td><td>(8.7)</td></tr>
<tr><td>25</td><td>Louisiana</td><td>(11.9)</td><td>18</td><td>Texas</td><td>(10.7)</td></tr>
<tr><td>12</td><td>Maine</td><td>(6.5)</td><td>19</td><td>Maryland</td><td>(11.0)</td></tr>
<tr><td>19</td><td>Maryland</td><td>(11.0)</td><td>20</td><td>New Mexico</td><td>(11.1)</td></tr>
<tr><td>37</td><td>Massachusetts</td><td>(15.7)</td><td>21</td><td>Indiana</td><td>(11.2)</td></tr>
<tr><td>31</td><td>Michigan</td><td>(13.4)</td><td>22</td><td>Montana</td><td>(11.3)</td></tr>
<tr><td>40</td><td>Minnesota</td><td>(19.9)</td><td>22</td><td>New York</td><td>(11.3)</td></tr>
<tr><td>33</td><td>Mississippi</td><td>(14.5)</td><td>24</td><td>Iowa</td><td>(11.7)</td></tr>
<tr><td>30</td><td>Missouri</td><td>(13.2)</td><td>25</td><td>Louisiana</td><td>(11.9)</td></tr>
<tr><td>22</td><td>Montana</td><td>(11.3)</td><td>26</td><td>Tennessee</td><td>(12.1)</td></tr>
<tr><td>40</td><td>Nebraska</td><td>(19.9)</td><td>26</td><td>Wyoming</td><td>(12.1)</td></tr>
<tr><td>49</td><td>Nevada</td><td>(29.7)</td><td>28</td><td>Kentucky</td><td>(12.2)</td></tr>
<tr><td>3</td><td>New Hampshire</td><td>6.8</td><td>29</td><td>California</td><td>(12.7)</td></tr>
<tr><td>14</td><td>New Jersey</td><td>(8.0)</td><td>30</td><td>Missouri</td><td>(13.2)</td></tr>
<tr><td>20</td><td>New Mexico</td><td>(11.1)</td><td>31</td><td>Michigan</td><td>(13.4)</td></tr>
<tr><td>22</td><td>New York</td><td>(11.3)</td><td>32</td><td>Florida</td><td>(14.1)</td></tr>
<tr><td>9</td><td>North Carolina</td><td>(6.0)</td><td>33</td><td>Kansas</td><td>(14.5)</td></tr>
<tr><td>7</td><td>North Dakota</td><td>(3.8)</td><td>33</td><td>Mississippi</td><td>(14.5)</td></tr>
<tr><td>37</td><td>Ohio</td><td>(15.7)</td><td>35</td><td>Wisconsin</td><td>(14.6)</td></tr>
<tr><td>39</td><td>Oklahoma</td><td>(19.7)</td><td>36</td><td>Pennsylvania</td><td>(15.2)</td></tr>
<tr><td>44</td><td>Oregon</td><td>(23.0)</td><td>37</td><td>Massachusetts</td><td>(15.7)</td></tr>
<tr><td>36</td><td>Pennsylvania</td><td>(15.2)</td><td>37</td><td>Ohio</td><td>(15.7)</td></tr>
<tr><td>5</td><td>Rhode Island</td><td>(0.1)</td><td>39</td><td>Oklahoma</td><td>(19.7)</td></tr>
<tr><td>4</td><td>South Carolina</td><td>2.0</td><td>40</td><td>Minnesota</td><td>(19.9)</td></tr>
<tr><td>2</td><td>South Dakota</td><td>7.8</td><td>40</td><td>Nebraska</td><td>(19.9)</td></tr>
<tr><td>26</td><td>Tennessee</td><td>(12.1)</td><td>42</td><td>Colorado</td><td>(20.8)</td></tr>
<tr><td>18</td><td>Texas</td><td>(10.7)</td><td>43</td><td>Utah</td><td>(21.1)</td></tr>
<tr><td>43</td><td>Utah</td><td>(21.1)</td><td>44</td><td>Oregon</td><td>(23.0)</td></tr>
<tr><td>17</td><td>Vermont</td><td>(8.7)</td><td>45</td><td>Hawaii</td><td>(23.8)</td></tr>
<tr><td>11</td><td>Virginia</td><td>(6.3)</td><td>46</td><td>Arizona</td><td>(25.0)</td></tr>
<tr><td>47</td><td>Washington</td><td>(25.6)</td><td>47</td><td>Washington</td><td>(25.6)</td></tr>
<tr><td>16</td><td>West Virginia</td><td>(8.4)</td><td>48</td><td>Idaho</td><td>(26.3)</td></tr>
<tr><td>35</td><td>Wisconsin</td><td>(14.6)</td><td>49</td><td>Nevada</td><td>(29.7)</td></tr>
<tr><td>26</td><td>Wyoming</td><td>(12.1)</td><td>50</td><td>Alaska</td><td>(32.5)</td></tr>
<tr><td></td><td></td><td></td><td></td><td>District of Columbia</td><td>(15.4)</td></tr>
</table>

Source: Reported data from the Federal Bureau of Investigation
"Crime in the United States 2008" (Uniform Crime Reports, September 14, 2009, http://www.fbi.gov/ucr/ucr.htm)
*Includes the theft or attempted theft of a self-propelled vehicle. Excludes motorboats, construction equipment, airplanes, and farming equipment.

Crimes in Urban Areas in 2008

National Urban Total = 10,582,191 Crimes*

ALPHA ORDER

ALPHA ORDER

RANK	STATE	CRIMES	% of USA
18	Alabama	199,317	1.9%
45	Alaska	19,653	0.2%
10	Arizona	303,619	2.9%
27	Arkansas	112,016	1.1%
1	California	1,255,451	11.9%
23	Colorado	153,005	1.4%
32	Connecticut	90,830	0.9%
39	Delaware	32,910	0.3%
3	Florida	858,658	8.1%
6	Georgia	406,953	3.8%
38	Hawaii	34,356	0.3%
41	Idaho	32,024	0.3%
NA	Illinois**	NA	NA
16	Indiana	221,906	2.1%
35	Iowa	75,924	0.7%
30	Kansas	100,419	0.9%
29	Kentucky	102,952	1.0%
21	Louisiana	176,651	1.7%
42	Maine	29,483	0.3%
14	Maryland	228,277	2.2%
20	Massachusetts	185,133	1.7%
9	Michigan	322,064	3.0%
24	Minnesota	138,813	1.3%
34	Mississippi	77,897	0.7%
13	Missouri	232,601	2.2%
44	Montana	20,398	0.2%
36	Nebraska	52,843	0.5%
28	Nevada	104,747	1.0%
43	New Hampshire	29,265	0.3%
15	New Jersey	227,477	2.1%
33	New Mexico	85,111	0.8%
4	New York	450,185	4.3%
7	North Carolina	362,778	3.4%
49	North Dakota	11,750	0.1%
5	Ohio	408,799	3.9%
25	Oklahoma	135,105	1.3%
26	Oregon	126,989	1.2%
8	Pennsylvania	333,311	3.1%
40	Rhode Island	32,380	0.3%
19	South Carolina	189,686	1.8%
47	South Dakota	13,563	0.1%
11	Tennessee	269,936	2.6%
2	Texas	1,066,538	10.1%
31	Utah	95,400	0.9%
48	Vermont	13,317	0.1%
17	Virginia	202,262	1.9%
12	Washington	256,739	2.4%
37	West Virginia	40,619	0.4%
22	Wisconsin	158,952	1.5%
46	Wyoming	13,832	0.1%

RANK ORDER

RANK	STATE	CRIMES	% of USA
1	California	1,255,451	11.9%
2	Texas	1,066,538	10.1%
3	Florida	858,658	8.1%
4	New York	450,185	4.3%
5	Ohio	408,799	3.9%
6	Georgia	406,953	3.8%
7	North Carolina	362,778	3.4%
8	Pennsylvania	333,311	3.1%
9	Michigan	322,064	3.0%
10	Arizona	303,619	2.9%
11	Tennessee	269,936	2.6%
12	Washington	256,739	2.4%
13	Missouri	232,601	2.2%
14	Maryland	228,277	2.2%
15	New Jersey	227,477	2.1%
16	Indiana	221,906	2.1%
17	Virginia	202,262	1.9%
18	Alabama	199,317	1.9%
19	South Carolina	189,686	1.8%
20	Massachusetts	185,133	1.7%
21	Louisiana	176,651	1.7%
22	Wisconsin	158,952	1.5%
23	Colorado	153,005	1.4%
24	Minnesota	138,813	1.3%
25	Oklahoma	135,105	1.3%
26	Oregon	126,989	1.2%
27	Arkansas	112,016	1.1%
28	Nevada	104,747	1.0%
29	Kentucky	102,952	1.0%
30	Kansas	100,419	0.9%
31	Utah	95,400	0.9%
32	Connecticut	90,830	0.9%
33	New Mexico	85,111	0.8%
34	Mississippi	77,897	0.7%
35	Iowa	75,924	0.7%
36	Nebraska	52,843	0.5%
37	West Virginia	40,619	0.4%
38	Hawaii	34,356	0.3%
39	Delaware	32,910	0.3%
40	Rhode Island	32,380	0.3%
41	Idaho	32,024	0.3%
42	Maine	29,483	0.3%
43	New Hampshire	29,265	0.3%
44	Montana	20,398	0.2%
45	Alaska	19,653	0.2%
46	Wyoming	13,832	0.1%
47	South Dakota	13,563	0.1%
48	Vermont	13,317	0.1%
49	North Dakota	11,750	0.1%
NA	Illinois**	NA	NA
	District of Columbia	38,720	0.4%

Source: CQ Press using reported data from the Federal Bureau of Investigation
   "Crime in the United States 2008" (Uniform Crime Reports, September 14, 2009, http://www.fbi.gov/ucr/ucr.htm)
*Estimated totals for urban areas, defined by the F.B.I. as Metropolitan Statistical Areas and other cities outside such areas.
National total includes those states listed as not available. Includes murder, rape, robbery, aggravated assault, burglary,
larceny-theft, and motor vehicle theft.
**Not available.

Urban Crime Rate in 2008

National Urban Rate = 3,862.7 Crimes per 100,000 Population*

ALPHA ORDER

RANK	STATE	RATE
3	Alabama	5,075.2
16	Alaska	4,271.3
8	Arizona	4,869.6
4	Arkansas	5,070.5
30	California	3,468.9
33	Colorado	3,348.8
39	Connecticut	3,048.3
13	Delaware	4,527.4
7	Florida	4,921.6
10	Georgia	4,751.2
24	Hawaii	3,790.6
46	Idaho	2,586.5
NA	Illinois**	NA
21	Indiana	4,042.1
34	Iowa	3,338.0
20	Kansas	4,054.9
31	Kentucky	3,461.0
9	Louisiana	4,834.1
43	Maine	2,819.9
18	Maryland	4,218.5
42	Massachusetts	2,849.2
28	Michigan	3,660.4
37	Minnesota	3,151.7
19	Mississippi	4,130.6
12	Missouri	4,585.8
25	Montana	3,703.2
27	Nebraska	3,690.2
15	Nevada	4,396.2
49	New Hampshire	2,308.9
44	New Jersey	2,619.9
5	New Mexico	4,967.5
47	New York	2,432.2
6	North Carolina	4,947.5
45	North Dakota	2,617.5
22	Ohio	4,012.2
14	Oklahoma	4,458.2
23	Oregon	3,796.4
40	Pennsylvania	2,926.7
38	Rhode Island	3,081.5
2	South Carolina	5,146.9
48	South Dakota	2,351.2
1	Tennessee	5,227.7
11	Texas	4,695.1
26	Utah	3,692.7
36	Vermont	3,222.5
41	Virginia	2,917.4
17	Washington	4,222.1
35	West Virginia	3,304.1
32	Wisconsin	3,364.7
29	Wyoming	3,651.2

RANK ORDER

RANK	STATE	RATE
1	Tennessee	5,227.7
2	South Carolina	5,146.9
3	Alabama	5,075.2
4	Arkansas	5,070.5
5	New Mexico	4,967.5
6	North Carolina	4,947.5
7	Florida	4,921.6
8	Arizona	4,869.6
9	Louisiana	4,834.1
10	Georgia	4,751.2
11	Texas	4,695.1
12	Missouri	4,585.8
13	Delaware	4,527.4
14	Oklahoma	4,458.2
15	Nevada	4,396.2
16	Alaska	4,271.3
17	Washington	4,222.1
18	Maryland	4,218.5
19	Mississippi	4,130.6
20	Kansas	4,054.9
21	Indiana	4,042.1
22	Ohio	4,012.2
23	Oregon	3,796.4
24	Hawaii	3,790.6
25	Montana	3,703.2
26	Utah	3,692.7
27	Nebraska	3,690.2
28	Michigan	3,660.4
29	Wyoming	3,651.2
30	California	3,468.9
31	Kentucky	3,461.0
32	Wisconsin	3,364.7
33	Colorado	3,348.8
34	Iowa	3,338.0
35	West Virginia	3,304.1
36	Vermont	3,222.5
37	Minnesota	3,151.7
38	Rhode Island	3,081.5
39	Connecticut	3,048.3
40	Pennsylvania	2,926.7
41	Virginia	2,917.4
42	Massachusetts	2,849.2
43	Maine	2,819.9
44	New Jersey	2,619.9
45	North Dakota	2,617.5
46	Idaho	2,586.5
47	New York	2,432.2
48	South Dakota	2,351.2
49	New Hampshire	2,308.9
NA	Illinois**	NA
	District of Columbia	6,542.4

Source: CQ Press using reported data from the Federal Bureau of Investigation
"Crime in the United States 2008" (Uniform Crime Reports, September 14, 2009, http://www.fbi.gov/ucr/ucr.htm)
*Estimated rates for urban areas, defined by the F.B.I. as Metropolitan Statistical Areas and other cities outside such areas.
National rate includes those states listed as not available. Includes murder, rape, robbery, aggravated assault, burglary,
larceny-theft, and motor vehicle theft.
**Not available.

Percent of Crimes Occurring in Urban Areas in 2008

National Percent = 94.9% of Crimes*

<table>
<tr><td colspan="3">ALPHA ORDER</td><td colspan="3">RANK ORDER</td></tr>
<tr><td>RANK</td><td>STATE</td><td>PERCENT</td><td>RANK</td><td>STATE</td><td>PERCENT</td></tr>
<tr><td>21</td><td>Alabama</td><td>94.3</td><td>1</td><td>Massachusetts</td><td>100.0</td></tr>
<tr><td>46</td><td>Alaska</td><td>79.9</td><td>1</td><td>New Jersey</td><td>100.0</td></tr>
<tr><td>6</td><td>Arizona</td><td>98.6</td><td>3</td><td>Rhode Island</td><td>99.7</td></tr>
<tr><td>33</td><td>Arkansas</td><td>90.4</td><td>4</td><td>California</td><td>99.2</td></tr>
<tr><td>4</td><td>California</td><td>99.2</td><td>5</td><td>New Hampshire</td><td>98.9</td></tr>
<tr><td>10</td><td>Colorado</td><td>97.0</td><td>6</td><td>Arizona</td><td>98.6</td></tr>
<tr><td>22</td><td>Connecticut</td><td>94.1</td><td>7</td><td>Maryland</td><td>97.7</td></tr>
<tr><td>38</td><td>Delaware</td><td>87.9</td><td>8</td><td>Texas</td><td>97.6</td></tr>
<tr><td>10</td><td>Florida</td><td>97.0</td><td>9</td><td>Utah</td><td>97.4</td></tr>
<tr><td>26</td><td>Georgia</td><td>93.5</td><td>10</td><td>Colorado</td><td>97.0</td></tr>
<tr><td>49</td><td>Hawaii</td><td>69.4</td><td>10</td><td>Florida</td><td>97.0</td></tr>
<tr><td>34</td><td>Idaho</td><td>90.2</td><td>12</td><td>Nevada</td><td>96.6</td></tr>
<tr><td>NA</td><td>Illinois**</td><td>NA</td><td>12</td><td>New York</td><td>96.6</td></tr>
<tr><td>16</td><td>Indiana</td><td>94.8</td><td>14</td><td>Washington</td><td>95.9</td></tr>
<tr><td>26</td><td>Iowa</td><td>93.5</td><td>15</td><td>Pennsylvania</td><td>94.9</td></tr>
<tr><td>19</td><td>Kansas</td><td>94.6</td><td>16</td><td>Indiana</td><td>94.8</td></tr>
<tr><td>43</td><td>Kentucky</td><td>83.7</td><td>17</td><td>Ohio</td><td>94.7</td></tr>
<tr><td>35</td><td>Louisiana</td><td>89.4</td><td>17</td><td>Oregon</td><td>94.7</td></tr>
<tr><td>40</td><td>Maine</td><td>87.1</td><td>19</td><td>Kansas</td><td>94.6</td></tr>
<tr><td>7</td><td>Maryland</td><td>97.7</td><td>20</td><td>Missouri</td><td>94.4</td></tr>
<tr><td>1</td><td>Massachusetts</td><td>100.0</td><td>21</td><td>Alabama</td><td>94.3</td></tr>
<tr><td>25</td><td>Michigan</td><td>93.7</td><td>22</td><td>Connecticut</td><td>94.1</td></tr>
<tr><td>41</td><td>Minnesota</td><td>85.4</td><td>22</td><td>New Mexico</td><td>94.1</td></tr>
<tr><td>44</td><td>Mississippi</td><td>82.2</td><td>24</td><td>Virginia</td><td>93.9</td></tr>
<tr><td>20</td><td>Missouri</td><td>94.4</td><td>25</td><td>Michigan</td><td>93.7</td></tr>
<tr><td>48</td><td>Montana</td><td>73.7</td><td>26</td><td>Georgia</td><td>93.5</td></tr>
<tr><td>30</td><td>Nebraska</td><td>93.1</td><td>26</td><td>Iowa</td><td>93.5</td></tr>
<tr><td>12</td><td>Nevada</td><td>96.6</td><td>26</td><td>Oklahoma</td><td>93.5</td></tr>
<tr><td>5</td><td>New Hampshire</td><td>98.9</td><td>29</td><td>Wisconsin</td><td>93.2</td></tr>
<tr><td>1</td><td>New Jersey</td><td>100.0</td><td>30</td><td>Nebraska</td><td>93.1</td></tr>
<tr><td>22</td><td>New Mexico</td><td>94.1</td><td>31</td><td>South Dakota</td><td>91.3</td></tr>
<tr><td>12</td><td>New York</td><td>96.6</td><td>32</td><td>Tennessee</td><td>91.2</td></tr>
<tr><td>39</td><td>North Carolina</td><td>87.2</td><td>33</td><td>Arkansas</td><td>90.4</td></tr>
<tr><td>36</td><td>North Dakota</td><td>88.9</td><td>34</td><td>Idaho</td><td>90.2</td></tr>
<tr><td>17</td><td>Ohio</td><td>94.7</td><td>35</td><td>Louisiana</td><td>89.4</td></tr>
<tr><td>26</td><td>Oklahoma</td><td>93.5</td><td>36</td><td>North Dakota</td><td>88.9</td></tr>
<tr><td>17</td><td>Oregon</td><td>94.7</td><td>37</td><td>Wyoming</td><td>88.0</td></tr>
<tr><td>15</td><td>Pennsylvania</td><td>94.9</td><td>38</td><td>Delaware</td><td>87.9</td></tr>
<tr><td>3</td><td>Rhode Island</td><td>99.7</td><td>39</td><td>North Carolina</td><td>87.2</td></tr>
<tr><td>42</td><td>South Carolina</td><td>85.3</td><td>40</td><td>Maine</td><td>87.1</td></tr>
<tr><td>31</td><td>South Dakota</td><td>91.3</td><td>41</td><td>Minnesota</td><td>85.4</td></tr>
<tr><td>32</td><td>Tennessee</td><td>91.2</td><td>42</td><td>South Carolina</td><td>85.3</td></tr>
<tr><td>8</td><td>Texas</td><td>97.6</td><td>43</td><td>Kentucky</td><td>83.7</td></tr>
<tr><td>9</td><td>Utah</td><td>97.4</td><td>44</td><td>Mississippi</td><td>82.2</td></tr>
<tr><td>45</td><td>Vermont</td><td>80.2</td><td>45</td><td>Vermont</td><td>80.2</td></tr>
<tr><td>24</td><td>Virginia</td><td>93.9</td><td>46</td><td>Alaska</td><td>79.9</td></tr>
<tr><td>14</td><td>Washington</td><td>95.9</td><td>47</td><td>West Virginia</td><td>78.8</td></tr>
<tr><td>47</td><td>West Virginia</td><td>78.8</td><td>48</td><td>Montana</td><td>73.7</td></tr>
<tr><td>29</td><td>Wisconsin</td><td>93.2</td><td>49</td><td>Hawaii</td><td>69.4</td></tr>
<tr><td>37</td><td>Wyoming</td><td>88.0</td><td>NA</td><td>Illinois**</td><td>NA</td></tr>
<tr><td></td><td></td><td></td><td></td><td>District of Columbia</td><td>100.0</td></tr>
</table>

Source: CQ Press using reported data from the Federal Bureau of Investigation
   "Crime in the United States 2008" (Uniform Crime Reports, September 14, 2009, http://www.fbi.gov/ucr/ucr.htm)
*Estimated percentages for urban areas, defined by the F.B.I. as Metropolitan Statistical Areas and other cities outside such areas. National percent includes those states listed as not available. Includes murder, rape, robbery, aggravated assault, burglary, larceny-theft, and motor vehicle theft.
**Not available.

Crimes in Rural Areas in 2008

National Rural Total = 567,736 Crimes*

ALPHA ORDER					RANK ORDER			
RANK	STATE	CRIMES	% of USA		RANK	STATE	CRIMES	% of USA
17	Alabama	12,137	2.1%		1	North Carolina	53,282	9.4%
33	Alaska	4,945	0.9%		2	South Carolina	32,688	5.8%
36	Arizona	4,360	0.8%		3	Georgia	28,366	5.0%
19	Arkansas	11,866	2.1%		4	Texas	26,596	4.7%
23	California	10,469	1.8%		5	Florida	26,541	4.7%
34	Colorado	4,666	0.8%		6	Tennessee	26,206	4.6%
29	Connecticut	5,684	1.0%		7	Ohio	23,060	4.1%
35	Delaware	4,534	0.8%		8	Michigan	21,687	3.8%
5	Florida	26,541	4.7%		9	Louisiana	20,923	3.7%
3	Georgia	28,366	5.0%		10	Kentucky	20,008	3.5%
14	Hawaii	15,160	2.7%		11	Pennsylvania	17,757	3.1%
40	Idaho	3,478	0.6%		12	Mississippi	16,884	3.0%
NA	Illinois**	NA	NA		13	New York	15,933	2.8%
18	Indiana	12,092	2.1%		14	Hawaii	15,160	2.7%
31	Iowa	5,285	0.9%		15	Missouri	13,803	2.4%
28	Kansas	5,721	1.0%		16	Virginia	13,254	2.3%
10	Kentucky	20,008	3.5%		17	Alabama	12,137	2.1%
9	Louisiana	20,923	3.7%		18	Indiana	12,092	2.1%
37	Maine	4,349	0.8%		19	Arkansas	11,866	2.1%
32	Maryland	5,281	0.9%		20	Wisconsin	11,596	2.0%
48	Massachusetts	0	0.0%		21	Washington	11,100	2.0%
8	Michigan	21,687	3.8%		22	West Virginia	10,956	1.9%
24	Minnesota	9,997	1.8%		23	California	10,469	1.8%
12	Mississippi	16,884	3.0%		24	Minnesota	9,997	1.8%
15	Missouri	13,803	2.4%		25	Oklahoma	9,463	1.7%
26	Montana	7,281	1.3%		26	Montana	7,281	1.3%
38	Nebraska	3,911	0.7%		27	Oregon	7,155	1.3%
39	Nevada	3,730	0.7%		28	Kansas	5,721	1.0%
46	New Hampshire	330	0.1%		29	Connecticut	5,684	1.0%
48	New Jersey	0	0.0%		30	New Mexico	5,357	0.9%
30	New Mexico	5,357	0.9%		31	Iowa	5,285	0.9%
13	New York	15,933	2.8%		32	Maryland	5,281	0.9%
1	North Carolina	53,282	9.4%		33	Alaska	4,945	0.9%
44	North Dakota	1,470	0.3%		34	Colorado	4,666	0.8%
7	Ohio	23,060	4.1%		35	Delaware	4,534	0.8%
25	Oklahoma	9,463	1.7%		36	Arizona	4,360	0.8%
27	Oregon	7,155	1.3%		37	Maine	4,349	0.8%
11	Pennsylvania	17,757	3.1%		38	Nebraska	3,911	0.7%
47	Rhode Island	90	0.0%		39	Nevada	3,730	0.7%
2	South Carolina	32,688	5.8%		40	Idaho	3,478	0.6%
45	South Dakota	1,291	0.2%		41	Vermont	3,298	0.6%
6	Tennessee	26,206	4.6%		42	Utah	2,543	0.4%
4	Texas	26,596	4.7%		43	Wyoming	1,878	0.3%
42	Utah	2,543	0.4%		44	North Dakota	1,470	0.3%
41	Vermont	3,298	0.6%		45	South Dakota	1,291	0.2%
16	Virginia	13,254	2.3%		46	New Hampshire	330	0.1%
21	Washington	11,100	2.0%		47	Rhode Island	90	0.0%
22	West Virginia	10,956	1.9%		48	Massachusetts	0	0.0%
20	Wisconsin	11,596	2.0%		48	New Jersey	0	0.0%
43	Wyoming	1,878	0.3%		NA	Illinois**	NA	NA
						District of Columbia	0	0.0%

Source: CQ Press using reported data from the Federal Bureau of Investigation
    "Crime in the United States 2008" (Uniform Crime Reports, September 14, 2009, http://www.fbi.gov/ucr/ucr.htm)
*Estimated totals for nonmetropolitan areas, defined by the F.B.I. as other than Metropolitan Statistical Areas and other cities
outside such areas. National total includes those states listed as not available. Includes murder, rape, robbery, aggravated
assault, burglary, larceny-theft, and motor vehicle theft.
**Not available.

Rural Crime Rate in 2008

National Rural Rate = 1,886.2 Crimes per 100,000 Population*

ALPHA ORDER

RANK	STATE	RATE
23	Alabama	1,652.1
11	Alaska	2,186.4
26	Arizona	1,644.0
15	Arkansas	1,836.2
14	California	1,852.4
37	Colorado	1,259.2
42	Connecticut	1,089.7
3	Delaware	3,101.7
4	Florida	3,010.8
7	Georgia	2,531.6
2	Hawaii	3,970.2
40	Idaho	1,217.3
NA	Illinois**	NA
35	Indiana	1,363.4
44	Iowa	726.0
18	Kansas	1,756.7
34	Kentucky	1,545.4
6	Louisiana	2,765.6
29	Maine	1,605.3
9	Maryland	2,375.6
47	Massachusetts	0.0
16	Michigan	1,800.2
38	Minnesota	1,225.2
30	Mississippi	1,603.8
25	Missouri	1,644.5
19	Montana	1,747.7
41	Nebraska	1,112.9
20	Nevada	1,715.2
45	New Hampshire	683.0
47	New Jersey	0.0
12	New Mexico	1,976.9
27	New York	1,624.0
5	North Carolina	2,819.4
43	North Dakota	763.4
17	Ohio	1,778.0
33	Oklahoma	1,546.6
28	Oregon	1,607.7
21	Pennsylvania	1,675.7
47	Rhode Island	0.0
1	South Carolina	4,114.9
46	South Dakota	567.9
8	Tennessee	2,492.7
24	Texas	1,650.8
22	Utah	1,662.9
31	Vermont	1,585.5
32	Virginia	1,584.9
10	Washington	2,369.5
13	West Virginia	1,872.5
36	Wisconsin	1,282.9
39	Wyoming	1,220.8

RANK ORDER

RANK	STATE	RATE
1	South Carolina	4,114.9
2	Hawaii	3,970.2
3	Delaware	3,101.7
4	Florida	3,010.8
5	North Carolina	2,819.4
6	Louisiana	2,765.6
7	Georgia	2,531.6
8	Tennessee	2,492.7
9	Maryland	2,375.6
10	Washington	2,369.5
11	Alaska	2,186.4
12	New Mexico	1,976.9
13	West Virginia	1,872.5
14	California	1,852.4
15	Arkansas	1,836.2
16	Michigan	1,800.2
17	Ohio	1,778.0
18	Kansas	1,756.7
19	Montana	1,747.7
20	Nevada	1,715.2
21	Pennsylvania	1,675.7
22	Utah	1,662.9
23	Alabama	1,652.1
24	Texas	1,650.8
25	Missouri	1,644.5
26	Arizona	1,644.0
27	New York	1,624.0
28	Oregon	1,607.7
29	Maine	1,605.3
30	Mississippi	1,603.8
31	Vermont	1,585.5
32	Virginia	1,584.9
33	Oklahoma	1,546.6
34	Kentucky	1,545.4
35	Indiana	1,363.4
36	Wisconsin	1,282.9
37	Colorado	1,259.2
38	Minnesota	1,225.2
39	Wyoming	1,220.8
40	Idaho	1,217.3
41	Nebraska	1,112.9
42	Connecticut	1,089.7
43	North Dakota	763.4
44	Iowa	726.0
45	New Hampshire	683.0
46	South Dakota	567.9
47	Massachusetts	0.0
47	New Jersey	0.0
47	Rhode Island	0.0
NA	Illinois**	NA

District of Columbia   0.0

Source: CQ Press using reported data from the Federal Bureau of Investigation
"Crime in the United States 2008" (Uniform Crime Reports, September 14, 2009, http://www.fbi.gov/ucr/ucr.htm)
*Estimated rates for nonmetropolitan areas, defined by the F.B.I. as other than Metropolitan Statistical Areas and other cities outside such areas. National rate includes those states listed as not available. Includes murder, rape, robbery, aggravated assault, burglary, larceny-theft, and motor vehicle theft.
**Not available.

Percent of Crimes Occurring in Rural Areas in 2008

National Percent = 5.1% of Crimes*

ALPHA ORDER				RANK ORDER		
RANK	STATE	PERCENT		RANK	STATE	PERCENT
29	Alabama	5.7		1	Hawaii	30.6
4	Alaska	20.1		2	Montana	26.3
44	Arizona	1.4		3	West Virginia	21.2
16	Arkansas	9.6		4	Alaska	20.1
46	California	0.8		5	Vermont	19.8
39	Colorado	3.0		6	Mississippi	17.8
27	Connecticut	5.9		7	Kentucky	16.3
11	Delaware	12.1		8	South Carolina	14.7
39	Florida	3.0		9	Maine	12.9
21	Georgia	6.5		10	North Carolina	12.8
1	Hawaii	30.6		11	Delaware	12.1
15	Idaho	9.8		12	Wyoming	12.0
NA	Illinois**	NA		13	North Dakota	11.1
34	Indiana	5.2		14	Louisiana	10.6
21	Iowa	6.5		15	Idaho	9.8
31	Kansas	5.4		16	Arkansas	9.6
7	Kentucky	16.3		17	Tennessee	8.8
14	Louisiana	10.6		18	South Dakota	8.7
9	Maine	12.9		19	Nebraska	6.9
43	Maryland	2.3		20	Wisconsin	6.8
48	Massachusetts	0.0		21	Georgia	6.5
24	Michigan	6.3		21	Iowa	6.5
25	Minnesota	6.2		21	Oklahoma	6.5
6	Mississippi	17.8		24	Michigan	6.3
30	Missouri	5.6		25	Minnesota	6.2
2	Montana	26.3		26	Virginia	6.1
19	Nebraska	6.9		27	Connecticut	5.9
37	Nevada	3.4		27	New Mexico	5.9
45	New Hampshire	1.1		29	Alabama	5.7
48	New Jersey	0.0		30	Missouri	5.6
27	New Mexico	5.9		31	Kansas	5.4
37	New York	3.4		32	Ohio	5.3
10	North Carolina	12.8		32	Oregon	5.3
13	North Dakota	11.1		34	Indiana	5.2
32	Ohio	5.3		35	Pennsylvania	5.1
21	Oklahoma	6.5		36	Washington	4.1
32	Oregon	5.3		37	Nevada	3.4
35	Pennsylvania	5.1		37	New York	3.4
47	Rhode Island	0.3		39	Colorado	3.0
8	South Carolina	14.7		39	Florida	3.0
18	South Dakota	8.7		41	Utah	2.6
17	Tennessee	8.8		42	Texas	2.4
42	Texas	2.4		43	Maryland	2.3
41	Utah	2.6		44	Arizona	1.4
5	Vermont	19.8		45	New Hampshire	1.1
26	Virginia	6.1		46	California	0.8
36	Washington	4.1		47	Rhode Island	0.3
3	West Virginia	21.2		48	Massachusetts	0.0
20	Wisconsin	6.8		48	New Jersey	0.0
12	Wyoming	12.0		NA	Illinois**	NA

District of Columbia 0.0

Source: CQ Press using reported data from the Federal Bureau of Investigation
    "Crime in the United States 2008" (Uniform Crime Reports, September 14, 2009, http://www.fbi.gov/ucr/ucr.htm)
*Estimated percentages for nonmetropolitan areas, defined by the F.B.I. as other than Metropolitan Statistical Areas and other cities outside such areas. National percent includes those states listed as not available. Includes murder, rape, robbery, aggravated assault, burglary, larceny-theft, and motor vehicle theft.
**Not available.

Violent Crimes in Urban Areas in 2008

National Urban Total = 1,320,279 Violent Crimes*

ALPHA ORDER

RANK	STATE	CRIMES	% of USA
20	Alabama	19,826	1.5%
38	Alaska	3,703	0.3%
14	Arizona	28,091	2.1%
26	Arkansas	13,129	1.0%
1	California	183,341	13.9%
24	Colorado	16,307	1.2%
30	Connecticut	10,031	0.8%
35	Delaware	5,410	0.4%
2	Florida	122,167	9.3%
7	Georgia	43,543	3.3%
41	Hawaii	2,575	0.2%
39	Idaho	3,098	0.2%
NA	Illinois**	NA	NA
19	Indiana	20,570	1.6%
32	Iowa	7,909	0.6%
29	Kansas	10,785	0.8%
28	Kentucky	10,827	0.8%
17	Louisiana	25,040	1.9%
45	Maine	1,354	0.1%
11	Maryland	34,750	2.6%
12	Massachusetts	29,174	2.2%
6	Michigan	47,889	3.6%
NA	Minnesota**	NA	NA
33	Mississippi	6,446	0.5%
15	Missouri	27,919	2.1%
43	Montana	1,524	0.1%
36	Nebraska	5,170	0.4%
22	Nevada	18,333	1.4%
42	New Hampshire	2,017	0.2%
13	New Jersey	28,351	2.1%
27	New Mexico	11,987	0.9%
4	New York	76,056	5.8%
10	North Carolina	38,146	2.9%
47	North Dakota	961	0.1%
9	Ohio	38,926	2.9%
23	Oklahoma	17,845	1.4%
31	Oregon	9,357	0.7%
5	Pennsylvania	49,478	3.7%
40	Rhode Island	2,606	0.2%
16	South Carolina	27,827	2.1%
44	South Dakota	1,404	0.1%
8	Tennessee	41,679	3.2%
3	Texas	120,362	9.1%
34	Utah	5,876	0.4%
48	Vermont	675	0.1%
21	Virginia	18,648	1.4%
18	Washington	21,054	1.6%
37	West Virginia	3,743	0.3%
25	Wisconsin	14,702	1.1%
46	Wyoming	1,028	0.1%

RANK ORDER

RANK	STATE	CRIMES	% of USA
1	California	183,341	13.9%
2	Florida	122,167	9.3%
3	Texas	120,362	9.1%
4	New York	76,056	5.8%
5	Pennsylvania	49,478	3.7%
6	Michigan	47,889	3.6%
7	Georgia	43,543	3.3%
8	Tennessee	41,679	3.2%
9	Ohio	38,926	2.9%
10	North Carolina	38,146	2.9%
11	Maryland	34,750	2.6%
12	Massachusetts	29,174	2.2%
13	New Jersey	28,351	2.1%
14	Arizona	28,091	2.1%
15	Missouri	27,919	2.1%
16	South Carolina	27,827	2.1%
17	Louisiana	25,040	1.9%
18	Washington	21,054	1.6%
19	Indiana	20,570	1.6%
20	Alabama	19,826	1.5%
21	Virginia	18,648	1.4%
22	Nevada	18,333	1.4%
23	Oklahoma	17,845	1.4%
24	Colorado	16,307	1.2%
25	Wisconsin	14,702	1.1%
26	Arkansas	13,129	1.0%
27	New Mexico	11,987	0.9%
28	Kentucky	10,827	0.8%
29	Kansas	10,785	0.8%
30	Connecticut	10,031	0.8%
31	Oregon	9,357	0.7%
32	Iowa	7,909	0.6%
33	Mississippi	6,446	0.5%
34	Utah	5,876	0.4%
35	Delaware	5,410	0.4%
36	Nebraska	5,170	0.4%
37	West Virginia	3,743	0.3%
38	Alaska	3,703	0.3%
39	Idaho	3,098	0.2%
40	Rhode Island	2,606	0.2%
41	Hawaii	2,575	0.2%
42	New Hampshire	2,017	0.2%
43	Montana	1,524	0.1%
44	South Dakota	1,404	0.1%
45	Maine	1,354	0.1%
46	Wyoming	1,028	0.1%
47	North Dakota	961	0.1%
48	Vermont	675	0.1%
NA	Illinois**	NA	NA
NA	Minnesota**	NA	NA
	District of Columbia	8,509	0.6%

Source: CQ Press using reported data from the Federal Bureau of Investigation
"Crime in the United States 2008" (Uniform Crime Reports, September 14, 2009, http://www.fbi.gov/ucr/ucr.htm)
*Estimated totals for urban areas, defined by the F.B.I. as Metropolitan Statistical Areas and other cities outside such areas.
National total includes those states listed as not available. Violent crimes are offenses of murder, forcible rape, robbery, and aggravated assault.
**Not available.

Urban Violent Crime Rate in 2008

National Urban Rate = 481.9 Violent Crimes per 100,000 Population*

ALPHA ORDER

RANK	STATE	RATE
18	Alabama	504.8
2	Alaska	804.8
19	Arizona	450.5
10	Arkansas	594.3
17	California	506.6
28	Colorado	356.9
32	Connecticut	336.7
5	Delaware	744.2
6	Florida	700.2
16	Georgia	508.4
36	Hawaii	284.1
41	Idaho	250.2
NA	Illinois**	NA
25	Indiana	374.7
29	Iowa	347.7
21	Kansas	435.5
26	Kentucky	364.0
8	Louisiana	685.2
48	Maine	129.5
9	Maryland	642.2
20	Massachusetts	449.0
13	Michigan	544.3
NA	Minnesota**	NA
31	Mississippi	341.8
12	Missouri	550.4
38	Montana	276.7
27	Nebraska	361.0
3	Nevada	769.4
47	New Hampshire	159.1
33	New Jersey	326.5
7	New Mexico	699.6
23	New York	410.9
15	North Carolina	520.2
45	North Dakota	214.1
24	Ohio	382.0
11	Oklahoma	588.8
37	Oregon	279.7
22	Pennsylvania	434.5
42	Rhode Island	248.0
4	South Carolina	755.1
43	South Dakota	243.4
1	Tennessee	807.2
14	Texas	529.9
44	Utah	227.4
46	Vermont	163.3
40	Virginia	269.0
30	Washington	346.2
35	West Virginia	304.5
34	Wisconsin	311.2
39	Wyoming	271.4

RANK ORDER

RANK	STATE	RATE
1	Tennessee	807.2
2	Alaska	804.8
3	Nevada	769.4
4	South Carolina	755.1
5	Delaware	744.2
6	Florida	700.2
7	New Mexico	699.6
8	Louisiana	685.2
9	Maryland	642.2
10	Arkansas	594.3
11	Oklahoma	588.8
12	Missouri	550.4
13	Michigan	544.3
14	Texas	529.9
15	North Carolina	520.2
16	Georgia	508.4
17	California	506.6
18	Alabama	504.8
19	Arizona	450.5
20	Massachusetts	449.0
21	Kansas	435.5
22	Pennsylvania	434.5
23	New York	410.9
24	Ohio	382.0
25	Indiana	374.7
26	Kentucky	364.0
27	Nebraska	361.0
28	Colorado	356.9
29	Iowa	347.7
30	Washington	346.2
31	Mississippi	341.8
32	Connecticut	336.7
33	New Jersey	326.5
34	Wisconsin	311.2
35	West Virginia	304.5
36	Hawaii	284.1
37	Oregon	279.7
38	Montana	276.7
39	Wyoming	271.4
40	Virginia	269.0
41	Idaho	250.2
42	Rhode Island	248.0
43	South Dakota	243.4
44	Utah	227.4
45	North Dakota	214.1
46	Vermont	163.3
47	New Hampshire	159.1
48	Maine	129.5
NA	Illinois**	NA
NA	Minnesota**	NA

District of Columbia   1,437.7

Source: CQ Press using reported data from the Federal Bureau of Investigation
"Crime in the United States 2008" (Uniform Crime Reports, September 14, 2009, http://www.fbi.gov/ucr/ucr.htm)
*Estimated rates for urban areas, defined by the F.B.I. as Metropolitan Statistical Areas and other cities outside such areas.
National rate includes those states listed as not available. Violent crimes are offenses of murder, forcible rape, robbery, and
aggravated assault.
**Not available.

Percent of Violent Crimes Occurring in Urban Areas in 2008

National Percent = 95.5% of Violent Crimes*

ALPHA ORDER

RANK	STATE	PERCENT
23	Alabama	93.9
43	Alaska	82.8
15	Arizona	96.7
32	Arkansas	91.3
4	California	99.0
17	Colorado	96.2
17	Connecticut	96.2
36	Delaware	88.1
13	Florida	96.8
23	Georgia	93.9
47	Hawaii	73.3
34	Idaho	88.9
NA	Illinois**	NA
16	Indiana	96.6
30	Iowa	92.8
26	Kansas	93.7
40	Kentucky	85.6
39	Louisiana	86.5
37	Maine	87.5
5	Maryland	98.2
1	Massachusetts	100.0
20	Michigan	95.5
NA	Minnesota**	NA
45	Mississippi	77.0
27	Missouri	93.6
48	Montana	61.0
20	Nebraska	95.5
9	Nevada	97.3
7	New Hampshire	97.5
1	New Jersey	100.0
28	New Mexico	93.0
6	New York	98.0
35	North Carolina	88.5
33	North Dakota	90.0
9	Ohio	97.3
28	Oklahoma	93.0
19	Oregon	96.0
12	Pennsylvania	96.9
3	Rhode Island	99.4
41	South Carolina	85.1
38	South Dakota	86.7
30	Tennessee	92.8
8	Texas	97.4
13	Utah	96.8
44	Vermont	80.0
25	Virginia	93.8
11	Washington	97.1
46	West Virginia	75.3
22	Wisconsin	95.3
42	Wyoming	83.2

RANK ORDER

RANK	STATE	PERCENT
1	Massachusetts	100.0
1	New Jersey	100.0
3	Rhode Island	99.4
4	California	99.0
5	Maryland	98.2
6	New York	98.0
7	New Hampshire	97.5
8	Texas	97.4
9	Nevada	97.3
9	Ohio	97.3
11	Washington	97.1
12	Pennsylvania	96.9
13	Florida	96.8
13	Utah	96.8
15	Arizona	96.7
16	Indiana	96.6
17	Colorado	96.2
17	Connecticut	96.2
19	Oregon	96.0
20	Michigan	95.5
20	Nebraska	95.5
22	Wisconsin	95.3
23	Alabama	93.9
23	Georgia	93.9
25	Virginia	93.8
26	Kansas	93.7
27	Missouri	93.6
28	New Mexico	93.0
28	Oklahoma	93.0
30	Iowa	92.8
30	Tennessee	92.8
32	Arkansas	91.3
33	North Dakota	90.0
34	Idaho	88.9
35	North Carolina	88.5
36	Delaware	88.1
37	Maine	87.5
38	South Dakota	86.7
39	Louisiana	86.5
40	Kentucky	85.6
41	South Carolina	85.1
42	Wyoming	83.2
43	Alaska	82.8
44	Vermont	80.0
45	Mississippi	77.0
46	West Virginia	75.3
47	Hawaii	73.3
48	Montana	61.0
NA	Illinois**	NA
NA	Minnesota**	NA

District of Columbia   100.0

Source: CQ Press using reported data from the Federal Bureau of Investigation

"Crime in the United States 2008" (Uniform Crime Reports, September 14, 2009, http://www.fbi.gov/ucr/ucr.htm)

*Estimated percentages for urban areas, defined by the F.B.I. as Metropolitan Statistical Areas and other cities outside such areas. National percent includes those states listed as not available. Violent crimes are offenses of murder, forcible rape, robbery, and aggravated assault.

**Not available.

Violent Crimes in Rural Areas in 2008

National Rural Total = 61,733 Violent Crimes*

ALPHA ORDER

RANK	STATE	CRIMES	% of USA
16	Alabama	1,285	2.1%
25	Alaska	771	1.2%
22	Arizona	968	1.6%
17	Arkansas	1,245	2.0%
11	California	1,832	3.0%
31	Colorado	639	1.0%
35	Connecticut	396	0.6%
26	Delaware	731	1.2%
3	Florida	4,098	6.6%
7	Georgia	2,841	4.6%
23	Hawaii	937	1.5%
37	Idaho	385	0.6%
NA	Illinois**	NA	NA
29	Indiana	713	1.2%
33	Iowa	611	1.0%
27	Kansas	720	1.2%
12	Kentucky	1,819	2.9%
4	Louisiana	3,904	6.3%
42	Maine	193	0.3%
30	Maryland	643	1.0%
47	Massachusetts	0	0.0%
8	Michigan	2,277	3.7%
NA	Minnesota**	NA	NA
9	Mississippi	1,927	3.1%
10	Missouri	1,900	3.1%
21	Montana	973	1.6%
38	Nebraska	246	0.4%
34	Nevada	504	0.8%
45	New Hampshire	52	0.1%
47	New Jersey	0	0.0%
24	New Mexico	909	1.5%
14	New York	1,529	2.5%
1	North Carolina	4,953	8.0%
44	North Dakota	107	0.2%
20	Ohio	1,071	1.7%
15	Oklahoma	1,339	2.2%
36	Oregon	390	0.6%
13	Pennsylvania	1,558	2.5%
46	Rhode Island	15	0.0%
2	South Carolina	4,864	7.9%
39	South Dakota	216	0.3%
5	Tennessee	3,218	5.2%
6	Texas	3,202	5.2%
41	Utah	194	0.3%
43	Vermont	169	0.3%
18	Virginia	1,234	2.0%
32	Washington	637	1.0%
19	West Virginia	1,225	2.0%
28	Wisconsin	719	1.2%
40	Wyoming	208	0.3%

RANK ORDER

RANK	STATE	CRIMES	% of USA
1	North Carolina	4,953	8.0%
2	South Carolina	4,864	7.9%
3	Florida	4,098	6.6%
4	Louisiana	3,904	6.3%
5	Tennessee	3,218	5.2%
6	Texas	3,202	5.2%
7	Georgia	2,841	4.6%
8	Michigan	2,277	3.7%
9	Mississippi	1,927	3.1%
10	Missouri	1,900	3.1%
11	California	1,832	3.0%
12	Kentucky	1,819	2.9%
13	Pennsylvania	1,558	2.5%
14	New York	1,529	2.5%
15	Oklahoma	1,339	2.2%
16	Alabama	1,285	2.1%
17	Arkansas	1,245	2.0%
18	Virginia	1,234	2.0%
19	West Virginia	1,225	2.0%
20	Ohio	1,071	1.7%
21	Montana	973	1.6%
22	Arizona	968	1.6%
23	Hawaii	937	1.5%
24	New Mexico	909	1.5%
25	Alaska	771	1.2%
26	Delaware	731	1.2%
27	Kansas	720	1.2%
28	Wisconsin	719	1.2%
29	Indiana	713	1.2%
30	Maryland	643	1.0%
31	Colorado	639	1.0%
32	Washington	637	1.0%
33	Iowa	611	1.0%
34	Nevada	504	0.8%
35	Connecticut	396	0.6%
36	Oregon	390	0.6%
37	Idaho	385	0.6%
38	Nebraska	246	0.4%
39	South Dakota	216	0.3%
40	Wyoming	208	0.3%
41	Utah	194	0.3%
42	Maine	193	0.3%
43	Vermont	169	0.3%
44	North Dakota	107	0.2%
45	New Hampshire	52	0.1%
46	Rhode Island	15	0.0%
47	Massachusetts	0	0.0%
47	New Jersey	0	0.0%
NA	Illinois**	NA	NA
NA	Minnesota**	NA	NA
	District of Columbia	0	0.0%

Source: Reported data from the Federal Bureau of Investigation
   "Crime in the United States 2008" (Uniform Crime Reports, September 14, 2009, http://www.fbi.gov/ucr/ucr.htm)
*Violent crimes are offenses of murder, forcible rape, robbery and aggravated assault. other cities outside such areas. National total includes those states listed as not available. Violent crimes are offenses of murder, forcible rape, robbery, and aggravated assault.
**Not available.

Rural Violent Crime Rate in 2008

National Rural Rate = 205.1 Violent Crimes per 100,000 Population*

<table>
<tr><td colspan="3">ALPHA ORDER</td><td colspan="3">RANK ORDER</td></tr>
<tr><th>RANK</th><th>STATE</th><th>RATE</th><th>RANK</th><th>STATE</th><th>RATE</th></tr>
<tr><td>24</td><td>Alabama</td><td>174.9</td><td>1</td><td>South Carolina</td><td>612.3</td></tr>
<tr><td>6</td><td>Alaska</td><td>340.9</td><td>2</td><td>Louisiana</td><td>516.0</td></tr>
<tr><td>5</td><td>Arizona</td><td>365.0</td><td>3</td><td>Delaware</td><td>500.1</td></tr>
<tr><td>21</td><td>Arkansas</td><td>192.7</td><td>4</td><td>Florida</td><td>464.9</td></tr>
<tr><td>8</td><td>California</td><td>324.2</td><td>5</td><td>Arizona</td><td>365.0</td></tr>
<tr><td>25</td><td>Colorado</td><td>172.4</td><td>6</td><td>Alaska</td><td>340.9</td></tr>
<tr><td>42</td><td>Connecticut</td><td>75.9</td><td>7</td><td>New Mexico</td><td>335.4</td></tr>
<tr><td>3</td><td>Delaware</td><td>500.1</td><td>8</td><td>California</td><td>324.2</td></tr>
<tr><td>4</td><td>Florida</td><td>464.9</td><td>9</td><td>Tennessee</td><td>306.1</td></tr>
<tr><td>12</td><td>Georgia</td><td>253.6</td><td>10</td><td>Maryland</td><td>289.2</td></tr>
<tr><td>13</td><td>Hawaii</td><td>245.4</td><td>11</td><td>North Carolina</td><td>262.1</td></tr>
<tr><td>32</td><td>Idaho</td><td>134.7</td><td>12</td><td>Georgia</td><td>253.6</td></tr>
<tr><td>NA</td><td>Illinois**</td><td>NA</td><td>13</td><td>Hawaii</td><td>245.4</td></tr>
<tr><td>40</td><td>Indiana</td><td>80.4</td><td>14</td><td>Montana</td><td>233.5</td></tr>
<tr><td>37</td><td>Iowa</td><td>83.9</td><td>15</td><td>Nevada</td><td>231.8</td></tr>
<tr><td>17</td><td>Kansas</td><td>221.1</td><td>16</td><td>Missouri</td><td>226.4</td></tr>
<tr><td>29</td><td>Kentucky</td><td>140.5</td><td>17</td><td>Kansas</td><td>221.1</td></tr>
<tr><td>2</td><td>Louisiana</td><td>516.0</td><td>18</td><td>Oklahoma</td><td>218.8</td></tr>
<tr><td>43</td><td>Maine</td><td>71.2</td><td>19</td><td>West Virginia</td><td>209.4</td></tr>
<tr><td>10</td><td>Maryland</td><td>289.2</td><td>20</td><td>Texas</td><td>198.7</td></tr>
<tr><td>46</td><td>Massachusetts</td><td>0.0</td><td>21</td><td>Arkansas</td><td>192.7</td></tr>
<tr><td>22</td><td>Michigan</td><td>189.0</td><td>22</td><td>Michigan</td><td>189.0</td></tr>
<tr><td>NA</td><td>Minnesota**</td><td>NA</td><td>23</td><td>Mississippi</td><td>183.0</td></tr>
<tr><td>23</td><td>Mississippi</td><td>183.0</td><td>24</td><td>Alabama</td><td>174.9</td></tr>
<tr><td>16</td><td>Missouri</td><td>226.4</td><td>25</td><td>Colorado</td><td>172.4</td></tr>
<tr><td>14</td><td>Montana</td><td>233.5</td><td>26</td><td>New York</td><td>155.8</td></tr>
<tr><td>44</td><td>Nebraska</td><td>70.0</td><td>27</td><td>Virginia</td><td>147.6</td></tr>
<tr><td>15</td><td>Nevada</td><td>231.8</td><td>28</td><td>Pennsylvania</td><td>147.0</td></tr>
<tr><td>34</td><td>New Hampshire</td><td>107.6</td><td>29</td><td>Kentucky</td><td>140.5</td></tr>
<tr><td>46</td><td>New Jersey</td><td>0.0</td><td>30</td><td>Washington</td><td>136.0</td></tr>
<tr><td>7</td><td>New Mexico</td><td>335.4</td><td>31</td><td>Wyoming</td><td>135.2</td></tr>
<tr><td>26</td><td>New York</td><td>155.8</td><td>32</td><td>Idaho</td><td>134.7</td></tr>
<tr><td>11</td><td>North Carolina</td><td>262.1</td><td>33</td><td>Utah</td><td>126.9</td></tr>
<tr><td>45</td><td>North Dakota</td><td>55.6</td><td>34</td><td>New Hampshire</td><td>107.6</td></tr>
<tr><td>38</td><td>Ohio</td><td>82.6</td><td>35</td><td>South Dakota</td><td>95.0</td></tr>
<tr><td>18</td><td>Oklahoma</td><td>218.8</td><td>36</td><td>Oregon</td><td>87.6</td></tr>
<tr><td>36</td><td>Oregon</td><td>87.6</td><td>37</td><td>Iowa</td><td>83.9</td></tr>
<tr><td>28</td><td>Pennsylvania</td><td>147.0</td><td>38</td><td>Ohio</td><td>82.6</td></tr>
<tr><td>46</td><td>Rhode Island</td><td>0.0</td><td>39</td><td>Vermont</td><td>81.2</td></tr>
<tr><td>1</td><td>South Carolina</td><td>612.3</td><td>40</td><td>Indiana</td><td>80.4</td></tr>
<tr><td>35</td><td>South Dakota</td><td>95.0</td><td>41</td><td>Wisconsin</td><td>79.5</td></tr>
<tr><td>9</td><td>Tennessee</td><td>306.1</td><td>42</td><td>Connecticut</td><td>75.9</td></tr>
<tr><td>20</td><td>Texas</td><td>198.7</td><td>43</td><td>Maine</td><td>71.2</td></tr>
<tr><td>33</td><td>Utah</td><td>126.9</td><td>44</td><td>Nebraska</td><td>70.0</td></tr>
<tr><td>39</td><td>Vermont</td><td>81.2</td><td>45</td><td>North Dakota</td><td>55.6</td></tr>
<tr><td>27</td><td>Virginia</td><td>147.6</td><td>46</td><td>Massachusetts</td><td>0.0</td></tr>
<tr><td>30</td><td>Washington</td><td>136.0</td><td>46</td><td>New Jersey</td><td>0.0</td></tr>
<tr><td>19</td><td>West Virginia</td><td>209.4</td><td>46</td><td>Rhode Island</td><td>0.0</td></tr>
<tr><td>41</td><td>Wisconsin</td><td>79.5</td><td>NA</td><td>Illinois**</td><td>NA</td></tr>
<tr><td>31</td><td>Wyoming</td><td>135.2</td><td>NA</td><td>Minnesota**</td><td>NA</td></tr>
<tr><td colspan="3"></td><td colspan="2">District of Columbia</td><td>0.0</td></tr>
</table>

Source: CQ Press using reported data from the Federal Bureau of Investigation
"Crime in the United States 2008" (Uniform Crime Reports, September 14, 2009, http://www.fbi.gov/ucr/ucr.htm)
*Estimated totals for urban areas, defined by the F.B.I. as Metropolitan Statistical Areas and other cities outside such areas.
National total includes those states listed as not available. Violent crimes are offenses of murder, forcible rape, robbery, and aggravated assault.
**Not available.

Percent of Violent Crimes Occurring in Rural Areas in 2008

National Percent = 4.5% of Violent Crimes*

ALPHA ORDER

RANK	STATE	PERCENT
25	Alabama	6.1
6	Alaska	17.2
34	Arizona	3.3
17	Arkansas	8.7
45	California	1.0
31	Colorado	3.8
31	Connecticut	3.8
13	Delaware	11.9
35	Florida	3.2
25	Georgia	6.1
2	Hawaii	26.7
15	Idaho	11.1
NA	Illinois**	NA
33	Indiana	3.4
18	Iowa	7.2
23	Kansas	6.3
9	Kentucky	14.4
10	Louisiana	13.5
12	Maine	12.5
44	Maryland	1.8
47	Massachusetts	0.0
28	Michigan	4.5
NA	Minnesota**	NA
4	Mississippi	23.0
22	Missouri	6.4
1	Montana	39.0
28	Nebraska	4.5
39	Nevada	2.7
42	New Hampshire	2.5
47	New Jersey	0.0
20	New Mexico	7.0
43	New York	2.0
14	North Carolina	11.5
16	North Dakota	10.0
39	Ohio	2.7
20	Oklahoma	7.0
30	Oregon	4.0
37	Pennsylvania	3.1
46	Rhode Island	0.6
8	South Carolina	14.9
11	South Dakota	13.3
18	Tennessee	7.2
41	Texas	2.6
35	Utah	3.2
5	Vermont	20.0
24	Virginia	6.2
38	Washington	2.9
3	West Virginia	24.7
27	Wisconsin	4.7
7	Wyoming	16.8

RANK ORDER

RANK	STATE	PERCENT
1	Montana	39.0
2	Hawaii	26.7
3	West Virginia	24.7
4	Mississippi	23.0
5	Vermont	20.0
6	Alaska	17.2
7	Wyoming	16.8
8	South Carolina	14.9
9	Kentucky	14.4
10	Louisiana	13.5
11	South Dakota	13.3
12	Maine	12.5
13	Delaware	11.9
14	North Carolina	11.5
15	Idaho	11.1
16	North Dakota	10.0
17	Arkansas	8.7
18	Iowa	7.2
18	Tennessee	7.2
20	New Mexico	7.0
20	Oklahoma	7.0
22	Missouri	6.4
23	Kansas	6.3
24	Virginia	6.2
25	Alabama	6.1
25	Georgia	6.1
27	Wisconsin	4.7
28	Michigan	4.5
28	Nebraska	4.5
30	Oregon	4.0
31	Colorado	3.8
31	Connecticut	3.8
33	Indiana	3.4
34	Arizona	3.3
35	Florida	3.2
35	Utah	3.2
37	Pennsylvania	3.1
38	Washington	2.9
39	Nevada	2.7
39	Ohio	2.7
41	Texas	2.6
42	New Hampshire	2.5
43	New York	2.0
44	Maryland	1.8
45	California	1.0
46	Rhode Island	0.6
47	Massachusetts	0.0
47	New Jersey	0.0
NA	Illinois**	NA
NA	Minnesota**	NA
	District of Columbia	0.0

Source: CQ Press using reported data from the Federal Bureau of Investigation
     "Crime in the United States 2008" (Uniform Crime Reports, September 14, 2009, http://www.fbi.gov/ucr/ucr.htm)
*Estimated totals for urban areas, defined by the F.B.I. as Metropolitan Statistical Areas and other cities outside such areas.
National total includes those states listed as not available. Violent crimes are offenses of murder, forcible rape, robbery, and
aggravated assault.
**Not available.

Murders in Urban Areas in 2008

National Urban Total = 15,243 Murders*

ALPHA ORDER

RANK	STATE	MURDERS	% of USA
16	Alabama	334	2.2%
41	Alaska	19	0.1%
13	Arizona	403	2.6%
27	Arkansas	132	0.9%
1	California	2,125	13.9%
25	Colorado	151	1.0%
29	Connecticut	114	0.7%
36	Delaware	51	0.3%
3	Florida	1,122	7.4%
6	Georgia	604	4.0%
42	Hawaii	18	0.1%
43	Idaho	15	0.1%
NA	Illinois**	NA	NA
18	Indiana	314	2.1%
35	Iowa	62	0.4%
31	Kansas	107	0.7%
29	Kentucky	114	0.7%
9	Louisiana	490	3.2%
40	Maine	23	0.2%
11	Maryland	483	3.2%
23	Massachusetts	167	1.1%
8	Michigan	517	3.4%
32	Minnesota	102	0.7%
20	Mississippi	186	1.2%
12	Missouri	418	2.7%
45	Montana	12	0.1%
34	Nebraska	63	0.4%
24	Nevada	154	1.0%
46	New Hampshire	11	0.1%
14	New Jersey	376	2.5%
28	New Mexico	124	0.8%
4	New York	820	5.4%
10	North Carolina	489	3.2%
48	North Dakota	3	0.0%
7	Ohio	522	3.4%
21	Oklahoma	183	1.2%
33	Oregon	77	0.5%
5	Pennsylvania	674	4.4%
39	Rhode Island	27	0.2%
19	South Carolina	253	1.7%
44	South Dakota	14	0.1%
14	Tennessee	376	2.5%
2	Texas	1,306	8.6%
38	Utah	38	0.2%
49	Vermont	2	0.0%
17	Virginia	317	2.1%
22	Washington	181	1.2%
37	West Virginia	44	0.3%
26	Wisconsin	133	0.9%
47	Wyoming	8	0.1%

RANK ORDER

RANK	STATE	MURDERS	% of USA
1	California	2,125	13.9%
2	Texas	1,306	8.6%
3	Florida	1,122	7.4%
4	New York	820	5.4%
5	Pennsylvania	674	4.4%
6	Georgia	604	4.0%
7	Ohio	522	3.4%
8	Michigan	517	3.4%
9	Louisiana	490	3.2%
10	North Carolina	489	3.2%
11	Maryland	483	3.2%
12	Missouri	418	2.7%
13	Arizona	403	2.6%
14	New Jersey	376	2.5%
14	Tennessee	376	2.5%
16	Alabama	334	2.2%
17	Virginia	317	2.1%
18	Indiana	314	2.1%
19	South Carolina	253	1.7%
20	Mississippi	186	1.2%
21	Oklahoma	183	1.2%
22	Washington	181	1.2%
23	Massachusetts	167	1.1%
24	Nevada	154	1.0%
25	Colorado	151	1.0%
26	Wisconsin	133	0.9%
27	Arkansas	132	0.9%
28	New Mexico	124	0.8%
29	Connecticut	114	0.7%
29	Kentucky	114	0.7%
31	Kansas	107	0.7%
32	Minnesota	102	0.7%
33	Oregon	77	0.5%
34	Nebraska	63	0.4%
35	Iowa	62	0.4%
36	Delaware	51	0.3%
37	West Virginia	44	0.3%
38	Utah	38	0.2%
39	Rhode Island	27	0.2%
40	Maine	23	0.2%
41	Alaska	19	0.1%
42	Hawaii	18	0.1%
43	Idaho	15	0.1%
44	South Dakota	14	0.1%
45	Montana	12	0.1%
46	New Hampshire	11	0.1%
47	Wyoming	8	0.1%
48	North Dakota	3	0.0%
49	Vermont	2	0.0%
NA	Illinois**	NA	NA
	District of Columbia	186	1.2%

Source: CQ Press using reported data from the Federal Bureau of Investigation
   "Crime in the United States 2008" (Uniform Crime Reports, September 14, 2009, http://www.fbi.gov/ucr/ucr.htm)
*Estimated totals for urban areas, defined by the F.B.I. as Metropolitan Statistical Areas and other cities outside such areas.
National total includes those states listed as not available. Includes nonnegligent manslaughter.
**Not available.

Urban Murder Rate in 2008

National Urban Rate = 5.6 Murders per 100,000 Population*

ALPHA ORDER

RANK	STATE	RATE
4	Alabama	8.5
28	Alaska	4.1
12	Arizona	6.5
15	Arkansas	6.0
17	California	5.9
32	Colorado	3.3
29	Connecticut	3.8
9	Delaware	7.0
14	Florida	6.4
8	Georgia	7.1
44	Hawaii	2.0
46	Idaho	1.2
NA	Illinois**	NA
20	Indiana	5.7
35	Iowa	2.7
26	Kansas	4.3
29	Kentucky	3.8
1	Louisiana	13.4
41	Maine	2.2
3	Maryland	8.9
36	Massachusetts	2.6
17	Michigan	5.9
39	Minnesota	2.3
2	Mississippi	9.9
5	Missouri	8.2
41	Montana	2.2
24	Nebraska	4.4
12	Nevada	6.5
47	New Hampshire	0.9
26	New Jersey	4.3
7	New Mexico	7.2
24	New York	4.4
11	North Carolina	6.7
48	North Dakota	0.7
22	Ohio	5.1
15	Oklahoma	6.0
39	Oregon	2.3
17	Pennsylvania	5.9
36	Rhode Island	2.6
10	South Carolina	6.9
38	South Dakota	2.4
6	Tennessee	7.3
20	Texas	5.7
45	Utah	1.5
49	Vermont	0.5
23	Virginia	4.6
33	Washington	3.0
31	West Virginia	3.6
34	Wisconsin	2.8
43	Wyoming	2.1

RANK ORDER

RANK	STATE	RATE
1	Louisiana	13.4
2	Mississippi	9.9
3	Maryland	8.9
4	Alabama	8.5
5	Missouri	8.2
6	Tennessee	7.3
7	New Mexico	7.2
8	Georgia	7.1
9	Delaware	7.0
10	South Carolina	6.9
11	North Carolina	6.7
12	Arizona	6.5
12	Nevada	6.5
14	Florida	6.4
15	Arkansas	6.0
15	Oklahoma	6.0
17	California	5.9
17	Michigan	5.9
17	Pennsylvania	5.9
20	Indiana	5.7
20	Texas	5.7
22	Ohio	5.1
23	Virginia	4.6
24	Nebraska	4.4
24	New York	4.4
26	Kansas	4.3
26	New Jersey	4.3
28	Alaska	4.1
29	Connecticut	3.8
29	Kentucky	3.8
31	West Virginia	3.6
32	Colorado	3.3
33	Washington	3.0
34	Wisconsin	2.8
35	Iowa	2.7
36	Massachusetts	2.6
36	Rhode Island	2.6
38	South Dakota	2.4
39	Minnesota	2.3
39	Oregon	2.3
41	Maine	2.2
41	Montana	2.2
43	Wyoming	2.1
44	Hawaii	2.0
45	Utah	1.5
46	Idaho	1.2
47	New Hampshire	0.9
48	North Dakota	0.7
49	Vermont	0.5
NA	Illinois**	NA
	District of Columbia	31.4

Source: CQ Press using reported data from the Federal Bureau of Investigation
   "Crime in the United States 2008" (Uniform Crime Reports, September 14, 2009, http://www.fbi.gov/ucr/ucr.htm)
*Estimated rates for urban areas, defined by the F.B.I. as Metropolitan Statistical Areas and other cities outside such areas.
National rate includes those states listed as not available. Includes nonnegligent manslaughter.
**Not available.

Percent of Murders Occurring in Urban Areas in 2008

National Percent = 93.7% of Murders*

<table>
<tr><td colspan="3">ALPHA ORDER</td><td colspan="3">RANK ORDER</td></tr>
<tr><td>RANK</td><td>STATE</td><td>PERCENT</td><td>RANK</td><td>STATE</td><td>PERCENT</td></tr>
<tr><td>18</td><td>Alabama</td><td>94.6</td><td>1</td><td>Massachusetts</td><td>100.0</td></tr>
<tr><td>44</td><td>Alaska</td><td>67.9</td><td>1</td><td>New Jersey</td><td>100.0</td></tr>
<tr><td>5</td><td>Arizona</td><td>99.0</td><td>1</td><td>North Dakota</td><td>100.0</td></tr>
<tr><td>37</td><td>Arkansas</td><td>81.5</td><td>4</td><td>California</td><td>99.2</td></tr>
<tr><td>4</td><td>California</td><td>99.2</td><td>5</td><td>Arizona</td><td>99.0</td></tr>
<tr><td>9</td><td>Colorado</td><td>96.2</td><td>6</td><td>New York</td><td>98.1</td></tr>
<tr><td>25</td><td>Connecticut</td><td>92.7</td><td>7</td><td>Maryland</td><td>98.0</td></tr>
<tr><td>30</td><td>Delaware</td><td>89.5</td><td>8</td><td>Utah</td><td>97.4</td></tr>
<tr><td>10</td><td>Florida</td><td>96.1</td><td>9</td><td>Colorado</td><td>96.2</td></tr>
<tr><td>16</td><td>Georgia</td><td>95.0</td><td>10</td><td>Florida</td><td>96.1</td></tr>
<tr><td>43</td><td>Hawaii</td><td>72.0</td><td>10</td><td>Ohio</td><td>96.1</td></tr>
<tr><td>45</td><td>Idaho</td><td>65.2</td><td>10</td><td>Pennsylvania</td><td>96.1</td></tr>
<tr><td>NA</td><td>Illinois**</td><td>NA</td><td>13</td><td>Indiana</td><td>96.0</td></tr>
<tr><td>13</td><td>Indiana</td><td>96.0</td><td>14</td><td>Michigan</td><td>95.4</td></tr>
<tr><td>36</td><td>Iowa</td><td>81.6</td><td>15</td><td>Texas</td><td>95.1</td></tr>
<tr><td>17</td><td>Kansas</td><td>94.7</td><td>16</td><td>Georgia</td><td>95.0</td></tr>
<tr><td>46</td><td>Kentucky</td><td>57.6</td><td>17</td><td>Kansas</td><td>94.7</td></tr>
<tr><td>24</td><td>Louisiana</td><td>93.0</td><td>18</td><td>Alabama</td><td>94.6</td></tr>
<tr><td>41</td><td>Maine</td><td>74.2</td><td>19</td><td>Nevada</td><td>94.5</td></tr>
<tr><td>7</td><td>Maryland</td><td>98.0</td><td>20</td><td>Washington</td><td>94.3</td></tr>
<tr><td>1</td><td>Massachusetts</td><td>100.0</td><td>21</td><td>Oregon</td><td>93.9</td></tr>
<tr><td>14</td><td>Michigan</td><td>95.4</td><td>22</td><td>Minnesota</td><td>93.6</td></tr>
<tr><td>22</td><td>Minnesota</td><td>93.6</td><td>23</td><td>Rhode Island</td><td>93.1</td></tr>
<tr><td>40</td><td>Mississippi</td><td>78.5</td><td>24</td><td>Louisiana</td><td>93.0</td></tr>
<tr><td>28</td><td>Missouri</td><td>91.9</td><td>25</td><td>Connecticut</td><td>92.7</td></tr>
<tr><td>48</td><td>Montana</td><td>52.2</td><td>26</td><td>Nebraska</td><td>92.6</td></tr>
<tr><td>26</td><td>Nebraska</td><td>92.6</td><td>27</td><td>Tennessee</td><td>92.2</td></tr>
<tr><td>19</td><td>Nevada</td><td>94.5</td><td>28</td><td>Missouri</td><td>91.9</td></tr>
<tr><td>34</td><td>New Hampshire</td><td>84.6</td><td>29</td><td>Wisconsin</td><td>91.1</td></tr>
<tr><td>1</td><td>New Jersey</td><td>100.0</td><td>30</td><td>Delaware</td><td>89.5</td></tr>
<tr><td>31</td><td>New Mexico</td><td>87.3</td><td>31</td><td>New Mexico</td><td>87.3</td></tr>
<tr><td>6</td><td>New York</td><td>98.1</td><td>32</td><td>Oklahoma</td><td>86.3</td></tr>
<tr><td>38</td><td>North Carolina</td><td>81.0</td><td>33</td><td>Virginia</td><td>86.1</td></tr>
<tr><td>1</td><td>North Dakota</td><td>100.0</td><td>34</td><td>New Hampshire</td><td>84.6</td></tr>
<tr><td>10</td><td>Ohio</td><td>96.1</td><td>35</td><td>South Carolina</td><td>83.0</td></tr>
<tr><td>32</td><td>Oklahoma</td><td>86.3</td><td>36</td><td>Iowa</td><td>81.6</td></tr>
<tr><td>21</td><td>Oregon</td><td>93.9</td><td>37</td><td>Arkansas</td><td>81.5</td></tr>
<tr><td>10</td><td>Pennsylvania</td><td>96.1</td><td>38</td><td>North Carolina</td><td>81.0</td></tr>
<tr><td>23</td><td>Rhode Island</td><td>93.1</td><td>39</td><td>Wyoming</td><td>80.0</td></tr>
<tr><td>35</td><td>South Carolina</td><td>83.0</td><td>40</td><td>Mississippi</td><td>78.5</td></tr>
<tr><td>47</td><td>South Dakota</td><td>53.8</td><td>41</td><td>Maine</td><td>74.2</td></tr>
<tr><td>27</td><td>Tennessee</td><td>92.2</td><td>42</td><td>West Virginia</td><td>73.3</td></tr>
<tr><td>15</td><td>Texas</td><td>95.1</td><td>43</td><td>Hawaii</td><td>72.0</td></tr>
<tr><td>8</td><td>Utah</td><td>97.4</td><td>44</td><td>Alaska</td><td>67.9</td></tr>
<tr><td>49</td><td>Vermont</td><td>11.8</td><td>45</td><td>Idaho</td><td>65.2</td></tr>
<tr><td>33</td><td>Virginia</td><td>86.1</td><td>46</td><td>Kentucky</td><td>57.6</td></tr>
<tr><td>20</td><td>Washington</td><td>94.3</td><td>47</td><td>South Dakota</td><td>53.8</td></tr>
<tr><td>42</td><td>West Virginia</td><td>73.3</td><td>48</td><td>Montana</td><td>52.2</td></tr>
<tr><td>29</td><td>Wisconsin</td><td>91.1</td><td>49</td><td>Vermont</td><td>11.8</td></tr>
<tr><td>39</td><td>Wyoming</td><td>80.0</td><td>NA</td><td>Illinois**</td><td>NA</td></tr>
<tr><td></td><td></td><td></td><td></td><td>District of Columbia</td><td>100.0</td></tr>
</table>

Source: CQ Press using reported data from the Federal Bureau of Investigation
    "Crime in the United States 2008" (Uniform Crime Reports, September 14, 2009, http://www.fbi.gov/ucr/ucr.htm)
*Estimated percentages for urban areas, defined by the F.B.I. as Metropolitan Statistical Areas and other cities outside such areas. National percent includes those states listed as not available. Includes nonnegligent manslaughter.
**Not available.

Murders in Rural Areas in 2008

National Rural Total = 1,029 Murders*

<table>
<tr><td colspan="4">ALPHA ORDER</td><td colspan="4">RANK ORDER</td></tr>
<tr><td>RANK</td><td>STATE</td><td>MURDERS</td><td>% of USA</td><td>RANK</td><td>STATE</td><td>MURDERS</td><td>% of USA</td></tr>
<tr><td>17</td><td>Alabama</td><td>19</td><td>1.8%</td><td>1</td><td>North Carolina</td><td>115</td><td>11.2%</td></tr>
<tr><td>30</td><td>Alaska</td><td>9</td><td>0.9%</td><td>2</td><td>Kentucky</td><td>84</td><td>8.2%</td></tr>
<tr><td>42</td><td>Arizona</td><td>4</td><td>0.4%</td><td>3</td><td>Texas</td><td>68</td><td>6.6%</td></tr>
<tr><td>12</td><td>Arkansas</td><td>30</td><td>2.9%</td><td>4</td><td>South Carolina</td><td>52</td><td>5.1%</td></tr>
<tr><td>19</td><td>California</td><td>17</td><td>1.7%</td><td>5</td><td>Mississippi</td><td>51</td><td>5.0%</td></tr>
<tr><td>37</td><td>Colorado</td><td>6</td><td>0.6%</td><td>5</td><td>Virginia</td><td>51</td><td>5.0%</td></tr>
<tr><td>30</td><td>Connecticut</td><td>9</td><td>0.9%</td><td>7</td><td>Florida</td><td>46</td><td>4.5%</td></tr>
<tr><td>37</td><td>Delaware</td><td>6</td><td>0.6%</td><td>8</td><td>Louisiana</td><td>37</td><td>3.6%</td></tr>
<tr><td>7</td><td>Florida</td><td>46</td><td>4.5%</td><td>8</td><td>Missouri</td><td>37</td><td>3.6%</td></tr>
<tr><td>10</td><td>Georgia</td><td>32</td><td>3.1%</td><td>10</td><td>Georgia</td><td>32</td><td>3.1%</td></tr>
<tr><td>35</td><td>Hawaii</td><td>7</td><td>0.7%</td><td>10</td><td>Tennessee</td><td>32</td><td>3.1%</td></tr>
<tr><td>33</td><td>Idaho</td><td>8</td><td>0.8%</td><td>12</td><td>Arkansas</td><td>30</td><td>2.9%</td></tr>
<tr><td>NA</td><td>Illinois**</td><td>NA</td><td>NA</td><td>13</td><td>Oklahoma</td><td>29</td><td>2.8%</td></tr>
<tr><td>24</td><td>Indiana</td><td>13</td><td>1.3%</td><td>14</td><td>Pennsylvania</td><td>27</td><td>2.6%</td></tr>
<tr><td>23</td><td>Iowa</td><td>14</td><td>1.4%</td><td>15</td><td>Michigan</td><td>25</td><td>2.4%</td></tr>
<tr><td>37</td><td>Kansas</td><td>6</td><td>0.6%</td><td>16</td><td>Ohio</td><td>21</td><td>2.0%</td></tr>
<tr><td>2</td><td>Kentucky</td><td>84</td><td>8.2%</td><td>17</td><td>Alabama</td><td>19</td><td>1.8%</td></tr>
<tr><td>8</td><td>Louisiana</td><td>37</td><td>3.6%</td><td>18</td><td>New Mexico</td><td>18</td><td>1.7%</td></tr>
<tr><td>33</td><td>Maine</td><td>8</td><td>0.8%</td><td>19</td><td>California</td><td>17</td><td>1.7%</td></tr>
<tr><td>29</td><td>Maryland</td><td>10</td><td>1.0%</td><td>20</td><td>New York</td><td>16</td><td>1.6%</td></tr>
<tr><td>47</td><td>Massachusetts</td><td>0</td><td>0.0%</td><td>20</td><td>West Virginia</td><td>16</td><td>1.6%</td></tr>
<tr><td>15</td><td>Michigan</td><td>25</td><td>2.4%</td><td>22</td><td>Vermont</td><td>15</td><td>1.5%</td></tr>
<tr><td>35</td><td>Minnesota</td><td>7</td><td>0.7%</td><td>23</td><td>Iowa</td><td>14</td><td>1.4%</td></tr>
<tr><td>5</td><td>Mississippi</td><td>51</td><td>5.0%</td><td>24</td><td>Indiana</td><td>13</td><td>1.3%</td></tr>
<tr><td>8</td><td>Missouri</td><td>37</td><td>3.6%</td><td>24</td><td>Wisconsin</td><td>13</td><td>1.3%</td></tr>
<tr><td>27</td><td>Montana</td><td>11</td><td>1.1%</td><td>26</td><td>South Dakota</td><td>12</td><td>1.2%</td></tr>
<tr><td>40</td><td>Nebraska</td><td>5</td><td>0.5%</td><td>27</td><td>Montana</td><td>11</td><td>1.1%</td></tr>
<tr><td>30</td><td>Nevada</td><td>9</td><td>0.9%</td><td>27</td><td>Washington</td><td>11</td><td>1.1%</td></tr>
<tr><td>43</td><td>New Hampshire</td><td>2</td><td>0.2%</td><td>29</td><td>Maryland</td><td>10</td><td>1.0%</td></tr>
<tr><td>47</td><td>New Jersey</td><td>0</td><td>0.0%</td><td>30</td><td>Alaska</td><td>9</td><td>0.9%</td></tr>
<tr><td>18</td><td>New Mexico</td><td>18</td><td>1.7%</td><td>30</td><td>Connecticut</td><td>9</td><td>0.9%</td></tr>
<tr><td>20</td><td>New York</td><td>16</td><td>1.6%</td><td>30</td><td>Nevada</td><td>9</td><td>0.9%</td></tr>
<tr><td>1</td><td>North Carolina</td><td>115</td><td>11.2%</td><td>33</td><td>Idaho</td><td>8</td><td>0.8%</td></tr>
<tr><td>47</td><td>North Dakota</td><td>0</td><td>0.0%</td><td>33</td><td>Maine</td><td>8</td><td>0.8%</td></tr>
<tr><td>16</td><td>Ohio</td><td>21</td><td>2.0%</td><td>35</td><td>Hawaii</td><td>7</td><td>0.7%</td></tr>
<tr><td>13</td><td>Oklahoma</td><td>29</td><td>2.8%</td><td>35</td><td>Minncsota</td><td>7</td><td>0.7%</td></tr>
<tr><td>40</td><td>Oregon</td><td>5</td><td>0.5%</td><td>37</td><td>Colorado</td><td>6</td><td>0.6%</td></tr>
<tr><td>14</td><td>Pennsylvania</td><td>27</td><td>2.6%</td><td>37</td><td>Delaware</td><td>6</td><td>0.6%</td></tr>
<tr><td>43</td><td>Rhode Island</td><td>2</td><td>0.2%</td><td>37</td><td>Kansas</td><td>6</td><td>0.6%</td></tr>
<tr><td>4</td><td>South Carolina</td><td>52</td><td>5.1%</td><td>40</td><td>Nebraska</td><td>5</td><td>0.5%</td></tr>
<tr><td>26</td><td>South Dakota</td><td>12</td><td>1.2%</td><td>40</td><td>Oregon</td><td>5</td><td>0.5%</td></tr>
<tr><td>10</td><td>Tennessee</td><td>32</td><td>3.1%</td><td>42</td><td>Arizona</td><td>4</td><td>0.4%</td></tr>
<tr><td>3</td><td>Texas</td><td>68</td><td>6.6%</td><td>43</td><td>New Hampshire</td><td>2</td><td>0.2%</td></tr>
<tr><td>46</td><td>Utah</td><td>1</td><td>0.1%</td><td>43</td><td>Rhode Island</td><td>2</td><td>0.2%</td></tr>
<tr><td>22</td><td>Vermont</td><td>15</td><td>1.5%</td><td>43</td><td>Wyoming</td><td>2</td><td>0.2%</td></tr>
<tr><td>5</td><td>Virginia</td><td>51</td><td>5.0%</td><td>46</td><td>Utah</td><td>1</td><td>0.1%</td></tr>
<tr><td>27</td><td>Washington</td><td>11</td><td>1.1%</td><td>47</td><td>Massachusetts</td><td>0</td><td>0.0%</td></tr>
<tr><td>20</td><td>West Virginia</td><td>16</td><td>1.6%</td><td>47</td><td>New Jersey</td><td>0</td><td>0.0%</td></tr>
<tr><td>24</td><td>Wisconsin</td><td>13</td><td>1.3%</td><td>47</td><td>North Dakota</td><td>0</td><td>0.0%</td></tr>
<tr><td>43</td><td>Wyoming</td><td>2</td><td>0.2%</td><td>NA</td><td>Illinois**</td><td>NA</td><td>NA</td></tr>
<tr><td></td><td></td><td></td><td></td><td></td><td>District of Columbia</td><td>0</td><td>0.0%</td></tr>
</table>

Source: Reported data from the Federal Bureau of Investigation
    "Crime in the United States 2008" (Uniform Crime Reports, September 14, 2009, http://www.fbi.gov/ucr/ucr.htm)
*Estimated totals for nonmetropolitan areas, defined by the F.B.I. as other than Metropolitan Statistical Areas and other cities outside such areas. National total includes those states listed as not available. Includes nonnegligent manslaughter.
**Not available.

Rural Murder Rate in 2008

National Rural Rate = 3.4 Murders per 100,000 Population*

RANK	STATE	RATE
26	Alabama	2.6
19	Alaska	4.0
38	Arizona	1.5
12	Arkansas	4.6
20	California	3.0
35	Colorado	1.6
34	Connecticut	1.7
16	Delaware	4.1
8	Florida	5.2
23	Georgia	2.9
32	Hawaii	1.8
24	Idaho	2.8
NA	Illinois**	NA
38	Indiana	1.5
31	Iowa	1.9
32	Kansas	1.8
3	Kentucky	6.5
9	Louisiana	4.9
20	Maine	3.0
13	Maryland	4.5
46	Massachusetts	0.0
30	Michigan	2.1
44	Minnesota	0.9
10	Mississippi	4.8
14	Missouri	4.4
26	Montana	2.6
40	Nebraska	1.4
16	Nevada	4.1
16	New Hampshire	4.1
46	New Jersey	0.0
2	New Mexico	6.6
35	New York	1.6
5	North Carolina	6.1
46	North Dakota	0.0
35	Ohio	1.6
11	Oklahoma	4.7
43	Oregon	1.1
28	Pennsylvania	2.5
46	Rhode Island	0.0
3	South Carolina	6.5
7	South Dakota	5.3
20	Tennessee	3.0
15	Texas	4.2
45	Utah	0.7
1	Vermont	7.2
5	Virginia	6.1
29	Washington	2.3
25	West Virginia	2.7
40	Wisconsin	1.4
42	Wyoming	1.3

RANK	STATE	RATE
1	Vermont	7.2
2	New Mexico	6.6
3	Kentucky	6.5
3	South Carolina	6.5
5	North Carolina	6.1
5	Virginia	6.1
7	South Dakota	5.3
8	Florida	5.2
9	Louisiana	4.9
10	Mississippi	4.8
11	Oklahoma	4.7
12	Arkansas	4.6
13	Maryland	4.5
14	Missouri	4.4
15	Texas	4.2
16	Delaware	4.1
16	Nevada	4.1
16	New Hampshire	4.1
19	Alaska	4.0
20	California	3.0
20	Maine	3.0
20	Tennessee	3.0
23	Georgia	2.9
24	Idaho	2.8
25	West Virginia	2.7
26	Alabama	2.6
26	Montana	2.6
28	Pennsylvania	2.5
29	Washington	2.3
30	Michigan	2.1
31	Iowa	1.9
32	Hawaii	1.8
32	Kansas	1.8
34	Connecticut	1.7
35	Colorado	1.6
35	New York	1.6
35	Ohio	1.6
38	Arizona	1.5
38	Indiana	1.5
40	Nebraska	1.4
40	Wisconsin	1.4
42	Wyoming	1.3
43	Oregon	1.1
44	Minnesota	0.9
45	Utah	0.7
46	Massachusetts	0.0
46	New Jersey	0.0
46	North Dakota	0.0
46	Rhode Island	0.0
NA	Illinois**	NA

	District of Columbia	0.0

Source: CQ Press using reported data from the Federal Bureau of Investigation
"Crime in the United States 2008" (Uniform Crime Reports, September 14, 2009, http://www.fbi.gov/ucr/ucr.htm)
*Estimated rates for nonmetropolitan areas, defined by the F.B.I. as other than Metropolitan Statistical Areas and other cities outside such areas. National rate includes those states listed as not available. Includes nonnegligent manslaughter.
**Not available.

Percent of Murders Occurring in Rural Areas in 2008

National Percent = 6.3% of Murders*

<table>
<tr><td colspan="3">ALPHA ORDER</td><td colspan="3">RANK ORDER</td></tr>
<tr><td>RANK</td><td>STATE</td><td>PERCENT</td><td>RANK</td><td>STATE</td><td>PERCENT</td></tr>
<tr><td>32</td><td>Alabama</td><td>5.4</td><td>1</td><td>Vermont</td><td>88.2</td></tr>
<tr><td>6</td><td>Alaska</td><td>32.1</td><td>2</td><td>Montana</td><td>47.8</td></tr>
<tr><td>45</td><td>Arizona</td><td>1.0</td><td>3</td><td>South Dakota</td><td>46.2</td></tr>
<tr><td>13</td><td>Arkansas</td><td>18.5</td><td>4</td><td>Kentucky</td><td>42.4</td></tr>
<tr><td>46</td><td>California</td><td>0.8</td><td>5</td><td>Idaho</td><td>34.8</td></tr>
<tr><td>41</td><td>Colorado</td><td>3.8</td><td>6</td><td>Alaska</td><td>32.1</td></tr>
<tr><td>25</td><td>Connecticut</td><td>7.3</td><td>7</td><td>Hawaii</td><td>28.0</td></tr>
<tr><td>20</td><td>Delaware</td><td>10.5</td><td>8</td><td>West Virginia</td><td>26.7</td></tr>
<tr><td>38</td><td>Florida</td><td>3.9</td><td>9</td><td>Maine</td><td>25.8</td></tr>
<tr><td>34</td><td>Georgia</td><td>5.0</td><td>10</td><td>Mississippi</td><td>21.5</td></tr>
<tr><td>7</td><td>Hawaii</td><td>28.0</td><td>11</td><td>Wyoming</td><td>20.0</td></tr>
<tr><td>5</td><td>Idaho</td><td>34.8</td><td>12</td><td>North Carolina</td><td>19.0</td></tr>
<tr><td>NA</td><td>Illinois**</td><td>NA</td><td>13</td><td>Arkansas</td><td>18.5</td></tr>
<tr><td>37</td><td>Indiana</td><td>4.0</td><td>14</td><td>Iowa</td><td>18.4</td></tr>
<tr><td>14</td><td>Iowa</td><td>18.4</td><td>15</td><td>South Carolina</td><td>17.0</td></tr>
<tr><td>33</td><td>Kansas</td><td>5.3</td><td>16</td><td>New Hampshire</td><td>15.4</td></tr>
<tr><td>4</td><td>Kentucky</td><td>42.4</td><td>17</td><td>Virginia</td><td>13.9</td></tr>
<tr><td>26</td><td>Louisiana</td><td>7.0</td><td>18</td><td>Oklahoma</td><td>13.7</td></tr>
<tr><td>9</td><td>Maine</td><td>25.8</td><td>19</td><td>New Mexico</td><td>12.7</td></tr>
<tr><td>43</td><td>Maryland</td><td>2.0</td><td>20</td><td>Delaware</td><td>10.5</td></tr>
<tr><td>47</td><td>Massachusetts</td><td>0.0</td><td>21</td><td>Wisconsin</td><td>8.9</td></tr>
<tr><td>36</td><td>Michigan</td><td>4.6</td><td>22</td><td>Missouri</td><td>8.1</td></tr>
<tr><td>28</td><td>Minnesota</td><td>6.4</td><td>23</td><td>Tennessee</td><td>7.8</td></tr>
<tr><td>10</td><td>Mississippi</td><td>21.5</td><td>24</td><td>Nebraska</td><td>7.4</td></tr>
<tr><td>22</td><td>Missouri</td><td>8.1</td><td>25</td><td>Connecticut</td><td>7.3</td></tr>
<tr><td>2</td><td>Montana</td><td>47.8</td><td>26</td><td>Louisiana</td><td>7.0</td></tr>
<tr><td>24</td><td>Nebraska</td><td>7.4</td><td>27</td><td>Rhode Island</td><td>6.9</td></tr>
<tr><td>31</td><td>Nevada</td><td>5.5</td><td>28</td><td>Minnesota</td><td>6.4</td></tr>
<tr><td>16</td><td>New Hampshire</td><td>15.4</td><td>29</td><td>Oregon</td><td>6.1</td></tr>
<tr><td>47</td><td>New Jersey</td><td>0.0</td><td>30</td><td>Washington</td><td>5.7</td></tr>
<tr><td>19</td><td>New Mexico</td><td>12.7</td><td>31</td><td>Nevada</td><td>5.5</td></tr>
<tr><td>44</td><td>New York</td><td>1.9</td><td>32</td><td>Alabama</td><td>5.4</td></tr>
<tr><td>12</td><td>North Carolina</td><td>19.0</td><td>33</td><td>Kansas</td><td>5.3</td></tr>
<tr><td>47</td><td>North Dakota</td><td>0.0</td><td>34</td><td>Georgia</td><td>5.0</td></tr>
<tr><td>38</td><td>Ohio</td><td>3.9</td><td>35</td><td>Texas</td><td>4.9</td></tr>
<tr><td>18</td><td>Oklahoma</td><td>13.7</td><td>36</td><td>Michigan</td><td>4.6</td></tr>
<tr><td>29</td><td>Oregon</td><td>6.1</td><td>37</td><td>Indiana</td><td>4.0</td></tr>
<tr><td>38</td><td>Pennsylvania</td><td>3.9</td><td>38</td><td>Florida</td><td>3.9</td></tr>
<tr><td>27</td><td>Rhode Island</td><td>6.9</td><td>38</td><td>Ohio</td><td>3.9</td></tr>
<tr><td>15</td><td>South Carolina</td><td>17.0</td><td>38</td><td>Pennsylvania</td><td>3.9</td></tr>
<tr><td>3</td><td>South Dakota</td><td>46.2</td><td>41</td><td>Colorado</td><td>3.8</td></tr>
<tr><td>23</td><td>Tennessee</td><td>7.8</td><td>42</td><td>Utah</td><td>2.6</td></tr>
<tr><td>35</td><td>Texas</td><td>4.9</td><td>43</td><td>Maryland</td><td>2.0</td></tr>
<tr><td>42</td><td>Utah</td><td>2.6</td><td>44</td><td>New York</td><td>1.9</td></tr>
<tr><td>1</td><td>Vermont</td><td>88.2</td><td>45</td><td>Arizona</td><td>1.0</td></tr>
<tr><td>17</td><td>Virginia</td><td>13.9</td><td>46</td><td>California</td><td>0.8</td></tr>
<tr><td>30</td><td>Washington</td><td>5.7</td><td>47</td><td>Massachusetts</td><td>0.0</td></tr>
<tr><td>8</td><td>West Virginia</td><td>26.7</td><td>47</td><td>New Jersey</td><td>0.0</td></tr>
<tr><td>21</td><td>Wisconsin</td><td>8.9</td><td>47</td><td>North Dakota</td><td>0.0</td></tr>
<tr><td>11</td><td>Wyoming</td><td>20.0</td><td>NA</td><td>Illinois**</td><td>NA</td></tr>
<tr><td></td><td></td><td></td><td></td><td>District of Columbia</td><td>0.0</td></tr>
</table>

Source: CQ Press using reported data from the Federal Bureau of Investigation
   "Crime in the United States 2008" (Uniform Crime Reports, September 14, 2009, http://www.fbi.gov/ucr/ucr.htm)
*Estimated percentages for nonmetropolitan areas, defined by the F.B.I. as other than Metropolitan Statistical Areas and other cities outside such areas. National percent includes those states listed as not available. Includes nonnegligent manslaughter.
**Not available.

Rapes in Urban Areas in 2008

National Urban Total = 81,959 Rapes*

ALPHA ORDER

RANK	STATE	RAPES	% of USA
18	Alabama	1,456	1.8%
38	Alaska	389	0.5%
14	Arizona	1,639	2.0%
21	Arkansas	1,230	1.5%
1	California	8,749	10.7%
9	Colorado	2,028	2.5%
34	Connecticut	611	0.7%
41	Delaware	292	0.4%
3	Florida	5,730	7.0%
10	Georgia	2,019	2.5%
45	Hawaii	203	0.2%
36	Idaho	493	0.6%
NA	Illinois**	NA	NA
16	Indiana	1,577	1.9%
32	Iowa	821	1.0%
23	Kansas	1,100	1.3%
30	Kentucky	896	1.1%
26	Louisiana	1,070	1.3%
40	Maine	326	0.4%
25	Maryland	1,089	1.3%
13	Massachusetts	1,736	2.1%
5	Michigan	3,768	4.6%
NA	Minnesota**	NA	NA
33	Mississippi	656	0.8%
17	Missouri	1,508	1.8%
46	Montana	188	0.2%
35	Nebraska	547	0.7%
27	Nevada	1,043	1.3%
39	New Hampshire	378	0.5%
22	New Jersey	1,122	1.4%
28	New Mexico	1,035	1.3%
7	New York	2,578	3.1%
11	North Carolina	1,953	2.4%
44	North Dakota	209	0.3%
4	Ohio	4,172	5.1%
20	Oklahoma	1,347	1.6%
24	Oregon	1,092	1.3%
6	Pennsylvania	3,124	3.8%
43	Rhode Island	272	0.3%
19	South Carolina	1,405	1.7%
37	South Dakota	390	0.5%
12	Tennessee	1,882	2.3%
2	Texas	7,695	9.4%
31	Utah	853	1.0%
48	Vermont	95	0.1%
15	Virginia	1,596	1.9%
8	Washington	2,489	3.0%
42	West Virginia	281	0.3%
29	Wisconsin	998	1.2%
47	Wyoming	152	0.2%

RANK ORDER

RANK	STATE	RAPES	% of USA
1	California	8,749	10.7%
2	Texas	7,695	9.4%
3	Florida	5,730	7.0%
4	Ohio	4,172	5.1%
5	Michigan	3,768	4.6%
6	Pennsylvania	3,124	3.8%
7	New York	2,578	3.1%
8	Washington	2,489	3.0%
9	Colorado	2,028	2.5%
10	Georgia	2,019	2.5%
11	North Carolina	1,953	2.4%
12	Tennessee	1,882	2.3%
13	Massachusetts	1,736	2.1%
14	Arizona	1,639	2.0%
15	Virginia	1,596	1.9%
16	Indiana	1,577	1.9%
17	Missouri	1,508	1.8%
18	Alabama	1,456	1.8%
19	South Carolina	1,405	1.7%
20	Oklahoma	1,347	1.6%
21	Arkansas	1,230	1.5%
22	New Jersey	1,122	1.4%
23	Kansas	1,100	1.3%
24	Oregon	1,092	1.3%
25	Maryland	1,089	1.3%
26	Louisiana	1,070	1.3%
27	Nevada	1,043	1.3%
28	New Mexico	1,035	1.3%
29	Wisconsin	998	1.2%
30	Kentucky	896	1.1%
31	Utah	853	1.0%
32	Iowa	821	1.0%
33	Mississippi	656	0.8%
34	Connecticut	611	0.7%
35	Nebraska	547	0.7%
36	Idaho	493	0.6%
37	South Dakota	390	0.5%
38	Alaska	389	0.5%
39	New Hampshire	378	0.5%
40	Maine	326	0.4%
41	Delaware	292	0.4%
42	West Virginia	281	0.3%
43	Rhode Island	272	0.3%
44	North Dakota	209	0.3%
45	Hawaii	203	0.2%
46	Montana	188	0.2%
47	Wyoming	152	0.2%
48	Vermont	95	0.1%
NA	Illinois**	NA	NA
NA	Minnesota**	NA	NA
	District of Columbia	186	0.2%

Source: CQ Press using reported data from the Federal Bureau of Investigation
"Crime in the United States 2008" (Uniform Crime Reports, September 14, 2009, http://www.fbi.gov/ucr/ucr.htm)
*Estimated totals for urban areas, defined by the F.B.I. as Metropolitan Statistical Areas and other cities outside such areas. National total includes those states listed as not available. Forcible rape is the carnal knowledge of a female forcibly and against her will. Attempts are included. However, statutory rape without force and other sex offenses are excluded.
**Not available.

Urban Rape Rate in 2008

National Urban Rate = 29.9 Rapes per 100,000 Population*

ALPHA ORDER

RANK	STATE	RATE
18	Alabama	37.1
1	Alaska	84.5
36	Arizona	26.3
4	Arkansas	55.7
38	California	24.2
6	Colorado	44.4
45	Connecticut	20.5
13	Delaware	40.2
25	Florida	32.8
39	Georgia	23.6
43	Hawaii	22.4
15	Idaho	39.8
NA	Illinois**	NA
32	Indiana	28.7
20	Iowa	36.1
6	Kansas	44.4
28	Kentucky	30.1
31	Louisiana	29.3
27	Maine	31.2
46	Maryland	20.1
34	Massachusetts	26.7
10	Michigan	42.8
NA	Minnesota**	NA
21	Mississippi	34.8
30	Missouri	29.7
22	Montana	34.1
16	Nebraska	38.2
9	Nevada	43.8
29	New Hampshire	29.8
48	New Jersey	12.9
3	New Mexico	60.4
47	New York	13.9
35	North Carolina	26.6
5	North Dakota	46.6
11	Ohio	40.9
6	Oklahoma	44.4
26	Oregon	32.6
33	Pennsylvania	27.4
37	Rhode Island	25.9
17	South Carolina	38.1
2	South Dakota	67.6
19	Tennessee	36.4
23	Texas	33.9
24	Utah	33.0
40	Vermont	23.0
40	Virginia	23.0
11	Washington	40.9
42	West Virginia	22.9
44	Wisconsin	21.1
14	Wyoming	40.1

RANK ORDER

RANK	STATE	RATE
1	Alaska	84.5
2	South Dakota	67.6
3	New Mexico	60.4
4	Arkansas	55.7
5	North Dakota	46.6
6	Colorado	44.4
6	Kansas	44.4
6	Oklahoma	44.4
9	Nevada	43.8
10	Michigan	42.8
11	Ohio	40.9
11	Washington	40.9
13	Delaware	40.2
14	Wyoming	40.1
15	Idaho	39.8
16	Nebraska	38.2
17	South Carolina	38.1
18	Alabama	37.1
19	Tennessee	36.4
20	Iowa	36.1
21	Mississippi	34.8
22	Montana	34.1
23	Texas	33.9
24	Utah	33.0
25	Florida	32.8
26	Oregon	32.6
27	Maine	31.2
28	Kentucky	30.1
29	New Hampshire	29.8
30	Missouri	29.7
31	Louisiana	29.3
32	Indiana	28.7
33	Pennsylvania	27.4
34	Massachusetts	26.7
35	North Carolina	26.6
36	Arizona	26.3
37	Rhode Island	25.9
38	California	24.2
39	Georgia	23.6
40	Vermont	23.0
40	Virginia	23.0
42	West Virginia	22.9
43	Hawaii	22.4
44	Wisconsin	21.1
45	Connecticut	20.5
46	Maryland	20.1
47	New York	13.9
48	New Jersey	12.9
NA	Illinois**	NA
NA	Minnesota**	NA

District of Columbia   31.4

Source: CQ Press using reported data from the Federal Bureau of Investigation
"Crime in the United States 2008" (Uniform Crime Reports, September 14, 2009, http://www.fbi.gov/ucr/ucr.htm)
*Estimated rates for urban areas, defined by the F.B.I. as Metropolitan Statistical Areas and other cities outside such areas.
National rate includes those states listed as not available. Forcible rape is the carnal knowledge of a female forcibly and against her will. Attempts are included. However, statutory rape without force and other sex offenses are excluded.
**Not available.

Percent of Rapes Occurring in Urban Areas in 2008

National Percent = 92.1% of Rapes*

<table>
<tr><td colspan="3">ALPHA ORDER</td><td colspan="3">RANK ORDER</td></tr>
<tr><th>RANK</th><th>STATE</th><th>PERCENT</th><th>RANK</th><th>STATE</th><th>PERCENT</th></tr>
<tr><td>30</td><td>Alabama</td><td>90.0</td><td>1</td><td>Massachusetts</td><td>100.0</td></tr>
<tr><td>34</td><td>Alaska</td><td>88.2</td><td>1</td><td>New Jersey</td><td>100.0</td></tr>
<tr><td>5</td><td>Arizona</td><td>98.0</td><td>3</td><td>California</td><td>98.3</td></tr>
<tr><td>34</td><td>Arkansas</td><td>88.2</td><td>4</td><td>Rhode Island</td><td>98.2</td></tr>
<tr><td>3</td><td>California</td><td>98.3</td><td>5</td><td>Arizona</td><td>98.0</td></tr>
<tr><td>6</td><td>Colorado</td><td>96.7</td><td>6</td><td>Colorado</td><td>96.7</td></tr>
<tr><td>27</td><td>Connecticut</td><td>90.7</td><td>6</td><td>New Hampshire</td><td>96.7</td></tr>
<tr><td>42</td><td>Delaware</td><td>79.8</td><td>8</td><td>Maryland</td><td>96.6</td></tr>
<tr><td>10</td><td>Florida</td><td>95.9</td><td>9</td><td>Texas</td><td>96.0</td></tr>
<tr><td>20</td><td>Georgia</td><td>92.0</td><td>10</td><td>Florida</td><td>95.9</td></tr>
<tr><td>48</td><td>Hawaii</td><td>55.6</td><td>11</td><td>Utah</td><td>95.5</td></tr>
<tr><td>32</td><td>Idaho</td><td>89.5</td><td>12</td><td>Washington</td><td>94.7</td></tr>
<tr><td>NA</td><td>Illinois**</td><td>NA</td><td>13</td><td>Nevada</td><td>94.6</td></tr>
<tr><td>23</td><td>Indiana</td><td>91.7</td><td>14</td><td>Oregon</td><td>94.5</td></tr>
<tr><td>18</td><td>Iowa</td><td>92.5</td><td>15</td><td>Ohio</td><td>94.4</td></tr>
<tr><td>19</td><td>Kansas</td><td>92.4</td><td>16</td><td>Nebraska</td><td>93.8</td></tr>
<tr><td>47</td><td>Kentucky</td><td>63.6</td><td>17</td><td>Missouri</td><td>93.4</td></tr>
<tr><td>36</td><td>Louisiana</td><td>86.9</td><td>18</td><td>Iowa</td><td>92.5</td></tr>
<tr><td>36</td><td>Maine</td><td>86.9</td><td>19</td><td>Kansas</td><td>92.4</td></tr>
<tr><td>8</td><td>Maryland</td><td>96.6</td><td>20</td><td>Georgia</td><td>92.0</td></tr>
<tr><td>1</td><td>Massachusetts</td><td>100.0</td><td>20</td><td>New York</td><td>92.0</td></tr>
<tr><td>41</td><td>Michigan</td><td>83.7</td><td>22</td><td>Oklahoma</td><td>91.9</td></tr>
<tr><td>NA</td><td>Minnesota**</td><td>NA</td><td>23</td><td>Indiana</td><td>91.7</td></tr>
<tr><td>45</td><td>Mississippi</td><td>73.7</td><td>24</td><td>Tennessee</td><td>91.3</td></tr>
<tr><td>17</td><td>Missouri</td><td>93.4</td><td>25</td><td>New Mexico</td><td>90.9</td></tr>
<tr><td>46</td><td>Montana</td><td>63.9</td><td>26</td><td>Virginia</td><td>90.8</td></tr>
<tr><td>16</td><td>Nebraska</td><td>93.8</td><td>27</td><td>Connecticut</td><td>90.7</td></tr>
<tr><td>13</td><td>Nevada</td><td>94.6</td><td>28</td><td>South Dakota</td><td>90.3</td></tr>
<tr><td>6</td><td>New Hampshire</td><td>96.7</td><td>29</td><td>North Dakota</td><td>90.1</td></tr>
<tr><td>1</td><td>New Jersey</td><td>100.0</td><td>30</td><td>Alabama</td><td>90.0</td></tr>
<tr><td>25</td><td>New Mexico</td><td>90.9</td><td>31</td><td>Pennsylvania</td><td>89.8</td></tr>
<tr><td>20</td><td>New York</td><td>92.0</td><td>32</td><td>Idaho</td><td>89.5</td></tr>
<tr><td>39</td><td>North Carolina</td><td>85.5</td><td>33</td><td>Wisconsin</td><td>89.1</td></tr>
<tr><td>29</td><td>North Dakota</td><td>90.1</td><td>34</td><td>Alaska</td><td>88.2</td></tr>
<tr><td>15</td><td>Ohio</td><td>94.4</td><td>34</td><td>Arkansas</td><td>88.2</td></tr>
<tr><td>22</td><td>Oklahoma</td><td>91.9</td><td>36</td><td>Louisiana</td><td>86.9</td></tr>
<tr><td>14</td><td>Oregon</td><td>94.5</td><td>36</td><td>Maine</td><td>86.9</td></tr>
<tr><td>31</td><td>Pennsylvania</td><td>89.8</td><td>38</td><td>South Carolina</td><td>85.8</td></tr>
<tr><td>4</td><td>Rhode Island</td><td>98.2</td><td>39</td><td>North Carolina</td><td>85.5</td></tr>
<tr><td>38</td><td>South Carolina</td><td>85.8</td><td>40</td><td>Wyoming</td><td>84.4</td></tr>
<tr><td>28</td><td>South Dakota</td><td>90.3</td><td>41</td><td>Michigan</td><td>83.7</td></tr>
<tr><td>24</td><td>Tennessee</td><td>91.3</td><td>42</td><td>Delaware</td><td>79.8</td></tr>
<tr><td>9</td><td>Texas</td><td>96.0</td><td>43</td><td>West Virginia</td><td>77.6</td></tr>
<tr><td>11</td><td>Utah</td><td>95.5</td><td>44</td><td>Vermont</td><td>74.8</td></tr>
<tr><td>44</td><td>Vermont</td><td>74.8</td><td>45</td><td>Mississippi</td><td>73.7</td></tr>
<tr><td>26</td><td>Virginia</td><td>90.8</td><td>46</td><td>Montana</td><td>63.9</td></tr>
<tr><td>12</td><td>Washington</td><td>94.7</td><td>47</td><td>Kentucky</td><td>63.6</td></tr>
<tr><td>43</td><td>West Virginia</td><td>77.6</td><td>48</td><td>Hawaii</td><td>55.6</td></tr>
<tr><td>33</td><td>Wisconsin</td><td>89.1</td><td>NA</td><td>Illinois**</td><td>NA</td></tr>
<tr><td>40</td><td>Wyoming</td><td>84.4</td><td>NA</td><td>Minnesota**</td><td>NA</td></tr>
<tr><td></td><td></td><td></td><td></td><td>District of Columbia</td><td>100.0</td></tr>
</table>

Source: CQ Press using reported data from the Federal Bureau of Investigation
"Crime in the United States 2008" (Uniform Crime Reports, September 14, 2009, http://www.fbi.gov/ucr/ucr.htm)
*Estimated percentages for urban areas, defined by the F.B.I. as Metropolitan Statistical Areas and other cities outside such areas. National percent includes those states listed as not available. Forcible rape is the carnal knowledge of a female forcibly and against her will. Attempts are included. However, statutory rape without force and other sex offenses are excluded.
**Not available.

Rapes in Rural Areas in 2008

National Rural Total = 7,041 Rapes*

RANK	STATE	RAPES	% of USA
17	Alabama	161	2.3%
35	Alaska	52	0.7%
41	Arizona	34	0.5%
13	Arkansas	165	2.3%
18	California	154	2.2%
29	Colorado	70	1.0%
32	Connecticut	63	0.9%
28	Delaware	74	1.1%
7	Florida	242	3.4%
12	Georgia	176	2.5%
14	Hawaii	162	2.3%
34	Idaho	58	0.8%
NA	Illinois**	NA	NA
19	Indiana	143	2.0%
30	Iowa	67	1.0%
26	Kansas	90	1.3%
2	Kentucky	512	7.3%
14	Louisiana	162	2.3%
36	Maine	49	0.7%
39	Maryland	38	0.5%
47	Massachusetts	0	0.0%
1	Michigan	734	10.4%
NA	Minnesota**	NA	NA
8	Mississippi	234	3.3%
23	Missouri	107	1.5%
24	Montana	106	1.5%
40	Nebraska	36	0.5%
33	Nevada	59	0.8%
45	New Hampshire	13	0.2%
47	New Jersey	0	0.0%
25	New Mexico	104	1.5%
10	New York	223	3.2%
4	North Carolina	331	4.7%
44	North Dakota	23	0.3%
6	Ohio	247	3.5%
22	Oklahoma	119	1.7%
31	Oregon	64	0.9%
3	Pennsylvania	354	5.0%
46	Rhode Island	5	0.1%
9	South Carolina	233	3.3%
37	South Dakota	42	0.6%
11	Tennessee	180	2.6%
5	Texas	319	4.5%
38	Utah	40	0.6%
42	Vermont	32	0.5%
14	Virginia	162	2.3%
20	Washington	139	2.0%
27	West Virginia	81	1.2%
21	Wisconsin	122	1.7%
43	Wyoming	28	0.4%

RANK	STATE	RAPES	% of USA
1	Michigan	734	10.4%
2	Kentucky	512	7.3%
3	Pennsylvania	354	5.0%
4	North Carolina	331	4.7%
5	Texas	319	4.5%
6	Ohio	247	3.5%
7	Florida	242	3.4%
8	Mississippi	234	3.3%
9	South Carolina	233	3.3%
10	New York	223	3.2%
11	Tennessee	180	2.6%
12	Georgia	176	2.5%
13	Arkansas	165	2.3%
14	Hawaii	162	2.3%
14	Louisiana	162	2.3%
14	Virginia	162	2.3%
17	Alabama	161	2.3%
18	California	154	2.2%
19	Indiana	143	2.0%
20	Washington	139	2.0%
21	Wisconsin	122	1.7%
22	Oklahoma	119	1.7%
23	Missouri	107	1.5%
24	Montana	106	1.5%
25	New Mexico	104	1.5%
26	Kansas	90	1.3%
27	West Virginia	81	1.2%
28	Delaware	74	1.1%
29	Colorado	70	1.0%
30	Iowa	67	1.0%
31	Oregon	64	0.9%
32	Connecticut	63	0.9%
33	Nevada	59	0.8%
34	Idaho	58	0.8%
35	Alaska	52	0.7%
36	Maine	49	0.7%
37	South Dakota	42	0.6%
38	Utah	40	0.6%
39	Maryland	38	0.5%
40	Nebraska	36	0.5%
41	Arizona	34	0.5%
42	Vermont	32	0.5%
43	Wyoming	28	0.4%
44	North Dakota	23	0.3%
45	New Hampshire	13	0.2%
46	Rhode Island	5	0.1%
47	Massachusetts	0	0.0%
47	New Jersey	0	0.0%
NA	Illinois**	NA	NA
NA	Minnesota**	NA	NA
	District of Columbia	0	0.0%

Source: Reported data from the Federal Bureau of Investigation
"Crime in the United States 2008" (Uniform Crime Reports, September 14, 2009, http://www.fbi.gov/ucr/ucr.htm)
*Estimated totals for nonmetropolitan areas, defined by the F.B.I. as other than Metropolitan Statistical Areas and other cities outside such areas. National total includes those states listed as not available. Forcible rape is the carnal knowledge of a female forcibly and against her will. Attempts are included. However, statutory rape without force and other sex offenses are excluded. **Not available.

Rural Rape Rate in 2008

National Rural Rate = 23.4 Rapes per 100,000 Population*

ALPHA ORDER

RANK	STATE	RATE
20	Alabama	21.9
17	Alaska	23.0
40	Arizona	12.8
15	Arkansas	25.5
11	California	27.2
27	Colorado	18.9
42	Connecticut	12.1
2	Delaware	50.6
10	Florida	27.5
35	Georgia	15.7
3	Hawaii	42.4
22	Idaho	20.3
NA	Illinois**	NA
34	Indiana	16.1
45	Iowa	9.2
9	Kansas	27.6
4	Kentucky	39.5
21	Louisiana	21.4
30	Maine	18.1
32	Maryland	17.1
46	Massachusetts	0.0
1	Michigan	60.9
NA	Minnesota**	NA
19	Mississippi	22.2
41	Missouri	12.7
16	Montana	25.4
44	Nebraska	10.2
12	Nevada	27.1
13	New Hampshire	26.9
46	New Jersey	0.0
5	New Mexico	38.4
18	New York	22.7
31	North Carolina	17.5
43	North Dakota	11.9
26	Ohio	19.0
24	Oklahoma	19.4
37	Oregon	14.4
6	Pennsylvania	33.4
46	Rhode Island	0.0
8	South Carolina	29.3
28	South Dakota	18.5
32	Tennessee	17.1
23	Texas	19.8
14	Utah	26.2
36	Vermont	15.4
24	Virginia	19.4
7	Washington	29.7
38	West Virginia	13.8
39	Wisconsin	13.5
29	Wyoming	18.2

RANK ORDER

RANK	STATE	RATE
1	Michigan	60.9
2	Delaware	50.6
3	Hawaii	42.4
4	Kentucky	39.5
5	New Mexico	38.4
6	Pennsylvania	33.4
7	Washington	29.7
8	South Carolina	29.3
9	Kansas	27.6
10	Florida	27.5
11	California	27.2
12	Nevada	27.1
13	New Hampshire	26.9
14	Utah	26.2
15	Arkansas	25.5
16	Montana	25.4
17	Alaska	23.0
18	New York	22.7
19	Mississippi	22.2
20	Alabama	21.9
21	Louisiana	21.4
22	Idaho	20.3
23	Texas	19.8
24	Oklahoma	19.4
24	Virginia	19.4
26	Ohio	19.0
27	Colorado	18.9
28	South Dakota	18.5
29	Wyoming	18.2
30	Maine	18.1
31	North Carolina	17.5
32	Maryland	17.1
32	Tennessee	17.1
34	Indiana	16.1
35	Georgia	15.7
36	Vermont	15.4
37	Oregon	14.4
38	West Virginia	13.8
39	Wisconsin	13.5
40	Arizona	12.8
41	Missouri	12.7
42	Connecticut	12.1
43	North Dakota	11.9
44	Nebraska	10.2
45	Iowa	9.2
46	Massachusetts	0.0
46	New Jersey	0.0
46	Rhode Island	0.0
NA	Illinois**	NA
NA	Minnesota**	NA

District of Columbia | 0.0

Source: CQ Press using reported data from the Federal Bureau of Investigation
 "Crime in the United States 2008" (Uniform Crime Reports, September 14, 2009, http://www.fbi.gov/ucr/ucr.htm)
*Estimated rates for nonmetropolitan areas, defined by the F.B.I. as other than Metropolitan Statistical Areas and other cities outside such areas. National rate includes those states listed as not available. Forcible rape is the carnal knowledge of a female forcibly and against her will. Attempts are included. However, statutory rape without force and other sex offenses are excluded. **Not available.

Percent of Rapes Occurring in Rural Areas in 2008

National Percent = 7.9% of Rapes*

ALPHA ORDER

RANK	STATE	PERCENT
19	Alabama	10.0
14	Alaska	11.8
44	Arizona	2.0
14	Arkansas	11.8
46	California	1.7
42	Colorado	3.3
22	Connecticut	9.3
7	Delaware	20.2
39	Florida	4.1
28	Georgia	8.0
1	Hawaii	44.4
17	Idaho	10.5
NA	Illinois**	NA
26	Indiana	8.3
31	Iowa	7.5
30	Kansas	7.6
2	Kentucky	36.4
12	Louisiana	13.1
12	Maine	13.1
41	Maryland	3.4
47	Massachusetts	0.0
8	Michigan	16.3
NA	Minnesota**	NA
4	Mississippi	26.3
32	Missouri	6.6
3	Montana	36.1
33	Nebraska	6.2
36	Nevada	5.4
42	New Hampshire	3.3
47	New Jersey	0.0
24	New Mexico	9.1
28	New York	8.0
10	North Carolina	14.5
20	North Dakota	9.9
34	Ohio	5.6
27	Oklahoma	8.1
35	Oregon	5.5
18	Pennsylvania	10.2
45	Rhode Island	1.8
11	South Carolina	14.2
21	South Dakota	9.7
25	Tennessee	8.7
40	Texas	4.0
38	Utah	4.5
5	Vermont	25.2
23	Virginia	9.2
37	Washington	5.3
6	West Virginia	22.4
16	Wisconsin	10.9
9	Wyoming	15.6

RANK ORDER

RANK	STATE	PERCENT
1	Hawaii	44.4
2	Kentucky	36.4
3	Montana	36.1
4	Mississippi	26.3
5	Vermont	25.2
6	West Virginia	22.4
7	Delaware	20.2
8	Michigan	16.3
9	Wyoming	15.6
10	North Carolina	14.5
11	South Carolina	14.2
12	Louisiana	13.1
12	Maine	13.1
14	Alaska	11.8
14	Arkansas	11.8
16	Wisconsin	10.9
17	Idaho	10.5
18	Pennsylvania	10.2
19	Alabama	10.0
20	North Dakota	9.9
21	South Dakota	9.7
22	Connecticut	9.3
23	Virginia	9.2
24	New Mexico	9.1
25	Tennessee	8.7
26	Indiana	8.3
27	Oklahoma	8.1
28	Georgia	8.0
28	New York	8.0
30	Kansas	7.6
31	Iowa	7.5
32	Missouri	6.6
33	Nebraska	6.2
34	Ohio	5.6
35	Oregon	5.5
36	Nevada	5.4
37	Washington	5.3
38	Utah	4.5
39	Florida	4.1
40	Texas	4.0
41	Maryland	3.4
42	Colorado	3.3
42	New Hampshire	3.3
44	Arizona	2.0
45	Rhode Island	1.8
46	California	1.7
47	Massachusetts	0.0
47	New Jersey	0.0
NA	Illinois**	NA
NA	Minnesota**	NA

District of Columbia	0.0

Source: CQ Press using reported data from the Federal Bureau of Investigation
"Crime in the United States 2008" (Uniform Crime Reports, September 14, 2009, http://www.fbi.gov/ucr/ucr.htm)
*Estimated percentages for nonmetropolitan areas, defined by the F.B.I. as other than Metropolitan Statistical Areas and other cities outside such areas. National percent includes those states listed as not available. Forcible rape is the carnal knowledge of a female forcibly and against her will. Attempts are included. However, statutory rape without force and other sex offenses are excluded. **Not available.

Robberies in Urban Areas in 2008

National Urban Total = 436,696 Robberies*

RANK	STATE	ROBBERIES	% of USA
17	Alabama	7,229	1.7%
41	Alaska	612	0.1%
13	Arizona	9,675	2.2%
29	Arkansas	2,665	0.6%
1	California	69,230	15.9%
28	Colorado	3,351	0.8%
25	Connecticut	3,854	0.9%
33	Delaware	1,745	0.4%
3	Florida	35,863	8.2%
7	Georgia	17,109	3.9%
38	Hawaii	928	0.2%
44	Idaho	228	0.1%
NA	Illinois**	NA	NA
14	Indiana	7,457	1.7%
37	Iowa	1,236	0.3%
34	Kansas	1,659	0.4%
26	Kentucky	3,783	0.9%
22	Louisiana	5,768	1.3%
43	Maine	327	0.1%
9	Maryland	13,118	3.0%
18	Massachusetts	7,069	1.6%
10	Michigan	12,898	3.0%
24	Minnesota	4,151	1.0%
30	Mississippi	2,662	0.6%
15	Missouri	7,342	1.7%
45	Montana	152	0.0%
36	Nebraska	1,282	0.3%
19	Nevada	6,432	1.5%
42	New Hampshire	416	0.1%
11	New Jersey	12,701	2.9%
32	New Mexico	2,117	0.5%
4	New York	31,706	7.3%
8	North Carolina	13,602	3.1%
49	North Dakota	71	0.0%
6	Ohio	18,606	4.3%
27	Oklahoma	3,652	0.8%
31	Oregon	2,606	0.6%
5	Pennsylvania	18,702	4.3%
39	Rhode Island	879	0.2%
21	South Carolina	5,987	1.4%
46	South Dakota	112	0.0%
12	Tennessee	10,657	2.4%
2	Texas	37,579	8.6%
35	Utah	1,411	0.3%
48	Vermont	79	0.0%
16	Virginia	7,261	1.7%
20	Washington	6,292	1.4%
40	West Virginia	802	0.2%
23	Wisconsin	5,097	1.2%
47	Wyoming	84	0.0%

RANK	STATE	ROBBERIES	% of USA
1	California	69,230	15.9%
2	Texas	37,579	8.6%
3	Florida	35,863	8.2%
4	New York	31,706	7.3%
5	Pennsylvania	18,702	4.3%
6	Ohio	18,606	4.3%
7	Georgia	17,109	3.9%
8	North Carolina	13,602	3.1%
9	Maryland	13,118	3.0%
10	Michigan	12,898	3.0%
11	New Jersey	12,701	2.9%
12	Tennessee	10,657	2.4%
13	Arizona	9,675	2.2%
14	Indiana	7,457	1.7%
15	Missouri	7,342	1.7%
16	Virginia	7,261	1.7%
17	Alabama	7,229	1.7%
18	Massachusetts	7,069	1.6%
19	Nevada	6,432	1.5%
20	Washington	6,292	1.4%
21	South Carolina	5,987	1.4%
22	Louisiana	5,768	1.3%
23	Wisconsin	5,097	1.2%
24	Minnesota	4,151	1.0%
25	Connecticut	3,854	0.9%
26	Kentucky	3,783	0.9%
27	Oklahoma	3,652	0.8%
28	Colorado	3,351	0.8%
29	Arkansas	2,665	0.6%
30	Mississippi	2,662	0.6%
31	Oregon	2,606	0.6%
32	New Mexico	2,117	0.5%
33	Delaware	1,745	0.4%
34	Kansas	1,659	0.4%
35	Utah	1,411	0.3%
36	Nebraska	1,282	0.3%
37	Iowa	1,236	0.3%
38	Hawaii	928	0.2%
39	Rhode Island	879	0.2%
40	West Virginia	802	0.2%
41	Alaska	612	0.1%
42	New Hampshire	416	0.1%
43	Maine	327	0.1%
44	Idaho	228	0.1%
45	Montana	152	0.0%
46	South Dakota	112	0.0%
47	Wyoming	84	0.0%
48	Vermont	79	0.0%
49	North Dakota	71	0.0%
NA	Illinois**	NA	NA
	District of Columbia	4,430	1.0%

Source: CQ Press using reported data from the Federal Bureau of Investigation
"Crime in the United States 2008" (Uniform Crime Reports, September 14, 2009, http://www.fbi.gov/ucr/ucr.htm)
*Estimated totals for urban areas, defined by the F.B.I. as Metropolitan Statistical Areas and other cities outside such areas.
National total includes those states listed as not available. Robbery is the taking or attempting to take anything of value by force or threat of force.
**Not available.

Urban Robbery Rate in 2008

National Urban Rate = 159.4 Robberies per 100,000 Population*

ALPHA ORDER

RANK	STATE	RATE
9	Alabama	184.1
22	Alaska	133.0
16	Arizona	155.2
26	Arkansas	120.6
7	California	191.3
37	Colorado	73.3
23	Connecticut	129.3
3	Delaware	240.1
5	Florida	205.6
6	Georgia	199.7
32	Hawaii	102.4
48	Idaho	18.4
NA	Illinois**	NA
21	Indiana	135.8
41	Iowa	54.3
38	Kansas	67.0
24	Kentucky	127.2
15	Louisiana	157.8
43	Maine	31.3
2	Maryland	242.4
28	Massachusetts	108.8
17	Michigan	146.6
33	Minnesota	94.2
20	Mississippi	141.2
19	Missouri	144.7
44	Montana	27.6
34	Nebraska	89.5
1	Nevada	269.9
42	New Hampshire	32.8
18	New Jersey	146.3
25	New Mexico	123.6
11	New York	171.3
8	North Carolina	185.5
49	North Dakota	15.8
10	Ohio	182.6
27	Oklahoma	120.5
36	Oregon	77.9
13	Pennsylvania	164.2
35	Rhode Island	83.7
14	South Carolina	162.5
46	South Dakota	19.4
4	Tennessee	206.4
12	Texas	165.4
40	Utah	54.6
47	Vermont	19.1
30	Virginia	104.7
31	Washington	103.5
39	West Virginia	65.2
29	Wisconsin	107.9
45	Wyoming	22.2

RANK ORDER

RANK	STATE	RATE
1	Nevada	269.9
2	Maryland	242.4
3	Delaware	240.1
4	Tennessee	206.4
5	Florida	205.6
6	Georgia	199.7
7	California	191.3
8	North Carolina	185.5
9	Alabama	184.1
10	Ohio	182.6
11	New York	171.3
12	Texas	165.4
13	Pennsylvania	164.2
14	South Carolina	162.5
15	Louisiana	157.8
16	Arizona	155.2
17	Michigan	146.6
18	New Jersey	146.3
19	Missouri	144.7
20	Mississippi	141.2
21	Indiana	135.8
22	Alaska	133.0
23	Connecticut	129.3
24	Kentucky	127.2
25	New Mexico	123.6
26	Arkansas	120.6
27	Oklahoma	120.5
28	Massachusetts	108.8
29	Wisconsin	107.9
30	Virginia	104.7
31	Washington	103.5
32	Hawaii	102.4
33	Minnesota	94.2
34	Nebraska	89.5
35	Rhode Island	83.7
36	Oregon	77.9
37	Colorado	73.3
38	Kansas	67.0
39	West Virginia	65.2
40	Utah	54.6
41	Iowa	54.3
42	New Hampshire	32.8
43	Maine	31.3
44	Montana	27.6
45	Wyoming	22.2
46	South Dakota	19.4
47	Vermont	19.1
48	Idaho	18.4
49	North Dakota	15.8
NA	Illinois**	NA

District of Columbia — 748.5

Source: CQ Press using reported data from the Federal Bureau of Investigation
  "Crime in the United States 2008" (Uniform Crime Reports, September 14, 2009, http://www.fbi.gov/ucr/ucr.htm)
*Estimated rates for urban areas, defined by the F.B.I. as Metropolitan Statistical Areas and other cities outside such areas.
National rate includes those states listed as not available. Robbery is the taking or attempting to take anything of value by
force or threat of force.
**Not available.

Percent of Robberies Occurring in Urban Areas in 2008

National Percent = 98.8% of Robberies*

ALPHA ORDER				RANK ORDER		
RANK	STATE	PERCENT		RANK	STATE	PERCENT
31	Alabama	98.4		1	Massachusetts	100.0
38	Alaska	94.9		1	New Jersey	100.0
4	Arizona	99.8		1	Rhode Island	100.0
36	Arkansas	97.4		4	Arizona	99.8
4	California	99.8		4	California	99.8
7	Colorado	99.6		4	New York	99.8
27	Connecticut	98.6		7	Colorado	99.6
38	Delaware	94.9		8	Michigan	99.5
23	Florida	98.9		8	Texas	99.5
27	Georgia	98.6		10	Maryland	99.4
49	Hawaii	85.5		10	Minnesota	99.4
41	Idaho	94.6		10	Missouri	99.4
NA	Illinois**	NA		10	Nevada	99.4
21	Indiana	99.0		10	Ohio	99.4
21	Iowa	99.0		10	Wisconsin	99.4
30	Kansas	98.5		16	New Hampshire	99.3
42	Kentucky	94.5		16	Utah	99.3
37	Louisiana	96.2		18	Oklahoma	99.2
32	Maine	98.2		19	Pennsylvania	99.1
10	Maryland	99.4		19	Washington	99.1
1	Massachusetts	100.0		21	Indiana	99.0
8	Michigan	99.5		21	Iowa	99.0
10	Minnesota	99.4		23	Florida	98.9
48	Mississippi	88.3		24	Nebraska	98.7
10	Missouri	99.4		24	Oregon	98.7
47	Montana	88.4		24	Tennessee	98.7
24	Nebraska	98.7		27	Connecticut	98.6
10	Nevada	99.4		27	Georgia	98.6
16	New Hampshire	99.3		27	North Dakota	98.6
1	New Jersey	100.0		30	Kansas	98.5
35	New Mexico	97.5		31	Alabama	98.4
4	New York	99.8		32	Maine	98.2
38	North Carolina	94.9		33	Wyoming	97.7
27	North Dakota	98.6		34	Virginia	97.6
10	Ohio	99.4		35	New Mexico	97.5
18	Oklahoma	99.2		36	Arkansas	97.4
24	Oregon	98.7		37	Louisiana	96.2
19	Pennsylvania	99.1		38	Alaska	94.9
1	Rhode Island	100.0		38	Delaware	94.9
44	South Carolina	90.7		38	North Carolina	94.9
43	South Dakota	93.3		41	Idaho	94.6
24	Tennessee	98.7		42	Kentucky	94.5
8	Texas	99.5		43	South Dakota	93.3
16	Utah	99.3		44	South Carolina	90.7
46	Vermont	88.8		45	West Virginia	90.2
34	Virginia	97.6		46	Vermont	88.8
19	Washington	99.1		47	Montana	88.4
45	West Virginia	90.2		48	Mississippi	88.3
10	Wisconsin	99.4		49	Hawaii	85.5
33	Wyoming	97.7		NA	Illinois**	NA
					District of Columbia	100.0

Source: CQ Press using reported data from the Federal Bureau of Investigation
"Crime in the United States 2008" (Uniform Crime Reports, September 14, 2009, http://www.fbi.gov/ucr/ucr.htm)
*Estimated percentages for urban areas, defined by the F.B.I. as Metropolitan Statistical Areas and other cities outside such areas. National percent includes those states listed as not available. Robbery is the taking or attempting to take anything of value by force or threat of force.
**Not available.

Robberies in Rural Areas in 2008

National Rural Total = 5,159 Robberies*

ALPHA ORDER

RANK	STATE	ROBBERIES	% of USA
14	Alabama	117	2.3%
29	Alaska	33	0.6%
34	Arizona	22	0.4%
21	Arkansas	70	1.4%
12	California	155	3.0%
37	Colorado	14	0.3%
25	Connecticut	53	1.0%
16	Delaware	93	1.8%
3	Florida	410	7.9%
5	Georgia	248	4.8%
11	Hawaii	158	3.1%
38	Idaho	13	0.3%
NA	Illinois**	NA	NA
19	Indiana	75	1.5%
39	Iowa	12	0.2%
33	Kansas	25	0.5%
7	Kentucky	221	4.3%
6	Louisiana	226	4.4%
43	Maine	6	0.1%
18	Maryland	85	1.6%
47	Massachusetts	0	0.0%
22	Michigan	66	1.3%
32	Minnesota	26	0.5%
4	Mississippi	354	6.9%
26	Missouri	48	0.9%
35	Montana	20	0.4%
36	Nebraska	17	0.3%
27	Nevada	41	0.8%
44	New Hampshire	3	0.1%
47	New Jersey	0	0.0%
23	New Mexico	55	1.1%
20	New York	72	1.4%
1	North Carolina	732	14.2%
46	North Dakota	1	0.0%
15	Ohio	113	2.2%
30	Oklahoma	31	0.6%
28	Oregon	35	0.7%
10	Pennsylvania	171	3.3%
47	Rhode Island	0	0.0%
2	South Carolina	612	11.9%
42	South Dakota	8	0.2%
13	Tennessee	143	2.8%
9	Texas	174	3.4%
40	Utah	10	0.2%
40	Vermont	10	0.2%
8	Virginia	176	3.4%
23	Washington	55	1.1%
17	West Virginia	87	1.7%
31	Wisconsin	29	0.6%
45	Wyoming	2	0.0%

RANK ORDER

RANK	STATE	ROBBERIES	% of USA
1	North Carolina	732	14.2%
2	South Carolina	612	11.9%
3	Florida	410	7.9%
4	Mississippi	354	6.9%
5	Georgia	248	4.8%
6	Louisiana	226	4.4%
7	Kentucky	221	4.3%
8	Virginia	176	3.4%
9	Texas	174	3.4%
10	Pennsylvania	171	3.3%
11	Hawaii	158	3.1%
12	California	155	3.0%
13	Tennessee	143	2.8%
14	Alabama	117	2.3%
15	Ohio	113	2.2%
16	Delaware	93	1.8%
17	West Virginia	87	1.7%
18	Maryland	85	1.6%
19	Indiana	75	1.5%
20	New York	72	1.4%
21	Arkansas	70	1.4%
22	Michigan	66	1.3%
23	New Mexico	55	1.1%
23	Washington	55	1.1%
25	Connecticut	53	1.0%
26	Missouri	48	0.9%
27	Nevada	41	0.8%
28	Oregon	35	0.7%
29	Alaska	33	0.6%
30	Oklahoma	31	0.6%
31	Wisconsin	29	0.6%
32	Minnesota	26	0.5%
33	Kansas	25	0.5%
34	Arizona	22	0.4%
35	Montana	20	0.4%
36	Nebraska	17	0.3%
37	Colorado	14	0.3%
38	Idaho	13	0.3%
39	Iowa	12	0.2%
40	Utah	10	0.2%
40	Vermont	10	0.2%
42	South Dakota	8	0.2%
43	Maine	6	0.1%
44	New Hampshire	3	0.1%
45	Wyoming	2	0.0%
46	North Dakota	1	0.0%
47	Massachusetts	0	0.0%
47	New Jersey	0	0.0%
47	Rhode Island	0	0.0%
NA	Illinois**	NA	NA
	District of Columbia	0	0.0%

Source: Reported data from the Federal Bureau of Investigation
"Crime in the United States 2008" (Uniform Crime Reports, September 14, 2009, http://www.fbi.gov/ucr/ucr.htm)
*Estimated totals for nonmetropolitan areas, defined by the F.B.I. as other than Metropolitan Statistical Areas and other cities outside such areas. National total includes those states listed as not available. Robbery is the taking or attempting to take anything of value by force or threat of force.
**Not available.

Rural Robbery Rate in 2008

National Rural Rate = 17.1 Robberies per 100,000 Population*

ALPHA ORDER

RANK	STATE	RATE
16	Alabama	15.9
18	Alaska	14.6
26	Arizona	8.3
21	Arkansas	10.8
9	California	27.4
39	Colorado	3.8
23	Connecticut	10.2
2	Delaware	63.6
3	Florida	46.5
10	Georgia	22.1
4	Hawaii	41.4
38	Idaho	4.5
NA	Illinois**	NA
25	Indiana	8.5
44	Iowa	1.6
28	Kansas	7.7
14	Kentucky	17.1
8	Louisiana	29.9
43	Maine	2.2
6	Maryland	38.2
47	Massachusetts	0.0
33	Michigan	5.5
41	Minnesota	3.2
7	Mississippi	33.6
32	Missouri	5.7
35	Montana	4.8
35	Nebraska	4.8
13	Nevada	18.9
31	New Hampshire	6.2
47	New Jersey	0.0
12	New Mexico	20.3
29	New York	7.3
5	North Carolina	38.7
46	North Dakota	0.5
24	Ohio	8.7
34	Oklahoma	5.1
27	Oregon	7.9
15	Pennsylvania	16.1
47	Rhode Island	0.0
1	South Carolina	77.0
40	South Dakota	3.5
19	Tennessee	13.6
21	Texas	10.8
30	Utah	6.5
35	Vermont	4.8
11	Virginia	21.0
20	Washington	11.7
17	West Virginia	14.9
41	Wisconsin	3.2
45	Wyoming	1.3

RANK ORDER

RANK	STATE	RATE
1	South Carolina	77.0
2	Delaware	63.6
3	Florida	46.5
4	Hawaii	41.4
5	North Carolina	38.7
6	Maryland	38.2
7	Mississippi	33.6
8	Louisiana	29.9
9	California	27.4
10	Georgia	22.1
11	Virginia	21.0
12	New Mexico	20.3
13	Nevada	18.9
14	Kentucky	17.1
15	Pennsylvania	16.1
16	Alabama	15.9
17	West Virginia	14.9
18	Alaska	14.6
19	Tennessee	13.6
20	Washington	11.7
21	Arkansas	10.8
21	Texas	10.8
23	Connecticut	10.2
24	Ohio	8.7
25	Indiana	8.5
26	Arizona	8.3
27	Oregon	7.9
28	Kansas	7.7
29	New York	7.3
30	Utah	6.5
31	New Hampshire	6.2
32	Missouri	5.7
33	Michigan	5.5
34	Oklahoma	5.1
35	Montana	4.8
35	Nebraska	4.8
35	Vermont	4.8
38	Idaho	4.5
39	Colorado	3.8
40	South Dakota	3.5
41	Minnesota	3.2
41	Wisconsin	3.2
43	Maine	2.2
44	Iowa	1.6
45	Wyoming	1.3
46	North Dakota	0.5
47	Massachusetts	0.0
47	New Jersey	0.0
47	Rhode Island	0.0
NA	Illinois**	NA
	District of Columbia	0.0

Source: CQ Press using reported data from the Federal Bureau of Investigation
"Crime in the United States 2008" (Uniform Crime Reports, September 14, 2009, http://www.fbi.gov/ucr/ucr.htm)
*Estimated rates for nonmetropolitan areas, defined by the F.B.I. as other than Metropolitan Statistical Areas and other cities outside such areas. National rate includes those states listed as not available. Robbery is the taking or attempting to take anything of value by force or threat of force.
**Not available.

Percent of Robberies Occurring in Rural Areas in 2008

National Percent = 1.2% of Robberies*

ALPHA ORDER

RANK	STATE	PERCENT
19	Alabama	1.6
10	Alaska	5.1
44	Arizona	0.2
14	Arkansas	2.6
44	California	0.2
43	Colorado	0.4
21	Connecticut	1.4
10	Delaware	5.1
27	Florida	1.1
21	Georgia	1.4
1	Hawaii	14.5
9	Idaho	5.4
NA	Illinois**	NA
28	Indiana	1.0
28	Iowa	1.0
20	Kansas	1.5
8	Kentucky	5.5
13	Louisiana	3.8
18	Maine	1.8
35	Maryland	0.6
47	Massachusetts	0.0
41	Michigan	0.5
35	Minnesota	0.6
2	Mississippi	11.7
35	Missouri	0.6
3	Montana	11.6
24	Nebraska	1.3
35	Nevada	0.6
33	New Hampshire	0.7
47	New Jersey	0.0
15	New Mexico	2.5
44	New York	0.2
10	North Carolina	5.1
21	North Dakota	1.4
35	Ohio	0.6
32	Oklahoma	0.8
24	Oregon	1.3
30	Pennsylvania	0.9
47	Rhode Island	0.0
6	South Carolina	9.3
7	South Dakota	6.7
24	Tennessee	1.3
41	Texas	0.5
33	Utah	0.7
4	Vermont	11.2
16	Virginia	2.4
30	Washington	0.9
5	West Virginia	9.8
35	Wisconsin	0.6
17	Wyoming	2.3

RANK ORDER

RANK	STATE	PERCENT
1	Hawaii	14.5
2	Mississippi	11.7
3	Montana	11.6
4	Vermont	11.2
5	West Virginia	9.8
6	South Carolina	9.3
7	South Dakota	6.7
8	Kentucky	5.5
9	Idaho	5.4
10	Alaska	5.1
10	Delaware	5.1
10	North Carolina	5.1
13	Louisiana	3.8
14	Arkansas	2.6
15	New Mexico	2.5
16	Virginia	2.4
17	Wyoming	2.3
18	Maine	1.8
19	Alabama	1.6
20	Kansas	1.5
21	Connecticut	1.4
21	Georgia	1.4
21	North Dakota	1.4
24	Nebraska	1.3
24	Oregon	1.3
24	Tennessee	1.3
27	Florida	1.1
28	Indiana	1.0
28	Iowa	1.0
30	Pennsylvania	0.9
30	Washington	0.9
32	Oklahoma	0.8
33	New Hampshire	0.7
33	Utah	0.7
35	Maryland	0.6
35	Minnesota	0.6
35	Missouri	0.6
35	Nevada	0.6
35	Ohio	0.6
35	Wisconsin	0.6
41	Michigan	0.5
41	Texas	0.5
43	Colorado	0.4
44	Arizona	0.2
44	California	0.2
44	New York	0.2
47	Massachusetts	0.0
47	New Jersey	0.0
47	Rhode Island	0.0
NA	Illinois**	NA
	District of Columbia	0.0

Source: CQ Press using reported data from the Federal Bureau of Investigation
"Crime in the United States 2008" (Uniform Crime Reports, September 14, 2009, http://www.fbi.gov/ucr/ucr.htm)
*Estimated percentages for nonmetropolitan areas, defined by the F.B.I. as other than Metropolitan Statistical Areas and other cities outside such areas. National percent includes those states listed as not available. Robbery is the taking or attempting to take anything of value by force or threat of force.
**Not available.

Aggravated Assaults in Urban Areas in 2008

National Urban Total = 786,381 Aggravated Assaults*

ALPHA ORDER

RANK	STATE	ASSAULTS	% of USA
21	Alabama	10,807	1.4%
38	Alaska	2,683	0.3%
15	Arizona	16,374	2.1%
25	Arkansas	9,102	1.2%
1	California	103,237	13.1%
22	Colorado	10,777	1.4%
33	Connecticut	5,452	0.7%
35	Delaware	3,322	0.4%
2	Florida	79,452	10.1%
8	Georgia	23,811	3.0%
42	Hawaii	1,426	0.2%
40	Idaho	2,362	0.3%
NA	Illinois**	NA	NA
20	Indiana	11,222	1.4%
31	Iowa	5,790	0.7%
28	Kansas	7,919	1.0%
30	Kentucky	6,034	0.8%
14	Louisiana	17,712	2.3%
47	Maine	678	0.1%
12	Maryland	20,060	2.6%
10	Massachusetts	20,202	2.6%
5	Michigan	30,706	3.9%
29	Minnesota	7,075	0.9%
37	Mississippi	2,942	0.4%
13	Missouri	18,651	2.4%
44	Montana	1,172	0.1%
36	Nebraska	3,278	0.4%
23	Nevada	10,704	1.4%
43	New Hampshire	1,212	0.2%
17	New Jersey	14,152	1.8%
26	New Mexico	8,711	1.1%
4	New York	40,952	5.2%
9	North Carolina	22,102	2.8%
47	North Dakota	678	0.1%
16	Ohio	15,626	2.0%
18	Oklahoma	12,663	1.6%
32	Oregon	5,582	0.7%
7	Pennsylvania	26,978	3.4%
41	Rhode Island	1,428	0.2%
11	South Carolina	20,182	2.6%
45	South Dakota	888	0.1%
6	Tennessee	28,764	3.7%
3	Texas	73,782	9.4%
34	Utah	3,574	0.5%
49	Vermont	499	0.1%
24	Virginia	9,474	1.2%
19	Washington	12,092	1.5%
39	West Virginia	2,616	0.3%
27	Wisconsin	8,474	1.1%
46	Wyoming	784	0.1%

RANK ORDER

RANK	STATE	ASSAULTS	% of USA
1	California	103,237	13.1%
2	Florida	79,452	10.1%
3	Texas	73,782	9.4%
4	New York	40,952	5.2%
5	Michigan	30,706	3.9%
6	Tennessee	28,764	3.7%
7	Pennsylvania	26,978	3.4%
8	Georgia	23,811	3.0%
9	North Carolina	22,102	2.8%
10	Massachusetts	20,202	2.6%
11	South Carolina	20,182	2.6%
12	Maryland	20,060	2.6%
13	Missouri	18,651	2.4%
14	Louisiana	17,712	2.3%
15	Arizona	16,374	2.1%
16	Ohio	15,626	2.0%
17	New Jersey	14,152	1.8%
18	Oklahoma	12,663	1.6%
19	Washington	12,092	1.5%
20	Indiana	11,222	1.4%
21	Alabama	10,807	1.4%
22	Colorado	10,777	1.4%
23	Nevada	10,704	1.4%
24	Virginia	9,474	1.2%
25	Arkansas	9,102	1.2%
26	New Mexico	8,711	1.1%
27	Wisconsin	8,474	1.1%
28	Kansas	7,919	1.0%
29	Minnesota	7,075	0.9%
30	Kentucky	6,034	0.8%
31	Iowa	5,790	0.7%
32	Oregon	5,582	0.7%
33	Connecticut	5,452	0.7%
34	Utah	3,574	0.5%
35	Delaware	3,322	0.4%
36	Nebraska	3,278	0.4%
37	Mississippi	2,942	0.4%
38	Alaska	2,683	0.3%
39	West Virginia	2,616	0.3%
40	Idaho	2,362	0.3%
41	Rhode Island	1,428	0.2%
42	Hawaii	1,426	0.2%
43	New Hampshire	1,212	0.2%
44	Montana	1,172	0.1%
45	South Dakota	888	0.1%
46	Wyoming	784	0.1%
47	Maine	678	0.1%
47	North Dakota	678	0.1%
49	Vermont	499	0.1%
NA	Illinois**	NA	NA
	District of Columbia	3,707	0.5%

Source: CQ Press using reported data from the Federal Bureau of Investigation
"Crime in the United States 2008" (Uniform Crime Reports, September 14, 2009, http://www.fbi.gov/ucr/ucr.htm)
*Estimated totals for urban areas, defined by the F.B.I. as Metropolitan Statistical Areas and other cities outside such areas.
National total includes those states listed as not available. Aggravated assault is an attack for the purpose of inflicting severe bodily injury.
**Not available.

Urban Aggravated Assault Rate in 2008

National Urban Rate = 287.0 Aggravated Assaults per 100,000 Population*

ALPHA ORDER

RANK	STATE	RATE
20	Alabama	275.2
1	Alaska	583.1
21	Arizona	262.6
10	Arkansas	412.0
18	California	285.3
24	Colorado	235.9
34	Connecticut	183.0
6	Delaware	457.0
7	Florida	455.4
19	Georgia	278.0
39	Hawaii	157.3
33	Idaho	190.8
NA	Illinois**	NA
30	Indiana	204.4
22	Iowa	254.6
15	Kansas	319.8
31	Kentucky	202.9
5	Louisiana	484.7
49	Maine	64.8
11	Maryland	370.7
16	Massachusetts	310.9
13	Michigan	349.0
38	Minnesota	160.6
40	Mississippi	156.0
12	Missouri	367.7
27	Montana	212.8
25	Nebraska	228.9
8	Nevada	449.2
48	New Hampshire	95.6
37	New Jersey	163.0
4	New Mexico	508.4
26	New York	221.3
17	North Carolina	301.4
43	North Dakota	151.0
42	Ohio	153.4
9	Oklahoma	417.9
36	Oregon	166.9
23	Pennsylvania	236.9
46	Rhode Island	135.9
3	South Carolina	547.6
41	South Dakota	153.9
2	Tennessee	557.1
14	Texas	324.8
44	Utah	138.3
47	Vermont	120.7
45	Virginia	136.7
32	Washington	198.9
27	West Virginia	212.8
35	Wisconsin	179.4
29	Wyoming	206.9

RANK ORDER

RANK	STATE	RATE
1	Alaska	583.1
2	Tennessee	557.1
3	South Carolina	547.6
4	New Mexico	508.4
5	Louisiana	484.7
6	Delaware	457.0
7	Florida	455.4
8	Nevada	449.2
9	Oklahoma	417.9
10	Arkansas	412.0
11	Maryland	370.7
12	Missouri	367.7
13	Michigan	349.0
14	Texas	324.8
15	Kansas	319.8
16	Massachusetts	310.9
17	North Carolina	301.4
18	California	285.3
19	Georgia	278.0
20	Alabama	275.2
21	Arizona	262.6
22	Iowa	254.6
23	Pennsylvania	236.9
24	Colorado	235.9
25	Nebraska	228.9
26	New York	221.3
27	Montana	212.8
27	West Virginia	212.8
29	Wyoming	206.9
30	Indiana	204.4
31	Kentucky	202.9
32	Washington	198.9
33	Idaho	190.8
34	Connecticut	183.0
35	Wisconsin	179.4
36	Oregon	166.9
37	New Jersey	163.0
38	Minnesota	160.6
39	Hawaii	157.3
40	Mississippi	156.0
41	South Dakota	153.9
42	Ohio	153.4
43	North Dakota	151.0
44	Utah	138.3
45	Virginia	136.7
46	Rhode Island	135.9
47	Vermont	120.7
48	New Hampshire	95.6
49	Maine	64.8
NA	Illinois**	NA

District of Columbia 626.4

Source: CQ Press using reported data from the Federal Bureau of Investigation
"Crime in the United States 2008" (Uniform Crime Reports, September 14, 2009, http://www.fbi.gov/ucr/ucr.htm)
*Estimated rates for urban areas, defined by the F.B.I. as Metropolitan Statistical Areas and other cities outside such areas.
National rate includes those states listed as not available. Aggravated assault is an attack for the purpose of inflicting severe bodily injury.
**Not available.

Percent of Aggravated Assaults Occurring Urban Areas in 2008

National Percent = 94.2% of Aggravated Assaults*

ALPHA ORDER

RANK	STATE	PERCENT
28	Alabama	91.6
45	Alaska	79.9
20	Arizona	94.7
33	Arkansas	90.3
4	California	98.6
18	Colorado	95.2
17	Connecticut	95.3
37	Delaware	85.6
13	Florida	95.9
31	Georgia	90.9
47	Hawaii	70.0
35	Idaho	88.5
NA	Illinois**	NA
13	Indiana	95.9
26	Iowa	91.8
23	Kansas	93.0
36	Kentucky	85.8
41	Louisiana	83.6
40	Maine	83.9
5	Maryland	97.5
1	Massachusetts	100.0
16	Michigan	95.5
24	Minnesota	92.8
48	Mississippi	69.6
28	Missouri	91.6
49	Montana	58.4
21	Nebraska	94.6
10	Nevada	96.4
6	New Hampshire	97.3
1	New Jersey	100.0
25	New Mexico	92.2
7	New York	97.1
38	North Carolina	85.4
34	North Dakota	89.1
15	Ohio	95.8
28	Oklahoma	91.6
19	Oregon	95.1
10	Pennsylvania	96.4
3	Rhode Island	99.4
41	South Carolina	83.6
39	South Dakota	85.2
31	Tennessee	90.9
9	Texas	96.5
12	Utah	96.2
43	Vermont	81.7
26	Virginia	91.8
8	Washington	96.6
46	West Virginia	71.5
22	Wisconsin	93.9
43	Wyoming	81.7

RANK ORDER

RANK	STATE	PERCENT
1	Massachusetts	100.0
1	New Jersey	100.0
3	Rhode Island	99.4
4	California	98.6
5	Maryland	97.5
6	New Hampshire	97.3
7	New York	97.1
8	Washington	96.6
9	Texas	96.5
10	Nevada	96.4
10	Pennsylvania	96.4
12	Utah	96.2
13	Florida	95.9
13	Indiana	95.9
15	Ohio	95.8
16	Michigan	95.5
17	Connecticut	95.3
18	Colorado	95.2
19	Oregon	95.1
20	Arizona	94.7
21	Nebraska	94.6
22	Wisconsin	93.9
23	Kansas	93.0
24	Minnesota	92.8
25	New Mexico	92.2
26	Iowa	91.8
26	Virginia	91.8
28	Alabama	91.6
28	Missouri	91.6
28	Oklahoma	91.6
31	Georgia	90.9
31	Tennessee	90.9
33	Arkansas	90.3
34	North Dakota	89.1
35	Idaho	88.5
36	Kentucky	85.8
37	Delaware	85.6
38	North Carolina	85.4
39	South Dakota	85.2
40	Maine	83.9
41	Louisiana	83.6
41	South Carolina	83.6
43	Vermont	81.7
43	Wyoming	81.7
45	Alaska	79.9
46	West Virginia	71.5
47	Hawaii	70.0
48	Mississippi	69.6
49	Montana	58.4
NA	Illinois**	NA

District of Columbia 100.0

Source: CQ Press using reported data from the Federal Bureau of Investigation
"Crime in the United States 2008" (Uniform Crime Reports, September 14, 2009, http://www.fbi.gov/ucr/ucr.htm)
*Estimated percentages for urban areas, defined by the F.B.I. as Metropolitan Statistical Areas and other cities outside such areas. National percent includes those states listed as not available. Aggravated assault is an attack for the purpose of inflicting severe bodily injury.
**Not available.

Aggravated Assaults in Rural Areas in 2008

National Rural Total = 48,504 Aggravated Assaults*

ALPHA ORDER

RANK	STATE	ASSAULTS	% of USA
17	Alabama	988	2.0%
24	Alaska	677	1.4%
19	Arizona	908	1.9%
18	Arkansas	980	2.0%
9	California	1,506	3.1%
30	Colorado	549	1.1%
38	Connecticut	271	0.6%
27	Delaware	558	1.2%
4	Florida	3,400	7.0%
7	Georgia	2,385	4.9%
25	Hawaii	610	1.3%
36	Idaho	306	0.6%
NA	Illinois**	NA	NA
33	Indiana	482	1.0%
31	Iowa	518	1.1%
26	Kansas	599	1.2%
16	Kentucky	1,002	2.1%
3	Louisiana	3,479	7.2%
43	Maine	130	0.3%
32	Maryland	510	1.1%
48	Massachusetts	0	0.0%
10	Michigan	1,452	3.0%
29	Minnesota	551	1.1%
11	Mississippi	1,288	2.7%
8	Missouri	1,708	3.5%
21	Montana	836	1.7%
39	Nebraska	188	0.4%
35	Nevada	395	0.8%
46	New Hampshire	34	0.1%
48	New Jersey	0	0.0%
22	New Mexico	732	1.5%
12	New York	1,218	2.5%
2	North Carolina	3,775	7.8%
45	North Dakota	83	0.2%
23	Ohio	690	1.4%
13	Oklahoma	1,160	2.4%
37	Oregon	286	0.6%
15	Pennsylvania	1,006	2.1%
47	Rhode Island	8	0.0%
1	South Carolina	3,967	8.2%
41	South Dakota	154	0.3%
5	Tennessee	2,863	5.9%
6	Texas	2,641	5.4%
42	Utah	143	0.3%
44	Vermont	112	0.2%
20	Virginia	845	1.7%
34	Washington	432	0.9%
14	West Virginia	1,041	2.1%
28	Wisconsin	555	1.1%
40	Wyoming	176	0.4%

RANK ORDER

RANK	STATE	ASSAULTS	% of USA
1	South Carolina	3,967	8.2%
2	North Carolina	3,775	7.8%
3	Louisiana	3,479	7.2%
4	Florida	3,400	7.0%
5	Tennessee	2,863	5.9%
6	Texas	2,641	5.4%
7	Georgia	2,385	4.9%
8	Missouri	1,708	3.5%
9	California	1,506	3.1%
10	Michigan	1,452	3.0%
11	Mississippi	1,288	2.7%
12	New York	1,218	2.5%
13	Oklahoma	1,160	2.4%
14	West Virginia	1,041	2.1%
15	Pennsylvania	1,006	2.1%
16	Kentucky	1,002	2.1%
17	Alabama	988	2.0%
18	Arkansas	980	2.0%
19	Arizona	908	1.9%
20	Virginia	845	1.7%
21	Montana	836	1.7%
22	New Mexico	732	1.5%
23	Ohio	690	1.4%
24	Alaska	677	1.4%
25	Hawaii	610	1.3%
26	Kansas	599	1.2%
27	Delaware	558	1.2%
28	Wisconsin	555	1.1%
29	Minnesota	551	1.1%
30	Colorado	549	1.1%
31	Iowa	518	1.1%
32	Maryland	510	1.1%
33	Indiana	482	1.0%
34	Washington	432	0.9%
35	Nevada	395	0.8%
36	Idaho	306	0.6%
37	Oregon	286	0.6%
38	Connecticut	271	0.6%
39	Nebraska	188	0.4%
40	Wyoming	176	0.4%
41	South Dakota	154	0.3%
42	Utah	143	0.3%
43	Maine	130	0.3%
44	Vermont	112	0.2%
45	North Dakota	83	0.2%
46	New Hampshire	34	0.1%
47	Rhode Island	8	0.0%
48	Massachusetts	0	0.0%
48	New Jersey	0	0.0%
NA	Illinois**	NA	NA
	District of Columbia	0	0.0%

Source: Reported data from the Federal Bureau of Investigation
"Crime in the United States 2008" (Uniform Crime Reports, September 14, 2009, http://www.fbi.gov/ucr/ucr.htm)
*Estimated totals for nonmetropolitan areas, defined by the F.B.I. as other than Metropolitan Statistical Areas and other cities outside such areas. National total includes those states listed as not available. Aggravated assault is an attack for the purpose of inflicting severe bodily injury.
**Not available.

Rural Aggravated Assault Rate in 2008

National Rural Rate = 161.1 Aggravated Assaults per 100,000 Population*

ALPHA ORDER

RANK	STATE	RATE
23	Alabama	134.5
6	Alaska	299.3
5	Arizona	342.4
21	Arkansas	151.7
9	California	266.5
22	Colorado	148.2
44	Connecticut	52.0
4	Delaware	381.7
3	Florida	385.7
11	Georgia	212.9
20	Hawaii	159.7
28	Idaho	107.1
NA	Illinois**	NA
40	Indiana	54.3
34	Iowa	71.2
16	Kansas	183.9
33	Kentucky	77.4
2	Louisiana	459.9
45	Maine	48.0
10	Maryland	229.4
47	Massachusetts	0.0
26	Michigan	120.5
37	Minnesota	67.5
25	Mississippi	122.3
12	Missouri	203.5
13	Montana	200.7
42	Nebraska	53.5
17	Nevada	181.6
35	New Hampshire	70.4
47	New Jersey	0.0
8	New Mexico	270.1
24	New York	124.1
14	North Carolina	199.8
46	North Dakota	43.1
43	Ohio	53.2
15	Oklahoma	189.6
38	Oregon	64.3
30	Pennsylvania	94.9
47	Rhode Island	0.0
1	South Carolina	499.4
36	South Dakota	67.7
7	Tennessee	272.3
19	Texas	163.9
31	Utah	93.5
41	Vermont	53.8
29	Virginia	101.0
32	Washington	92.2
18	West Virginia	177.9
39	Wisconsin	61.4
27	Wyoming	114.4

RANK ORDER

RANK	STATE	RATE
1	South Carolina	499.4
2	Louisiana	459.9
3	Florida	385.7
4	Delaware	381.7
5	Arizona	342.4
6	Alaska	299.3
7	Tennessee	272.3
8	New Mexico	270.1
9	California	266.5
10	Maryland	229.4
11	Georgia	212.9
12	Missouri	203.5
13	Montana	200.7
14	North Carolina	199.8
15	Oklahoma	189.6
16	Kansas	183.9
17	Nevada	181.6
18	West Virginia	177.9
19	Texas	163.9
20	Hawaii	159.7
21	Arkansas	151.7
22	Colorado	148.2
23	Alabama	134.5
24	New York	124.1
25	Mississippi	122.3
26	Michigan	120.5
27	Wyoming	114.4
28	Idaho	107.1
29	Virginia	101.0
30	Pennsylvania	94.9
31	Utah	93.5
32	Washington	92.2
33	Kentucky	77.4
34	Iowa	71.2
35	New Hampshire	70.4
36	South Dakota	67.7
37	Minnesota	67.5
38	Oregon	64.3
39	Wisconsin	61.4
40	Indiana	54.3
41	Vermont	53.8
42	Nebraska	53.5
43	Ohio	53.2
44	Connecticut	52.0
45	Maine	48.0
46	North Dakota	43.1
47	Massachusetts	0.0
47	New Jersey	0.0
47	Rhode Island	0.0
NA	Illinois**	NA

District of Columbia   0.0

Source: CQ Press using reported data from the Federal Bureau of Investigation
  "Crime in the United States 2008" (Uniform Crime Reports, September 14, 2009, http://www.fbi.gov/ucr/ucr.htm)
*Estimated rates for nonmetropolitan areas, defined by the F.B.I. as other than Metropolitan Statistical Areas and other cities
outside such areas. National rate includes those states listed as not available. Aggravated assault is an attack for the purpose
of inflicting severe bodily injury.
**Not available.

Percent of Aggravated Assaults Occurring in Rural Areas in 2008

National Percent = 5.8% of Aggravated Assaults*

ALPHA ORDER

RANK	STATE	PERCENT
20	Alabama	8.4
5	Alaska	20.1
30	Arizona	5.3
17	Arkansas	9.7
46	California	1.4
32	Colorado	4.8
33	Connecticut	4.7
13	Delaware	14.4
36	Florida	4.1
18	Georgia	9.1
3	Hawaii	30.0
15	Idaho	11.5
NA	Illinois**	NA
36	Indiana	4.1
23	Iowa	8.2
27	Kansas	7.0
14	Kentucky	14.2
8	Louisiana	16.4
10	Maine	16.1
45	Maryland	2.5
48	Massachusetts	0.0
34	Michigan	4.5
26	Minnesota	7.2
2	Mississippi	30.4
20	Missouri	8.4
1	Montana	41.6
29	Nebraska	5.4
39	Nevada	3.6
44	New Hampshire	2.7
48	New Jersey	0.0
25	New Mexico	7.8
43	New York	2.9
12	North Carolina	14.6
16	North Dakota	10.9
35	Ohio	4.2
20	Oklahoma	8.4
31	Oregon	4.9
39	Pennsylvania	3.6
47	Rhode Island	0.6
8	South Carolina	16.4
11	South Dakota	14.8
18	Tennessee	9.1
41	Texas	3.5
38	Utah	3.8
6	Vermont	18.3
23	Virginia	8.2
42	Washington	3.4
4	West Virginia	28.5
28	Wisconsin	6.1
6	Wyoming	18.3

RANK ORDER

RANK	STATE	PERCENT
1	Montana	41.6
2	Mississippi	30.4
3	Hawaii	30.0
4	West Virginia	28.5
5	Alaska	20.1
6	Vermont	18.3
6	Wyoming	18.3
8	Louisiana	16.4
8	South Carolina	16.4
10	Maine	16.1
11	South Dakota	14.8
12	North Carolina	14.6
13	Delaware	14.4
14	Kentucky	14.2
15	Idaho	11.5
16	North Dakota	10.9
17	Arkansas	9.7
18	Georgia	9.1
18	Tennessee	9.1
20	Alabama	8.4
20	Missouri	8.4
20	Oklahoma	8.4
23	Iowa	8.2
23	Virginia	8.2
25	New Mexico	7.8
26	Minnesota	7.2
27	Kansas	7.0
28	Wisconsin	6.1
29	Nebraska	5.4
30	Arizona	5.3
31	Oregon	4.9
32	Colorado	4.8
33	Connecticut	4.7
34	Michigan	4.5
35	Ohio	4.2
36	Florida	4.1
36	Indiana	4.1
38	Utah	3.8
39	Nevada	3.6
39	Pennsylvania	3.6
41	Texas	3.5
42	Washington	3.4
43	New York	2.9
44	New Hampshire	2.7
45	Maryland	2.5
46	California	1.4
47	Rhode Island	0.6
48	Massachusetts	0.0
48	New Jersey	0.0
NA	Illinois**	NA

District of Columbia 0.0

Source: CQ Press using reported data from the Federal Bureau of Investigation
"Crime in the United States 2008" (Uniform Crime Reports, September 14, 2009, http://www.fbi.gov/ucr/ucr.htm)
*Estimated percentages for nonmetropolitan areas, defined by the F.B.I. as other than Metropolitan Statistical Areas and other cities outside such areas. National percent includes those states listed as not available. Aggravated assault is an attack for the purpose of inflicting severe bodily injury.
**Not available.

Property Crimes in Urban Areas in 2008

National Urban Total = 9,261,912 Property Crimes*

ALPHA ORDER

RANK ORDER

RANK	STATE	CRIMES	% of USA
18	Alabama	179,491	1.9%
45	Alaska	15,950	0.2%
9	Arizona	275,528	3.0%
27	Arkansas	98,887	1.1%
1	California	1,072,110	11.6%
24	Colorado	136,698	1.5%
32	Connecticut	80,799	0.9%
42	Delaware	27,500	0.3%
3	Florida	736,491	8.0%
6	Georgia	363,410	3.9%
38	Hawaii	31,781	0.3%
40	Idaho	28,926	0.3%
NA	Illinois**	NA	NA
14	Indiana	201,336	2.2%
35	Iowa	68,015	0.7%
29	Kansas	89,634	1.0%
28	Kentucky	92,125	1.0%
21	Louisiana	151,611	1.6%
41	Maine	28,129	0.3%
16	Maryland	193,527	2.1%
20	Massachusetts	155,959	1.7%
10	Michigan	274,175	3.0%
23	Minnesota	138,813	1.5%
34	Mississippi	71,451	0.8%
13	Missouri	204,682	2.2%
44	Montana	18,874	0.2%
36	Nebraska	47,673	0.5%
31	Nevada	86,414	0.9%
43	New Hampshire	27,248	0.3%
15	New Jersey	199,126	2.1%
33	New Mexico	73,124	0.8%
4	New York	374,129	4.0%
7	North Carolina	324,632	3.5%
49	North Dakota	10,789	0.1%
5	Ohio	369,873	4.0%
26	Oklahoma	117,260	1.3%
25	Oregon	117,632	1.3%
8	Pennsylvania	283,833	3.1%
39	Rhode Island	29,774	0.3%
19	South Carolina	161,859	1.7%
48	South Dakota	12,159	0.1%
12	Tennessee	228,257	2.5%
2	Texas	946,176	10.2%
30	Utah	89,524	1.0%
47	Vermont	12,642	0.1%
17	Virginia	183,614	2.0%
11	Washington	235,685	2.5%
37	West Virginia	36,876	0.4%
22	Wisconsin	144,250	1.6%
46	Wyoming	12,804	0.1%

RANK	STATE	CRIMES	% of USA
1	California	1,072,110	11.6%
2	Texas	946,176	10.2%
3	Florida	736,491	8.0%
4	New York	374,129	4.0%
5	Ohio	369,873	4.0%
6	Georgia	363,410	3.9%
7	North Carolina	324,632	3.5%
8	Pennsylvania	283,833	3.1%
9	Arizona	275,528	3.0%
10	Michigan	274,175	3.0%
11	Washington	235,685	2.5%
12	Tennessee	228,257	2.5%
13	Missouri	204,682	2.2%
14	Indiana	201,336	2.2%
15	New Jersey	199,126	2.1%
16	Maryland	193,527	2.1%
17	Virginia	183,614	2.0%
18	Alabama	179,491	1.9%
19	South Carolina	161,859	1.7%
20	Massachusetts	155,959	1.7%
21	Louisiana	151,611	1.6%
22	Wisconsin	144,250	1.6%
23	Minnesota	138,813	1.5%
24	Colorado	136,698	1.5%
25	Oregon	117,632	1.3%
26	Oklahoma	117,260	1.3%
27	Arkansas	98,887	1.1%
28	Kentucky	92,125	1.0%
29	Kansas	89,634	1.0%
30	Utah	89,524	1.0%
31	Nevada	86,414	0.9%
32	Connecticut	80,799	0.9%
33	New Mexico	73,124	0.8%
34	Mississippi	71,451	0.8%
35	Iowa	68,015	0.7%
36	Nebraska	47,673	0.5%
37	West Virginia	36,876	0.4%
38	Hawaii	31,781	0.3%
39	Rhode Island	29,774	0.3%
40	Idaho	28,926	0.3%
41	Maine	28,129	0.3%
42	Delaware	27,500	0.3%
43	New Hampshire	27,248	0.3%
44	Montana	18,874	0.2%
45	Alaska	15,950	0.2%
46	Wyoming	12,804	0.1%
47	Vermont	12,642	0.1%
48	South Dakota	12,159	0.1%
49	North Dakota	10,789	0.1%
NA	Illinois**	NA	NA
	District of Columbia	30,211	0.3%

Source: CQ Press using reported data from the Federal Bureau of Investigation
  "Crime in the United States 2008" (Uniform Crime Reports, September 14, 2009, http://www.fbi.gov/ucr/ucr.htm)
*Estimated totals for urban areas, defined by the F.B.I. as Metropolitan Statistical Areas and other cities outside such areas.
National total includes those states listed as not available. Property crimes are offenses of burglary, larceny-theft, and motor vehicle theft.
**Not available.

Urban Property Crime Rate in 2008

National Urban Rate = 3,380.7 Property Crimes per 100,000 Population*

ALPHA ORDER

RANK	STATE	RATE
1	Alabama	4,570.4
24	Alaska	3,466.5
5	Arizona	4,419.1
2	Arkansas	4,476.2
37	California	2,962.3
35	Colorado	2,991.9
39	Connecticut	2,711.7
16	Delaware	3,783.1
9	Florida	4,221.4
8	Georgia	4,242.8
23	Hawaii	3,506.5
45	Idaho	2,336.3
NA	Illinois**	NA
17	Indiana	3,667.4
36	Iowa	2,990.2
20	Kansas	3,619.4
31	Kentucky	3,097.1
11	Louisiana	4,148.9
40	Maine	2,690.4
21	Maryland	3,576.4
44	Massachusetts	2,400.2
30	Michigan	3,116.1
29	Minnesota	3,151.7
15	Mississippi	3,788.8
12	Missouri	4,035.3
26	Montana	3,426.5
28	Nebraska	3,329.1
19	Nevada	3,626.7
47	New Hampshire	2,149.8
46	New Jersey	2,293.4
7	New Mexico	4,267.8
49	New York	2,021.3
3	North Carolina	4,427.2
43	North Dakota	2,403.4
18	Ohio	3,630.1
14	Oklahoma	3,869.3
22	Oregon	3,516.6
42	Pennsylvania	2,492.3
38	Rhode Island	2,833.5
6	South Carolina	4,391.9
48	South Dakota	2,107.8
4	Tennessee	4,420.5
10	Texas	4,165.3
25	Utah	3,465.2
32	Vermont	3,059.1
41	Virginia	2,648.5
13	Washington	3,875.9
34	West Virginia	2,999.6
33	Wisconsin	3,053.5
27	Wyoming	3,379.8

RANK ORDER

RANK	STATE	RATE
1	Alabama	4,570.4
2	Arkansas	4,476.2
3	North Carolina	4,427.2
4	Tennessee	4,420.5
5	Arizona	4,419.1
6	South Carolina	4,391.9
7	New Mexico	4,267.8
8	Georgia	4,242.8
9	Florida	4,221.4
10	Texas	4,165.3
11	Louisiana	4,148.9
12	Missouri	4,035.3
13	Washington	3,875.9
14	Oklahoma	3,869.3
15	Mississippi	3,788.8
16	Delaware	3,783.1
17	Indiana	3,667.4
18	Ohio	3,630.1
19	Nevada	3,626.7
20	Kansas	3,619.4
21	Maryland	3,576.4
22	Oregon	3,516.6
23	Hawaii	3,506.5
24	Alaska	3,466.5
25	Utah	3,465.2
26	Montana	3,426.5
27	Wyoming	3,379.8
28	Nebraska	3,329.1
29	Minnesota	3,151.7
30	Michigan	3,116.1
31	Kentucky	3,097.1
32	Vermont	3,059.1
33	Wisconsin	3,053.5
34	West Virginia	2,999.6
35	Colorado	2,991.9
36	Iowa	2,990.2
37	California	2,962.3
38	Rhode Island	2,833.5
39	Connecticut	2,711.7
40	Maine	2,690.4
41	Virginia	2,648.5
42	Pennsylvania	2,492.3
43	North Dakota	2,403.4
44	Massachusetts	2,400.2
45	Idaho	2,336.3
46	New Jersey	2,293.4
47	New Hampshire	2,149.8
48	South Dakota	2,107.8
49	New York	2,021.3
NA	Illinois**	NA

District of Columbia 5,104.6

Source: CQ Press using reported data from the Federal Bureau of Investigation
"Crime in the United States 2008" (Uniform Crime Reports, September 14, 2009, http://www.fbi.gov/ucr/ucr.htm)
*Estimated rates for urban areas, defined by the F.B.I. as Metropolitan Statistical Areas and other cities outside such areas.
National rate includes those states listed as not available. Property crimes are offenses of burglary, larceny-theft, and
motor vehicle theft.
**Not available.

Percent of Property Crimes Occurring in Urban Areas in 2008

National Percent = 94.8% of Property Crimes*

ALPHA ORDER

RANK	STATE	PERCENT
21	Alabama	94.3
46	Alaska	79.3
6	Arizona	98.8
34	Arkansas	90.3
4	California	99.2
10	Colorado	97.1
23	Connecticut	93.9
39	Delaware	87.9
11	Florida	97.0
27	Georgia	93.4
49	Hawaii	69.1
34	Idaho	90.3
NA	Illinois**	NA
15	Indiana	94.7
25	Iowa	93.6
15	Kansas	94.7
43	Kentucky	83.5
36	Louisiana	89.9
40	Maine	87.1
7	Maryland	97.7
1	Massachusetts	100.0
27	Michigan	93.4
29	Minnesota	93.3
44	Mississippi	82.7
19	Missouri	94.5
48	Montana	75.0
31	Nebraska	92.9
12	Nevada	96.4
5	New Hampshire	99.0
1	New Jersey	100.0
21	New Mexico	94.3
13	New York	96.3
41	North Carolina	87.0
37	North Dakota	88.8
20	Ohio	94.4
26	Oklahoma	93.5
17	Oregon	94.6
17	Pennsylvania	94.6
3	Rhode Island	99.7
42	South Carolina	85.3
32	South Dakota	91.9
33	Tennessee	90.9
8	Texas	97.6
9	Utah	97.4
45	Vermont	80.2
23	Virginia	93.9
14	Washington	95.7
47	West Virginia	79.1
30	Wisconsin	93.0
38	Wyoming	88.5

RANK ORDER

RANK	STATE	PERCENT
1	Massachusetts	100.0
1	New Jersey	100.0
3	Rhode Island	99.7
4	California	99.2
5	New Hampshire	99.0
6	Arizona	98.8
7	Maryland	97.7
8	Texas	97.6
9	Utah	97.4
10	Colorado	97.1
11	Florida	97.0
12	Nevada	96.4
13	New York	96.3
14	Washington	95.7
15	Indiana	94.7
15	Kansas	94.7
17	Oregon	94.6
17	Pennsylvania	94.6
19	Missouri	94.5
20	Ohio	94.4
21	Alabama	94.3
21	New Mexico	94.3
23	Connecticut	93.9
23	Virginia	93.9
25	Iowa	93.6
26	Oklahoma	93.5
27	Georgia	93.4
27	Michigan	93.4
29	Minnesota	93.3
30	Wisconsin	93.0
31	Nebraska	92.9
32	South Dakota	91.9
33	Tennessee	90.9
34	Arkansas	90.3
34	Idaho	90.3
36	Louisiana	89.9
37	North Dakota	88.8
38	Wyoming	88.5
39	Delaware	87.9
40	Maine	87.1
41	North Carolina	87.0
42	South Carolina	85.3
43	Kentucky	83.5
44	Mississippi	82.7
45	Vermont	80.2
46	Alaska	79.3
47	West Virginia	79.1
48	Montana	75.0
49	Hawaii	69.1
NA	Illinois**	NA

District of Columbia 100.0

Source: CQ Press using reported data from the Federal Bureau of Investigation
"Crime in the United States 2008" (Uniform Crime Reports, September 14, 2009, http://www.fbi.gov/ucr/ucr.htm)
*Estimated percentages for urban areas, defined by the F.B.I. as Metropolitan Statistical Areas and other cities outside such areas. National percent includes those states listed as not available. Property crimes are offenses of burglary, larceny-theft, and motor vehicle theft.
**Not available.

Property Crimes Occurring in Rural Areas in 2008

National Rural Total = 506,003 Property Crimes*

ALPHA ORDER

RANK	STATE	CRIMES	% of USA
19	Alabama	10,852	2.1%
33	Alaska	4,174	0.8%
38	Arizona	3,392	0.7%
20	Arkansas	10,621	2.1%
24	California	8,637	1.7%
35	Colorado	4,027	0.8%
28	Connecticut	5,288	1.0%
36	Delaware	3,803	0.8%
6	Florida	22,443	4.4%
3	Georgia	25,525	5.0%
14	Hawaii	14,223	2.8%
41	Idaho	3,093	0.6%
NA	Illinois**	NA	NA
17	Indiana	11,379	2.2%
30	Iowa	4,674	0.9%
29	Kansas	5,001	1.0%
9	Kentucky	18,189	3.6%
10	Louisiana	17,019	3.4%
34	Maine	4,156	0.8%
31	Maryland	4,638	0.9%
48	Massachusetts	0	0.0%
8	Michigan	19,410	3.8%
22	Minnesota	9,997	2.0%
12	Mississippi	14,957	3.0%
16	Missouri	11,903	2.4%
27	Montana	6,308	1.2%
37	Nebraska	3,665	0.7%
39	Nevada	3,226	0.6%
46	New Hampshire	278	0.1%
48	New Jersey	0	0.0%
32	New Mexico	4,448	0.9%
13	New York	14,404	2.8%
1	North Carolina	48,329	9.6%
44	North Dakota	1,363	0.3%
7	Ohio	21,989	4.3%
25	Oklahoma	8,124	1.6%
26	Oregon	6,765	1.3%
11	Pennsylvania	16,199	3.2%
47	Rhode Island	75	0.0%
2	South Carolina	27,824	5.5%
45	South Dakota	1,075	0.2%
5	Tennessee	22,988	4.5%
4	Texas	23,394	4.6%
42	Utah	2,349	0.5%
40	Vermont	3,129	0.6%
15	Virginia	12,020	2.4%
21	Washington	10,463	2.1%
23	West Virginia	9,731	1.9%
18	Wisconsin	10,877	2.1%
43	Wyoming	1,670	0.3%

RANK ORDER

RANK	STATE	CRIMES	% of USA
1	North Carolina	48,329	9.6%
2	South Carolina	27,824	5.5%
3	Georgia	25,525	5.0%
4	Texas	23,394	4.6%
5	Tennessee	22,988	4.5%
6	Florida	22,443	4.4%
7	Ohio	21,989	4.3%
8	Michigan	19,410	3.8%
9	Kentucky	18,189	3.6%
10	Louisiana	17,019	3.4%
11	Pennsylvania	16,199	3.2%
12	Mississippi	14,957	3.0%
13	New York	14,404	2.8%
14	Hawaii	14,223	2.8%
15	Virginia	12,020	2.4%
16	Missouri	11,903	2.4%
17	Indiana	11,379	2.2%
18	Wisconsin	10,877	2.1%
19	Alabama	10,852	2.1%
20	Arkansas	10,621	2.1%
21	Washington	10,463	2.1%
22	Minnesota	9,997	2.0%
23	West Virginia	9,731	1.9%
24	California	8,637	1.7%
25	Oklahoma	8,124	1.6%
26	Oregon	6,765	1.3%
27	Montana	6,308	1.2%
28	Connecticut	5,288	1.0%
29	Kansas	5,001	1.0%
30	Iowa	4,674	0.9%
31	Maryland	4,638	0.9%
32	New Mexico	4,448	0.9%
33	Alaska	4,174	0.8%
34	Maine	4,156	0.8%
35	Colorado	4,027	0.8%
36	Delaware	3,803	0.8%
37	Nebraska	3,665	0.7%
38	Arizona	3,392	0.7%
39	Nevada	3,226	0.6%
40	Vermont	3,129	0.6%
41	Idaho	3,093	0.6%
42	Utah	2,349	0.5%
43	Wyoming	1,670	0.3%
44	North Dakota	1,363	0.3%
45	South Dakota	1,075	0.2%
46	New Hampshire	278	0.1%
47	Rhode Island	75	0.0%
48	Massachusetts	0	0.0%
48	New Jersey	0	0.0%
NA	Illinois**	NA	NA
	District of Columbia	0	0.0%

Source: Reported data from the Federal Bureau of Investigation
   "Crime in the United States 2008" (Uniform Crime Reports, September 14, 2009, http://www.fbi.gov/ucr/ucr.htm)
*Estimated totals for nonmetropolitan areas, defined by the F.B.I. as other than Metropolitan Statistical Areas and other cities outside such areas. National total includes those states listed as not available. Property crimes are offenses of burglary, larceny-theft, and motor vehicle theft.
**Not available.

Rural Property Crime Rate in 2008

National Rural Rate = 1,681.1 Property Crimes per 100,000 Population*

<table>
<tr><td colspan="3">ALPHA ORDER</td><td colspan="3">RANK ORDER</td></tr>
<tr><td>RANK</td><td>STATE</td><td>RATE</td><td>RANK</td><td>STATE</td><td>RATE</td></tr>
<tr><td>26</td><td>Alabama</td><td>1,477.2</td><td>1</td><td>Hawaii</td><td>3,724.8</td></tr>
<tr><td>11</td><td>Alaska</td><td>1,845.5</td><td>2</td><td>South Carolina</td><td>3,502.6</td></tr>
<tr><td>35</td><td>Arizona</td><td>1,279.0</td><td>3</td><td>Delaware</td><td>2,601.6</td></tr>
<tr><td>14</td><td>Arkansas</td><td>1,643.6</td><td>4</td><td>North Carolina</td><td>2,557.3</td></tr>
<tr><td>21</td><td>California</td><td>1,528.2</td><td>5</td><td>Florida</td><td>2,545.9</td></tr>
<tr><td>38</td><td>Colorado</td><td>1,086.7</td><td>6</td><td>Georgia</td><td>2,278.1</td></tr>
<tr><td>42</td><td>Connecticut</td><td>1,013.8</td><td>7</td><td>Louisiana</td><td>2,249.6</td></tr>
<tr><td>3</td><td>Delaware</td><td>2,601.6</td><td>8</td><td>Washington</td><td>2,233.5</td></tr>
<tr><td>5</td><td>Florida</td><td>2,545.9</td><td>9</td><td>Tennessee</td><td>2,186.6</td></tr>
<tr><td>6</td><td>Georgia</td><td>2,278.1</td><td>10</td><td>Maryland</td><td>2,086.4</td></tr>
<tr><td>1</td><td>Hawaii</td><td>3,724.8</td><td>11</td><td>Alaska</td><td>1,845.5</td></tr>
<tr><td>40</td><td>Idaho</td><td>1,082.5</td><td>12</td><td>Ohio</td><td>1,695.4</td></tr>
<tr><td>NA</td><td>Illinois**</td><td>NA</td><td>13</td><td>West Virginia</td><td>1,663.1</td></tr>
<tr><td>34</td><td>Indiana</td><td>1,283.0</td><td>14</td><td>Arkansas</td><td>1,643.6</td></tr>
<tr><td>44</td><td>Iowa</td><td>642.0</td><td>15</td><td>New Mexico</td><td>1,641.4</td></tr>
<tr><td>18</td><td>Kansas</td><td>1,535.6</td><td>16</td><td>Michigan</td><td>1,611.1</td></tr>
<tr><td>32</td><td>Kentucky</td><td>1,404.9</td><td>17</td><td>Utah</td><td>1,536.0</td></tr>
<tr><td>7</td><td>Louisiana</td><td>2,249.6</td><td>18</td><td>Kansas</td><td>1,535.6</td></tr>
<tr><td>19</td><td>Maine</td><td>1,534.0</td><td>19</td><td>Maine</td><td>1,534.0</td></tr>
<tr><td>10</td><td>Maryland</td><td>2,086.4</td><td>20</td><td>Pennsylvania</td><td>1,528.7</td></tr>
<tr><td>47</td><td>Massachusetts</td><td>0.0</td><td>21</td><td>California</td><td>1,528.2</td></tr>
<tr><td>16</td><td>Michigan</td><td>1,611.1</td><td>22</td><td>Oregon</td><td>1,520.1</td></tr>
<tr><td>36</td><td>Minnesota</td><td>1,225.2</td><td>23</td><td>Montana</td><td>1,514.1</td></tr>
<tr><td>30</td><td>Mississippi</td><td>1,420.7</td><td>24</td><td>Vermont</td><td>1,504.2</td></tr>
<tr><td>31</td><td>Missouri</td><td>1,418.1</td><td>25</td><td>Nevada</td><td>1,483.4</td></tr>
<tr><td>23</td><td>Montana</td><td>1,514.1</td><td>26</td><td>Alabama</td><td>1,477.2</td></tr>
<tr><td>41</td><td>Nebraska</td><td>1,042.9</td><td>27</td><td>New York</td><td>1,468.2</td></tr>
<tr><td>25</td><td>Nevada</td><td>1,483.4</td><td>28</td><td>Texas</td><td>1,452.1</td></tr>
<tr><td>45</td><td>New Hampshire</td><td>575.4</td><td>29</td><td>Virginia</td><td>1,437.4</td></tr>
<tr><td>47</td><td>New Jersey</td><td>0.0</td><td>30</td><td>Mississippi</td><td>1,420.7</td></tr>
<tr><td>15</td><td>New Mexico</td><td>1,641.4</td><td>31</td><td>Missouri</td><td>1,418.1</td></tr>
<tr><td>27</td><td>New York</td><td>1,468.2</td><td>32</td><td>Kentucky</td><td>1,404.9</td></tr>
<tr><td>4</td><td>North Carolina</td><td>2,557.3</td><td>33</td><td>Oklahoma</td><td>1,327.8</td></tr>
<tr><td>43</td><td>North Dakota</td><td>707.8</td><td>34</td><td>Indiana</td><td>1,283.0</td></tr>
<tr><td>12</td><td>Ohio</td><td>1,695.4</td><td>35</td><td>Arizona</td><td>1,279.0</td></tr>
<tr><td>33</td><td>Oklahoma</td><td>1,327.8</td><td>36</td><td>Minnesota</td><td>1,225.2</td></tr>
<tr><td>22</td><td>Oregon</td><td>1,520.1</td><td>37</td><td>Wisconsin</td><td>1,203.3</td></tr>
<tr><td>20</td><td>Pennsylvania</td><td>1,528.7</td><td>38</td><td>Colorado</td><td>1,086.7</td></tr>
<tr><td>47</td><td>Rhode Island</td><td>0.0</td><td>39</td><td>Wyoming</td><td>1,085.6</td></tr>
<tr><td>2</td><td>South Carolina</td><td>3,502.6</td><td>40</td><td>Idaho</td><td>1,082.5</td></tr>
<tr><td>46</td><td>South Dakota</td><td>472.9</td><td>41</td><td>Nebraska</td><td>1,042.9</td></tr>
<tr><td>9</td><td>Tennessee</td><td>2,186.6</td><td>42</td><td>Connecticut</td><td>1,013.8</td></tr>
<tr><td>28</td><td>Texas</td><td>1,452.1</td><td>43</td><td>North Dakota</td><td>707.8</td></tr>
<tr><td>17</td><td>Utah</td><td>1,536.0</td><td>44</td><td>Iowa</td><td>642.0</td></tr>
<tr><td>24</td><td>Vermont</td><td>1,504.2</td><td>45</td><td>New Hampshire</td><td>575.4</td></tr>
<tr><td>29</td><td>Virginia</td><td>1,437.4</td><td>46</td><td>South Dakota</td><td>472.9</td></tr>
<tr><td>8</td><td>Washington</td><td>2,233.5</td><td>47</td><td>Massachusetts</td><td>0.0</td></tr>
<tr><td>13</td><td>West Virginia</td><td>1,663.1</td><td>47</td><td>New Jersey</td><td>0.0</td></tr>
<tr><td>37</td><td>Wisconsin</td><td>1,203.3</td><td>47</td><td>Rhode Island</td><td>0.0</td></tr>
<tr><td>39</td><td>Wyoming</td><td>1,085.6</td><td>NA</td><td>Illinois**</td><td>NA</td></tr>
</table>

District of Columbia   0.0

Source: CQ Press using reported data from the Federal Bureau of Investigation
   "Crime in the United States 2008" (Uniform Crime Reports, September 14, 2009, http://www.fbi.gov/ucr/ucr.htm)
*Estimated rates for nonmetropolitan areas, defined by the F.B.I. as other than Metropolitan Statistical Areas and other cities outside such areas. National rate includes those states listed as not available. Property crimes are offenses of burglary, larceny-theft, and motor vehicle theft.
**Not available.

Percent of Property Crimes Occurring in Rural Areas in 2008

National Percent = 5.2% of Property Crimes*

ALPHA ORDER

RANK	STATE	PERCENT
28	Alabama	5.7
4	Alaska	20.7
44	Arizona	1.2
15	Arkansas	9.7
46	California	0.8
40	Colorado	2.9
26	Connecticut	6.1
11	Delaware	12.1
39	Florida	3.0
22	Georgia	6.6
1	Hawaii	30.9
15	Idaho	9.7
NA	Illinois**	NA
34	Indiana	5.3
25	Iowa	6.4
34	Kansas	5.3
7	Kentucky	16.5
14	Louisiana	10.1
10	Maine	12.9
43	Maryland	2.3
48	Massachusetts	0.0
22	Michigan	6.6
21	Minnesota	6.7
6	Mississippi	17.3
31	Missouri	5.5
2	Montana	25.0
19	Nebraska	7.1
38	Nevada	3.6
45	New Hampshire	1.0
48	New Jersey	0.0
28	New Mexico	5.7
37	New York	3.7
9	North Carolina	13.0
13	North Dakota	11.2
30	Ohio	5.6
24	Oklahoma	6.5
32	Oregon	5.4
32	Pennsylvania	5.4
47	Rhode Island	0.3
8	South Carolina	14.7
18	South Dakota	8.1
17	Tennessee	9.1
42	Texas	2.4
41	Utah	2.6
5	Vermont	19.8
26	Virginia	6.1
36	Washington	4.3
3	West Virginia	20.9
20	Wisconsin	7.0
12	Wyoming	11.5

RANK ORDER

RANK	STATE	PERCENT
1	Hawaii	30.9
2	Montana	25.0
3	West Virginia	20.9
4	Alaska	20.7
5	Vermont	19.8
6	Mississippi	17.3
7	Kentucky	16.5
8	South Carolina	14.7
9	North Carolina	13.0
10	Maine	12.9
11	Delaware	12.1
12	Wyoming	11.5
13	North Dakota	11.2
14	Louisiana	10.1
15	Arkansas	9.7
15	Idaho	9.7
17	Tennessee	9.1
18	South Dakota	8.1
19	Nebraska	7.1
20	Wisconsin	7.0
21	Minnesota	6.7
22	Georgia	6.6
22	Michigan	6.6
24	Oklahoma	6.5
25	Iowa	6.4
26	Connecticut	6.1
26	Virginia	6.1
28	Alabama	5.7
28	New Mexico	5.7
30	Ohio	5.6
31	Missouri	5.5
32	Oregon	5.4
32	Pennsylvania	5.4
34	Indiana	5.3
34	Kansas	5.3
36	Washington	4.3
37	New York	3.7
38	Nevada	3.6
39	Florida	3.0
40	Colorado	2.9
41	Utah	2.6
42	Texas	2.4
43	Maryland	2.3
44	Arizona	1.2
45	New Hampshire	1.0
46	California	0.8
47	Rhode Island	0.3
48	Massachusetts	0.0
48	New Jersey	0.0
NA	Illinois**	NA

District of Columbia   0.0

Source: CQ Press using reported data from the Federal Bureau of Investigation
   "Crime in the United States 2008" (Uniform Crime Reports, September 14, 2009, http://www.fbi.gov/ucr/ucr.htm)
*Estimated percentages for nonmetropolitan areas, defined by the F.B.I. as other than Metropolitan Statistical Areas and other cities outside such areas. National percent includes those states listed as not available. Property crimes are offenses of burglary, larceny-theft, and motor vehicle theft.
**Not available.

Burglaries in Urban Areas in 2008

National Urban Total = 2,056,896 Burglaries*

ALPHA ORDER

RANK	STATE	BURGLARIES	% of USA
13	Alabama	46,832	2.3%
46	Alaska	2,059	0.1%
10	Arizona	55,166	2.7%
22	Arkansas	29,884	1.5%
1	California	234,643	11.4%
24	Colorado	27,357	1.3%
35	Connecticut	13,481	0.7%
41	Delaware	5,567	0.3%
3	Florida	180,756	8.8%
5	Georgia	93,412	4.5%
38	Hawaii	6,370	0.3%
39	Idaho	5,887	0.3%
NA	Illinois**	NA	NA
14	Indiana	45,318	2.2%
33	Iowa	14,877	0.7%
32	Kansas	18,061	0.9%
28	Kentucky	21,744	1.1%
17	Louisiana	38,171	1.9%
42	Maine	5,108	0.2%
19	Maryland	37,512	1.8%
20	Massachusetts	36,094	1.8%
7	Michigan	68,329	3.3%
26	Minnesota	23,523	1.1%
29	Mississippi	19,977	1.0%
15	Missouri	41,900	2.0%
45	Montana	2,301	0.1%
37	Nebraska	7,912	0.4%
27	Nevada	23,119	1.1%
43	New Hampshire	4,144	0.2%
16	New Jersey	40,401	2.0%
30	New Mexico	19,680	1.0%
8	New York	61,710	3.0%
6	North Carolina	91,777	4.5%
49	North Dakota	1,712	0.1%
4	Ohio	95,555	4.6%
21	Oklahoma	32,109	1.6%
31	Oregon	18,963	0.9%
11	Pennsylvania	53,449	2.6%
40	Rhode Island	5,750	0.3%
18	South Carolina	37,640	1.8%
47	South Dakota	2,055	0.1%
9	Tennessee	56,757	2.8%
2	Texas	221,410	10.8%
34	Utah	14,068	0.7%
44	Vermont	2,322	0.1%
23	Virginia	28,803	1.4%
12	Washington	48,793	2.4%
36	West Virginia	8,320	0.4%
25	Wisconsin	24,221	1.2%
48	Wyoming	1,839	0.1%

RANK ORDER

RANK	STATE	BURGLARIES	% of USA
1	California	234,643	11.4%
2	Texas	221,410	10.8%
3	Florida	180,756	8.8%
4	Ohio	95,555	4.6%
5	Georgia	93,412	4.5%
6	North Carolina	91,777	4.5%
7	Michigan	68,329	3.3%
8	New York	61,710	3.0%
9	Tennessee	56,757	2.8%
10	Arizona	55,166	2.7%
11	Pennsylvania	53,449	2.6%
12	Washington	48,793	2.4%
13	Alabama	46,832	2.3%
14	Indiana	45,318	2.2%
15	Missouri	41,900	2.0%
16	New Jersey	40,401	2.0%
17	Louisiana	38,171	1.9%
18	South Carolina	37,640	1.8%
19	Maryland	37,512	1.8%
20	Massachusetts	36,094	1.8%
21	Oklahoma	32,109	1.6%
22	Arkansas	29,884	1.5%
23	Virginia	28,803	1.4%
24	Colorado	27,357	1.3%
25	Wisconsin	24,221	1.2%
26	Minnesota	23,523	1.1%
27	Nevada	23,119	1.1%
28	Kentucky	21,744	1.1%
29	Mississippi	19,977	1.0%
30	New Mexico	19,680	1.0%
31	Oregon	18,963	0.9%
32	Kansas	18,061	0.9%
33	Iowa	14,877	0.7%
34	Utah	14,068	0.7%
35	Connecticut	13,481	0.7%
36	West Virginia	8,320	0.4%
37	Nebraska	7,912	0.4%
38	Hawaii	6,370	0.3%
39	Idaho	5,887	0.3%
40	Rhode Island	5,750	0.3%
41	Delaware	5,567	0.3%
42	Maine	5,108	0.2%
43	New Hampshire	4,144	0.2%
44	Vermont	2,322	0.1%
45	Montana	2,301	0.1%
46	Alaska	2,059	0.1%
47	South Dakota	2,055	0.1%
48	Wyoming	1,839	0.1%
49	North Dakota	1,712	0.1%
NA	Illinois**	NA	NA
	District of Columbia	3,788	0.2%

Source: CQ Press using reported data from the Federal Bureau of Investigation
   "Crime in the United States 2008" (Uniform Crime Reports, September 14, 2009, http://www.fbi.gov/ucr/ucr.htm)
*Estimated totals for urban areas, defined by the F.B.I. as Metropolitan Statistical Areas and other cities outside such areas.
National total includes those states listed as not available. Burglary is the unlawful entry of a structure to commit a felony or theft. Attempts are included.
**Not available.

Urban Burglary Rate in 2008

National Urban Rate = 750.8 Burglaries per 100,000 Population*

ALPHA ORDER				RANK ORDER		
RANK	STATE	RATE		RANK	STATE	RATE
3	Alabama	1,192.5		1	Arkansas	1,352.7
43	Alaska	447.5		2	North Carolina	1,251.6
15	Arizona	884.8		3	Alabama	1,192.5
1	Arkansas	1,352.7		4	New Mexico	1,148.6
27	California	648.3		5	Tennessee	1,099.2
28	Colorado	598.8		6	Georgia	1,090.6
42	Connecticut	452.4		7	Oklahoma	1,059.5
20	Delaware	765.8		8	Mississippi	1,059.3
10	Florida	1,036.0		9	Louisiana	1,044.6
6	Georgia	1,090.6		10	Florida	1,036.0
23	Hawaii	702.8		11	South Carolina	1,021.3
39	Idaho	475.5		12	Texas	974.7
NA	Illinois**	NA		13	Nevada	970.3
17	Indiana	825.5		14	Ohio	937.8
26	Iowa	654.1		15	Arizona	884.8
22	Kansas	729.3		16	Missouri	826.1
21	Kentucky	731.0		17	Indiana	825.5
9	Louisiana	1,044.6		18	Washington	802.4
37	Maine	488.6		19	Michigan	776.6
24	Maryland	693.2		20	Delaware	765.8
31	Massachusetts	555.5		21	Kentucky	731.0
19	Michigan	776.6		22	Kansas	729.3
35	Minnesota	534.1		23	Hawaii	702.8
8	Mississippi	1,059.3		24	Maryland	693.2
16	Missouri	826.1		25	West Virginia	676.8
44	Montana	417.7		26	Iowa	654.1
32	Nebraska	552.5		27	California	648.3
13	Nevada	970.3		28	Colorado	598.8
49	New Hampshire	326.9		29	Oregon	566.9
41	New Jersey	465.3		30	Vermont	561.9
4	New Mexico	1,148.6		31	Massachusetts	555.5
48	New York	333.4		32	Nebraska	552.5
2	North Carolina	1,251.6		33	Rhode Island	547.2
46	North Dakota	381.4		34	Utah	544.5
14	Ohio	937.8		35	Minnesota	534.1
7	Oklahoma	1,059.5		36	Wisconsin	512.7
29	Oregon	566.9		37	Maine	488.6
40	Pennsylvania	469.3		38	Wyoming	485.4
33	Rhode Island	547.2		39	Idaho	475.5
11	South Carolina	1,021.3		40	Pennsylvania	469.3
47	South Dakota	356.2		41	New Jersey	465.3
5	Tennessee	1,099.2		42	Connecticut	452.4
12	Texas	974.7		43	Alaska	447.5
34	Utah	544.5		44	Montana	417.7
30	Vermont	561.9		45	Virginia	415.5
45	Virginia	415.5		46	North Dakota	381.4
18	Washington	802.4		47	South Dakota	356.2
25	West Virginia	676.8		48	New York	333.4
36	Wisconsin	512.7		49	New Hampshire	326.9
38	Wyoming	485.4		NA	Illinois**	NA
					District of Columbia	640.0

Source: CQ Press using reported data from the Federal Bureau of Investigation
 "Crime in the United States 2008" (Uniform Crime Reports, September 14, 2009, http://www.fbi.gov/ucr/ucr.htm)
*Estimated rates for urban areas, defined by the F.B.I. as Metropolitan Statistical Areas and other cities outside such areas.
National rate includes those states listed as not available. Burglary is the unlawful entry of a structure to commit a felony or theft. Attempts are included.
**Not available.

Percent of Burglaries Occurring in Urban Areas in 2008

National Percent = 92.6% of Burglaries*

<table>
<tr><td colspan="3">ALPHA ORDER</td><td colspan="3">RANK ORDER</td></tr>
<tr><td>RANK</td><td>STATE</td><td>PERCENT</td><td>RANK</td><td>STATE</td><td>PERCENT</td></tr>
<tr><td>17</td><td>Alabama</td><td>92.9</td><td>1</td><td>Massachusetts</td><td>100.0</td></tr>
<tr><td>49</td><td>Alaska</td><td>63.5</td><td>1</td><td>New Jersey</td><td>100.0</td></tr>
<tr><td>5</td><td>Arizona</td><td>97.7</td><td>1</td><td>Rhode Island</td><td>100.0</td></tr>
<tr><td>31</td><td>Arkansas</td><td>88.7</td><td>4</td><td>California</td><td>98.7</td></tr>
<tr><td>4</td><td>California</td><td>98.7</td><td>5</td><td>Arizona</td><td>97.7</td></tr>
<tr><td>6</td><td>Colorado</td><td>96.8</td><td>6</td><td>Colorado</td><td>96.8</td></tr>
<tr><td>29</td><td>Connecticut</td><td>89.8</td><td>7</td><td>New Hampshire</td><td>96.7</td></tr>
<tr><td>38</td><td>Delaware</td><td>82.4</td><td>8</td><td>Maryland</td><td>96.6</td></tr>
<tr><td>10</td><td>Florida</td><td>95.9</td><td>9</td><td>Texas</td><td>96.2</td></tr>
<tr><td>18</td><td>Georgia</td><td>92.8</td><td>10</td><td>Florida</td><td>95.9</td></tr>
<tr><td>47</td><td>Hawaii</td><td>67.9</td><td>11</td><td>Utah</td><td>95.8</td></tr>
<tr><td>34</td><td>Idaho</td><td>87.9</td><td>12</td><td>Nevada</td><td>95.7</td></tr>
<tr><td>NA</td><td>Illinois**</td><td>NA</td><td>13</td><td>New York</td><td>93.9</td></tr>
<tr><td>14</td><td>Indiana</td><td>93.2</td><td>14</td><td>Indiana</td><td>93.2</td></tr>
<tr><td>26</td><td>Iowa</td><td>90.4</td><td>14</td><td>Ohio</td><td>93.2</td></tr>
<tr><td>19</td><td>Kansas</td><td>92.1</td><td>16</td><td>Washington</td><td>93.0</td></tr>
<tr><td>44</td><td>Kentucky</td><td>75.4</td><td>17</td><td>Alabama</td><td>92.9</td></tr>
<tr><td>32</td><td>Louisiana</td><td>88.1</td><td>18</td><td>Georgia</td><td>92.8</td></tr>
<tr><td>42</td><td>Maine</td><td>78.3</td><td>19</td><td>Kansas</td><td>92.1</td></tr>
<tr><td>8</td><td>Maryland</td><td>96.6</td><td>19</td><td>Michigan</td><td>92.1</td></tr>
<tr><td>1</td><td>Massachusetts</td><td>100.0</td><td>21</td><td>Missouri</td><td>91.5</td></tr>
<tr><td>19</td><td>Michigan</td><td>92.1</td><td>21</td><td>Oklahoma</td><td>91.5</td></tr>
<tr><td>30</td><td>Minnesota</td><td>89.1</td><td>23</td><td>Pennsylvania</td><td>91.2</td></tr>
<tr><td>43</td><td>Mississippi</td><td>76.8</td><td>24</td><td>Oregon</td><td>90.8</td></tr>
<tr><td>21</td><td>Missouri</td><td>91.5</td><td>25</td><td>New Mexico</td><td>90.6</td></tr>
<tr><td>46</td><td>Montana</td><td>69.1</td><td>26</td><td>Iowa</td><td>90.4</td></tr>
<tr><td>27</td><td>Nebraska</td><td>90.2</td><td>27</td><td>Nebraska</td><td>90.2</td></tr>
<tr><td>12</td><td>Nevada</td><td>95.7</td><td>28</td><td>Virginia</td><td>90.0</td></tr>
<tr><td>7</td><td>New Hampshire</td><td>96.7</td><td>29</td><td>Connecticut</td><td>89.8</td></tr>
<tr><td>1</td><td>New Jersey</td><td>100.0</td><td>30</td><td>Minnesota</td><td>89.1</td></tr>
<tr><td>25</td><td>New Mexico</td><td>90.6</td><td>31</td><td>Arkansas</td><td>88.7</td></tr>
<tr><td>13</td><td>New York</td><td>93.9</td><td>32</td><td>Louisiana</td><td>88.1</td></tr>
<tr><td>39</td><td>North Carolina</td><td>82.2</td><td>32</td><td>Wisconsin</td><td>88.1</td></tr>
<tr><td>41</td><td>North Dakota</td><td>81.3</td><td>34</td><td>Idaho</td><td>87.9</td></tr>
<tr><td>14</td><td>Ohio</td><td>93.2</td><td>35</td><td>Tennessee</td><td>87.3</td></tr>
<tr><td>21</td><td>Oklahoma</td><td>91.5</td><td>36</td><td>South Dakota</td><td>84.6</td></tr>
<tr><td>24</td><td>Oregon</td><td>90.8</td><td>37</td><td>Wyoming</td><td>84.2</td></tr>
<tr><td>23</td><td>Pennsylvania</td><td>91.2</td><td>38</td><td>Delaware</td><td>82.4</td></tr>
<tr><td>1</td><td>Rhode Island</td><td>100.0</td><td>39</td><td>North Carolina</td><td>82.2</td></tr>
<tr><td>40</td><td>South Carolina</td><td>81.9</td><td>40</td><td>South Carolina</td><td>81.9</td></tr>
<tr><td>36</td><td>South Dakota</td><td>84.6</td><td>41</td><td>North Dakota</td><td>81.3</td></tr>
<tr><td>35</td><td>Tennessee</td><td>87.3</td><td>42</td><td>Maine</td><td>78.3</td></tr>
<tr><td>9</td><td>Texas</td><td>96.2</td><td>43</td><td>Mississippi</td><td>76.8</td></tr>
<tr><td>11</td><td>Utah</td><td>95.8</td><td>44</td><td>Kentucky</td><td>75.4</td></tr>
<tr><td>48</td><td>Vermont</td><td>67.1</td><td>45</td><td>West Virginia</td><td>75.2</td></tr>
<tr><td>28</td><td>Virginia</td><td>90.0</td><td>46</td><td>Montana</td><td>69.1</td></tr>
<tr><td>16</td><td>Washington</td><td>93.0</td><td>47</td><td>Hawaii</td><td>67.9</td></tr>
<tr><td>45</td><td>West Virginia</td><td>75.2</td><td>48</td><td>Vermont</td><td>67.1</td></tr>
<tr><td>32</td><td>Wisconsin</td><td>88.1</td><td>49</td><td>Alaska</td><td>63.5</td></tr>
<tr><td>37</td><td>Wyoming</td><td>84.2</td><td>NA</td><td>Illinois**</td><td>NA</td></tr>
<tr><td></td><td></td><td></td><td></td><td>District of Columbia</td><td>100.0</td></tr>
</table>

Source: CQ Press using reported data from the Federal Bureau of Investigation
"Crime in the United States 2008" (Uniform Crime Reports, September 14, 2009, http://www.fbi.gov/ucr/ucr.htm)
*Estimated percentages for urban areas, defined by the F.B.I. as Metropolitan Statistical Areas and other cities outside such areas. National percent includes those states listed as not available. Burglary is the unlawful entry of a structure to commit a felony or theft. Attempts are included.
**Not available.

Burglaries in Rural Areas in 2008

National Rural Total = 165,300 Burglaries*

ALPHA ORDER				RANK ORDER			
RANK	STATE	BURGLARIES	% of USA	RANK	STATE	BURGLARIES	% of USA
17	Alabama	3,576	2.2%	1	North Carolina	19,825	12.0%
35	Alaska	1,181	0.7%	2	Texas	8,713	5.3%
33	Arizona	1,315	0.8%	3	South Carolina	8,327	5.0%
15	Arkansas	3,810	2.3%	4	Tennessee	8,249	5.0%
20	California	3,192	1.9%	5	Florida	7,711	4.7%
39	Colorado	899	0.5%	6	Georgia	7,217	4.4%
30	Connecticut	1,530	0.9%	7	Kentucky	7,095	4.3%
34	Delaware	1,193	0.7%	8	Ohio	6,989	4.2%
5	Florida	7,711	4.7%	9	Mississippi	6,047	3.7%
6	Georgia	7,217	4.4%	10	Michigan	5,847	3.5%
22	Hawaii	3,009	1.8%	11	Pennsylvania	5,171	3.1%
41	Idaho	814	0.5%	12	Louisiana	5,149	3.1%
NA	Illinois**	NA	NA	13	New York	4,025	2.4%
18	Indiana	3,327	2.0%	14	Missouri	3,888	2.4%
28	Iowa	1,573	1.0%	15	Arkansas	3,810	2.3%
29	Kansas	1,551	0.9%	16	Washington	3,685	2.2%
7	Kentucky	7,095	4.3%	17	Alabama	3,576	2.2%
12	Louisiana	5,149	3.1%	18	Indiana	3,327	2.0%
31	Maine	1,414	0.9%	19	Wisconsin	3,258	2.0%
32	Maryland	1,337	0.8%	20	California	3,192	1.9%
47	Massachusetts	0	0.0%	21	Virginia	3,190	1.9%
10	Michigan	5,847	3.5%	22	Hawaii	3,009	1.8%
24	Minnesota	2,887	1.7%	23	Oklahoma	2,972	1.8%
9	Mississippi	6,047	3.7%	24	Minnesota	2,887	1.7%
14	Missouri	3,888	2.4%	25	West Virginia	2,746	1.7%
38	Montana	1,031	0.6%	26	New Mexico	2,033	1.2%
40	Nebraska	863	0.5%	27	Oregon	1,916	1.2%
37	Nevada	1,037	0.6%	28	Iowa	1,573	1.0%
46	New Hampshire	142	0.1%	29	Kansas	1,551	0.9%
47	New Jersey	0	0.0%	30	Connecticut	1,530	0.9%
26	New Mexico	2,033	1.2%	31	Maine	1,414	0.9%
13	New York	4,025	2.4%	32	Maryland	1,337	0.8%
1	North Carolina	19,825	12.0%	33	Arizona	1,315	0.8%
43	North Dakota	394	0.2%	34	Delaware	1,193	0.7%
8	Ohio	6,989	4.2%	35	Alaska	1,181	0.7%
23	Oklahoma	2,972	1.8%	36	Vermont	1,140	0.7%
27	Oregon	1,916	1.2%	37	Nevada	1,037	0.6%
11	Pennsylvania	5,171	3.1%	38	Montana	1,031	0.6%
47	Rhode Island	0	0.0%	39	Colorado	899	0.5%
3	South Carolina	8,327	5.0%	40	Nebraska	863	0.5%
44	South Dakota	375	0.2%	41	Idaho	814	0.5%
4	Tennessee	8,249	5.0%	42	Utah	614	0.4%
2	Texas	8,713	5.3%	43	North Dakota	394	0.2%
42	Utah	614	0.4%	44	South Dakota	375	0.2%
36	Vermont	1,140	0.7%	45	Wyoming	345	0.2%
21	Virginia	3,190	1.9%	46	New Hampshire	142	0.1%
16	Washington	3,685	2.2%	47	Massachusetts	0	0.0%
25	West Virginia	2,746	1.7%	47	New Jersey	0	0.0%
19	Wisconsin	3,258	2.0%	47	Rhode Island	0	0.0%
45	Wyoming	345	0.2%	NA	Illinois**	NA	NA
					District of Columbia	0	0.0%

Source: Reported data from the Federal Bureau of Investigation
"Crime in the United States 2008" (Uniform Crime Reports, September 14, 2009, http://www.fbi.gov/ucr/ucr.htm)
*Estimated totals for nonmetropolitan areas, defined by the F.B.I. as other than Metropolitan Statistical Areas and other cities outside such areas. National total includes those states listed as not available. Burglary is the unlawful entry of a structure to commit a felony or theft. Attempts are included.
**Not available.

Rural Burglary Rate in 2008

National Rural Rate = 549.2 Burglaries per 100,000 Population*

ALPHA ORDER

RANK	STATE	RATE
23	Alabama	486.8
19	Alaska	522.2
21	Arizona	495.8
12	Arkansas	589.6
14	California	564.8
42	Colorado	242.6
38	Connecticut	293.3
4	Delaware	816.1
3	Florida	874.7
10	Georgia	644.1
5	Hawaii	788.0
39	Idaho	284.9
NA	Illinois**	NA
34	Indiana	375.1
44	Iowa	216.1
27	Kansas	476.3
15	Kentucky	548.0
9	Louisiana	680.6
20	Maine	521.9
11	Maryland	601.4
47	Massachusetts	0.0
25	Michigan	485.3
36	Minnesota	353.8
13	Mississippi	574.4
29	Missouri	463.2
40	Montana	247.5
41	Nebraska	245.6
26	Nevada	476.8
37	New Hampshire	293.9
47	New Jersey	0.0
8	New Mexico	750.2
31	New York	410.3
1	North Carolina	1,049.0
45	North Dakota	204.6
18	Ohio	538.9
24	Oklahoma	485.7
30	Oregon	430.5
22	Pennsylvania	488.0
47	Rhode Island	0.0
2	South Carolina	1,048.2
46	South Dakota	165.0
7	Tennessee	784.6
17	Texas	540.8
32	Utah	401.5
15	Vermont	548.0
33	Virginia	381.5
6	Washington	786.6
28	West Virginia	469.3
35	Wisconsin	360.4
43	Wyoming	224.3

RANK ORDER

RANK	STATE	RATE
1	North Carolina	1,049.0
2	South Carolina	1,048.2
3	Florida	874.7
4	Delaware	816.1
5	Hawaii	788.0
6	Washington	786.6
7	Tennessee	784.6
8	New Mexico	750.2
9	Louisiana	680.6
10	Georgia	644.1
11	Maryland	601.4
12	Arkansas	589.6
13	Mississippi	574.4
14	California	564.8
15	Kentucky	548.0
15	Vermont	548.0
17	Texas	540.8
18	Ohio	538.9
19	Alaska	522.2
20	Maine	521.9
21	Arizona	495.8
22	Pennsylvania	488.0
23	Alabama	486.8
24	Oklahoma	485.7
25	Michigan	485.3
26	Nevada	476.8
27	Kansas	476.3
28	West Virginia	469.3
29	Missouri	463.2
30	Oregon	430.5
31	New York	410.3
32	Utah	401.5
33	Virginia	381.5
34	Indiana	375.1
35	Wisconsin	360.4
36	Minnesota	353.8
37	New Hampshire	293.9
38	Connecticut	293.3
39	Idaho	284.9
40	Montana	247.5
41	Nebraska	245.6
42	Colorado	242.6
43	Wyoming	224.3
44	Iowa	216.1
45	North Dakota	204.6
46	South Dakota	165.0
47	Massachusetts	0.0
47	New Jersey	0.0
47	Rhode Island	0.0
NA	Illinois**	NA

District of Columbia 0.0

Source: CQ Press using reported data from the Federal Bureau of Investigation
  "Crime in the United States 2008" (Uniform Crime Reports, September 14, 2009, http://www.fbi.gov/ucr/ucr.htm)
*Estimated rates for nonmetropolitan areas, defined by the F.B.I. as other than Metropolitan Statistical Areas and other cities outside such areas. National rate includes those states listed as not available. Burglary is the unlawful entry of a structure to commit a felony or theft. Attempts are included.
**Not available.

Percent of Burglaries Occurring in Rural Areas in 2008

National Percent = 7.4% of Burglaries*

ALPHA ORDER

RANK	STATE	PERCENT
33	Alabama	7.1
1	Alaska	36.5
45	Arizona	2.3
19	Arkansas	11.3
46	California	1.3
44	Colorado	3.2
21	Connecticut	10.2
12	Delaware	17.6
40	Florida	4.1
32	Georgia	7.2
3	Hawaii	32.1
16	Idaho	12.1
NA	Illinois**	NA
35	Indiana	6.8
24	Iowa	9.6
30	Kansas	7.9
6	Kentucky	24.6
17	Louisiana	11.9
8	Maine	21.7
42	Maryland	3.4
47	Massachusetts	0.0
30	Michigan	7.9
20	Minnesota	10.9
7	Mississippi	23.2
28	Missouri	8.5
4	Montana	30.9
23	Nebraska	9.8
38	Nevada	4.3
43	New Hampshire	3.3
47	New Jersey	0.0
25	New Mexico	9.4
37	New York	6.1
11	North Carolina	17.8
9	North Dakota	18.7
35	Ohio	6.8
28	Oklahoma	8.5
26	Oregon	9.2
27	Pennsylvania	8.8
47	Rhode Island	0.0
10	South Carolina	18.1
14	South Dakota	15.4
15	Tennessee	12.7
41	Texas	3.8
39	Utah	4.2
2	Vermont	32.9
22	Virginia	10.0
34	Washington	7.0
5	West Virginia	24.8
17	Wisconsin	11.9
13	Wyoming	15.8

RANK ORDER

RANK	STATE	PERCENT
1	Alaska	36.5
2	Vermont	32.9
3	Hawaii	32.1
4	Montana	30.9
5	West Virginia	24.8
6	Kentucky	24.6
7	Mississippi	23.2
8	Maine	21.7
9	North Dakota	18.7
10	South Carolina	18.1
11	North Carolina	17.8
12	Delaware	17.6
13	Wyoming	15.8
14	South Dakota	15.4
15	Tennessee	12.7
16	Idaho	12.1
17	Louisiana	11.9
17	Wisconsin	11.9
19	Arkansas	11.3
20	Minnesota	10.9
21	Connecticut	10.2
22	Virginia	10.0
23	Nebraska	9.8
24	Iowa	9.6
25	New Mexico	9.4
26	Oregon	9.2
27	Pennsylvania	8.8
28	Missouri	8.5
28	Oklahoma	8.5
30	Kansas	7.9
30	Michigan	7.9
32	Georgia	7.2
33	Alabama	7.1
34	Washington	7.0
35	Indiana	6.8
35	Ohio	6.8
37	New York	6.1
38	Nevada	4.3
39	Utah	4.2
40	Florida	4.1
41	Texas	3.8
42	Maryland	3.4
43	New Hampshire	3.3
44	Colorado	3.2
45	Arizona	2.3
46	California	1.3
47	Massachusetts	0.0
47	New Jersey	0.0
47	Rhode Island	0.0
NA	Illinois**	NA

District of Columbia   0.0

Source: CQ Press using reported data from the Federal Bureau of Investigation
   "Crime in the United States 2008" (Uniform Crime Reports, September 14, 2009, http://www.fbi.gov/ucr/ucr.htm)
*Estimated percentages for nonmetropolitan areas, defined by the F.B.I. as other than Metropolitan Statistical Areas and other cities outside such areas. National percent includes those states listed as not available. Burglary is the unlawful entry of a structure to commit a felony or theft. Attempts are included.
**Not available.

Larceny-Thefts in Urban Areas in 2008

National Urban Total = 6,285,483 Larceny-Thefts*

ALPHA ORDER

RANK	STATE	THEFTS	% of USA
18	Alabama	119,978	1.9%
45	Alaska	12,648	0.2%
9	Arizona	183,574	2.9%
30	Arkansas	63,288	1.0%
1	California	645,917	10.3%
24	Colorado	96,074	1.5%
31	Connecticut	58,761	0.9%
43	Delaware	19,663	0.3%
3	Florida	493,799	7.9%
6	Georgia	232,194	3.7%
41	Hawaii	21,473	0.3%
40	Idaho	21,631	0.3%
NA	Illinois**	NA	NA
15	Indiana	139,427	2.2%
32	Iowa	49,177	0.8%
28	Kansas	64,518	1.0%
29	Kentucky	64,278	1.0%
23	Louisiana	100,720	1.6%
38	Maine	22,073	0.4%
17	Maryland	130,968	2.1%
21	Massachusetts	107,128	1.7%
10	Michigan	170,599	2.7%
22	Minnesota	105,947	1.7%
34	Mississippi	46,171	0.7%
13	Missouri	142,989	2.3%
44	Montana	15,540	0.2%
36	Nebraska	35,831	0.6%
33	Nevada	47,696	0.8%
39	New Hampshire	21,733	0.3%
16	New Jersey	138,545	2.2%
35	New Mexico	45,837	0.7%
4	New York	287,760	4.6%
7	North Carolina	209,958	3.3%
49	North Dakota	8,348	0.1%
5	Ohio	246,914	3.9%
26	Oklahoma	75,087	1.2%
25	Oregon	87,867	1.4%
8	Pennsylvania	208,798	3.3%
42	Rhode Island	20,867	0.3%
20	South Carolina	109,149	1.7%
48	South Dakota	9,372	0.1%
12	Tennessee	154,294	2.5%
2	Texas	641,244	10.2%
27	Utah	68,397	1.1%
47	Vermont	9,906	0.2%
14	Virginia	142,482	2.3%
11	Washington	159,336	2.5%
37	West Virginia	26,200	0.4%
19	Wisconsin	109,159	1.7%
46	Wyoming	10,378	0.2%

RANK ORDER

RANK	STATE	THEFTS	% of USA
1	California	645,917	10.3%
2	Texas	641,244	10.2%
3	Florida	493,799	7.9%
4	New York	287,760	4.6%
5	Ohio	246,914	3.9%
6	Georgia	232,194	3.7%
7	North Carolina	209,958	3.3%
8	Pennsylvania	208,798	3.3%
9	Arizona	183,574	2.9%
10	Michigan	170,599	2.7%
11	Washington	159,336	2.5%
12	Tennessee	154,294	2.5%
13	Missouri	142,989	2.3%
14	Virginia	142,482	2.3%
15	Indiana	139,427	2.2%
16	New Jersey	138,545	2.2%
17	Maryland	130,968	2.1%
18	Alabama	119,978	1.9%
19	Wisconsin	109,159	1.7%
20	South Carolina	109,149	1.7%
21	Massachusetts	107,128	1.7%
22	Minnesota	105,947	1.7%
23	Louisiana	100,720	1.6%
24	Colorado	96,074	1.5%
25	Oregon	87,867	1.4%
26	Oklahoma	75,087	1.2%
27	Utah	68,397	1.1%
28	Kansas	64,518	1.0%
29	Kentucky	64,278	1.0%
30	Arkansas	63,288	1.0%
31	Connecticut	58,761	0.9%
32	Iowa	49,177	0.8%
33	Nevada	47,696	0.8%
34	Mississippi	46,171	0.7%
35	New Mexico	45,837	0.7%
36	Nebraska	35,831	0.6%
37	West Virginia	26,200	0.4%
38	Maine	22,073	0.4%
39	New Hampshire	21,733	0.3%
40	Idaho	21,631	0.3%
41	Hawaii	21,473	0.3%
42	Rhode Island	20,867	0.3%
43	Delaware	19,663	0.3%
44	Montana	15,540	0.2%
45	Alaska	12,648	0.2%
46	Wyoming	10,378	0.2%
47	Vermont	9,906	0.2%
48	South Dakota	9,372	0.1%
49	North Dakota	8,348	0.1%
NA	Illinois**	NA	NA
	District of Columbia	19,958	0.3%

Source: CQ Press using reported data from the Federal Bureau of Investigation
"Crime in the United States 2008" (Uniform Crime Reports, September 14, 2009, http://www.fbi.gov/ucr/ucr.htm)
*Estimated totals for urban areas, defined by the F.B.I. as Metropolitan Statistical Areas and other cities outside such areas.
National total includes those states listed as not available. Larceny-theft is the unlawful taking of property without use of force, violence, or fraud. Attempts are included. Motor vehicle thefts are excluded.
**Not available.

Urban Larceny-Theft Rate in 2008

National Urban Rate = 2,294.3 Larceny-Thefts per 100,000 Population*

ALPHA ORDER

RANK	STATE	RATE
1	Alabama	3,055.0
12	Alaska	2,748.9
4	Arizona	2,944.3
5	Arkansas	2,864.8
43	California	1,784.7
35	Colorado	2,102.8
39	Connecticut	1,972.1
15	Delaware	2,705.0
7	Florida	2,830.3
14	Georgia	2,710.9
29	Hawaii	2,369.2
44	Idaho	1,747.1
NA	Illinois**	NA
21	Indiana	2,539.7
31	Iowa	2,162.0
20	Kansas	2,605.2
32	Kentucky	2,160.9
11	Louisiana	2,756.2
34	Maine	2,111.2
26	Maryland	2,420.3
46	Massachusetts	1,648.7
40	Michigan	1,938.9
27	Minnesota	2,405.5
24	Mississippi	2,448.3
10	Missouri	2,819.1
9	Montana	2,821.2
22	Nebraska	2,502.2
37	Nevada	2,001.8
45	New Hampshire	1,714.6
48	New Jersey	1,595.7
16	New Mexico	2,675.3
49	New York	1,554.7
6	North Carolina	2,863.3
41	North Dakota	1,859.6
25	Ohio	2,423.3
23	Oklahoma	2,477.7
18	Oregon	2,626.8
42	Pennsylvania	1,833.4
38	Rhode Island	1,985.8
3	South Carolina	2,961.6
47	South Dakota	1,624.6
2	Tennessee	2,988.1
8	Texas	2,822.9
17	Utah	2,647.5
28	Vermont	2,397.1
36	Virginia	2,055.2
19	Washington	2,620.3
33	West Virginia	2,131.2
30	Wisconsin	2,310.7
13	Wyoming	2,739.4

RANK ORDER

RANK	STATE	RATE
1	Alabama	3,055.0
2	Tennessee	2,988.1
3	South Carolina	2,961.6
4	Arizona	2,944.3
5	Arkansas	2,864.8
6	North Carolina	2,863.3
7	Florida	2,830.3
8	Texas	2,822.9
9	Montana	2,821.2
10	Missouri	2,819.1
11	Louisiana	2,756.2
12	Alaska	2,748.9
13	Wyoming	2,739.4
14	Georgia	2,710.9
15	Delaware	2,705.0
16	New Mexico	2,675.3
17	Utah	2,647.5
18	Oregon	2,626.8
19	Washington	2,620.3
20	Kansas	2,605.2
21	Indiana	2,539.7
22	Nebraska	2,502.2
23	Oklahoma	2,477.7
24	Mississippi	2,448.3
25	Ohio	2,423.3
26	Maryland	2,420.3
27	Minnesota	2,405.5
28	Vermont	2,397.1
29	Hawaii	2,369.2
30	Wisconsin	2,310.7
31	Iowa	2,162.0
32	Kentucky	2,160.9
33	West Virginia	2,131.2
34	Maine	2,111.2
35	Colorado	2,102.8
36	Virginia	2,055.2
37	Nevada	2,001.8
38	Rhode Island	1,985.8
39	Connecticut	1,972.1
40	Michigan	1,938.9
41	North Dakota	1,859.6
42	Pennsylvania	1,833.4
43	California	1,784.7
44	Idaho	1,747.1
45	New Hampshire	1,714.6
46	Massachusetts	1,648.7
47	South Dakota	1,624.6
48	New Jersey	1,595.7
49	New York	1,554.7
NA	Illinois**	NA
	District of Columbia	3,372.2

Source: CQ Press using reported data from the Federal Bureau of Investigation
   "Crime in the United States 2008" (Uniform Crime Reports, September 14, 2009, http://www.fbi.gov/ucr/ucr.htm)
*Estimated rates for urban areas, defined by the F.B.I. as Metropolitan Statistical Areas and other cities outside such areas.
National rate includes those states listed as not available. Larceny-theft is the unlawful taking of property without use of force,
violence, or fraud. Attempts are included. Motor vehicle thefts are excluded.
**Not available.

Percent of Larceny-Thefts Occurring in Urban Areas in 2008

National Percent = 95.4% of Larceny-Thefts*

ALPHA ORDER

RANK	STATE	PERCENT
21	Alabama	94.9
46	Alaska	83.0
6	Arizona	99.1
35	Arkansas	91.3
5	California	99.3
11	Colorado	97.1
25	Connecticut	94.6
41	Delaware	89.4
10	Florida	97.4
30	Georgia	93.4
49	Hawaii	68.2
34	Idaho	91.5
NA	Illinois**	NA
20	Indiana	95.1
22	Iowa	94.7
16	Kansas	95.4
42	Kentucky	87.1
37	Louisiana	90.3
38	Maine	89.8
8	Maryland	97.7
1	Massachusetts	100.0
32	Michigan	93.1
27	Minnesota	94.3
44	Mississippi	85.5
18	Missouri	95.3
48	Montana	76.6
30	Nebraska	93.4
14	Nevada	96.2
4	New Hampshire	99.5
1	New Jersey	100.0
15	New Mexico	95.8
12	New York	96.7
40	North Carolina	89.5
36	North Dakota	91.1
22	Ohio	94.7
26	Oklahoma	94.5
18	Oregon	95.3
16	Pennsylvania	95.4
3	Rhode Island	99.8
43	South Carolina	86.6
29	South Dakota	93.7
33	Tennessee	92.4
7	Texas	98.0
8	Utah	97.7
45	Vermont	84.5
22	Virginia	94.7
13	Washington	96.4
47	West Virginia	81.0
28	Wisconsin	94.0
39	Wyoming	89.6

RANK ORDER

RANK	STATE	PERCENT
1	Massachusetts	100.0
1	New Jersey	100.0
3	Rhode Island	99.8
4	New Hampshire	99.5
5	California	99.3
6	Arizona	99.1
7	Texas	98.0
8	Maryland	97.7
8	Utah	97.7
10	Florida	97.4
11	Colorado	97.1
12	New York	96.7
13	Washington	96.4
14	Nevada	96.2
15	New Mexico	95.8
16	Kansas	95.4
16	Pennsylvania	95.4
18	Missouri	95.3
18	Oregon	95.3
20	Indiana	95.1
21	Alabama	94.9
22	Iowa	94.7
22	Ohio	94.7
22	Virginia	94.7
25	Connecticut	94.6
26	Oklahoma	94.5
27	Minnesota	94.3
28	Wisconsin	94.0
29	South Dakota	93.7
30	Georgia	93.4
30	Nebraska	93.4
32	Michigan	93.1
33	Tennessee	92.4
34	Idaho	91.5
35	Arkansas	91.3
36	North Dakota	91.1
37	Louisiana	90.3
38	Maine	89.8
39	Wyoming	89.6
40	North Carolina	89.5
41	Delaware	89.4
42	Kentucky	87.1
43	South Carolina	86.6
44	Mississippi	85.5
45	Vermont	84.5
46	Alaska	83.0
47	West Virginia	81.0
48	Montana	76.6
49	Hawaii	68.2
NA	Illinois**	NA

District of Columbia 100.0

Source: CQ Press using reported data from the Federal Bureau of Investigation
   "Crime in the United States 2008" (Uniform Crime Reports, September 14, 2009, http://www.fbi.gov/ucr/ucr.htm)
*Estimated percentages for urban areas, defined by the F.B.I. as Metropolitan Statistical Areas and other cities outside such areas. National percent includes those states listed as not available. Larceny-theft is the unlawful taking of property without use of force, violence, or fraud. Attempts are included. Motor vehicle thefts are excluded.
**Not available.

Larceny-Thefts in Rural Areas in 2008

National Rural Total = 303,390 Larceny-Thefts*

ALPHA ORDER

RANK	STATE	THEFTS	% of USA
19	Alabama	6,499	2.1%
33	Alaska	2,598	0.9%
41	Arizona	1,647	0.5%
22	Arkansas	6,015	2.0%
25	California	4,468	1.5%
31	Colorado	2,876	0.9%
28	Connecticut	3,352	1.1%
36	Delaware	2,339	0.8%
5	Florida	13,159	4.3%
3	Georgia	16,484	5.4%
11	Hawaii	10,019	3.3%
37	Idaho	2,019	0.7%
NA	Illinois**	NA	NA
16	Indiana	7,188	2.4%
32	Iowa	2,730	0.9%
29	Kansas	3,110	1.0%
13	Kentucky	9,530	3.1%
9	Louisiana	10,847	3.6%
35	Maine	2,514	0.8%
30	Maryland	3,015	1.0%
48	Massachusetts	0	0.0%
8	Michigan	12,569	4.1%
20	Minnesota	6,375	2.1%
15	Mississippi	7,861	2.6%
17	Missouri	7,043	2.3%
24	Montana	4,737	1.6%
34	Nebraska	2,544	0.8%
39	Nevada	1,885	0.6%
46	New Hampshire	120	0.0%
48	New Jersey	0	0.0%
38	New Mexico	2,018	0.7%
12	New York	9,924	3.3%
1	North Carolina	24,658	8.1%
44	North Dakota	816	0.3%
4	Ohio	13,872	4.6%
26	Oklahoma	4,335	1.4%
27	Oregon	4,320	1.4%
10	Pennsylvania	10,143	3.3%
47	Rhode Island	32	0.0%
2	South Carolina	16,915	5.6%
45	South Dakota	632	0.2%
7	Tennessee	12,721	4.2%
6	Texas	12,853	4.2%
42	Utah	1,599	0.5%
40	Vermont	1,818	0.6%
14	Virginia	7,900	2.6%
23	Washington	6,003	2.0%
21	West Virginia	6,137	2.0%
18	Wisconsin	6,969	2.3%
43	Wyoming	1,199	0.4%

RANK ORDER

RANK	STATE	THEFTS	% of USA
1	North Carolina	24,658	8.1%
2	South Carolina	16,915	5.6%
3	Georgia	16,484	5.4%
4	Ohio	13,872	4.6%
5	Florida	13,159	4.3%
6	Texas	12,853	4.2%
7	Tennessee	12,721	4.2%
8	Michigan	12,569	4.1%
9	Louisiana	10,847	3.6%
10	Pennsylvania	10,143	3.3%
11	Hawaii	10,019	3.3%
12	New York	9,924	3.3%
13	Kentucky	9,530	3.1%
14	Virginia	7,900	2.6%
15	Mississippi	7,861	2.6%
16	Indiana	7,188	2.4%
17	Missouri	7,043	2.3%
18	Wisconsin	6,969	2.3%
19	Alabama	6,499	2.1%
20	Minnesota	6,375	2.1%
21	West Virginia	6,137	2.0%
22	Arkansas	6,015	2.0%
23	Washington	6,003	2.0%
24	Montana	4,737	1.6%
25	California	4,468	1.5%
26	Oklahoma	4,335	1.4%
27	Oregon	4,320	1.4%
28	Connecticut	3,352	1.1%
29	Kansas	3,110	1.0%
30	Maryland	3,015	1.0%
31	Colorado	2,876	0.9%
32	Iowa	2,730	0.9%
33	Alaska	2,598	0.9%
34	Nebraska	2,544	0.8%
35	Maine	2,514	0.8%
36	Delaware	2,339	0.8%
37	Idaho	2,019	0.7%
38	New Mexico	2,018	0.7%
39	Nevada	1,885	0.6%
40	Vermont	1,818	0.6%
41	Arizona	1,647	0.5%
42	Utah	1,599	0.5%
43	Wyoming	1,199	0.4%
44	North Dakota	816	0.3%
45	South Dakota	632	0.2%
46	New Hampshire	120	0.0%
47	Rhode Island	32	0.0%
48	Massachusetts	0	0.0%
48	New Jersey	0	0.0%
NA	Illinois**	NA	NA
	District of Columbia	0	0.0%

Source: Reported data from the Federal Bureau of Investigation
"Crime in the United States 2008" (Uniform Crime Reports, September 14, 2009, http://www.fbi.gov/ucr/ucr.htm)
*Estimated totals for nonmetropolitan areas, defined by the F.B.I. as other than Metropolitan Statistical Areas and other cities outside such areas. National total includes those states listed as not available. Larceny-theft is the unlawful taking of property without use of force, violence, or fraud. Attempts are included. Motor vehicle thefts are excluded.
**Not available.

Rural Larceny-Theft Rate in 2008

National Rural Rate = 1,008.0 Larceny-Thefts per 100,000 Population*

ALPHA ORDER

RANK	STATE	RATE
24	Alabama	884.6
11	Alaska	1,148.7
42	Arizona	621.0
22	Arkansas	930.8
30	California	790.6
33	Colorado	776.1
41	Connecticut	642.6
3	Delaware	1,600.1
4	Florida	1,492.7
5	Georgia	1,471.2
1	Hawaii	2,623.8
40	Idaho	706.6
NA	Illinois**	NA
28	Indiana	810.5
44	Iowa	375.0
20	Kansas	955.0
37	Kentucky	736.1
6	Louisiana	1,433.8
23	Maine	928.0
7	Maryland	1,356.3
47	Massachusetts	0.0
16	Michigan	1,043.3
31	Minnesota	781.3
35	Mississippi	746.7
27	Missouri	839.1
12	Montana	1,137.0
38	Nebraska	723.9
26	Nevada	866.8
46	New Hampshire	248.4
47	New Jersey	0.0
36	New Mexico	744.7
17	New York	1,011.5
8	North Carolina	1,304.8
43	North Dakota	423.7
13	Ohio	1,069.6
39	Oklahoma	708.5
18	Oregon	970.7
19	Pennsylvania	957.2
47	Rhode Island	0.0
2	South Carolina	2,129.3
45	South Dakota	278.0
10	Tennessee	1,210.0
29	Texas	797.8
15	Utah	1,045.6
25	Vermont	874.0
21	Virginia	944.7
9	Washington	1,281.5
14	West Virginia	1,048.9
34	Wisconsin	771.0
32	Wyoming	779.4

RANK ORDER

RANK	STATE	RATE
1	Hawaii	2,623.8
2	South Carolina	2,129.3
3	Delaware	1,600.1
4	Florida	1,492.7
5	Georgia	1,471.2
6	Louisiana	1,433.8
7	Maryland	1,356.3
8	North Carolina	1,304.8
9	Washington	1,281.5
10	Tennessee	1,210.0
11	Alaska	1,148.7
12	Montana	1,137.0
13	Ohio	1,069.6
14	West Virginia	1,048.9
15	Utah	1,045.6
16	Michigan	1,043.3
17	New York	1,011.5
18	Oregon	970.7
19	Pennsylvania	957.2
20	Kansas	955.0
21	Virginia	944.7
22	Arkansas	930.8
23	Maine	928.0
24	Alabama	884.6
25	Vermont	874.0
26	Nevada	866.8
27	Missouri	839.1
28	Indiana	810.5
29	Texas	797.8
30	California	790.6
31	Minnesota	781.3
32	Wyoming	779.4
33	Colorado	776.1
34	Wisconsin	771.0
35	Mississippi	746.7
36	New Mexico	744.7
37	Kentucky	736.1
38	Nebraska	723.9
39	Oklahoma	708.5
40	Idaho	706.6
41	Connecticut	642.6
42	Arizona	621.0
43	North Dakota	423.7
44	Iowa	375.0
45	South Dakota	278.0
46	New Hampshire	248.4
47	Massachusetts	0.0
47	New Jersey	0.0
47	Rhode Island	0.0
NA	Illinois**	NA

District of Columbia 0.0

Source: CQ Press using reported data from the Federal Bureau of Investigation
"Crime in the United States 2008" (Uniform Crime Reports, September 14, 2009, http://www.fbi.gov/ucr/ucr.htm)
*Estimated rates for nonmetropolitan areas, defined by the F.B.I. as other than Metropolitan Statistical Areas and other cities outside such areas. National rate includes those states listed as not available. Larceny-theft is the unlawful taking of property without use of force, violence, or fraud. Attempts are included. Motor vehicle thefts are excluded.
**Not available.

Percent of Larceny-Thefts Occurring in Rural Areas in 2008

National Percent = 4.6% of Larceny-Thefts*

<table>
<tr><td colspan="3">ALPHA ORDER</td><td colspan="3">RANK ORDER</td></tr>
<tr><td>RANK</td><td>STATE</td><td>PERCENT</td><td>RANK</td><td>STATE</td><td>PERCENT</td></tr>
<tr><td>29</td><td>Alabama</td><td>5.1</td><td>1</td><td>Hawaii</td><td>31.8</td></tr>
<tr><td>4</td><td>Alaska</td><td>17.0</td><td>2</td><td>Montana</td><td>23.4</td></tr>
<tr><td>44</td><td>Arizona</td><td>0.9</td><td>3</td><td>West Virginia</td><td>19.0</td></tr>
<tr><td>15</td><td>Arkansas</td><td>8.7</td><td>4</td><td>Alaska</td><td>17.0</td></tr>
<tr><td>45</td><td>California</td><td>0.7</td><td>5</td><td>Vermont</td><td>15.5</td></tr>
<tr><td>39</td><td>Colorado</td><td>2.9</td><td>6</td><td>Mississippi</td><td>14.5</td></tr>
<tr><td>25</td><td>Connecticut</td><td>5.4</td><td>7</td><td>South Carolina</td><td>13.4</td></tr>
<tr><td>9</td><td>Delaware</td><td>10.6</td><td>8</td><td>Kentucky</td><td>12.9</td></tr>
<tr><td>40</td><td>Florida</td><td>2.6</td><td>9</td><td>Delaware</td><td>10.6</td></tr>
<tr><td>19</td><td>Georgia</td><td>6.6</td><td>10</td><td>North Carolina</td><td>10.5</td></tr>
<tr><td>1</td><td>Hawaii</td><td>31.8</td><td>11</td><td>Wyoming</td><td>10.4</td></tr>
<tr><td>16</td><td>Idaho</td><td>8.5</td><td>12</td><td>Maine</td><td>10.2</td></tr>
<tr><td>NA</td><td>Illinois**</td><td>NA</td><td>13</td><td>Louisiana</td><td>9.7</td></tr>
<tr><td>30</td><td>Indiana</td><td>4.9</td><td>14</td><td>North Dakota</td><td>8.9</td></tr>
<tr><td>26</td><td>Iowa</td><td>5.3</td><td>15</td><td>Arkansas</td><td>8.7</td></tr>
<tr><td>33</td><td>Kansas</td><td>4.6</td><td>16</td><td>Idaho</td><td>8.5</td></tr>
<tr><td>8</td><td>Kentucky</td><td>12.9</td><td>17</td><td>Tennessee</td><td>7.6</td></tr>
<tr><td>13</td><td>Louisiana</td><td>9.7</td><td>18</td><td>Michigan</td><td>6.9</td></tr>
<tr><td>12</td><td>Maine</td><td>10.2</td><td>19</td><td>Georgia</td><td>6.6</td></tr>
<tr><td>41</td><td>Maryland</td><td>2.3</td><td>19</td><td>Nebraska</td><td>6.6</td></tr>
<tr><td>48</td><td>Massachusetts</td><td>0.0</td><td>21</td><td>South Dakota</td><td>6.3</td></tr>
<tr><td>18</td><td>Michigan</td><td>6.9</td><td>22</td><td>Wisconsin</td><td>6.0</td></tr>
<tr><td>23</td><td>Minnesota</td><td>5.7</td><td>23</td><td>Minnesota</td><td>5.7</td></tr>
<tr><td>6</td><td>Mississippi</td><td>14.5</td><td>24</td><td>Oklahoma</td><td>5.5</td></tr>
<tr><td>31</td><td>Missouri</td><td>4.7</td><td>25</td><td>Connecticut</td><td>5.4</td></tr>
<tr><td>2</td><td>Montana</td><td>23.4</td><td>26</td><td>Iowa</td><td>5.3</td></tr>
<tr><td>19</td><td>Nebraska</td><td>6.6</td><td>26</td><td>Ohio</td><td>5.3</td></tr>
<tr><td>36</td><td>Nevada</td><td>3.8</td><td>26</td><td>Virginia</td><td>5.3</td></tr>
<tr><td>46</td><td>New Hampshire</td><td>0.5</td><td>29</td><td>Alabama</td><td>5.1</td></tr>
<tr><td>48</td><td>New Jersey</td><td>0.0</td><td>30</td><td>Indiana</td><td>4.9</td></tr>
<tr><td>35</td><td>New Mexico</td><td>4.2</td><td>31</td><td>Missouri</td><td>4.7</td></tr>
<tr><td>38</td><td>New York</td><td>3.3</td><td>31</td><td>Oregon</td><td>4.7</td></tr>
<tr><td>10</td><td>North Carolina</td><td>10.5</td><td>33</td><td>Kansas</td><td>4.6</td></tr>
<tr><td>14</td><td>North Dakota</td><td>8.9</td><td>33</td><td>Pennsylvania</td><td>4.6</td></tr>
<tr><td>26</td><td>Ohio</td><td>5.3</td><td>35</td><td>New Mexico</td><td>4.2</td></tr>
<tr><td>24</td><td>Oklahoma</td><td>5.5</td><td>36</td><td>Nevada</td><td>3.8</td></tr>
<tr><td>31</td><td>Oregon</td><td>4.7</td><td>37</td><td>Washington</td><td>3.6</td></tr>
<tr><td>33</td><td>Pennsylvania</td><td>4.6</td><td>38</td><td>New York</td><td>3.3</td></tr>
<tr><td>47</td><td>Rhode Island</td><td>0.2</td><td>39</td><td>Colorado</td><td>2.9</td></tr>
<tr><td>7</td><td>South Carolina</td><td>13.4</td><td>40</td><td>Florida</td><td>2.6</td></tr>
<tr><td>21</td><td>South Dakota</td><td>6.3</td><td>41</td><td>Maryland</td><td>2.3</td></tr>
<tr><td>17</td><td>Tennessee</td><td>7.6</td><td>41</td><td>Utah</td><td>2.3</td></tr>
<tr><td>43</td><td>Texas</td><td>2.0</td><td>43</td><td>Texas</td><td>2.0</td></tr>
<tr><td>41</td><td>Utah</td><td>2.3</td><td>44</td><td>Arizona</td><td>0.9</td></tr>
<tr><td>5</td><td>Vermont</td><td>15.5</td><td>45</td><td>California</td><td>0.7</td></tr>
<tr><td>26</td><td>Virginia</td><td>5.3</td><td>46</td><td>New Hampshire</td><td>0.5</td></tr>
<tr><td>37</td><td>Washington</td><td>3.6</td><td>47</td><td>Rhode Island</td><td>0.2</td></tr>
<tr><td>3</td><td>West Virginia</td><td>19.0</td><td>48</td><td>Massachusetts</td><td>0.0</td></tr>
<tr><td>22</td><td>Wisconsin</td><td>6.0</td><td>48</td><td>New Jersey</td><td>0.0</td></tr>
<tr><td>11</td><td>Wyoming</td><td>10.4</td><td>NA</td><td>Illinois**</td><td>NA</td></tr>
<tr><td></td><td></td><td></td><td></td><td>District of Columbia</td><td>0.0</td></tr>
</table>

Source: CQ Press using reported data from the Federal Bureau of Investigation
"Crime in the United States 2008" (Uniform Crime Reports, September 14, 2009, http://www.fbi.gov/ucr/ucr.htm)
*Estimated percentages for nonmetropolitan areas, defined by the F.B.I. as other than Metropolitan Statistical Areas and other cities outside such areas. National percent includes those states listed as not available. Larceny-theft is the unlawful taking of property without use of force, violence, or fraud. Attempts are included. Motor vehicle thefts are excluded.
**Not available.

Motor Vehicle Thefts in Urban Areas in 2008

National Urban Total = 919,533 Motor Vehicle Thefts*

ALPHA ORDER					RANK ORDER			
RANK	STATE	THEFTS	% of USA		RANK	STATE	THEFTS	% of USA
22	Alabama	12,681	1.4%		1	California	191,550	20.8%
43	Alaska	1,243	0.1%		2	Texas	83,522	9.1%
5	Arizona	36,788	4.0%		3	Florida	61,936	6.7%
33	Arkansas	5,715	0.6%		4	Georgia	37,804	4.1%
1	California	191,550	20.8%		5	Arizona	36,788	4.0%
19	Colorado	13,267	1.4%		6	Michigan	35,247	3.8%
28	Connecticut	8,557	0.9%		7	Washington	27,556	3.0%
40	Delaware	2,270	0.2%		8	Ohio	27,404	3.0%
3	Florida	61,936	6.7%		9	Maryland	25,047	2.7%
4	Georgia	37,804	4.1%		10	New York	24,659	2.7%
36	Hawaii	3,938	0.4%		11	North Carolina	22,897	2.5%
41	Idaho	1,408	0.2%		12	Pennsylvania	21,586	2.3%
NA	Illinois**	NA	NA		13	New Jersey	20,180	2.2%
16	Indiana	16,591	1.8%		14	Missouri	19,793	2.2%
35	Iowa	3,961	0.4%		15	Tennessee	17,206	1.9%
31	Kansas	7,055	0.8%		16	Indiana	16,591	1.8%
32	Kentucky	6,103	0.7%		17	Nevada	15,599	1.7%
21	Louisiana	12,720	1.4%		18	South Carolina	15,070	1.6%
45	Maine	948	0.1%		19	Colorado	13,267	1.4%
9	Maryland	25,047	2.7%		20	Massachusetts	12,737	1.4%
20	Massachusetts	12,737	1.4%		21	Louisiana	12,720	1.4%
6	Michigan	35,247	3.8%		22	Alabama	12,681	1.4%
27	Minnesota	9,343	1.0%		23	Virginia	12,329	1.3%
34	Mississippi	5,303	0.6%		24	Wisconsin	10,870	1.2%
14	Missouri	19,793	2.2%		25	Oregon	10,802	1.2%
44	Montana	1,033	0.1%		26	Oklahoma	10,064	1.1%
37	Nebraska	3,930	0.4%		27	Minnesota	9,343	1.0%
17	Nevada	15,599	1.7%		28	Connecticut	8,557	0.9%
42	New Hampshire	1,371	0.1%		29	New Mexico	7,607	0.8%
13	New Jersey	20,180	2.2%		30	Utah	7,059	0.8%
29	New Mexico	7,607	0.8%		31	Kansas	7,055	0.8%
10	New York	24,659	2.7%		32	Kentucky	6,103	0.7%
11	North Carolina	22,897	2.5%		33	Arkansas	5,715	0.6%
47	North Dakota	729	0.1%		34	Mississippi	5,303	0.6%
8	Ohio	27,404	3.0%		35	Iowa	3,961	0.4%
26	Oklahoma	10,064	1.1%		36	Hawaii	3,938	0.4%
25	Oregon	10,802	1.2%		37	Nebraska	3,930	0.4%
12	Pennsylvania	21,586	2.3%		38	Rhode Island	3,157	0.3%
38	Rhode Island	3,157	0.3%		39	West Virginia	2,356	0.3%
18	South Carolina	15,070	1.6%		40	Delaware	2,270	0.2%
46	South Dakota	732	0.1%		41	Idaho	1,408	0.2%
15	Tennessee	17,206	1.9%		42	New Hampshire	1,371	0.1%
2	Texas	83,522	9.1%		43	Alaska	1,243	0.1%
30	Utah	7,059	0.8%		44	Montana	1,033	0.1%
49	Vermont	414	0.0%		45	Maine	948	0.1%
23	Virginia	12,329	1.3%		46	South Dakota	732	0.1%
7	Washington	27,556	3.0%		47	North Dakota	729	0.1%
39	West Virginia	2,356	0.3%		48	Wyoming	587	0.1%
24	Wisconsin	10,870	1.2%		49	Vermont	414	0.0%
48	Wyoming	587	0.1%		NA	Illinois**	NA	NA
						District of Columbia	6,465	0.7%

Source: CQ Press using reported data from the Federal Bureau of Investigation
   "Crime in the United States 2008" (Uniform Crime Reports, September 14, 2009, http://www.fbi.gov/ucr/ucr.htm)
*Estimated totals for urban areas, defined by the F.B.I. as Metropolitan Statistical Areas and other cities outside such areas.
National total includes those states listed as not available. Motor vehicle theft includes the theft or attempted theft of a
self-propelled vehicle. Excludes motorboats, construction equipment, airplanes, and farming equipment.
**Not available.

Urban Motor Vehicle Theft Rate in 2008

National Urban Rate = 335.6 Motor Vehicle Thefts per 100,000 Population*

ALPHA ORDER

RANK	STATE	RATE
17	Alabama	322.9
29	Alaska	270.1
2	Arizona	590.0
31	Arkansas	258.7
3	California	529.3
23	Colorado	290.4
24	Connecticut	287.2
19	Delaware	312.3
13	Florida	355.0
7	Georgia	441.4
8	Hawaii	434.5
46	Idaho	113.7
NA	Illinois**	NA
21	Indiana	302.2
41	Iowa	174.1
25	Kansas	284.9
35	Kentucky	205.2
14	Louisiana	348.1
49	Maine	90.7
4	Maryland	462.9
36	Massachusetts	196.0
10	Michigan	400.6
34	Minnesota	212.1
26	Mississippi	281.2
11	Missouri	390.2
39	Montana	187.5
27	Nebraska	274.4
1	Nevada	654.7
47	New Hampshire	108.2
32	New Jersey	232.4
6	New Mexico	444.0
44	New York	133.2
19	North Carolina	312.3
42	North Dakota	162.4
30	Ohio	269.0
16	Oklahoma	332.1
17	Oregon	322.9
38	Pennsylvania	189.5
22	Rhode Island	300.4
9	South Carolina	408.9
45	South Dakota	126.9
15	Tennessee	333.2
12	Texas	367.7
28	Utah	273.2
48	Vermont	100.2
40	Virginia	177.8
5	Washington	453.2
37	West Virginia	191.6
33	Wisconsin	230.1
43	Wyoming	154.9

RANK ORDER

RANK	STATE	RATE
1	Nevada	654.7
2	Arizona	590.0
3	California	529.3
4	Maryland	462.9
5	Washington	453.2
6	New Mexico	444.0
7	Georgia	441.4
8	Hawaii	434.5
9	South Carolina	408.9
10	Michigan	400.6
11	Missouri	390.2
12	Texas	367.7
13	Florida	355.0
14	Louisiana	348.1
15	Tennessee	333.2
16	Oklahoma	332.1
17	Alabama	322.9
17	Oregon	322.9
19	Delaware	312.3
19	North Carolina	312.3
21	Indiana	302.2
22	Rhode Island	300.4
23	Colorado	290.4
24	Connecticut	287.2
25	Kansas	284.9
26	Mississippi	281.2
27	Nebraska	274.4
28	Utah	273.2
29	Alaska	270.1
30	Ohio	269.0
31	Arkansas	258.7
32	New Jersey	232.4
33	Wisconsin	230.1
34	Minnesota	212.1
35	Kentucky	205.2
36	Massachusetts	196.0
37	West Virginia	191.6
38	Pennsylvania	189.5
39	Montana	187.5
40	Virginia	177.8
41	Iowa	174.1
42	North Dakota	162.4
43	Wyoming	154.9
44	New York	133.2
45	South Dakota	126.9
46	Idaho	113.7
47	New Hampshire	108.2
48	Vermont	100.2
49	Maine	90.7
NA	Illinois**	NA

District of Columbia 1,092.4

Source: CQ Press using reported data from the Federal Bureau of Investigation
"Crime in the United States 2008" (Uniform Crime Reports, September 14, 2009, http://www.fbi.gov/ucr/ucr.htm)
*Estimated rates for urban areas, defined by the F.B.I. as Metropolitan Statistical Areas and other cities outside such areas.
National rate includes those states listed as not available. Motor vehicle theft includes the theft or attempted theft of a
self-propelled vehicle. Excludes motorboats, construction equipment, airplanes, and farming equipment.
**Not available.

Percent of Motor Vehicle Thefts Occurring in Urban Areas in 2008

National Percent = 96.1% of Motor Vehicle Thefts*

<table>
<tr><td colspan="3">ALPHA ORDER</td><td colspan="3">RANK ORDER</td></tr>
<tr><td>RANK</td><td>STATE</td><td>PERCENT</td><td>RANK</td><td>STATE</td><td>PERCENT</td></tr>
<tr><td>26</td><td>Alabama</td><td>94.2</td><td>1</td><td>Massachusetts</td><td>100.0</td></tr>
<tr><td>46</td><td>Alaska</td><td>75.9</td><td>1</td><td>New Jersey</td><td>100.0</td></tr>
<tr><td>5</td><td>Arizona</td><td>98.8</td><td>3</td><td>California</td><td>99.5</td></tr>
<tr><td>36</td><td>Arkansas</td><td>87.8</td><td>4</td><td>Maryland</td><td>98.9</td></tr>
<tr><td>3</td><td>California</td><td>99.5</td><td>5</td><td>Arizona</td><td>98.8</td></tr>
<tr><td>9</td><td>Colorado</td><td>98.1</td><td>5</td><td>New Hampshire</td><td>98.8</td></tr>
<tr><td>18</td><td>Connecticut</td><td>95.5</td><td>7</td><td>Rhode Island</td><td>98.7</td></tr>
<tr><td>35</td><td>Delaware</td><td>89.3</td><td>8</td><td>New York</td><td>98.2</td></tr>
<tr><td>13</td><td>Florida</td><td>97.5</td><td>9</td><td>Colorado</td><td>98.1</td></tr>
<tr><td>19</td><td>Georgia</td><td>95.4</td><td>9</td><td>Nevada</td><td>98.1</td></tr>
<tr><td>45</td><td>Hawaii</td><td>76.7</td><td>9</td><td>Utah</td><td>98.1</td></tr>
<tr><td>39</td><td>Idaho</td><td>84.4</td><td>12</td><td>Texas</td><td>97.9</td></tr>
<tr><td>NA</td><td>Illinois**</td><td>NA</td><td>13</td><td>Florida</td><td>97.5</td></tr>
<tr><td>23</td><td>Indiana</td><td>95.1</td><td>14</td><td>Michigan</td><td>97.3</td></tr>
<tr><td>33</td><td>Iowa</td><td>91.4</td><td>14</td><td>Washington</td><td>97.3</td></tr>
<tr><td>19</td><td>Kansas</td><td>95.4</td><td>16</td><td>Pennsylvania</td><td>96.1</td></tr>
<tr><td>44</td><td>Kentucky</td><td>79.6</td><td>17</td><td>Ohio</td><td>96.0</td></tr>
<tr><td>30</td><td>Louisiana</td><td>92.6</td><td>18</td><td>Connecticut</td><td>95.5</td></tr>
<tr><td>43</td><td>Maine</td><td>80.6</td><td>19</td><td>Georgia</td><td>95.4</td></tr>
<tr><td>4</td><td>Maryland</td><td>98.9</td><td>19</td><td>Kansas</td><td>95.4</td></tr>
<tr><td>1</td><td>Massachusetts</td><td>100.0</td><td>21</td><td>Missouri</td><td>95.3</td></tr>
<tr><td>14</td><td>Michigan</td><td>97.3</td><td>21</td><td>Oregon</td><td>95.3</td></tr>
<tr><td>29</td><td>Minnesota</td><td>92.7</td><td>23</td><td>Indiana</td><td>95.1</td></tr>
<tr><td>40</td><td>Mississippi</td><td>83.5</td><td>24</td><td>New Mexico</td><td>95.0</td></tr>
<tr><td>21</td><td>Missouri</td><td>95.3</td><td>25</td><td>Wisconsin</td><td>94.4</td></tr>
<tr><td>49</td><td>Montana</td><td>65.7</td><td>26</td><td>Alabama</td><td>94.2</td></tr>
<tr><td>27</td><td>Nebraska</td><td>93.8</td><td>27</td><td>Nebraska</td><td>93.8</td></tr>
<tr><td>9</td><td>Nevada</td><td>98.1</td><td>28</td><td>Virginia</td><td>93.0</td></tr>
<tr><td>5</td><td>New Hampshire</td><td>98.8</td><td>29</td><td>Minnesota</td><td>92.7</td></tr>
<tr><td>1</td><td>New Jersey</td><td>100.0</td><td>30</td><td>Louisiana</td><td>92.6</td></tr>
<tr><td>24</td><td>New Mexico</td><td>95.0</td><td>31</td><td>Oklahoma</td><td>92.5</td></tr>
<tr><td>8</td><td>New York</td><td>98.2</td><td>32</td><td>South Dakota</td><td>91.5</td></tr>
<tr><td>37</td><td>North Carolina</td><td>85.6</td><td>33</td><td>Iowa</td><td>91.4</td></tr>
<tr><td>41</td><td>North Dakota</td><td>82.7</td><td>34</td><td>Tennessee</td><td>89.5</td></tr>
<tr><td>17</td><td>Ohio</td><td>96.0</td><td>35</td><td>Delaware</td><td>89.3</td></tr>
<tr><td>31</td><td>Oklahoma</td><td>92.5</td><td>36</td><td>Arkansas</td><td>87.8</td></tr>
<tr><td>21</td><td>Oregon</td><td>95.3</td><td>37</td><td>North Carolina</td><td>85.6</td></tr>
<tr><td>16</td><td>Pennsylvania</td><td>96.1</td><td>38</td><td>South Carolina</td><td>85.4</td></tr>
<tr><td>7</td><td>Rhode Island</td><td>98.7</td><td>39</td><td>Idaho</td><td>84.4</td></tr>
<tr><td>38</td><td>South Carolina</td><td>85.4</td><td>40</td><td>Mississippi</td><td>83.5</td></tr>
<tr><td>32</td><td>South Dakota</td><td>91.5</td><td>41</td><td>North Dakota</td><td>82.7</td></tr>
<tr><td>34</td><td>Tennessee</td><td>89.5</td><td>42</td><td>Wyoming</td><td>82.3</td></tr>
<tr><td>12</td><td>Texas</td><td>97.9</td><td>43</td><td>Maine</td><td>80.6</td></tr>
<tr><td>9</td><td>Utah</td><td>98.1</td><td>44</td><td>Kentucky</td><td>79.6</td></tr>
<tr><td>48</td><td>Vermont</td><td>70.8</td><td>45</td><td>Hawaii</td><td>76.7</td></tr>
<tr><td>28</td><td>Virginia</td><td>93.0</td><td>46</td><td>Alaska</td><td>75.9</td></tr>
<tr><td>14</td><td>Washington</td><td>97.3</td><td>47</td><td>West Virginia</td><td>73.5</td></tr>
<tr><td>47</td><td>West Virginia</td><td>73.5</td><td>48</td><td>Vermont</td><td>70.8</td></tr>
<tr><td>25</td><td>Wisconsin</td><td>94.4</td><td>49</td><td>Montana</td><td>65.7</td></tr>
<tr><td>42</td><td>Wyoming</td><td>82.3</td><td>NA</td><td>Illinois**</td><td>NA</td></tr>
<tr><td></td><td></td><td></td><td></td><td>District of Columbia</td><td>100.0</td></tr>
</table>

Source: CQ Press using reported data from the Federal Bureau of Investigation
    "Crime in the United States 2008" (Uniform Crime Reports, September 14, 2009, http://www.fbi.gov/ucr/ucr.htm)
*Estimated percentages for urban areas, defined by the F.B.I. as Metropolitan Statistical Areas and other cities outside such areas. National percent includes those states listed as not available. Motor vehicle theft includes the theft or attempted theft of a self-propelled vehicle. Excludes motorboats, construction equipment, airplanes, and farming equipment.
**Not available.

Motor Vehicle Thefts in Rural Areas in 2008

National Rural Total = 37,313 Motor Vehicle Thefts*

<table>
<tr><td colspan="4">ALPHA ORDER</td><td colspan="4">RANK ORDER</td></tr>
<tr><th>RANK</th><th>STATE</th><th>THEFTS</th><th>% of USA</th><th>RANK</th><th>STATE</th><th>THEFTS</th><th>% of USA</th></tr>
<tr><td>21</td><td>Alabama</td><td>777</td><td>2.1%</td><td>1</td><td>North Carolina</td><td>3,846</td><td>10.3%</td></tr>
<tr><td>31</td><td>Alaska</td><td>395</td><td>1.1%</td><td>2</td><td>South Carolina</td><td>2,582</td><td>6.9%</td></tr>
<tr><td>28</td><td>Arizona</td><td>430</td><td>1.2%</td><td>3</td><td>Tennessee</td><td>2,018</td><td>5.4%</td></tr>
<tr><td>20</td><td>Arkansas</td><td>796</td><td>2.1%</td><td>4</td><td>Texas</td><td>1,828</td><td>4.9%</td></tr>
<tr><td>13</td><td>California</td><td>977</td><td>2.6%</td><td>5</td><td>Georgia</td><td>1,824</td><td>4.9%</td></tr>
<tr><td>39</td><td>Colorado</td><td>252</td><td>0.7%</td><td>6</td><td>Florida</td><td>1,573</td><td>4.2%</td></tr>
<tr><td>29</td><td>Connecticut</td><td>406</td><td>1.1%</td><td>7</td><td>Kentucky</td><td>1,564</td><td>4.2%</td></tr>
<tr><td>36</td><td>Delaware</td><td>271</td><td>0.7%</td><td>8</td><td>Hawaii</td><td>1,195</td><td>3.2%</td></tr>
<tr><td>6</td><td>Florida</td><td>1,573</td><td>4.2%</td><td>9</td><td>Ohio</td><td>1,128</td><td>3.0%</td></tr>
<tr><td>5</td><td>Georgia</td><td>1,824</td><td>4.9%</td><td>10</td><td>Mississippi</td><td>1,049</td><td>2.8%</td></tr>
<tr><td>8</td><td>Hawaii</td><td>1,195</td><td>3.2%</td><td>11</td><td>Louisiana</td><td>1,023</td><td>2.7%</td></tr>
<tr><td>37</td><td>Idaho</td><td>260</td><td>0.7%</td><td>12</td><td>Michigan</td><td>994</td><td>2.7%</td></tr>
<tr><td>NA</td><td>Illinois**</td><td>NA</td><td>NA</td><td>13</td><td>California</td><td>977</td><td>2.6%</td></tr>
<tr><td>17</td><td>Indiana</td><td>864</td><td>2.3%</td><td>14</td><td>Missouri</td><td>972</td><td>2.6%</td></tr>
<tr><td>32</td><td>Iowa</td><td>371</td><td>1.0%</td><td>15</td><td>Virginia</td><td>930</td><td>2.5%</td></tr>
<tr><td>33</td><td>Kansas</td><td>340</td><td>0.9%</td><td>16</td><td>Pennsylvania</td><td>885</td><td>2.4%</td></tr>
<tr><td>7</td><td>Kentucky</td><td>1,564</td><td>4.2%</td><td>17</td><td>Indiana</td><td>864</td><td>2.3%</td></tr>
<tr><td>11</td><td>Louisiana</td><td>1,023</td><td>2.7%</td><td>18</td><td>West Virginia</td><td>848</td><td>2.3%</td></tr>
<tr><td>40</td><td>Maine</td><td>228</td><td>0.6%</td><td>19</td><td>Oklahoma</td><td>817</td><td>2.2%</td></tr>
<tr><td>35</td><td>Maryland</td><td>286</td><td>0.8%</td><td>20</td><td>Arkansas</td><td>796</td><td>2.1%</td></tr>
<tr><td>48</td><td>Massachusetts</td><td>0</td><td>0.0%</td><td>21</td><td>Alabama</td><td>777</td><td>2.1%</td></tr>
<tr><td>12</td><td>Michigan</td><td>994</td><td>2.7%</td><td>22</td><td>Washington</td><td>775</td><td>2.1%</td></tr>
<tr><td>23</td><td>Minnesota</td><td>735</td><td>2.0%</td><td>23</td><td>Minnesota</td><td>735</td><td>2.0%</td></tr>
<tr><td>10</td><td>Mississippi</td><td>1,049</td><td>2.8%</td><td>24</td><td>Wisconsin</td><td>650</td><td>1.7%</td></tr>
<tr><td>14</td><td>Missouri</td><td>972</td><td>2.6%</td><td>25</td><td>Montana</td><td>540</td><td>1.4%</td></tr>
<tr><td>25</td><td>Montana</td><td>540</td><td>1.4%</td><td>26</td><td>Oregon</td><td>529</td><td>1.4%</td></tr>
<tr><td>38</td><td>Nebraska</td><td>258</td><td>0.7%</td><td>27</td><td>New York</td><td>455</td><td>1.2%</td></tr>
<tr><td>34</td><td>Nevada</td><td>304</td><td>0.8%</td><td>28</td><td>Arizona</td><td>430</td><td>1.2%</td></tr>
<tr><td>47</td><td>New Hampshire</td><td>16</td><td>0.0%</td><td>29</td><td>Connecticut</td><td>406</td><td>1.1%</td></tr>
<tr><td>48</td><td>New Jersey</td><td>0</td><td>0.0%</td><td>30</td><td>New Mexico</td><td>397</td><td>1.1%</td></tr>
<tr><td>30</td><td>New Mexico</td><td>397</td><td>1.1%</td><td>31</td><td>Alaska</td><td>395</td><td>1.1%</td></tr>
<tr><td>27</td><td>New York</td><td>455</td><td>1.2%</td><td>32</td><td>Iowa</td><td>371</td><td>1.0%</td></tr>
<tr><td>1</td><td>North Carolina</td><td>3,846</td><td>10.3%</td><td>33</td><td>Kansas</td><td>340</td><td>0.9%</td></tr>
<tr><td>42</td><td>North Dakota</td><td>153</td><td>0.4%</td><td>34</td><td>Nevada</td><td>304</td><td>0.8%</td></tr>
<tr><td>9</td><td>Ohio</td><td>1,128</td><td>3.0%</td><td>35</td><td>Maryland</td><td>286</td><td>0.8%</td></tr>
<tr><td>19</td><td>Oklahoma</td><td>817</td><td>2.2%</td><td>36</td><td>Delaware</td><td>271</td><td>0.7%</td></tr>
<tr><td>26</td><td>Oregon</td><td>529</td><td>1.4%</td><td>37</td><td>Idaho</td><td>260</td><td>0.7%</td></tr>
<tr><td>16</td><td>Pennsylvania</td><td>885</td><td>2.4%</td><td>38</td><td>Nebraska</td><td>258</td><td>0.7%</td></tr>
<tr><td>46</td><td>Rhode Island</td><td>43</td><td>0.1%</td><td>39</td><td>Colorado</td><td>252</td><td>0.7%</td></tr>
<tr><td>2</td><td>South Carolina</td><td>2,582</td><td>6.9%</td><td>40</td><td>Maine</td><td>228</td><td>0.6%</td></tr>
<tr><td>45</td><td>South Dakota</td><td>68</td><td>0.2%</td><td>41</td><td>Vermont</td><td>171</td><td>0.5%</td></tr>
<tr><td>3</td><td>Tennessee</td><td>2,018</td><td>5.4%</td><td>42</td><td>North Dakota</td><td>153</td><td>0.4%</td></tr>
<tr><td>4</td><td>Texas</td><td>1,828</td><td>4.9%</td><td>43</td><td>Utah</td><td>136</td><td>0.4%</td></tr>
<tr><td>43</td><td>Utah</td><td>136</td><td>0.4%</td><td>44</td><td>Wyoming</td><td>126</td><td>0.3%</td></tr>
<tr><td>41</td><td>Vermont</td><td>171</td><td>0.5%</td><td>45</td><td>South Dakota</td><td>68</td><td>0.2%</td></tr>
<tr><td>15</td><td>Virginia</td><td>930</td><td>2.5%</td><td>46</td><td>Rhode Island</td><td>43</td><td>0.1%</td></tr>
<tr><td>22</td><td>Washington</td><td>775</td><td>2.1%</td><td>47</td><td>New Hampshire</td><td>16</td><td>0.0%</td></tr>
<tr><td>18</td><td>West Virginia</td><td>848</td><td>2.3%</td><td>48</td><td>Massachusetts</td><td>0</td><td>0.0%</td></tr>
<tr><td>24</td><td>Wisconsin</td><td>650</td><td>1.7%</td><td>48</td><td>New Jersey</td><td>0</td><td>0.0%</td></tr>
<tr><td>44</td><td>Wyoming</td><td>126</td><td>0.3%</td><td>NA</td><td>Illinois**</td><td>NA</td><td>NA</td></tr>
<tr><td></td><td></td><td></td><td></td><td></td><td>District of Columbia</td><td>0</td><td>0.0%</td></tr>
</table>

Source: Reported data from the Federal Bureau of Investigation
"Crime in the United States 2008" (Uniform Crime Reports, September 14, 2009, http://www.fbi.gov/ucr/ucr.htm)
*Estimated totals for nonmetropolitan areas, defined by the F.B.I. as other than Metropolitan Statistical Areas and other cities outside such areas. National total includes those states listed as not available. Motor vehicle theft includes the theft or attempted theft of a self-propelled vehicle. Excludes motorboats, construction equipment, airplanes, and farming equipment.
**Not available.

Rural Motor Vehicle Theft Rate in 2008

National Rural Rate = 124.0 Motor Vehicle Thefts per 100,000 Population*

ALPHA ORDER

RANK	STATE	RATE
25	Alabama	105.8
7	Alaska	174.6
11	Arizona	162.1
19	Arkansas	123.2
8	California	172.9
42	Colorado	68.0
39	Connecticut	77.8
5	Delaware	185.4
6	Florida	178.4
10	Georgia	162.8
2	Hawaii	313.0
29	Idaho	91.0
NA	Illinois**	NA
28	Indiana	97.4
43	Iowa	51.0
26	Kansas	104.4
20	Kentucky	120.8
15	Louisiana	135.2
33	Maine	84.2
18	Maryland	128.7
47	Massachusetts	0.0
35	Michigan	82.5
30	Minnesota	90.1
27	Mississippi	99.6
22	Missouri	115.8
17	Montana	129.6
40	Nebraska	73.4
14	Nevada	139.8
45	New Hampshire	33.1
47	New Jersey	0.0
12	New Mexico	146.5
44	New York	46.4
3	North Carolina	203.5
38	North Dakota	79.5
32	Ohio	87.0
16	Oklahoma	133.5
21	Oregon	118.9
34	Pennsylvania	83.5
47	Rhode Island	0.0
1	South Carolina	325.0
46	South Dakota	29.9
4	Tennessee	191.9
23	Texas	113.5
31	Utah	88.9
36	Vermont	82.2
24	Virginia	111.2
9	Washington	165.4
13	West Virginia	144.9
41	Wisconsin	71.9
37	Wyoming	81.9

RANK ORDER

RANK	STATE	RATE
1	South Carolina	325.0
2	Hawaii	313.0
3	North Carolina	203.5
4	Tennessee	191.9
5	Delaware	185.4
6	Florida	178.4
7	Alaska	174.6
8	California	172.9
9	Washington	165.4
10	Georgia	162.8
11	Arizona	162.1
12	New Mexico	146.5
13	West Virginia	144.9
14	Nevada	139.8
15	Louisiana	135.2
16	Oklahoma	133.5
17	Montana	129.6
18	Maryland	128.7
19	Arkansas	123.2
20	Kentucky	120.8
21	Oregon	118.9
22	Missouri	115.8
23	Texas	113.5
24	Virginia	111.2
25	Alabama	105.8
26	Kansas	104.4
27	Mississippi	99.6
28	Indiana	97.4
29	Idaho	91.0
30	Minnesota	90.1
31	Utah	88.9
32	Ohio	87.0
33	Maine	84.2
34	Pennsylvania	83.5
35	Michigan	82.5
36	Vermont	82.2
37	Wyoming	81.9
38	North Dakota	79.5
39	Connecticut	77.8
40	Nebraska	73.4
41	Wisconsin	71.9
42	Colorado	68.0
43	Iowa	51.0
44	New York	46.4
45	New Hampshire	33.1
46	South Dakota	29.9
47	Massachusetts	0.0
47	New Jersey	0.0
47	Rhode Island	0.0
NA	Illinois**	NA

District of Columbia 0.0

Source: CQ Press using reported data from the Federal Bureau of Investigation
   "Crime in the United States 2008" (Uniform Crime Reports, September 14, 2009, http://www.fbi.gov/ucr/ucr.htm)
*Estimated rates for nonmetropolitan areas, defined by the F.B.I. as other than Metropolitan Statistical Areas and other cities outside such areas. National rate includes those states listed as not available. Motor vehicle theft includes the theft or attempted theft of a self-propelled vehicle. Excludes motorboats, construction equipment, airplanes, and farming equipment.
**Not available.

Percent of Motor Vehicle Thefts Occurring in Rural Areas in 2008

National Percent = 3.9% of Motor Vehicle Thefts*

ALPHA ORDER

RANK	STATE	PERCENT
24	Alabama	5.8
4	Alaska	24.1
44	Arizona	1.2
14	Arkansas	12.2
47	California	0.5
39	Colorado	1.9
32	Connecticut	4.5
15	Delaware	10.7
37	Florida	2.5
30	Georgia	4.6
5	Hawaii	23.3
11	Idaho	15.6
NA	Illinois**	NA
27	Indiana	4.9
17	Iowa	8.6
30	Kansas	4.6
6	Kentucky	20.4
20	Louisiana	7.4
7	Maine	19.4
46	Maryland	1.1
48	Massachusetts	0.0
35	Michigan	2.7
21	Minnesota	7.3
10	Mississippi	16.5
28	Missouri	4.7
1	Montana	34.3
23	Nebraska	6.2
39	Nevada	1.9
44	New Hampshire	1.2
48	New Jersey	0.0
26	New Mexico	5.0
42	New York	1.8
13	North Carolina	14.4
9	North Dakota	17.3
33	Ohio	4.0
19	Oklahoma	7.5
28	Oregon	4.7
34	Pennsylvania	3.9
43	Rhode Island	1.3
12	South Carolina	14.6
18	South Dakota	8.5
16	Tennessee	10.5
38	Texas	2.1
39	Utah	1.9
2	Vermont	29.2
22	Virginia	7.0
35	Washington	2.7
3	West Virginia	26.5
25	Wisconsin	5.6
8	Wyoming	17.7

RANK ORDER

RANK	STATE	PERCENT
1	Montana	34.3
2	Vermont	29.2
3	West Virginia	26.5
4	Alaska	24.1
5	Hawaii	23.3
6	Kentucky	20.4
7	Maine	19.4
8	Wyoming	17.7
9	North Dakota	17.3
10	Mississippi	16.5
11	Idaho	15.6
12	South Carolina	14.6
13	North Carolina	14.4
14	Arkansas	12.2
15	Delaware	10.7
16	Tennessee	10.5
17	Iowa	8.6
18	South Dakota	8.5
19	Oklahoma	7.5
20	Louisiana	7.4
21	Minnesota	7.3
22	Virginia	7.0
23	Nebraska	6.2
24	Alabama	5.8
25	Wisconsin	5.6
26	New Mexico	5.0
27	Indiana	4.9
28	Missouri	4.7
28	Oregon	4.7
30	Georgia	4.6
30	Kansas	4.6
32	Connecticut	4.5
33	Ohio	4.0
34	Pennsylvania	3.9
35	Michigan	2.7
35	Washington	2.7
37	Florida	2.5
38	Texas	2.1
39	Colorado	1.9
39	Nevada	1.9
39	Utah	1.9
42	New York	1.8
43	Rhode Island	1.3
44	Arizona	1.2
44	New Hampshire	1.2
46	Maryland	1.1
47	California	0.5
48	Massachusetts	0.0
48	New Jersey	0.0
NA	Illinois**	NA

District of Columbia 0.0

Source: CQ Press using reported data from the Federal Bureau of Investigation
"Crime in the United States 2008" (Uniform Crime Reports, September 14, 2009, http://www.fbi.gov/ucr/ucr.htm)
*Estimated percentages for nonmetropolitan areas, defined by the F.B.I. as other than Metropolitan Statistical Areas and other cities outside such areas. National percent includes those states listed as not available. Motor vehicle theft includes the theft or attempted theft of a self-propelled vehicle. Excludes motorboats, construction equipment, airplanes, and farming equipment.
**Not available.

Crimes Reported at Universities and Colleges in 2008

National Total = 88,432 Reported Crimes*

<table>
<tr><td colspan="4">ALPHA ORDER</td><td colspan="4">RANK ORDER</td></tr>
<tr><td>RANK</td><td>STATE</td><td>CRIMES</td><td>% of USA</td><td>RANK</td><td>STATE</td><td>CRIMES</td><td>% of USA</td></tr>
<tr><td>23</td><td>Alabama</td><td>1,413</td><td>1.6%</td><td>1</td><td>California</td><td>12,382</td><td>14.0%</td></tr>
<tr><td>41</td><td>Alaska</td><td>243</td><td>0.3%</td><td>2</td><td>Texas</td><td>8,923</td><td>10.1%</td></tr>
<tr><td>10</td><td>Arizona</td><td>2,708</td><td>3.1%</td><td>3</td><td>Florida</td><td>4,020</td><td>4.5%</td></tr>
<tr><td>24</td><td>Arkansas</td><td>1,398</td><td>1.6%</td><td>4</td><td>North Carolina</td><td>3,764</td><td>4.3%</td></tr>
<tr><td>1</td><td>California</td><td>12,382</td><td>14.0%</td><td>5</td><td>Massachusetts</td><td>3,724</td><td>4.2%</td></tr>
<tr><td>20</td><td>Colorado</td><td>1,764</td><td>2.0%</td><td>6</td><td>Ohio</td><td>3,676</td><td>4.2%</td></tr>
<tr><td>29</td><td>Connecticut</td><td>944</td><td>1.1%</td><td>7</td><td>Georgia</td><td>3,598</td><td>4.1%</td></tr>
<tr><td>36</td><td>Delaware</td><td>459</td><td>0.5%</td><td>8</td><td>Michigan</td><td>3,518</td><td>4.0%</td></tr>
<tr><td>3</td><td>Florida</td><td>4,020</td><td>4.5%</td><td>9</td><td>Virginia</td><td>3,335</td><td>3.8%</td></tr>
<tr><td>7</td><td>Georgia</td><td>3,598</td><td>4.1%</td><td>10</td><td>Arizona</td><td>2,708</td><td>3.1%</td></tr>
<tr><td>NA</td><td>Hawaii**</td><td>NA</td><td>NA</td><td>11</td><td>New York</td><td>2,498</td><td>2.8%</td></tr>
<tr><td>NA</td><td>Idaho**</td><td>NA</td><td>NA</td><td>12</td><td>New Jersey</td><td>2,442</td><td>2.8%</td></tr>
<tr><td>NA</td><td>Illinois**</td><td>NA</td><td>NA</td><td>13</td><td>Tennessee</td><td>2,318</td><td>2.6%</td></tr>
<tr><td>16</td><td>Indiana</td><td>2,016</td><td>2.3%</td><td>14</td><td>Pennsylvania</td><td>2,273</td><td>2.6%</td></tr>
<tr><td>32</td><td>Iowa</td><td>638</td><td>0.7%</td><td>15</td><td>South Carolina</td><td>2,108</td><td>2.4%</td></tr>
<tr><td>30</td><td>Kansas</td><td>717</td><td>0.8%</td><td>16</td><td>Indiana</td><td>2,016</td><td>2.3%</td></tr>
<tr><td>18</td><td>Kentucky</td><td>1,910</td><td>2.2%</td><td>17</td><td>Maryland</td><td>1,931</td><td>2.2%</td></tr>
<tr><td>19</td><td>Louisiana</td><td>1,788</td><td>2.0%</td><td>18</td><td>Kentucky</td><td>1,910</td><td>2.2%</td></tr>
<tr><td>37</td><td>Maine</td><td>381</td><td>0.4%</td><td>19</td><td>Louisiana</td><td>1,788</td><td>2.0%</td></tr>
<tr><td>17</td><td>Maryland</td><td>1,931</td><td>2.2%</td><td>20</td><td>Colorado</td><td>1,764</td><td>2.0%</td></tr>
<tr><td>5</td><td>Massachusetts</td><td>3,724</td><td>4.2%</td><td>21</td><td>Wisconsin</td><td>1,493</td><td>1.7%</td></tr>
<tr><td>8</td><td>Michigan</td><td>3,518</td><td>4.0%</td><td>22</td><td>Missouri</td><td>1,475</td><td>1.7%</td></tr>
<tr><td>31</td><td>Minnesota</td><td>709</td><td>0.8%</td><td>23</td><td>Alabama</td><td>1,413</td><td>1.6%</td></tr>
<tr><td>33</td><td>Mississippi</td><td>635</td><td>0.7%</td><td>24</td><td>Arkansas</td><td>1,398</td><td>1.6%</td></tr>
<tr><td>22</td><td>Missouri</td><td>1,475</td><td>1.7%</td><td>25</td><td>Washington</td><td>1,309</td><td>1.5%</td></tr>
<tr><td>43</td><td>Montana</td><td>165</td><td>0.2%</td><td>26</td><td>Utah</td><td>1,234</td><td>1.4%</td></tr>
<tr><td>38</td><td>Nebraska</td><td>379</td><td>0.4%</td><td>27</td><td>Oklahoma</td><td>1,199</td><td>1.4%</td></tr>
<tr><td>34</td><td>Nevada</td><td>494</td><td>0.6%</td><td>28</td><td>New Mexico</td><td>1,042</td><td>1.2%</td></tr>
<tr><td>NA</td><td>New Hampshire**</td><td>NA</td><td>NA</td><td>29</td><td>Connecticut</td><td>944</td><td>1.1%</td></tr>
<tr><td>12</td><td>New Jersey</td><td>2,442</td><td>2.8%</td><td>30</td><td>Kansas</td><td>717</td><td>0.8%</td></tr>
<tr><td>28</td><td>New Mexico</td><td>1,042</td><td>1.2%</td><td>31</td><td>Minnesota</td><td>709</td><td>0.8%</td></tr>
<tr><td>11</td><td>New York</td><td>2,498</td><td>2.8%</td><td>32</td><td>Iowa</td><td>638</td><td>0.7%</td></tr>
<tr><td>4</td><td>North Carolina</td><td>3,764</td><td>4.3%</td><td>33</td><td>Mississippi</td><td>635</td><td>0.7%</td></tr>
<tr><td>39</td><td>North Dakota</td><td>315</td><td>0.4%</td><td>34</td><td>Nevada</td><td>494</td><td>0.6%</td></tr>
<tr><td>6</td><td>Ohio</td><td>3,676</td><td>4.2%</td><td>35</td><td>Rhode Island</td><td>470</td><td>0.5%</td></tr>
<tr><td>27</td><td>Oklahoma</td><td>1,199</td><td>1.4%</td><td>36</td><td>Delaware</td><td>459</td><td>0.5%</td></tr>
<tr><td>NA</td><td>Oregon**</td><td>NA</td><td>NA</td><td>37</td><td>Maine</td><td>381</td><td>0.4%</td></tr>
<tr><td>14</td><td>Pennsylvania</td><td>2,273</td><td>2.6%</td><td>38</td><td>Nebraska</td><td>379</td><td>0.4%</td></tr>
<tr><td>35</td><td>Rhode Island</td><td>470</td><td>0.5%</td><td>39</td><td>North Dakota</td><td>315</td><td>0.4%</td></tr>
<tr><td>15</td><td>South Carolina</td><td>2,108</td><td>2.4%</td><td>40</td><td>West Virginia</td><td>292</td><td>0.3%</td></tr>
<tr><td>45</td><td>South Dakota</td><td>0</td><td>0.0%</td><td>41</td><td>Alaska</td><td>243</td><td>0.3%</td></tr>
<tr><td>13</td><td>Tennessee</td><td>2,318</td><td>2.6%</td><td>42</td><td>Vermont</td><td>181</td><td>0.2%</td></tr>
<tr><td>2</td><td>Texas</td><td>8,923</td><td>10.1%</td><td>43</td><td>Montana</td><td>165</td><td>0.2%</td></tr>
<tr><td>26</td><td>Utah</td><td>1,234</td><td>1.4%</td><td>44</td><td>Wyoming</td><td>151</td><td>0.2%</td></tr>
<tr><td>42</td><td>Vermont</td><td>181</td><td>0.2%</td><td>45</td><td>South Dakota</td><td>0</td><td>0.0%</td></tr>
<tr><td>9</td><td>Virginia</td><td>3,335</td><td>3.8%</td><td>NA</td><td>Hawaii**</td><td>NA</td><td>NA</td></tr>
<tr><td>25</td><td>Washington</td><td>1,309</td><td>1.5%</td><td>NA</td><td>Idaho**</td><td>NA</td><td>NA</td></tr>
<tr><td>40</td><td>West Virginia</td><td>292</td><td>0.3%</td><td>NA</td><td>Illinois**</td><td>NA</td><td>NA</td></tr>
<tr><td>21</td><td>Wisconsin</td><td>1,493</td><td>1.7%</td><td>NA</td><td>New Hampshire**</td><td>NA</td><td>NA</td></tr>
<tr><td>44</td><td>Wyoming</td><td>151</td><td>0.2%</td><td>NA</td><td>Oregon**</td><td>NA</td><td>NA</td></tr>
<tr><td></td><td></td><td></td><td></td><td></td><td>District of Columbia**</td><td>NA</td><td>NA</td></tr>
</table>

Source: CQ Press using reported data from the Federal Bureau of Investigation
"Crime in the United States 2008" (Uniform Crime Reports, September 14, 2009, http://www.fbi.gov/ucr/ucr.htm)
*Includes murder, rape, robbery, aggravated assault, burglary, larceny-theft, and motor vehicle theft. Total is only for states shown separately. Many states had incomplete reports.
**Not available.

Crime Rate Reported at Universities and Colleges in 2008

National Rate = 1,354.8 Reported Crimes per 100,000 Enrollment*

<table>
<tr><td colspan="3">ALPHA ORDER</td><td colspan="3">RANK ORDER</td></tr>
<tr><th>RANK</th><th>STATE</th><th>RATE</th><th>RANK</th><th>STATE</th><th>RATE</th></tr>
<tr><td>24</td><td>Alabama</td><td>1,291.3</td><td>1</td><td>New Mexico</td><td>2,237.6</td></tr>
<tr><td>40</td><td>Alaska</td><td>968.9</td><td>2</td><td>New York</td><td>2,154.8</td></tr>
<tr><td>8</td><td>Arizona</td><td>1,724.4</td><td>3</td><td>Connecticut</td><td>2,015.5</td></tr>
<tr><td>6</td><td>Arkansas</td><td>1,858.0</td><td>4</td><td>Rhode Island</td><td>1,973.4</td></tr>
<tr><td>22</td><td>California</td><td>1,341.5</td><td>5</td><td>Delaware</td><td>1,904.7</td></tr>
<tr><td>29</td><td>Colorado</td><td>1,218.4</td><td>6</td><td>Arkansas</td><td>1,858.0</td></tr>
<tr><td>3</td><td>Connecticut</td><td>2,015.5</td><td>7</td><td>Georgia</td><td>1,797.5</td></tr>
<tr><td>5</td><td>Delaware</td><td>1,904.7</td><td>8</td><td>Arizona</td><td>1,724.4</td></tr>
<tr><td>31</td><td>Florida</td><td>1,190.5</td><td>9</td><td>Maryland</td><td>1,688.2</td></tr>
<tr><td>7</td><td>Georgia</td><td>1,797.5</td><td>10</td><td>North Carolina</td><td>1,654.9</td></tr>
<tr><td>NA</td><td>Hawaii**</td><td>NA</td><td>11</td><td>Indiana</td><td>1,639.2</td></tr>
<tr><td>NA</td><td>Idaho**</td><td>NA</td><td>12</td><td>Kentucky</td><td>1,609.1</td></tr>
<tr><td>NA</td><td>Illinois**</td><td>NA</td><td>13</td><td>Maine</td><td>1,541.5</td></tr>
<tr><td>11</td><td>Indiana</td><td>1,639.2</td><td>14</td><td>Louisiana</td><td>1,509.0</td></tr>
<tr><td>42</td><td>Iowa</td><td>938.7</td><td>15</td><td>South Carolina</td><td>1,491.6</td></tr>
<tr><td>37</td><td>Kansas</td><td>1,062.4</td><td>16</td><td>Vermont</td><td>1,478.9</td></tr>
<tr><td>12</td><td>Kentucky</td><td>1,609.1</td><td>17</td><td>Mississippi</td><td>1,417.9</td></tr>
<tr><td>14</td><td>Louisiana</td><td>1,509.0</td><td>18</td><td>Massachusetts</td><td>1,409.9</td></tr>
<tr><td>13</td><td>Maine</td><td>1,541.5</td><td>19</td><td>Ohio</td><td>1,404.8</td></tr>
<tr><td>9</td><td>Maryland</td><td>1,688.2</td><td>20</td><td>Montana</td><td>1,382.8</td></tr>
<tr><td>18</td><td>Massachusetts</td><td>1,409.9</td><td>21</td><td>New Jersey</td><td>1,369.9</td></tr>
<tr><td>30</td><td>Michigan</td><td>1,214.4</td><td>22</td><td>California</td><td>1,341.5</td></tr>
<tr><td>34</td><td>Minnesota</td><td>1,112.1</td><td>23</td><td>Tennessee</td><td>1,329.5</td></tr>
<tr><td>17</td><td>Mississippi</td><td>1,417.9</td><td>24</td><td>Alabama</td><td>1,291.3</td></tr>
<tr><td>36</td><td>Missouri</td><td>1,078.1</td><td>25</td><td>Nebraska</td><td>1,286.9</td></tr>
<tr><td>20</td><td>Montana</td><td>1,382.8</td><td>26</td><td>Washington</td><td>1,250.6</td></tr>
<tr><td>25</td><td>Nebraska</td><td>1,286.9</td><td>27</td><td>Texas</td><td>1,246.7</td></tr>
<tr><td>44</td><td>Nevada</td><td>869.6</td><td>28</td><td>Virginia</td><td>1,242.3</td></tr>
<tr><td>NA</td><td>New Hampshire**</td><td>NA</td><td>29</td><td>Colorado</td><td>1,218.4</td></tr>
<tr><td>21</td><td>New Jersey</td><td>1,369.9</td><td>30</td><td>Michigan</td><td>1,214.4</td></tr>
<tr><td>1</td><td>New Mexico</td><td>2,237.6</td><td>31</td><td>Florida</td><td>1,190.5</td></tr>
<tr><td>2</td><td>New York</td><td>2,154.8</td><td>32</td><td>North Dakota</td><td>1,145.3</td></tr>
<tr><td>10</td><td>North Carolina</td><td>1,654.9</td><td>33</td><td>Pennsylvania</td><td>1,139.3</td></tr>
<tr><td>32</td><td>North Dakota</td><td>1,145.3</td><td>34</td><td>Minnesota</td><td>1,112.1</td></tr>
<tr><td>19</td><td>Ohio</td><td>1,404.8</td><td>35</td><td>West Virginia</td><td>1,083.8</td></tr>
<tr><td>38</td><td>Oklahoma</td><td>1,018.8</td><td>36</td><td>Missouri</td><td>1,078.1</td></tr>
<tr><td>NA</td><td>Oregon**</td><td>NA</td><td>37</td><td>Kansas</td><td>1,062.4</td></tr>
<tr><td>33</td><td>Pennsylvania</td><td>1,139.3</td><td>38</td><td>Oklahoma</td><td>1,018.8</td></tr>
<tr><td>4</td><td>Rhode Island</td><td>1,973.4</td><td>39</td><td>Wisconsin</td><td>970.0</td></tr>
<tr><td>15</td><td>South Carolina</td><td>1,491.6</td><td>40</td><td>Alaska</td><td>968.9</td></tr>
<tr><td>45</td><td>South Dakota</td><td>0.0</td><td>41</td><td>Utah</td><td>962.9</td></tr>
<tr><td>23</td><td>Tennessee</td><td>1,329.5</td><td>42</td><td>Iowa</td><td>938.7</td></tr>
<tr><td>27</td><td>Texas</td><td>1,246.7</td><td>43</td><td>Wyoming</td><td>934.9</td></tr>
<tr><td>41</td><td>Utah</td><td>962.9</td><td>44</td><td>Nevada</td><td>869.6</td></tr>
<tr><td>16</td><td>Vermont</td><td>1,478.9</td><td>45</td><td>South Dakota</td><td>0.0</td></tr>
<tr><td>28</td><td>Virginia</td><td>1,242.3</td><td>NA</td><td>Hawaii**</td><td>NA</td></tr>
<tr><td>26</td><td>Washington</td><td>1,250.6</td><td>NA</td><td>Idaho**</td><td>NA</td></tr>
<tr><td>35</td><td>West Virginia</td><td>1,083.8</td><td>NA</td><td>Illinois**</td><td>NA</td></tr>
<tr><td>39</td><td>Wisconsin</td><td>970.0</td><td>NA</td><td>New Hampshire**</td><td>NA</td></tr>
<tr><td>43</td><td>Wyoming</td><td>934.9</td><td>NA</td><td>Oregon**</td><td>NA</td></tr>
<tr><td></td><td></td><td></td><td></td><td>District of Columbia**</td><td>NA</td></tr>
</table>

Source: CQ Press using reported data from the Federal Bureau of Investigation
   "Crime in the United States 2008" (Uniform Crime Reports, September 14, 2009, http://www.fbi.gov/ucr/ucr.htm)
*Includes murder, rape, robbery, aggravated assault, burglary, larceny-theft, and motor vehicle theft. National rate is only for states shown separately. Many states had incomplete reports.
**Not available.

Crimes Reported at Universities and Colleges as a Percent of All Crimes in 2008

National Percent = 0.85% of Crimes*

<table>
<tr><td colspan="3">ALPHA ORDER</td><td colspan="3">RANK ORDER</td></tr>
<tr><td>RANK</td><td>STATE</td><td>PERCENT</td><td>RANK</td><td>STATE</td><td>PERCENT</td></tr>
<tr><td>33</td><td>Alabama</td><td>0.67</td><td>1</td><td>North Dakota</td><td>2.38</td></tr>
<tr><td>15</td><td>Alaska</td><td>0.99</td><td>2</td><td>Massachusetts</td><td>2.01</td></tr>
<tr><td>22</td><td>Arizona</td><td>0.88</td><td>3</td><td>Kentucky</td><td>1.55</td></tr>
<tr><td>9</td><td>Arkansas</td><td>1.13</td><td>3</td><td>Virginia</td><td>1.55</td></tr>
<tr><td>16</td><td>California</td><td>0.98</td><td>5</td><td>Rhode Island</td><td>1.45</td></tr>
<tr><td>11</td><td>Colorado</td><td>1.12</td><td>6</td><td>Utah</td><td>1.26</td></tr>
<tr><td>16</td><td>Connecticut</td><td>0.98</td><td>7</td><td>Delaware</td><td>1.23</td></tr>
<tr><td>7</td><td>Delaware</td><td>1.23</td><td>8</td><td>New Mexico</td><td>1.15</td></tr>
<tr><td>43</td><td>Florida</td><td>0.45</td><td>9</td><td>Arkansas</td><td>1.13</td></tr>
<tr><td>26</td><td>Georgia</td><td>0.83</td><td>9</td><td>Maine</td><td>1.13</td></tr>
<tr><td>NA</td><td>Hawaii**</td><td>NA</td><td>11</td><td>Colorado</td><td>1.12</td></tr>
<tr><td>NA</td><td>Idaho**</td><td>NA</td><td>12</td><td>Vermont</td><td>1.09</td></tr>
<tr><td>NA</td><td>Illinois**</td><td>NA</td><td>13</td><td>New Jersey</td><td>1.07</td></tr>
<tr><td>24</td><td>Indiana</td><td>0.86</td><td>14</td><td>Michigan</td><td>1.02</td></tr>
<tr><td>30</td><td>Iowa</td><td>0.79</td><td>15</td><td>Alaska</td><td>0.99</td></tr>
<tr><td>32</td><td>Kansas</td><td>0.68</td><td>16</td><td>California</td><td>0.98</td></tr>
<tr><td>3</td><td>Kentucky</td><td>1.55</td><td>16</td><td>Connecticut</td><td>0.98</td></tr>
<tr><td>20</td><td>Louisiana</td><td>0.90</td><td>18</td><td>Wyoming</td><td>0.96</td></tr>
<tr><td>9</td><td>Maine</td><td>1.13</td><td>19</td><td>South Carolina</td><td>0.95</td></tr>
<tr><td>26</td><td>Maryland</td><td>0.83</td><td>20</td><td>Louisiana</td><td>0.90</td></tr>
<tr><td>2</td><td>Massachusetts</td><td>2.01</td><td>20</td><td>North Carolina</td><td>0.90</td></tr>
<tr><td>14</td><td>Michigan</td><td>1.02</td><td>22</td><td>Arizona</td><td>0.88</td></tr>
<tr><td>44</td><td>Minnesota</td><td>0.44</td><td>22</td><td>Wisconsin</td><td>0.88</td></tr>
<tr><td>33</td><td>Mississippi</td><td>0.67</td><td>24</td><td>Indiana</td><td>0.86</td></tr>
<tr><td>37</td><td>Missouri</td><td>0.60</td><td>25</td><td>Ohio</td><td>0.85</td></tr>
<tr><td>37</td><td>Montana</td><td>0.60</td><td>26</td><td>Georgia</td><td>0.83</td></tr>
<tr><td>33</td><td>Nebraska</td><td>0.67</td><td>26</td><td>Maryland</td><td>0.83</td></tr>
<tr><td>42</td><td>Nevada</td><td>0.46</td><td>26</td><td>Oklahoma</td><td>0.83</td></tr>
<tr><td>NA</td><td>New Hampshire**</td><td>NA</td><td>29</td><td>Texas</td><td>0.82</td></tr>
<tr><td>13</td><td>New Jersey</td><td>1.07</td><td>30</td><td>Iowa</td><td>0.79</td></tr>
<tr><td>8</td><td>New Mexico</td><td>1.15</td><td>31</td><td>Tennessee</td><td>0.78</td></tr>
<tr><td>40</td><td>New York</td><td>0.54</td><td>32</td><td>Kansas</td><td>0.68</td></tr>
<tr><td>20</td><td>North Carolina</td><td>0.90</td><td>33</td><td>Alabama</td><td>0.67</td></tr>
<tr><td>1</td><td>North Dakota</td><td>2.38</td><td>33</td><td>Mississippi</td><td>0.67</td></tr>
<tr><td>25</td><td>Ohio</td><td>0.85</td><td>33</td><td>Nebraska</td><td>0.67</td></tr>
<tr><td>26</td><td>Oklahoma</td><td>0.83</td><td>36</td><td>Pennsylvania</td><td>0.65</td></tr>
<tr><td>NA</td><td>Oregon**</td><td>NA</td><td>37</td><td>Missouri</td><td>0.60</td></tr>
<tr><td>36</td><td>Pennsylvania</td><td>0.65</td><td>37</td><td>Montana</td><td>0.60</td></tr>
<tr><td>5</td><td>Rhode Island</td><td>1.45</td><td>39</td><td>West Virginia</td><td>0.57</td></tr>
<tr><td>19</td><td>South Carolina</td><td>0.95</td><td>40</td><td>New York</td><td>0.54</td></tr>
<tr><td>45</td><td>South Dakota</td><td>0.00</td><td>41</td><td>Washington</td><td>0.49</td></tr>
<tr><td>31</td><td>Tennessee</td><td>0.78</td><td>42</td><td>Nevada</td><td>0.46</td></tr>
<tr><td>29</td><td>Texas</td><td>0.82</td><td>43</td><td>Florida</td><td>0.45</td></tr>
<tr><td>6</td><td>Utah</td><td>1.26</td><td>44</td><td>Minnesota</td><td>0.44</td></tr>
<tr><td>12</td><td>Vermont</td><td>1.09</td><td>45</td><td>South Dakota</td><td>0.00</td></tr>
<tr><td>3</td><td>Virginia</td><td>1.55</td><td>NA</td><td>Hawaii**</td><td>NA</td></tr>
<tr><td>41</td><td>Washington</td><td>0.49</td><td>NA</td><td>Idaho**</td><td>NA</td></tr>
<tr><td>39</td><td>West Virginia</td><td>0.57</td><td>NA</td><td>Illinois**</td><td>NA</td></tr>
<tr><td>22</td><td>Wisconsin</td><td>0.88</td><td>NA</td><td>New Hampshire**</td><td>NA</td></tr>
<tr><td>18</td><td>Wyoming</td><td>0.96</td><td>NA</td><td>Oregon**</td><td>NA</td></tr>
<tr><td></td><td></td><td></td><td></td><td>District of Columbia**</td><td>NA</td></tr>
</table>

Source: CQ Press using reported data from the Federal Bureau of Investigation
    "Crime in the United States 2008" (Uniform Crime Reports, September 14, 2009, http://www.fbi.gov/ucr/ucr.htm)
*Includes murder, rape, robbery, aggravated assault, burglary, larceny-theft, and motor vehicle theft. National percent is only for states shown separately. Many states had incomplete reports.
**Not available.

Violent Crimes Reported at Universities and Colleges in 2008

National Total = 2,672 Reported Violent Crimes*

ALPHA ORDER

RANK	STATE	CRIMES	% of USA
16	Alabama	61	2.3%
35	Alaska	9	0.3%
18	Arizona	60	2.2%
16	Arkansas	61	2.3%
1	California	406	15.2%
21	Colorado	47	1.8%
29	Connecticut	23	0.9%
30	Delaware	20	0.7%
4	Florida	123	4.6%
12	Georgia	87	3.3%
NA	Hawaii**	NA	NA
NA	Idaho**	NA	NA
NA	Illinois**	NA	NA
25	Indiana	33	1.2%
23	Iowa	39	1.5%
32	Kansas	19	0.7%
22	Kentucky	43	1.6%
5	Louisiana	115	4.3%
38	Maine	8	0.3%
7	Maryland	111	4.2%
3	Massachusetts	165	6.2%
13	Michigan	80	3.0%
43	Minnesota	0	0.0%
35	Mississippi	9	0.3%
20	Missouri	48	1.8%
34	Montana	10	0.4%
40	Nebraska	4	0.1%
33	Nevada	13	0.5%
NA	New Hampshire**	NA	NA
10	New Jersey	95	3.6%
24	New Mexico	36	1.3%
19	New York	54	2.0%
9	North Carolina	107	4.0%
41	North Dakota	1	0.0%
15	Ohio	69	2.6%
26	Oklahoma	30	1.1%
NA	Oregon**	NA	NA
11	Pennsylvania	91	3.4%
38	Rhode Island	8	0.3%
8	South Carolina	108	4.0%
43	South Dakota	0	0.0%
14	Tennessee	74	2.8%
2	Texas	212	7.9%
35	Utah	9	0.3%
43	Vermont	0	0.0%
6	Virginia	113	4.2%
27	Washington	25	0.9%
30	West Virginia	20	0.7%
27	Wisconsin	25	0.9%
41	Wyoming	1	0.0%

RANK ORDER

RANK	STATE	CRIMES	% of USA
1	California	406	15.2%
2	Texas	212	7.9%
3	Massachusetts	165	6.2%
4	Florida	123	4.6%
5	Louisiana	115	4.3%
6	Virginia	113	4.2%
7	Maryland	111	4.2%
8	South Carolina	108	4.0%
9	North Carolina	107	4.0%
10	New Jersey	95	3.6%
11	Pennsylvania	91	3.4%
12	Georgia	87	3.3%
13	Michigan	80	3.0%
14	Tennessee	74	2.8%
15	Ohio	69	2.6%
16	Alabama	61	2.3%
16	Arkansas	61	2.3%
18	Arizona	60	2.2%
19	New York	54	2.0%
20	Missouri	48	1.8%
21	Colorado	47	1.8%
22	Kentucky	43	1.6%
23	Iowa	39	1.5%
24	New Mexico	36	1.3%
25	Indiana	33	1.2%
26	Oklahoma	30	1.1%
27	Washington	25	0.9%
27	Wisconsin	25	0.9%
29	Connecticut	23	0.9%
30	Delaware	20	0.7%
30	West Virginia	20	0.7%
32	Kansas	19	0.7%
33	Nevada	13	0.5%
34	Montana	10	0.4%
35	Alaska	9	0.3%
35	Mississippi	9	0.3%
35	Utah	9	0.3%
38	Maine	8	0.3%
38	Rhode Island	8	0.3%
40	Nebraska	4	0.1%
41	North Dakota	1	0.0%
41	Wyoming	1	0.0%
43	Minnesota	0	0.0%
43	South Dakota	0	0.0%
43	Vermont	0	0.0%
NA	Hawaii**	NA	NA
NA	Idaho**	NA	NA
NA	Illinois**	NA	NA
NA	New Hampshire**	NA	NA
NA	Oregon**	NA	NA
	District of Columbia**	NA	NA

Source: CQ Press using reported data from the Federal Bureau of Investigation
"Crime in the United States 2008" (Uniform Crime Reports, September 14, 2009, http://www.fbi.gov/ucr/ucr.htm)
*Includes murder, rape, robbery, and aggravated assault. Total is only for states shown separately. Many states had incomplete reports.
**Not available.

Violent Crime Rate Reported at Universities and Colleges in 2008

National Rate = 40.9 Reported Violent Crimes per 100,000 Enrollment*

<u>ALPHA ORDER</u>

RANK	STATE	RATE
11	Alabama	55.7
24	Alaska	35.9
21	Arizona	38.2
5	Arkansas	81.1
17	California	44.0
27	Colorado	32.5
13	Connecticut	49.1
4	Delaware	83.0
22	Florida	36.4
18	Georgia	43.5
NA	Hawaii**	NA
NA	Idaho**	NA
NA	Illinois**	NA
32	Indiana	26.8
10	Iowa	57.4
30	Kansas	28.2
23	Kentucky	36.2
1	Louisiana	97.1
28	Maine	32.4
2	Maryland	97.0
9	Massachusetts	62.5
31	Michigan	27.6
43	Minnesota	0.0
37	Mississippi	20.1
25	Missouri	35.1
3	Montana	83.8
39	Nebraska	13.6
36	Nevada	22.9
NA	New Hampshire**	NA
12	New Jersey	53.3
6	New Mexico	77.3
15	New York	46.6
14	North Carolina	47.0
42	North Dakota	3.6
33	Ohio	26.4
34	Oklahoma	25.5
NA	Oregon**	NA
16	Pennsylvania	45.6
26	Rhode Island	33.6
7	South Carolina	76.4
43	South Dakota	0.0
19	Tennessee	42.4
29	Texas	29.6
40	Utah	7.0
43	Vermont	0.0
20	Virginia	42.1
35	Washington	23.9
8	West Virginia	74.2
38	Wisconsin	16.2
41	Wyoming	6.2

<u>RANK ORDER</u>

RANK	STATE	RATE
1	Louisiana	97.1
2	Maryland	97.0
3	Montana	83.8
4	Delaware	83.0
5	Arkansas	81.1
6	New Mexico	77.3
7	South Carolina	76.4
8	West Virginia	74.2
9	Massachusetts	62.5
10	Iowa	57.4
11	Alabama	55.7
12	New Jersey	53.3
13	Connecticut	49.1
14	North Carolina	47.0
15	New York	46.6
16	Pennsylvania	45.6
17	California	44.0
18	Georgia	43.5
19	Tennessee	42.4
20	Virginia	42.1
21	Arizona	38.2
22	Florida	36.4
23	Kentucky	36.2
24	Alaska	35.9
25	Missouri	35.1
26	Rhode Island	33.6
27	Colorado	32.5
28	Maine	32.4
29	Texas	29.6
30	Kansas	28.2
31	Michigan	27.6
32	Indiana	26.8
33	Ohio	26.4
34	Oklahoma	25.5
35	Washington	23.9
36	Nevada	22.9
37	Mississippi	20.1
38	Wisconsin	16.2
39	Nebraska	13.6
40	Utah	7.0
41	Wyoming	6.2
42	North Dakota	3.6
43	Minnesota	0.0
43	South Dakota	0.0
43	Vermont	0.0
NA	Hawaii**	NA
NA	Idaho**	NA
NA	Illinois**	NA
NA	New Hampshire**	NA
NA	Oregon**	NA
	District of Columbia**	NA

Source: CQ Press using reported data from the Federal Bureau of Investigation
"Crime in the United States 2008" (Uniform Crime Reports, September 14, 2009, http://www.fbi.gov/ucr/ucr.htm)
*Includes murder, rape, robbery, and aggravated assault. National rate is only for states shown separately. Many states had incomplete reports.
**Not available.

Violent Crimes Reported at Universities and Colleges as a Percent of All Violent Crimes in 2008
National Percent = 0.85% of Violent Crimes*

ALPHA ORDER

RANK	STATE	PERCENT
15	Alabama	0.29
22	Alaska	0.20
21	Arizona	0.21
5	Arkansas	0.42
19	California	0.22
16	Colorado	0.28
19	Connecticut	0.22
11	Delaware	0.33
37	Florida	0.10
23	Georgia	0.19
NA	Hawaii**	NA
NA	Idaho**	NA
NA	Illinois**	NA
28	Indiana	0.16
4	Iowa	0.46
25	Kansas	0.17
9	Kentucky	0.34
6	Louisiana	0.40
3	Maine	0.52
13	Maryland	0.31
1	Massachusetts	0.57
28	Michigan	0.16
43	Minnesota	0.00
36	Mississippi	0.11
28	Missouri	0.16
6	Montana	0.40
40	Nebraska	0.07
40	Nevada	0.07
NA	New Hampshire**	NA
9	New Jersey	0.34
16	New Mexico	0.28
40	New York	0.07
18	North Carolina	0.25
38	North Dakota	0.09
25	Ohio	0.17
28	Oklahoma	0.16
NA	Oregon**	NA
24	Pennsylvania	0.18
13	Rhode Island	0.31
11	South Carolina	0.33
43	South Dakota	0.00
28	Tennessee	0.16
25	Texas	0.17
34	Utah	0.15
43	Vermont	0.00
1	Virginia	0.57
35	Washington	0.12
6	West Virginia	0.40
28	Wisconsin	0.16
39	Wyoming	0.08

RANK ORDER

RANK	STATE	PERCENT
1	Massachusetts	0.57
1	Virginia	0.57
3	Maine	0.52
4	Iowa	0.46
5	Arkansas	0.42
6	Louisiana	0.40
6	Montana	0.40
6	West Virginia	0.40
9	Kentucky	0.34
9	New Jersey	0.34
11	Delaware	0.33
11	South Carolina	0.33
13	Maryland	0.31
13	Rhode Island	0.31
15	Alabama	0.29
16	Colorado	0.28
16	New Mexico	0.28
18	North Carolina	0.25
19	California	0.22
19	Connecticut	0.22
21	Arizona	0.21
22	Alaska	0.20
23	Georgia	0.19
24	Pennsylvania	0.18
25	Kansas	0.17
25	Ohio	0.17
25	Texas	0.17
28	Indiana	0.16
28	Michigan	0.16
28	Missouri	0.16
28	Oklahoma	0.16
28	Tennessee	0.16
28	Wisconsin	0.16
34	Utah	0.15
35	Washington	0.12
36	Mississippi	0.11
37	Florida	0.10
38	North Dakota	0.09
39	Wyoming	0.08
40	Nebraska	0.07
40	Nevada	0.07
40	New York	0.07
43	Minnesota	0.00
43	South Dakota	0.00
43	Vermont	0.00
NA	Hawaii**	NA
NA	Idaho**	NA
NA	Illinois**	NA
NA	New Hampshire**	NA
NA	Oregon**	NA
	District of Columbia**	NA

Source: CQ Press using reported data from the Federal Bureau of Investigation
"Crime in the United States 2008" (Uniform Crime Reports, September 14, 2009, http://www.fbi.gov/ucr/ucr.htm)
*Includes murder, rape, robbery, and aggravated assault. National percent is only for states shown separately. Many states had incomplete reports.
**Not available.

Property Crimes Reported at Universities and Colleges in 2008

National Total = 85,760 Reported Property Crimes*

ALPHA ORDER

RANK	STATE	CRIMES	% of USA
23	Alabama	1,352	1.6%
41	Alaska	234	0.3%
10	Arizona	2,648	3.1%
24	Arkansas	1,337	1.6%
1	California	11,976	14.0%
19	Colorado	1,717	2.0%
29	Connecticut	921	1.1%
36	Delaware	439	0.5%
3	Florida	3,897	4.5%
7	Georgia	3,511	4.1%
NA	Hawaii**	NA	NA
NA	Idaho**	NA	NA
NA	Illinois**	NA	NA
16	Indiana	1,983	2.3%
33	Iowa	599	0.7%
31	Kansas	698	0.8%
17	Kentucky	1,867	2.2%
20	Louisiana	1,673	2.0%
38	Maine	373	0.4%
18	Maryland	1,820	2.1%
6	Massachusetts	3,559	4.1%
8	Michigan	3,438	4.0%
30	Minnesota	709	0.8%
32	Mississippi	626	0.7%
22	Missouri	1,427	1.7%
43	Montana	155	0.2%
37	Nebraska	375	0.4%
34	Nevada	481	0.6%
NA	New Hampshire**	NA	NA
12	New Jersey	2,347	2.7%
28	New Mexico	1,006	1.2%
11	New York	2,444	2.8%
4	North Carolina	3,657	4.3%
39	North Dakota	314	0.4%
5	Ohio	3,607	4.2%
27	Oklahoma	1,169	1.4%
NA	Oregon**	NA	NA
14	Pennsylvania	2,182	2.5%
35	Rhode Island	462	0.5%
15	South Carolina	2,000	2.3%
45	South Dakota	0	0.0%
13	Tennessee	2,244	2.6%
2	Texas	8,711	10.2%
26	Utah	1,225	1.4%
42	Vermont	181	0.2%
9	Virginia	3,222	3.8%
25	Washington	1,284	1.5%
40	West Virginia	272	0.3%
21	Wisconsin	1,468	1.7%
44	Wyoming	150	0.2%

RANK ORDER

RANK	STATE	CRIMES	% of USA
1	California	11,976	14.0%
2	Texas	8,711	10.2%
3	Florida	3,897	4.5%
4	North Carolina	3,657	4.3%
5	Ohio	3,607	4.2%
6	Massachusetts	3,559	4.1%
7	Georgia	3,511	4.1%
8	Michigan	3,438	4.0%
9	Virginia	3,222	3.8%
10	Arizona	2,648	3.1%
11	New York	2,444	2.8%
12	New Jersey	2,347	2.7%
13	Tennessee	2,244	2.6%
14	Pennsylvania	2,182	2.5%
15	South Carolina	2,000	2.3%
16	Indiana	1,983	2.3%
17	Kentucky	1,867	2.2%
18	Maryland	1,820	2.1%
19	Colorado	1,717	2.0%
20	Louisiana	1,673	2.0%
21	Wisconsin	1,468	1.7%
22	Missouri	1,427	1.7%
23	Alabama	1,352	1.6%
24	Arkansas	1,337	1.6%
25	Washington	1,284	1.5%
26	Utah	1,225	1.4%
27	Oklahoma	1,169	1.4%
28	New Mexico	1,006	1.2%
29	Connecticut	921	1.1%
30	Minnesota	709	0.8%
31	Kansas	698	0.8%
32	Mississippi	626	0.7%
33	Iowa	599	0.7%
34	Nevada	481	0.6%
35	Rhode Island	462	0.5%
36	Delaware	439	0.5%
37	Nebraska	375	0.4%
38	Maine	373	0.4%
39	North Dakota	314	0.4%
40	West Virginia	272	0.3%
41	Alaska	234	0.3%
42	Vermont	181	0.2%
43	Montana	155	0.2%
44	Wyoming	150	0.2%
45	South Dakota	0	0.0%
NA	Hawaii**	NA	NA
NA	Idaho**	NA	NA
NA	Illinois**	NA	NA
NA	New Hampshire**	NA	NA
NA	Oregon**	NA	NA
	District of Columbia**	NA	NA

Source: CQ Press using reported data from the Federal Bureau of Investigation
"Crime in the United States 2008" (Uniform Crime Reports, September 14, 2009, http://www.fbi.gov/ucr/ucr.htm)
*Includes burglary, larceny-theft, and motor vehicle theft. Total is only for states shown separately. Many states had incomplete reports.
**Not available.

Property Crime Rate Reported at Universities and Colleges in 2008

National Rate = 1,313.8 Reported Property Crimes per 100,000 Enrollment*

ALPHA ORDER

RANK	STATE	RATE
25	Alabama	1,235.6
41	Alaska	933.0
8	Arizona	1,686.2
6	Arkansas	1,776.9
22	California	1,297.5
30	Colorado	1,185.9
3	Connecticut	1,966.4
5	Delaware	1,821.7
31	Florida	1,154.0
7	Georgia	1,754.0
NA	Hawaii**	NA
NA	Idaho**	NA
NA	Illinois**	NA
9	Indiana	1,612.3
43	Iowa	881.3
36	Kansas	1,034.3
12	Kentucky	1,572.9
16	Louisiana	1,412.0
13	Maine	1,509.1
11	Maryland	1,591.1
19	Massachusetts	1,347.4
29	Michigan	1,186.8
33	Minnesota	1,112.1
17	Mississippi	1,397.8
35	Missouri	1,043.0
21	Montana	1,299.0
24	Nebraska	1,273.3
44	Nevada	846.7
NA	New Hampshire**	NA
20	New Jersey	1,316.6
1	New Mexico	2,160.3
2	New York	2,108.2
10	North Carolina	1,607.8
32	North Dakota	1,141.7
18	Ohio	1,378.5
38	Oklahoma	993.3
NA	Oregon**	NA
34	Pennsylvania	1,093.7
4	Rhode Island	1,939.8
15	South Carolina	1,415.2
45	South Dakota	0.0
23	Tennessee	1,287.0
27	Texas	1,217.0
39	Utah	955.9
14	Vermont	1,478.9
28	Virginia	1,200.2
26	Washington	1,226.7
37	West Virginia	1,009.6
40	Wisconsin	953.8
42	Wyoming	928.7

RANK ORDER

RANK	STATE	RATE
1	New Mexico	2,160.3
2	New York	2,108.2
3	Connecticut	1,966.4
4	Rhode Island	1,939.8
5	Delaware	1,821.7
6	Arkansas	1,776.9
7	Georgia	1,754.0
8	Arizona	1,686.2
9	Indiana	1,612.3
10	North Carolina	1,607.8
11	Maryland	1,591.1
12	Kentucky	1,572.9
13	Maine	1,509.1
14	Vermont	1,478.9
15	South Carolina	1,415.2
16	Louisiana	1,412.0
17	Mississippi	1,397.8
18	Ohio	1,378.5
19	Massachusetts	1,347.4
20	New Jersey	1,316.6
21	Montana	1,299.0
22	California	1,297.5
23	Tennessee	1,287.0
24	Nebraska	1,273.3
25	Alabama	1,235.6
26	Washington	1,226.7
27	Texas	1,217.0
28	Virginia	1,200.2
29	Michigan	1,186.8
30	Colorado	1,185.9
31	Florida	1,154.0
32	North Dakota	1,141.7
33	Minnesota	1,112.1
34	Pennsylvania	1,093.7
35	Missouri	1,043.0
36	Kansas	1,034.3
37	West Virginia	1,009.6
38	Oklahoma	993.3
39	Utah	955.9
40	Wisconsin	953.8
41	Alaska	933.0
42	Wyoming	928.7
43	Iowa	881.3
44	Nevada	846.7
45	South Dakota	0.0
NA	Hawaii**	NA
NA	Idaho**	NA
NA	Illinois**	NA
NA	New Hampshire**	NA
NA	Oregon**	NA
	District of Columbia**	NA

Source: CQ Press using reported data from the Federal Bureau of Investigation
"Crime in the United States 2008" (Uniform Crime Reports, September 14, 2009, http://www.fbi.gov/ucr/ucr.htm)
*Includes burglary, larceny-theft, and motor vehicle theft. National rate is only for states shown separately. Many states had incomplete reports.
**Not available.

Property Crimes Reported at Universities and Colleges as a Percent of All Property Crimes in 2008
National Percent = 0.94% of Property Crimes*

ALPHA ORDER

RANK	STATE	PERCENT
36	Alabama	0.71
13	Alaska	1.16
22	Arizona	0.95
9	Arkansas	1.22
16	California	1.11
9	Colorado	1.22
17	Connecticut	1.07
6	Delaware	1.40
43	Florida	0.51
28	Georgia	0.90
NA	Hawaii**	NA
NA	Idaho**	NA
NA	Illinois**	NA
24	Indiana	0.93
31	Iowa	0.82
32	Kansas	0.74
3	Kentucky	1.69
20	Louisiana	0.99
13	Maine	1.16
26	Maryland	0.92
2	Massachusetts	2.28
12	Michigan	1.17
44	Minnesota	0.48
35	Mississippi	0.72
37	Missouri	0.66
39	Montana	0.62
33	Nebraska	0.73
41	Nevada	0.54
NA	New Hampshire**	NA
11	New Jersey	1.18
8	New Mexico	1.30
38	New York	0.63
21	North Carolina	0.98
1	North Dakota	2.58
26	Ohio	0.92
24	Oklahoma	0.93
NA	Oregon**	NA
33	Pennsylvania	0.73
5	Rhode Island	1.55
18	South Carolina	1.05
45	South Dakota	0.00
30	Tennessee	0.89
28	Texas	0.90
7	Utah	1.33
15	Vermont	1.15
4	Virginia	1.65
42	Washington	0.52
40	West Virginia	0.58
22	Wisconsin	0.95
19	Wyoming	1.04

RANK ORDER

RANK	STATE	PERCENT
1	North Dakota	2.58
2	Massachusetts	2.28
3	Kentucky	1.69
4	Virginia	1.65
5	Rhode Island	1.55
6	Delaware	1.40
7	Utah	1.33
8	New Mexico	1.30
9	Arkansas	1.22
9	Colorado	1.22
11	New Jersey	1.18
12	Michigan	1.17
13	Alaska	1.16
13	Maine	1.16
15	Vermont	1.15
16	California	1.11
17	Connecticut	1.07
18	South Carolina	1.05
19	Wyoming	1.04
20	Louisiana	0.99
21	North Carolina	0.98
22	Arizona	0.95
22	Wisconsin	0.95
24	Indiana	0.93
24	Oklahoma	0.93
26	Maryland	0.92
26	Ohio	0.92
28	Georgia	0.90
28	Texas	0.90
30	Tennessee	0.89
31	Iowa	0.82
32	Kansas	0.74
33	Nebraska	0.73
33	Pennsylvania	0.73
35	Mississippi	0.72
36	Alabama	0.71
37	Missouri	0.66
38	New York	0.63
39	Montana	0.62
40	West Virginia	0.58
41	Nevada	0.54
42	Washington	0.52
43	Florida	0.51
44	Minnesota	0.48
45	South Dakota	0.00
NA	Hawaii**	NA
NA	Idaho**	NA
NA	Illinois**	NA
NA	New Hampshire**	NA
NA	Oregon**	NA
	District of Columbia**	NA

Source: CQ Press using reported data from the Federal Bureau of Investigation
   "Crime in the United States 2008" (Uniform Crime Reports, September 14, 2009, http://www.fbi.gov/ucr/ucr.htm)
*Includes burglary, larceny-theft, and motor vehicle theft. National percent is only for states shown separately. Many states had incomplete reports.
**Not available.

Crimes in 2004

National Total = 11,679,474 Crimes*

ALPHA ORDER

RANK	STATE	CRIMES	% of USA
21	Alabama	201,664	1.7%
46	Alaska	26,331	0.2%
12	Arizona	320,155	2.7%
28	Arkansas	124,725	1.1%
1	California	1,416,369	12.1%
22	Colorado	197,443	1.7%
33	Connecticut	104,055	0.9%
43	Delaware	32,361	0.3%
3	Florida	850,895	7.3%
7	Georgia	416,873	3.6%
38	Hawaii	63,738	0.5%
40	Idaho	42,251	0.4%
5	Illinois	472,851	4.0%
17	Indiana	232,223	2.0%
35	Iowa	94,274	0.8%
29	Kansas	120,101	1.0%
30	Kentucky	115,361	1.0%
18	Louisiana	227,997	2.0%
42	Maine	33,104	0.3%
16	Maryland	241,435	2.1%
23	Massachusetts	187,639	1.6%
9	Michigan	359,542	3.1%
25	Minnesota	168,770	1.4%
32	Mississippi	109,548	0.9%
14	Missouri	252,855	2.2%
44	Montana	29,938	0.3%
37	Nebraska	66,905	0.6%
31	Nevada	112,594	1.0%
45	New Hampshire	28,860	0.2%
15	New Jersey	242,256	2.1%
36	New Mexico	92,976	0.8%
4	New York	507,648	4.3%
8	North Carolina	393,572	3.4%
50	North Dakota	13,051	0.1%
6	Ohio	458,124	3.9%
26	Oklahoma	167,107	1.4%
24	Oregon	177,199	1.5%
10	Pennsylvania	350,609	3.0%
41	Rhode Island	33,839	0.3%
19	South Carolina	223,616	1.9%
48	South Dakota	16,204	0.1%
13	Tennessee	296,104	2.5%
2	Texas	1,132,256	9.7%
34	Utah	103,409	0.9%
49	Vermont	15,272	0.1%
20	Virginia	220,976	1.9%
11	Washington	322,167	2.8%
39	West Virginia	51,436	0.4%
27	Wisconsin	158,258	1.4%
47	Wyoming	18,052	0.2%

RANK ORDER

RANK	STATE	CRIMES	% of USA
1	California	1,416,369	12.1%
2	Texas	1,132,256	9.7%
3	Florida	850,895	7.3%
4	New York	507,648	4.3%
5	Illinois	472,851	4.0%
6	Ohio	458,124	3.9%
7	Georgia	416,873	3.6%
8	North Carolina	393,572	3.4%
9	Michigan	359,542	3.1%
10	Pennsylvania	350,609	3.0%
11	Washington	322,167	2.8%
12	Arizona	320,155	2.7%
13	Tennessee	296,104	2.5%
14	Missouri	252,855	2.2%
15	New Jersey	242,256	2.1%
16	Maryland	241,435	2.1%
17	Indiana	232,223	2.0%
18	Louisiana	227,997	2.0%
19	South Carolina	223,616	1.9%
20	Virginia	220,976	1.9%
21	Alabama	201,664	1.7%
22	Colorado	197,443	1.7%
23	Massachusetts	187,639	1.6%
24	Oregon	177,199	1.5%
25	Minnesota	168,770	1.4%
26	Oklahoma	167,107	1.4%
27	Wisconsin	158,258	1.4%
28	Arkansas	124,725	1.1%
29	Kansas	120,101	1.0%
30	Kentucky	115,361	1.0%
31	Nevada	112,594	1.0%
32	Mississippi	109,548	0.9%
33	Connecticut	104,055	0.9%
34	Utah	103,409	0.9%
35	Iowa	94,274	0.8%
36	New Mexico	92,976	0.8%
37	Nebraska	66,905	0.6%
38	Hawaii	63,738	0.5%
39	West Virginia	51,436	0.4%
40	Idaho	42,251	0.4%
41	Rhode Island	33,839	0.3%
42	Maine	33,104	0.3%
43	Delaware	32,361	0.3%
44	Montana	29,938	0.3%
45	New Hampshire	28,860	0.2%
46	Alaska	26,331	0.2%
47	Wyoming	18,052	0.2%
48	South Dakota	16,204	0.1%
49	Vermont	15,272	0.1%
50	North Dakota	13,051	0.1%
	District of Columbia	34,486	0.3%

Source: CQ Press using reported data from the Federal Bureau of Investigation
"Crime in the United States 2005" (Uniform Crime Reports, September 2006, http://www.fbi.gov/ucr/ucr.htm)
*Revised figures. Includes murder, rape, robbery, aggravated assault, burglary, larceny-theft, and motor vehicle theft.

Percent Change in Number of Crimes: 2004 to 2008

National Percent Change = 4.5% Decrease*

RANK	STATE	PERCENT CHANGE
6	Alabama	4.9
33	Alaska	(6.6)
26	Arizona	(3.8)
17	Arkansas	(0.7)
38	California	(10.6)
48	Colorado	(20.1)
34	Connecticut	(7.2)
1	Delaware	15.7
8	Florida	4.0
7	Georgia	4.4
49	Hawaii	(22.3)
46	Idaho	(16.0)
30	Illinois	(5.6)
12	Indiana	0.8
44	Iowa	(13.9)
39	Kansas	(11.6)
4	Kentucky	6.6
41	Louisiana	(13.3)
10	Maine	2.2
22	Maryland	(3.3)
18	Massachusetts	(1.3)
28	Michigan	(4.4)
24	Minnesota	(3.7)
42	Mississippi	(13.5)
20	Missouri	(2.6)
35	Montana	(7.5)
45	Nebraska	(15.2)
24	Nevada	(3.7)
9	New Hampshire	2.5
32	New Jersey	(6.1)
21	New Mexico	(2.7)
36	New York	(8.2)
5	North Carolina	5.7
11	North Dakota	1.3
31	Ohio	(5.7)
42	Oklahoma	(13.5)
50	Oregon	(24.3)
14	Pennsylvania	0.1
27	Rhode Island	(4.0)
16	South Carolina	(0.6)
37	South Dakota	(8.3)
15	Tennessee	0.0
23	Texas	(3.5)
29	Utah	(5.3)
2	Vermont	8.8
19	Virginia	(2.5)
47	Washington	(16.9)
13	West Virginia	0.3
3	Wisconsin	7.8
40	Wyoming	(13.0)

RANK	STATE	PERCENT CHANGE
1	Delaware	15.7
2	Vermont	8.8
3	Wisconsin	7.8
4	Kentucky	6.6
5	North Carolina	5.7
6	Alabama	4.9
7	Georgia	4.4
8	Florida	4.0
9	New Hampshire	2.5
10	Maine	2.2
11	North Dakota	1.3
12	Indiana	0.8
13	West Virginia	0.3
14	Pennsylvania	0.1
15	Tennessee	0.0
16	South Carolina	(0.6)
17	Arkansas	(0.7)
18	Massachusetts	(1.3)
19	Virginia	(2.5)
20	Missouri	(2.6)
21	New Mexico	(2.7)
22	Maryland	(3.3)
23	Texas	(3.5)
24	Minnesota	(3.7)
24	Nevada	(3.7)
26	Arizona	(3.8)
27	Rhode Island	(4.0)
28	Michigan	(4.4)
29	Utah	(5.3)
30	Illinois	(5.6)
31	Ohio	(5.7)
32	New Jersey	(6.1)
33	Alaska	(6.6)
34	Connecticut	(7.2)
35	Montana	(7.5)
36	New York	(8.2)
37	South Dakota	(8.3)
38	California	(10.6)
39	Kansas	(11.6)
40	Wyoming	(13.0)
41	Louisiana	(13.3)
42	Mississippi	(13.5)
42	Oklahoma	(13.5)
44	Iowa	(13.9)
45	Nebraska	(15.2)
46	Idaho	(16.0)
47	Washington	(16.9)
48	Colorado	(20.1)
49	Hawaii	(22.3)
50	Oregon	(24.3)

District of Columbia 12.3

Source: CQ Press using reported data from the Federal Bureau of Investigation
"Crime in the United States 2005" (Uniform Crime Reports, September 2006, http://www.fbi.gov/ucr/ucr.htm)
*Revised figures. Includes murder, rape, robbery, aggravated assault, burglary, larceny-theft, and motor vehicle theft.

Crime Rate in 2004

National Rate = 3,977.3 Crimes per 100,000 Population*

<table>
<tr><td colspan="3">ALPHA ORDER</td><td colspan="3">RANK ORDER</td></tr>
<tr><td>RANK</td><td>STATE</td><td>RATE</td><td>RANK</td><td>STATE</td><td>RATE</td></tr>
<tr><td>16</td><td>Alabama</td><td>4,456.3</td><td>1</td><td>Arizona</td><td>5,577.7</td></tr>
<tr><td>22</td><td>Alaska</td><td>4,003.2</td><td>2</td><td>South Carolina</td><td>5,326.8</td></tr>
<tr><td>1</td><td>Arizona</td><td>5,577.7</td><td>3</td><td>Washington</td><td>5,190.3</td></tr>
<tr><td>15</td><td>Arkansas</td><td>4,535.4</td><td>4</td><td>Louisiana</td><td>5,059.1</td></tr>
<tr><td>24</td><td>California</td><td>3,951.7</td><td>5</td><td>Hawaii</td><td>5,050.1</td></tr>
<tr><td>20</td><td>Colorado</td><td>4,290.5</td><td>6</td><td>Texas</td><td>5,038.6</td></tr>
<tr><td>37</td><td>Connecticut</td><td>2,973.9</td><td>7</td><td>Tennessee</td><td>5,024.4</td></tr>
<tr><td>25</td><td>Delaware</td><td>3,898.6</td><td>8</td><td>Oregon</td><td>4,934.0</td></tr>
<tr><td>9</td><td>Florida</td><td>4,894.3</td><td>9</td><td>Florida</td><td>4,894.3</td></tr>
<tr><td>13</td><td>Georgia</td><td>4,674.5</td><td>10</td><td>New Mexico</td><td>4,885.8</td></tr>
<tr><td>5</td><td>Hawaii</td><td>5,050.1</td><td>11</td><td>Nevada</td><td>4,826.4</td></tr>
<tr><td>36</td><td>Idaho</td><td>3,028.4</td><td>12</td><td>Oklahoma</td><td>4,742.6</td></tr>
<tr><td>29</td><td>Illinois</td><td>3,719.8</td><td>13</td><td>Georgia</td><td>4,674.5</td></tr>
<tr><td>28</td><td>Indiana</td><td>3,729.5</td><td>14</td><td>North Carolina</td><td>4,608.3</td></tr>
<tr><td>34</td><td>Iowa</td><td>3,192.6</td><td>15</td><td>Arkansas</td><td>4,535.4</td></tr>
<tr><td>17</td><td>Kansas</td><td>4,393.4</td><td>16</td><td>Alabama</td><td>4,456.3</td></tr>
<tr><td>44</td><td>Kentucky</td><td>2,785.3</td><td>17</td><td>Kansas</td><td>4,393.4</td></tr>
<tr><td>4</td><td>Louisiana</td><td>5,059.1</td><td>18</td><td>Missouri</td><td>4,390.2</td></tr>
<tr><td>46</td><td>Maine</td><td>2,517.4</td><td>19</td><td>Maryland</td><td>4,341.3</td></tr>
<tr><td>19</td><td>Maryland</td><td>4,341.3</td><td>20</td><td>Colorado</td><td>4,290.5</td></tr>
<tr><td>39</td><td>Massachusetts</td><td>2,928.4</td><td>21</td><td>Utah</td><td>4,271.9</td></tr>
<tr><td>31</td><td>Michigan</td><td>3,558.3</td><td>22</td><td>Alaska</td><td>4,003.2</td></tr>
<tr><td>32</td><td>Minnesota</td><td>3,311.4</td><td>23</td><td>Ohio</td><td>4,001.0</td></tr>
<tr><td>27</td><td>Mississippi</td><td>3,776.5</td><td>24</td><td>California</td><td>3,951.7</td></tr>
<tr><td>18</td><td>Missouri</td><td>4,390.2</td><td>25</td><td>Delaware</td><td>3,898.6</td></tr>
<tr><td>33</td><td>Montana</td><td>3,229.9</td><td>26</td><td>Nebraska</td><td>3,828.2</td></tr>
<tr><td>26</td><td>Nebraska</td><td>3,828.2</td><td>27</td><td>Mississippi</td><td>3,776.5</td></tr>
<tr><td>11</td><td>Nevada</td><td>4,826.4</td><td>28</td><td>Indiana</td><td>3,729.5</td></tr>
<tr><td>48</td><td>New Hampshire</td><td>2,221.4</td><td>29</td><td>Illinois</td><td>3,719.8</td></tr>
<tr><td>43</td><td>New Jersey</td><td>2,789.3</td><td>30</td><td>Wyoming</td><td>3,568.4</td></tr>
<tr><td>10</td><td>New Mexico</td><td>4,885.8</td><td>31</td><td>Michigan</td><td>3,558.3</td></tr>
<tr><td>45</td><td>New York</td><td>2,632.9</td><td>32</td><td>Minnesota</td><td>3,311.4</td></tr>
<tr><td>14</td><td>North Carolina</td><td>4,608.3</td><td>33</td><td>Montana</td><td>3,229.9</td></tr>
<tr><td>50</td><td>North Dakota</td><td>2,051.1</td><td>34</td><td>Iowa</td><td>3,192.6</td></tr>
<tr><td>23</td><td>Ohio</td><td>4,001.0</td><td>35</td><td>Rhode Island</td><td>3,133.5</td></tr>
<tr><td>12</td><td>Oklahoma</td><td>4,742.6</td><td>36</td><td>Idaho</td><td>3,028.4</td></tr>
<tr><td>8</td><td>Oregon</td><td>4,934.0</td><td>37</td><td>Connecticut</td><td>2,973.9</td></tr>
<tr><td>42</td><td>Pennsylvania</td><td>2,828.8</td><td>38</td><td>Virginia</td><td>2,953.7</td></tr>
<tr><td>35</td><td>Rhode Island</td><td>3,133.5</td><td>39</td><td>Massachusetts</td><td>2,928.4</td></tr>
<tr><td>2</td><td>South Carolina</td><td>5,326.8</td><td>40</td><td>Wisconsin</td><td>2,875.5</td></tr>
<tr><td>49</td><td>South Dakota</td><td>2,102.8</td><td>41</td><td>West Virginia</td><td>2,837.7</td></tr>
<tr><td>7</td><td>Tennessee</td><td>5,024.4</td><td>42</td><td>Pennsylvania</td><td>2,828.8</td></tr>
<tr><td>6</td><td>Texas</td><td>5,038.6</td><td>43</td><td>New Jersey</td><td>2,789.3</td></tr>
<tr><td>21</td><td>Utah</td><td>4,271.9</td><td>44</td><td>Kentucky</td><td>2,785.3</td></tr>
<tr><td>47</td><td>Vermont</td><td>2,458.4</td><td>45</td><td>New York</td><td>2,632.9</td></tr>
<tr><td>38</td><td>Virginia</td><td>2,953.7</td><td>46</td><td>Maine</td><td>2,517.4</td></tr>
<tr><td>3</td><td>Washington</td><td>5,190.3</td><td>47</td><td>Vermont</td><td>2,458.4</td></tr>
<tr><td>41</td><td>West Virginia</td><td>2,837.7</td><td>48</td><td>New Hampshire</td><td>2,221.4</td></tr>
<tr><td>40</td><td>Wisconsin</td><td>2,875.5</td><td>49</td><td>South Dakota</td><td>2,102.8</td></tr>
<tr><td>30</td><td>Wyoming</td><td>3,568.4</td><td>50</td><td>North Dakota</td><td>2,051.1</td></tr>
<tr><td></td><td></td><td></td><td></td><td>District of Columbia</td><td>6,222.2</td></tr>
</table>

Source: CQ Press using reported data from the Federal Bureau of Investigation
   "Crime in the United States 2005" (Uniform Crime Reports, September 2006, http://www.fbi.gov/ucr/ucr.htm)
*Revised figures. Includes murder, rape, robbery, aggravated assault, burglary, larceny-theft, and motor vehicle theft.

Percent Change in Crime Rate: 2004 to 2008

National Percent Change = 7.8% Decrease*

ALPHA ORDER

RANK	STATE	PERCENT CHANGE
6	Alabama	1.8
31	Alaska	(10.5)
40	Arizona	(15.1)
18	Arkansas	(4.3)
36	California	(12.8)
49	Colorado	(25.6)
29	Connecticut	(7.3)
1	Delaware	10.0
11	Florida	(1.3)
17	Georgia	(3.9)
48	Hawaii	(23.9)
47	Idaho	(23.1)
28	Illinois	(7.0)
13	Indiana	(1.6)
41	Iowa	(15.3)
38	Kansas	(13.8)
4	Kentucky	3.4
34	Louisiana	(11.5)
5	Maine	2.1
19	Maryland	(4.5)
15	Massachusetts	(2.7)
16	Michigan	(3.4)
22	Minnesota	(6.0)
39	Mississippi	(14.6)
20	Missouri	(5.1)
33	Montana	(11.4)
44	Nebraska	(16.9)
37	Nevada	(13.6)
7	New Hampshire	1.2
24	New Jersey	(6.1)
26	New Mexico	(6.7)
30	New York	(9.2)
14	North Carolina	(2.1)
8	North Dakota	0.5
22	Ohio	(6.0)
43	Oklahoma	(16.3)
50	Oregon	(28.3)
10	Pennsylvania	(0.3)
12	Rhode Island	(1.4)
27	South Carolina	(6.8)
35	South Dakota	(12.2)
21	Tennessee	(5.2)
32	Texas	(10.8)
42	Utah	(16.2)
2	Vermont	8.8
24	Virginia	(6.1)
46	Washington	(21.2)
9	West Virginia	0.2
3	Wisconsin	5.4
45	Wyoming	(17.3)

RANK ORDER

RANK	STATE	PERCENT CHANGE
1	Delaware	10.0
2	Vermont	8.8
3	Wisconsin	5.4
4	Kentucky	3.4
5	Maine	2.1
6	Alabama	1.8
7	New Hampshire	1.2
8	North Dakota	0.5
9	West Virginia	0.2
10	Pennsylvania	(0.3)
11	Florida	(1.3)
12	Rhode Island	(1.4)
13	Indiana	(1.6)
14	North Carolina	(2.1)
15	Massachusetts	(2.7)
16	Michigan	(3.4)
17	Georgia	(3.9)
18	Arkansas	(4.3)
19	Maryland	(4.5)
20	Missouri	(5.1)
21	Tennessee	(5.2)
22	Minnesota	(6.0)
22	Ohio	(6.0)
24	New Jersey	(6.1)
24	Virginia	(6.1)
26	New Mexico	(6.7)
27	South Carolina	(6.8)
28	Illinois	(7.0)
29	Connecticut	(7.3)
30	New York	(9.2)
31	Alaska	(10.5)
32	Texas	(10.8)
33	Montana	(11.4)
34	Louisiana	(11.5)
35	South Dakota	(12.2)
36	California	(12.8)
37	Nevada	(13.6)
38	Kansas	(13.8)
39	Mississippi	(14.6)
40	Arizona	(15.1)
41	Iowa	(15.3)
42	Utah	(16.2)
43	Oklahoma	(16.3)
44	Nebraska	(16.9)
45	Wyoming	(17.3)
46	Washington	(21.2)
47	Idaho	(23.1)
48	Hawaii	(23.9)
49	Colorado	(25.6)
50	Oregon	(28.3)

District of Columbia 5.1

Source: CQ Press using reported data from the Federal Bureau of Investigation
"Crime in the United States 2005" (Uniform Crime Reports, September 2006, http://www.fbi.gov/ucr/ucr.htm)
*Revised figures. Includes murder, rape, robbery, aggravated assault, burglary, larceny-theft, and motor vehicle theft.

Violent Crimes in 2004

National Total = 1,360,088 Violent Crimes*

ALPHA ORDER

RANK	STATE	CRIMES	% of USA
22	Alabama	19,324	1.4%
40	Alaska	4,159	0.3%
16	Arizona	28,952	2.1%
26	Arkansas	13,814	1.0%
1	California	189,175	13.9%
24	Colorado	17,121	1.3%
33	Connecticut	10,113	0.7%
39	Delaware	5,105	0.4%
2	Florida	123,754	9.1%
9	Georgia	40,217	3.0%
42	Hawaii	3,213	0.2%
41	Idaho	3,452	0.3%
5	Illinois	69,365	5.1%
21	Indiana	20,294	1.5%
35	Iowa	8,499	0.6%
31	Kansas	10,330	0.8%
32	Kentucky	10,152	0.7%
17	Louisiana	28,844	2.1%
46	Maine	1,364	0.1%
10	Maryland	38,961	2.9%
15	Massachusetts	29,489	2.2%
7	Michigan	49,737	3.7%
27	Minnesota	13,751	1.0%
34	Mississippi	8,568	0.6%
18	Missouri	28,226	2.1%
43	Montana	2,723	0.2%
37	Nebraska	5,393	0.4%
25	Nevada	14,379	1.1%
45	New Hampshire	2,202	0.2%
14	New Jersey	30,943	2.3%
28	New Mexico	13,081	1.0%
4	New York	84,914	6.2%
12	North Carolina	38,244	2.8%
50	North Dakota	558	0.0%
11	Ohio	38,787	2.9%
23	Oklahoma	17,635	1.3%
30	Oregon	10,724	0.8%
6	Pennsylvania	50,998	3.7%
44	Rhode Island	2,673	0.2%
13	South Carolina	33,160	2.4%
47	South Dakota	1,319	0.1%
8	Tennessee	41,113	3.0%
3	Texas	121,554	8.9%
36	Utah	5,647	0.4%
49	Vermont	713	0.1%
20	Virginia	20,608	1.5%
19	Washington	21,330	1.6%
38	West Virginia	5,110	0.4%
29	Wisconsin	11,548	0.8%
48	Wyoming	1,163	0.1%

RANK ORDER

RANK	STATE	CRIMES	% of USA
1	California	189,175	13.9%
2	Florida	123,754	9.1%
3	Texas	121,554	8.9%
4	New York	84,914	6.2%
5	Illinois	69,365	5.1%
6	Pennsylvania	50,998	3.7%
7	Michigan	49,737	3.7%
8	Tennessee	41,113	3.0%
9	Georgia	40,217	3.0%
10	Maryland	38,961	2.9%
11	Ohio	38,787	2.9%
12	North Carolina	38,244	2.8%
13	South Carolina	33,160	2.4%
14	New Jersey	30,943	2.3%
15	Massachusetts	29,489	2.2%
16	Arizona	28,952	2.1%
17	Louisiana	28,844	2.1%
18	Missouri	28,226	2.1%
19	Washington	21,330	1.6%
20	Virginia	20,608	1.5%
21	Indiana	20,294	1.5%
22	Alabama	19,324	1.4%
23	Oklahoma	17,635	1.3%
24	Colorado	17,121	1.3%
25	Nevada	14,379	1.1%
26	Arkansas	13,814	1.0%
27	Minnesota	13,751	1.0%
28	New Mexico	13,081	1.0%
29	Wisconsin	11,548	0.8%
30	Oregon	10,724	0.8%
31	Kansas	10,330	0.8%
32	Kentucky	10,152	0.7%
33	Connecticut	10,113	0.7%
34	Mississippi	8,568	0.6%
35	Iowa	8,499	0.6%
36	Utah	5,647	0.4%
37	Nebraska	5,393	0.4%
38	West Virginia	5,110	0.4%
39	Delaware	5,105	0.4%
40	Alaska	4,159	0.3%
41	Idaho	3,452	0.3%
42	Hawaii	3,213	0.2%
43	Montana	2,723	0.2%
44	Rhode Island	2,673	0.2%
45	New Hampshire	2,202	0.2%
46	Maine	1,364	0.1%
47	South Dakota	1,319	0.1%
48	Wyoming	1,163	0.1%
49	Vermont	713	0.1%
50	North Dakota	558	0.0%
	District of Columbia	7,590	0.6%

Source: Reported data from the Federal Bureau of Investigation
"Crime in the United States 2005" (Uniform Crime Reports, September 2006, http://www.fbi.gov/ucr/ucr.htm)
*Revised figures. Violent crimes are offenses of murder, forcible rape, robbery, and aggravated assault.

Percent Change in Number of Violent Crimes: 2004 to 2008

National Percent Change = 1.6% Increase*

ALPHA ORDER

RANK	STATE	PERCENT CHANGE
13	Alabama	9.2
16	Alaska	7.6
29	Arizona	0.4
21	Arkansas	4.1
40	California	(2.1)
35	Colorado	(1.0)
22	Connecticut	3.1
6	Delaware	20.3
24	Florida	2.0
8	Georgia	15.3
12	Hawaii	9.3
27	Idaho	0.9
41	Illinois	(2.3)
20	Indiana	4.9
32	Iowa	0.2
11	Kansas	11.4
4	Kentucky	24.6
31	Louisiana	0.3
9	Maine	13.4
50	Maryland	(9.2)
36	Massachusetts	(1.1)
27	Michigan	0.9
34	Minnesota	(0.2)
41	Mississippi	(2.3)
19	Missouri	5.6
46	Montana	(8.3)
29	Nebraska	0.4
3	Nevada	31.0
45	New Hampshire	(6.0)
47	New Jersey	(8.4)
37	New Mexico	(1.4)
48	New York	(8.6)
10	North Carolina	12.7
1	North Dakota	91.4
22	Ohio	3.1
15	Oklahoma	8.8
49	Oregon	(9.1)
33	Pennsylvania	0.1
39	Rhode Island	(1.9)
37	South Carolina	(1.4)
5	South Dakota	22.8
13	Tennessee	9.2
25	Texas	1.7
17	Utah	7.5
7	Vermont	18.4
44	Virginia	(3.5)
25	Washington	1.7
43	West Virginia	(2.8)
2	Wisconsin	33.5
18	Wyoming	6.3

RANK ORDER

RANK	STATE	PERCENT CHANGE
1	North Dakota	91.4
2	Wisconsin	33.5
3	Nevada	31.0
4	Kentucky	24.6
5	South Dakota	22.8
6	Delaware	20.3
7	Vermont	18.4
8	Georgia	15.3
9	Maine	13.4
10	North Carolina	12.7
11	Kansas	11.4
12	Hawaii	9.3
13	Alabama	9.2
13	Tennessee	9.2
15	Oklahoma	8.8
16	Alaska	7.6
17	Utah	7.5
18	Wyoming	6.3
19	Missouri	5.6
20	Indiana	4.9
21	Arkansas	4.1
22	Connecticut	3.1
22	Ohio	3.1
24	Florida	2.0
25	Texas	1.7
25	Washington	1.7
27	Idaho	0.9
27	Michigan	0.9
29	Arizona	0.4
29	Nebraska	0.4
31	Louisiana	0.3
32	Iowa	0.2
33	Pennsylvania	0.1
34	Minnesota	(0.2)
35	Colorado	(1.0)
36	Massachusetts	(1.1)
37	New Mexico	(1.4)
37	South Carolina	(1.4)
39	Rhode Island	(1.9)
40	California	(2.1)
41	Illinois	(2.3)
41	Mississippi	(2.3)
43	West Virginia	(2.8)
44	Virginia	(3.5)
45	New Hampshire	(6.0)
46	Montana	(8.3)
47	New Jersey	(8.4)
48	New York	(8.6)
49	Oregon	(9.1)
50	Maryland	(9.2)

District of Columbia   12.1

Source: CQ Press using reported data from the Federal Bureau of Investigation
"Crime in the United States 2005" (Uniform Crime Reports, September 2006, http://www.fbi.gov/ucr/ucr.htm)
*Revised figures. Violent crimes are offenses of murder, forcible rape, robbery, and aggravated assault.

Violent Crime Rate in 2004

National Rate = 463.2 Violent Crimes per 100,000 Population*

RANK	STATE (ALPHA ORDER)	RATE		RANK	STATE (RANK ORDER)	RATE
22	Alabama	427.0		1	South Carolina	789.9
7	Alaska	632.3		2	Florida	711.8
13	Arizona	504.4		3	Maryland	700.6
14	Arkansas	502.3		4	Tennessee	697.6
12	California	527.8		5	New Mexico	687.4
25	Colorado	372.0		6	Louisiana	640.0
34	Connecticut	289.0		7	Alaska	632.3
9	Delaware	615.0		8	Nevada	616.4
2	Florida	711.8		9	Delaware	615.0
19	Georgia	451.0		10	Illinois	545.7
39	Hawaii	254.6		11	Texas	540.9
41	Idaho	247.4		12	California	527.8
10	Illinois	545.7		13	Arizona	504.4
29	Indiana	325.9		14	Arkansas	502.3
35	Iowa	287.8		15	Oklahoma	500.5
24	Kansas	377.9		16	Michigan	492.2
42	Kentucky	245.1		17	Missouri	490.1
6	Louisiana	640.0		18	Massachusetts	460.2
49	Maine	103.7		19	Georgia	451.0
3	Maryland	700.6		20	North Carolina	447.8
18	Massachusetts	460.2		21	New York	440.4
16	Michigan	492.2		22	Alabama	427.0
38	Minnesota	269.8		23	Pennsylvania	411.5
32	Mississippi	295.4		24	Kansas	377.9
17	Missouri	490.1		25	Colorado	372.0
33	Montana	293.8		26	New Jersey	356.3
30	Nebraska	308.6		27	Washington	343.6
8	Nevada	616.4		28	Ohio	338.7
47	New Hampshire	169.5		29	Indiana	325.9
26	New Jersey	356.3		30	Nebraska	308.6
5	New Mexico	687.4		31	Oregon	298.6
21	New York	440.4		32	Mississippi	295.4
20	North Carolina	447.8		33	Montana	293.8
50	North Dakota	87.7		34	Connecticut	289.0
28	Ohio	338.7		35	Iowa	287.8
15	Oklahoma	500.5		36	West Virginia	281.9
31	Oregon	298.6		37	Virginia	275.5
23	Pennsylvania	411.5		38	Minnesota	269.8
40	Rhode Island	247.5		39	Hawaii	254.6
1	South Carolina	789.9		40	Rhode Island	247.5
46	South Dakota	171.2		41	Idaho	247.4
4	Tennessee	697.6		42	Kentucky	245.1
11	Texas	540.9		43	Utah	233.3
43	Utah	233.3		44	Wyoming	229.9
48	Vermont	114.8		45	Wisconsin	209.8
37	Virginia	275.5		46	South Dakota	171.2
27	Washington	343.6		47	New Hampshire	169.5
36	West Virginia	281.9		48	Vermont	114.8
45	Wisconsin	209.8		49	Maine	103.7
44	Wyoming	229.9		50	North Dakota	87.7
					District of Columbia	1,369.4

Source: Reported data from the Federal Bureau of Investigation
"Crime in the United States 2005" (Uniform Crime Reports, September 2006, http://www.fbi.gov/ucr/ucr.htm)
*Revised figures. Violent crimes are offenses of murder, forcible rape, robbery, and aggravated assault.

Percent Change in Violent Crime Rate: 2004 to 2008

National Percent Change = 1.9% Decrease*

ALPHA ORDER

RANK	STATE	PERCENT CHANGE
12	Alabama	6.0
16	Alaska	3.1
48	Arizona	(11.4)
25	Arkansas	0.2
36	California	(4.5)
44	Colorado	(7.8)
17	Connecticut	3.0
7	Delaware	14.4
32	Florida	(3.2)
11	Georgia	6.2
10	Hawaii	7.1
42	Idaho	(7.6)
35	Illinois	(3.7)
21	Indiana	2.4
27	Iowa	(1.4)
9	Kansas	8.7
3	Kentucky	20.8
20	Louisiana	2.5
8	Maine	13.3
47	Maryland	(10.3)
29	Massachusetts	(2.4)
22	Michigan	1.9
30	Minnesota	(2.6)
33	Mississippi	(3.6)
18	Missouri	2.9
49	Montana	(12.2)
28	Nebraska	(1.6)
6	Nevada	17.5
41	New Hampshire	(7.3)
45	New Jersey	(8.4)
38	New Mexico	(5.5)
46	New York	(9.6)
14	North Carolina	4.4
1	North Dakota	89.9
19	Ohio	2.8
13	Oklahoma	5.2
50	Oregon	(13.9)
26	Pennsylvania	(0.4)
24	Rhode Island	0.8
42	South Carolina	(7.6)
5	South Dakota	17.6
15	Tennessee	3.6
39	Texas	(6.1)
37	Utah	(4.9)
4	Vermont	18.4
40	Virginia	(7.1)
33	Washington	(3.6)
31	West Virginia	(2.9)
2	Wisconsin	30.6
23	Wyoming	0.9

RANK ORDER

RANK	STATE	PERCENT CHANGE
1	North Dakota	89.9
2	Wisconsin	30.6
3	Kentucky	20.8
4	Vermont	18.4
5	South Dakota	17.6
6	Nevada	17.5
7	Delaware	14.4
8	Maine	13.3
9	Kansas	8.7
10	Hawaii	7.1
11	Georgia	6.2
12	Alabama	6.0
13	Oklahoma	5.2
14	North Carolina	4.4
15	Tennessee	3.6
16	Alaska	3.1
17	Connecticut	3.0
18	Missouri	2.9
19	Ohio	2.8
20	Louisiana	2.5
21	Indiana	2.4
22	Michigan	1.9
23	Wyoming	0.9
24	Rhode Island	0.8
25	Arkansas	0.2
26	Pennsylvania	(0.4)
27	Iowa	(1.4)
28	Nebraska	(1.6)
29	Massachusetts	(2.4)
30	Minnesota	(2.6)
31	West Virginia	(2.9)
32	Florida	(3.2)
33	Mississippi	(3.6)
33	Washington	(3.6)
35	Illinois	(3.7)
36	California	(4.5)
37	Utah	(4.9)
38	New Mexico	(5.5)
39	Texas	(6.1)
40	Virginia	(7.1)
41	New Hampshire	(7.3)
42	Idaho	(7.6)
42	South Carolina	(7.6)
44	Colorado	(7.8)
45	New Jersey	(8.4)
46	New York	(9.6)
47	Maryland	(10.3)
48	Arizona	(11.4)
49	Montana	(12.2)
50	Oregon	(13.9)

District of Columbia	5.0

Source: CQ Press using reported data from the Federal Bureau of Investigation
  "Crime in the United States 2005" (Uniform Crime Reports, September 2006, http://www.fbi.gov/ucr/ucr.htm)
*Revised figures. Violent crimes are offenses of murder, forcible rape, robbery, and aggravated assault.

Murders in 2004

National Total = 16,148 Murders*

ALPHA ORDER

RANK	STATE	MURDERS	% of USA
20	Alabama	254	1.6%
39	Alaska	37	0.2%
13	Arizona	414	2.6%
26	Arkansas	176	1.1%
1	California	2,392	14.8%
23	Colorado	201	1.2%
33	Connecticut	100	0.6%
43	Delaware	28	0.2%
3	Florida	946	5.9%
8	Georgia	613	3.8%
40	Hawaii	33	0.2%
41	Idaho	31	0.2%
5	Illinois	780	4.8%
18	Indiana	316	2.0%
37	Iowa	44	0.3%
31	Kansas	122	0.8%
21	Kentucky	236	1.5%
9	Louisiana	574	3.6%
45	Maine	18	0.1%
11	Maryland	521	3.2%
28	Massachusetts	171	1.1%
7	Michigan	643	4.0%
32	Minnesota	113	0.7%
22	Mississippi	227	1.4%
17	Missouri	354	2.2%
42	Montana	30	0.2%
38	Nebraska	40	0.2%
27	Nevada	172	1.1%
46	New Hampshire	17	0.1%
14	New Jersey	392	2.4%
29	New Mexico	169	1.0%
4	New York	889	5.5%
10	North Carolina	532	3.3%
50	North Dakota	8	0.0%
12	Ohio	506	3.1%
25	Oklahoma	186	1.2%
34	Oregon	90	0.6%
6	Pennsylvania	650	4.0%
44	Rhode Island	26	0.2%
19	South Carolina	286	1.8%
46	South Dakota	17	0.1%
16	Tennessee	357	2.2%
2	Texas	1,364	8.4%
36	Utah	46	0.3%
48	Vermont	16	0.1%
15	Virginia	390	2.4%
24	Washington	190	1.2%
35	West Virginia	68	0.4%
30	Wisconsin	154	1.0%
49	Wyoming	11	0.1%

RANK ORDER

RANK	STATE	MURDERS	% of USA
1	California	2,392	14.8%
2	Texas	1,364	8.4%
3	Florida	946	5.9%
4	New York	889	5.5%
5	Illinois	780	4.8%
6	Pennsylvania	650	4.0%
7	Michigan	643	4.0%
8	Georgia	613	3.8%
9	Louisiana	574	3.6%
10	North Carolina	532	3.3%
11	Maryland	521	3.2%
12	Ohio	506	3.1%
13	Arizona	414	2.6%
14	New Jersey	392	2.4%
15	Virginia	390	2.4%
16	Tennessee	357	2.2%
17	Missouri	354	2.2%
18	Indiana	316	2.0%
19	South Carolina	286	1.8%
20	Alabama	254	1.6%
21	Kentucky	236	1.5%
22	Mississippi	227	1.4%
23	Colorado	201	1.2%
24	Washington	190	1.2%
25	Oklahoma	186	1.2%
26	Arkansas	176	1.1%
27	Nevada	172	1.1%
28	Massachusetts	171	1.1%
29	New Mexico	169	1.0%
30	Wisconsin	154	1.0%
31	Kansas	122	0.8%
32	Minnesota	113	0.7%
33	Connecticut	100	0.6%
34	Oregon	90	0.6%
35	West Virginia	68	0.4%
36	Utah	46	0.3%
37	Iowa	44	0.3%
38	Nebraska	40	0.2%
39	Alaska	37	0.2%
40	Hawaii	33	0.2%
41	Idaho	31	0.2%
42	Montana	30	0.2%
43	Delaware	28	0.2%
44	Rhode Island	26	0.2%
45	Maine	18	0.1%
46	New Hampshire	17	0.1%
46	South Dakota	17	0.1%
48	Vermont	16	0.1%
49	Wyoming	11	0.1%
50	North Dakota	8	0.0%
	District of Columbia	198	1.2%

Source: Reported data from the Federal Bureau of Investigation
   "Crime in the United States 2005" (Uniform Crime Reports, September 2006, http://www.fbi.gov/ucr/ucr.htm)
*Revised figures. Includes nonnegligent manslaughter.

Percent Change in Number of Murders: 2004 to 2008

National Percent Change = 0.8% Increase*

ALPHA ORDER				RANK ORDER		
RANK	STATE	PERCENT CHANGE		RANK	STATE	PERCENT CHANGE
6	Alabama	39.0		1	Delaware	103.6
48	Alaska	(24.3)		2	Iowa	72.7
24	Arizona	(1.7)		3	Maine	72.2
34	Arkansas	(8.0)		4	Nebraska	70.0
38	California	(10.5)		5	South Dakota	52.9
44	Colorado	(21.9)		6	Alabama	39.0
9	Connecticut	23.0		7	Missouri	28.5
1	Delaware	103.6		8	Florida	23.5
8	Florida	23.5		9	Connecticut	23.0
19	Georgia	3.8		10	Tennessee	14.3
47	Hawaii	(24.2)		11	Oklahoma	14.0
49	Idaho	(25.8)		12	North Carolina	13.5
21	Illinois	1.3		13	Rhode Island	11.5
20	Indiana	3.5		14	Pennsylvania	7.8
2	Iowa	72.7		15	Ohio	7.3
33	Kansas	(7.4)		16	South Carolina	6.6
43	Kentucky	(16.1)		17	Vermont	6.3
35	Louisiana	(8.2)		18	Mississippi	4.4
3	Maine	72.2		19	Georgia	3.8
30	Maryland	(5.4)		20	Indiana	3.5
25	Massachusetts	(2.3)		21	Illinois	1.3
41	Michigan	(15.7)		22	Washington	1.1
26	Minnesota	(3.5)		23	Texas	0.7
18	Mississippi	4.4		24	Arizona	(1.7)
7	Missouri	28.5		25	Massachusetts	(2.3)
45	Montana	(23.3)		26	Minnesota	(3.5)
4	Nebraska	70.0		27	New Jersey	(4.1)
28	Nevada	(5.2)		28	Nevada	(5.2)
46	New Hampshire	(23.5)		28	Wisconsin	(5.2)
27	New Jersey	(4.1)		30	Maryland	(5.4)
42	New Mexico	(16.0)		31	Virginia	(5.6)
32	New York	(6.0)		32	New York	(6.0)
12	North Carolina	13.5		33	Kansas	(7.4)
50	North Dakota	(62.5)		34	Arkansas	(8.0)
15	Ohio	7.3		35	Louisiana	(8.2)
11	Oklahoma	14.0		36	Oregon	(8.9)
36	Oregon	(8.9)		37	Wyoming	(9.1)
14	Pennsylvania	7.8		38	California	(10.5)
13	Rhode Island	11.5		39	West Virginia	(11.8)
16	South Carolina	6.6		40	Utah	(15.2)
5	South Dakota	52.9		41	Michigan	(15.7)
10	Tennessee	14.3		42	New Mexico	(16.0)
23	Texas	0.7		43	Kentucky	(16.1)
40	Utah	(15.2)		44	Colorado	(21.9)
17	Vermont	6.3		45	Montana	(23.3)
31	Virginia	(5.6)		46	New Hampshire	(23.5)
22	Washington	1.1		47	Hawaii	(24.2)
39	West Virginia	(11.8)		48	Alaska	(24.3)
28	Wisconsin	(5.2)		49	Idaho	(25.8)
37	Wyoming	(9.1)		50	North Dakota	(62.5)
					District of Columbia	(6.1)

Source: CQ Press using reported data from the Federal Bureau of Investigation
   "Crime in the United States 2005" (Uniform Crime Reports, September 2006, http://www.fbi.gov/ucr/ucr.htm)
*Revised figures. Includes nonnegligent manslaughter.

Murder Rate in 2004

National Rate = 5.5 Murders per 100,000 Population*

ALPHA ORDER

RANK	STATE	RATE
18	Alabama	5.6
18	Alaska	5.6
6	Arizona	7.2
10	Arkansas	6.4
9	California	6.7
28	Colorado	4.4
34	Connecticut	2.9
31	Delaware	3.4
20	Florida	5.4
7	Georgia	6.9
37	Hawaii	2.6
42	Idaho	2.2
13	Illinois	6.1
24	Indiana	5.1
47	Iowa	1.5
26	Kansas	4.5
17	Kentucky	5.7
1	Louisiana	12.7
48	Maine	1.4
2	Maryland	9.4
36	Massachusetts	2.7
10	Michigan	6.4
42	Minnesota	2.2
4	Mississippi	7.8
13	Missouri	6.1
32	Montana	3.2
41	Nebraska	2.3
5	Nevada	7.4
49	New Hampshire	1.3
26	New Jersey	4.5
3	New Mexico	8.9
25	New York	4.6
12	North Carolina	6.2
49	North Dakota	1.3
28	Ohio	4.4
21	Oklahoma	5.3
39	Oregon	2.5
22	Pennsylvania	5.2
40	Rhode Island	2.4
8	South Carolina	6.8
42	South Dakota	2.2
13	Tennessee	6.1
13	Texas	6.1
46	Utah	1.9
37	Vermont	2.6
22	Virginia	5.2
33	Washington	3.1
30	West Virginia	3.8
35	Wisconsin	2.8
42	Wyoming	2.2

RANK ORDER

RANK	STATE	RATE
1	Louisiana	12.7
2	Maryland	9.4
3	New Mexico	8.9
4	Mississippi	7.8
5	Nevada	7.4
6	Arizona	7.2
7	Georgia	6.9
8	South Carolina	6.8
9	California	6.7
10	Arkansas	6.4
10	Michigan	6.4
12	North Carolina	6.2
13	Illinois	6.1
13	Missouri	6.1
13	Tennessee	6.1
13	Texas	6.1
17	Kentucky	5.7
18	Alabama	5.6
18	Alaska	5.6
20	Florida	5.4
21	Oklahoma	5.3
22	Pennsylvania	5.2
22	Virginia	5.2
24	Indiana	5.1
25	New York	4.6
26	Kansas	4.5
26	New Jersey	4.5
28	Colorado	4.4
28	Ohio	4.4
30	West Virginia	3.8
31	Delaware	3.4
32	Montana	3.2
33	Washington	3.1
34	Connecticut	2.9
35	Wisconsin	2.8
36	Massachusetts	2.7
37	Hawaii	2.6
37	Vermont	2.6
39	Oregon	2.5
40	Rhode Island	2.4
41	Nebraska	2.3
42	Idaho	2.2
42	Minnesota	2.2
42	South Dakota	2.2
42	Wyoming	2.2
46	Utah	1.9
47	Iowa	1.5
48	Maine	1.4
49	New Hampshire	1.3
49	North Dakota	1.3
	District of Columbia	35.7

Source: Reported data from the Federal Bureau of Investigation
"Crime in the United States 2005" (Uniform Crime Reports, September 2006, http://www.fbi.gov/ucr/ucr.htm)
*Revised figures. Includes nonnegligent manslaughter.

Percent Change in Murder Rate: 2004 to 2008

National Percent Change = 1.8% Decrease*

ALPHA ORDER

RANK	STATE	PERCENT CHANGE
6	Alabama	35.7
46	Alaska	(26.8)
35	Arizona	(12.5)
32	Arkansas	(10.9)
37	California	(13.4)
48	Colorado	(27.3)
8	Connecticut	20.7
1	Delaware	91.2
9	Florida	18.5
22	Georgia	(4.3)
47	Hawaii	(26.9)
49	Idaho	(31.8)
18	Illinois	0.0
18	Indiana	0.0
3	Iowa	66.7
33	Kansas	(11.1)
42	Kentucky	(19.3)
25	Louisiana	(6.3)
2	Maine	71.4
26	Maryland	(6.4)
21	Massachusetts	(3.7)
40	Michigan	(15.6)
24	Minnesota	(4.5)
16	Mississippi	3.8
7	Missouri	26.2
44	Montana	(25.0)
4	Nebraska	65.2
39	Nevada	(14.9)
43	New Hampshire	(23.1)
23	New Jersey	(4.4)
41	New Mexico	(19.1)
27	New York	(6.5)
15	North Carolina	4.8
50	North Dakota	(61.5)
14	Ohio	6.8
11	Oklahoma	9.4
34	Oregon	(12.0)
13	Pennsylvania	7.7
10	Rhode Island	16.7
18	South Carolina	0.0
5	South Dakota	45.5
12	Tennessee	8.2
30	Texas	(8.2)
45	Utah	(26.3)
16	Vermont	3.8
31	Virginia	(9.6)
27	Washington	(6.5)
36	West Virginia	(13.2)
29	Wisconsin	(7.1)
38	Wyoming	(13.6)

RANK ORDER

RANK	STATE	PERCENT CHANGE
1	Delaware	91.2
2	Maine	71.4
3	Iowa	66.7
4	Nebraska	65.2
5	South Dakota	45.5
6	Alabama	35.7
7	Missouri	26.2
8	Connecticut	20.7
9	Florida	18.5
10	Rhode Island	16.7
11	Oklahoma	9.4
12	Tennessee	8.2
13	Pennsylvania	7.7
14	Ohio	6.8
15	North Carolina	4.8
16	Mississippi	3.8
16	Vermont	3.8
18	Illinois	0.0
18	Indiana	0.0
18	South Carolina	0.0
21	Massachusetts	(3.7)
22	Georgia	(4.3)
23	New Jersey	(4.4)
24	Minnesota	(4.5)
25	Louisiana	(6.3)
26	Maryland	(6.4)
27	New York	(6.5)
27	Washington	(6.5)
29	Wisconsin	(7.1)
30	Texas	(8.2)
31	Virginia	(9.6)
32	Arkansas	(10.9)
33	Kansas	(11.1)
34	Oregon	(12.0)
35	Arizona	(12.5)
36	West Virginia	(13.2)
37	California	(13.4)
38	Wyoming	(13.6)
39	Nevada	(14.9)
40	Michigan	(15.6)
41	New Mexico	(19.1)
42	Kentucky	(19.3)
43	New Hampshire	(23.1)
44	Montana	(25.0)
45	Utah	(26.3)
46	Alaska	(26.8)
47	Hawaii	(26.9)
48	Colorado	(27.3)
49	Idaho	(31.8)
50	North Dakota	(61.5)
	District of Columbia	(12.0)

Source: CQ Press using reported data from the Federal Bureau of Investigation
   "Crime in the United States 2005" (Uniform Crime Reports, September 2006, http://www.fbi.gov/ucr/ucr.htm)
*Revised figures. Includes nonnegligent manslaughter.

Rapes in 2004

National Total = 95,089 Rapes*

ALPHA ORDER

RANK	STATE	RAPES	% of USA
20	Alabama	1,742	1.8%
39	Alaska	558	0.6%
15	Arizona	1,896	2.0%
28	Arkansas	1,183	1.2%
1	California	9,615	10.1%
14	Colorado	1,945	2.0%
36	Connecticut	755	0.8%
41	Delaware	357	0.4%
3	Florida	6,612	7.0%
10	Georgia	2,387	2.5%
44	Hawaii	333	0.4%
38	Idaho	594	0.6%
6	Illinois	4,220	4.4%
17	Indiana	1,803	1.9%
35	Iowa	782	0.8%
30	Kansas	1,142	1.2%
27	Kentucky	1,238	1.3%
21	Louisiana	1,616	1.7%
46	Maine	315	0.3%
25	Maryland	1,317	1.4%
18	Massachusetts	1,794	1.9%
4	Michigan	5,482	5.8%
13	Minnesota	2,123	2.2%
29	Mississippi	1,161	1.2%
23	Missouri	1,479	1.6%
47	Montana	273	0.3%
37	Nebraska	620	0.7%
34	Nevada	954	1.0%
40	New Hampshire	466	0.5%
24	New Jersey	1,331	1.4%
32	New Mexico	1,039	1.1%
7	New York	3,608	3.8%
11	North Carolina	2,339	2.5%
48	North Dakota	177	0.2%
5	Ohio	4,744	5.0%
22	Oklahoma	1,557	1.6%
26	Oregon	1,283	1.3%
8	Pennsylvania	3,535	3.7%
45	Rhode Island	320	0.3%
19	South Carolina	1,772	1.9%
43	South Dakota	336	0.4%
12	Tennessee	2,282	2.4%
2	Texas	8,388	8.8%
33	Utah	967	1.0%
49	Vermont	160	0.2%
16	Virginia	1,816	1.9%
9	Washington	2,857	3.0%
42	West Virginia	346	0.4%
31	Wisconsin	1,136	1.2%
50	Wyoming	112	0.1%

RANK ORDER

RANK	STATE	RAPES	% of USA
1	California	9,615	10.1%
2	Texas	8,388	8.8%
3	Florida	6,612	7.0%
4	Michigan	5,482	5.8%
5	Ohio	4,744	5.0%
6	Illinois	4,220	4.4%
7	New York	3,608	3.8%
8	Pennsylvania	3,535	3.7%
9	Washington	2,857	3.0%
10	Georgia	2,387	2.5%
11	North Carolina	2,339	2.5%
12	Tennessee	2,282	2.4%
13	Minnesota	2,123	2.2%
14	Colorado	1,945	2.0%
15	Arizona	1,896	2.0%
16	Virginia	1,816	1.9%
17	Indiana	1,803	1.9%
18	Massachusetts	1,794	1.9%
19	South Carolina	1,772	1.9%
20	Alabama	1,742	1.8%
21	Louisiana	1,616	1.7%
22	Oklahoma	1,557	1.6%
23	Missouri	1,479	1.6%
24	New Jersey	1,331	1.4%
25	Maryland	1,317	1.4%
26	Oregon	1,283	1.3%
27	Kentucky	1,238	1.3%
28	Arkansas	1,183	1.2%
29	Mississippi	1,161	1.2%
30	Kansas	1,142	1.2%
31	Wisconsin	1,136	1.2%
32	New Mexico	1,039	1.1%
33	Utah	967	1.0%
34	Nevada	954	1.0%
35	Iowa	782	0.8%
36	Connecticut	755	0.8%
37	Nebraska	620	0.7%
38	Idaho	594	0.6%
39	Alaska	558	0.6%
40	New Hampshire	466	0.5%
41	Delaware	357	0.4%
42	West Virginia	346	0.4%
43	South Dakota	336	0.4%
44	Hawaii	333	0.4%
45	Rhode Island	320	0.3%
46	Maine	315	0.3%
47	Montana	273	0.3%
48	North Dakota	177	0.2%
49	Vermont	160	0.2%
50	Wyoming	112	0.1%
	District of Columbia	222	0.2%

Source: Reported data from the Federal Bureau of Investigation
"Crime in the United States 2005" (Uniform Crime Reports, September 2006, http://www.fbi.gov/ucr/ucr.htm)
*Revised figures. Forcible rape is the carnal knowledge of a female forcibly and against her will. Assaults or attempts to commit rape by force or threat of force are included. However, statutory rape without force and other sex offenses are excluded.

Percent Change in Number of Rapes: 2004 to 2008

National Percent Change = 6.4% Decrease*

ALPHA ORDER				RANK ORDER		
RANK	STATE	PERCENT CHANGE		RANK	STATE	PERCENT CHANGE
28	Alabama	(7.2)		1	Wyoming	60.7
47	Alaska	(21.0)		2	North Dakota	31.1
39	Arizona	(11.8)		3	South Dakota	28.6
5	Arkansas	17.9		4	Maine	19.0
30	California	(7.4)		5	Arkansas	17.9
12	Colorado	7.9		6	Nevada	15.5
38	Connecticut	(10.7)		7	Kentucky	13.7
16	Delaware	2.5		8	Iowa	13.6
36	Florida	(9.7)		9	Hawaii	9.6
33	Georgia	(8.0)		9	New Mexico	9.6
9	Hawaii	9.6		11	Missouri	9.2
28	Idaho	(7.2)		12	Colorado	7.9
19	Illinois	(2.4)		13	Montana	7.7
24	Indiana	(4.6)		14	West Virginia	4.6
8	Iowa	13.6		15	Kansas	4.2
15	Kansas	4.2		16	Delaware	2.5
7	Kentucky	13.7		17	Wisconsin	(1.4)
50	Louisiana	(23.8)		18	Pennsylvania	(1.6)
4	Maine	19.0		19	Illinois	(2.4)
41	Maryland	(14.4)		19	North Carolina	(2.4)
21	Massachusetts	(3.2)		21	Massachusetts	(3.2)
45	Michigan	(17.9)		21	Virginia	(3.2)
42	Minnesota	(15.0)		23	Texas	(4.5)
49	Mississippi	(23.3)		24	Indiana	(4.6)
11	Missouri	9.2		25	Oklahoma	(5.8)
13	Montana	7.7		26	Nebraska	(6.0)
26	Nebraska	(6.0)		27	Ohio	(6.9)
6	Nevada	15.5		28	Alabama	(7.2)
44	New Hampshire	(16.1)		28	Idaho	(7.2)
43	New Jersey	(15.7)		30	California	(7.4)
9	New Mexico	9.6		31	South Carolina	(7.6)
48	New York	(22.4)		32	Utah	(7.7)
19	North Carolina	(2.4)		33	Georgia	(8.0)
2	North Dakota	31.1		33	Washington	(8.0)
27	Ohio	(6.9)		35	Tennessee	(9.6)
25	Oklahoma	(5.8)		36	Florida	(9.7)
37	Oregon	(9.9)		37	Oregon	(9.9)
18	Pennsylvania	(1.6)		38	Connecticut	(10.7)
40	Rhode Island	(13.4)		39	Arizona	(11.8)
31	South Carolina	(7.6)		40	Rhode Island	(13.4)
3	South Dakota	28.6		41	Maryland	(14.4)
35	Tennessee	(9.6)		42	Minnesota	(15.0)
23	Texas	(4.5)		43	New Jersey	(15.7)
32	Utah	(7.7)		44	New Hampshire	(16.1)
46	Vermont	(20.6)		45	Michigan	(17.9)
21	Virginia	(3.2)		46	Vermont	(20.6)
33	Washington	(8.0)		47	Alaska	(21.0)
14	West Virginia	4.6		48	New York	(22.4)
17	Wisconsin	(1.4)		49	Mississippi	(23.3)
1	Wyoming	60.7		50	Louisiana	(23.8)
					District of Columbia	(16.2)

Source: CQ Press using reported data from the Federal Bureau of Investigation
"Crime in the United States 2005" (Uniform Crime Reports, September 2006, http://www.fbi.gov/ucr/ucr.htm)
*Revised figures. Forcible rape is the carnal knowledge of a female forcibly and against her will. Assaults or attempts to commit rape by force or threat of force are included. However, statutory rape without force and other sex offenses are excluded.

Rape Rate in 2004

National Rate = 32.4 Rapes per 100,000 Population*

ALPHA ORDER

RANK	STATE	RATE
19	Alabama	38.5
1	Alaska	84.8
27	Arizona	33.0
7	Arkansas	43.0
36	California	26.8
10	Colorado	42.3
46	Connecticut	21.6
7	Delaware	43.0
20	Florida	38.0
36	Georgia	26.8
39	Hawaii	26.4
9	Idaho	42.6
26	Illinois	33.2
31	Indiana	29.0
38	Iowa	26.5
12	Kansas	41.8
28	Kentucky	29.9
22	Louisiana	35.9
43	Maine	24.0
44	Maryland	23.7
33	Massachusetts	28.0
3	Michigan	54.3
13	Minnesota	41.7
16	Mississippi	40.0
41	Missouri	25.7
30	Montana	29.5
25	Nebraska	35.5
15	Nevada	40.9
22	New Hampshire	35.9
50	New Jersey	15.3
2	New Mexico	54.6
49	New York	18.7
35	North Carolina	27.4
34	North Dakota	27.8
14	Ohio	41.4
5	Oklahoma	44.2
24	Oregon	35.7
32	Pennsylvania	28.5
29	Rhode Island	29.6
11	South Carolina	42.2
6	South Dakota	43.6
18	Tennessee	38.7
21	Texas	37.3
17	Utah	39.9
40	Vermont	25.8
42	Virginia	24.3
4	Washington	46.0
48	West Virginia	19.1
47	Wisconsin	20.6
45	Wyoming	22.1

RANK ORDER

RANK	STATE	RATE
1	Alaska	84.8
2	New Mexico	54.6
3	Michigan	54.3
4	Washington	46.0
5	Oklahoma	44.2
6	South Dakota	43.6
7	Arkansas	43.0
7	Delaware	43.0
9	Idaho	42.6
10	Colorado	42.3
11	South Carolina	42.2
12	Kansas	41.8
13	Minnesota	41.7
14	Ohio	41.4
15	Nevada	40.9
16	Mississippi	40.0
17	Utah	39.9
18	Tennessee	38.7
19	Alabama	38.5
20	Florida	38.0
21	Texas	37.3
22	Louisiana	35.9
22	New Hampshire	35.9
24	Oregon	35.7
25	Nebraska	35.5
26	Illinois	33.2
27	Arizona	33.0
28	Kentucky	29.9
29	Rhode Island	29.6
30	Montana	29.5
31	Indiana	29.0
32	Pennsylvania	28.5
33	Massachusetts	28.0
34	North Dakota	27.8
35	North Carolina	27.4
36	California	26.8
36	Georgia	26.8
38	Iowa	26.5
39	Hawaii	26.4
40	Vermont	25.8
41	Missouri	25.7
42	Virginia	24.3
43	Maine	24.0
44	Maryland	23.7
45	Wyoming	22.1
46	Connecticut	21.6
47	Wisconsin	20.6
48	West Virginia	19.1
49	New York	18.7
50	New Jersey	15.3
	District of Columbia	40.1

Source: Reported data from the Federal Bureau of Investigation
    "Crime in the United States 2005" (Uniform Crime Reports, September 2006, http://www.fbi.gov/ucr/ucr.htm)
*Revised figures. Forcible rape is the carnal knowledge of a female forcibly and against her will. Assaults or attempts to commit rape by force or threat of force are included. However, statutory rape without force and other sex offenses are excluded.

Percent Change in Rape Rate: 2004 to 2008

National Percent Change = 9.6% Decrease*

ALPHA ORDER				RANK ORDER		
RANK	STATE	PERCENT CHANGE		RANK	STATE	PERCENT CHANGE
28	Alabama	(9.9)		1	Wyoming	52.9
49	Alaska	(24.2)		2	North Dakota	30.2
46	Arizona	(22.1)		3	South Dakota	23.2
5	Arkansas	13.7		4	Maine	18.8
27	California	(9.7)		5	Arkansas	13.7
15	Colorado	0.5		6	Iowa	11.7
29	Connecticut	(10.6)		7	Kentucky	10.4
17	Delaware	(2.6)		8	Hawaii	7.2
34	Florida	(14.2)		9	Missouri	6.2
38	Georgia	(15.3)		10	New Mexico	5.1
8	Hawaii	7.2		11	West Virginia	4.7
37	Idaho	(15.0)		12	Nevada	3.7
19	Illinois	(3.9)		13	Montana	3.1
21	Indiana	(6.9)		14	Kansas	1.7
6	Iowa	11.7		15	Colorado	0.5
14	Kansas	1.7		16	Pennsylvania	(2.1)
7	Kentucky	10.4		17	Delaware	(2.6)
47	Louisiana	(22.3)		18	Wisconsin	(3.4)
4	Maine	18.8		19	Illinois	(3.9)
39	Maryland	(15.6)		20	Massachusetts	(4.6)
20	Massachusetts	(4.6)		21	Indiana	(6.9)
42	Michigan	(17.1)		22	Ohio	(7.0)
41	Minnesota	(17.0)		22	Virginia	(7.0)
50	Mississippi	(24.3)		24	Nebraska	(7.9)
9	Missouri	6.2		25	Oklahoma	(9.0)
13	Montana	3.1		26	North Carolina	(9.5)
24	Nebraska	(7.9)		27	California	(9.7)
12	Nevada	3.7		28	Alabama	(9.9)
43	New Hampshire	(17.3)		29	Connecticut	(10.6)
40	New Jersey	(15.7)		30	Rhode Island	(10.8)
10	New Mexico	5.1		31	Texas	(11.8)
48	New York	(23.0)		32	Washington	(12.8)
26	North Carolina	(9.5)		33	South Carolina	(13.3)
2	North Dakota	30.2		34	Florida	(14.2)
22	Ohio	(7.0)		34	Tennessee	(14.2)
25	Oklahoma	(9.0)		36	Oregon	(14.6)
36	Oregon	(14.6)		37	Idaho	(15.0)
16	Pennsylvania	(2.1)		38	Georgia	(15.3)
30	Rhode Island	(10.8)		39	Maryland	(15.6)
33	South Carolina	(13.3)		40	New Jersey	(15.7)
3	South Dakota	23.2		41	Minnesota	(17.0)
34	Tennessee	(14.2)		42	Michigan	(17.1)
31	Texas	(11.8)		43	New Hampshire	(17.3)
44	Utah	(18.3)		44	Utah	(18.3)
45	Vermont	(20.9)		45	Vermont	(20.9)
22	Virginia	(7.0)		46	Arizona	(22.1)
32	Washington	(12.8)		47	Louisiana	(22.3)
11	West Virginia	4.7		48	New York	(23.0)
18	Wisconsin	(3.4)		49	Alaska	(24.2)
1	Wyoming	52.9		50	Mississippi	(24.3)
				District of Columbia		(21.7)

Source: CQ Press using reported data from the Federal Bureau of Investigation
  "Crime in the United States 2005" (Uniform Crime Reports, September 2006, http://www.fbi.gov/ucr/ucr.htm)
*Revised figures. Forcible rape is the carnal knowledge of a female forcibly and against her will. Assaults or attempts to commit rape by force or threat of force are included. However, statutory rape without force and other sex offenses are excluded.

Robberies in 2004

National Total = 401,470 Robberies*

ALPHA ORDER

RANK	STATE	ROBBERIES	% of USA
20	Alabama	6,042	1.5%
43	Alaska	447	0.1%
14	Arizona	7,721	1.9%
32	Arkansas	2,372	0.6%
1	California	61,768	15.4%
27	Colorado	3,739	0.9%
24	Connecticut	4,188	1.0%
35	Delaware	1,343	0.3%
4	Florida	29,997	7.5%
8	Georgia	13,656	3.4%
39	Hawaii	944	0.2%
45	Idaho	241	0.1%
5	Illinois	22,582	5.6%
19	Indiana	6,373	1.6%
37	Iowa	1,160	0.3%
34	Kansas	1,812	0.5%
28	Kentucky	3,268	0.8%
18	Louisiana	6,564	1.6%
44	Maine	289	0.1%
10	Maryland	12,772	3.2%
15	Massachusetts	7,484	1.9%
12	Michigan	11,336	2.8%
25	Minnesota	4,070	1.0%
31	Mississippi	2,503	0.6%
17	Missouri	6,630	1.7%
46	Montana	233	0.1%
38	Nebraska	1,138	0.3%
23	Nevada	4,905	1.2%
42	New Hampshire	500	0.1%
9	New Jersey	13,076	3.3%
33	New Mexico	2,062	0.5%
3	New York	33,506	8.3%
11	North Carolina	11,782	2.9%
50	North Dakota	43	0.0%
7	Ohio	17,429	4.3%
29	Oklahoma	3,090	0.8%
30	Oregon	2,751	0.7%
6	Pennsylvania	18,474	4.6%
41	Rhode Island	731	0.2%
22	South Carolina	5,468	1.4%
47	South Dakota	112	0.0%
13	Tennessee	8,863	2.2%
2	Texas	35,817	8.9%
36	Utah	1,236	0.3%
48	Vermont	78	0.0%
16	Virginia	6,899	1.7%
21	Washington	5,866	1.5%
40	West Virginia	774	0.2%
26	Wisconsin	4,067	1.0%
49	Wyoming	67	0.0%

RANK ORDER

RANK	STATE	ROBBERIES	% of USA
1	California	61,768	15.4%
2	Texas	35,817	8.9%
3	New York	33,506	8.3%
4	Florida	29,997	7.5%
5	Illinois	22,582	5.6%
6	Pennsylvania	18,474	4.6%
7	Ohio	17,429	4.3%
8	Georgia	13,656	3.4%
9	New Jersey	13,076	3.3%
10	Maryland	12,772	3.2%
11	North Carolina	11,782	2.9%
12	Michigan	11,336	2.8%
13	Tennessee	8,863	2.2%
14	Arizona	7,721	1.9%
15	Massachusetts	7,484	1.9%
16	Virginia	6,899	1.7%
17	Missouri	6,630	1.7%
18	Louisiana	6,564	1.6%
19	Indiana	6,373	1.6%
20	Alabama	6,042	1.5%
21	Washington	5,866	1.5%
22	South Carolina	5,468	1.4%
23	Nevada	4,905	1.2%
24	Connecticut	4,188	1.0%
25	Minnesota	4,070	1.0%
26	Wisconsin	4,067	1.0%
27	Colorado	3,739	0.9%
28	Kentucky	3,268	0.8%
29	Oklahoma	3,090	0.8%
30	Oregon	2,751	0.7%
31	Mississippi	2,503	0.6%
32	Arkansas	2,372	0.6%
33	New Mexico	2,062	0.5%
34	Kansas	1,812	0.5%
35	Delaware	1,343	0.3%
36	Utah	1,236	0.3%
37	Iowa	1,160	0.3%
38	Nebraska	1,138	0.3%
39	Hawaii	944	0.2%
40	West Virginia	774	0.2%
41	Rhode Island	731	0.2%
42	New Hampshire	500	0.1%
43	Alaska	447	0.1%
44	Maine	289	0.1%
45	Idaho	241	0.1%
46	Montana	233	0.1%
47	South Dakota	112	0.0%
48	Vermont	78	0.0%
49	Wyoming	67	0.0%
50	North Dakota	43	0.0%
	District of Columbia	3,202	0.8%

Source: Reported data from the Federal Bureau of Investigation
"Crime in the United States 2005" (Uniform Crime Reports, September 2006, http://www.fbi.gov/ucr/ucr.htm)
*Revised figures. Robbery is the taking or attempting to take anything of value by force or threat of force.

Percent Change in Number of Robberies: 2004 to 2008

National Percent Change = 10.1% Increase*

ALPHA ORDER				RANK ORDER		
RANK	STATE	PERCENT CHANGE		RANK	STATE	PERCENT CHANGE
12	Alabama	21.6		1	North Dakota	67.4
2	Alaska	44.3		2	Alaska	44.3
8	Arizona	25.6		3	Delaware	36.9
19	Arkansas	15.3		4	Nevada	32.0
27	California	12.3		5	Wyoming	28.4
48	Colorado	(10.0)		6	Georgia	27.1
45	Connecticut	(6.7)		7	Wisconsin	26.0
3	Delaware	36.9		8	Arizona	25.6
13	Florida	20.9		9	Kentucky	22.5
6	Georgia	27.1		10	Tennessee	21.9
21	Hawaii	15.0		11	North Carolina	21.7
40	Idaho	0.0		12	Alabama	21.6
34	Illinois	6.5		13	Florida	20.9
18	Indiana	18.2		14	South Carolina	20.7
31	Iowa	7.6		15	Mississippi	20.5
46	Kansas	(7.1)		16	Rhode Island	20.2
9	Kentucky	22.5		17	Oklahoma	19.2
47	Louisiana	(8.7)		18	Indiana	18.2
20	Maine	15.2		19	Arkansas	15.3
37	Maryland	3.4		20	Maine	15.2
44	Massachusetts	(5.5)		21	Hawaii	15.0
24	Michigan	14.4		21	Utah	15.0
38	Minnesota	2.6		23	West Virginia	14.9
15	Mississippi	20.5		24	Michigan	14.4
28	Missouri	11.5		25	Nebraska	14.1
50	Montana	(26.2)		25	Vermont	14.1
25	Nebraska	14.1		27	California	12.3
4	Nevada	32.0		28	Missouri	11.5
49	New Hampshire	(16.2)		29	Washington	8.2
41	New Jersey	(2.9)		30	Virginia	7.8
36	New Mexico	5.3		31	Iowa	7.6
43	New York	(5.2)		32	Ohio	7.4
11	North Carolina	21.7		33	South Dakota	7.1
1	North Dakota	67.4		34	Illinois	6.5
32	Ohio	7.4		35	Texas	5.4
17	Oklahoma	19.2		36	New Mexico	5.3
42	Oregon	(4.0)		37	Maryland	3.4
39	Pennsylvania	2.2		38	Minnesota	2.6
16	Rhode Island	20.2		39	Pennsylvania	2.2
14	South Carolina	20.7		40	Idaho	0.0
33	South Dakota	7.1		41	New Jersey	(2.9)
10	Tennessee	21.9		42	Oregon	(4.0)
35	Texas	5.4		43	New York	(5.2)
21	Utah	15.0		44	Massachusetts	(5.5)
25	Vermont	14.1		45	Connecticut	(6.7)
30	Virginia	7.8		46	Kansas	(7.1)
29	Washington	8.2		47	Louisiana	(8.7)
23	West Virginia	14.9		48	Colorado	(10.0)
7	Wisconsin	26.0		49	New Hampshire	(16.2)
5	Wyoming	28.4		50	Montana	(26.2)

District of Columbia   38.4

Source: CQ Press using reported data from the Federal Bureau of Investigation
   "Crime in the United States 2005" (Uniform Crime Reports, September 2006, http://www.fbi.gov/ucr/ucr.htm)
*Revised figures. Robbery is the taking or attempting to take anything of value by force or threat of force.

Robbery Rate in 2004

National Rate = 136.7 Robberies per 100,000 Population*

ALPHA ORDER			RANK ORDER		
RANK	STATE	RATE	RANK	STATE	RATE
17	Alabama	133.5	1	Maryland	229.7
36	Alaska	68.0	2	Nevada	210.3
16	Arizona	134.5	3	Illinois	177.6
28	Arkansas	86.3	4	New York	173.8
6	California	172.3	5	Florida	172.5
30	Colorado	81.3	6	California	172.3
19	Connecticut	119.7	7	Delaware	161.8
7	Delaware	161.8	8	Texas	159.4
5	Florida	172.5	9	Georgia	153.1
9	Georgia	153.1	10	Ohio	152.2
34	Hawaii	74.8	11	New Jersey	150.6
46	Idaho	17.3	12	Tennessee	150.4
3	Illinois	177.6	13	Pennsylvania	149.1
24	Indiana	102.4	14	Louisiana	145.7
42	Iowa	39.3	15	North Carolina	138.0
38	Kansas	66.3	16	Arizona	134.5
32	Kentucky	78.9	17	Alabama	133.5
14	Louisiana	145.7	18	South Carolina	130.3
45	Maine	22.0	19	Connecticut	119.7
1	Maryland	229.7	20	Massachusetts	116.8
20	Massachusetts	116.8	21	Missouri	115.1
22	Michigan	112.2	22	Michigan	112.2
31	Minnesota	79.9	23	New Mexico	108.4
28	Mississippi	86.3	24	Indiana	102.4
21	Missouri	115.1	25	Washington	94.5
44	Montana	25.1	26	Virginia	92.2
39	Nebraska	65.1	27	Oklahoma	87.7
2	Nevada	210.3	28	Arkansas	86.3
43	New Hampshire	38.5	28	Mississippi	86.3
11	New Jersey	150.6	30	Colorado	81.3
23	New Mexico	108.4	31	Minnesota	79.9
4	New York	173.8	32	Kentucky	78.9
15	North Carolina	138.0	33	Oregon	76.6
50	North Dakota	6.8	34	Hawaii	74.8
10	Ohio	152.2	35	Wisconsin	73.9
27	Oklahoma	87.7	36	Alaska	68.0
33	Oregon	76.6	37	Rhode Island	67.7
13	Pennsylvania	149.1	38	Kansas	66.3
37	Rhode Island	67.7	39	Nebraska	65.1
18	South Carolina	130.3	40	Utah	51.1
47	South Dakota	14.5	41	West Virginia	42.7
12	Tennessee	150.4	42	Iowa	39.3
8	Texas	159.4	43	New Hampshire	38.5
40	Utah	51.1	44	Montana	25.1
49	Vermont	12.6	45	Maine	22.0
26	Virginia	92.2	46	Idaho	17.3
25	Washington	94.5	47	South Dakota	14.5
41	West Virginia	42.7	48	Wyoming	13.2
35	Wisconsin	73.9	49	Vermont	12.6
48	Wyoming	13.2	50	North Dakota	6.8
				District of Columbia	577.7

Source: Reported data from the Federal Bureau of Investigation
  "Crime in the United States 2005" (Uniform Crime Reports, September 2006, http://www.fbi.gov/ucr/ucr.htm)
*Revised figures. Robbery is the taking or attempting to take anything of value by force or threat of force.

Percent Change in Robbery Rate: 2004 to 2008

National Percent Change = 6.3% Increase*

ALPHA ORDER

RANK	STATE	PERCENT CHANGE
10	Alabama	18.1
2	Alaska	38.2
25	Arizona	10.9
24	Arkansas	11.0
26	California	9.6
48	Colorado	(16.2)
43	Connecticut	(6.8)
3	Delaware	30.1
18	Florida	14.7
11	Georgia	17.0
21	Hawaii	12.7
45	Idaho	(8.7)
30	Illinois	5.0
14	Indiana	15.3
29	Iowa	5.9
47	Kansas	(9.4)
7	Kentucky	18.9
42	Louisiana	(6.7)
16	Maine	15.0
34	Maryland	2.0
43	Massachusetts	(6.8)
13	Michigan	15.5
38	Minnesota	0.1
7	Mississippi	18.9
27	Missouri	8.6
50	Montana	(29.1)
23	Nebraska	11.8
9	Nevada	18.4
49	New Hampshire	(17.4)
40	New Jersey	(2.9)
37	New Mexico	1.0
41	New York	(6.2)
22	North Carolina	12.6
1	North Dakota	64.7
28	Ohio	7.1
14	Oklahoma	15.3
46	Oregon	(9.0)
35	Pennsylvania	1.7
4	Rhode Island	23.6
20	South Carolina	13.0
32	South Dakota	2.8
12	Tennessee	15.6
39	Texas	(2.6)
36	Utah	1.6
19	Vermont	13.5
31	Virginia	3.8
33	Washington	2.5
17	West Virginia	14.8
5	Wisconsin	23.3
6	Wyoming	22.0

RANK ORDER

RANK	STATE	PERCENT CHANGE
1	North Dakota	64.7
2	Alaska	38.2
3	Delaware	30.1
4	Rhode Island	23.6
5	Wisconsin	23.3
6	Wyoming	22.0
7	Kentucky	18.9
7	Mississippi	18.9
9	Nevada	18.4
10	Alabama	18.1
11	Georgia	17.0
12	Tennessee	15.6
13	Michigan	15.5
14	Indiana	15.3
14	Oklahoma	15.3
16	Maine	15.0
17	West Virginia	14.8
18	Florida	14.7
19	Vermont	13.5
20	South Carolina	13.0
21	Hawaii	12.7
22	North Carolina	12.6
23	Nebraska	11.8
24	Arkansas	11.0
25	Arizona	10.9
26	California	9.6
27	Missouri	8.6
28	Ohio	7.1
29	Iowa	5.9
30	Illinois	5.0
31	Virginia	3.8
32	South Dakota	2.8
33	Washington	2.5
34	Maryland	2.0
35	Pennsylvania	1.7
36	Utah	1.6
37	New Mexico	1.0
38	Minnesota	0.1
39	Texas	(2.6)
40	New Jersey	(2.9)
41	New York	(6.2)
42	Louisiana	(6.7)
43	Connecticut	(6.8)
43	Massachusetts	(6.8)
45	Idaho	(8.7)
46	Oregon	(9.0)
47	Kansas	(9.4)
48	Colorado	(16.2)
49	New Hampshire	(17.4)
50	Montana	(29.1)

District of Columbia   29.6

Source: CQ Press using reported data from the Federal Bureau of Investigation
"Crime in the United States 2005" (Uniform Crime Reports, September 2006, http://www.fbi.gov/ucr/ucr.htm)
*Revised figures. Robbery is the taking or attempting to take anything of value by force or threat of force.

Aggravated Assaults in 2004

National Total = 847,381 Aggravated Assaults*

ALPHA ORDER

RANK	STATE	ASSAULTS	% of USA
23	Alabama	11,286	1.3%
40	Alaska	3,117	0.4%
16	Arizona	18,921	2.2%
25	Arkansas	10,083	1.2%
1	California	115,400	13.6%
24	Colorado	11,236	1.3%
34	Connecticut	5,070	0.6%
39	Delaware	3,377	0.4%
2	Florida	86,199	10.2%
12	Georgia	23,561	2.8%
43	Hawaii	1,903	0.2%
41	Idaho	2,586	0.3%
5	Illinois	41,783	4.9%
21	Indiana	11,802	1.4%
31	Iowa	6,513	0.8%
29	Kansas	7,254	0.9%
33	Kentucky	5,410	0.6%
13	Louisiana	20,090	2.4%
48	Maine	742	0.1%
10	Maryland	24,351	2.9%
14	Massachusetts	20,040	2.4%
6	Michigan	32,276	3.8%
28	Minnesota	7,445	0.9%
35	Mississippi	4,677	0.6%
15	Missouri	19,763	2.3%
42	Montana	2,187	0.3%
37	Nebraska	3,595	0.4%
27	Nevada	8,348	1.0%
45	New Hampshire	1,219	0.1%
17	New Jersey	16,144	1.9%
26	New Mexico	9,811	1.2%
4	New York	46,911	5.5%
11	North Carolina	23,591	2.8%
50	North Dakota	330	0.0%
18	Ohio	16,108	1.9%
19	Oklahoma	12,802	1.5%
30	Oregon	6,600	0.8%
8	Pennsylvania	28,339	3.3%
44	Rhode Island	1,596	0.2%
9	South Carolina	25,634	3.0%
47	South Dakota	854	0.1%
7	Tennessee	29,611	3.5%
3	Texas	75,985	9.0%
38	Utah	3,398	0.4%
49	Vermont	459	0.1%
22	Virginia	11,503	1.4%
20	Washington	12,417	1.5%
36	West Virginia	3,922	0.5%
32	Wisconsin	6,191	0.7%
46	Wyoming	973	0.1%

RANK ORDER

RANK	STATE	ASSAULTS	% of USA
1	California	115,400	13.6%
2	Florida	86,199	10.2%
3	Texas	75,985	9.0%
4	New York	46,911	5.5%
5	Illinois	41,783	4.9%
6	Michigan	32,276	3.8%
7	Tennessee	29,611	3.5%
8	Pennsylvania	28,339	3.3%
9	South Carolina	25,634	3.0%
10	Maryland	24,351	2.9%
11	North Carolina	23,591	2.8%
12	Georgia	23,561	2.8%
13	Louisiana	20,090	2.4%
14	Massachusetts	20,040	2.4%
15	Missouri	19,763	2.3%
16	Arizona	18,921	2.2%
17	New Jersey	16,144	1.9%
18	Ohio	16,108	1.9%
19	Oklahoma	12,802	1.5%
20	Washington	12,417	1.5%
21	Indiana	11,802	1.4%
22	Virginia	11,503	1.4%
23	Alabama	11,286	1.3%
24	Colorado	11,236	1.3%
25	Arkansas	10,083	1.2%
26	New Mexico	9,811	1.2%
27	Nevada	8,348	1.0%
28	Minnesota	7,445	0.9%
29	Kansas	7,254	0.9%
30	Oregon	6,600	0.8%
31	Iowa	6,513	0.8%
32	Wisconsin	6,191	0.7%
33	Kentucky	5,410	0.6%
34	Connecticut	5,070	0.6%
35	Mississippi	4,677	0.6%
36	West Virginia	3,922	0.5%
37	Nebraska	3,595	0.4%
38	Utah	3,398	0.4%
39	Delaware	3,377	0.4%
40	Alaska	3,117	0.4%
41	Idaho	2,586	0.3%
42	Montana	2,187	0.3%
43	Hawaii	1,903	0.2%
44	Rhode Island	1,596	0.2%
45	New Hampshire	1,219	0.1%
46	Wyoming	973	0.1%
47	South Dakota	854	0.1%
48	Maine	742	0.1%
49	Vermont	459	0.1%
50	North Dakota	330	0.0%
	District of Columbia	3,968	0.5%

Source: Reported data from the Federal Bureau of Investigation
"Crime in the United States 2005" (Uniform Crime Reports, September 2006, http://www.fbi.gov/ucr/ucr.htm)
*Revised figures. Aggravated assault is an attack for the purpose of inflicting severe bodily injury.

Percent Change in Number of Aggravated Assaults: 2004 to 2008

National Percent Change = 1.5% Decrease*

ALPHA ORDER				RANK ORDER		
RANK	STATE	PERCENT CHANGE		RANK	STATE	PERCENT CHANGE
19	Alabama	4.5		1	North Dakota	130.6
15	Alaska	7.8		2	Wisconsin	45.8
42	Arizona	(8.7)		3	Vermont	33.1
29	Arkansas	0.0		4	Nevada	33.0
43	California	(9.2)		5	Kentucky	30.1
26	Colorado	0.8		6	South Dakota	22.0
9	Connecticut	12.9		7	Kansas	17.4
8	Delaware	14.9		8	Delaware	14.9
37	Florida	(3.9)		9	Connecticut	12.9
10	Georgia	11.2		10	Georgia	11.2
16	Hawaii	7.0		11	North Carolina	9.7
20	Idaho	3.2		12	Utah	9.4
40	Illinois	(7.1)		13	Maine	8.9
31	Indiana	(0.8)		14	Oklahoma	8.0
34	Iowa	(3.1)		15	Alaska	7.8
7	Kansas	17.4		16	Hawaii	7.0
5	Kentucky	30.1		17	Tennessee	6.8
18	Louisiana	5.5		18	Louisiana	5.5
13	Maine	8.9		19	Alabama	4.5
50	Maryland	(15.5)		20	Idaho	3.2
26	Massachusetts	0.8		21	Missouri	3.0
30	Michigan	(0.4)		22	Minnesota	2.4
22	Minnesota	2.4		23	New Hampshire	2.2
44	Mississippi	(9.6)		24	Ohio	1.3
21	Missouri	3.0		25	Washington	0.9
41	Montana	(8.2)		26	Colorado	0.8
35	Nebraska	(3.6)		26	Massachusetts	0.8
4	Nevada	33.0		28	Texas	0.6
23	New Hampshire	2.2		29	Arkansas	0.0
49	New Jersey	(12.3)		30	Michigan	(0.4)
36	New Mexico	(3.8)		31	Indiana	(0.8)
46	New York	(10.1)		32	Pennsylvania	(1.3)
11	North Carolina	9.7		32	Wyoming	(1.3)
1	North Dakota	130.6		34	Iowa	(3.1)
24	Ohio	1.3		35	Nebraska	(3.6)
14	Oklahoma	8.0		36	New Mexico	(3.8)
48	Oregon	(11.1)		37	Florida	(3.9)
32	Pennsylvania	(1.3)		38	South Carolina	(5.8)
45	Rhode Island	(10.0)		39	West Virginia	(6.8)
38	South Carolina	(5.8)		40	Illinois	(7.1)
6	South Dakota	22.0		41	Montana	(8.2)
17	Tennessee	6.8		42	Arizona	(8.7)
28	Texas	0.6		43	California	(9.2)
12	Utah	9.4		44	Mississippi	(9.6)
3	Vermont	33.1		45	Rhode Island	(10.0)
47	Virginia	(10.3)		46	New York	(10.1)
25	Washington	0.9		47	Virginia	(10.3)
39	West Virginia	(6.8)		48	Oregon	(11.1)
2	Wisconsin	45.8		49	New Jersey	(12.3)
32	Wyoming	(1.3)		50	Maryland	(15.5)

District of Columbia   (6.6)

Source: CQ Press using reported data from the Federal Bureau of Investigation
"Crime in the United States 2005" (Uniform Crime Reports, September 2006, http://www.fbi.gov/ucr/ucr.htm)
*Revised figures. Aggravated assault is an attack for the purpose of inflicting severe bodily injury.

Aggravated Assault Rate in 2004

National Rate = 288.6 Aggravated Assaults per 100,000 Population*

ALPHA ORDER

RANK	STATE	RATE
22	Alabama	249.4
5	Alaska	473.9
14	Arizona	329.6
9	Arkansas	366.7
16	California	322.0
23	Colorado	244.2
41	Connecticut	144.9
8	Delaware	406.8
4	Florida	495.8
21	Georgia	264.2
38	Hawaii	150.8
34	Idaho	185.4
15	Illinois	328.7
32	Indiana	189.5
27	Iowa	220.6
20	Kansas	265.4
44	Kentucky	130.6
6	Louisiana	445.8
49	Maine	56.4
7	Maryland	437.9
18	Massachusetts	312.8
17	Michigan	319.4
40	Minnesota	146.1
36	Mississippi	161.2
12	Missouri	343.1
25	Montana	235.9
29	Nebraska	205.7
11	Nevada	357.8
47	New Hampshire	93.8
33	New Jersey	185.9
2	New Mexico	515.6
24	New York	243.3
19	North Carolina	276.2
50	North Dakota	51.9
42	Ohio	140.7
10	Oklahoma	363.3
35	Oregon	183.8
26	Pennsylvania	228.6
39	Rhode Island	147.8
1	South Carolina	610.6
46	South Dakota	110.8
3	Tennessee	502.5
13	Texas	338.1
43	Utah	140.4
48	Vermont	73.9
37	Virginia	153.8
30	Washington	200.0
28	West Virginia	216.4
45	Wisconsin	112.5
31	Wyoming	192.3

RANK ORDER

RANK	STATE	RATE
1	South Carolina	610.6
2	New Mexico	515.6
3	Tennessee	502.5
4	Florida	495.8
5	Alaska	473.9
6	Louisiana	445.8
7	Maryland	437.9
8	Delaware	406.8
9	Arkansas	366.7
10	Oklahoma	363.3
11	Nevada	357.8
12	Missouri	343.1
13	Texas	338.1
14	Arizona	329.6
15	Illinois	328.7
16	California	322.0
17	Michigan	319.4
18	Massachusetts	312.8
19	North Carolina	276.2
20	Kansas	265.4
21	Georgia	264.2
22	Alabama	249.4
23	Colorado	244.2
24	New York	243.3
25	Montana	235.9
26	Pennsylvania	228.6
27	Iowa	220.6
28	West Virginia	216.4
29	Nebraska	205.7
30	Washington	200.0
31	Wyoming	192.3
32	Indiana	189.5
33	New Jersey	185.9
34	Idaho	185.4
35	Oregon	183.8
36	Mississippi	161.2
37	Virginia	153.8
38	Hawaii	150.8
39	Rhode Island	147.8
40	Minnesota	146.1
41	Connecticut	144.9
42	Ohio	140.7
43	Utah	140.4
44	Kentucky	130.6
45	Wisconsin	112.5
46	South Dakota	110.8
47	New Hampshire	93.8
48	Vermont	73.9
49	Maine	56.4
50	North Dakota	51.9
	District of Columbia	715.9

Source: Reported data from the Federal Bureau of Investigation
"Crime in the United States 2005" (Uniform Crime Reports, September 2006, http://www.fbi.gov/ucr/ucr.htm)
*Revised figures. Aggravated assault is an attack for the purpose of inflicting severe bodily injury.

Percent Change in Aggravated Assault Rate: 2004 to 2008

National Percent Change = 4.9% Decrease*

ALPHA ORDER

RANK	STATE	PERCENT CHANGE
17	Alabama	1.4
14	Alaska	3.3
50	Arizona	(19.3)
28	Arkansas	(3.7)
43	California	(11.5)
33	Colorado	(6.1)
8	Connecticut	12.8
9	Delaware	9.2
40	Florida	(8.8)
15	Georgia	2.4
12	Hawaii	4.8
32	Idaho	(5.6)
39	Illinois	(8.5)
26	Indiana	(3.2)
30	Iowa	(4.8)
7	Kansas	14.5
4	Kentucky	26.2
11	Louisiana	7.8
10	Maine	8.9
49	Maryland	(16.6)
24	Massachusetts	(0.6)
21	Michigan	0.7
23	Minnesota	0.0
41	Mississippi	(10.7)
22	Missouri	0.4
45	Montana	(12.0)
31	Nebraska	(5.5)
5	Nevada	19.3
19	New Hampshire	1.0
46	New Jersey	(12.3)
38	New Mexico	(7.7)
42	New York	(11.1)
16	North Carolina	1.6
1	North Dakota	128.5
19	Ohio	1.0
13	Oklahoma	4.5
48	Oregon	(15.8)
25	Pennsylvania	(1.7)
37	Rhode Island	(7.5)
44	South Carolina	(11.7)
6	South Dakota	17.0
18	Tennessee	1.3
36	Texas	(7.1)
27	Utah	(3.3)
3	Vermont	33.0
47	Virginia	(13.7)
29	Washington	(4.4)
35	West Virginia	(6.9)
2	Wisconsin	42.6
34	Wyoming	(6.3)

RANK ORDER

RANK	STATE	PERCENT CHANGE
1	North Dakota	128.5
2	Wisconsin	42.6
3	Vermont	33.0
4	Kentucky	26.2
5	Nevada	19.3
6	South Dakota	17.0
7	Kansas	14.5
8	Connecticut	12.8
9	Delaware	9.2
10	Maine	8.9
11	Louisiana	7.8
12	Hawaii	4.8
13	Oklahoma	4.5
14	Alaska	3.3
15	Georgia	2.4
16	North Carolina	1.6
17	Alabama	1.4
18	Tennessee	1.3
19	New Hampshire	1.0
19	Ohio	1.0
21	Michigan	0.7
22	Missouri	0.4
23	Minnesota	0.0
24	Massachusetts	(0.6)
25	Pennsylvania	(1.7)
26	Indiana	(3.2)
27	Utah	(3.3)
28	Arkansas	(3.7)
29	Washington	(4.4)
30	Iowa	(4.8)
31	Nebraska	(5.5)
32	Idaho	(5.6)
33	Colorado	(6.1)
34	Wyoming	(6.3)
35	West Virginia	(6.9)
36	Texas	(7.1)
37	Rhode Island	(7.5)
38	New Mexico	(7.7)
39	Illinois	(8.5)
40	Florida	(8.8)
41	Mississippi	(10.7)
42	New York	(11.1)
43	California	(11.5)
44	South Carolina	(11.7)
45	Montana	(12.0)
46	New Jersey	(12.3)
47	Virginia	(13.7)
48	Oregon	(15.8)
49	Maryland	(16.6)
50	Arizona	(19.3)

District of Columbia (12.5)

Source: CQ Press using reported data from the Federal Bureau of Investigation
   "Crime in the United States 2005" (Uniform Crime Reports, September 2006, http://www.fbi.gov/ucr/ucr.htm)
*Revised figures. Aggravated assault is an attack for the purpose of inflicting severe bodily injury.

Property Crimes in 2004

National Total = 10,319,386 Property Crimes*

<table>
<tr><td colspan="4">ALPHA ORDER</td><td colspan="4">RANK ORDER</td></tr>
<tr><td>RANK</td><td>STATE</td><td>CRIMES</td><td>% of USA</td><td>RANK</td><td>STATE</td><td>CRIMES</td><td>% of USA</td></tr>
<tr><td>21</td><td>Alabama</td><td>182,340</td><td>1.8%</td><td>1</td><td>California</td><td>1,227,194</td><td>11.9%</td></tr>
<tr><td>46</td><td>Alaska</td><td>22,172</td><td>0.2%</td><td>2</td><td>Texas</td><td>1,010,702</td><td>9.8%</td></tr>
<tr><td>12</td><td>Arizona</td><td>291,203</td><td>2.8%</td><td>3</td><td>Florida</td><td>727,141</td><td>7.0%</td></tr>
<tr><td>28</td><td>Arkansas</td><td>110,911</td><td>1.1%</td><td>4</td><td>New York</td><td>422,734</td><td>4.1%</td></tr>
<tr><td>1</td><td>California</td><td>1,227,194</td><td>11.9%</td><td>5</td><td>Ohio</td><td>419,337</td><td>4.1%</td></tr>
<tr><td>22</td><td>Colorado</td><td>180,322</td><td>1.7%</td><td>6</td><td>Illinois</td><td>403,486</td><td>3.9%</td></tr>
<tr><td>34</td><td>Connecticut</td><td>93,942</td><td>0.9%</td><td>7</td><td>Georgia</td><td>376,656</td><td>3.6%</td></tr>
<tr><td>43</td><td>Delaware</td><td>27,256</td><td>0.3%</td><td>8</td><td>North Carolina</td><td>355,328</td><td>3.4%</td></tr>
<tr><td>3</td><td>Florida</td><td>727,141</td><td>7.0%</td><td>9</td><td>Michigan</td><td>309,805</td><td>3.0%</td></tr>
<tr><td>7</td><td>Georgia</td><td>376,656</td><td>3.6%</td><td>10</td><td>Washington</td><td>300,837</td><td>2.9%</td></tr>
<tr><td>38</td><td>Hawaii</td><td>60,525</td><td>0.6%</td><td>11</td><td>Pennsylvania</td><td>299,611</td><td>2.9%</td></tr>
<tr><td>40</td><td>Idaho</td><td>38,799</td><td>0.4%</td><td>12</td><td>Arizona</td><td>291,203</td><td>2.8%</td></tr>
<tr><td>6</td><td>Illinois</td><td>403,486</td><td>3.9%</td><td>13</td><td>Tennessee</td><td>254,991</td><td>2.5%</td></tr>
<tr><td>15</td><td>Indiana</td><td>211,929</td><td>2.1%</td><td>14</td><td>Missouri</td><td>224,629</td><td>2.2%</td></tr>
<tr><td>35</td><td>Iowa</td><td>85,775</td><td>0.8%</td><td>15</td><td>Indiana</td><td>211,929</td><td>2.1%</td></tr>
<tr><td>29</td><td>Kansas</td><td>109,771</td><td>1.1%</td><td>16</td><td>New Jersey</td><td>211,313</td><td>2.0%</td></tr>
<tr><td>30</td><td>Kentucky</td><td>105,209</td><td>1.0%</td><td>17</td><td>Maryland</td><td>202,474</td><td>2.0%</td></tr>
<tr><td>19</td><td>Louisiana</td><td>199,153</td><td>1.9%</td><td>18</td><td>Virginia</td><td>200,368</td><td>1.9%</td></tr>
<tr><td>41</td><td>Maine</td><td>31,740</td><td>0.3%</td><td>19</td><td>Louisiana</td><td>199,153</td><td>1.9%</td></tr>
<tr><td>17</td><td>Maryland</td><td>202,474</td><td>2.0%</td><td>20</td><td>South Carolina</td><td>190,456</td><td>1.8%</td></tr>
<tr><td>24</td><td>Massachusetts</td><td>158,150</td><td>1.5%</td><td>21</td><td>Alabama</td><td>182,340</td><td>1.8%</td></tr>
<tr><td>9</td><td>Michigan</td><td>309,805</td><td>3.0%</td><td>22</td><td>Colorado</td><td>180,322</td><td>1.7%</td></tr>
<tr><td>25</td><td>Minnesota</td><td>155,019</td><td>1.5%</td><td>23</td><td>Oregon</td><td>166,475</td><td>1.6%</td></tr>
<tr><td>31</td><td>Mississippi</td><td>100,980</td><td>1.0%</td><td>24</td><td>Massachusetts</td><td>158,150</td><td>1.5%</td></tr>
<tr><td>14</td><td>Missouri</td><td>224,629</td><td>2.2%</td><td>25</td><td>Minnesota</td><td>155,019</td><td>1.5%</td></tr>
<tr><td>44</td><td>Montana</td><td>27,215</td><td>0.3%</td><td>26</td><td>Oklahoma</td><td>149,472</td><td>1.4%</td></tr>
<tr><td>37</td><td>Nebraska</td><td>61,512</td><td>0.6%</td><td>27</td><td>Wisconsin</td><td>146,710</td><td>1.4%</td></tr>
<tr><td>32</td><td>Nevada</td><td>98,215</td><td>1.0%</td><td>28</td><td>Arkansas</td><td>110,911</td><td>1.1%</td></tr>
<tr><td>45</td><td>New Hampshire</td><td>26,658</td><td>0.3%</td><td>29</td><td>Kansas</td><td>109,771</td><td>1.1%</td></tr>
<tr><td>16</td><td>New Jersey</td><td>211,313</td><td>2.0%</td><td>30</td><td>Kentucky</td><td>105,209</td><td>1.0%</td></tr>
<tr><td>36</td><td>New Mexico</td><td>79,895</td><td>0.8%</td><td>31</td><td>Mississippi</td><td>100,980</td><td>1.0%</td></tr>
<tr><td>4</td><td>New York</td><td>422,734</td><td>4.1%</td><td>32</td><td>Nevada</td><td>98,215</td><td>1.0%</td></tr>
<tr><td>8</td><td>North Carolina</td><td>355,328</td><td>3.4%</td><td>33</td><td>Utah</td><td>97,762</td><td>0.9%</td></tr>
<tr><td>50</td><td>North Dakota</td><td>12,493</td><td>0.1%</td><td>34</td><td>Connecticut</td><td>93,942</td><td>0.9%</td></tr>
<tr><td>5</td><td>Ohio</td><td>419,337</td><td>4.1%</td><td>35</td><td>Iowa</td><td>85,775</td><td>0.8%</td></tr>
<tr><td>26</td><td>Oklahoma</td><td>149,472</td><td>1.4%</td><td>36</td><td>New Mexico</td><td>79,895</td><td>0.8%</td></tr>
<tr><td>23</td><td>Oregon</td><td>166,475</td><td>1.6%</td><td>37</td><td>Nebraska</td><td>61,512</td><td>0.6%</td></tr>
<tr><td>11</td><td>Pennsylvania</td><td>299,611</td><td>2.9%</td><td>38</td><td>Hawaii</td><td>60,525</td><td>0.6%</td></tr>
<tr><td>42</td><td>Rhode Island</td><td>31,166</td><td>0.3%</td><td>39</td><td>West Virginia</td><td>46,326</td><td>0.4%</td></tr>
<tr><td>20</td><td>South Carolina</td><td>190,456</td><td>1.8%</td><td>40</td><td>Idaho</td><td>38,799</td><td>0.4%</td></tr>
<tr><td>48</td><td>South Dakota</td><td>14,885</td><td>0.1%</td><td>41</td><td>Maine</td><td>31,740</td><td>0.3%</td></tr>
<tr><td>13</td><td>Tennessee</td><td>254,991</td><td>2.5%</td><td>42</td><td>Rhode Island</td><td>31,166</td><td>0.3%</td></tr>
<tr><td>2</td><td>Texas</td><td>1,010,702</td><td>9.8%</td><td>43</td><td>Delaware</td><td>27,256</td><td>0.3%</td></tr>
<tr><td>33</td><td>Utah</td><td>97,762</td><td>0.9%</td><td>44</td><td>Montana</td><td>27,215</td><td>0.3%</td></tr>
<tr><td>49</td><td>Vermont</td><td>14,559</td><td>0.1%</td><td>45</td><td>New Hampshire</td><td>26,658</td><td>0.3%</td></tr>
<tr><td>18</td><td>Virginia</td><td>200,368</td><td>1.9%</td><td>46</td><td>Alaska</td><td>22,172</td><td>0.2%</td></tr>
<tr><td>10</td><td>Washington</td><td>300,837</td><td>2.9%</td><td>47</td><td>Wyoming</td><td>16,889</td><td>0.2%</td></tr>
<tr><td>39</td><td>West Virginia</td><td>46,326</td><td>0.4%</td><td>48</td><td>South Dakota</td><td>14,885</td><td>0.1%</td></tr>
<tr><td>27</td><td>Wisconsin</td><td>146,710</td><td>1.4%</td><td>49</td><td>Vermont</td><td>14,559</td><td>0.1%</td></tr>
<tr><td>47</td><td>Wyoming</td><td>16,889</td><td>0.2%</td><td>50</td><td>North Dakota</td><td>12,493</td><td>0.1%</td></tr>
<tr><td></td><td></td><td></td><td></td><td></td><td>District of Columbia</td><td>26,896</td><td>0.3%</td></tr>
</table>

Source: Reported data from the Federal Bureau of Investigation
  "Crime in the United States 2005" (Uniform Crime Reports, September 2006, http://www.fbi.gov/ucr/ucr.htm)
*Revised figures. Property crimes are offenses of burglary, larceny-theft, and motor vehicle theft.

Percent Change in Number of Property Crimes: 2004 to 2008

National Percent Change = 5.3% Decrease*

ALPHA ORDER				RANK ORDER		
RANK	STATE	PERCENT CHANGE		RANK	STATE	PERCENT CHANGE
6	Alabama	4.4		1	Delaware	14.8
36	Alaska	(9.2)		2	Vermont	8.3
25	Arizona	(4.2)		3	Wisconsin	5.7
15	Arkansas	(1.3)		4	North Carolina	5.0
38	California	(11.9)		5	Kentucky	4.9
48	Colorado	(22.0)		6	Alabama	4.4
34	Connecticut	(8.4)		6	Florida	4.4
1	Delaware	14.8		8	Georgia	3.3
6	Florida	4.4		8	New Hampshire	3.3
8	Georgia	3.3		10	Maine	1.7
49	Hawaii	(24.0)		11	West Virginia	0.6
46	Idaho	(17.5)		12	Indiana	0.4
30	Illinois	(6.2)		13	Pennsylvania	0.1
12	Indiana	0.4		14	South Carolina	(0.4)
42	Iowa	(15.3)		15	Arkansas	(1.3)
39	Kansas	(13.8)		16	Massachusetts	(1.4)
5	Kentucky	4.9		17	Tennessee	(1.5)
42	Louisiana	(15.3)		18	Maryland	(2.1)
10	Maine	1.7		19	Virginia	(2.4)
18	Maryland	(2.1)		20	North Dakota	(2.7)
16	Massachusetts	(1.4)		21	New Mexico	(2.9)
27	Michigan	(5.2)		22	Missouri	(3.6)
23	Minnesota	(4.0)		23	Minnesota	(4.0)
41	Mississippi	(14.4)		24	Texas	(4.1)
22	Missouri	(3.6)		25	Arizona	(4.2)
32	Montana	(7.5)		25	Rhode Island	(4.2)
45	Nebraska	(16.5)		27	Michigan	(5.2)
35	Nevada	(8.7)		28	New Jersey	(5.8)
8	New Hampshire	3.3		29	Utah	(6.0)
28	New Jersey	(5.8)		30	Illinois	(6.2)
21	New Mexico	(2.9)		31	Ohio	(6.6)
33	New York	(8.1)		32	Montana	(7.5)
4	North Carolina	5.0		33	New York	(8.1)
20	North Dakota	(2.7)		34	Connecticut	(8.4)
31	Ohio	(6.6)		35	Nevada	(8.7)
44	Oklahoma	(16.1)		36	Alaska	(9.2)
50	Oregon	(25.3)		37	South Dakota	(11.1)
13	Pennsylvania	0.1		38	California	(11.9)
25	Rhode Island	(4.2)		39	Kansas	(13.8)
14	South Carolina	(0.4)		40	Wyoming	(14.3)
37	South Dakota	(11.1)		41	Mississippi	(14.4)
17	Tennessee	(1.5)		42	Iowa	(15.3)
24	Texas	(4.1)		42	Louisiana	(15.3)
29	Utah	(6.0)		44	Oklahoma	(16.1)
2	Vermont	8.3		45	Nebraska	(16.5)
19	Virginia	(2.4)		46	Idaho	(17.5)
47	Washington	(18.2)		47	Washington	(18.2)
11	West Virginia	0.6		48	Colorado	(22.0)
3	Wisconsin	5.7		49	Hawaii	(24.0)
40	Wyoming	(14.3)		50	Oregon	(25.3)

District of Columbia	12.3

Source: CQ Press using reported data from the Federal Bureau of Investigation
  "Crime in the United States 2005" (Uniform Crime Reports, September 2006, http://www.fbi.gov/ucr/ucr.htm)
*Revised figures. Property crimes are offenses of burglary, larceny-theft, and motor vehicle theft.

Property Crime Rate in 2004

National Rate = 3,514.1 Property Crimes per 100,000 Population*

ALPHA ORDER

RANK	STATE	RATE
17	Alabama	4,029.3
27	Alaska	3,370.9
1	Arizona	5,073.3
16	Arkansas	4,033.1
25	California	3,423.9
19	Colorado	3,918.5
37	Connecticut	2,684.9
29	Delaware	3,283.6
13	Florida	4,182.5
10	Georgia	4,223.5
3	Hawaii	4,795.5
36	Idaho	2,781.0
30	Illinois	3,174.1
26	Indiana	3,403.6
34	Iowa	2,904.8
18	Kansas	4,015.5
41	Kentucky	2,540.2
7	Louisiana	4,419.1
45	Maine	2,413.7
22	Maryland	3,640.7
42	Massachusetts	2,468.2
31	Michigan	3,066.1
32	Minnesota	3,041.6
24	Mississippi	3,481.1
20	Missouri	3,900.1
33	Montana	2,936.1
23	Nebraska	3,519.6
11	Nevada	4,210.0
48	New Hampshire	2,051.9
43	New Jersey	2,433.0
12	New Mexico	4,198.4
47	New York	2,192.5
14	North Carolina	4,160.5
49	North Dakota	1,963.4
21	Ohio	3,662.3
9	Oklahoma	4,242.1
4	Oregon	4,635.4
44	Pennsylvania	2,417.3
35	Rhode Island	2,886.0
5	South Carolina	4,536.9
50	South Dakota	1,931.6
8	Tennessee	4,326.8
6	Texas	4,497.7
15	Utah	4,038.6
46	Vermont	2,343.6
38	Virginia	2,678.2
2	Washington	4,846.7
40	West Virginia	2,555.8
39	Wisconsin	2,665.7
28	Wyoming	3,338.5

RANK ORDER

RANK	STATE	RATE
1	Arizona	5,073.3
2	Washington	4,846.7
3	Hawaii	4,795.5
4	Oregon	4,635.4
5	South Carolina	4,536.9
6	Texas	4,497.7
7	Louisiana	4,419.1
8	Tennessee	4,326.8
9	Oklahoma	4,242.1
10	Georgia	4,223.5
11	Nevada	4,210.0
12	New Mexico	4,198.4
13	Florida	4,182.5
14	North Carolina	4,160.5
15	Utah	4,038.6
16	Arkansas	4,033.1
17	Alabama	4,029.3
18	Kansas	4,015.5
19	Colorado	3,918.5
20	Missouri	3,900.1
21	Ohio	3,662.3
22	Maryland	3,640.7
23	Nebraska	3,519.6
24	Mississippi	3,481.1
25	California	3,423.9
26	Indiana	3,403.6
27	Alaska	3,370.9
28	Wyoming	3,338.5
29	Delaware	3,283.6
30	Illinois	3,174.1
31	Michigan	3,066.1
32	Minnesota	3,041.6
33	Montana	2,936.1
34	Iowa	2,904.8
35	Rhode Island	2,886.0
36	Idaho	2,781.0
37	Connecticut	2,684.9
38	Virginia	2,678.2
39	Wisconsin	2,665.7
40	West Virginia	2,555.8
41	Kentucky	2,540.2
42	Massachusetts	2,468.2
43	New Jersey	2,433.0
44	Pennsylvania	2,417.3
45	Maine	2,413.7
46	Vermont	2,343.6
47	New York	2,192.5
48	New Hampshire	2,051.9
49	North Dakota	1,963.4
50	South Dakota	1,931.6
	District of Columbia	4,852.8

Source: Reported data from the Federal Bureau of Investigation
"Crime in the United States 2005" (Uniform Crime Reports, September 2006, http://www.fbi.gov/ucr/ucr.htm)
*Revised figures. Property crimes are offenses of burglary, larceny-theft, and motor vehicle theft.

Percent Change in Property Crime Rate: 2004 to 2008

National Percent Change = 8.6% Decrease*

RANK	STATE	PERCENT CHANGE
7	Alabama	1.3
33	Alaska	(13.0)
37	Arizona	(15.4)
18	Arkansas	(4.9)
35	California	(14.1)
49	Colorado	(27.3)
29	Connecticut	(8.4)
1	Delaware	9.2
10	Florida	(1.0)
18	Georgia	(4.9)
48	Hawaii	(25.5)
47	Idaho	(24.4)
28	Illinois	(7.6)
12	Indiana	(2.0)
40	Iowa	(16.7)
39	Kansas	(15.9)
5	Kentucky	1.7
34	Louisiana	(13.5)
6	Maine	1.6
15	Maryland	(3.4)
13	Massachusetts	(2.8)
17	Michigan	(4.3)
23	Minnesota	(6.3)
38	Mississippi	(15.5)
22	Missouri	(6.1)
31	Montana	(11.3)
43	Nebraska	(18.2)
42	Nevada	(18.1)
4	New Hampshire	1.9
20	New Jersey	(5.7)
27	New Mexico	(6.9)
30	New York	(9.1)
13	North Carolina	(2.8)
16	North Dakota	(3.5)
26	Ohio	(6.8)
45	Oklahoma	(18.9)
50	Oregon	(29.2)
9	Pennsylvania	(0.3)
11	Rhode Island	(1.6)
25	South Carolina	(6.7)
36	South Dakota	(14.8)
24	Tennessee	(6.6)
32	Texas	(11.4)
41	Utah	(16.9)
2	Vermont	8.3
21	Virginia	(6.0)
46	Washington	(22.5)
8	West Virginia	0.5
3	Wisconsin	3.4
44	Wyoming	(18.6)

RANK	STATE	PERCENT CHANGE
1	Delaware	9.2
2	Vermont	8.3
3	Wisconsin	3.4
4	New Hampshire	1.9
5	Kentucky	1.7
6	Maine	1.6
7	Alabama	1.3
8	West Virginia	0.5
9	Pennsylvania	(0.3)
10	Florida	(1.0)
11	Rhode Island	(1.6)
12	Indiana	(2.0)
13	Massachusetts	(2.8)
13	North Carolina	(2.8)
15	Maryland	(3.4)
16	North Dakota	(3.5)
17	Michigan	(4.3)
18	Arkansas	(4.9)
18	Georgia	(4.9)
20	New Jersey	(5.7)
21	Virginia	(6.0)
22	Missouri	(6.1)
23	Minnesota	(6.3)
24	Tennessee	(6.6)
25	South Carolina	(6.7)
26	Ohio	(6.8)
27	New Mexico	(6.9)
28	Illinois	(7.6)
29	Connecticut	(8.4)
30	New York	(9.1)
31	Montana	(11.3)
32	Texas	(11.4)
33	Alaska	(13.0)
34	Louisiana	(13.5)
35	California	(14.1)
36	South Dakota	(14.8)
37	Arizona	(15.4)
38	Mississippi	(15.5)
39	Kansas	(15.9)
40	Iowa	(16.7)
41	Utah	(16.9)
42	Nevada	(18.1)
43	Nebraska	(18.2)
44	Wyoming	(18.6)
45	Oklahoma	(18.9)
46	Washington	(22.5)
47	Idaho	(24.4)
48	Hawaii	(25.5)
49	Colorado	(27.3)
50	Oregon	(29.2)

District of Columbia — 5.2

Source: CQ Press using reported data from the Federal Bureau of Investigation
   "Crime in the United States 2005" (Uniform Crime Reports, September 2006, http://www.fbi.gov/ucr/ucr.htm)
*Revised figures. Property crimes are offenses of burglary, larceny-theft, and motor vehicle theft.

Burglaries in 2004

National Total = 2,144,446 Burglaries*

ALPHA ORDER

RANK	STATE	BURGLARIES	% of USA
15	Alabama	44,666	2.1%
45	Alaska	3,773	0.2%
12	Arizona	56,885	2.7%
24	Arkansas	30,151	1.4%
1	California	245,903	11.5%
23	Colorado	33,010	1.5%
35	Connecticut	15,959	0.7%
42	Delaware	5,669	0.3%
3	Florida	166,332	7.8%
6	Georgia	82,992	3.9%
38	Hawaii	10,827	0.5%
40	Idaho	7,671	0.4%
7	Illinois	76,088	3.5%
17	Indiana	42,168	2.0%
34	Iowa	17,928	0.8%
32	Kansas	20,146	0.9%
29	Kentucky	25,902	1.2%
14	Louisiana	45,359	2.1%
41	Maine	6,341	0.3%
20	Maryland	36,704	1.7%
22	Massachusetts	34,497	1.6%
9	Michigan	64,233	3.0%
27	Minnesota	28,048	1.3%
28	Mississippi	27,661	1.3%
19	Missouri	40,472	1.9%
46	Montana	3,515	0.2%
39	Nebraska	9,826	0.5%
31	Nevada	23,142	1.1%
44	New Hampshire	4,979	0.2%
18	New Jersey	41,030	1.9%
33	New Mexico	19,924	0.9%
8	New York	70,696	3.3%
4	North Carolina	101,193	4.7%
50	North Dakota	2,040	0.1%
5	Ohio	96,518	4.5%
21	Oklahoma	35,244	1.6%
25	Oregon	30,072	1.4%
13	Pennsylvania	54,443	2.5%
43	Rhode Island	5,465	0.3%
16	South Carolina	43,739	2.0%
48	South Dakota	3,148	0.1%
11	Tennessee	60,386	2.8%
2	Texas	220,118	10.3%
36	Utah	15,225	0.7%
47	Vermont	3,435	0.2%
26	Virginia	28,759	1.3%
10	Washington	60,632	2.8%
37	West Virginia	10,994	0.5%
30	Wisconsin	23,854	1.1%
49	Wyoming	2,738	0.1%

RANK ORDER

RANK	STATE	BURGLARIES	% of USA
1	California	245,903	11.5%
2	Texas	220,118	10.3%
3	Florida	166,332	7.8%
4	North Carolina	101,193	4.7%
5	Ohio	96,518	4.5%
6	Georgia	82,992	3.9%
7	Illinois	76,088	3.5%
8	New York	70,696	3.3%
9	Michigan	64,233	3.0%
10	Washington	60,632	2.8%
11	Tennessee	60,386	2.8%
12	Arizona	56,885	2.7%
13	Pennsylvania	54,443	2.5%
14	Louisiana	45,359	2.1%
15	Alabama	44,666	2.1%
16	South Carolina	43,739	2.0%
17	Indiana	42,168	2.0%
18	New Jersey	41,030	1.9%
19	Missouri	40,472	1.9%
20	Maryland	36,704	1.7%
21	Oklahoma	35,244	1.6%
22	Massachusetts	34,497	1.6%
23	Colorado	33,010	1.5%
24	Arkansas	30,151	1.4%
25	Oregon	30,072	1.4%
26	Virginia	28,759	1.3%
27	Minnesota	28,048	1.3%
28	Mississippi	27,661	1.3%
29	Kentucky	25,902	1.2%
30	Wisconsin	23,854	1.1%
31	Nevada	23,142	1.1%
32	Kansas	20,146	0.9%
33	New Mexico	19,924	0.9%
34	Iowa	17,928	0.8%
35	Connecticut	15,959	0.7%
36	Utah	15,225	0.7%
37	West Virginia	10,994	0.5%
38	Hawaii	10,827	0.5%
39	Nebraska	9,826	0.5%
40	Idaho	7,671	0.4%
41	Maine	6,341	0.3%
42	Delaware	5,669	0.3%
43	Rhode Island	5,465	0.3%
44	New Hampshire	4,979	0.2%
45	Alaska	3,773	0.2%
46	Montana	3,515	0.2%
47	Vermont	3,435	0.2%
48	South Dakota	3,148	0.1%
49	Wyoming	2,738	0.1%
50	North Dakota	2,040	0.1%
	District of Columbia	3,946	0.2%

Source: Reported data from the Federal Bureau of Investigation
"Crime in the United States 2005" (Uniform Crime Reports, September 2006, http://www.tbı.gov/ucr/ucr.htm)
*Revised figures. Burglary is the unlawful entry of a structure to commit a felony or theft. Attempts are included.

Percent Change in Number of Burglaries: 2004 to 2008

National Percent Change = 3.6% Increase*

RANK	STATE	PERCENT CHANGE
8	Alabama	12.9
46	Alaska	(14.1)
29	Arizona	(0.7)
9	Arkansas	11.8
32	California	(3.3)
47	Colorado	(14.4)
37	Connecticut	(5.9)
2	Delaware	19.2
6	Florida	13.3
1	Georgia	21.3
43	Hawaii	(13.4)
42	Idaho	(12.6)
23	Illinois	3.8
4	Indiana	15.4
40	Iowa	(8.2)
31	Kansas	(2.7)
10	Kentucky	11.3
34	Louisiana	(4.5)
25	Maine	2.9
17	Maryland	5.8
20	Massachusetts	4.6
3	Michigan	15.5
36	Minnesota	(5.8)
37	Mississippi	(5.9)
7	Missouri	13.1
35	Montana	(5.2)
41	Nebraska	(10.7)
22	Nevada	4.4
45	New Hampshire	(13.9)
30	New Jersey	(1.5)
13	New Mexico	9.0
39	New York	(7.0)
12	North Carolina	10.3
24	North Dakota	3.2
16	Ohio	6.2
28	Oklahoma	(0.5)
50	Oregon	(30.6)
14	Pennsylvania	7.7
18	Rhode Island	5.2
19	South Carolina	5.1
49	South Dakota	(22.8)
14	Tennessee	7.7
21	Texas	4.5
33	Utah	(3.6)
26	Vermont	0.8
11	Virginia	11.2
43	Washington	(13.4)
27	West Virginia	0.7
5	Wisconsin	15.2
48	Wyoming	(20.2)

RANK	STATE	PERCENT CHANGE
1	Georgia	21.3
2	Delaware	19.2
3	Michigan	15.5
4	Indiana	15.4
5	Wisconsin	15.2
6	Florida	13.3
7	Missouri	13.1
8	Alabama	12.9
9	Arkansas	11.8
10	Kentucky	11.3
11	Virginia	11.2
12	North Carolina	10.3
13	New Mexico	9.0
14	Pennsylvania	7.7
14	Tennessee	7.7
16	Ohio	6.2
17	Maryland	5.8
18	Rhode Island	5.2
19	South Carolina	5.1
20	Massachusetts	4.6
21	Texas	4.5
22	Nevada	4.4
23	Illinois	3.8
24	North Dakota	3.2
25	Maine	2.9
26	Vermont	0.8
27	West Virginia	0.7
28	Oklahoma	(0.5)
29	Arizona	(0.7)
30	New Jersey	(1.5)
31	Kansas	(2.7)
32	California	(3.3)
33	Utah	(3.6)
34	Louisiana	(4.5)
35	Montana	(5.2)
36	Minnesota	(5.8)
37	Connecticut	(5.9)
37	Mississippi	(5.9)
39	New York	(7.0)
40	Iowa	(8.2)
41	Nebraska	(10.7)
42	Idaho	(12.6)
43	Hawaii	(13.4)
43	Washington	(13.4)
45	New Hampshire	(13.9)
46	Alaska	(14.1)
47	Colorado	(14.4)
48	Wyoming	(20.2)
49	South Dakota	(22.8)
50	Oregon	(30.6)

District of Columbia	(4.0)

Source: CQ Press using reported data from the Federal Bureau of Investigation
"Crime in the United States 2005" (Uniform Crime Reports, September 2006, http://www.fbi.gov/ucr/ucr.htm)
*Revised figures. Burglary is the unlawful entry of a structure to commit a felony or theft. Attempts are included.

Burglary Rate in 2004

National Rate = 730.3 Burglaries per 100,000 Population*

ALPHA ORDER

RANK	STATE	RATE
10	Alabama	987.0
32	Alaska	573.6
9	Arizona	991.0
2	Arkansas	1,096.4
22	California	686.1
20	Colorado	717.3
42	Connecticut	456.1
23	Delaware	683.0
13	Florida	956.7
15	Georgia	930.6
16	Hawaii	857.8
36	Idaho	549.8
31	Illinois	598.6
24	Indiana	677.2
29	Iowa	607.1
19	Kansas	737.0
28	Kentucky	625.4
6	Louisiana	1,006.5
40	Maine	482.2
25	Maryland	660.0
38	Massachusetts	538.4
26	Michigan	635.7
35	Minnesota	550.3
14	Mississippi	953.6
21	Missouri	702.7
48	Montana	379.2
33	Nebraska	562.2
8	Nevada	992.0
47	New Hampshire	383.2
41	New Jersey	472.4
3	New Mexico	1,047.0
49	New York	366.7
1	North Carolina	1,184.9
50	North Dakota	320.6
17	Ohio	842.9
7	Oklahoma	1,000.2
18	Oregon	837.3
43	Pennsylvania	439.3
39	Rhode Island	506.1
4	South Carolina	1,041.9
45	South Dakota	408.5
5	Tennessee	1,024.7
11	Texas	979.5
27	Utah	628.9
34	Vermont	552.9
46	Virginia	384.4
12	Washington	976.8
30	West Virginia	606.5
44	Wisconsin	433.4
37	Wyoming	541.2

RANK ORDER

RANK	STATE	RATE
1	North Carolina	1,184.9
2	Arkansas	1,096.4
3	New Mexico	1,047.0
4	South Carolina	1,041.9
5	Tennessee	1,024.7
6	Louisiana	1,006.5
7	Oklahoma	1,000.2
8	Nevada	992.0
9	Arizona	991.0
10	Alabama	987.0
11	Texas	979.5
12	Washington	976.8
13	Florida	956.7
14	Mississippi	953.6
15	Georgia	930.6
16	Hawaii	857.8
17	Ohio	842.9
18	Oregon	837.3
19	Kansas	737.0
20	Colorado	717.3
21	Missouri	702.7
22	California	686.1
23	Delaware	683.0
24	Indiana	677.2
25	Maryland	660.0
26	Michigan	635.7
27	Utah	628.9
28	Kentucky	625.4
29	Iowa	607.1
30	West Virginia	606.5
31	Illinois	598.6
32	Alaska	573.6
33	Nebraska	562.2
34	Vermont	552.9
35	Minnesota	550.3
36	Idaho	549.8
37	Wyoming	541.2
38	Massachusetts	538.4
39	Rhode Island	506.1
40	Maine	482.2
41	New Jersey	472.4
42	Connecticut	456.1
43	Pennsylvania	439.3
44	Wisconsin	433.4
45	South Dakota	408.5
46	Virginia	384.4
47	New Hampshire	383.2
48	Montana	379.2
49	New York	366.7
50	North Dakota	320.6
	District of Columbia	712.0

Source: Reported data from the Federal Bureau of Investigation
"Crime in the United States 2005" (Uniform Crime Reports, September 2006, http://www.fbi.gov/ucr/ucr.htm)
*Revised figures. Burglary is the unlawful entry of a structure to commit a felony or theft. Attempts are included.

Percent Change in Burglary Rate: 2004 to 2008

National Percent Change = 0.1% Increase*

ALPHA ORDER

RANK	STATE	PERCENT CHANGE
7	Alabama	9.6
44	Alaska	(17.7)
39	Arizona	(12.3)
10	Arkansas	7.6
31	California	(5.7)
47	Colorado	(20.3)
32	Connecticut	(6.0)
2	Delaware	13.4
11	Florida	7.5
5	Georgia	11.6
43	Hawaii	(15.1)
46	Idaho	(20.0)
20	Illinois	2.3
4	Indiana	12.6
38	Iowa	(9.8)
30	Kansas	(5.0)
9	Kentucky	8.0
27	Louisiana	(2.4)
18	Maine	2.7
15	Maryland	4.5
17	Massachusetts	3.2
1	Michigan	16.6
36	Minnesota	(8.1)
34	Mississippi	(7.1)
6	Missouri	10.2
37	Montana	(9.2)
40	Nebraska	(12.5)
33	Nevada	(6.4)
42	New Hampshire	(15.0)
25	New Jersey	(1.5)
15	New Mexico	4.5
35	New York	(8.0)
21	North Carolina	2.1
19	North Dakota	2.4
14	Ohio	5.9
29	Oklahoma	(3.7)
50	Oregon	(34.2)
12	Pennsylvania	7.2
8	Rhode Island	8.1
25	South Carolina	(1.5)
49	South Dakota	(26.0)
21	Tennessee	2.1
28	Texas	(3.4)
41	Utah	(14.7)
23	Vermont	0.8
13	Virginia	7.1
45	Washington	(18.0)
24	West Virginia	0.6
3	Wisconsin	12.7
48	Wyoming	(24.2)

RANK ORDER

RANK	STATE	PERCENT CHANGE
1	Michigan	16.6
2	Delaware	13.4
3	Wisconsin	12.7
4	Indiana	12.6
5	Georgia	11.6
6	Missouri	10.2
7	Alabama	9.6
8	Rhode Island	8.1
9	Kentucky	8.0
10	Arkansas	7.6
11	Florida	7.5
12	Pennsylvania	7.2
13	Virginia	7.1
14	Ohio	5.9
15	Maryland	4.5
15	New Mexico	4.5
17	Massachusetts	3.2
18	Maine	2.7
19	North Dakota	2.4
20	Illinois	2.3
21	North Carolina	2.1
21	Tennessee	2.1
23	Vermont	0.8
24	West Virginia	0.6
25	New Jersey	(1.5)
25	South Carolina	(1.5)
27	Louisiana	(2.4)
28	Texas	(3.4)
29	Oklahoma	(3.7)
30	Kansas	(5.0)
31	California	(5.7)
32	Connecticut	(6.0)
33	Nevada	(6.4)
34	Mississippi	(7.1)
35	New York	(8.0)
36	Minnesota	(8.1)
37	Montana	(9.2)
38	Iowa	(9.8)
39	Arizona	(12.3)
40	Nebraska	(12.5)
41	Utah	(14.7)
42	New Hampshire	(15.0)
43	Hawaii	(15.1)
44	Alaska	(17.7)
45	Washington	(18.0)
46	Idaho	(20.0)
47	Colorado	(20.3)
48	Wyoming	(24.2)
49	South Dakota	(26.0)
50	Oregon	(34.2)

District of Columbia (10.1)

Source: CQ Press using reported data from the Federal Bureau of Investigation
   "Crime in the United States 2005" (Uniform Crime Reports, September 2006, http://www.fbi.gov/ucr/ucr.htm)
*Revised figures. Burglary is the unlawful entry of a structure to commit a felony or theft. Attempts are included.

Larceny-Thefts in 2004

National Total = 6,937,089 Larceny-Thefts*

ALPHA ORDER					RANK ORDER			
RANK	STATE	THEFTS	% of USA		RANK	STATE	THEFTS	% of USA
21	Alabama	123,650	1.8%		1	California	728,687	10.5%
46	Alaska	16,159	0.2%		2	Texas	696,507	10.0%
12	Arizona	179,012	2.6%		3	Florida	482,484	7.0%
30	Arkansas	74,242	1.1%		4	New York	311,036	4.5%
1	California	728,687	10.5%		5	Illinois	287,025	4.1%
22	Colorado	123,308	1.8%		6	Ohio	282,168	4.1%
32	Connecticut	66,770	1.0%		7	Georgia	249,426	3.6%
45	Delaware	19,285	0.3%		8	North Carolina	227,147	3.3%
3	Florida	482,484	7.0%		9	Pennsylvania	214,199	3.1%
7	Georgia	249,426	3.6%		10	Washington	196,972	2.8%
38	Hawaii	41,078	0.6%		11	Michigan	194,988	2.8%
40	Idaho	28,389	0.4%		12	Arizona	179,012	2.6%
5	Illinois	287,025	4.1%		13	Tennessee	169,828	2.4%
16	Indiana	148,670	2.1%		14	Missouri	158,264	2.3%
34	Iowa	62,214	0.9%		15	Virginia	154,154	2.2%
28	Kansas	81,115	1.2%		16	Indiana	148,670	2.1%
31	Kentucky	70,535	1.0%		17	New Jersey	139,977	2.0%
18	Louisiana	134,080	1.9%		18	Louisiana	134,080	1.9%
41	Maine	24,096	0.3%		19	South Carolina	130,991	1.9%
20	Maryland	129,888	1.9%		20	Maryland	129,888	1.9%
26	Massachusetts	101,605	1.5%		21	Alabama	123,650	1.8%
11	Michigan	194,988	2.8%		22	Colorado	123,308	1.8%
24	Minnesota	113,453	1.6%		23	Oregon	117,868	1.7%
33	Mississippi	65,440	0.9%		24	Minnesota	113,453	1.6%
14	Missouri	158,264	2.3%		25	Wisconsin	111,482	1.6%
42	Montana	22,082	0.3%		26	Massachusetts	101,605	1.5%
37	Nebraska	46,399	0.7%		27	Oklahoma	101,271	1.5%
35	Nevada	52,438	0.8%		28	Kansas	81,115	1.2%
44	New Hampshire	19,723	0.3%		29	Utah	74,889	1.1%
17	New Jersey	139,977	2.0%		30	Arkansas	74,242	1.1%
36	New Mexico	52,069	0.8%		31	Kentucky	70,535	1.0%
4	New York	311,036	4.5%		32	Connecticut	66,770	1.0%
8	North Carolina	227,147	3.3%		33	Mississippi	65,440	0.9%
50	North Dakota	9,516	0.1%		34	Iowa	62,214	0.9%
6	Ohio	282,168	4.1%		35	Nevada	52,438	0.8%
27	Oklahoma	101,271	1.5%		36	New Mexico	52,069	0.8%
23	Oregon	117,868	1.7%		37	Nebraska	46,399	0.7%
9	Pennsylvania	214,199	3.1%		38	Hawaii	41,078	0.6%
43	Rhode Island	21,623	0.3%		39	West Virginia	31,566	0.5%
19	South Carolina	130,991	1.9%		40	Idaho	28,389	0.4%
48	South Dakota	10,890	0.2%		41	Maine	24,096	0.3%
13	Tennessee	169,828	2.4%		42	Montana	22,082	0.3%
2	Texas	696,507	10.0%		43	Rhode Island	21,623	0.3%
29	Utah	74,889	1.1%		44	New Hampshire	19,723	0.3%
49	Vermont	10,537	0.2%		45	Delaware	19,285	0.3%
15	Virginia	154,154	2.2%		46	Alaska	16,159	0.2%
10	Washington	196,972	2.8%		47	Wyoming	13,352	0.2%
39	West Virginia	31,566	0.5%		48	South Dakota	10,890	0.2%
25	Wisconsin	111,482	1.6%		49	Vermont	10,537	0.2%
47	Wyoming	13,352	0.2%		50	North Dakota	9,516	0.1%
						District of Columbia	14,542	0.2%

Source: Reported data from the Federal Bureau of Investigation
   "Crime in the United States 2005" (Uniform Crime Reports, September 2006, http://www.fbi.gov/ucr/ucr.htm)
*Revised figures. Larceny-theft is the unlawful taking of property without use of force, violence, or fraud. Attempts are included. Motor vehicle thefts are excluded.

Percent Change in Larceny-Thefts: 2004 to 2008

National Percent Change = 5.0% Decrease*

ALPHA ORDER

ALPHA ORDER

RANK	STATE	PERCENT CHANGE
12	Alabama	2.3
27	Alaska	(5.7)
8	Arizona	3.5
31	Arkansas	(6.7)
38	California	(10.7)
47	Colorado	(19.8)
32	Connecticut	(7.0)
1	Delaware	14.1
5	Florida	5.1
15	Georgia	(0.3)
50	Hawaii	(23.3)
43	Idaho	(16.7)
32	Illinois	(7.0)
18	Indiana	(1.4)
41	Iowa	(16.6)
41	Kansas	(16.6)
6	Kentucky	4.6
44	Louisiana	(16.8)
14	Maine	2.0
10	Maryland	3.2
4	Massachusetts	5.4
28	Michigan	(6.1)
16	Minnesota	(1.0)
46	Mississippi	(17.4)
25	Missouri	(5.2)
37	Montana	(8.2)
45	Nebraska	(17.3)
26	Nevada	(5.4)
3	New Hampshire	10.8
16	New Jersey	(1.0)
35	New Mexico	(8.1)
24	New York	(4.3)
9	North Carolina	3.3
22	North Dakota	(3.7)
34	Ohio	(7.6)
48	Oklahoma	(21.6)
49	Oregon	(21.8)
13	Pennsylvania	2.2
21	Rhode Island	(3.3)
23	South Carolina	(3.8)
35	South Dakota	(8.1)
19	Tennessee	(1.7)
28	Texas	(6.1)
30	Utah	(6.5)
2	Vermont	11.3
20	Virginia	(2.4)
40	Washington	(16.1)
11	West Virginia	2.4
7	Wisconsin	4.2
39	Wyoming	(13.3)

RANK ORDER

RANK	STATE	PERCENT CHANGE
1	Delaware	14.1
2	Vermont	11.3
3	New Hampshire	10.8
4	Massachusetts	5.4
5	Florida	5.1
6	Kentucky	4.6
7	Wisconsin	4.2
8	Arizona	3.5
9	North Carolina	3.3
10	Maryland	3.2
11	West Virginia	2.4
12	Alabama	2.3
13	Pennsylvania	2.2
14	Maine	2.0
15	Georgia	(0.3)
16	Minnesota	(1.0)
16	New Jersey	(1.0)
18	Indiana	(1.4)
19	Tennessee	(1.7)
20	Virginia	(2.4)
21	Rhode Island	(3.3)
22	North Dakota	(3.7)
23	South Carolina	(3.8)
24	New York	(4.3)
25	Missouri	(5.2)
26	Nevada	(5.4)
27	Alaska	(5.7)
28	Michigan	(6.1)
28	Texas	(6.1)
30	Utah	(6.5)
31	Arkansas	(6.7)
32	Connecticut	(7.0)
32	Illinois	(7.0)
34	Ohio	(7.6)
35	New Mexico	(8.1)
35	South Dakota	(8.1)
37	Montana	(8.2)
38	California	(10.7)
39	Wyoming	(13.3)
40	Washington	(16.1)
41	Iowa	(16.6)
41	Kansas	(16.6)
43	Idaho	(16.7)
44	Louisiana	(16.8)
45	Nebraska	(17.3)
46	Mississippi	(17.4)
47	Colorado	(19.8)
48	Oklahoma	(21.6)
49	Oregon	(21.8)
50	Hawaii	(23.3)

District of Columbia 37.2

Source: CQ Press using reported data from the Federal Bureau of Investigation
"Crime in the United States 2005" (Uniform Crime Reports, September 2006, http://www.fbi.gov/ucr/ucr.htm)
*Revised figures. Larceny-theft is the unlawful taking of property without use of force, violence, or fraud. Attempts are included. Motor vehicle thefts are excluded.

Larceny-Theft Rate in 2004

National Rate = 2,362.3 Larceny-Thefts per 100,000 Population*

ALPHA ORDER

RANK	STATE	RATE
16	Alabama	2,732.4
23	Alaska	2,456.7
5	Arizona	3,118.7
17	Arkansas	2,699.7
35	California	2,033.1
18	Colorado	2,679.5
39	Connecticut	1,908.3
27	Delaware	2,323.3
13	Florida	2,775.2
12	Georgia	2,796.8
2	Hawaii	3,254.7
34	Idaho	2,034.8
28	Illinois	2,257.9
24	Indiana	2,387.7
32	Iowa	2,106.9
9	Kansas	2,967.2
43	Kentucky	1,703.0
8	Louisiana	2,975.1
40	Maine	1,832.4
26	Maryland	2,335.6
47	Massachusetts	1,585.7
38	Michigan	1,929.8
31	Minnesota	2,226.1
29	Mississippi	2,256.0
14	Missouri	2,747.9
25	Montana	2,382.3
20	Nebraska	2,654.9
30	Nevada	2,247.8
48	New Hampshire	1,518.1
46	New Jersey	1,611.7
15	New Mexico	2,736.1
45	New York	1,613.2
19	North Carolina	2,659.7
49	North Dakota	1,495.5
22	Ohio	2,464.3
11	Oklahoma	2,874.1
1	Oregon	3,282.0
42	Pennsylvania	1,728.2
37	Rhode Island	2,002.3
4	South Carolina	3,120.4
50	South Dakota	1,413.1
10	Tennessee	2,881.7
6	Texas	3,099.5
7	Utah	3,093.7
44	Vermont	1,696.1
33	Virginia	2,060.5
3	Washington	3,173.4
41	West Virginia	1,741.5
36	Wisconsin	2,025.6
21	Wyoming	2,639.3

RANK ORDER

RANK	STATE	RATE
1	Oregon	3,282.0
2	Hawaii	3,254.7
3	Washington	3,173.4
4	South Carolina	3,120.4
5	Arizona	3,118.7
6	Texas	3,099.5
7	Utah	3,093.7
8	Louisiana	2,975.1
9	Kansas	2,967.2
10	Tennessee	2,881.7
11	Oklahoma	2,874.1
12	Georgia	2,796.8
13	Florida	2,775.2
14	Missouri	2,747.9
15	New Mexico	2,736.1
16	Alabama	2,732.4
17	Arkansas	2,699.7
18	Colorado	2,679.5
19	North Carolina	2,659.7
20	Nebraska	2,654.9
21	Wyoming	2,639.3
22	Ohio	2,464.3
23	Alaska	2,456.7
24	Indiana	2,387.7
25	Montana	2,382.3
26	Maryland	2,335.6
27	Delaware	2,323.3
28	Illinois	2,257.9
29	Mississippi	2,256.0
30	Nevada	2,247.8
31	Minnesota	2,226.1
32	Iowa	2,106.9
33	Virginia	2,060.5
34	Idaho	2,034.8
35	California	2,033.1
36	Wisconsin	2,025.6
37	Rhode Island	2,002.3
38	Michigan	1,929.8
39	Connecticut	1,908.3
40	Maine	1,832.4
41	West Virginia	1,741.5
42	Pennsylvania	1,728.2
43	Kentucky	1,703.0
44	Vermont	1,696.1
45	New York	1,613.2
46	New Jersey	1,611.7
47	Massachusetts	1,585.7
48	New Hampshire	1,518.1
49	North Dakota	1,495.5
50	South Dakota	1,413.1
	District of Columbia	2,623.8

Source: Reported data from the Federal Bureau of Investigation
"Crime in the United States 2005" (Uniform Crime Reports, September 2006, http://www.fbi.gov/ucr/ucr.htm)
*Revised figures. Larceny-theft is the unlawful taking of property without use of force, violence, or fraud. Attempts are included. Motor vehicle thefts are excluded.

Percent Change in Larceny-Theft Rate: 2004 to 2008

National Percent Change = 8.3% Decrease*

ALPHA ORDER

RANK	STATE	PERCENT CHANGE
12	Alabama	(0.7)
29	Alaska	(9.6)
28	Arizona	(8.6)
31	Arkansas	(10.1)
35	California	(13.0)
49	Colorado	(25.2)
23	Connecticut	(7.0)
3	Delaware	8.5
11	Florida	(0.3)
26	Georgia	(8.2)
48	Hawaii	(24.9)
46	Idaho	(23.7)
27	Illinois	(8.4)
16	Indiana	(3.7)
41	Iowa	(17.9)
43	Kansas	(18.7)
10	Kentucky	1.5
37	Louisiana	(15.0)
6	Maine	1.9
8	Maryland	1.8
4	Massachusetts	4.0
19	Michigan	(5.1)
15	Minnesota	(3.3)
42	Mississippi	(18.5)
24	Missouri	(7.6)
33	Montana	(12.0)
44	Nebraska	(18.9)
38	Nevada	(15.2)
2	New Hampshire	9.4
14	New Jersey	(1.0)
32	New Mexico	(11.9)
20	New York	(5.3)
17	North Carolina	(4.4)
18	North Dakota	(4.5)
25	Ohio	(7.9)
47	Oklahoma	(24.1)
50	Oregon	(25.9)
8	Pennsylvania	1.8
12	Rhode Island	(0.7)
30	South Carolina	(9.8)
33	South Dakota	(12.0)
22	Tennessee	(6.7)
36	Texas	(13.3)
39	Utah	(17.3)
1	Vermont	11.3
21	Virginia	(6.1)
45	Washington	(20.4)
5	West Virginia	2.3
6	Wisconsin	1.9
40	Wyoming	(17.7)

RANK ORDER

RANK	STATE	PERCENT CHANGE
1	Vermont	11.3
2	New Hampshire	9.4
3	Delaware	8.5
4	Massachusetts	4.0
5	West Virginia	2.3
6	Maine	1.9
6	Wisconsin	1.9
8	Maryland	1.8
8	Pennsylvania	1.8
10	Kentucky	1.5
11	Florida	(0.3)
12	Alabama	(0.7)
12	Rhode Island	(0.7)
14	New Jersey	(1.0)
15	Minnesota	(3.3)
16	Indiana	(3.7)
17	North Carolina	(4.4)
18	North Dakota	(4.5)
19	Michigan	(5.1)
20	New York	(5.3)
21	Virginia	(6.1)
22	Tennessee	(6.7)
23	Connecticut	(7.0)
24	Missouri	(7.6)
25	Ohio	(7.9)
26	Georgia	(8.2)
27	Illinois	(8.4)
28	Arizona	(8.6)
29	Alaska	(9.6)
30	South Carolina	(9.8)
31	Arkansas	(10.1)
32	New Mexico	(11.9)
33	Montana	(12.0)
33	South Dakota	(12.0)
35	California	(13.0)
36	Texas	(13.3)
37	Louisiana	(15.0)
38	Nevada	(15.2)
39	Utah	(17.3)
40	Wyoming	(17.7)
41	Iowa	(17.9)
42	Mississippi	(18.5)
43	Kansas	(18.7)
44	Nebraska	(18.9)
45	Washington	(20.4)
46	Idaho	(23.7)
47	Oklahoma	(24.1)
48	Hawaii	(24.9)
49	Colorado	(25.2)
50	Oregon	(25.9)

	District of Columbia	28.5

Source: CQ Press using reported data from the Federal Bureau of Investigation
"Crime in the United States 2005" (Uniform Crime Reports, September 2006, http://www.fbi.gov/ucr/ucr.htm)
*Revised figures. Larceny-theft is the unlawful taking of property without use of force, violence, or fraud. Attempts are included. Motor vehicle thefts are excluded.

Motor Vehicle Thefts in 2004

National Total = 1,237,851 Motor Vehicle Thefts*

ALPHA ORDER

RANK	STATE	THEFTS	% of USA
25	Alabama	14,024	1.1%
43	Alaska	2,240	0.2%
4	Arizona	55,306	4.5%
36	Arkansas	6,518	0.5%
1	California	252,604	20.4%
17	Colorado	24,004	1.9%
29	Connecticut	11,213	0.9%
42	Delaware	2,302	0.2%
3	Florida	78,325	6.3%
6	Georgia	44,238	3.6%
31	Hawaii	8,620	0.7%
41	Idaho	2,739	0.2%
10	Illinois	40,373	3.3%
20	Indiana	21,091	1.7%
37	Iowa	5,633	0.5%
32	Kansas	8,510	0.7%
30	Kentucky	8,772	0.7%
21	Louisiana	19,714	1.6%
46	Maine	1,303	0.1%
11	Maryland	35,882	2.9%
19	Massachusetts	22,048	1.8%
5	Michigan	50,584	4.1%
26	Minnesota	13,518	1.1%
34	Mississippi	7,879	0.6%
15	Missouri	25,893	2.1%
45	Montana	1,618	0.1%
38	Nebraska	5,287	0.4%
18	Nevada	22,635	1.8%
44	New Hampshire	1,956	0.2%
13	New Jersey	30,306	2.4%
33	New Mexico	7,902	0.6%
8	New York	41,002	3.3%
14	North Carolina	26,988	2.2%
47	North Dakota	937	0.1%
9	Ohio	40,651	3.3%
27	Oklahoma	12,957	1.0%
22	Oregon	18,535	1.5%
12	Pennsylvania	30,969	2.5%
39	Rhode Island	4,078	0.3%
24	South Carolina	15,726	1.3%
48	South Dakota	847	0.1%
16	Tennessee	24,777	2.0%
2	Texas	94,077	7.6%
35	Utah	7,648	0.6%
50	Vermont	587	0.0%
23	Virginia	17,455	1.4%
7	Washington	43,233	3.5%
40	West Virginia	3,766	0.3%
28	Wisconsin	11,374	0.9%
49	Wyoming	799	0.1%

RANK ORDER

RANK	STATE	THEFTS	% of USA
1	California	252,604	20.4%
2	Texas	94,077	7.6%
3	Florida	78,325	6.3%
4	Arizona	55,306	4.5%
5	Michigan	50,584	4.1%
6	Georgia	44,238	3.6%
7	Washington	43,233	3.5%
8	New York	41,002	3.3%
9	Ohio	40,651	3.3%
10	Illinois	40,373	3.3%
11	Maryland	35,882	2.9%
12	Pennsylvania	30,969	2.5%
13	New Jersey	30,306	2.4%
14	North Carolina	26,988	2.2%
15	Missouri	25,893	2.1%
16	Tennessee	24,777	2.0%
17	Colorado	24,004	1.9%
18	Nevada	22,635	1.8%
19	Massachusetts	22,048	1.8%
20	Indiana	21,091	1.7%
21	Louisiana	19,714	1.6%
22	Oregon	18,535	1.5%
23	Virginia	17,455	1.4%
24	South Carolina	15,726	1.3%
25	Alabama	14,024	1.1%
26	Minnesota	13,518	1.1%
27	Oklahoma	12,957	1.0%
28	Wisconsin	11,374	0.9%
29	Connecticut	11,213	0.9%
30	Kentucky	8,772	0.7%
31	Hawaii	8,620	0.7%
32	Kansas	8,510	0.7%
33	New Mexico	7,902	0.6%
34	Mississippi	7,879	0.6%
35	Utah	7,648	0.6%
36	Arkansas	6,518	0.5%
37	Iowa	5,633	0.5%
38	Nebraska	5,287	0.4%
39	Rhode Island	4,078	0.3%
40	West Virginia	3,766	0.3%
41	Idaho	2,739	0.2%
42	Delaware	2,302	0.2%
43	Alaska	2,240	0.2%
44	New Hampshire	1,956	0.2%
45	Montana	1,618	0.1%
46	Maine	1,303	0.1%
47	North Dakota	937	0.1%
48	South Dakota	847	0.1%
49	Wyoming	799	0.1%
50	Vermont	587	0.0%
	District of Columbia	8,408	0.7%

Source: Reported data from the Federal Bureau of Investigation
   "Crime in the United States 2005" (Uniform Crime Reports, September 2006, http://www.fbi.gov/ucr/ucr.htm)
*Revised figures. Includes the theft or attempted theft of a self-propelled vehicle. Excludes motorboats, construction equipment, airplanes, and farming equipment.

Percent Change in Number of Motor Vehicle Thefts: 2004 to 2008

National Percent Change = 22.7% Decrease*

ALPHA ORDER

RANK	STATE	PERCENT CHANGE
9	Alabama	(4.0)
34	Alaska	(26.9)
42	Arizona	(32.7)
5	Arkansas	(0.1)
31	California	(23.8)
50	Colorado	(43.7)
26	Connecticut	(20.1)
2	Delaware	10.4
22	Florida	(18.9)
15	Georgia	(10.4)
48	Hawaii	(40.5)
47	Idaho	(39.1)
23	Illinois	(19.3)
21	Indiana	(17.2)
30	Iowa	(23.1)
18	Kansas	(13.1)
17	Kentucky	(12.6)
41	Louisiana	(30.3)
14	Maine	(9.7)
38	Maryland	(29.4)
49	Massachusetts	(42.2)
36	Michigan	(28.4)
33	Minnesota	(25.4)
24	Mississippi	(19.4)
25	Missouri	(19.8)
8	Montana	(2.8)
27	Nebraska	(20.8)
39	Nevada	(29.7)
37	New Hampshire	(29.1)
43	New Jersey	(33.4)
3	New Mexico	1.3
45	New York	(38.7)
7	North Carolina	(0.9)
11	North Dakota	(5.9)
40	Ohio	(29.8)
20	Oklahoma	(16.0)
46	Oregon	(38.9)
35	Pennsylvania	(27.4)
28	Rhode Island	(21.5)
1	South Carolina	12.2
10	South Dakota	(5.5)
29	Tennessee	(22.4)
13	Texas	(9.3)
11	Utah	(5.9)
6	Vermont	(0.3)
32	Virginia	(24.0)
44	Washington	(34.5)
19	West Virginia	(14.9)
3	Wisconsin	1.3
16	Wyoming	(10.8)

RANK ORDER

RANK	STATE	PERCENT CHANGE
1	South Carolina	12.2
2	Delaware	10.4
3	New Mexico	1.3
3	Wisconsin	1.3
5	Arkansas	(0.1)
6	Vermont	(0.3)
7	North Carolina	(0.9)
8	Montana	(2.8)
9	Alabama	(4.0)
10	South Dakota	(5.5)
11	North Dakota	(5.9)
11	Utah	(5.9)
13	Texas	(9.3)
14	Maine	(9.7)
15	Georgia	(10.4)
16	Wyoming	(10.8)
17	Kentucky	(12.6)
18	Kansas	(13.1)
19	West Virginia	(14.9)
20	Oklahoma	(16.0)
21	Indiana	(17.2)
22	Florida	(18.9)
23	Illinois	(19.3)
24	Mississippi	(19.4)
25	Missouri	(19.8)
26	Connecticut	(20.1)
27	Nebraska	(20.8)
28	Rhode Island	(21.5)
29	Tennessee	(22.4)
30	Iowa	(23.1)
31	California	(23.8)
32	Virginia	(24.0)
33	Minnesota	(25.4)
34	Alaska	(26.9)
35	Pennsylvania	(27.4)
36	Michigan	(28.4)
37	New Hampshire	(29.1)
38	Maryland	(29.4)
39	Nevada	(29.7)
40	Ohio	(29.8)
41	Louisiana	(30.3)
42	Arizona	(32.7)
43	New Jersey	(33.4)
44	Washington	(34.5)
45	New York	(38.7)
46	Oregon	(38.9)
47	Idaho	(39.1)
48	Hawaii	(40.5)
49	Massachusetts	(42.2)
50	Colorado	(43.7)

District of Columbia (23.1)

Source: CQ Press using reported data from the Federal Bureau of Investigation
"Crime in the United States 2005" (Uniform Crime Reports, September 2006, http://www.fbi.gov/ucr/ucr.htm)
*Revised figures. Includes the theft or attempted theft of a self-propelled vehicle. Excludes motorboats, construction equipment, airplanes, and farming equipment.

Motor Vehicle Theft Rate in 2004

National Rate = 421.5 Motor Vehicle Thefts per 100,000 Population*

ALPHA ORDER

RANK	STATE	RATE
30	Alabama	309.9
23	Alaska	340.6
2	Arizona	963.5
36	Arkansas	237.0
3	California	704.8
7	Colorado	521.6
25	Connecticut	320.5
32	Delaware	277.3
11	Florida	450.5
10	Georgia	496.0
5	Hawaii	683.0
42	Idaho	196.3
26	Illinois	317.6
24	Indiana	338.7
43	Iowa	190.8
29	Kansas	311.3
39	Kentucky	211.8
13	Louisiana	437.4
49	Maine	99.1
6	Maryland	645.2
22	Massachusetts	344.1
9	Michigan	500.6
34	Minnesota	265.2
33	Mississippi	271.6
12	Missouri	449.6
44	Montana	174.6
31	Nebraska	302.5
1	Nevada	970.3
46	New Hampshire	150.6
21	New Jersey	348.9
16	New Mexico	415.2
38	New York	212.7
27	North Carolina	316.0
47	North Dakota	147.3
20	Ohio	355.0
19	Oklahoma	367.7
8	Oregon	516.1
35	Pennsylvania	249.9
17	Rhode Island	377.6
18	South Carolina	374.6
48	South Dakota	109.9
14	Tennessee	420.4
15	Texas	418.6
28	Utah	315.9
50	Vermont	94.5
37	Virginia	233.3
4	Washington	696.5
40	West Virginia	207.8
41	Wisconsin	206.7
45	Wyoming	157.9

RANK ORDER

RANK	STATE	RATE
1	Nevada	970.3
2	Arizona	963.5
3	California	704.8
4	Washington	696.5
5	Hawaii	683.0
6	Maryland	645.2
7	Colorado	521.6
8	Oregon	516.1
9	Michigan	500.6
10	Georgia	496.0
11	Florida	450.5
12	Missouri	449.6
13	Louisiana	437.4
14	Tennessee	420.4
15	Texas	418.6
16	New Mexico	415.2
17	Rhode Island	377.6
18	South Carolina	374.6
19	Oklahoma	367.7
20	Ohio	355.0
21	New Jersey	348.9
22	Massachusetts	344.1
23	Alaska	340.6
24	Indiana	338.7
25	Connecticut	320.5
26	Illinois	317.6
27	North Carolina	316.0
28	Utah	315.9
29	Kansas	311.3
30	Alabama	309.9
31	Nebraska	302.5
32	Delaware	277.3
33	Mississippi	271.6
34	Minnesota	265.2
35	Pennsylvania	249.9
36	Arkansas	237.0
37	Virginia	233.3
38	New York	212.7
39	Kentucky	211.8
40	West Virginia	207.8
41	Wisconsin	206.7
42	Idaho	196.3
43	Iowa	190.8
44	Montana	174.6
45	Wyoming	157.9
46	New Hampshire	150.6
47	North Dakota	147.3
48	South Dakota	109.9
49	Maine	99.1
50	Vermont	94.5

| | District of Columbia | 1,517.0 |

Source: Reported data from the Federal Bureau of Investigation
"Crime in the United States 2005" (Uniform Crime Reports, September 2006, http://www.fbi.gov/ucr/ucr.htm)
*Revised figures. Includes the theft or attempted theft of a self-propelled vehicle. Excludes motorboats, construction equipment, airplanes, and farming equipment.

Percent Change in Motor Vehicle Theft Rate: 2004 to 2008

National Percent Change = 25.3% Decrease*

ALPHA ORDER

RANK	STATE	PERCENT CHANGE
8	Alabama	(6.8)
37	Alaska	(29.9)
45	Arizona	(40.6)
6	Arkansas	(3.8)
30	California	(25.7)
50	Colorado	(47.5)
23	Connecticut	(20.1)
2	Delaware	4.9
28	Florida	(23.1)
19	Georgia	(17.5)
46	Hawaii	(41.7)
49	Idaho	(44.2)
25	Illinois	(20.5)
21	Indiana	(19.2)
29	Iowa	(24.4)
14	Kansas	(15.2)
14	Kentucky	(15.2)
36	Louisiana	(28.8)
12	Maine	(9.9)
40	Maryland	(30.3)
48	Massachusetts	(43.0)
34	Michigan	(27.6)
33	Minnesota	(27.2)
24	Mississippi	(20.4)
26	Missouri	(21.9)
9	Montana	(6.9)
27	Nebraska	(22.4)
42	Nevada	(37.0)
38	New Hampshire	(30.0)
41	New Jersey	(33.4)
5	New Mexico	(2.8)
44	New York	(39.4)
10	North Carolina	(8.2)
7	North Dakota	(6.7)
38	Ohio	(30.0)
20	Oklahoma	(18.8)
47	Oregon	(42.1)
35	Pennsylvania	(27.8)
22	Rhode Island	(19.4)
1	South Carolina	5.2
11	South Dakota	(9.5)
31	Tennessee	(26.4)
17	Texas	(16.2)
18	Utah	(16.8)
3	Vermont	(0.3)
32	Virginia	(26.8)
43	Washington	(37.9)
13	West Virginia	(15.0)
4	Wisconsin	(1.0)
14	Wyoming	(15.2)

RANK ORDER

RANK	STATE	PERCENT CHANGE
1	South Carolina	5.2
2	Delaware	4.9
3	Vermont	(0.3)
4	Wisconsin	(1.0)
5	New Mexico	(2.8)
6	Arkansas	(3.8)
7	North Dakota	(6.7)
8	Alabama	(6.8)
9	Montana	(6.9)
10	North Carolina	(8.2)
11	South Dakota	(9.5)
12	Maine	(9.9)
13	West Virginia	(15.0)
14	Kansas	(15.2)
14	Kentucky	(15.2)
14	Wyoming	(15.2)
17	Texas	(16.2)
18	Utah	(16.8)
19	Georgia	(17.5)
20	Oklahoma	(18.8)
21	Indiana	(19.2)
22	Rhode Island	(19.4)
23	Connecticut	(20.1)
24	Mississippi	(20.4)
25	Illinois	(20.5)
26	Missouri	(21.9)
27	Nebraska	(22.4)
28	Florida	(23.1)
29	Iowa	(24.4)
30	California	(25.7)
31	Tennessee	(26.4)
32	Virginia	(26.8)
33	Minnesota	(27.2)
34	Michigan	(27.6)
35	Pennsylvania	(27.8)
36	Louisiana	(28.8)
37	Alaska	(29.9)
38	New Hampshire	(30.0)
38	Ohio	(30.0)
40	Maryland	(30.3)
41	New Jersey	(33.4)
42	Nevada	(37.0)
43	Washington	(37.9)
44	New York	(39.4)
45	Arizona	(40.6)
46	Hawaii	(41.7)
47	Oregon	(42.1)
48	Massachusetts	(43.0)
49	Idaho	(44.2)
50	Colorado	(47.5)

District of Columbia (28.0)

Source: CQ Press using reported data from the Federal Bureau of Investigation
  "Crime in the United States 2005" (Uniform Crime Reports, September 2006, http://www.fbi.gov/ucr/ucr.htm)
*Revised figures. Includes the theft or attempted theft of a self-propelled vehicle. Excludes motorboats, construction equipment, airplanes, and farming equipment.

Hate Crimes in 2008

National Total = 7,783 Reported Hate Crimes*

ALPHA ORDER

RANK	STATE	HATE CRIMES	% of USA
43	Alabama	11	0.1%
47	Alaska	8	0.1%
12	Arizona	185	2.4%
25	Arkansas	91	1.2%
1	California	1,381	17.7%
17	Colorado	149	1.9%
13	Connecticut	164	2.1%
31	Delaware	58	0.7%
15	Florida	153	2.0%
45	Georgia	9	0.1%
NA	Hawaii**	NA	NA
39	Idaho	30	0.4%
19	Illinois	120	1.5%
30	Indiana	61	0.8%
38	Iowa	33	0.4%
20	Kansas	113	1.5%
28	Kentucky	64	0.8%
27	Louisiana	67	0.9%
29	Maine	63	0.8%
21	Maryland	100	1.3%
6	Massachusetts	333	4.3%
4	Michigan	560	7.2%
13	Minnesota	164	2.1%
49	Mississippi	4	0.1%
22	Missouri	99	1.3%
40	Montana	24	0.3%
43	Nebraska	11	0.1%
23	Nevada	94	1.2%
33	New Hampshire	44	0.6%
2	New Jersey	744	9.6%
45	New Mexico	9	0.1%
3	New York	570	7.3%
18	North Carolina	124	1.6%
42	North Dakota	16	0.2%
5	Ohio	345	4.4%
32	Oklahoma	51	0.7%
11	Oregon	187	2.4%
26	Pennsylvania	68	0.9%
37	Rhode Island	35	0.4%
15	South Carolina	153	2.0%
35	South Dakota	42	0.5%
8	Tennessee	255	3.3%
9	Texas	246	3.2%
36	Utah	40	0.5%
41	Vermont	20	0.3%
7	Virginia	263	3.4%
10	Washington	239	3.1%
34	West Virginia	43	0.6%
24	Wisconsin	92	1.2%
48	Wyoming	6	0.1%

RANK ORDER

RANK	STATE	HATE CRIMES	% of USA
1	California	1,381	17.7%
2	New Jersey	744	9.6%
3	New York	570	7.3%
4	Michigan	560	7.2%
5	Ohio	345	4.4%
6	Massachusetts	333	4.3%
7	Virginia	263	3.4%
8	Tennessee	255	3.3%
9	Texas	246	3.2%
10	Washington	239	3.1%
11	Oregon	187	2.4%
12	Arizona	185	2.4%
13	Connecticut	164	2.1%
13	Minnesota	164	2.1%
15	Florida	153	2.0%
15	South Carolina	153	2.0%
17	Colorado	149	1.9%
18	North Carolina	124	1.6%
19	Illinois	120	1.5%
20	Kansas	113	1.5%
21	Maryland	100	1.3%
22	Missouri	99	1.3%
23	Nevada	94	1.2%
24	Wisconsin	92	1.2%
25	Arkansas	91	1.2%
26	Pennsylvania	68	0.9%
27	Louisiana	67	0.9%
28	Kentucky	64	0.8%
29	Maine	63	0.8%
30	Indiana	61	0.8%
31	Delaware	58	0.7%
32	Oklahoma	51	0.7%
33	New Hampshire	44	0.6%
34	West Virginia	43	0.6%
35	South Dakota	42	0.5%
36	Utah	40	0.5%
37	Rhode Island	35	0.4%
38	Iowa	33	0.4%
39	Idaho	30	0.4%
40	Montana	24	0.3%
41	Vermont	20	0.3%
42	North Dakota	16	0.2%
43	Alabama	11	0.1%
43	Nebraska	11	0.1%
45	Georgia	9	0.1%
45	New Mexico	9	0.1%
47	Alaska	8	0.1%
48	Wyoming	6	0.1%
49	Mississippi	4	0.1%
NA	Hawaii**	NA	NA
	District of Columbia	42	0.5%

Source: Reported data from the Federal Bureau of Investigation
"Hate Crime Statistics, 2008" (Uniform Crime Reports, November 23, 2009, www.fbi.gov/ucr/hc2008/index.html)
*Figures are for reporting law enforcement agencies. Participating agencies covered 89 percent of the U.S. population. Fifty-one percent of the incidents were motivated by racial bias, 19.5 percent by religious bias, 11.5 percent by ethnicity/national origin bias, and 16.7 percent by sexual-orientation bias.
**Not available.

Rate of Hate Crimes in 2008

National Rate = 2.9 Hate Crimes Reported per 100,000 Population*

ALPHA ORDER

RANK	STATE	RATE
49	Alabama	0.4
25	Alaska	2.8
24	Arizona	2.9
19	Arkansas	3.3
12	California	3.8
23	Colorado	3.1
9	Connecticut	4.7
2	Delaware	6.6
45	Florida	0.8
35	Georgia	1.6
NA	Hawaii**	NA
30	Idaho	2.0
37	Illinois	1.5
30	Indiana	2.0
42	Iowa	1.1
7	Kansas	4.9
33	Kentucky	1.7
26	Louisiana	2.7
8	Maine	4.8
32	Maryland	1.8
5	Massachusetts	5.2
4	Michigan	5.7
12	Minnesota	3.8
48	Mississippi	0.5
33	Missouri	1.7
29	Montana	2.5
39	Nebraska	1.4
16	Nevada	3.6
11	New Hampshire	3.9
1	New Jersey	8.6
45	New Mexico	0.8
19	New York	3.3
39	North Carolina	1.4
26	North Dakota	2.7
12	Ohio	3.8
39	Oklahoma	1.4
6	Oregon	5.0
47	Pennsylvania	0.6
19	Rhode Island	3.3
17	South Carolina	3.4
3	South Dakota	6.1
10	Tennessee	4.1
44	Texas	1.0
37	Utah	1.5
19	Vermont	3.3
17	Virginia	3.4
15	Washington	3.7
28	West Virginia	2.6
35	Wisconsin	1.6
42	Wyoming	1.1

RANK ORDER

RANK	STATE	RATE
1	New Jersey	8.6
2	Delaware	6.6
3	South Dakota	6.1
4	Michigan	5.7
5	Massachusetts	5.2
6	Oregon	5.0
7	Kansas	4.9
8	Maine	4.8
9	Connecticut	4.7
10	Tennessee	4.1
11	New Hampshire	3.9
12	California	3.8
12	Minnesota	3.8
12	Ohio	3.8
15	Washington	3.7
16	Nevada	3.6
17	South Carolina	3.4
17	Virginia	3.4
19	Arkansas	3.3
19	New York	3.3
19	Rhode Island	3.3
19	Vermont	3.3
23	Colorado	3.1
24	Arizona	2.9
25	Alaska	2.8
26	Louisiana	2.7
26	North Dakota	2.7
28	West Virginia	2.6
29	Montana	2.5
30	Idaho	2.0
30	Indiana	2.0
32	Maryland	1.8
33	Kentucky	1.7
33	Missouri	1.7
35	Georgia	1.6
35	Wisconsin	1.6
37	Illinois	1.5
37	Utah	1.5
39	Nebraska	1.4
39	North Carolina	1.4
39	Oklahoma	1.4
42	Iowa	1.1
42	Wyoming	1.1
44	Texas	1.0
45	Florida	0.8
45	New Mexico	0.8
47	Pennsylvania	0.6
48	Mississippi	0.5
49	Alabama	0.4
NA	Hawaii**	NA

District of Columbia   7.1

Source: CQ Press using reported data from the Federal Bureau of Investigation
"Hate Crime Statistics, 2008" (Uniform Crime Reports, November 23, 2009, www.fbi.gov/ucr/hc2008/index.html)
*Figures are for reporting law enforcement agencies. Participating agencies covered 89 percent of the U.S. population. Fifty-one percent of the incidents were motivated by racial bias, 19.5 percent by religious bias, 11.5 percent by ethnicity/national origin bias, and 16.7 percent by sexual-orientation bias.
**Not available.

Consumer Fraud Complaints in 2008

National Total = 909,388 Complaints*

ALPHA ORDER				RANK ORDER			
RANK	STATE	COMPLAINTS	% of USA	RANK	STATE	COMPLAINTS	% of USA
24	Alabama	11,417	1.3%	1	California	106,623	11.7%
46	Alaska	2,253	0.2%	2	Texas	60,633	6.7%
14	Arizona	20,610	2.3%	3	Florida	57,472	6.3%
34	Arkansas	5,492	0.6%	4	New York	44,996	4.9%
1	California	106,623	11.7%	5	Pennsylvania	30,711	3.4%
16	Colorado	17,755	2.0%	6	Illinois	30,578	3.4%
28	Connecticut	8,552	0.9%	7	Ohio	29,506	3.2%
43	Delaware	2,630	0.3%	8	Georgia	27,470	3.0%
3	Florida	57,472	6.3%	9	New Jersey	24,830	2.7%
8	Georgia	27,470	3.0%	10	Virginia	24,695	2.7%
41	Hawaii	3,689	0.4%	11	North Carolina	23,128	2.5%
39	Idaho	3,970	0.4%	12	Michigan	22,805	2.5%
6	Illinois	30,578	3.4%	13	Washington	21,730	2.4%
20	Indiana	15,159	1.7%	14	Arizona	20,610	2.3%
33	Iowa	5,895	0.6%	15	Maryland	19,585	2.2%
32	Kansas	7,101	0.8%	16	Colorado	17,755	2.0%
29	Kentucky	8,173	0.9%	17	Missouri	17,056	1.9%
26	Louisiana	8,978	1.0%	18	Tennessee	15,893	1.7%
42	Maine	3,138	0.3%	19	Massachusetts	15,515	1.7%
15	Maryland	19,585	2.2%	20	Indiana	15,159	1.7%
19	Massachusetts	15,515	1.7%	21	Minnesota	13,259	1.5%
12	Michigan	22,805	2.5%	22	Wisconsin	13,142	1.4%
21	Minnesota	13,259	1.5%	23	Oregon	12,584	1.4%
36	Mississippi	4,498	0.5%	24	Alabama	11,417	1.3%
17	Missouri	17,056	1.9%	25	South Carolina	10,556	1.2%
45	Montana	2,410	0.3%	26	Louisiana	8,978	1.0%
37	Nebraska	4,353	0.5%	27	Nevada	8,953	1.0%
27	Nevada	8,953	1.0%	28	Connecticut	8,552	0.9%
38	New Hampshire	3,985	0.4%	29	Kentucky	8,173	0.9%
9	New Jersey	24,830	2.7%	30	Oklahoma	8,099	0.9%
35	New Mexico	4,807	0.5%	31	Utah	7,345	0.8%
4	New York	44,996	4.9%	32	Kansas	7,101	0.8%
11	North Carolina	23,128	2.5%	33	Iowa	5,895	0.6%
50	North Dakota	1,041	0.1%	34	Arkansas	5,492	0.6%
7	Ohio	29,506	3.2%	35	New Mexico	4,807	0.5%
30	Oklahoma	8,099	0.9%	36	Mississippi	4,498	0.5%
23	Oregon	12,584	1.4%	37	Nebraska	4,353	0.5%
5	Pennsylvania	30,711	3.4%	38	New Hampshire	3,985	0.4%
44	Rhode Island	2,417	0.3%	39	Idaho	3,970	0.4%
25	South Carolina	10,556	1.2%	40	West Virginia	3,709	0.4%
49	South Dakota	1,333	0.1%	41	Hawaii	3,689	0.4%
18	Tennessee	15,893	1.7%	42	Maine	3,138	0.3%
2	Texas	60,633	6.7%	43	Delaware	2,630	0.3%
31	Utah	7,345	0.8%	44	Rhode Island	2,417	0.3%
47	Vermont	1,535	0.2%	45	Montana	2,410	0.3%
10	Virginia	24,695	2.7%	46	Alaska	2,253	0.2%
13	Washington	21,730	2.4%	47	Vermont	1,535	0.2%
40	West Virginia	3,709	0.4%	48	Wyoming	1,397	0.2%
22	Wisconsin	13,142	1.4%	49	South Dakota	1,333	0.1%
48	Wyoming	1,397	0.2%	50	North Dakota	1,041	0.1%
					District of Columbia	2,685	0.3%

Source: Federal Trade Commission, Consumer Sentinel
"Consumer Fraud and Identify Theft Complaint Data, January - December 2008" (February 2009, http://www.ftc.gov/sentinel/)
*Total includes complaints not shown by state. Total does not include identity theft or "Do Not Call" registry complaints.

Rate of Consumer Fraud Complaints in 2008

National Rate = 299.1 Complaints per 100,000 Population*

ALPHA ORDER

RANK	STATE	RATE
29	Alabama	244.9
6	Alaska	328.3
8	Arizona	317.1
46	Arkansas	192.3
12	California	290.1
1	Colorado	359.5
30	Connecticut	244.3
11	Delaware	301.2
9	Florida	313.6
16	Georgia	283.6
14	Hawaii	286.4
19	Idaho	260.5
36	Illinois	237.0
35	Indiana	237.7
45	Iowa	196.3
23	Kansas	253.4
47	Kentucky	191.4
44	Louisiana	203.5
34	Maine	238.4
2	Maryland	347.6
33	Massachusetts	238.8
41	Michigan	228.0
22	Minnesota	254.0
50	Mississippi	153.1
13	Missouri	288.5
26	Montana	249.1
31	Nebraska	244.1
3	Nevada	344.3
10	New Hampshire	302.9
15	New Jersey	286.0
32	New Mexico	242.2
39	New York	230.9
24	North Carolina	250.8
49	North Dakota	162.3
20	Ohio	256.9
42	Oklahoma	222.4
4	Oregon	332.0
28	Pennsylvania	246.7
40	Rhode Island	230.0
37	South Carolina	235.6
48	South Dakota	165.8
21	Tennessee	255.7
25	Texas	249.2
17	Utah	268.4
27	Vermont	247.1
7	Virginia	317.9
5	Washington	331.8
43	West Virginia	204.4
38	Wisconsin	233.5
18	Wyoming	262.3

RANK ORDER

RANK	STATE	RATE
1	Colorado	359.5
2	Maryland	347.6
3	Nevada	344.3
4	Oregon	332.0
5	Washington	331.8
6	Alaska	328.3
7	Virginia	317.9
8	Arizona	317.1
9	Florida	313.6
10	New Hampshire	302.9
11	Delaware	301.2
12	California	290.1
13	Missouri	288.5
14	Hawaii	286.4
15	New Jersey	286.0
16	Georgia	283.6
17	Utah	268.4
18	Wyoming	262.3
19	Idaho	260.5
20	Ohio	256.9
21	Tennessee	255.7
22	Minnesota	254.0
23	Kansas	253.4
24	North Carolina	250.8
25	Texas	249.2
26	Montana	249.1
27	Vermont	247.1
28	Pennsylvania	246.7
29	Alabama	244.9
30	Connecticut	244.3
31	Nebraska	244.1
32	New Mexico	242.2
33	Massachusetts	238.8
34	Maine	238.4
35	Indiana	237.7
36	Illinois	237.0
37	South Carolina	235.6
38	Wisconsin	233.5
39	New York	230.9
40	Rhode Island	230.0
41	Michigan	228.0
42	Oklahoma	222.4
43	West Virginia	204.4
44	Louisiana	203.5
45	Iowa	196.3
46	Arkansas	192.3
47	Kentucky	191.4
48	South Dakota	165.8
49	North Dakota	162.3
50	Mississippi	153.1
	District of Columbia	453.7

Source: Federal Trade Commission, Consumer Sentinel
"Consumer Fraud and Identify Theft Complaint Data, January - December 2008" (February 2009, http://www.ftc.gov/sentinel/)
*Total includes complaints not shown by state. Total does not include identity theft or "Do Not Call" registry complaints.

Average Amount Paid by Consumers to Fraudulent Organizations in 2008

National Average = $3,403*

ALPHA ORDER

RANK	STATE	AVERAGE PAID
38	Alabama	$1,711
49	Alaska	1,257
12	Arizona	2,913
46	Arkansas	1,509
5	California	4,119
2	Colorado	6,809
34	Connecticut	1,788
39	Delaware	1,703
3	Florida	4,570
11	Georgia	3,001
8	Hawaii	3,245
35	Idaho	1,779
15	Illinois	2,653
47	Indiana	1,455
36	Iowa	1,765
45	Kansas	1,542
9	Kentucky	3,226
33	Louisiana	1,793
13	Maine	2,894
1	Maryland	9,383
41	Massachusetts	1,646
26	Michigan	2,166
7	Minnesota	3,341
16	Mississippi	2,645
44	Missouri	1,617
50	Montana	990
21	Nebraska	2,401
4	Nevada	4,172
32	New Hampshire	1,813
14	New Jersey	2,683
27	New Mexico	2,063
17	New York	2,560
31	North Carolina	1,824
42	North Dakota	1,621
28	Ohio	2,054
37	Oklahoma	1,723
29	Oregon	2,052
24	Pennsylvania	2,277
18	Rhode Island	2,479
22	South Carolina	2,327
6	South Dakota	3,799
10	Tennessee	3,100
23	Texas	2,302
19	Utah	2,464
43	Vermont	1,619
25	Virginia	2,276
20	Washington	2,428
40	West Virginia	1,681
30	Wisconsin	1,834
48	Wyoming	1,422

RANK ORDER

RANK	STATE	AVERAGE PAID
1	Maryland	$9,383
2	Colorado	6,809
3	Florida	4,570
4	Nevada	4,172
5	California	4,119
6	South Dakota	3,799
7	Minnesota	3,341
8	Hawaii	3,245
9	Kentucky	3,226
10	Tennessee	3,100
11	Georgia	3,001
12	Arizona	2,913
13	Maine	2,894
14	New Jersey	2,683
15	Illinois	2,653
16	Mississippi	2,645
17	New York	2,560
18	Rhode Island	2,479
19	Utah	2,464
20	Washington	2,428
21	Nebraska	2,401
22	South Carolina	2,327
23	Texas	2,302
24	Pennsylvania	2,277
25	Virginia	2,276
26	Michigan	2,166
27	New Mexico	2,063
28	Ohio	2,054
29	Oregon	2,052
30	Wisconsin	1,834
31	North Carolina	1,824
32	New Hampshire	1,813
33	Louisiana	1,793
34	Connecticut	1,788
35	Idaho	1,779
36	Iowa	1,765
37	Oklahoma	1,723
38	Alabama	1,711
39	Delaware	1,703
40	West Virginia	1,681
41	Massachusetts	1,646
42	North Dakota	1,621
43	Vermont	1,619
44	Missouri	1,617
45	Kansas	1,542
46	Arkansas	1,509
47	Indiana	1,455
48	Wyoming	1,422
49	Alaska	1,257
50	Montana	990

| | District of Columbia | 3,277 |

Source: Federal Trade Commission, Consumer Sentinel
"Consumer Fraud and Identify Theft Complaint Data, January - December 2008" (February 2009, http://www.ftc.gov/sentinel/)
*Average amount is based on the total number of fraud complaints where amount paid was reported by consumers. Organizations include internet auctions, foreign money offers, catalog sales, prizes, lotteries, and other internet services. In 2008, 257 consumers each reported an amount paid of $1 million or more.

Identity Theft Complaints in 2008

National Total = 313,982 Complaints*

ALPHA ORDER

RANK	STATE	COMPLAINTS	% of USA
21	Alabama	4,342	1.4%
45	Alaska	490	0.2%
8	Arizona	9,683	3.1%
33	Arkansas	2,068	0.7%
1	California	51,140	16.3%
17	Colorado	4,983	1.6%
27	Connecticut	3,031	1.0%
41	Delaware	759	0.2%
3	Florida	24,440	7.8%
6	Georgia	10,748	3.4%
43	Hawaii	711	0.2%
38	Idaho	867	0.3%
5	Illinois	13,726	4.4%
19	Indiana	4,589	1.5%
36	Iowa	1,347	0.4%
34	Kansas	2,005	0.6%
30	Kentucky	2,396	0.8%
22	Louisiana	3,819	1.2%
44	Maine	623	0.2%
15	Maryland	5,412	1.7%
16	Massachusetts	5,408	1.7%
9	Michigan	8,363	2.7%
23	Minnesota	3,528	1.1%
31	Mississippi	2,367	0.8%
20	Missouri	4,433	1.4%
46	Montana	450	0.1%
37	Nebraska	1,055	0.3%
25	Nevada	3,275	1.0%
41	New Hampshire	759	0.2%
11	New Jersey	8,181	2.6%
32	New Mexico	2,081	0.7%
4	New York	22,647	7.2%
12	North Carolina	7,609	2.4%
50	North Dakota	229	0.1%
10	Ohio	8,237	2.6%
29	Oklahoma	2,696	0.9%
28	Oregon	2,937	0.9%
7	Pennsylvania	10,723	3.4%
40	Rhode Island	824	0.3%
24	South Carolina	3,292	1.0%
48	South Dakota	272	0.1%
18	Tennessee	4,982	1.6%
2	Texas	31,708	10.1%
35	Utah	1,775	0.6%
47	Vermont	296	0.1%
13	Virginia	6,349	2.0%
14	Washington	5,855	1.9%
39	West Virginia	866	0.3%
26	Wisconsin	3,152	1.0%
49	Wyoming	250	0.1%

RANK ORDER

RANK	STATE	COMPLAINTS	% of USA
1	California	51,140	16.3%
2	Texas	31,708	10.1%
3	Florida	24,440	7.8%
4	New York	22,647	7.2%
5	Illinois	13,726	4.4%
6	Georgia	10,748	3.4%
7	Pennsylvania	10,723	3.4%
8	Arizona	9,683	3.1%
9	Michigan	8,363	2.7%
10	Ohio	8,237	2.6%
11	New Jersey	8,181	2.6%
12	North Carolina	7,609	2.4%
13	Virginia	6,349	2.0%
14	Washington	5,855	1.9%
15	Maryland	5,412	1.7%
16	Massachusetts	5,408	1.7%
17	Colorado	4,983	1.6%
18	Tennessee	4,982	1.6%
19	Indiana	4,589	1.5%
20	Missouri	4,433	1.4%
21	Alabama	4,342	1.4%
22	Louisiana	3,819	1.2%
23	Minnesota	3,528	1.1%
24	South Carolina	3,292	1.0%
25	Nevada	3,275	1.0%
26	Wisconsin	3,152	1.0%
27	Connecticut	3,031	1.0%
28	Oregon	2,937	0.9%
29	Oklahoma	2,696	0.9%
30	Kentucky	2,396	0.8%
31	Mississippi	2,367	0.8%
32	New Mexico	2,081	0.7%
33	Arkansas	2,068	0.7%
34	Kansas	2,005	0.6%
35	Utah	1,775	0.6%
36	Iowa	1,347	0.4%
37	Nebraska	1,055	0.3%
38	Idaho	867	0.3%
39	West Virginia	866	0.3%
40	Rhode Island	824	0.3%
41	Delaware	759	0.2%
41	New Hampshire	759	0.2%
43	Hawaii	711	0.2%
44	Maine	623	0.2%
45	Alaska	490	0.2%
46	Montana	450	0.1%
47	Vermont	296	0.1%
48	South Dakota	272	0.1%
49	Wyoming	250	0.1%
50	North Dakota	229	0.1%
	District of Columbia	979	0.3%

Source: Federal Trade Commission, Consumer Sentinel
   "Consumer Fraud and Identify Theft Complaint Data, January - December 2008" (February 2009, http://www.ftc.gov/sentinel/)
*Total includes complaints not shown by state. Total does not include consumer fraud or "Do Not Call" registry complaints.

Rate of Identity Theft Complaints in 2008

National Rate = 103.3 Complaints per 100,000 Population*

ALPHA ORDER

RANK	STATE	RATE
13	Alabama	93.1
34	Alaska	71.4
1	Arizona	149.0
30	Arkansas	72.4
2	California	139.1
10	Colorado	100.9
16	Connecticut	86.6
15	Delaware	86.9
3	Florida	133.3
7	Georgia	111.0
42	Hawaii	55.2
39	Idaho	56.9
8	Illinois	106.4
31	Indiana	72.0
48	Iowa	44.9
33	Kansas	71.6
40	Kentucky	56.1
16	Louisiana	86.6
45	Maine	47.3
11	Maryland	96.1
20	Massachusetts	83.2
19	Michigan	83.6
35	Minnesota	67.6
23	Mississippi	80.5
27	Missouri	75.0
47	Montana	46.5
37	Nebraska	59.2
5	Nevada	126.0
38	New Hampshire	57.7
12	New Jersey	94.2
9	New Mexico	104.9
6	New York	116.2
21	North Carolina	82.5
49	North Dakota	35.7
32	Ohio	71.7
28	Oklahoma	74.0
26	Oregon	77.5
18	Pennsylvania	86.1
25	Rhode Island	78.4
29	South Carolina	73.5
50	South Dakota	33.8
24	Tennessee	80.2
4	Texas	130.3
36	Utah	64.9
44	Vermont	47.6
22	Virginia	81.7
14	Washington	89.4
43	West Virginia	47.7
41	Wisconsin	56.0
46	Wyoming	46.9

RANK ORDER

RANK	STATE	RATE
1	Arizona	149.0
2	California	139.1
3	Florida	133.3
4	Texas	130.3
5	Nevada	126.0
6	New York	116.2
7	Georgia	111.0
8	Illinois	106.4
9	New Mexico	104.9
10	Colorado	100.9
11	Maryland	96.1
12	New Jersey	94.2
13	Alabama	93.1
14	Washington	89.4
15	Delaware	86.9
16	Connecticut	86.6
16	Louisiana	86.6
18	Pennsylvania	86.1
19	Michigan	83.6
20	Massachusetts	83.2
21	North Carolina	82.5
22	Virginia	81.7
23	Mississippi	80.5
24	Tennessee	80.2
25	Rhode Island	78.4
26	Oregon	77.5
27	Missouri	75.0
28	Oklahoma	74.0
29	South Carolina	73.5
30	Arkansas	72.4
31	Indiana	72.0
32	Ohio	71.7
33	Kansas	71.6
34	Alaska	71.4
35	Minnesota	67.6
36	Utah	64.9
37	Nebraska	59.2
38	New Hampshire	57.7
39	Idaho	56.9
40	Kentucky	56.1
41	Wisconsin	56.0
42	Hawaii	55.2
43	West Virginia	47.7
44	Vermont	47.6
45	Maine	47.3
46	Wyoming	46.9
47	Montana	46.5
48	Iowa	44.9
49	North Dakota	35.7
50	South Dakota	33.8
	District of Columbia	165.4

Source: Federal Trade Commission, Consumer Sentinel
"Consumer Fraud and Identify Theft Complaint Data, January - December 2008" (February 2009, http://www.ftc.gov/sentinel/)
*Total includes complaints not shown by state. Total does not include consumer fraud or "Do Not Call" registry complaints.

Rate of Internet Crime Complaints in 2008

National Rate = 78.7 Complaints per 100,000 Population*

<table>
<tr><td colspan="3">ALPHA ORDER</td><td colspan="3">RANK ORDER</td></tr>
<tr><th>RANK</th><th>STATE</th><th>RATE</th><th>RANK</th><th>STATE</th><th>RATE</th></tr>
<tr><td>40</td><td>Alabama</td><td>64.3</td><td>1</td><td>Alaska</td><td>337.6</td></tr>
<tr><td>1</td><td>Alaska</td><td>337.6</td><td>2</td><td>Colorado</td><td>135.5</td></tr>
<tr><td>6</td><td>Arizona</td><td>101.5</td><td>3</td><td>Nevada</td><td>113.1</td></tr>
<tr><td>45</td><td>Arkansas</td><td>60.2</td><td>4</td><td>Maryland</td><td>111.6</td></tr>
<tr><td>9</td><td>California</td><td>95.1</td><td>5</td><td>Washington</td><td>106.0</td></tr>
<tr><td>2</td><td>Colorado</td><td>135.5</td><td>6</td><td>Arizona</td><td>101.5</td></tr>
<tr><td>38</td><td>Connecticut</td><td>65.1</td><td>7</td><td>Oregon</td><td>101.0</td></tr>
<tr><td>29</td><td>Delaware</td><td>69.8</td><td>8</td><td>New Jersey</td><td>95.3</td></tr>
<tr><td>10</td><td>Florida</td><td>92.4</td><td>9</td><td>California</td><td>95.1</td></tr>
<tr><td>33</td><td>Georgia</td><td>67.3</td><td>10</td><td>Florida</td><td>92.4</td></tr>
<tr><td>16</td><td>Hawaii</td><td>84.9</td><td>11</td><td>Virginia</td><td>90.5</td></tr>
<tr><td>13</td><td>Idaho</td><td>88.8</td><td>12</td><td>Wyoming</td><td>89.0</td></tr>
<tr><td>42</td><td>Illinois</td><td>62.4</td><td>13</td><td>Idaho</td><td>88.8</td></tr>
<tr><td>21</td><td>Indiana</td><td>72.9</td><td>14</td><td>Kansas</td><td>87.9</td></tr>
<tr><td>46</td><td>Iowa</td><td>54.3</td><td>15</td><td>New Hampshire</td><td>86.6</td></tr>
<tr><td>14</td><td>Kansas</td><td>87.9</td><td>16</td><td>Hawaii</td><td>84.9</td></tr>
<tr><td>46</td><td>Kentucky</td><td>54.3</td><td>17</td><td>Utah</td><td>82.3</td></tr>
<tr><td>44</td><td>Louisiana</td><td>60.8</td><td>18</td><td>Vermont</td><td>78.1</td></tr>
<tr><td>23</td><td>Maine</td><td>72.2</td><td>19</td><td>New Mexico</td><td>74.0</td></tr>
<tr><td>4</td><td>Maryland</td><td>111.6</td><td>20</td><td>Nebraska</td><td>73.6</td></tr>
<tr><td>31</td><td>Massachusetts</td><td>69.1</td><td>21</td><td>Indiana</td><td>72.9</td></tr>
<tr><td>39</td><td>Michigan</td><td>64.8</td><td>22</td><td>Missouri</td><td>72.4</td></tr>
<tr><td>32</td><td>Minnesota</td><td>68.5</td><td>23</td><td>Maine</td><td>72.2</td></tr>
<tr><td>50</td><td>Mississippi</td><td>44.3</td><td>24</td><td>Montana</td><td>71.7</td></tr>
<tr><td>22</td><td>Missouri</td><td>72.4</td><td>24</td><td>Tennessee</td><td>71.7</td></tr>
<tr><td>24</td><td>Montana</td><td>71.7</td><td>26</td><td>Rhode Island</td><td>71.3</td></tr>
<tr><td>20</td><td>Nebraska</td><td>73.6</td><td>27</td><td>Texas</td><td>70.4</td></tr>
<tr><td>3</td><td>Nevada</td><td>113.1</td><td>28</td><td>Pennsylvania</td><td>69.9</td></tr>
<tr><td>15</td><td>New Hampshire</td><td>86.6</td><td>29</td><td>Delaware</td><td>69.8</td></tr>
<tr><td>8</td><td>New Jersey</td><td>95.3</td><td>30</td><td>North Carolina</td><td>69.2</td></tr>
<tr><td>19</td><td>New Mexico</td><td>74.0</td><td>31</td><td>Massachusetts</td><td>69.1</td></tr>
<tr><td>35</td><td>New York</td><td>66.8</td><td>32</td><td>Minnesota</td><td>68.5</td></tr>
<tr><td>30</td><td>North Carolina</td><td>69.2</td><td>33</td><td>Georgia</td><td>67.3</td></tr>
<tr><td>48</td><td>North Dakota</td><td>49.9</td><td>34</td><td>West Virginia</td><td>67.1</td></tr>
<tr><td>41</td><td>Ohio</td><td>63.4</td><td>35</td><td>New York</td><td>66.8</td></tr>
<tr><td>37</td><td>Oklahoma</td><td>66.4</td><td>36</td><td>South Carolina</td><td>66.6</td></tr>
<tr><td>7</td><td>Oregon</td><td>101.0</td><td>37</td><td>Oklahoma</td><td>66.4</td></tr>
<tr><td>28</td><td>Pennsylvania</td><td>69.9</td><td>38</td><td>Connecticut</td><td>65.1</td></tr>
<tr><td>26</td><td>Rhode Island</td><td>71.3</td><td>39</td><td>Michigan</td><td>64.8</td></tr>
<tr><td>36</td><td>South Carolina</td><td>66.6</td><td>40</td><td>Alabama</td><td>64.3</td></tr>
<tr><td>49</td><td>South Dakota</td><td>48.4</td><td>41</td><td>Ohio</td><td>63.4</td></tr>
<tr><td>24</td><td>Tennessee</td><td>71.7</td><td>42</td><td>Illinois</td><td>62.4</td></tr>
<tr><td>27</td><td>Texas</td><td>70.4</td><td>42</td><td>Wisconsin</td><td>62.4</td></tr>
<tr><td>17</td><td>Utah</td><td>82.3</td><td>44</td><td>Louisiana</td><td>60.8</td></tr>
<tr><td>18</td><td>Vermont</td><td>78.1</td><td>45</td><td>Arkansas</td><td>60.2</td></tr>
<tr><td>11</td><td>Virginia</td><td>90.5</td><td>46</td><td>Iowa</td><td>54.3</td></tr>
<tr><td>5</td><td>Washington</td><td>106.0</td><td>46</td><td>Kentucky</td><td>54.3</td></tr>
<tr><td>34</td><td>West Virginia</td><td>67.1</td><td>48</td><td>North Dakota</td><td>49.9</td></tr>
<tr><td>42</td><td>Wisconsin</td><td>62.4</td><td>49</td><td>South Dakota</td><td>48.4</td></tr>
<tr><td>12</td><td>Wyoming</td><td>89.0</td><td>50</td><td>Mississippi</td><td>44.3</td></tr>
<tr><td colspan="3"></td><td colspan="2">District of Columbia</td><td>119.6</td></tr>
</table>

Source: The Internet Crime Complaint Center (IC3)
    "2008 Internet Crime Report" (http://www.ic3.gov/media/annualreports.aspx)
*These rates are based on the residence of individuals filing complaints. National figure is a weighted average calculated by the editors.

Rate of Internet Crime Perpetrators in 2008

National Rate = 29.2 Perpetrators per 100,000 Population*

ALPHA ORDER

RANK	STATE	RATE
34	Alabama	19.9
14	Alaska	30.9
10	Arizona	37.8
45	Arkansas	16.1
9	California	40.1
18	Colorado	27.0
22	Connecticut	25.4
5	Delaware	45.8
4	Florida	48.0
15	Georgia	30.0
7	Hawaii	44.6
30	Idaho	20.5
26	Illinois	23.9
38	Indiana	19.2
49	Iowa	14.4
36	Kansas	19.5
44	Kentucky	16.3
46	Louisiana	15.0
11	Maine	33.1
24	Maryland	25.1
27	Massachusetts	22.3
31	Michigan	20.4
40	Minnesota	18.4
50	Mississippi	10.0
32	Missouri	20.2
3	Montana	54.5
28	Nebraska	22.1
1	Nevada	80.8
23	New Hampshire	25.3
16	New Jersey	29.6
47	New Mexico	14.8
6	New York	45.5
39	North Carolina	18.6
12	North Dakota	32.7
33	Ohio	20.1
40	Oklahoma	18.4
19	Oregon	26.3
37	Pennsylvania	19.4
13	Rhode Island	31.3
42	South Carolina	18.3
17	South Dakota	27.5
34	Tennessee	19.9
25	Texas	24.6
8	Utah	41.1
21	Vermont	25.9
29	Virginia	21.0
2	Washington	55.4
43	West Virginia	17.2
47	Wisconsin	14.8
19	Wyoming	26.3

RANK ORDER

RANK	STATE	RATE
1	Nevada	80.8
2	Washington	55.4
3	Montana	54.5
4	Florida	48.0
5	Delaware	45.8
6	New York	45.5
7	Hawaii	44.6
8	Utah	41.1
9	California	40.1
10	Arizona	37.8
11	Maine	33.1
12	North Dakota	32.7
13	Rhode Island	31.3
14	Alaska	30.9
15	Georgia	30.0
16	New Jersey	29.6
17	South Dakota	27.5
18	Colorado	27.0
19	Oregon	26.3
19	Wyoming	26.3
21	Vermont	25.9
22	Connecticut	25.4
23	New Hampshire	25.3
24	Maryland	25.1
25	Texas	24.6
26	Illinois	23.9
27	Massachusetts	22.3
28	Nebraska	22.1
29	Virginia	21.0
30	Idaho	20.5
31	Michigan	20.4
32	Missouri	20.2
33	Ohio	20.1
34	Alabama	19.9
34	Tennessee	19.9
36	Kansas	19.5
37	Pennsylvania	19.4
38	Indiana	19.2
39	North Carolina	18.6
40	Minnesota	18.4
40	Oklahoma	18.4
42	South Carolina	18.3
43	West Virginia	17.2
44	Kentucky	16.3
45	Arkansas	16.1
46	Louisiana	15.0
47	New Mexico	14.8
47	Wisconsin	14.8
49	Iowa	14.4
50	Mississippi	10.0

District of Columbia   81.3

Source: The Internet Crime Complaint Center (IC3)
"2008 Internet Crime Report" (http://www.ic3.gov/media/annualreports.aspx)
*These rates are based on the residence of known perpetrators. National figure is a weighted average calculated by the editors.

VIII. APPENDIX

Population in 2009

National Total = 307,006,550*

ALPHA ORDER

RANK	STATE	POPULATION	% of USA
23	Alabama	4,708,708	1.5%
47	Alaska	698,473	0.2%
14	Arizona	6,595,778	2.1%
32	Arkansas	2,889,450	0.9%
1	California	36,961,664	12.0%
22	Colorado	5,024,748	1.6%
29	Connecticut	3,518,288	1.1%
45	Delaware	885,122	0.3%
4	Florida	18,537,969	6.0%
9	Georgia	9,829,211	3.2%
42	Hawaii	1,295,178	0.4%
39	Idaho	1,545,801	0.5%
5	Illinois	12,910,409	4.2%
16	Indiana	6,423,113	2.1%
30	Iowa	3,007,856	1.0%
33	Kansas	2,818,747	0.9%
26	Kentucky	4,314,113	1.4%
25	Louisiana	4,492,076	1.5%
41	Maine	1,318,301	0.4%
19	Maryland	5,699,478	1.9%
15	Massachusetts	6,593,587	2.1%
8	Michigan	9,969,727	3.2%
21	Minnesota	5,266,214	1.7%
31	Mississippi	2,951,996	1.0%
18	Missouri	5,987,580	2.0%
44	Montana	974,989	0.3%
38	Nebraska	1,796,619	0.6%
35	Nevada	2,643,085	0.9%
40	New Hampshire	1,324,575	0.4%
11	New Jersey	8,707,739	2.8%
36	New Mexico	2,009,671	0.7%
3	New York	19,541,453	6.4%
10	North Carolina	9,380,884	3.1%
48	North Dakota	646,844	0.2%
7	Ohio	11,542,645	3.8%
28	Oklahoma	3,687,050	1.2%
27	Oregon	3,825,657	1.2%
6	Pennsylvania	12,604,767	4.1%
43	Rhode Island	1,053,209	0.3%
24	South Carolina	4,561,242	1.5%
46	South Dakota	812,383	0.3%
17	Tennessee	6,296,254	2.1%
2	Texas	24,782,302	8.1%
34	Utah	2,784,572	0.9%
49	Vermont	621,760	0.2%
12	Virginia	7,882,590	2.6%
13	Washington	6,664,195	2.2%
37	West Virginia	1,819,777	0.6%
20	Wisconsin	5,654,774	1.8%
50	Wyoming	544,270	0.2%

RANK ORDER

RANK	STATE	POPULATION	% of USA
1	California	36,961,664	12.0%
2	Texas	24,782,302	8.1%
3	New York	19,541,453	6.4%
4	Florida	18,537,969	6.0%
5	Illinois	12,910,409	4.2%
6	Pennsylvania	12,604,767	4.1%
7	Ohio	11,542,645	3.8%
8	Michigan	9,969,727	3.2%
9	Georgia	9,829,211	3.2%
10	North Carolina	9,380,884	3.1%
11	New Jersey	8,707,739	2.8%
12	Virginia	7,882,590	2.6%
13	Washington	6,664,195	2.2%
14	Arizona	6,595,778	2.1%
15	Massachusetts	6,593,587	2.1%
16	Indiana	6,423,113	2.1%
17	Tennessee	6,296,254	2.1%
18	Missouri	5,987,580	2.0%
19	Maryland	5,699,478	1.9%
20	Wisconsin	5,654,774	1.8%
21	Minnesota	5,266,214	1.7%
22	Colorado	5,024,748	1.6%
23	Alabama	4,708,708	1.5%
24	South Carolina	4,561,242	1.5%
25	Louisiana	4,492,076	1.5%
26	Kentucky	4,314,113	1.4%
27	Oregon	3,825,657	1.2%
28	Oklahoma	3,687,050	1.2%
29	Connecticut	3,518,288	1.1%
30	Iowa	3,007,856	1.0%
31	Mississippi	2,951,996	1.0%
32	Arkansas	2,889,450	0.9%
33	Kansas	2,818,747	0.9%
34	Utah	2,784,572	0.9%
35	Nevada	2,643,085	0.9%
36	New Mexico	2,009,671	0.7%
37	West Virginia	1,819,777	0.6%
38	Nebraska	1,796,619	0.6%
39	Idaho	1,545,801	0.5%
40	New Hampshire	1,324,575	0.4%
41	Maine	1,318,301	0.4%
42	Hawaii	1,295,178	0.4%
43	Rhode Island	1,053,209	0.3%
44	Montana	974,989	0.3%
45	Delaware	885,122	0.3%
46	South Dakota	812,383	0.3%
47	Alaska	698,473	0.2%
48	North Dakota	646,844	0.2%
49	Vermont	621,760	0.2%
50	Wyoming	544,270	0.2%
	District of Columbia	599,657	0.2%

Source: U.S. Bureau of the Census
"Population Estimates" (December 23, 2009, http://www.census.gov/popest/estimates.php)
*Resident population.

Population in 2008

National Total = 304,374,846*

ALPHA ORDER

RANK	STATE	POPULATION	% of USA
23	Alabama	4,677,464	1.5%
47	Alaska	688,125	0.2%
15	Arizona	6,499,377	2.1%
32	Arkansas	2,867,764	0.9%
1	California	36,580,371	12.0%
22	Colorado	4,935,213	1.6%
29	Connecticut	3,502,932	1.2%
45	Delaware	876,211	0.3%
4	Florida	18,423,878	6.1%
9	Georgia	9,697,838	3.2%
42	Hawaii	1,287,481	0.4%
39	Idaho	1,527,506	0.5%
5	Illinois	12,842,954	4.2%
16	Indiana	6,388,309	2.1%
30	Iowa	2,993,987	1.0%
33	Kansas	2,797,375	0.9%
26	Kentucky	4,287,931	1.4%
25	Louisiana	4,451,513	1.5%
41	Maine	1,319,691	0.4%
19	Maryland	5,658,655	1.9%
14	Massachusetts	6,543,595	2.1%
8	Michigan	10,002,486	3.3%
21	Minnesota	5,230,567	1.7%
31	Mississippi	2,940,212	1.0%
18	Missouri	5,956,335	2.0%
44	Montana	968,035	0.3%
38	Nebraska	1,781,949	0.6%
35	Nevada	2,615,772	0.9%
40	New Hampshire	1,321,872	0.4%
11	New Jersey	8,663,398	2.8%
36	New Mexico	1,986,763	0.7%
3	New York	19,467,789	6.4%
10	North Carolina	9,247,134	3.0%
48	North Dakota	641,421	0.2%
7	Ohio	11,528,072	3.8%
28	Oklahoma	3,644,025	1.2%
27	Oregon	3,782,991	1.2%
6	Pennsylvania	12,566,368	4.1%
43	Rhode Island	1,053,502	0.3%
24	South Carolina	4,503,280	1.5%
46	South Dakota	804,532	0.3%
17	Tennessee	6,240,456	2.1%
2	Texas	24,304,290	8.0%
34	Utah	2,727,343	0.9%
49	Vermont	621,049	0.2%
12	Virginia	7,795,424	2.6%
13	Washington	6,566,073	2.2%
37	West Virginia	1,814,873	0.6%
20	Wisconsin	5,627,610	1.8%
50	Wyoming	532,981	0.2%

RANK ORDER

RANK	STATE	POPULATION	% of USA
1	California	36,580,371	12.0%
2	Texas	24,304,290	8.0%
3	New York	19,467,789	6.4%
4	Florida	18,423,878	6.1%
5	Illinois	12,842,954	4.2%
6	Pennsylvania	12,566,368	4.1%
7	Ohio	11,528,072	3.8%
8	Michigan	10,002,486	3.3%
9	Georgia	9,697,838	3.2%
10	North Carolina	9,247,134	3.0%
11	New Jersey	8,663,398	2.8%
12	Virginia	7,795,424	2.6%
13	Washington	6,566,073	2.2%
14	Massachusetts	6,543,595	2.1%
15	Arizona	6,499,377	2.1%
16	Indiana	6,388,309	2.1%
17	Tennessee	6,240,456	2.1%
18	Missouri	5,956,335	2.0%
19	Maryland	5,658,655	1.9%
20	Wisconsin	5,627,610	1.8%
21	Minnesota	5,230,567	1.7%
22	Colorado	4,935,213	1.6%
23	Alabama	4,677,464	1.5%
24	South Carolina	4,503,280	1.5%
25	Louisiana	4,451,513	1.5%
26	Kentucky	4,287,931	1.4%
27	Oregon	3,782,991	1.2%
28	Oklahoma	3,644,025	1.2%
29	Connecticut	3,502,932	1.2%
30	Iowa	2,993,987	1.0%
31	Mississippi	2,940,212	1.0%
32	Arkansas	2,867,764	0.9%
33	Kansas	2,797,375	0.9%
34	Utah	2,727,343	0.9%
35	Nevada	2,615,772	0.9%
36	New Mexico	1,986,763	0.7%
37	West Virginia	1,814,873	0.6%
38	Nebraska	1,781,949	0.6%
39	Idaho	1,527,506	0.5%
40	New Hampshire	1,321,872	0.4%
41	Maine	1,319,691	0.4%
42	Hawaii	1,287,481	0.4%
43	Rhode Island	1,053,502	0.3%
44	Montana	968,035	0.3%
45	Delaware	876,211	0.3%
46	South Dakota	804,532	0.3%
47	Alaska	688,125	0.2%
48	North Dakota	641,421	0.2%
49	Vermont	621,049	0.2%
50	Wyoming	532,981	0.2%
	District of Columbia	590,074	0.2%

Source: U.S. Bureau of the Census
   "Population Estimates" (December 23, 2009, http://www.census.gov/popest/estimates.php)
*Resident population. Revised estimates.

Population in 2004

National Total = 293,045,739*

ALPHA ORDER				RANK ORDER			
RANK	STATE	POPULATION	% of USA	RANK	STATE	POPULATION	% of USA
23	Alabama	4,512,190	1.5%	1	California	35,558,419	12.1%
47	Alaska	661,569	0.2%	2	Texas	22,418,319	7.7%
17	Arizona	5,759,425	2.0%	3	New York	19,297,933	6.6%
32	Arkansas	2,746,161	0.9%	4	Florida	17,375,259	5.9%
1	California	35,558,419	12.1%	5	Illinois	12,645,295	4.3%
22	Colorado	4,599,681	1.6%	6	Pennsylvania	12,388,368	4.2%
29	Connecticut	3,474,610	1.2%	7	Ohio	11,464,593	3.9%
45	Delaware	826,639	0.3%	8	Michigan	10,089,305	3.4%
4	Florida	17,375,259	5.9%	9	Georgia	8,913,676	3.0%
9	Georgia	8,913,676	3.0%	10	New Jersey	8,611,530	2.9%
42	Hawaii	1,252,782	0.4%	11	North Carolina	8,531,283	2.9%
39	Idaho	1,391,718	0.5%	12	Virginia	7,468,914	2.5%
5	Illinois	12,645,295	4.3%	13	Massachusetts	6,451,279	2.2%
14	Indiana	6,214,454	2.1%	14	Indiana	6,214,454	2.1%
30	Iowa	2,941,358	1.0%	15	Washington	6,184,289	2.1%
33	Kansas	2,730,765	0.9%	16	Tennessee	5,916,762	2.0%
26	Kentucky	4,147,970	1.4%	17	Arizona	5,759,425	2.0%
24	Louisiana	4,489,327	1.5%	18	Missouri	5,758,444	2.0%
40	Maine	1,308,253	0.4%	19	Maryland	5,542,659	1.9%
19	Maryland	5,542,659	1.9%	20	Wisconsin	5,511,385	1.9%
13	Massachusetts	6,451,279	2.2%	21	Minnesota	5,079,344	1.7%
8	Michigan	10,089,305	3.4%	22	Colorado	4,599,681	1.6%
21	Minnesota	5,079,344	1.7%	23	Alabama	4,512,190	1.5%
31	Mississippi	2,886,006	1.0%	24	Louisiana	4,489,327	1.5%
18	Missouri	5,758,444	2.0%	25	South Carolina	4,201,306	1.4%
44	Montana	925,887	0.3%	26	Kentucky	4,147,970	1.4%
38	Nebraska	1,742,184	0.6%	27	Oregon	3,573,505	1.2%
35	Nevada	2,328,703	0.8%	28	Oklahoma	3,514,449	1.2%
41	New Hampshire	1,292,766	0.4%	29	Connecticut	3,474,610	1.2%
10	New Jersey	8,611,530	2.9%	30	Iowa	2,941,358	1.0%
36	New Mexico	1,891,829	0.6%	31	Mississippi	2,886,006	1.0%
3	New York	19,297,933	6.6%	32	Arkansas	2,746,161	0.9%
11	North Carolina	8,531,283	2.9%	33	Kansas	2,730,765	0.9%
48	North Dakota	636,303	0.2%	34	Utah	2,438,915	0.8%
7	Ohio	11,464,593	3.9%	35	Nevada	2,328,703	0.8%
28	Oklahoma	3,514,449	1.2%	36	New Mexico	1,891,829	0.6%
27	Oregon	3,573,505	1.2%	37	West Virginia	1,803,302	0.6%
6	Pennsylvania	12,388,368	4.2%	38	Nebraska	1,742,184	0.6%
43	Rhode Island	1,071,414	0.4%	39	Idaho	1,391,718	0.5%
25	South Carolina	4,201,306	1.4%	40	Maine	1,308,253	0.4%
46	South Dakota	774,283	0.3%	41	New Hampshire	1,292,766	0.4%
16	Tennessee	5,916,762	2.0%	42	Hawaii	1,252,782	0.4%
2	Texas	22,418,319	7.7%	43	Rhode Island	1,071,414	0.4%
34	Utah	2,438,915	0.8%	44	Montana	925,887	0.3%
49	Vermont	618,145	0.2%	45	Delaware	826,639	0.3%
12	Virginia	7,468,914	2.5%	46	South Dakota	774,283	0.3%
15	Washington	6,184,289	2.1%	47	Alaska	661,569	0.2%
37	West Virginia	1,803,302	0.6%	48	North Dakota	636,303	0.2%
20	Wisconsin	5,511,385	1.9%	49	Vermont	618,145	0.2%
50	Wyoming	502,988	0.2%	50	Wyoming	502,988	0.2%
					District of Columbia	579,796	0.2%

Source: U.S. Bureau of the Census
   "Population Estimates" (December 23, 2009, http://www.census.gov/popest/estimates.php)
*Resident population. Revised estimates.

Population 10 to 17 Years Old in 2008

National Total = 32,868,515

ALPHA ORDER

RANK	STATE	POPULATION	% of USA
23	Alabama	504,388	1.5%
47	Alaska	80,135	0.2%
13	Arizona	719,442	2.2%
33	Arkansas	308,853	0.9%
1	California	4,167,634	12.7%
22	Colorado	513,425	1.6%
29	Connecticut	381,714	1.2%
45	Delaware	91,094	0.3%
4	Florida	1,782,831	5.4%
9	Georgia	1,096,653	3.3%
42	Hawaii	122,548	0.4%
38	Idaho	177,035	0.5%
5	Illinois	1,418,760	4.3%
14	Indiana	707,584	2.2%
32	Iowa	319,690	1.0%
34	Kansas	305,582	0.9%
26	Kentucky	448,289	1.4%
24	Louisiana	492,628	1.5%
41	Maine	131,237	0.4%
19	Maryland	607,629	1.8%
16	Massachusetts	659,021	2.0%
8	Michigan	1,123,548	3.4%
21	Minnesota	560,269	1.7%
31	Mississippi	338,168	1.0%
18	Missouri	640,054	1.9%
44	Montana	100,950	0.3%
37	Nebraska	193,551	0.6%
35	Nevada	284,805	0.9%
40	New Hampshire	141,033	0.4%
11	New Jersey	933,699	2.8%
36	New Mexico	217,278	0.7%
3	New York	2,026,449	6.2%
10	North Carolina	967,363	2.9%
48	North Dakota	64,446	0.2%
7	Ohio	1,249,659	3.8%
27	Oklahoma	391,183	1.2%
28	Oregon	389,457	1.2%
6	Pennsylvania	1,291,420	3.9%
43	Rhode Island	107,302	0.3%
25	South Carolina	472,244	1.4%
46	South Dakota	87,232	0.3%
17	Tennessee	657,587	2.0%
2	Texas	2,818,336	8.6%
30	Utah	340,090	1.0%
49	Vermont	62,778	0.2%
12	Virginia	802,896	2.4%
15	Washington	692,815	2.1%
39	West Virginia	175,673	0.5%
20	Wisconsin	599,032	1.8%
50	Wyoming	55,973	0.2%

RANK ORDER

RANK	STATE	POPULATION	% of USA
1	California	4,167,634	12.7%
2	Texas	2,818,336	8.6%
3	New York	2,026,449	6.2%
4	Florida	1,782,831	5.4%
5	Illinois	1,418,760	4.3%
6	Pennsylvania	1,291,420	3.9%
7	Ohio	1,249,659	3.8%
8	Michigan	1,123,548	3.4%
9	Georgia	1,096,653	3.3%
10	North Carolina	967,363	2.9%
11	New Jersey	933,699	2.8%
12	Virginia	802,896	2.4%
13	Arizona	719,442	2.2%
14	Indiana	707,584	2.2%
15	Washington	692,815	2.1%
16	Massachusetts	659,021	2.0%
17	Tennessee	657,587	2.0%
18	Missouri	640,054	1.9%
19	Maryland	607,629	1.8%
20	Wisconsin	599,032	1.8%
21	Minnesota	560,269	1.7%
22	Colorado	513,425	1.6%
23	Alabama	504,388	1.5%
24	Louisiana	492,628	1.5%
25	South Carolina	472,244	1.4%
26	Kentucky	448,289	1.4%
27	Oklahoma	391,183	1.2%
28	Oregon	389,457	1.2%
29	Connecticut	381,714	1.2%
30	Utah	340,090	1.0%
31	Mississippi	338,168	1.0%
32	Iowa	319,690	1.0%
33	Arkansas	308,853	0.9%
34	Kansas	305,582	0.9%
35	Nevada	284,805	0.9%
36	New Mexico	217,278	0.7%
37	Nebraska	193,551	0.6%
38	Idaho	177,035	0.5%
39	West Virginia	175,673	0.5%
40	New Hampshire	141,033	0.4%
41	Maine	131,237	0.4%
42	Hawaii	122,548	0.4%
43	Rhode Island	107,302	0.3%
44	Montana	100,950	0.3%
45	Delaware	91,094	0.3%
46	South Dakota	87,232	0.3%
47	Alaska	80,135	0.2%
48	North Dakota	64,446	0.2%
49	Vermont	62,778	0.2%
50	Wyoming	55,973	0.2%
	District of Columbia	47,053	0.1%

Source: CQ Press using data from U.S. Bureau of the Census
"Population Estimates Data Sets" (http://www.census.gov/popest/datasets.html)

Sources

Administrative Office of the U.S. Courts
One Columbus Circle, NE
Washington, DC 20544
202-502-2600
www.uscourts.gov

Bureau of Justice Assistance
810 Seventh Street, NW
4th Floor
Washington, DC 20531
202-616-6500
www.ojp.usdoj.gov/BJA/

Bureau of Justice Statistics
810 Seventh Street, NW
Washington, DC 20531
202-307-0765
http://bjs.ojp.usdoj.gov/

Bureau of the Census
4600 Silver Hill Road
Washington, DC 20233
301-763-4636
www.census.gov

Child Welfare Information Gateway
Children's Bureau ACYF
1250 Maryland Avenue, SW
8th Floor
Washington, DC 20024
800-394-3366
www.childwelfare.gov

Children's Bureau
Administration for Children & Families; HHS
370 L'Enfant Promenade, SW
Washington, DC 20447
202-401-9215
www.acf.hhs.gov

Drug Enforcement Administration
Mail Stop: AES
8701 Morrissette Drive
Springfield, VA 22152
202-307-1000
www.dea.gov

Federal Bureau of Investigation
J. Edgar Hoover Building
935 Pennsylvania Avenue, NW
Washington, DC 20535
202-324-3000
www.fbi.gov

Identity Theft Data Clearinghouse
FTC Consumer Response Center
600 Pennsylvania Avenue, NW
Washington, DC 20580
202-326-2222
www.ftc.gov/sentinel

Juvenile Justice Clearinghouse
P.O. Box 6000
Rockville, MD 20849
800-851-3420
www.ojjdp.ncjrs.org

NAACP Legal Defense Fund, Inc.
99 Hudson Street
Suite 1600
New York, NY 10013
212-965-2200
www.naacpldf.org

National Archive of Criminal Justice Data
ICPSR—University of Michigan
P.O. Box 1248
Ann Arbor, MI 48106
734-647-5000 or 800-999-0960
www.icpsr.umich.edu/NACJD/

National Association of State Alcohol and Drug Abuse Directors, Inc.
1025 Connecticut Avenue, NW
Suite 605
Washington, DC 20036
202-293-0090
www.nasadad.org

National Center for State Courts
300 Newport Avenue
Williamsburg, VA 23185
800-616-6164
www.ncsc.org

National Criminal Justice Reference Service (NCJRS)
Box 6000
Rockville, MD 20849
800-851-3420
www.ncjrs.org

National Institute of Justice
810 Seventh Street, NW
Washington, DC 20531
202-307-2942
www.ojp.usdoj.gov/nij

Office of Juvenile Justice and Delinquency Prevention
801 Seventh Street, NW
Washington, DC 20531
202-307-5911
202-307-5911

Parents for Megan's Law
PO Box 145
Stony Brook, NY 11790
631-689-2672
www.parentsformeganslaw.com

Substance Abuse and Mental Health Services Administration
U.S. Department of Health and Human Services
P.O. Box 2345
Rockville, MD 20847
877-726-4727
www.samhsa.gov

Index

8163